GREENS
CRIMINAL LAW
STATUTES
2001/2002

D1323281

AUSTRALIA
LBC Information Services—Sydney

CANADA and USA
Carswell—Toronto

NEW ZEALAND
Brooker's—Auckland

SINGAPORE and MALAYSIA
Sweet & Maxwell Asia
Singapore and Kuala Lumpur

Reprinted from *Renton & Brown's Criminal Procedure Legislation*,
published in looseleaf form and updated three times a year by W. Green,
the Scottish Law Publisher

The following paperback titles are also available in the series:

Family Law Statues 2000/2001
Conveyancing Statutes 2001/2002
Mercantile Statutes 2001/2002
Sheriff Court Rules 2001/2002
Solicitors Professional Handbook 2001/2002

GREENS
CRIMINAL LAW
STATUTES
2001/2002

Reprinted from
Renton & Brown's Criminal Procedure Legislation

EDINBURGH
W. GREEN/Sweet & Maxwell
2001

Published in 2001 by W. Green & Son Ltd
21 Alva Street
Edinburgh EH2 4PS

Printed in Great Britain by Athenaeum Press,
Gateshead, Tyne & Wear

No natural forests were destroyed to make this product;
only farmed timber was used and replanted

A CIP catalogue record for this book is available from the British Library
ISBN 0 414 01426 X

© W. Green & Son Ltd 2001

CONTENTS

DIVISION A

PART I—PRIMARY STATUTES

PART II—MISCELLANEOUS STATUTES

DIVISION B

ACTS OF ADJOURNAL, ETC

CRIMINAL JUSTICE (INTERNATIONAL CO-OPERATION) ACT 1990*

(1990 c. 5)

An Act to enable the United Kingdom to co-operate with other countries in criminal proceedings and investigations; to enable the United Kingdom to join with other countries in implementing the Vienna Convention against Illicit Traffic in Narcotic Drugs and Psychotropic Substances; and to provide for the seizure, detention and forfeiture of drug trafficking money imported or exported in cash.   [5th April 1990]

PART I

CRIMINAL PROCEEDINGS AND INVESTIGATIONS

Mutual service of process

Service of overseas process in United Kingdom

1.—(1) This section has effect where the Secretary of State receives from the government of, or other authority in, a country or territory outside the United Kingdom—
    (a) a summons or other process requiring a person to appear as defendant or attend as a witness in criminal proceedings in that country or territory; or
    (b) a document issued by a court exercising criminal jurisdiction in that country or territory and recording a decision of the court made in the exercise of that jurisdiction,
together with a request for it to be served on a person in the United Kingdom.
    (2) The Secretary of State or, where the person to be served is in Scotland,

the Lord Advocate may cause the process or document to be served by post or, if the request is for personal service, direct the chief officer of police for the area in which that person appears to be to cause it to be personally served on him.

(3) Service by virtue of this section of any such process as is mentioned in subsection (1)(a) above shall not impose any obligation under the law of any part of the United Kingdom to comply with it.

(4) Any such process served by virtue of this section shall be accompanied by a notice—

(a) stating the effect of subsection (3) above;

(b) indicating that the person on whom it is served may wish to seek advice as to the possible consequences of his failing to comply with the process under the law of the country or territory where it was issued; and

(c) indicating that under that law he may not, as a witness, be accorded the same rights and privileges as would be accorded to him in criminal proceedings in the United Kingdom.

(5) Where a chief officer of police is directed under this section to cause any process or document to be served he shall after it has been served forthwith inform the Secretary of State or, as the case may be, the Lord Advocate when and how it was served and (if possible) furnish him with a receipt signed by the person on whom it was served; and if the chief officer has been unable to cause the process or document to be served he shall forthwith inform the Secretary of State or, as the case may be, the Lord Advocate of that fact and of the reason.

(6) In the application of this section to Northern Ireland for references to a chief officer of police there shall be substituted references to the Chief Constable of the Royal Ulster Constabulary.

Service of United Kingdom process overseas

2.—(1) Process of the following descriptions, that is to say—

(a) a summons requiring a person charged with an offence to appear before a court in the United Kingdom; and

(b) a summons or order requiring a person to attend before a court in the United Kingdom for the purpose of giving evidence in criminal proceedings,

may be issued or made notwithstanding that the person in question is outside the United Kingdom and may be served outside the United Kingdom in accordance with arrangements made by the Secretary of State.

(2) In relation to Scotland subsection (1) above applies to any document which may competently be served on any accused person or on any person who may give evidence in criminal proceedings.

(3) Service of any process outside the United Kingdom by virtue of this section shall not impose any obligation under the law of any part of the United Kingdom to comply with it and accordingly failure to do so shall not constitute contempt of any court or be a ground for issuing a warrant to secure the attendance of the person in question or, in Scotland, for imposing any penalty.

(4) Subsection (3) above is without prejudice to the service of any process (with the usual consequences for non-compliance) on the person in question if subsequently effected in the United Kingdom.

Mutual provision of evidence

Overseas evidence for use in United Kingdom

3.—(1) Where on an application made in accordance with subsection (2) below it appears to a justice of the peace or a judge or, in Scotland, to a sheriff or a judge—

(a) that an offence has been committed or that there are reasonable grounds for suspecting that an offence has been committed; and

(b) that proceedings in respect of the offence have been instituted or that the offence is being investigated,

he may issue a letter ("a letter of request") requesting assistance in obtaining outside the United Kingdom such evidence as is specified in the letter for use in the proceedings or investigation.

(2) An application under subsection (1) above may be made by a prosecuting authority or, if proceedings have been instituted, by the person charged in those proceedings.

(3) A prosecuting authority which is for the time being designated for the purposes of this section by an order made by the Secretary of State by statutory instrument may itself issue a letter of request if—

(a) it is satisfied as to the matters mentioned in subsection (1)(a) above; and

(b) the offence in question is being investigated or the authority has instituted proceedings in respect of it.

(4) Subject to subsection (5) below, a letter of request shall be sent to the Secretary of State for transmission either—

(a) to a court or tribunal specified in the letter and exercising jurisdiction in the place where the evidence is to be obtained; or

(b) to any authority recognised by the government of the country or territory in question as the appropriate authority for receiving requests for assistance of the kind to which this section applies.

(5) In cases of urgency a letter of request may be sent direct to such a court or tribunal as is mentioned in subsection (4)(a) above.

(6) In this section "evidence" includes documents and other articles.

(7) Evidence obtained by virtue of a letter of request shall not without the consent of such an authority as is mentioned in subsection (4)(b) above be used for any purpose other than that specified in the letter; and when any document or other article obtained pursuant to a letter of request is no longer required for that purpose (or for any other purpose for which such consent has been obtained), it shall be returned to such an authority unless that authority indicates that the document or article need not be returned.

(8) In exercising the discretion conferred by section 25 of the Criminal Justice Act 1988 (exclusion of evidence otherwise admissible) in relation to a statement contained in evidence taken pursuant to a letter of request the court shall have regard—

(a) to whether it was possible to challenge the statement by questioning the person who made it; and

(b) if proceedings have been instituted, to whether the local law allowed the parties to the proceedings to be legally represented when the evidence was being taken.

(9) In Scotland evidence obtained by virtue of a letter of request shall, without being sworn to by witnesses, be received in evidence in so far as that can be done without unfairness to either party.

(10) In the application of this section to Northern Ireland for the reference in subsection (1) to a justice of the peace there shall be substituted a reference to a resident magistrate and for the reference in subsection (8) to section 25 of the Criminal Justice (Evidence, Etc.) (Northern Ireland) Order 1988.

United Kingdom evidence for use overseas

4.—This section has effect where the Secretary of State receives—

(a) from a court or tribunal exercising criminal jurisdiction in a country or territory outside the United Kingdom or a prosecuting authority in such a country or territory; or

(b) from any other authority in such a country or territory which appears to him to have the function of making requests of the kind to which this section applies,

a request for assistance in obtaining evidence in the United Kingdom in connection with criminal proceedings that have been instituted, or a criminal investigation that is being carried on, in that country or territory.

(2) If the Secretary of State or, if the evidence is to be obtained in Scotland, the Lord Advocate is satisfied—

(a) that an offence under the law of the country or territory in question has been committed or that there are reasonable grounds for suspecting that such an offence has been committed; and

(b) that proceedings in respect of that offence have been instituted in that country or territory or that an investigation into that offence is being carried on there,

he may, if he thinks fit, by a notice in writing nominate a court in England, Wales or Northern Ireland or, as the case may be, Scotland to receive such of the evidence to which the request relates as may appear to the court to be appropriate for the purpose of giving effect to the request.

(3) Where it appears to the Secretary of State or, as the case may be, the Lord Advocate that the request relates to a fiscal offence in respect of which proceedings have not yet been instituted he shall not exercise his powers under subsection (2) above unless—

(a) the request is from a country or territory which is a member of the Commonwealth or is made pursuant to a treaty to which the United Kingdom is a party; or

(b) he is satisfied that the conduct constituting the offence would constitute an offence of the same or a similar nature if it had occurred in the United Kingdom.

(4) For the purpose of satisfying himself as to the matters mentioned in subsection (2)(a) and (b) above the Secretary of State or, as the case may be, the Lord Advocate shall regard as conclusive a certificate issued by such authority in the country or territory in question as appears to him to be appropriate.

(5) In this section "evidence" includes documents and other articles.

(6) Schedule 1 to this Act shall have effect with respect to the proceedings before a nominated court in pursuance of a notice under subsection (2) above.

Transfer of United Kingdom prisoner to give evidence or assist investigation overseas

5.—(1) The Secretary of State may, if he thinks fit, issue a warrant providing for any person ("a prisoner") serving a sentence in a prison or other institution to which the Prison Act 1952 or the Prisons (Scotland) Act 1989 applies to be transferred to a country or territory outside the United Kingdom for the purpose—

(a) of giving evidence in criminal proceedings there; or

(b) of being identified in, or otherwise by his presence assisting, such proceedings or the investigation of an offence.

(2) No warrant shall be issued under this section in respect of any prisoner unless he has consented to being transferred as mentioned in subsection (1) above and that consent may be given either—

(a) by the prisoner himself; or

(b) in circumstances in which it appeas to the Secretary of State inappropriate, by reason of the prisoner's physical or mental condition or his youth, for him to act for himself, by a person appearing to the Secretary of State to be an appropriate person to act on his behalf;

but a consent once given shall not be capable of being withdrawn after the issue of the warrant.

(3) The effect of a warrant under this section shall be to authorise—

(a) the taking of the prisoner to a place in the United Kingdom and his delivery at a place of departure from the United Kingdom into the custody of a person representing the appropriate authority of the country or territory to which the prisoner is to be transferred; and

(b) the bringing of the prisoner back to the United Kingdom and his transfer in custody to the place where he is liable to be detained under the sentence to which he is subject.

(4) Where a warrant has been issued in respect of a prisoner under this section he shall be deemed to be in legal custody at any time when, being in the United Kingdom or on board a British ship, British aircraft or British hovercraft, he is being taken under the warrant to or from any place or being kept in custody under the warrant.

(5) A person authorised by or for the purposes of the warrant to take the prisoner to or from any place or to keep him in custody shall have all the powers, authority, protection and privileges—

(a) of a constable in the part of the United Kingdom in which that person is for the time being; or

(b) if he is outside the United Kingdom, of a constable in the part of the United Kingdom to or from which the prisoner is to be taken under the warrant.

(6) If the prisoner escapes or is unlawfully at large, he may be arrested without warrant by a constable and taken to any place to which he may be taken under the warrant issued under this section.

(7) In subsection (4) above—

"British aircraft" means a British-controlled aircraft within the meaning of section 92 of the Civil Aviation Act 1982 (application of criminal law to aircraft) or one of Her Majesty's aircraft;

"British hovercraft" means a British-controlled hovercraft within the meaning of that section as applied in relation to hovercraft by virtue of provisions made under the Hovercraft Act 1968 or one of Her Majesty's hovercraft;

"British ship" means a British ship for the purposes of the Merchant Shipping Acts 1894 to 1988 or one of Her Majesty's ships;

and in this subsection references to Her Majesty's aircraft, hovercraft or ships are references to aircraft, hovercraft or, as the case may be, ships belonging to or exclusively employed in the service of Her Majesty in right of the Government of the United Kingdom.

(8) In subsection (6) above "constable", in relation to any part of the United Kingdom, means any person who is a constable in that or any other part of the United Kingdom or any person who, at the place in question has, under any enactment including subsection (5) above, the powers of a constable in that or any other part of the United Kingdom.

(9) This section applies to a person in custody awaiting trial or sentence and a person committed to prison for default in paying a fine as it applies to a prisoner and the reference in subsection (3)(b) above to a sentence shall be construed accordingly.

(10) In the application of this section to Northern Ireland for the reference in subsection (1) to the Prison Act 1952 there shall be substituted a reference to the Prison Act (Northern Ireland) 1953.

Transfer of overseas prisoner to give evidence or assist investigation in the United Kingdom

6.—(1) This section has effect where—

(a) a witness order has been made or a witness summons or citation issued in criminal proceedings in the United Kingdom in respect of a person ("a prisoner") who is detained in custody in a country or territory outside the United Kingdom by virtue of a sentence or order of a court or tribunal exercising criminal jurisdiction in that country or territory; or

(b) it appears to the Secretary of State that it is desirable for a prisoner to be identified in, or otherwise by his presence to assist, such proceedings or the investigation in the United Kingdom of an offence.

(2) If the Secretary of State is satisfied that the appropriate authority in the country or territory where the prisoner is detained will make arrangements for him to come to the United Kingdom to give evidence pursuant to the witness order, witness summons or citation or, as the case may be, for the purpose mentioned in subsection (1)(b) above, he may issue a warrant under this section.

(3) No warrant shall be issued under this section in respect of any prisoner unless he has consented to being brought to the United Kingdom to give evidence as aforesaid or, as the case may be, for the purpose mentioned in subsection (1)(b) above but a consent once given shall not be capable of being withdrawn after the issue of the warrant.

(4) The effect of the warrant shall be to authorise—

(a) the bringing of the prisoner to the United Kingdom;

(b) the taking of the prisoner to, and his detention in custody at, such place or places in the United Kingdom as are specified in the warrant; and

(c) the returning of the prisoner to the country or territory from which he has come.

(5) Subsections (4) to (8) of section 5 above shall have effect in relation to a warrant issued under this section as they have effect in relation to a warrant issued under that section.

(6) A person shall not be subject to the Immigration Act 1971 in respect of his entry into or presence in the United Kingdom in pursuance of a warrant under this section but if the warrant ceases to have effect while he is still in the United Kingdom—

(a) he shall be treated for the purposes of that Act as if he has then illegally entered the United Kingdom; and

(b) the provisions of Schedule 2 to that Act shall have effect accordingly except that paragraph 20(1) (liability of carrier for expenses of custody etc. of illegal entrant) shall not have effect in relation to directions for his removal given by virtue of this subsection.

(7) This section applies to a person detained in custody in a country or territory outside the United Kingdom in consequence of having been transferred there—

(a) from the United Kingdom under the Repatriation of Prisoners Act 1984; or

(b) under any similar provision or arrangement from any other country or territory,

as it applies to a person detained as mentioned in subsection (1) above.

Additional co-operation powers

7. [Not reproduced in this work]

Search etc. for material relevant to overseas investigation: Scotland

8.—(1) If, on an application made by the procurator fiscal, it appears to the sheriff—

(a) that there are reasonable grounds for believing that an offence under the law of a country or territory outside the United Kingdom has been committed; and

(b) that the conduct constituting that offence would constitute an offence punishable by imprisonment if it had occurred in Scotland,

the sheriff shall have the like power to grant warrant authorising entry, search and seizure by any constable as he would have at common law in respect of any offence punishable at common law in Scotland.

(2) No application for a warrant shall be made by virtue of subsection (1) above except in pursuance of a direction given by the Lord Advocate in response to a request received by the Secretary of State—

(a) from a court or tribunal exercising criminal jurisdiction in the overseas country or territory in question or a prosecuting authority in that country or territory; or

(b) from any other authority in that country or territory which appears to him to have the function of making requests for the purpose of this section,

and any evidence seized by the constable by virtue of this section shall be furnished by him to the Lord Advocate for transmission to that court, tribunal or authority.

(3) If in order to comply with the request it is necessary for any such evidence to be accompanied by any certificate, affidavit or other verifying document the constable shall also furnish for transmission such document of that nature as may be specified in the direction given by the Lord Advocate.

(4) Where the evidence consists of a document the original or a copy shall be transmitted, and where it consists of any other article the article itself or a description, photograph or other representation of it shall be transmitted, as may be necessary in order to comply with the request.

(5) The Treasury may by order direct that any powers to enter, search or seize granted by virtue of subsection (1) above which may be exercised by a constable shall also be exercisable by, or by any person acting under the direction of, an officer commissioned by the Commissioners of Customs and Excise under section 6(3) of the Customs and Excise Management Act 1979; and the Secretary of State may by order direct that any of those powers shall also be exercisable by a person of any other description specified in the order.

(6) An order under subsection (5) above shall be made by statutory instrument subject to annulment in pursuance of a resolution of either House of Parliament.

Enforcement of overseas forfeiture orders

9.—(1) Her Majesty may by Order in Council provide for the enforcement in the United Kingdom of any order which—

(a) is made by a court in a country or territory outside the United Kingdom designated for the purposes of this section by the Order in Council; and

(b) is for the forfeiture and destruction, or the forfeiture and other disposal, of anything in respect of which an offence to which this section applies has been committed or which was used in connection with the commission of such an offence.

(2) Without prejudice to the generality of subsection (1) above an Order in Council under this section may provide for the registration by a court in the United Kingdom of any order as a condition of its enforcement and prescribe requirements to be satisfied before an order can be registered.

(3) An Order in Council under this section may include such supplementary and incidental provisions as appear to Her Majesty to be necessary or expedient and may apply for the purposes of the Order (with such modifications as appear to Her Majesty to be appropriate) any provisions relating to confiscation or forfeiture orders under any other enactment.

(4) An Order in Council under this section may make different provision for different cases.

(5) No Order in Council shall be made under this section unless a draft of it has been laid before and approved by a resolution of each House of Parliament.

(6) This section applies to any offence which corresponds to or is similar to an offence under the Misuse of Drugs Act 1971, a drug trafficking offence as defined in section 38(1) of the Drug Trafficking Offences Act 1986, an offence to which section 1 of the Criminal Justice (Scotland) Act 1987 relates or an offence to which Part VI of the Criminal Justice Act 1988 applies.

Supplementary

Rules of court

10.—(1) Provision may be made by rules of court for any purpose for which it appears to the authority having power to make the rules that it is necessary or expedient that provision should be made in connection with any of the provisions of this Part of this Act.

(2) Rules made for the purposes of Schedule 1 to this Act may, in particular, make provision with respect to the persons entitled to appear or take part in the proceedings to which that Schedule applies and for excluding the public from any such proceedings.

(3) An Order in Council under section 9 above may authorise the making of rules of court for any purpose specified in the Order.

(4) Rules of court made under this section by the High Court in Scotland shall be made by Act of Adjournal.

(5) This section is without prejudice to the generality of any existing power to make rules.

Application to courts-martial etc.

11.—(1) Section 2 above applies also to a summons requiring a person charged with a civil offence to appear before a service court (whether or not in the United Kingdom) or to attend before such a court for the purpose of giving evidence in proceedings for such an offence; and a warrant may be issued under section 6 above where—

(a) such a summons has been issued in respect of a prisoner within the meaning of that section; or

(b) it appears to the Secretary of State that it is desirable for such a prisoner to be identified in, otherwise by his presence to assist, such proceedings or the investigation of such an offence.

(2) Section 5 above applies also to a person serving a sentence of detention imposed by a service court or detained in custody awaiting trial by such a court.

(3) In this section "a civil offence" has the same meaning as in the Army Act 1955, the Air Force Act 1955 and the Naval Discipline Act 1957 and "service court" means a court-martial constituted under any of those Acts or a Standing Civilian Court.

SCHEDULE 1

Section 4(6)

UNITED KINGDOM EVIDENCE FOR USE OVERSEAS: PROCEEDINGS OF NOMINATED COURT

Securing attendance of witnesses

1. The court shall have the like powers for securing the attendance of a witness for the purpose of the proceedings as it has for the purpose of other proceedings before the court.

2. In Scotland the court shall have power to issue a warrant to officers of law to cite witnesses for the purpose of the proceedings and section 320 of the Criminal Procedure (Scotland) Act 1975 shall apply in relation to such a witness.

Power to administer oaths

3. The court may in the proceedings take evidence on oath.

Privilege of witnesses

4.—(1) A person shall not be compelled to give in the proceedings any evidence which he could not be compelled to give—

    (a) in criminal proceedings in the part of the United Kingdom in which the nominated court exercises jurisdiction; or

    (b) subject to sub-paragraph (2) below, in criminal proceedings in the country or territory from which the request for the evidence has come.

(2) Sub-paragraph (1)(b) above shall not apply unless the claim of the person questioned to be exempt from giving the evidence is conceded by the court, tribunal or authority which made the request.

(3) Where such a claim made by any person is not conceded as aforesaid he may (subject to the other provisions of this paragraph) be required to give the evidence to which the claim relates but the evidence shall not be transmitted to the court, tribunal or authority which requested it if a court in the country or territory in question, on the matter being referred to it, upholds the claim.

(4) Without prejudice to sub-paragraph (1) above a person shall not be compelled under this Schedule to give any evidence if his doing so would be prejudicial to the security of the United Kingdom; and a certificate signed by or on behalf of the Secretary of State or, where the court is in Scotland, by or on behalf of the Lord Advocate to the effect that it would be so prejudicial for that person to do so shall be conclusive evidence of that fact.

(5) Without prejudice to sub-paragraph (1) above a person shall not be compelled under this Schedule to give any evidence in his capacity as an officer or servant of the Crown.

(6) In this paragraph references to giving evidence include references to answering any question and to producing any document or other article and the reference in sub-paragraph (3) above to the transmission of evidence given by a person shall be construed accordingly.

Transmission of evidence

5.—(1) The evidence received by the court shall be furnished to the Secretary of State or, in Scotland, the Lord Advocate for transmission to the court, tribunal or authority that made the request.

(2) If in order to comply with the request it is necessary for the evidence to be accompanied by any certificate, affidavit or other verifying document, the court shall also furnish for transmission such document of that nature as may be specified in the notice nominating the court.

(3) Where the evidence consists of a document the original or a copy shall be transmitted, and where it consists of any other article the article itself or a description, photograph or other representation of it shall be transmitted, as may be necessary in order to comply with the request.

Supplementary

6. For the avoidance of doubt it is hereby declared that the Bankers Books' Evidence Act 1879 applies to the proceedings as it applies to other proceedings before the court.

7. No order for costs shall be made in the proceedings.

SCHEDULE 2

Sections 12 and 13

*   *   *

PRISONERS AND CRIMINAL PROCEEDINGS (SCOTLAND) ACT 1993

(1993 c. 9)

36. Evidence as to taking or destruction of eggs.
37. Evidence by certificate.

Part III

An Act to amend the law of Scotland with respect to the detention, transfer and release of persons serving sentences of imprisonment etc. or committed or remanded in custody; to make further provision as regards evidence and procedure in criminal proceedings in Scotland; and for connected purposes.   [29th March 1993]

Part I

Detention, Transfer and Release of Offenders

Early release

Release of short-term, long-term and life prisoners

1.—[2](1) Subject to section 26A(4) of this Act as soon as a short-term prisoner has served one-half of his sentence the Secretary of State shall, without prejudice to any supervised release order to which the prisoner is subject, release him unconditionally.

[2](2) As soon as a long-term prisoner has served two-thirds of his sentence, the Secretary of State shall release him on licence unless he has before that time been so released, in relation to that sentence, under any provision of this Act.

[1](3) After a long-term prisoner has served one-half of his sentence the Secretary of State shall, if recommended to do so by the Parole Board under this section, release him on licence.

[4](3A) Subsections (1) to (3) above are subject to section 1A of this Act.

[3](4) If recommended to do so by the Parole Board under this section, the Secretary of State may, after consultation with—

(a) the Lord Justice General, whom failing the Lord Justice Clerk; and
(b) if available, the trial judge,

release on licence a life prisoner who is not a designated life prisoner.

(5) The Parole Board shall not make a recommendation under subsection (4) above unless the Secretary of State has referred the case to the Board for its advice.

(6) Notwithstanding the foregoing provisions of this section, the Secretary of State shall not release a person who is serving—

(a) a sentence of imprisonment for a term and one or more sentences of imprisonment for life; or

(b) more than one sentence of imprisonment for life,

unless and until the requirements of those provisions are satisfied in respect of each of those sentences.

(7) A person to whom subsection (6) above applies shall, when released on licence under this section, be released on a single licence under subsection (4) above.

[1](8) Schedule 1 to this Act, which makes special provision as respects the release of persons serving both a sentence of imprisonment imposed on conviction of an offence and a term of imprisonment or detention referred to in section 5(1)(a) or (b) of this Act, shall have effect.

NOTES

[1]As amended by S.I. 1995 No. 911.

[2]As amended by the Crime and Disorder Act 1998 (c. 37), Sched. 8, para. 98.

[3]As amended by the 1997 Punishment Act, Sched. 1, para. 14(2)(b) (effective October 20, 1997: S.I. 1997 No. 2323).

[4]Inserted by the Crime and Disorder Act 1998 (c. 37), Sched. 8, para. 98.

Application to persons serving more than one sentence

[1]**1A.** Where a prisoner has been sentenced to two or more terms of imprisonment which are wholly or partly concurrent and do not fall to be treated as a single term by virtue of section 27(5) of this Act—

(a) nothing in this Part of this Act shall require the Secretary of State to release him in respect of any of the terms unless and until the Secretary of State is required to release him in respect of each of the other terms;

(b) nothing in this Part of this Act shall require the Secretary of State or the Parole Board to consider his release in respect of any of the terms unless and until the Secretary of State or the Parole Board is required to consider his release, or the Secretary of State is required to release him, in respect of each of the other terms; and

(c) where he is released on licence under this Part of this Act, he shall be on a single licence which—

(i) shall (unless revoked) remain in force until the date on which he would (but for his release) have served in full all the sentences in respect of which he has been so released; and

(ii) shall be subject to such conditions as may be specified or required by this Part of this Act in respect of any of the sentences.

NOTE

[1]Inserted by the Crime and Disorder Act 1998 (c. 37): s.111(1) (effective September 30, 1998, S.I. 1998 No. 2327).

Duty to release discretionary life prisoners

2.—[3](1) In this Part of this Act "designated life prisoner", subject to subsection (9)(a) below and except where the context otherwise requires, means a person—

(a) sentenced to life imprisonment for an offence for which, subject to paragraph (b) below, such a sentence is not the sentence fixed by law;

(b) whose sentence was imposed under section 205A(2) of the 1995 Act (imprisonment for life on further conviction for certain offences); or

(c) whose sentence was imposed in respect of a murder committed by him before he attained the age of 18 years,

and in respect of whom the court which sentenced him for that offence made the order mentioned in subsection (2) below.

[1,2](2) The order referred to in subsection (1) above is an order that subsections (4) and (6) below shall apply to the designated life prisoner as soon as he has served such part of his sentence ("the designated part") as is specified in the order, being such part as the court considers appropriate taking into account—

    (a) the seriousness of the offence, or of the offence combined with other offences associated with it;

    (b) any previous conviction of the designated life prisoner; and

  [4](c) where appropriate, the matters mentioned in paragraphs (a) and (b) of section 196(1) of the 1995 Act.

[1](3) Where a court which imposes life imprisonment for an offence such as is mentioned in subsection (1) above decides not to make such order as is mentioned in subsection (2) above, it shall state its reasons for so deciding; and for the purposes of any appeal or review, any such order and any such decision shall each constitute part of a person's sentence within the meaning of the 1995 Act.

[1](4) Where this subsection applies, the Secretary of State shall, if directed to do so by the Parole Board, release a designated life prisoner on licence.

(5) The Parole Board shall not give a direction under subsection (4) above unless—

    (a) the Secretary of State has referred the prisoner's case to the Board; and

    (b) the Board is satisfied that it is no longer necessary for the protection of the public that the prisoner should be confined.

[1](6) Where this subsection applies, a designated life prisoner may, subject to subsection (7) below, at any time require the Secretary of State to refer his case to the Parole Board.

(7) No requirement shall be made under subsection (6) above—

    (a) where the prisoner is also serving a sentence of imprisonment for a term, before he has served one-half of that sentence; and

    (b) where less than two years has elapsed since the disposal of any (or the most recent if more than one) previous reference of his case to the Board under subsection (5)(a) or (6) above or under section 17(3) of this Act.

[1](8) In determining for the purposes of subsection (4) or (6) above whether a designated life prisoner has served the designated part of his sentence, no account shall be taken of any time during which he was unlawfully at large.

(9) Where a life prisoner is serving two or more sentences of imprisonment for life—

  [1](a) he is a designated life prisoner only if the requirements of subsection (1) above are satisfied in respect of each of those sentences;

  [1](b) notwithstanding the terms of any order under subsection (2) above, subsections (4) and (6) above shall not apply to him until he has served the designated part of each of those sentences; and

    (c) he shall, if released on licence under subsection (4) above, be so released on a single licence.

NOTES

[1]As amended by the 1997 Punishment Act, Sched. 1, para. 14(3) (effective October 20, 1997: S.I. 1997 No. 2323).

[2]As amended by the 1997 Punishment Act, Sched. 3 (effective October 20, 1997: S.I. 1997 No. 2323).

[3]Substituted by the 1997 Punishment Act, s.16(1)(a) (effective August 1, 1997: S.I. 1997 No.1712).

[4]Inserted by the 1997 Punishment Act, s.16(1)(b) (effective August 1, 1997: S.I. 1997 No.1712).

Power to release prisoners on compassionate grounds

3.—(1) The Secretary of State may at any time, if satisfied that there are compassionate grounds justifying the release of a person serving a sentence of imprisonment, release him on licence.

(2) Before so releasing any long-term prisoner or any life prisoner, the Secretary of State shall consult the Parole Board unless the circumstances are such as to render consultation impracticable.

(3) The release of a person under subsection (1) above shall not constitute release for the purpose of a supervised release order.

Re-release of prisoners serving extended sentences

[1]**3A.**—(1) This section applies to a prisoner serving an extended sentence within the meaning of section 210A of the 1995 Act (extended sentences) who has been recalled to prison under section 17(1) of this Act.

(2) Subject to subsection (3) below, a prisoner to whom this section applies may require the Secretary of State to refer his case to the Parole Board—

    (a) where his case has previously been referred to the Parole Board under this section or section 17(3) of this Act, not less than one year following the disposal of that referral;

    (b) in any one case, at any time.

(3) Where a prisoner to whom this section applies is subject to another sentence which is not treated as a single sentence with the extended sentence, the Secretary of State shall not be required to refer his case to the Parole Board before he has served one half of that other sentence.

(4) Where the case of a prisoner to whom this section applies is referred to the Parole Board under this section or section 17(3) of this Act, the Board shall, if it is satisfied that it is no longer necessary for the protection of the public from serious harm that the prisoner should be confined (but not otherwise), direct that he should be released.

(5) If the Parole Board gives a direction under subsection (4) above, the Secretary of State shall release the prisoner on licence.

NOTE
[1]Inserted by the Crime and Disorder Act 1998 (c. 37), s.88 (effective September 30, 1998: S.I. 1998 No. 2327).

Persons detained under Mental Health (Scotland) Act 1984

4.—(1) Notwithstanding that a transfer direction and a restriction direction (those expressions having the same meanings as in the Mental Health (Scotland) Act 1984) have been given in respect of a person serving a sentence of imprisonment, this Part of this Act shall apply to the person as if he continued to serve that sentence while detained in, and as if he had not been removed to, hospital.

[1](1A) This part of this Act shall apply to a person conveyed to and detained in a hospital pursuant to a hospital directed under section 59A of the 1995 Act as if, while so detained, he was serving the sentence of imprisonment imposed on him at the time at which that direction was made.

(2) In section 71(7)(a) of the said Act of 1984 (categories of prisoner who may be transferred to hospital), the words "in criminal proceedings" shall cease to have effect.

(3) For sections 74 and 75 of the said Act of 1984 there shall be substituted the following section—

    "Further provision as to transfer directions and restriction directions

    74.—(1) This subsection applies where a transfer direction and a restriction direction have been given in respect of a person—

        (a) serving a sentence of imprisonment; or

   (b) who is detained (other than in respect of a criminal offence)
        under or by virtue of the Immigration Act 1971,
if the Secretary of State is satisfied, at a time when the person would but
for those directions be, by virtue of the circumstance mentioned in
paragraph (a) or (b) above, in prison or being detained other than in a
hospital, as to the matters mentioned in subsection (2) below.

   [1](1A) This Part of this Act shall apply to a person conveyed to and
detained in a hospital pursuant to a hospital direction under section 59A
of the 1995 Act as if, while so detained, he was serving the sentence of
imprisonment imposed on him at the time at which that direction was
made.

   (2) The matters referred to in subsection (1) above are—
   (a) that either—
        (i) the person is not suffering from mental disorder of a nature
        or degree which makes it appropriate for him to be liable to be
        detained in a hospital for medical treatment; or
        (ii) that it is not necessary for the health or safety of the person
        or for the protection of other persons that he should receive such
        treatment; and
   (b) that it is not appropriate for the person to remain liable to be
        recalled to hospital for further treatment.

   (3) Where subsection (1) above applies, the Secretary of State shall
by warrant direct that the person be remitted to any prison or other
institution or place in which he might have been detained had he not
been removed to hospital and that he be dealt with there as if he had not
been so removed.

   (4) Where subsection (1) above does not apply only because the
Secretary of State is not satisfied as to the matter mentioned in
subsection (2)(b) above, he may either—
   (a) by warrant give such direction as is mentioned in subsection (3)
        above; or
   (b) decide that the person shall continue to be detained in hospital.

   (5) If a direction is given under subsection (3) or (4)(a) above, then on
the person's arrival in the prison or other institution or place to which
remitted by virtue of that subsection the transfer direction and the
restriction direction shall cease to have effect.

   (6) This subsection applies where a transfer direction and a restriction direction have been given in respect of such person as is mentioned
in subsection (1) above and he has thereafter been released under Part I
of the Prisoners and Criminal Proceedings (Scotland) Act 1993.

   (7) Where subsection (6) above applies—
   (a) the transfer direction and the restriction direction shall forthwith
        cease to have effect; and
   (b) the person shall thereupon be discharged from hospital unless a
        report is furnished in respect of him under subsection (9) below.

   (8) A transfer direction or restriction direction given in respect of a
person detained (other than in respect of a criminal offence) under or
by virtue of the Immigration Act 1971 shall, if it does not first cease to
have effect under subsection (5) above or under section 65(2) of this
Act, cease to have effect when his liability to be so detained comes to an
end.

   (9) Not earlier than 28 days before a restriction direction given in
respect of a person ceases to have effect other than by virtue of
subsection (8) above, the responsible medical officer shall obtain from
another medical practitioner a report on the condition of the person in
the prescribed form and thereafter shall assess the need for the
detention of the person to be continued; and, if it appears to the
responsible medical officer that it is necessary in the interests of the

health or safety of the person or for the protection of others that the person should continue to be liable to be detained in hospital, the officer shall furnish to the managers of the hospital where the person is liable to be detained and to the Mental Welfare Commission a report to that effect in the prescribed form along with the report of the other medical practitioner.

(10) Where a report has been furnished under subsection (9) above the person shall, after the restriction direction ceases to have effect, be treated as if he had, on the date on which the restriction direction ceased to have effect, been admitted to the hospital in pursuance of an application for admission; but the provisions of sections 30(5) and (6) and 35 of this Act shall apply to the person and that report as they apply to a patient the authority for whose detention in hospital has been renewed in pursuance of subsection (4) of, and to a report under subsection (3) of, the said section 30.

(11) For the purposes of section 40(2) of the Prisons (Scotland) Act 1989 (discounting from sentence periods while unlawfully at large) a person who, having been transferred to hospital in pursuance of a transfer direction from a prison or young offenders institution, is at large in circumstances in which he is liable to be taken into custody under any provision of this Act, shall be treated as unlawfully at large and absent from the prison or young offenders institution.

(12) In this section "prescribed" means prescribed by regulations made by the Secretary of State.".

NOTE
[1]Inserted by the Crime and Disorder Act 1998 (c. 37), Sched. 8, para. 99(1) and (2) (effective from January 1, 1998).

Fine defaulters and persons in contempt of court

[2]**5.**—(1) Subject to section 1(8) of this Act and to subsections (2) to (4) below, this Part of this Act (except sections 1(3), 16 and 27(5)) applies to a person on whom imprisonment, or as the case may be detention in a young offenders institution, has been imposed—

[1](a) under section 219 of the 1995 Act (imprisonment for non-payment of fine) or, by virtue of that section, under section 207 of that Act (detention of young offenders);

(b) for contempt of court,

as it applies to a person sentenced to imprisonment, or on whom detention has been imposed, on conviction of an offence; and references in this Part of this Act to prisoners (whether short-term or long-term), or to prison, imprisonment, detention or sentences of imprisonment shall be construed accordingly.

(2) Where section 1(1) or (2) of this Act applies to a person by virtue of subsection (1) above, that section shall be construed as requiring the Secretary of State to release the person unconditionally as soon as, in the case of—

(a) a short-term prisoner, he has served one-half of his term of imprisonment; or

(b) a long-term prisoner, he has served two-thirds of his term of imprisonment,

and if during the term in question the prisoner is both released under section 3 of this Act and subsequently recalled under section 17(1) thereof, the period during which he is thereby lawfully at large shall be taken, for the purposes of paragraph (a) or (b) above, to be a period of imprisonment served.

(3) Notwithstanding subsection (1) above, section 11 of this Act shall not apply to a person to whom this Part of this Act applies by virtue of that

subsection but whose release on licence is under section 3 of this Act; and that licence shall (unless revoked) remain in force only until the date on which, by virtue of subsection (2) above, his release would have been required had he not been released earlier.

[3](4) Where a person has had imposed on him two or more terms of imprisonment or detention mentioned in subsection (1)(a) or (b) above, sections 1A and 27(5) of this Act shall apply to those terms as if they were terms of imprisonment.

NOTES
[1]As substituted by the 1995 C.P. Act, Sched. 4.
[2]As amended by the Crime and Disorder Act 1998 (c. 37), Sched. 8, para. 100 (effective September 30, 1998: S.I. 1998 No. 2327).
[3]Inserted by the Crime and Disorder Act 1998 (c. 37), Sched. 8, para. 100 (effective September 30, 1998: S.I. 1988 No. 2327).

Application to young offenders and to children detained without limit of time

6.—(1) This Part of this Act applies—
(a) to persons on whom detention in a young offenders institution (other than detention without limit of time or for life) has been imposed under section 207(2) of the 1995 Act as the Part applies to persons serving equivalent sentences of imprisonment; and
(b) to—
    [1](i) persons sentenced under section 205(1) to (3) of that Act to be detained without limit of time or for life;
    [1](ii) children sentenced to be detained without limit of time under section 208 of that Act; and
    (iii) persons on whom detention without limit of time or for life is imposed under section 207(2) of that Act,
as the Part applies to persons sentenced to imprisonment for life, and references in the Part (except in this section, sections 1(8) and 5(1) and paragraph 1(b) of Schedule 1) to prisoners (whether short-term, long-term or life) or to prison, imprisonment or sentences of imprisonment shall be construed accordingly.

[1](2) A child detained without limit of time under section 208 of the 1975 Act may, on the recommendation of the Parole Board made at any time, be released on licence by the Secretary of State.

(3) The Secretary of State may, after consultation with the Parole Board, by order provide that, in relation to all children detained without limit of time under section 208 of the 1995 Act or to such class of those children as may be specified in the order, this section shall have effect subject to the modification that, in subsection (2), for the word "may" there shall be substituted the word "shall".

NOTE
[1]As amended by the 1995 C.P. Act, Sched. 4.

Children detained in solemn proceedings

[4]**7.**—[1](1) Where a child is detained under section 208 of the 1995 Act (detention of children convicted on indictment) and the period specified in the sentence—
(a) is less than four years, he shall be released on licence by the Secretary of State as soon as (following commencement of the sentence) half the period so specified has elapsed;

(b) is of four or more years, he shall be so released as soon as (following such commencement) two thirds of the period so specified has elapsed unless he has before that time been so released, in relation to that sentence, under any provision of this Act.

(1A) The Secretary of State may by order provide—

(a) that the reference to—

(i) four years, in paragraph (a) of subsection (1) above; or

(ii) four or more years, in paragraph (b) of that subsection, shall be construed as a reference to such other period as may be specified in the order;

(b) that the reference to—

(i) half, in the said paragraph (a); or

(ii) two thirds, in the said paragraph (b),

shall be construed as a reference to such other proportion of the period specified in the sentence as may be specified in the order.

(1B) An order under subsection (1A) above may make such transitional provision as appears to the Secretary of State necessary or expedient in connection with any provision made by the order.

[1](2) A child detained under section 208 of the 1995 Act or in pursuance of an order under subsection (3) below may, on the recommendation of the Parole Board made at any time, be released on licence by the Secretary of State.

[4](2A) This subsection applies where a child detained under section 208 of the 1995 Act is sentenced, while so detained, to a determinate term of detention in a young offenders institution or imprisonment and, by virtue of section 27(5) of this Act, such terms of detention or imprisonment are treated as single term.

[4](2B) In a case where subsection (2A) applies and the single term mentioned in that subsection is less than four years, the provisions of this section shall apply.

[4](2C) In a case where subsection (2A) applies and the single term mentioned in that subsection is of four or more years—

(a) section 6 of this Act shall apply to him as if the single term were an equivalent sentence of detention in a young offenders institution, if that term is served in such an institution; and

(b) the provisions of this Act shall apply to him as if the single term were an equivalent sentence of imprisonment, if that term is served in a remand centre or a prison.

(3) If, after release under subsection (1) or (2) above and before the date on which the entire period specified in the sentence elapses (following commencement of the sentence), a child commits an offence in respect of which it is competent to impose imprisonment on a person aged 21 years or more (other than an offence in respect of which imprisonment for life is mandatory) and, whether before or after that date, pleads guilty to or is found guilty of it a court may, instead of or in addition to making any other order in respect of that plea or finding—

(a) in a case other than that mentioned in paragraph (b) below, order that he be returned to detention for the whole or any part of the period which—

(i) begins with the date of the order for his return; and

(ii) is equal in length to the period between the date on which the new offence was committed and the date on which that entire period so elapses; and

(b) in a case where that court is inferior to the court which imposed the sentence, refer the case to the superior court in question; and a court to which a case is so referred may make such order with regard to it as is mentioned in paragraph (a) above.

(4) The period for which a child is ordered under subsection (3) above to be returned to detention—

(a) shall be taken to be a sentence of detention for the purposes of this Act and of any appeal; and

(b) shall, as the court making that order may direct, either be served before and be followed by, or be served concurrently with, any sentence imposed for the new offence (being in either case disregarded in determining the appropriate length of that sentence).

[4](4A) Where an order under subsection (3) above is made, the making of the order shall, if there is in force a licence relating to the person in respect of whom the order is made, have the effect of revoking that licence.

[5](5) Without prejudice to section 6(1)(b)(ii) of this Act, section 3, 11(1), 12, 17 and 20(2) of this Act apply to children detained under section 208 of the 1995 Act as they apply to long-term prisoners; and references in those sections of this Act to prisoners, or to prison, imprisonment or sentences of imprisonment shall be construed and sections 1A and 27 shall apply accordingly.

(6) The Secretary of State may, after consultation with the Parole Board, by order provide that, in relation to all children detained under section 208 of the 1995 Act or to such class of those children as may be specified in the order, this section shall have effect subject to the modification that, in subsection (2), for the word "may" there shall be substituted the word "shall".

(7) In the foregoing provisions of this section any reference to a child being detained does not include a reference to his being detained without limit of time.

NOTES

[1]As amended by the 1995 C.P. Act, Sched. 4.

[2]As amended by the Criminal Justice and Public Order Act 1994 (c. 33), s.130.

[3]As amended by the 1995 C.P. Act, Sched. 4 and by the Criminal Justice Act 1993 (c. 36), s.75.

[4]Inserted by the Crime and Disorder Act 1998 (c. 37), Sched. 8, para. 101 (effective September 30, 1998: S.I. 1998 No. 2327).

[5]As amended by the above Act, Sched. 8, para. 101(d) (effective September 30, 1998: S.I. 1998 No. 2327).

Children detained in summary proceedings

8. [Repealed by the 1995 C.P. Act, Sched. 5.]

Persons liable to removal from the United Kingdom

9.—(1) In relation to a long-term prisoner who is liable to removal from the United Kingdom, section 1(3) of this Act shall have effect as if the words ", if recommended to do so by the Parole Board," were omitted.

(2) In relation to a person who is liable to removal from the United Kingdom, section 12 of this Act shall have effect as if subsection (2) were omitted.

(3) For the purposes of this section, a person is liable to removal from the United Kingdom if he—

(a) is liable to deportation under section 3(5) of the Immigration Act 1971 and has been notified of a decision to make a deportation order against him;

(b) is liable to deportation under section 3(6) of that Act;

(c) has been notified of a decision to refuse him leave to enter the United Kingdom; or

(d) is an illegal immigrant within the meaning of section 33(1) of that Act.

Life prisoners transferred to Scotland

10.—[3](1) In a case where a transferred life prisoner transferred from England and Wales (whether before or after the commencement of this enactment) is a life prisoner to whom section 28 of the Crime (Sentences) Act 1997 (duty to release certain life prisoners) applies, this Part of this Act except sections 1(4) and 2(9) shall apply as if—

(a) the prisoner were a designated life prisoner within the meaning of section 2 of this Act; and

(b) the designated part of his sentence within the meaning of that section were the relevant part specified in an order or direction made under the said section 28.

[1](2) In the case of any other transferred life prisoner, except such case as is mentioned in paragraph 7 of Schedule 6 to this Act, subsection (3) below applies where the Lord Justice General, whom failing the Lord Justice Clerk, certifies his opinion that, if the prisoner had been sentenced for his offence in Scotland after the commencement of section 2 of this Act, the court by which he was so sentenced would have ordered that that section should apply to him as soon as he had served a part of his sentence specified in the certificate.

(3) In a case to which this subsection applies, this Part of this Act except sections 1(4) and 2(9) shall apply as if—

[4](a) the transferred life prisoner were a designated life prisoner within the meaning of section 2 of this Act; and

[4](b) the designated part of his sentence within the meaning of that section were the part specified in the certificate.

(4) In this section "transferred life prisoner" means a person—

[1,2](a) on whom a court in a country or territory outside Scotland or a court-martial, has or in the case of a sentence imposed by a court-martial in Scotland to a prison in Scotland (in either case whether before or after the commencement of this section) imposed one or more sentences of imprisonment or detention for an indeterminate period; and

[1,2,5](b) who has been transferred to Scotland (whether before or after the commencement of this section), in pursuance of—

(i) an order made by the Secretary of State under paragraph 1 of Schedule 1 to the Crime (Sentences) Act 1997 or section 2 of the Colonial Prisoners Removal Act 1884; or

(ii) a warrant issued by the Secretary of State under the Repatriation of Prisoners Act 1984,

(iii) rules made under section 122(1)(a) of the Army Act 1955 (imprisonment and detention rules); or

(iv) rules made under section 122(1)(a) of the Air Force Act 1955 (imprisonment and detention rules); or

(v) a determination made under section 81(3) of the Naval Discipline Act 1957 (place of imprisonment or detention)

there to serve, or to serve the remainder of, his sentence or sentences; and in this subsection "prison" has the same meaning as in the 1989 Act.

(5) Where a transferred life prisoner has been transferred to Scotland to serve the whole or part of two or more sentences referred to in subsection (4)(a) above—

[4](a) he shall be treated as a designated life prisoner (within the meaning of section 2 of this Act) for the purposes of subsection (3) above only if

the requirements of subsection (2) above are satisfied in respect of each of those sentences; and

[4](b) notwithstanding the terms of any order under the said section 28 of the Crime (Sentences) Act 1997 or of any certificate under subsection (2) above, subsections (4) and (6) of section 2 of this Act shall not apply to him until he has served the relevant part of each of those sentences.

NOTES

[1]As amended by the Criminal Justice Act 1993 (c. 36), s.76.

[2]As amended by the Criminal Justice and Public Order Act 1994 (c. 33), s.133.

[3]As substituted by the 1997 Punishment Act, Sched. 1, para. 14(8) (effective October 20, 1997: S.I. No. 2323).

[4]As amended by the 1997 Punishment Act, Sched. 1, para. 14(8) (effective October 20, 1997: S.I. No. 2323).

[5]As amended by the Crime (Sentences) Act 1997, Sched. 4 (effective October 1, 1997: S.I. 1997 No. 2200).

Duration of licence

11.—(1) Where a long-term prisoner is released on licence under this Part of this Act, the licence shall (unless revoked) remain in force until the entire period specified in his sentence (reckoned from the commencement of the sentence) has elapsed.

(2) Where a life prisoner is so released, the licence shall (unless revoked) remain in force until his death.

[2](3) [*Repealed by the 1998 Act, Sched. 8, para. 102.*]

[2](4) [*As above.*]

NOTES

[1]As amended by the 1995 C.P. Act, Sched. 4; and as amended by S.I. 1995 No. 911.

[2]Repeal of subss. (3) and (4) by the Crime and Disorder Act 1998 (c. 37), Sched. 8, para. 102 (effective September 30, 1998: S.I. 1998 No. 2327).

Conditions in licence

12.—(1) A person released on licence under this Part of this Act shall comply with such conditions as may be specified in that licence by the Secretary of State.

(2) Without prejudice to the generality of subsection (1) above and to the power of the Secretary of State under subsection (3) below to vary or cancel any condition, a licence granted under this Part of this Act shall include a condition requiring that the person subject to it—

[4](a) shall be under the supervision of a relevant officer of such local authority, or of an officer of a local probation board appointed for or assigned to such petty sessions area, as may be specified in the licence; and

(b) shall comply with such requirements as that officer may specify for the purposes of the supervision.

[3](3) The Secretary of State may from time to time under subsection (1) above insert, vary or cancel a condition in a licence granted under this Part of this Act; but in the case of a long-term or life prisoner no licence condition shall be included on release or subsequently inserted, varied or cancelled except—

[1,2](a) in the case of the inclusion or subsequent insertion, variation or cancellation of a condition in the licence of a long-term or designated life prisoner, in accordance with the recommendations of the Parole Board; and

(b) in any other case, after consulting the Board.

(4) For the purposes of subsection (3) above, the Secretary of State shall be treated as having consulted the Parole Board about a proposal to include, insert, vary or cancel a condition in any case if he has consulted the Board about the implementation of proposals of that description generally or in that class of case.

NOTES

[1]As amended by the Criminal Justice and Public Order 1994 (c. 33), s.131.

[2,3]As amended by the 1997 Punishment Act, Sched. 1, para. 14(10)(b); prospective amendment by the 1997 Punishment Act, Sched. 1, para. 14(10)(a).

[4]As amended by the Criminal Justice and Court Services Act 2000 (c. 43), s.74 and Sched. 7, para. 4. Brought into force by the Criminal Justice and Court Services Act 2000 (Commencement No. 4) Order 2001 (S.I. 2001 No. 919 (C. 33)), art. 2(f)(i) (effective April 1, 2001).

Supervision of persons released on licence

13. The Secretary of State may make rules for regulating the supervision of any description of person released, under this Part of this Act, on licence.

Supervised release of short-term prisoners

14.—(1) [*Repealed by the 1995 C.P. Act, Sched. 5.*]

(2) [*Repealed by the 1998 Act, Sched. 8, para. 103* (effective September 30, 1998: S.I. 1998 No. 2327).]

(3) [*As above.*]

[2](4) The Secretary of State shall, not later than thirty days before the date of release of a short-term prisoner who is subject to a supervised release order, designate—

(a) the local authority for the area where the prisoner proposes to reside after release;

(b) the local authority for the area where the place from which he is to be released is situated; or

(c) the justices for the petty sessions area where he proposes to reside after release,

as the appropriate authority or, as the case may be, justices for the purposes of the order.

(5) As soon as practicable after designating a local authority or justices under subsection (4) above the Secretary of State shall—

(a) inform the prisoner in writing of the designation; and

[1,3](b) send to the authority or, as the case may be, to the clerk to the justices a copy of the supervised release order and of the relevant documents and information received by the Secretary of State by virtue of section 209(6)(b) of the 1995 Act.

NOTES

[1]As amended by the 1995 C.P. Act, Sched. 4.

[2]As amended by the 1997 Punishment Act, Sched. 1, para. 14(11)(a).

[3]Prospectively amended by the Access to Justice 1999 (c. 22), s.90 and Sched. 13, para. 170.

Variation of supervised release order etc.

15.—(1) A person released subject to a supervised release order, or his supervising officer, may request the Secretary of State that a local authority or the justices for a petty sessions area (in this section referred to as the "second" designee) be designated under this subsection as the appropriate authority or justices for the purposes of the order in place of that or those for the time being designated under section 14(4) of this Act or this subsection (the "first" designee) if the person resides or proposes to reside in the area of the second designee.

(2) The Secretary of State shall, if he designates the second designee in accordance with the request, determine the date from which the designation shall have effect.

(3) As soon as practicable after a designation is made under subsection (1) above—

(a) the Secretary of State shall—

(i) inform the person subject to the supervised release order, the first designee and the second designee that the designation has been made and of the date determined under subsection (2) above; and

(ii) send a copy of the supervised release order to the second designee; and

(b) the first designee shall send to the second designee the relevant documents and information received by the first designee by virtue of section 14(5)(b) of this Act (or by virtue of this paragraph).

[1](4) The court which made a supervised release order may, on an application under this subsection by a person subject to the order (whether or not he has been released before the application is made) or by his supervising officer (or, if the person is not yet released, but a local authority stands or justices stand designated as the appropriate authority or justices in respect of the order, by a relevant officer of that authority or, as the case may be, an officer of a local probation board appointed for or assigned to the petty sessions area)—

(a) amend, vary or cancel any requirement specified in or by virtue of the order;

(b) insert in the order a requirement specified for the purpose mentioned in section 209(3)(b) of the 1995 Act,

whether or not such amendment, variation, cancellation or insertion accords with what is sought by the applicant; but the period during which the person is to be under supervision shall not thereby be increased beyond any period which could have been specified in making the order.

(5) If an application under subsection (4) above is by the supervising officer (or other relevant officer or probation officer) alone, the court shall cite the person who is subject to the order to appear before the court and shall not proceed under that subsection until it has explained to the person, in as straightforward a way as is practicable, the effect of any proposed amendment, variation, cancellation or insertion.

(6) The clerk of the court by which an amendment, variation, cancellation or insertion is made under subsection (4) above shall forthwith send a copy of the resultant order to the person subject to it and to the supervising officer.

NOTE
[1]As amended by the Criminal Justice and Court Services Act 2000 (c. 43), s.74 and Sched. 7, para. 4. Brought into force by the Criminal Justice and Court Services Act 2000 (Commencement No. 4) Order 2001 (S.I. 2001 No. 919 (C. 33)), art. 2(f)(i) (effective April 1, 2001).

Commission of offence by released prisoner

16.—[3](1) This section applies to a short-term or long-term prisoner sentenced to a term of imprisonment (in this section referred to as "the original sentence") by a court in Scotland and released at any time under this Part of this Act or Part II of the Criminal Justice Act 1991 if—

(a) before the date on which he would (but for his release) have served his sentence in full, he commits an offence punishable with imprisonment (other than an offence in respect of which imprisonment for life is mandatory); and

(b) whether before or after that date, he pleads guilty to or is found guilty of that offence (in this section referred to as "the new offence") in a court in Scotland or England and Wales.

(2) Where the court mentioned in subsection (1)(b) above is in Scotland it may, instead of or in addition to making any other order in respect of the plea or finding—

(a) in a case other than that mentioned in paragraph (b) below, order the person to be returned to prison for the whole or any part of the period which—

(i) begins with the date of the order for his return; and

(ii) is equal in length to the period between the date on which the new offence was committed and the date mentioned in subsection (1)(a) above; and

(b) in a case where that court is inferior to the court which imposed the sentence mentioned in the said subsection (1)(a), refer the case to the superior court in question; and a court to which a case is so referred may make such order with regard to it as is mentioned in paragraph (a) above.

(3) Where the court mentioned in subsection (1)(b) above is in England and Wales it may, instead of or in addition to making any other order in respect of the plea or finding, refer the case to the court which imposed the original sentence and shall, if it does so, send to that court such particulars of that case as may be relevant.

(4) The court to which a case is referred under subsection (3) above may make such an order as is mentioned in subsection (2)(a) above in respect of the person.

(5) The period for which a person to whom this section applies is ordered under subsection (2) or (4) above to be returned to prison—

(a) shall be taken to be a sentence of imprisonment for the purposes of this Act and of any appeal; and

(b) shall, as the court making that order may direct, either be served before and be followed by, or be served concurrently with, any sentence of imprisonment imposed for the new offence (being in either case disregarded in determining the appropriate length of that sentence).

[1](6) In exercising its powers under section 118(4) or 189(1) and (2) of the 1995 Act, the court hearing an appeal against an order under subsection (2) or (4) above may, if it thinks fit and notwithstanding subsection (2)(a), substitute for the period specified in the order a period not exceeding the period between the date on which the person was released and the date mentioned in subsection (1)(a) above.

[2](7) Where an order under subsection (2) or (4) above is made in respect of a person released on licence—

[3](a) the making of the order shall, if the licence is in force when the order is made, have the effect of revoking the licence;

(b) [*Repealed by the 1998 Act, Sched. 8, para. 104(3).*]

[4](8) Where a prisoner has been sentenced to two or more terms of imprisonment which are wholly or partly concurrent and do not fall to be treated as a single term by virtue of section 27(5) of this Act, the date mentioned in subsection (1)(a) above shall be taken to be that on which he would (but for his release) have served all of the sentences in full.

NOTES
[1]As amended by the 1995 C.P. Act, Sched. 4.

[2]Substituted by the 1995 C.P. Act, Sched. 4.

[3]Amended by the Crime and Disorder Act 1998 (c. 37), Sched. 8, para. 104 (effective September 30, 1998: S.I. 1998 No. 2327).

[4]Inserted by the Crime and Disorder Act 1998 (c. 37), s.111(2) (effective September 30, 1998: S.I. 1998 No. 2327).

Revocation of licence

17.—(1) Where—

[1](a) a long-term or life prisoner has been released on licence under this
Part of this Act, the Secretary of State shall revoke that licence and
recall him to prison—

(i) if recommended to do so by the Parole Board; or

(ii) if revocation and recall are, in the opinion of the Secretary of
State, expedient in the public interest and it is not practicable to await
such recommendation;

(b) a short-term prisoner has been so released, the Secretary of State may
revoke his licence and recall him to prison if satisfied that his health or
circumstances have so changed that were he in prison his release
under section 3(1) of this Act would no longer be justified.

(2) A person recalled under subsection (1) above shall, on his return to
prison, be informed of the reasons for his recall and that he has the right to
make written representations to the Secretary of State in that regard.

(3) The Secretary of State shall refer to the Parole Board the case of—

(a) a person recalled under subsection (1)(a)(i) above who makes
representations under subsection (2) above; or

(b) a person recalled under subsection (1)(a)(ii) above.

(4) Where on a reference under subsection (3) above the Parole Board
directs a prisoner's immediate release on licence, the Secretary of State shall
under this section give effect to that direction.

[2](4A) Where the case of a prisoner to whom section 3A of this Act applies
is referred to the Parole Board under subsection (3) above, subsection (4) of
that section shall apply to that prisoner in place of subsection (4) above.

(5) On the revocation of the licence of any person under the foregoing
provisions of this section, he shall be liable to be detained in pursuance of his
sentence and, if at large, shall be deemed to be unlawfully at large.

(6) A licence under this Part of this Act, other than the licence of a life
prisoner, shall be revoked by the Secretary of State if all conditions in it have
been cancelled; and where a person's licence has been revoked under this
subsection the person shall be treated in all respects as if released
unconditionally.

NOTES
[1]As amended by S.I. 1997 No. 911.
[2]Inserted by the Crime and Disorder Act 1998 (c. 37), Sched. 8, para. 105 (effective
September 30, 1998: S.I. 1998 No. 2327).

Breach of supervised release order

18.—[1](1) Where it appears to the court which imposed a supervised
release order on a person, on information from an appropriate officer, that
the person has failed to comply with a requirement specified in or by virtue
of that order, the court may—

(a) issue a warrant for the arrest of the person; or

(b) issue a citation requiring the person to appear before the court at such
time as may be specified in the citation.

(2) If it is proved to the satisfaction of the court before which a person is
brought, or appears, in pursuance of a warrant or citation issued under
subsection (1) above that there has been such failure as is mentioned in that
subsection, the court may—

(a) order him to be returned to prison for the whole or any part of the
period which—

(i) begins with the date of the order for his return; and

(ii) is equal in length to the period between the date of the first
proven failure referred to in the statement mentioned in subsection

(1) above and the date on which supervision under the supervised release order would have ceased; or

(b) do anything in respect of the supervised release order that might have been done under section 15(4) of this Act on an application under that subsection in relation to that order.

(3) For the purposes of subsection (2) above, evidence of one witness shall be sufficient evidence.

(4) As soon as the period for which a person is ordered under subsection (2) above to be returned to prison expires, the Secretary of State shall release him unconditionally.

(5) For the purposes of this Act, any such period as is mentioned in subsection (4) above is neither a sentence nor a part of a sentence.

²(6) The following are "appropriate officers" for the purposes of subsection (1) above—

(a) the person's supervising officer;

(b) the chief social work officer of a local authority which is designated under section 14(4) or 15(1) of this Act as the appropriate authority for the purposes of the order;

(c) any officer appointed by that chief social work officer for the purposes of this section.

Notes
¹As amended by the 1995 Justice Act, Sched. 6, para. 179(4).
²As amended by the Local Government etc. (Scotland) Act 1994 (c. 39), Sched. 13.

Appeals in respect of decisions relating to supervised release orders

19.—(1) Within two weeks after a determination by a court—

(a) on an application under section 15(4); or

(b) under section 18(2),

of this Act, or within such longer period as the High Court may allow, the person subject to the supervised release order may lodge a written note of appeal with the Clerk of Justiciary, who shall send a copy to the court which made the determination and to the Secretary of State.

(2) A note of appeal under subsection (1) above shall be as nearly as possible in such form as may be prescribed by Act of Adjournal and shall contain a full statement of all the grounds of appeal; and except by leave of the High Court on cause shown it shall not be competent for an appellant to found any aspect of his appeal on a ground not contained in the note of appeal.

The Parole Board for Scotland

20.—(1) There shall continue to be a body to be known as the Parole Board for Scotland, which shall discharge the functions conferred on it by, or by virtue of, this Part of this Act.

(2) It shall be the duty of the Board to advise the Secretary of State with respect to any matter referred to it by him which is connected with the early release or recall of prisoners.

(3) The Secretary of State may, after consultation with the Board, by order provide that, in relation to such class of case as may be specified in the order, this Act shall have effect subject to the modifications that—

¹(a) in subsection (3) of section 1, for the word "may" there shall be substituted the word "shall" so however that nothing in this paragraph shall affect the operation of that subsection as it has effect in relation to a long-term prisoner who is liable to removal from the United Kingdom (within the meaning of section 9 of this Act);

(b) in section 12—

(i) in subsection (3)(a), after the words "licence of a" there shall be inserted the words "long-term or"; and

(ii) subsection (4) shall be omitted; and

(c) in section 17(1)(a), for the word "may" there shall be substituted the word "shall".

[1](4) The Secretary of State may by rules make provision with respect to the proceedings of the Board, including provision—

(a) authorising cases to be dealt with in whole or in part by a prescribed number of members of the Board in accordance with such procedure as may be prescribed;

(b) requiring cases to be dealt with at prescribed times; and

(c) as to what matters may be taken into account by the Board (or by such number) in dealing with a case,

and rules under this section may make different provision for different classes of prisoner.

(5) The Secretary of State may give the Board directions as to the matters to be taken into account by it in discharging its functions under this Part of this Act; and in giving any such directions the Secretary of State shall in particular have regard to—

(a) the need to protect the public from serious harm from offenders; and

(b) the desirability of preventing the commission by offenders of further offences and of securing their rehabilitation.

(6) The supplementary provisions in Schedule 2 to this Act shall have effect with respect to the Board.

NOTE

[1]Inserted by the Crime and Disorder Act 1998 (c. 37), Sched. 8, para. 106 (effective September 30, 1998: S.I. 1998 No. 2327).

Parole advisers

21.—(1) The Secretary of State may appoint under this section persons (to be known as "parole advisers") to give advice to prisoners, or former prisoners, who wish to make representations to the Secretary of State or to the Parole Board as regards any matter concerning their release on licence under this Part of this Act or their return to prison or detention by virtue of this Part of this Act.

(2) The Secretary of State shall pay to parole advisers such remuneration and allowances as he may with the consent of the Treasury determine.

Miscellaneous

Place of confinement of prisoners

22. For section 10 of the 1989 Act (place of confinement of prisoners) there shall be substituted the following section—

"Place of confinement of prisoners

10.—(1) A prisoner may be lawfully confined in any prison.

(2) Prisoners shall be committed to such prisons as the Secretary of State may from time to time direct, and may be moved by the Secretary of State from any prison to any other prison.

(3) The foregoing provisions of this section are without prejudice to section 11 of this Act and section 241 of the 1995 Act (transfer of prisoner in connection with hearing of appeal).".

Transfer of young offenders to prison or remand centre

23. After section 20 of the 1989 Act there shall be inserted the following section—

"Transfer of young offenders to prison or remand centre

20A.—(1) Subject to section 21 of this Act, an offender sentenced to detention in a young offenders institution shall be detained in such an institution unless a direction under subsection (2) below is in force in relation to him.

(2) The Secretary of State may from time to time direct that an offender sentenced to detention in a young offenders institution shall be detained in a prison or remand centre instead of in a young offenders institution, but if the offender is under 18 years of age at the time of the direction, only for a temporary purpose.

(3) Where an offender is detained in a prison or remand centre by virtue of subsection (2) above, any rules under section 39 of this Act which apply in relation to persons detained in that place shall apply to that offender; but subject to the foregoing and to subsection (4) below, the provisions of the 1995 Act, the Prisoners and Criminal Proceedings (Scotland) Act 1993 and this Act relating to the treatment and supervision of persons sentenced to detention in a young offenders institution shall continue to apply to the offender.

(4) Where an offender referred to in subsection (3) above attains the age of 21 years, subsection (3) of section 21 of this Act shall apply to him as if he had been transferred to prison under that section.".

Additional days for disciplinary offences

24. The following subsection shall be added at the end of section 39 of the 1989 Act (rules for the management of prisons and other institutions)—

"(7) Rules made under this section may provide for the award of additional days, not exceeding in aggregate one-sixth of the prisoner's sentence—

   (a) to a short-term or long-term prisoner within the meaning of Part I of the Prisoners and Criminal Proceedings (Scotland) Act 1993; or

   (b) conditionally on his eventually becoming such a prisoner, to a person remanded in custody,

where he is guilty, under such rules, of a breach of discipline.".

Provision in prison rules for directions

25. The following subsections shall be added at the end of section 39 of the 1989 Act (rules for the management of prisons and other institutions) after the subsection added by section 24 of this Act—

"(8) Without prejudice to any power to make standing orders or to issue directions or any other kind of instruction, rules made under this section may authorise the Secretary of State to supplement the rules by making provision by directions for any purpose specified in the rules; and rules so made or directions made by virtue of this subsection may authorise the governor, or any other officer, of a prison, or some other person or class of persons specified in the rules or directions, to exercise a discretion in relation to the purpose so specified.

(9) Rules made under this section may permit directions made by virtue of subsection (8) above to derogate (but only to such extent, or in such manner, as may be specified in the rules) from provisions of rules so made and so specified.

(10) Any reference, however expressed, in any enactment other than this section to rules made under this section shall be construed as including a reference to directions made by virtue of subsection (8) above.

(11) Directions made by virtue of subsection (8) above shall be published by the Secretary of State in such manner as he considers appropriate.".

Further amendment of Mental Health (Scotland) Act 1984

26. In section 73 of the Mental Health (Scotland) Act 1984, subsection (3) (which provides for the continued detention in hospital of persons moved there by virtue of a transfer order while awaiting trial etc. even where that order has ceased to have effect) shall cease to have effect.

Extended sentences

Extended sentences

[1]**26A.**—(1) This section applies to a prisoner who, on or after the date on which section 87 of the Crime and Disorder Act 1998 comes into force, has been made subject to an extended sentence within the meaning of section 210A of the 1995 Act (extended sentences).

(2) Subject to the provisions of this section, this Part of this Act, except section 1A, shall apply in relation to extended sentences as if any reference to a sentence or term of imprisonment was a reference to the custodial term of an extended sentence.

(3) Where a prisoner subject to an extended sentence is released on licence under this Part the licence shall, subject to any revocation under section 17 of this Act, remain in force until the end of the extension period.

(4) Where, apart from this subsection, a prisoner subject to an extended sentence would be released unconditionally—

(a) he shall be released on licence; and
(b) the licence shall, subject to any revocation under section 17 of this Act, remain in force until the end of the extension period.

(5) The extension period shall be taken to begin as follows—

(a) for the purposes of subsection (3) above, on the day following the date on which, had there been no extension period, the prisoner would have ceased to be on licence in respect of the custodial term;
(b) for the purposes of subsection (4) above, on the date on which, apart from that subsection, he would have been released unconditionally.

(6) Subject to section 1A(c) of this Act and section 210A(3) of the 1995 Act and to any direction by the court which imposes an extended sentence, where a prisoner is subject to two or more extended sentences, the extension period which is taken to begin in accordance with subsection (5) above shall be the aggregate of the extension period of each of those sentences.

(7) For the purposes of sections 12(3) and 17(1) of this Act, and subject to subsection (8) below, the question whether a prisoner is a long-term or short-term prisoner shall be determined by reference to the extended sentence.

(8) Where a short-term prisoner serving an extended sentence in respect of a sexual offence is released on licence under subsection (4)(a) above, the provisions of section 17 of this Act shall apply to him as if he was a long-term prisoner.

(9) In relation to a prisoner subject to an extended sentence, the reference in section 17(5) of this Act to his sentence shall be construed as a reference to the extended sentence.

(10) For the purposes of this section "custodial term", "extension period" and "imprisonment" shall have the same meaning as in section 210A of the 1995 Act.

(11) In section 1A(c) and section 16(1)(a) of this Act, the reference to the date on which a prisoner would have served his sentence in full shall mean, in relation to a prisoner subject to an extended sentence, the date on which the extended sentence, as originally imposed by the court, would expire.

NOTE
[1]Inserted by the Crime and Disorder Act 1998 (c. 37), s.87 (effective September 30, 1998: S.I. 1998 No. 2327).

Interpretation of Part I

27.—(1) In this Part of this Act, except where the context otherwise requires—

"court" does not include a court-martial;

"discretionary life prisoner" has the meaning given by section 2 of this Act;

"life prisoner" means a person serving a sentence of imprisonment for life;

[1]"local authority" means a council constituted under section 2 of the Local Government etc. (Scotland) Act 1994;

[6]"local probation board" means a local probation board established under section 4 of the Criminal Justice and Court Services Act 2000;

"long-term prisoner" means a person serving a sentence of imprisonment for a term of four years or more;

"Parole Board" means the Parole Board for Scotland;

[3]"petty sessions area" has the same meaning as in the Justices of the Peace Act 1997;

"relevant officer", in relation to a local authority, means an officer of that authority employed by them in the discharge of their functions under section 27(1) of the Social Work (Scotland) Act 1968 (supervision and care of persons put on probation or released from prison etc.);

"short-term prisoner" means a person serving a sentence of imprisonment for a term of less than four years;

[2]"supervised release order" has the meaning given by section 209 (as inserted by section 14 of this Act) of the 1995 Act but includes any order under subsection (2) of the said section 14; and

[2]"supervising officer" has the meaning given by the said section 209.

(2) The Secretary of State may by order provide—

(a) that the references to four years in the definitions of "long-term prisoner" and "short-term prisoner" in subsection (1) above shall be construed as references to such other period as may be specified in the order;

(b) that any reference in this Part of this Act to a particular proportion of a prisoner's sentence shall be construed as a reference to such other proportion of a prisoner's sentence as may be so specified.

(3) An order under subsection (2) above may make such transitional provisions as appear to the Secretary of State necessary or expedient in connection with any provision made by the order.

(4) For the purposes of this Part of this Act so far as relating to licences or persons released on licence, the age of any person at the time when sentence was passed on him shall be deemed to have been that which appears to the Secretary of State to have been his age at that time.

[4](5) For the purposes of any reference, however expressed, in this Part of this Act to the term of imprisonment or other detention to which a person has been sentenced or which, or any part of which, he has served, consecutive terms and terms which are wholly or partly concurrent shall be treated as a single term if—

(a) the sentences were passed at the same time; or

(b) where the sentences were passed at different times, the person has not been released under this Part of this Act at any time during the period beginning with passing of the first sentence and ending with the passing of the last.

(6) If additional days are awarded in accordance with rules made under

section 39(7) of the 1989 Act (and are not remitted in accordance with such rules), the period which the prisoner (or eventual prisoner) must serve before becoming entitled to or eligible for release shall be extended by those additional days.

(7) Where (but for this subsection) a prisoner would, under any provision of this Act or of the 1995 Act, fall to be released on or by a day which is a Saturday, Sunday or public holiday he shall instead be released on or by the last preceding day which is not a Saturday, Sunday or public holiday.

[5](8) For the purposes of this section "public holiday" means any day on which, in the opinion of the Secretary of State, public offices or other facilities likely to be of use to the prisoner in the area in which he is likely to be following his discharge from prison will be closed.

NOTES
[1]As amended by the Local Government etc. (Scotland) Act 1994 (c. 39), Sched. 13.
[2]As amended by the 1995 C.P. Act, Sched. 4.
[3]As amended by the Justices of the Peace Act 1997 (c. 25), s.73(2) and Sched. 5, para. 33.
[4]Substituted by the Crime and Disorder Act 1998 (c. 37), s.111(3) (effective September 30, 1998: S.I. 1998 No. 2327).
[5]Inserted by above Act, s.119 and Schedule 8, para. 107 (effective September 30, 1998: S.I. 1998 No. 2327).
[6] Inserted by the Criminal Justice and Court Services Act 2000 (c. 43), s.74 and Sched. 7, para. 118. Brought into force by the Criminal Justice and Court Services Act 2000 (Commencement No. 4) Order 2001 (S.I. 2001 No. 919 (C. 33)), art. 2(f)(ii) (effective April 1, 2001).

PART II

CRIMINAL PROCEEDINGS

Evidence

Prints, samples etc. in criminal investigations
28.—[Repealed by the 1995 C.P. Act, Sched. 5].

Evidence from documents
29. [Repealed by the 1995 C.P. Act, Sched. 5.]

Admissibility of audio and video records
30.—[Repealed by the 1995 C.P. Act, Sched. 5.]

Transcript of customs interview sufficient evidence
31. [Repealed by the 1995 C.P. Act, Sched. 5.]

Evidence from abroad through television links in solemn proceedings
32. [Repealed by the 1995 C.P. Act, Sched. 5.]

Evidence of children on commission
33. [Repealed by the 1995 C.P. Act, Sched. 5.]

Concealment by screen of accused from child giving evidence
34. [Repealed by the 1995 C.P. Act, Sched. 5.]

Circumstances in which application under section 33 or 34 may be granted or on transfer be deemed granted, etc.

35. [Repealed by the 1995 C.P. Act, Sched. 5.]

Evidence as to taking or destruction of eggs

36. After section 19 of the Wildlife and Countryside Act 1981 there shall be inserted the following section—

"Evidence in Scotland as to taking or destruction of eggs
19A. In any proceedings in Scotland for an offence under section 1(1)(c) of, or by virtue of section 3(1)(a)(iii) of, this Act, the accused may be convicted on the evidence of one witness.".

Evidence by certificate

37. [Repealed by the 1995 C.P. Act, Sched. 5.]

Procedure

Adjournment for inquiry etc. in summary proceedings at first calling

38. [Repealed by the 1995 C.P. Act, Sched. 5.]

New circumstances on notice of which preliminary diet may be ordered

39. [Repealed by the 1995 C.P. Act, Sched. 5.]

Taking of other proceedings while jury out

40. [Repealed by the 1995 C.P. Act, Sched. 5.]

Date of commencement of sentence

41. [Repealed by the 1995 C.P. Act, Sched. 5.]

Appeal by Lord Advocate against sentence in solemn proceedings etc.

42. [Repealed by the 1995 C.P. Act, Sched. 5.]

Prosecutor's consent to or application for setting aside of conviction

43. [Repealed by the 1995 C.P. Act, Sched. 5.]

PART III

GENERAL

Expenses

44. There shall be paid out of money provided by Parliament—
(a) any sums required by the Secretary of State for defraying the expenses of the Parole Board for Scotland;
(b) any expenses incurred by the Secretary of State under section 21(2) of this Act;

(c) any administrative expenses incurred by the Secretary of State under this Act; and

(d) any increase attributable to this Act in the sums payable out of money so provided under any other Act.

Rules and orders

45.—(1) The power of the Secretary of State to make rules and orders under this Act shall be exercisable by statutory instrument.

(2) Any rule made under section 13 or 20(4) of this Act shall be subject to annulment in pursuance of a resolution of either House of Parliament.

[1](3) An order shall not be made under section 6(3), 7(1A) or (6), 20(3) or 27(2) of this Act unless a draft of the order has been laid before Parliament and approved by a resolution of each House of Parliament.

NOTE
[1] As amended by the Criminal Justice and Public Order Act 1994 (c. 33), s.130.

Interpretation

46. [1] In this Act—

"the 1980 Act" means the Criminal Justice (Scotland) Act 1980; and
"the 1989 Act" means the Prisons (Scotland) Act 1989.
[2] "the 1995 Act" means the Criminal Procedure (Scotland) Act 1995.

NOTES
[1] As amended by the 1995 C.P. Act, Sched. 5.
[2] As inserted by the 1995 C.P. Act, Sched. 4.

Minor and consequential amendments, transitional provisions, savings and repeals

47.—(1) The enactments mentioned in Schedule 5 to this Act shall have effect subject to the amendments there specified (being minor amendments and amendments consequential on the preceding provisions of this Act).

(2) The transitional provisions and savings contained in Schedule 6 to this Act shall have effect; but nothing in this subsection shall be taken as prejudicing the operation of sections 16 and 17 of the Interpretation Act 1978 (effect of repeals).

(3) The enactments mentioned in Part I of Schedule 7 to this Act (which include some that are spent or no longer of practical utility) are hereby repealed to the extent specified in the third column of that Part and the instruments mentioned in Part II of that Schedule are hereby revoked to the extent specified in the third column of that Part.

Short title, commencement and extent

48.—(1) This Act may be cited as the Prisoners and Criminal Proceedings (Scotland) Act 1993.

(2) Subject to subsection (4) below, this Act shall come into force on such day as the Secretary of State may by order made by statutory instrument appoint, and different days may be appointed for different provisions and for different purposes.

(3) An order under subsection (2) above may make such transitional provisions and savings as appear to the Secretary of State necessary or expedient in connection with any provision brought into force by the order.

(4) This section and, in so far as relating to paragraph 5 of Schedule 5 to this Act, section 47(1) of this Act shall come into force on the day on which this Act is passed.

(5) Subject to subsection (6) below, this Act extends to Scotland only.

(6) This section and the following provisions of this Act also extend to England and Wales—

section 12(2);

section 14(4);

section 15;

section 16(1) and (3);

section 27;

section 46; and

in section 47, subsection (1) in so far as relating to paragraphs 1(38) and 3 of Schedule 5, and subsection (3) in so far as relating to the entry in Schedule 7 in respect of the Criminal Justice Act 1991.

(7) Nothing in subsection (5) above affects the extent of this Act in so far as it amends or repeals any provision of the Army Act 1955, the Air Force Act 1955 or the Naval Discipline Act 1957.

SCHEDULES

SCHEDULE 1

Section 1(8)

CONSECUTIVE AND CONCURRENT TERMS OF IMPRISONMENT

General

1. This Schedule applies as respects the release of a person on whom there has been imposed—

(a) a term of imprisonment on conviction of an offence ("his offence term"); and

(b) a term of imprisonment or detention mentioned in section 5(1)(a) or (b) of this Act ("his non-offence term").

Consecutive terms of imprisonment

2. Where his offence term and his non-offence term are consecutive—

(a) his offence term shall be taken to precede his non-offence term;

(b) notwithstanding section 1(1) to (3) of this Act, he shall not be released when he has served the proportion of his offence term mentioned in whichever of those subsections is (or are) relevant to the term in question but when he falls to be released by virtue of the application of section 5 of this Act to his non-offence term; and

(c) his non-offence term shall be taken as beginning on the date on which he would have been released under section 1(1) to (3) but for sub-paragraph (b) above.

Wholly concurrent terms of imprisonment

3. Where his offence term and his non-offence term are wholly concurrent—

(a) only the offence term shall be taken into account for the purposes of the provisions of this Part of this Act relating to his release; but

(b) he shall not be released under section 1(3) of this Act.

Partly concurrent terms of imprisonment

4. Where his offence term and his non-offence term are partly concurrent—

(a) section 1(1) or (2), or as the case may be those provisions as modified by section 5(2), of this Act shall apply in relation to the term which is due to expire later and shall not apply to the term which is due to expire first; and

(b) if the term due to expire later is his offence term, section 1(3) of this Act shall apply in relation to it only if the person has served such proportion of his non-offence term as would, but for sub-paragraph (a) above, entitle him to release under section 1(1) or (2), as modified by section 5(2), of this Act.

NOTE

[1]Prospective repeal by the 1997 Punishment Act, Sched. 1, para. 14(17), Sched. 3.

SCHEDULE 2

Section 20(6)

THE PAROLE BOARD

Membership

1. The Parole Board shall consist of a chairman and not less than four other members appointed by the Secretary of State.
2. The Parole Board shall include among its members—
(a) a Lord Commissioner of Justiciary;
(b) a registered medical practitioner who is a psychiatrist;
(c) a person appearing to the Secretary of State to have knowledge and experience of the supervision or aftercare of discharged prisoners; and
(d) a person appearing to the Secretary of State to have made a study of the causes of delinquency or the treatment of offenders.
3. A member of the Parole Board shall hold and vacate office under the terms of the instrument by which he is appointed, but may at any time resign his office; and a person who ceases to hold office as a member of the Parole Board shall be eligible for reappointment.

Remuneration and allowances

4. There shall be paid to the members of the Board such remuneration and allowances as the Secretary of State may with the consent of the Treasury determine.
5. The expenses of the Board under paragraph 4 above and any other expenses incurred by the Board in discharging the functions mentioned in section 20(1) of this Act shall be defrayed by the Secretary of State.

Reports

6. The Board shall as soon as practicable after the end of each year make to the Secretary of State a report on the performance of its functions during that year, and the Secretary of State shall lay a copy of the report before Parliament.

SCHEDULE 3

Section 29

[Repealed by the 1995 C.P. Act, Sched. 5.]

SCHEDULE 4

Section 37

[Repealed by the 1995 C.P. Act, Sched. 5.]

SCHEDULE 5

Section 47(1)

MINOR AND CONSEQUENTIAL AMENDMENTS

Criminal Procedure (Scotland) Act 1975 (c. 21)

[Repealed by the 1995 C.P. Act, Sched. 5.]

Mental Health (Scotland) Act 1984 (c. 36)

2.—(1) Section 65 of the Mental Health (Scotland) Act 1984 (appeal to sheriff by patient in respect of whom restriction direction has been given) shall be amended as follows.

(2) In subsection (1)(b), for the words "in the event of the patient's not being released on licence or discharged under supervision under subsection (2)(b)(ii) of this section he" there shall be substituted the words "the patient".

(3) For subsection (2) there shall be substituted the following subsection—

"(2) If the sheriff notifies the Secretary of State—

(a) that the patient would be entitled to be absolutely discharged, the Secretary of State shall by warrant direct that the patient be remitted to any prison or other institution or place in which he might have been detained had he not been removed to hospital and that he shall be dealt with there as if he had not been so removed;

(b) that the patient would be entitled to be conditionally discharged, the Secretary of State may—

(i) by warrant give such direction as is mentioned in paragraph (a) above; or

(ii) decide that the patient should continue to be detained in a hospital,

and (if a direction is given under this subsection) on the person's arrival in the prison or other institution or place to which remitted by virtue of this subsection, the restriction direction, together with the transfer direction given in respect of the person, shall cease to have effect.".

Repatriation of Prisoners Act 1984 (c. 47)

3.—(1) The Repatriation of Prisoners Act 1984 shall be amended as follows.

(2) In section 2 (transfer of prisoners out of United Kingdom), in subsection (4)(b), for sub-paragraph (ii) there shall be substituted the following sub-paragraph—

"(ii) released on licence under section 1(2), (3) or (4), 2(4) or 7(1) or (2) of the Prisoners and Criminal Proceedings (Scotland) Act 1993;".

(3) In section 3 (transfer of prisoners into United Kingdom), after subsection (8) there shall be inserted the following subsection—

"(9) The provisions contained by virtue of subsection (1)(c) above in a warrant under this Act shall, in the case of a person who is a transferred life prisoner for the purposes of section 48 of the Criminal Justice Act 1991 or section 10 of the Prisoners and Criminal Proceedings (Scotland) Act 1993 (life prisoners transferred to England and Wales or, as the case may be, Scotland) include provision specifying the part of his sentence which is treated by virtue of section 48 or section 10 as the relevant part of his sentence.".

(4) In the Schedule (operation of certain enactments in relation to prisoners transferred into United Kingdom), in paragraph 2, for sub-paragraph (1) there shall be substituted the following sub-paragraphs—

"(1) In determining for the purposes of any of the enactments relating to release on licence whether the prisoner has at any time served a particular proportion or part of his sentence specified in that provision, the prisoner's sentence shall, subject to sub-paragraph (2) below, be deemed to begin with the day on which the relevant provisions take effect.

(1A) In sub-paragraph (1) above "the enactments relating to release on licence" means—

(a) sections 33(1)(b) and (2), 34(3) and (5), 35(1) and 37(1) and (2) of the Criminal Justice Act 1991; and

(b) sections 1(2) and (3), 2(2) and (7) and 7(1) of the Prisoners and Criminal Proceedings (Scotland) Act 1993.";

and the amendment made to sub-paragraph (2) of that paragraph by paragraph 35(3)(b) of Schedule 11 to the Criminal Justice Act 1991 shall extend also to Scotland.

(5) For paragraph 3 of the Schedule there shall be substituted the following paragraph—

"3. Where the relevant provisions include provision equivalent to a sentence in relation to which section 35(2) of the Criminal Justice Act 1991 or, as the case may be, section 1(4) of the Prisoners and Criminal Proceedings (Scotland) Act 1993 (power to release life prisoners who are not discretionary life prisoners) applies, section 35(2) or, as the case may be, section 1(4) shall have effect as if the reference to consulting the trial judge were omitted.".

Legal Aid (Scotland) Act 1986 (c. 47)

4. In section 21(1) of the Legal Aid (Scotland) Act 1986 (definition of "criminal legal aid"), after paragraph (a) (but before the word "and" which immediately follows that paragraph) there shall be inserted the following paragraph—

"(aa) any case the referral of which is required, under section 2(6) of the Prisoners and Criminal Proceedings (Scotland) Act 1993, by a discretionary life prisoner;".

Road Traffic Offenders Act 1988 (c. 53)

5. In section 12(4) of the Road Traffic Offenders Act 1988, as proposed to be inserted by paragraph 85 of Schedule 4 to the Road Traffic Act 1991 (proof of identity of driver in summary proceedings for certain road traffic offences), for the words "Road Traffic Act 1988" in the first place where they occur there shall be substituted the words "this Act".

Prisons (Scotland) Act 1989 (c. 45)

6.—(1) The Prisons (Scotland) Act 1989 shall be amended as follows.

(2) In section 12 (photographing and measuring of prisoners)—

(a) for the words "The Secretary of State may make regulations as to" there shall be substituted the words "Rules under section 39 of this Act may provide for"; and

(b) the words "such regulations" shall cease to have effect.

(3) In section 14(1) (legalised police cells), after the word "under" there shall be inserted the words "section 39 of".

(4) In section 19 (provisions of 1989 Act applying to remand centres and young offenders institutions)—

(a) in subsection (3), for the words "the rules" there shall be substituted the words "rules under section 39 of this Act"; and

(b) in subsection (4), in sub-paragraph (iii) of the proviso—

(i) for the words "paragraphs (i) and (ii)" there shall be substituted the words "paragraph (i)"; and

(ii) for the words "of the Secretary of State" there shall be substituted the words "under section 39 of this Act".

(5) In section 21 (transfer to prison of persons over 21 etc.)—

(a) in subsection (1), after the word "section" there shall be inserted the words "but without prejudice to section 20A(2) of this Act"; and

(b) in subsection (3), after the words "1995 Act" there shall be inserted the words "the Prisoners and Criminal Proceedings (Scotland) Act 1993".

(6) In section 39(1) (rules for the management of prisons and other institutions)—

(a) the word "and", where it occurs for the third time, shall cease to have effect; and

(b) at the end there shall be added the words "and for any other matter as respects which it is provided in this Act that rules may be made under this section".

(7) In section 40(2) (no account to be taken, in calculating period of liability to detention, of period when unlawfully at large)—

(a) after the word "institution", where it first occurs, there shall be inserted the words "or committed to a prison or remand centre";

(b) after the word "sentence" there shall be inserted the words "or committal";

(c) for the words "or young offenders institution" there shall be substituted the words ", young offenders institution or remand centre"; and

(d) after the words "so detained," there shall be inserted the words "or the date on or by which a term or period of imprisonment or detention elapses or has been served,".

(8) In section 42(2) (procedure in relation to statutory instruments containing regulations or rules), for the words from "regulations" to the end there shall be substituted the words "an order made under section 37(1) or rules made under section 39 of this Act shall be subject to annulment in pursuance of a resolution of either House of Parliament".

(9) In section 43 (interpretation)—

(a) in subsection (1), the definition of "sentence of imprisonment" shall cease to have effect; and

(b) in subsection (2), the words "(other than in section 25)" shall cease to have effect.

SCHEDULE 6

Section 47(2)

Transitional Provisions and Savings

1. In this Schedule—

"existing provisions" means such provisions as relate to the detention or release of persons and are amended or repealed by this Act, as they had effect immediately before such amendment or repeal except that an amendment or repeal effected by any enactment shall apply for the purposes of the existing provisions if expressly stated to do so;

[6]"new provisions" means sections 1 to 21 and 27 of this Act (together with the provisions of the 1975 Act and of the Mental Health (Scotland) Act 1984 which so relate and are so amended by this Act and the Repatriation of Prisoners Act 1984 as it has effect by virtue of paragraphs 6 and 7 of Schedule 2 to the Crime (Sentences) Act 1997);

"existing child detainee" means any child ("child" having the meaning assigned to that expression by section 30 of the Social Work (Scotland) Act 1968) who, at the relevant date, is detained under section 206 of the 1975 Act other than without limit of time or is detained in residential care by virtue of section 413 of the 1995 Act;

"existing licensee" means any person who, before the relevant date, has been released on licence under the 1989 Act;

[1]"existing life prisoner" means any person (other than a transferred life prisoner) who, at the relevant date, is serving—
  (a) a sentence of imprisonment for life;
  (b) a sentence of detention without limit of time or for life under section 205 of the 1995 Act;
  (c) a sentence of detention without limit of time under section 206 of that Act; or
  (d) a period of detention without limit of time or for life under section 207(2) of that Act;

"existing prisoner" means any person who, at the relevant date, is serving—
  (a) a sentence of imprisonment; or
  (b) a sentence of detention in a young offenders institution; and

[6]"relevant date" means the date of commencement of the new provisions.

2.—(1) Subject to sub-paragraph (2), to the following provisions of this Schedule and to the exception in the definition of "existing provisions" in paragraph 1 above, the existing provisions shall continue to apply to persons sentenced (or on whom detention has been imposed) before that date.

[2](2) Section 3 of this Act, and sections 12 and 17 of this Act in so far as relating to a licence granted, or person released, by virtue of this sub-paragraph, shall apply irrespective of the date on which a person is sentenced (or on which detention is imposed on him).

3. An existing prisoner whose sentence is for a term of less than two years and who, by the relevant date, has served—
  (a) one-half or more of that sentence, shall be released unconditionally by the Secretary of State on that date;
  (b) less than one-half of that sentence, shall be so released as soon as he has served one-half of that sentence.

4.—(1) An existing child detainee whose sentence under section 206 of the 1995 Act is for a period—
  (a) of less than four years and who, by the relevant date, has served—
    (i) one-half or more of that sentence, shall be released on licence by the Secretary of State on that date;
    (ii) less than one-half of that sentence, shall be so released as soon as he has served one-half of that sentence;
  (b) of four years or more and who, by the relevant date, has served—
    (i) two-thirds or more of that sentence, shall be released on licence by the Secretary of State on that date;
    (ii) less than two-thirds of that sentence, shall be so released as soon as he has served two-thirds of that sentence.

(2) An existing child detainee detained under section 206 of the 1995 Act may, on the recommendation of the Parole Board made at any time, be released on licence by the Secretary of State.

5.—(1) An existing child detainee who, by the relevant date, has completed—
  (a) one-half or more of a period of detention in residential care for which he has been committed, shall be released from such care on that date;
  (b) less than one-half of that period, shall be so released as soon as he has completed one-half of that period,
but until the entire such period has elapsed may be required by the appropriate local authority to submit to supervision in accordance with such conditions as they consider appropriate.

(2) Where a child released under sub-paragraph (1) above is subject to a supervision requirement within the meaning of the Social Work (Scotland) Act 1968, the effect of that requirement shall commence, or as the case may be resume, upon such release.

6.—(1) This paragraph applies where, in the case of an existing life prisoner, the Lord Justice General, whom failing the Lord Justice Clerk, after consultation with the trial judge, if available, certifies his opinion that, if section 2 of this Act had been in force at the time when the prisoner was sentenced, the court by which he was sentenced would have ordered that that section should apply to him as soon as he had served a part of his sentence specified in the certificate.

⁸(2) In a case to which this paragraph applies, sections 1 to 27 of this Act except sections 1(4) and 2(9) shall apply as if—

(a) the existing life prisoner were a designated life prisoner within the meaning of section 2 of this Act; and

(b) the designated part of his sentence within the meaning of that section were the part specified in the certificate.

⁸(3) Where a person is serving two or more sentences of imprisonment for life or detention without limit of time or for life—

(a) he shall be treated as a designated life prisoner within the meaning of section 2 of this Act only if the requirements of sub-paragraph (1) above are satisfied in respect of each of those sentences; and

(b) notwithstanding the terms of any certificate under that sub-paragraph, subsections (4) and (6) of section 2 shall not apply to him until he has served the designated part of each of those sentences.

⁷6A—(1) This paragraph applies where a prisoner sentenced before the relevant date to a sentence of imprisonment for life for an offence the sentence for which is not fixed by law has been (whether before, on or after that date) released on licence under the 1989 Act.

⁸(2) Without prejudice to section 22(6) of the 1989 Act, in a case to which this paragraph applies, the new provisions shall apply as if the prisoner were a designated life prisoner, within the meaning of section 2 of this Act, whose licence has been granted under subsection (4) of that section of this Act on his having served the designated part of his sentence.

6B—(1) This paragraph applies where—

¹⁰(a) an existing prisoner was, at the relevant date, serving a sentence or sentences of imprisonment, on conviction of an offence, passed before that date and that sentence was for a term of, or as the case may be those sentences fall to be treated as for a single term of, two or more years;

¹⁰(b) on or after the date on which section 111 of the Crime and Disorder Act 1998 comes into force he is, or has been, sentenced to a further term or terms of imprisonment, on conviction of an offence, to be served consecutively to, or concurrently with, the sentence or sentences mentioned in head (a) above; and

¹⁰(c) he has not at any time prior to the passing of the sentence or sentences mentioned in head (b) above been released from the sentence or sentences mentioned in head (a) above under the existing provisions.

(2) In a case to which this paragraph applies—

(a) the sentence or sentences mentioned in head (b) of sub-paragraph (1) above shall be treated as a single term with the sentences mentioned in head (a) of that sub-paragraph and that single term as imposed on or after the relevant date (so however that nothing in the foregoing provisions of this head shall affect the application of sections 39(7) (which makes provision as respects the award of additional days for breaches of discipline) and 24 (which makes provision as respects remission for good conduct) of the 1989 Act); and

(b) the new provisions shall apply accordingly, except that—

(i) where the prisoner is a long-term prisoner by virtue only of the aggregation provided for in head (a) of this sub-paragraph, he shall be released unconditionally on the same day as he would have been but for that aggregation;

(ii) where, notwithstanding the aggregation so provided for, the prisoner remains a short-term prisoner, subsection (1) of section 1 of this Act shall in its application be construed as subject to the qualification that the prisoner shall be released no earlier than he would have been but for that aggregation;

(iii) that section shall in its application be construed as if for subsection (3) there were substituted—

"(3) Without prejudice to subsection (1) above and to sub-paragraph (2)(b)(i) of paragraph 6B of Schedule 6 to this Act, after a prisoner to whom that paragraph applies has either served one-third of the sentence, or as the case may be sentences, mentioned in sub-paragraph (1)(a) of that paragraph, or (if it results in a later date of release) has served twelve months of that sentence or those sentences, the Secretary of State may, if recommended to do so by the Parole Board under this section, release him on licence; and where such a prisoner has been released on licence under section 22 of the 1989 Act, that licence shall be deemed to have been granted by virtue of this subsection.";

(iv) section 11(1) shall in its application be construed as if the sentence referred to were the further term or terms mentioned in head (b) of sub-paragraph (1) above; and

(v) section 16 shall in its application be construed as if the original sentence (within the meaning of that section) were the further term or terms so mentioned.

[1]6C—(1) This paragraph applies where—

(a) an existing prisoner was, at the relevant date, serving a sentence or sentences of imprisonment, on conviction of an offence, passed before that date;

(b) on or after the date on which section 111 of the Crime and Disorder Act 1998 comes into force he is, or has been, sentenced to a further term or terms of imprisonment on conviction of an offence, to be served wholly or partly concurrently with the sentence or sentences mentioned in head (a); and

(c) the sentences do not fall to be treated as a single term by virtue of paragraph 6B(2)(a) above.

(2) In a case to which this paragraph applies the Secretary of State shall not release, or be required to consider the release of, the prisoner unless and until the requirements for release, or for consideration of his release, of the new and the existing provisions are satisfied in relation to each sentence to which they respectively apply.

(3) In a case to which this paragraph applies the Parole Board shall not be required to consider the release of the prisoner unless and until the requirements for release, or for consideration for release, of the new and the existing provisions are satisfied in relation to each sentence to which they respectively apply.

(4) In a case to which this paragraph applies, where the prisoner is released on licence, he shall be on a single licence which—

(a) shall (unless revoked) remain in force until the later of—

(i) the date on which he would have been discharged from prison on remission of part of his sentence or sentences under the existing provisions if, after his release, he had not forfeited remission of any part of that sentence under those provisions; or

(ii) the date on which he would (but for his release) have served in full all the sentences in respect of which he was released on licence and which were imposed after the relevant date; and

(b) shall be deemed to be granted under the new provisions and, subject to sub-paragraph (5) below, those provisions so far as relating to conditions of licences, and recall or return to prison, shall apply as they apply in respect of a prisoner on licence in respect of a sentence passed after the relevant date.

(5) In the application of section 16 to a person whose licence is deemed to be granted under the new provisions by virtue of sub-paragraph (4)(b) above, the reference to the original sentence (within the meaning of that section) shall be construed as a reference to the further term or terms mentioned in head (b) of sub-paragraph (1) above.

(6) Subject to subsection (7) below, the amendments made by subsections (1) to (5) above apply where one or more of the sentences concerned was passed after the commencement of this section.

(7) Where the terms of two or more sentences passed before the commencement of this section have been treated, by virtue of section 27(5) of, or paragraph 6B of Schedule 6 to, the 1993 Act, as a single term for the purposes of Part I of that Act, they shall continue to be so treated after that commencement.

(8) In relation to a prisoner released on licence at any time under section 16(7)(b) of the 1993 Act, section 17(1)(a) of that Act shall have effect as if after the word "Act" there were inserted the words "or a short term prisoner has been released on licence by virtue of section 16(7)(b) of this Act.

[2]6D—(1) Where a prisoner released on licence is treated by the virtue of the provisions of this or any other enactment as a prisoner whose licence was granted under section 2(4) of this Act, the validity of his licence shall not be affected by the absence in the licence of such a condition as is specified in section 12(2) of this Act.

7. In the case of a transferred life prisoner who is a designated life prisoner for the purposes of Part II of the Criminal Justice Act 1991 by virtue of section 48 of or paragraph 9 of Schedule 12 to that Act, subsection (3) of section 10 of this Act applies and the certificate mentioned in paragraph (b) of that subsection is the certificate under the said section 48 or paragraph 9.

[4]8. Unless revoked by virtue of paragraph 10 of this Schedule, a licence under—

(a) paragraph 4(1)(a)(i) or (b)(i) above shall remain in force until at least twelve months have elapsed after the date of release and until the entire period of sentence has elapsed;

(b) paragraph 4(1)(a)(ii) or (b)(ii) above shall remain in force until a date determined by the Parole Board, being a date not later than the date by which the entire period of sentence has elapsed.

9. Section 12 of this Act shall apply in respect of a licence granted under this Schedule.

[5]10. Section 17 of this Act shall apply in respect of a release on licence under paragraph 4 of this Schedule as that section applies in respect of the release on licence, under Part I of this Act, of a long-term prisoner.

NOTES

[1]As amended by the Criminal Justice Act 1993 (c. 36), s.76.
[2]As amended by the Criminal Justice Act 1993 (c. 36), s.75.
[3]Substituted by the Criminal Justice Act 1993 (c. 36), s.76.
[4]As amended by the Criminal Justice and Public Order Act 1994 (c. 33), s.130.
[5]Inserted by the Criminal Justice and Public Order Act 1994 (c. 33), s.130.
[6]As amended by the Criminal Justice and Public Order Act 1994 (c. 33), s.134.
[7]As amended by the Criminal Justice and Public Order Act 1994 (c. 33), s.135.
[8]As amended by the 1997 Punishment Act, Sched. 1, para. 14(18).
[9]As amended by the Crimes (Sentences) Act 1997 (c. 43), Sched. 4, para. 16(2).
[10]As amended by the Crime and Disorder Act 1998 (c. 37), s.111(4) (effective September 30, 1998: S.I. 1998 No. 2327).
[11]Inserted by the Crime and Disorder Act 1998 (c. 37), s.111(5) (effective September 30, 1998: S.I. 1998 No. 2327).
[12]Inserted by the Crime and Disorder At 1998 (c. 37), s.119 and Sched. 8, para. 108 (effective September 30, 1998: S.I. 1998 No. 2327).

SCHEDULE 7

Section 47(3)

REPEALS AND REVOCATIONS

PART I

REPEALS

Chapter	Short title	Extent of repeal
1 Edw. 8 & 1 Geo. 6 c. 37.	The Children and Young Persons (Scotland) Act 1937.	In section 57(3), the words "or section 25 of the Prisons (Scotland) Act 1989".
3 & 4 Eliz 2 c. 18.	The Army Act 1955.	Section 71AA(6B). In Schedule 5A, paragraph 10(6B).
3 & 4 Eliz. 2 c. 19.	The Air Force Act 1955. Section 71AA(6B).	In Schedule 5A, paragraph 10(6B).
5 & 6 Eliz. 2 c. 53.	The Naval Discipline Act 1957.	Section 43AA(6B). In Schedule 4A, paragraph 10(6B).
1963 c. 39.	The Criminal Justice (Scotland) Act 1963.	In paragraph 13 of Schedule 1, the words "(and, if that person is released from such a prison under the said section 214(7) or 423(7), section 30(3) of the Prisons (Scotland) Act 1989)".
1965 c. 20.	The Criminal Evidence Act 1965.	The whole Act.
1969 c. 48.	The Post Office Act 1969.	Section 93(4).
1975 c. 21.	The Criminal Procedure (Scotland) Act 1975.	In section 108(2), the word "and" at the end of paragraph (b). Section 207(11). Section 212. Section 214. In section 270(2), the words "of two weeks or any extension thereof authorised by the High Court". Section 289D(1A)(e). Section 328. In section 413(1) the words "for such period, not exceeding one year, as the sheriff may determine". Section 415(11). Section 421. Section 423.

Chapter	Short title	Extent of repeal
1980 c. 55.	The Law Reform (Miscellaneous Provisions) (Scotland) Act 1980.	In part I of Schedule 1, in Group B, paragraph (v).
1980 c. 62.	The Criminal Justice (Scotland) Act 1980.	In section 2, in subsection (5), paragraph (c) and the proviso to that paragraph; and in subsection (6) the words "or (c)". In Schedule 3, paragraph 12.
1981 c. 49.	The Contempt of Court Act 1981.	Section 15(6).
1984 c. 36.	The Mental Health (Scotland) Act 1984.	In section 71, subsection (2)(b); and in subsection (7)(a), the words "in criminal proceedings". Section 73(3).
1987 c. 41.	The Criminal Justice (Scotland) Act 1987.	Section 62(1). In Schedule 1, paragraph 19.
1989 c. 45.	The Prisons (Scotland) Act 1989.	In section 12, the words "such regulations". Section 16(1). Section 18. In section 19(4), in paragraph (b), the word "24,"; and in the proviso, sub-paragraph (ii). In section 21(3), the proviso. Sections 22 to 32. In section 39, in subsection (1) the word "and" where it occurs for the third time; and subsection (4). In section 42, in subsection (1) the words "22(2), 30(6) or (7), 32(5) or"; and subsections (3) and (4). In section 43, in subsection (1), the definitions of "local review committee", "Parole Board" and "sentence of imprisonment"; in subsection (2), the words "(other than in section 25)"; and in subsection (5), the words "(other than in section 30)". Schedule 1. In Schedule 2, paragraphs 1, 3 to 5, 8, 13 to 15, 17 and 18.
1991 c. 53.	The Criminal Justice Act 1991.	In Schedule 11, in paragraph 35, sub-paragraphs (2), (3)(a) and (4).

Part II

Revocations

Year and number	Title	Extent of revocation
S.I. 1952/565.	The Prison (Scotland) Rules 1952.	Rule 9.
S.I. 1976/1889.	The Prison (Scotland) Amendment Rules 1976.	The whole rules.

CRIMINAL LAW (CONSOLIDATION) (SCOTLAND) ACT 1995

(1995 c. 39)

ARRANGEMENT OF SECTIONS

PART I

SEXUAL OFFENCES

Incest and related offences

General

53. Short title, commencement and extent.

An Act to consolidate for Scotland certain enactments creating offences and relating to criminal law there. [8th November 1995]

PART I

SEXUAL OFFENCES

Incest and related offences

Incest

1.—(1) Any male person who has sexual intercourse with a person related to him in a degree specified in column 1 of the Table set out at the end of this subsection, or any female person who has sexual intercourse with a person related to her in a degree specified in column 2 of that Table, shall be guilty of incest, unless the accused proves that he or she—

   (a) did not know and had no reason to suspect that the person with whom he or she had sexual intercourse was related in a degree so specified; or

   (b) did not consent to have sexual intercourse, or to have sexual intercourse with that person; or

   (c) was married to that person, at the time when the sexual intercourse took place, by a marriage entered into outside Scotland and recognised as valid by Scots law.

Table

Degrees of Relationship

Column 1	Column 2
1. Relationships by consanguinity	
Mother	Father
Daughter	Son
Grandmother	Grandfather
Grand-daughter	Grandson
Sister	Brother
Aunt	Uncle
Niece	Nephew
Great grandmother	Great grandfather
Great grand-daughter	Great grandson
2. Relationships by adoption	
Adoptive mother or former adoptive mother.	Adoptive father or former adoptive father.
Adopted daughter or former adopted daughter.	Adopted son or former adopted son.

(2) For the purpose of this section, a degree of relationship exists in the case of a degree specified in paragraph 1 of the Table—

   (a) whether it is of the full blood or the half blood; and

   (b) even where traced through or to any person whose parents are not or have not been married to one another.

(3) For the avoidance of doubt sexual intercourse between persons who

are not related to each other in a degree referred to in subsection (1) above is not incest.

Intercourse with step-child

2. Any step-parent or former step-parent who has sexual intercourse with his or her step-child or former step-child shall be guilty of an offence if that step-child is either under the age of 21 years or has at any time before attaining the age of 18 years lived in the same household and been treated as a child of his or her family, unless the accused proves that he or she—
  (a) did not know and had no reason to suspect that the person with whom he or she had sexual intercourse was a step-child or former step-child; or
  (b) believed on reasonable grounds that that person was of or over the age of 21 years; or
  (c) did not consent to have sexual intercourse, or to have sexual intercourse with that person; or
  (d) was married to that person, at the time when the sexual intercourse took place, by a marriage entered into outside Scotland and recognised as valid by Scots law.

Intercourse of person in position of trust with child under 16

3.—(1) Any person of or over the age of 16 years who—
  (a) has sexual intercourse with a child under the age of 16 years;
  (b) is a member of the same household as that child; and
  (c) is in a position of trust or authority in relation to that child,
shall be guilty of an offence, unless the accused proves that subsection (2) below applies in his or her case.
  (2) This subsection applies where the accused—
  (a) believed on reasonable grounds that the person with whom he or she had sexual intercourse was of or over the age of 16 years; or
  (b) did not consent to have sexual intercourse, or to have sexual intercourse with that person; or
  (c) was married to that person, at the time when the sexual intercourse took place, by a marriage entered into outside Scotland and recognised as valid by Scots law.

Proceedings and penalties for offences under sections 1 to 3

4.—(1) Proceedings in respect of an offence under section 1, 2 or 3 of this Act may be brought on indictment or, if the Lord Advocate so directs, on a summary complaint before the sheriff.
  (2) Summary proceedings in pursuance of this section may be commenced at any time within the period of 6 months from the date on which evidence sufficient in the opinion of the Lord Advocate to justify the proceedings comes to his knowledge.
  (3) Subsection (3) of section 136 of the Criminal Procedure (Scotland) Act 1995 (date of commencement of summary proceedings) shall have effect for the purposes of subsection (2) above as it has effect for the purposes of that section.
  (4) For the purposes of subsection (2) above, a certificate of the Lord Advocate as to the date on which the evidence in question came to his knowledge is conclusive evidence of the date on which it did so.
  (5) Subject to subsection (6) below, a person guilty of an offence under section 1, 2 or 3 of this Act shall be liable—
  (a) on conviction on indictment, to imprisonment for any term of imprisonment up to and including life imprisonment; and
  (b) on summary conviction, to imprisonment for a term not exceeding '3' months.

(6) Before passing sentence on a person convicted of any such offence, the court shall—

(a) obtain information about that person's circumstances from an officer of a local authority or otherwise and consider that information; and

(b) take into account any information before it which is relevant to his character and to his physical and mental condition.

(7) In subsection (6) above, "local authority" has the meaning assigned to it by section 1(2) of the Social Work (Scotland) Act 1968.

Offences against children

Intercourse with girl under 16

5.—(1) Any person who has unlawful sexual intercourse with any girl under the age of 13 years shall be liable on conviction on indictment to imprisonment for life.

[1](2) Any person who attempts to have unlawful sexual intercourse with any girl under the age of 13 years shall be liable on conviction on indictment to imprisonment for a term not exceeding ten years or on summary conviction to imprisonment for a term not exceeding three months.

[2](3) Without prejudice to sections 1 to 4 of this Act, any person who has, or attempts to have, unlawful sexual intercourse with any girl of or over the age of 13 years and under the age of 16 years shall be liable on conviction on indictment to imprisonment for a term not exceeding ten years or on summary conviction to imprisonment for a term not exceeding three months.

(4) No prosecution shall be commenced for an offence under subsection (3) above more than one year after the commission of the offence.

(5) It shall be a defence to a charge under subsection (3) above that the person so charged—

(a) had reasonable cause to believe that the girl was his wife; or

(b) being a man under the age of 24 years who had not previously been charged with a like offence, had reasonable cause to believe that the girl was of or over the age of 16 years.

(6) In subsection (5) above, "a like offence" means an offence under—

(a) subsection (3) above; or

(b) section 4(1) or 10(1) of the Sexual Offences (Scotland) Act 1976 or section 5 or 6 of the Criminal Law Amendment Act 1885 (the enactments formerly creating the offences mentioned in subsection (3) above and section 9(1) of this Act); or

(c) section 6 of the Sexual Offences Act 1956 (the provision for England and Wales corresponding to subsection (3) above), or with an attempt to commit such an offence; or

(d) section 9(1) of this Act.

(7) For the purposes of subsection (4) above, a prosecution shall be deemed to commence on the date on which a warrant to apprehend or to cite the accused is granted, if such warrant is executed without undue delay.

NOTES

[1]Substituted by the Crime and Punishment (Scotland) Act 1997 (c. 48) s.14(1).

[2]Substituted by the Crime and Punishment (Scotland) Act 1997 (c. 48) s.62(1) and Sched. 1, para. 18(2)(b) and commenced by the Crime and Punishment (Scotland) Act 1997 (Commencement and Transitional Provisions) Order 1997 (S.I. 1997 No. 1712), para. 3 (August 1, 1997).

Indecent behaviour towards girl between 12 and 16

[1]**6.** Any person who uses towards a girl of or over the age of 12 years and under the age of 16 years any lewd, indecent or libidinous practice or behaviour which, if used towards a girl under the age of 12 years, would have constituted an offence at common law shall, whether the girl consented to

such practice or behaviour or not, be liable on conviction on indictment to imprisonment for a term not exceeding ten years or on summary conviction to imprisonment for a term not exceeding three months.

NOTE
[1]Substituted by the Crime and Punishment (Scotland) Act 1997 (c. 48) s.14(2).

Procuring, prostitution etc.

Procuring

7.—(1) Any person who procures or attempts to procure—
(a) any woman under 21 years of age or girl to have unlawful sexual intercourse with any other person or persons in any part of the world; or
(b) any woman or girl to become a common prostitute in any part of the world; or
(c) any woman or girl to leave the United Kingdom, with intent that she may become an inmate of or frequent a brothel elsewhere; or
(d) any woman or girl to leave her usual place of abode in the United Kingdom, with intent that she may, for the purposes of prostitution, become an inmate of or frequent a brothel in any part of the world,
shall be liable on conviction on indictment to imprisonment for a term not exceeding two years or on summary conviction to imprisonment for a term not exceeding three months.
(2) Any person who—
(a) by threats or intimidation procures or attempts to procure any woman or girl to have any unlawful sexual intercourse in any part of the world; or
(b) by false pretences or false representations procures any woman or girl to have any unlawful sexual intercourse in any part of the world; or
(c) applies or administers to, or causes to be taken by, any woman or girl any drug, matter or thing, with intent to stupefy or overpower so as thereby to enable any person to have unlawful sexual intercourse with such woman or girl,
shall be liable on conviction on indictment to imprisonment for a term not exceeding two years or on summary conviction to imprisonment for a term not exceeding three months.
[1](3) A man who induces a married woman to permit him to have sexual intercourse with her by impersonating her husband shall be deemed to be guilty of rape.
(4) A constable may arrest without a warrant any person whom he has good cause to suspect of having committed, or of attempting to commit, any offence under subsection (1) above.

NOTE
[1]Inserted by the Crime and Punishment (Scotland) Act 1997 (c. 48), s.62(1) and Sched. 1, para. 18(3); commenced by the Crime and Punishment (Scotland) Act 1997 (Commencement and Transitional Provisions) Order 1997 (S.I. 1997 No. 1712) para. 3 (August 1, 1997).

Abduction and unlawful detention

8.—(1) Any person who, with intent that any unmarried girl under the age of 18 years should have unlawful sexual intercourse with men or with a particular man, takes or causes to be taken such girl out of the possession and against the will of her father or mother, or any other person having the lawful care or charge of her, shall be liable on conviction on indictment to imprisonment for a term not exceeding two years or on summary conviction to imprisonment for a term not exceeding three months.
(2) It shall be a defence to any charge under subsection (1) above that the

person so charged had reasonable cause to believe that the girl was of or over the age of 18 years.

(3) Any person who detains any woman or girl against her will—

(a) in or upon any premises with intent that she may have unlawful sexual intercourse with men or with a particular man; or

(b) in any brothel,

shall be liable on conviction on indictment to imprisonment for a term not exceeding two years or on summary conviction to imprisonment for a term not exceeding three months.

(4) Where a woman or girl is in or upon any premises for the purpose of having unlawful sexual intercourse, or is in a brothel, a person shall be deemed to detain such woman or girl in or upon such premises or brothel if, with intent to compel or induce her to remain in or upon the premises or brothel, he withholds from her any wearing apparel or other property belonging to her or, where wearing apparel has been lent or otherwise supplied to the woman or girl by or by the direction of such person, he threatens the woman or girl with legal proceedings if she takes away with her the wearing apparel so lent or supplied.

(5) No legal proceedings, whether civil or criminal, shall be taken against a woman or girl mentioned in subsection (4) above for taking away or being found in possession of any such wearing apparel as was necessary to enable her to leave such premises or brothel mentioned in that subsection.

Permitting girl to use premises for intercourse

9.—(1) Any person who, being the owner or occupier of any premises, or having, or acting or assisting in, the management or control of any premises, induces or knowingly suffers any girl of such age as is mentioned in this subsection to resort to or be in or upon such premises for the purpose of having unlawful sexual intercourse with men or with a particular man—

(a) if such girl is under the age of 13 years, shall be liable on conviction on indictment to imprisonment for life; and

(b) if such girl is of or over the age of 13 years and under the age of 16 years, shall be liable on conviction on indictment to imprisonment for a term not exceeding two years or on summary conviction to imprisonment for a term not exceeding three months.

(2) It shall be a defence to a charge under this section that the person so charged, being a man under the age 24 years who had not previously been charged with a like offence, had reasonable cause to believe that the girl was of or over the age of 16 years.

(3) In subsection (2) above, "a like offence" means an offence under—

(a) subsection (1) above; or

(b) section 5(3) of this Act; or

(c) section 4(1) or 10(1) of the Sexual Offences (Scotland) Act 1976 or section 5 or 6 of the Criminal Law Amendment Act 1885 (the enactments formerly creating the offences mentioned in paragraphs (a) and (b) above).

Seduction, prostitution, etc., of girl under 16

10.—(1) If any person having parental responsibilities (within the meaning of section 1(3) of the Children (Scotland) Act 1995), in relation to, or having charge or care of a girl under the age of 16 years causes or encourages—

(a) the seduction or prostitution of;

(b) unlawful sexual intercourse with; or

(c) the commission of an indecent assault upon,

her he shall be liable on conviction on indictment to imprisonment for a term not exceeding two years or on summary conviction to imprisonment for a term not exceeding three months.

(2) For the purposes of this section, a person shall be deemed to have caused or encouraged the matters mentioned in paragraphs (a) to (c) of subsection (1) above upon a girl who has been seduced or indecently assaulted, or who has had unlawful sexual intercourse or who has become a prostitute, if he has knowingly allowed her to consort with, or to enter or continue in the employment of, any prostitute or person of known immoral character.

(3) Subsections (1) and (2) above shall apply to a contravention of section 6 of this Act in like manner as they apply to an indecent assault, and any reference to the commission of such an assault or to being indecently assaulted shall be construed accordingly.

(4) Where on the trial of any offence under this Part of this Act it is proved to the satisfaction of the court that the seduction or prostitution of a girl under the age of 16 years has been caused, encouraged or favoured by her father, mother or guardian it shall be in the power of the court to divest such person of all authority over her, and to appoint any person or persons willing to take charge of such girl to be her guardian until she has attained the age of 21 years, or such lower age as the court may direct.

(5) The High Court of Justiciary shall have the power from time to time to rescind or vary an order under subsection (4) above by the appointment of any other person or persons as such guardian, or in any other respect.

Trading in prostitution and brothel-keeping

11.—(1) Every male person who—
(a) knowingly lives wholly or in part on the earnings of prostitution; or
(b) in any public place persistently solicits or importunes for immoral purposes,
shall be liable on conviction on indictment to imprisonment for a term not exceeding two years or on summary conviction to imprisonment for a term not exceeding six months.

(2) If it is made to appear to a court of summary jurisdiction by information on oath that there is reason to suspect that any house or any part of a house is used by a female for purposes of prostitution, and that any male person residing in or frequenting the house is living wholly or in part on the earnings of the prostitute, the court may issue a warrant authorising a constable to enter and search the house and to arrest that male person.

(3) Where a male person is proved to live with or to be habitually in the company of a prostitute, or is proved to have exercised control, direction or influence over the movements of a prostitute in such a manner as to show that he is aiding, abetting or compelling her prostitution with any other person, or generally, he shall, unless he can satisfy the court to the contrary, be deemed to be knowingly living on the earnings of prostitution.

(4) Every female who is proved to have, for the purposes of gain, exercised control, direction or influence over the movements of a prostitute in such a manner as to show that she is aiding, abetting or compelling her prostitution with any other person, or generally, shall be liable to the penalties set out in subsection (1) above.

(5) Any person who—
(a) keeps or manages or acts or assists in the management of a brothel; or
(b) being the tenant, lessee, occupier or person in charge of any premises, knowingly permits such premises or any part thereof to be used as a brothel or for the purposes of habitual prostitution; or
(c) being the lessor or landlord of any premises, or the agent of such lessor or landlord, lets the same or any part thereof with the knowledge that such premises or some part thereof are or is to be used

as a brothel, or is wilfully a party to the continued use of such premises or any part thereof as a brothel,

shall be guilty of an offence.

(6) A person convicted of an offence under subsection (5) above shall be liable—

    (a) in the sheriff court to a fine not exceeding level 4 on the standard scale or to imprisonment for a term not exceeding six months; and

    (b) in the district court to a fine not exceeding level 3 on the standard scale or to imprisonment for a term not exceeding three months,

or, in either case, to both such fine and imprisonment.

Allowing child to be in brothel

12.—(1) If any person having parental responsibilities (within the meaning of section 1(3) of the Children (Scotland) Act 1995), in relation to, or having charge or care of a child who has attained the age of four years and is under the age of 16 years, allows that child to reside in or to frequent a brothel, he shall be liable on conviction on indictment, or on summary conviction, to a fine not exceeding level 2 on the standard scale or alternatively, or in default of payment of such a fine, or in addition thereto, to imprisonment for a term not exceeding six months.

(2) Nothing in this section shall affect the liability of a person to be indicted under section 9 of this Act, but upon the trial of a person under that section it shall be lawful for the jury, if they are satisfied that he is guilty of an offence under this section, to find him guilty of that offence.

Homosexual offences

Homosexual offences

13.—[1](1) Subject to the provisions of this section, a homosexual act in private shall not be an offence provided that the parties consent thereto and have attained the age of sixteen years.

(2) An act which would otherwise be treated for the purpose of this Act as being done in private shall not be so treated if done—

    (a) when more than two persons take part or are present; or

    (b) in a lavatory to which the public have, or are permitted to have, access whether on payment or otherwise.

(3) A male person who is suffering from mental deficiency which is of such a nature or degree that he is incapable of living an independent life or of guarding himself against serious exploitation cannot in law give any consent which, by virtue of subsection (1) above, would prevent a homosexual act from being an offence; but a person shall not be convicted on account of the incapacity of such a male person to consent, of an offence consisting of such an act if he proves that he did not know and had no reason to suspect that male person to be suffering from such mental deficiency.

(4) In this section, a "homosexual act" means sodomy or an act of gross indecency or shameless indecency by one male person with another male person.

(5) Subject to subsection (3) above, it shall be an offence to commit or to be party to the commission of, or to procure or attempt to procure the commission of a homosexual act—

    (a) otherwise than in private;

    (b) without the consent of both parties to the act; or

    [1](c) with a person under the age of sixteen years.

(6) It shall be an offence to procure or attempt to procure the commission of a homosexual act between two other male persons.

(7) A person who commits or is party to the commission of an offence under subsection (5) or subsection (6) above shall be liable on conviction on

indictment to imprisonment for a term not exceeding two years or to a fine or to both and on summary conviction to imprisonment for a term not exceeding 3 months, or to a fine not exceeding the prescribed sum (within the meaning of section 225(8) of the Criminal Procedure (Scotland) Act 1995).

[1](8) It shall be a defence to a charge of committing a homosexual act under subsection (5)(c) above that the person so charged being under the age of 24 years who had not previously been charged with a like offence, had reasonable cause to believe that the other person was of or over the age of sixteen years.

[2](8A) A person under the age of sixteen years does not commit an offence under subsection (5)(a) or (c) above if he commits or is party to the commission of a homosexual act with a person who has attained that age.

(9) A person who knowingly lives wholly or in part on the earnings of another from male prostitution or who solicits or importunes any male person for the purpose of procuring the commission of a homosexual act within the meaning of subsection (4) above shall be liable—

(a) on summary conviction to imprisonment for a term not exceeding six months; or

(b) on conviction on indictment to imprisonment for a term not exceeding two years.

(10) Premises shall be treated for the purposes of sections 11(1) and 12 of this Act as a brothel if people resort to it for the purposes of homosexual acts within the meaning of subsection (4) above in circumstances in which resort thereto for heterosexual practices would have led to its being treated as a brothel for the purposes of those sections.

(11) No proceedings for—

(a) the offences mentioned in subsections (5) and (6) above; and

(b) any offence under subsection (9) above which consists of soliciting or importuning any male person for the purpose of procuring the commission of a homosexual act,

shall be commenced after the expiration of twelve months from the date on which that offence was committed.

NOTES
[1]As amended by the Sexual Offences (Amendment) Act 2000 (c. 44), s.1(3). Brought into force by the Sexual Offences (Amendment) Act 2000 (Commencement No.2) Order 2000 (S.S.I. 2000 452 (C. 18)), art.2 (effective January 8, 2001).
[2]Inserted by the Sexual Offences (Amendment) Act 2000 (c. 44), s.2(4). Brought into force as above.

Miscellaneous

Power, on indictment for rape, etc., to convict of other offences

14. If, in the trial of an indictment for rape or an offence under section 5(1) of this Act, the jury—

(a) are not satisfied that the accused is guilty of the charge or of an attempt to commit the charge; but

(b) are satisfied that the accused is guilty of an offence under section 5(2) or (3) or 7(2) or (3) of this Act, or of an indecent assault,

the jury may acquit the accused of the charge mentioned in paragraph (a) above, and find him guilty of such offence as is mentioned in paragraph (b) or of an indecent assault, and the accused shall be liable to be punished in the same manner as if he had been convicted upon an indictment for such offence or for indecent assault.

Defence to charge or indecent assault

15. It shall be a defence to a charge of indecent assault committed against a girl under the age of 16 years that the person so charged has reasonable cause to believe that the girl was his wife.

Power of search

16.—(1) If it appears to a justice on information on oath by any parent, relative or guardian of any woman or girl, or any other person who, in the opinion of the justice, is *bona fide* acting in the interest of any woman or girl, that there is reasonable cause to suspect that such woman or girl is unlawfully detained for immoral purposes by any person in any place within the jurisdiction of the justice, he may issue a warrant authorising any person named therein to search for, and, when found, to take to and detain in a place of safety, such woman or girl until she can be brought before a justice, and the justice before whom such woman or girl is brought may cause her to be delivered up to her parents or guardians, or otherwise dealt with as circumstances may permit and require.

(2) The justice issuing such warrant may, by the same or any other warrant, cause any person accused of so unlawfully detaining such woman or girl to be apprehended and brought before a justice, and proceedings to be taken for punishing such person according to law.

(3) A woman or girl shall be deemed to be unlawfully detained for immoral purposes is she is so detained for the purpose of having unlawful sexual intercourse with men or with a particular man, and she—

    (a) is under the age of 16 years; or

    (b) if of or over the age of 16 years and under the age of 18 years, is so detained against her will, or against the will of her father or mother or of any other person having the lawful care or charge of her; or

    (c) if of or over the age of 18 years, is so detained against her will.

(4) Any person authorised by warrant under this section to search for any woman or girl so detained as aforesaid may enter (if need be by force) any house, building, or other place specified in the warrant, and may remove the woman or girl therefrom.

(5) Every warrant issued under this section shall be addressed to and executed by a constable, who shall be accompanied by the parent, relative, or guardian or other person giving the information, if that person so desires, unless the justice directs otherwise.

(6) In this section, "justice" has the same meaning as in section 307 of the Criminal Procedure (Scotland) Act 1995.

Conspiracy or incitement to commit certain sexual acts outside the United Kingdom

[1,2]**16A.**—(1) This section applies to any act done by a person in Scotland which would amount to the offence of incitement to commit a listed sexual offence but for the fact that what he had in view is intended to occur in a country or territory outside the United Kingdom.

[2](2) Where a person does an act to which this section applies, what he had in view shall be treated as the listed sexual offence mentioned in subsection (1) above and he shall, accordingly, be guilty of, as the case may be, incitement to commit the listed sexual offence.

[2](3) A person is guilty of an offence by virtue of this section only if what he had in view would involve the commission of an offence under the law in force in the country or territory where the whole or any part of it was intended to take place, and conduct punishable under the law in force in the country or territory is an offence under that law for the purposes of this section however it is described in that law.

(4) Subject to subsection (6) below, a condition specified in subsection (3)

above shall be taken to be satisfied unless, not later than such time as the High Court may, by Act of Adjournal, prescribe, the accused serves on the prosecutor a notice—

    (a) stating that, on the facts as alleged with respect to the relevant conduct, the condition is not in his opinion satisfied;

    (b) setting out the grounds for his opinion; and

    (c) requiring the prosecutor to prove that the condition is satisfied.

[2](5) In subsection (4) above "the relevant conduct" means what the accused had in view.

(6) The court, if it thinks fit, may permit the accused to require the prosecutor to prove that the condition mentioned in subsection (4) above is satisfied without the prior service of a notice under that subsection.

(7) In proceedings on indictment, the question whether a condition is satisfied shall be determined by the judge alone.

(8) Any act of incitement by means of a message (however communicated) is to be treated as done in Scotland if the message is sent or received in Scotland.

(9) In this section "listed sexual offence" means any of the following—

    (a) rape of a girl under the age of 16;

    (b) indecent assault of a person under the age of 16;

    (c) lewd and libidinous conduct;

    (d) shamelessly indecent conduct involving a person under the age of 16;

    (e) sodomy with or against a boy under the age of 16;

    (f) an offence under section 5(1) or (2) of this Act (unlawful sexual intercourse with a girl under the age of 13);

    (g) an offence under section 5(3) of this Act (unlawful sexual intercourse with a girl under the age of 16);

    (h) an offence under section 6 of this Act (indecent behaviour towards a girl between the age of 12 and 16);

    (i) an offence under section 13(5) or (6) of this Act where the homosexual act involves a person under the age of 16 (prohibition on certain homosexual acts).

NOTES

[1]Inserted by the Sexual Offences (Conspiracy and Incitement) Act 1996 (c. 29), s.6.

[2]As amended by the Criminal Justice (Terrorism and Conspiracy) Act 1998 (c. 40), Sched. 1, para. 8 (effective September 9, 1998).

Commission of certain sexual acts outside the United Kingdom

[1] **16B.**—(1) Subject to subsection (2) below, any act done by a person in a country or territory outside the United Kingdom which—

    (a) constituted an offence under the law in force in that country or territory; and

    (b) would constitute a listed sexual offence if it had been done in Scotland, shall constitute that sexual offence.

(2) No proceedings shall by virtue of this section be brought against any person unless he was at the commencement of this section, or has subsequently become, a British citizen or resident in the United Kingdom.

(3) An act punishable under the law in force in any country or territory constitutes an offence under that law for the purposes of subsection (1) above, however it is described in that law.

(4) Subject to subsection (5) below, the condition in subsection (1)(a) above shall be taken to be satisfied unless, not later than may be prescribed by Act of Adjournal, the accused serves on the prosecutor a notice—

    (a) stating that, on the facts as alleged with respect to the act in question, the condition is not in his opinion satisfied;

    (b) setting out the grounds for that opinion; and

(c) requiring the prosecutor to prove that it is satisfied.

(5) The court, if it thinks fit, may permit the accused to require the prosecutor to prove that the condition is satisfied without the prior service of a notice under subsection (4) above.

(6) In proceedings on indictment, the question whether the condition is satisfied is to be decided by the judge alone.

(7) Subject to subsection (8) below, in this section "listed sexual offence" means any of the following—

   (a) rape of a girl under the age of 16;

   (b) indecent assault of a person under the age of 16;

   (c) lewd, indecent or libidinous behaviour or practices;

   (d) shamelessly indecent conduct involving a person under the age of 16;

   (e) sodomy with or against a boy under the age of 16;

   (f) an offence under section 5(1) or (2) of this Act (unlawful sexual intercourse with a girl under the age of 13);

   (g) an offence under section 5(3) of this Act (unlawful sexual intercourse with a girl under the age of 16);

   (h) an offence under section 6 of this Act (indecent behaviour towards a girl between the age of 12 and 16);

   (i) an offence under section 13(5) or (6) of this Act where the homosexual act involves a person under the age of 16 (prohibition on certain homosexual acts); and

   (j) an offence under section 52 of the Civic Government (Scotland) Act 1982 (taking and distribution of indecent images of children).

(8) "Listed sexual offence" includes—

   (a) conspiracy or incitement to commit any such offence; and

   (b) any offence under section 293(2) of the Criminal Procedure (Scotland) Act 1995 (aiding and abetting etc. the commission of statutory offences) relating to any offence mentioned in subsection (7)(f) to (j) above.

NOTE

[1]Inserted by the Sex Offenders Act 1997 (c. 51), s.8 (effective September 1, 1997, S.I. 1997 No. 1920).

Liability to other criminal proceedings

17. This Part of this Act shall not exempt any person from any proceedings for an offence which is punishable at common law, or under any enactment other than this Part, but nothing in this Part of this Act shall enable a person to be punished twice for the same offence.

PART II

Sporting Events: Control of Alcohol etc.

Designation of sports grounds and sporting events

18.—(1) Subject to subsection (2) below, the Secretary of State may for the purposes of this Part of this Act by order designate—

   (a) a sports ground or a class of sports ground;

   (b) a sporting event, or a class of sporting event, at that ground or at any of that class of ground;

   (c) a sporting event, or a class of sporting event, taking place outside Great Britain.

(2) An order under this section shall not apply to a sporting event at which all the participants take part without financial or material reward and to which all spectators are admitted free of charge; but this subsection is without prejudice to the order's validity as respects any other sporting event.

(3) The power to make an order under subsection (1) above shall be

exercisable by statutory instrument which shall be subject to annulment in pursuance of a resolution of either House of Parliament.

Alcohol on vehicles

19.—(1) Where a public service vehicle or railway passenger vehicle is being operated for the principal purpose of conveying passengers for the whole or part of a journey to or from a designated sporting event, then—

(a) any person in possession of alcohol on the vehicle shall be guilty of an offence and liable on summary conviction to imprisonment for a period not exceeding 60 days or a fine not exceeding level 3 on the standard scale or both;

(b) if alcohol is being carried on the vehicle and the vehicle is on hire to a person, he shall, subject to subsection (7) below, be guilty of an offence and liable on summary conviction to a fine not exceeding level 3 on the standard scale; and

(c) any person who is drunk on the vehicle shall be guilty of an offence and liable on summary conviction to a fine not exceeding level 2 on the standard scale.

(2) Notwithstanding section 92 of the Licensing (Scotland) Act 1976 (restriction on carriage of alcoholic liquor in crates on contract carriages), but subject to subsection (7) below, if the operator of a public service vehicle which is being operated as mentioned in subsection (1) above, either by himself or by his employee or agent permits alcohol to be carried on the vehicle, the operator and, as the case may be, the employee or agent shall be guilty of an offence and liable on summary conviction to a fine not exceeding level 3 on the standard scale.

[1](3) This subsection applies to a motor vehicle which is not a public service vehicle but which is adapted to carry more than 8 passengers and is being operated for the principal purpose of conveying two or more passengers for the whole or part of a journey to or from a designated sporting event.

(4) Any person in possession of alcohol on a vehicle to which subsection (3) above applies shall be guilty of an offence and liable on summary conviction to imprisonment for a period not exceeding 60 days or a fine not exceeding level 3 on the standard scale or both.

(5) Any person who is drunk on a vehicle to which subsection (3) above applies shall be guilty of an offence and liable on summary conviction to a fine not exceeding level 2 on the standard scale.

(6) Any person who permits alcohol to be carried on a vehicle to which subsection (3) above applies and—

(a) is the driver of the vehicle; or

(b) where he is not its driver, is the keeper of the vehicle, the employee or agent of the keeper, a person to whom it is made available (by hire, loan or otherwise) by the keeper or the keeper's employee or agent, or the employee or agent of a person to whom it is so made available,

shall, subject to subsection (7) below, be guilty of an offence and liable on summary conviction to a fine not exceeding level 3 on the standard scale.

(7) Where a person is charged with an offence under subsection (1)(b), (2) or (6) above, it shall be a defence for him to prove that the alcohol was carried on the vehicle without his consent or connivance and that he did all he reasonably could to prevent such carriage.

NOTE

[1]Amended by the Crime and Punishment (Scotland) Act 1997 s.62(1) and Sched. 1, para. 18(4); commenced by the Crime and Punishment (Scotland) Act 1997 (Commencement and Transitional Provisions) Order 1997 (S.I. 1997 No. 1713) para. 3 (August 1, 1997).

Sporting events: controls

20.—(1) Any person who—

(a) is in possession of a controlled container in; or

(b) while in possession of a controlled container, attempts to enter,

the relevant area of a designated sports ground at any time during the period of a designated sporting event shall be guilty of an offence and liable on summary conviction to imprisonment for a period not exceeding 60 days or to a fine not exceeding level 3 on the standard scale or both.

(2) Any person who—

(a) is in possession of alcohol in; or

(b) while in possession of alcohol, attempts to enter,

the relevant area of a designated sports ground at any time during the period of a designated sporting event, shall be guilty of an offence and liable on summary conviction to imprisonment for a period not exceeding 60 days or to a fine not exceeding level 3 on the standard scale or both.

(3) Any person who has entered the relevant area of a designated sports ground and is in possession of a controlled article or substance at any time during the period of a designated sporting event shall be guilty of an offence.

(4) Any person who, while in possession of a controlled article or substance, attempts to enter the relevant area of a designated sports ground at any time during the period of a designated sporting event at the ground shall be guilty of an offence.

(5) A person guilty of an offence under subsection (3) or (4) above shall be liable on summary conviction to imprisonment for a period not exceeding 60 days or to a fine not exceeding level 3 on the standard scale or both.

(6) It shall be a defence for a person charged with an offence under subsection (3) or (4) above to show that he had been lawful authority to be in possession of the controlled article or substance.

(7) Any person who—

(a) is drunk in; or

(b) while drunk, attempts to enter,

the relevant area of a designated sports ground at any time during the period of a designated sporting event shall be guilty of an offence and liable on summary conviction to a fine not exceeding level 2 on the standard scale.

(8) In this section—

"controlled article or substance" means—

(a) any article or substance whose main purpose is the emission of a flare for purposes of illuminating or signalling (as opposed to igniting or heating) or the emission of smoke or a visible gas; and in particular it includes distress flares, fog signals, and pellets and capsules intended to be used as fumigators or for testing pipes, but not matches, cigarette lighters or heaters; and

(b) any article which is a firework.

"controlled container" means any bottle, can or other portable container, whether open or sealed, which is, or was, in its original manufactured state, capable of containing liquid and is made from such material or is of such construction, or is so adapted, that if it were thrown at or propelled against a person it would be capable of causing some injury to that person; but the term does not include a container holding a medicinal product for a medicinal purpose.

"medicinal product" and "medicinal purpose" have the meanings assigned to those terms by section 130 of the Medicines Act 1968.

Police powers of enforcement

21. For the purpose of enforcing the provisions of this Part of this Act, a constable shall have the power without warrant—

(a) to enter a designated sports ground at any time during the period of a designated sporting event;

(b) to search a person who he has reasonable grounds to suspect is committing or has committed an offence under this Part of this Act;

(c) to stop and search a vehicle where he has reasonable grounds to suspect that an offence under section 19 of this Act is being or has been committed;

(d) to arrest a person who he has reasonable grounds to suspect is committing or has committed an offence under this Part of this Act;

(e) to seize and detain—

    (i) with its contents (if any), a controlled container as defined in section 20(8) of this Act, or

    [1](ii) with its contents, any other container if he has reasonable grounds to suspect that those contents are or include alcohol; or

    (iii) a controlled article or substance as defined in section 20(8) of this Act.

NOTE

[1]Inserted by the Crime and Punishment (Scotland) Act 1997 (c. 48) s.62(1) and Sched. 1, para 18(5); commenced by the Crime and Punishment (Scotland) Act 1997 (Commencement and Transitional Provisions) Order 1997 (S.I. 1997 No. 1712) para. 3 (August 1, 1997).

Presumption as to contents of container

22. Section 127 of the Licensing (Scotland) Act 1976 (presumption as to contents of container) shall apply for the purposes of any trial in connection with an alleged contravention of any provision of this Part of this Act as it applies for the purposes of any trial in connection with an alleged contravention of any provision of that Act.

Interpretation of Part II

23. In this Part of this Act, unless the context otherwise requires—

"advertised" means announced in any written or printed document or in any broadcast announcement;

"alcohol" means alcoholic liquor as defined in section 139 of the Licensing (Scotland) Act 1976;

"designated" means designated by the Secretary of State by order under section 18 of this Act, and "designated sporting event" includes a sporting event designated under section 9(3)(a) of the Sporting Events (Control of Alcohol) Etc. Act 1985;

"keeper", in relation to a vehicle, means the person having the duty to take out a licence for it under section 1(1) of the Vehicles Excise and Registration Act 1994;

[1]"motor vehicle" means a mechanically propelled vehicle intended or adapted for use on roads;

"period of a designated sporting event" means the period commencing two hours before the start and ending one hour after the end of a designated sporting event, except that where the event is advertised as to start at a particular time but is delayed or postponed in includes, and where for any reason an event does not take place it means, the period commencing two hours before and ending one hour after, that particular time;

"public service vehicle" has the same meaning as in the Public Passenger Vehicles Act 1981 and "operator" in relation to such a vehicle means—

    (a) the driver if he owns the vehicle; and

    (b) in any case the person for whom the driver works (whether under a contract of employment or any other description of contract personally to do work);

"railway passenger vehicle" has the same meaning as in the Licensing (Scotland) Act 1976;

"relevant area" means any part of a sports ground—

(a) to which spectators attending a designated sporting event are granted access on payment; or

(b) from which a designated sporting event may be viewed directly;

"sporting event" means any physical competitive activity at a sports ground, and includes any such activity which has been advertised as to, but does not, take place; and

"sports ground" means any place whatsoever which is designed, or is capable of being adapted, for the holding of sporting events in respect of which spectators are accommodated.

NOTE

[1]Inserted by the Crime and Punishment (Scotland) Act 1997 (c. 48), s.62(1) and Sched. 1, para. 18(6); commenced by the Crime and Punishment (Scotland) Act 1997 (Commencement and Transitional Provisions) Order 1997 (S.I. 1997 No. 1712) para. 3 (August 1, 1997).

PART III

DETENTION BY CUSTOMS OFFICERS

Detention and questioning by customs officers

24.—(1) Where an officer has reasonable grounds for suspecting that a person has committed or is committing an offence punishable by imprisonment relating to an assigned matter, the officer may, for the purpose of facilitating the carrying out of investigations—

(a) into the offence; and

(b) as to whether criminal proceedings should be instigated against the person,

detain that person and take him as quickly as is reasonably practicable to a customs office or other premises and may thereafter for that purpose take him to any other place and, subject to the following provisions of this section, the detention may continue at the customs office or, as the case may be, the other premises or place.

(2) Detention under subsection (1) above shall be terminated not more than six hours after it begins or (if earlier)—

(a) when the person is arrested;

(b) when he is detained in pursuance of any other enactment or subordinate instrument; or

(c) where there are no longer such grounds as are mentioned in the said subsection (1),

and when a person has been detained under subsection (1) above, he shall be informed immediately upon the termination of his detention in accordance with this subsection that his detention has been terminated.

(3) Where a person has been detained under subsection (1) above, he shall not thereafter be detained under that subsection on the same grounds or on any grounds arising out of the same circumstances.

[1](4) Where a person has previously been detained in pursuance of any other enactment or subordinate instrument, and is detained under subsection (1) above on the same grounds or on grounds arising from the same circumstances as those which led to his earlier detention, the period of six hours mentioned in subsection (2) above shall be reduced by the length of that earlier detention.

(5) At the time when an officer detains a person under subsection (1) above, he shall inform the person of his suspicion, of the general nature of the offence which he suspects has been or is being committed and of the reason for the detention; and there shall be recorded—

(a) the place where detention begins and the customs office or other premises to which the person is taken;

(b) any other place to which the person is, during the detention, thereafter taken;

(c) the general nature of the suspected offence;

(d) the time when detention under subsection (1) above begins and the time of the person's arrival at the customs office or other premises;

(e) the time when the person is informed of his rights in terms of subsection (8) below and of section 25(1) of this Act and the identity of the officer so informing him;

(f) where the person requests such intimation to be sent as is specified in the said section 25(1), the time when such request is—
  (i) made;
  (ii) complied with; and

(g) the time of the person's release from detention or, where instead of being released he is—
  (i) further detained under section 26 of this Act, the time of commencement of the further detention; or
  (ii) arrested in respect of the alleged offence, the time of such arrest.

(6) Where a person is detained under subsection (1) above, an officer may—
  (i) made;
  (ii) complied with; and

(g) the time of the person's release from detention or, where instead of being released he is—
  (i) further detained under section 26 of this Act, the time of commencement of the further detention; or
  (ii) arrested in respect of the alleged offence, the time of such arrest.

(6) Where a person is detained under subsection (1) above, an officer may—

(a) without prejudice to any existing rule of law as regards the admissibility in evidence of an answer given, put questions to him in relation to the suspected offence;

(b) exercise the same powers of search as are available following an arrest.

(7) An officer may use reasonable force in exercising any power conferred by subsection (1) or (6)(b) above.

(8) A person detained under subsection (1) above shall be under no obligation to answer any question other than to give his name and address, and an officer shall so inform him both on so detaining him and on arrival at the customs office or other premises.

(9) In this section and in sections 25 and 26 of this Act "assigned matter" and "officer" have the meanings given to them by section 1 of the Customs and Excise Management Act 1979, and "customs office" means a place for the time being occupied by Her Majesty's Customs and Excise.

NOTE
[1]Substituted by the Crime and Disorder Act 1998 (c. 37), s.110 (effective September 30, 1998: S.I. 1998 No. 2327).

Right to have someone informed when detained

25.—(1) Without prejudice to section 17 the Criminal Procedure (Scotland) Act 1995 (intimation to solicitor following arrest), a person who, not being a person in respect of whose detention subsection (2) below applies, is being detained under section 24 of this Act and has been taken to a customs office or other premises or place shall be entitled to have intimation of his

detention and of the customs office or other premises or place sent to a solicitor and to one other person reasonably named by him without delay or, where some delay is necessary in the interest of the investigation or the prevention of crime or the apprehension of offenders, with no more delay than is so necessary; and the person shall be informed of such entitlement—
  (a) on arrival at the customs office or other premises; or
  (b) where he is not detained until after such arrival, on such detention.
  (2) Without prejudice to the said section 17, an officer shall, where a person who is being detained as is mentioned in subsection (1) above appears to him to be a child, send without delay such information as is mentioned in that subsection to that person's parent if known; and the parent—
  (a) in a case where there is reasonable cause to suspect that he has been involved in the alleged offence in respect of which the person has been detained, may; and
  (b) in any other case shall,
be permitted access to the person.
  (3) The nature and extent of any access permitted under subsection (2), above shall be subject to any restriction essential for the furtherance of the investigation or the well-being of the person.
  (4) In subsection (2) above—
  (a) "child" means a person under 16 years of age; and
  (b) "parent" includes a guardian and any person who has the care of a child.

Detention in connection with certain drug smuggling offences

26.—(1) Where an officer has reasonable grounds for suspecting—
  (a) that a person has committed or is committing a relevant offence; and
  (b) that, in connection with the commission of such an offence, a controlled drug is secreted in the person's body,
a superior officer may, notwithstanding that the person has been or is being detained in pursuance of any other enactment or subordinate instrument, authorise the detention of the person at a customs office or other premises in accordance with this section.
  (2) Subject to subsection (7) below, where a person is detained under subsection (1) above or is further detained in pursuance of a warrant under subsection (4) below he shall—
  (a) provide such specimens of blood or urine for analysis;
  (b) submit to such intimate searches, to be carried out by a registered medical practitioner;
  (c) submit to such other test or examinations prescribed by the Secretary of State by regulations made under this paragraph to be carried out by, or under the supervision of, a registered medical practitioner,
as the officer may reasonably require; and regulations under paragraph (c) above shall be made by statutory instrument subject to annulment in pursuance of a resolution of either House of Parliament.
  (3) Subject to subsection (4) below, detention under subsection (1) above shall be terminated not more than 24 hours after it begins, or (if earlier)—
  (a) when the person is arrested;
  (b) when he is detained in pursuance of any other enactment or subordinate instrument; or
  (c) where there are no longer such grounds as are mentioned in subsection (1),
and, when a person has been detained under subsection (1), he shall, unless further detained in pursuance of a warrant under subsection (4) below, be informed immediately upon the termination of his detention in accordance with this subsection that his detention has been terminated.

(4) Where a person is detained under subsection (1) above and either—

(a) he has failed or refused—

(i) to provide a specimen in pursuance of paragraph (a) of subsection (2) above; or

(ii) to submit to any search, test or examination referred to in paragraph (b) or (c) of that subsection; or

(b) as a result of anything done in pursuance of the said subsection (2) the officer continues to have reasonable grounds for suspecting—

(i) that the person has committed or is committing a relevant offence; and

(ii) that a controlled drug is secreted in the person's body,

the procurator fiscal may, at the request of a superior officer, apply to the sheriff for a warrant for the further detention of the person at a customs office or other premises for an additional period of not more than 7 days; and if the sheriff is satisfied that there has been such failure or refusal as is mentioned in paragraph (a) above or, as the case may be, that there are reasonable grounds as mentioned in paragraph (b) above he may grant a warrant for such further detention.

(5) Detention in pursuance of a warrant under subsection (4) above shall be terminated at the end of the period of 7 days mentioned in that subsection or (if earlier)—

(a) when the person is arrested;

(b) when he is detained in pursuance of any other enactment or subordinate instrument; or

(c) where there are no longer such grounds as are mentioned in paragraph (b) of that subsection,

and when a person has been detained in pursuance of a warrant under subsection (4), he shall be informed immediately on the termination of his detention in accordance with this subsection that his detention has been terminated.

(6) Subject to subsection (7) below, the question whether it is to be a specimen of blood or a specimen of urine which is to be provided in pursuance of subsection (2) above shall be decided by the officer making the requirement.

(7) A person may be required, in pursuance of subsection (2) above—

(a) to provide a specimen of blood; or

(b) to submit to any search, test or examination,

only if a registered medical practitioner is of the opinion that there are no medical reasons for not making such a requirement; and, if a requirement to provide a specimen of blood is made, the specimen may be taken only by a registered medical practitioner.

(8) Subsections (3), (5), (6) and (8) of section 24 of this Act shall apply in respect of a person detained under this section as they apply in respect of a person detained under the said section 24; and, except as regards a requirement under subsection (2) above, an officer may use reasonable force in exercising any power conferred by this section.

(9) Section 25 of this Act shall, subject to the following modifications, apply in respect of a person detained under this section as it applies to a person detained under section 24 of this Act—

(a) any delay in informing a solicitor and one other person of such detention as is mentioned in subsection (1) of the said section 25 shall not extend longer than the period of 24 hours from the start of the detention, and shall only be permitted on the authorisation of a superior officer;

(b) the person detained shall be entitled to consult a solicitor at any time without delay, and he shall be informed of such entitlement at the commencement of the detention, but, if a superior officer considers it necessary in the interest of the investigation or the prevention of crime or the apprehension of offenders, he may authorise a delay not extending longer than the period of 24 hours from the start of the detention; and

(c) paragraph (a) of subsection (2) of the said section 25 shall cease to apply at the end of the period of 24 hours from the start of the detention,

but any delay authorised by virtue of this subsection shall be for no longer than is necessary in the interest of the investigation or the prevention of crime or the apprehension of offenders.

(10) Without prejudice to section 20(2) of the Interpretation Act 1978, the references in section 24(5) of this Act to section 25(1) of this Act shall be construed as including references to subsection (9) above; and the requirement to record certain matters under the said section 24(5) shall include a requirement to record the time when a person detained makes a request to consult a solicitor and the time when the solicitor is contacted for the purpose of arranging a consultation.

(11) In this section—

"controlled drug" has the meaning assigned by section 2 of the Misuse of Drugs Act 1971;

"intimate search" means a search which consists of the physical examination of a person's body orifices;

"relevant offence" means an offence involving a controlled drug under any of the following provisions of the Customs and Excise Management Act 1979—

(a) section 50(2) or (3) (importation etc. of prohibited goods);
(b) section 68(2) (exportation etc. of prohibited goods);
(c) section 170(1) (possession or dealing with prohibited goods);
(d) section 170(2) (being concerned in evasion or attempt at evasion of a prohibition);

[1]"superior officer" means an officer whose title is specified for the purpose of this section by the Treasury in an order made by statutory instrument subject to annulment in pursuance of a resolution of either House of Parliament.

NOTE

[1]Substituted by the Crime and Punishment (Scotland) Act 1997 (c. 48) s.62(1) and Sched. 1, para. 18(8) with effect from August 1, 1997 in terms of the Crime and Punishment (Scotland) Act 1997 (Commencement and Transitional Provisions) Order 1997 (S.I. 1997 No. 1712) para. 3.

PART IV

INVESTIGATION OF SERIOUS OR COMPLEX FRAUD

Lord Advocate's direction

27.—(1) Where it appears to the Lord Advocate—

(a) that a suspected offence may involve serious or complex fraud; and
(b) that, for the purpose of investigating the affairs or any aspect of the affairs of any person, there is good reason to do so,

he may give a direction under this section.

(2) The Lord Advocate may also give a direction under this section by virtue of section 4(2B) of the Criminal Justice (International Co-operation) Act 1990 or on a request being made to him by the Attorney-General of the Isle of Man, Jersey or Guernsey acting under legislation corresponding to this Part of this Act.

(3) Where a direction is given under this section, this Part of this Act shall apply as regards the investigation of the offence; and any person (other than a constable) nominated by the Lord Advocate either generally or in respect of a particular case (in this Part of this Act referred to as "a nominated

officer") shall be entitled to exercise the powers and functions conferred by this Part of this Act.

(4) A direction under this section shall be signed by the Lord Advocate.

Powers of investigation

28.—(1) A nominated officer may by notice in writing require the person whose affairs are to be investigated ("the person under investigation") or any other person who he has reason to believe has relevant information to answer questions or otherwise furnish information with respect to any matter relevant to the investigation at a specified place and either at a specified time or forthwith.

(2) A nominated officer may by notice in writing require the person under investigation or any other person to produce at such place as may be specified in the notice and either forthwith or at such time as may be so specified any specified documents which appear to a nominated officer to relate to any matter relevant to the investigation or any documents of a specified description which appear to him so to relate; and—

    (a) if any such documents are produced, a nominated officer may—

        (i) take copies or extracts from them;

        (ii) require the person producing them to provide an explanation of any of them;

    (b) if any such documents are not produced, a nominated officer may require the person who was required to produce them to state, to the best of his knowledge and belief, where they are.

(3) Where, on a petition presented by the procurator fiscal, the sheriff is satisfied, in relation to any documents, that there are reasonable grounds for believing—

    (a) that—

        (i) a person has failed to comply with an obligation under this section to produce them;

        (ii) it is not practicable to serve a notice under subsection (2) above in relation to them; or

        (iii) the service of such a notice in relation to them might seriously prejudice the investigation; and

    (b) that they are on premises specified in the petition,

he may issue such a warrant as is mentioned in subsection (4) below.

(4) The warrant referred to in subsection (3) above is a warrant authorising a constable together with any other persons named in the warrant—

    (a) to enter (using such force as is reasonably necessary for the purpose) and search the premises; and

    (b) to take possession of any documents appearing to be documents of the description specified in the petition or to take in relation to any documents so appearing any other steps which may appear to be necessary for preserving them and preventing interference with them.

(5) A statement by a person in response to a requirement imposed by virtue of this section may only be used in evidence against him—

    (a) in a prosecution for an offence under section 44(2) of this Act; or

    (b) in a prosecution for some other offence where in giving evidence he makes a statement inconsistent with it.

[[1] (5A) However, the statement may not be used against that person by virtue of paragraph (b) of subsection (5) unless evidence relating to it is adduced, or a question relating to it is asked, by or on behalf of that person in the proceedings arising out of the prosecution.]

(6) A person shall not under this section be required to disclose any

information or produce any document which is an item subject to legal privilege within the meaning of section 33 of this Act; except that a lawyer may be required to furnish the name and address of his client.

(7) No person shall be bound to comply with any requirement imposed by a person exercising power by virtue of a nomination under section 27(3) of this Act unless he has, if required to do so, produced evidence of his authority.

(8) Any evidence obtained by the Lord Advocate by virtue of section 4(2B) of the Criminal Justice (International Co-operation) Act 1990 shall be furnished by him to the Secretary of State for transmission to the overseas authority in compliance with whose request (in the following subsections referred to as the "relevant request") it was so obtained.

(9) If, in order to comply with the relevant request, it is necessary for that evidence to be accompanied by any certificate, affidavit or other verifying document, the Lord Advocate shall also furnish for transmission such document of that nature as appears to him to be appropriate.

(10) Where any evidence obtained by virtue of section 4(2B) of the said Act of 1990 consists of a document, the original or a copy shall be transmitted and where it consists of any other article, the article itself or a description, photograph or other representation of it shall be transmitted, as may be necessary in order to comply with the relevant request.

(11) In this section—

"documents" includes information recorded in any form and, in relation to information recorded otherwise than in legible form, references to its production include references to producing a copy of the information in legible form;

"evidence", in relation to a relevant request, includes documents and other articles; and

"premises" has the same meaning as in section 33 of this Act.

(2) This section and sections 27 and 29 of this Act shall apply to England and Wales and Northern Ireland; and for the purposes of such application any reference—

(a) to the sheriff shall be construed as a reference to a justice of the peace; and

(b) to a petition presented by the procurator fiscal shall be construed—

(i) in England and Wales as a reference to an information laid by a nominated officer;

(ii) in Northern Ireland as a reference to a complaint laid by a nominated officer.

NOTE
[1] Prospectively amended by the Youth Justice and Criminal Evidence Act 1999 (c.23), s.59 and Sched. 3, para. 25.

Offences in relation to investigations under section 28

29.—(1) Where any person—

(a) knows or suspects that an investigation under section 28 of this Act is being carried out or is likely to be carried out; and

(b) falsifies, conceals, destroys or otherwise disposes of, or causes or permits the falsification, concealment, destruction or disposal of documents which he knows or suspects or has reasonable grounds to suspect are or would be relevant to such an investigation,

he shall be guilty of an offence.

(2) In proceedings against a person for an offence under subsection (1) above, it shall be a defence to prove—

(a) that he did not know or suspect that by acting as he did he was likely to prejudice the investigation; or

(b) that he had lawful authority or reasonable excuse for acting as he did.

(3) A person guilty of an offence under subsection (1) above shall be liable—

(a) on conviction on indictment, to imprisonment for a term not exceeding seven years or to a fine or to both; and

(b) on summary conviction, to imprisonment for a term not exceeding six months or to a fine not exceeding the statutory maximum or to both.

(4) Any person who fails to comply with a requirement imposed on him under the said section 28 shall be guilty of an offence and liable on summary conviction to imprisonment for a term not exceeding six months or to a fine not exceeding level 5 on the standard scale or to both.

(5) In proceedings against a person for an offence under subsection (4) above, it shall be a defence to prove that he had a reasonable excuse for acting as he did.

Disclosure of information

30.—(1) Where any information subject to an obligation of secrecy under the Taxes Management Act 1970 has been disclosed by the Commissioners of Inland Revenue or an officer of those Commissioners for the purposes of any prosecution of an offence relating to inland revenue, that information may be disclosed by the Lord Advocate for the purposes of any prosecution of an offence—

(a) in respect of which a direction has been given under section 27(1)(a) of this Act; or

(b) relating to inland revenue,

but not otherwise.

(2) Where any information is subject to an obligation of secrecy imposed by or under any enactment other than an enactment contained in the Taxes Management Act 1970, the obligation shall not have effect to prohibit the disclosure of that information to a nominated officer but any information disclosed by virtue of this subsection may only be disclosed by the Lord Advocate for the purpose of a prosecution in Scotland or elsewhere.

(3) Without prejudice to his power to enter into an agreement apart from this subsection, the Lord Advocate may enter into an agreement for the supply of information to or by him subject, in either case, to an obligation not to disclose the information concerned otherwise than for a specified purpose.

(4) Subject to subsections (1) and (2) above and to any provision of an agreement for the supply of information which restricts the disclosure of the information supplied, information obtained by a nominated officer may be disclosed—

(a) to any government department, or any Northern Ireland Department, or other authority or body discharging its functions on behalf of the Crown (including the Crown in right of Her Majesty's Government in Northern Ireland);

(b) to any competent authority;

(c) for the purposes of any prosecution in Scotland or elsewhere; and

(d) for the purposes of assisting any public or other authority for the time being designated for the purpose of this paragraph by an order made by the Secretary of State to discharge any functions which are specified in the order.

(5) The following are competent authorities for the purposes of subsection (4) above—

(a) an inspector appointed under Part XIV of the Companies Act 1985 or Part XV of the Companies (Northern Ireland) Order 1986;

(b) the Accountant in Bankruptcy;

(c) an Official Receiver;

(d) the Official Receiver for Northern Ireland;

(e) a person appointed to carry out an investigation under section 55 of the Building Societies Act 1986;

(f) a body administering a compensation scheme under section 54 of the Financial Services Act 1986;

(g) an inspector appointed under section 94 of that Act;

(h) a person exercising powers by virtue of section 106 of that Act;

(j) an inspector appointed under section 177 of that Act or any corresponding enactment having effect in Northern Ireland;

(k) a person appointed by the Bank of England under section 41 of the Banking Act 1987 to carry out an investigation and make a report;

(l) a person exercising powers by virtue of section 44(2) of the Insurance Companies Act 1982;

(m) any body having supervisory, regulatory or disciplinary functions in relation to any profession or any area of commercial activity; and

(n) any person or body having, under the law of any country or territory outside the United Kingdom, functions corresponding to any of the functions of any person or body mentioned in any of the foregoing paragraphs.

(6) An order under subsection (4)(d) above may impose conditions subject to which, and otherwise restrict the circumstances in which, information may be disclosed under that paragraph.

PART V

DRUG TRAFFICKING

Investigations and disclosure of information

Order to make material available

31.—(1) The procurator fiscal may, for the purpose of an investigation into drug trafficking, apply to the sheriff for an order under subsection (2) below in relation to particular material or material of a particular description.

(2) If on such an application the sheriff is satisfied that the conditions in subsection (4) below are fulfilled, he may, subject to section 35(11) of this Act, make an order that the person who appears to him to be in possession of the material to which the application relates shall—

(a) produce it to a constable or person commissioned by the Commissioners of Customs and Excise for him to take away; or

(b) give a constable or person so commissioned access to it,

within such period as the order may specify.

(3) The period to be specified in an order under subsection (2) above shall be seven days unless it appears to the sheriff that a longer or shorter period would be appropriate in the particular circumstances of the application.

(4) The conditions referred to in subsection (2) above are—

(a) that there are reasonable grounds for suspecting that a specified person has carried on, or has derived financial or other rewards from, drug trafficking;

(b) that there are reasonable grounds for suspecting that the material to which the application relates—

(i) is likely to be of substantial value (whether by itself or together with other material) to the investigation for the purpose of which the application is made; and

(ii) does not consist of or include items subject to legal privilege; and

    (c) that there are reasonable grounds for believing that it is in the public interest, having regard—
        (i) to the benefit likely to accrue to the investigation if the material is obtained; and
        (ii) to the circumstances under which the person in possession of the material holds it,
    that the material should be produced or that access to it should be given.

(5) Where the sheriff makes an order under subsection (2)(b) above in relation to material on any premises he may, on the application of the procurator fiscal, order any person who appears to him to be entitled to grant entry to the premises to allow a constable or person commissioned as aforesaid to enter the premises to obtain access to the material.

(6) Provision may be made by rules of court as to—
    (a) the discharge and variation of orders under this section, and
    (b) proceedings relating to such orders.

(7) Where the material to which an application under this section relates consists of information contained in a computer—
    (a) an order under subsection (2)(a) above shall have effect as an order to produce the material in a form in which it can be taken away and in which it is visible and legible; and
    (b) an order under subsection (2)(b) above shall have effect as an order to give access to the material in a form in which it is visible and legible.

(8) An order under subsection (2) above—
    (a) shall not confer any right to production of, or access to, items subject to legal privilege;
    (b) shall have effect notwithstanding any obligation as to secrecy or other restriction upon the disclosure of information imposed by statute or otherwise; and
    (c) may be made in relation to material in the possession of an authorised government department.

Authority for search

32.—(1) The procurator fiscal may, for the purpose of an investigation into drug trafficking, apply to the sheriff for a warrant under this section in relation to specified premises.

(2) On such application the sheriff may issue a warrant authorising a constable, or person commissioned by the Commissioners of Customs and Excise, to enter and search the premises if the sheriff is satisfied—
    (a) that an order made under section 31 of this Act in relation to material on the premises has not been complied with; or
    (b) that the conditions in subsection (3) below are fulfilled; or
    (c) that the conditions in subsection (4) below are fulfilled.

(3) The conditions referred to in subsection (2)(b) above are—
    (a) that there are reasonable grounds for suspecting that a specified person has carried on, or has derived financial or other rewards from, drug trafficking; and
    (b) that the conditions in subsection (4)(b) and (c) of section 31 of this Act are fulfilled in relation to any material on the premises; and
    (c) that it would not be appropriate to make an order under that section in relation to the material because—
        (i) it is not practicable to communicate with any person entitled to produce the material; or
        (ii) it is not practicable to communicate with any person entitled to grant access to the material or entitled to grant entry to the premises on which the material is situated; or

(iii) the investigation for the purposes of which the application is made might be seriously prejudiced unless a constable or person commissioned as aforesaid could secure immediate access to the material.

(4) The conditions referred to in subsection (2)(c) above are—

(a) that there are reasonable grounds for suspecting that a specified person has carried on, or has derived financial or other rewards from, drug trafficking; and

(b) that there are reasonable grounds for suspecting that there is on the premises material relating to the specified person or to drug trafficking which is likely to be of substantial value (whether by itself or together with other material) to the investigation for the purpose of which the application is made, but that the material cannot at the time of the application be particularised; and

(c) that—

    (i) it is not practicable to communicate with any person entitled to grant entry to the premises; or

    (ii) entry to the premises will not be granted unless a warrant is produced; or

    (iii) the investigation for the purpose of which the application is made might be seriously prejudiced unless a constable or person commissioned as aforesaid arriving at the premises could secure immediate entry to them.

(5) Where a constable or person commissioned as aforesaid has entered premises in the execution of a warrant issued under this section, he may seize and retain any material, other than items subject to legal privilege, which is likely to be of substantial value (whether by itself or together with other material) to the investigation for the purpose of which the warrant was issued.

Interpretation of sections 31 and 32

33. In sections 31 and 32 of this Act—

"items subject to legal privilege" means—

    (a) communications between a professional legal adviser and his client; or

    (b) communications made in connection with or in contemplation of legal proceedings and for the purposes of these proceedings,

being communications which would in legal proceedings be protected from disclosure by virtue of any rule of law relating to the confidentiality of communications; and

"premises" includes any place and, in particular, includes—

    (a) any vehicle, vessel, aircraft or hovercraft;

    (b) any offshore installation within the meaning of section 1 of the Mineral Workings (Offshore Installations) Act 1971; and

    (c) any tent or moveable structure.

Prosecution by order of the Commissioners of Customs and Excise

34.—(1) Summary proceedings for a specified offence may be instituted by order of the Commissioners and shall, if so instituted, be commenced in the name of an officer.

(2) In the case of the death, removal, discharge or absence of the officer in whose name any proceedings for a specified offence were commenced, those proceedings may be continued by another officer.

(3) Where the Commissioners investigate, or propose to investigate, any matter with a view to determining—

(a) whether there are grounds for believing that a specified offence has been committed; or

(b) whether a person should be prosecuted for a specified offence,
that matter shall be treated as an assigned matter within the meaning of the
Customs and Excise Management Act 1979.

(4) Nothing in this section shall be taken—

(a) to prevent any person (including any officer) who has power to arrest,
detain or prosecute any person for a specified offence from doing so;
or

(b) to prevent a court from proceeding to deal with a person brought
before it following his arrest by an officer for a specified offence, even
though the proceedings have not been instituted by an order made
under subsection (1) above.

(5) In this section—

"the Commissioners" means the Commissioners of Customs and
Excise;

"officer" means a person commissioned by the Commissioners; and

"specified offence" means—

(a) an offence under section 36, 37, 38, 39 or 40 of this Act or
section 14 of the Criminal Justice (International Co- operation) Act 1990 (concealing or transferring proceeds of drug
trafficking);

(b) attempting to commit, conspiracy to commit or incitement to
commit, any such offence; or

(c) any other offence of a kind prescribed in regulations made by
the Secretary of State for the purposes of this section.

(6) Regulations under subsection (5) above shall be made by statutory
instrument subject to annulment in pursuance of a resolution of either
House of Parliament.

Disclosure of information held by government departments

35.—(1) Subject to subsection (4) below, the Court of Session may on an
application by the Lord Advocate order any material mentioned in
subsection (3) below which is in the possession of an authorised government
department to be produced to the Court within such period as the Court may
specify.

(2) The power to make an order under subsection (1) above is exercisable
if—

(a) the powers conferred on the Court by subsection (1) of section 28 of
the Proceeds of Crime (Scotland) Act 1995 are exercisable by virtue
of subsection (2) of section 29 of that Act; or

(b) those powers are exercisable by virtue of subsection (3) of the said
section 29 and the Court has made a restraint order (within the
meaning of section 28 of that Act) which has not been recalled.

(3) The material referred to in subsection (1) above is any material
which—

(a) has been submitted to an officer of an authorised government
department by a person who holds, or has at any time held, realisable
property (within the meaning of section 4 of the said Act of 1995);

(b) has been made by an officer of an authorised government department
in relation to such a person; or

(c) is correspondence which passed between an officer of an authorised
government department and such a person,

and an order under that subsection may require the production of all such
material or of a particular description of such material, being material in the
possession of the department concerned.

(4) An order under subsection (1) above shall not require the production
of any material unless it appears to the Court of Session that the material is
likely to contain information that would facilitate the exercise of the powers

conferred on the Court by section 28 of the said Act of 1995 or paragraph 1 or 12 of Schedule 1 to that Act or on an administrator appointed under sub-paragraph (1) of the said paragraph 1.

(5) The Court may by order authorise the disclosure to such an administrator of any material produced under subsection (1) above or any part of such material; but the Court shall not make an order under this subsection unless a reasonable opportunity has been given for an officer of the department to make representations to the Court.

(6) Material disclosed in pursuance of an order under subsection (5) above may, subject to any conditions contained in the order, be further disclosed for the purposes of the functions under the said Act of 1995 of the administrator or the High Court.

(7) The Court of Session may by order authorise the disclosure to a person mentioned in subsection (8) below of any material produced under subsection (1) above or any part of such material; but the Court shall not make an order under this subsection unless—

(a) a reasonable opportunity has been given for an officer of the department to make representations to the Court; and

(b) it appears to the Court that the material is likely to be of substantial value in exercising functions relating to drug trafficking.

(8) The persons referred to in subsection (7) above are—

(a) a constable;

(b) the Lord Advocate or any procurator fiscal; and

(c) a person commissioned by the Commissioners of Customs and Excise.

(9) Material disclosed in pursuance of an order under subsection (7) above may, subject to any conditions contained in the order, be further disclosed for the purposes of functions relating to drug trafficking.

(10) Material may be produced or disclosed in pursuance of this section notwithstanding any obligation as to secrecy or other restriction upon the disclosure of information imposed by statute or otherwise.

(11) An order under subsection (1) above and, in the case of material in the possession of an authorised government department, an order under section 31(2) of this Act may require any officer of the department (whether named in the order or not) who may for the time being be in possession of the material concerned to comply with such order; and any such order shall be served as if the proceedings were civil proceedings against the department.

(12) The person on whom an order under subsection (1) above is served—

(a) shall take all reasonable steps to bring it to the attention of the officer concerned; and

(b) if the order is not brought to that officer's attention within the period referred to in subsection (1) above, shall report the reasons for the failure to the Court of Session,

and it shall also be the duty of any other officer of the department in receipt of the order to take such steps as are mentioned in paragraph (a) above.

Offences

Offence of prejudicing investigation

36.—(1) A person who, knowing or suspecting that an investigation into drug trafficking is taking place, does anything which is likely to prejudice the investigation is guilty of an offence.

(2) In proceedings against a person for an offence under subsection (1) above, it is a defence to prove—

(a) that he did not know or suspect, or have reasonable grounds to suspect, that by acting as he did he was likely to prejudice the investigation; or

(b) that he had lawful authority or reasonable excuse for acting as he did.

(3) Nothing in subsection (1) above makes it an offence for a professional legal adviser to disclose any information or other matter—

    (a) to, or to a representative of, a client of his in connection with the giving by the adviser of legal advice to the client; or

    (b) to any person—

        (i) in contemplation of, or in connection with, legal proceedings; and

        (ii) for the purpose of those proceedings.

(4) Subsection (3) above does not apply in relation to any information or other matter which is disclosed with a view to furthering any criminal purpose.

(5) A person guilty of an offence under subsection (1) above shall be liable—

    (a) on conviction on indictment, to imprisonment for a term not exceeding five years or to a fine or to both; and

    (b) on summary conviction, to imprisonment for a term not exceeding six months or to a fine not exceeding the statutory maximum or to both.

Acquisition, possession or use of proceeds of drug trafficking

37.—(1) A person is guilty of an offence if, knowing that any property is, or in whole or in part directly or indirectly represents, another person's proceeds of drug trafficking, he acquires or uses that property or has possession of it.

(2) It is a defence to a charge of committing an offence under this section that the person charged acquired or used the property or had possession of it for adequate consideration.

(3) For the purposes of subsection (2) above—

    (a) a person acquires property for inadequate consideration if the value of the consideration is significantly less than the value of the property; and

    (b) a person uses or has possession of property for inadequate consideration if the value of the consideration is significantly less than the value of his use or possession of the property.

(4) The provision for any person of services or goods which are of assistance to him in drug trafficking shall not be treated as consideration for the purposes of subsection (2) above.

(5) Where a person discloses to a constable or to a person commissioned by the Commissioners of Customs and Excise a suspicion or belief that any property is, or in whole or in part directly or indirectly represents, another person's proceeds of drug trafficking, or discloses to a constable or a person so commissioned any matter on which such a suspicion or belief is based—

    (a) the disclosure shall not be treated as a breach of any restriction upon the disclosure of information imposed by statute or otherwise; and

    (b) if he does any act in relation to the property in contravention of subsection (1) above, he does not commit an offence under this section if—

        (i) the disclosure is made before he does the act concerned and the act is done with the consent of the constable or person so commissioned, or

        (ii) the disclosure is made after he does the act, but on his initiative and as soon as it is reasonable for him to make it.

(6) For the purposes of this section having possession of any property shall be taken to be doing an act in relation to it.

(7) In proceedings against a person for an offence under this section, it is a defence to prove that—

(a) he intended to disclose to a constable or a person so commissioned such a suspicion, belief or matter as is mentioned in subsection (5) above; but

(b) there is reasonable excuse for his failure to make the disclosure in accordance with paragraph (b) of that subsection.

(8) In the case of a person who was in employment at the relevant time, subsections (5) and (7) above shall have effect in relation to disclosures, and intended disclosures, to the appropriate person in accordance with the procedure established by his employer for the making of such disclosures as they have effect in relation to disclosures, and intended disclosures, to a constable or a person so commissioned.

(9) A person guilty of an offence under this section is liable—

(a) on summary conviction, to imprisonment for a term not exceeding six months or to a fine not exceeding the statutory maximum or to both; or

(b) on conviction on indictment, to imprisonment for a term not exceeding fourteen years or to a fine or to both.

(10) No constable, person so commissioned or other person shall be guilty of an offence under this section in respect of anything done by him in the course of acting in connection with the enforcement, or intended enforcement, of any provision of this Act or of any other enactment relating to drug trafficking or the proceeds of such trafficking.

Offence of assisting another to retain the proceeds of drug trafficking

38.—(1) Subject to subsection (3)(b) below, a person shall be guilty of an offence if, knowing or suspecting that another person (in this section referred to as "A") is a person who carries on, or has carried on, or has derived financial or other rewards from, drug trafficking, he enters into, or is otherwise concerned in, an arrangement whereby—

(a) the retention or control, by or on behalf of A, of A's proceeds of drug trafficking is facilitated (whether by concealment, removal from the jurisdiction, transfer to nominees or otherwise); or

(b) A's proceeds of drug trafficking—
   (i) are used to secure that funds are placed at A's disposal; or
   (ii) are used for A's benefit to acquire property by way of investment.

(2) In this section, references to proceeds of drug trafficking shall be construed as including any property which, whether in whole or in part, directly or indirectly constitutes such proceeds.

(3) Where a person discloses to a constable or to a person commissioned by the Commissioners of Customs and Excise a suspicion or belief that any funds or investments are derived from or used in connection with drug trafficking or discloses to a constable or a person so commissioned any matter on which such a suspicion or belief is based—

(a) the disclosure shall not be treated as a breach of any restriction imposed by statute or otherwise on the disclosure of information; and

(b) if the disclosure relates to an arrangement entry into which, or concern in which, by the person would (but for this paragraph) contravene subsection (1) above, he does not commit an offence under that subsection if—
   (i) the disclosure is made before, with the consent of the constable or as the case may be of the person so commissioned, he enters into, or becomes concerned in, that arrangement; or
   (ii) though made after he enters into, or becomes concerned in, that arrangement, it is made on his own initiative and as soon as it is reasonable for him to do so.

(4) In proceedings against a person for an offence under subsection (1) above, it shall be a defence to prove—

(a) that he did not know or suspect that the arrangement related to any person's proceeds of drug trafficking; or

(b) that he did not know or suspect that by the arrangement the retention or control by or on behalf of A of any property was facilitated or, as the case may be, that by the arrangement any property was used as mentioned in subsection (1) above; or

(c) that—

    (i) he intended to disclose to a constable or to a person commissioned as aforesaid such a suspicion, belief or matter as is mentioned in subsection (3) above in relation to the arrangement; but

    (ii) there is reasonable excuse for his failure to make disclosure in accordance with paragraph (b) of that subsection.

(5) In the case of a person who was in employment at the relevant time, subsections (3) and (4) above shall have effect in relation to disclosures, and intended disclosures, to the appropriate person in accordance with the procedure established by his employer for the making of such disclosures as they have effect in relation to disclosures, and intended disclosures, to a constable or a person commissioned as aforesaid.

(6) A person guilty of an offence under subsection (1) above shall be liable—

(a) on conviction on indictment, to imprisonment for a term not exceeding fourteen years or to a fine or to both; and

(b) on summary conviction, to imprisonment for a term not exceeding six months or to a fine not exceeding the statutory maximum or to both.

Failure to disclose knowledge or suspicion of money laundering

39.—(1) A person is guilty of an offence if—

(a) he knows, or suspects, that another person is engaged in drug money laundering;

(b) the information, or other matter, on which that knowledge or suspicion is based came to his attention in the course of his trade, profession, business or employment; and

(c) he does not disclose the information or other matter to a constable or to a person commissioned by the Commissioners of Customs and Excise as soon as is reasonably practicable after it comes to his attention.

(2) Subsection (1) above does not make it an offence for a professional legal adviser to fail to disclose any information or other matter which has come to him in privileged circumstances.

(3) It is a defence to a charge of committing an offence under this section that the person charged had a reasonable excuse for not disclosing the information or other matter in question.

(4) Where a person discloses to a constable or a person so commissioned—

(a) his suspicion or belief that another person is engaged in drug money laundering; or

(b) any information or other matter on which that suspicion or belief is based,

the disclosure shall not be treated as a breach of any restriction imposed by statute or otherwise.

(5) Without prejudice to subsection (3) or (4) above, in the case of a person who was in employment at the relevant time, it is a defence to a

charge of committing an offence under this section that he disclosed the information or other matter in question to the appropriate person in accordance with the procedure established by his employer for the making of such disclosures.

(6) A disclosure to which subsection (5) above applies shall not be treated as a breach of any restriction imposed by statute or otherwise.

(7) In this section "drug money laundering" means doing any act which constitutes an offence under—

(a) section 37 or 38 of this Act; or

(b) section 14 of the Criminal Justice (International Co-operation) Act 1990 (concealing or transferring proceeds of drug trafficking),

or, in the case of an act done otherwise than in Scotland, would constitute such an offence if done in Scotland.

(8) For the purposes of subsection (7) above, having possession of any property shall be taken to be doing an act in relation to it.

(9) For the purposes of this section, any information or other matter comes to a professional legal adviser in privileged circumstances if it is communicated, or given, to him—

(a) by, or by a representative of, a client of his in connection with the giving by the adviser of legal advice to the client;

(b) by, or by a representative of, a person seeking legal advice from the adviser; or

(c) by any person—

(i) in contemplation of, or in connection with, legal proceedings; and

(ii) for the purpose of those proceedings.

(10) No information or other matter shall be treated as coming to a professional legal adviser in privileged circumstances if it is communicated or given with a view to furthering any criminal purpose.

(11) A person guilty of an offence under this section shall be liable—

(a) on summary conviction, to imprisonment for a term not exceeding six months or a fine not exceeding the statutory maximum or to both, or

(b) on conviction on indictment, to imprisonment for a term not exceeding five years or a fine, or to both.

Tipping-off

40.—(1) A person is guilty of an offence if—

(a) he knows or suspects that a constable or a person commissioned by the Commissioners of Customs and Excise is acting, or is proposing to act, in connection with an investigation which is being, or is about to be, conducted into drug money laundering within the meaning of subsections (7) and (8) of section 39 of this Act; and

(b) he discloses to any other person information or any other matter which is likely to prejudice that investigation, or proposed investigation.

(2) A person is guilty of an offence if—

(a) he knows or suspects that a disclosure has been made to a constable, or a person so commissioned, under section 37, 38 or 39 of this Act; and

(b) he discloses to any other person information or any other matter which is likely to prejudice any investigation which might be conducted following the disclosure.

(3) A person is guilty of an offence if—

(a) he knows or suspects that a disclosure of a kind mentioned in section 37(8), 38(5) or 39(5) of this Act has been made; and

(b) he discloses to any person information or any other matter which is likely to prejudice any investigation which might be conducted following the disclosure.

(4) Nothing in subsections (1) to (3) above makes it an offence for a professional legal adviser to disclose any information or other matter—

(a) to, or to a representative of, a client of his in connection with the giving by the adviser of legal advice to the client; or

(b) to any person—

    (i) in contemplation of, or in connection with, legal proceedings; and

    (ii) for the purpose of those proceedings.

(5) Subsection (4) above does not apply in relation to any information or other matter which is disclosed with a view to furthering any criminal purpose.

(6) In proceedings against a person for an offence under subsection (1), (2) or (3) above, it is a defence to prove that he did not know or suspect that the disclosure was likely to be prejudicial in the way mentioned in that subsection.

(7) A person guilty of an offence under this section shall be liable—

(a) on summary conviction, to imprisonment for a term not exceeding six months or a fine not exceeding the statutory maximum or to both, or

(b) on conviction on indictment, to imprisonment for a term not exceeding five years or a fine, or to both.

(8) No constable, person so commissioned or other person shall be guilty of an offence under this section in respect of anything done by him in the course of acting in connection with the enforcement, or intended enforcement, of any provision of this Act or of any other enactment relating to drug trafficking or the proceeds of such trafficking.

Offences relating to controlled drugs: fines

41.—(1) Without prejudice to section 211(7) of the Criminal Procedure (Scotland) Act 1995 (fines) but subject to section 10(3)(a) of the Proceeds of Crime (Scotland) Act 1995, where a person is convicted on indictment of an offence to which this section relates and sentenced in respect of that offence to a period of imprisonment or detention, the Court where—

(a) paragraph (b) below does not apply shall, unless it is satisfied that for any reason it would be inappropriate to do so, also impose a fine;

(b) it makes a confiscation order under section 1(1) of the Proceeds of Crime (Scotland) Act 1995 as regards the person, may also impose a fine.

(2) In determining the amount of a fine imposed under paragraph (a) of subsection (1) above, the Court shall have regard to any profits likely to have been made by the person from the crime in respect of which he has been convicted.

(3) This section relates to an offence which is a drug trafficking offence within the meaning of the said last mentioned Act of 1995.

(4) Where in any proceedings a fine has been imposed by virtue of subsection (1) above as regards a person and a period of imprisonment or detention is imposed on him in default of payment of its amount (or as the case may be of an instalment thereof), that period shall run from the expiry of any other period of imprisonment or detention (not being one of life imprisonment or detention for life) imposed on him in the proceedings.

(5) The reference in subsection (4) above to "any other period of imprisonment or detention imposed" includes (without prejudice to the generality of the expression) a reference to such a period imposed on default of payment of a fine (or instalment thereof) or of a confiscation order (or instalment thereof); but only where that default has occurred before the

warrant for imprisonment is issued for the default in relation to the fine imposed by virtue of subsection (1) of this section.

Extension of certain offences to Crown servants and exemptions for regulators etc.

42.—(1) The Secretary of State may by regulations provide that, in such circumstances as may be prescribed, sections 36 to 40 of this Act shall apply to such persons in the public service of the Crown, or such categories of person in that service, as may be prescribed.

(2) Section 39 of this Act shall not apply to—

(a) any person designated by regulations made by the Secretary of State for the purpose of this paragraph; or

(b) in such circumstances as may be prescribed, any person who falls within such category of person as may be prescribed for the purpose of this paragraph.

(3) The Secretary of State may designate, for the purpose of paragraph (a) of subsection (2) above, any person appearing to him to be performing regulatory, supervisory, investigative or registration functions.

(4) The categories of person prescribed by the Secretary of State, for the purpose of paragraph (b) of subsection (2) above, shall be such categories of person connected with the performance by any designated person of regulatory, supervisory, investigative or registration functions as he considers it appropriate to prescribe.

(5) In this section—

"the Crown" includes the Crown in right of Her Majesty's Government in Northern Ireland; and

"prescribed" means prescribed by regulations made by the Secretary of State.

(6) The power to make regulations under this section shall be exercisable by statutory instrument.

(7) Any such instrument shall be subject to annulment in pursuance of a resolution of either House of Parliament.

Interpretation of Part V

43.—(1) In this Part of this Act (except where the context otherwise requires)—

"authorised government department" means a government department which is an authorised department for the purposes of the Crown Proceedings Act 1947;

"confiscation order" means an order under section 1(1), 11(4), 12(3) or 13 of the Proceeds of Crime (Scotland) Act 1995; and

"drug trafficking" has the same meaning as in the said Act of 1995.

(2) This Part of this Act shall (except where the context otherwise requires) be construed as one with the Criminal Procedure (Scotland) Act 1995.

(3) This Part of this Act applies to property whether it is situated in Scotland or elsewhere.

(4) References in this Part of this Act—

(a) to offences include a reference to offences committed before the commencement of section 1 of the Criminal Justice (Scotland) Act 1987; but nothing in this Act imposes any duty or confers any power on any court in or in connection with proceedings against a person for an offence to which that section relates instituted before the commencement of that section;

(b) to anything received in connection with drug trafficking include a reference to anything received both in that connection and in some other connection; and

(c) to property held by a person include a reference to property vested in the interim or permanent trustee in his sequestration or in his trustee in bankruptcy or liquidator.

PART VI

MISCELLANEOUS AND GENERAL

False oaths etc.

False statements and declarations

44.—(1) Any person who—

(a) is required or authorised by law to make a statement on oath for any purpose; and

(b) being lawfully sworn, wilfully makes a statement which is material for that purpose and which he knows to be false or does not believe to be true,

shall be guilty of an offence and liable on conviction to imprisonment for a term not exceeding five years or to a fine or to both such fine and imprisonment.

(2) Any person who knowingly and wilfully makes, otherwise than on oath, a statement false in a material particular, and the statement is made—

(a) in a statutory declaration; or

(b) in an abstract, account, balance sheet, book, certificate, declaration, entry, estimate, inventory, notice, report, return or other document which he is authorised or required to make, attest or verify by, under or in pursuance of any public general Act of Parliament for the time being in force; or

(c) in any oral declaration or oral answer which he is authorised or required to make by, under or in pursuance of any public general Act of Parliament for the time being in force; or

(d) in any declaration not falling within paragraph (a), (b) or (c) above which he is required to make by an order under section 2 of the Evidence (Proceedings in Other Jurisdictions) Act 1975,

shall be guilty of an offence and liable on conviction to imprisonment for a term not exceeding two years or to a fine or to both such fine and imprisonment.

(3) Any person who—

(a) procures or attempts to procure himself to be registered on any register or roll kept under or in pursuance of any Act of Parliament for the time being in force of persons qualified by law to practise any vocation or calling; or

(b) procures or attempts to procure a certificate of the registration of any person on any such register or roll,

by wilfully making or producing or causing to be made or produced either verbally or in writing, any declaration, certificate or representation which he knows to be false or fraudulent, shall be guilty of an offence and be liable on conviction to imprisonment for a term not exceeding 12 months or to a fine or to both such fine and imprisonment.

(4) Subsection (2) above applies to any oral statement made for the purpose of any entry in a register kept in pursuance of any Act of Parliament as it applies to the statements mentioned in that subsection.

Provisions supplementary to section 44

[1]**45.**—(1) Any person who aids, abets, counsels, procures or suborns another person to commit an offence against section 44 of this Act shall be liable to be proceeded against, indicted, tried and punished as if he were a principal offender.

(2) Any person who incites or attempts to procure or suborn another person to commit an offence against that section shall be guilty of an offence and be liable on conviction to imprisonment or to a fine or to both such fine and imprisonment.

(3) Nothing in section 44 and 46(1) of this Act and subsections (1) and (2) above shall affect the common law relating to the crime of perjury or to any crime or offence involving falsehood, fraud or wilful imposition, or the liability of any person to be prosecuted for any such crime or offence, provided that no person shall be liable in respect of the same matter to be punished both at common law and under these sections.

(4) Where the making of a false statement is not only an offence under the said sections 44 or 46(1) or under subsection (1) or (2) above, but also by virtue of some other Act is a corrupt practice or subjects the offender to any forfeiture or disqualification or to any penalty other than imprisonment or a fine, the liability of the offender under these sections shall be in addition to and not in substitution for his liability under such other Act.

(5) Where the making of a false statement is by any other Act whether passed before or after the commencement of this Act, made punishable on summary conviction, proceedings may be taken either under such other Act or under this Act.

NOTES
[1]Substituted by the Crime and Punishment (Scotland) Act 1997 (c. 48) s.62(1) and Sched. 1, para. 18(8) with effect from August 1, 1997 in terms of the Crime and Punishment (Scotland) Act 1997 (Commencement and Transitional Provisions) Order 1997 (S.I. 1997 No. 1712) para. 3.

Proceedings

46.—(1) For the purposes of any proceedings at common law for perjury or of any proceedings for a contravention of section 44(1) of this Act—
- (a) the forms and ceremonies used in administering an oath shall be immaterial if the court or person before whom the oath is taken has power to administer an oath for the purpose of verifying the statement in question, and if the oath has been administered in a form and with ceremonies which the person taking the oath has accepted without objection or has declared to be binding on him;
- (b) an affirmation or declaration made in lieu of an oath shall be of the like effect in all respects as if it had been made on oath.

(2) Where an offence against section 44 of this Act is committed in any place outside the United Kingdom, the offender may be proceeded against, tried and punished in any place in Scotland where he was apprehended or is in custody as if the offence had been committed in that place; and for all purposes incidental to or consequential on the trial or punishment of the offence, it shall be deemed to have been committed in that place.

(3) Any summary criminal proceedings for an offence against section 44 of this Act may, notwithstanding anything in the Criminal Procedure (Scotland) Act 1995, be commenced at any time within one year from the date of the commission of the offence, or within three months from the date when evidence sufficient in the opinion of the Lord Advocate to justify the proceedings comes to his knowledge whichever period last expires; and for the purposes of this section a certificate purporting to be signed by or on behalf of the Lord Advocate as to the date on which such evidence as aforesaid came to his knowledge shall be conclusive evidence thereof.

(4) In sections 44 and 45 of this Act and in this section, the expression "statutory declaration" means a declaration made by virtue of the Statutory Declarations Act 1835 or of any enactment (including subordinate legislation) applying or extending the provisions of that Act.

Offensive weapons

Prohibition of the carrying of offensive weapons

47.—(1) Any person who without lawful authority or reasonable excuse, the proof whereof shall lie on him, has with him in any public place any offensive weapon shall be guilty of an offence, and shall be liable—

    (a) on summary conviction, to imprisonment for a term not exceeding six months or a fine not exceeding the statutory maximum, or both;

    [1](b) on conviction on indictment, to imprisonment for a term not exceeding four years or a fine, or both.

(2) Where any person is convicted of an offence under subsection (1) above the court may make an order for the forfeiture or disposal of any weapon in respect of which the offence was committed.

(3) A constable may arrest without warrant any person whom he has reasonable cause to believe to be committing an offence under subsection (1) above, if the constable is not satisfied as to that person's identity or place of residence, or has reasonable cause to believe that it is necessary to arrest him in order to prevent the commission by him of any other offence in the course of committing which an offensive weapon might be used.

[2](4) In this section "public place" includes any road within the meaning of the Roads (Scotland) Act 1984 and any other premises or place to which at the material time the public have or are permitted to have access, whether on payment or otherwise; and "offensive weapon" means any article made or adapted for use for causing injury to the person, or intended by the person having it with him for such use by him or by some other person.

NOTES
[1]Amended by the Offensive Weapons Act 1996 (c. 26), s.2(2).
[2]Amended by the Offensive Weapons Act 1996 (c. 26), s.5.

Search for offensive weapons

48.—(1) Where a constable has reasonable grounds for suspecting that any person is carrying an offensive weapon and has committed or is committing an offence under section 47 of this Act, the constable may search that person without warrant, and detain him for such time as is reasonably required to permit the search to be carried out; and he shall inform the person of the reason for such detention.

(2) Any person who—

    (a) intentionally obstructs a constable in the exercise of the constable's powers under subsection (1) above; or

    (b) conceals from a constable acting in the exercise of those powers an offensive weapon,

shall be guilty of an offence and liable on summary conviction to a fine not exceeding level 4 on the standard scale.

(3) A constable may arrest without warrant any person who he has reason to believe has committed an offence under subsection (2) above.

(4) In this section, "offensive weapon" has the same meaning as in the said section 47.

Offence of having in public place article with blade or point

49.—(1) Subject to subsections (4) and (5) below, any person who has an article to which this section applies with him in a public place shall be guilty of an offence and liable—

    (a) on summary conviction, to imprisonment for a term not exceeding six months or a fine not exceeding the statutory maximum or both; and

(b) on conviction on indictment, to imprisonment for a term not exceeding two years or a fine or both.

(2) Subject to subsection (3) below, this section applies to any article which has a blade or is sharply pointed.

(3) This section does not apply to a folding pocketknife if the cutting edge of its blade does not exceed three inches (7.62 centimetres).

(4) It shall be a defence for a person charged with an offence under subsection (1) above to prove that he had good reason or lawful authority for having the article with him in the public place.

(5) Without prejudice to the generality of subsection (4) above, it shall be a defence for a person charged with an offence under subsection (1) above to prove that he had the article with him—

(a) for use at work;
(b) for religious reasons; or
(c) as part of any national costume.

(6) Where a person is convicted of an offence under subsection (1) above the court may make an order for the forfeiture of any article to which the offence relates, and any article forfeited under this subsection shall (subject to section 193 of the Criminal Procedure (Scotland) Act 1995 (suspension of forfeiture etc., pending appeal)) be disposed of as the court may direct.

(7) In this section "public place" includes any place to which at the material time the public have or are permitted access, whether on payment or otherwise.

Offence of having article with blade or point (or offensive weapon) on school premises

[1]**49A.**—(1) Any person who has an article to which section 49 of this Act applies with him on school premises shall be guilty of an offence.

(2) Any person who has an offensive weapon within the meaning of section 47 of this Act with him on school premises shall be guilty of an offence.

(3) It shall be a defence for a person charged with an offence under subsection (1) or (2) above to prove that he had good reason or lawful authority for having the article or weapon with him on the premises in question.

(4) Without prejudice to the generality of subsection (3) above, it shall be a defence for a person charged with an offence under subsection (1) or (2) above to prove that he had the article or weapon in question with him—

(a) for use at work,
(b) for educational purposes,
(c) for religious reasons, or
(d) as part of any national costume.

(5) A person guilty of an offence—
(a) under subsection (1) above shall be liable—

(i) on summary conviction to imprisonment for a term not exceeding six months, or a fine not exceeding the statutory maximum, or both;

(ii) on conviction on indictment, to imprisonment for a term not exceeding two years, or a fine, or both;

(b) under subsection (2) above shall be liable—

(i) on summary conviction, to imprisonment for a term not exceeding six months, or a fine not exceeding the statutory maximum, or both;

(ii) on conviction on indictment, to imprisonment for a term not exceeding four years, or a fine, or both.

(6) In this section and section 49B of this Act, "school premises" means land used for the purpose of a school excluding any land occupied solely as a

dwelling by a person employed at the school; and "school" has the meaning given by section 135(1) of the Education (Scotland) Act 1980.

NOTE
[1]Inserted by the Offensive Weapons Act 1996 (c. 26), s.4(3).

Power of entry to search for articles with blade or point and offensive weapons

[1]**49B.**—(1) A constable may enter school premises and search those premises and any person on those premises for—
  (a) any article to which section 49 of this Act applies, or
  (b) any offensive weapon within the meaning of section 47 of this Act,
if he has reasonable grounds for suspecting that an offence under section 49A of this Act is being, or has been, committed.
  (2) If in the course of a search under this section a constable discovers an article or weapon which he has reasonable grounds for believing to be an article or weapon of a kind described in subsection (1) above, he may seize it.
  (3) The constable may use reasonable force, if necessary, in the exercise of the power of entry conferred by this section.
  (4) Subsections (1) to (3) above shall come into force on such day as the Secretary of State may by order made by statutory instrument appoint.

NOTE
[1]Inserted by the Offensive Weapons Act 1996 (c. 26), s.4(3).

Extension of constable's power to stop, search and arrest without warrant

50.—(1) Where a constable has reasonable grounds for suspecting that a person has with him an article to which section 49 of this Act applies and has committed or is committing an offence under subsection (1) of that section, the constable may search that person without warrant and detain him for such time as is reasonably required to permit the search to be carried out.
  (2) A constable who detains a person under subsection (1) above shall inform him of the reason for his detention.
  [1](3) Where a constable has reasonable cause to believe that a person has committed or is committing an offence under section 49(1) or section 49A(1) or (2) of this Act and the constable—
  (a) having requested that person to give his name or address or both—
    (i) is not given the information requested; or
    (ii) is not satisfied that such information as is given is correct; or
  (b) has reasonable cause to believe that it is necessary to arrest him in order to prevent the commission by him of any other offence in the course of committing which an article to which that section applies might be used,
he may arrest that person without warrant.
  (4) Any person who—
  (a) intentionally obstructs a constable in the exercise of the constable's powers under subsection (1) above; or
  (b) conceals from a constable acting in the exercise of those powers an article to which section 49 of this Act applies,
shall be guilty of an offence and liable on summary conviction to a fine not exceeding level 3 on the standard scale.
  (5) Where a constable has reasonable cause to believe that a person has committed or is committing an offence under subsection (4) above he may arrest that person without warrant.

NOTE
[1]As amended by the Offensive Weapons Act 1996 (c. 26), s.2(2).

Racially-aggravated harassment

[1]**50A.**—(1) A person is guilty of an offence under this section if he—

(a) pursues a racially-aggravated course of conduct which amounts to harassment of a person and—

(i) is intended to amount to harassment of that person; or

(ii) occurs in circumstances where it would appear to a reasonable person that it would amount to harassment of that person; or

(b) acts in a manner which is racially aggravated and which causes, or is intended to cause, a person alarm or distress.

(2) For the purposes of this section a course of conduct or an action is racially aggravated if—

(a) immediately before, during or immediately after carrying out the course of conduct or action the offender evinces towards the person affected malice and ill-will based on that person's membership (or presumed membership) of a racial group; or

(b) the course of conduct or action is motivated (wholly or partly) by malice and ill-will towards members of a racial group based on their membership of that group.

(3) In subsection (2)(a) above—

"membership", in relation to a racial group, includes association with members of that group;

"presumed" means presumed by the offender.

(4) It is immaterial for the purposes of paragraph (a) or (b) of subsection (2) above whether or not the offender's malice and ill-will is also based, to any extent, on—

(a) the fact or presumption that any person or group of persons belongs to any religious group; or

(b) any other factor not mentioned in that paragraph.

(5) A person who is guilty of an offence under this section shall—

(a) on summary conviction, be liable to a fine not exceeding the statutory maximum, or imprisonment for a period not exceeding six months, or both such fine and such imprisonment; and

(b) on conviction on indictment, be liable to a fine or to imprisonment for a period not exceeding seven years, or both such fine and such imprisonment.

(6) In this section—

"conduct" includes speech;

"harassment" of a person includes causing the person alarm or distress;

"racial group" means a group of persons defined by reference to race, colour, nationality (including citizenship) or ethnic or national origins,

and a course of conduct must involve conduct on at least two occasions.

NOTE

[1]Inserted by the Crime and Disorder Act 1998 (c. 37), s.33 (effective September 30, 1998: S.I. 1998 No. 2327).

Reset

Reset

51. Criminal resetting of property shall not be limited to the receiving of property taken by theft or robbery, but shall extend to the receiving of property appropriated by breach of trust and embezzlement and by falsehood, fraud and wilful imposition.

Vandalism

52.—(1) Subject to subsection (2) below, any person who, without reasonable excuse, wilfully or recklessly destroys or damages any property belonging to another shall be guilty of the offence of vandalism.

(2) It shall not be competent to charge acts which constitute the offence of wilful fire-raising as vandalism under this section.

(3) Any person convicted of the offence of vandalism shall be liable on summary conviction—

    (a) in the district court, to imprisonment for a term not exceeding 60 days, or to a fine not exceeding level 3 on the standard scale, or to both;

    (b) in the sheriff court—

        (i) for a first such offence, to imprisonment for a term not exceeding 3 months, or to a fine not exceeding the prescribed sum (within the meaning of section 225(8) of the Criminal Procedure (Scotland) Act 1995), or to both; and

        (ii) for any subsequent such offence, to imprisonment for a term not exceeding 6 months, or to the fine mentioned in sub-paragraph (i) above, or to both.

General

Short title, commencement and extent

53.—(1) This Act may be cited as the Criminal Law (Consolidation) (Scotland) Act 1995.

(2) This Act shall come into force on 1 April 1996.

(3) Subject to subsection (4) below, this Act extends only to Scotland.

(4) Section 35(10) to (12) of this Act extends also to England and Wales and sections 27 to 29 of this Act and this section extend also to England and Wales and Northern Ireland.

TABLE OF DERIVATIONS

Notes:

1. This Table shows the derivation of the provisions of the Bill.

2. The following abbreviations are used in the Table:—

Acts of Parliament

1933	=	False Oaths (Scotland) Act 1933 (c. 20)
1976	=	Sexual Offences (Scotland) Act 1976 (c. 67)
1980	=	Criminal Justice (Scotland) Act 1980 (c. 62)
1987	=	Criminal Justice (Scotland) Act 1987 (c. 41)
1988	=	Criminal Justice Act 1988 (c. 33)
1993	=	Criminal Justice Act 1993 (c. 36)
1994	=	Drug Trafficking Act 1994 (c. 37)
1995	=	Criminal Justice (Scotland) Act 1995 (c. 20)
1995CP	=	Criminal Justice (Consequential Provisions) (Scotland) Act 1995 (c. 40)
1995CLC	=	Criminal Law (Consolidation) (Scotland) Act 1995 (c. 39)

Provision	Derivation
1	1976 s.2A; Incest and Related Offences (Scotland) Act 1986 (c. 36) s.1
2	1976 s.2B; Incest and Related Offences (Scotland) Act 1986 (c. 36) s.1
3	1976 s.2C; Incest and Related Offences (Scotland) Act 1986 (c. 36) s.1
4	1976 s.2D; Incest and Related Offences (Scotland) Act 1986 (c. 36) s.1; 1987 Sch. 2
5(1), (2)	1976 s.3
(3)–(7)	1976 s.4; Incest and Related Offences (Scotland) Act 1986 (c. 36) Sch. 1 §.4; Criminal Justice (Scotland) Act 1995 (c. 20) Sch. 6 §
6	1976 s.5
7(1)	1976 s.1
(2), (3)	1976 s.2
(4)	1976 s.17
8(1), (2)	1976 s.8
(3)–(5)	1976 s.9
9	1976 s.10
10	1976 s.11
11(1)–(4)	1976 s.12
(5), (6)	1976 s.13(1)
12	1976 s.14; Criminal Procedure (Scotland) Act 1975 (c. 21) Sch. 7A; Criminal Law Act 1977 (c. 45) Sch. 11
13	1980 s.80; Mental Health (Scotland) Act 1984 (c. 36) Sch. 5; Criminal Justice and Public Order Act 1994 (c. 33) ss.145(2), 146(2)
14	1976 s.15
15	1976 s.6
16	1976 s.18
17	1976 s.19
18	1980 s.68; Sporting Events (Control of Alcohol etc.) Act 1985 (c. 57) s.10
19(1)	1980 s.69
(2)	1980 s.70
(3)–(6)	1980 s.70A; Public Order Act 1986 (c. 64) Sch. 1 §.10
(7)	1980 s.71; Public Order Act 1986 (c. 64) Sch. 1 §.11
20(1)	1980 s.72(1)
(2)	1980 s.73
(3)–(6)	1980 s.72A(1)–(4); Public Order Act 1986 (c. 64) Sch. 1 §.14
(7)	1980 s.74
(8)	1980 ss.72(2), (3), 72A(5); Public Order Act 1986 (c. 64) Sch. 1 §.14
21	1980 s.75; Public Order Act 1986 (c. 64) Sch. 1 §.12
22	1980 s.76; Law Reform (Miscellaneous Provisions) (Scotland) Act 1990 (c. 40) Sch. 8 §.3
23	1980 s.77; Sporting Events (Control of Alcohol etc.) Act 1985 (c. 57) s.10; Public Order Act 1986 (c. 64) Sch. 1 §.13
24	1987 s.48; Criminal Justice and Public Order Act 1994 (c. 33) s.129(4), (5)
25	1987 s.49; Criminal Justice and Public Order Act 1994 (c. 33) s.129(6); Children (Scotland) Act 1995 (c. 36) Sch. 3 §.[39]
26	1987 s.50
27	1987 s.51; Criminal Justice and Public Order Act 1994 (c. 33) s.164(3)
28	1987 s.52; 1988 Sch. 15 §.117; Criminal Justice and Public Order Act 1994 (c. 33) s.164(4)
29	1987 s.53

Provision	Derivation
30	1987 s.54; 1988 Sch. 15 §.111; S.I. 1989/2405 Sch. 9 Pt. II §.58
31	1987 s.38; 1988 Sch. 5 §.23
32	1987 s.39
33	1987 s.40
34	1987 s.40A; 1993 s.20(2)
35	1987 s.41
36	1987 s.42; 1993 s.26(2)
37	1987 s.42A; 1993 s.17(1)
38	1987 s.43; 1993 s.19(2), (3)
39	1987 s.43A; 1993 s.19(1)L
40	1987 s.43B; 1993 s.19(1)
41	1987 s.44
42	1987 s.46A; 1993 Sch. 4 §.2
43	1987 s.47(1)(part)–(4)
44(1) (2) (3) (4)	1933 s.1; Criminal procedure (Scotland) Act 1975 s.221(1) 1933 s.2; Evidence (Proceedings in Other Jurisdictions) Act 1975 (c. 35) Sch.1 1933 s.3 Criminal Justice (Scotland) Act 1949 (c. 94) s.42(1)
45(1), (2) (3)–(5)	1933 s.4 1933 s.6
46(1) (2) (3) (4)	1933 s.7(1) 1933 s.5 Criminal Justice (Scotland) Act 1949 (c. 94) s.42(2) 1933 s.7(2)
47	Prevention of Crime Act 1953 (c. 14) s.1; Criminal Procedure (Scotland) Act 1975 (c. 21) ss.193A, 298B; Roads (Scotland) Act 1984 (c. 54) Sch. 9 §.42; Criminal Justice Act 1988 (c. 33) Sch. 8 §.16
48	1980 s.4
49	Carrying of Knives (Scotland) Act 1993 (c. 13) s.1; Council Directive 80/181 (Approximation of Laws Relating to Units of Measurement)
50	Carrying of Knives (Scotland) Act 1993 (c. 13) s.2
51	Criminal Procedure (Scotland) Act 1975 (c. 21) s.59
52	1980 s.78
53(1), (2) (3), (4)	Drafting 1987 s.72(1), (4)

TABLE OF DESTINATIONS

FALSE OATHS (SCOTLAND) ACT 1933
(c.20)

1933	1995
s.1	s.44(1)
2	44(2)
3	44(3)
4	45(1), (2)
5	46(2)
6	45(3)–(5)
7(1)	46(1)
7(2)	46(2)

CRIMINAL JUSTICE (SCOTLAND) ACT 1949
c.94

1949	1995
s.42(1)	s.44(4)
(2)	46(2)

PREVENTION OF CRIME ACT 1953
(c.14)

1953	1995
s.1	s.47

CRIMINAL PROCEDURE (SCOTLAND) ACT 1975
(c.21)

1975	1995
s.59	s.51
193A	47
221(1)	44(1)
298B	47
Sched. 7A	s.12

EVIDENCE (PROCEEDINGS IN OTHER JURISDICTIONS) ACT 1975
(c.35)

1975	1995
Sched. 1	s.44(2)

SEXUAL OFFENCES (SCOTLAND) ACT 1976
(c.67)

1976	1995	1976	1995	1976	1995
s.1	s.7(1)	s.4	s.5(3)–(7)	s.12	s.11(1)–(4)
2	7(2), (3)	5	6	13(1)	11(5), (6)
2A	1	6	15	14	12
2B	2	8	8(1), (2)	15	14
2C	3	9	8(3)–(5)	17	7(4)
2D	4	10	9	18	16
3	5(1), (2)	11	10	19	17

CRIMINAL LAW ACT 1977
(c.45)

1977	1995
Sched. 11	s.12

CRIMINAL JUSTICE (SCOTLAND) ACT 1980
(c.62)

1980	1995	1980	1995	1980	1995
s.4	s.48	s.72(1)	s.20(1)	s.74	s.20(7)
68	18	(2)	20(8)	75	21
69	19(1)	72(3)	20(8)	76	22
70	19(2)	72A(1)–(4)	20(3)–(6)	77	23
70A	19(3)–(6)	(5)	20(8)	78	52
71	19(7)	73	20(2)	80	13

MENTAL HEALTH (SCOTLAND) ACT 1984
(c.36)

1984	1995
Sched. 5	13

ROADS (SCOTLAND) ACT 1984
(c.54)

1984	1995
Sched. 9, para. 42	47

SPORTING EVENTS (CONTROL OF ALCOHOL ETC.) ACT 1985
(c.57)

1985	1995
s.10	18, 23

INCEST AND RELATED OFFENCES (SCOTLAND) ACT 1986
(c.36)

1986	1995
s.1	ss.1, 2, 3, 4
Sched. 1, para. 4	s.5(3)–(7)

PUBLIC ORDER ACT 1986
(c.64)

1986	1995
Sched. 1,	
para. 10	s.19(3)–(6)
para. 11	19(7)
para. 12	21
para. 13	23
para. 14	s 20(3)–(6), 20(8)

CRIMINAL JUSTICE (SCOTLAND) ACT 1987
(c.41)

1987	1995	1987	1995	1987	1995
s.38	s.31	s.43	s.38	s.49	s.25
39	s.32	43A	39	50	26
40	33	43B	40	51	27
40A	34	44	41	52	28
41	35	46A	42	53	29
42	36	47(1)part–			
		(4)	43	54	30
42A	37	48	24	72(1)	53(3)

CRIMINAL PROCEDURE
(CONSEQUENTIAL PROVISIONS)
(SCOTLAND) ACT 1995*

(1995 c. 40)

ARRANGEMENT OF SECTIONS

An Act to make provision for repeals, consequential amendments, transitional and transitory matters and savings in connection with the consolidation of enactments in the Criminal Procedure (Scotland) Act 1995, the Proceeds of Crime (Scotland) Act 1995 and the Criminal Law (Consolidation) (Scotland) Act 1995.　　　　[8th November 1995]

Interpretation

1. In this Act—
　　"the consolidating Acts" means the Principal Act, the Proceeds of Crime (Scotland) Act 1995, the Criminal Law (Consolidation) (Scotland) Act 1995 and, so far as it reproduces the effect of the repealed enactments, this Act;
　　"the Principal Act" means the Criminal Procedure (Scotland) Act 1995"; and
　　"the repealed enactments" means the enactments repealed by this Act.

Continuity of the law

2.—(1) The substitution of the consolidating Acts for the repealed enactments does not affect the continuity of the law.

(2) Anything done or having effect as if done under or for the purposes of a provision of the repealed enactments has effect, if it could have been done under or for the purposes of the corresponding provision of the consolidating Acts, as if done under or for the purposes of that provision.

(3) Any reference, whether express or implied, in any enactment, instrument or document to a provision of the consolidating Acts shall, so far as the context permits, be construed as including, in relation to the times, circumstances and purposes in relation to which the corresponding provision of the repealed enactments has effect, a reference to that corresponding provision.

(4) Any reference, whether express or implied, in any enactment,

instrument or document to a provision of the repealed enactments shall be construed, so far as is required for continuing its effect, as including a reference to the corresponding provision of the consolidating Acts.

Rationalisation of penalties

3.—(1) Schedule 1 to this Act shall have effect for the purpose of setting or altering or enabling the Secretary of State to set or alter the penalties or maximum penalties in respect of certain offences or classes or descriptions of offences.

(2) Schedule 2 to this Act shall have effect for the purpose of amending the enactments there specified for the purposes of and in accordance with the provisions of the said Schedule 1.

Transitional, transitory and savings

4. The transitional provisions, transitory modifications and savings contained in Schedule 3 to this Act shall have effect.

Minor and consequential amendments

5. The enactments mentioned in Schedule 4 to this Act shall have effect subject to the amendments there specified being amendments consequential on this Act.

Repeals

6.—(1) The enactments mentioned in Schedule 5 to this Act are hereby repealed to the extent specified in the third column of that Schedule.

(2) Without prejudice to section 16(1)(a) of the Interpretation Act 1978, the repeal by this Act of the provisions of the Criminal Procedure (Scotland) Act 1975 specified in Schedule 6 to this Act shall not revive any rule of law or practice having effect before the coming into force of the Criminal Procedure (Scotland) Act 1887.

Short title, interpretation, commencement and extent

7.—(1) This Act may be cited as the Criminal Procedure (Consequential Provisions) (Scotland) Act 1995.

(2) This Act shall come into force on 1 April 1996.

(3) Subject to subsections (4) and (5) below, this Act extends to Scotland only.

(4) Paragraph 5 of Schedule 3 to this Act and this section also extend to England and Wales and Northern Ireland.

(5) Any amendment contained in Schedule 4 to this Act of any enactment which extends to England and Wales or Northern Ireland shall also so extend.

SCHEDULES

Section 3(1)   SCHEDULE 1

SETTING AND ALTERATION OF CERTAIN PENALTIES

Amendments relating to penalties and mode of trial for offences made triable only summarily

1.—(1) The enactments specified in column 2 of Part I of Schedule 2 to this Act (which relate to the modes of trial of, and the maximum penalties for, the offences which are by section 292 of the Principal Act made triable only summarily) shall continue to have effect subject to the amendments specified in column 3 of that Part.

(2) The said amendments have the effect of altering the maximum penalties available on summary conviction of those offences as well as making alterations consequential on their becoming triable only summarily; and in that Part, column 4 shows the maximum penalties resulting from the amendments.

Penalties on summary conviction for offences triable either summarily or on indictment

2.—(1) Where an offence created by a relevant enactment may be tried either on indictment or summarily, the penalty or maximum penalty on summary conviction shall, to the extent that it included, immediately before the commencement of section 55 of the Criminal Justice Act 1982, a penalty or maximum penalty mentioned in column 1 of the Table below, be amended so as to substitute as a maximum penalty the corresponding penalty set forth in column 2 thereof (unless provision is expressly made by any enactment for a larger penalty or maximum penalty on summary conviction)—

Column 1	Column 2
Penalty or maximum penalty at commencement of section 55 of Criminal Justice Act 1982	New maximum penalty
1. Fine (other than a fine specified in paragraph 3 below, or a fine in respect of each period of a specified length during which a continuing offence is committed).	1. Fine not exceeding the prescribed sum.
2. Imprisonment for a period exceeding 3 months.	2. Imprisonment for a period not exceeding 3 months.
3. Fine in respect of a specified quantity or number of things.	3. Fine not exceeding the prescribed sum in respect of each such quantity or number.
4. Fine exceeding £100 in respect of each period of a specified length during which a continuing offence is committed.	4. Fine not exceeding £100 in respect of each such period.

(2) Where by virtue of a relevant enactment, a person summarily convicted of any offence to which sub-paragraph (1) above relates would, apart from this paragraph, be liable to a fine or a maximum fine of one amount in the case of a first conviction and of a different amount in the case of a second or subsequent conviction, sub-paragraph (1) above shall apply irrespective of whether the conviction is a first, second or subsequent one.

(3) Sub-paragraph (1) above is without prejudice to section 5 of the Principal Act (6 months' imprisonment competent for certain offences).

(4) In this paragraph "relevant enactment" means an enactment contained in the Criminal Law Act 1977 or in any other Act (including this Act).

(5) Sub-paragraph (1) of paragraph 7 below shall not affect so much of any enactment as (in whatever words) provides for a person to be made liable, on summary conviction, to a fine or a maximum fine for each period of a specified length during which a continuing offence is committed.

(6) Where an enactment to which sub-paragraph (1) of the said paragraph 7 below applies provides for a person to be made liable to a penalty or a maximum penalty on summary conviction of an offence triable either on indictment or summarily which includes a fine or a maximum fine in respect of a specified quantity or a specified number of things, that sub-paragraph shall apply to that fine or maximum fine.

(7) Sub-paragraph (1) above shall not apply on summary conviction of any of the offences mentioned in sub-paragraph (2) of paragraph 11 below.

Increase of fines for certain summary offences

3.—(1) The enactments specified in column 2 of Part II of Schedule 2 to this Act, which relate to the maximum fines for the offences mentioned (and broadly described) in column I of that Schedule, shall have effect as if the maximum fine that may be imposed on summary conviction of any offence so mentioned were a fine not exceeding the amount specified in column 4 of that Schedule instead of a fine not exceeding the amount specified in column 3 of that Schedule (being the amount of the maximum fine in respect of the offence immediately before the passing of the Criminal Law Act 1977), but this sub-paragraph shall not alter the maximum daily fine, if any, provided for by any of those enactments.

(2) In section 203 of the Local Government (Scotland) Act 1973 (offences against byelaws), except as applied to byelaws made under any provision contained in a local or private Act other than by a local authority, for any reference to £20 there shall be substituted a reference to £50.

(3) Subject to sub-paragraph (4) below, this sub-paragraph applies to any pre-1949 enactment however framed or worded which—

(a) as regards any summary offence makes a person liable on conviction thereof to a fine of, or not exceeding, a specified amount less than £50 which has not been altered since the end of 1948 (and is not altered by this Act); or

(b) confers power by subordinate instrument to make a person, as regards any summary offence (whether or not created by the instrument), liable on conviction thereof to a fine of, or a maximum fine of, less than £50 which has not been altered since the end of 1948 (and is not altered by this Act).

(4) Sub-paragraph (3) above does not apply to any offence to which section 292(2)(b) of the Principal Act applies (offences triable only summarily other than by virtue of express provision).

(5) Every enactment to which sub-paragraph (3) above applies shall have effect as if for the specified amount less than £50 there mentioned there were substituted—

(a) £25 if the specified amount is less than £20; or

(b) £50 if the specified amount is not less than £20.

(6) Where, by virtue of any enactment to which sub-paragraph (3) above applies by virtue of sub-sub-paragraph (a) of that sub-paragraph, a person convicted, of a summary offence would, apart from this paragraph, be liable to a fine, or maximum fine, of one amount in the case of a first conviction and of a different amount in the case of a second or subsequent conviction, sub-paragraph (5) above shall apply separately in relation to each specified amount less than £50, even if this produces the same instead of different amounts for different convictions.

(7) Sub-paragraph (3) above does not apply to so much of any enactment as in whatever words, makes a person liable or provides for a person to be made liable, on summary conviction, to a fine or a maximum fine for each period of a specified length during which a continuing offence is committed.

(8) Where an enactment to which sub-paragraph (3) above applies provides or confers a power to provide for, on conviction of an offence triable only summarily, a fine or a maximum fine in respect of a specified quantity or a specified number of things, "the specified amount" for the purposes of subsection (5) above is the fine or maximum fine so provided or for which provision may be made.

(9) In sub-paragraph (3) above "pre-1949 enactment" means an enactment passed before 1st January 1949 or an enactment passed on or after that date which whether directly or, through successive re-enactments, indirectly re-enacts with or without modification an enactment passed before that date.

(10) In this paragraph, "enactment" does not include an enactment contained in an order, regulation or other instrument made under an Act.

Penalties for first and subsequent convictions of summary offences to be the same

4.—(1) Subject to sub-paragraphs (2) to (4) and (6) below, this paragraph applies where any enactment—

(a) makes a person liable on conviction of an offence triable only summarily to a penalty or a maximum penalty; or

(b) confers a power by subordinate instrument to make a person liable on conviction of an offence triable only summarily (whether or not created by the instrument) to a penalty or a maximum penalty,

which is different in the case of a second or subsequent conviction from the penalty or maximum penalty provided or for which provision may be made in the case of a first conviction.

(2) Where the penalty or maximum penalty for an offence to which section 292(2)(b) of the Principal Act applies has not been altered by any enactment passed or made after 29th July 1977 (the date of the passing of the Criminal Law Act 1977), this paragraph applies as if the amount referred to in sub-paragraph (5)(a) below were the greatest amount to which a person would have been liable on any conviction immediately before that date.

(3) Where any enactment—

(a) provides or confers a power to provide for a penalty or a maximum penalty which would, but for the operation of paragraph 3(5) above, be different in the case of a second or subsequent conviction from the penalty or maximum penalty provided for or for which provision may be made in the case of a first conviction; and

(b) otherwise fulfils the conditions of sub-paragraph (1) above;

this paragraph applies to that penalty or maximum penalty as if the amount referred to in sub-paragraph (5)(a) below were the greatest amount to which a person would have been liable or could have been made liable on any conviction immediately before 17th July 1978 (the date of coming into force of section 289C of the Criminal Procedure (Scotland) Act 1975).

(4) This paragraph does not apply to—

(a) section 5(3) of the Principal Act (imprisonment for certain offences);

(b) section 78 of the Criminal Justice (Scotland) Act 1980 (vandalism); or

(c) an enactment mentioned in Part III of Schedule 2 to this Act.

(5) Where this paragraph applies the maximum penalty to which a person is or may be made liable by or under the enactment in the case of any conviction shall be either or both of—

(a) a fine not exceeding the greatest amount;

(b) imprisonment for a term not exceeding the longest term (if any),

to which an offender would have been liable or could have been made liable on any conviction (whether the first or a second or subsequent conviction) by or under the enactment immediately before the relevant date.

(6) This paragraph does not affect the penalty which may be imposed in respect of an offence committed before the relevant date.

(7) In sub-paragraphs (5) and (6) above "the relevant date" means—

(a) in relation to an offence created by or under an Act or, as the case may be, to conviction of such an offence, 11th April 1983; and

(b) in relation to an offence created under a subordinate instrument or, as the case may be, to conviction of such an offence, 12th October 1988.

Increases of fines for certain summary offences

5.—(1) Subject to sub-paragraphs (3) to (8) and (10) below, this paragraph applies where any Act passed on or before 29th July 1977 (the date of the passing of the Criminal Law Act 1977)—

(a) makes a person liable on conviction of an offence triable only summarily to a fine or a maximum fine which is less than £1,000; or

(b) confers a power by subordinate instrument to make a person liable on conviction of an offence triable only summarily (whether or not created by the instrument) to a fine or a maximum fine which is less than £1,000, or a fine or a maximum fine which shall not exceed an amount of less than £1,000,

and the fine or maximum fine which may be imposed or, as the case may be, for which the subordinate instrument may provide has not been altered by any provision mentioned in sub-paragraph (2) below.

(2) The provisions referred to in sub-paragraph (1) above are—

(a) paragraph 1 above;

(b) paragraph 3 above (except where paragraph 4(3) above applies);

(c) section 30(3) of the Criminal Law Act 1977;

(d) an enactment passed or made after 29th July 1977 and before 11th April 1983.

(3) In the case of an offence to which section 292(2)(b) of the Principal Act applies, sub-paragraphs (2)(a) to (c) above do not apply and the fine or the maximum fine referred to in sub-paragraph (9) below is the fine or the maximum fine for the offence immediately before 29th July 1977 as amended, where applicable, by paragraph 4 above.

(4) This paragraph also applies where any enactment—

(a) is contained in a consolidation Act passed after 29th July 1977 and before 11th April 1983; and

(b) otherwise fulfils the conditions of sub-paragraph (1) above as amended by sub-paragraph (3) above where it applies; and

(c) is a re-enactment (with or without modification) of an enactment passed on or before 29th July 1977.

(5) Subject to sub-paragraph (10) below, where an Act provides or confers a power to provide for, on conviction of an offence triable only summarily, a fine or a maximum fine in respect of a specified quantity or a specified number of things, that fine or maximum fine is the fine or, as the case may be, the maximum fine for the purposes of this paragraph.

(6) Where an Act to which this paragraph applies provides or confers a power to provide different fines or maximum fines in relation to different circumstances or persons of different descriptions, such fines or maximum fines are to be treated separately for the purposes of this paragraph.

(7) This paragraph also applies where the penalties or maximum penalties provided or for which provision may be made by or under an Act on first and on second or subsequent conviction of an offence have been made the same by operation of paragraph 4 above; and in that case the fine or the maximum fine referred to in sub-paragraph (9) below is the maximum fine to which a person is or may be made liable by virtue of that paragraph.

(8) This paragraph does not apply in the case of—

(a) so much of any Act as (in whatever words) makes a person liable or provides for a person to be made liable to a fine or a maximum fine for each period of a specified length during which a continuing offence is committed;

(b) section 67(3) of the Transport Act 1962;

(c) sections 42(1) and 47(1) of the Road Traffic Act 1988;

(d) an enactment mentioned in Schedule 1 to the British Railways Act 1977 to the extent that the enactment was amended by section 13(1) of that Act;

(e) an enactment mentioned in Part III of Schedule 2 to this Act or in Schedule 2 to the Criminal Justice Act 1982.

(9) Where this paragraph applies, the fine or, as the case may be, the maximum fine to which a person is or may be made liable by or under the Act shall be increased to the amount shown in column 2 of the Table below opposite the band in column 1 within which the fine or the maximum fine referred to in sub-paragraph (1) above falls.

Column 1	Column 2
Fine or maximum fine	Increased amount
Under £25	£25
Under £50 but not less than £25	£50
Under £200 but not less than £50	£200
Under £400 but not less than £200	£500
Under £1,000 but not less than £400	£1,000

(10) Where an Act to which this paragraph applies provides or confers a power to provide for, on conviction of an offence triable only summarily, a fine or a maximum fine in respect of a specified quantity or a specified number of things but also provides or confers a power to provide for an alternative fine or maximum fine as regards the offence, sub-paragraph (9) above shall have effect to increase—
(a) the alternative fine; and
(b) any amount that the Act provides or confers a power to provide for as the maximum which a fine as regards the offence may not exceed,
as well as the fine or maximum fine which it has effect to increase by virtue of sub-paragraph (5) above.

Standard scale: amendment of enactments

6.—(1) Subject to sub-paragraph (5) below, where—
(a) an enactment to which sub-paragraph (2) below applies either—
(i) makes a person liable on conviction of an offence triable only summarily (whether created by that enactment or otherwise) to a fine or a maximum fine; or
(ii) confers a power by subordinate instrument to make a person liable on conviction of an offence triable only summarily (whether or not created by the instrument) to a fine or a maximum fine; and
(b) the amount of the fine or the maximum fine is, whether by virtue of that enactment or otherwise, an amount shown in the second column of the standard scale,
for the reference in the enactment to the amount of the fine or maximum fine there shall be substituted a reference to the level on the standard scale shown in the first column thereof as corresponding to the amount in the second column thereof referred to in sub-sub-paragraph (b) above.

(2) This sub-paragraph applies to an enactment in any Act passed before 11th April 1983.

(3) Subject to sub-paragraph (4) below, where an Act provides or confers a power to provide for, on conviction of an offence triable only summarily, a fine or a maximum fine in respect of a specified quantity or a specified number of things, that fine or maximum fine is the fine or, as the case may be, the maximum fine for the purposes of this paragraph.

(4) Where an Act provides or confers a power to provide for, on conviction of an offence triable only summarily, a fine or a maximum fine in respect of a specified quantity or a specified number of things but also provides or confers a power to provide for an alternative fine or maximum fine as regards the offence the fine or the maximum fine for the purposes of this paragraph is—
(a) the alternative fine; and
(b) any amount that the Act provides or confers a power to provide for as the maximum which a fine as regards the offence may not exceed,
as well as the fine or maximum fine referred to in sub-paragraph (3) above.

(5) Sub-paragraph (1) above does not apply to so much of any Act as (in whatever words) makes a person liable or provides for a person to be made liable to a fine or a maximum fine for each period of a specified length during which a continuing offence is committed.

(6) Where an enactment to which sub-paragraph (2) above applies confers a power such as is mentioned in sub-paragraph (1)(a)(ii) above, the power shall be construed as a power to make a person liable to a fine or, as the case may be, a maximum fine of the amount corresponding to the level on the standard scale to which the enactment refers by virtue of sub-paragraph (1) above or of a lesser amount.

(7) Subject to sub-paragraph (9) below, where under a relevant subordinate instrument the fine or maximum fine on conviction of a summary offence specified in the instrument is an amount shown in the second column of the standard scale, the reference in the instrument to the amount of the fine or maximum fine shall be construed as a reference to the level in the first column of the standard scale corresponding to that amount.

(8) In sub-paragraph (7) above, "relevant subordinate instrument" means any instrument made by virtue of an enactment after 30th April 1984 and before 12th October 1988 (the date of commencement of section 66 of the Criminal Justice (Scotland) Act 1987).

(9) Sub-paragraph (7) above shall not affect so much of any instrument as (in whatever words) makes a person liable on summary conviction to a fine not exceeding a specified amount for each period of a specified length during which a continuing offence is continued after conviction or the occurrence of any other specified event.

(10) Where there is—

(a) under any enactment (however framed or worded) contained in an Act passed before 12th October 1988,

(b) under any instrument (however framed or worded) made by virtue of such an enactment,

a power to provide by subordinate instrument that a person, as regards any summary offence (whether or not created by the instrument) shall be liable on conviction to a fine, a person may be so made liable to a fine not exceeding a specified level on the standard scale.

(11) Sub-paragraph (10) above has effect in relation to exercises of powers before as well as after 12th October 1988.

Statutory maximum as penalty in respect of summary conviction for offences in subordinate instruments

7.—(1) Where there is, under any enactment (however framed or worded) contained in an Act passed before the relevant date, a power by subordinate instrument to create a criminal offence triable either on indictment or summarily the maximum fine which may, in the exercise of the power, be authorised on summary conviction shall, by virtue of this paragraph, be the statutory maximum (unless some larger maximum fine can be authorised on summary conviction of such an offence by virtue of an enactment other than this sub-paragraph).

(2) Where there is, under any enactment (however framed or worded) contained in an Act passed before the relevant date, a power to create offences triable either on indictment or summarily by subordinate instrument, the maximum fine on summary conviction for such an offence may be expressed as a fine not exceeding the statutory maximum.

(3) Sub-paragraphs (1) and (2) above shall have effect in relation to any exercise of such power before as well as after the relevant date.

(4) Where an offence created by a subordinate instrument made before the relevant date may be tried either on indictment or summarily, the maximum fine which may be imposed on summary conviction shall by virtue of this sub-paragraph be the statutory maximum (unless the offence is one for which by virtue of the instrument a larger maximum fine may be imposed on summary conviction).

(5) Where a person summarily convicted of any offence to which sub-paragraph (4) above relates would, apart from this paragraph, be liable to a fine or to a maximum fine of an amount in the case of a first conviction and of a different amount in the case of a second or subsequent conviction, sub-paragraph (4) above shall apply irrespective of whether the conviction is a first, second or subsequent one.

(6) Sub-paragraph (4) above shall not affect so much of any instrument as (in whatever words) makes a person liable on summary conviction to a fine not exceeding a specified amount for each period of a specified length during which a continuing offence is continued after conviction or the occurrence of any other specified event.

(7) Nothing in this paragraph shall affect the punishment for an offence committed before the relevant date.

(8) In this paragraph "the relevant date" means 12th October 1988 (the date of commencement of section 66 of the Criminal Justice (Scotland) Act 1987).

Fines under secondary subordinate instruments

8.—(1) This paragraph applies to any instrument (however framed or worded) which—

(a) was made before 11th April 1983 (the date of commencement of Part IV of the Criminal Justice Act 1982); and

(b) confers on any authority other than a harbour authority a power by subordinate instrument to make a person, as regards any summary offence (whether or not created by the latter instrument), liable on conviction to a maximum fine of a specified amount not exceeding £1,000,

but does not affect so much of any such instrument as (in whatever words) confers a power by subordinate instrument to make a person liable on conviction to a fine for each period of a specified length during which a continuing offence is continued.

(2) The maximum fine to which a subordinate instrument made by virtue of an instrument to

which this paragraph applies may provide that a person shall be liable on conviction of a summary offence is—

(a) if the specified amount is less than £25, level 1 on the standard scale;
(b) if it is £25 or more but less than £50, level 2;
(c) if it is £50 or more but less than £200, level 3;
(d) if it is £200 or more but less than £400, level 4; and
(e) if it is £400 or more, level 5.

(3) Subject to sub-paragraph (5) below, where an instrument to which this paragraph applies confers a power by subordinate instrument to make a person, as regards a summary offence, liable on conviction to a fine in respect of a specified quantity or a specified number of things, that shall be treated for the purposes of this paragraph as being the maximum fine to which a person may be made liable by virtue of the instrument.

(4) Where an instrument to which this paragraph applies confers a power to provide for different maximum fines in relation to different circumstances or persons of different descriptions, the amount specified as those maximum fines are to be treated separately for the purposes of this paragraph.

(5) Where an instrument to which this paragraph applies confers a power by subordinate instrument to make a person, as regards a summary offence, liable on conviction to a fine in respect of a specified quantity or a specified number of things but also confers a power by subordinate instrument to make a person, as regards such an offence, liable on conviction to an alternative fine, this paragraph shall have effect in relation—

(a) to the alternative fine; and
(b) to any amount that the instrument specifies as the maximum fine for which a subordinate
    instrument made in the exercise of the power conferred by it may provide,

as well as in relation to the fine mentioned in sub-paragraph (3) above.

Fines on summary conviction for offences under subordinate instruments: conversion to references to levels on scale

9.—(1) Where an instrument which was made under an enactment on or after 11th April 1983 but before 12th October 1988 (the date of commencement of section 54 of the Criminal Justice Act 1988) confers on any authority other than a harbour authority a power by subordinate instrument to make a person liable on summary conviction to a fine of an amount shown in the second column of the standard scale, as that scale had effect when the instrument was made, a reference to the level in the first column of the standard scale which then corresponded to that amount shall be substituted for the reference in the instrument conferring the power to the amount of the fine.

(2) This paragraph shall not affect so much of any instrument as (in whatever words) makes a person liable on summary conviction to a maximum fine not exceeding a specified amount for each period of a specified length during which a continuing offence is continued.

Part III of Schedule 2

10.—(1) The enactments specified in column 1 of Part III of Schedule 2 to this Act, which relate to the penalties or the maximum penalties for the offences mentioned in those enactments, shall be amended in accordance with the amendments specified in column 2 of that Part, which have the effect of altering the penalties on summary conviction of the said offences and placing the fines on a level on the standard scale; and in that Part column 3 shows the penalties or, as the case may be, maximum penalties resulting from the amendments.

(2) Sub-paragraph (1) above does not affect the penalty which may be imposed in respect of an offence committed before 11th April 1983.

Alteration of penalties on summary conviction of certain offences under the Misuse of Drugs Act 1971

11.—(1) The Misuse of Drugs Act 1971 shall be amended as follows—

(a) in the entries in Schedule 4 showing the punishment that may be imposed on persons
    summarily convicted of offences mentioned in sub-paragraph (2)(b) below, for "6
    months" there shall be substituted "3 months"; and
(b) in the entry in Schedule 4 relating to section 5(2)—
        (i) for "6 months" (being the maximum punishment on summary conviction of an
        offence under that section where a Class B drug was involved) there shall be
        substituted "3 months", and
        (ii) for "6 months" being the maximum punishment on summary conviction of
        such an offence where a Class C drug was involved there shall be substituted "3
        months".

(2) The offences to which (as provided in paragraph 2(7) above) paragraph 2(1) above does not apply are—

(a) offences under section 5(2) of the Misuse of Drugs Act 1971 (having possession of a controlled drug) where the controlled drug in relation to which the offence was committed was a Class B or Class C drug;

(b) offences under the following provisions of that Act, where the controlled drug in relation to which the offence was committed was a Class C drug, namely—

  (i) section 4(2) (production, or being concerned in the production, of a controlled drug);

  (ii) section 4(3) (supplying or offering a controlled drug or being concerned in the doing of either activity by another);

  (iii) section 5(3) (having possession of a controlled drug with intent to supply it to another);

  (iv) section 8 (being the occupier, or concerned in the management, of premises and permitting or suffering certain activities to take place there);

  (v) section 12(6) (contravention of direction prohibiting practitioner etc. from possessing, supplying etc. controlled drugs); or

  (vi) section 13(3) (contravention of direction prohibiting practitioner etc. from prescribing, supplying etc. controlled drugs).

(3) In this paragraph "controlled drug", "Class B drug" and "Class C drug" have the same meaning as in the Misuse of Drugs Act 1971.

Transitional provisions and savings

12.—(1) The following transitional provisions and savings relating to the provisions contained in this Schedule shall have effect.

(2) For the purposes of paragraph 3(2) above, any provision in force at 17th July 1978 (the date of coming into force of subsection (3) of section 289C of the Criminal Procedure (Scotland) Act 1975) which—

(a) is contained in any byelaw made by virtue of section 203 of the Local Government (Scotland) Act 1973 but not that section as applied to byelaws made under any provision contained in a local or private Act other than by a local authority; and

(b) specified £20 as the maximum fine which may be imposed on summary conviction in respect of a contravention of, or offence under, any byelaw mentioned in that provision,

shall have effect as if it specified £50 instead, but with no change by virtue of this sub-paragraph in the maximum daily fine, if any, for which it provides.

(3) Paragraph 5 above does not affect the penalty which may be imposed in respect of an offence committed before 11th April 1983.

SCHEDULE 2

INCREASE IN CERTAIN PENALTIES

PART I

OFFENCES MADE TRIABLE ONLY SUMMARILY, AND RELATED AMENDMENTS

(1) Offence	(2) Enactment	(3) Amendment	(4) Penalties
NIGHT POACHING ACT 1828 (C. 69) Offences under section 1 (taking or destroying game or rabbits by night or entering land for that purpose).	Section 1.	For the words from "such offender" onwards substitute "he shall be liable on summary conviction to a fine not exceeding level 3 on the standard scale".	Level 3 on the standard scale.
PUBLIC MEETING ACT 1908 (C. 66) Offences under section 1(1) (endeavour to break up a public meeting).	Section 1(1).	After "offence" add "shall on summary conviction be liable to imprisonment for a term not exceeding 6 months or to a fine not exceeding level 5 on the standard scale or to both".	6 months or level 5 on the standard scale or both.
POST OFFICE ACT 1953 (C. 36) Offences under section 56 (criminal diversions of letters from addressee).	Section 56(1).	For the words "guilty" onwards substitute "liable on summary conviction to a fine not exceeding level 4 on the standard scale or to imprisonment for a term not exceeding six months or to both".	Level 4 on the standard scale or 6 months or both.

(1) Offence	(2) Enactment	(3) Amendment	(4) Penalties
BETTING, GAMING AND LOTTERIES ACT 1963 (C. 2) Offences under the following provisions – section 7 (restriction of betting on dog racecourses); section 10(5) (advertising licensed betting offices); section 11(6) (person holding bookmaker's or betting agency permit employing a person disqualified from holding such a permit); section 18(2) (making unauthorised charges to bookmakers on licensed track); section 19 (occupiers of licensed tracks not to have any interest in bookmaker thereon); section 21 (betting with young persons); section 22 (betting circulars not to be sent to young persons).	Section 52.	For paragraphs (a) and (b) of subsection (2) (penalties for certain offences) substitute "on summary conviction to a fine not exceeding level 5 on the standard scale or to imprisonment for a term not exceeding six months or to both".	Level 5 on the standard scale or 6 months or both.
THEATRES ACT 1968 (C. 54) Offences under section 6 (provocation of breach of the peace by means of public performance of play).	Section 6(2).	For paragraphs (a) and (b) substitute "on summary conviction to a fine not exceeding level 5 on the standard scale or to imprisonment for a term not exceeding six months or to both".	6 months or level 5 on the standard scale or both".

PART II

INCREASE OF FINES FOR CERTAIN SUMMARY OFFENCES

(1) Enactment creating offence	(2) Penalty enactment	(3) Old maximum fine	(4) New maximum fine
...	Section 1(1) (as amended by section 3 of the Protection of Animals (Amendment) Act 1954).	£50	Level 4 on the standard scale.
PROTECTION OF ANIMALS ACT 1934 (C. 21) Offences under section 1(1) (prohibition of certain public contests, performances and exhibitions with horses or bulls).	Section 2.	£100	Level 4 on the standard scale.
PUBLIC ORDER ACT 1936 (1 Edw. 8 & 1 Geo. 6) (C. 6) Offences under section 1(1) (wearing uniform signifying association with political organisation).	Section 7(2).	£50	Level 4 on the standard scale.
CHILDREN AND YOUNG PERSONS (SCOTLAND) ACT 1937 (C. 37) Offences under section 46(2) (publication of matters identifying juveniles in court proceedings)	Section 46(2).	£50	Level 4 on the standard scale.
CINEMATOGRAPH FILMS (ANIMALS) ACT 1937 (C. 59) Offences under section 1(1) (prohibition of films in production of which suffering has been caused to animals).	Section 1(3).	£100	Level 4 on the standard scale.
ARCHITECTS REGISTRATION ACT 1938 (C. 54) Offences under section 1 (unregistered persons using title of architect).	Section 3.	£50	Level 4 on the standard scale.
NURSING HOMES REGISTRATION (SCOTLAND) ACT 1938 (C. 73) Any offence under the Act for which no express penalty is provided, except an offence under section 1(4).	Section 8 (as amended by Schedule 3 to the Criminal Justice Act 1967).	£20	Level 4 on the standard scale.

(1) Enactment creating offence	(2) Penalty enactment	(3) Old maximum fine	(4) New maximum fine
FIRE SERVICES ACT 1947 (C. 41) Offences under section 31(1) (giving false fire alarm).	Section 31(1) (as amended by Schedule 3 to the Criminal Justice Act 1967).	£50	Level 4 on the standard scale.
NATIONAL ASSISTANCE ACT 1948 (C. 29) Offences under section 55(2) (obstruction).	Section 55(2) (as amended by Schedule 3 to the Criminal Justice Act 1967).	£10 for a first offence and £20 for a second or subsequent offence.	Level 4 on the standard scale.
AGRICULTURE (SCOTLAND) ACT 1948 (C. 45) Offences under section 50(1) (prohibition of night shooting and use of spring traps).	Section 50(2).	£20 for a first offence and £50 for a second or subsequent offence.	Level 3 on the standard scale.
Offences under section 50A(1) (open trapping of hares and rabbits).	Section 50A(2).	£20 for a first offence and £50 for a second or subsequent offence.	Level 3 on the standard scale.
DOCKING AND NICKING OF HORSES ACT 1949 (C. 70) Offences under section 1(1) (prohibition of docking or nicking horses).	Section 1(3).	£25	Level 3 on the standard scale.
Offences under section 2(3) (offences in connection with importation of docked horses).	Section 2(3).	£25	Level 3 on the standard scale.
Offences under section 2(4) (making of false statement).	Section 2(4).	£25	Level 3 on the standard scale.
COCKFIGHTING ACT 1952 (C. 59) Offences under section 1(1) (possession of appliances for use in fighting of domestic fowl).	Section 1(1).	£25	Level 3 on the standard scale.

(1) Enactment creating offence	(2) Penalty enactment	(3) Old maximum fine	(4) New maximum fine
DOGS (PROTECTION OF LIVESTOCK) ACT 1953 (C. 28) Offences under section 1(1) (owning or keeping a dog which worries livestock).	Section 1(6) (as amended by Schedule 3 to the Criminal Justice Act 1967).	£20 for a first offence and £50 for a second or subsequent offence in respect of the same dog.	Level 3 on the standard scale.
PESTS ACT 1954 (C. 68) Offences under section 12 (spreading of myxomatosis).	Section 12.	£20 for a first offence and £50 for a second or subsequent offence in respect of the same dog.	Level 3 on the standard scale.
ANIMAL (CRUEL POISONS) ACT 1962 (C. 26) Offences under section 1 (offences in connection with use of prohibited poison for destroying animals).	Section 1.	£50	Level 3 on the standard scale.
POLICE (SCOTLAND) ACT 1967 (C. 77) Offences under section 41(1) (assaults on constable etc.), where the offender has not, within the period of two years immediately preceding the offence been convicted of an offence against the section.	Section 41(1).	£50	Level 4 on the standard scale.
SEA FISHERIES (SHELLFISH ACT) 1967 (C. 83) Offences under section 7(4) (using prohibited fishing implements etc. in an area of fishery or oyster bed to which section applies).	Section 7(4).	£2 for a first offence, £5 for a second offence and £10 for a third or subsequent offence.	Level 3 on the standard scale.
ABORTION ACT 1967 (C. 87) Offences under section 2(3) (contravening or failing to comply with regulations as to notification).	Section 2(3).	£100	Level 5 on the standard scale.
AGRICULTURE (MISCELLANEOUS PROVISIONS) ACT 1968 (C. 34) Offences under the following provisions— section 1(1) (prevention of unnecessary pain and distress to livestock); section 2(2) (breach of regulations with respect to welfare of livestock).	Section 7(1).	£100 for a first offence and £200 for a second or subsequent offence.	Level 4 on the standard scale.

(1) Enactment creating offence	(2) Penalty enactment	(3) Old maximum fine	(4) New maximum fine
SOCIAL WORK (SCOTLAND) ACT 1968 (C. 49) Offences under section 6(5) (obstructing officer in exercise of power under section 6).	Section 6(5).	£10 for a first offence and £50 for a second or subsequent offence.	Level 4 on the standard scale.
Offences under section 60(3) (failure to comply with regulations etc. in respect of the control of residential and other establishments).	Section 60(3).	£50	Level 4 on the standard scale.
Offences under section 61(3) (carrying on establishment without registration).	Section 61(3).	£50 for a first offence and £100 for a second or subsequent offence.	Level 4 on the standard scale.
Offences under section 62(6) (failure to comply with a condition of the registration of an establishment).	Section 62(6).	£50 for a first offence and £100 for a second or subsequent offence.	Level 4 on the standard scale.
Offences under section 65(4) (obstructing officer in exercise of power under section 65).	Section 65(4).	£10 for a first offence and £50 for a second or subsequent offence.	Level 4 on the standard scale.
GAMING ACT 1968 (C. 65) Offences under section 8(5) (gaming in a street or public place).	Section 8(5).	£50.	Level 4 on the standard scale.
EMPLOYERS' LIABILITY (COMPULSORY INSURANCE) ACT 1969 (C. 57) Offences under section 4(3) (offences in relation to certificates of insurance).	Section 4(3).	£50.	Level 3 on the standard scale.
Offences under section 5 (employer failing to insure employee).	Section 5.	£200.	Level 4 on the standard scale.
CONSERVATION OF SEALS ACT 1970 (C. 30) Any offence under the Act, except an offence under section 11(7).	Section 5(2).	£50 for a first offence and £100 for a second or subsequent offence.	Level 4 on the standard scale.
MISUSE OF DRUGS ACT 1971 (C. 38) Offences under section 17(3) (failure to comply with notice requiring information relating to prescribing supply etc. of drugs).	Schedule 4.	£100.	Level 3 on the standard scale.

(1) Enactment creating offence	(2) Penalty enactment	(3) Old maximum fine	(4) New maximum fine
POISONS ACT 1972 (C. 66) Any offence under section 8(1) (contravention of provisions of sections 1 to 7, other than section 6(4), or of the Poisons rules).	Section 8(1).	£50.	Level 4 on the standard scale.
Offences under section 6(4) (using title etc. falsely to suggest entitlement to sell poison).	Section 6(4).	£20.	Level 2 on the standard scale.
Offences under section 9(8) (obstructing an inspector etc.).	Section 9(8).	£5.	Level 2 on the standard scale.
HEALTH AND SAFETY AT WORK ETC. ACT 1974 (C. 37) Offences under the following provisions— ²section 33(1)(d) ... section 33(1)(e) (contravening requirement imposed by inspector) where the requirement contravened was imposed under section 20; section 33(1)(f) (prevening etc, any other person from appearing before inspector); section 33(1)(h) (intentionally obstructing an inspector); section 33(1)(n) (falsely pretending to be an inspector).	Section 33(2).	£400.	Level 5 on the standard scale.
SALMON AND FRESHWATER FISHERIES ACT 1975 (C. 51) Offences against any provision of the Act not specified in the table in Part I of Schedule 4.	Paragraph 1(2) of Schedule 4.	£50 for a first offence and £100 for a second or subsequent offence.	Level 4 on the standard scale.
Offences under section 1 (fishing with certain instruments for salmon, trout or freshwater fish and possessing certain instruments for fishing for such fish) if not acting with another.	The Table in Part I of Schedule 4.	£50 for a first offence and £100 for a second or subsequent offence.	Level 4 on the standard scale.
Offences under section 19(2) (fishing for salmon during the annual close season or weekly close time).	The said Table.	£100 for a first offence and £200 for a second or subsequent offence.	Level 4 on the standard scale.

(1) Enactment creating offence	(2) Penalty enactment	(3) Old maximum fine	(4) New maximum fine
Offences under section 19(4) (fishing for trout during the annual close season or weekly close time).	The said Table.	£100 for a first offence and £200 for a second or subsequent offence.	Level 4 on the standard scale.
Offences under section 19(6) (fishing for freshwater fish during the annual close season for freshwater fish and fishing for eels by means of a rod and line during that season).	The said Table.	£100 for a first offence and £200 for a second or subsequent offence.	Level 4 on the standard scale.
Offences under section 19(7) (fishing for rainbow trout during the annual close season for rainbow trout and fishing for eels by means of a rod and line during that season).	The said Table.	£100 for a first offence and £200 for a second or subsequent offence.	Level 4 on the standard scale.
Offences under section 21 (prohibition on use of certain devices at certain times).	The said Table.	£100 for a first offence and £200 for a second or subsequent offence.	Level 4 on the standard scale.
Offences under section 27 (fishing for fish otherwise than under the authority of a licence and possessing an unlicensed instrument with intent to use it for fishing) if not acting with another.	The said Table.	£50 for a first offence and £100 for a second or subsequent offence.	Level 4 on the standard scale.

NOTE

[1] Repealed by the Crime and Punishment (Scotland) Act 1997 (c. 48) s.62(1) and Sched. 1, para. 19(2) with effect from August 1, 1997 in terms of S.I. 1997 No. 1712, para. 3.

[2] Repealed by the Health and Safety, the Lifts Regulations 1997 (S.I. 1997 No.831) Reg.19, Sched. 15, para. 1 (effective July 1, 1997).

PART III

FINES TO BE ALTERED OTHER THAN IN ACCORDANCE WITH PARAGRAPHS 4 AND 5 OF SCHEDULE 1

(1) Enactment	(2) Amendment	(3) New penalty
MILITARY LANDS ACT 1892 (C. 43) Section 17(2) (offences against byelaws).	For "five pounds" substitute "level 2 on the standard scale".	Level 2 on the standard scale.
PROTECTION OF ANIMALS (SCOTLAND) ACT 1912 (C. 14) Section 7 (selling poisoned grain or placing on any land matter rendered poisonous).	For "ten pounds" substitute "level 4 on the standard scale".	Level 4 on the standard scale.
LAND DRAINAGE (SCOTLAND) ACT 1930 (C. 20) ¹Section 4 (obstruction of person exercising power of entry).	...	...
LAND DRAINAGE (SCOTLAND) ACT 1941 (C. 13) Section 2(2) (obstruction of person exercising power of entry).	For "twenty pounds" substitute "level 3 on the standard scale".	Level 3 on the standard scale.
PUBLIC HEALTH (SCOTLAND) ACT 1945 (C. 15) Section 1(5) (contravention of regulations as to treatment and spread of certain deseases).	For "one hundred pounds" substitute "level 5 on the standard scale".	Level 5 on the standard scale and £50 per day during which the offence continues.
FIRE SERVICES ACT 1947 (C. 41) Section 14(5) (improper use of fire hydrant).	For "ten pounds" substitute "level 2 on the standard scale".	Level 2 on the standard scale.
Section 30(2) (obstructing a member of a fire brigade).	For "twenty-five pounds" substitute "level 3 on the standard scale".	Level 3 on the standard scale.
...	...	...
...	...	...
...	...	...

(1) Enactment	(2) Amendment	(3) New penalty
LAND DRAINAGE (SCOTLAND) ACT 1958 (C. 24) Section 11(4) (obstruction of person exercising power of entry)	For the words from "five pounds" to the end substitute "level 3 on the standard scale".	Level 3 on the standard scale.
BETTING, GAMING AND LOTTERIES ACT 1963 (C. 2) Section 28(10) (disclosing information about bookmaker's business).	For "one hundred pounds" substitute "level 4 on the standard scale".	Level 4 on the standard scale.
PLANT VARIETIES AND SEEDS ACT 1964 (C. 14) Section 25(9) (obstructing an authorised person).	For "twenty pounds" substitute "level 3 on the standard scale".	Level 3 on the standard scale.
Section 27(1) (tampering with samples).	For "one hundred pounds" substitute "level 5 on the standard scale".	Level 5 on the standard scale or 3 months or both.
AGRICULTURE AND HORTICULTURE ACT 1964 (C. 28) Section 20(1) (obstruction, etc. of authorised officer).	For "twenty pounds" substitute "level 3 on the standard scale".	Level 3 on the standard scale.
Section 20(2) (offences under Part III).	For the words from "one hundred pounds" to "two hundred and fifty pounds" substitute "level 5 on the standard scale".	Level 5 on the standard scale or 3 months or both.
INDUSTRIAL AND PROVIDENT SOCIETIES ACT 1965 (C. 12) Section 61 (general offences).	For "five pounds" substitute "level 3 on the standard scale".	Level 3 on the standard scale.
RIVERS (PREVENTION OF POLLUTION) (SCOTLAND) ACT 1965 (C. 13) Section 11(2) (unauthorised disclosure of information).	For the words from "one hundred pounds" to the end substitute "level 5 on the standard scale".	Level 5 on the standard scale.
FORESTRY ACT 1967 (C. 10) Section 24(4) (failure to comply with felling licence).	For "£50" substitute "level 5 on the standard scale".	Level 5 on the standard scale.
Section 46(5) (offences against byelaws).	In paragraph (a) for "£10" substitute "level 2 on the standard scale", and in paragraph (b) for "£5" substitute "level 2 on the standard scale".	Level 2 on the standard scale and 50 pence per day during which the offence continues.
Section 48(3) (obstruction of Forestry Commission officers).	For "£5" substitute "level 3 on the standard scale".	Level 3 on the standard scale.

(1) Enactment	(2) Amendment	(3) New penalty
POLICE (SCOTLAND) ACT 1967 (C. 77)		
Section 43(1) (impersonating a police officer).	For "fifty pounds" substitute "level 4 on the standard scale".	Level 4 on the standard scale or 3 months.
Section 44(5) (offences by constables).	For "ten pounds" substitute "level 3 on the standard scale".	Level 3 on the standard scale or 60 days.
AGRICULTURE (MISCELLANEOUS PROVISIONS) ACT 1968 (C. 34)		
Section 7(2) (obstructing officer authorised to carry out welfare inspections).	For "twenty pounds" substitute "level 3 on the standard scale".	Level 3 on the standard scale.
SALE OF VENISON (SCOTLAND) ACT 1968 (C. 38)		
Section 1(4) (contravention of provisions regarding registration of venison dealers).	For "£20" substitute "level 3 on the standard scale".	Level 3 on the standard scale.
Section 2(4) (failure to keep records, etc.).	For "£20" substitute "level 2 on the standard scale".	Level 2 on the standard scale.
SEWERAGE (SCOTLAND) ACT 1968 (C. 47)		
Section 44 (failure to provide information, etc.).	For "£20" substitute "level 3 on the standard scale".	Level 3 on the standard scale.
Section 48(9) (obstruction of person having right of entry).	For "£20" substitute "level 3 on the standard scale".	Level 3 on the standard scale and £5 per day which the offence continues.
Section 50(3) (unauthorised disclosure of information).	For the words from "£100" to the end substitute "level 5 on the standard scale".	Level 5 on the standard scale.
TRANSPORT ACT 1968 (C. 73)		
Section 97A(1) (tachograph offences).	For "£200" substitute "level 4 on the standard scale".	Level 4 on the standard scale.
Section 97A(2) (failure by employer to secure compliance with section 97A(1)(a)).	For "£200" substitute "level 4 on the standard scale".	Level 4 on the standard scale.
ROAD TRAFFIC (FOREIGN VEHICLES) ACT 1972 (C. 27)		
Section 3(1) (disobeying prohibition on a goods vehicle).	For "£200" substitute "level 5 on the standard scale".	Level 5 on the standard scale.
EDUCATION (SCOTLAND) ACT 1980 (C. 44)		
Section 43(1) (contravention of section 35, 41 or 42).	For the words from "in the case" where first occurring to "£50" where thirdly occurring substitute "to a fine not exceeding level 3 on the standard scale".	Level 3 on the standard scale or 1 month or both.

(1) Enactment	(2) Amendment	(3) New penalty
Section 66(3) (obstruction of inspectors).	For the words from "£20" to "£50" substitute "level 4 on the standard scale".	Level 4 on the standard scale or 3 months or both.
Section 98(2) (failure to register independent school, etc.).	For the words "£20" to "£50" substitute "level 4 on the standard scale".	Level 4 on the standard scale or 3 months or both.
Section 101(2) (using disqualified premises).	For the words from "£20" to "£50" substitute level 4 on the standard scale.	Level 4 on the standard scale or 3 months or both.
Section 101(3) (disqualified person acting as proprietor of independent school, etc.).	For the words from "£20" to "£50" substitute "level 4 on the standard scale".	Level 4 on the standard scale or 3 months or both.
WATER (SCOTLAND) ACT 1980 (C. 45) Section 38(7) (obstruction of person exercising power of entry).	For "£25" substitute "level 3 on the standard scale".	Level 3 on the standard scale.
Section 64(2) (failure to provide information, etc.).	For "£25" substitute "level 3 on the standard scale".	Level 3 on the standard scale.
Section 72(3) (penalty which may be provided for contravention of byelaws).	For "the sum of £400" substitute "level 4 on the standard scale".	Level 4 on the standard scale and £50 per day during which the offence continues.
Section 93(7) (failure to provide information, etc.).	For "£200" substitute "level 4 on the standard scale".	Level 4 on the standard scale and £20 per day during which the offence continues.
Paragraph 10(3) of Schedule 4 (offences relating to construction of reservoirs).	For the words from "£50" where first occurring to "continued" substitute "level 3 on the standard scale".	Level 3 on the standard scale.
Paragraph 28 of Schedule 4 (obstruction of person exercising power of entry).	For the words "£25" substitute "level 3 on the standard scale".	Level 3 on the standard scale.

NOTE
[1] Repealed by the Flood Prevention and Land Drainage (Scotland) Act 1997 (c.36) s.8, Sched.

SCHEDULE 3

TRANSITIONAL PROVISIONS, TRANSITORY MODIFICATIONS AND SAVINGS

PART I

General saving for old savings

1. The repeal by this Act of an enactment previously repealed subject to savings (whether or not in the repealing enactment) does not affect the continued operation of those savings.

Documents referring to repealed enactments

2. Any document made served or issued after this Act comes into force which contains a reference to any of the repealed enactments shall be construed, except so far as the contrary intention appears, as referring or, as the context may require, including a reference to the corresponding provision of the consolidating Acts.

Provisions relating to the coming into force of other provisions

3.—(1) The repeal by this Act of a provision providing for or relating to the coming into force of a provision reproduced in the consolidating Acts does not affect the operation of the first provision, in so far as it remains capable of having effect, in relation to the enactment reproducing the second provision.

(2) The repeal by this Act of a power to make provision or savings in preparation for or in connection with the coming into force of a provision reproduced in the consolidating Acts does not affect the power, in so far as it remains capable of having effect, in relation to the enactment reproducing the second provision.

PART II

SPECIFIC PROVISIONS

Local government reform

4.—(1) At any time before 1 April 1996 or the coming into force of section 1 of the Local Government etc. (Scotland) Act 1994, whichever is the later, in section 206 of the Principal Act, for subsection (6) there shall be substituted the following subsection—

"(6) In this section the expression "police authority" means a regional or islands council, except that where there is an amalgamation scheme under the Police (Scotland) Act 1967 in force it means a joint police committee."

(2) Until the date on which paragraph 71 of Schedule 13 to the said Act of 1994 comes into force, the reference in section 17(5)(a) of the Proceeds of Crime (Scotland) Act 1995 to a joint police board shall be construed as a reference to a joint police committee.

The Principal Reporter

5. Until the coming into force of section 127 of the Local Government etc. (Scotland) Act 1994, for any reference in any provision of the Principal Act to the Principal Reporter there shall be substituted a reference to the reporter of the local authority in whose area any child referred to in that provision resides.

Penalties

6.—(1) The repeal by this Act of any enactment—
(a) by virtue of which the penalty which may be imposed in respect of any offence is altered; but
(b) which provides that the penalty in respect of such an offence committed before a particular date shall not be so altered,
shall not affect the penalty which may be imposed in respect of an offence mentioned in paragraph (b) above.

(2) The periods of imprisonment set forth in subsection (2) of section 219 of the Principal Act shall apply to the non-payment of any sum imposed under that section by a court under a statute or order passed or made before 1 June 1909, notwithstanding that that statute or order fixes any other period of imprisonment.

District court procedure

7. The repeal by this Act of section 4 of the District Courts (Scotland) Act 1975 shall not affect the rules of procedure and practice in the district court.

Detention of children in summary proceedings

8. Notwithstanding the repeal by Schedule 2 of the Criminal Justice (Scotland) Act 1987 of section 58A of the Children and Young Persons (Scotland) Act 1937, any child who, before 1 April 1988 (the date of commencement of section 59 of the said Act of 1987), had been ordered to be detained pursuant to the directions of the Secretary of State under section 413 of the Criminal Procedure (Scotland) Act 1975—

(a) shall, while so detained after such date, continue to be deemed to be in legal custody; and

(b) may at any time be released conditionally or unconditionally by the Secretary of State, and any such child conditionally released shall be liable to recall on the directions of the Secretary of State and if he fails to comply with any condition of his release he may be apprehended without warrant and taken to the place from which he was released.

Effect of probation and absolute discharge

9. Subsections (1) and (2) of section 246 of the Principal Act shall not affect the operation, in relation to an offender as mentioned in those subsections, of any enactment which was in force as at the commencement of section 9(3)(b) of the Criminal Justice (Scotland) Act 1949 and is expressed to extend to persons dealt with under section 1(1) of the Probation of Offenders Act 1907 as well as to convicted persons.

Restriction on discharge of hospital order

10. Until the coming into force of section 54 of the Criminal Justice (Scotland) Act 1995, in section 59 of the Principal Act for the words "without limit of time" there shall be substituted the words "either without limit of time or during such period as may be specified in the order".

Aiding and abetting

11. Subsection (2) of section 293 of the Principal Act shall not apply in respect of any offence committed before 1 October 1987 (the date of commencement of section 64 of the Criminal Justice (Scotland) Act 1987).

Penal servitude and hard labour

12.—(1) Any enactment which confers power on a court to pass a sentence of penal servitude in any case shall be construed, subject to sub-paragraph (3) below, as conferring power to pass a sentence of imprisonment for a term not exceeding the maximum term of penal servitude for which a sentence could have been passed in that case immediately before 12 June 1950.

(2) Any enactment which confers power on a court to pass a sentence of imprisonment with hard labour in any case shall be construed as conferring power to pass a sentence of imprisonment for a term not exceeding the term for which a sentence of imprisonment with hard labour could have been passed in that case immediately before 12 June 1950.

(3) Nothing in sub-paragraph (1) above shall be construed as empowering a court, other than the High Court, to pass a sentence of imprisonment for a term exceeding two years.

Supervised attendance orders

13.—(1) In section 235 of the Principal Act, paragraph (b) of subsection (3) shall also apply to an offender where, having been convicted of an offence, he has had imposed on him a fine which (or any part or instalment of which) he has failed to pay and the court, prior to 1 April 1991 (the date of commencement of section 62 of the Law Reform (Miscellaneous Provisions) (Scotland) Act 1990), has imposed on him a period of imprisonment under paragraph (a) of subsection (1) of section 219 of the Principal Act but he has not served any of that period of imprisonment.

(2) Where, in respect of an offender, a court makes a supervised attendance order in circumstances where paragraph (b) of the said subsection (3) applies as mentioned in sub-paragraph (1) above, the making of that order shall have the effect of discharging the sentence of imprisonment imposed on the offender.

Hearsay evidence

14. Nothing in the sections 259 to 261 of the Principal Act shall apply to—

(a) proceedings commenced; or

(b) where the proceedings consist of an application to the sheriff by virtue of section 42(2)(c) of the Social Work (Scotland) Act 1968 or by virtue of Chapter 3 of Part II of the Children (Scotland) Act 1995, an application made,

before sections 17 to 20 of the Criminal Justice (Scotland) Act 1995 came into force; and, for the purposes of paragraph (a) above, solemn proceedings are commenced when the indictment is served.

Confiscation of proceeds of crime, etc.

15.—(1) Where a person is charged with an offence in relation to which provision is made by Part I of the Proceeds of Crime (Scotland) Act 1995, being an offence committed before the coming into force of Chapter I of Part II of the Criminal Justice (Scotland) Act 1995, Part I of the said Proceeds of Crime (Scotland) Act shall not affect the powers of the court in the event of his being convicted of the offence.

(2) Where a person is charged with an offence committed before the coming into force of Part II of the Proceeds of Crime (Scotland) Act 1995, in the event of his being convicted of the offence, the court shall be entitled to exercise the powers conferred by section 223 or section 436 of the Criminal Procedure (Scotland) Act 1975, but not the powers conferred by that Part.

(3) Paragraph (b) of section 2(4) of the Proceeds of Crime (Scotland) Act 1995 shall not apply in the case of an offence committed before the coming into force of Chapter I of Part II of the Criminal Justice (Scotland) Act 1995.

(4) In any case in which, notwithstanding the coming into force of the Bankruptcy (Scotland) Act 1985, the Bankruptcy (Scotland) Act 1913 applies to a sequestration, paragraph 1(2) of Schedule 2 to the Proceeds of Crime (Scotland) Act 1995 shall have effect as if for sub-sub-paragraphs (a) and (b) thereof there were substituted the following paragraphs—

"(a) property comprised in the whole property of the debtor which vests in the trustee under section 97 of the Bankruptcy (Scotland) Act 1913,

(b) any income of the bankrupt which has been ordered, under subsection (2) of section 98 of that Act, to be paid to the trustee or any estate which, under subsection (1) of that section, vests in the trustee,",

and paragraph 1(3) of that Schedule shall have effect as if, for the reference in it to the said Act of 1985, there were substituted a reference to the said Act of 1913.

(5) In any case in which a petition in bankruptcy was presented, or a receiving order or adjudication in bankruptcy was made, before 29 December 1986 (the date on which the Insolvency Act 1986 came into force), paragraph 2(2) to (5) of Schedule 2 to the Proceeds of Crime (Scotland) Act 1995 shall have effect with the following modifications—

(a) for references to the bankrupt's estate for the purposes of Part IX of the said Act of 1986 there are substituted references to the property of the bankrupt for the purposes of the Bankruptcy Act 1914;

(b) for references to the said Act of 1986 and to sections 280(2)(c), 286, 339, and 423 of that Act there are respectively substituted references to the said Act of 1914 and to sections 26(2), 8, 27 and 42 of that Act;

(c) the references in subsection (4) to an interim receiver appointed as there mentioned include, where a receiving order has been made, a reference to the receiver constituted by virtue of section 7 of the said Act of 1914, and

(d) subsection (2)(b) is omitted.

(6) In any case in which a winding up of a company commenced, or is treated as having commenced, before 29 December 1986, paragraph 3(2) to (6) of the said Schedule 2 shall have effect with the substitution for references to the said Act of 1986 of references to the Companies Act 1985.

(7) In any case in which a receiver was appointed as is mentioned in sub-paragraph (1) of paragraph 4 of the said Schedule 2 before 29 December 1986, sub-paragraphs (2) to (4) of that paragraph have effect with the substitution for references to the said Act of 1986 of references to the Companies Act 1985.

Criminal Justice (Scotland) Act 1995 (c. 20)

16.—(1) Any enactment repealed by this Act which has been amended by any provision of the Criminal Justice (Scotland) Act 1995 which has not been brought into force at the commencement of this Act shall, notwithstanding such repeal, continue to have effect until such provision is brought into force as if it had not been so repealed or amended.

(2) Any provision of the consolidating Acts which re-enacts any enactment contained in the said Criminal Justice (Scotland) Act which has not been brought into force at the commencement of this Act shall be of no effect until such enactment is brought into force.

(3) The repeal by this Act of any enactment contained in the Criminal Justice (Scotland) Act 1995 which has not been brought into force shall not have effect until such enactment is brought into force.

Children (Scotland) Act 1995 (c. 36)

17. Any enactment repealed by this Act which has been amended by any provision of the Children (Scotland) Act 1995 which has not been brought into force at the commencement of

this Act shall, notwithstanding such repeal, continue to have effect until such provision is brought into force as if it had not been so repealed or amended.

False oaths

18. Where an offence mentioned in section 45(5) of the Criminal Law (Consolidation) (Scotland) Act 1995 is, by any Act passed before 28 June 1933, as originally enacted, made punishable only on summary conviction, it shall remain only so punishable.

SCHEDULE 4

MINOR AND CONSEQUENTIAL AMENDMENTS

Jurors (Scotland) Act 1825 (c. 22)

1. In section 3 of the Jurors (Scotland) Act 1825 (sheriff principal to maintain lists of potential jurors)
(a) the existing provision shall become subsection (1);
(b) in that subsection, for the word "designations" there shall be substituted "addresses"; and
(c) after that subsection there shall be inserted the following subsections—

"(2) For the purpose of maintaining lists of potential jurors under subsection (1) above, a sheriff principal may require any person in the sheriff court district in question who appears to him to be qualified and liable to serve as a juror to provide such information, and in such form, as the Secretary of State may by order prescribe.

(3) A statutory instrument containing an order prescribed by virtue of subsection (2) above shall be subject to annulment pursuant to a resolution of either House of Parliament.

(4) Any person who fails to comply with a requirement under subsection (2) above shall be guilty of an offence and liable on summary conviction to a fine not exceeding level 1 on the standard scale.

(5) In proceedings against a person for an offence under subsection (4) above it is a defence to prove that he had reasonable excuse for the failure."

Bankers' Books Evidence Act 1879 (c. 11)

2. In section 6 of the Bankers' Books Evidence Act 1879 (case in which banker not compellable to produce book), after the word "1988" there shall be inserted the words "or Schedule 8 to the Criminal Procedure (Scotland) Act 1995".

The Children and Young Persons (Scotland) Act 1937 (c. 37)

3.—(1) The Children and Young Persons (Scotland) Act 1937, shall be amended as follows.
(2) After 62 there shall be inserted the following section—

"Register of children found guilty of offences
63. In addition to any other register required by law, a separate register of children found guilty of offences and of children discharged on bond or put on probation shall be kept for every summary court by the chief constable or other person charged with the duty of keeping registers of convictions. The register shall apply to children of such age, and shall include such particulars, as may be directed by the Secretary of State, and it shall be the duty of the keeper of the register, within seven days after any such child has been dealt with by the court, to transmit a copy of the entry relating to the child to the education authority for the area in which the child resides."
(3) Before section 104 there shall be added the following section—

"Proof of age a defence
103. Where a person is charged with an offence under this Act in respect of a person apparently under a specified age, it shall be a defence to prove that the person was actually of or over that age."

The Trade Marks Act 1938 (c. 22)

4. In section 58B of the Trade Marks Act 1938 (delivery up of offending goods and material), in subsection (6) for the words "Chapter II of Part II of the Criminal Justice

(Scotland) Act 1995" there shall be substituted the words "Part II of the Proceeds of Crime (Scotland) Act 1995."

The Backing of Warrants (Republic of Ireland) Act 1965 (c. 45)

5. In section 8(1)(b) of the Backing of Warrants (Republic of Ireland) Act 1965 (rules of court), for the words "section 457ZA of the Criminal Procedure (Scotland) Act 1975" there shall be substituted the words "section 306 of the Criminal Procedure (Scotland) Act 1995".

Social Work (Scotland) Act 1968 (c. 49)

6.—(1) The Social Work (Scotland) Act 1968 shall be amended as follows.

(2) In subsection (1B) of section 5 (powers of Secretary of State), for paragraph (f) there shall be substituted the following paragraph—

"(f) section 51 of the Criminal Procedure (Scotland) Act 1995;".

(3) In subsection (1) of section 6A (power to hold inquiries) for sub-paragraph (ii) of paragraph (d) there shall be substituted—

"(ii) section 44 or 208 of the Criminal Procedure (Scotland) Act 1995;".

¹ ...

(b) in paragraph (b)(iii) for the words "the Community Service by Offenders (Scotland) Act 1978" there shall be substituted the words "section 238 of the Criminal Procedure (Scotland) Act 1995";

(c) in paragraph (b)(iv) for the words "section 62 of the Law Reform (Miscellaneous Provisions) (Scotland) Act 1990" there shall be substituted the words "section 235 of the said Act of 1995"; and

(d) after sub-paragraph (iv) of paragraph (b) there shall be inserted the following sub-paragraphs—

"(v) without prejudice to sub-paragraphs (i) to (iv) above, persons in their area who are subject to a supervision and treatment order made under section 57(2)(d) of the Criminal Procedure (Scotland) Act 1995; and

(vi) persons in their area aged 16 and 17 years who are subject to a supervision requirement imposed in relation to the commission of any offence by that person; and

(vii) persons in their area who are charged with, but not prosecuted for, any offence and are referred to the local authority by the procurator fiscal or the Lord Advocate; and".

Sea Fisheries Act 1968 (c. 77)

7. In section 13(2) of the Sea Fisheries Act 1968 (power to award compensation), for "£400" there shall be substituted the words "level 5 on the standard scale".

European Communities Act 1972 (c. 68)

8. In subsection (1) of section 11 of the European Communities Act 1972 (making a false statement before the European Court) for the words "section 1 of the False Oaths (Scotland) Act 1933" there shall be substituted the words "section 44(1) of the Criminal Law (Consolidation) (Scotland) Act 1995".

Fair Trading Act 1973 (c. 41)

9. In subsection (3) of section 129 of the Fair Trading Act 1973 (time-limit for prosecutions)—

(a) for the words "section 331 of the Criminal Procedure (Scotland) Act 1975" there shall be substituted the words "section 136 of the Criminal Procedure (Scotland) Act 1995" and

(b) for the words "subsection (3) of the said section 331" there shall be substituted the words "subsection (3) of the said section 136".

Fatal Accidents and Sudden Deaths Inquiry (Scotland) Act 1976 (c. 14)

10. In section 2(3) of the Fatal Accidents and Sudden Deaths Inquiry (Scotland) Act 1976 for "£25" there shall be substituted the words "level 3 on the standard scale".

Freshwater and Salmon Fisheries (Scotland) Act 1976 (c. 22)

11. In subsection (9) of section 1 of the Freshwater and Salmon Fisheries (Scotland) Act 1976 for the words "the operation of section 312(o) of the Criminal Procedure (Scotland) Act 1975" there shall be substituted the words "paragraph 10 of Schedule 3 to the Criminal Procedure (Scotland) Act 1995".

Restrictive Trade Practices Act 1976 (c. 34)

12.—(1) The Restrictive Trade Practices Act 1976 shall be amended as follows.

(2) In subsection (3) of section 39 (time limit for prosecution) the words "section 331 of the Criminal Procedure (Scotland) Act 1975" there shall be substituted the words "section 136 of the Criminal Procedure (Scotland) Act 1995".

(3) In subsection (6) of section 41 (time limit for prosecution of offences relating to disclosure of documents)—

(a) for the words "section 331 of the Criminal Procedure (Scotland) Act 1975" there shall be substituted the words "section 136 of the Criminal Procedure (Scotland) Act 1995"; and

(b) for the words "subsection (3) of the said section 331" there shall be substituted the words "subsection (3) of the said section 136".

International Carriage of Perishable Foodstuffs Act 1976 (c. 58)

13. In subsection (2) of section 12 of the International Carriage of Perishable Foodstuffs Act 1976 for the words "section 331 of the Criminal Procedure (Scotland) Act 1975" there shall be substituted the words "section 136 of the Criminal Procedure (Scotland) Act 1995".

Marriage (Scotland) Act 1977 (c. 15)

14. In subsection (3) of section 24 of the Marriage (Scotland) Act 1977 for the words "section 331 of the Criminal Procedure (Scotland) Act 1975 (date of commencement of summary proceedings)" there shall be substituted the words "section 136 of the Criminal Procedure (Scotland) Act 1995 (time limit for certain offences)".

Refuse Disposal (Amenity) Act 1978 (c. 3)

15. In subsection (3) of section 2 of the Refuse Disposal (Amenity) Act 1978 for the words "section 462(1) of the Criminal Procedure (Scotland) Act 1975" there shall be substituted the words "section 307(1) of the Criminal Procedure (Scotland) Act 1995".
[1]...

Interpretation Act 1978 (c. 30)

17. In Schedule 1 to the Interpretation Act 1978—

(a) in paragraph (b) of the definition of "the standard scale" for the words "section 289G of the Criminal Procedure (Scotland) Act 1975" there shall be substituted the words "section 225(1) of the Criminal Procedure (Scotland) Act 1995"; and

(b) in paragraph (b) of the definition of "statutory maximum" for the words "section 289B(6) of the Criminal Procedure (Scotland) Act 1975" there shall be substituted the words "section 225(8) of the Criminal Procedure (Scotland) Act 1995".

Customs and Excise Management Act 1979 (c. 2)

18.—(1) The Customs and Excise Management Act 1979 shall be amended as follows.

(2) In subsection (6) of section 118A (duty of revenue traders to keep records), in paragraph (d) for the words "Schedule 3 to the Prisoners and Criminal Evidence (Scotland) Act 1993" there shall be substituted the words "Schedule 8 to the Criminal Procedure (Scotland) Act 1995".

(3) In subsection (3) of section 118C (search warrant) for the words "section 462 of the Criminal Procedure (Scotland) Act 1975" there shall be substituted the words "section 307 of the Criminal Procedure (Scotland) Act 1995".

(4) In subsection (1) of section 118D (order for access to certain information) for the words "section 462 of the Criminal Procedure (Scotland) Act 1975" there shall be substituted the words "section 307 of the Criminal Procedure (Scotland) Act 1995".

(5) In subsection (2) of section 171, in paragraph (b) for the words from "section 289B" to the end of the paragraph there shall be substituted the words "subsection (8) of section 225 of the Criminal Procedure (Scotland) Act 1995 (£5,000 or other sum substituted by order under subsection (4) of that section)".

Customs and Excise Duties (General Reliefs) Act 1979 (c. 3)

19. In subsection (3) of section 15 of the Customs and Excise Duties (General Reliefs) Act 1979, in paragraph (b) for the words from "section 289B" to the end of the paragraph there shall

be substituted the words "subsection (8) of section 225 of the Criminal Procedure (Scotland) Act 1995 (£5,000 or other sum substituted by order under subsection (4) of that section)".

Alcoholic Liquor Duties Act 1979 (c. 4)

20. In subsection (1) of section 4 of the Alcoholic Liquor Duties Act 1979, in the definition of "the prescribed sum", in paragraph (b) for the words from "section 289B" to the end of the paragraph there shall be substituted the words "subsection (8) of section 225 of the Criminal Procedure (Scotland) Act 1995 (£5,000 or other sum substituted by order under subsection (4) of that section)".

Hydrocarbon Oil Duties Act 1979 (c. 5)

21. In subsection (1) of section 27 of the Hydrocarbon Oil Duties Act 1979, in the definition of "the prescribed sum", in paragraph (b) for the words from "section 289B" to the end of the paragraph there shall be substituted the words "subsection (8) of section 225 of the Criminal Procedure (Scotland) Act 1995 (£5,000 or other sum substituted by order under subsection (4) of that section)".

Credit Unions Act 1979 (c. 34)

22. In subsection (1) of section 31 of the Credit Unions Act 1979, in the definition of "statutory maximum", in paragraph (b) for the words from "section 289B" to the end of the paragraph there shall be substituted the words "subsection (8) of section 225 of the Criminal Procedure (Scotland) Act 1995".

Estate Agents Act 1979 (c. 38)

23. In subsection (1) of section 33 of the Estate Agents Act 1979, in the definition of "the statutory maximum", in paragraph (b) for the words "section 289B of the Criminal Procedure (Scotland) Act 1975" there shall be substituted the words "subsection (8) of section 225 of the Criminal Procedure (Scotland) Act 1995".

Ancient Monuments and Archaeological Areas Act 1979 (c. 46)

24.—(1) The Ancient Monuments and Archaeological Areas Act 1979 shall be amended as follows.

(2) In section 59, for the words "section 331 of the Criminal Procedure (Scotland) Act 1975" there shall be substituted the words "section 136 of the Criminal Procedure (Scotland) Act 1995".

(3) In subsection (1) of section 61, in the definition of "the statutory maximum" in sub-paragraph (i) of paragraph (b) for the words from "section 289B" to the end of the sub-paragraph there shall be substituted the words "subsection (8) of section 225 of the Criminal Procedure (Scotland) Act 1995 (that is to say £5,000 or another sum fixed by order under subsection (4) of that section for that purpose)".

Isle of Man Act 1979 (c. 58)

25. In subsection (4) of section 5 of the Isle of Man Act 1979, for the words "section 462(1) of the Criminal Procedure (Scotland) Act 1975" there shall be substituted the words "section 307(1) of the Criminal Procedure (Scotland) Act 1995".

Reserve Forces Act 1980 (c. 9)

26. In subsection (2) of section 144 of the Reserve Forces Act 1980, in paragraph (b) for the words "section 289B of the Criminal Procedure (Scotland) Act 1975" there shall be substituted the words "section 225(8) of the Criminal Procedure (Scotland) Act 1995".

Protection of Trading Interests Act 1980 (c. 11)

27. In subsection (5) of section 3 of the Protection of Trading Interests Act 1980, in paragraph (b) for the words "section 289B of the Criminal Procedure (Scotland) Act 1975" there shall be substituted the words "section 225(8) of the Criminal Procedure (Scotland) Act 1995".

Competition Act 1980 (c. 21)

28. In subsection (7) of section 19 of the Competition Act 1980, in paragraph (b) for the words "section 289B of the Criminal Procedure (Scotland) Act 1975" there shall be substituted the words "section 225(8) of the Criminal Procedure (Scotland) Act 1995".

Licensed Premises (Exclusion of Certain Persons) Act 1980 (c. 32)

29. In subsection (2) of section 1 of the Licensed Premises (Exclusion of Certain Persons) Act 1980, in paragraph (c) for the words from "sections" to "1975" there shall be substituted the words "sections 228, 246(2) and (3) and 247 of the Criminal Procedure (Scotland) Act 1995".

Water (Scotland) Act 1980 (c. 45)

30. In subsection (4) of section 75 of the Water (Scotland) Act 1980, for the words "section 289B(6) of the Criminal Procedure (Scotland) Act 1975" there shall be substituted the words "section 225(8) of the Criminal Procedure (Scotland) Act 1995".

Solicitors (Scotland) Act 1980 (c. 46)

31. In subsection (1) of section 25A of the Solicitors (Scotland) Act 1980 (rights of audience) for the words from "section 250" to "1975" there shall be substituted the words "section 103(8) of the Criminal Procedure (Scotland) Act 1995 (right of solicitor to appear before single judge)".

Law Reform (Miscellaneous Provisions) (Scotland) Act 1980 (c. 55)

32.—(1) The Law Reform (Miscellaneous Provisions) (Scotland) Act 1980 shall be amended as follows.
(2) After subsection (5) of section 1 (persons excused from jury service for good reason) there shall be inserted the following subsection—
"(5A) Where the clerk of court has, under subsection (5) above, excused a person from jury service in any criminal proceedings he shall, unless he considers there to be exceptional circumstances which make it inappropriate to do so, within one year of the date of that excusal cite that person to attend for jury service in criminal proceedings."
(3) In subsection (6) of that section, for paragraph (c) there shall be substituted the following—
"(c) section 85(8) or 88(7) of the Criminal Procedure (Scotland) Act 1995,".
(4) In Schedule 1 (ineligibility for and disqualification and excusal from jury service)—
(a) in Part I (persons ineligible), in paragraph (p) of Group B for the words "section 462(1) of the Criminal Procedure (Scotland) Act 1975" there shall be substituted the words "section 307(1) of the Criminal Procedure (Scotland) Act 1995";
(b) in Part II (persons disqualified from jury service), at the end of paragraph (b) there shall be inserted—
"(c) in respect of jury service in any criminal proceedings, persons who are on bail in or in connection with criminal proceedings in any part of the United Kingdom."; and
(c) in Part III (persons excusable as of right), at the end of Group D there shall be inserted—

"GROUP DD

Members of certain religious bodies

In respect of jury service in any criminal proceedings, practising members of religious societies or orders the tenets or beliefs of which are incompatible with jury service."

Criminal Justice (Scotland) Act 1980 (c. 62)

33. In subsection (10) of section 80 of the Criminal Justice (Scotland) Act 1980, for the words "section 289B of the 1975 Act" there shall be substituted the words "section 225(8) of the Criminal Procedure (Scotland) Act 1995".

Local Government, Planning and Land Act 1980 (c. 65)

34. In subsection (14) of section 167 of the Local Government, Planning and Land Act 1980, in paragraph (b) of the definition of "the statutory maximum" for the words "section 289B of the Criminal Procedure (Scotland) Act 1975" there shall be substituted the words "section 225(8) of the Criminal Procedure (Scotland) Act 1995".

Animal Health Act 1981 (c. 22)

35. In subsection (2) of section 92 of the Animal Health Act 1981, for the words "section 284 of the Criminal Procedure (Scotland) Act 1975" there shall be substituted the words "section 7(6) of the Criminal Procedure (Scotland) Act 1995".

Contempt of Court Act 1981 (c. 49)

36.—(1) Section 15 of the Contempt of Court Act 1981 (penalties for contempt in Scottish proceedings) shall be amended as follows.
(2) In subsection (2)—
(a) in paragraph (a) for "£500" there shall be substituted the words "level 4 on the standard scale"; and
(b) in paragraph (b) for "£200" there shall be substituted the words "level 4 on the standard scale".
(3) For subsections (3) and (4) there shall be substituted the following—
"(3) The following provisions of the Criminal Procedure (Scotland) Act 1995 shall apply in relation to persons found guilty of contempt of court in Scottish proceedings as they apply in relation to persons convicted of offences—
(a) in every case, section 207 (restrictions on detention of young offenders);
(b) in any case to which paragraph (b) of subsection (2) above does not apply, sections 58, 59 and 61 (persons suffering from mental disorder);
and in any case to which the said paragraph (b) does apply, subsection (5) below shall have effect."
(4) In subsection (5)—
(a) for the words "section 286 of the Criminal Procedure (Scotland) Act 1975" there shall be substituted the words "section 7(9) and (10) of the Criminal Procedure (Scotland) Act 1995"; and
(b) for the words "section 376(1)" there shall be substituted the words "section 58(1)".

The Matrimonial Homes (Family Protection) (Scotland) Act 1981 (c. 59)

37. In section 17 of the Matrimonial Homes (Family Protection) (Scotland) Act 1981 (procedure after arrest)—
(a) in subsection (2) for the words "section 10 of the Bail (Scotland) Act 1980" there shall be substituted the words "section 8 of the Criminal Procedure (Scotland) Act 1995"; and
(b) in subsection (3) for the words from the beginning to "1980" there shall be substituted the words "Subsections (1) to (3) of section 15 of the said Act of 1995".

Betting and Gaming Duties Act 1981 (c. 63)

38. In subsection (1) of section 33 of the Betting and Gaming Duties Act 1981 in the definition of "the prescribed sum", in paragraph (b) for the words from "section 289B" to the end of the paragraph there shall be substituted the words "subsection (8) of section 225 of the Criminal Procedure (Scotland) Act 1995 (£5,000 or other sum substituted by order under subsection (4) of that section)".

Civil Aviation Act 1982 (c. 16)

39. In subsection (1) of section 105 of the Civil Aviation Act 1982, in the definition of "the statutory maximum" for paragraph (b) there shall be substituted the following—
"(b) in Scotland, the prescribed sum within the meaning of subsection (8) of section 225 of the Criminal Procedure (Scotland) Act 1995 (that is to say £5,000 or another sum fixed by order under subsection (4) of that section);".

Oil and Gas Enterprise Act 1982 (c. 23)

40. In subsection (1) of section 28 of the Oil and Gas Enterprise Act 1982, in the definition of "the statutory maximum" for paragraph (b) there shall be substituted the following—
"(b) in Scotland, the prescribed sum within the meaning of subsection (8) of section 225 of the Criminal Procedure (Scotland) Act 1995 (that is to say £5,000 or another sum fixed by order under subsection (4) of that section);".

Iron and Steel Act 1982 (c. 25)

41. In subsection (1) of section 37 of the Iron and Steel Act 1982, in the definition of "the statutory maximum" for paragraph (b) there shall be substituted the following—
"(b) in Scotland, the prescribed sum within the meaning of subsection (8) of section 225 of the Criminal Procedure (Scotland) Act 1995 (that is to say £5,000 or another sum fixed by order under subsection (4) of that section);".

Civil Jurisdiction and Judgments Act 1982 (c. 27)

42. In subsection (4A) of section 18 of the Civil Jurisdiction and Judgments Act 1982 (enforcement of U.K. judgments in other parts of U.K.) for the words from "Part I of the Criminal Justice (Scotland) Act 1987" to the end there shall be substituted the words "the Proceeds of Crime (Scotland) Act 1995".

Aviation Security Act 1982 (c. 36)

43. In subsection (1) of section 38 of the Aviation Security Act 1982, in the definition of "the statutory maximum" for paragraph (b) there shall be substituted the following—
"(b) in Scotland, the prescribed sum within the meaning of subsection (8) of section 225 of the Criminal Procedure (Scotland) Act 1995 (that is to say £5,000 or another sum fixed by order under subsection (4) of that section);".

Civic Government (Scotland) Act 1982 (c. 45)

44.—(1) The Civic Government (Scotland) Act 1982 shall be amended as follows.
(2) In subsection (8) of section 51, in the definition of "prescribed sum" for the words "section 289B of the Criminal Procedure (Scotland) Act 1975" there shall be substituted the words "section 225(8) of the Criminal Procedure (Scotland) Act 1995".
(3) In subsection (3) of section 52, for the words "section 289B of the Criminal Procedure (Scotland) Act 1975" there shall be substituted the words "section 225(8) of the Criminal Procedure (Scotland) Act 1995".

Insurance Companies Act 1982 (c. 50)

45.—(1) The Insurance Companies Act 1982 shall be amended as follows.
(2) In subsection (3) of section 14, in paragraph (b)(ii) for the words "section 289B of the Criminal Procedure (Scotland) Act 1975" there shall be substituted the words "section 225(8) of the Criminal Procedure (Scotland) Act 1995".
(3) In subsection (2) of section 71, in paragraph (b)(ii) for the words "section 289B of the Criminal Procedure (Scotland) Act 1975" there shall be substituted the words "section 225(8) of the Criminal Procedure (Scotland) Act 1995".
(4) In subsection (1) of section 81, in paragraph (b)(ii) for the words "section 289B of the Criminal Procedure (Scotland) Act 1975" there shall be substituted the words "section 225(8) of the Criminal Procedure (Scotland) Act 1995".
(5) In subsection (4) of section 92, for the words "section 74 of the Criminal Procedure (Scotland) Act 1975" there shall be substituted the words "section 70 of the Criminal Procedure (Scotland) Act 1995".
(6) In subsection (4) of section 94 for the words "section 331 of the Criminal Procedure (Scotland) Act 1975" there shall be substituted the words "section 136 of the Criminal Procedure (Scotland) Act 1995".
(7) In subsection (5) of that section for the words "section 331 of the said Act of 1975" there shall be substituted the words "section 136 of the said Act of 1995".

Industrial Development Act 1982 (c. 52)

46. In Schedule 1 to the Industrial Development Act 1982, in paragraph 4(2) for the words "section 331 of the Criminal Procedure (Scotland) Act 1975" there shall be substituted the words "section 136 of the Criminal Procedure (Scotland) Act 1995".

Car Tax Act 1983 (c. 53)

47. In Schedule 1 to the Car Tax Act 1983, in paragraph 7(3) for the words "section 462 of the Criminal Procedure (Scotland) Act 1975" there shall be substituted the words "section 307 of the Criminal Procedure (Scotland) Act 1995".

Telecommunications Act 1984 (c. 12)

48.—(1) The Telecommunications Act 1984 shall be amended as follows.
(2) In subsection (2) of section 81, for the words from "section 310" to "1975 Act" there shall

be substituted the words "section 134 of the Criminal Procedure (Scotland) Act 1995 (in this section referred to as "the 1995 Act")".

(3) In subsection (8) of that section, for the words from "and section 452(4)(a)" to the end there shall be substituted the words "and section 182(5)(a) to (e) of the 1995 Act shall apply to appeals under this section as it applies to appeals such as are mentioned in section 176(1) of that Act".

(4) In Schedule 3 (penalties and mode of trial under the Wireless Telegraphy Act 1949), in paragraph 3(b) for the words "Chapter II of Part II of the Criminal Justice (Scotland) Act 1995" there shall be substituted the words "Part II of the Proceeds of Crime (Scotland) Act 1995".

Road Traffic Regulation Act 1984 (c. 27)

49. In subsection (2) of section 110 of the Road Traffic Regulation Act 1984—
(a) for the words "section 331 of the Criminal Procedure (Scotland) Act 1975" there shall be substituted the words "section 136 of the Criminal Procedure (Scotland) Act 1995"; and
(b) for the words "section 331" where they second occur there shall be substituted the words "section 136".

Mental Health (Scotland) Act 1984 (c. 36)

50.—(1) The Mental Health (Scotland) Act 1984 shall be amended as follows.
(2) In section 60 (effect of hospital orders)—
(a) in subsection (1) for the words "section 175 or 376 of the Criminal Procedure (Scotland) Act 1975" there shall be substituted the words "section 58 of the Criminal Procedure (Scotland) Act 1995"; and
(b) in subsection (3) for the words "section 178(3) or 379(3) of the said Act of 1975" there shall be substituted the words "section 59(3) of the said Act of 1995".

(3) In subsection (1) of section 61 (effect of guardianship orders) for the words "section 175 or 376 of the Criminal Procedure (Scotland) Act 1975" there shall be substituted the words "section 58 of the Criminal Procedure (Scotland) Act 1995".

(4) In subsection (1) of section 62 (effect of restriction orders), for the words "section 178 or 397 of the Criminal Procedure (Scotland) Act 1975" there shall be substituted the words "section 59 of the Criminal Procedure (Scotland) Act 1995".

(5) In subsection (3) of section 69 (persons ordered to be kept in custody during Her Majesty's pleasure), for the words from "an order" to the end there shall be substituted "a hospital order together with a restriction order".

(6) In subsection (7) of section 71 (removal to hospital of persons serving sentences of imprisonment etc.), in paragraph (a) for the words from "section 174" to "1975" there shall be substituted the words "section 54, 57, 118 or 190 of the Criminal Procedure (Scotland) Act 1995".

(7) In section 73 (provision as to persons removed to hospital while awaiting trial etc.)—
(a) in subsection (1), for the words from "section 174ZC" to "1975" there shall be substituted the words "section 53, 57, 58 or 59 of the Criminal Procedure (Scotland) Act 1995"; and
¹...

(8) In section 76 (interpretation of Part VI) for the words "section 178(3) or 379(3) of the Criminal Procedure (Scotland) Act 1975" there shall be substituted the words "section 59(3) of the Criminal Procedure (Scotland) Act 1995".

(9) After section 121 there shall be inserted the following section—

"Warrants for arrest of escaped mental patients.

121A.—(1) On an application being made to a justice alleging that any person is a convicted mental patient liable to be retaken under section 18, 38(7) or 138 of the Mental Health Act 1983, section 28, 44 or 121 of the this Act or section 30 or 108 of the Mental Health Act (Northern Ireland) 1961 (retaking of mental patients who are absent without leave or have escaped from custody), the justice may issue a warrant to arrest him and bring him before any sheriff.

(2) Where a person is brought before a sheriff in pursuance of a warrant for his arrest under this section, the sheriff shall, if satisfied that he is the person named in the warrant and if satisfied that he is a convicted mental patient as mentioned in subsection (1) above, order him to be kept in custody or detained in a place of safety pending his admission to hospital.

(3) Section 137 of the Mental Health Act 1983 and section 107 of the Mental Health Act (Northern Ireland) 1961 (custody, conveyance and detention of certain mental patients)

shall apply to a convicted mental patient required by this section to be conveyed to any place or to be kept in custody or detained in a place of safety as they apply to a person required by or by virtue of the said Act of 1983 or 1961, as the case may be, to be so conveyed, kept or detained.

(4) In this section—

"convicted mental patient" means a person liable after being convicted of an offence to be detained under Part III of the Mental Health Act 1983, Part VI of this Act, Part III of the Mental Health Act (Northern Ireland) 1961 or section 52, 59(1) to (10) or 60 of the Criminal Procedure (Scotland) Act 1995 in pursuance of a hospital order or transfer direction together with an order or direction restricting his discharge or a person liable to be detained under section 38 of the said Act of 1983;

"place of safety" has the same meaning as in Part III of the said Act of 1983 or Part III of the said Act of 1961 or section 297 of the said Act of 1995, as the case may be."

(10) In section 125—

(a) in the definition of "hospital order" and "guardianship order" for the words "section 175 or 376 of the Criminal Procedure (Scotland) Act 1975" there shall be substituted the words "section 58 of the Criminal Procedure (Scotland) Act 1995";

(b) in the definition of "restriction order" for the words "section 178 or 379 of the Criminal Procedure (Scotland) Act 1975" there shall be substituted the words "section 59 of the Criminal Procedure (Scotland) Act 1995"; and

(c) in subsection (4) for the words from "section 174" to "1975" there shall be substituted the words "section 54, 57, 58 or 59 of the Criminal Procedure (Scotland) Act 1995".

Video Recordings Act 1984 (c. 39)

51. In subsection (1) of section 16C of the Video Recordings Act 1984 (sheriff's jurisdiction), for the words "section 287 of the Criminal Procedure (Scotland) Act 1975" there shall be substituted the words "section 9 of the Criminal Procedure (Scotland) Act 1995".

Repatriation of Prisoners Act 1984 (c. 47)

52. The Schedule to the Repatriation of Prisoners Act 1984 shall be amended as follows—

(a) in paragraph 4(2) for the words "section 207 or 415 of the Criminal Procedure (Scotland) Act 1975" there shall be substituted the words "section 207 of the Criminal Procedure (Scotland) Act 1995";

(b) in paragraph 5(3) for "1975" there shall be substituted "1995".

Foster Children (Scotland) Act 1984 (c. 56)

53.—(1) The Foster Children (Scotland) Act 1984 shall be amended as follows.

(2) In section 7, in paragraph (c) of subsection (1) for the words "Criminal Procedure (Scotland) Act 1975" there shall be substituted the words "Criminal Procedure (Scotland) Act 1995".

[1] ...

Rent (Scotland) Act 1984 (c. 58)

54. In subsection (1) of section 115 of the Rent (Scotland) Act 1984, in the definition of—

(a) "the standard scale" for the words "section 289G of the Criminal Procedure (Scotland) Act 1975" there shall be substituted the words "section 225(1) of the Criminal Procedure (Scotland) Act 1995"; and

(b) "the statutory maximum" for the words "section 289B(6) of the Criminal Procedure (Scotland) Act 1975" there shall be substituted the words "section 225(8) of the Criminal Procedure (Scotland) Act 1995".

Police and Criminal Evidence Act 1984 (c. 60)

55. In subsection (3) of section 75 of the Police and Criminal Evidence Act 1984—

(a) for the words "section 392 of the Criminal Procedure (Scotland) Act 1975" there shall be substituted the words "section 247 of the Criminal Procedure (Scotland) Act 1995"; and

(b) for the words "section 182 or section 183 of the said Act of 1975" there shall be substituted the words "section 228 or section 246(3) of the said Act of 1995".

Companies Act 1985 (c. 6)

56.—(1) The Companies Act 1985 shall be amended as follows.

(2) In section 440, for the words "section 52 of the Criminal Justice (Scotland) Act 1987" there shall be substituted the words "section 28 of the Criminal Law (Consolidation) (Scotland) Act 1995".

(3) In subsection (3) of section 731, for the words "section 331 of the Criminal Procedure (Scotland) Act 1975" there shall be substituted the words "section 136 of the Criminal Procedure (Scotland) Act 1995".

(4) In subsection (4) of section 734, for the words "section 74 of the Criminal Procedure (Scotland) Act 1975" there shall be substituted the words "section 70 of the Criminal Procedure (Scotland) Act 1995".

Surrogacy Arrangements Act 1985 (c. 49)

57. In subsection (6) of section 4 of the Surrogacy Arrangements Act 1985, for the words "section 331(1) of the Criminal Procedure (Scotland) Act 1975" there shall be substituted the words "section 136(1) of the Criminal Procedure (Scotland) Act 1995".

The Bankruptcy (Scotland) Act 1985 (c. 66)

58.—(1) The Bankruptcy (Scotland) Act 1985 shall be amended as follows.

(2) In section 5(4) (meaning of qualified creditor), for the words "or by section 114(1) of the Criminal Justice (Scotland) Act 1995" there shall be substituted the words "or by section 49(1) of the Proceeds of Crime (Scotland) Act 1995".

(3) In section 7(1) (meaning of apparent insolvency), in the definition of "confiscation order", for the words "or by section 114(1) of the Criminal Justice (Scotland) Act 1995" there shall be substituted the words "or by section 49(1) of the Proceeds of Crime (Scotland) Act 1995".

(4) In subsection (2) of section 55 (effect of discharge of bankrupt on certain liabilities), after paragraph (a) there shall be inserted the following paragraphs—

"(aa) any liability to pay a fine imposed in a district court;

(ab) any liability under a compensation order within the meaning of section 249 of the Criminal Procedure (Scotland) Act 1995;".

(5) In subsection (2) of section 68, for the words "section 331 of the Criminal Procedure (Scotland) Act 1975" there shall be substituted the words "section 136 of the Criminal Procedure (Scotland) Act 1995".

Animals (Scientific Procedures) Act 1986 (c. 14)

59. In subsection (4) of section 26 of the Animals (Scientific Procedures) Act 1986, for the words "section 331 of the Criminal Procedure (Scotland) Act 1975" there shall be substituted the words "section 136 of the Criminal Procedure (Scotland) Act 1995".

Consumer Safety (Amendment) Act 1986 (c. 29)

60.—(1) The Consumer Safety (Amendment) Act 1986 shall be amended as follows.

(2) In subsection (3) of section 7, for "1975" there shall be substituted "1995".

(3) In section 10 for the words "section 452(4)(a) to (e) of the Criminal Procedure (Scotland) Act 1975" there shall be substituted the words "section 182(5)(a) to (e) of the Criminal Procedure (Scotland) Act 1995".

Insolvency Act 1986 (c. 45)

61. In subsection (3) of section 431 of the Insolvency Act 1986, for the words "section 331 of the Criminal Procedure (Scotland) Act 1975" there shall be substituted the words "section 136 of the Criminal Procedure (Scotland) Act 1995".

Company Directors Disqualification Act 1986 (c. 46)

62. In subsection (1) of section 8 of the Company Directors Disqualification Act 1986, for the words "section 52 of the Criminal Justice (Scotland) Act 1987" there shall be substituted the words "section 28 of the Criminal Law (Consolidation) (Scotland) Act 1995".

Legal Aid (Scotland) Act 1986 (c. 47)

63.—(1) The Legal Aid (Scotland) Act 1986 shall be amended as follows.

(2) In subsection (4) of section 21, for the words "section 462 of the Criminal Procedure (Scotland) Act 1975" there shall be substituted the words "section 307 of the Criminal Procedure (Scotland) Act 1995".

(3) In subsection (1) of section 22 (circumstances in which criminal legal aid automatically available), after paragraph (d) there shall be inserted the following paragraphs—

"(da) in relation to any proceedings under solemn or summary procedure whereby the court determines (whether or not on a plea by the accused person) whether he is insane so that his trial cannot proceed or continue;

(db) in relation to an examination of facts held under section 55 of the Criminal Procedure (Scotland) Act 1995 and the disposal of the case following such examination of facts;

(dc) in relation to any appeal under section 62 or 63 (appeal by, respectively, accused or prosecutor in case involving insanity) of that Act of 1995;"

(4) In subsection (2) of section 23, for the words from "section 41(2)(b)" to the end there shall be substituted the words "section 204(4)(b) of the Criminal Procedure (Scotland) Act 1995".

(5) In subsection (1) of section 25 (legal aid in criminal appeals)—

(a) after the word "sentence" there shall be inserted the words ", other disposal"; and

(b) at the end there shall be inserted the words "other than an appeal in relation to which section 22(1)(dc) of this Act applies".

(6) In subsection (2) of that section—

(a) in paragraph (a) after the word "below," there shall be inserted the words "the Board is satisfied"; and

(b) for paragraph (b) and the preceding "and" there shall be substituted the following paragraphs—

"(b) in the case of an appeal under section 106(1) or 175(2) of the Criminal Procedure (Scotland) Act 1995, leave to appeal is granted; and

(c) in the case of an appeal under any other provision of that Act, where the applicant is the appellant, the Board is satisfied that in all the circumstances of the case it is in the interests of justice that the applicant should receive criminal legal aid."

(7) After the said subsection (2) there shall be inserted the following subsection—

"(2A) Where the Board has refused an application for criminal legal aid on the ground that it is not satisfied as mentioned in subsection (2)(c) above the High Court may, at any time prior to the disposal of an appeal, whether or not on application made to it, notwithstanding such refusal determine that it is in the interests of justice that the applicant should receive criminal legal aid in connection with the appeal, and the Board shall forthwith make such legal aid available to him."

(8) For subsection (5) there shall be substituted the following subsections—

"(5) Subsections (2)(a), (3) and (4) above shall apply to an application for criminal legal aid in connection with consideration under section 107, 180 or 187 of the Criminal Procedure (Scotland) Act 1995 whether to grant leave to appeal as if—

(a) in subsection (2)(a), for the words "of the appeal" there were substituted the words "in connection with consideration whether to grant leave to appeal"; and

(b) in subsection (4), after the word "is" there were inserted the words "subject to leave being granted,".

(6) Subsections (2)(a) and (c) and (2A) to (4) above shall apply to an application for criminal legal aid in connection with a petition to the *nobile officium* of the High Court of Justiciary (whether arising in the course of any proceedings or otherwise) as they apply for the purposes of subsection (1) above.

(7) Subsections (2)(a), (3) and (4) above shall apply to an application for criminal legal aid in connection with a reference by the Secretary of State under section 124 of the Criminal Procedure (Scotland) Act 1995 as they apply for the purposes of subsection (1) above."

(9) In subsection (3) of section 30 (application of section 25 to legal aid in contempt proceedings),—

(a) before the words "Section 25" there shall be inserted the words "Subsections (2)(a) and (c), (2A) to (4) and (6) of";

(b) for the words "it applies" there shall be substituted the words "they apply";

(c) after the word "sentence" there shall be substituted the words ", other disposal";

(d) after the word "application" there shall be inserted the following paragraph—

"(za) in subsection (2a) of that section, the reference to the High Court shall include a reference to the Court of Session;"; and

(e) in paragraph (b) for the word "(5)" there shall be substituted the word "(6)".

(10) In subsection (2) of section 35, for the words "section 331 of the Criminal Procedure (Scotland) Act 1975" there shall be substituted the words "section 136 of the Criminal Procedure (Scotland) Act 1995".

Social Security Act 1986 (c. 50)

64. In subsection (5) of section 56 of the Social Security Act 1986—
(a) for the words "section 331 of the Criminal Procedure (Scotland) Act 1975" there shall be substituted the words "section 136 of the Criminal Procedure (Scotland) Act 1995"; and
(b) for the words "section 331 of the said Act of 1975" there shall be substituted the words "section 136 of the said Act of 1995".

Building Societies Act 1986 (c. 53)

65. In subsection (5) of section 111 of the Building Societies Act 1986, for the words "section 331(3) of the Criminal Procedure (Scotland) Act 1975" there shall be substituted the words "section 136(3) of the Criminal Procedure (Scotland) Act 1995".

Financial Services Act 1986 (c. 60)

66. In subsection (4) of section 203 of the Financial Services Act 1986, for the words "section 74 of the Criminal Procedure (Scotland) Act 1975" there shall be substituted the words "section 70 of the Criminal Procedure (Scotland) Act 1995".

Banking Act 1987 (c. 22)

67.—(1) The Banking Act 1987 shall be amended as follows.
(2) In subsection (3) of section 97, for the words "section 331 of the Criminal Procedure (Scotland) Act 1975" there shall be substituted the words "section 136 of the Criminal Procedure (Scotland) Act 1995"
(3) In subsection (4) of section 98, for the words "section 74 of the Criminal Procedure (Scotland) Act 1975" there shall be substituted the words "section 70 of the Criminal Procedure (Scotland) Act 1995".

Consumer Protection Act 1987 (c. 43)

68. In subsection (8) of section 17 of the Consumer Protection Act 1987, for the words from "and section 452(4)(a) to (e)" to the end there shall be substituted the words "and section 182(5)(a) to (e) of the Criminal Procedure (Scotland) Act 1995 shall apply to an appeal under this subsection as it applies to a stated case under Part X of that Act".

The Criminal Justice Act 1988 (c. 33)

69.—(1) The Criminal Justice Act 1988 shall be amended as follows.
(2) In section 74(2)(c) (meaning of realisable property) for the words "Chapter II of Part II of the Criminal Justice (Scotland) Act 1995" there shall be substituted the words "Part II of the Proceeds of Crime (Scotland) Act 1995".
(3) In subsection (10) of section 77 (restraint orders) for the words "Part II of the Criminal Justice (Scotland) Act 1995" there shall be substituted the words "the Proceeds of Crime (Scotland) Act 1995".
(4) In section 89(2)(b) (compensation), for sub-paragraph (ii) there shall be substituted the following sub-paragraph—
"(ii) an order of the Court of Session under section 32, 33, 34 or 35 of the Proceeds of Crime (Scotland) Act 1995."

The Copyright, Designs and Patents Act 1988 (c. 48)

70.—(1) The Copyright, Designs and Patents Act 1988 shall be amended as follows.
(2) In section 108(6) (order for delivery up in criminal proceedings) for the words "Chapter II of Part II of the Criminal Justice (Scotland) Act 1995" there shall be substituted the words "Part II of the Proceeds of Crime (Scotland) Act 1995".
(3) In section 199(6) (order for delivery up in criminal proceedings) for the words "Chapter II of Part II of the Criminal Justice (Scotland) Act 1995" there shall be substituted the words "Part II of the Proceeds of Crime (Scotland) Act 1995".

Road Traffic Offenders Act 1988 (c. 53)

71.—(1) The Road Traffic Offenders Act 1988 shall be amended as follows.
(2) In subsection (5) of section 6 (time limit for commencement of summary proceedings), for the words "section 331 of the Criminal Procedure (Scotland) Act 1975" there shall be substituted the words "section 136 of the Criminal Procedure (Scotland) Act 1995".
(3) In subsection (6) of section 24 (alternative verdicts) for the words "sections 61, 63, 64, 312

and 457A of the Criminal Procedure (Scotland) Act 1975" there shall be substituted the words "sections 295, 138(4), 256 and 293 of and Schedule 3 to the Criminal Procedure (Scotland) Act 1995".

(4) In subsection (2) of section 31 (taking account of endorsation) for the words "section 357(1) of the Criminal Procedure (Scotland) Act 1975" there shall be substituted the words "section 166(1) to (6) of the Criminal Procedure (Scotland) Act 1995".

(5) In subsection (6) of section 32 (extracts of licensing records) for the words "section 357(1) of the Criminal Procedure (Scotland) Act 1975" there shall be substituted the words "section 166(1) to (6) of the Criminal Procedure (Scotland) Act 1995".

(6) After section 33 of the Road Traffic Offenders Act 1988 (fine and imprisonment), there shall be inserted the following section—

"Forfeiture of vehicles: Scotland.

33A.—(1) Where a person commits an offence to which this subsection applies by—

(a) driving, attempting to drive, or being in charge of a vehicle; or

(b) failing to comply with a requirement made under section 7 of the Road Traffic Act 1988 (failure to provide specimen for analysis or laboratory test) in the course of an investigation into whether the offender had committed an offence while driving, attempting to drive or being in charge of a vehicle, or

(c) failing, as the driver of a vehicle, to comply with subsections (2) and (3) of section 170 of the Road Traffic Act 1988 (duty to stop and give information or report accident),

the court may, on an application under this subsection, make an order forfeiting the vehicle concerned, and any vehicle forfeited under this subsection shall be disposed of as the court may direct.

(2) Subsection (1) above applies—

(a) to an offence under the Road Traffic Act 1988 which is punishable with imprisonment; and

(b) to an offence of culpable homicide.

(3) An application under subsection (1) above shall be at the instance of the prosecutor made when he moves for sentence (or, if the person has been remitted for sentence under section 195 of the Criminal Procedure (Scotland) Act 1995) made before sentence is pronounced.

(4) Where—

(a) the court is satisfied, on an application under this subsection by the prosecutor—

(i) that proceedings have been, or are likely to be, instituted against a person in Scotland for an offence to which subsection (1) above applies allegedly committed in the manner specified in paragraph (a), (b) or (c) of that subsection; and

(ii) that there is reasonable cause to believe that a vehicle specified in the application is to be found in a place or in premises so specified; and

(b) it appears to the court that there are reasonable grounds for thinking that in the event of the person being convicted of the offence an order under subsection (1) above might be made in relation to the vehicle,

the court may grant a warrant authorising a person named therein to enter and search the place or premises and seize the vehicle.

(5) Where the court has made an order under subsection (1) above for the forfeiture of a vehicle, the court or any justice may, if satisfied on evidence on oath—

(a) that there is reasonable cause to believe that the vehicle is to be found in any place or premises; and

(b) that admission to the place or premises has been refused or that a refusal of such admission is apprehended,

issue a warrant of search which may be executed according to law.

(6) In relation to summary proceedings, the reference in subsection (5) above to a justice includes a reference to the sheriff and to a magistrate.

(7) Part II of the Proceeds of Crime (Scotland) Act 1995 shall not apply in respect of a vehicle in relation to which this section applies.

(8) This section extends to Scotland only."

(7) In subsection (3) of section 46 (combination of disqualification and endorsement with probation etc)—

(a) in paragraph (b) for the words from "section 182" to the end there shall be substituted the words "section 228 (probation) or 246(2) or (3) (absolute discharge) of the Criminal Procedure (Scotland) Act 1995"; and

(b) for the words from "section 191" to the end of the subsection there shall be substituted the words "section 247 of that Act shall not apply".

(8) In section 60—

(a) in subsection (4) for the words "section 315 of the Criminal Procedure (Scotland) Act 1975" there shall be substituted the words "section 140 of the Criminal Procedure (Scotland) Act 1995";

(b) in subsection (5) for the words "Part II" there shall be substituted the words "Part IX"; and

(c) in subsection (6)—

    (i) in paragraph (b) for the words "section 312" where they first occur there shall be substituted the words "section 140(4)";

    (ii) in that paragraph for the words "paragraphs (a) to (z) of section 312 of" there shall be substituted the words "section 255 of and Schedule 3 to"; and

    (iii) paragraph (c) shall cease to have effect.

(9) In subsection (7) of section 64 (commencement of proceedings against owner of vehicle) for the words "section 331(1) of the Criminal Procedure (Scotland) Act 1975" there shall be substituted the words "section 136(1) of the Criminal Procedure (Scotland) Act 1995".

(10) In subsection (1) of section 89 (interpretation), in the definition of "court of summary jurisdiction" for the words "section 462(1) of the Criminal Procedure (Scotland) Act 1975" there shall be substituted the words "section 307(1) of the Criminal Procedure (Scotland) Act 1995".

Prevention of Terrorism (Temporary Provisions) Act 1989 (c. 4)

72.—(1) The Prevention of Terrorism (Temporary Provisions) Act 1989 shall be amended as follows.

(2) In section 15 (supplementary provisions relating to arrest and detention)—

(a) in subsection (7) for paragraph (a) there shall be substituted the following paragraph—

"(a) section 135(3) of the Criminal Procedure (Scotland) Act 1995;"; and

(b) in subsection (8) for the words "Section 295(1) of the Criminal Procedure (Scotland) Act 1975" there shall be substituted the words "Section 22(1) and (3) of the Criminal Procedure (Scotland) Act 1995".

(3) In Schedule 4—

(a) in paragraph 16—

    (i) in sub-paragraph (1), paragraph (b) shall cease to have effect;

    (ii) in sub-paragraph (2)(b) the words "where granted under sub-paragraph (1)(a) above," shall cease to have effect; and

    (iii) in sub-paragraphs (5) and (6), the words "or arrestment", in each place where they occur, shall cease to have effect; and

(b) after paragraph 16 there shall be inserted the following paragraph—

"16A.—(1) On the application of the prosecutor, the court may, in respect of moveable property affected by a restraint order (whether such property generally or particular such property), grant warrant for arrestment if the property would be arrestable if the person entitled to it were a debtor.

(2) A warrant under sub-paragraph (1) above shall have effect as if granted on the dependence of an action for debt at the instance of the prosecutor against the person and may be executed, recalled, loosed or restricted accordingly.

(3) The fact that an arrestment has been executed under sub-paragraph (2) above in respect of property shall not prejudice the exercise of an administrator's powers under or for the purposes of this Part of this Schedule in respect of that property.

(4) No arrestment executed under sub-paragraph (2) above shall have effect once, or in so far as, the restraint order affecting the property in respect of which the warrant for such arrestment has been granted has ceased to have effect in respect of that property; and the prosecutor shall apply to the court for an order recalling, or as the case may be, restricting the arrestment accordingly."

(c) in paragraph 19 (enforcement in Scotland of orders made elsewhere in the British Isles)—

    (i) in sub-paragraph (5), for the words "and 16" there shall be substituted ", 16 and (subject to sub-paragraph (5A) below) 16A"; and

    (ii) after sub-paragraph (5) there shall be inserted the following sub-paragraph—

"(5A) In its application by virtue of sub-paragraph (5) above paragraph 16A above shall have effect with the following modifications—

(a) for the references to the prosecutor there shall be substituted references to the Lord Advocate; and

(b) for the references to the court there shall be substituted references to the Court of Session."

Note
[1] Prospectively replaced by the Terrorism Act 2000 (c. 11), s.125 and Sched. 16 Part I.

Extradition Act 1989 (c. 33)

73. In subsection (13) of section 10 of the Extradition Act 1989 (bail in connection with appeal)—
  (a) for the words "section 446(2) of the Criminal Procedure (Scotland) Act 1975" there shall be substituted the words "section 177(2) and (3) of the Criminal Procedure (Scotland) Act 1995"; and
  (a) for the words "section 446(2) of the Criminal Procedure (Scotland) Act 1975" there shall be substituted the words "section 177(2) and (3) of the Criminal Procedure (Scotland) Act 1995"; and
  (b) for the words "section 444" there shall be substituted the words "section 176".

Companies Act 1989 (c. 40)

74.—(1) The Companies Act 1989 shall be amended as follows.
  (2) In subsection (4) of section 44 (jurisdiction and procedure for offences) for the words "section 74 of the Criminal Procedure (Scotland) Act 1975" there shall be substituted the words "section 70 of the Criminal Procedure (Scotland) Act 1995".
  (3) In subsection (4) of section 91 (jurisdiction and procedure for offences) for the words "section 74 of the Criminal Procedure (Scotland) Act 1975" there shall be substituted the words "section 70 of the Criminal Procedure (Scotland) Act 1995".

Prisons (Scotland) Act 1989 (c. 45)

75.—(1) The Prisons (Scotland) Act 1989 shall be amended as follows.
  (2) In subsection (1) of section 11 (removal of prisoners for judicial and other purposes), for the words "section 279 of the 1975 Act" there shall be substituted the words "section 132 of the 1995 Act".
  (3) In subsection (3) of section 21 (transfer to prison of young offenders) for the words "the 1975 Act" where they first occur there shall be substituted the words "the 1995 Act".
  (4) In section 39 (prison rules)—
  (a) in subsection (5), for the words "section 279 of the 1975 Act" there shall be substituted the words "section 132 of the 1995 Act"; and
  (b) in subsection (7), for the words "section 206 of the 1975 Act" there shall be substituted the words "section 208 of the 1995 Act".
  (5) For subsection (3) of section 40 (persons unlawfully at large) there shall be substituted the following subsection—
    "(3) In this section—
    (a) any reference to a person sentenced to imprisonment shall be construed as including a reference to any person sentenced or ordered to be detained under section 44, 205 or 208 of the 1995 Act;
    (b) any reference to a prison shall be construed as including a reference to a place where the person is liable to be detained under the sentence or order; and
    (c) any reference to a sentence shall be construed as including a reference to an order under the said section 44."
  (6) After section 40 there shall be added the following section—

"Warrants for arrest of escaped prisoners
  40A.—(1) On an application being made to a justice alleging that any person is an offender unlawfully at large from a prison or other institution to which this Act or, as the case may be the Prison Act 1952 or the Prison Act (Northern Ireland) 1953 applies in which he is required to be detained after being convicted of an offence, the justice may issue a warrant to arrest him and bring him before any sheriff.
  (2) Where a person is brought before a sheriff in pursuance of a warrant for his arrest under this section, the sheriff shall, if satisfied that he is the person named in the warrant and if satisfied that he is an offender unlawfully at large as mentioned in subsection (1) above, order him to be returned to the prison or other institution where he is required or liable to be detained."

(7) In subsection (1) of section 43 (interpretation) for the definition of "the 1975 Act" there shall be substituted the following—
" "the 1995 Act" means the Criminal Procedure (Scotland) Act 1995;".

The Criminal Justice (International Co-operation) Act 1990 (c. 5)

76.—(1) The Criminal Justice (International Co-operation) Act 1990 shall be amended as follows.

(2) In subsection (6) of section 9 (enforcement of overseas forfeiture orders) for the words from "an offence", in the second place where they occur, to the end there shall be substituted the words "an offence to which Part VI of the Criminal Justice Act 1988 applies or an offence to which Part I of the Proceeds of Crime (Scotland) Act 1995 applies or an offence in respect of which a suspended forfeiture order may be made under section 18 of the said Act of 1995".

(3) In paragraph 2 of Schedule 1, for the words "section 320 of the Criminal Procedure (Scotland) Act 1975" there shall be substituted the words "section 156 of the Criminal Procedure (Scotland) Act 1995".

Computer Misuse Act 1990 (c. 18)

77. In subsection (7) of section 13 of the Computer Misuse Act 1990, for the words "section 331 of the Criminal Procedure (Scotland) Act 1975" there shall be substituted the words "section 136 of the Criminal Procedure (Scotland) Act 1995".

Law Reform (Miscellaneous Provisions) (Scotland) Act 1990 (c. 40)

78. In subsection (4) of section 20 of the Law Reform (Miscellaneous Provisions) (Scotland) Act 1990 (destination of fine imposed for professional misconduct) for the words "section 203 of the Criminal Procedure (Scotland) Act 1975" there shall be substituted the words "section 211(5) of the Criminal Procedure (Scotland) Act 1995".

The Northern Ireland (Emergency Provisions) Act 1991 (c. 24)

79. In section 50(2) of the Northern Ireland (Emergency Provisions) Act 1991 (realisable property, value and gifts), for paragraph (e) there shall be substituted the following paragraph—
"(e) Part II of the Proceeds of Crime (Scotland) Act 1995".

Criminal Justice Act 1991 (c. 53)

[1]80.—(1) The Criminal Justice Act 1991 shall be amended as follows.
(2) In subsection (3) of section 24 (deduction of fines from income support)—
(a) in paragraph (a) for the words "section 196(2) of the Criminal Procedure (Scotland) Act 1975" there shall be substituted the words "section 211(4) of the Criminal Procedure (Scotland) Act 1995";
(b) in paragraph (b) for the words "section 66 of the Criminal Justice (Scotland) Act 1980" there shall be substituted the words "section 252 of the Criminal Procedure (Scotland) Act 1995"; and
(c) in paragraph (c) for the words "section 403(1)(a) or (b) of the Criminal Procedure (Scotland) Act 1975" there shall be substituted the words "section 222(1)(a) or (b) of the Criminal Procedure (Scotland) Act 1995".

NOTE
[1]As amended by the Powers of Criminal Courts (Sentencing) Act 2000 (c. 6), s.165 and Sched. 12, Part I.

Dangerous Dogs Act 1991 (c. 65)

81. In subsection (9) of section 4 of the Dangerous Dogs Act 1991 (destruction and disqualification orders)—
(a) for the words "section 411 of the Criminal Procedure (Scotland) Act 1975" there shall be substituted the words "section 221 of the Criminal Procedure (Scotland) Act 1995"; and
(b) for the words "Part II" there shall be substituted the words "Part XI".

Social Security Administration Act 1992 (c. 5)

82. In subsection (7) of section 116 of the Social Security Administration Act 1992—
(a) for the words "section 331 of the Criminal Procedure (Scotland) Act 1975" there shall be substituted the words "section 136 of the Criminal Procedure (Scotland) Act 1995"; and

(b) for the words "section 331 of the said Act of 1975" there shall be substituted the words "section 136 of the said Act of 1995".

Timeshare Act 1992 (c. 35)

83. In subsection (3) of section 11 of the Timeshare Act 1992 (prosecution time limit), for the words "section 331 of the Criminal Procedure (Scotland) Act 1975" there shall be substituted the words "section 136 of the Criminal Procedure (Scotland) Act 1995".

Friendly Societies Act 1992 (c. 40)

84. In subsection (5) of section 107 of the Friendly Societies Act 1992 (prosecution time limit), for the words "section 331(1) of the Criminal Procedure (Scotland) Act 1975" there shall be substituted the words "section 136(1) of the Criminal Procedure (Scotland) Act 1995".

Trade Union and Labour Relations (Consolidation) Act 1992 (c. 52)

85. In subsection (6) of section 45A of the Trade Union and Labour Relations (Consolidation) Act 1992 (prosecution time limit), for the words "section 331 of the Criminal Procedure (Scotland) Act 1975" there shall be substituted the words "section 136 of the Criminal Procedure (Scotland) Act 1995".

Prisoners and Criminal Proceedings (Scotland) Act 1993 (c. 9)

86.—(1) The Prisoners and Criminal Proceedings (Scotland) Act 1993 shall be amended as follows.

(2) Subject to any specific amendment under this paragraph, for the words "1975 Act" where they occur there shall be substituted the words "1995 Act".

(3) In subsection (1) of section 5 (fine defaulters) for paragraph (a) there shall be substituted the following paragraph—

"(a) under section 219 of the 1995 Act (imprisonment for non-payment of fine) or, by virtue of that section, under section 207 of that Act (detention of young offenders);".

(4) Section 6 (application of Part to young offenders etc) shall be amended as follows—

(a) in paragraph (a) for the words "section 207(2) or 415(2)" there shall be substituted the words "section 207(2)";

(b) for the words "section 205" there shall be substituted the words "section 205(1) to (3)";

(c) for the words "section 206" where they occur there shall be substituted the words "section 208"; and

(d) for the words "section 207(2)" there shall be substituted the words "section 207(2)".

(5) In section 7 (children detained in solemn proceedings) for the words "section 206" where they occur there shall be substituted the words "section 208".

(6) In section 11 (duration of licence)—

(a) in subsection (3), for the words "section 212A" there shall be substituted the words "section 209"; and

(b) in paragraph (b) of that subsection, for the words from "the" in the second place where it occurs to the end there shall be substituted—

"there has elapsed—

(i) a period (reckoned from the date on which he was ordered to be returned to prison under or by virtue of subsection (2)(a) of that section) equal in length to the period between the date on which the new offence was committed and the date on which he would (but for his release) have served the original sentence in full; or

(ii) subject to subsection (4) below, a total period equal in length to the period for which he was so ordered to be returned to prison together with, so far as not concurrent with that period, any term of imprisonment to which he was sentenced in respect of the new offence,

whichever results in the later date.

(4) In subsection (3)(b) above, "the original sentence" and "the new offence" have the same meanings as in section 16 of this Act."

(7) Section 14 (supervised release of short term prisoners) shall be amended as follows—

(a) in subsection (2)—

(i) for the words "section 212A(1)" there shall be substituted the words "section 209(1)"; and

(ii) for the words "section 212A(2) to (6)" there shall be substituted the words "section 209(3) to (7)";

(b) in subsection (3) for the words "section 212A(2)" there shall be substituted the words "section 209(3)"; and

(c) in subsection (5) for the words "section 212A(5)(b)" there shall be substituted the words "section 209(6)(b)".

(8) In subsection (4) of section 15 (variation of supervised release order) for the words "section 212A(2)(b)" there shall be substituted the words "section 209(3)(b)"

(9) In section 16 (commission of offence by released prisoner)—

(a) in subsection (6), for the words "section 254(3) or 453C(1)" there shall be substituted the words "section 118(4) or 189(1) and (2)"; and

(b) for subsection (7) there shall be substituted the following subsection—

"(7) Where an order under subsection (2) or (4) above is made in respect of a person released on licence—

(a) the making of the order shall have the effect of revoking the licence; and

(b) if the sentence comprising—

(i) the period for which the person is ordered to be returned to prison; and

(ii) so far as not concurrent with that period, any term of imprisonment to which he is sentenced in respect of the new offence,

is six months or more but less than four years, section 1(1) of this Act shall apply in respect of that sentence as if for the word "unconditionally" there were substituted the words "on licence"."

(10) In subsection (1) of section 27 (interpretation of Part I), for the words "section 212A" where they occur there shall be substituted the words "section 209".

(11) In section 46 (interpretation) the definition of "the 1975 Act" shall cease to have effect and at the end there shall be inserted the following definition—

" "the 1995 Act" means the Criminal Procedure (Scotland) Act 1995".

Agriculture Act 1993 (c. 37)

87. In subsection (5) of section 52 of the Agriculture Act 1993 (prosecution time limit) for the words "section 331 of the Criminal Procedure (Scotland) Act 1975" there shall be substituted the words "section 136 of the Criminal Procedure (Scotland) Act 1995".

Railways Act 1993 (c. 43)

88. In subsection (5) of section 148 of the Railways Act 1993 (prosecution time limit) for the words "section 331 of the Criminal Procedure (Scotland) Act 1975" there shall be substituted the words "section 136 of the Criminal Procedure (Scotland) Act 1995".

Finance Act 1994 (c. 9)

89.—(1) The Finance Act 1994 shall be amended as follows.

(2) In subsection (2) of section 22 (records and rules of evidence), in paragraph (d) for the words "Schedule 3 to the Prisoners and Criminal Proceedings (Scotland) Act 1993" there shall be substituted the words "Schedule 8 to the Criminal Procedure (Scotland) Act 1995".

(3) In subsection (3) of section 25 (order for production of documents), for the words "section 462 of the Criminal Procedure (Scotland) Act 1975" there shall be substituted the words "section 308 of the Criminal Procedure (Scotland) Act 1995".

(4) In Schedule 7 (insurance premium tax)—

(a) in paragraph 1(6)(d), for the words "Schedule 3 to the Prisoners and Criminal Proceedings (Scotland) Act 1993" there shall be substituted the words "Schedule 8 to the Criminal Procedure (Scotland) Act 1995"; and

(b) in paragraph 4(2), for the words "section 462 of the Criminal Procedure (Scotland) Act 1975" there shall be substituted the words "section 308 of the Criminal Procedure (Scotland) Act 1995".

Vehicle Excise and Registration Act 1994 (c. 22)

90.—(1) The Vehicle Excise and Registration Act 1994 shall be amended as follows.

(2) In subsection (1) of section 32 (effect of certain orders) for paragraph (b) there shall be substituted the following paragraph—

"(b) or an order under section 228 of the Criminal Procedure (Scotland) Act 1995 placing him on probation or under 246(3) of that Act discharging him absolutely, or".

(3) In subsection (1) of section 41 (effect of certain orders) for paragraph (b) there shall be substituted the following paragraph—

"(b) or an order under section 228 of the Criminal Procedure (Scotland) Act 1995 placing him on probation or under 246(2) or (3) of that Act discharging him absolutely, or".

(4) In subsection (4) of section 48 (time limit for proceedings) for the words "section 331 of the Criminal Procedure (Scotland) Act 1975" there shall be substituted the words "section 136 of the Criminal Procedure (Scotland) Act 1995".

91. In Schedule 11 of the Value Added Tax Act 1994—
(a) in paragraph 10(3) (power of entry and search) for the words "section 462 of the Criminal Procedure (Scotland) Act 1975" there shall be substituted the words "section 308 of the Criminal Procedure (Scotland) Act 1995"; and
(b) in paragraph 11(1) (access to certain information) for the words "section 462 of the Criminal Procedure (Scotland) Act 1975" there shall be substituted the words "section 308 of the Criminal Procedure (Scotland) Act 1995".

Trade Marks Act 1994 (c. 26)

92.—(1) The Trade Marks Act 1994 shall be amended as follows.
(2) In subsection (1) of section 96 (prosecution time limit) for the words "section 331 of the Criminal Procedure (Scotland) Act 1975" there shall be substituted the words "section 136 of the Criminal Procedure (Scotland) Act 1995".
(3) In section 98 (forfeiture)—
(a) in subsection (2) for the words "section 310 of the Criminal Procedure (Scotland) Act 1975" there shall be substituted the words "section 134 of the Criminal Procedure (Scotland) Act 1995";
(b) in subsection (6) for the words "Criminal Procedure (Scotland) Act 1975" there shall be substituted the words "Criminal Procedure (Scotland) Act 1995";
(c) in subsection (9) for the words "section 452(4)(a) to (e) of the Criminal Procedure (Scotland) Act 1975" there shall be substituted the words "section 182(5)(a) to (e) of the Criminal Procedure (Scotland) Act 1995"; and
(d) in subsection (11) for the words "Criminal Procedure (Scotland) Act 1975" there shall be substituted the words "Criminal Procedure (Scotland) Act 1995".

Criminal Justice and Public Order Act 1994 (c. 33)

93.—(1) The Criminal Justice and Public Order Act 1994 shall be amended as follows.
(2) In subsection (5) of section 25 (restriction on bail) in the definition of "the relevant enactments", for paragraph (b) there shall be substituted the following paragraph—
"(b) as respects Scotland, sections 205(1) to (3) and 208 of the Criminal Procedure (Scotland) Act 1995;".
(3) In section 102 (provision of prisoner escorts)—
(a) in paragraph (b) of subsection (3), for the words "Criminal Procedure (Scotland) Act 1975" there shall be substituted the words "Criminal Procedure (Scotland) Act 1995"; and
(b) in subsection (6)—
(i) in the definition of "hospital order", for the words "section 174, 174A, 175, 375A or 376 of the Act of 1975" there shall be substituted the words "section 53, 54 or 58 of the Act of 1995"; and
(ii) in the definition of "warrant", for the words "Act of 1975" there shall be substituted the words "Act of 1995".
(4) In subsection (4) of section 104 (powers and duties of prison custody officers), for the words "section 395(2) of the Criminal Procedure (Scotland) Act 1975" there shall be substituted the words "section 212 of the Criminal Procedure (Scotland) Act 1995".
(5) In subsection (1) of section 117 (interpretation of Chapter), in the definition of "prisoner" for the words "section 215 or 426 of the Criminal Procedure (Scotland) Act 1975" there shall be substituted the words "section 295 of the Criminal Procedure (Scotland) Act 1995".
(6) In section 138 (which supplements section 137 relating to cross-border powers of arrest)—
(a) in subsection (2), for the words from "subsections (2) to (7)" to "1993" there shall be substituted the words "subsections (2) to (8) of section 14 (detention and questioning at police station), subsections (1), (2) and (4) to (6) of section 15 (rights of person arrested or detained) and section 18 (prints, samples etc. in criminal investigations) of the Criminal Procedure (Scotland) Act 1995";
(b) in subsection (6)—
(i) for the words "sections 2 and 3 of the Criminal Justice (Scotland) Act 1980" there shall be substituted the words "sections 14 and 15 of the said Act of 1995";
(ii) in paragraph (a), for the words "in section 2" there shall be substituted the words "in section 14" and for the words "in subsections (4) and (7)" there shall be substituted the words "in subsections (6) and (9)"; and
(iii) in paragraph (b), for the words "in section 3(1)" there shall be substituted the words "in subsections (1) and (2) of section 15".

The Drug Trafficking Act 1994 (c. 37)

94.—(1) The Drug Trafficking Act 1994 shall be amended as follows.

(2) In subsection (7) of section 4 (assessing the proceeds of drug trafficking), for paragraphs (b) and (c) there shall be substituted the following—
    "(b) the Proceeds of Crime (Scotland) Act 1995;".

(3) In subsection (3) of section 6 (meaning of realisable property) for paragraph (e) there shall be substituted the following—
    "(e) Part II of the Proceeds of Crime (Scotland) Act 1995 (forfeiture of property used in crime);"

    (4) In subsection (2) of section 18 (compensation) for sub-paragraph (ii) of paragraph (b) there shall be substituted the following—
        "(ii) an order of the Court of Session under section 32, 33, 34 or 35 of the Proceeds of Crime (Scotland) Act 1995 (recognition and enforcement of orders under this Act and inhibition and arrestment of property affected by restraint orders);".

(5) In subsection (10) of section 26 (restraint orders) for the words from "Part I" to the end of the subsection there shall be substituted the words "the Proceeds of Crime (Scotland) Act 1995, and in relation to such an order "realisable property" has the same meaning as in that Act".

(6) In section 37 (recognition and enforcement of certain Scottish orders and functions)—
(a) in subsection (1)—
        (i) after the words "expedient for the purpose" there shall be inserted the words "in connection with a drug trafficking offence within the meaning of the Proceeds of Crime (Scotland) Act 1995";
        (ii) in paragraph (a) for the words "Part I of the Criminal Justice (Scotland) Act 1987" there shall be substituted the words "that Act";
        (iii) in each of paragraphs (a) and (b) where they occur, the words "that Part of" shall cease to have effect;
(b) in subsection (2)—
        (i) in paragraph (a), in sub-paragraph (i) for the words "section 13 of the Criminal Justice (Scotland) Act 1987" there shall be substituted the words "Schedule 1 to the Proceeds of Crime (Scotland) Act 1995" and in sub-paragraph (ii) the words "Part I of" shall cease to have effect;
        (ii) in each of paragraphs (b) and (c) where they occur, the words "that Part of" shall cease to have effect.

(7) In subsection (2) of section 48 (interpretation of Part II), in paragraph (a) for the words "Part I of the Criminal Justice (Scotland) Act 1987" there shall be substituted the words "the Proceeds of Crime (Scotland) Act 1995".

Local Government etc. (Scotland) Act 1994 (c. 39)

95.—(1) The Local Government etc. (Scotland) Act 1994 shall be amended as follows.

(2) In subsection (1) of section 127 (the Principal Reporter), for the words "Criminal Procedure (Scotland) Act 1975" there shall be substituted the words "Criminal Procedure (Scotland) Act 1995".

(3) In each of subsections (3) and (8) of section 128 (Scottish Children's Reporter Administration), for the words "Criminal Procedure (Scotland) Act 1975" there shall be substituted the words "Criminal Procedure (Scotland) Act 1995".

(4) In subsection (1) of section 130 (annual report of Principal Reporter), for the words "Criminal Procedure (Scotland) Act 1975" there shall be substituted the words "Criminal Procedure (Scotland) Act 1995".

Deregulation and Contracting Out Act 1994 (c. 40)

96. In subsection (2) of section 2 of the Deregulation and Contracting Out Act 1994, for paragraph (b) there shall be substituted the following paragraph—
    "(b) section 292(6) and (7) of the Criminal Procedure (Scotland) Act 1995,".

Children (Scotland) Act 1995 (c. 36)

97.—(1) The Children (Scotland) Act 1995 shall be amended as follows.

(2) In subsection (2) of section 45 (attendance of child etc. at hearing), in paragraph (a) for the words "Schedule 1 of the Criminal Procedure (Scotland) Act 1975" there shall be substituted the words "Schedule I of the Criminal Procedure (Scotland) Act 1995".

(3) In section 50 (treatment of child's case on remission by court)—

(a) in subsection (1), for the words "section 173, 372 or 373 of the Criminal Procedure (Scotland) Act 1975" there shall be substituted "section 49 of the Criminal Procedure (Scotland) Act 1995"; and

(b) in subsection (2), for the words "the said section 373" there shall be substituted "subsection (7) of the said section 49".

(4) In subsection (2) of section 52 (children requiring compulsory supervision)—

(a) in paragraph (d) for the words "Schedule 1 of the Criminal Procedure (Scotland) Act 1975" there shall be substituted the words "Schedule 1 of the Criminal Procedure (Scotland) Act 1995"; and

(b) in paragraph (g), for the words "sections 2A to 2C of the Sexual Offences (Scotland) Act 1976" there shall be substituted "sections 1 to 3 of the Criminal Law (Consolidation) (Scotland) Act 1995".

(5) In subsection (7) of section 53 (information for Principal Reporter) for the words "section 462 of the Criminal Procedure (Scotland) Act 1975" there shall be substituted the words "section 307 of the Criminal Procedure (Scotland) Act 1995".

(6) In section 63(1) (duty of Principal Reporter where informed by constable of detention of a child) for the words "section 296(3) of the Criminal Procedure (Scotland) Act 1975" there shall be substituted "section 43(5) of the Criminal Procedure (Scotland) Act 1995".

(7) In section 78 (powers of arrest)—

(a) in subsection (8), for the words "Criminal Procedure (Scotland) Act 1975" there shall be substituted the words "Criminal Procedure (Scotland) Act 1995";

(b) in subsection (11), for the words "section 10 of the Bail etc, (Scotland) Act 1980" there shall be substituted the words "section 8 of the said Act of 1995"; and

(c) in subsection (12), for the words "Subsections (1) and (3) of section 3 of the Criminal Justice (Scotland) Act 1980" there shall be substituted the words "Subsections (1), (2) and (4) of section 15 of the said Act of 1995".

Pensions Act 1995 (c. 26)

98. In subsection (5) of section 100 of the Pensions Act 1995 (warrants) for the words "Criminal Procedure (Scotland) Act 1975" there shall be substituted the words "Criminal Procedure (Scotland) Act 1995".

Note

99. The amendments made by this Schedule to—

(a) the Sea Fisheries Act 1968;

(b) the Fatal Accidents and Sudden Deaths Inquiry (Scotland) Act 1976; and

(c) section 15(2) of the Contempt of Court Act 1981,

are in substitution for amendments made to those enactments by section 56 of and Schedule 7 to the Criminal Justice Act 1988 which are repealed by this Act.

NOTE
[1]Deleted by the Crime and Punishment (Scotland) Act 1997 (c. 48) s.62(1) and Sched. 1, para. 19(3) with effect from August 1, 1997 in terms of S.I. 1997 No. 1712.

Section 6   SCHEDULE 5

REPEALS

Chapter	Short title	Extent of repeal
11 Geo. 4 & 1 Wm. 4 c. 69	The Court of Session Act 1830	Section 18
50 & 51 Vict. c. 35	The Criminal Procedure (Scotland) Act 1887	The whole Act
4 & 5 Geo. 5 c. 582	The Criminal Justice Administration Act 1914	Section 28(3)
12, 13 & 14 Geo. 6, c. 94	The Criminal Justice (Scotland) Act 1949	The whole Act
1 & 2 Eliz. 2, c. 14	The Prevention of Crime Act 1953	Section 1

Chapter	Short title	Extent of repeal
2 & 3 Eliz. 2, c. 48	The Summary Jurisdiction (Scotland) Act 1954	The whole Act
1968 c. 49	The Social Work (Scotland) Act 1968	Section 31(1)
1975 c. 20	The District Courts (Scotland) Act 1975	Sections 2 to 4 Section 6 In Schedule 1, paragraph 27
1975 c. 21	The Criminal Procedure (Scotland) Act 1975	The whole Act
1977 c. 45	The Criminal Law Act 1977	In Schedule 6, the entries relating to the Criminal Procedure (Scotland) Act 1975 In Schedule 7, paragraph 2 Schedule 11
1978 c. 29	The National Health Service (Scotland) Act 1978	In Schedule 16, paragraph 41
1978 c. 49	The Community Service by Offenders (Scotland) Act 1978	Sections 1 to 8 Sections 10 to 13 Section 15 In Schedule 2, paragraphs 2 and 3
1979 c. 16	The Criminal Evidence Act 1979	In section 1(1) the words "sections 141 and 346 of the Criminal Procedure (Scotland) Act 1975"
1980 c. 4	The Bail (Scotland) Act 1980	The whole Act
1980 c. 62	The Criminal Justice (Scotland) Act 1980	Sections 1 to 3 Sections 4 to 7 Sections 9 to 43 Section 45(1) Sections 46 to 50 Sections 52 to 54 Sections 58 to 67 Part V Sections 78 and 80 Schedules 1 to 4 In Schedule 7, paragraphs 25 to 78
1981 c. 45	The Forgery and Counterfeiting Act 1981	Section 26
1982 c. 48	The Criminal Justice Act 1982	Part IV Schedules 6 and 7
1982 c. 49	The Transport Act 1982	In section 40, paragraph (c) of subsection (5)
1984 c. 39	The Video Recordings Act 1984	Section 20
1985 c. 66	The Bankruptcy (Scotland) Act 1985	In section 5(4) the words "by section 1(1) of the Criminal Justice (Scotland) Act 1987" In section 7(1) the words "by section 1(1) of the Criminal Justice (Scotland) Act 1987"
1985 c. 73	The Law Reform (Miscellaneous Provisions) (Scotland) Act 1985	Section 21 Sections 36 and 37 Section 40 Section 43 Section 45 In Schedule 2, paragraphs 16 to 20 and paragraph 23 In Schedule 3, paragraphs 1, 3 and 4
1987 c. 41	The Criminal Justice (Scotland) Act 1987	Part I Sections 56 to 68 In Schedule 1, paragraphs 4 to 18

Chapter	Short title	Extent of repeal
1988 c. 53	The Road Traffic Offenders Act 1988	In section 60, paragraph (c) of subsection (6)
1988 c. 54	The Road Traffic (Consequential Provisions) Act 1988	In Schedule 3, paragraph 34
1990 c. 5	The Criminal Justice (International Co-operation) Act 1990	Section 15 In Schedule 4, paragraph 5
1990 c. 40	The Law Reform (Miscellaneous Provisions) (Scotland) Act 1990	Sections 56 and 57 Section 62 Schedule 6
1991 c. 53	The Criminal Justice Act 1991	In Schedule 3, paragraph 8
1991 c. 62	The Armed Forces Act 1991	In Schedule 2, paragraph 9(2)
1993 c. 9	The Prisoners and Criminal Proceedings (Scotland) Act 1993	Section 8 Section 14(1) Sections 28 to 35 Sections 37 to 43 In section 46, the definition of "the 1975 Act" Schedules 3 and 4 In Schedule 5, paragraph 1
1993 c. 13	The Carrying of Knives etc. (Scotland) Act 1993	The whole Act
1993 c. 36	The Criminal Justice Act 1993Sections 68 and 69 In Schedule 5, paragraph 2	
1994 c. 33	The Criminal Justice and Public Order Act 1994	
Section 47(4) In section 129, subsections (1) to (3) Section 132 In section 157, subsection (7)		
1994 c. 37	The Drug Trafficking Act 1994	In section 37, the words "that Part of" where they occur and in paragraph (a)(ii) of subsection (2) the words "Part I of".
1995 c. 20	The Criminal Justice (Scotland) Act 1995	The whole Act
1995 c. 36	The Children (Scotland) Act 1995.	Section 49 In Schedule 4, paragraphs 24, 27 and 29.

Section 6(2)   SCHEDULE 6

PROVISIONS REPEALED WITH SAVINGS

In section 43, the words from "and it shall not be necessary" to the end.
Section 45.
Section 46.
Section 47.
Section 52.
Section 53.

In section 54 the words from "and it shall not be necessary to specify" to the end.

In section 55, the words "it shall not be necessary to set forth the document or any part of it in such indictment".

Section 56.

Section 57.

In section 109, the words from the beginning to "except that".

In section 111, the words "it shall not be necessary that a new warrant should be granted for the incarceration of the accused, but".

Section 124 (except the proviso).

Section 222.

PROCEEDS OF CRIME (SCOTLAND) ACT 1995

(1995 c. 43)

ARRANGEMENT OF SECTIONS

PART I

CONFISCATION OF THE PROCEEDS OF CRIME

Confiscation orders

PART II

FORFEITURE OF PROPERTY USED IN CRIME

PART III

RESTRAINT ORDERS

An Act to consolidate as regards Scotland certain enactments relating to the confiscation of the proceeds of, and forfeiture of property used in, crime.
[8th November 1995]

PART I

CONFISCATION OF THE PROCEEDS OF CRIME

Confiscation orders

General provision

1.—(1) Subject to the provisions of this Part, where in respect of any offence to which this Part applies—
  (a) the accused is convicted, whether in solemn or summary proceedings; or
  (b) in the case of summary proceedings (without proceeding to conviction) an order is made discharging him absolutely,
the court, on the application of the prosecutor, may make an order (a "confiscation order") requiring the accused to pay such sum as the court thinks fit.

¹(2) This Part applies to any offence which has been prosecuted—
  (a) on indictment; or
  (b) on summary complaint if the offence is punishable by a fine of an amount greater than the amount corresponding to level 5 on the standard scale or by imprisonment for a period longer than 3 months or by both such fine and imprisonment,
but it does not apply to an offence under Part III of the 1989 Act (financial assistance for terrorism).

(3) A confiscation order shall not be made unless the court orders some other disposal (including an absolute discharge) in respect of the accused.

(4) Except where the offence is a drug trafficking offence, the court may make a confiscation order against an accused only if it is satisfied that he has benefited from the commission of the offence concerned.

(5) The sum which a confiscation order requires an accused to pay in the case of a drug trafficking offence shall be an amount not exceeding—

(a) subject to paragraph (b) below, what the court assesses to be the value of the proceeds of the person's drug trafficking; or

(b) if the court is satisfied that the amount that might be realised in terms of this Act at the time the confiscation order is made has a value less than that of the proceeds of the person's drug trafficking, what it assesses to be that amount.

(6) The sum which a confiscation order requires an accused to pay in the case of an offence not mentioned in subsection (5) above, must not exceed the lesser of—

(a) the amount of the benefit—

(i) from the commission of the offence; or

(ii) where section 2(4) of this Act applies, from the commission of the offence and any other offence, not being a drug trafficking offence, to which this Part of this Act applies; and

(b) the amount that might be realised at the time the order is made.

(7) Any application under this section shall be made—

(a) in proceedings on indictment, when the prosecutor moves for sentence or, if the accused is remitted for sentence under section 195 of the 1995 Act, before sentence is pronounced; and

(b) in summary proceedings, following the conviction of the accused.

(8) For the purposes of any appeal or review, a confiscation order is a sentence.

NOTE

[1] Prospectively amended by the Terrorism Act 2000 (c. 11), s.125 and Sched. 15, para. 11.

Benefit from commission of offence

2.—(1) For the purposes of this Part of this Act, an accused shall be held to have benefited from the commission of an offence if in connection with its commission he has obtained, directly or indirectly, any property or other economic advantage.

(2) Subject to subsection (4) below, in determining whether an accused has benefited from the commission of an offence and, if he has, the amount referred to in section 1(6)(a)(i) of this Act, the court may make the following assumptions, except in so far as he proves either of them, on the balance of probabilities, to be incorrect—

(a) that any property or other economic advantage which has been obtained by him since the relevant date has been obtained in connection with the commission of the offence; and

(b) that any expenditure by him since the relevant date was met out of property or other economic advantage obtained in connection with the commission of the offence.

(3) In subsection (2) above "the relevant date" means—

(a) the date of the offence; or

(b) if the offence is found to have been committed over a period of time, the date occurring at the beginning of that period.

(4) Where—

(a) the application for the confiscation order has been made in respect of two or more offences; or

(b) during the relevant period the accused has been convicted of at least one other offence to which this Part of this Act applies,

the court may, in determining the amount referred to in section 1(6)(a)(ii) of this Act, make the assumptions set out in subsection (5) below, except in so far as the accused proves either of those assumptions, on the balance of probabilities, to be incorrect.

(5) Those assumptions are—

(a) that any property or economic advantage which has been obtained by the accused during the relevant period has been obtained in connection with the commission of an offence to which this Part of this Act applies; and

(b) that any expenditure by him during the relevant period was met out of property or other economic advantage obtained in connection with the commission of such an offence.

(6) In subsections (4) and (5) above, "the relevant period" means the period of six years ending with the date on which proceedings were instituted against the accused for the offence in respect of which the application for the confiscation order has been made.

(7) In this Act, "property" means any property wherever situated, whether heritable or moveable or whether corporeal or incorporeal.

Assessing the proceeds of drug trafficking

3.—(1) For the purposes of this Act—

(a) any payments or other rewards received by a person at any time (whether before or after the commencement of this Act) in connection with drug trafficking carried on by him or another are his proceeds of drug trafficking, and

(b) the value of his proceeds of drug trafficking is the aggregate of the values of the payments or other rewards.

(2) Without prejudice to section 9 of this Act the court may, in making an assessment as regards a person under section 1(5) of this Act, make the following assumptions, except in so far as any of them may be shown to be incorrect in that person's case—

(a) that any property appearing to the court—

    (i) to have been held by him at any time since his conviction; or, as the case may be,

    (ii) to have been transferred to him at any time since a date six years before his being indicted, or being served with the complaint, was received by him, at the earliest time at which he appears to the court to have held it, as a payment or reward in connection with drug trafficking carried on by him;

(b) that any expenditure of his since the date mentioned in paragraph (a)(ii) above was met out of payments received by him in connection with drug trafficking carried on by him, and

(c) that, for the purpose of valuing any property received or assumed to have been received by him at any time as such a reward, he received the property free of any other interests in it.

(3) Subsection (2) above does not apply if the only offence by virtue of which the assessment is being made is an offence under section 14 of the Criminal Justice (International Co-operation) Act 1990 or section 37 or 38 of the Criminal Law (Consolidation) (Scotland) Act 1995.

(4) The court shall, in making an assessment as regards a person under section 1(5) of this Act, leave out of account any of his proceeds of drug trafficking that are shown to the court to have been taken into account in a case where a confiscation order (whether under this Act or under and within the meaning of—

(a) section 2 of the 1994 Act; or

(b) any corresponding provision in Northern Ireland),

has previously been made against him.

Realisable property

4.—(1) In this Act "realisable property" means, subject to subsection (2) below—

    (a) the whole estate wherever situated of a person—

        (i) against whom proceedings have been instituted for an offence to which this Part of this Act applies; or

        (ii) in espect of whom a restraint order has been made by virtue of section 29(3) of this Act;

    (b) the whole estate wherever situated of a person to whom any person whose whole estate is realisable by virtue of paragraph (a) above has (directly or indirectly and whether in one transaction or in a series of transactions) made a gift caught by this Part of this Act or, as the case may be, an implicative gift;

    (c) any other property in the possession or under the control of a person mentioned in paragraph (a) or (b) above; and

    (d) any income or estate vesting in a person mentioned in paragraph (a) or (b) above.

(2) Property is not realisable if—

    (a) held on trust by a person mentioned in subsection (1)(a) or (b) above for a person not so mentioned;

    (b) a suspended forfeiture order is in force in respect of the property; or

    (c) it is, for the time being, subject to a restraint order made in respect of other proceedings.

(3) For the purposes of this Part of this Act, the amount that might be realised at the time a confiscation order is made in respect of a person is—

    (a) in relation to an offence which is not a drug trafficking offence, subject to section 7(5) of this Act, the total value at that time of all his realisable property, and of all gifts caught by this Part which have been made by him, less any amount due by him at that time in respect of any compensation order under section 249 of the 1995 Act made before the confiscation order; and

    (b) in relation to a drug trafficking offence, the total value at that time of all his realisable property and all implicative gifts which have been made by him.

(4) In assessing the value of realisable property (other than money) of a person in respect of whom it proposes to make a confiscation order, the court shall have regard to the likely market value of the property at the date on which the order would be made; but it may also have regard to any security or real burden which would require to be discharged in realising the property or to any other factors which might reduce the amount recoverable by such realisation.

(5) In assessing the value of realisable property of a person whose estate has been sequestrated, or who has been adjudged bankrupt in England and Wales or Northern Ireland, the court shall take into account the extent to which the property is subject to, as the case may be, sequestration or bankruptcy procedure by virtue of paragraph 1 or 2 of Schedule 2 to this Act.

(6) Without prejudice to section 2(7) of this Act, the court may, for the purposes of section 1(5)(b) of this Act, disregard the amount (or part of the amount) of an implicative gift if it considers it improbable that such amount (or part) could be realised.

Gifts caught by Part I

5.—(1) A gift is caught by this Part of this Act if—

    (a) it was made by the accused—

(i) in contemplation of, or after, the commission of the offence; or, if more than one,

(ii) in contemplation of any of the offences or after the commission of the earlier or the earliest of the offences,

to which the proceedings mentioned in section 4(1)(a)(i) of this Act for the time being relate, not being drug trafficking offences; or

(b) where subsection (4) of section 2 of this Act applies, it was made by the accused within the relevant period within the meaning of subsection (6) of that section.

(2) The value of a gift caught by this Part of this Act shall be assessed in accordance with section 7 of this Act.

(3) At any time before the realisation of property which is or represents a gift caught by this Part of this Act, the recipient of the gift may apply to the court for an order under this subsection, and, if the court is satisfied, on the balance of probabilities—

(a) that the person received the gift not knowing, not suspecting and not having reasonable grounds to suspect that the gift was made in contemplation of, or after, the commission of the offence or, if more than one, in contemplation of any of the offences or after the commission of the earlier or the earliest of the offences to which the proceedings for the time being relate; and

(b) that he was not associated with the giver in the commission of the offence; and

(c) that he would suffer hardship if the application were not granted,

it may make an order declaring that the gift or a part of the gift shall not be caught by this Part of this Act and that the property or part of the property of the recipient of the gift shall not be, or shall cease to be, realisable for the purposes of this Part of this Act and, if a confiscation order has already been made, varying that order accordingly, where necessary.

(4) An appeal shall lie to the High Court at the instance of—

(a) the applicant against the refusal;

(b) the prosecutor against the granting,

of an application under subsection (3) above, and the High Court in determining such an appeal may make such order as could have been made by the court on an application under that subsection.

(5) The procedure in an appeal under this section shall be the same as the procedure in an appeal against sentence.

Implicative gifts

6.—(1) In this Act references to an "implicative gift" are references to a gift (whether made before or after the commencement of this Act)—

(a) made not more than six years before the date on which, in respect of a person suspected of, or charged with, a drug trafficking offence, the proceedings were commenced or a restraint order was made (whichever first occurs); or

(b) made at any time if the gift was of property—

(i) received by the giver in connection with drug trafficking carried on by him or another, or

(ii) which, in whole or in part, directly or indirectly represented in the giver's hands property received by him in that connection.

(2) The value of an implicative gift shall be assessed in accordance with section 7 of this Act.

(3) Where the court is satisfied, on the application of a person in receipt of an implicative gift made before or after a confiscation order has been made—

(a) that the person received the gift not knowing, not suspecting and not having reasonable grounds to suspect that the giver was in any way concerned in drug trafficking; and

(b) that he is not, and has never been, associated with the giver in drug trafficking; and

(c) that he would suffer hardship if the application were not granted,

it may make an order declaring that the gift or a part of the gift shall not be an implicative gift and that the property or part of the property of the recipient of the gift shall not be, or shall cease to be, realisable for the purposes of this Part of this Act and, if a confiscation order has already been made, varying that order accordingly, where necessary.

(4) An appeal shall lie to the High Court at the instance of—

(a) the applicant against the refusal;

(b) the prosecutor against the granting,

of an application under subsection (3) above on the ground that there has been a miscarriage of justice.

(5) The procedure in an appeal under this section shall be the same as the procedure in an appeal against sentence.

Gifts: valuation

7.—(1) In assessing the value of—

(a) a gift caught by this Part of this Act; or

(b) an implicative gift,

the court shall, subject to subsections (4) to (6) below, take it to be the greater of the values specified in subsections (2) and (3) below.

(2) The value specified in this subsection is the value of the gift when received adjusted to take account of subsequent changes in the value of money.

(3) The value specified in this subsection is both of the following—

(a) the likely market value, on the date on which the confiscation order is to be made, of—

  (i) the gift, if retained; or

  (ii) where the recipient of the gift retains only part of it, the retained part, and any property or part of any property which, directly or indirectly, represents the gift; or

  (iii) where the recipient of the gift retains no part of it, any property or part of any property which, directly or indirectly, represents the gift; and

(b) the value of any other property and any other economic advantage which by reason of the making of the gift the recipient of the gift has obtained, directly or indirectly, prior to the date on which the confiscation order is to be made, adjusted to take account of subsequent changes in the value of money.

(4) The circumstances in which the accused is to be treated as making a gift include those where he transfers an interest in property to another person directly or indirectly for a consideration the value of which is significantly less than the value of that interest at the time of transfer; and in those circumstances the value of the gift shall be the difference between the value of that consideration and the value of that interest at the time of transfer, adjusted to take account of subsequent changes in the value of money.

(5) Where a gift was in the form of money and the recipient of the gift shows that, on the balance of probabilities, the money or any of it has not been used to purchase goods or services or to earn interest or any other return, the value of the gift or such part of it as has not been so used shall be taken to be the face value of the money or, as the case may be, unused amount of the money.

(6) The court may, notwithstanding the foregoing provisions of this section, disregard the amount (or part of the amount) of a gift caught by this Part of this Act if it considers it improbable that such amount (or part) could be realised.

Making of confiscation orders

8.—(1) If the court decides to make a confiscation order, it shall determine the amount to be payable thereunder before making any decision as to—
    (a) imposing a fine on the accused;
    (b) making any order involving any payment by him.
(2) Where a court makes a confiscation order against an accused in any proceedings, it shall, in respect of any offence of which he is convicted in those proceedings, take account of the order before—
    (a) imposing any fine on him;
    (b) making any order involving any other payment by him,
but subject to that, the court shall leave the order out of account in determining the appropriate sentence or other manner of dealing with the accused.

(3) No enactment restricting the power of a court which deals with an accused in a particular way from dealing with him also in any other way shall, by reason only of the making of a confiscation order (or the postponement of a decision as regards making such an order), have the effect of restricting the court in dealing with the accused in any way it considers appropriate in respect of an offence.

(4) Where a court makes both a confiscation order and a compensation order under section 249 of the 1995 Act against the same person in the same proceedings in relation to the same offence and the offence involves the misappropriation of property, it shall direct that the compensation shall be paid first out of any sums applied towards the satisfaction of the confiscation order.

Statements relevant to making confiscation orders

9.—(1) Where the prosecutor applies for the making of a confiscation order, the prosecutor may lodge with the clerk of court a statement as to any matters relevant—
    (a) in connection with a drug trafficking offence, to the assessment of the value of the accused's proceeds of drug trafficking; and
    (b) in connection with any other offence—
        (i) to determining whether the accused has benefited for the purposes of section 1(6)(a) of this Act; or
        (ii) to an assessment of the value of the accused's benefit from the commission of the offence.
(2) Without prejudice to section 256 of the 1995 Act, if the accused accepts to any extent any allegation in the statement lodged under subsection (1) above, the court may, for the purpose of such determination or assessment as is mentioned in paragraph (a) or (b) of that subsection, treat his acceptance as conclusive of the matters to which it relates.
(3) Where—
    (a) a statement is lodged under subsection (1) above; and
    (b) the court is satisfied that a copy of that statement has been served on the accused,
the court may require the accused to indicate, within such period as the court may specify, to what extent he accepts each allegation in the statement and, in so far as he does not accept any such allegation, to indicate the basis of such non-acceptance.
(4) If the accused fails in any respect to comply with a requirement under subsection (3) above, he may be treated for the purposes of this section as

accepting every allegation in the statement apart from any allegation in respect of which he has complied with the requirement.

(5) Without prejudice to section 256 of the 1995 Act, where—

(a) there is lodged with the clerk of court by the accused a statement as to any matters relevant to determining the amount that might be realised at the time the confiscation order is made; and

(b) the prosecutor accepts to any extent any allegation in the statement,

the court may, for the purposes of that determination, treat that acceptance as conclusive of the matters to which it relates.

(6) Without prejudice to section 10(1) of this Act, where—

(a) any allegation in the statement lodged under subsection (1) above is challenged by the accused, or

(b) the basis of the non-acceptance by the accused of any such allegation is challenged by the prosecutor,

the court shall consider the matters being challenged at a hearing.

(7) Where the judge presiding at a hearing held under subsection (6) above is not the trial judge he may, on the application of either party, if he considers that it would be in the interests of justice to do so, adjourn the hearing to a date when the trial judge is available.

(8) No acceptance by a person under this section that any payment or other reward was received by him in connection with drug trafficking carried on by him or another shall be admissible in evidence in any proceedings, whether in Scotland or elsewhere, in respect of an offence.

Postponed confiscation orders

10.—(1) If the court considers—

(a) that it has some, but not sufficient, relevant information for the purpose of enabling it to come to a decision as to whether to make a confiscation order; or

(b) that it does not have sufficient relevant information to enable it to come to a decision as to the amount to be payable under the confiscation order,

it may, subject as the case may be to subsection (6) or (10) below, postpone that decision for a period not exceeding 6 months after the date of conviction for the purpose of enabling further information to be obtained.

(2) Without prejudice to sections 201 and 202 of the 1995 Act, the court may notwithstanding postponement under subsection (1) above and subject to subsection (3) below, proceed, on the prosecutor's motion therefor, to sentence or to otherwise deal with the accused in respect of the conviction.

(3) Where the court proceeds as mentioned in subsection (2) above—

(a) no fine shall be imposed on the accused; and

(b) no order shall be made involving any other payment by him,

in relation to the conviction before the decision whether to make a confiscation order is taken.

(4) Where in the case of conviction on indictment a decision has been postponed under subsection (1) above for a period, any intention to appeal under section 106 of the 1995 Act against conviction or against both conviction and any sentence passed during that period in respect of the conviction, shall be intimated under section 109(1) of the 1995 Act not within 2 weeks of the final determination of the proceedings but within 2 weeks of—

(a) in the case of an appeal against conviction where there has been no such sentence, the day on which the period of postponement commences;

(b) in any other case, the day on which such sentence is passed in open court.

(5) Notwithstanding any appeal of which intimation has been given by

virtue of subsection (4) above, a person may appeal under section 106 of the 1995 Act against the confiscation order (if the decision is to make one) or against any other sentence passed, after the period of postponement, in respect of the conviction.

(6) If during the period of postponement intimation is given by virtue of subsection (4) above by the person, the High Court may, on the application of the prosecutor, extend that period to a date up to 3 months after the date of disposal of the appeal.

(7) This subsection applies where in the case of summary conviction a decision has been postponed under subsection (1) above for a period.

(8) Where subsection (7) above applies and the offender appeals under section 175 of the 1995 Act against conviction or against both conviction and any sentence passed during the period of postponement—

(a) his application for a stated case shall be made not within one week of the final determination of the proceedings but within one week of the day mentioned in paragraph (a) or (b) of subsection (4) above;

(b) his draft stated case shall be prepared and issued not within 3 weeks of the final determination of the proceedings but within 3 weeks of the said day.

(9) Where subsection (7) above applies, then, notwithstanding any appeal against conviction or sentence or both, the offender may appeal under section 175(2)(b), and the prosecutor may appeal under section 175(3)(b), of the 1995 Act against any confiscation order or against any other sentence passed, after the period of postponement, in respect of the conviction.

(10) Where subsection (7) above applies, then, if during the period of postponement the offender applies for a stated case or lodges a note of appeal, the High Court may, on the application of the prosecutor, extend the period of postponement to a date up to 3 months after the date of disposal of the appeal.

Increase in benefit or realisable property

11.—(1) This section applies where the court which made a confiscation order is satisfied, on an application made by the prosecutor, that at the time the application is made—

(a) in the case of a drug trafficking offence, the value of the proceeds of the person's drug trafficking, or the amount that might be realised, is greater than—

    (i) the value of the proceeds of his drug trafficking; or, as the case may be,

    (ii) the amount that might be realised; or

(b) in any other case, the benefit for the purposes of section 1(6)(a) of this Act, or the amount that might be realised, is greater than—

    (i) the benefit; or, as the case may be,

    (ii) the amount that might be realised,

which was taken into account when the order was made.

(2) The considerations by reference to which the court may be satisfied as mentioned in subsection (1) above shall include—

(a) the value of the proceeds of the person's drug trafficking or, as the case may be, the benefit was greater than was taken into account when the confiscation order was made or has increased in value since the confiscation order was made; or

(b) further proceeds of drug trafficking have or benefit has been obtained since the confiscation order was made; or

(c) the value of realisable property was greater than was taken into account when the confiscation order was made; or

(d) any realisable property taken into account at the time when the confiscation order was made has subsequently increased in value; or

(e) that the amount, or part of the amount, of a gift which was disregarded under section 7(6) of this Act could now be realised.

(3) An application under subsection (1) above shall be made as soon as is reasonably practicable after the relevant information becomes available to the prosecutor but in any event within 6 years commencing with the date when the person was convicted of the offence.

(4) Where this section applies—

(a) the court may make a new confiscation order for the payment of such sum as appears to the court to be appropriate having regard to what is now shown to be the benefit or the amount that might be realised; and

(b) if the earlier confiscation order has not been satisfied then the court, in making the new confiscation order, shall recall the earlier order and may take into account the amount unpaid (including any interest payable by virtue of section 15(1) of this Act) under the earlier order.

(5) Subsection (4) above applies to an offence which is not a drug trafficking offence notwithstanding that any matters in relation to the making of the confiscation order are, by virtue of section 9(2) or (5) of this Act, to be treated as conclusive.

(6) Section 9 of this Act shall, subject to any necessary modifications, apply in relation to the making of a new confiscation order in pursuance of this section as it applies where the prosecutor has applied for the making of a confiscation order under section 1 of this Act.

(7) The assumptions mentioned in, as the case may be, section 3(2) or 2(2) and (5) of this Act shall not apply for the purposes of this section.

Realisable property inadequate to meet payments under confiscation order

12.—(1) This section applies where the court which made a confiscation order is satisfied on the balance of probabilities, on an application made to it by the accused or the prosecutor, that the value of the realisable property is inadequate to meet any amount unpaid (including any interest payable by virtue of section 15(1) of this Act) under the confiscation order.

(2) When considering whether the value of the realisable property is inadequate the court—

(a) shall, unless already taken into account under section 4(5) of this Act, take into account the extent to which property of a person whose estate has been sequestrated or who has been adjudged bankrupt is or has been included in the bankrupt's estate for the purposes of the Bankruptcy (Scotland) Act 1985 or Part IX of the Insolvency Act 1986; and

(b) may disregard any inadequacy which appears to it to be attributable, wholly or partly, to anything done by the accused for the purpose of protecting the realisable property from realisation.

(3) Where this section applies, the court shall recall the confiscation order and make a new confiscation order for the payment of such sum of a lesser amount than that for which the original order was made which appears to the court to be appropriate having regard to—

(a) the value of the realisable property as determined under subsection (1) above; and

(b) any amount paid in pursuance of the original order.

(4) Section 9 of this Act shall, subject to any necessary modifications, apply in relation to an application under this section as it applies where the prosecutor has applied for the making of a confiscation order under section 1 of this Act.

Confiscation orders where proceeds of crime discovered at later date

13.—(1) This section applies where no confiscation order has been made in relation to an offence under section 1 or 10 of this Act.

(2) Where the court, on an application made to it by the prosecutor under this section, is satisfied—

    (a) that a person convicted of—

        (i) an offence other than a drug trafficking offence has benefited in connection with the commission of the offence concerned; or

        (ii) a drug trafficking offence was in receipt of the proceeds of drug trafficking in respect of that offence;

    (b) that the information necessary to enable a confiscation order to be made on the date on which an application under section 1 of this Act was or could have been made was not available to the prosecutor,

it may make a confiscation order in relation to that person.

(3) An application under this section shall be made as soon as is reasonably practicable after the relevant information becomes available to the prosecutor but in any event not later than 6 years after the date when the person was convicted of the offence.

(4) In determining the sum to be payable under a confiscation order made in pursuance of this section, the court shall take into account—

    (a) any order involving any payment by the offender;

    (b) any suspended forfeiture order or an order for forfeiture under any other enactment made in respect of the offender,

which forms part of the sentence already imposed for the offence concerned.

(5) Sections 1(3) and 8(1), (2) and (4) of this Act shall not apply in relation to a confiscation order made in pursuance of this section.

(6) Section 9 of this Act shall, subject to any necessary modifications, apply in relation to the making of a confiscation order in pursuance of this section as it applies where the prosecutor has applied for the making of a confiscation order under section 1 of this Act.

(7) Where the court makes a confiscation order in pursuance of this section and a compensation order has been made under section 249 of the 1995 Act in respect of misappropriation of property by the offender, the court shall direct that compensation shall first be paid out of any sums applied towards the satisfaction of the confiscation order to the extent of any sums outstanding in respect of the compensation order.

(8) The assumptions mentioned in, as the case may be, section 2(2) and (5) or 3(2) of this Act shall not apply for the purposes of this section.

(9) In determining the sum to be payable as mentioned in subsection (4) above in connection with a drug trafficking offence, the court may take into account any payment or other reward received by the offender on or after the date of conviction, but only if the prosecutor satisfies the court that it was received by the offender in connection with drug trafficking carried on by the offender or another on or before that date.

(10) In this section "the court" means the court which had jurisdiction in respect of the offence concerned to make a confiscation order under section 1 of this Act.

Application of provisions relating to fines to enforcement of confiscation orders

14.—(1) Section 211(3) to (6) of the 1995 Act and the other provisions of that Act specified in subsection (2) below shall, subject to the qualifications mentioned in that subsection, apply in relation to confiscation orders as they apply in relation to fines; and section 91 of the Magistrates' Courts Act 1980 and Article 96 of the Magistrates' Courts (Northern Ireland) Order 1981 (provisions relating to transfer of fines from Scotland etc.) shall be construed accordingly.

(2) The provisions of the 1995 Act mentioned in subsection (1) above are—

   (a) section 214, provided that—
       (i) any allowance under that section of time (or further time) for payment; or
       (ii) any order of payment by instalments,
shall be without prejudice to the exercise by any administrator appointed in relation to the confiscation order of his powers and duties under this Act; and the court may, pending such exercise,
any decision as to refusing or allowing time (or further time) for payment or, as the case may be, making an order of payment by instalments;

   (b) section 215, subject to the like proviso as in paragraph (a) above;

   (c) section 216, but as if subsection (1)—
       (i) gave the prosecutor an opportunity to be heard at any enquiry thereunder; and
       (ii) applied whether the offender was in prison or not;

   (d) section 217;

   (e) section 218(2) and (3);

   (f) section 219, provided that—
       (i) where a court imposes a period of imprisonment both in respect of a fine and of a confiscation order the amounts in respect of which the period is imposed shall, for the purposes of subsection (2) of that section, be aggregated; and
       (ii) before imposing a period of imprisonment to which there is a liability by virtue of that section the court shall, if an administrator has been appointed in relation to the confiscation order, require a report from him as to whether and in what way he is likely to exercise his powers and duties under this Act and shall take that report into account; and the court may, pending such exercise, postpone any decision as to such imposition;

   (g) section 220, except that the reference in subsection (1) of that section to the person paying a sum to the governor of the prison under conditions prescribed by rules made under the Prisons (Scotland) Act 1989 shall be construed as including a reference to an administrator appointed in relation to the confiscation order making such payment under this Act in respect of the person;

   (h) section 221, provided that an order of recovery by civil diligence shall not be made under the section where an administrator is appointed in relation to the confiscation order;

   (i) section 222; except that for the purposes of that section "confiscation order" in subsection (1) above shall be construed as including such an order within the meaning of the 1994 Act or of any corresponding provision in Northern Ireland;

   (j) section 223;

   (k) section 224.

(3) Where a court, by virtue of subsection (1) above, orders the sum due under a confiscation order to be recovered by civil diligence under section 221 of the 1995 Act, any arrestment executed by a prosecutor under subsection (2) of section 33 of this Act shall be deemed to have been executed by the court as if that subsection authorised such execution.

(4) Where in any proceedings a confiscation order has been made as regards a person and a period of imprisonment or detention is imposed on him in default of payment of its amount (or as the case may be of an instalment thereof), that period shall run from the expiry of any other period of imprisonment or detention (not being one of life imprisonment or detention for life) imposed on him in the proceedings.

(5) The reference in subsection (4) above to "any other period of imprisonment or detention imposed" includes (without prejudice to the generality of the expression) a reference to such a period on default of

payment of a fine (or instalment thereof); but only where that default had occurred before the warrant for imprisonment is issued for the default in relation to the order.

Interest on sums unpaid under confiscation orders

15.—(1) If any sum required to be paid by a person under a confiscation order is not paid when it is required to be paid (whether forthwith on the making of the order or at a time specified under section 214(1) of the 1995 Act) that person shall be liable to pay interest on that sum for the period for which it remains unpaid and the amount of the interest shall for the purposes of enforcement be treated as part of the amount to be recovered from him under the confiscation order.

(2) The sheriff may, on the application of the prosecutor, increase the term of imprisonment or detention fixed in respect of the confiscation order under section 214(2) of the 1995 Act if the effect of subsection (1) above is to increase the maximum period applicable in relation to the order under section 219(2) of the 1995 Act.

(3) The rate of interest under subsection (1) above shall be the rate payable under a decree of the Court of Session.

Exercise of powers

Exercise of powers by court or administrator

16.—(1) This section applies to the powers as regards realisable property conferred on the court by sections 28, 29, 31, 32 and 33 of and paragraphs 1, 4, and 12 of Schedule 1 to this Act in relation to confiscation orders and on an administrator by that Schedule.

(2) Subject to the following provisions of this section, the powers shall be exercised with a view to making available for satisfying the confiscation order or, as the case may be, any confiscation order that may be made in the case of a person mentioned in section 4(1)(a) of this Act the value for the time being of realisable property held by any person by the realisation of such property.

(3) In the case of realisable property held by a person by virtue only of having received a gift made directly or indirectly by the accused which is caught by this Part of this Act, the powers shall be exercised with a view to realising no more than the value of the gift as assessed under section 7 of this Act.

(4) The powers shall be exercised with a view to allowing any person other than a person mentioned in paragraph (a) and, in relation to a drug trafficking offence, paragraph (b) of section 4(1) of this Act or the recipient of any such gift to retain or recover the value of any property held by him.

(5) An order may be made or other action taken in respect of a debt owed by the Crown.

(6) In exercising those powers, no account shall be taken of any obligations of such a person or of the recipient of any such gift which conflict with the obligation to satisfy the confiscation order.

(7) Subsections (2) to (6) of section 31 of the 1994 Act (exercise of powers by High Court etc.) shall apply as regards the powers conferred on the court by sections 35, 36, 37 and 38 of this Act as those subsections apply as regards the powers conferred on the High Court (within the meaning that expression has in relation to England and Wales) by the sections mentioned in subsection (1) of the said section 31.

Compensation

Compensation

17.—(1) Subject to subsection (3) below, if proceedings are instituted against a person for an offence to which this Part of this Act applies, and either—

    (a) the proceedings do not result in his conviction for any such offence, or

    (b) where he is convicted of one or more such offences—

        (i) the conviction or convictions concerned are quashed (and no conviction for any such offence is substituted); or

        (ii) he is pardoned by Her Majesty in respect of the conviction or convictions concerned,

the court may, on an application by a person who held property which was realisable property, order compensation to be paid to the applicant if, having regard to all the circumstances, it considers it appropriate to do so.

(2) Subsection (1) above is without prejudice to any right which may otherwise exist to institute proceedings in respect of delictual liability disclosed by such circumstances as are mentioned in paragraphs (a) and (b) of subsection (3) below.

(3) The court shall not order compensation to be paid under subsection (1) above in any case unless satisfied—

    (a) that there has been some serious default on the part of a person concerned in the investigation of the offence or offences concerned, being a person mentioned in subsection (5) below, and that, but for that default, the proceedings would not have been instituted or continued; and

    (b) that the applicant has suffered loss or damage in consequence of anything done in relation to the property under section 28, 29, 31, 32, 33 or 42 of or Schedule 1 to this Act or by virtue of section 37 of the 1994 Act (recognition and enforcement in England and Wales of orders and functions under this Act).

(4) The amount of compensation to be paid under this section shall be such as the court thinks just in all the circumstances of the case.

(5) Compensation payable under this section shall be paid, where the person in default was—

    (a) a constable of a police force within the meaning of the Police (Scotland) Act 1967, by the police authority or joint police board for the police area for which that force is maintained;

    (b) a constable other than is mentioned in paragraph (a) above, but with the powers of such a constable, by the body under whose authority he acts;

    (c) a procurator fiscal or was acting on behalf of the Lord Advocate, by the Lord Advocate;

    (d) a person commissioned by the Commissioners of Customs and Excise, by those Commissioners; and

    (e) an officer of the Commissioners of Inland Revenue, by those Commissioners.

(6) An application for compensation under this section shall be made not later than three years after the conclusion of the proceedings in respect of which the confiscation order was made; and subsection (6) of section 29 of this Act shall apply for the purpose of determining when proceedings are concluded for the purposes of this subsection as it applies for the purposes of that section.

(7) In this section, "the court" means the Court of Session or the sheriff exercising his civil jurisdiction.

Investigation and disclosure of information

Order to make material available

18.—(1) The procurator fiscal may, for the purpose of an investigation into whether a person has benefited from the commission of an offence to which this Part of this Act applies and as to the amount of that benefit, apply to the sheriff for an order under subsection (2) below in relation to particular material or material of a particular description.

(2) If on such an application the sheriff is satisfied that the conditions in subsection (4) below are fulfilled, he may, subject to section 20(11) of this Act, make an order that the person who appears to him to be in possession of the material to which the application relates shall—

(a) produce it to a constable for him to take away; or

(b) give a constable access to it,

within such period as the order may specify.

(3) The period to be specified in an order under subsection (2) above shall be seven days unless it appears to the sheriff that a longer or shorter period would be appropriate in the particular circumstances of the application.

(4) The conditions referred to in subsection (2) above are—

(a) that there are reasonable grounds for suspecting that a specified person has benefited from the commission of an offence to which this Part of this Act applies;

(b) that there are reasonable grounds for suspecting that the material to which the application relates—

(i) is likely to be of substantial value (whether by itself or together with other material) to the investigation for the purpose of which the application is made; and

(ii) does not consist of or include items subject to legal privilege; and

(c) that there are reasonable grounds for believing that it is in the public interest, having regard—

(i) to the benefit likely to accrue to the investigation if the material is obtained; and

(ii) to the circumstances under which the person in possession of the material holds it,

that the material should be produced or that access to it should be given.

(5) Where the sheriff makes an order under subsection (2)(b) above in relation to material on any premises he may, on the application of the procurator fiscal, order any person who appears to him to be entitled to grant entry to the premises to allow a constable to enter the premises to obtain access to the material.

(6) An application under subsection (1) or (5) above may be made *ex parte* in chambers.

(7) Provision may be made by rules of court as to—

(a) the discharge add variation of orders under this section, and

(b) proceedings relating to such orders.

(8) Where the material to which an application under this section relates consists of information contained in a computer—

(a) an order under subsection (2)(a) above shall have effect as an order to produce the material in a form in which it can be taken away and in which it is visible and legible; and

(b) an order under subsection (2)(b) above shall have effect as an order to give access to the material in a form in which it is visible and legible.

(9) An order under subsection (2) above—

(a) shall not confer any right to production of, or access to, items subject to legal privilege;

(b) shall have effect notwithstanding any obligation as to secrecy or other restriction upon the disclosure of information imposed by statute or otherwise; and

(c) may be made in relation to material in the possession of an authorised government department;

and in this subsection "authorised government department" means a government department which is an authorised department for the purposes of the Crown Proceedings Act 1947.

(10) In this section—

(a) "items subject to legal privilege" and "premises" have the same meanings as in section 33 of the Criminal Law (Consolidation) (Scotland) Act 1995; and

(b) references to a person benefiting from the commission of an offence to which this Part of this Act applies, in relation to conduct which is not such an offence but which would have been if it had occurred in Scotland, shall be construed in accordance with section 2 of this Act as if that conduct had so occurred.

(11) This section and sections 19 and 20 of this Act do not apply to investigations into drug trafficking.

[1](12) In this section "constable" includes a person commissioned by the Commissioners of Customs and Excise.

NOTE
[1]Inserted by the Crime and Disorder Act 1998 (c. 37), Sched. 8, para. 115 (effective September 30, 1998: S.I. 1998 No. 2327).

Authority for search

19.—(1) The procurator fiscal may, for the purpose of an investigation into whether a person has benefited from the commission of an offence to which this Part of this Act applies and as to the amount of that benefit, apply to the sheriff for a warrant under this section in relation to specified premises.

(2) On such application the sheriff may issue a warrant authorising a constable to enter and search the premises if the sheriff is satisfied—

(a) that an order made under section 18 of this Act in relation to material on the premises has not been complied with; or

(b) that the conditions in subsection (3) below are fulfilled; or

(c) that the conditions in subsection (4) below are fulfilled.

(3) The conditions referred to in subsection (2)(b) above are—

(a) that there are reasonable grounds for suspecting that a specified person has benefited from the commission of an offence to which this Part of this Act applies; and

(b) that the conditions in section 18(4)(b) and (c) of this Act are fulfilled in relation to any material on the premises; and

(c) that it would not be appropriate to make an order under that section in relation to the material because—

(i) it is not practicable to communicate with any person entitled to produce the material; or

(ii) it is not practicable to communicate with any person entitled to grant access to the material or entitled to grant entry to the premises on which the material is situated; or

(iii) the investigation for the purposes of which the application is made might be seriously prejudiced unless a constable could secure immediate access to the material.

(4) The conditions referred to in subsection (2)(c) above are—

(a) that there are reasonable grounds for suspecting that a specified person has benefited from the commission of an offence to which this Part of this Act applies; and

(b) that there are reasonable grounds for suspecting that there is on the premises material relating to the specified person, or to the question whether that person has so benefited or the amount of that benefit, which is likely to be of substantial value (whether by itself or together with other material) to the investigation for the purpose of which the application is made, but that the material cannot at the time of the application be particularised; and

(c) that—

(i) it is not practicable to communicate with any person entitled to grant entry to the premises; or

(ii) entry to the premises will not be granted unless a warrant is produced; or

(iii) the investigation for the purpose of which the application is made might be seriously prejudiced unless a constable arriving at the premises could secure immediate entry to them.

(5) Where a constable has entered premises in the execution of a warrant issued under this section, he may seize and retain any material, other than items subject to legal privilege, which is likely to be of substantial value (whether by itself or together with other material) to the investigation for the purpose of which the warrant was issued.

[1](6) Subsections (10) and (12) of section 18 of this Act shall apply for the purposes of this section as they apply for the purposes of that section.

NOTE
[1]Amended by the Crime and Disorder Act 1998 (c. 37), Sched. 8, para. 116 (effective September 30, 1998: S.I. 1998 No. 2327).

Disclosure of information held by government departments

20.—(1) Subject to subsection (4) below, the Court of Session may on an application by the Lord Advocate order any material mentioned in subsection (3) below which is in the possession of an authorised government department to be produced to the Court within such period as the Court may specify.

(2) The power to make an order under subsection (1) above is exercisable if—

(a) the powers conferred on the Court by section 28(1)(a) of this Act are exercisable by virtue of section 29(2) of this Act; or

(b) those powers are exercisable by virtue of section 29(3) of this Act and the Court has made a restraint order which has not been recalled.

(3) The material referred to in subsection (1) above is any material which—

(a) has been submitted to an officer of an authorised government department by a person who holds, or has at any time held, realisable property;

(b) has been made by an officer of an authorised government department in relation to such a person; or

(c) is correspondence which passed between an officer of an authorised government department and such a person;

and an order under that subsection may require the production of all such material or of a particular description of such material, being material in the possession of the department concerned.

(4) An order under subsection (1) above shall not require the production of any material unless it appears to the Court of Session that the material is likely to contain information that would facilitate the exercise of the powers conferred on the Court by section 28(1)(a) of or paragraph 1 or 12 of Schedule 1 to this Act or on an administrator appointed under paragraph 1(1) of that Schedule.

(5) The Court may by order authorise the disclosure to such an

administrator of any material produced under subsection (1) above or any part of such material; but the Court shall not make an order under this subsection unless a reasonable opportunity has been given for an officer of the department to make representations to the Court.

(6) Material disclosed in pursuance of an order under subsection (5) above may, subject to any conditions contained in the order, be further disclosed for the purposes of the functions under this Act of the administrator or the High Court.

(7) The Court of Session may by order authorise the disclosure to a person mentioned in subsection (8) below of any material produced under subsection (1) above or any part of such material; but the Court shall not make an order under this subsection unless—

(a) a reasonable opportunity has been given for an officer of the department to make representations to the Court; and

(b) it appears to the Court that the material is likely to be of substantial value in exercising functions relating to the investigation of crime.

(8) The persons referred to in subsection (7) above are—

(a) a constable;

(b) the Lord Advocate or any procurator fiscal; and

(c) an officer within the meaning of the Customs and Excise Management Act 1979.

(9) Material disclosed in pursuance of an order under subsection (7) above may, subject to any conditions contained in the order, be further disclosed for the purposes of functions relating to the investigation of crime or whether any person has benefited from the commission of an offence to which this Part of this Act applies or the amount of that benefit.

(10) Material may be produced or disclosed in pursuance of this section notwithstanding any obligation as to secrecy or other restriction upon the disclosure of information imposed by statute or otherwise.

(11) An order under subsection (1) above and, in the case of material in the possession of an authorised government department, an order under section 18(2) of this Act may require any officer of the department (whether named in the order or not) who may for the time being be in possession of the material concerned to comply with such order; and any such order shall be served as if the proceedings were civil proceedings against the department.

(12) Where any requirement is included in any order by virtue of subsection (11) above, the person on whom the order is served—

(a) shall take all reasonable steps to bring it to the attention of the officer concerned; and

(b) if the order is not brought to that officer's attention within the period referred to in subsection (1) above, shall report the reasons for the failure to the Court of Session,

and it shall also be the duty of any other officer of the department in receipt of the order to take such steps as are mentioned in paragraph (a) above.

(13) In this section "authorised government department" means a government department which is an authorised department for the purposes of the Crown Proceedings Act 1947; and subsection (10) of section 18 of this Act shall apply for the purposes of this section as it applies for the purposes of that section.

PART II

FORFEITURE OF PROPERTY USED IN CRIME

Suspended forfeiture order

21.—(1) This section applies where in respect of any offence—

(a) the accused is convicted, whether in solemn or summary proceedings; or

(b) in the case of summary proceedings, (without proceeding to conviction) an order is made discharging him absolutely.

(2) Where this section applies, the court may, if it is satisfied on the application of the prosecutor that any property which was at the time of the offence or of the accused's apprehension in his ownership or possession or under his control—

(a) has been used for the purpose of committing, or facilitating the commission of, any offence; or

(b) was intended to be used for that purpose,

make an order (a "suspended forfeiture order") in respect of that property.

(3) Any application under this section shall be made—

(a) in proceedings on indictment, when the prosecutor moves for sentence or if the accused is remitted for sentence under section 195 of the 1995 Act, before sentence is pronounced; and

(b) in summary proceedings, following upon the conviction of the accused or, as the case may be, the finding that he committed the offence with which he was charged.

(4) If the prosecutor knows or reasonably suspects the identity of a person (other than the accused) as being the owner of, or otherwise having an interest in, the property to which the suspended forfeiture order relates, he shall intimate that fact to the court on making the application and the order shall name that person as a person having an interest or suspected of having an interest in the property.

(5) Any reference in this Part of this Act to facilitating the commission of an offence shall include a reference to the taking of any steps after it has been committed for the purpose of disposing of any property to which it relates or of avoiding apprehension or detection.

(6) Where, by itself, the use of property constitutes an offence in whole or in part, that property shall be regarded for the purpose of subsection (2)(a) above as used for the purpose of committing the offence, unless the enactment which created the offence expressly excludes the application of this section.

(7) Subject to subsection (8) below, where the accused is convicted of an offence under any enactment, the court shall not be precluded from making a suspended forfeiture order in respect of any property by reason only that the property would not be liable to forfeiture under that enactment.

(8) Subsection (7) above shall not apply—

(a) if the enactment concerned expressly excludes the application of this section; or

(b) to any property which has been used or has been intended to be used as mentioned in subsection (2)(a) or (b) above in relation to the offence of which the accused has been convicted, if the enactment concerned specifies the category of property which is to be liable to forfeiture thereunder, and the category so specified does not include the category of property which has been used or has been intended to be used as aforesaid.

(9) Where the court makes both a suspended forfeiture order and a compensation order under section 249 of the 1995 Act against the same accused in the same proceedings, it may order that, in the event of the property subject to the suspended forfeiture order being forfeited under section 24 of this Act, the proceeds of sale of that property shall be first directed towards satisfaction of the compensation order.

(10) As soon as may be after a suspended forfeiture order has been made, the prosecutor—

(a) shall notify in writing any person named in the order in pursuance of subsection (4) above that the order has been made, and that the person so notified may be entitled to apply to the court for—

(i) the order to be recalled under section 25 of this Act; or

(ii) a direction under section 26 of this Act; and
(b) if the property in respect of which the order has been made includes heritable property in Scotland, shall cause a certified copy of the order to be recorded in the General Register of Sasines or as the case may be registered in the Land Register of Scotland; and
(c) if the court directs him to do so, shall insert a notice in the Edinburgh Gazette or in such other newspaper or journal as appears to the court to be appropriate specifying the terms of the suspended forfeiture order.

(11) Any property in respect of which a suspended forfeiture order is made shall be taken into the possession of or placed under the control of the clerk of court until—
(a) the order is recalled; or
(b) the property is forfeited to the Crown and disposed of under section 24 of this Act or forfeited to another person under that section.

(12) For the purposes of any appeal or review a suspended forfeiture order is a sentence.

(13) In this section "the court" does not include a district court, whether or not constituted by a stipendiary magistrate.

Forfeiture: district court

22.—(1) Where, in respect of any offence tried in the district court, the accused is convicted or (without proceeding to conviction) an order is made discharging him absolutely the court may, if it is satisfied on the application of the prosecutor that any moveable property which was at the time of the offence or of the accused's apprehension in his ownership or possession or under his control—
(a) has been used for the purpose of committing, or facilitating the commission of, any offence; or
(b) was intended to be used for that purpose,
order that the property shall be forfeited to and vest in the Crown or such other person as the court may direct.

(2) Any application under subsection (1) above shall be made following upon the conviction of the accused or, as the case may be, the finding that he committed the offence with which he was charged.

(3) Where, by itself, the use of property constitutes an offence in whole or in part, that property shall be regarded for the purpose of subsection (1)(a) above as used for the purpose of committing the offence, unless the enactment which created the offence expressly excludes the application of this section.

(4) Subject to subsection (5) below, where the accused is convicted of an offence under any enactment, the court shall not be precluded from making an order under subsection (1) above in respect of any property by reason only that the property would not be liable to forfeiture under that enactment.

(5) Subsection (4) above shall not apply—
(a) if the enactment concerned expressly excludes the application of this section; or
(b) to any property which has been used or has been intended to be used as mentioned in subsection (1)(a) or (b) above in relation to the offence of which the accused has been convicted, if the enactment concerned specifies the category of property which is to be liable to forfeiture thereunder, and the category so specified does not include the category of property which has been used or has been intended to be used as aforesaid.

(6) Where the court makes—

(a) an order under subsection (1) above that property shall be forfeited to the Crown; and

(b) a compensation order under section 249 of the 1995 Act,

against the same accused in the same proceedings, it may order that the proceeds of sale of the property forfeited by virtue of subsection (1) above shall be first directed towards satisfaction of the compensation order.

(7) For the purposes of any appeal or review an order under subsection (1) above is a sentence.

(8) In this section "the court" means the district court.

Warrant to search for and seize property

23.—(1) Where—

(a) the sheriff is satisfied, on an application being made to him by the prosecutor—

(i) that proceedings have been, or are likely to be, instituted against a person in Scotland for an offence; and

(ii) that there is reasonable cause to believe that property specified in the application is to be found in a place or in premises specified in the application; and

(b) it appears to him that there are reasonable grounds for thinking that in the event of the person being convicted of the offence a suspended forfeiture order might be made in relation to the property,

he may grant a warrant authorising a person named therein to enter and search the place or premises and seize the property.

(2) Where a court has made a suspended forfeiture order in respect of any property, if it is satisfied on the application of the prosecutor—

(a) that there is reasonable cause to believe that the property is to be found in any place or premises; and

(b) that admission to the place or premises has been refused or that it is reasonably believed that such admission will be refused,

it may grant a warrant authorising a person named therein to enter and search the place or premises and seize the property.

(3) An application for a warrant under subsection (2) above may be made at the same time as an application for a suspended forfeiture order.

Forfeiture of property subject to suspended forfeiture order

24.—(1) Subject to the following provisions of this section, property in respect of which a suspended forfeiture order has been made shall be forfeited to and vest in the Crown, or such other person as the court may direct, as follows—

(a) heritable property situated in Scotland shall be forfeited at the end of the period of 6 months commencing with the date on which a certified copy of the suspended forfeiture order is recorded in the General Register of Sasines or, as the case may be, registered in the Land Register of Scotland;

(b) heritable property situated outside Scotland shall be forfeited at the end of the period of six months commencing with the date of the making of the suspended forfeiture order;

(c) moveable property shall be forfeited at the end of the period of 60 days commencing with the date of the making of the suspended forfeiture order.

(2) Notwithstanding subsection (1)(c) above, moveable property which is certified by the prosecutor as being—

(a) of a perishable or dangerous nature;

(b) of no commercial value; or

(c) property which cannot lawfully be sold, supplied or possessed, shall be forfeited immediately after the making of the suspended forfeiture order.

(3) If an application for recall or variation of the suspended forfeiture order concerned has been made under section 25 of this Act, there shall be no forfeiture of property mentioned in paragraph (a), (b) or (c) of subsection (1) above unless and until whichever is the later of the following occurs—

    (a) the application is finally disposed of in favour of the prosecutor; or

    (b) the period mentioned in that paragraph has expired.

(4) Without prejudice to subsection (2) above, in the event of an appeal against conviction or sentence, there shall be no forfeiture of property until whichever is the later of the following occurs—

    (a) the appeal, if it is proceeded with, is determined in favour of the prosecutor; or

    (b) the period mentioned in paragraph (a) or, as the case may be, (b) or (c) of subsection (1) above has expired.

(5) Property which has been forfeited to the Crown under this section shall be dealt with by the Crown in such manner as seems to it to be appropriate.

(6) A certificate by the clerk of court that property was forfeited to and vested in the Crown, or another person, under this section on the date specified in the certificate shall be conclusive evidence of that fact; and, in the case of a certificate in respect of heritable property situated in Scotland, the prosecutor shall, forthwith, cause a certified copy of the certificate to be recorded in the General Register of Sasines or, as the case may be, registered in the Land Register of Scotland.

Recall or variation of suspended forfeiture order

25.—(1) The court shall, on an application being made to it under this section by a person other than the accused, recall a suspended forfeiture order in relation to any property or an interest in property if—

    (a) it is satisfied by the applicant on the balance of probabilities that he is the owner of the property or otherwise has an interest in it; and

    (b) subsection (2) or subsection (3) below is applicable.

(2) This subsection applies if the court is not satisfied by the prosecutor that—

    (a) where the applicant was the owner of or otherwise had an interest in the property before the commission of the offence in connection with which the suspended forfeiture order was made, he—

        (i) knew or ought to have known that the property was intended to be used for the purpose of committing, or facilitating the commission of, the offence, and

        (ii) did not take all the steps which were reasonable for him to take to prevent such intended use; or

    (b) where he has become the owner of, or has otherwise acquired an interest in, the property after the commission of the offence, the applicant knew or ought to have known that the property had been intended to be, or had been, so used.

(3) This subsection applies if the court is satisfied as mentioned in subsection (2) above, but it appears to the court that, in all the circumstances of the case, forfeiture of the property would be excessive or inappropriate.

(4) Where an order ("a recalling order") recalling a suspended forfeiture order relates to heritable property situated in Scotland, the prosecutor shall, as soon as may be after the recalling order has been made, cause a certified copy of the recalling order to be recorded in the General Register of Sasines or, as the case may be, registered in the Land Register of Scotland.

(5) Where the prosecutor believes that the person named in the suspended forfeiture order in pursuance of section 21(4) of this Act is not the owner of, or does not otherwise have an interest in, the property concerned then—

    (a) if he does not know who the true owner is, or who otherwise truly has the interest, he may apply to the court under this section for an order varying the suspended forfeiture order by deleting that name from it;

    (b) if he does know or reasonably suspects the identity of the true owner or the person who otherwise truly has the interest ("the correct person"), he may apply to the court under this section for an order varying the suspended forfeiture order by substituting the name of the correct person for that of the person so named.

(6) Where no person is named in the suspended forfeiture order in pursuance of section 21(4) of this Act but the prosecutor later comes to believe that a person is, or may be, the owner of, or otherwise has or may have an interest in, the property concerned, he may apply to the court for an order varying the suspended forfeiture order by naming that person as a person having or being suspected of having such an interest.

(7) The court shall grant any application made in pursuance of subsection (5) or (6) above; and sections 21(10) and 24 of this Act shall apply in relation to an order varying a suspended forfeiture order in accordance with an application under subsection (5) or (6) above as they apply in relation to a suspended forfeiture order.

(8) An application under this section may be made at any time before the property concerned is forfeited to the Crown or another person under section 24 of this Act.

(9) The court shall not be entitled in considering any application under this section to review the sentence passed, or any probation order or order of discharge made, in respect of the offence concerned otherwise than as provided by this section.

(10) In this section "the court" means the court which made the suspended forfeiture order.

Property wrongly forfeited: return or compensation

    26.—(1) Where the court, on an application being made to it by a person other than the accused—

    (a) is satisfied by the applicant on the balance of probabilities that in relation to any property forfeited to the Crown or another person under section 24 of this Act or by virtue of an order for forfeiture made under any other enactment he was the owner of, or a person otherwise having an interest in, the property immediately before such forfeiture; and

    (b) subsection (3) or (4) below is applicable,

it shall make an order under subsection (2) below.

(2) An order under this subsection shall direct the Crown or, as the case may be, the other person, if the applicant—

    (a) was the owner of the property, to return it to him if reasonably practicable to do so or, if not, to pay compensation to him of an amount determined under subsection (5) below; or

    (b) otherwise had an interest in the property, to pay compensation to him of an amount corresponding to the value of such interest.

(3) This subsection applies if the court is not satisfied that—

    (a) where the applicant was the owner of or otherwise had an interest in the property before the commission of the offence in connection with which the suspended forfeiture order or order for forfeiture was made, he knew or ought to have known that the property was intended to be used for the purpose of committing, or facilitating the commission of, the offence, and did not take all the steps which were reasonable for him to take to prevent such intended use; or

    (b) where the applicant has become the owner of, or has otherwise acquired an interest in, the property after the commission of the offence, he knew or ought to have known that the property had been intended to be, or had been, so used.

(4) This subsection applies if the court is satisfied as mentioned in subsection (3) above, but it appears to the court that, in all the circumstances of the case, forfeiture of the property would be excessive or inappropriate.

(5) For the purposes of subsection (2) above, the amount determined under this subsection shall be an amount equal to the amount of any consideration received for the property or the value of any such consideration at the time of the disposal, or, if no consideration was received, an amount equal to the value of the property at the time of the disposal.

(6) An application under subsection (1) shall be made not later than three years after the date on which the property was forfeited as mentioned in subsection (1)(a) above.

(7) Where, after property has been forfeited by virtue of section 24 of this Act, the prosecutor comes to believe that the person named in the suspended forfeiture order in pursuance of section 21(4) of this Act is not the owner of, or a person otherwise having an interest in, the property concerned, then—

(a) whether he knows who the true owner was, or who the person truly with the interest was, or not, he shall forthwith notify the court in writing of that belief; and

(b) if he does know or reasonably suspects the identity of the person who was the true owner or who truly had the interest, he shall forthwith notify that person in writing that he may be entitled to apply to the court for a direction under this section.

(8) Where no person has been named in the suspended forfeiture order in pursuance of section 21(4) of this Act or in a variation order under section 25(5) of this Act but, after the property concerned has been forfeited under section 24 of this Act, the prosecutor comes to believe that a person was or might have been the owner of, or otherwise had or might have had an interest in, the property concerned, he shall forthwith notify—

(a) the court of his belief; and

(b) that person in writing that he may be entitled to apply to the court for a direction under this section.

(9) The court shall not be entitled in considering any application under this section to review the sentence passed, or any probation order or order of discharge made, in respect of the offence concerned otherwise than as provided by this section.

(10) In this section "the court" means the court which made the suspended forfeiture order or order for forfeiture.

Appeal against court decision under section 25(1) or 26(1)

27.—(1) An appeal shall lie to the High Court of Justiciary at the instance of—

(a) the applicant against the refusal;

(b) the prosecutor against the granting,

of an application under section 25(1) or 26(1) of this Act, and the High Court in determining such an appeal may make such order as could have been made by the court on an application under that section.

(2) The procedure in an appeal under this section shall be the same as the procedure in an appeal against sentence.

(3) Where a suspended forfeiture order relating to heritable property situated in Scotland is recalled on appeal to the High Court of Justiciary, the prosecutor shall, as soon as may be after the appeal has been disposed of, cause a certified copy of the interlocutor of the Court to be recorded in the General Register of Sasines or, as the case may be, registered in the Land Register of Scotland.

PART III

RESTRAINT ORDERS

Restraint orders

28.—(1) The court may, on the application of the prosecutor, make an order (in this Part of this Act referred to as a "restraint order") in the circumstances mentioned in—

(a) section 29(2) or (3) of this Act interdicting—

(i) any person named in the order from dealing with his realisable property; or

(ii) that person and any person named in the order as appearing to the court to have received from him a gift caught by Part I of this Act or, as the case may be, an implicative gift from dealing with their own, or the other's, realisable property,

(whenever that property was acquired and whether it is described in the order or not); and

(b) section 30(1) of this Act interdicting any person named in the order from dealing with any property which is, or is liable to be, the subject of a suspended forfeiture order.

(2) A restraint order made under subsection (1)(a) above may contain conditions and exceptions to which the interdict shall be subject and in particular—

(a) may provide for the release to the person named in the order of such reasonable living expenses as the court thinks fit; and

(b) shall provide for the release of property in so far as it is required to meet reasonable legal expenses payable or likely to be payable in relation to proceedings—

(i) as regards the offence by virtue of which the restraint order has been made; or

(ii) as regards a confiscation order made on conviction of the offence.

(3) A restraint order shall—

(a) be made on an *ex parte* application which shall be heard in chambers; and

(b) without prejudice to the time when it becomes effective, be intimated to each person affected by it.

(4) For the purposes of this Part of this Act, dealing with property includes (without prejudice to the generality of the expression)—

(a) making a payment to any person in reduction of the amount of a debt;

(b) removing the property from the jurisdiction of the court; and

(c) transferring or disposing of the property.

(5) Where the court has made a restraint order (including a restraint order made under and within the meaning of the 1994 Act), a constable or a person commissioned by the Commissioners of Customs and Excise may, for the purpose of preventing any property subject to the order being removed—

(a) in the case of a restraint order made in connection with a drug trafficking offence (including a drug trafficking offence within the meaning of the 1994 Act) from Great Britain;

(b) in any other case, the jurisdiction of the court,

seize that property.

(6) Property seized under subsection (5) above shall be dealt with in accordance with the directions of the court which made the order.

(7) In this Part of this Act, "the court" means where, as regards the criminal proceedings in question, a trial diet or a diet fixed for the purposes of section 76 of the 1995 Act is intended to be held, is being or has been held—

(a) in the High Court of Justiciary, the Court of Session;

(b) in the sheriff court, a sheriff of that court exercising his civil jurisdiction.

(8) The court may, where it has granted a restraint order, interdict a person not subject to that order from dealing with property affected by it while it is in force.

(9) Subsections (2)(a) and (3)(a) above shall apply in relation to an interdict under subsection (8) above as they apply in relation to subsection (1) above; and subsections (1), (2), (4) and (5) of section 31 of this Act shall apply in relation to an interdict under subsection (8) above as they apply in relation to a restraint order.

(10) Without prejudice to the time when it becomes effective, an interdict under subsection (8) above shall be intimated to each person affected by it.

Restraint orders in relation to realisable property

29.—(1) A restraint order under section 28(1)(a) of this Act may be made in the circumstances mentioned in either subsection (2) or (3) below.

(2) For the purposes of this subsection, the circumstances are—

(a) proceedings have been instituted against an accused in Scotland for an offence to which Part I of this Act applies;

(b) the proceedings have not been concluded; and

(c) either a confiscation order has been made or it appears to the court that, in the event of his conviction of the offence, there are reasonable grounds for thinking that a confiscation order may be made in those proceedings.

(3) For the purposes of this subsection, the circumstances are that the court is satisfied that—

(a) it is proposed to institute proceedings within 28 days against a person suspected of such an offence and it appears to the court that, in the event of his conviction of the offence, there are reasonable grounds for thinking that a confiscation order may be made in those proceedings; or

(b) the prosecutor has made, or proposes within 28 days to make, an application under section 11 or, as the case may be, section 13 of this Act in relation to that person in respect of the offence, and it appears to the court that there are reasonable grounds for thinking that the application may be granted.

(4) Where the court has made a restraint order in the circumstances mentioned in subsection (3)(a) or (b) above and no proceedings have been instituted or application made within 28 days as mentioned in that subsection, the prosecutor shall forthwith apply to the court for the recall of the order and the court shall grant the application.

(5) When proceedings for the offence or, as the case may be, proceedings on an application under section 11 or 13 of this Act are concluded, the prosecutor shall forthwith apply to the court for recall of the order and the court shall grant the application.

(6) For the purposes of this section, proceedings are concluded as regards an offence where—

(a) the trial diet is deserted *simpliciter*;

(b) the accused is acquitted or, under section 65 or 147 of the 1995 Act, discharged or liberated;

(c) the High Court of Justiciary or, as the case may be, the sheriff sentences or otherwise deals with him without making a confiscation order and without postponing a decision as regards making such an order;

(d) after such postponement as is mentioned in paragraph (c) above, the High Court of Justiciary or, as the case may be, the sheriff decides not to make a confiscation order;

(e) his conviction is quashed; or

(f) a confiscation order made in the proceedings is satisfied (whether by payment of the amount due under the order or by the accused serving imprisonment in default).

(7) For the purposes of this section, proceedings on an application under section 11 or 13 of this Act are concluded—

(a) when the application is refused; or

(b) where the application is granted, when a confiscation order made in the proceedings is satisfied (whether by payment of the amount due under the order or by the accused serving imprisonment in default).

Restraint orders in relation to forfeitable property

30.—(1) A restraint order may be made in respect of a person under section 28(1)(b) where—

(a) proceedings have been instituted against him in Scotland for an offence;

(b) the proceedings have not been concluded; and

(c) a suspended forfeiture order has been made in respect of the property concerned or it appears to the court that, in the event of his conviction of the offence, there are reasonable grounds for thinking that a suspended forfeiture order may be made in those proceedings.

(2) A restraint order may also be made where the court is satisfied that it is proposed to institute proceedings in respect of an offence within 28 days and it appears to the court that, in the event of his conviction of the offence, there are reasonable grounds for thinking that a suspended forfeiture order may be made in those proceedings.

(3) Where the court has made a restraint order by virtue of subsection (2) above, and no proceedings have been instituted within 28 days as mentioned in that subsection, the prosecutor shall forthwith apply to the court for the recall of the order and the court shall grant the application.

(4) When proceedings for the offence are concluded, the prosecutor shall forthwith apply to the court for recall of the order and the court shall grant the application.

(5) For the purposes of this section, proceedings are concluded as regards an offence where—

(a) the trial is deserted *simpliciter*;

(b) the accused is acquitted or, under section 65 or 147 of the 1995 Act, discharged or liberated;

(c) the High Court of Justiciary or, as the case may be, the sheriff sentences or otherwise deals with him without making a suspended forfeiture order;

(d) his conviction is quashed;

(e) a suspended forfeiture order made in the proceedings is recalled or varied so as to exclude from forfeiture any property to which the restraint order relates; or

(f) the property, or part of the property, to which the restraint order relates is forfeited.

Variation and recall of restraint orders

31.—(1) Subject to subsections (2) and (3) below, the court may, at the instance of—

(a) the prosecutor, at any time vary or recall a restraint order in relation to any person or to any property;

(b) any person having an interest, at any time vary or recall a restraint order in relation to the person or to any property.

(2) On an application made under subsection (1)(b) above by a person

named in a restraint order as having received a gift caught by Part I of this Act or, as the case may be, an implicative gift, the court may recall the order in relation to that person if it is satisfied on the balance of probabilities—

    (a) that he received the gift not knowing, not suspecting and not having reasonable grounds to suspect that the gift was made in contemplation of, or after, the commission of the offence or if more than one, in contemplation of any of the offences or after the commission of the earlier or the earliest of the offences to which the proceedings for the time being relate; and

    (b) that he was not associated with the giver in the commission of the offence; and

    (c) that he would suffer hardship if the order were not recalled.

(3) Where an application has been made under subsection (1) above for the variation or recall of a restraint order, any property in relation to which the restraint order was made shall not be realised during the period beginning with the making of the application and ending with the determination of the application by the court.

(4) The court may, where it has recalled a restraint order as mentioned in subsection (1)(b) or (2) above, order that property of the person at whose instance it was recalled shall cease to be realisable or, as the case may be, liable to forfeiture.

(5) The prosecutor or any person having an interest may reclaim or appeal to the Court of Session against an interlocutor refusing, varying or recalling or refusing to vary or recall a restraint order, within such period as may be prescribed by Act of Sederunt.

(6) Where, in relation to a restraint order which is recalled, interdict has been granted under section 28(8) of this Act, the clerk of court shall, on the restraint order being recalled, forthwith so inform each person so interdicted.

Inhibition of property affected by restraint order or by interdict

32.—(1) On the application of the Lord Advocate, the Court of Session may in respect of heritable realisable property in Scotland affected by a restraint order (whether such property generally or particular such property) grant warrant for inhibition against any person interdicted by the order or, in relation to that property, under section 28(8) of this Act; and subject to the provisions of this Part of this Act, the warrant—

    (a) shall have effect as if granted on the dependence of an action for debt at the instance of the Lord Advocate against the person and may be executed, recalled, loosed or restricted accordingly; and

    (b) shall have the effect of letters of inhibition and shall forthwith be registered by the Lord Advocate in the Register of Inhibitions and Adjudications.

(2) Section 155 of the Titles to Land Consolidation (Scotland) Act 1868 (effective date of inhibition) shall apply in relation to an inhibition for which warrant has been granted under subsection (1) above as that section applies to an inhibition by separate letters or contained in a summons.

(3) In the application of section 158 of that Act of 1868 (recall of inhibition) to such an inhibition as is mentioned in subsection (2) above, that section to a particular Lord Ordinary shall be construed as references to any Lord Ordinary.

(4) The fact that an inhibition has been executed under subsection (1) above in respect of property shall not prejudice the exercise of an administrator's powers under or for the purposes of this Part of this Act in respect of that property.

(5) No inhibition executed under subsection (1) above shall have effect once, or in so far as, the restraint order affecting the property in respect of

which the warrant for the inhibition has been granted has ceased to have effect in respect of that property; and the Lord Advocate shall—

(a) apply for the recall, or as the case may be restriction, of the inhibition; and

(b) ensure that the recall, or restriction, of an inhibition on such application is reflected in the Register of Inhibitions and Adjudications.

Arrestment of property affected by restraint order

33.—(1) On the application of the prosecutor, the court may, in respect of moveable property affected by a restraint order (whether such property generally or particular such property), grant warrant for arrestment if the property would be arrestable if the person entitled to it were a debtor.

(2) A warrant under subsection (1) above shall have effect as if granted on the dependence of an action for debt at the instance of the prosecutor against the person and may be executed, recalled, loosed or restricted accordingly.

(3) The fact that an arrestment has been executed under subsection (2) above in respect of property shall not prejudice the exercise of an administrator's powers under or for the purposes of this Act in respect of that property.

(4) No arrestment executed under subsection (2) above shall have effect once, or in so far as, the restraint order affecting the property in respect of which the warrant for such arrestment has been granted has ceased to have effect in respect of that property; and the prosecutor shall apply to the court for an order recalling, or as the case may be, restricting the arrestment accordingly.

Administrators

34. Schedule 1 to this Act shall have effect as regards the appointment of administrators under this Act.

PART IV

RECIPROCAL ARRANGEMENTS FOR ENFORCEMENT OF ORDERS

Recognition and enforcement of orders made in England and Wales

35.—(1) An order to which this section applies shall, subject to this section and section 36 of this Act, have effect in the law of Scotland but shall be enforced in Scotland only in accordance with this section and that section.

(2) A receiver's functions under or for the purposes of section 77, 80 or 81 of the 1988 Act or section 26, 29 or 30 of the 1994 Act shall, subject to this section and section 36 of this Act, have effect in the law of Scotland.

(3) If an order to which this section applies is registered under this section—

(a) the Court of Session shall have, in relation to its enforcement, the same power;

(b) proceedings for or with respect to its enforcement may be taken, and

(c) proceedings for or with respect to any contravention of such an order (whether before or after such registration) may be taken,

as if the order had originally been made in that Court.

(4) Nothing in this section enables any provision of an order which empowers a receiver to do anything in Scotland under section 80(3)(a) of the 1988 Act or section 29(3)(a) of the 1994 Act to have effect in the law of Scotland.

(5) The orders to which this section applies are orders of the High Court—

(a) made under section 77, 78 or 81 of the 1988 Act or section 26, 29, 30 or 59 of the 1994 Act;

    (b) relating to the exercise by that Court of its powers under those sections; or

    (c) relating to receivers in the performance of their functions under the said section 77, 78 or 81 of the 1988 Act or the said section 26, 29 or 30 of the 1994 Act,

but not including an order in proceedings for enforcement of any such order.

    (6) References in this section to an order under—

    (a) section 77 of the 1988 Act include references to a discharge under section 76(4) of that Act; or

    (b) section 26 of the 1994 Act include references to a discharge under section 25(5) of that Act,

of such an order.

    (7) In this section and in section 36 of this Act, "order" means any order, direction or judgment (by whatever name called).

    (8) Nothing in any order of the High Court under section 80(6) of the 1988 Act or section 29(6) of the 1994 Act prejudices any enactment or rule of law in respect of the recording of deeds relating to heritable property in Scotland or the registration of interests in such property.

    (9) In this Part, "High Court" means the High Court of England and Wales.

Act	Section	Nature of Order
Criminal Justice Act 1988	77	Restraint Order
Criminal Justice Act 1988	78	Charging Order
Criminal Justice Act 1988	81	Directions as to application of proceeds of realisation of estate
Drug Trafficking Act 1994	26	Restraint Order
Drug Trafficking Act 1994	29	Appointment of a receiver and associated orders
Drug Trafficking Act 1994	30	Directions as to application of proceeds of realisation of estate
Drug Trafficking Act 1994	59	Order that government departments should disclose information

    (b) Orders relating to the exercise by that court of its powers under the sections specified in (a).

    (c) Orders relating to receivers in the performance of their functions under those sections.

Provisions supplementary to section 35

    36.—(1) The Court of Session shall, on application made to it in accordance with rules of court for registration of an order to which section 35 of this Act applies, direct that the order shall, in accordance with such rules, be registered in that Court.

    (2) Subsections (1) and (3) of section 35 of this Act and subsection (1) above are subject to any provision made by rules of court—

    (a) as to the manner in which and conditions subject to which that section applies are to be enforced in Scotland;

    (b) for the sisting of proceedings for enforcement of such an order;

    (c) for the modification or cancellation of the registration of such an order if the order is modified or revoked or ceases to have effect.

    (3) This section and section 35 of this Act are without prejudice to any enactment or rule of law as to the effect of notice or the want of it in relation to orders of the High Court.

(4) The Court of Session shall have the like power to make an order under section 1 of the Administration of Justice (Scotland) Act 1972 (extended power to order inspection of documents etc.) in relation to proceedings brought or likely to be brought under—

(a) Part VI of the 1988 Act; or

(b) the 1994 Act,

in the High Court as if those proceedings were brought or were likely to be brought in the Court of Session.

(5) The Court of Session may, additionally, for the purpose of—

(a) assisting the achievement in Scotland of the purposes of orders to which section 35 of this Act applies;

(b) assisting receivers performing functions thereunder or for the purposes of section 77, 80 or 81 of the 1988 Act or section 26, 29 or 30 of the 1994 Act,

make such orders and do otherwise as seems to it appropriate.

(6) A document purporting to be a copy of an order under or for the purposes of—

(a) Part VI of the 1988 Act; or

(b) the 1994 Act,

by the High Court and to be certified as such by a proper officer of that Court shall, in Scotland, be sufficient evidence of the order.

Inhibition of Scottish property affected by order registered under section 35

37.—(1) On the application of the Lord Advocate, the Court of Session may in respect of heritable realisable property in Scotland affected by a restraint order registered under section 35 of this Act (whether such property generally or particular such property) grant warrant for inhibition against any person with an interest in that property; and the warrant—

(a) shall have effect as if granted on the dependence of an action for debt at the instance of the Lord Advocate against the person and may be executed, recalled, loosed or restricted accordingly;

(b) shall have the effect of letters of inhibition and shall forthwith be registered by the Lord Advocate in the Register of Inhibitions and Adjudications.

(2) Section 155 of the Titles to Land Consolidation (Scotland) Act 1868 (effective date of inhibition) shall apply in relation to an inhibition for which warrant has been granted under subsection (1) above as that section applies to an inhibition by separate letters or contained in a summons.

(3) In the application of section 158 of that Act of 1868 (recall of inhibition) to such an inhibition as is mentioned in subsection (2) above, references in that section to a particular Lord Ordinary shall be construed as references to any Lord Ordinary.

(4) The fact that an inhibition has been executed under subsection (1) above, in respect of property shall not prejudice the exercise of a receiver's powers under or for the purposes of—

(a) section 77, 80 or 81 of the 1988 Act; or

(b) section 26, 29 or 30 of the 1994 Act,

in respect of that property.

(5) No inhibition executed under subsection (1) above shall have effect once, or in so far as, the restraint order affecting the property in respect of which the warrant for the inhibition has been granted has ceased to have effect in respect of that property; and the Lord Advocate shall—

(a) apply for the recall, or as the case may be restriction, of the inhibition; and

(b) ensure that the recall, or restriction, of an inhibition on such application is reflected in the Register of Inhibitions and Adjudications.

(6) Any power of the Court of Session to recall, loose or restrict inhibitions shall, in relation to an order containing an inhibition under subsection (1) above and without prejudice to any other consideration lawfully applying to the exercise of the power, be exercised with a view to achieving the purposes specified in section 80 of the 1988 Act or, as the case may be, section 31 of the 1994 Act.

Arrestment of Scottish property affected by order registered under section 35

38.—(1) On the application of the Lord Advocate, the Court of Session may, in respect of moveable property affected by a restraint order registered under section 35 of this Act (whether such property generally or particular such property), grant warrant for arrestment if the property would be arrestable if the person entitled to it were a debtor.

(2) A warrant under subsection (1) above shall have effect as if granted on the dependence of an action for debt at the instance of the Lord Advocate against the person and may be executed, recalled, loosed or restricted accordingly.

(3) The fact that an arrestment has been executed under subsection (2) above in respect of property shall not prejudice the exercise of a receiver's powers under or for the purposes of—

(a) section 77, 80 or 81 of the 1988 Act; or

(b) section 26, 29 or 30 of the 1994 Act,

in respect of that property.

(4) No arrestment executed under subsection (2) above shall have effect once, or in so far as, the restraint order affecting the property in respect of which the warrant for such arrestment has been granted has ceased to have effect in respect of that property; and the Lord Advocate shall apply to the Court of Session for an order recalling, or as the case may be, restricting the arrestment accordingly.

(5) Any power of the Court of Session to recall, loose or restrict arrestments shall, in relation to an arrestment proceeding upon a warrant under subsection (1) above and without prejudice to any other consideration lawfully applying to the exercise of the power, be exercised with a view to achieving the purposes specified in section 80 of the 1988 Act or, as the case may be, section 31 of the 1994 Act.

Enforcement of Northern Ireland orders

39.—(1) Her Majesty may by Order in Council provide that, for the purposes of Part III of and Schedules 1 and 2 to this Act, this Act shall have effect as if—

(a) references to confiscation orders included a reference to orders made by courts in Northern Ireland which appear to Her Majesty to correspond to confiscation orders;

(b) references to—

(i) offences to which Part I of this Act applies; or

(ii) drug trafficking offences,

included a reference to any offence under the law of Northern Ireland (not being an offence to which that Part applies) which appears to Her Majesty to correspond to such an offence; and

(c) such other modifications were made as may be specified in the Order in Council, being modifications which appear to Her Majesty to be requisite or desirable having regard to procedural differences which may for the time being exist between Scotland and Northern Ireland; and without prejudice to the generality of this paragraph modifications may include provision as to the circumstances in which proceedings in Northern Ireland are to be treated for the purposes of those sections as instituted or as concluded.

(2) An Order in Council under this section may provide for the provisions mentioned in subsection (1) above to have effect in relation to anything done or to be done in Northern Ireland subject to such further modifications as may be specified in the Order.

(3) An Order in Council under this section may contain such incidental, consequential and transitional provisions as Her Majesty considers expedient.

(4) An Order in Council under this section may, in particular, provide for section 18 of the Civil Jurisdiction and Judgements Act 1982 (enforcement of United Kingdom judgments in other parts of the United Kingdom) not to apply in relation to such orders made in connection with drug trafficking offences as may be prescribed by the Order.

(5) An Order in Council under this section shall be subject to annulment in pursuance of a resolution of either House of Parliament.

Enforcement of orders made outside United Kingdom

40.—(1) Her Majesty may by Order in Council—

(a) direct in relation to a country or territory outside the United Kingdom designated by the Order that, subject to such modifications as may be specified, Part I of this Act and Part III of this Act so far as it relates to realisable property shall apply in relation to external confiscation orders and to proceedings which have been or are to be instituted in the designated country and may result in an external confiscation order being made there;

(b) make—

(i) such provision as to evidence or proof of any matter for the purposes of this section and section 41 of this Act; and

(ii) such incidental, consequential and transitional provision,

as appears to Her Majesty to be expedient.

(2) In this Part of this Act—

"designated country" means a country or territory designated by an Order in Council made under this section; and

"external confiscation order" means an order made by a court in a designated country for the purpose of recovering payments or other rewards or property or other economic advantage received in connection with—

(a) an offence corresponding with or similar to an offence to which Part I of this Act applies; or

(b) drug trafficking,

or the value of such payments, property, reward or economic advantage.

(3) An Order in Council under this section may make different provision for different cases or classes of case.

(4) The power to make an Order in Council under this section includes power to modify Part I of this Act or Part III of this Act so far as it relates to realisable property in such a way as to confer power on a person to exercise a discretion.

(5) An Order in Council under this section shall be subject to annulment in pursuance of a resolution of either House of Parliament.

Registration of external confiscation orders

41.—(1) On an application made by or on behalf of the Government of a designated country, the Court of Session may register an external confiscation order made there if—

(a) it is satisfied that at the time of registration the order is in force and not subject to appeal;

(b) it is satisfied, where the person against whom the order is made did not appear in the proceedings, that he received notice of the proceedings in sufficient time to enable him to defend them; and

(c) it is of the opinion that enforcing the order in Scotland would not be contrary to the interests of justice.

(2) In subsection (1) above "appeal" includes—

(a) any proceedings by way of discharging or setting aside a judgment; and

(b) an application for a new trial or a stay of execution.

(3) The Court of Session shall cancel the registration of an external confiscation order if it appears to the court that the order has been satisfied by payment of the amount due under it or by the person against whom it was made serving imprisonment in default of payment or by any other means.

Enforcement of Scottish orders in England and Wales

42.—(1) Her Majesty may by Order in Council make such provision as Her Majesty considers expedient for the purpose—

(a) of enabling property in England and Wales which is realisable property to be used or realised for the payment of any amount payable under a confiscation order made in connection with an offence to which Part I of this Act applies;

(b) of securing that, where no such confiscation order has been made, property in England and Wales which is realisable property is available, in the event that such an order is so made, to be used or realised for the payment of any amount payable under it; and

[1](c) of enabling the enforcement in England and Wales of restraint orders, suspended forfeiture orders and forfeiture orders under any enactment other than the 1989 Act.

(2) Without prejudice to the generality of the power conferred by subsection (1) above, an Order in Council under this section may—

(a) provide that, subject to any specific conditions, such description of orders made under or for the purposes of Part I, II or III of this Act so far as it relates to realisable property shall have effect in the law of England and Wales;

(b) provide that, subject to any specified conditions, the functions of a person appointed under Schedule 1 to this Act shall have effect in the law of England and Wales;

(c) make provision—

(i) for the registration in the High Court of such descriptions of orders made under or for the purposes of Part I, II or III of this Act so far as it relates to realisable property as may be specified; and

(ii) for the High Court to have, in relation to the enforcement of orders made under or for the purposes of Part I, II or III of this Act so far as it so relates which are so registered, such powers as may be specified; and

(d) make provision as to the proof in England and Wales of orders made under or for the purposes of Part I, II or III of this Act so far as it so relates.

(3) In subsection (2) above "specified" means specified in an Order in Council under this section.

(4) An Order in Council under this section may amend or apply, with or without modifications, any enactment.

(5) An Order in Council under this section may contain such incidental, consequential and transitional provisions as Her Majesty considers expedient.

(6) An Order in Council under this section shall be subject to annulment in pursuance of a resolution of either House of Parliament.

<small>Note</small>
   [1]Prospectively amended by the Terrorism Act 2000 (c. 11), s.125 and Sched. 15, para. 11.

Order in Council as regards taking of action in designated country

43.—(1) Her Majesty may by Order in Council make such provision in connection with the taking of action in a designated country in consequence of the making of a restraint order, confiscation order or suspended forfeiture order under this Act or a forfeiture order under any other enactment as appears to Her Majesty to be expedient.

(2) Without prejudice to the generality of subsection (1) above, the provision contained in an Order in Council made under this section may include a direction that in such circumstances as may be specified proceeds arising out of action taken in a designated country with a view to satisfying a confiscation order which are retained there shall nevertheless be treated as reducing the amount payable under the confiscation order to such extent as may be specified.

(3) An Order in Council under this section may amend or apply, with or without modifications, any enactment.

(4) Subsections (1)(b), (3) and (5) of section 40 of this Act shall apply in respect of Orders in Council under this section as they apply in respect of Orders in Council under that section.

Part V

Miscellaneous and General

Sequestration etc. of person holding realisable or forfeitable property

44.—(1) Schedule 2 to this Act shall have effect in relation to the sequestration, bankruptcy, winding up or receivership of persons or, as the case may be, companies holding realisable or forfeitable property.

(2) In this section and in that Schedule "forfeitable property" means property which is or is liable to be the subject of a suspended forfeiture order.

Disposal of family home under Part I or II

45.—(1) This section applies where—
(a) a confiscation order has been made in relation to any person and the prosecutor has not satisfied the court that—
    (i) in the case of an order made in connection with a drug trafficking offence, the person's interest in his family home has been acquired by means of the proceeds of drug trafficking; or
    (ii) in any other case, the person's interest in his family home has been acquired by means of the benefit derived from the commission of the offence concerned; or
(b) a person's family home has been forfeited to the Crown under section 24 of this Act.

(2) Where this section applies, then, before the Crown disposes of any right or interest in the person's family home it shall—
(a) obtain the relevant consent; or
(b) where it is unable to do so, apply to the court for authority to carry out the disposal.

(3) On an application being made to it under subsection (2)(b) above, the court, after having regard to all the circumstances of the case including—
(a) the needs and financial resources of the spouse or former spouse of the person concerned;

(b) the needs and financial resources of any child of the family;

(c) the length of the period during which the family home has been used as a residence by any of the persons referred to in paragraph (a) or (b) above,

may refuse to grant the application or may postpone the granting of the application for such period (not exceeding 12 months) as it may consider reasonable in the circumstances or may grant the application subject to such conditions as it may prescribe.

(4) Subsection (3) above shall apply—

(a) to an action for division and sale of the family home of the person concerned; or

(b) to an action for the purpose of obtaining vacant possession of that home,

brought by the Crown as it applies to an application under subsection (2)(b) above and, for the purposes of this subsection, any reference in the said subsection (3) to the granting of the application shall be construed as a reference to the granting of decree in the action.

(5) In this section—

"family home", in relation to any person (in this subsection referred to as "the relevant person") means any property in which the relevant person has or had (whether alone or in common with any other person) a right or interest, being property which is occupied as a residence by the relevant person and his or her spouse or by the relevant person's spouse or former spouse (in any case with or without a child of the family) or by the relevant person with a child of the family;

"child of the family" includes any child or grandchild of either the relevant person or his or her spouse or former spouse, and any person who has been treated by either the relevant person or his or her spouse or former spouse as if he or she were a child of the relevant person, spouse or former spouse, whatever the age of such a child, grandchild or person may be; and

"relevant consent" means in relation to the disposal of any right or interest in a family home—

(a) in a case where the family home is occupied by the spouse or former spouse of the relevant person, the consent of the spouse or, as the case may be, of the former spouse, whether or not the family home is also occupied by the relevant person;

(b) where paragraph (a) above does not apply, in a case where the family home is occupied by the relevant person with a child of the family, the consent of the relevant person.

Forfeiture of property where accused has died

46.—(1) This section applies where at any time after criminal proceedings have been instituted against an accused for an offence to which Part I of this Act applies and before the accused has been sentenced or otherwise dealt with in the proceedings he dies.

(2) The Court of Session, if it is satisfied beyond reasonable doubt on an application being made to it by the Lord Advocate—

(a) that the accused committed the offence; and

(b) that there is property—

(i) which the accused had obtained, directly or indirectly, in connection with the commission of the offence or, as the case may be, in connection with drug trafficking; or

(ii) which is a gift caught by Part I of this Act or, as the case may be, an implicative gift, may, subject to subsection (5) below, make an order which shall have the effect of forfeiting that property.

(3) The Court of Session may, without prejudice to any other power available to it, at any time before the determination of the case, allow an amendment of the application under subsection (2) above if the amendment is of a type which could competently have been made in an indictment or complaint under section 96 or 159 of the 1995 Act in the criminal proceedings.

(4) An application under subsection (2) above shall be made as soon as is reasonably practicable after the relevant information becomes available to the Lord Advocate, but, in any event, within 6 years commencing with the date of death of the accused.

(5) An application under subsection (2) above in relation to property such as is mentioned in paragraph (b)(ii) of that subsection shall be served on the recipient of the gift and, if he satisfies the Court on the balance of probabilities—

(a) that he received the gift not knowing, not suspecting and not having reasonable grounds to suspect that the gift was made in contemplation of, or after, the commission of the offence or, if more than one, in contemplation of any of the offences or after the commission of the earlier or the earliest of the offences to which the proceedings for the time being relate; and

(b) that he was not associated with the giver in the commission of the offence; and

(c) that he would suffer hardship if the application were granted,

the Court may refuse to make an order as mentioned in that subsection; and in the application of this subsection to an implicative gift, any reference to the commission of the offence shall be construed as a reference to the drug trafficking and the reference in paragraph (b) above to the earlier or earliest of more than one offence shall be construed as a reference to the beginning of the drug trafficking.

(6) Where property has been forfeited under this section, then, if the Court of Session, on an application being made to it is satisfied by the applicant on the balance of probabilities that he was the owner of, or otherwise had an interest in, the property immediately before such forfeiture, it shall make an order under subsection (7) below.

(7) An order under this subsection shall direct the Crown, if the applicant—

(a) was the owner of the property, to return it to him if it is reasonably practicable to do so or, if not, to pay compensation to him of an amount determined under subsection (8) below; or

(b) otherwise had an interest in the property, to pay compensation to him of an amount corresponding to the value of such interest.

(8) For the purposes of subsection (7) above, the amount determined under this subsection shall be an amount equal to the amount of any consideration received for the property or the value of any such consideration at the time of the disposal, or, if no consideration was received, an amount equal to the value of the property at the time of the disposal.

(9) Property which has been forfeited under this section shall be dealt with by the Crown in such manner as seems to it to be appropriate.

(10) Where a restraint order is not in force in respect of a person when he dies in the circumstances mentioned in subsection (1) above, the Court of Session may, on the application of the Lord Advocate, in so far as the property concerned is—

(a) heritable property in Scotland, make an order inhibiting any person; and

(b) moveable property, grant warrant for arrestment if the property would be arrestable if the person entitled to it were a debtor.

(11) Paragraphs (a) and (b) of subsection (1) and subsections (2) to (5) of section 32 of this Act shall, subject to any necessary modifications, apply for the purposes of subsection (10)(a) above as they apply for the purposes of that section.

(12) Subsections (2) to (4) of section 33 of this Act shall, subject to any necessary modifications, apply for the purposes of subsection (10)(b) above as they apply for the purposes of that section.

(13) Proceedings under this section are civil proceedings for the purposes of section 10 of the Law Reform (Miscellaneous Provisions) (Scotland) Act 1968.

Construction of certain enactments

47.—(1) Section 28 of the Bankruptcy Act 1914 (effect of order of discharge) shall have effect as if amounts payable under confiscation orders were debts excepted under subsection (1)(a) of that section.

(2) In section 1(2)(a) of the Rehabilitation of Offenders Act 1974 (failure to pay fines etc. not to prevent person becoming rehabilitated) the reference to a fine or other sum adjudged to be paid by or on a conviction does not include a reference to an amount payable under a confiscation order.

(3) Section 55(2) of the Bankruptcy (Scotland) Act 1985 (discharge of debtor not to release him from liabilities in respect of fines, etc.) shall have effect as if the reference to a fine included a reference to a confiscation order.

(4) Section 281(4) of the Insolvency Act 1986 (discharge of bankrupt not to release him from liabilities in respect of fines, etc.) shall have effect as if the reference to a fine included a reference to a confiscation order.

Service and notice

48. Subject to the provisions of this Act, provision may be made by rules of court as to the giving of notice required for the purposes of this Act in so far as it is connected with drug trafficking or the effecting of service so required; and different provision may be so made for different cases or classes of case and for different circumstances or classes of circumstance.

Interpretation

[1]**49.**—(1) In this Act, unless the context otherwise requires—
"the 1988 Act" means the Criminal Justice Act 1988;
"the 1989 Act" means the Prevention of Terrorism (Temporary Provisions) Act 1989;
"the 1994 Act" means the Drug Trafficking Act 1994;
"the 1995 Act" means the Criminal Procedure (Scotland) Act 1995;
"accused" includes a person against whom criminal proceedings have been instituted in relation to the commission of an offence and a person convicted of an offence;
"clerk of court" includes the sheriff clerk;
"confiscation order" means an order made under section 1(1), 11(4), 12(3) or 13 of this Act;
"interest", in relation to property, includes right;
"property" has the meaning assigned by section 2 of this Act;
"realisable property" has the meaning assigned by section 4 of this Act;
"restraint order" means an order made under section 28 of this Act;
"suspended forfeiture order" means an order made under section 21(2) of this Act.

(2) In this Act, "drug trafficking" means, subject to subsections (3) and (4) below, doing or being concerned in any of the following, whether in Scotland or elsewhere—

(a) producing or supplying a controlled drug where the production or supply contravenes section 4(1) of the Misuse of Drugs Act 1971;

(b) transporting or storing such a drug where possession of it contravenes section 5(1) of that Act;

(c) importing or exporting such a drug where the importation or exportation is prohibited by section 3(1) of that Act;

(d) producing, supplying, transporting, storing, importing or exporting such a drug in contravention of a corresponding law ("corresponding law" having the meaning assigned by section 36(1) of that Act);

(e) manufacturing or supplying a scheduled substance within the meaning of section 12 of the Criminal Justice (International Co-operation) Act 1990 where the manufacture or supply is an offence under that section;

(f) acquiring, having possession of or using property in contravention of section 37 of the Criminal Law (Consolidation) (Scotland) Act 1995;

(g) concealing or transferring the proceeds of drug trafficking in contravention of section 14 of the said Act of 1990;

(h) using any ship for illicit traffic in controlled drugs in contravention of section 19 of the said Act of 1990.

(3) Drug trafficking also includes, whether in Scotland or elsewhere, entering into or being otherwise concerned in any arrangement whereby—

(a) the retention or control by or on behalf of another person of the other person's proceeds of drug trafficking is facilitated, or

(b) the proceeds of drug trafficking by another person are used to secure that funds are placed at the other person's disposal or are used for the other person's benefit to acquire property by way of investment.

(4) In paragraphs (e) to (g) of subsection (2) above, references to conduct in contravention of the enactments mentioned in those paragraphs include conduct which would contravene the enactments if it took place in Scotland.

(5) In this Act a "drug trafficking offence" means any of the following—

(a) an offence under—

(i) section 4(2) (production, or being concerned in production, of controlled drug);

(ii) section 4(3) (supply of, or offer to supply, or being concerned in supply of, controlled drug);

(iii) section 5(3) (possession of controlled drug with intent to supply); or

(iv) section 20 (assisting in, or inducing commission of, certain drug related offences punishable under foreign law),

of the Misuse of Drugs Act 1971;

(b) in connection with a prohibition or restriction on importation and exportation having effect by virtue of section 3 of the said Act of 1971, an offence under section 50(2) or (3) (improper importation), 68(2) (improper exportation) or 170 (fraudulent evasion of duty etc.) of the Customs and Excise Management Act 1979;

(c) an offence under section 37 of the Criminal Law (Consolidation) (Scotland) Act 1995;

(d) an offence under section 38 of the said Act of 1995;

(e) an offence under section 12, 14 or 19 of the Criminal Justice (International Co-operation) Act 1990;

(f) an offence of conspiring, inciting or attempting to commit an offence mentioned in paragraph (a), (b), (c) or (e) above.

(6) For the purposes of this Act proceedings for an offence are instituted against a person—

(a) on his arrest without warrant;

(b) when he is charged with the offence without being arrested;

(c) when a warrant to arrest him is granted;

(d) when a warrant to cite him is granted;

(e) in summary proceedings, on the first calling of the case; or

(f) when a petition is intimated to him or an indictment or a complaint is served on him,

and, where the application of this subsection would result in there being more than one time for the institution of proceedings, they shall be taken to be instituted at the earliest of those times.

(7) Any reference in this Act to a conviction of an offence includes a reference to a finding that the offence has been committed.

NOTE

[1]Prospectively amended by the Terrorism Act 2000 (c. 11), s.125 and Sched. 15, para. 11.

Short title, commencement and extent

50.—(1) This Act may be cited as the Proceeds of Crime (Scotland) Act 1995.

(2) This Act shall come into force on 1 April 1996.

(3) Subject to subsections (4) and (5) below, this Act extends only to Scotland.

(4) Section 44 of and Schedule 2 to this Act and this section extend to England and Wales as well as to Scotland.

(5) Section 42 of this Act extends only to England and Wales.

SCHEDULES

Section 34   SCHEDULE 1

ADMINISTRATORS

Appointment of administrators

1.—(1) On the application of the prosecutor the court may as regards property—

(a) affected by a restraint order or a suspended forfeiture order, appoint a person to manage, or otherwise deal with, the property; or

(b) where a suspended forfeiture order or a confiscation order has been made, appoint a person (or empower an appointee under paragraph (a) above) to realise the property,

in accordance with the court's directions and may (whether on making the appointment or from time to time) require any person having possession of the property to give possession of it to the appointee (any such appointee being in this Act referred to as an "administrator").

(2) A requirement under sub-paragraph (1) above—

(a) subject to paragraph (b) below, may relate to the property generally or to particular such property and may be subject to such exceptions and conditions as may be specified by the court;

(b) shall relate to property mentioned in paragraph (b) of section 4(1) of this Act only if expressly stated so to do and then only in so far as the person in whom such property is vested is named in the requirement as being subject to it.

(3) On a requirement being imposed under sub-paragraph (1) above—

(a) the clerk of court shall forthwith notify—

(i) the person in respect of whom the restraint order, or as the case may be the suspended forfeiture order or confiscation order, has been made; and

(ii) any other person named in the requirement as being subject to it; and

(b) any dealing of or with such person in relation to the property shall be of no effect in a question with the administrator unless whoever dealt with the person had, at the time when the dealing occurred, no knowledge of the appointment.

(4) The court, at the instance of any person having an interest, may at any time—

(a) vary or withdraw a requirement imposed under sub-paragraph (1) above; or

(b) without prejudice to paragraph 4 below or to the powers and duties of an administrator pending a decision under this sub-sub-paragraph, on cause shown, remove the administrator from office.

(5) On the death or resignation of the administrator, or on his removal from office under sub-paragraph (4)(b) above or paragraph 5 below, the court shall appoint a new administrator.

(6) Such of the property (if any) as was, by virtue of paragraph 2(3) below, vested in the

administrator who has died, resigned or been removed shall forthwith vest in the new administrator; and any requirement imposed under sub-paragraph (1) above shall, on the person subject to the requirement being notified in writing of the appointment by the appointee, apply in relation to the appointee instead of in relation to his predecessor.

(7) The administration of property by an administrator shall be deemed continuous notwithstanding any temporary vacancy in that office.

(8) Any appointment under this paragraph shall be on such conditions as to caution as the accountant of court may think fit to impose; but the premium of any bond of caution or other security thereby required of the administrator shall be treated as part of his outlays in his actings as such.

(9) Without prejudice to paragraph 5 below, section 6 of the Judicial Factors (Scotland) Act 1889 (supervision of judicial factors) shall not apply in relation to an appointment under this section.

Functions of administrators

2.—(1) Subject to paragraph 5 below, an administrator—

(a) shall be entitled to take possession of, and if appointed (or empowered) under paragraph 1(1)(b) above where a confiscation order has been made shall as soon as practicable take possession of, the property as regards which he has been appointed and of any document which both—
> (i) is in the possession or control of the person (in this paragraph referred to as "A") in whom the property is vested (or would be vested but for an order made under sub-paragraph (3) below); and
> (ii) relates to the property or to A's assets, business or financial affairs;

(b) shall be entitled to have access to, and to copy, any document relating to the property or to A's assets, business or financial affairs and not in such possession or control as is mentioned in sub-sub-paragraph (a) above;

(c) may bring, defend or continue any legal proceedings relating to the property;

(d) may borrow money in so far as it is necessary to do so to safeguard the property and may for the purposes of such borrowing create a security over any part of the property;

(e) may, if the administrator considers that to do so would be beneficial for the management or realisation of the property—
> (i) carry on any business of A;
> (ii) exercise any right of A as holder of securities in a company;
> (iii) grant a lease of the property or take on lease any other property; or
> (iv) enter into any contract, or execute any deed, as regards the property or as regards A's business;

(f) may, where any right, option or other power forms part of A's estate, make payments or incur liabilities with a view to—
> (i) obtaining property which is the subject of; or
> (ii) maintaining,

the right, option or power;

(g) may effect or maintain insurance policies as regards the property on A's business;

(h) where he has been appointed under paragraph 1(1)(b) above may, where A has an uncompleted title to any heritable estate, complete title thereto;
Provided that completion of title in A's name shall not validate by accretion any unperfected right in favour of any person other than the administrator;

(j) may sell, purchase or exchange property or discharge any security for an obligation due to A:
Provided that it shall be incompetent for the administrator or an associate of his (within the meaning of section 74 of the Bankruptcy (Scotland) Act 1985) to purchase any of A's property in pursuance of this paragraph;

(k) may claim, vote and draw dividends in the sequestration of the estate (or bankruptcy or liquidation) of a debtor of A and may accede to a voluntary trust deed for creditors of such a debtor;

(l) may discharge any of his functions through agents or employees;
Provided that the administrator shall be personally liable to meet the fees and expenses of any such agent or employee out of such remuneration as is payable to the administrator by virtue of paragraph 6(1) and (3) below;

(m) may take such professional advice as he may consider requisite for the proper discharge of his functions;

(n) may at any time apply to the court for directions as regards the discharge of his functions;

(o) may exercise any power specifically conferred on him by the court, whether such conferral was at the time of his appointment or on his subsequent application to the court in that regard; and

(p) may do anything incidental to the above powers and duties.

(2) Subject to the proviso to sub-paragraph (1)(j) above—

(a) a person dealing with an administrator in good faith and for value shall not require to determine whether the administrator is acting within the powers mentioned in that subsection; and

(b) the validity of any title shall not be challengeable by reason only of the administrator having acted outwith those powers.

(3) The exercise of a power mentioned in any of sub-paragraphs (1)(c) to (k) above shall be in A's name except where and in so far as an order made by the court under this sub-paragraph (either on its own motion or on the application of the administrator) has vested the property in the administrator (or in his predecessor in that office).

Money received by administrator

3.—(1) Subject to sub-paragraph (2) below, all money received by an administrator in the exercise of his functions shall be deposited by him, in the name (unless vested in the administrator by virtue of paragraph 2(3) above) of the holder of the property realised, in an appropriate bank or institution.

(2) The administrator may at any time retain in his hands a sum not exceeding £200 or such other sum as may be prescribed by the Secretary of State by regulations made by statutory instrument.

(3) In sub-paragraph (1) above, "appropriate bank or institution" means a bank or institution mentioned in section 2(1) of the Banking Act 1979 or for the time being specified in Schedule 1 to that Act.

Application of proceeds of realisation and other sums

4.—(1) This paragraph applies only to an administrator appointed to realise property where a confiscation order has been made.

(2) Subject to sub-paragraph (3) below, sums in the hands of an administrator which are—

(a) proceeds of a realisation of property under paragraph 1 above, and

(b) other property held by the person in respect of whom the confiscation order was made,

shall first be applied in payment of any expenses to the payment of which a person is entitled under paragraph 5(2) of Schedule 2 to this Act and then shall, after such payments (if any) as the court may direct have been made out of those proceeds and sums, be applied on the person's behalf towards the satisfaction of the confiscation order.

(3) If, after the amount payable under the confiscation order has been fully paid, any such proceeds and sums remain in the hands of the administrator, he shall distribute them—

(a) among such of those who held property which has been realised under this Act, and

(b) in such proportions,

as the court may, after giving such persons an opportunity to be heard as regards the matter, direct.

(4) The receipt of any sum by a sheriff clerk on account of an amount payable under a confiscation order shall reduce the amount so payable, but the sheriff clerk shall apply the money—

(a) first, in payment of any expenses to the payment of which a person is entitled under paragraph 5(2) of Schedule 2 to this Act but which were not paid to him under sub-paragraph (2) above;

(b) next, in payment of the administrator's remuneration and expenses;

(c) next, in reimbursement of any sums paid by the Lord Advocate under paragraph 8(2) below;

(d) next, in accordance with any direction given by the court under section 8(4) or 13(7) of this Act,

and the balance shall be payable and recoverable (or as the case may be disposed of) under section 211(5) or (6) of the 1995 Act (destination of fines) as applied by section 14 of this Act.

Supervision of administrators

5.—(1) The accountant of court shall supervise the performance by administrators of the functions conferred on them by Part I of this Act; and in particular an administrator proposing to exercise functions conferred by any of paragraphs 2(1)(c) to (p) above shall first obtain the consent of the accountant of court to such exercise.

(2) If it appears to the accountant of court that an administrator has, without reasonable cause, failed to perform a duty imposed on him by any provision of section 16 of this Act or of this Schedule, he shall report the matter to the court which, after giving the administrator an opportunity to be heard as regards the matter, may remove the administrator from office, censure him or make such other order as the circumstances of the case may appear to the court to require.

Accounts and remuneration of administrator

6.—(1) The administrator shall keep such accounts in relation to his intromissions with the property as regards which he is appointed as the court may require and shall lodge these accounts with the accountant of court at such times as may be fixed by the court in that regard; and the accountant of court shall audit the accounts and issue a determination as to the amount of outlays and, on the basis mentioned in sub-paragraph (3) below, remuneration payable to the administrator in respect of those intromissions.

(2) Not later than two weeks after the issuing of a determination under sub-paragraph (1) above, the administrator or the Lord Advocate may appeal against it to the court.

(3) The basis for determining the amount of remuneration payable to the administrator shall be the value of the work reasonably undertaken by him, regard being had to the extent of the responsibilities involved.

(4) The accountant of court may authorise the administrator to pay without taxation an account in respect of legal services incurred by the administrator.

Effect of appointment of administrator on diligence

7. Without prejudice to sections 32 and 33 of this Act—
(a) no arrestment or poinding of property executed on or after an appointment as regards the property under paragraph 1 above shall be effectual to create a preference for the arrester or poinder and any such property so arrested or poinded, or the proceeds of sale thereof, shall be handed over to the administrator;
(b) no poinding of the ground in respect of property on or after such appointment shall be effectual in a question with the administrator except for the interest on the debt of a secured creditor, being interest for the current half-yearly term and arrears of interest for one year immediately before the commencement of that term;
(c) it shall be incompetent on or after such appointment for any other person to raise or insist in an adjudication against the property or to be confirmed as executor-creditor on that property; and
(d) no inhibition on property which takes effect on or after such appointment shall be effectual to create a preference for the inhibitor in a question with the administrator.

Further provision as to administrators

8.—(1) Where an administrator takes any action—
(a) in relation to property as regards which he has not been appointed, being action which he would be entitled to take if he had been so appointed,
(b) believing, and having reasonable grounds for believing, that he is entitled to take that action in relation to that property,
he shall not be liable to any person in respect of any loss or damage resulting from his action except in so far as the loss or damage is caused by his negligence.

(2) Any amount due in respect of the remuneration and expenses of an administrator appointed under this Schedule shall, unless in a case where a confiscation order has been made there are sums available to be applied in payment of it under paragraph 4(4)(b) above, be paid by the Lord Advocate.

(3) Any disposal of property under paragraph 1 above to a person taking in good faith shall vest the ownership of the property in that person.

Discharge of administrator

9. After an administrator has lodged his final accounts under paragraph 6(1) above, he may apply to the accountant of court to be discharged from office; and such discharge, if granted, shall have the effect of freeing him from all liability (other than liability arising from fraud) in respect of any act or omission of his in exercising the functions conferred on him by this Act.

Compensation

10.—(1) Where the court, on an application made to it by a person other than the accused or the recipient of a gift caught by Part I of this Act or an implicative gift, is satisfied on the balance of probabilities that in relation to any property realised under paragraph 1 above he was the owner of, or a person otherwise having an interest in, the property immediately before such realisation, it shall make an order directing the Crown to pay to that person compensation of an amount equal to the consideration received for the property or, as the case may be, interest or the value of any such consideration at the time of such realisation, or, if no consideration was received, an amount equal to the value of the property or interest at the time of the realisation.

(2) An application under this paragraph shall be made not later than three years after the conclusion of the proceedings in respect of which the confiscation order was made.

(3) Subsection (6) of section 29 of this Act shall apply for the purpose of determining for the purposes of this paragraph whether proceedings are concluded as it applies for the purposes of that section.

Rules of court as regards accountant of court's supervision etc of administrators

11. Without prejudice to section 5 of the Court of Session Act 1988 (power to regulate procedure etc. by Act of Sederunt), provision may be made by rules of court as regards (or as regards any matter incidental to) the accountant of court's powers and duties under this Act in relation to the functions of administrators.

Power to facilitate realisation

12.—(1) Without prejudice to any enactment or rule of law in respect of the recording of deeds relating to heritable property or the registration of interests therein, the court, to facilitate realisation under paragraph 1 above, may—
(a) order any person (in this paragraph referred to as "A") holding an interest in property, not being such person (in this paragraph referred to as "B") as is mentioned in paragraph (a) or (b) of section 4(1) or section 21 of this Act, to make such payment to an administrator appointed to realise estate comprising an interest of B in that property as the court may direct and may, subject to such payment being made—
   (i) authorise the administrator to transfer B's interest to A or to discharge it in favour of A; or
   (ii) itself by order transfer or discharge B's interest; or
(b) by order—
   (i) transfer A's interest to B; or
   (ii) discharge it in favour of B,
on the administrator making such payment to A out of that estate in respect of A's interest as the court may direct.

(2) The court may make such incidental provision in relation to any exercise of powers conferred on it by sub-paragraph (1) above as it considers appropriate; but it shall not exercise those powers without giving such persons as hold an interest in the property reasonable opportunity to make representations to it in that regard.

Section 44   SCHEDULE 2

SEQUESTRATION ETC. OF PERSONS HOLDING REALISABLE OR FORFEITABLE PROPERTY

Sequestration of person holding realisable or forfeitable property

1.—(1) Where the estate of a person who holds realisable or forfeitable property is sequestrated—
(a) property, other than heritable property situated in Scotland, for the time being subject to a restraint order made before the date of sequestration (within the meaning of section 12(4) of the 1985 Act) and heritable property situated in Scotland for the time being subject to a restraint order recorded in the General Register of Sasines or, as the case may be, registered in the Land Register of Scotland before such date of sequestration; and
(b) any proceeds of property realised by virtue of paragraph 1 of Schedule 1 to this Act for the time being in the hands of an administrator appointed under that paragraph,
is excluded from the debtor's estate for the purposes of that Act.

(2) Where an award of sequestration has been made, the powers conferred on the court by sections 28 to 33 and 35 to 38 of and the said Schedule 1 to this Act or on an administrator appointed under paragraph 1 of that Schedule shall not be exercised in relation to—
(a) property comprised in the whole estate of the debtor (within the meaning of section 31(8) of the 1985 Act); or
(b) any income of the debtor which has been ordered, under subsection (2) of section 32 of that Act, to be paid to the permanent trustee or any estate which, under subsection (10) of

section 31 of that Act or subsection (6) of the said section 32 of that Act, vests in the permanent trustee,

and it shall not be competent to submit a claim in relation to the confiscation order to the permanent trustee in accordance with section 48 of that Act.

(3) Nothing in the 1985 Act shall be taken as restricting, or enabling the restriction of, the exercise of the powers so conferred.

(4) Where, during the period before sequestration is awarded, an interim trustee stands appointed under section 2(5) of the 1985 Act and any property in the debtor's estate is subject to a restraint order, the powers conferred on the interim trustee by virtue of that Act do not apply to property for the time being subject to the restraint order.

(5) Where the estate of a person is sequestrated and he has directly or indirectly made a gift caught by Part I of this Act or an implicative gift—

(a) no decree shall, at any time when proceedings as regards an offence to which Part I of this Act applies or, as the case may be, a drug trafficking offence have been instituted against him and have not been concluded or when property of the person to whom the gift was made is subject to a restraint order, be granted under section 34 or 36 of the 1985 Act (gratuitous alienations and unfair preferences) in respect of the making of the gift; and

(b) any decree granted under either of the said sections 34 and 36 after the conclusion of the proceedings shall take into account any realisation under this Act of property held by the person to whom the gift was made.

Bankruptcy in England and Wales of person holding realisable or forfeitable property

2.—(1) Where a person who holds realisable or forfeitable property is adjudged bankrupt—

(a) property, other than heritable property situated in Scotland, for the time being subject to a restraint order made before the order adjudging him bankrupt and heritable property situated in Scotland for the time being subject to a restraint order recorded in the General Register of Sasines or, as the case may be, registered in the Land Register of Scotland before the order adjudging him bankrupt was made; and

(b) any proceeds of property realised by virtue of paragraph 1 of Schedule 1 to this Act for the time being in the hands of an administrator appointed under that paragraph,

is excluded from the bankrupt's estate for the purposes of Part IX of the Insolvency Act 1986.

(2) Where a person has been adjudged bankrupt, the powers conferred on the court by sections 28 to 33 and 35 to 38 of and the said Schedule 1 to this Act or on an administrator appointed under paragraph 1 of that Schedule shall not be exercised in relation to—

(a) property for the time being comprised in the bankrupt's estate for the purposes of the said Part IX;

(b) property in respect of which his trustee in bankruptcy may (without leave of the court) serve a notice under section 307, 308 or 308A of the Insolvency Act 1986 (after-acquired property and tools, clothes, etc. exceeding value of reasonable replacement and certain tenancies); and

(c) property which is to be applied for the benefit of creditors of the bankrupt by virtue of a condition imposed under section 280(2)(c) of the Insolvency Act 1986.

(3) Nothing in the Insolvency Act 1986 shall be taken as restricting, or enabling the restriction of, the exercise of the powers so conferred.

(4) Where, in the case of a debtor, an interim receiver stands appointed under section 286 of the Insolvency Act 1986 and any property of the debtor is subject to a restraint order the powers conferred on the receiver by virtue of that Act do not apply to property for the time being subject to the restraint order.

(5) Where a person is adjudged bankrupt and has directly or indirectly made a gift caught by Part I of this Act or an implicative gift—

(a) no order shall, at any time when proceedings for an offence to which Part VI of the Criminal Justice Act 1988 applies or, as the case may be a drug trafficking offence have been instituted against him and have not been concluded or when property of the person to whom the gift was made is subject to a restraint order, be made under section 339 or 423 of the Insolvency Act 1986 (avoidance of certain transactions) in respect of the making of the gift, and

(b) any order made under either of those sections after the conclusion of the proceedings shall take into account any realisation under this Act of property held by the person to whom the gift was made.

Winding up of company holding realisable or forfeitable property

3.—(1) Where realisable or forfeitable property is held by a company and an order for the winding up of the company has been made or a resolution has been passed by the company for the voluntary winding up, the functions of the liquidator (or any provisional liquidator) shall not be exercisable in relation to—

    (a) property, other than heritable property situated in Scotland, for the time being subject to a restraint order made before the relevant time and heritable property situated in Scotland for the time being subject to a restraint order recorded in the General Register of Sasines or, as the case may be, registered in the Land Register of Scotland before the relevant time; and

    (b) any proceeds of property realised by virtue of paragraph 1 of Schedule 1 to this Act for the time being in the hands of an administrator appointed under that paragraph.

(2) Where, in the case of a company, such an order has been made or such a resolution has been passed, the powers conferred on the court by sections 28 to 33 and 35 to 38 of and the said Schedule 1 to this Act or on an administrator appointed under paragraph 1 of that Schedule shall not be exercised in relation to any realisable or forfeitable property held by the company in relation to which the functions of the liquidator are exercisable—

    (a) so as to inhibit the liquidator from exercising those functions for the purpose of distributing any property held by the company to the company's creditors; or

    (b) so as to prevent the payment out of any property of expenses (including the remuneration of the liquidator or any provisional liquidator) properly incurred in the winding up in respect of the property.

(3) Nothing in the Insolvency Act 1986 shall be taken as restricting, or enabling the restriction of, the exercise of the powers so conferred.

(4) For the purposes of the application of Parts IV and V of the Insolvency Act 1986 (winding up of registered companies and winding up of unregistered companies) to a company which the court has jurisdiction to wind up, a person is not a creditor in so far as any sum due to him by the company is due in respect of a confiscation order (whether under this Act or under and within the meaning of section 2 of the Drug Trafficking Act 1994 or any corresponding provision in Northern Ireland).

(5) Where an order for the winding up of a company has been made or a resolution has been passed by a company for its voluntary winding up and before the relevant time the company has directly or indirectly made a gift caught by Part I of this Act or an implicative gift—

    (a) no order or, as the case may be, decree shall, at any time when proceedings as regards an offence to which that Part applies or, as the case may be a drug trafficking offence have been instituted against the company and have not been concluded or when property of the person to whom the gift was made is subject to a restraint order, be made under section 238 or 239 of the Insolvency Act 1986 (transactions at an undervalue and preferences) or granted under section 242 or 243 of that Act (gratuitous alienations and unfair preferences) in respect of the making of the gift; and

    (b) any order made under either of the said sections 242 and 243 or decree granted under either of the said sections 242 or 243 after the conclusion of the proceedings shall take into account any realisation under Part I of this Act of property held by the person to whom the gift was made.

(6) In this paragraph—

    "company" means any company which may be wound up under the Insolvency Act 1986; and

    "the relevant time" means—

        (a) where no order for the winding up of the company has been made, the time of the passing of the resolution for voluntary winding up;

        (b) where such an order has been made and, before the presentation of the petition for the winding up of the company by the court, such a resolution had been passed by the company, the time of the passing of the resolution; and

        (c) in any other case where such an order has been made, the time of the making of the order.

Property subject to floating charge

4.—(1) Where any property held subject to a floating charge by a company is realisable or forfeitable property and a receiver has been appointed by, or on the application of, the holder of the charge, the powers of the receiver in relation to the property so held shall not be exercisable in relation to—

    (a) so much of it, not being heritable property situated in Scotland, as is for the time being subject to a restraint order made before the appointment of the receiver and so much of it, being heritable property situated in Scotland, as is for the time being subject to a restraint order recorded in the General Register of Sasines or, as the case may be, registered in the Land Register of Scotland before such appointment; and

(b) any proceeds of property realised by virtue of paragraph 1 of Schedule 1 to this Act for the time being in the hands of an administrator appointed under that paragraph.

(2) Where, in the case of a company, such an appointment has been made, the powers conferred on the court by sections 28 to 33 and 35 to 38 of and the said Schedule 1 to this Act or on an administrator appointed under paragraph 1 of that Schedule shall not be exercised in relation to any realisable property held by the company in relation to which the powers of the receiver are exercisable—

(a) so as to inhibit the receiver from exercising his powers for the purpose of distributing any property held by the company to the company's creditors; or

(b) so as to prevent the payment out of any property of expenses (including the remuneration of the receiver) properly incurred in the exercise of the receiver's powers in respect of the property.

(3) Nothing in the Insolvency Act 1986, shall be taken as restricting, or enabling the restriction of, the exercise of the powers so conferred.

(4) In this paragraph—

"company" has the same meaning as in paragraph 3 above; and

"floating charge" includes a floating charge within the meaning given by section 462 of the Companies Act 1985 (power of incorporated company to create floating charge).

Insolvency practitioners dealing with property subject to restraint order

5.—(1) Without prejudice to the generality of any enactment contained in the Insolvency Act 1986 or in the 1985 Act, where

(a) any person acting as an insolvency practitioner seizes or disposes of any property in relation to which his functions are, because that property is for the time being subject to a restraint order, not exercisable; and

(b) at the time of the seizure or disposal he believes, and has reasonable grounds for believing, that he is entitled (whether in pursuance of a court order or otherwise) to seize or dispose of that property,

he shall not be liable to any person in respect of any loss or damage resulting from the seizure or disposal except in so far as the loss or damage is caused by the insolvency practitioner's negligence; and the insolvency practitioner shall have a lien on the property, or the proceeds of its sale, for such of his expenses as were incurred in connection with the liquidation, sequestration or other proceedings in relation to which the seizure or disposal purported to take place and for so much of his remuneration as may reasonably be assigned for his actings in connection with those proceedings.

(2) Any person who, acting as an insolvency practitioner, incurs expenses—

(a) in respect of such realisable property as is mentioned in sub-paragraph (1)(a) above and in so doing does not know and has no reasonable grounds to believe that the property is for the time being subject to a restraint order; or

(b) other than in respect of such realisable property as is so mentioned, being expenses which, but for the effect of a restraint order, might have been met by taking possession of and realising the property,

shall be entitled (whether or not he has seized or disposed of that property so as to have a lien under sub-paragraph (1) above) to payment of those expenses under paragraph 4(2) or (4)(a) of Schedule 1 to this Act.

(3) In the foregoing provisions of this paragraph, the expression "acting as an insolvency practitioner" shall be construed in accordance with section 388 (interpretation) of the said Act of 1986 except that for the purposes of such construction the reference in subsection (2)(a) of that section to a permanent or interim trustee in a sequestration shall be taken to include a reference to a trustee in a sequestration and subsection (5) of that section shall be disregarded; and the expression shall also comprehend the official receiver acting as receiver or manager of the property.

Interpretation

6.—(1) In this Schedule "the 1985 Act" means the Bankruptcy (Scotland) Act 1985.

(2) References in this Schedule to the conclusion of proceedings, except for the purposes of paragraph 2(5) above, shall be construed—

(a) as regards property subject to a restraint order under section 28(1)(a) of this Act, in accordance with section 29(6) of this Act; and

(b) as regards property subject to a restraint order under section 28(1)(b) of this Act, in accordance with section 30(5) of this Act.

(3) References in this Schedule to property held by a person include a reference to property

vested in the interim or permanent trustee in his sequestration or in his trustee in bankruptcy or liquidation.

TABLE OF DERIVATIONS

Notes:

1. This Table shows the derivation of the provisions of the Bill.
2. The following abbreviations are used in the Table:—

Acts of Parliament

1987	=	*Criminal Justice (Scotland) Act 1987 (c. 41)*
1988	=	*Criminal Justice Act 1988 (c. 33)*
1993	=	*Criminal Justice Act 1993 (c. 36)*
1994	=	*Drug Trafficking Act 1994 (c. 37)*
1995	=	*Criminal Justice (Scotland) Act 1995 (1995 c. 20)*
1995 CP	=	*Criminal Procedure (Consequential Provisions) (Scotland) Act (1995 c. 40)*
1995 CLC	=	*Criminal Law (Consolidation) (Scotland) Act 1995 (1995 c. 39)*

Provision	Derivation
1(1)	1987 s.1(1); 1995 s.70(1), Sch. 5 §.2
(2)	1987 s.1(2); 1995 s.70(2), Sch. 5 §.2
(3)	1987 s.1(2B); 1995 s.70(3), Sch. 5 §.2
(4)	1995 s.70(4)
(5)	1987 s.1(1); 1995 s.70(5), Sch. 5 §.2
(6)	1987 s.1(2A); 1995 s.70(6), Sch. 5 §.2
(7)	1987 s.1(4); 1995 s.70(7)
2	1995 s.71
3	1987 s.3; 1994 Sch. 1 §.12; 1995 Sch. 5 §.4
4(1)	1987 s.5(1); 1995 s.72(1), Sch. 5 §.6
(2)	1987 s.5(2); 1995 s.72(2), Sch. 5 §.6
(3)	1987 s.5(4); 1995 s.72(3), Sch. 5 §.6
(4)	1987 s.5(5); 1995 s.72(4), Sch. 5 §.6
(5)	1987 s.5(5); 1995 s.72(5), Sch. 5 §.6
(6)	1987 s.5(7); 1995 Sch. 5 §.6
5(1)	1995 s.73(1)
(2)	1995 s.73(2)(part)
(3)	1995 s.73(6)
(4)	1995 s.73(7)
(5)	1995 s.73(8)
6(1)	1987 s.6(1); Law Reform (Miscellaneous Provisions) (Scotland) Act 1990 (c. 40) Sch. 8 §.37; 1995 Sch. 5 §.7
(2)	1987 s.6(2)(part); 1995 Sch. 5 §.7
(3)	1987 s.5(7A); 1995 Sch. 5 §.6
(4)	1987 s.5(7B); 1995 Sch. 5 §.6
(5)	1987 s.5(7C); 1995 Sch. 5 §.6
7(1)	1987 s.6(2)(part); 1995 s.73(2)(part), Sch. 5 §.7
(2)	1987 s.6(2)(part); 1995 s.73(2)(part), Sch. 5 §.7
(3)	1987 s.6(2)(part); 1995 s.73(2)(part), Sch. 5 §.7
(4)	1987 s.6(3); 1995 s.73(3), Sch. 5 §.7
(5)	1987 s.6(3A); 1995 s.73(4), Sch. 5 §.7
(6)	1995 s.73(5)
8(1)	1987 s.1(2C); 1995 s.74(1), Sch. 5 §.2
(2)	1987 s.1(2D); 1995 s.74(2), Sch. 5 §.2
(3)	1987 s.1(5); 1995 s.74(3), Sch. 5 §.2
(4)	1987 s.1(2E); 1995 s.74(4), Sch. 5 §.2
9(1)	1987 s.4(1)(part); 1995 s.75(1), Sch. 5 §.5
(2)	1987 s.4(1)(part); 1995 s.75(2), Sch. 5 §.5
(3)	1987 s.4(2); 1995 s.75(3), Sch. 5 §.5
(4)	1987 s.4(3); 1995 s.75(4)
(5)	1987 s.4(4); 1995 s.75(5), Sch. 5 §.5
(6)	1987 s.4(6); 1995 s.75(6), Sch. 5 §.5
(7)	1995 s.75(7)

Section A—Legislation

Provision	Derivation
(8)	1987 s.4(5)
10	1987 s.2; 1995 s.76, Sch. 5 §.3
11	1987 s.6A; 1995 s.77, Sch. 5 §.8
12	1987 s.25; 1995 s.78, Sch. 23
13(1)	1987 s.6B(1); 1995 s.79(1), Sch. 5 §.8
(2)	1987 s.6B(2); 1995 s.79(2), Sch. 5 §.8
(3)	1987 s.6B(3); 1995 s.79(3), Sch. 5 §.8
(4)	1987 s.6B(4); 1995 s.79(4), Sch. 5 §.8
(5)	1987 s.6B(7); 1995 s.79(5), Sch. 5 §.8
(6)	1987 s.6B(6); 1995 s.79(6), Sch. 5 §.8
(7)	1987 s.6B(9); 1995 s.79(7), Sch. 5 §.8
(8)	1987 s.6B(8); 1995 s.79(8), Sch. 5 §.8
(9)	1987 s.6B(5); 1995 Sch. 5 §.8
(10)	1987 s.6B(10); 1995 s.79(9), Sch. 5 §.8
14	1987 s.7; 1994 Sch. 1 §.13; 1995 s.80, Sch. 5 §.9
15	Criminal Justice (International Co-operation) Act 1990 (c. 5) s.15; 1995 s.81
16	1987 s.23; 1995 s.82, Sch. 5 §.21
17(1)	1987 s.26(1); 1995 s.83(1), Sch. 5 §.24
(2)	1987 s.26(1A); 1995 s.83(2), Sch. 5 §.24
(3)	1987 s.26(2); 1995 s.83(3), Sch. 5 §.24
(4)	1987 s.26(3); 1995 s.83(4), Sch. 5 §.24
(5)	1987 s.26(4); 1995 s.83(5), Sch. 5 §.24
(6)	1987 s.26(6), 47(5); 1995 s.83(6), Sch. 5 §.24
(7)	1987 s.47(1); 1995 s.83(7), Sch. 5 §.33
18	1995 s.18
19	1995 s.19
20	1995 s.20
21	1995 s.84
22	1995 s.85
23	1995 s.86
24	1995 s.87
25	1995 s.88
26	1995 s.89
27	1995 s.90
28(1)	1987 s.8(1); 1995 s.91(1), Sch. 5 §.11
(2)	1987 s.8(2); 1995 s.91(2), Sch. 5 §.11
(3)	1987 s.8(7); 1995 s.91(3), Sch. 5 §.11
(4)	1987 s.8(8); 1995 s.91(4), Sch. 5 §.11
(5)	1987 s.10(1); 1994 Sch. 1 §.14; 1995 s.91(5)
(6)	1987 s.10(2); 1995 s.91(6)
(7)	1987 s.8(9); 1995 s.91(7), Sch. 5 §.11
(8)	1987 s.12(1); 1995 s.91(8), Sch. 5 §.14
(9)	1987 s.12(2); 1995 s.91(9)
(10)	1987 s.12(3); 1995 s.91(10), Sch. 5 §.14
29(1)	1995 s.92(1); Drafting
(2)	1987 s.8(3); 1995 s.92(2), Sch. 5 §.11
(3)	1987 s.8(4); 1995 s.92(3), Sch. 5 §.11
(4)	1987 s.8(5); 1995 s.92(4), Sch. 5 §.11
(5)	1987 s.8(6); 1995 s.92(5), Sch. 5 §.11
(6)	1987 s.47(5); 1995 s.92(6), Sch. 5 §.33
(7)	1987 s.8(10); 1995 s.92(7), Sch. 5 §.11
30	1995 s.93
31	1987 s.9; 1995 s.94, Sch. 5 §.11
32	1987 s.11; 1995 s.95, Sch. 5 §.12
33	1987 s.11A; 1995 s.96, Sch. 5 §.13
34	1995 s.97; Drafting
35	1987 s.27; 1994 Sch. 1 §.18; 1995 s.98
36	1987 s.28; 1994 Sch. 1 §.19; 1995 s.99
37	1987 s.28A; 1995 s.100, Sch. 5 §.2

Provision	Derivation
38	1987 s.28B; 1995 s.101, Sch. 5 §.25
39(1)	1987 s.29(1); 1995 s.102(1)
(2)	1987 s.29(2); 1995 s.102(2)
(3)	1987 s.29(3); 1995 s.102(3)
(4)	1987 s.29(3A); 1993 s.22(2)
(5)	1987 s.29(4); 1993 s.21(3); 1995 s.102(4)
40	1987 s.30; Law Reform Miscellaneous Provisions (Scotland) Act 1990 (c. 40) s.63; 1993 s.21(3); 1995 s.103
41	1987 s.30A; Law Reform Miscellaneous Provisions (Scotland) Act 1990 (c. 40) s.63; 1995 s.104
42	1995 s.105
43	1987 s.32; 1995 s.106, Sch. 5 §.27
44	1995 s.107; Drafting
45	1987 s.7A; 1995 s.108, Sch. 5 §.10
46	1987 s.37A; 1995 s.109, Sch. 5 §.32
47(1)	1987 s.45(1); 1995 s.110(4)
(2)	1987 s.45(2); 1995 s.110(5)
(3)	1987 s.45(5); 1995 s.110(7)
(4)	1987 s.45(4); 1995 s.110(6)
48	1987 s.46
49(1)	1995 s.111(1)
(2)	1987 s.1(6); 1988 Sch. 5 §.19; 1990 Sch. 4 §.5; 1993 s.24(13)
(3)	1987 s.1(6)
(4)	1987 s.1(7); 1993 s.24(15)
(5)	1987 s.1(6); 1990 Sch. 4 §.5; 1993 s.24(14)
(6)	1987 ss.5(3), 8(12); 1995 s.111(3), Sch. 5 §s.6, 11
(7)	1987 s.47(6); 1995 s.111(4), Sch. 5 §.33
50(1), (2)	Drafting
(3)–(5)	1995 s.115(4)–(6)
Sch. 1	
§.1	1987 s.13; 1995 Sch. 3 §.1, Sch. 5 §.15
§.2	1987 s.14; 1995 Sch. 3 §.2, Sch. 5 §.16
§.3	1987 s.15; 1995 Sch. 3 §.3
§.4	1987 s.16; 1988 Sch. 5 §.21; 1995 Sch. 3 §.4, Sch. 5 §.17
§.5	1987 s.17; 1995 Sch. 3 §.5, Sch. 5 §.18
§.6	1987 s.18; 1995 Sch. 3 §.6, Sch. 5 §.19
§.7	1987 s.19; 1995 Sch. 3 §.7
§.8	1987 s.20; 1995 Sch. 3 §.8, Sch. 5 §.20
§.9	1987 s.21; 1995 Sch. 3 §.9
§.10	1987 s.26(5), (6), 47(5); 1995 Sch. 3 §.10
§.11	1987 s.22; 1995 Sch. 5 §.11
§.12	1987 s.24; 1995 Sch. 5 §.12
Sch. 2	1
§.1	1987 s.33; Housing Act 1988 (c. 50) Sch. 17 §.81; 1995 Sch. 4 §.1, Sch. 5 §.28
§.2	1987 s.34; 1988 Sch. 5 §.22; Housing Act 1988 (c. 50) Sch. 17 §.81; 1995 Sch. 4 §.2, Sch. 5 §.29
§.3	1987 s.35; 1995 Sch. 4 §.3, Sch. 5 §.30
§.4	1987 s.36; 1995 Sch. 4 §.4, Sch. 5 §.31
§.5	1987 s.37; 1995 Sch. 4 §.5, Sch. 5 §.32
§.6	1987 s.47(1), (4); 1995 Sch. 4 §.6

TABLE OF DESTINATIONS

CRIMINAL JUSTICE (SCOTLAND) ACT 1987
(c.41)

CRIMINAL JUSTICE ACT 1988
(c.33)

HOUSING ACT 1988
(c.50)

1988	1995
Sched. 17,	Sched. 2,
para. 81	para. 1
	para. 2

CRIMINAL JUSTICE (INTERNATIONAL CO-OPERATION) ACT 1990
(c.5)

1990	1995
s.15	s.15
Sched. 4,	
para. 5	49(2)–(5)

LAW REFORM (MISCELLANEOUS PROVISIONS) (SCOTLAND) ACT 1990
(c.40)

1990	1995
s.63	ss.40, 41
Sched. 8,	
para. 37	s.6(1)

CRIMINAL JUSTICE ACT 1993
(c.36)

1993	1995
s.21(3)	ss.39(5), 40
22(2)	39(4)
24(13)	49(2)
(14)	49(5)
(15)	49(4)

DRUG TRAFFICKING ACT 1994
(c.37)

1994	1995
Sched. 1,	
para. 12	s.3
para. 13	14
para. 14	28(5)
para. 18	35
para. 19	36

CRIMINAL JUSTICE (SCOTLAND) ACT 1995
(c.20)

CRIMINAL PROCEDURE (SCOTLAND) ACT 1995

(1995 c. 46)

ARRANGEMENT OF SECTIONS

PART I

CRIMINAL COURTS

JURISDICTION AND POWERS

The High Court

PART II

POLICE FUNCTIONS

Lord Advocate's instructions

Division A—Legislation

83. Transfer of sheriff court solemn proceedings.

Jurors for sittings

84. Juries: returns of jurors and preparation of lists.
85. Juries: citation and attendance of jurors.
86. Jurors: excusal and objections.

Non-availability of judge

87. Non-availability of judge.

Jury for trial

88. Plea of not guilty, balloting and swearing of jury, etc.
89. Jury to be informed of special defence.
90. Death or illness of jurors.

Trial

91. Trial to be continuous.
92. Trial in presence of accused.
93. Record of trial.
94. Transcripts of record and documentary productions.
95. Verdict by judge alone.
96. Amendment of indictment.
97. No case to answer.
98. Defence to speak last.
99. Seclusion of jury to consider verdict.

Verdict and conviction

100. Verdict of jury.
101. Previous convictions: solemn proceedings.
102. Interruption of trial for other proceedings.

PART VIII

APPEALS FROM SOLEMN PROCEEDINGS

103. Appeal sittings.
104. Power of High Court in appeals.
105. Appeal against refusal of application.
106. Right of appeal.
106A. Appeal against automatic sentences where earlier conviction quashed.
107. Leave to appeal.
108. Lord Advocate's appeal against sentence.
108A. Lord Advocate's appeal against decision not to impose automatic sentence in certain cases.
109. Intimation of intention to appeal.
110. Note of appeal.
111. Provisions supplementary to sections 109 and 110.
112. Admission of appellant to bail.
113. Judge's report.
114. Applications made orally or in writing.
115. Presentation of appeal in writing.
116. Abandonment of appeal.
117. Presence of appellant or applicant at hearing.
118. Disposal of appeals.
119. Provision where High Court authorises new prosecution.
120. Appeals: supplementary provisions.
121. Suspension of disqualification, forfeiture, etc.
121A. Suspension of certain sentences pending determination of appeal.
122. Fines and caution.
123. Lord Advocate's reference.
124. Finality of proceedings and Secretary of State's reference.
125. Reckoning of time spent pending appeal.

PART IX

SUMMARY PROCEEDINGS

General

Complaints

Citation

Children

Companies

First diet

Pre-trial procedure

Failure of accused to appear

Non-availability of judge

Trial diet

PART X

APPEALS FROM SUMMARY PROCEEDINGS

General

Stated case

New prosecution

Appeals against sentence

Disposal of appeals

Miscellaneous

PART XA

SCOTTISH CRIMINAL CASES REVIEW COMMISSION

The Scottish Criminal Cases Review Commission

PART XII

EVIDENCE

PART XIV

An Act to consolidate certain enactments relating to criminal procedure in Scotland. [8th November 1995]

PART I

CRIMINAL COURTS

JURISDICTION AND POWERS

The High Court

Judges in the High Court

1.—(1) The Lord President of the Court of Session shall be the Lord Justice General and shall perform his duties as the presiding judge of the High Court.

(2) Every person who is appointed to the office of one of the Senators of the College of Justice in Scotland shall, by virtue of such appointment, be a Lord Commissioner of Justiciary in Scotland.

(3) If any difference arises as to the rotation of judges in the High Court, it shall be determined by the Lord Justice General, whom failing by the Lord Justice Clerk.

(4) Any Lord Commissioner of Justiciary may preside alone at the trial of an accused before the High Court.

(5) Without prejudice to subsection (4) above, in any trial of difficulty or importance it shall be competent for two or more judges in the High Court to preside for the whole or any part of the trial.

Fixing of High Court sittings

2.—(1) The High Court shall sit at such times and places as the Lord Justice General, whom failing the Lord Justice Clerk, may, after consultation with the Lord Advocate, determine.

(2) Without prejudice to subsection (1) above, the High Court shall hold such additional sittings as the Lord Advocate may require.

(3) Where an accused has been cited to attend a sitting of the High Court, the prosecutor may, at any time before the commencement of his trial, apply to the Court to transfer the case to another sitting of the High Court; and a single judge of the High Court may—

(a) after giving the accused or his counsel an opportunity to be heard; or

(b) on the joint application of all parties,

make an order for the transfer of the case.

(4) Where no cases have been indicted for a sitting of the High Court or if it is no longer expedient that a sitting should take place, it shall not be necessary for the sitting to take place.

(5) If any case remains indicted for a sitting which does not take place in pursuance of subsection (4) above, subsection (3) above shall apply in relation to the transfer of any other such case to another sitting.

Solemn courts: general

Jurisdiction and powers of solemn courts

3.—(1) The jurisdiction and powers of all courts of solemn jurisdiction, except so far as altered or modified by any enactment passed after the commencement of this Act, shall remain as at the commencement of this Act.

(2) Any crime or offence which is triable on indictment may be tried by the High Court sitting at any place in Scotland.

(3) The sheriff shall, without prejudice to any other or wider power conferred by statute, not be entitled, on the conviction on indictment of an accused, to pass a sentence of imprisonment for a term exceeding three years.

(4) Subject to subsection (5) below, where under any enactment passed or made before 1st January 1988 (the date of commencement of section 58 of the Criminal Justice (Scotland) Act 1987) an offence is punishable on conviction on indictment by imprisonment for a term exceeding two years but the enactment either expressly or impliedly restricts the power of the sheriff to impose a sentence of imprisonment for a term exceeding two years, it shall be competent for the sheriff to impose a sentence of imprisonment for a term exceeding two but not exceeding three years.

(5) Nothing in subsection (4) above shall authorise the imposition by the sheriff of a sentence in excess of the sentence specified by the enactment as the maximum sentence which may be imposed on conviction of the offence.

(6) Subject to any express exclusion contained in any enactment, it shall be lawful to indict in the sheriff court all crimes except murder, treason, rape and breach of duty by magistrates.

The sheriff

Territorial jurisdiction of sheriff

4.—(1) Subject to the provisions of this section, the jurisdiction of the sheriffs, within their respective sheriffdoms shall extend to and include all navigable rivers, ports, harbours, creeks, shores and anchoring grounds in or adjoining such sheriffdoms and includes all criminal maritime causes and proceedings (including those applying to persons furth of Scotland) provided that the accused is, by virtue of any enactment or rule of law, subject to the jurisdiction of the sheriff before whom the case or proceeding is raised.

(2) Where an offence is alleged to have been committed in one district in a sheriffdom, it shall be competent to try that offence in a sheriff court in any other district in that sheriffdom.

(3) It shall not be competent for the sheriff to try any crime committed on the seas which it would not be competent for him to try if the crime had been committed on land.

(4) The sheriff shall have a concurrent jurisdiction with every other court of summary jurisdiction in relation to all offences competent for trial in such courts.

The sheriff: summary jurisdiction and powers

5.—(1) The sheriff, sitting as a court of summary jurisdiction, shall continue to have all the jurisdiction and powers exercisable by him at the commencement of this Act.

(2) The sheriff shall, without prejudice to any other or wider powers conferred by statute, have power on convicting any person of a common law offence—

(a) to impose a fine not exceeding the prescribed sum;
(b) to ordain the accused to find caution for good behaviour for any period not exceeding 12 months to an amount not exceeding the prescribed sum either in lieu of or in addition to a fine or in addition to imprisonment;
(c) failing payment of such fine, or on failure to find such caution, to award imprisonment in accordance with section 219 of this Act;
(d) to impose imprisonment, for any period not exceeding three months.

(3) Where a person is convicted by the sheriff of—

(a) a second or subsequent offence inferring dishonest appropriation of property, or attempt thereat; or
(b) a second or subsequent offence inferring personal violence,

he may, without prejudice to any wider powers conferred by statute, be sentenced to imprisonment for any period not exceeding six months.

(4) It shall be competent to prosecute summarily in the sheriff court the following offences—

(a) uttering a forged document;
(b) wilful fire-raising;
(c) robbery; and
(d) assault with intent to rob.

District courts

District courts: area, constitution and prosecutor

6.—(1) Each commission area shall be the district of a district court, and the places at which a district court sits and, subject to section 8 of this Act, the days and times when it sits at any given place, shall be determined by the local authority; and in determining where and when a district court should sit, the local authority shall have regard to the desirability of minimising the expense and inconvenience occasioned to those directly involved, whether as parties or witnesses, in the proceedings before the court.

(2) The jurisdiction and powers of the district court shall be exercisable by a stipendiary magistrate or by one or more justices, and no decision of the court shall be questioned on the ground that it was not constituted as

required by this subsection unless objection was taken on that ground by or on behalf of a party to the proceedings not later than the time when the proceedings or the alleged irregularity began.

(3) All prosecutions in a commission area shall proceed at the instance of the procurator fiscal.

(4) The procurator fiscal for an area which includes a commission area shall have all the powers and privileges conferred on a district prosecutor by section 6 of the District Courts (Scotland) Act 1975.

(5) The prosecutions authorised by the said Act of 1975 under complaint by the procurator fiscal shall be without prejudice to complaints at the instance of any other person entitled to make the same.

(6) In this section—

"commission area" means the area of a local authority;

"justice" means a justice of the peace appointed or deemed to have been appointed under section 9 of the said Act of 1975; and

"local authority" means a council constituted under section 2 of the Local Government (Scotland) Act 1994.

District court: jurisdiction and powers

7.—(1) A district court shall continue to have all the jurisdiction and powers exercisable by it at the commencement of this Act.

(2) Where several offences, which if committed in one commission area could be tried under one complaint, are alleged to have been committed in different commission areas, proceedings may be taken for all or any of those offences under one complaint before the district court of any one of such commission areas, and any such offence may be dealt with, heard, tried, determined, adjudged and punished as if the offence had been wholly committed within the jurisdiction of that court.

(3) Except in so far as any enactment (including this Act or an enactment passed after this Act) otherwise provides, it shall be competent for a district court to try any statutory offence which is triable summarily.

(4) It shall be competent, whether or not the accused has been previously convicted of an offence inferring dishonest appropriation of property, for any of the following offences to be tried in the district court—

(a) theft or reset of theft;

(b) falsehood, fraud or wilful imposition;

(c) breach of trust or embezzlement,

where (in any such case) the amount concerned does not exceed level 4 on the standard scale.

(5) A district court when constituted by a stipendiary magistrate shall, in addition to the jurisdiction and powers mentioned in subsection (1) above, have the summary criminal jurisdiction and powers of a sheriff.

(6) The district court shall, without prejudice to any other or wider powers conferred by statute, be entitled on convicting of a common law offence—

(a) to impose imprisonment for any period not exceeding 60 days;

(b) to impose a fine not exceeding level 4 on the standard scale;

(c) to ordain the accused (in lieu of or in addition to such imprisonment or fine) to find caution for good behaviour for any period not exceeding six months and to an amount not exceeding level 4 on the standard scale;

(d) failing payment of such fine or on failure to find such caution, to award imprisonment in accordance with section 219 of this Act,

but in no case shall the total period of imprisonment imposed in pursuance of this subsection exceed 60 days.

(7) Without prejudice to any other or wider power conferred by any enactment, it shall not be competent for a district court, as respects any statutory offence—

(a) to impose a sentence of imprisonment for a period exceeding 60 days;

(b) to impose a fine of an amount exceeding level 4 on the standard scale; or

(c) to ordain an accused person to find caution for any period exceeding six months or to an amount exceeding level 4 on the standard scale.

(8) The district court shall not have jurisdiction to try or to pronounce sentence in the case of any person—

(a) found within its jurisdiction, and brought before it accused or suspected of having committed any offence at any place beyond its jurisdiction; or

(b) brought before it accused or suspected of having committed within its jurisdiction any of the following offences—

(i) murder, culpable homicide, robbery, rape, wilful fire-raising, or attempted wilful fire-raising;

(ii) theft by housebreaking, or housebreaking with intent to steal;

(iii) theft or reset, falsehood fraud or wilful imposition, breach of trust or embezzlement, where the value of the property is an amount exceeding level 4 on the standard scale;

(iv) assault causing the fracture of a limb, assault with intent to ravish, assault to the danger of life, or assault by stabbing;

(v) uttering forged documents or uttering forged bank or banker's notes, or offences under the Acts relating to coinage.

(9) Without prejudice to subsection (8) above, where either in the preliminary investigation or in the course of the trial of any offence it appears that the offence is one which—

(a) cannot competently be tried in the court before which an accused is brought; or

(b) in the opinion of the court in view of the circumstances of the case, should be dealt with by a higher court,

the court may take cognizance of the offence and commit the accused to prison for examination for any period not exceeding four days.

(10) Where an accused is committed as mentioned in subsection (9) above, the prosecutor in the court which commits the accused shall forthwith give notice of the committal to the procurator fiscal of the district within which the offence was committed or to such other official as is entitled to take cognizance of the offence in order that the accused may be dealt with according to law.

Sittings of sheriff and district courts

Sittings of sheriff and district courts

8.—(1) Notwithstanding any enactment or rule of law, a sheriff court or a district court—

(a) shall not be required to sit on any Saturday or Sunday or on a day which by virtue of subsection (2) or (3) below is a court holiday; but

(b) may sit on any day for the disposal of criminal business.

(2) A sheriff principal may in an order made under section 17(1)(b) of the Sheriff Courts (Scotland) Act 1971 prescribe in respect of criminal business not more than 10 days, other than Saturdays and Sundays, in a calendar year as court holidays in the sheriff courts within his jurisdiction; and may in the like manner prescribe as an additional court holiday any day which has been proclaimed, under section 1(3) of the Banking and Financial Dealings Act 1971, to be a bank holiday either throughout the United Kingdom or in a place or locality in the United Kingdom within his jurisdiction.

(3) Notwithstanding section 6(1) of this Act, a sheriff principal may, after consultation with the appropriate local authority, prescribe not more than 10 days, other than Saturdays and Sundays, in a calendar year as court holidays

in the district courts within his jurisdiction; and he may, after such consultation, prescribe as an additional holiday any day which has been proclaimed, under section 1(3) of the said Banking and Financial Dealings Act 1971, to be a bank holiday either throughout the United Kingdom or in a place or locality in the United Kingdom within his jurisdiction.

(4) A sheriff principal may in pursuance of subsection (2) or (3) above prescribe different days as court holidays in relation to different sheriff or district courts.

Territorial jurisdiction: general

Boundaries of jurisdiction

9.—(1) Where an offence is committed in any harbour, river, arm of the sea or other water (tidal or otherwise) which runs between or forms the boundary of the jurisdiction of two or more courts, the offence may be tried by any one of such courts.

(2) Where an offence is committed on the boundary of the jurisdiction of two or more courts, or within the distance of 500 metres of any such boundary, or partly within the jurisdiction of one court and partly within the jurisdiction of another court or courts, the offence may be tried by any one of such courts.

(3) Where an offence is committed against any person or in respect of any property in or on any carriage, cart or vehicle employed in a journey by road or railway, or on board any vessel employed in a river, loch, canal or inland navigation, the offence may be tried by any court through whose jurisdiction the carriage, cart, vehicle or vessel passed in the course of the journey or voyage during which the offence was committed.

(4) Where several offences, which if committed in one sheriff court district could be tried under one indictment or complaint, are alleged to have been committed by any person in different sheriff court districts, the accused may be tried for all or any of those offences under one indictment or complaint before the sheriff of any one of such sheriff court districts.

(5) Where an offence is authorised by this section to be tried by any court, it may be dealt with, heard, tried, determined, adjudged and punished as if the offence had been committed wholly within the jurisdiction of such court.

Crimes committed in different districts

10.—(1) Where a person is alleged to have committed in more than one sheriff court district a crime or crimes to which subsection (2) below applies, he may be indicted to the sheriff court of such one of those districts as the Lord Advocate determines.

(2) This subsection applies to—

(a) a crime committed partly in one sheriff court district and partly in another;

(b) crimes connected with each other but committed in different sheriff court districts;

(c) crimes committed in different sheriff court districts in succession which, if they had been committed in one such district, could have been tried under one indictment.

(3) Where, in pursuance of subsection (1) above, a case is tried in the sheriff court of any sheriff court district, the procurator fiscal of that district shall have power to prosecute in that case even if the crime was in whole or in part committed in a different district, and the procurator fiscal shall have the like powers in relation to such case, whether before, during or after the trial, as he has in relation to a case arising out of a crime or crimes committed wholly within his own district.

Certain offences committed outside Scotland

11.—(1) Any British citizen or British subject who in a country outside the United Kingdom does any act or makes any omission which if done or made in Scotland would constitute the crime of murder or of culpable homicide shall be guilty of the same crime and subject to the same punishment as if the act or omission had been done or made in Scotland.

(2) Any British citizen or British subject employed in the service of the Crown who, in a foreign country, when acting or purporting to act in the course of his employment, does any act or makes any omission which if done or made in Scotland would constitute an offence punishable on indictment shall be guilty of the same offence and subject to the same punishment, as if the act or omission had been done or made in Scotland.

(3) A person may be proceeded against, indicted, tried and punished for an offence to which this section applies—

(a) in any sheriff court district in Scotland in which he is apprehended or is in custody; or

(b) in such sheriff court district as the Lord Advocate may determine, as if the offence had been committed in that district, and the offence shall, for all purposes incidental to or consequential on the trial or punishment thereof, be deemed to have been committed in that district.

(4) Any person who—

(a) has in his possession in Scotland property which he has stolen in any other part of the United Kingdom; or

(b) in Scotland receives property stolen in any other part of the United Kingdom,

may be dealt with, indicted, tried and punished in Scotland in like manner as if he had stolen it in Scotland.

(5) Where a person in any part of the United Kingdom outside Scotland—

(a) steals or attempts to steal any mail-bag or postal packet in the course of its transmission by post, or any of the contents of such a mail-bag or postal packet; or

(b) in stealing or with intent to steal any such mail-bag or postal packet or any of its contents commits any robbery, attempted robbery or assault with intent to rob,

he is guilty of the offence mentioned in paragraph (a) or (b) as if he had committed it in Scotland and shall be liable to be prosecuted, tried and punished there without proof that the offence was committed there.

(6) Any expression used in subsection (5) and in the Postal Services Act 2000 has the same meaning in that subsection as it has in that Act.

NOTE
[1]Inserted by the Postal Services Act 2000 (c.26), s.127(4) and Sched. 8, para. 24. Brought into force by the Postal Services Act 2000 (Commencement No. 1 and Transitional Provisions) Order 2000 (S.I. 2000 No. 2957 (C.88)), art. 2(3) and Sched. 3 (effective March 26, 2001).

Conspiracy to commit offences outside the United Kingdom

11A.—(1) This section applies to any act done by a person in Scotland which would amount to conspiracy to commit an offence but for the fact that the criminal purpose is intended to occur in a country or territory outside the United Kingdom.

(2) Where a person does an act to which this section applies, the criminal purpose shall be treated as the offence mentioned in subsection (1) above and he shall, accordingly, be guilty of conspiracy to commit the offence.

(3) A person is guilty of an offence by virtue of this section only if the criminal purpose would involve at some stage—

(a) an act by him or another party to the conspiracy; or

(b) the happening of some other event,

constituting an offence under the law in force in the country or territory where the act or other event was intended to take place; and conduct punishable under the law in force in the country or territory is an offence under that law for the purposes of this section however it is described in that law.

(4) Subject to subsection (6) below, a condition specified in subsection (3) above shall be taken to be satisfied unless, not later than such time as the High Court may, by Act of Adjournal, prescribe, the accused serves on the prosecutor a notice—

    (a) stating that, on the facts as alleged with respect to the relevant conduct, the condition is not in his opinion satisfied;

    (b) setting out the grounds for his opinion; and

    (c) requiring the prosecutor to prove that the condition is satisfied.

(5) In subsection (4) above "the relevant conduct" means the agreement to effect the criminal purpose.

(6) The court may permit the accused to require the prosecutor to prove that the condition mentioned in subsection (4) above is satisfied without the prior service of a notice under that subsection.

(7) In proceedings on indictment, the question whether a condition is satisfied shall be determined by the judge alone.

(8) Nothing in this section—

    (a) applies to an act done before the day on which the Criminal Justice (Terrorism and Conspiracy) Act 1998 was passed, or

    (b) imposes criminal liability on any person acting on behalf of, or holding office under, the Crown.

PART II

POLICE FUNCTIONS

Lord Advocate's instructions

Instructions by Lord Advocate as to reporting of offences

12. The Lord Advocate may, from time to time, issue instructions to a chief constable with regard to the reporting, for consideration of the question of prosecution, of offences alleged to have been committed within the area of such chief constable, and it shall be the duty of a chief constable to whom any such instruction is issued to secure compliance therewith.

Detention and questioning

Powers relating to suspects and potential witnesses

13.—(1) Where a constable has reasonable grounds for suspecting that a person has committed or is committing an offence at any place, he may require—

    (a) that person, if the constable finds him at that place or at any place where the constable is entitled to be, to give his name and address and may ask him for an explanation of the circumstances which have given rise to the constable's suspicion;

    (b) any other person whom the constable finds at that place or at any place where the constable is entitled to be and who the constable believes has information relating to the offence, to give his name and address.

(2) The constable may require the person mentioned in paragraph (a) of subsection (1) above to remain with him while he (either or both)—

    (a) subject to subsection (3) below, verifies any name and address given by the person;

(b) notes any explanation proffered by the person.

(3) The constable shall exercise his power under paragraph (a) of subsection (2) above only where it appears to him that such verification can be obtained quickly.

(4) A constable may use reasonable force to ensure that the person mentioned in paragraph (a) of subsection (1) above remains with him.

(5) A constable shall inform a person, when making a requirement of that person under—

(a) paragraph (a) of subsection (1) above, of his suspicion and of the general nature of the offence which he suspects that the person has committed or is committing;

(b) paragraph (b) of subsection (1) above, of his suspicion, of the general nature of the offence which he suspects has been or is being committed and that the reason for the requirement is that he believes the person has information relating to the offence;

(c) subsection (2) above, why the person is being required to remain with him;

(d) either of the said subsections, that failure to comply with the requirement may constitute an offence.

(6) A person mentioned in—

(a) paragraph (a) of subsection (1) above who having been required—

    (i) under that subsection to give his name and address; or

    (ii) under subsection (2) above to remain with a constable,

fails, without reasonable excuse, to do so, shall be guilty of an offence and liable on summary conviction to a fine not exceeding level 3 on the standard scale;

(b) paragraph (b) of the said subsection (1) who having been required under that subsection to give his name and address fails, without reasonable excuse, to do so shall be guilty of an offence and liable on summary conviction to a fine not exceeding level 2 on the standard scale.

(7) A constable may arrest without warrant any person who he has reasonable grounds for suspecting has committed an offence under subsection (6) above.

Detention and questioning at police station

14.—(1) Where a constable has reasonable grounds for suspecting that a person has committed or is committing an offence punishable by imprisonment, the constable may, for the purpose of facilitating the carrying out of investigations—

(a) into the offence; and

(b) as to whether criminal proceedings should be instigated against the person,

detain that person and take him as quickly as is reasonably practicable to a police station or other premises and may thereafter for that purpose take him to any other place and, subject to the following provisions of this section, the detention may continue at the police station or, as the case may be, the other premises or place.

(2) Detention under subsection (1) above shall be terminated not more than six hours after it begins or (if earlier)—

(a) when the person is arrested;

(b) when he is detained in pursuance of any other enactment; or

(c) where there are no longer such grounds as are mentioned in the said subsection (1),

and when a person has been detained under subsection (1) above, he shall be informed immediately upon the termination of his detention in accordance with this subsection that his detention has been terminated.

(3) Where a person has been released at the termination of a period of detention under subsection (1) above he shall not thereafter be detained, under that subsection, on the same grounds or on any grounds arising out of the same circumstances.

(4) Subject to subsection (5) below, where a person has previously been detained in pursuance of any other enactment, and is detained under subsection (1) above on the same grounds or on grounds arising from the same circumstances as those which led to his earlier detention, the period of six hours mentioned in subsection (2) above shall be reduced by the length of that earlier detention.

(5) Subsection (4) above shall not apply in relation to detention under section 41(3) of the Prisons (Scotland) Act 1989 (detention in relation to introduction etc. into prison of prohibited article), but where a person was detained under section 41(3) immediately prior to his detention under subsection (1) above the period of six hours mentioned in subsection (2) above shall be reduced by the length of that earlier detention.

(6) At the time when a constable detains a person under subsection (1) above, he shall inform the person of his suspicion, of the general nature of the offence which he suspects has been or is being committed and of the reason for the detention; and there shall be recorded—

    (a) the place where detention begins and the police station or other premises to which the person is taken;

    (b) any other place to which the person is, during the detention, thereafter taken;

    (c) the general nature of the suspected offence;

    (d) the time when detention under subsection (1) above begins and the time of the person's arrival at the police station or other premises;

    (e) the time when the person is informed of his rights in terms of subsection (9) below and of subsection (1)(b) of section 15 of this Act and the identity of the constable so informing him;

    (f) where the person requests such intimation to be sent as is specified in section 15(1)(b) of this Act, the time when such request is—

        (i) made;

        (ii) complied with; and

    (g) the time of the person's release from detention or, where instead of being released he is arrested in respect of the alleged offence, the time of such arrest.

(7) Where a person is detained under subsection (1) above, a constable may—

    (a) without prejudice to any relevant rule of law as regards the admissibility in evidence of any answer given, put questions to him in relation to the suspected offence;

    (b) exercise the same powers of search as are available following an arrest.

(8) A constable may use reasonable force in exercising any power conferred by subsection (1), or by paragraph (b) of subsection (7), above.

(9) A person detained under subsection (1) above shall be under no obligation to answer any question other than to give his name and address, and a constable shall so inform him both on so detaining him and on arrival at the police station or other premises.

Rights of person arrested or detained

15.—(1) Without prejudice to section 17 of this Act, a person who, not being a person in respect of whose custody or detention subsection (4) below applies—

(a) has been arrested and is in custody in a police station or other premises, shall be entitled to have intimation of his custody and of the place where he is being held sent to a person reasonably named by him;

(b) is being detained under section 14 of this Act and has been taken to a police station or other premises or place, shall be entitled to have intimation of his detention and of the police station or other premises or place sent to a solicitor and to one other person reasonably named by him,

without delay or, where some delay is necessary in the interest of the investigation or the prevention of crime or the apprehension of offenders, with no more delay than is so necessary.

(2) A person shall be informed of his entitlement under subsection (1) above—

(a) on arrival at the police station or other premises; or

(b) where he is not arrested, or as the case may be detained, until after such arrival, on such arrest or detention.

(3) Where the person mentioned in paragraph (a) of subsection (1) above requests such intimation to be sent as is specified in that paragraph there shall be recorded the time when such request is—

(a) made;

(b) complied with.

(4) Without prejudice to the said section 17, a constable shall, where a person who has been arrested and is in such custody as is mentioned in paragraph (a) of subsection (1) above or who is being detained as is mentioned in paragraph (b) of that subsection appears to him to be a child, send without delay such intimation as is mentioned in the said paragraph (a), or as the case may be paragraph (b), to that person's parent if known; and the parent—

(a) in a case where there is reasonable cause to suspect that he has been involved in the alleged offence in respect of which the person has been arrested or detained, may; and

(b) in any other case shall,

be permitted access to the person.

(5) The nature and extent of any access permitted under subsection (4) above shall be subject to any restriction essential for the furtherance of the investigation or the well-being of the person.

(6) In subsection (4) above—

(a) "child" means a person under 16 years of age; and

[1](b) "parent" includes guardian and any person who has the care of a child.

NOTE

[1]Substituted by the Crime and Punishment (Scotland) Act 1997 (c. 48) s.62(1) and Sched. 1, para. 21 with effect from August 1, by the Crime and Punishment (Scotland) Act 1997 (Commencement and Transitional Provisions) Order 1997 (S.I. 1997 No. 1712) para. 3.

Drunken persons: power to take to designated place

16.—(1) Where a constable has power to arrest a person without a warrant for any offence and the constable has reasonable grounds for suspecting that that person is drunk, the constable may, if he thinks fit, take him to any place designated by the Secretary of State for the purposes of this section as a place suitable for the care of drunken persons.

(2) A person shall not by virtue of this section be liable to be detained in any such place as is mentioned in subsection (1) above, but the exercise in his case of the power conferred by this section shall not preclude his being charged with any offence.

Right of accused to have access to solicitor

17.—(1) Where an accused has been arrested on any criminal charge, he shall be entitled immediately upon such arrest—
  (a) to have intimation sent to a solicitor that his professional assistance is required by the accused, and informing the solicitor—
      (i) of the place where the person is being detained;
      (ii) whether the person is to be liberated; and
      (iii) if the person is not to be liberated, the court to which he is to be taken and the date when he is to be so taken; and
  (b) to be told what rights there are under—
      (i) paragraph (a) above;
      (ii) subsection (2) below; and
      (iii) section 35(1) and (2) of this Act.
(2) The accused and the solicitor shall be entitled to have a private interview before the examination or, as the case may be, first appearance.

Prints and samples

Prints, samples etc. in criminal investigations

[4]**18.**—(1) This section applies where a person has been arrested and is in custody or is detained under section 14(1) of this Act.
[1,5](2) A constable may take from the person, or require the person to provide him with, such relevant physical data as the constable may, having regard to the circumstances of the suspected offence in respect of which the person has been arrested or detained, reasonably consider it appropriate to take.
[2](3) Subject to subsection (4) below, all record of any relevant physical data taken from or provided by a person under subsection (2) above, all samples taken under subsection (6) below and all information derived from such samples shall be destroyed as soon as possible following a decision not to institute criminal proceedings against the person or on the conclusion of such proceedings otherwise than with a conviction or an order under section 246(3) of this Act.
(4) The duty under subsection (3) above to destroy samples taken under subsection (6) below and information derived from such samples shall not apply—
  (a) where the destruction of the sample or the information could have the effect of destroying any sample, or any information derived therefrom, lawfully held in relation to a person other than the person from whom the sample was taken; or
  (b) where the record, sample or information in question is of the same kind as a record, a sample or, as the case may be, information lawfully held by or on behalf of any police force in relation to the person.
(5) No sample, or information derived from a sample, retained by virtue of subsection (4) above shall be used—
  (a) in evidence against the person from whom the sample was taken; or
  (b) for the purposes of the investigation of any offence.
(6) A constable may, with the authority of an officer of a rank no lower than inspector, take from the person—
  (a) from the hair of an external part of the body other than pubic hair, by means of cutting, combing or plucking, a sample of hair or other material;
  (b) from a fingernail or toenail or from under any such nail, a sample of nail or other material;

   (c) from an external part of the body, by means of swabbing or rubbing, a sample of blood or other body fluid, of body tissue or of other material;

   (d) from the inside of the mouth, by means of swabbing, a sample of saliva or other material.

     (7) A constable may use reasonable force in exercising any power conferred by subsection (2) or (6) above.

     [3](7A) For the purposes of this section and sections 19 and 20 of this Act "relevant physical data" means any—

   (a) fingerprint;

   (b) palm print;

   (c) print or impression other than those mentioned in paragraph (a) and (b) above, of an external part of the body;

   (d) record of a person's on an external part of the body created by a device approved by the Secretary of State.

   (7B) The Secretary of State by order made by statutory instrument may approve a device for the purpose of creating such records as are mentioned in paragraph (d) of subsection (7A) above.

   (8) Nothing in this section shall prejudice—

   (a) any power of search;

   (b) any power to take possession of evidence where there is imminent danger of its being lost or destroyed; or

   (c) any power to take prints, impressions or samples under the authority of a warrant.

NOTES

[1]Substituted by the Crime and Punishment (Scotland) Act 1997 (c. 48), s.47(1))(a) with effect from August 1, 1997 in terms of the Crime and Punishment (Scotland) ACt 1997 (Commencement and Transitional Provisions) Order 1997 (S.I. 1997 No. 1712) para. 3.

[2]Substituted by the Crime and Disorder Act 1998 (c. 37), Sched. 8, para. 117(1) and (2) (effective August 1, 1997: S.I. 1998 No. 2327).

[3]Inserted by s.47(1)(d) of the 1997 Act with effect from August 1, 1997 in terms of the Order above.

[4]Prospectively amended by the Terrorism Act 2000 (c.11), s.47 and Sched. 8, para. 20(1).

[5]Prospectively substituted by the Terrorism Act 2000 (c.11), s.47 and Sched. 8, para. 20(2).

Prints, samples etc. in criminal investigations: supplementary provisions

   19.—(1) This section applies where a person convicted of an offence—

[1](a) has not, since the conviction, had taken from him, or been required to provide, any relevant physical data or had any impression or sample taken from him; or

[1](b) has at any time had—

     (i) taken from him or been required (whether under paragraph (a) above or under section 18 or 19A of this Act or otherwise) to provide any physical data; or

     (ii) any impression or sample taken from him,

   which was not suitable for the means of analysis for which the data were taken or required or the impression or sample was taken or, though suitable, was insufficient (either in quantity or in quality) to enable information to be obtained by that means of analysis.

   (2) Where this section applies, a constable may, within the permitted period—

[2](a) take from on require the convicted person to provide him with such relevant physical data as he reasonably considers it appropriate to take or, as the case may be, require the provision of;

   (b) with the authority of an officer of a rank no lower than inspector, take from the person any sample mentioned in any of paragraphs (a) to (d) of subsection (6) of section 18 of this Act by the means specified in that paragraph in relation to that sample.

(3) A constable—

(a) may require the convicted person to attend a police station for the purposes of subsection (2) above;

(b) may, where the convicted person is in legal custody by virtue of section 295 of this Act, exercise the powers conferred by subsection (2) above in relation to the person in the place where he is for the time being.

(4) In subsection (2) above, "the permitted period" means—

(a) in a case to which paragraph (a) of subsection (1) above applies, the period of one month beginning with the date of the conviction;

³(b) in a case to which paragraph (b) of that subsection applies, the period of one month beginning with the date on which a constable of the police force which instructed the analysis receives written intimation that the relevant physical data were or the sample was unsuitable or, as the case may be, insufficient as mentioned in that paragraph.

(5) A requirement under subsection (3)(a) above—

(a) shall give the person at least seven days' notice of the date on which he is required to attend;

(b) may direct him to attend at a specified time of day or between specified times of day.

(6) Any constable may arrest without warrant a person who fails to comply with a requirement under subsection (3)(a) above.

Notes

¹Substituted by the Crime and Punishment (Scotland) Act 1997 (c. 48) s.47(2)(a) with effect from August 1, 1997 in terms of the Crime and Punishment (Scotland) Act 1997 (Commencement and Transitional Provisions) Order 1997 (S.I. 1997 No. 1712) para. 3

²Substituted by the above Act s.47(2)(b) with effect from August 1, 1997 as provided by the Order above.

³Amended by the above Act s.47(2)(c) with effect from August 1, 1997 as provided by the Order above.

Use of prints, samples etc.

20. Without prejudice to any power to do so apart from this section, relevant physical data, impressions and samples lawfully held by or on behalf of any police force or in connection with or as a result of an investigation of an offence and information derived therefrom may be checked against other such data, impressions, samples and information.

Schedule 1 offences

Schedule 1 offences: power of constable to take offender into custody

21.—(1) Without prejudice to any other powers of arrest, a constable may take into custody without warrant—

(a) any person who within his view commits any of the offences mentioned in Schedule 1 to this Act, if the constable does not know and cannot ascertain his name and address;

(b) any person who has committed, or whom he had reason to believe to have committed, any of the offences mentioned in that Schedule, if the constable does not know and cannot ascertain his name and address or has reasonable ground for believing that he will abscond.

(2) Where a person has been arrested under this section, the officer in charge of a police station may—

(a) liberate him upon a written undertaking, signed by him and certified by the said officer, in terms of which that person undertakes to appear at a specified court at a specified time; or

(b) liberate him without any such undertaking; or

(c) refuse to liberate him, and such refusal and the detention of that person until his case is tried in the usual form shall not subject the officer to any claim whatsoever.

(3) A person in breach of an undertaking given by him under subsection (2)(a) above without reasonable excuse shall be guilty of an offence and liable to the following penalties—

(a) a fine not exceeding level 3 on the standard scale; and

(b) imprisonment for a period—

    (i) where conviction is in the district court, not exceeding 60 days; or

    (ii) in any other case, not exceeding 3 months.

(4) The penalties provided for in subsection (3) above may be imposed in addition to any other penalty which it is competent for the court to impose, notwithstanding that the total of penalties imposed may exceed the maximum penalty which it is competent to impose in respect of the original offence.

(5) In any proceedings relating to an offence under this section, a writing, purporting to be such an undertaking as is mentioned in subsection (2)(a) above and bearing to be signed and certified, shall be sufficient evidence of the terms of the undertaking given by the arrested person.

Police liberation

Liberation by police

22.—(1) Where a person has been arrested and charged with an offence which may be tried summarily, the officer in charge of a police station may—

(a) liberate him upon a written undertaking, signed by him and certified by the officer, in terms of which the person undertakes to appear at a specified court at a specified time; or

(b) liberate him without any such undertaking; or

(c) refuse to liberate him.

(2) A person in breach of an undertaking given by him under subsection (1) above without reasonable excuse shall be guilty of an offence and liable on summary conviction to the following penalties—

(a) a fine not exceeding level 3 on the standard scale; and

(b) imprisonment for a period—

    (i) where conviction is in the district court, not exceeding 60 days; or

    (ii) where conviction is in the sheriff court, not exceeding 3 months.

(3) The refusal of the officer in charge to liberate a person under subsection (1)(c) above and the detention of that person until his case is tried in the usual form shall not subject the officer to any claim whatsoever.

(4) The penalties provided for in subsection (2) above may be imposed in addition to any other penalty which it is competent for the court to impose, notwithstanding that the total of penalties imposed may exceed the maximum penalty which it is competent to impose in respect of the original offence.

(5) In any proceedings relating to an offence under this section, a writing, purporting to be such an undertaking as is mentioned in subsection (1)(a) above and bearing to be signed and certified, shall be sufficient evidence of the terms of the undertaking given by the arrested person.

PART III

BAIL

Consideration of bail on first appearance

[1]**22A.**—(1) On the first occasion on which—

(a) a person accused on petition is brought before the sheriff prior to committal until liberated in due course of law; or

(b) a person charged on complaint with an offence is brought before a judge having jurisdiction to try the offence,

the sheriff or, as the case may be, the judge shall, after giving that person and the prosecutor an opportunity to be heard and within the period specified in subsection (2) below, either admit or refuse to admit that person to bail.

(2) That period is the period of 24 hours beginning with the time when the person accused or charged is brought before the sheriff or judge.

(3) If, by the end of that period, the sheriff or judge has not admitted or refused to admit the person accused or charged to bail, then that person shall be forthwith liberated.

(4) This section applies whether or not the person accused or charged is in custody when that person is brought before the sheriff or judge.

NOTE
[1]Inserted by the Bail, Judicial Appointments etc. (Scotland) Act 2000 (asp 9), s.1.

Bail applications

23.—[1](1) Any person accused on petition of a crime shall be entitled immediately, on any (other than the first) occasion on which he is brought before the sheriff prior to his committal until liberated in due course of law, to apply to the sheriff for bail, and the prosecutor shall be entitled to be heard against any such application.

(2) The sheriff shall be entitled in his discretion to refuse such application before the person accused is committed until liberated in due course of law.

(3) Where an accused is admitted to bail without being committed until liberated in due course of law, it shall not be necessary so to commit him, and it shall be lawful to serve him with an indictment or complaint without his having been previously so committed.

(4) Where bail is refused before committal until liberation in due course of law on an application under subsection (1) above, the application for bail may be renewed after such committal.

[2](5) Any sheriff having jurisdiction to try the offence or to commit the accused until liberated in due course of law may, at his discretion, on the application of any person who has been committed until liberation in due course of law for any crime or offence, and having given the prosecutor an opportunity to be heard, admit or refuse to admit the person to bail.

[3](6) Any person charged on complaint with an offence shall, on any (other than the first) occasion on which he is brought before a judge having jurisdiction to try the offence, be entitled to apply to the judge for bail and the prosecutor shall be entitled to be heard against any such application.

(7) An application under subsection (5) or (6) above shall be disposed of within 24 hours after its presentation to the judge, failing which the accused shall be forthwith liberated.

(8) This section applies whether or not the accused is in custody at the time he appears for disposal of his application.

NOTES
[1]As amended by the Bail, Judicial Appointments etc. (Scotland) Act (asp 9), s.12 and Sched., para. 7(1)(a).

[2]As amended by the Bail, Judicial Appointments etc. (Scotland) Act (asp 9), s.12 and Sched., para. 7(1)(b).
[3]Substituted by the Bail, Judicial Appointments etc. (Scotland) Act (asp 9), s.12 and Sched., para. 7(1)(c).

Bail and liberation where person already in custody

[1]**23A.**—(1) A person may be admitted to bail under section 22A or 23 of this Act although in custody—
    (a) having been refused bail in respect of another crime or offence; or
    (b) serving a sentence of imprisonment.
(2) A decision to admit a person to bail by virtue of subsection (1) above does not liberate the person from the custody mentioned in that subsection.
(3) The liberation under section 22A(3) or 23(7) of this Act of a person who may be admitted to bail by virtue of subsection (1) above does not liberate that person from the custody mentioned in that subsection.

NOTE
[1]Inserted by the Bail, Judicial Appointments etc. (Scotland) Act 2000 (asp 9), s.1.

Bail and bail conditions

24.—[1](1) All crimes and offences are bailable.
(2) Nothing in this Act shall affect the right of the Lord Advocate or the High Court to admit to bail any person charged with any crime or offence.
(3) It shall not be lawful to grant bail or release for a pledge or deposit of money, and—
    (a) release on bail may be granted only on conditions which subject to subsection (6) below, shall not include a pledge or deposit of money;
    (b) liberation may be granted by the police under section 21, 22 or 43 of this Act.
(4) In granting bail the court or, as the case may be, the Lord Advocate shall impose on the accused—
    (a) the standard conditions; and
    (b) such further conditions as the court or, as the case may be, the Lord Advocate considers necessary to secure—
        (i) that the standard conditions are observed; and
        (ii) that the accused makes himself available for the purpose of participating in an identification parade or of enabling any print, impression or sample to be taken from him.
(5) The standard conditions referred to in subsection (4) above are conditions that the accused—
    (a) appears at the appointed time at every diet relating to the offence with which he is charged of which he is given due notice;
    (b) does not commit an offence while on bail;
    (c) does not interfere with witnesses or otherwise obstruct the course of justice whether in relation to himself or any other person; and
    (d) makes himself available for the purpose of enabling enquiries or a report to be made to assist the court in dealing with him for the offence with which he is charged.
(6) The court or, as the case may be, the Lord Advocate may impose as one of the conditions of release on bail a requirement that the accused or a cautioner on his behalf deposits a sum of money in court, but only where the court or, as the case may be, the Lord Advocate is satisfied that the imposition of such condition is appropriate to the special circumstances of the case.
(7) In any enactment, including this Act and any enactment passed after this Act—

(a) any reference to bail shall be construed as a reference to release on conditions in accordance with this Act or to conditions imposed on bail, as the context requires;

(b) any reference to an amount of bail fixed shall be construed as a reference to conditions, including a sum required to be deposited under subsection (6) above;

(c) any reference to finding bail or finding sufficient bail shall be construed as a reference to acceptance of conditions imposed or the finding of a sum required to be deposited under subsection (6) above.

(8) In this section and sections 25 and 27 to 29 of this Act, references to an accused and to appearance at a diet shall include references respectively to an appellant and to appearance at the court on the day fixed for the hearing of an appeal.

NOTE
[1]As amended by the Bail, Judicial Appointments etc. (Scotland) Act 2000 (asp 9), s.3(1).

Bail conditions: supplementary

25.—(1) The court shall specify in the order granting bail, a copy of which shall be given to the accused—

(a) the conditions imposed; and

(b) an address, within the United Kingdom (being the accused's normal place of residence or such other place as the court may, on cause shown, direct) which, subject to subsection (2) below, shall be his proper domicile of citation.

(2) The court may on application in writing by the accused while he is on bail alter the address specified in the order granting bail, and this new address shall, as from such date as the court may direct, become his proper domicile of citation; and the court shall notify the accused of its decision on any application under this subsection.

(3) In this section "proper domicile of citation" means the address at which the accused may be cited to appear at any diet relating to the offence with which he is charged or an offence charged in the same proceedings as that offence or to which any other intimation or document may be sent; and any citation at or the sending of an intimation or document to the proper domicile of citation shall be presumed to have been duly carried out.

Bail: circumstances where not available

26.—[*Deleted by s.4 of the Bail, Judicial Appointments etc. (Scotland) Act 2000 (asp 9)*]

Breach of bail conditions: offences

27.—(1) Subject to subsection (7) below, an accused who having been granted bail fails without reasonable excuse—

(a) to appear at the time and place appointed for any diet of which he has been given due notice; or

(b) to comply with any other condition imposed on bail,

shall, subject to subsection (3) below, be guilty of an offence and liable on conviction to the penalties specified in subsection (2) below.

(2) The penalties mentioned in subsection (1) above are—

(a) a fine not exceeding level 3 on the standard scale; and

(b) imprisonment for a period—

(i) where conviction is in the district court, not exceeding 60 days; or

(ii) in any other case, not exceeding 3 months.

(3) Where, and to the extent that, the failure referred to in subsection (1)(b) above consists in the accused having committed an offence while on

bail (in this section referred to as "the subsequent offence"), he shall not be guilty of an offence under that subsection but, subject to subsection (4) below, the court which sentences him for the subsequent offence shall, in determining the appropriate sentence or disposal for that offence, have regard to—

    (a) the fact that the offence was committed by him while on bail and the number of bail orders to which he was subject when the offence was committed;

    (b) any previous conviction of the accused of an offence under subsection (1)(b) above; and

    (c) the extent to which the sentence or disposal in respect of any previous conviction of the accused differed, by virtue of this subsection, from that which the court would have imposed but for this subsection.

    (4) The court shall not, under subsection (3) above, have regard to the fact that the subsequent offence was committed while the accused was on bail unless that fact is libelled in the indictment or, as the case may be, specified in the complaint.

    [1](4A) The fact that the subsequent offence was committed while the accused was on bail shall, unless challenged—

    (a) in the case of proceedings on indictment, by giving notice of a preliminary objection under paragraph (b) of section 72(1) of this Act or under that paragraph as applied by section 71(2) of this Act; or

    (b) in summary proceedings, by preliminary objection before his plea is recorded,

be held as admitted.

    (5) Where the maximum penalty in respect of the subsequent offence is specified by or by virtue of any enactment, that maximum penalty shall, for the purposes of the court's determination, by virtue of subsection (3) above, of the appropriate sentence or disposal in respect of that offence, be increased—

    (a) where it is a fine, by the amount for the time being equivalent to level 3 on the standard scale; and

    (b) where it is a period of imprisonment—

        (i) as respects a conviction in the High Court or the sheriff court, by 6 months; and

        (ii) as respects a conviction in the district court, by 60 days,

notwithstanding that the maximum penalty as so increased exceeds the penalty which it would otherwise be competent for the court to impose.

    (6) Where the sentence or disposal in respect of the subsequent offence is, by virtue of subsection (3) above, different from that which the court would have imposed but for that subsection, the court shall state the extent of and the reasons for that difference.

    (7) An accused who having been granted bail in relation to solemn proceedings fails without reasonable excuse to appear at the time and place appointed for any diet of which he has been given due notice (where such diet is in respect of solemn proceedings) shall be guilty of an offence and liable on conviction on indictment to the following penalties—

    (a) a fine; and

    (b) imprisonment for a period not exceeding two years.

    (8) At any time before the trial of an accused under solemn procedure for the original offence, it shall be competent—

    (a) to amend the indictment to include an additional charge of an offence under this section;

    (b) to include in the list of witnesses or productions relating to the original offence, witnesses or productions relating to the offence under this section.

    (9) The penalties provided for in subsection (2) above may be imposed in addition to any other penalty which it is competent for the court to impose,

notwithstanding that the total of penalties imposed may exceed the maximum penalty which it is competent to impose in respect of the original offence.

(10) A court which finds an accused guilty of an offence under this section may remit the accused for sentence in respect of that offence to any court which is considering the original offence.

(11) In this section "the original offence" means the offence with which the accused was charged when he was granted bail or an offence charged in the same proceedings as that offence.

NOTE
[1]Inserted by the Criminal Procedure and Investigations Act 1996 (c. 25), s.73(2).

Breach of bail conditions: arrest of offender, etc.

28.—(1) A constable may arrest without warrant an accused who has been released on bail where the constable has reasonable grounds for suspecting that the accused has broken, is breaking, or is likely to break any condition imposed on his bail.

(2) An accused who is arrested under this section shall wherever practicable be brought before the court to which his application for bail was first made not later than in the course of the first day after his arrest, such day not being, subject to subsection (3) below, a Saturday, a Sunday or a court holiday prescribed for that court under section 8 of this Act.

(3) Nothing in subsection (2) above shall prevent an accused being brought before a court on a Saturday, a Sunday or such a court holiday where the court is, in pursuance of the said section 8, sitting on such day for the disposal of criminal business.

(4) Where an accused is brought before a court under subsection (2) or (3) above, the court, after hearing the parties, may—

(a) recall the order granting bail;
(b) release the accused under the original order granting bail; or
(c) vary the order granting bail so as to contain such conditions as the court thinks it necessary to impose to secure that the accused complies with the requirements of paragraphs (a) to (d) of section 24(5) of this Act.

(5) The same rights of appeal shall be available against any decision of the court under subsection (4) above as were available against the original order of the court relating to bail.

(6) For the purposes of this section and section 27 of this Act, an extract from the minute of proceedings, containing the order granting bail and bearing to be signed by the clerk of court, shall be sufficient evidence of the making of that order and of its terms and of the acceptance by the accused of the conditions imposed under section 24 of this Act.

Bail: monetary conditions

29.—(1) Without prejudice to section 27 of this Act, where the accused or a cautioner on his behalf has deposited a sum of money in court under section 24(6) of this Act, then—

(a) if the accused fails to appear at the time and place appointed for any diet of which he has been given due notice, the court may, on the motion of the prosecutor, immediately order forfeiture of the sum deposited;
(b) if the accused fails to comply with any other condition imposed on bail, the court may, on conviction of an offence under section 27(1)(b) of this Act and on the motion of the prosecutor, order forfeiture of the sum deposited.

(2) If the court is satisfied that it is reasonable in all the circumstances to do so, it may recall an order made under subsection (1)(a) above and direct that

the money forfeited shall be refunded, and any decision of the court under this subsection shall be final and not subject to review.

(3) A cautioner, who has deposited a sum of money in court under section 24(6) of this Act, shall be entitled, subject to subsection (4) below, to recover the sum deposited at any diet of the court at which the accused appears personally.

(4) Where the accused has been charged with an offence under section 27(1)(b) of this Act, nothing in subsection (3) above shall entitle a cautioner to recover the sum deposited unless and until—

(a) the charge is not proceeded with; or
(b) the accused is acquitted of the charge; or
(c) on the accused's conviction of the offence, the court has determined not to order forfeiture of the sum deposited.

(5) The references in subsections (1)(b) and (4)(c) above to conviction of an offence shall include references to the making of an order in respect of the offence under section 246(3) of this Act.

Bail review

30.—(1) This section applies where a court has refused to admit a person to bail or, where a court has so admitted a person, the person has failed to accept the conditions imposed or that a sum required to be deposited under section 24(6) of this Act has not been so deposited.

(2) A court shall, on the application of any person mentioned in subsection (1) above, have power to review its decision to admit to bail or its decision as to the conditions imposed and may, on cause shown, admit the person to bail or, as the case may be, fix bail on different conditions.

(3) An application under this section, where it relates to the original decision of the court, shall not be made before the fifth day after that decision and, where it relates to a subsequent decision, before the fifteenth day thereafter.

(4) Nothing in this section shall affect any right of a person to appeal against the decision of a court in relation to admitting to bail or to the conditions imposed.

Bail review on prosecutor's application

31.—(1) On an application by the prosecutor at any time after a court has granted bail to a person the court may, where the prosecutor puts before the court material information which was not available to it when it granted bail to that person, review its decision.

(2) On receipt of an application under subsection (1) above the court shall—

(a) intimate the application to the person granted bail;
(b) fix a diet for hearing the application and cite that person to attend the diet; and
(c) where it considers that the interests of justice so require, grant warrant to arrest that person.

(3) On hearing an application under subsection (1) above the court may—

(a) withdraw the grant of bail and remand the person in question in custody; or
(b) grant bail, or continue the grant of bail, either on the same or on different conditions.

(4) Nothing in the foregoing provisions of this section shall affect any right of appeal against the decision of a court in relation to bail.

Bail appeal

32.—[1](1) Where, in any case, bail is refused or where the accused is dissatisfied with the amount of bail fixed, he may appeal to the High Court which may, in its discretion order intimation to the Lord Advocate or, as the case may be, the prosecutor.

³(2) Where, in any case, is granted, or, in summary proceedings an accused is ordained to appear, the public prosecutor, if dissatisfied—

(a) with the decision allowing bail;

(b) with the amount of bail fixed; or

(c) in summary proceedings, that the accused has been ordained to appear,

may appeal to the High Court, and the applicant shall not be liberated, subject to subsection (7) below, until the appeal by the prosecutor is disposed of.

(3) Written notice of appeal shall be immediately given to the opposite party by a party appealing under this section.

(4) An appeal under this section shall be disposed of by the High Court or any Lord Commissioner of Justiciary in court or in chambers after such inquiry and hearing of parties as shall seem just.

²(5) Where an accused in an appeal under this section is under 21 years of age, section 51 of this Act shall apply to the High Court or, as the case may be, the Lord Commissioner of Justiciary when disposing of the appeal as it applies to a court when remanding or committing a person of the accused's age for trial or sentence.

(6) In the event of the appeal of the public prosecutor under this section being refused, the court may award expenses against him.

²(7) When an appeal is taken by the public prosecutor either against the grant of bail or against the amount fixed, the accused to whom bail has been granted shall, if the bail fixed has been found by him, be liberated after 72 hours from the granting of the bail, whether the appeal has been disposed of or not, unless the High Court grants an order for his further detention in custody.

(8) In computing the period mentioned in subsection (7) above, Sundays and public holidays, whether general or court holidays, shall be excluded.

(9) When an appeal is taken under this section by the prosecutor in summary proceedings against the fact that the accused has been ordained to appear, subsections (7) and (8) above shall apply as they apply in the case of an appeal against the granting of bail or the amount fixed.

(10) Notice to the governor of the prison of the issue of an order such as is mentioned in subsection (7) above within the time mentioned in that subsection bearing to be sent by the Clerk of Justiciary or the Crown Agent shall be sufficient warrant for the detention of the applicant pending arrival of the order in due course of post.

NOTES

¹Substituted by the Bail, Judicial Appointments etc. (Scotland) Act 2000 (asp 9), s.4.

²As amended by the Bail, Judicial Appointments etc. (Scotland) Act 2000 (asp 9), s.12 and Sched., para. 7(2)(a).

³As amended by the Bail, Judicial Appointments etc. (Scotland) Act 2000 (asp 9), s.12 and Sched., para. 7(2)(b).

Bail: no fees exigible

33. No clerks fees, court fees or other fees or expenses shall be exigible from or awarded against an accused in respect of a decision on bail under section 22A above, an application for bail or of the appeal of such a decision or application to the High Court.

NOTE

¹As amended by the Bail, Judicial Appointments etc. (Scotland) Act (asp 9), s.12 and Sched., para. 7(3)(a) and (b).

PART IV

PETITION PROCEDURE

Warrants

Petition for warrant

34.—(1) A petition for warrant to arrest and commit a person suspected of or charged with crime may be in the forms—
  (a) set out in Schedule 2 to this Act; or
  (b) prescribed by Act of Adjournal,
or as nearly as may be in such form; and Schedule 3 to this Act shall apply to any such petition as it applies to the indictment.
  (2) If on the application of the procurator fiscal, a sheriff is satisfied that there is reasonable ground for suspecting that an offence has been or is being committed by a body corporate, the sheriff shall have the like power to grant warrant for the citation of witnesses and the production of documents and articles as he would have if a petition charging an individual with the commission of the offence were presented to him.

Judicial examination

Judicial examination

35.—(1) The accused's solicitor shall be entitled to be present at the examination.
  (2) The sheriff may delay the examination for a period not exceeding 48 hours from and after the time of the accused's arrest, in order to allow time for the attendance of the solicitor.
  (3) Where the accused is brought before the sheriff for examination on any charge and he or his solicitor intimates that he does not desire to emit a declaration in regard to such a charge, it shall be unnecessary to take a declaration, and, subject to section 36 of this Act, the accused may be committed for further examination or until liberated in due course of law without a declaration being taken.
  (4) Nothing in subsection (3) above shall prejudice the right of the accused subsequently to emit a declaration on intimating to the prosecutor his desire to do so; and that declaration shall be taken in further examination.
  (5) Where, subsequent to examination or further examination on any charge, the prosecutor desires to question the accused as regards an extrajudicial confession, whether or not a full admission, allegedly made by him to or in the hearing of a constable, which is relevant to the charge and as regards which he has not previously been examined, the accused may be brought before the sheriff for further examination.
  (6) Where the accused is brought before the sheriff for further examination the sheriff may delay that examination for a period not exceeding 24 hours in order to allow time for the attendance of the accused's' solicitor.
  (7) Any proceedings before the sheriff in examination or further examination shall be conducted in chambers and outwith the presence of any co-accused.
  (8) This section applies to procedure on petition, without prejudice to the accused being tried summarily by the sheriff for any offence in respect of which he has been committed until liberated in due course of law.

Judicial examination: questioning by prosecutor

36.—(1) Subject to the following provisions of this section, an accused on being brought before the sheriff for examination on any charge (whether the first or a further examination) may be questioned by the prosecutor in so far as such questioning is directed towards eliciting any admission, denial, explanation, justification or comment which the accused may have as regards anything to which subsections (2) to (4) below apply.

(2) This subsection applies to matters averred in the charge, and the particular aims of a line of questions under this subsection shall be to determine—

    (a) whether any account which the accused can give ostensibly discloses a defence; and

    (b) the nature and particulars of that defence.

(3) This subsection applies to the alleged making by the accused, to or in the hearing of a constable, of an extrajudicial confession (whether or not a full admission) relevant to the charge, and questions under this subsection may only be put if the accused has, before the examination, received from the prosecutor or from a constable a written record of the confession allegedly made.

(4) This subsection applies to what is said in any declaration emitted in regard to the charge by the accused at examination.

(5) The prosecutor shall, in framing questions in exercise of his power under subsection (1) above, have regard to the following principles—

    (a) the question should not be designed to challenge the truth of anything said by the accused;

    (b) there should be no reiteration of a question which the accused has refused to answer at the examination; and

    (c) there should be no leading questions,

and the sheriff shall ensure that all questions are fairly put to, and understood by, the accused.

(6) The accused shall be told by the sheriff—

    (a) where he is represented by a solicitor at the judicial examination, that he may consult that solicitor before answering any question; and

    (b) that if he answers any question put to him at the examination under this section in such a way as to disclose an ostensible defence, the prosecutor shall be under the duty imposed by subsection (10) below.

(7) With the permission of the sheriff, the solicitor for the accused may ask the accused any question the purpose of which is to clarify any ambiguity in an answer given by the accused to the prosecutor at the examination or to give the accused an opportunity to answer any question which he has previously refused to answer.

(8) An accused may decline to answer a question under subsection (1) above; and, where he is subsequently tried on the charge mentioned in that subsection or on any other charge arising out of the circumstances which gave rise to the charge so mentioned, his having so declined may be commented upon by the prosecutor, the judge presiding at the trial, or any co-accused, only where and in so far as the accused (or any witness called on his behalf) in evidence avers something which could have been stated appropriately in answer to that question.

(9) The procedure in relation to examination under this section shall be prescribed by Act of Adjournal.

(10) Without prejudice to any rule of law, on the conclusion of an examination under this section the prosecutor shall secure the investigation, to such extent as is reasonably practicable, of any ostensible defence disclosed in the course of the examination.

(11) The duty imposed by subsection (10) above shall not apply as respects

any ostensible defence which is not reasonably capable of being investigated.

Judicial examination: record of proceedings

37.—(1) The prosecutor shall provide for a verbatim record to be made by means of shorthand notes or by mechanical means of all questions to and answers and declarations by the accused in examination, or further examination, under sections 35 and 36 of this Act.

(2) A shorthand writer shall—

(a) sign the shorthand notes taken by him of the questions, answers and declarations mentioned in subsection (1) above and certify the notes as being complete and correct; and

(b) retain the notes.

(3) A person recording the questions, answers and declarations mentioned in subsection (1) above by mechanical means shall—

(a) certify that the record is true and complete;

(b) specify in the certificate the proceedings to which the record relates; and

(c) retain the record.

(4) The prosecutor shall require the person who made the record mentioned in subsection (1) above, or such other competent person as he may specify, to make a transcript of the record in legible form; and that person shall—

(a) comply with the requirement;

(b) certify the transcript as being a complete and correct transcript of the record purporting to have been made and certified, and in the case of shorthand notes signed, by the person who made the record; and

(c) send the transcript to the prosecutor.

(5) A transcript certified under subsection (4)(b) above shall, subject to section 38(1) of this Act, be deemed for all purposes to be a complete and correct record of the questions, answers and declarations mentioned in subsection (1) above.

(6) Subject to subsections (7) to (9) below, within 14 days of the date of examination or further examination, the prosecutor shall—

(a) serve a copy of the transcript on the accused examined; and

(b) serve a further such copy on the solicitor (if any) for that accused.

(7) Where at the time of further examination a trial diet is already fixed and the interval between the further examination and that diet is not sufficient to allow of the time limits specified in subsection (6) above and subsection (1) of section 38 of this Act, the sheriff shall (either or both)—

(a) direct that those subsections shall apply in the case with such modifications as to time limits as he shall specify;

(b) subject to subsection (8) below, postpone the trial diet.

(8) Postponement under paragraph (b) of subsection (7) above alone shall only be competent where the sheriff considers that to proceed under paragraph (a) of that subsection alone, or paragraphs (a) and (b) together, would not be practicable.

[1](9) Any time limit mentioned in subsection (6) above and subsection (1) of section 38 of this Act (including any such time limit as modified by a direction under subsection (7) above) may be extended, in respect of the case, by the High Court; and an application to the High Court for any such extension shall be disposed of by the High Court or any Lord Commissioner of Justiciary in court or in chambers.

(10) A copy of—

(a) a transcript required by paragraph (a) of subsection (6) above to be served on an accused or by paragraph (b) of that subsection to be served on his solicitor; or

(b) a notice required by paragraph (a) of section 38(1) of this Act to be served on an accused or on the prosecutor,

shall be served in such manner as may be prescribed by Act of Adjournal; and a written execution purporting to be signed by the person who served such transcript or notice, together with, where appropriate, the relevant post office receipt shall be sufficient evidence of service of such a copy.

NOTE

[1] As amended by the Act of Adjournal (Extention of Time Limit for Service of Transcript of Examination) 1998 No. 2635: effective December 1, 1998).

Judicial examination: rectification of record of proceedings

38.—(1) Subject to subsections (7) to (9) of section 37 of this Act, where notwithstanding the certification mentioned in subsection (5) of that section the accused or the prosecutor is of the opinion that a transcript served under paragraph (a) of subsection (6) of that section contains an error or is incomplete he may—

(a) within 10 days of service under the said paragraph (a), serve notice of such opinion on the prosecutor or as the case may be the accused; and

(b) within 14 days of service under paragraph (a) of this subsection, apply to the sheriff for the error or incompleteness to be rectified,

and the sheriff shall within 7 days of the application hear the prosecutor and the accused in chambers and may authorise rectification.

(2) Where—

(a) the person on whom notice is served under paragraph (a) of subsection (1) above agrees with the opinion to which that notice relates the sheriff may dispense with such hearing;

(b) the accused neither attends, nor secures that he is represented at, such hearing it shall, subject to paragraph (a) above, nevertheless proceed.

(3) In so far as it is reasonably practicable so to arrange, the sheriff who deals with any application made under subsection (1) above shall be the sheriff before whom the examination or further examination to which the application relates was conducted.

(4) Any decision of the sheriff, as regards rectification under subsection (1) above, shall be final.

Judicial examination: charges arising in different districts

39.—(1) An accused against whom there are charges in more than one sheriff court district may be brought before the sheriff of any one such district at the instance of the procurator fiscal of such district for examination on all or any of the charges.

(2) Where an accused is brought for examination as mentioned in subsection (1) above, he may be dealt with in every respect as if all of the charges had arisen in the district where he is examined.

(3) This section is without prejudice to the power of the Lord Advocate under section 10 of this Act to determine the court before which the accused shall be tried on such charges.

Committal

Committal until liberated in due course of law

40.—(1) Every petition shall be signed and no accused shall be committed until liberated in due course of law for any crime or offence without a warrant in writing expressing the particular charge in respect of which he is committed.

(2) Any such warrant for imprisonment which either proceeds on an unsigned petition or does not express the particular charge shall be null and void.

(3) The accused shall immediately be given a true copy of the warrant for imprisonment signed by the constable or person executing the warrant before imprisonment or by the prison officer receiving the warrant.

PART V

CHILDREN AND YOUNG PERSONS

Age of criminal responsibility

41. It shall be conclusively presumed that no child under the age of eight years can be guilty of any offence.

Prosecution of children

42.—(1) No child under the age of 16 years shall be prosecuted for any offence except on the instructions of the Lord Advocate, or at his instance; and no court other than the High Court and the sheriff court shall have jurisdiction over a child under the age of 16 years for an offence.

(2) Where a child is charged with any offence, his parent or guardian may in any case, and shall, if he can be found and resides within a reasonable distance, be required to attend at the court before which the case is heard or determined during all the stages of the proceedings, unless the court is satisfied that it would be unreasonable to require his attendance.

(3) Where the child is arrested, the constable by whom he is arrested or the police officer in charge of the police station to which he is brought shall cause the parent or guardian of the child, if he can be found, to be warned to attend at the court before which the child will appear.

(4) For the purpose of enforcing the attendance of a parent or guardian and enabling him to take part in the proceedings and enabling orders to be made against him, rules may be made under section 305 of this Act, for applying, with the necessary adaptations and modifications, such of the provisions of this Act relating to summary proceedings as appear appropriate for the purpose.

(5) The parent or guardian whose attendance is required under this section is—

(a) the parent who has parental responsibilities or parental rights (within the meaning of sections 1(3) and 2(4) respectively of the Children (Scotland) Act 1995) in relation to the child; or

(b) the guardian having actual possession and control of him.

(6) The attendance of the parent of a child shall not be required under this section in any case where the child was before the institution of the proceedings removed from the care or charge of his parent by an order of a court.

(7) Where a child is to be brought before a court, notification of the day and time when, and the nature of the charge on which, the child is to be so brought shall be sent by the chief constable of the area in which the offence is alleged to have been committed to the local authority for the area in which the court will sit.

(8) Where a local authority receive notification under subsection (7) above they shall make such investigations and submit to the court a report which shall contain such information as to the home surroundings of the child as appear to them will assist the court in the disposal of his case, and the report shall contain information, which the appropriate education authority shall have a duty to supply, as to the school record, health and character of the child.

(9) Any child detained in a police station, or being conveyed to or from any criminal court, or waiting before or after attendance in such court, shall be prevented from associating with an adult (not being a relative) who is

charged with any offence other than an offence with which the child is jointly charged.

(10) Any female child shall, while detained, being conveyed or waiting as mentioned in subsection (9) above, be kept under the care of a woman.

Arrangements where children arrested

43.—[1](1) Where a person who is apparently a child is apprehended, with or without warrant, and cannot be brought forthwith before a sheriff, a police officer of the rank of inspector or above or the officer in charge of the police station to which he is brought, shall inquire into the case, and, subject to subsection (3) below, may liberate him—

 (a) on a written undertaking being entered into by him or his parent or guardian that he will attend at a court and at a time specified in the undertaking; or

 (b) unconditionally liberate him on a written undertaking being entered into by him or his parent or guardian that he will attend at the hearing of the charge.

(2) An undertaking mentioned in subsection (1) above shall be signed by the child or, as the case may be, the parent or guardian and shall be certified by the officer mentioned in that subsection.

(3) A person shall not be liberated under subsection (1) where—

 (a) the charge is one of homicide or other grave crime;

 (b) it is necessary in his interest to remove him from association with any reputed criminal or prostitute; or

 (c) the officer has reason to believe that his liberation would defeat the ends of justice.

(4) Where a person who is apparently a child having been apprehended is not liberated as mentioned in subsection (1) above, the police officer referred to in that subsection shall cause him to be kept in a place of safety other than a police station until he can be brought before a sheriff unless the officer certifies—

 (a) that it is impracticable to do so;

 (b) that he is of so unruly a character that he cannot safely be so detained; or

 (c) that by reason of his state of health or of his mental or bodily condition it is inadvisable so to detain him,

and the certificate shall be produced to the court before which he is brought.

(5) Where a person who is apparently a child has not been liberated as mentioned in subsection (1) above but has been kept under subsection (4) above, and it is decided not to proceed with the charge against him, a constable shall so inform the Principal Reporter.

[2,3](6) Any person, who without reasonable excuse fails to appear at the court and at the time specified in the undertaking entered into by him or on his behalf under subsection (1) above, shall be guilty of an offence, and liable on summary conviction of any charge made against him at the time he was liberated under that subsection in addition to any other penalty which it is competent for the court to impose on him, to a fine not exceeding level 3 on the standard scale.

(7) In any proceedings relating to an offence under this section, a writing, purporting to be such an undertaking as is mentioned in subsection (1) above and bearing to be signed and certified, shall be sufficient evidence of the undertaking given by the accused.

NOTES

[1]Substituted by the Crime and Punishment (Scotland) Act 1997 (c. 48) s.55(2) with effect from August 1, 1997 in terms of the Crime and Punishment (Scotland) Act 1997 (Commencement and Transitional Provisions) Order 1997 (S.I. 1997 No. 1712) para. 3.

[2]Subsituted by the 1997 Act s.55(3) with effect from August 1, 1997 by the above Order.
[3]Inserted by s.55(3) of said Act with effect from August 1, 1997 a above.

Detention of children

44.—(1) Where a child appears before the sheriff in summary proceedings and pleads guilty to, or is found guilty of, an offence to which this section applies, the sheriff may order that he be detained in residential accommodation provided under Part II of the Children (Scotland) Act 1995 by the appropriate local authority for such period not exceeding one year as may be specified in the order in such place (in any part of the United Kingdom) as the local authority may, from time to time, consider appropriate.

(2) This section applies to any offence in respect of which it is competent to impose imprisonment on a person of the age of 21 years or more.

(3) Where a child in respect of whom an order is made under this section is detained by the appropriate local authority, that authority shall have the same powers and duties in respect of the child as they would have if he were subject to a supervision requirement.

[1](4) Where a child in respect of whom an order is made under this section is also subject to a supervision requirement ... the supervision requirement shall be of no effect during any period for which he is required to be detained under the order.

(5) The Secretary of State may, by regulations made by statutory instrument subject to annulment in pursuance of a resolution of either House of Parliament, make such provision as he considers necessary as regards the detention in secure accommodation of children in respect of whom orders have been made under this section.

[1](6) ...
[1](7) ...
[1](8) ...
[1](9) ...

[1](10) Where a local authority consider it appropriate that a child in respect of whom an order has been made under subsection (1) above should be detained in a place in any part of the United Kingdom outside Scotland, the order shall be a like authority as in Scotland to the person in charge of the place to restrict the child's liberty to such an extent as that person may consider appropriate having regard to the terms of the order.

(11) In this section—
"the appropriate local authority" means—
    (a) where the child usually resides in Scotland, the local authority for the area in which he usually resides;
    (b) in any other case, the local authority for the area in which the offence was committed; and
"secure accommodation" has the meaning assigned to it in Part II of the Children (Scotland) Act 1995.

NOTE
[1]Deleted by the Crime and Punishment (Scotland) Act 1997 (c. 48) s.62(1) and Sched. 1, para. 21(3) with effect from August 1, 1997 in terms of the Crime and Punishment (Scotland) Act 1997 (Commencement and Transitional Provisions) Order 1997 (S.I. 1997 No. 1712) para. 3.

Security for child's good behaviour

45.—(1) Where a child has been charged with an offence the court may order his parent or guardian to give security for his co-operation in securing the child's good behaviour.

(2) Subject to subsection (3) below, an order under this section shall not be made unless the parent or guardian has been given the opportunity of being heard.

(3) Where a parent or guardian has been required to attend and fails to do so, the court may make an order under this section.

(4) Any sum ordered to be paid by a parent or guardian on the forfeiture of any security given under this section may be recovered from him by civil diligence or imprisonment in like manner as if the order had been made on the conviction of the parent or guardian of the offence with which the child was charged.

(5) In this section "parent" means either of the child's parents, if that parent has parental responsibilities or parental rights (within the meaning of sections 1(3) and 2(4) respectively of the Children (Scotland) Act 1995) in relation to him.

Presumption and determination of age of child

46.—[1](1) Where a person charged with an offence whose age is not specified in the indictment or complaint in relation to that offence is brought before a court other than for the purpose of giving evidence, and it appears to the court that he is a child, the court shall make due enquiry as to the age of that person, and for that purpose shall take such evidence as may be forthcoming at the hearing of the case, and the age presumed or declared by the court to be the age of that person shall, for the purposes of this Act or the Children and Young Persons (Scotland) Act 1937, be deemed to be the true age of that person.

(2) The court in making any inquiry in pursuance of subsection (1) above shall have regard to the definition of child for the purposes of this Act.

[1](3) Without prejudice to section 255A of this Act, where in an indictment or complaint for—

(a) an offence under the Children and Young Persons (Scotland) Act 1937;

(b) any of the offences mentioned in paragraphs 3 and 4 of Schedule 1 to this Act; or

(c) an offence under section 1, 10(1) to (3) or 12 of the Criminal Law (Consolidation) (Scotland) Act 1995,

it is alleged that the person by or in respect of whom the offence was committed was a child or was under or had attained any specified age, and he appears to the court to have been at the date of the commission of the alleged offence a child, or to have been under or to have attained the specified age, as the case may be, he shall for the purposes of this Act or the Children and Young Persons (Scotland) Act 1937 or Part I of the Criminal Law (Consolidation) (Scotland) Act 1995 be presumed at that date to have been a child or to have been under or to have attained that age, as the case may be, unless the contrary is proved.

(4) Where, in an indictment or complaint for an offence under the Children and Young Persons (Scotland) Act 1937 or any of the offences mentioned in Schedule 1 to this Act, it is alleged that the person in respect of whom the offence was committed was a child or was a young person, it shall not be a defence to prove that the person alleged to have been a child was a young person or the person alleged to have been a young person was a child in any case where the acts constituting the alleged offence would equally have been an offence if committed in respect of a young person or child respectively.

(5) An order or judgement of the court shall not be invalidated by any subsequent proof that—

(a) the age of a person mentioned in subsection (1) above has not been correctly stated to the court; or

(b) the court was not informed that at the material time the person was subject to a supervision requirement or that his case had been referred to a children's hearing by virtue of regulations made under the Children (Scotland) Act 1995 for the purpose of giving effect to orders made in different parts of the United Kingdom.

(6) Where it appears to the court that a person mentioned in subsection (1) above has attained the age of 17 years, he shall for the purposes of this Act or the Children and Young Persons (Scotland) Act 1937 be deemed not to be a child.

(7) In subsection (3) above, references to a child (other than a child charged with an offence) shall be construed as references to a child under the age of 17 years; but except as aforesaid references in this section to a child shall be construed as references to a child within the meaning of section 307 of this Act.

NOTE
[1]Inserted by the Crime and Punishment (Scotland) Act 1995 (c. 48) s.62(1) and Sched. 1, para. 21(4) with effect from August 1, 1997 by the Crime and Punishment (Scotland) Act 1997 (Commencement and Transitional Provisions) Order 1997 (S.I. 1997 No. 1712) para. 3.

Restriction on report of proceedings involving children

47.—(1) Subject to subsection (3) below, no newspaper report of any proceedings in a court shall reveal the name, address or school, or include any particulars calculated to lead to the identification, of any person under the age of 16 years concerned in the proceedings, either—

(a) as being a person against or in respect of whom the proceedings are taken; or

(b) as being a witness in the proceedings.

(2) Subject to subsection (3) below, no picture which is, or includes, a picture of a person under the age of 16 years concerned in proceedings as mentioned in subsection (1) above shall be published in any newspaper in a context relevant to the proceedings.

(3) The requirements of subsections (1) and (2) above shall be applied in any case mentioned in any of the following paragraphs to the extent specified in that paragraph—

(a) where a person under the age of 16 years is concerned in the proceedings as a witness only and no one against whom the proceedings are taken is under the age of 16 years, the requirements shall not apply unless the court so directs;

(b) where, at any stage of the proceedings, the court, if it is satisfied that it is in the public interest so to do, directs that the requirements (including the requirements as applied by a direction under para- graph (a) above) shall be dispensed with to such extent as the court may specify; and

(c) where the Secretary of State, after completion of the proceedings, if satisfied as mentioned in paragraph (b) above, by order dispenses with the requirements to such extent as may be specified in the order.

(4) This section shall, with the necessary modifications, apply in relation to sound and television programmes included in a programme service (within the meaning of the Broadcasting Act 1990) as it applies in relation to newspapers.

(5) A person who publishes matter in contravention of this section shall be guilty of an offence and liable on summary conviction to a fine not exceeding level 4 of the standard scale.

(6) In this section, references to a court shall not include a court in England, Wales or Northern Ireland.

Power to refer certain children to reporter

48.—(1) A court by or before which a person is convicted of having committed an offence to which this section applies may refer—

(a) a child in respect of whom an offence mentioned in paragraph (a) or
   (b) of subsection (2) below has been committed; or
(b) any child who is, or who is likely to become, a member of the same
   household as the person who has committed an offence mentioned in
   paragraph (b) or (c) of that subsection or the person in respect of
   whom the offence so mentioned was committed,

to the Principal Reporter, and certify that the offence shall be a ground
established for the purposes of Chapter 3 of Part II of the Children
(Scotland) Act 1995.

(2) This section applies to an offence—
(a) under section 21 of the Children and Young Persons (Scotland) Act
   1937;
(b) mentioned in Schedule 1 to this Act; or
(c) in respect of a person aged 17 years or over which constitutes the
   crime of incest.

Reference or remit to children's hearing

49.—(1) Where a child who is not subject to a supervision requirement
pleads guilty to, or is found guilty of, an offence the court—
(a) instead of making an order on that plea or finding, may remit the case
   to the Principal Reporter to arrange for the disposal of the case by a
   children's hearing; or
(b) on that plea or finding may request the Principal Reporter to arrange
   a children's hearing for the purposes of obtaining their advice as to the
   treatment of the child.

(2) Where a court has acted in pursuance of paragraph (b) of subsection
(1) above, the court, after consideration of the advice received from the
children's hearing may, as it thinks proper, itself dispose of the case or remit
the case as mentioned in paragraph (a) of that subsection.

(3) Where a child who is subject to a supervision requirement pleads guilty
to, or is found guilty of, an offence the court dealing with the case if it is—
   (a) the High Court, may; and
 ²(b) the sheriff or district court, shall,
request the Principal Reporter to arrange a children's hearing for the
purpose of obtaining their advice as to the treatment of the child, and on
consideration of that advice may, as it thinks proper, itself dispose of the case
or remit the case as mentioned in subsection (1)(a) above.

¹(4) Subject to any appeal against any decision to remit made under
subsection (1)(a) or (7)(b) below, where a court has remitted a case to the
Principal Reporter under this section, the jurisdiction of the court in respect
of the child shall cease, and his case shall stand referred to a children's
hearing.

(5) Nothing in this section shall apply to a case in respect of an offence the
sentence for which is fixed by law.

(6) Where a person who is—
(a) not subject to a supervision requirement;
(b) over the age of 16; and
(c) not within six months of attaining the age of 18,
is charged summarily with an offence and pleads guilty to, or has been found
guilty of, the offence the court may request the Principal Reporter to
arrange a children's hearing for the purpose of obtaining their advice as to
the treatment of the person.

(7) On consideration of any advice obtained under subsection (6) above,
the court may, as it thinks proper—
(a) itself dispose of the case; or

(b) where the hearing have so advised, remit the case to the Principal Reporter for the disposal of the case by a children's hearing.

NOTES

[1]Inserted by s.23(a) of the Crime and Punishment (Scotland) Act 1997 with effect from August 1, 1997 in terms of the Crime and Punishment (Scotland) Act (Commencement and Transitional Provisions) Order 1997 (S.I. 1997 No. 1712) Art. 3.

[2]Inserted by the Crime and Disorder Act 1998 (c. 37), Sched. 8, para. 118 (effective September 30, 1998: S.I. 1998 No. 2327).

Children and certain proceedings

50.—[1](1) No child under 14 years of age (other than an infant in arms) shall be permitted to be present in court during any proceedings against any other person charged with an offence unless his presence is required as a witness or otherwise for the purposes of justice or the Court consents to his presence.

(2) Any child present in court when, under subsection (1) above, he is not to be permitted to be so shall be ordered to be removed.

(3) Where, in any proceedings in relation to an offence against, or any conduct contrary to, decency or morality, a person who, in the opinion of the court, is a child is called as a witness, the court may direct that all or any persons, not being—

(a) members or officers of the court;
(b) parties to the case before the court, their counsel or solicitors or persons otherwise directly concerned in the case;
(c) *bona fide* representatives of news gathering or reporting organisations present for the purpose of the preparation of contemporaneous reports of the proceedings; or
(d) such other persons as the court may specially authorise to be present,

shall be excluded from the court during the taking of the evidence of that witness.

(4) The powers conferred on a court by subsection (3) above shall be in addition and without prejudice to any other powers of the court to hear proceedings *in camera*.

(5) Where in any proceedings relating to any of the offences mentioned in Schedule 1 to this Act, the court is satisfied that the attendance before the court of any person under the age of 17 years in respect of whom the offence is alleged to have been committed is not essential to the just hearing of the case, the case may be proceeded with and determined in the absence of that person.

(6) Every court in dealing with a child who is brought before it as an offender shall have regard to the welfare of the child and shall in a proper case take steps for removing him from undesirable surroundings.

NOTE

[1]As amended by the Access to Justice Act 1999 (c. 22), s.73(2) (effective September 27, 1999).

Remand and committal of children and young persons

51.—(1) Where a court remands or commits for trial or for sentence a person under 21 years of age who is charged with or convicted of an offence and is not released on bail or ordained to appear, then, except as otherwise expressly provided by this section, the following provisions shall have effect—

[1](a) subject to paragraph (b) below, if he is under 16 years of age the court shall, instead of committing him to prison, commit him to the local authority which it considers appropriate to be detained—

       (i) where the court so requires, in secure accommodation within the meaning of Part II of the Children (Scotland) Act 1995; and

       (ii) in any other case, in a suitable place of safety chosen by the authority;

[2](aa) if the person is over 16 years of age and subject to a supervision requirement, the court may, instead of committing him to prison, commit him to the local authority which it considers appropriate to be detained as mentioned in sub-paragraphs (i) or (ii) of paragraph (a) above;

[3](b) if he is a person of over 16 years of age to whom paragraph (aa) above does not apply, or a child under 16 years of age but over 14 years of age who is certified by the court to be unruly or depraved, and the court has been notified by the Secretary of State that a remand centre is available for the reception from that court of persons of his class or description, he shall be committed to a remand centre instead of being committed to prison.

(2) Where any person is committed to a local authority or to a remand centre under any provision of this Act, that authority or centre shall be specified in the warrant, and he shall be detained by the authority or in the centre for the period for which he is committed or until he is liberated in due course of law.

(3) Where any person has been committed to a local authority under any provision of this Act, the court by which he was committed, if the person so committed is not less than 14 years of age and it appears to the court that he is unruly or depraved, may revoke the committal and commit the said person—

    (a) if the court has been notified that a remand centre is available for the reception from that court of persons of his class or description, to a remand centre; and

    (b) if the court has not been so notified, to a prison.

[4](4) Where in the case of a person under 16 years of age who has been committed to prison or to a remand centre under this section, the sheriff is satisfied that his detention in prison or a remand centre is no longer necessary, he may revoke the committal and commit the person to the local authority which he considers appropriate to be detained—

    (a) where the court so requires, in secure accommodation within the meaning of Part II of the Children (Scotland) Act 1995; and

    (b) in any other case, in a suitable place of safety chosen by the authority.

[5](4A) The local authority which may be appropriate in relation to a power to commit a person under paragraphs (a) or (aa) of subsection (1) or subsection (4) above may, without prejudice to the generality of those powers, be—

    (a) the local authority for the area in which the court is situated;

    (b) if the person is usually resident in Scotland, the local authority for the area in which he is usually resident;

    (c) if the person is subject to a supervision requirement, the relevant local authority within the meaning of Part II of the Children (Scotland) Act 1995 in relation to that requirement.

NOTES

[1]Substituted by the Crime and Punishment (Scotland) Act 1997 (c. 48) s.56(2)(a) with effect from August 1, 1997 in terms of the Crime and Punishment (Scotland) Act 1997 (Commencement and Transitional Provisions) Order 1997 (S.I. 1997 No. 1712) para. 3.

[2]Inserted by s.56(2)(b) of the above Act with effect from August 1, 1997 in terms of the above Order.

[3]Inserted by s.56(2)(c) of the above Act and in terms of the above Order.

[4]Substituted by s.56(3) of the above Act and in terms of the above Order.

⁵Inserted by s.52(4) of the above Act and in terms of the above Order.

PART VI

MENTAL DISORDER

Committal of mentally disordered persons

Power of court to commit to hospital an accused suffering from mental disorder

52.—(1) Where it appears to the prosecutor in any court before which a person is charged with an offence that the person may be suffering from mental disorder, it shall be the duty of the prosecutor to bring before the court such evidence as may be available of the mental condition of that person.

(2) Where a court remands or commits for trial a person charged with any offence who appears to the court to be suffering from mental disorder, and the court is satisfied that a hospital is available for his admission and suitable for his detention, the court may, instead of remanding him in custody, commit him to that hospital.

(3) Where an accused is committed to a hospital as mentioned in subsection (2) above, the hospital shall be specified in the warrant, and if the responsible medical officer is satisfied that he is suffering from mental disorder of a nature or degree which warrants his admission to a hospital under Part V of the Mental Health (Scotland) Act 1984, he shall be detained in the hospital specified in the warrant for the period for which he is remanded or the period of committal, unless before the expiration of that period he is liberated in due course of law.

(4) When the responsible medical officer has examined the person so detained he shall report the result of that examination to the court and, where the report is to the effect that the person is not suffering from mental disorder of such a nature or degree as aforesaid, the court may commit him to any prison or other institution to which he might have been committed had he not been committed to hospital or may otherwise deal with him according to law.

(5) No person shall be committed to a hospital under this section except on the written or oral evidence of a registered medical practitioner.

(6) Without prejudice to subsection (4) above, the court may review an order under subsection (2) above on the ground that there has been a change of circumstances since the order was made and, on such review—

(a) where the court considers that such an order is no longer required in relation to a person, it shall revoke the order and may deal with him in such way mentioned in subsection (4) above as the court thinks appropriate;

(b) in any other case, the court may—
 (i) confirm or vary the order; or
 (ii) revoke the order and deal with him in such way mentioned in subsection (4) above as the court considers appropriate.

(7) Subsections (2) to (5) above shall apply to the review of an order under subsection (6) above as they apply to the making of an order under subsection (2) above.

Interim hospital orders

Interim hospital orders

53.—¹,³(1) Where, in the case of a person to whom this section applies the court is satisfied on the written or oral evidence of two medical practitioners (complying with section 61 of this Act)—

(a) that the offender is suffering from mental disorder within the meaning of section 1(2) of the Mental Health (Scotland) Act 1984; and

(b) that there is reason to suppose—

　　(i) that the mental disorder from which the offender is suffering is such that it may be appropriate for a hospital order to be made in his case; and

　　(ii) that, having regard to section 58(5) of this Act, the hospital to be specified in any such hospital order may be a State hospital,

the court may, before making a hospital order or dealing with the offender in some other way including imposing a sentence of imprisonment and making a hospital direction, make an order (to be known as "an interim hospital order") authorising his admission to and detention in a state hospital or such other hospital as for special reasons the court may specify in the order.

³(2) ...

²(3) An interim hospital order shall not be made in respect of an offender unless the court is satisfied that the hospital which is to be specified in the order, in the event of such an order being made by the court, is available for his admission thereto within 7 days of the making of such an order.

¹(4) Where a court makes an interim hospital order it shall not at that time make any other order for detention or impose a fine or pass sentence of imprisonment or make a probation order or a community service order in respect of the offence, but may make any other order which it has power to make apart from this section.

²(5) The court by which an interim hospital order is made may include in the order such direction as it thinks fit for the conveyance of the offender to a place of safety and his detention therein pending his admission to the hospital within the period of 7 days referred to in subsection (3) above.

¹(5A) Subsections (1) and (4) of section 60 of the Mental Health (Scotland) Act 1984 shall apply to an interim hospital order as they apply to a hospital order.

¹,³(6) An interim hospital order—

(a) shall be in force for such period, not exceeding 12 weeks, as the court may specify when making the order; but

(b) may be renewed for further periods of not more than 28 days at a time if it appears to the court on the written or oral evidence of the responsible medical officer that the continuation of the order is warranted,

but no such order shall continue in force for more than twelve months in all and the court shall terminate the order if it makes a hospital order in respect of the offender or decides, after considering the written or oral evidence of the responsible medical officer, to deal with the offender in some other way including imposing a sentence of imprisonment and making a hospital direction.

(7) An interim hospital order may be renewed under subsection (6) above without the offender being brought before the court if he is represented by counsel or a solicitor and his counsel or solicitor is given an opportunity of being heard.

(8) If an offender absconds from a hospital in which he is detained in pursuance of an interim hospital order, or while being conveyed to or from such a hospital, he may be arrested without warrant by a constable and shall, after being arrested, be brought as soon as practicable before the court which made the order; and the court may thereupon terminate the order and deal with him in any way in which it could have dealt with him if no such order had been made.

(9) When an interim hospital order ceases to have effect in relation to an offender the court may deal with him in any way (other than by making a new interim hospital order) in which it could have dealt with him if no such order had been made.

(10) The power conferred on the court by this section is without prejudice to the power of the court under section 200(1) of this Act to remand a person in order that an inquiry may be made into his physical or mental condition.

(11) This section applies to any person—

(a) convicted in the High Court or the sheriff court of an offence punishable with imprisonment (other than an offence the sentence for which is fixed by law);

(b) charged on complaint in the sheriff court if the sheriff is satisfied that he did the act or made the omission charged but does not convict him; or

(c) remitted to the sheriff court from the district court under section 58(10) of this Act if the sheriff is satisfied as mentioned in paragraph (b) above.

(12) In this section "the court" means—

(a) the High Court, as regards a person—

    (i) convicted on indictment in that court; or

    (ii) convicted on indictment in the sheriff court and remitted for sentence to the High Court; and

(b) the sheriff court, as regards a person—

    (i) convicted in the sheriff court and not remitted as mentioned in paragraph (a)(ii) above; or

    (ii) referred to in paragraph (b) or (c) of subsection (11) above.

NOTES

[1] As amended by the Crime and Punishment (Scotland) Act 1997 (c. 48) s.62(1) Sched. 1, and para. 21(5) with effect from January 1, 1998 by the Crime and Punishment (Scotland) Act 1997 (Commencement No. 2 and Transitional Provisions) Order 1997 (S.I. 1997 No. 2323) para. 3.

[2] Substituted by the Act and Order above mentioned.

[3] Amended by the Crime and Punishment (Scotland) Act 1997 (c. 48) ss.10 and 11 with effect from January 1, 1998 by the Crime and Punishment (Scotland) Act 1997 (Commencement No. 2 and Transitional Provisions) Order 1997 (S.I. 1997 No. 2323) Art. 4 Sched. 2.

Insanity in bar of trial

Insanity in bar of trial

54.—(1) Where the court is satisfied, on the written or oral evidence of two medical practitioners, that a person charged with the commission of an offence is insane so that his trial cannot proceed or, if it has commenced, cannot continue, the court shall, subject to subsection (2) below—

(a) make a finding to that effect and state the reasons for that finding;

(b) discharge the trial diet and order that a diet (in this Act referred to as an "an examination of facts") be held under section 55 of this Act; and

(c) remand the person in custody or on bail or, where the court is satisfied—

    (i) on the written or oral evidence of two medical practitioners, that he is suffering from mental disorder of a nature or degree which warrants his admission to hospital under Part V of the Mental Health (Scotland) Act 1984; and

    (ii) that a hospital is available for his admission and suitable for his detention,

make an order (in this section referred to as a "temporary hospital order") committing him to that hospital until the conclusion of the examination of facts.

(2) Subsection (1) above is without prejudice to the power of the court, on an application by the prosecutor, to desert the diet *pro loco et tempore*.

(3) The court may, before making a finding under subsection (1) above as to the insanity of a person, adjourn the case in order that investigation of his mental condition may be carried out.

(4) The court which made a temporary hospital order may, at any time

while the order is in force, review the order on the ground that there has been a change of circumstances since the order was made and, on such review—

    (a) where the court considers that such an order is no longer required in relation to a person, it shall revoke the order and may remand him in custody or on bail;

    (b) in any other case, the court may—

        (i) confirm or vary the order; or

        (ii) revoke the order and make such other order, under subsection (1)(c) above or any other provision of this Act, as the court considers appropriate.

(5) Where it appears to a court that it is not practicable or appropriate for the accused to be brought before it for the purpose of determining whether he is insane so that his trial cannot proceed, then, if no objection to such a course is taken by or on behalf of the accused, the court may order that the case be proceeded with in his absence.

(6) Where evidence is brought before the court that the accused was insane at the time of doing the act or making the omission constituting the offence with which he is charged and he is acquitted, the court shall—

    (a) in proceedings on indictment, direct the jury to find; or

    (b) in summary proceedings, state,

whether the accused was insane at such time as aforesaid, and, if so, to declare whether he was acquitted on account of his insanity at that time.

(7) It shall not be competent for a person charged summarily in the sheriff court to found on a plea of insanity standing in bar of trial unless, before the first witness for the prosecution is sworn, he gives notice to the prosecutor of the plea and of the witnesses by whom he proposes to maintain it; and where such notice is given, the court shall, if the prosecutor so moves, adjourn the case.

(8) In this section, "the court" means—

    (a) as regards a person charged on indictment, the High Court or the sheriff court;

    (b) as regards a person charged summarily, the sheriff court.

Examination of facts

Examination of facts

55.—(1) At an examination of facts ordered under section 54(1)(b) of this Act the court shall, on the basis of the evidence (if any) already given in the trial and such evidence, or further evidence, as may be led by either party, determine whether it is satisfied—

    (a) beyond reasonable doubt, as respects any charge on the indictment or, as the case may be, the complaint in respect of which the accused was being or was to be tried, that he did the act or made the omission constituting the offence; and

    (b) on the balance of probabilities, that there are no grounds for acquitting him.

(2) Where the court is satisfied as mentioned in subsection (1) above, it shall make a finding to that effect.

(3) Where the court is not so satisfied it shall, subject to subsection (4) below, acquit the person of the charge.

(4) Where, as respects a person acquitted under subsection (3) above, the court is satisfied as to the matter mentioned in subsection (1)(a) above but it appears to the court that the person was insane at the time of doing the act or making the omission constituting the offence, the court shall state whether the acquittal is on the ground of such insanity.

(5) Where it appears to the court that it is not practical or appropriate for

the accused to attend an examination of facts the court may, if no objection is taken by or on behalf of the accused, order that the examination of facts shall proceed in his absence.

(6) Subject to the provisions of this section, section 56 of this Act and any Act of Adjournal the rules of evidence and procedure and the powers of the court shall, in respect of an examination of facts, be as nearly as possible those applicable in respect of a trial.

(7) For the purposes of the application to an examination of facts of the rules and powers mentioned in subsection (6) above, an examination of facts—

    (a) commences when the indictment or, as the case may be, complaint is called; and

    (b) concludes when the court—

        (i) acquits the person under subsection (3) above;

        (ii) makes an order under subsection (2) of section 57 of this Act; or

        (iii) decides, under paragraph (e) of that subsection, not to make an order.

Examination of facts: supplementary provisions

56.—(1) An examination of facts ordered under section 54(1)(b) of this Act may, where the order is made at the trial diet, be held immediately following the making of the order and, where it is so held, the citation of the accused and any witness to the trial diet shall be a valid citation to the examination of facts.

(2) Where an examination of facts is ordered in connection with proceedings on indictment, a warrant for citation of an accused and witnesses under section 66(1) of this Act shall be sufficient warrant for citation to an examination of facts.

(3) Where an accused person is not legally represented at an examination of facts the court shall appoint counsel or a solicitor to represent his interests.

(4) The court may, on the motion of the prosecutor and after hearing the accused, order that the examination of facts shall proceed in relation to a particular charge, or particular charges, in the indictment or, as the case may be, complaint in priority to other such charges.

(5) The court may, on the motion of the prosecutor and after hearing the accused, at any time desert the examination of facts *pro loco et tempore* as respects either the whole indictment or, as the case may be, complaint or any charge therein.

(6) Where, and to the extent that, an examination of facts has, under subsection (5) above, been deserted *pro loco et tempore*—

    (a) in the case of proceedings on indictment, the Lord Advocate may, at any time, raise and insist in a new indictment; or

    (b) in the case of summary proceedings, the prosecutor may at any time raise a fresh libel,

notwithstanding any time limit which would otherwise apply in respect of prosecution of the alleged offence.

(7) If, in a case where a court has made a finding under subsection (2) of section 55 of this Act, a person is subsequently charged, whether on indictment or on a complaint, with an offence arising out of the same act or omission as is referred to in subsection (1) of that section, any order made, under section 57(2) of this Act shall, with effect from the commencement of the later proceedings, cease to have effect.

(8) For the purposes of subsection (7) above, the later proceedings are commenced when the indictment or, as the case may be, the complaint is served.

Disposal in case of insanity

Disposal of case where accused found to be insane

¹**57.**—(1) This section applies where—

(a) a person is, by virtue of section 54(6) or 55(3) of this Act, acquitted on the ground of his insanity at the time of the act or omission; or

(b) following an examination of facts under section 55, a court makes a finding under subsection (2) of that section.

(2) Subject to subsection (3) below, where this section applies the court may, as it thinks fit—

(a) make an order (which shall have the same effect as a hospital order) that the person be detained in such hospital as the court may specify;

(b) in addition to making an order under paragraph (a) above, make an order (which shall have the same effect as a restriction order) that the person shall, without limit of time, be subject to the special restrictions set out in section 62(1) of the Mental Health (Scotland) Act 1984;

(c) make an order (which shall have the same effect as a guardianship order) placing the person under the guardianship of a local authority or of a person approved by a local authority;

(d) make a supervision and treatment order (within the meaning of paragraph 1(1) of Schedule 4 to this Act); or

(e) make no order.

(3) Where the offence with which the person was charged is murder, the court shall make orders under both paragraphs (a) and (b) of subsection (2) above in respect of that person.

(4) Sections 58(1), (2) and (4) to (7) and 59 and 61 of this Act shall have effect in relation to the making, terms and effect of an order under paragraph (a), (b) or (c) of subsection (2) above as those provisions have effect in relation to the making, terms and effect of, respectively, a hospital order, a restriction order and a guardianship order as respects a person convicted of an offence, other than an offence the sentence for which is fixed by law, punishable by imprisonment.

(5) Schedule 4 to this Act shall have effect as regards supervision and treatment orders.

NOTE
¹Prospectively amended by the Adults with Incapacity (Scotland) Act 2000 (asp 4), s.88 and Sched. 5, para. 26.

Hospital orders and guardianship

Order for hospital admission or guardianship

³**58.**—(1) Where a person is convicted in the High Court or the sheriff court of an offence, other than an offence the sentence for which is fixed by law, punishable by that court with imprisonment, and the following conditions are satisfied, that is to say—

(a) the court is satisfied, on the written or oral evidence of two medical practitioners (complying with section 61 of this Act) that the grounds set out in—

(i) section 17(1); or, as the case may be

(ii) section 36(a),

of the Mental Health (Scotland) Act 1984 apply in relation to the offender;

(b) the court is of the opinion, having regard to all the circumstances including the nature of the offence and the character and antecedents of the offender and to the other available methods of dealing with him, that the most suitable method of disposing of the case is by means of an order under this section,

subject to subsection (2) below, the court may by order authorise his admission to and detention in such hospital as may be specified in the order or, as the case may be, place him under the guardianship of such local authority or of such other person approved by a local authority as may be so specified.

(2) Where the case is remitted by the sheriff to the High Court for sentence under any enactment, the power to make an order under subsection (1) above shall be exercisable by that court.

(3) Where in the case of a person charged summarily in the sheriff court with an act or omission constituting an offence the court would have power, on convicting him, to make an order under subsection (1) above, then, if it is satisfied that the person did the act or made the omission charged, the court may, if it thinks fit, make such an order without convicting him.

[1](4) An order for the admission of a person to a hospital (in this Act, referred to as "a hospital order") shall not be made under this section in respect of an offender or of a person to whom subsection (3) above applies unless the court is satisfied that that hospital, in the event of such an order being made by the court, is available for his admission thereto within 7 days of the making of such an order.

(5) A State hospital shall not be specified in a hospital order in respect of the detention of a person unless the court is satisfied, on the evidence of the medical practitioners which is taken into account under paragraph (a) of subsection (1) above, that the offender, on account of his dangerous, violent or criminal propensities, requires treatment under conditions of special security, and cannot suitably be cared for in a hospital other than a State hospital.

(6) An order placing a person under the guardianship of a local authority or of any other person (in this Act referred to as "a guardianship order") shall not be made under this section unless the court is satisfied—

(a) after taking into consideration the evidence of a mental health officer, that it is necessary in the interests of the welfare of the person that he should be placed under guardianship; and

(b) that that authority or person is willing to receive that person into guardianship.

[2](7) A hospital order or guardianship order shall specify the form of mental disorder, being mental illness (including personality disorder) or mental handicap or both, from which, upon the evidence taken into account under paragraph (a) of subsection (1) above, the offender is found by the court to be suffering; and no such order shall be made unless the offender is described by each of the practitioners, whose evidence is taken into account as aforesaid, as suffering from the same form of mental disorder, whether or not he is also described by either of them as suffering from the other form.

(8) Where an order is made under this section, the court shall not pass sentence of imprisonment or impose a fine or make a probation order or a community service order in respect of the offence, but may make any other order which the court has power to make apart from this section; and for the purposes of this subsection "sentence of imprisonment" includes any sentence or order for detention.

[1](9) The court by which a hospital order is made may give such directions as it thinks fit for the conveyance of the patient to a place of safety and his detention therein pending his admission to the hospital within the period of 7 days referred to in subsection (4) above; but a direction for the conveyance of a patient to a residential establishment shall not be given unless the court is satisfied that the authority is willing to receive the patient therein.

(10) Where a person is charged before the district court with an act or

omission constituting an offence punishable with imprisonment, the district court, if it appears to it that that person may be suffering from mental disorder, shall remit him to the sheriff court in the manner provided by section 7(9) and (10) of this Act, and the sheriff court shall, on any such remit being made, have the like power to make an order under subsection (1) above in respect of him as if he had been charged before that court with the said act or omission as an offence, or in dealing with him may exercise the like powers as the district court.

(11) Section 58A of this Act shall have effect as regards guardianship orders made under subsection (1) of this section.

NOTES
[1]Amended by the Crime and Punishment (Scotland) Act 1997 (c. 48), s.62(1) and Sched. 1 para. 21(6), with effect from January 1, 1998 in terms of the Crime and Punishment (Scotland) Act 1997 (Commencement No. 2 and Transitional and Consequential Provisions) Order 1997 (S.I. 1997 No. 2323) Art. 4, Sched. 2.)
[2] As amended by the Mental Health (Public Safety and Appeals) (Scotland) Act 1999 (asp 1), s.3(b) (effective September 13, 1999).
[3]Prospectively amended by the Adults with Incapacity (Scotland) Act 2000 (asp 4), s.88 and Sched. 5, para. 26.
[4]Prospectively inserted by the Adults with Incapacity (Scotland) Act 2000 (asp 4), s.88 and Sched. 5, para. 26.

[[1]Application of Adults with Incapacity (Scotland) Act 2000

58A.—(1) Subject to the provisions of this section, the provisions of Parts 1, 5, 6 and 7 of the Adults with Incapacity (Scotland) Act 2000 (asp 4) ("the 2000 Act") apply—

(a) to a guardian appointed by an order of the court under section 57(2)(c), 58(1) or 58(1A) of this Act (in this section referred to as a "guardianship order") whether appointed before or after the coming into force of these provisions, as they apply to a guardian with powers relating to the personal welfare of an adult appointed under section 58 of that Act;

(b) to a person authorised under an intervention order under section 60A of this Act as they apply to a person so authorised under section 53 of that Act.

(2) In making a guardianship order the court shall have regard to any regulations made by the Scottish Ministers under section 64(11) of the 2000 Act and—

(a) shall confer powers, which it shall specify in the order, relating only to the personal welfare of the person;

(b) may appoint a joint guardian;

(c) may appoint a substitute guardian;

(d) may make such consequential or ancillary order, provision or direction as it considers appropriate.

(3) Without prejudice to the generality of subsection (2), or to any other powers conferred by this Act, the court may—

(a) make any order granted by it subject to such conditions and restrictions as appear to it to be appropriate;

(b) order that any reports relating to the person who will be the subject of the order be lodged with the court or that the person be assessed or interviewed and that a report of such assessment or interview be lodged;

(c) make such further inquiry or call for such further information as appears to it to be appropriate;

(d) make such interim order as appears to it to be appropriate pending the disposal of the proceedings.

(4) Where the court makes a guardianship order it shall forthwith send a

copy of the interlocutor containing the order to the Public Guardian who shall—

    (a) enter prescribed particulars of the appointment in the register maintained by him under section 6(2)(b)(iv) of the 2000 Act;

    (b) unless he considers that the notification would be likely to pose a serious risk to the person's health notify the person of the appointment of the guardian; and

    (c) notify the local authority and the Mental Welfare Commission of the terms of the interlocutor.

(5) A guardianship order shall continue in force for a period of 3 years or such other period (including an indefinite period) as, on cause shown, the court may determine.

(6) Where any proceedings for the appointment of a guardian under section 57(2)(c) or 58(1) of this Act have been commenced and not determined before the date of coming into force of section 84 of, and paragraph 26 of schedule 5 to, the Adults with Incapacity (Scotland) Act 2000 (asp 4) they shall be determined in accordance with this Act as it was immediately in force before that date.]

NOTE
  [1]Prospectively inserted by the Adults with Incapacity (Scotland) Act 2000 (asp 4), s.84.

Hospital orders: restrictions on discharge

[1]**59.**—(1) Where a hospital order is made in respect of a person, and it appears to the court—

    (a) having regard to the nature of the offence with which he is charged;

    (b) the antecedents of the person; and

    (c) the risk that as a result of his mental disorder he would commit offences if set at large,

that it is necessary for the protection of the public from serious harm so to do, the court may, subject to the provisions of this section, further order that the person shall be subject to the special restrictions set out in section 62(1) of the Mental Health (Scotland) Act 1984, without limit of time.

(2) An order under this section (in this Act referred to as "a restriction order") shall not be made in the case of any person unless the medical practitioner approved by the Health Board for the purposes of section 20 or section 39 of the Mental Health (Scotland) Act 1984, whose evidence is taken into account by the court under section 58(1)(a) of this Act, has given evidence orally before the court.

(3) Where a restriction order is in force in respect of a patient, a guardianship order shall not be made in respect of him; and where the hospital order relating to him ceases to have effect by virtue of section 60(3) of the Mental Health (Scotland) Act 1984 on the making of another hospital order, that order shall have the same effect in relation to the restriction order as the previous hospital order, but without prejudice to the power of the court making that other hospital order to make another restriction order to have effect on the expiration of the previous such order.

NOTE
  [1]Prospectively amended by the Adults with Incapacity (Scotland) Act 2000 (asp 4), s.88 and Sched. 6.

Hospital directions

[1]**59A.**—(1) Subject to subsection (2) and (3) below, where a person is convicted on indictment in the High Court or in the sheriff court of an offence punishable by imprisonment, the court may, in addition to any sentence of imprisonment which it has the power or the duty to impose, by a direction under this subsection (in this act referred to as a "hospital

direction") authorise his admission to and detention in such hospital as may be specified in the direction.

(2) Subsection (1) above shall not apply where the person convicted is a child.

(3) A hospital direction shall not be made unless—

(a) the court is satisfied on the written or oral evidence of two medical practitioners complying with section 61 of this Act) that the grounds set out in section 17(1) of the Mental Health (Scotland) Act 1984 apply in relation to the offender;

²(b) the medical practitioners mentioned in paragraph (a) above each describe the person as suffering from the same form of mental disorder, being mental illness (including personality disorder) or mental handicap, whether or not he is also described by either of them as suffering from the other form; and

(c) the court is satisfied that the hospital to be specified in the direction can admit the person in respect of whom it is to be made within 7 days of the direction being made.

(4) A State hospital shall not be specified in a hospital direction in respect of the detention of a person unless the court is satisfied, on the evidence of the medical practitioners which is taken into account under paragraphs (a) and (b) of subsection (3) above, that the person—

(a) on account of his dangerous or violent or criminal propensities requires treatment under conditions of special security; and

(b) cannot suitably be cared for in a hospital other than a State hospital.

(5) A hospital direction shall specify the form of mental disorder from which, upon the evidence taken into account under paragraphs (a) and (b) of subsection (3) above, the person in respect of whom it is made is found to be suffering.

(6) The court by which a hospital direction is made may give such additional directions as it thinks fit for the conveyance of the person in respect of whom it is made to a place of safety and for his detention in that place pending his admission to hospital within the period mentioned in paragraph (c) of subsection (3) above.

(7) The court shall not make an additional direction under subsection (6) above directing the conveyance of the person concerned to a place of safety which is a residential establishment unless it is satisfied that the managers of that establishment are willing to receive him in the establishment.

NOTES

¹Inserted by the Crime and Punishment (Scotland) Act 1997 (c. 48) s.6 with effect from January 1, 1998 by the Crime and Punishment (Scotland) Act 1997 (Commencement No. 2 and Transitional and Consequential Provisions) Order 1997 (S.I. 1997 No. 2323) Art. 4, Sched. 2.

² As amended by the Mental Health (Public Safety and Appeals) (Scotland) Act 1999 (asp 1), s.3(b) (effective September 13, 1999).

Appeals against hospital orders

¹**60.** Where a hospital order, interim hospital order (but not a renewal thereof), guardianship order, a restriction order or a hospital direction has been made by a court in respect of a person charged or brought before it, he may without prejudice to any other form of appeal under any rule of law (or, where an interim hospital order has been made, to any right of appeal against any other order or sentence which may be imposed), appeal against that order or, as the case may be, direction in the same manner as against sentence.

NOTES

¹As amended by the Crime and Punishment (Scotland) Act 1997 (c. 48) s.6(2) with effect from January 1, by the Crime and Punishment (Scotland) Act 1997 (Commencement No. 2 and Transitional Provisions) Order 1997 (S.I. 1997 No. 2323) Art. 4, Sched. 2.

Appeal by prosecutor against hospital orders etc.

[1, 2]**60A.**—(1) This section applies where the court, in respect of a person charged or brought before it, has made—
    (a) an order under any of paragraphs (a) to (d) of subsection (2) of section 57 of this Act or such a decision as is mentioned in paragraph (e) of that subsection; or
    (b) a hospital order, guardianship order, restriction order or a hospital direction.

(2) Where this section applies, the prosecutor may appeal against any such order, decision or direction as is mentioned in subsection (1) above—
    (a) if it appears to him that the order, decision or direction was inappropriate; or
    (b) on a point of law,
and an appeal under this section shall be treated in the same manner as an appeal against sentence under section 108 of this Act.

NOTES
[1]Inserted by the Crime and Punishment (Scotland) Act 1997 (c. 48) s.22 with effect from January 1, 1998 by the Crime and Punishment (Scotland) Act 1997 (Commencement No. 2 and Transitional and Consequential Provisions) Order 1997 (S.I. 1997, No. 2323) Art. 4, Sched. 2.
    [2]Prospectively amended by the Adults with Incapacity (Scotland) Act 2000 (asp 4), s.88 and Sched. 5, para. 26.

Medical evidence

Requirements as to medical evidence

[3]**61.**[1]—(1) Of the medical practitioners whose evidence is taken into account in making a finding under section 54(1)(a) of this Act or under any of the relevant provisions, at least one shall be a practitioner approved for the purposes of section 20 or section 39 of the Mental Health (Scotland) Act 1984 by a Health Board as having special experience in the diagnosis or treatment of mental disorder.

[2](1A) Of the medical practitioners whose evidence is taken into account under section 53(1), 54(1)(c), 58(1)(a)(i) or 59A(3)(a) and (b) of this Act, at least one shall be employed at the hospital which is to be specified in the order or, as the case may be, direction.

[1](2) Written or oral evidence given for the purposes of any of the relevant provisions shall include a statement as to whether the person giving the evidence is related to the accused and of any pecuniary interest which that person may have in the admission of the accused to hospital or his reception into guardianship.

[1](3) For the purposes of making a finding under section 54(1)(a) of this Act or of any of the relevant provisions a report in writing purporting to be signed by a medical practitioner may, subject to the provisions of this section, be received in evidence without proof of the signature or qualifications of the practitioner; but the court may, in any case, require that the practitioner by whom such a report was signed be called to give oral evidence.

(4) Where any such report as aforesaid is tendered in evidence, otherwise than by or on behalf of the accused, then—
    (a) if the accused is represented by counsel or solicitor, a copy of the report shall be given to his counsel or solicitor;
    (b) if the accused is not so represented, the substance of the report shall be disclosed to the accused or, where he is a child under 16 years of age, to his parent or guardian if present in court;
    (c) in any case, the accused may require that the practitioner by whom the report was signed be called to give oral evidence, and evidence to

rebut the evidence contained in the report may be called by or on behalf of the accused,

and where the court is of the opinion that further time is necessary in the interests of the accused for consideration of that report, or the substance of any such report, it shall adjourn the case.

(5) For the purpose of calling evidence to rebut the evidence contained in any such report as aforesaid, arrangements may be made by or on behalf of an accused person detained in a hospital or, as respects a report for the purposes of the said section 54(1), remanded in custody for his examination by any medical practitioner, and any such examination may he made in private.

²(6) In this section the "relevant provisions" means sections 53(1), 54(1)(c), 58(1)(a) and 59A(3)(a) and (b) of this Act.

NOTES

¹As amended by the Crime and Punishment (Scotland) Act 1997 (c. 48) s.10(2) with effect from January 1, 1998 by the Crime and Punishment (Scotland) Act 1997 (Commencement No. 2 and Transitional and Consequential Provisions) Order 1997 (S.I. 1997 No. 2323) Art. 4, Sched. 2.

²As inserted by the above in Note 1.

³Prospectively amended by the Adults with Incapacity (Scotland) Act 2000 (asp 4), s.88 and Sched. 5, para. 26.

Appeals under Part VI

Appeal by accused in case involving insanity

62.—(1) A person may appeal to the High Court against—
  (a) a finding made under section 54(1) of this Act that he is insane so that his trial cannot proceed or continue, or the refusal of the court to make such a finding;
  (b) a finding under section 55(2) of this Act; or
  (c) an order made under section 57(2) of this Act.
(2) An appeal under subsection (1) above shall be—
  (a) in writing; and
  (b) lodged—
      (i) in the case of an appeal under paragraph (a) of that subsection, not later than seven days after the date of the finding or refusal which is the subject of the appeal;
      (ii) in the case of an appeal under paragraph (b), or both paragraphs (b) and (c) of that subsection, not later than 28 days after the conclusion of the examination of facts;
      (iii) in the case of an appeal under paragraph (c) of that subsection against an order made on an acquittal, by virtue of section 54(6) or 55(3) of this Act, on the ground of insanity at the time of the act or omission, not later than 14 days after the date of the acquittal;
      (iv) in the case of an appeal under that paragraph against an order made on a finding under section 55(2), not later than 14 days after the conclusion of the examination of facts,
  or within such longer period as the High Court may, on cause shown, allow.
(3) Where the examination of facts was held in connection with proceedings on indictment, subsections (1)(a) and (2)(b)(i) above are without prejudice to section 74(1) of this Act.
(4) Where an appeal is taken under subsection (1) above, the period from the date on which the appeal was lodged until it is withdrawn or disposed of shall not count towards any time limit applying in respect of the case.
(5) An appellant in an appeal under this section shall be entitled to be

present at the hearing of the appeal unless the High Court determines that his presence is not practicable or appropriate.

(6) In disposing of an appeal under subsection (1) above the High Court may——

(a) affirm the decision of the court of first instance;

[1](b) make any other finding, order or other disposal which that court could have made at the time when it made the finding or order which is the subject of the appeal; or

(c) remit the case to that court with such directions in the matter as the High Court thinks fit.

(7) Section 60 of this Act shall not apply in relation to any order as respects which a person has a right of appeal under subsection (1)(c) above.

NOTE

[1]As amended by the Crime and Punishment (Scotland) Act 1997 (c. 48) Sched. 1, para. 21(7) with effect from January 1, 1997 (Commencement No. 2 and Transitional and Consequential Provisions) Order 1997 (S.I. 1997 No. 2323) Art. 4, Sched. 2.

Appeal by prosecutor in case involving insanity

63.—(1) The prosecutor may appeal to the High Court on a point of law against——

(a) a finding under subsection (1) of section 54 of this Act that an accused is insane so that his trial cannot proceed or continue;

(b) an acquittal on the ground of insanity at the time of the act or omission by virtue of subsection (6) of that section;

(c) an acquittal under section 55(3) of this Act (whether or not on the ground of insanity at the time of the act or omission); or

[2](d) ...

(2) An appeal under subsection (1) above shall be—

(a) in writing; and

(b) lodged—

(i) in the case of an appeal under paragraph (a) or (b) of that subsection, not later than seven days after the finding or, as the case may be, the acquittal which is the subject of the appeal;

(ii) in the case of an appeal under paragraph (c) of that subsection, not later than seven days after the conclusion of the examination of facts,

or within such longer period as the High Court may, on cause shown, allow.

(3) Where the examination of facts was held in connection with proceedings on indictment, subsections (1)(a) and (2)(b)(i) above are without prejudice to section 74(1) of this Act.

(4) A respondent in an appeal under this subsection shall be entitled to be present at the hearing of the appeal unless the High Court determines that his presence is not practicable or appropriate.

(5) In disposing of an appeal under subsection (1) above the High Court may—

(a) affirm the decision of the court of first instance;

[1](b) make any other finding, order or disposal which that court could have made at the time when it made the finding [2]or acquittal which is the subject of the appeal; or

(c) remit the case to that court with such directions in the matter as the High Court thinks fit.

(6) In this section, "the prosecutor" means, in relation to proceedings on indictment, the Lord Advocate.

NOTES

[1]As amended by the Crime and Punishment (Scotland) Act 1997 (c.48) Sched. 1, para. 21(8) with effect from January 1, 1998 by the Crime and Punishment (Scotland) Act 1997

(Commencement No. 2 and Transitional and Consequential Provisions) Order 1997 (S.I. 1997 No. 2323) Art. 4, Sched. 2.
[2]As repealed by the above in Note 1.

PART VII

SOLEMN PROCEEDINGS

The indictment

Prosecution on indictment

64.—(1) All prosecutions for the public interest before the High Court or before the sheriff sitting with a jury shall proceed on indictment in name of Her Majesty's Advocate.

(2) The indictment may be in the forms—

(a) set out in Schedule 2 to this Act; or

(b) prescribed by Act of Adjournal,

or as nearly as may be in such form.

(3) Indictments in proceedings before the High Court shall be signed by the Lord Advocate or one of his deputes.

(4) Indictments in proceedings before the sheriff sitting with a jury shall be signed by the procurator fiscal, and the words "By Authority of Her Majesty's Advocate" shall be prefixed to the signature of the procurator fiscal.

(5) The principal record and service copies of indictments and all notices of citation, lists of witnesses, productions and jurors, and all other official documents required in a prosecution on indictment may be either written or printed or partly written and partly printed.

(6) Schedule 3 to this Act shall have effect as regards indictments under this Act.

Prevention of delay in trials

65.—(1) Subject to subsections (2) and (3) below, an accused shall not be tried on indictment for any offence unless the trial is commenced within a period of 12 months of the first appearance of the accused on petition in respect of the offence; and, failing such commencement within that period, the accused

[1](a) shall be discharged forthwith from any indictment as respects the offence; and

(b) shall not at any time be proceeded against on indictment as respects the offence.

(2) Nothing in subsection (1) above shall bar the trial of an accused for whose arrest a warrant has been granted for failure to appear at a diet in the case.

(3) On an application made for the purpose, the sheriff or, where an indictment has been served on the accused in respect of the High Court, a single judge of that court, may on cause shown extend the said period of 12 months.

[1](3A) An application under subsection (3) shall not be made at any time when an appeal made with leave under s.74(1) of this Act has not been disposed of by the High Court.

(4) Subject to subsections (5) to (9) below, an accused who is committed for any offence until liberated in due course of law shall not be detained by virtue of that committal for a total period of more than—

(a) 80 days, unless within that period the indictment is served on him, which failing he shall be liberated forthwith; or

(b) 110 days, unless the trial of the case is commenced within that period, which failing he shall be liberated forthwith and thereafter he shall be for ever free from all question or process for that offence.

(5) Subject to subsection (6) below, a single judge of the High Court, may, on an application made to him for the purpose, for any sufficient cause extend the period mentioned in subsection (4)(a) above.

(6) An application under subsection (5) above shall not be granted if the judge is satisfied that, but for some fault on the part of the prosecution, the indictment could have been served within the period of 80 days.

(7) A single judge of the High Court may, on an application made to him for the purpose, extend the period mentioned in subsection (4)(b) above where he is satisfied that delay in the commencement of the trial is due to—

(a) the illness of the accused or of a judge;

(b) the absence or illness of any necessary witness;

(c) any other sufficient cause which is not attributable to any fault on the part of the prosecutor.

(8) The grant or refusal of any application to extend the periods mentioned in this section may be appealed against by note of appeal presented to the High Court; and that Court may affirm, reverse or amend the determination made on such application.

(9) For the purposes of this section, a trial shall be taken to commence when the oath is administered to the jury.

(10) In calculating the period of 12 months specified in subsections (1) and (3) above there shall be left out of account any period during which the accused is detained, other than while serving a sentence of imprisonment or detention, in any other part of the United Kingdom or in any of the Channel Islands or the Isle of Man in any prison or other institution or place mentioned in subsection (1) or (1A) of section 29 of the Criminal Justice Act 1961 (transfer of prisoners for certain judicial purposes).

NOTE

[1]Inserted by the Crime and Punishment (Scotland) Act 1997 Sched. 1, para. 21(9) with effect from August 1, 1997 in terms of the Crime and Punishment (Scotland) Act 1997 (Commencement and Transitional Provisions) Order 1997 (S.I. 1997 No. 1712) para. 21(9).

Service and lodging of indictment, etc.

66.—(1) When a sitting of the sheriff court or of the High Court has been appointed to be held for the trial of persons accused on indictment—

(a) where the trial diet is to be held in the sheriff court, the sheriff clerk; and

(b) where the trial diet is to be held in the High Court, the Clerk of Justiciary,

shall issue a warrant to officers of law to cite the accused, witnesses and jurors, in such form as may be prescribed by Act of Adjournal, or as nearly as may be in such form, and such warrant authenticated by the signature of such clerk, or a duly certified copy thereof, shall be a sufficient warrant for such citation.

(2) The execution of the citation against an accused, witness or juror shall be in such form as may be prescribed by Act of Adjournal, or as nearly as may be in such form.

(3) A witness may be cited by sending the citation to the witness by ordinary or registered post or by the recorded delivery service and a written execution in the form prescribed by Act of Adjournal or as nearly as may be in such form, purporting to be signed by the person who served such citation together with, where appropriate, the relevant post office receipt shall be sufficient evidence of such citation.

(4) The accused shall be served with a copy of the indictment and of the list

of the names and addresses of the witnesses to be adduced by the prosecution.

(5) Except in a case to which section 76 of this Act applies, the prosecutor shall on or before the date of service of the indictment lodge the record copy of the indictment with the clerk of court before which the trial is to take place, together with a copy of the list of witnesses and a copy of the list of productions.

(6) Except where the indictment is served under section 76(1) of this Act, a notice shall be served on the accused with the indictment calling upon him to appear and answer to the indictment—

(a) where the case is to be tried in the sheriff court, at a first diet not less than 15 clear days after the service of the indictment and not less than 10 clear days before the trial diet; and

(b) at a trial diet (either in the High Court or in the sheriff court) not less than 29 clear days after the service of the indictment and notice.

(7) Service of the indictment, lists of witnesses and productions, and any notice or intimation to the accused, and the citation of witnesses, whether for precognition or trial, may be effected by any officer of law.

(8) No objection to the service of an indictment or to the citation of a witness shall be upheld on the ground that the officer who effected service or executed the citation was not at the time in possession of the warrant of citation, and it shall not be necessary to produce the execution of citation of an indictment.

(9) The citation of witnesses may be effected by any officer of law duly authorised; and in any proceedings, the evidence on oath of the officer shall, subject to subsection (10) below, be sufficient evidence of the execution of the citation.

(10) A court shall not issue a warrant to apprehend a witness who fails to appear at a diet to which he has been duly cited unless the court is satisfied that the witness received the citation or that its contents came to his knowledge.

(11) No objection to the competency of the officer who served the indictment to give evidence in respect of such service shall be upheld on the ground that his name is not included in the list of witnesses served on the accused.

(12) Any deletion or correction made before service on the record or service copy of an indictment shall be sufficiently authenticated by the initials of the person who has signed, or could by law have signed, the indictment.

(13) Any deletion or correction made on a service copy of an indictment, or on any notice of citation, postponement, adjournment or other notice required to be served on an accused shall be sufficiently authenticated by the initials of any procurator fiscal or of the person serving the same.

(14) Any deletion or correction made on any execution of citation or notice of other document requiring to be served shall be sufficiently authenticated by the initials of the person serving the same.

Witnesses

67.—(1) The list of witnesses shall consist of the names of the witnesses together with an address at which they can be contacted for the purposes of precognition.

(2) It shall not be necessary to include in the list of witnesses the names of any witnesses to the declaration of the accused or the names of any witnesses to prove that an extract conviction applies to the accused, but witnesses may be examined in regard to these matters without previous notice.

(3) Any objection in respect of misnomer or misdescription of—

(a) any person named in the indictment; or

    (b) any witness in the list of witnesses, shall be intimated in writing to the court before which the trial is to take place, to the prosecutor and to any other accused, where the case is to be tried in the sheriff court, at or before the first diet and, where the case is to be tried in the High Court, not less than ten clear days before the trial diet; and, except on cause shown, no such objection shall be admitted at the trial diet unless so intimated.

    (4) Where such intimation has been given or cause is shown and the court is satisfied that the accused making the objection has not been supplied with sufficient information to enable him to identify the person named in the indictment or to find such witness in sufficient time to precognosce him before the trial, the court may grant such remedy by postponement, adjournment or otherwise as appears to it to be appropriate.

    (5) Without prejudice to—

    (a) any enactment or rule of law permitting the prosecutor to examine any witness not included in the list of witnesses; or

    (b) subsection (6) below,

in any trial it shall be competent with the leave of the court for the prosecutor to examine any witness or to put in evidence any production not included in the lists lodged by him, provided that written notice, containing in the case of a witness his name and address as mentioned in subsection (1) above, has been given to the accused not less than two clear days before the day on which the jury is sworn to try the case.

    (6) It shall be competent for the prosecutor to examine any witness or put in evidence any production included in any list or notice lodged by the accused, and it shall be competent for an accused to examine any witness or put in evidence any production included in any list or notice lodged by the prosecutor or by a co-accused.

    [1]**67A.**—(1) This section applies where a prosecutor has obtained a warrant to cite a witness for precognition and has served a citation for precognition on the witness.

    (2) Where this section applies, a witness who—

    (a) fails without reasonable excuse, after receiving at least 48 hours notice, to attend for precognition by a prosecutor at the time and place mentioned in the citation served on him; or

    (b) refuses when so cited to give information within his knowledge regarding any matter relative to the commission of the offence in relation to which such precognition is taken,

shall be guilty of an offence and shall be liable on summary conviction to a fine not exceeding level 3 on the standard scale or to a term of imprisonment not exceeding 21 days.

NOTE

[1]Inserted by the Crime and Punishment (Scotland) Act 1997 (c. 48) s.57(1) with effect from August 1, 1997 in terms of the Crime and Punishment (Scotland) Act 1997 (Commencement and Transitional Provisions) Order 1997 (S.I. 1997 No. 1712) para. 5.

Productions

    68.—(1) The list of productions shall include the record, made under section 37 of this Act (incorporating any rectification authorised under section 38(1) of this Act), of proceedings at the examination of the accused.

    (2) The accused shall be entitled to see the productions according to the existing law and practice in the office of the sheriff clerk of the district in which the court of the trial diet is situated or, where the trial diet is to be in the High Court in Edinburgh, in the Justiciary Office.

    (3) Where a person who has examined a production is adduced to give

evidence with regard to it and the production has been lodged at least eight days before the trial diet, it shall not be necessary to prove—

    (a) that the production was received by him in the condition in which it was taken possession of by the procurator fiscal or the police and returned by him after his examination of it to the procurator fiscal or the police; or

    (b) that the production examined by him is that taken possession of by the procurator fiscal or the police,

unless the accused, at least four days before the trial diet, gives in accordance with subsection (4) below written notice that he does not admit that the production was received or returned as aforesaid or, as the case may be, that it is that taken possession of as aforesaid.

    (4) The notice mentioned in subsection (3) above shall be given—

    (a) where the accused is cited to the High Court for the trial diet, to the Crown Agent; and

    (b) where he is cited to the sheriff court for the trial diet, to the procurator fiscal.

Notice of previous convictions

    69.—(1) No mention shall be made in the indictment of previous convictions, nor shall extracts of previous convictions be included in the list of productions annexed to the indictment.

    (2) If the prosecutor intends to place before the court any previous conviction, he shall cause to be served on the accused along with the indictment a notice in the form set out in an Act of Adjournal or as nearly as may be in such form, and any conviction specified in the notice shall be held to apply to the accused unless he gives, in accordance with subsection (3) below, written intimation objecting to such conviction on the ground that it does not apply to him or is otherwise inadmissible.

    (3) Intimation objecting to a conviction under subsection (2) above shall be given—

    (a) where the accused is cited to the High Court for the trial diet, to the Crown Agent; or

    (b) where the accused is cited to the sheriff court for the trial diet, to the procurator fiscal,

at least five clear days before the first day of the sitting in which the trial diet is to be held.

    (4) Where notice is given by the accused under section 76 of this Act of his intention to plead guilty and the prosecutor intends to place before the court any previous conviction, he shall cause to be served on the accused along with the indictment a notice in the form set out in an Act of Adjournal or as nearly as may be in such form.

    (5) Where the accused pleads guilty at any diet, no objection to any conviction of which notice has been served on him under this section shall be entertained unless he has, at least two clear days before the diet, given intimation to the procurator fiscal of the district to the court of which the accused is cited for the diet.

Proceedings against bodies corporate

    70.—(1) This section applies to proceedings on indictment against a body corporate.

    (2) The indictment may be served by delivery of a copy of the indictment together with notice to appear at the registered office or, if there is no registered office or the registered office is not in the United Kingdom, at the principal place of business in the United Kingdom of the body corporate.

    (3) Where a letter containing a copy of the indictment has been sent by registered post or by the recorded delivery service to the registered office or

principal place of business of the body corporate, an acknowledgement or certificate of the delivery of the letter issued by the Post Office shall be sufficient evidence of the delivery of the letter at the registered office or place of business on the day specified in such acknowledgement or certificate.

(4) A body corporate may, for the purpose of—

(a) stating objections to the competency or relevancy of the indictment or proceedings; or

(b) tendering a plea of guilty or not guilty; or

(c) making a statement in mitigation of sentence,

appear by a representative of the body corporate.

(5) Where at the trial diet the body corporate does not appear as mentioned in subsection (4) above, or by counsel or a solicitor, the court shall, on the motion of the prosecutor, if it is satisfied that subsection (2) above has been complied with, proceed to hear and dispose of the case in the absence of the body corporate.

(6) Where a body corporate is sentenced to a fine, the fine may be recovered in like manner in all respects as if a copy of the sentence certified by the clerk of the court were an extract decree of the Court of Session for the payment of the amount of the fine by the body corporate to the Queen's and Lord Treasurer's Remembrancer.

(7) Nothing in section 77 of this Act shall require a plea tendered by or on behalf of a body corporate to be signed.

(8) In this section, "representative", in relation to a body corporate, means an officer or employee of the body corporate duly appointed by it for the purpose of the proceedings; and a statement in writing purporting to be signed by the managing director of, or by any person having or being one of the persons having the management of the affairs of the body corporate, to the effect that the person named in the statement has been appointed the representative of the body corporate for the purpose of any proceedings to which this section applies shall be sufficient evidence of such appointment.

Pre-trial proceedings

First diet

71.—(1) At a first diet the court shall, so far as is reasonably practicable, ascertain whether the case is likely to proceed to trial on the date assigned as the trial diet and, in particular—

(a) the state of preparation of the prosecutor and of the accused with respect to their cases; and

(b) the extent to which the prosecutor and the accused have complied with the duty under section 257(1) of this Act.

(2) In addition to the matters mentioned in subsection (1) above the court shall, at a first diet, consider any matter mentioned in any of paragraphs (a) to (d) of section 72(1) of this Act of which a party has, not less than two clear days before the first diet, given notice to the court and to the other parties.

(3) At a first diet the court may ask the prosecutor and the accused any question in connection with any matter which it is required to ascertain or consider under subsection (1) or (2) above.

(4) The accused shall attend a first diet of which he has been given notice and the court may, if he fails to do so, grant a warrant to apprehend him.

(5) A first diet may proceed notwithstanding the absence of the accused.

(6) The accused shall, at the first diet, be required to state how he pleads to the indictment, and section 77 of this Act shall apply where he tenders a plea of guilty.

(7) Where at a first diet the court concludes that the case is unlikely to proceed to trial on the date assigned for the trial diet, the court—

(a) shall, unless having regard to previous proceedings in the case it considers it inappropriate to do so, postpone the trial diet; and

(b) may fix a further first diet.

(8) Subject to subsection (7) above, the court may, if it considers it appropriate to do so, adjourn a first diet.

(9) In this section "the court" means the sheriff court.

Preliminary diet: notice

72.—(1) Subject to subsections (4) and (5) below, where a party to a case which is to be tried in the High Court within the appropriate period gives written notice to the court and to the other parties—

(a) that he intends to raise—
  (i) a matter relating to the competency or relevancy of the indictment; or
  (ii) an objection to the validity of the citation against him, on the ground of any discrepancy between the record copy of the indictment and the copy served on him, or on account of any error or deficiency in such service copy or in the notice of citation;

(b) that he intends—
  (i) to submit a plea in bar of trial;
  (ii) to apply for separation or conjunction of charges or trials;
  (iii) to raise a preliminary objection under section 255 of this Act; or
  (iv) to make an application under section 278(2) of this Act;

(c) that there are documents the truth of the contents of which ought to be admitted, or that there is any other matter which in his view ought to be agreed;

(d) that there is some point, as regards any matter not mentioned in paragraph (a) to (c) above, which could in his opinion be resolved with advantage before the trial and that he therefore applies for a diet to be held before the trial diet,

the court shall in a case to which paragraph (a) above applies, and in any other case may, order that there be a diet before the trial diet, and a diet ordered under this subsection is in this Act referred to as a "preliminary diet".

(2) A party giving notice under subsection (1) above shall specify in the notice the matter or, as the case may be, the grounds of submission or the point to which the notice relates.

(3) The fact that a preliminary diet has been ordered on a particular notice under subsection (1) above shall not preclude the court's consideration at that diet of any other such notice as is mentioned in that subsection, which has been intimated to the court and to the other parties at least 24 hours before that diet.

(4) Subject to subsection (5) below, the court may on ordering a preliminary diet postpone the trial diet for a period not exceeding 21 days; and any such postponement (including postponement for a period which by virtue of the said subsection (5) exceeds 21 days) shall not count towards any time limit applying in respect of the case.

(5) Any period mentioned in subsection (4) above may be extended by the High Court in respect of the case.

(6) In subsection (1) above, "appropriate period" means as regards notice—

(a) under paragraph (a) of that subsection, the period of 15 clear days after service of the indictment;

(b) under paragraph (b) of that subsection, the period from service of the indictment to 10 clear days before the trial diet; and

(c) under paragraph (c) or (d) of that subsection, the period from service of the indictment to the trial diet.

Preliminary diet: procedure

73.—(1) Where a preliminary diet is ordered, subject to subsection (2) below, the accused shall attend it, and he shall be required at the conclusion of the diet to state how he pleads to the indictment.

(2) The court may permit the diet to proceed notwithstanding the absence of an accused.

(3) At a preliminary diet the court shall, in addition to disposing of any matter specified in a notice given under subsection (1) of section 72 of this Act or referred to in subsection (3) of that section, ascertain, so far as is reasonably practicable, whether the case is likely to proceed to trial on the date assigned as the trial diet and, in particular—

(a) the state of preparation of the prosecutor and of the accused with respect to their cases; and

(b) the extent to which the prosecutor and the accused have complied with the duty under section 257(1) of this Act.

(4) At a preliminary diet the court may ask the prosecutor and the accused any question in connection with any matter specified in a notice under subsection (1) of the said section 72 or referred to in subsection (3) of that section or which it is required to ascertain under subsection (3) above.

(5) Where at a preliminary diet the court concludes that the case is unlikely to proceed to trial on the date assigned for the trial diet, the court—

(a) shall, unless having regard to previous proceedings in the case it considers it inappropriate to do so, postpone the trial diet; and

(b) may fix a further preliminary diet.

(6) Subject to subsection (5) above, the court may, if it considers it appropriate to do so, adjourn a preliminary diet.

(7) Where an objection is taken to the relevancy of the indictment under subsection (1)(a)(i) of the said section 72, the clerk of court shall minute whether the objection is sustained or repelled and sign the minute.

(8) In subsection (1) above, the reference to the accused shall, without prejudice to section 6(c) of the Interpretation Act 1978, in any case where there is more than one accused include a reference to all of them.

Appeals in connection with preliminary diets

74.—(1) Without prejudice to—

(a) any right of appeal under section 106 or 108 of this Act; and

(b) section 131 of this Act,

and subject to subsection (2) below, a party may with the leave of the court of first instance (granted either on the motion of the party or *ex proprio motu*) in accordance with such procedure as may be prescribed by Act of Adjournal, appeal to the High Court against a decision at a first diet or a preliminary diet.

(2) An appeal under subsection (1) above—

(a) may not be taken against a decision to adjourn the first or, as the case may be, preliminary diet or to postpone the trial diet;

(b) must be taken not later than 2 days after the decision.

(3) Where an appeal is taken under subsection (1) above, the High Court may postpone the trial diet for such period as appears to it to be appropriate and may, if it thinks fit, direct that such period (or some part of it) shall not count towards any time limit applying in respect of the case.

(4) In disposing of an appeal under subsection (1) above the High Court—

¹(a) may affirm the decision of the court of first instance or may remit the case to it with such directions in the matter as it thinks fit;

(b) where the court of first instance has dismissed the indictment or any part of it, may reverse that decision and direct that the court of first instance fix a trial diet, if it has not already fixed one as regards so much of the indictment as it has not dismissed; and

²(c) may on cause shown extend the period mentioned in section 65(1) of this Act.

NOTES

¹Words deleted by the Crime and Punishment (Scotland) Act 1997 (c. 48), s.62(1) Sched. 1, para. 21(10)(a) with effect from August 1, 1997 as provided by the Crime and Punishment (Scotland) Act 1997 (Commencement and Transitional Provisions) Order 1997 (S.I. 1997 No. 1712) Art. 3 and Sched. 1.

²Inserted by para. 21(10)(b) of the above-mentioned Act with effect from August 1, 1997 in terms of the above Order.

Computation of certain periods

75. Where the last day of any period mentioned in section 66(6), 67(3), 72 or 74 of this Act falls on a Saturday, Sunday or court holiday, such period shall extend to and include the next day which is not a Saturday, Sunday or court holiday.

Plea of guilty

Procedure where accused desires to plead guilty

76.—(1) Where an accused intimates in writing to the Crown Agent that he intends to plead guilty and desires to have his case disposed of at once, the accused may be served with an indictment (unless one has already been served) and a notice to appear at a diet of the appropriate court not less than four clear days after the date of the notice; and it shall not be necessary to lodge or give notice of any list of witnesses or productions.

(2) In subsection (1) above, "appropriate court" means—

(a) in a case where at the time of the intimation mentioned in that subsection an indictment had not been served, either the High Court or the sheriff court; and

(b) in any other case, the court specified in the notice served under section 66(6) of this Act on the accused.

(3) If at any such diet the accused pleads not guilty to the charge or pleads guilty only to a part of the charge, and the prosecutor declines to accept such restricted plea, the diet shall be deserted *pro loco et tempore* and thereafter the cause may proceed in accordance with the other provisions of this Part of this Act; except that in a case mentioned in paragraph (b) of subsection (2) above the court may postpone the trial diet and the period of such postponement shall not count towards any time limit applying in respect of the case.

Plea of guilty

77.—(1) Where at any diet the accused tenders a plea of guilty to the indictment or any part thereof he shall do so in open court and, subject to section 70(7) of this Act, shall, if he is able to do so, sign a written copy of the plea; and the judge shall countersign such copy.

(2) Where the plea is to part only of the charge and the prosecutor does not accept the plea, such non-acceptance shall be recorded.

(3) Where an accused charged on indictment with any offence tenders a

plea of guilty to any other offence of which he could competently be found guilty on the trial of the indictment, and that plea is accepted by the prosecutor, it shall be competent to convict the accused of the offence to which he has so pled guilty and to sentence him accordingly.

Notice by accused

Special defences, incrimination and notice of witnesses, etc.

78.—(1) It shall not be competent for an accused to state a special defence or to lead evidence calculated to exculpate the accused by incriminating a co-accused unless—

(a) a plea of special defence or, as the case may be, notice of intention to lead such evidence has been lodged and intimated in writing in accordance with subsection (3) below—

   (i) where the accused is cited to the High Court for the trial diet, to the Crown Agent; and

   (ii) where he is cited to the sheriff court for the trial diet, to the procurator fiscal,

and to any co-accused not less than 10 clear days before the trial diet; or

(b) the court, on cause shown, otherwise directs.

(2) Subsection (1) above shall apply to a defence of automatism or coercion as if it were a special defence.

(3) A plea or notice is lodged and intimated in accordance with this subsection—

(a) where the accused is cited to the High Court for the trial diet, by lodging the plea or notice with the Clerk of Justiciary and by intimating the plea or notice to the Crown Agent and to any co-accused not less than 10 clear days before the trial diet;

(b) where the accused is cited to the sheriff court for the trial diet, by lodging the plea or notice with the sheriff clerk and by intimating it to the procurator fiscal and to any co-accused at or before the first diet.

(4) It shall not be competent for the accused to examine any witnesses or to put in evidence any productions not included in the lists lodged by the prosecutor unless—

(a) written notice of the names and addresses of such witnesses and of such productions has been given—

   (i) where the case is to be tried in the sheriff court, to the procurator fiscal of the district of the trial diet at or before the first diet; and

   (ii) where the case is to be tried in the High Court, to the Crown Agent at least ten clear days before the day on which the jury is sworn; or

(b) the court, on cause shown, otherwise directs.

(5) A copy of every written notice required by subsection (4) above shall be lodged by the accused with the sheriff clerk of the district in which the trial diet is to be held, or in any case the trial diet of which is to be held in the High Court in Edinburgh with the Clerk of Justiciary, at or before the trial diet, for the use of the court.

Preliminary pleas

79.—(1) Except by leave of the court on cause shown, no application, matter or point mentioned in subsection (1) of section 72 of this Act or that subsection as applied by section 71 of this Act shall be made, raised or submitted by an accused unless his intention to do so has been stated in a notice under the said subsection (1) or, as the case may be, under subsection (2) of the said section 71.

(2) No discrepancy, error or deficiency such as is mentioned in paragraph

(a)(ii) of subsection (1) of the said section 72 or that subsection as applied by the said section 71 shall entitle the accused to object to plead to the indictment unless the court is satisfied that the discrepancy, error or deficiency tended substantially to mislead and prejudice the accused.

Alteration, etc, of diet

Alteration and postponement of trial diet

80.—(1) Where an indictment is not brought to trial at the trial diet and a warrant for a subsequent sitting of the court on a day within two months after the date of the trial diet has been issued under section 66(1) of this Act by the clerk of court, the court may adjourn the trial diet to the subsequent sitting, and the warrant shall have effect as if the trial diet had originally been fixed for the date of the subsequent sitting.

(2) At any time before the trial diet, a party may apply to the court before which the trial is to take place for postponement of the trial diet.

(3) Subject to subsection (4) below, after hearing all the parties the court may discharge the trial diet and either fix a new trial diet or give leave to the prosecutor to serve a notice fixing a new trial diet.

(4) Where all the parties join in an application to postpone the trial diet, the court may proceed under subsection (3) above without hearing the parties.

(5) Where there is a hearing under this section the accused shall attend it, unless the court permits the hearing to proceed notwithstanding the absence of the accused.

(6) In subsection (5) above, the reference to the accused shall, without prejudice to section 6(c) of the Interpretation Act 1978, in any case where there is more than one accused include a reference to all of them.

Procedure where trial does not take place

81.—(1) Where at the trial diet—

(a) the diet has been deserted *pro loco et tempore* for any cause; or

(b) an indictment is for any cause not brought to trial and no order has been given by the court postponing such trial or appointing it to be held at a subsequent date at some other sitting of the court,

it shall be lawful at any time within nine clear days after the last day of the sitting in which the trial diet was to be held to give notice to the accused on another copy of the indictment to appear to answer the indictment at a further diet either in the High Court or in the sheriff court when the charge is one that can be lawfully tried in that court, notwithstanding that the original citation to a trial diet was to a different court.

(2) Without prejudice to subsection (1) above, where a trial diet has been deserted *pro loco et tempore* and the court has appointed a further trial diet to be held on a subsequent date at the same sitting the accused shall require to appear and answer the indictment at that further diet.

(3) The prosecutor shall not raise a fresh libel in a case where the court has deserted the trial *simpliciter* and its decision in that regard has not been reversed on appeal.

(4) The notice referred to in subsection (1) above shall be in the form prescribed by Act of Adjournal or as nearly as may be in such form.

(5) The further diet specified in the notice referred to in subsection (1) above shall be not earlier than nine clear days from the giving of the notice.

[1,2](6) On or before the day on which notice referred to in subsection (1) above is given, a list of jurors shall be prepared, ... and kept by the sheriff clerk of the district to which the notice applies in the manner provided in section 85(2) of this Act.

(7) The warrant issued under section 66(1) of this Act shall be sufficient warrant for the citation of accused and witnesses to the further diet.

NOTES

[1]Deleted by the Crime and Punishment (Scotland) Act 1997 (c. 48), s.62(1) and Sched. 1, para. 21(11) with effect from August 1, 1997 in terms of the Crime and Punishment (Scotland) Act 1997 (Commencement and Transitional Provisions) Order 1997 (S.I. 1997 No. 1712) para. 3.

[2]Inserted by the above Act and Schedule and commenced as above.

Desertion or postponement where accused in custody

82. Where—
  (a) a diet is deserted *pro loco et tempore*;
  (b) a diet is postponed or adjourned; or
  (c) an order is issued for the trial to take place at a different place from that first given notice of,
the warrant of committal on which the accused is at the time in custody till liberated in due course of law shall continue in force.

Transfer of sheriff court solemn proceedings

83.—[1](1) Where an accused person has been cited to attend a sitting of the sheriff court the prosecutor may, at any time before the commencement of his trial, apply to the sheriff to adjourn the trial and transfer it to a sitting of a sheriff court, appointed as mentioned in section 66(1) of this Act, in any other district in that sheriffdom.

[2](2) On an application under subsection (1) above the sheriff may—
  (a) after giving the accused or his counsel or solicitor an opportunity to be heard; or
  (b) on the joint application of the parties,
adjourn the trial and make an order for the transfer of the trial as mentioned in subsection (1) above.

[3](3) Where a warrant to cite any person to attend a sitting of the sheriff court has been issued by the sheriff clerk under section 66(1) of this Act and the trial has been adjourned and transferred by an order under subsection (2) above, the warrant shall have effect as if the trial diet had originally been fixed for the court, and the date of the sitting of that court, to which the trial is so transferred.

NOTES

[1]Substituted by the Crime and Punishment (Scotland) Act 1997 (c. 48), s.62(1) and Sched. 1, para. 21(12)(a) with effect from August 1, 1997 in terms of the Crime and Punishment (Scotland) Act 1997 (Commencement and Transitional Provisions) Order 1997 (S.I. 1997 No. 1712) para. 3.

[2]Inserted by s.62(1) and Sched. 1, para. 21(12)(b) of the above Act with effect from August 1, 1997 by mean of the above Order.

[3]Inserted by s.62(1) and Sched. 1, para. 21(12)(c) of the above Act with effect from August 1, 1997 in terms of the above Order.

Jurors for sittings

Juries: returns of jurors and preparation of lists

84.—(1) For the purposes of a trial, the sheriff principal shall return such number of jurors as he thinks fit or, in relation to a trial in the High Court, such other number as the Lord Justice Clerk or any Lord Commissioner of Justiciary may direct.

(2) The Lord Justice General, whom failing the Lord Justice Clerk, may give directions as to the areas from which and the proportions in which jurors are to be summoned for trials to be held in the High Court, and for any such trial the sheriff principal of the sheriffdom in which the trial is to take place shall requisition the required number of jurors from the areas and in the proportions so specified.

(3) Where a sitting of the High Court is to be held at a town in which the

High Court does not usually sit, the jury summoned to try any case in such a sitting shall be summoned from the list of potential jurors of the sheriff court district in which the town is situated.

(4) For the purpose of a trial in the sheriff court, the clerk of court shall be furnished with a list of names from lists of potential jurors of the sheriff court district in which the court is held containing the number of persons required.

(5) The sheriff principal, in any return of jurors made by him to a court, shall take the names in regular order, beginning at the top of the list of potential jurors in each of the sheriff court districts, as required; and as often as a juror is returned to him, he shall mark or cause to be marked, in the list of potential jurors of the respective sheriff court districts the date when any such juror was returned to serve; and in any such return he shall commence with the name immediately after the last in the preceding return, without regard to the court to which the return was last made, and taking the subsequent names in the order in which they are entered, as directed by this subsection, and so to the end of the lists respectively.

(6) Where a person whose name has been entered in the lists of potential jurors dies, or ceases to be qualified to serve as a juror, the sheriff principal, in making returns of jurors in accordance with the Jurors (Scotland) Act 1825, shall pass over the name of that person, but the date at which his name has been so passed over, and the reason therefor, shall be entered at the time in the lists of potential jurors.

(7) Only the lists returned in accordance with this section by the sheriffs principal to the clerks of court shall be used for the trials for which they were required.

(8) The persons to serve as jurors at sittings of the High Court shall be listed and their names and addresses shall be inserted in one roll to be signed by the judge, and the list made up under this section shall be known as the "list of assize".

(9) When more than one case is set down for trial at a sitting of the High Court, it shall not be necessary to prepare more than one list of assize, and such list shall be authenticated by the signature of a judge of the Court, and shall be the list of assize for the trial of all parties cited to that particular sitting; and the persons included in such list shall be summoned to serve generally for the trials of all the accused cited to the sitting, and only one general execution of citation shall be returned against them; and a copy of the list of assize, certified by one of the clerks of court, shall have the like effect, for all purposes for which the list may be required, as the principal list of assize authenticated as aforesaid.

(10) No irregularity in—
(a) making up the lists in accordance with the provisions of this Act;
(b) transmitting the lists;
(c) the warrant of citation;
(d) summoning jurors; or
(e) in returning any execution of citation,
shall constitute an objection to jurors whose names are included in the jury list, subject to the ruling of the court in relation to the effect of an objection as to any criminal act by which jurors may be returned to serve in any case contrary to this Act or the Jurors (Scotland) Act 1825.

Juries: citation and attendance of jurors

85.—[1](1) It shall not be necessary to serve any list of jurors upon the accused ...
[1](2) A list of jurors shall—
(a) contain not less than 30 names;

(b) be prepared under the directions of the clerk of the court before which the trial is to take place;

(c) be kept at the office of the sheriff clerk of the district in which the court of the trial diet is situated; and

(d) be headed "List of Assize for the sitting of the High Court of Justiciary (or the sheriff court of. at.) on the. of.".

(2A) The clerk of the court before which the trial is to take place shall, on an application made to him by or on behalf of an accused, supply the accused, free of charge on the day on which the trial diet is called, and before the oath has been administered to the jurors for the trial of the accused, with a copy of a list of jurors prepared under subsection (2) above.

(2B) Where an accused has been supplied under subsection (2A) above with a list of jurors—

(a) neither he nor any person acting on his behalf shall make a copy of that list, or any part thereof; and

(b) he or his representatives shall return the list to the clerk of the court after the oath has been administered to the jurors for his trial.

(2C) A person who fails to comply with subsection (2B) above shall be guilty of an offence and shall be liable on summary conviction to a fine not exceeding level 1 on the standard scale.

(3) It shall not be necessary to summon all the jurors contained in any list of jurors under this Act, but it shall be competent to summon such jurors only, commencing from the top of the list, as may be necessary to ensure a sufficient number for the trial of the cases which remain for trial at the date of the citation of the jurors, and such number shall be fixed by the clerk of the court in which the trial diet is to be called, or in any case in the High Court by the Clerk of Justiciary, and the jurors who are not so summoned shall be placed upon the next list issued, until they have attended to serve.

(4) The sheriff clerk of the sheriffdom in which a sitting of the High Court is to be held or the sheriff clerk of the sheriff court district in which any juror is to be cited where the citation is for a trial before a sheriff, shall fill up and sign a proper citation addressed to each such juror, and shall cause the same to be transmitted to him by letter, sent to him at his place of residence as stated in the lists of potential jurors by registered post or recorded delivery or to be served on him by an officer of law; and a certificate under the hand of such sheriff clerk of the citation of any jurors or juror in the manner provided in this subsection shall be a legal citation.

(5) The sheriff clerk of the sheriffdom in which a sitting of the High Court is to be held shall issue citations to the whole jurors required for the sitting, whether the jurors reside in that or in any other sheriffdom.

(6) Persons cited to attend as jurors may, unless they have been excused in respect thereof under section 1 of the Law Reform (Miscellaneous Provisions) (Scotland) Act 1980, be fined up to level 3 on the standard scale if they fail to attend in compliance with the citation.

(7) A fine imposed under subsection (6) above may, on application, be remitted—

(a) by a Lord Commissioner of Justiciary where imposed in the High Court;

(b) by the sheriff court where imposed in the sheriff court,

and no court fees or expenses shall be exigible in respect of any such application.

(8) A person shall not be exempted by sex or marriage from the liability to serve as a juror.

NOTE

[1] As amended by the Crime and Punishment (Scotland) Act 1997 (c. 48), s.58 with effect from August 1, 1997 (Commencement and Transitional Provisions) Order 1997, (S.I. 1997 No. 1712) para. 3.

Jurors: excusal and objections

86.—(1) Where, before a juror is sworn to serve, the parties jointly apply for him to be excused the court shall, notwithstanding that no reason is given in the application, excuse that juror from service.

(2) Nothing in subsection (1) above shall affect the right of the accused or the prosecutor to object to any juror on cause shown.

(3) If any objection is taken to a juror on cause shown and such objection is founded on the want of sufficient qualification as provided by section 1(1) of the Law Reform (Miscellaneous Provisions) (Scotland) Act 1980, such objection shall be proved only by the oath of the juror objected to.

(4) No objection to a juror shall be competent after he has been sworn to serve.

Non-availability of judge

Non-availability of judge

87.—(1) Where the court is unable to proceed owing to the death, illness or absence of the presiding judge, the clerk of court may convene the court (if necessary) and—

  (a) in a case where no evidence has been led, adjourn the diet and any other diet appointed for that sitting to—

    (i) a time later the same day, or a date not more than seven days later, when he believes a judge will be available; or

    (ii) a later sitting not more than two months after the date of the adjournment; or

  (b) in a case where evidence has been led—

    (i) adjourn the diet and any other diet appointed for that sitting to a time later the same day, or a date not more than seven days later, when he believes a judge will be available; or

    (ii) with the consent of the parties, desert the diet *pro loco et tempore.*

(2) Where a diet has been adjourned under sub-paragraph (i) of either paragraph (a) or paragraph (b) of subsection (1) above the clerk of court may, where the conditions of that subsection continue to be satisfied, further adjourn the diet under that sub-paragraph; but the total period of such adjournments shall not exceed seven days.

(3) Where a diet has been adjourned under subsection (1)(b)(i) above the court may, at the adjourned diet—

  (a) further adjourn the diet; or

  (b) desert the diet *pro loco et tempore.*

(4) Where a diet is deserted in pursuance of subsection (1)(b)(ii) or (3)(b) above, the Lord Advocate may raise and insist in a new indictment, and—

  (a) where the accused is in custody it shall not be necessary to grant a new warrant for his incarceration, and the warrant or commitment on which he is at the time in custody till liberation in due course of law shall continue in force; and

  (b) where the accused is at liberty on bail, his bail shall continue in force.

Jury for trial

Plea of not guilty, balloting and swearing of jury, etc.

88.—(1) Where the accused pleads not guilty, the clerk of court shall record that fact and proceed to ballot the jury.

(2) The jurors for the trial shall be chosen in open court by ballot from the list of persons summoned in such manner as shall be prescribed by Act of Adjournal, and the persons so chosen shall be the jury to try the accused, and their names shall be recorded in the minutes of the proceedings.

(3) It shall not be competent for the accused or the prosecutor to object to a juror on the ground that the juror has not been duly cited to attend.

(4) Notwithstanding subsection (1) above, the jurors chosen for any particular trial may, when that trial is disposed of, without a new ballot serve on the trials of other accused, provided that—

    (a) the accused and the prosecutor consent;

    (b) the names of the jurors are contained in the list of jurors; and

    (c) the jurors are duly sworn to serve on each successive trial.

(5) When the jury has been balloted, the clerk of court shall inform the jury of the charge against the accused—

    (a) by reading the words of the indictment (with the substitution of the third person for the second); or

    (b) if the presiding judge, because of the length or complexity of the indictment, so directs, by reading to the jury a summary of the charge approved by the judge,

and copies of the indictment shall be provided for each member of the jury without lists of witnesses or productions.

(6) After reading the charge as mentioned in subsection (5) above and any special defence as mentioned in section 89(1) of this Act, the clerk of court shall administer the oath in common form.

(7) The court may excuse a juror from serving on a trial where the juror has stated the ground for being excused in open court.

(8) Where a trial which is proceeding is adjourned from one day to another, the jury shall not be secluded during the adjournment, unless, on the motion of the prosecutor or the accused or *ex proprio motu* the court sees fit to order that the jury be kept secluded.

Jury to be informed of special defence

89.—(1) Subject to subsection (2) below, where the accused has lodged a plea of special defence, the clerk of court shall, after informing the jury, in accordance with section 88(5) of this Act, of the charge against the accused, and before administering the oath, read to the jury the plea of special defence.

(2) Where the presiding judge on cause shown so directs, the plea of special defence shall not be read over to the jury in accordance with subsection (1) above; and in any such case the judge shall inform the jury of the lodging of the plea and of the general nature of the special defence.

(3) Copies of a plea of special defence shall be provided for each member of the jury.

Death or illness of jurors

90.—(1) Where in the course of a trial—

    (a) a juror dies; or

    (b) the court is satisfied that it is for any reason inappropriate for any juror to continue to serve as a juror,

the court may in its discretion, on an application made by the prosecutor or an accused, direct that the trial shall proceed before the remaining jurors (if they are not less than twelve in number), and where such direction is given the remaining jurors shall be deemed in all respects to be a properly constituted jury for the purpose of the trial and shall have power to return a verdict accordingly whether unanimous or, subject to subsection (2) below, by majority.

(2) The remaining jurors shall not be entitled to return a verdict of guilty by majority unless at least eight of their number are in favour of such verdict and if, in any such case, the remaining jurors inform the court that—

    (a) fewer than eight of their number are in favour of a verdict of guilty; and

(b) there is not a majority in favour of any other verdict,
they shall be deemed to have returned a verdict of not guilty.

Trial

Trial to be continuous

91. Every trial shall proceed from day to day until it is concluded unless the court sees cause to adjourn over a day or days.

Trial in presence of accused

92.—(1) Without prejudice to section 54 of this Act, and subject to subsection (2) below, no part of a trial shall take place outwith the presence of the accused.

(2) If during the course of his trial an accused so misconducts himself that in the view of the court a proper trial cannot take place unless he is removed, the court may order—

(a) that he is removed from the court for so long as his conduct makes it necessary; and

(b) that the trial proceeds in his absence,

but if he is not legally represented the court shall appoint counsel or a solicitor to represent his interests during such absence.

(3) From the commencement of the leading of evidence in a trial for rape or the like the judge may, if he thinks fit, cause all persons other than the accused and counsel and solicitors to be removed from the court-room.

Record of trial

93.—(1) The proceedings at the trial of any person who, if convicted, is entitled to appeal under Part VIII of this Act, shall be recorded by means of shorthand notes or by mechanical means.

(2) A shorthand writer shall—

(a) sign the shorthand notes taken by him of such proceedings and certify them as being complete and correct; and

(b) retain the notes.

(3) A person recording such proceedings by mechanical means shall—

(a) certify that the record is true and complete;

(b) specify in the certificate the proceedings or, as the case may be, the part of the proceedings to which the record relates; and

(c) retain the record.

(4) The cost of making a record under subsection (1) above shall be defrayed, in accordance with scales of payment fixed for the time being by Treasury, out of money provided by Parliament.

(5) In subsection (1) above "proceedings at the trial" means the whole proceedings including, without prejudice to that generality—

(a) discussions—

   (i) on any objection to the relevancy of the indictment;

   (ii) with respect to any challenge of jurors; and

   (iii) on all questions arising in the course of the trial;

(b) the decision of the court on any matter referred to in paragraph (a) above;

(c) the evidence led at the trial;

(d) any statement made by or on behalf of the accused whether before or after the verdict;

(e) the judge's charge to the jury;

(f) the speeches of counsel or agent;

(g) the verdict of the jury;
(h) the sentence by the judge.

Transcripts of record and documentary productions

94.—(1) The Clerk of Justiciary may direct that a transcript of a record made under section 93(1) of this Act, or any part thereof, be made and delivered to him for the use of any judge.

(2) Subject to subsection (3) below, the Clerk of Justiciary shall, if requested to do so by—

(a) the Secretary of State; or
(b) any other person on payment of such charges as may be fixed for the time being by Treasury,

direct that such a transcript be made and sent to the person who requested it.

(3) The Secretary of State may, after consultation with the Lord Justice General, by order made by statutory instrument provide that in any class of proceedings specified in the order the Clerk of Justiciary shall only make a direction under subsection (2)(b) above if satisfied that the person requesting the transcript is of a class of person so specified and, if purposes for which the transcript may be used are so specified, intends to use it only for such a purpose; and different purposes may be so specified for different classes of proceedings or classes of person.

(4) Where subsection (3) above applies as respects a direction, the person to whom the transcript is sent shall, if purposes for which that transcript may be used are specified by virtue of that subsection, use it only for such a purpose.

(5) A statutory instrument containing an order under subsection (3) above shall be subject to annulment in pursuance of a resolution of either House of Parliament.

(6) A direction under subsection (1) or (2) above may require that the transcript be made by the person who made the record or by such competent person as may be specified in the direction; and that person shall comply with the direction.

(7) A transcript made in compliance with a direction under subsection (1) or (2) above—

(a) shall be in legible form; and
(b) shall be certified by the person making it as being a correct and complete transcript of the whole or, as the case may be, the part of the record purporting to have been made and certified, and in the case of shorthand notes signed, by the person who made the record.

(8) The cost of making a transcript in compliance with a direction under subsection (1) or (2)(a) above shall be defrayed, in accordance with scales of payment fixed for the time being by the Treasury, out of money provided by Parliament.

(9) The Clerk of Justiciary shall, on payment of such charges as may be fixed for the time being by the Treasury, provide a copy of any documentary production lodged in connection with an appeal under this Part of this Act to such of the following persons as may request it—

(a) the prosecutor;
(b) any person convicted in the proceedings;
(c) any other person named in, or immediately affected by, any order made in the proceedings; and
(d) any person authorised to act on behalf of any of the persons mentioned in paragraphs (a) to (c) above.

Verdict by judge alone

95.—(1) Where, at any time after the jury has been sworn to serve in a trial, the prosecutor intimates to the court that he does not intend to proceed in respect of an offence charged in the indictment, the judge shall acquit the accused of that offence and the trial shall proceed only in respect of any other offence charged in the indictment.

(2) Where, at any time after the jury has been sworn to serve in a trial, the accused intimates to the court that he is prepared to tender a plea of guilty as libelled, or such other plea as the Crown is prepared to accept, in respect of any offence charged in the indictment, the judge shall accept the plea tendered and shall convict the accused accordingly.

(3) Where an accused is convicted under subsection (2) above of an offence—

(a) the trial shall proceed only in respect of any other offence charged in the indictment; and

(b) without prejudice to any other power of the court to adjourn the case or to defer sentence, the judge shall not sentence him or make any other order competent following conviction until a verdict has been returned in respect of every other offence mentioned in paragraph (a) above.

Amendment of indictment

96.—(1) No trial shall fail or the ends of justice be allowed to be defeated by reason of any discrepancy or variance between the indictment and the evidence.

(2) It shall be competent at any time prior to the determination of the case, unless the court see just cause to the contrary, to amend the indictment by deletion, alteration or addition, so as to—

(a) cure any error or defect in it;

(b) meet any objection to it; or

(c) cure any discrepancy or variance between the indictment and the evidence.

(3) Nothing in this section shall authorise an amendment which changes the character of the offence charged, and, if it appears to the court that the accused may in any way be prejudiced in his defence on the merits of the case by any amendment made under this section, the court shall grant such remedy to the accused by adjournment or otherwise as appears to the court to be just.

(4) An amendment made under this section shall be sufficiently authenticated by the initials of the clerk of the court.

No case to answer

97.—(1) Immediately after the close of the evidence for the prosecution, the accused may intimate to the court his desire to make a submission that he has no case to answer both—

(a) on an offence charged in the indictment; and

(b) on any other offence of which he could be convicted under the indictment.

(2) If, after hearing both parties, the judge is satisfied that the evidence led by the prosecution is insufficient in law to justify the accused being convicted of the offence charged in respect of which the submission has been made or of such other offence as is mentioned, in relation to that offence, in paragraph (b) of subsection (1) above, he shall acquit him of the offence charged in respect of which the submission has been made and the trial shall proceed only in respect of any other offence charged in the indictment.

(3) If, after hearing both parties, the judge is not satisfied as is mentioned in subsection (2) above, he shall reject the submission and the trial shall proceed, with the accused entitled to give evidence and call witnesses, as if such submission had not been made.

(4) A submission under subsection (1) above shall be heard by the judge in the absence of the jury.

Defence to speak last

98. In any trial the accused or, where he is legally represented, his counsel or solicitor shall have the right to speak last.

Seclusion of jury to consider verdict

99.—(1) When the jury retire to consider their verdict, the clerk of court shall enclose the jury in a room by themselves and, except in so far as provided for, or is made necessary, by an instruction under subsection (4) below, neither he nor any other person shall be present with the jury after they are enclosed.

(2) Except in so far as is provided for, or is made necessary, by an instruction under subsection (4) below, until the jury intimate that they are ready to return their verdict—

    (a) subject to subsection (3) below, no person shall visit the jury or communicate with them; and

    (b) no juror shall come out of the jury room other than to receive or seek a direction from the judge or to make a request—

        (i) for an instruction under subsection (4)(a), (c) or (d) below; or

        (ii) regarding any matter in the cause.

(3) Nothing in paragraph (a) of subsection (2) above shall prohibit the judge, or any person authorised by him for the purpose, communicating with the jury for the purposes—

    (a) of giving a direction, whether or not sought under paragraph (b) of that subsection; or

    (b) responding to a request made under that paragraph.

(4) The judge may give such instructions as he considers appropriate as regards—

    (a) the provision of meals and refreshments for the jury;

    (b) the making of arrangements for overnight accommodation for the jury and for their continued seclusion if such accommodation is provided;

    (c) the communication of a personal or business message, unconnected with any matter in the cause, from a juror to another person (or vice versa); or

    (d) the provision of medical treatment, or other assistance, immediately required by a juror.

(5) If the prosecutor or any other person contravenes the provisions of this section, the accused shall be acquitted of the crime with which he is charged.

(6) During the period in which the jury are retired to consider their verdict, the judge may sit in any other proceedings; and the trial shall not fail by reason only of his so doing.

Verdict and conviction

Verdict of jury

100.—(1) The verdict of the jury, whether the jury are unanimous or not, shall be returned orally by the foreman of the jury unless the court directs a written verdict to be returned.

(2) Where the jury are not unanimous in their verdict, the foreman shall announce that fact so that the relative entry may be made in the record.

(3) The verdict of the jury may be given orally through the foreman of the

jury after consultation in the jury box without the necessity for the jury to retire.

Previous convictions: solemn proceedings

101.—(1) Previous convictions against the accused shall not be laid before the jury, nor shall reference be made to them in presence of the jury before the verdict is returned.

(2) Nothing in subsection (1) above shall prevent the prosecutor—

(a) asking the accused questions tending to show that he has been convicted of an offence other than that with which he is charged, where he is entitled to do so under section 266 of this Act; or

(b) leading evidence of previous convictions where it is competent to do so under section 270 of this Act, and nothing in this section or in section 69 of this Act shall prevent evidence of previous convictions being led in any case where such evidence is competent in support of a substantive charge.

(3) Previous convictions shall not be laid before the presiding judge until the prosecutor moves for sentence, and in that event the prosecutor shall lay before the judge a copy of the notice referred to in subsection (2) or (4) of section 69 of this Act.

(4) On the conviction of the accused it shall be competent for the court, subject to subsection (5) below, to amend a notice of previous convictions so laid by deletion or alteration for the purpose of curing any error or defect.

[1](5) ...

(6) Any conviction which is admitted in evidence by the court shall be entered in the record of the trial.

(7) Where a person is convicted of an offence, the court may have regard to any previous conviction in respect of that person in deciding on the disposal of the case.

(8) Where any such intimation as is mentioned in section 69 of this Act is given by the accused, it shall be competent to prove any previous conviction included in a notice under that section in the manner specified in section 285 of this Act, and the provisions of the said section shall apply accordingly.

NOTE
[1]As amended by the Crime and Punishment (Scotland) Act 1997 (c. 48) s.31 with effect from August 1, 1997 (Commencement and Transitional Provisions) Order 1997 (S.I. 1997 No. 1712) para. 3.

Interruption of trial for other proceedings

102.—(1) When the jury have retired to consider their verdict, and the diet in another criminal cause has been called, then, subject to subsection (3) below, if it appears to the judge presiding at the trial to be appropriate, he may interrupt the proceedings in such other cause—

(a) in order to receive the verdict of the jury in the preceding trial, and thereafter to dispose of the case;

(b) to give a direction to the jury in the preceding trial upon any matter upon which the jury may wish a direction from the judge or to hear any request from the jury regarding any matter in the cause.

(2) Where in any case the diet of which has not been called, the accused intimates to the clerk of court that he is prepared to tender a plea of guilty as libelled or such qualified plea as the Crown is prepared to accept, or where a case is remitted to the High Court for sentence, then, subject to subsection (3) below, any trial then proceeding may be interrupted for the purpose of receiving such plea or dealing with the remitted case and pronouncing sentence or otherwise disposing of any such case.

(3) In no case shall any proceedings in the preceding trial take place in the presence of the jury in the interrupted trial, but in every case that jury shall be directed to retire by the presiding judge.

(4) On the interrupted trial being resumed the diet shall be called *de novo*.

(5) In any case an interruption under this section shall not be deemed an irregularity, nor entitle the accused to take any objection to the proceedings.

PART VIII

APPEALS FROM SOLEMN PROCEEDINGS

Appeal sittings

103.—(1) The High Court shall hold both during session and during vacation such sittings as are necessary for the disposal of appeals and other proceedings under this Part of this Act.

(2) Subject to subsection (3) below, for the purpose of hearing and determining any appeal or other proceeding under this Part of this Act three of the Lords Commissioners of Justiciary shall be a quorum of the High Court, and the determination of any question under this Part of this Act by the court shall be according to the votes of the majority of the members of the court sitting, including the presiding judge, and each judge so sitting shall be entitled to pronounce a separate opinion.

[1](3) For the purpose of hearing and determining any appeal under section 106(1)(b) to (e) of this Act, or any proceeding connected therewith, two of the Lords Commissioners of Justiciary shall be a quorum of the High Court, and each judge shall be entitled to pronounce a separate opinion; but where the two Lords Commissioners of Justiciary are unable to reach agreement on the disposal of the appeal, or where they consider it appropriate, the appeal shall be heard and determined in accordance with subsection (2) above.

[1](4) Subsections (1) to (3) above shall apply to cases certified to the High Court by a single judge of the said court and to appeals by way of advocation in like manner as they apply to appeals under this Part of this Act.

(5) The powers of the High Court under this Part of this Act—

(a) to extend the time within which intimation of intention to appeal and note of appeal may be given;

(b) to allow the appellant to be present at any proceedings in cases where he is not entitled to be present without leave; and

(c) to admit an appellant to bail,

may be exercised by any judge of the High Court, sitting and acting wherever convenient, in the same manner as they may be exercised by the High Court, and subject to the same provisions.

(6) Where a judge acting under subsection (5) above refuses an application by an appellant to exercise under that subsection any power in his favour, the appellant shall be entitled to have the application determined by the High Court.

[1](7) Subject to subsections (5) and (6) above and without prejudice to it, preliminary and interlocutory proceedings incidental to any appeal or application may be disposed of by a single judge.

(8) In all proceedings before a judge under section (5) above, and in all preliminary and interlocutory proceedings and applications except such as are heard before the full court, the parties may be represented and appear by a solicitor alone.

NOTE
[1]As amended by the Crime and Punishment (Scotland) Act 1997 (c. 48), s.62(1) and Sched. 1, para. 21(13) with effect from August 1, 1997 in terms of the Crime and Punishment (Scotland)

Act 1997 (Commencement and Transitional Provisions) Order 1997 (S.I. 1997 No. 1712) para. 3.

Power of High Court in appeals

104.—(1) Without prejudice to any existing power of the High Court, it may for the purposes of an appeal under section 106(1) or 108 of this Act—
- (a) order the production of any document or other thing connected with the proceedings;
- (b) hear any evidence relevant to any alleged miscarriage of justice or order such evidence to be heard by a judge of the High Court or by such other person as it may appoint for that purpose;
- (c) take account of any circumstances relevant to the case which were not before the trial judge;
- (d) remit to any fit person to enquire and report in regard to any matter or circumstance affecting the appeal;
- (e) appoint a person with expert knowledge to act as assessor to the High Court in any case where it appears to the court that such expert knowledge is required for the proper determination of the case.

(2) The evidence of any witnesses ordered to be examined before the High Court or before any judge of the High Court or other person appointed by the High Court shall be taken in accordance with the existing law and practice as to the taking of evidence in criminal trials in Scotland.

(3) The appellant or applicant and the respondent or counsel on their behalf shall be entitled to be present at and take part in any examination of any witness to which this section relates.

Appeal against refusal of application

105.—(1) When an application or applications have been dealt with by a judge of the High Court, under section 103(5) of this Act, the Clerk of Justiciary shall—
- (a) notify to the applicant the decision in the form prescribed by Act of Adjournal or as nearly as may be in such form; and
- (b) where all or any of such applications have been refused, forward to the applicant the prescribed form for completion and return forthwith if he desires to have the application or applications determined by the High Court as fully constituted for the hearing of appeals under this Part of this Act.

(2) Where the applicant does not desire a determination as mentioned in subsection (1)(b) above, or does not return within five days to the Clerk the form duly completed by him, the refusal of his application or applications by the judge shall be final.

(3) Where an applicant who desires a determination by the High Court as mentioned in subsection (1)(b) above—
- (a) is not legally represented, he may be present at the hearing and determination by the High Court of the application;
- (b) is legally represented, he shall not be entitled to be present without leave of the court.

(4) When an applicant duly completes and returns to the Clerk of Justiciary within the prescribed time the form expressing a desire to be present at the hearing and determination by the court of the applications mentioned in this section, the form shall be deemed to be an application by the applicant for leave to be so present, and the Clerk of Justiciary, on receiving the form, shall take the necessary steps for placing the application before the court.

(5) If the application to be present is refused by the court, the Clerk of Justiciary shall notify the applicant; and if the application is granted, he shall

notify the applicant and the Governor of the prison where the applicant is in custody and the Secretary of State.

(6) For the purpose of constituting a Court of Appeal, the judge who has refused any application may sit as a member of the court, and take part in determining the application.

Right of appeal

106.—(1) Any person convicted on indictment may, with leave granted in accordance with section 107 of this Act, appeal in accordance with this Part of this Act, to the High Court—

  (a) against such conviction;

  (b) subject to subsection (2) below, against the sentence passed on such conviction;

²(bb) against any decision not to exercise the power conferred by section 205A(3) or 205B(3) of this Act;

  (c) against his absolute discharge or admonition;

  (d) against any probation order or any community service order;

³(da) against any decision to remit made under section 49(1)(a) of this Act;

  (e) against any order deferring sentence; or

  (f) against both such conviction and, subject to subsection (2) below, such sentence or disposal or order.

(2) There shall be no appeal against any sentence fixed by law.

¹(3) By an appeal under subsection (1) above a person may bring under review of the High Court any alleged miscarriage of justice, which may include such a miscarriage based on—

  (a) subject to subsections (3A) to (3D) below, the existence and significance of evidence which was not heard at the original proceedings; and

  (b) the jury's having returned a verdict which no reasonable jury, properly directed, could have returned.

(3A) Evidence such as is mentioned in subsection (3)(a) above may found an appeal only where there is a reasonable explanation of why it was not so heard.

(3B) Where the explanation referred to in subsection (3A) above or, as the case may be, (3C) below is that the evidence was not admissible at the time of the original proceedings, but is admissible at the time of the appeal, the court may admit that evidence if it appears to the court that it would be in the interests of justice to do so.

(3C) Without prejudice to subsection (3A) above, where evidence such as is mentioned in paragraph (a) of subsection (3) above is evidence—

  (a) which is—

    (i) from a person; or

    (ii) of a statement (within the meaning of section 259(1) of this Act) by a person,

  who gave evidence at the original proceedings; and

  (b) which is different from, or additional to, the evidence so given,

it may not found an appeal unless there is a reasonable explanation as to why the evidence now sought to be adduced was not given by that person at those proceedings, which explanation is itself supported by independent evidence.

(3D) For the purposes of subsection (3C) above, "independent evidence" means evidence which—

  (a) was not heard at the original proceedings;

  (b) is from a source independent of the person referred to in subsection (3C) above; and

  (c) is accepted by the court as being credible and reliable.

(4) Any document, production or other thing lodged in connection with the proceedings on the trial of any person who, if convicted, is entitled or

may be authorised to appeal under this Part of this Act, shall, in accordance with subsections (5) to (9) below, be kept in the custody of the court in which the conviction took place.

(5) All documents and other productions produced at the trial of a convicted person shall be kept in the custody of the court of trial in such manner as it may direct until any period allowed under or by virtue of this Part of this Act for lodging intimation of intention to appeal has elapsed.

(6) Where no direction is given as mentioned in subsection (5) above, such custody shall be in the hands of the sheriff clerk of the district of the court of the second diet to whom the clerk of court shall hand them over at the close of the trial, unless otherwise ordered by the High Court on an intimation of intention to appeal being lodged, and if within such period there has been such lodgement under this Part of this Act, they shall be so kept until the appeal, if it is proceeded with, is determined.

(7) Notwithstanding subsections (5) and (6) above, the judge of the court in which the conviction took place may, on cause shown, grant an order authorising any of such documents or productions to be released on such conditions as to custody and return as he may deem it proper to prescribe.

(8) All such documents or other productions so retained in custody or released and returned shall, under supervision of the custodian thereof, be made available for inspection and for the purpose of making copies of documents or productions to a person who has lodged an intimation of intention to appeal or as the case may be, to the convicted person's counsel or agent, and to the Crown Agent and the procurator fiscal or his deputes.

(9) Where no intimation of intention to appeal is lodged within the period mentioned in subsection (6) above, all such documents and productions shall be dealt with as they are dealt with according to the existing law and practice at the conclusion of a trial; and they shall be so dealt with if, there having been such intimation, the appeal is not proceeded with.

NOTES

[1]As amended by the Crime and Punishment (Scotland) Act 1997 (c. 48), s.17 with effect from August 1, 1997 in terms of the Crime and Punishment (Scotland) Act 1997 (Commencement and Transitional Provisions) Order 1997 (S.I. 1997 No. 1712) para. 3.

[2]Inserted by the Crime and Punishment (Scotland) Act 1997 (c. 48), s.18 with effect from October 20, 1997 in terms of the Crime and Punishment (Scotland) Act 1997 (Commencement No. 2 and Transitional Provisions) Order 1997 (S.I. 1997 No. 2323) Art. 3, Sched. 1; amended by the Crime and Disorder Act 1998 (c. 37), Sched. 8, para. 119 (effective September 30, 1998: S.I. 1998 No. 2327).

[3]Inserted by the Crime and Punishment (Scotland) Act 1997 (c. 48), s.23 with effect from August 1, 1997 in terms of the Crime and Punishment (Scotland) Act 1997 (Commencement and Transitional Provisions) Order 1997 (S.I. 1997 No. 1712) para. 3.

Appeal against automatic sentences where earlier conviction quashed

[1]**106A.**[2][(1) This subsection applies where—
  (a) a person has been sentenced under section 205A(2) of this Act;
  (b) he had, at the time at which the offence for which he was so sentenced was committed, only one previous conviction for a qualifying offence or a relevant offence within the meaning of that section; and
  (c) after he has been so sentenced, the conviction mentioned in paragraph (b) above has been quashed.]
(2) This subsection applies where—
  (a) a person has been sentenced under section 205B(2) of this Act;
  (b) he had, at the time at which the offence for which he was so sentenced was committed, only two previous convictions for class A drug trafficking offences within the meaning of that section; and
  (c) after he has been so sentenced, one of the convictions mentioned in paragraph (b) above has been quashed.
[3](3) Where subsection (1) or (2) above applies, the person may appeal

under section 106(1)(b) of this Act against the sentence imposed on him under [section 205A(2) or, as the case may be], 205B(2) of this Act.

(4) An appeal under section 106(1)(b) of this Act by virtue of subsection (3) above—

(a) may be made notwithstanding that the person has previously appealed under that section; and

(b) shall be lodged within two weeks of the quashing of the conviction as mentioned in subsection (1)(c) or, as the case may be, (2)(c) above.

(5) Where an appeal is made under section 106(1)(b) by virtue of this section, the following provisions of this Act shall not apply in relation to such an appeal, namely—

(a) section 121; and

(b) section 126.

NOTES

[1]Inserted by the Crime and Punishment (Scotland) Act 1997 (c. 48) s.19 with effect from October 20, 1997 in terms of the Crime and Punishment (Scotland) Act 1997 (Commencement No. 2 and Transitional Provisions) Order 1997 (S.I. 1997 No. 2323) Art. 3, Sched. 1.

[2]Prospective insertion by the above.

[3]Inserted by the above and effective except in so far as it refers to section 205(A)(2) of the 1995 Act.

Leave to appeal

107.—(1) The decision whether to grant leave to appeal for the purposes of section 106(1) of this Act shall be made by a judge of the High Court who shall—

(a) if he considers that the documents mentioned in subsection (2) below disclose arguable grounds of appeal, grant leave to appeal and make such comments in writing as he considers appropriate; and

(b) in any other case—

(i) refuse leave to appeal and give reasons in writing for the refusal; and

(ii) where the appellant is on bail and the sentence imposed on his conviction is one of imprisonment, grant a warrant to apprehend and imprison him.

(2) The documents referred to in subsection (1) above are—

(a) the note of appeal lodged under section 110(1)(a) of this Act;

(b) in the case of an appeal against conviction or sentence in a sheriff court, the certified copy or, as the case may be, the record of the proceedings at the trial;

(c) where the judge who presided at the trial furnishes a report under section 113 of this Act, that report; and

(d) where, by virtue of section 94(1) of this Act, a transcript of the charge to the jury of the judge who presided at the trial is delivered to the Clerk of Justiciary, that transcript.

(3) A warrant granted under subsection (1)(b)(ii) above shall not take effect until the expiry of the period of 14 days mentioned in subsection (4) below without an application to the High Court for leave to appeal having been lodged by the appellant under that subsection.

(4) Where leave to appeal is refused under subsection (1) above the appellant may, within 14 days of intimation under subsection (10) below, apply to the High Court for leave to appeal.

(5) In deciding an application under subsection (4) above the High Court shall—

(a) if, after considering the documents mentioned in subsection (2) above and the reasons for the refusal, the court is of the opinion that there are arguable grounds of appeal, grant leave to appeal and make such comments in writing as the court considers appropriate; and

(b) in any other case—
   (i) refuse leave to appeal and give reasons in writing for the refusal; and
   (ii) where the appellant is on bail and the sentence imposed on his conviction is one of imprisonment, grant a warrant to apprehend and imprison him.

(6) Consideration whether to grant leave to appeal under subsection (1) or (5) above shall take place in chambers without the parties being present.

(7) Comments in writing made under subsection (1)(a) or (5)(a) above may, without prejudice to the generality of that provision, specify the arguable grounds of appeal (whether or not they are contained in the note of appeal) on the basis of which leave to appeal is granted.

(8) Where the arguable grounds of appeal are specified by virtue of subsection (7) above it shall not, except by leave of the High Court on cause shown, be competent for the appellant to found any aspect of his appeal on any ground of appeal contained in the note of appeal but not so specified.

(9) Any application by the appellant for the leave of the High Court under subsection (8) above—
   (a) shall be made not less than seven days before the date fixed for the hearing of the appeal; and
   (b) shall, not less that seven days before that date, be intimated by the appellant to the Crown Agent.

(10) The Clerk of Justiciary shall forthwith intimate—
   (a) a decision under subsection (1) or (5) above; and
   (b) in the case of a refusal of leave to appeal, the reasons for the decision,
to the appellant or his solicitor and to the Crown Agent.

NOTE
[1]Inserted by the Crime and Punishment (Scotland) Act 1997 (c. 48) Sched. 1, para. 21(15) with effect from August 1, 1997 in terms of the Crime and Punishment (Scotland) Act 1997 (Commencement and Transitional Provisions) Order 1997 (S.I. 1997 No. 1712) para. 3.

Lord Advocate's right of appeal against disposal

[1]**108.**—(1) Where a person has been convicted on indictment, the Lord Advocate may, in accordance with subsection (2) below, appeal against any of the following disposals, namely—
   (a) a sentence passed on conviction;
   (b) a decision under section 209(1)(b) of this Act not to make a supervised release order;
   (c) a decision under section 234A(2) of this Act not to make a non-harassment order;
   (d) a probation order;
   (e) a community service order;
   (f) a decision to remit to the Principal Reporter made under section 49(1)(a) of this Act;
   (g) an order deferring sentence;
   (h) an admonition; or
   (i) an absolute discharge.

(2) An appeal under subsection (1) above may be made—
   (a) on a point of law;
   (b) where it appears to the Lord Advocate, in relation to an appeal under—
      (i) paragraph (a), (h) or (i) of that subsection, that the disposal was unduly lenient;
      (ii) paragraph (b) or (c) of that subsection, that the decision not to make the order in question was inappropriate;

(iii) paragraph (d) or (e) of that subsection, that the making of the order concerned was unduly lenient or was on unduly lenient terms;

(iv) under paragraph (f) of that subsection, that the decision to remit was inappropriate;

(v) under paragraph (g) of that subsection, that the deferment of sentence was inappropriate or was on unduly lenient conditions.

NOTE

[1]Substituted by the Crime and Punishment (Scotland) Act 1997 (c. 48), s.21 with effect from August 1, 1997 in terms of the Crime and Punishment (Scotland) Act 1997 (Commencement and Transitional Provisions) Order 1997 (S.I. 1997 No. 1712) para. 3.

Lord Advocate's appeal against decision not to impose automatic sentence in certain cases

[1]**108A.** Where the court has exercised the power conferred by section 205A(3) or 205B(3) of this Act, the Lord Advocate may appeal against that decision.

NOTE

[1]Inserted by the Crime and Punishment (Scotland) Act 1997 (c. 48), s.18(2) with effect from October 20, 1997 in terms of the Crime and Punishment (Scotland) Act 1997 (Commencement No. 2 and Transitional Provisions) Order 1997 (S.I. 1997 No. 2323) Art. 3, Sched. 1; as amended by the Crime and Disorder Act 1998 (c. 37), Sched. 8, para. 120 (effective September 30, 1998: S.I. 1998 No. 2327).

Intimation of intention to appeal

109.—(1) Subject to section 111(2) of this Act and to section 10 of the Proceeds of Crime (Scotland) Act 1995 (postponed confiscation orders), where a person desires to appeal under section 106(1)(a) or (f) of this Act, he shall within two weeks of the final determination of the proceedings, lodge with the Clerk of Justiciary written intimation of intention to appeal which shall identify the proceedings and be in as nearly as may be the form prescribed by Act of Adjournal.

(2) A copy of intimation given under subsection (1) above shall be sent to the Crown Agent.

(3) On intimation under subsection (1) above being lodged by a person in custody, the Clerk of Justiciary shall give notice of the intimation to the Secretary of State.

(4) Subject to subsection (5) below, for the purposes of subsection (1) above and section 106(5) to (7) of this Act, proceedings shall be deemed finally determined on the day on which sentence is passed in open court.

(5) Where in relation to an appeal under section 106(1)(a) of this Act sentence is deferred under section 202 of this Act, the proceedings shall be deemed finally determined on the day on which sentence is first so deferred in open court.

(6) Without prejudice to section 10 of the said Act of 1995, the reference in subsection (4) above to "the day on which sentence is passed in open court" shall, in relation to any case in which, under subsection (1) of that section, a decision has been postponed for a period, be construed as a reference to the day on which that decision is made, whether or not a confiscation order is then made or any other sentence is then passed.

Note of appeal

110.—(1) Subject to section 111(2) of this Act—

[1](a) within six weeks of lodging intimation of intention to appeal or, in the case of an appeal under section 106(1)(b) to (e) of this Act, within two weeks of the appropriate date (being, and the case may be, the date on

which sentence was passed, the order disposing of the case was made, sentence was deferred or the previous conviction was quashed as mentioned in section 106A(1)(c) or (2)(c) of this Act) (or, as the case may be, of the making of the order disposing of the case or deferring sentence) in open court, the convicted person may lodge a written note of appeal with the Clerk of Justiciary who shall send a copy to the judge who presided at the trial and to the Crown Agent; or, as the case may be,

(b) within four weeks of the passing of the sentence in open court, the Lord Advocate may lodge such a note with the Clerk of Justiciary, who shall send a copy to the said judge and to the convicted person or that person's solicitor.

(2) The period of six weeks mentioned in paragraph (a) of subsection (1) above may be extended, before it expires, by the Clerk of Justiciary.

(3) A note of appeal shall—
(a) identify the proceedings;
(b) contain a full statement of all the grounds of appeal; and
(c) be in as nearly as may be the form prescribed by Act of Adjournal.

(4) Except by leave of the High Court on cause shown, it shall not be competent for an appellant to found any aspect of his appeal on a ground not contained in the note of appeal.

(5) Subsection (4) above shall not apply as respects any ground of appeal specified as an arguable ground of appeal by virtue of subsection (7) of section 107 of this Act.

(6) On a note of appeal under section 106(1)(b) to (e) of this Act being lodged by an appellant in custody the Clerk of Justiciary shall give notice of that fact to the Secretary of State.

NOTE
[1]As amended by the Crime and Punishment (Scotland) Act 1997 (c. 48), s.19(2) with effect from October 20, 1997 in terms of the Crime and Punishment (Scotland) Act 1997 (Commencement No. 2 and Transitional Provisions) Order 1997 (S.I. 1997 No. 2323) Art. 3, Sched. 1.

Provisions supplementary to sections 109 and 110

111.—(1) Where the last day of any period mentioned in sections 109(1) and 110(1) of this Act falls on a day on which the office of the Clerk of Justiciary is closed, such period shall extend to and include the next day on which such office is open.

(2) Any period mentioned in section 109(1) or 110(1)(a) of this Act may be extended at any time by the High Court in respect of any convicted person; and an application for such extension may be made under this subsection and shall be in as nearly as may be the form prescribed by Act of Adjournal.

Admission of appellant to bail

112.—(1) Subject to subsection (2) below, the High Court may, if it thinks fit, on the application of a convicted person, admit him to bail pending the determination of—
(a) his appeal; or
[1](b) any relevant appeal by the Lord Advocate under section 108 or 108A of this Act.

(2) The High Court shall not admit a convicted person to bail under subsection (1) above unless—
(a) where he is the appellant and has not lodged a note of appeal in accordance with section 110(1)(a) of this Act, the application for bail states reasons why it should be granted and sets out the proposed grounds of appeal; or

(b) where the Lord Advocate is the appellant, the application for bail states reasons why it should be granted,

and, in either case, the High Court considers there to be exceptional circumstances justifying admitting the convicted person to bail.

(3) A person who is admitted to bail under subsection (1) above shall, unless the High Court otherwise directs, appear personally in court on the day or days fixed for the hearing of the appeal.

(4) Where an appellant fails to appear personally in court as mentioned in subsection (3) above, the court may—

    (a) if he is the appellant—

        (i) decline to consider the appeal; and

        (ii) dismiss it summarily; or

    (b) whether or not he is the appellant—

        (i) consider and determine the appeal; or

        (ii) without prejudice to section 27 of this Act, make such other order as the court thinks fit.

(5) For the purposes of subsections (1), (3) and (4) above, "appellant" includes not only a person who has lodged a note of appeal but also one who has lodged an intimation of intention to appeal.

[2](6) Subject to subsection (7) below, the High Court may, if it thinks fit, on the application of a convicted person, admit him to bail pending the determination of any appeal under paragraph 13(a) of Schedule 6 to the Scotland Act 1998 and the disposal of the proceedings by the High Court thereafter.

[2](7) The High Court shall not admit a convicted person to bail under subsection (6) above unless the application for bail states reasons why it should be granted and the High Court considers there to be exceptional circumstances justifying admitting the convicted person to bail.

[2](8) A person who is admitted to bail under subsection (6) above shall, unless the High Court otherwise directs, appear personally in the High Court at any subsequent hearing in the High Court in relation to the proceedings; and if he fails to do so the court may, without prejudice to section 27 of this Act, make such order as it thinks fit.

NOTES

[1]As amended by the Crime and Punishment (Scotland) Act 1997 (c. 48), s.18(3) with effect from October 20, 1997 in terms of the Crime and Punishment (Scotland) Act 1997 (Commencement No. 2 and Transitional Provisions) Order 1997 (S.I. 1997 No. 2323) Art. 3, Sched. 1.

[2]Inserted by the Scotland Act 1998 (Consequential Modifications) (No.1) Order 1999 (S.I. 1999 No.1042) art.3, Sched.1, para.13 (effective May 6, 1999).

Judge's report

113.—(1) As soon as is reasonably practicable after receiving the copy note of appeal sent to him under section 110(1) of this Act, the judge who presided at the trial shall furnish the Clerk of Justiciary with a written report giving the judge's opinion on the case generally and on the grounds contained in the note of appeal.

(2) The Clerk of Justiciary shall send a copy of the judge's report—

    (a) to the convicted person or his solicitor;

    (b) to the Crown Agent; and

    [1](c) in a case referred under Part XA of this Act, to the Commission.

(3) Where the judge's report is not furnished as mentioned in subsection (1) above, the High Court may call for the report to be furnished within such period as it may specify or, if it thinks fit, hear and determine the appeal without the report.

(4) Subject to subsection (2) above, the report of the judge shall be available only to the High Court, the parties and, on such conditions as may

be prescribed by Act of Adjournal, such other persons or classes of persons as may be so prescribed.

NOTE
[1]As amended by the Crime and Punishment (Scotland) Act 1997, Sched. 1, para. 21(16) (effective April 1, 1999: S.I. 1999 No. 652).

Applications made orally or in writing

114. Subject to any provision of this Part of this Act to the contrary, any application to the High Court may be made by the appellant or respondent as the case may be or by counsel on his behalf, orally or in writing.

Presentation of appeal in writing

115.—(1) If an appellant, other than the Lord Advocate, desires to present his case and his argument in writing instead of orally he shall, at least four days before the diet fixed for the hearing of the appeal—
  (a) intimate this desire to the Clerk of Justiciary;
  (b) lodge with the Clerk of Justiciary three copies of his case and argument; and
  (c) send a copy of the intimation, case and argument to the Crown Agent.
(2) Any case or argument presented as mentioned in subsection (1) above shall be considered by the High Court.
(3) Unless the High Court otherwise directs, the respondent shall not make a written reply to a case and argument presented as mentioned in subsection (1) above, but shall reply orally at the diet fixed for the hearing of the appeal.
(4) Unless the High Court otherwise allows, an appellant who has presented his case and argument in writing shall not be entitled to submit in addition an oral argument to the court in support of the appeal.

Abandonment of appeal

116.—(1) An appellant may abandon his appeal by lodging with the Clerk of Justiciary a notice of abandonment in as nearly as may be the form prescribed by Act of Adjournal; and on such notice being lodged the appeal shall be deemed to have been dismissed by the court.
[1](2) A person who has appealed against both conviction and sentence (or, as the case may be, against both conviction and a decision such as is mentioned in section 106(1)(bb) or both conviction and disposal or order) may abandon the appeal in so far as it is against conviction and may proceed with it against sentence (or, as the case may be, decision, disposal or order) alone.

NOTE
[1]As amended by the Crime and Punishment (Scotland) Act 1997 (c. 48), s.18(4) with effect from October 20, 1997 in terms of the Crime and Punishment (Scotland) Act 1997 (Commencement No. 2 and Transitional Provisions) Order 1997 (S.I. 1997 No. 2323) Art. 3, Sched. 1.

Presence of appellant or applicant at hearing

117.—(1) Where an appellant or applicant is in custody the Clerk of Justiciary shall notify—
  (a) the appellant or applicant;
  (b) the Governor of the prison in which the appellant or applicant then is; and
  (c) the Secretary of State,
of the probable day on which the appeal or application will be heard.
(2) The Secretary of State shall take steps to transfer the appellant or

applicant to a prison convenient for his appearance before the High Court at such reasonable time before the hearing as shall enable him to consult his legal adviser, if any.

(3) A convicted appellant, notwithstanding that he is in custody, shall be entitled to be present if he desires it, at the hearing of his appeal.

(4) When an appellant or applicant is to be present at any diet—

(a) before the High Court or any judge of that court; or

(b) for the taking of additional evidence before a person appointed for that purpose under section 104(1)(b) of this Act, or

(c) for an examination or investigation by a special commissioner in terms of section 104(1)(d) of this Act,

the Clerk of Justiciary shall give timeous notice to the Secretary of State, in the form prescribed by Act of Adjournal or as nearly as may be in such form.

(5) A notice under subsection (4) above shall be sufficient warrant to the Secretary of State for transmitting the appellant or applicant in custody from prison to the place where the diet mentioned in that subsection or any subsequent diet is to be held and for reconveying him to prison at the conclusion of such diet.

(6) The appellant or applicant shall appear at any diet mentioned in subsection (4) above in ordinary civilian clothes.

(7) Where the Lord Advocate is the appellant, subsections (1) to (6) above shall apply in respect of the convicted person, if in custody, as they apply to an appellant or applicant in custody.

(8) The Secretary of State shall, on notice under subsection (4) above from the Clerk of Justiciary, ensure that sufficient male and female prison officers attend each sitting of the court, having regard to the list of appeals for the sitting.

(9) When the High Court fixes the date for the hearing of an appeal or of an application under section 111(2) of this Act, the Clerk of Justiciary shall give notice to the Crown Agent and to the solicitor of the convicted person, or to the convicted person himself if he has no known solicitor.

Disposal of appeals

118.—(1) The High Court may, subject to subsection (4) below, dispose of an appeal against conviction by—

(a) affirming the verdict of the trial court;

(b) setting aside the verdict of the trial court and either quashing the conviction or, subject to subsection (2) below, substituting therefor an amended verdict of guilty; or

(c) setting aside the verdict of the trial court and quashing the conviction and granting authority to bring a new prosecution in accordance with section 119 of this Act.

(2) An amended verdict of guilty substituted under subsection (1) above must be one which could have been returned on the indictment before the trial court.

(3) In setting aside, under subsection (1) above, a verdict the High Court may quash any sentence imposed on the appellant (or, as the case may be, any disposal or order made) as respects the indictment, and—

(a) in a case where it substitutes an amended verdict of guilty, whether or not the sentence (or disposal or order) related to the verdict set aside; or

(b) in any other case, where the sentence (or disposal or order) did not so relate,

may pass another (but not more severe) sentence or make another (but not more severe) disposal or order in substitution for the sentence, disposal or order so quashed.

(4) The High Court may, subject to subsection (5) below, dispose of an appeal against sentence by—

(a) affirming such sentence; or

¹(b) if the Court thinks that, having regard to all the circumstances, including any evidence such as is mentioned in section 106(3) of this Act, a different sentence should have been passed, quashing the sentence and passing another sentence whether more or less severe in substitution therefor,

and, in this subsection, "appeal against sentence" shall, without prejudice to the generality of the expression, be construed as including an appeal under section 106(1)(bb) to (e), and any appeal under section 108, of this Act; and other references to sentence shall be construed accordingly.

²(4A) On an appeal under section 108A of this Act, the High Court may dispose of the appeal—

(a) by affirming the decision and any sentence or order passed;

(b) where it is of the opinion mentioned in section 205A(3) or, as the case may be, 205B(3) of this Act but it considers that a different sentence or order should have been passed, by affirming the decision but quashing any sentence or order passed and passing another sentence or order whether more or less severe in substitution therefor; or

(c) in any other case, by setting aside the decision appealed against and any sentence or order passed by the trial court and where the decision appealed against was taken under—

(i) subsection (3) of section 205A of this Act, by passing the sentence mentioned in subsection (2) of that section;

(ii) subsection (3) of section 205B of this Act, by passing a sentence of imprisonment of at least the length mentioned in subsection (2) of that section; or

(iii) [*Repealed by the 1998 Act, Sched. 8, para. 121.*]

(5) In relation to any appeal under section 106(1) of this Act, the High Court shall, where it appears to it that the appellant committed the act charged against him but that he was insane when he did so, dispose of the appeal by—

(a) setting aside the verdict of the trial court and substituting therefor a verdict of acquittal on the ground of insanity; and

(b) quashing any sentence imposed on the appellant (or disposal or order made) as respects the indictment and—

(i) making, in respect of the appellant, any order mentioned in section 57(2)(a) to (d) of this Act; or

(ii) making no order.

(6) Subsections (3) and (4) of section 57 of this Act shall apply to an order made under subsection (5)(b)(i) above as they apply to an order made under subsection (2) of that section.

(7) In disposing of an appeal under section 106(1)(b) to (f) or 108 of this Act the High Court may, without prejudice to any other power in that regard, pronounce an opinion on the sentence or other disposal or order which is appropriate in any similar case.

(8) No conviction, sentence, judgment, order of court or other proceeding whatsoever in or for the purposes of solemn proceedings under this Act—

(a) shall be quashed for want of form; or

(b) where the accused had legal assistance in his defence, shall be suspended or set aside in respect of any objections to—

(i) the relevancy of the indictment, or the want of specification therein; or

(ii) the competency or admission or rejection of evidence at the trial in the inferior court, unless such objections were timeously stated.

[3](9) The High Court may give its reasons for the disposal of any appeal in writing without giving those reasons orally.

NOTES

[1]As amended by the Crime and Punishment (Scotland) Act 1997 (c. 48), Sched. 1, para. 21(17) with effect from August 1, 1997 in terms of the Crime and Punishment (Scotland) Act 1997 (Commencement and Transitional Provisions) Order 1997 (S.I. 1997 No. 1712) para. 3. As amended by the Crime and Punishment (Scotland) Act 1997 (c. 48), s.18(5) with effect from October 20, 1997 in terms of the Crime and Punishment (Scotland) Act 1997 (Commencement No. 2 and Transitional Provisions) Order 1997 (S.I. 1997 No. 2323) Art. 3, Sched. 1.

[2]Inserted by the Crime and Punishment (Scotland) Act 1997 (c. 48), s.18(5) with effect from October 20, 1997 in terms of the Crime and Punishment (Scotland) Act 1997 (Commencement No. 2 and Transitional Provisions) Order 1997 (S.I. 1997 No. 2323) Art. 3, Sched. 1.

[3]Inserted by the Crime and Punishment (Scotland) Act 1997 (c. 48), Sched. 1, para. 21(17) with effect from August 1, 1997 in terms of the Crime and Punishment (Scotland) Act 1997 (Commencement and Transitional Provisions) Order 1997 (S.I. 1997 No. 1712) para. 3.

Provision where High Court authorises new prosecution

119.—(1) Subject to subsection (2) below, where authority is granted under section 118(1)(c) of this Act, a new prosecution may be brought charging the accused with the same or any similar offence arising out of the same facts; and the proceedings out of which the appeal arose shall not be a bar to such new prosecution.

(2) In a new prosecution under this section the accused shall not be charged with an offence more serious than that of which he was convicted in the earlier proceedings.

(3) No sentence may be passed on conviction under the new prosecution which could not have been passed on conviction under the earlier proceedings.

(4) A new prosecution may be brought under this section, notwithstanding that any time limit, other than the time limit mentioned in subsection (5) below, for the commencement of such proceedings has elapsed.

(5) Proceedings in a prosecution under this section shall be commenced within two months of the date on which authority to bring the prosecution was granted.

(6) In proceedings in a new prosecution under this section it shall, subject to subsection (7) below, be competent for either party to lead any evidence which it was competent for him to lead in the earlier proceedings.

(7) The indictment in a new prosecution under this section shall identify any matters as respects which the prosecutor intends to lead evidence by virtue of subsection (6) above which would not have been competent but for that subsection.

(8) For the purposes of subsection (5) above, proceedings shall be deemed to be commenced—

   (a) in a case where a warrant to apprehend or to cite the accused is executed without unreasonable delay, on the date on which the warrant is granted; and

   (b) in any other case, on the date on which the warrant is executed.

(9) Where the two months mentioned in subsection (5) above elapse and no new prosecution has been brought under this section, the order under section 118(1)(c) of this Act setting aside the verdict shall have the effect, for all purposes, of an acquittal.

(10) On granting authority under section 118(1)(c) of this Act to bring a new prosecution, the High Court shall, after giving the parties an opportunity of being heard, order the detention of the accused person in custody or admit him to bail.

(11) Subsections (4)(b) and (7) to (9) of section 65 of this Act (prevention of delay in trials) shall apply to an accused person who is detained under

subsection (10) above as they apply to an accused person detained by virtue of being committed until liberated in due course of law.

Appeals: supplementary provisions

120.—(1) Where—
(a) intimation of the diet appointed for the hearing of the appeal has been made to the appellant;
(b) no appearance is made by or on behalf of an appellant at the diet; and
(c) no case or argument in writing has been timeously lodged,
the High Court shall dispose of the appeal as if it had been abandoned.

(2) The power of the High Court to pass any sentence under this Part of this Act may be exercised notwithstanding that the appellant (or, where the Lord Advocate is the appellant, the convicted person) is for any reason not present.

(3) When the High Court has heard and dealt with any application under this Part of this Act, the Clerk of Justiciary shall (unless it appears to him unnecessary so to do) give to the applicant if he is in custody and has not been present at the hearing of such application notice of the decision of the court in relation to the said application.

(4) On the final determination of any appeal under this Part of this Act or of any matter under section 103(5) of this Act, the Clerk of Justiciary shall give notice of such determination—
(a) to the appellant or applicant if he is in custody and has not been present at such final determination;
(b) to the clerk of the court in which the conviction took place; and
(c) to the Secretary of State.

Suspension of disqualification, forfeiture, etc.

121.—(1) Any disqualification, forfeiture or disability which attaches to a person by reason of a conviction shall not attach—
(a) for the period of four weeks from the date of the verdict against him; or
[1](b) where an intimation of intention to appeal or, in the case of an appeal under section 106(1)(b) to (e), 108 or 108A of this Act, a note of appeal is lodged, until the appeal, if it is proceeded with, is determined.

(2) The destruction or forfeiture or any order for the destruction or forfeiture of any property, matter or thing which is the subject of or connected with any prosecution following upon a conviction shall be suspended—
(a) for the period of four weeks after the date of the verdict in the trial; or
[1](b) where an intimation of intention to appeal or, in the case of an appeal under section 106(1)(b) to (e), 108 or 108A of this Act, a note of appeal is lodged, until the appeal, if it is proceeded with, is determined.

(3) This section does not apply in the case of any disqualification, destruction or forfeiture or order for destruction or forfeiture under or by virtue of any enactment which makes express provision for the suspension of the disqualification, destruction or forfeiture or order for destruction or forfeiture pending the determination of an appeal against conviction or sentence.

[1](4) Where, upon conviction, a fine has been imposed on a person or a compensation order has been made against him under section 249 of this Act, then, for a period of four weeks from the date of the verdict against such person or, in the event of an intimation of intention to appeal (or in the case of an appeal under section 106(1)(b) to (e), 108 or 108A of this Act a note of

appeal) being lodged under this Part of this Act, until such appeal, if it is proceeded with, is determined—

(a) the fine or compensation order shall not be enforced against that person and he shall not be liable to make any payment in respect of the fine or compensation order; and

(b) any money paid by that person under the compensation order shall not be paid by the clerk of court to the person entitled to it under subsection (9) of the said section 249.

[2](5) In this section—

(a) "appeal" includes an appeal under paragraph 13(a) of Schedule 6 to the Scotland Act 1998; and

(b) in relation to such an appeal, references to an appeal being determined are to be read as references to the disposal of the proceedings by the High Court following determination of the appeal.

Notes

[1]As amended by the Crime and Punishment (Scotland) Act 1997 (c. 48) s.18(6) with effect from October 20, 1997 in terms of the Crime and Punishment (Scotland) Act 1997 (Commencement No. 2 and Transitional Provisions) Order 1997 S.I. 2323, Art. 3, Sched. 1.

[2]Inserted by the Scotland Act 1998 (Consequential Modifications) (No.1) Order 1999 (S.I. 1999 No.1042) art.3, Sched.1, para.13(3) (effective May 6, 1999).

Suspension of certain sentences pending determination of appeal

[1]**121A.**—(1) Where an intimation of intention to appeal or, in the case of an appeal under section 106(1)(b) to (e), 108 or 108A of this Act, a note of appeal is lodged, the court may on the application of the appellant direct that the whole, or any remaining part, of a relevant sentence shall be suspended until the appeal, if it is proceeded with, is determined.

(2) Where the court has directed the suspension of the whole or any remaining part of a person's relevant sentence, the person shall, unless the High Court otherwise directs, appear personally in court on the day or days fixed for the hearing of the appeal.

(3) Where a person fails to appear personally in court as mentioned in subsection (2) above, the court may—

(a) if he is the appellant—

(i) decline to consider the appeal; and

(ii) dismiss it summarily; or

(b) whether or not he is the appellant—

(i) consider and determine the appeal; or

(ii) make such other order as the court thinks fit.

(4) In this section "relevant sentence" means any one or more of the following—

(a) a probation order;

(b) a supervised attendance order made under section 236(6) of this Act;

(c) a community service order;

[2](d) a restriction of liberty order.

[3](5) Subsections (1), (2) and (4) above apply to an appeal under paragraph 13(a) of Schedule 6 to the Scotland Act 1998 and, in relation to such an appeal—

(a) references to an appeal being determined are to be read as references to the disposal of the proceedings by the High Court following determination of the appeal; and

(b) the reference in subsection (2) to the hearing of the appeal is to be read as a reference to any subsequent hearing in the High Court in relation to the proceedings.

[3](6) Where a person fails to appear personally in court as mentioned in subsection (2) as read with subsection (5) above, the court may make such order as it thinks fit.

¹Inserted by the Crime and Punishment (Scotland) Act 1997 (c. 48), s.24 with effect from August 1, 1997 in terms of the Crime and Punishment (Scotland) Act 1997 (Commencement and Transitional Provisions) Order 1997 (S.I. 1997 No. 1712) para. 3.

²Inserted by the Crime and Punishment (Scotland) Act 1997 (c. 48), s.24 (effective July 1, 1998: S.I. 1998 No. 2323).

³Inserted by the Scotland Act 1998 (Consequential Modifications) (No.1) Order 1999 (S.I. 1999 No.1042) art.3, Sched.1, para.13(4) (effective May 6, 1999).

Fines and caution

122.—(1) Where a person has on conviction been sentenced to payment of a fine and in default of payment to imprisonment, the person lawfully authorised to receive the fine shall, on receiving it, retain it until the determination of any appeal in relation to the conviction or sentence.

(2) If a person sentenced to payment of a fine remains in custody in default of payment of the fine he shall be deemed, for the purposes of this Part of this Act, to be a person sentenced to imprisonment.

(3) An appellant who has been sentenced to the payment of a fine, and has paid it in accordance with the sentence, shall, in the event of his appeal being successful, be entitled, subject to any order of the High Court, to the return of the sum paid or any part of it.

¹(4) A convicted person who has been sentenced to the payment of a fine and has duly paid it shall, if an appeal against sentence by the Lord Advocate or any appeal by the Lord Advocate or the Advocate General for Scotland under paragraph 13(a) of Schedule 6 to the Scotland Act 1998 results in the sentence being quashed and no fine, or a lesser fine than that paid, being imposed, be entitled, subject to any order of the High Court, to the return of the sum paid or as the case may be to the return of the amount by which that sum exceeds the amount of the lesser fine.

²(5) In subsections (1) and (3) above, "appeal" includes an appeal under paragraph 13(a) of Schedule 6 to the Scotland Act 1998.

NOTES
¹As amended by the Scotland Act 1998 (Consequential Modifications) (No.1) Order 1999 (S.I. 1999 No.1042) art.3, Sched.1, para.13(5)(a) (effective May 6, 1999).

²Inserted by the Scotland Act 1998 (Consequential Modifications) (No.1) Order 1999 (S.I. 1999 No.1042) art.3, Sched.1, para.13(5)(b) (effective May 6, 1999).

Lord Advocate's reference

123.—(1) Where a person tried on indictment is acquitted or convicted of a charge, the Lord Advocate may refer a point of law which has arisen in relation to that charge to the High Court for their opinion; and the Clerk of Justiciary shall send to the person and to any solicitor who acted for the person at the trial, a copy of the reference and intimation of the date fixed by the Court for a hearing.

(2) The person may, not later than seven days before the date so fixed, intimate in writing to the Clerk of Justiciary and to the Lord Advocate either—

(a) that he elects to appear personally at the hearing; or

(b) that he elects to be represented thereat by counsel,

but, except by leave of the Court on cause shown, and without prejudice to his right to attend, he shall not appear or be represented at the hearing other than by and in conformity with an election under this subsection.

(3) Where there is no intimation under subsection (2)(b) above, the High Court shall appoint counsel to act at the hearing as *amicus curiae*.

(4) The costs of representation elected under subsection (2)(b) above or of an appointment under subsection (3) above shall, after being taxed by the Auditor of the Court of Session, be paid by the Lord Advocate.

(5) The opinion on the point referred under subsection (1) above shall not affect the acquittal or, as the case may be, conviction in the trial.

Finality of proceedings and Secretary of State's reference

124.—[1](1) Nothing in this Part or Part XA of this Act shall affect the prerogative of mercy.

[1,2](2) Subject to Part XA of this Act and paragraph 13(a) of Schedule 6 to the Scotland Act 1998, every interlocutor and sentence pronounced by the High Court under this Part of this Act shall be final and conclusive and not subject to review by any court whatsoever and, except for the purposes of an appeal under paragraph 13(a) of that Schedule, it shall be incompetent to stay or suspend any execution or diligence issuing from the High Court under this Part of this Act.

(3)–(5) [*Repealed by the Crime and Punishment (Scotland) Act 1997, Sched. 1, para. 21(18) and Sched. 3 (effective April 1, 1999: S.I. 1999 No. 652).*]

NOTES

[1]As amended by the Crime and Punishment (Scotland) Act 1997, Sched. 1, para. 21(18).
[2]As amended by the Scotland Act 1998 (Consequential Modifications) (No.1) Order 1999 (S.I. 1999 No.1042) art.3, Sched.1, para.13(6) (effective May 6, 1999).

Reckoning of time spent pending appeal

125.—(1) Subject to subsection (2) below, where a convicted person is admitted to bail under section 112 of this Act, the period beginning with the date of his admission to bail and ending on the date of his readmission to prison in consequence of the determination or abandonment of—

(a) his appeal; or, as the case may be,
[1](b) any relevant appeal by the Lord Advocate under section 108 or 108A of this Act,

shall not be reckoned as part of any term of imprisonment under his sentence.

[1](2) The time, including any period consequent on the recall of bail during which an appellant is in custody pending the determination of his appeal or, as the case may be, of any relevant appeal by the Lord Advocate under section 108 or 108A of this Act shall, subject to any direction which the High Court may give to the contrary, be reckoned as part of any term of imprisonment under his sentence.

(3) Subject to any direction which the High Court may give to the contrary, imprisonment of an appellant or, where the appellant is the Lord Advocate, of a convicted person—

(a) who is in custody in consequence of the conviction or sentence appealed against, shall be deemed to run as from the date on which the sentence was passed;
(b) who is in custody other than in consequence of such conviction or sentence, shall be deemed to run or to be resumed as from the date on which his appeal was determined or abandoned;
(c) who is not in custody, shall be deemed to run or to be resumed as from the date on which he is received into prison under the sentence.

(4) In this section references to a prison and imprisonment shall include respectively references to a young offenders institution or place of safety or, as respects a child sentenced to be detained under section 208 of this Act, the place directed by the Secretary of State and to detention in such institution, centre or place of safety, or, as respects such a child, place directed by the Secretary of State and any reference to a sentence shall be construed as a reference to a sentence passed by the court imposing sentence or by the High Court on appeal as the case may require.

NOTE

[1]As amended by the Crime and Punishment (Scotland) Act 1997 (c. 48), s.18(7) with effect from October 20, 1997 in terms of the Crime and Punishment (Scotland) Act 1997 (Commencement and Transitional Provisions) Order 1997 (S.I. 1997 No. 2323) Art. 3, Sched. 1.

Extract convictions

126. No extract conviction shall be issued—

(a) during the period of four weeks after the day on which the conviction took place, except in so far as it is required as a warrant for the detention of the person convicted under any sentence which has been pronounced against him; nor

[1](b) where an intimation of intention to appeal or, in the case of an appeal under section 106(1)(b) to (e), 108 or 108A of this Act, a note of appeal is lodged, until the appeal, if it is proceeded with, is determined.

NOTE

[1]As amended by the Crime and Punishment (Scotland) Act 1997 (c. 48), s.18(8) with effect from October 20, 1997 in terms of the Crime and Punishment (Scotland) Act 1997 (Commencement and Transitional Provisions) Order 1997 S.I. 2323, Art. 3, Sched. 1.

Forms in relation to appeals

127.—(1) The Clerk of Justiciary shall furnish the necessary forms and, instructions in relation to intimations of intention to appeal, notes of appeal or notices of application under this Part of this Act to—

(a) any person who demands them; and

(b) to officers of courts, governors of prisons, and such other officers or persons as he thinks fit.

(2) The governor of a prison shall cause the forms and instructions mentioned in subsection (1) above to be placed at the disposal of prisoners desiring to appeal or to make any application under this Part of this Act.

(3) The governor of a prison shall, if requested to do so by a prisoner, forwarded on the prisoner's behalf to the Clerk of Justiciary any intimation, note or notice mentioned in subsection (1) above given by the prisoner.

Fees and expenses

128. Except as otherwise provided in this Part of this Act, no court fees, or other fees or expenses shall be exigible from or awarded against an appellant or applicant in respect of an appeal or application under this Part of this Act.

Non-compliance with certain provisions may be waived

129.—(1) Non-compliance with—

(a) the provisions of this Act set out in subsection (3) below; or

(b) any rule of practice for the time being in force under this Part of this Act relating to appeals,

shall not prevent the further prosecution of an appeal if the High Court or a judge thereof considers it just and proper that the non-compliance is waived or, in the manner directed by the High Court or judge, remedied by amendment or otherwise.

(2) Where the High Court or a judge thereof directs that the non-compliance is to be remedied, and the remedy is carried out, the appeal shall proceed.

(3) The provisions of this Act referred to in subsection (1) above are:—

section 94

section 103(1), (4), (6) and (7)

section 104(2) and (3)

section 105

section 106(4)
section 111
section 114
section 115
section 116
section 117
section 120(1), (3) and (4)
section 121
section 122
section 126
section 128.

(4) This section does not apply to any rule of practice relating to appeals under section 60 of this Act.

Bill of suspension not competent

130. It shall not be competent to appeal to the High Court by bill of suspension against any conviction, sentence, judgement or order pronounced in any proceedings on indictment in the sheriff court.

Prosecution appeal by bill of advocation

131.—(1) Without prejudice to section 74 of this Act, the prosecutor's right to bring a decision under review of the High Court by way of bill of advocation in accordance with existing law and practice shall extend to the review of a decision of any court of solemn jurisdiction.

(2) Where a decision to which a bill of advocation relates is reversed on the review of the decision the prosecutor may, whether or not there has already been a trial diet at which evidence has been led, proceed against the accused by serving him with an indictment containing, subject to subsection (3) below, the charge or charges which were affected by the decision.

(3) The wording of the charge or charges referred to in subsection (2) above shall be as it was immediately before the decision appealed against.

Interpretation of Part VIII

132. In this Part of this Act, unless the context otherwise requires—

"appellant" includes a person who has been convicted and desires to appeal under this Part of the Act;

"sentence" includes any order of the High Court made on conviction with reference to the person convicted or his wife or children, and any recommendation of the High Court as to the making of a deportation order in the case of a person convicted and the power of the High Court to pass a sentence includes a power to make any such order of the court or recommendation, and a recommendation so made by the High Court shall have the same effect for the purposes of Articles 20 and 21 of the Aliens Order 1953 as the certificate and recommendation of the convicting court.

PART IX

SUMMARY PROCEEDINGS

General

Application of Part IX of Act

133.—(1) This Part of this Act applies to summary proceedings in respect of any offence which might prior to the passing of this Act, or which may under the provisions of this or any Act, whether passed before or after the passing of this Act, be tried summarily.

(2) Without prejudice to subsection (1) above, this Part of this Act also applies to procedure in all courts of summary jurisdiction in so far as they have jurisdiction in respect of—

(a) any offence or the recovery of a penalty under any enactment or rule of law which does not exclude summary procedure as well as, in accordance with section 211(3) and (4) of this Act, to the enforcement of a fine imposed in solemn proceedings; and

(b) any order *ad factum praestandum*, or other order of court or warrant competent to a court of summary jurisdiction.

(3) Where any statute provides for summary proceedings to be taken under any public general or local enactment, such proceedings shall be taken under this Part of this Act.

(4) Nothing in this Part of this Act shall—

(a) extend to any complaint or other proceeding under or by virtue of any statutory provision for the recovery of any rate, tax, or impost whatsoever; or

(b) affect any right to raise any civil proceedings.

(5) Except where any enactment otherwise expressly provides, all prosecutions under this Part of this Act shall be brought at the instance of the procurator fiscal.

Incidental applications

134.—(1) This section applies to any application to a court for any warrant or order of court—

(a) as incidental to proceedings by complaint; or

(b) where a court has power to grant any warrant or order of court, although no subsequent proceedings by complaint may follow thereon.

(2) An application to which this section applies may be made by petition at the instance of the prosecutor in the form prescribed by Act of Adjournal.

(3) Where it is necessary for the execution of a warrant or order granted under this section, warrant to break open shut and lockfast places shall be implied.

Warrants of apprehension and search

135.—(1) A warrant of apprehension or search may be in the form prescribed by Act of Adjournal or as nearly as may be in such form, and any warrant of apprehension or search shall, where it is necessary for its execution, imply warrant to officers of law to break open shut and lockfast places.

(2) A warrant of apprehension of an accused in the form mentioned in subsection (1) above shall imply warrant to officers of law to search for and to apprehend the accused, and to bring him before the court issuing the warrant, or before any other court competent to deal with the case, to answer to the charge on which such warrant is granted, and, in the meantime, until he can be so brought, to detain him in a police station, police cell, or other convenient place.

(3) A person apprehended under a warrant or by virtue of power under any enactment or rule of law shall wherever practicable be brought before a court competent to deal with the case not later than in the course of the first day after he is taken into custody.

(4) The reference in subsection (3) above to the first day after he is taken into custody shall not include a Saturday, a Sunday or a court holiday prescribed for that court under section 8 of this Act; but nothing in this subsection shall prevent a person being brought before the court on a Saturday, a Sunday or such a court holiday where the court is, in pursuance of the said section 8, sitting on such day for the disposal of criminal business.

(5) A warrant of apprehension or other warrant shall not be required for the purpose of bringing before the court an accused who has been apprehended without a written warrant or who attends without apprehension in answer to any charge made against him.

Time limit for certain offences

136.—(1) Proceedings under this Part of this Act in respect of any offence to which this section applies shall be commenced—
  (a) within six months after the contravention occurred;
  (b) in the case of a continuous contravention, within six months after the
      last date of such contravention,
and it shall be competent in a prosecution of a contravention mentioned in paragraph (b) above to include the entire period during which the contravention occurred.

(2) This section applies to any offence triable only summarily and consisting of the contravention of any enactment, unless the enactment fixes a different time limit.

(3) For the purposes of this section proceedings shall be deemed to be commenced on the date on which a warrant to apprehend or to cite the accused is granted, if the warrant is executed without undue delay.

Alteration of diets

137.—(1) Where a diet has been fixed in a summary prosecution, it shall be competent for the court, on a joint application in writing by the parties or their solicitors, to discharge the diet and fix an earlier diet in lieu.

(2) Where the prosecutor and the accused make joint application to the court (orally or in writing) for postponement of a diet which has been fixed, the court shall discharge the diet and fix a later diet in lieu unless the court considers that it should not do so because there has been unnecessary delay on the part of one of more of the parties.

(3) Where all the parties join in an application under subsection (2) above, the court may proceed under that subsection without hearing the parties.

(4) Where the prosecutor has intimated to the accused that he desires to postpone or accelerate a diet which has been fixed, and the accused refuses, or any of the accused refuse, to make a joint application to the court for that purpose, the prosecutor may make an incidental application for that purpose under section 134 of this Act; and after giving the parties an opportunity to be heard, the court may discharge the diet and fix a later diet or, as the case may be, an earlier diet in lieu.

(5) Where an accused had intimated to the prosecutor and to all the other accused that he desires such postponement or acceleration and the prosecutor refuses, or any of the other accused refuse, to make a joint application to the court for that purpose, the accused who has so intimated may apply to the court for that purpose; and, after giving the parties an opportunity to be heard, the court may discharge the diet and fix a later diet or, as the case may be, an earlier diet in lieu.

Complaints

Complaints

138.—(1) All proceedings under this Part of this Act for the trial of offences or recovery of penalties shall be instituted by complaint signed by the prosecutor or by a solicitor on behalf of a prosecutor other than the procurator fiscal.

(2) The complaint shall be in the form—
  (a) set out in Schedule 5 to this Act; or
  (b) prescribed by Act of Adjournal,

or as nearly as may be in such form.

(3) A solicitor may appear for and conduct any prosecution on behalf of a prosecutor other than the procurator fiscal.

(4) Schedule 3 to this Act shall have effect as regards complaints under this Act.

Complaints: orders and warrants

139.—(1) On any complaint under this Part of this Act being laid before a judge of the court in which the complaint is brought, he shall have power on the motion of the prosecutor—

(a) to pronounce an order assigning a diet for the disposal of the case to which the accused may be cited as mentioned in section 141 of this Act;

(b) to grant warrant to apprehend the accused where this appears to the judge expedient;

(c) to grant warrant to search the person, dwelling-house and repositories of the accused and any place where he may be found for any documents, articles, or property likely to afford evidence of his guilt of, or guilty participation in, any offence charged in the complaint, and to take possession of such documents, articles or property;

(d) to grant any other order or warrant of court or warrant which may be competent in the circumstances.

(2) The power of a judge under subsection (1) above—

(a) to pronounce an order assigning a diet for the disposal of the case may be exercised on his behalf by the clerk of court;

(b) to grant a warrant to apprehend the accused shall be exercisable notwithstanding that there is power whether at common law or under any Act to apprehend him without a warrant.

Citation

Citation

140.—[1](1) This Act shall be a sufficient warrant for

[1](a) the citation of witnesses for precognition by the prosecutor, whether or not any person has been charged with the offence in relation to which the precognition is taken; and

(b) the citation of the accused and witnesses in a summary prosecution to any ordinary sitting of the court or to any special diet fixed by the court or any adjournment thereof.

(2) Such citation shall be in the form prescribed by Act of Adjournal or as nearly as may be in such form and shall, in the case of the accused, proceed on an induciae of at least 48 hours unless in the special circumstances of the case the court fixes a shorter induciae.

[2](3) . . .

NOTES
[1]Inserted by the Crime and Punishment (Scotland) Act 1997 (c. 48) s.57(2) with effect from August 1, 1997 in terms of the Crime and Punishment (Scotland) Act 1997 (Commencement and Transitional Provisions) Order 1997 (S.I. 1997 No. 1712) para. 3.
[2]Deleted by s.57(2)(b) of the Act above in terms of the above Order.

Manner of citation

141.—(1) The citation of the accused and witnesses in a summary prosecution to any ordinary sitting of the court or to any special diet fixed by the court or to any adjourned sitting or diet shall be effected by delivering the citation to him personally or leaving it for him at his dwelling-house or place of business with a resident or, as the case may be, employee at that place or, where he has no known dwelling-house or place of business, at any other place in which he may be resident at the time.

(2) Notwithstanding subsection (1) above, citation may also be effected—

(a) where the accused or witness is the master of, or a seaman or person employed in a vessel, if the citation is left with a person on board the vessel and connected with it;

(b) where the accused is a partnership, association or body corporate—

(i) if the citation is left at its ordinary place of business with a partner, director, secretary or other official; or

(ii) if it is cited in the same manner as if the proceedings were in a civil court; or

(c) where the accused is a body of trustees, if the citation is left with any one of them who is resident in Scotland or with their known solicitor in Scotland.

[1](3) Subject to subsection (4) below, the citation of the accused or a witness to a sitting or diet or adjourned sitting or diet as mentioned in subsection (1) above shall be effective if it is — ...

[2](a) in the case of the accused signed by the prosecutor and sent by post in a registered envelope or through the recorded delivery service; and

[2](b) in the case of a witness, sent by or on behalf of the prosecutor by ordinary post,

to the dwelling-house or place of business of the accused or witness or, if he has no known dwelling-house or place of business, to any other place in which he may be resident at the time.

(4) Where the accused fails to appear at a diet or sitting or adjourned diet or sitting to which he has been cited in the manner provided by this section, subsections (3) and (5) to (7) of section 150 of this Act shall not apply unless it is proved to the court that he received the citation or that its contents came to his knowledge.

(5) The production in court of any letter or other communication purporting to be written by or on behalf of an accused who has been cited as mentioned in subsection (3) above in such terms as to infer that the contents of such citation came to his knowledge, shall be admissible as evidence of that fact for the purposes of subsection (4) above.

[2](5A) The citation of a witness to a sitting or diet or adjourned sitting or diet as mentioned in subsection (1) above shall be effective if it is sent by the accused's solicitor by ordinary post to the dwelling house or place of business of the witness or if he has no known dwelling house or place of business, to any other place in which he may be resident at the time.

(6) When the citation of any person is effected by post in terms of this section or any other provision of this Act to which this section is applied, the induciae shall be reckoned from 24 hours after the time of posting.

(7) It shall be sufficient evidence that a citation has been sent by post in terms of this section or any other provision of this Act mentioned in subsection (6) above, if there is produced in court a written execution, signed by the person who signed the citation in the form prescribed by Act of Adjournal, or as nearly as may be in such form, together with the post office receipt for the relative registered or recorded delivery letter.

NOTES

[1]Delected by the Crime and Punishment (Scotland) Act 1997 (c. 48) s.62(1) and Sched. 1, para. 21(19)(a) with effect from August 1, 1997 in terms of the Crime and Punishment (Scotland) Act 1997 (Commencement and Transitional Provisions) Order 1997 (S.I. 1997 No. 1712) para. 3.

[2]Inserted by the 1997 Act s.62(1) and Sched. 1, para. 21(19)(a) with effect from August 1, 1997 in terms of the above Order.

³Inserted by the 1997 Act s.62(1) and Sched. 1, para. 21(19)(b) with effect from August 1, 1997 in terms of the above Order.

Children

Summary proceedings against children

142.—(1) Where summary proceedings are brought in respect of an offence alleged to have been committed by a child, the sheriff shall sit either in a different building or room from that in which he usually sits or on different days from those on which other courts in the building are engaged in criminal proceedings: and no person shall be present at any sitting for the purposes of such proceedings except—

(a) members and officers of the court;

(b) parties to the case before the court, their solicitors and counsel, and witnesses and other persons directly concerned in that case;

(c) *bona fide* representatives of news gathering or reporting organisations present for the purpose of the preparation of contemporaneous reports of the proceedings;

(d) such other persons as the court may specially authorise to be present.

(2) A sheriff sitting summarily for the purpose of hearing a charge against, or an application relating to, a person who is believed to be a child may, if he thinks fit to do so, proceed with the hearing and determination of the charge or application, notwithstanding that it is discovered that the person in question is not a child.

(3) When a sheriff sitting summarily has remanded a child for information to be obtained with respect to him, any sheriff sitting summarily in the same place—

(a) may in his absence extend the period for which he is remanded provided that he appears before a sheriff or a justice at least once every 21 days;

(b) when the required information has been obtained, may deal with him finally,

and where the sheriff by whom he was originally remanded has recorded a finding that he is guilty of an offence charged against him it shall not be necessary for any court which subsequently deals with him under this subsection to hear evidence as to the commission of that offence, except in so far as it may consider that such evidence will assist the court in determining the manner in which he should be dealt with.

(4) Any direction in any enactment that a charge shall be brought before a juvenile court shall be construed as a direction that he shall be brought before the sheriff sitting as a court of summary jurisdiction, and no such direction shall be construed as restricting the powers of any justice or justices to entertain an application for bail or for a remand, and to hear such evidence as may be necessary for that purpose.

(5) This section does not apply to summary proceedings before the sheriff in respect of an offence where a child has been charged jointly with a person who is not a child.

Companies

Prosecution of companies, etc.

143.—(1) Without prejudice to any other or wider powers conferred by statute, this section shall apply in relation to the prosecution by summary procedure of a partnership, association, body corporate or body of trustees.

(2) Proceedings may be taken against the partnership, association body corporate or body of trustees in their corporate capacity, and in that event any penalty imposed shall be recovered by civil diligence in accordance with section 221 of this Act.

(3) Proceedings may be taken against an individual representative of a partnership, association or body corporate as follows:—

    (a) in the case of a partnership or firm, any one of the partners, or the manager or the person in charge or locally in charge of its affairs;

    (b) in the case of an association or body corporate, the managing director or the secretary or other person in charge, or locally in charge, of its affairs,

may be dealt with as if he was the person offending, and the offence shall be deemed to be the offence of the partnership, association or body corporate.

First diet

Procedure at first diet

144.—(1) Where the accused is present at the first calling of the case in a summary prosecution and—

    (a) the complaint has been served on him, or

    (b) the complaint or the substance thereof has been read to him, or

    (c) he has legal assistance in his defence,

he shall, unless the court adjourns the case under the section 145 of this Act and subject to subsection (4) below, be asked to plead to the charge.

(2) Where the accused is not present at a calling of the case in a summary prosecution and either—

    (a) the prosecutor produces to the court written intimation that the accused pleads not guilty or pleads guilty and the court is satisfied that the intimation has been made or authorised by the accused; or

    (b) counsel or a solicitor, or a person not being counsel or a solicitor who satisfies the court that he is authorised by the accused, appears on behalf of the accused and tenders a plea of not guilty or a plea of guilty,

subsection (3) below shall apply.

(3) Where this subsection applies—

    (a) in the case of a plea of not guilty, this Part of this Act except section 146(2) shall apply in like manner as if the accused had appeared and tendered the plea; and

    (b) in the case of a plea of guilty, the court may, if the prosecutor accepts the plea, proceed to hear and dispose of the case in the absence of the accused in like manner as if he had appeared and pled guilty, or may, if it thinks fit, continue the case to another diet and require the attendance of the accused with a view to pronouncing sentence in his presence.

(4) Any objection to the competency or relevancy of a summary complaint or the proceedings thereon, or any denial that the accused is the person charged by the police with the offence shall be stated before the accused pleads to the charge or any plea is tendered on his behalf.

(5) No objection or denial such as is mentioned in subsection (4) above shall be allowed to be stated or issued at any future diet in the case except with the leave of the court, which may be granted only on cause shown.

(6) Where in pursuance of subsection (3)(b) above the court proceeds to hear and dispose of a case in the absence of the accused, it shall not pronounce a sentence of imprisonment or of detention in a young offenders institution, remand centre or other establishment.

(7) In this section a reference to a plea of guilty shall include a reference to a plea of guilty to only part of the charge, but where a plea of guilty to only part of a charge is not accepted by the prosecutor it shall be deemed to be a plea of not guilty.

(8) It shall not be competent for any person appearing to answer a complaint, or for counsel or a solicitor appearing for the accused in his

absence, to plead want of due citation or informality therein or in the execution thereof.

(9) In this section, a reference to the first calling of a case includes a reference to any adjourned diet fixed by virtue of section 145 of this Act.

Adjournment for inquiry at first calling

145.—(1) Without prejudice to section 150(1) to (7) of this Act, at the first calling of a case in a summary prosecution the court may, in order to allow time for inquiry into the case or for any other cause which it considers reasonable, adjourn the case under this section, for such period as it considers appropriate, without calling on the accused to plead to any charge against him but remanding him in custody or on bail or ordaining him to appear at the diet thus fixed; and, subject to subsections (2) and (3) below, the court may from time to time so adjourn the case.

(2) Where the accused is remanded in custody, the total period for which he is so remanded under this section shall not exceed 21 days and no one period of adjournment shall, except on special cause shown, exceed 7 days.

(3) Where the accused is remanded on bail or ordained to appear, no one period of adjournment shall exceed 28 days.

Plea of not guilty

146.—(1) This section applies where the accused in a summary prosecution—

(a) pleads not guilty to the charge; or

(b) pleads guilty to only part of the charge and the prosecutor does not accept the partial plea.

(2) The court may proceed to trial at once unless either party moves for an adjournment and the court considers it expedient to grant it.

(3) The court may adjourn the case for trial to as early a diet as is consistent with the just interest of both parties, and the prosecutor shall, if requested by the accused, furnish him with a copy of the complaint if he does not already have one.

(4) Where the accused is brought before the court from custody the court shall inform the accused of his right to an adjournment of the case for not less than 48 hours and if he requests such adjournment before the prosecutor has commenced his proof, subject to subsection (5) below, the adjournment shall be granted.

(5) Where the court considers that it is necessary to secure the examination of witnesses who otherwise would not be available, the case may proceed to trial at once or on a shorter adjournment than 48 hours.

(6) Where the accused is in custody, he may be committed to prison or to legalised police cells or to any other place to which he may lawfully be committed pending trial—

(a) if he is neither granted bail nor ordained to appear; or

(b) if he is granted bail on a condition imposed under section 24(6) of this Act that a sum of money is deposited in court, until the accused or a cautioner on his behalf has so deposited that sum.

(7) The court may from time to time at any stage of the case on the motion of either party or *ex proprio motu* grant such adjournment as may be necessary for the proper conduct of the case, and where from any cause a diet has to be continued from day to day it shall not be necessary to intimate the continuation to the accused.

(8) It shall not be necessary for the prosecutor to establish a charge or part of a charge to which the accused pleads guilty.

(9) The court may, in any case where it considers it expedient, permit any witness for the defence to be examined prior to evidence for the prosecution having been led or concluded, but in any such case the accused shall be

entitled to lead additional evidence after the case for the prosecution is closed.

Pre-trial procedure

Prevention of delay in trials

147.—(1) Subject to subsections (2) and (3) below, a person charged with an offence in summary proceedings shall not be detained in that respect for a total of more than 40 days after the bringing of the complaint in court unless his trial is commenced within that period, failing which he shall be liberated forthwith and thereafter he shall be for ever free from all question or process for that offence.

(2) The sheriff may, on application made to him for the purpose, extend the period mentioned in subsection (1) above and order the accused to be detained awaiting trial for such period as he thinks fit where he is satisfied that delay in the commencement of the trial is due to—

   (a) the illness of the accused or of a judge;

   (b) the absence or illness of any necessary witness; or

   (c) any other sufficient cause which is not attributable to any fault on the part of the prosecutor.

(3) The grant or refusal of any application to extend the period mentioned in subsection (1) above may be appealed against by note of appeal presented to the High Court; and that Court may affirm, reverse or amend the determination made on such application.

(4) For the purposes of this section, a trial shall be taken to commence when the first witness is sworn.

Intermediate diet

148.—(1) The court may, when adjourning a case for trial in terms of section 146(3) of this Act, and may also, at any time thereafter, whether before, on or after any date assigned as a trial diet, fix a diet (to be known as an intermediate diet) for the purpose of ascertaining, so far as is reasonably practicable, whether the case is likely to proceed to trial on any date assigned as a trial diet and, in particular—

   (a) the state of preparation of the prosecutor and of the accused with respect to their cases;

   (b) whether the accused intends to adhere to the plea of not guilty; and

   (c) the extent to which the prosecutor and the accused have complied with the duty under section 257(1) of this Act.

(2) Where at an intermediate diet the court concludes that the case is unlikely to proceed to trial on the date assigned for the trial diet, the court—

   (a) shall, unless having regard to previous proceedings in the case it considers it inappropriate to do so, postpone the trial diet; and

   (b) may fix a further intermediate diet.

(3) Subject to subsection (2) above, the court may, if it considers it appropriate to do so, adjourn an intermediate diet.

(4) At an intermediate diet, the court may ask the prosecutor and the accused any question for the purposes mentioned in subsection (1) above.

(5) The accused shall attend an intermediate diet of which he has received intimation or to which he has been cited unless—

   (a) he is legally represented; and

   (b) the court considers that there are exceptional circumstances justifying him not attending.

(6) A plea of guilty may be tendered at the intermediate diet.

(7) The foregoing provisions of this section shall have effect as respects any court prescribed by the Secretary of State by order, in relation to proceedings commenced after such date as may be so prescribed, with the following modifications—

[1](a) in subsection (1), for the word "may" where it first appears there shall be substituted "shall, subject to subsection (1A) below,"; and

(b) after subsection (1) there shall be inserted the following subsections—

"(1A) If, on a joint application by the prosecutor and the accused made at any time before the commencement of the intermediate diet, the court considers it inappropriate to have such a diet, the duty under subsection (1) above shall not apply and the court shall discharge any such diet already fixed.

(1B) The court may consider an application under subsection (1A) above without hearing the parties.".

(8) An order under subsection (7) above shall be made by statutory instrument, which shall be subject to annulment in pursuance of a resolution of either House of Parliament.

NOTE

[1]As amended by the Criminal Procedure (Intermediate Diets) (Scotland) Act 1998 (c. 10) s.1 (effective April 8, 1998).

Alibi

149. It shall not be competent for the accused in a summary prosecution to found on a plea of alibi unless he gives, at any time before the first witness is sworn, notice to the prosecutor of the plea with particulars as to time and place and of the witnesses by whom it is proposed to prove it; and, on such notice being given, the prosecutor shall be entitled, if he so desires, to an adjournment of the case.

Failure of accused to appear

Failure of accused to appear

150.—(1) This section applies where the accused in a summary prosecution fails to appear at any diet of which he has received intimation, or to which he has been cited other than a diet which, by virtue of section 148(5) of this Act, he is not required to attend.

(2) The court may adjourn the proceedings to another diet, and order the accused to attend at such diet, and appoint intimation of the diet to be made to him.

(3) The court may grant warrant to apprehend the accused.

(4) Intimation under subsection (2) above shall be sufficiently given by an officer of law, or by letter signed by the clerk of court or prosecutor and sent to the accused at his last known address by registered post or by the recorded delivery service, and the production in court of the written execution of such officer or of an acknowledgement or certificate of the delivery of the letter issued by the Post Office shall be sufficient evidence of such intimation having been duly given.

(5) Where the accused is charged with a statutory offence for which a sentence of imprisonment cannot be imposed in the first instance, or where the statute founded on or conferring jurisdiction authorises procedure in the absence of the accused, the court, on the motion of the prosecutor and upon being satisfied that the accused has been duly cited, or has received due intimation of the diet where such intimation has been ordered, may subject to subsections (6) and (7) below, proceed to hear and dispose of the case in the absence of the accused.

(6) Unless the statute founded on authorises conviction in default of appearance, proof of the complaint must be led to the satisfaction of the court.

(7) In a case to which subsection (5) above applies, the court may, if it considers it expedient, allow counsel or a solicitor who satisfies the court that

he has authority from the accused so to do, to appear and plead for and defend him.

(8) An accused who without reasonable excuse fails to attend any diet of which he has been given due notice, shall be guilty of an offence and liable on summary conviction—

    (a) to a fine not exceeding level 3 on the standard scale; and

    (b) to a period of imprisonment not exceeding—

        (i) in the district court, 60 days; or

        (ii) in the sheriff court, 3 months.

(9) The penalties provided for in subsection (8) above may be imposed in addition to any other penalty which it is competent for the court to impose, notwithstanding that the total of penalties imposed may exceed the maximum penalty which it is competent to impose in respect of the original offence.

(10) An accused may be dealt with for an offence under subsection (8) above either at his diet of trial for the original offence or at a separate trial.

Non-availability of judge

• Death, illness or absence of judge

151.—(1) Where the court is unable to proceed owing to the death, illness or absence of the presiding judge, it shall be lawful for the clerk of court—

    (a) where the diet has not been called, to convene the court and adjourn the diet;

    (b) where the diet has been called but no evidence has been led, to adjourn the diet; and

    (c) where the diet has been called and evidence has been led—

        (i) with the agreement of the parties, to desert the diet *pro loco et tempore*; or

        (ii) to adjourn the diet.

(2) Where, under subsection (1)(c)(i) above, a diet has been deserted *pro loco et tempore*, any new prosecution charging the accused with the same or any similar offence arising out of the same facts shall be brought within two months of the date on which the diet was deserted notwithstanding that any other time limit for the commencement of such prosecution has elapsed.

(3) For the purposes of subsection (2) above, a new prosecution shall be deemed to commence on the date on which a warrant to apprehend or to cite the accused is granted, if such warrant is executed without undue delay.

Trial diet

Desertion of diet

152.—(1) It shall be competent at the diet of trial, at any time before the first witness is sworn, for the court, on the application of the prosecutor, to desert the diet *pro loco et tempore*.

(2) If, at a diet of trial, the court refuses an application by the prosecutor to adjourn the trial or to desert the diet *pro loco et tempore*, and the prosecutor is unable or unwilling to proceed with the trial, the court shall desert the diet *simpliciter*.

(3) Where the court has deserted a diet *simpliciter* under subsection (2) above (and the court's decision in that regard has not been reversed on appeal), it shall not be competent for the prosecutor to raise a fresh libel.

Trial in presence of accused

153.—(1) Without prejudice to section 150 of this Act, and subject to subsection (2) below, no part of a trial shall take place outwith the presence of the accused.

(2) If during the course of his trial an accused so misconducts himself that

in the view of the court a proper trial cannot take place unless he is removed, the court may order—

    (a) that he is removed from the court for so long as his conduct makes it necessary; and

    (b) that the trial proceeds in his absence,

but if he is not legally represented the court shall appoint counsel or a solicitor to represent his interests during such absence.

Proof of official documents

154.—[*Repealed by the Crime and Punishment (Scotland) Act s.28*]

Punishment of witness for contempt

155.—(1) If a witness in a summary prosecution—

    (a) wilfully fails to attend after being duly cited; or

    (b) unlawfully refuses to be sworn; or

    (c) after the oath has been administered to him refuses to answer any question which the court may allow; or

    (d) prevaricates in his evidence,

he shall be deemed guilty of contempt of court and be liable to be summarily punished forthwith for such contempt by a fine not exceeding level 3 on the standard scale or by imprisonment for any period not exceeding 21 days.

(2) Where punishment is summarily imposed as mentioned in subsection (1) above, the clerk of court shall enter in the record of the proceedings the acts constituting the contempt or the statements forming the prevarication.

(3) Subsections (1) and (2) above are without prejudice to the right of the prosecutor to proceed by way of formal complaint for any such contempt where a summary punishment, as mentioned in the said subsection (1), is not imposed.

(4) Any witness who, having been duly cited in accordance with section 140 of this Act—

    (a) fails without reasonable excuse, after receiving at least 48 hours' notice, to attend for precognition by a prosecutor at the time and place mentioned in the citation served on him; or

    (b) refuses when so cited to give information within his knowledge regarding any matter relative to the commission of the offence in relation to which such precognition is taken,

shall be liable to the like punishment as is provided in subsection (1) above.

Apprehension of witness

156.—(1) Where a witness, having been duly cited, fails to appear at the diet fixed for his attendance and no just excuse is offered by him or on his behalf, the court may, if it is satisfied that he received the citation or that its contents came to his knowledge, issue a warrant for his apprehension.

(2) Where the court is satisfied by evidence on oath that a witness is not likely to attend to give evidence without being compelled so to do, it may issue a warrant for his apprehension.

(3) A warrant of apprehension of a witness in the form mentioned in section 135(1) of this Act shall imply warrant to officers of law to search for and apprehend the witness, and to detain him in a police station, police cell, or other convenient place, until—

    (a) the date fixed for the hearing of the case; or

    (b) the date when security to the amount fixed under subsection (4) below is found,

whichever is the earlier.

(4) A witness apprehended under a warrant under subsection (1) or (2) above shall, wherever practicable, be brought immediately by the officer of law who executed that warrant before a justice, who shall fix such sum as he

considers appropriate as security for the appearance of the witness at all diets.

Record of proceedings

157.—(1) Proceedings in a summary prosecution shall be conducted summarily *viva voce* and, except where otherwise provided and subject to subsection (2) below, no record need be kept of the proceedings other than the complaint, or a copy of the complaint certified as a true copy by the procurator fiscal, the plea, a note of any documentary evidence produced, and the conviction and sentence or other finding of the court.

(2) Any objection taken to the competency or relevancy of the complaint or proceedings, or to the competency or admissibility of evidence, shall, if either party desires it, be entered in the record of the proceedings.

Interruption of summary proceedings for verdict in earlier trial

158. Where the sheriff is sitting in summary proceedings during the period in which the jury in a criminal trial in which he has presided are retired to consider their verdict, it shall be lawful, if he considers it appropriate to do so, to interrupt those proceedings—

(a) in order to receive the verdict of the jury and dispose of the cause to which it relates;

(b) to give a direction to the jury on any matter on which they may wish one from him, or to hear a request from them regarding any matter, and the interruption shall not affect the validity of the proceedings nor cause the instance to fall in respect of any person accused in the proceedings.

Amendment of complaint

159.—(1) It shall be competent at any time prior to the determination of the case, unless the court see just cause to the contrary, to amend the complaint or any notice of previous conviction relative thereto by deletion, alteration or addition, so as to—

(a) cure any error or defect in it;

(b) meet any objection to it; or

(c) cure any discrepancy or variance between the complaint or notice and the evidence.

(2) Nothing in this section shall authorise an amendment which changes the character of the offence charged, and, if it appears to the court that the accused may in any way be prejudiced in his defence on the merits of the case by any amendment made under this section, the court shall grant such remedy to the accused by adjournment or otherwise as appears to the court to be just.

(3) An amendment made under this section shall be sufficiently authenticated by the initials of the clerk of the court.

No case to answer

160.—(1) Immediately after the close of the evidence for the prosecution, the accused may intimate to the court his desire to make a submission that he has no case to answer both—

(a) on an offence charged in the complaint; and

(b) on any other offence of which he could be convicted under the complaint were the offence charged the only offence so charged.

(2) If, after hearing both parties, the judge is satisfied that the evidence led by the prosecution is insufficient in law to justify the accused being convicted of the offence charged in respect of which the submission has been made or of such other offence as is mentioned, in relation to that offence, in paragraph (b) of subsection (1) above, he shall acquit him of the offence

charged in respect of which the submission has been made and the trial shall proceed only in respect of any other offence charged in the complaint.

(3) If, after hearing both parties, the judge is not satisfied as is mentioned in subsection (2) above, he shall reject the submission and the trial shall proceed, with the accused entitled to give evidence and call witnesses, as if such submission had not been made.

Defence to speak last

161. In any trial the accused or, where he is legally represented, his counsel or solicitor shall have the right to speak last.

Verdict and conviction

Judges equally divided

162. In a summary prosecution in a court consisting of more than one judge, if the judges are equally divided in opinion as to the guilt of the accused, the accused shall be found not guilty of the charge or part thereof on which such division of opinion exists.

Conviction: miscellaneous provisions

163.—(1) Where imprisonment is authorised by the sentence of a court of summary jurisdiction, an extract of the finding and sentence in the form prescribed by Act of Adjournal shall be a sufficient warrant for the apprehension and commitment of the accused, and no such extract shall be void or liable to be set aside on account of any error or defect in point of form.

(2) In any proceedings in a court of summary jurisdiction consisting of more than one judge, the signature of one judge shall be sufficient in all warrants or other proceedings prior or subsequent to conviction, and it shall not be necessary that the judge so signing shall be one of the judges trying or dealing with the case otherwise.

Conviction of part of charge

164. A conviction of a part or parts only of the charge or charges libelled in a complaint shall imply dismissal of the rest of the complaint.

"Conviction" and "sentence" not to be used for children

165. The words "conviction" and "sentence" shall not be used in relation to children dealt with summarily and any reference in any enactment, whether passed before or after the commencement of this Act, to a person convicted, a conviction or a sentence shall in the case of a child be construed as including a reference to a person found guilty of an offence, a finding of guilt or an order made upon such a finding as the case may be.

Previous convictions: summary proceedings

166.—(1) This section shall apply where the accused in a summary prosecution has been previously convicted of any offence and the prosecutor has decided to lay a previous conviction before the court.

(2) A notice in the form prescribed by Act of Adjournal or as nearly as may be in such form specifying the previous conviction shall be served on the accused with the complaint where he is cited to a diet, and where he is in custody the complaint and such a notice shall be served on him before he is asked to plead.

(3) The previous conviction shall not be laid before the judge until he is satisfied that the charge is proved.

(4) If a plea of guilty is tendered or if, after a plea of not guilty, the accused is convicted the prosecutor shall lay the notice referred to in subsection (2) above before the judge, and—

(a) in a case where the plea of guilty is tendered in writing the accused shall be deemed to admit any previous conviction set forth in the notice, unless he expressly denies it in the writing by which the plea is tendered;

(b) in any other case the judge or the clerk of court shall ask the accused whether he admits the previous conviction,

and if such admission is made or deemed to be made it shall be entered in the record of the proceedings; and it shall not be necessary for the prosecutor to produce extracts of any previous convictions so admitted.

(5) Where the accused does not admit any previous conviction, the prosecutor unless he withdraws the conviction shall adduce evidence in proof thereof either then or at any other diet.

(6) A copy of any notice served on the accused under this section shall be entered in the record of the proceedings.

(7) Where a person is convicted of an offence, the court may have regard to any previous conviction in respect of that person in deciding on the disposal of the case.

(8) Nothing in this section shall prevent the prosecutor—

(a) asking the accused questions tending to show that the accused has been convicted of an offence other than that with which he is charged, where he is entitled to do so under section 266 of this Act; or

(b) leading evidence of previous convictions where it is competent to do so—

(i) as evidence in support of a substantive charge; or

(ii) under section 270 of this Act.

Forms of finding and sentence

167.—(1) Every sentence imposed by a court of summary jurisdiction shall unless otherwise provided be pronounced in open court in the presence of the accused, but need not be written out or signed in his presence.

(2) The finding and sentence and any order of a court of summary jurisdiction, as regards both offences at common law and offences under any enactment, shall be entered in the record of the proceedings in the form, as nearly as may be, prescribed by Act of Adjournal.

(3) The record of the proceedings shall be sufficient warrant for all execution on a finding, sentence or order and for the clerk of court to issue extracts containing such executive clauses as may be necessary for implement thereof.

(4) When imprisonment forms part of any sentence or other judgement, warrant for the apprehension and interim detention of the accused pending his being committed to prison shall, where necessary, be implied.

(5) Where a fine imposed by a court of summary jurisdiction is paid at the bar it shall not be necessary for the court to refer to the period of imprisonment applicable to the non-payment thereof.

(6) Where several charges at common law or under any enactment are embraced in one complaint, a cumulo penalty may be imposed in respect of all or any of such charges of which the accused is convicted.

[1](7) Subject to section 204A of this Act, a court of summary jurisdiction may frame—

(a) a sentence following on conviction; or

(b) an order for committal in default of payment of any sum of money or for contempt of court,

so as to take effect on the expiry of any previous sentence or order which, at the date of the later conviction or order, the accused is undergoing.

(8) It shall be competent at any time before imprisonment has followed on a sentence for the court to alter or modify it; but no higher sentence than that originally pronounced shall be competent, and—
   (a) the signature of the judge or clerk of court to any sentence shall be sufficient also to authenticate the findings on which such sentence proceeds; and
   (b) the power conferred by this subsection to alter or modify a sentence may be exercised without requiring the attendance of the accused.

NOTE
¹Inserted by the Crime and Disorder Act 1998 (c. 37), Sched. 8, para. 122 (effective September 30, 1998: S.I. 1998 No. 2327).

Caution

168.—(1) This section applies with regard to the finding, forfeiture, and recovery of caution in any proceedings under this Part of this Act.
   (2) Caution may be found by consignation of the amount with the clerk of court, or by bond of caution signed by the cautioner.
   (3) Where caution becomes liable to forfeiture, forfeiture may be granted by the court on the motion of the prosecutor, and, where necessary, warrant granted for the recovery of the caution.
   (4) Where a cautioner fails to pay the amount due under his bond within six days after he has received a charge to that effect, the court may—
   (a) order him to be imprisoned for the maximum period applicable in pursuance of section 219 of this Act to that amount or until payment is made; or
   (b) if it considers it expedient, on the application of the cautioner grant time for payment; or
   (c) instead of ordering imprisonment, order recovery by civil diligence in accordance with section 221 of this Act.

Detention in precincts of court

169.—(1) Where a court of summary jurisdiction has power to impose imprisonment or detention on an offender it may, in lieu of so doing and subject to subsection (2) below, order that the offender be detained within the precincts of the court or at any police station, till such hour, not later than eight in the evening on the day on which he is convicted, as the court may direct.
   (2) Before making an order under this section a court shall take into consideration the distance between the proposed place of detention and the offender's residence (if known to, or ascertainable by, the court), and shall not make any such order under this section as would deprive the offender of a reasonable opportunity of returning to his residence on the day on which the order is made.

Miscellaneous

Damages in respect of summary proceedings

170.—(1) No judge, clerk of court or prosecutor in the public interest shall be found liable by any court in damages for or in respect of any proceedings taken, act done, or judgment, decree or sentence pronounced in any summary proceedings under this Act, unless—
   (a) the person suing has suffered imprisonment in consequence thereof; and

(b) such proceedings, act, judgment, decree or sentence has been quashed; and

(c) the person suing specifically avers and proves that such proceeding, act, judgment, decree or sentence was taken, done or pronounced maliciously and without probable cause.

(2) No such liability as aforesaid shall be incurred or found where such judge, clerk of court or prosecutor establishes that the person suing was guilty of the offence in respect whereof he had been convicted, or on account of which he had been apprehended or had otherwise suffered, and that he had undergone no greater punishment than was assigned by law to such offence.

(3) No action to enforce such liability as aforesaid shall lie unless it is commenced within two months after the proceeding, act, judgment decree or sentence founded on, or in the case where the Act under which the action is brought fixes a shorter period, within that shorter period.

(4) In this section "judge" shall not include "sheriff", and the provisions of this section shall be without prejudice to the privileges and immunities possessed by sheriffs.

Recovery of penalties

171.—(1) All penalties, for the recovery of which no special provision has been made by any enactment may be recovered by the public prosecutor in any court having jurisdiction.

(2) Where a court has power to take cognisance of an offence the penalty attached to which is not defined, the punishment therefore shall be regulated by that applicable to common law offences in that court.

Forms of procedure

172.—(1) The forms of procedure for the purposes of summary proceedings under this Act and appeals therefrom shall be in such forms as are prescribed by Act of Adjournal or as nearly as may be in such forms.

(2) All warrants (other than warrants of apprehension or search), orders of court, and sentences may be signed either by the judge or by the clerk of court, and execution upon any warrant, order of court, or sentence may proceed either upon such warrant, order of court, or sentence itself or upon an extract thereof issued and signed by the clerk of court.

(3) Where, preliminary to any procedure, a statement on oath is required, the statement may be given before any judge, whether the subsequent procedure is in his court or another court.

PART X

APPEALS FROM SUMMARY PROCEEDINGS

General

Quorum of High Court in relation to appeals

173.—(1) For the purpose of hearing and determining any appeal under this Part of this Act, or any proceeding connected therewith, three of the Lords Commissioners of Justiciary shall be a quorum of the High Court, and the determination of any question under this Part of this Act by the court shall be according to the votes of the majority of the members of the court sitting, including the presiding judge, and each judge so sitting shall be entitled to pronounce a separate opinion.

(2) For the purpose of hearing and determining appeals under section 175(2)(b) or (c) of this Act, or any proceeding connected therewith, two of the Lords Commissioners of Justiciary shall be a quorum of the High Court,

and each judge shall be entitled to pronounce a separate opinion; but where the two Lords Commissioners of Justiciary are unable to reach agreement on the disposal of the appeal, or where they consider it appropriate, the appeal shall be heard and determined in accordance with subsection (1) above.

Appeals relating to preliminary pleas

174.—(1) Without prejudice to any right of appeal under section 175(1) to (6) or 191 of this Act, a party may, with the leave of the court (granted either on the motion of the party or *ex proprio motu*) and in accordance with such procedure as may be prescribed by Act of Adjournal, appeal to the High Court against a decision of the court of first instance (other than a decision not to grant leave under this subsection) which relates to such objection or denial as is mentioned in section 144(4) of this Act; but such appeal must be taken not later than two days after such decision.

(2) Where an appeal is taken under subsection (1) above, the High Court may postpone the trial diet (if one has been fixed) for such period as appears to it to be appropriate and may, if it thinks fit, direct that such period (or some part of it) shall not count towards any time limit applying in respect of the case.

(3) If leave to appeal under subsection (1) above is granted by the court it shall not proceed to trial at once under subsection (2) of section 146 of this Act; and subsection (3) of that section shall be construed as requiring sufficient time to be allowed for the appeal to be taken.

(4) In disposing of an appeal under subsection (1) above the High Court may affirm the decision of the court of first instance or may remit the case to it with such directions in the matter as it thinks fit; and where the court of first instance had dismissed the complaint, or any part of it, may reverse that decision and direct that the court of first instance fix a trial diet (if it has not already fixed one as regards so much of the complaint as it has not dismissed.)

Right of appeal

175.—(1) This section is without prejudice to any right of appeal under section 191 of this Act.

(2) Any person convicted, or found to have committed an offence, in summary proceedings may, with leave granted in accordance with section 180 or, as the case may be, 187 of this Act, appeal under this section to the High Court—

  (a) against such conviction, or finding;

  (b) against the sentence passed on such conviction;

  (c) against his absolute discharge or admonition or any probation order or any community service order or any order deferring sentence; or

[1](ca) against any decision to remit made under section 49(1)(a) or (7)(b) of this Act;

  (d) against both such conviction and such sentence or disposal or order.

(3) The prosecutor in summary proceedings may appeal under this section to the High Court on a point of law—

  (a) against an acquittal in such proceedings; or

  (b) against a sentence passed on conviction in such proceedings.

[2](4) The prosecutor in summary proceedings, in any class of case specified by order made by the Secretary of State, may, in accordance with subsection (4A) below, appeal to the High Court against any of the following disposals, namely—

  (a) a sentence passed on conviction;

  (b) a decision under section 209(1)(b) of this Act not to make a supervised release order;

   (c) a decision under section 234A(2) of this Act not to make a
      non-harassment order;
   (d) a probation order;
   (e) a community service order;
   (f) a decision to remit to the Principal Reporter made under section
      49(1)(a) or (7)(b) of this Act;
   (g) an order deferring sentence;
   (h) an admonition; or
   (i) an absolute discharge.
(4A) An appeal under subsection (4) above may be made—
   (a) on a point of law;
   (b) where it appears to the Lord Advocate, in relation to an appeal
      under—
       (i) paragraph (a), (h) or (i) of that subsection, that the disposal was
          unduly lenient;
      (ii) paragraph (b) or (c) of that subsection, that the decision not to
          make the order in question was inappropriate;
     (iii) paragraph (d) or (e) of that subsection, that the making of the
          order concerned was unduly lenient or was on unduly lenient
          terms;
     (iv) under paragraph (f) of that subsection, that the decision to remit
          was inappropriate;
      (v) under paragraph (g) of that subsection, that the deferment of
          sentence was inappropriate or was on unduly lenient conditions.
[3](5) By an appeal under subsection (2) above, an appellant may bring
under review of the High Court any alleged miscarriage of justice which may
include such a miscarriage based, subject to subsections (5A) to (5D) below,
on the existence and significance of evidence which was not heard at the
original proceedings.
   (5A) Evidence which was not heard at the original proceedings may found
an appeal only where there is a reasonable explanation of why it was not so
heard.
   (5B) Where the explanation referred to in subsection (5A) above or, as
the case may be, (5C) below is that the evidence was not admissible at the
time of the original proceedings, but is admissible at the time of the appeal,
the court may admit that evidence if it appears to the court that it would be in
the interests of justice to do so.
   [4](5C) Without prejudice to subsection (5A) above, where evidence such as
is mentioned subsection (5) above is evidence—
   (a) which is—
       (i) from a person; or
      (ii) of a statement (within the meaning of section 259(1) of this Act)
          by a person,
      who gave evidence at the original proceedings; and
   (b) which is different from, or additional to, the evidence so given,
it may not found an appeal unless there is a reasonable explanation as to why
the evidence now sought to be adduced was not given by that person at those
proceedings, which explanation is itself supported by independent evidence.
   (5D) For the purposes of subsection (5C) above, "independent evidence"
means evidence which—
   (a) was not heard at the original proceedings;
   (b) is from a source independent of the person referred to in subsection
      (5C) above; and
   (c) is accepted by the court as being credible and reliable.
   (5E) By an appeal against acquittal under subsection (3) above a
prosecutor may bring under review of the High Court any alleged
miscarriage of justice.
   (6) The power of the Secretary of State to make an order under subsection

(4) above shall be exercisable by statutory instrument; and any order so made shall be subject to annulment in pursuance of a resolution of either House of Parliament.

(7) Where a person desires to appeal under subsection (2)(a) or (d) or (3) above, he shall pursue such appeal in accordance with sections 176 to 179, 181 to 185, 188, 190 and 192(1) and (2) of this Act.

(8) A person who has appealed against both conviction and sentence, may abandon the appeal in so far as it is against conviction and may proceed with it against sentence alone, subject to such procedure as may be prescribed by Act of Adjournal.

(9) Where a convicted person or as the case may be a person found to have committed an offence desires to appeal under subsection (2)(b) or (c) above, or the prosecutor desires so to appeal by virtue of subsection (4) above, he shall pursue such appeal in accordance with sections 186, 189(1) to (6), 190 and 192(1) and (2) of this Act; but nothing in this section shall prejudice any right to proceed by bill of suspension, or as the case may be advocation, against an alleged fundamental irregularity relating to the imposition of sentence.

(10) Where any statute provides for an appeal from summary proceedings to be taken under any public general or local enactment, such appeal shall be taken under this Part of this Act.

NOTES

[1]Inserted by the Crime and Punishment (Scotland) Act 1997 (c. 48), s.23 with effect from August 1, 1997 in terms of the Crime and Punishment (Scotland) Act 1997 (Commencement and Transitional Provisions) Order 1997 (S.I. 1997 No. 1712) para. 3.

[2]Inserted by the Crime and Punishment (Scotland) Act 1997 (c. 48), s.21 with effect from August 1, 1997 in terms of the Crime and Punishment (Scotland) Act 1997 (Commencement and Transitional Provisions) Order 1997 (S.I. 1997 No. 1712) para. 3.

[3]Inserted by the Crime and Punishment (Scotland) Act 1997 (c. 48), s.17(2) with effect from August 1, 1997 in terms of the Crime and Punishment (Scotland) Act 1997 (Commencement and Transitional Provisions) Order 1997 (S.I. 1997 No. 1712) para. 3.

[4]As amended by the Crime and Disorder Act 1998 (c. 37), Sched. 8, para. 123 (effective September 30, 1998: S.I. 1998 No. 2327).

Stated case: manner and time of appeal

176.—(1) An appeal under section 175(2)(a) or (d) or (3) of this Act shall be by application for a stated case, which application shall—

    (a) be made within one week of the final determination of the proceedings;

    (b) contain a full statement of all the matters which the appellant desires to bring under review and, where the appeal is also against sentence or disposal or order, the ground of appeal against that sentence or disposal or order; and

    (c) be signed by the appellant or his solicitor and lodged with the clerk of court,

and a copy of the application shall, within the period mentioned in paragraph (a) above, be sent by the appellant to the respondent or the respondent's solicitor.

(2) The clerk of court shall enter in the record of the proceedings the date when an application under subsection (1) above was lodged.

(3) The appellant may, at any time within the period of three weeks mentioned in subsection (1) of section 179 of this Act, or within any further period afforded him by virtue of section 181(1) of this Act, amend any matter stated in his application or add a new matter; and he shall intimate any such amendment, or addition, to the respondent or the respondent's solicitor.

(4) Where such an application has been made by the person convicted, and the judge by whom he was convicted dies before signing the case or is

precluded by illness or other cause from doing so, it shall be competent for the convicted person to present a bill of suspension to the High Court and to bring under the review of that court any matter which might have been brought under review by stated case.

(5) The record of the procedure in the inferior court in an appeal mentioned in subsection (1) above shall be as nearly as may be in the form prescribed by Act of Adjournal.

Procedure where appellant in custody

177.—(1) If an appellant making an application under section 176 of this Act is in custody, the court of first instance may—

(a) grant bail;

(b) grant a sist of execution;

(c) make any other interim order.

(2) An application for bail shall be disposed of by the court within 24 hours after such application has been made.

(3) If bail is refused or the appellant is dissatisfied with the conditions imposed, he may, within 24 hours after the judgment of the court, appeal against it by a note of appeal written on the complaint and signed by himself or his solicitor, and the complaint and proceedings shall thereupon be transmitted to the Clerk of Justiciary, and the High Court or any judge thereof, either in court or in chambers, shall, after hearing parties, have power to review the decision of the inferior court and to grant bail on such conditions as the Court or judge may think fit, or to refuse bail.

(4) No clerks' fees, court fees or other fees or expenses shall be exigible from or awarded against an appellant in custody in respect of an appeal to the High Court against the conditions imposed or on account of refusal of bail by a court of summary jurisdiction.

(5) If an appellant who has been granted bail does not thereafter proceed with his appeal, the inferior court shall have power to grant warrant to apprehend and imprison him for such period of his sentence as at the date of his bail remained unexpired and, subject to subsection (6) below, such period shall run from the date of his imprisonment under the warrant or, on the application of the appellant, such earlier date as the court thinks fit, not being a date later than the date of expiry of any term or terms of imprisonment imposed subsequently to the conviction appealed against.

(6) Where an appellant who has been granted bail does not thereafter proceed with his appeal, the court from which the appeal was taken shall have power, where at the time of the abandonment of the appeal the person is in custody or serving a term or terms of imprisonment imposed subsequently to the conviction appealed against, to order that the sentence or, as the case may be, the unexpired portion of that sentence relating to that conviction should run from such date as the court may think fit, not being a date later than the date on which any term or terms of imprisonment subsequently imposed expired.

(7) The court shall not make an order under subsection (6) above to the effect that the sentence or, as the case may be, unexpired portion of the sentence shall run other than concurrently with the subsequently imposed term of imprisonment without first notifying the appellant of its intention to do so and considering any representations made by him or on his behalf.

[1](8) Subsections (6) and (7) of section 112 of this Act (bail pending determination of appeals under paragraph 13(a) of Schedule 6 to the Scotland Act 1998) shall apply to appeals arising in summary proceedings as they do to appeals arising in solemn proceedings.

NOTE

[1]Inserted by the Scotland Act 1998 (Consequential Modifications) (No.1) Order 1999 (S.I. 1999 No.1042) art.3, Sched.1, para.13(7) (effective May 6, 1999).

Stated case: preparation of draft

178.—(1) Within three weeks of the final determination of proceedings in respect of which an application for a stated case is made under section 176 of this Act—

(a) where the appeal is taken from the district court and the trial was presided over by a justice of the peace or justices of the peace, the Clerk of Court; or

(b) in any other case the judge who presided at the trial,

shall prepare a draft stated case, and the clerk of the court concerned shall forthwith issue the draft to the appellant or his solicitor and a duplicate thereof to the respondent or his solicitor.

(2) A stated case shall be, as nearly as may be, in the form prescribed by Act of Adjournal, and shall set forth the particulars of any matters competent for review which the appellant desires to bring under the review of the High Court, and of the facts, if any, proved in the case, and any point of law decided, and the grounds of the decision.

Stated case: adjustment and signature

179.—(1) Subject to section 181(1) of this Act, within three weeks of the issue of the draft stated case under section 178 of this Act, each party shall cause to be transmitted to the court and to the other parties or their solicitors a note of any adjustments he proposes be made to the draft case or shall intimate that he has no such proposal.

¹(2) The adjustments mentioned in subsection (1) above shall relate to evidence heard or purported to have been heard at the trial and not to such evidence as is mentioned in section 175(5) of this Act.

(3) Subject to section 181(1) of this Act, if the period mentioned in subsection (1) above has expired and the appellant has not lodged adjustments and has failed to intimate that he has no adjustments to propose, he shall be deemed to have abandoned his appeal; and subsection (5) of section 177 of this Act shall apply accordingly.

(4) If adjustments are proposed under subsection (1) above or if the judge desires to make any alterations to the draft case there shall, within one week of the expiry of the period mentioned in that subsection or as the case may be of any further period afforded under section 181(1) of this Act, be a hearing (unless the appellant has, or has been deemed to have, abandoned his appeal) for the purpose of considering such adjustments or alterations.

(5) Where a party neither attends nor secures that he is represented at a hearing under subsection (4) above, the hearing shall nevertheless proceed.

(6) Where at a hearing under subsection (4) above—

(a) any adjustment proposed under subsection (1) above by a party (and not withdrawn) is rejected by the judge; or

(b) any alteration proposed by the judge is not accepted by all the parties,

that fact shall be recorded in the minute of the proceedings of the hearing.

(7) Within two weeks of the date of the hearing under subsection (4) above or, where there is no hearing, within two weeks of the expiry of the period mentioned in subsection (1) above, the judge shall (unless the appellant has been deemed to have abandoned the appeal) state and sign the case and shall append to the case—

(a) any adjustment, proposed under subsection (1) above, which is rejected by him, a note of any evidence rejected by him which is alleged to support that adjustment and the reasons for his rejection of that adjustment and evidence; and

(b) a note of the evidence upon which he bases any finding of fact challenged, on the basis that it is unsupported by the evidence, by a party at the hearing under subsection (4) above.

(8) As soon as the case is signed under subsection (7) above the clerk of court—

(a) shall send the case to the appellant or his solicitor and a duplicate thereof to the respondent or his solicitor; and

(b) shall transmit the complaint, productions and any other proceedings in the cause to the Clerk of Justiciary.

(9) Subject to section 181(1) of this Act, within one week of receiving the case the appellant or his solicitor, as the case may be, shall cause it to be lodged with the Clerk of Justiciary.

(10) Subject to section 181(1) of this Act, if the appellant or his solicitor fails to comply with subsection (9) above the appellant shall be deemed to have abandoned the appeal; and subsection (5) of section 177 of this Act shall apply accordingly.

NOTE

[1] As amended by the Crime and Punishment (Scotland) Act 1997 (c. 48) Sched. 1, para. 21(20) with effect from August 1, 1997 in terms of the Crime and Punishment (Scotland) Act 1997 (Commencement and Transitional Provisions) Order 1997 (S.I. 1997 No. 1712) para. 3.

Leave to appeal against conviction etc.

180.—(1) The decision whether to grant leave to appeal for the purposes of section 175(2)(a) or (d) of this Act shall be made by a judge of the High Court who shall—

(a) if he considers that the documents mentioned in subsection (2) below disclose arguable grounds of appeal, grant leave to appeal and make such comments in writing as he considers appropriate; and

(b) in any other case—

(i) refuse leave to appeal and give reasons in writing for the refusal; and

(ii) where the appellant is on bail and the sentence imposed on his conviction is one of imprisonment, grant a warrant to apprehend and imprison him.

(2) The documents referred to in subsection (1) above are—

(a) the stated case lodged under subsection (9) of section 179 of this Act; and

(b) the documents transmitted to the Clerk of Justiciary under subsection (8)(b) of that section.

(3) A warrant granted under subsection (1)(b)(ii) above shall not take effect until the expiry of the period of 14 days mentioned in subsection (4) below without an application to the High Court for leave to appeal having been lodged by the appellant under that subsection.

(4) Where leave to appeal is refused under subsection (1) above the appellant may, within 14 days of intimation under subsection (10) below, apply to the High Court for leave to appeal.

(5) In deciding an application under subsection (4) above the High Court shall—

(a) if, after considering the documents mentioned in subsection (2) above and the reasons for the refusal, the court is of the opinion that there are arguable grounds of appeal, grant leave to appeal and make such comments in writing as the court considers appropriate; and

(b) in any other case—

(i) refuse leave to appeal and give reasons in writing for the refusal; and

(ii) where the appellant is on bail and the sentence imposed on his conviction is one of imprisonment, grant a warrant to apprehend and imprison him.

(6) The question whether to grant leave to appeal under subsection (1) or

(5) above shall be considered and determined in chambers without the parties being present.

(7) Comments in writing made under subsection (1)(a) or (5)(a) above may, without prejudice to the generality of that provision, specify the arguable grounds of appeal (whether or not they are contained in the stated case) on the basis of which leave to appeal is granted.

(8) Where the arguable grounds of appeal are specified by virtue of subsection (7) above it shall not, except by leave of the High Court on cause shown, be competent for the appellant to found any aspect of his appeal on any ground of appeal contained in the stated case but not so specified.

(9) Any application by the appellant for the leave of the High Court under subsection (8) above—

(a) shall be made not less than seven days before the date fixed for the hearing of the appeal; and

(b) shall, not less that seven days before that date, be intimated by the appellant to the Crown Agent.

(10) The Clerk of Justiciary shall forthwith intimate—

(a) a decision under subsection (1) or (5) above; and

(b) in the case of a refusal of leave to appeal, the reasons for the decision, to the appellant or his solicitor and to the Crown Agent.

Stated case: directions by High Court

181.—(1) Without prejudice to any other power of relief which the High Court may have, where it appears to that court on application made in accordance with subsection (2) below, that the applicant has failed to comply with any of the requirements of—

(a) subsection (1) of section 176 of this Act; or

(b) subsection (1) or (9) of section 179 of this Act,

the High Court may direct that such further period of time as it may think proper be afforded to the applicant to comply with any requirement of the aforesaid provisions.

(2) Any application for a direction under subsection (1) above shall be made in writing to the Clerk of Justiciary and shall state the ground for the application, and, in the case of an application for the purposes of paragraph (a) of subsection (1) above, notification of the application shall be made by the appellant or his solicitor to the clerk of the court from which the appeal is to be taken, and the clerk shall thereupon transmit the complaint, documentary productions and any other proceedings in the cause to the Clerk of Justiciary.

(3) The High Court shall dispose of any application under subsection (1) above in like manner as an application to review the decision of an inferior court on a grant of bail, but shall have power—

(a) to dispense with a hearing; and

(b) to make such enquiry in relation to the application as the court may think fit,

and when the High Court has disposed of the application the Clerk of Justiciary shall inform the clerk of the inferior court of the result.

Stated case: hearing of appeal

182.—(1) A stated case under this Part of this Act shall be heard by the High Court on such date as it may fix.

(2) For the avoidance of doubt, where an appellant, in his application under section 176(1) of this Act (or in a duly made amendment or addition to that application), refers to an alleged miscarriage of justice, but in stating a case under section 179(7) of this Act the inferior court is unable to take the allegation into account, the High Court may nevertheless have regard to the allegation at a hearing under subsection (1) above.

(3) Except by leave of the High Court on cause shown, it shall not be competent for an appellant to found any aspect of his appeal on a matter not contained in his application under section 176(1) of this Act (or in a duly made amendment or addition to that application).

(4) Subsection (3) above shall not apply as respects any ground of appeal specified as an arguable ground of appeal by virtue of subsection (7) of section 180 of this Act.

(5) Without prejudice to any existing power of the High Court, that court may in hearing a stated case—

- (a) order the production of any document or other thing connected with the proceedings;
- [1](b) hear any evidence relevant to any alleged miscarriage of justice or order such evidence to be heard by a judge at the High Court or by such other person as it may appoint for that purpose;
- (c) take account of any circumstances relevant to the case which were not before the trial judge;
- (d) remit to any fit person to enquire and report in regard to any matter or circumstance affecting the appeal;
- (e) appoint a person with expert knowledge to act as assessor to the High Court in any case where it appears to the court that such expert knowledge is required for the proper determination of the case;
- (f) take account of any matter proposed in any adjustment rejected by the trial judge and of the reasons for such rejection;
- (g) take account of any evidence contained in a note of evidence such as is mentioned in section 179(7) of this Act.

(6) The High Court may at the hearing remit the stated case back to the inferior court to be amended and returned.

NOTE

[1]As amended by the Crime and Punishment (Scotland) Act 1997 (c. 48) Sched. 1, para. 21(21) with effect from August 1, 1997 in terms of the Crime and Punishment (Scotland) Act 1997 (Commencement and Transitional Provisions) Order 1997 (S.I. 1997 No. 1712) para. 3.

Stated case: disposal of appeal

183.—(1) The High Court may, subject to subsection (3) below and to section 190(1) of this Act, dispose of a stated case by—

- (a) remitting the cause to the inferior court with its opinion and any direction thereon;
- (b) affirming the verdict of the inferior court;
- (c) setting aside the verdict of the inferior court and either quashing the conviction or, subject to subsection (2) below, substituting therefor an amended verdict of guilty; or
- (d) setting aside the verdict of the inferior court and granting authority to bring a new prosecution in accordance with section 185 of this Act.

(2) An amended verdict of guilty substituted under subsection (1)(c) above must be one which could have been returned on the complaint before the inferior court.

(3) The High Court shall, in an appeal—

- (a) against both conviction and sentence, subject to section 190(1) of this Act, dispose of the appeal against sentence; or
- (b) by the prosecutor, against sentence, dispose of the appeal,

by exercise of the power mentioned in section 189(1) of this Act.

(4) In setting aside, under subsection (1) above, a verdict the High Court may quash any sentence imposed on the appellant as respects the complaint, and—

- (a) in a case where it substitutes an amended verdict of guilty, whether or not the sentence related to the verdict set aside; or
- (b) in any other case, where the sentence did not so relate,

may pass another (but not more severe) sentence in substitution for the sentence so quashed.

(5) For the purposes of subsections (3) and (4) above, "sentence" shall be construed as including disposal or order.

(6) Where an appeal against acquittal is sustained, the High Court may—

(a) convict and, subject to subsection (7) below, sentence the respondent;

(b) remit the case to the inferior court with instructions to convict and sentence the respondent, who shall be bound to attend any diet fixed by the court for such purpose; or

(c) remit the case to the inferior court with their opinion thereon.

(7) Where the High Court sentences the respondent under subsection (6)(a) above it shall not in any case impose a sentence beyond the maximum sentence which could have been passed by the inferior court.

(8) Any reference in subsection (6) above to convicting and sentencing shall be construed as including a reference to—

(a) convicting and making some other disposal; or

(b) convicting and deferring sentence.

(9) The High Court shall have power in an appeal under this Part of this Act to award such expenses both in the High Court and in the inferior court as it may think fit.

(10) Where, following an appeal, other than an appeal under section 175(2)(b) or (3) of this Act, the appellant remains liable to imprisonment or detention under the sentence of the inferior court, or is so liable under a sentence passed in the appeal proceedings the High Court shall have the power where at the time of disposal of the appeal the appellant—

(a) was at liberty on bail, to grant warrant to apprehend and imprison or detain the appellant for a term, to run from the date of such apprehension, not longer than that part of the term or terms of imprisonment or detention specified in the sentence brought under review which remained unexpired at the date of liberation;

(b) is serving a term or terms of imprisonment or detention imposed in relation to a conviction subsequent to the conviction appealed against, to exercise the like powers in regard to him as may be exercised, in relation to an appeal which has been abandoned, by a court of summary jurisdiction in pursuance of section 177(6) of this Act.

Abandonment of appeal

184.—(1) An appellant in an appeal such as is mentioned in section 176(1) of this Act may at any time prior to lodging the case with the Clerk of Justiciary abandon his appeal by minute signed by himself or his solicitor, written on the complaint or lodged with the clerk of the inferior court, and intimated to the respondent or the respondent's solicitor, but such abandonment shall be without prejudice to any other competent mode of appeal, review, advocation or suspension.

(2) Subject to section 191 of this Act, on the case being lodged with the Clerk of Justiciary, the appellant shall be held to have abandoned any other mode of appeal which might otherwise have been open to him.

New prosecution

Authorisation of new prosecution

185.—(1) Subject to subsection (2) below, where authority is granted under section 183(1)(d) of this Act, a new prosecution may be brought charging the accused with the same or any similar offence arising out of the same facts; and the proceedings out of which the stated case arose shall not be a bar to such prosecution.

(2) In a new prosecution under this section the accused shall not be charged with an offence more serious than that of which he was convicted in the earlier proceedings.

(3) No sentence may be passed on conviction under the new prosecution which could not have been passed on conviction under the earlier proceedings.

(4) A new prosecution may be brought under this section, notwithstanding that any time limit (other than the time limit mentioned in subsection (5) below) for the commencement of such proceedings has elapsed.

(5) Proceedings in a prosecution under this section shall be commenced within two months of the date on which authority to bring the prosecution was granted.

(6) In proceedings in a new prosecution under this section it shall, subject to subsection (7) below, be competent for either party to lead any evidence which it was competent for him to lead in the earlier proceedings.

(7) The complaint in a new prosecution under this section shall identify any matters as respects which the prosecutor intends to lead evidence by virtue of subsection (6) above which would not have been competent but for that subsection.

(8) For the purposes of subsection (5) above, proceedings shall be deemed to be commenced—

(a) in a case where such warrant is executed without unreasonable delay, on the date on which a warrant to apprehend or to cite the accused is granted; and

(b) in any other case, on the date on which the warrant is executed.

(9) Where the two months mentioned in subsection (5) above elapse and no new prosecution has been brought under this section, the order under section 183(1)(d) of this Act setting aside the verdict shall have the effect, for all purposes, of an acquittal.

(10) On granting authority under section 183(1)(d) of this Act to bring a new prosecution, the High Court may, after giving the parties an opportunity of being heard, order the detention of the accused person in custody; but an accused person may not be detained by virtue of this subsection for a period of more than 40 days.

Appeals against sentence

Appeals against sentence only

186.—(1) An appeal under section 175(2)(b) or (c), or by virtue of section 175(4), of this Act shall be by note of appeal, which shall state the ground of appeal.

(2) The note of appeal shall, where the appeal is—

(a) under section 175(2)(b) or (c) be lodged, within one week of—

(i) the passing of the sentence; or

(ii) the making of the order disposing of the case or deferring sentence,

with the clerk of the court from which the appeal is to be taken; or

(b) by virtue of section 175(4) be so lodged within four weeks of such passing or making.

(3) The clerk of court on receipt of the note of appeal shall—

(a) send a copy of the note to the respondent or his solicitor; and

(b) obtain a report from the judge who sentenced the convicted person or, as the case may be, who disposed of the case or deferred sentence.

(4) Subject to subsection (5) below, the clerk of court shall within two weeks of the passing of the sentence or within two weeks of the disposal or order against which the appeal is taken—

(a) send to the Clerk of Justiciary the note of appeal, together with the report mentioned in subsection (3)(b) above, a certified copy of the complaint, the minute of proceedings and any other relevant documents; and

(b) send copies of that report to the appellant and respondent or their solicitors.

[1](5) Where a judge—

(a) is temporarily absent from duty for any cause;

(b) is a part-time sheriff; or

(c) is a justice of the peace,

the sheriff principal of the sheriffdom in which the judgment was pronounced may extend the period of two weeks specified in subsection (4) above for such period as he considers reasonable.

(6) Subject to subsection (4) above, the report mentioned in subsection (3)(b) above shall be available only to the High Court, the parties and, on such conditions as may be prescribed by Act of Adjournal, such other persons or classes of persons as may be so prescribed.

(7) Where the judge's report is not furnished within the period mentioned in subsection (4) above or such period as extended under subsection (5) above, the High Court may extend such period, or, if it thinks fit, hear and determine the appeal without the report.

(8) Section 181 of this Act shall apply where an appellant fails to comply with the requirement of subsection (2)(a) above as they apply where an applicant fails to comply with any of the requirements of section 176(1) of this Act.

(9) An appellant under section 175(2)(b) or (c), or by virtue of section 175(4), of this Act may at any time prior to the hearing of the appeal abandon his appeal by minute, signed by himself or his solicitor, lodged—

(a) in a case where the note of appeal has not yet been sent under subsection (4)(a) above to the Clerk of Justiciary, with the clerk of court;

(b) in any other case, with the Clerk of Justiciary,

and intimated to the respondent.

(10) Sections 176(5), 177 and 182(5)(a) to (e) of this Act shall apply to appeals under section 175(2)(b) or (c), or by virtue of section 175(4), of this Act as they apply to appeals under section 175(2)(a) or (d) of this Act, except that, for the purposes of such application to any appeal by virtue of section 175(4), references in subsections (1) to (4) of section 177 to the appellant shall be construed as references to the convicted person and subsections (6) and (7) of that section shall be disregarded.

NOTE

[1]As amended by the Bail, Judicial Appointments etc. (Scotland) Act (asp 9), s.12 and Sched., para. 7(4).

Leave to appeal against sentence

187.—(1) The decision whether to grant leave to appeal for the purposes of section 175(2)(b) or (c) of this Act shall be made by a judge of the High Court who shall—

(a) if he considers that the note of appeal and other documents sent to the Clerk of Justiciary under section 186(4)(a) of this Act disclose arguable grounds of appeal, grant leave to appeal and make such comments in writing as he considers appropriate; and

(b) in any other case—

(i) refuse leave to appeal and give reasons in writing for the refusal; and

(ii) where the appellant is on bail and the sentence imposed on his conviction is one of imprisonment, grant a warrant to apprehend and imprison him.

(2) A warrant granted under subsection (1)(b)(ii) above shall not take

effect until the expiry of the period of 14 days mentioned in subsection (3) below without an application to the High Court for leave to appeal having been lodged by the appellant under that subsection.

(3) Where leave to appeal is refused under subsection (1) above the appellant may, within 14 days of intimation under subsection (9) below, apply to the High Court for leave to appeal.

(4) In deciding an application under subsection (3) above the High Court shall—

(a) if, after considering the note of appeal and other documents mentioned in subsection (1) above and the reasons for the refusal, it is of the opinion that there are arguable grounds of appeal, grant leave to appeal and make such comments in writing as he considers appropriate; and

(b) in any other case—

(i) refuse leave to appeal and give reasons in writing for the refusal; and

(ii) where the appellant is on bail and the sentence imposed on his conviction is one of imprisonment, grant a warrant to apprehend and imprison him.

(5) The question whether to grant leave to appeal under subsection (1) or (4) above shall be considered and determined in chambers without the parties being present.

(6) Comments in writing made under subsection (1)(a) or (4)(a) above may, without prejudice to the generality of that provision, specify the arguable grounds of appeal (whether or not they are contained in the note of appeal) on the basis of which leave to appeal is granted.

(7) Where the arguable grounds of appeal are specified by virtue of subsection (6) above it shall not, except by leave of the High Court on cause shown, be competent for the appellant to found any aspect of his appeal on any ground of appeal contained in the note of appeal but not so specified.

(8) Any application by the appellant for the leave of the High Court under subsection (7) above—

(a) shall be made not less than seven days before the date fixed for the hearing of the appeal; and

(b) shall, not less that seven days before that date, be intimated by the appellant to the Crown Agent.

(9) The Clerk of Justiciary shall forthwith intimate—

(a) a decision under subsection (1) or (4) above; and

(b) in the case of a refusal of leave to appeal, the reasons for the decision,

to the appellant or his solicitor and to the Crown Agent.

Disposal of appeals

Setting aside conviction or sentence: prosecutor's consent or application

188.—(1) Without prejudice to section 175(3) or (4) of this Act, where—

(a) an appeal has been taken under section 175(2) of this Act or by suspension or otherwise and the prosecutor is not prepared to maintain the judgment appealed against he may, by a relevant minute, consent to the conviction or sentence or, as the case may be, conviction and sentence ("sentence" being construed in this section as including disposal or order) being set aside either in whole or in part; or

(b) no such appeal has been taken but the prosecutor is, at any time, not prepared to maintain the judgment on which a conviction is founded or the sentence imposed following such conviction he may, by a relevant minute, apply for the conviction or sentence or, as the case may be, conviction and sentence to be set aside.

(2) For the purposes of subsection (1) above, a "relevant minute" is a minute, signed by the prosecutor—
  (a) setting forth the grounds on which he is of the opinion that the judgment cannot be maintained; and
  (b) written on the complaint or lodged with the clerk of court.

(3) A copy of any minute under subsection (1) above shall be sent by the prosecutor to the convicted person or his solicitor and the clerk of court shall—
  (a) thereupon ascertain and note on the record, whether that person or solicitor desires to be heard by the High Court before the appeal, or as the case may be application, is disposed of; and
  (b) thereafter transmit the complaint and relative proceedings to the Clerk of Justiciary.

(4) The Clerk of Justiciary, on receipt of a complaint and relative proceedings transmitted under subsection (3) above, shall lay them before any judge of the High Court either in court or in chambers who, after hearing parties if they desire to be heard, may—
  (a) set aside the conviction or the sentence, or both, either in whole or in part and—
      (i) award such expenses to the convicted person, both in the High Court and in the inferior court, as the judge may think fit;
      (ii) where the conviction is set aside in part, pass another (but not more severe) sentence in substitution for the sentence imposed in respect of that conviction; and
      (iii) where the sentence is set aside, pass another (but not more severe) sentence; or
  (b) refuse to set aside the conviction or sentence or, as the case may be, conviction and sentence, in which case the complaint and proceedings shall be returned to the clerk of the inferior court.

(5) Where an appeal has been taken and the complaint and proceedings in respect of that appeal returned under subsection (4)(b) above, the appellant shall be entitled to proceed with the appeal as if it had been marked on the date of their being received by the clerk of the inferior court on such return.

(6) Where an appeal has been taken and a copy minute in respect of that appeal sent under subsection (3) above, the preparation of the draft stated case shall be delayed pending the decision of the High Court.

(7) The period from an application being made under subsection (1)(b) above until its disposal under subsection (4) above (including the day of application and the day of disposal) shall, in relation to the conviction to which the application relates, be disregarded in any computation of time specified in any provision of this Part of this Act.

Disposal of appeal against sentence

189.—(1) An appeal against sentence by note of appeal shall be heard by the High Court on such date as it may fix, and the High Court may, subject to section 190(1) of this Act, dispose of such appeal by—
  (a) affirming the sentence; or
  ¹(b) if the Court thinks that, having regard to all the circumstances, including any evidence such as is mentioned in section 175(5) of this Act, a different sentence should have been passed, quashing the sentence and, subject to subsection (2) below, passing another sentence, whether more or less severe, in substitution therefor.

(2) In passing another sentence under subsection (1)(b) above, the Court shall not in any case increase the sentence beyond the maximum sentence which could have been passed by the inferior court.

(3) The High Court shall have power in an appeal by note of appeal to award such expenses both in the High Court and in the inferior court as it may think fit.

(4) Where, following an appeal under section 175(2)(b) or (c), or by virtue of section 175(4), of this Act, the convicted person remains liable to imprisonment or detention under the sentence of the inferior court or is so liable under a sentence passed in the appeal proceedings, the High Court shall have power where at the time of disposal of the appeal the convicted person—

    (a) was at liberty on bail, to grant warrant to apprehend and imprison or detain the appellant for a term, to run from the date of such apprehension, not longer than that part of the term or terms of imprisonment or detention specified in the sentence brought under review which remained unexpired at the date of liberation; or

    (b) is serving a term or terms of imprisonment or detention imposed in relation to a conviction subsequent to the conviction in respect of which the sentence appealed against was imposed, to exercise the like powers in regard to him as may be exercised, in relation to an appeal which has been abandoned, by a court of summary jurisdiction in pursuance of section 177(6) of this Act.

(5) In subsection (1) above, "appeal against sentence" shall, without prejudice to the generality of the expression, be construed as including an appeal under section 175(2)(c), and any appeal by virtue of section 175(4), of this Act; and without prejudice to subsection (6) below, other references to sentence in that subsection and in subsection (4) above shall be construed accordingly.

(6) In disposing of any appeal in a case where the accused has not been convicted, the High Court may proceed to convict him; and where it does, the reference in subsection (4) above to the conviction in respect of which the sentence appealed against was imposed shall be construed as a reference to the disposal or order appealed against.

(7) In disposing of an appeal under section 175(2)(b) to (d), (3)(b) or (4) of this Act the High Court may, without prejudice to any other power in that regard, pronounce an opinion on the sentence or other disposal or order which is appropriate in any similar case.

NOTE
[1] As amended by the Crime and Punishment (Scotland) Act 1997 (c. 48) Sched. 1 para. 21(22) with effect from August 1, 1997 in terms of the Crime and Punishment (Scotland) Act 1997 (Commencement and Transitional Provisions) Order 1997 (S.I. 1997 No. 1712) para. 3.

Disposal of appeal where appellant insane

190.—(1) In relation to any appeal under section 175(2) of this Act, the High Court shall, where it appears to it that the appellant committed the act charged against him but that he was insane when he did so, dispose of the appeal by—

    (a) setting aside the verdict of the inferior court and substituting therefor a verdict of acquittal on the ground of insanity; and

    (b) quashing any sentence imposed on the appellant as respects the complaint and—

        (i) making, in respect of the appellant, any order mentioned in section 57(2)(a) to (d) of this Act; or

        (ii) making no order.

(2) Subsection (4) of section 57 of this Act shall apply to an order made under subsection (1)(b)(i) above as it applies to an order made under subsection (2) of that section.

Miscellaneous

Appeal by suspension or advocation on ground of miscarriage of justice

191.—(1) Notwithstanding section 184(2) of this Act, a party to a summary prosecution may, where an appeal under section 175 of this Act would be incompetent or would in the circumstances be inappropriate, appeal to the High Court, by bill of suspension against a conviction or, as the case may be, by advocation against an acquittal on the ground of an alleged miscarriage of justice in the proceedings.

(2) Where the alleged miscarriage of justice is referred to in an application under section 176(1) of this Act, for a stated case as regards the proceedings (or in a duly made amendment or addition to that application), an appeal under subsection (1) above shall not proceed without the leave of the High Court until the appeal to which the application relates has been finally disposed of or abandoned.

(3) Sections 182(5)(a) to (e), 183(1)(d) and (4) and 185 of this Act shall apply to appeals under this section as they apply to appeals such as are mentioned in section 176(1) of this Act.

(4) This section is without prejudice to any rule of law relating to bills of suspension or advocation in so far as such rule of law is not inconsistent with this section.

Appeals: miscellaneous provisions

192.—(1) Where an appellant has been granted bail, whether his appeal is under this Part of this Act or otherwise, he shall appear personally in court at the diet appointed for the hearing of the appeal.

(2) Where an appellant who has been granted bail does not appear at such a diet, the High Court shall either—
- (a) dispose of the appeal as if it had been abandoned (in which case subsection (5) of section 177 of this Act shall apply accordingly); or
- (b) on cause shown permit the appeal to be heard in his absence.

(3) No conviction, sentence, judgement, order of court or other proceeding whatsoever in or for the purposes of summary proceedings under this Act—
- (a) shall be quashed for want of form; or
- (b) where the accused had legal assistance in his defence, shall be suspended or set aside in respect of any objections to—
  - (i) the relevancy of the complaint, or to the want of specification therein; or
  - (ii) the competency or admission or rejection of evidence at the trial in the inferior court,
  unless such objections were timeously stated.

(4) The provisions regulating appeals shall, subject to the provisions of this Part of this Act, be without prejudice to any other mode of appeal competent.

(5) Any officer of law may serve any bill of suspension or other writ relating to an appeal.

Suspension of disqualification, forfeiture etc.

193.—(1) Where upon conviction of any person—
- (a) any disqualification, forfeiture or disability attaches to him by reason of such conviction; or
- (b) any property, matters or things which are the subject of the prosecution or connected therewith are to be or may be ordered to be destroyed or forfeited,

if the court before which he was convicted thinks fit, the disqualification, forfeiture or disability or, as the case may be, destruction or forfeiture or order for destruction or forfeiture shall be suspended pending the determination of any appeal against conviction or sentence (or disposal or order).

(2) Subsection (1) above does not apply in respect of any disqualification, forfeiture or, as the case may be, destruction or forfeiture or order for destruction or forfeiture under or by virtue of any enactment which contains express provision for the suspension of such disqualification, forfeiture or, as the case may be, destruction or forfeiture or order for destruction or forfeiture pending the determination of any appeal against conviction or sentence (or disposal or order).

(3) Where, upon conviction, a fine has been imposed upon a person or a compensation order has been made against him under section 249 of this Act—

(a) the fine or compensation order shall not be enforced against him and he shall not be liable to make any payment in respect of the fine or compensation order; and

(b) any money paid under the compensation order shall not be paid by the clerk of court to the entitled person under subsection (9) of that section,

pending the determination of any appeal against conviction or sentence (or disposal or order).

Suspension of certain sentences pending determination of appeal

[1]**193A.**—(1) Where a convicted person or the prosecutor appeals to the High Court under section 175 of this Act, the court may on the application of the appellant direct that the whole, or any remaining part, of a relevant sentence shall be suspended until the appeal, if it is proceeded with, is determined.

(2) Where the court has directed the suspension of the whole or any remaining part of a person's relevant sentence, the person shall, unless the High Court otherwise directs, appear personally in court on the day or days fixed for the hearing of the appeal.

(3) Where a person fails to appear personally in court as mentioned in subsection (2) above, the court may—

(a) if he is the appellant—
    (i) decline to consider the appeal; and
    (ii) dismiss it summarily; or
(b) whether or not he is the appellant—
    (i) consider and determine the appeal; or
    (ii) make such other order as the court thinks fit.

(4) In this section "relevant sentence" means any one or more of the following—

(a) a probation order;
(b) a supervised attendance order made under section 236(6) of this Act;
(c) a community service order;
[2](d) a restriction of liberty order.

NOTES
[1]Inserted by the Crime and Punishment (Scotland) Act 1997 (c. 48) s.24(2) with effect from August 1, 1997 in terms of the Crime and Punishment (Scotland) Act 1997 (Commencement and Transitional Provisions) Order 1997 (S.I. 1997 No. 1712) para. 3.
[2]Inserted by the Crime and Punishment (Scotland) Act 1997 (c. 48) s.24(2) (effective July 1, 1998: S.I. 1998 No. 2323).

Computation of time

194.—(1) If any period of time specified in any provision of this Part of this Act relating to appeals expires on a Saturday, Sunday or court holiday prescribed for the relevant court, the period shall be extended to expire on the next day which is not a Saturday, Sunday or such court holiday.

[1](2) Where a judge against whose judgment an appeal is taken—
(a) is temporarily absent from duty for any cause;
(b) is a part-time sheriff; or
(c) is a justice of the peace,
the sheriff principal of the sheriffdom in which the court at which the judgment was pronounced is situated may extend any period specified in sections 178(1) and 179(4) and (7) of this Act for such period as he considers reasonable.

(3) For the purposes of sections 176(1)(a) and 178(1) of this Act, summary proceedings shall be deemed to be finally determined on the day on which sentence is passed in open court; except that, where in relation to an appeal—
(a) under section 175(2)(a) or (3)(a); or
(b) in so far as it is against conviction, under section 175(2)(d),
of this Act sentence is deferred under section 202 of this Act, they shall be deemed finally determined on the day on which sentence is first so deferred in open court.

NOTE
[1]As amended by Bail, Judicial Appointments etc. (Scotland) Act (asp 9), s.12 and Sched., para. 7(5).

PART XA

SCOTTISH CRIMINAL CASES REVIEW COMMISSION

The Scottish Criminal Cases Review Commission

Scottish Criminal Cases Review Commission

[1]**194A.**—(1) There shall be established a body corporate to be known as the Scottish Criminal Cases Review Commission (in this Act referred to as "the Commission").

(2) The Commission shall not be regarded as the servant or agent of the Crown or as enjoying any status, immunity or privilege of the Crown; and the Commission's property shall not be regarded as property of, or held on behalf of, the Crown.

(3) The Commission shall consist of not fewer than three members.

(4) The members of the Commission shall be appointed by Her Majesty on the recommendation of the Secretary of State.

(5) At least one third of the members of the Commission shall be persons who are legally qualified; and for this purpose a person is legally qualified if he is an advocate or solicitor of at least ten years' standing.

(6) At least two thirds of the members of the Commission shall be persons who appear to the Secretary of State to have knowledge or experience of any aspect of the criminal justice system; and for the purposes of this subsection the criminal justice system includes, in particular, the investigation of offences and the treatment of offenders.

(7) Schedule 9A to this Act, which makes further provision as to the Commission, shall have effect.

NOTE
[1]Inserted by s.25 of the Crime and Punishment (Scotland) Act 1997 with effect from April 1, 1999 as provided by the Crime and Punishment (Scotland) Act 1997 (Commencement No. 5 and Transitional Provisions and Savings) Order 1999 (S.I. 1999 No. 652).

References to High Court

Cases dealt with on indictment

[1]**194B.**—[2](1) The Commission on the consideration of any conviction of a person or of the sentence (other than sentence of death) passed on a person

who has been convicted on indictment or complaint may, if they think fit, at any time, and whether or not an appeal against such conviction or sentence has previously been heard and determined by the High Court, refer the whole case to the High Court and the case shall be heard and determined, subject to any directions the High Court may make, as if it were an appeal under Part VIII or, as the case may be, Part X of this Act.

(2) The power of the Commission under this section to refer to the High Court the case of a person convicted shall be exercisable whether or not that person has petitioned for the exercise of Her Majesty's prerogative of mercy.

(3) This section shall apply in relation to a finding under section 55(2) and an order under section 57(2) of this Act as it applies, respectively, in relation to a conviction and a sentence.

(4) For the purposes of this section "person" includes a person who is deceased.

NOTES

[1]Inserted by s.25 of the Crime and Punishment (Scotland) Act 1997 with effect from April 1, 1999 as provided by the Crime and Punishment (Scotland) Act 1997 (Commencement No. 5 and Transitional Provisions and Savings) Order 1999 (S.I. 1999 No. 652).

[2]As amended by S.I. 1999 No. 1181, para. 3 (effective April 1, 1999).

Grounds for reference

[1]**194C.** The grounds upon which the Commission may refer a case to the High Court are that they believe—
  (a) that a miscarriage of justice may have occurred; and
  (b) that it is in the interests of justice that a reference should be made.

NOTE

[1]Inserted by s.25 of the Crime and Punishment (Scotland) Act 1997 with effect from April 1, 1999 as provided by the Crime and Punishment (Scotland) Act 1997 (Commencement No. 5 and Transitional Provisions and Savings) Order 1999 (S.I. 1999 No. 652).

Further provision as to references

[1]**194D.**—(1) A reference of a conviction, sentence or finding may be made under section 194B of this Act whether or not an application has been made by or on behalf of the person to whom it relates.

(2) In considering whether to make a reference the Commission shall have regard to—
  (a) any application or representations made to the Commission by or on behalf of the person to whom it relates;
  (b) any other representations made to the Commission in relation to it; and
  (c) any other matters which appear to the Commission to be relevant.

(3) In considering whether to make a reference the Commission may at any time refer to the High Court for the Court's opinion any point on which they desire the Court's assistance; and on a reference under this subsection the High Court shall consider the point referred and furnish the Commission with their opinion on the point.

(4) Where the Commission make a reference to the High Court under section 194B of this Act they shall—
  (a) give to the Court a statement of their reasons for making the reference; and
  (b) send a copy of the statement to every person who appears to them to be likely to be a party to any proceedings on the appeal arising from the reference.

(5) In every case in which—
  (a) an application has been made to the Commission by or on behalf of any person for the reference by them of any conviction, sentence or finding; but

(b) the Commission decide not to make a reference of the conviction, sentence or finding,

they shall give a statement of the reasons for their decision to the person who made the application.

NOTE

[1]Inserted by s.25 of the Crime and Punishment (Scotland) Act 1997 with effect from April 1, 1999 as provided by the Crime and Punishment (Scotland) Act 1997 (Commencement No. 5 and Transitional Provisions and Savings) Order 1999 (S.I. 1999 No. 652).

Extension of Commission's remit to summary cases

[1]**194E.**—(1) The Secretary of State may by order provide for this Part of this Act to apply in relation to convictions, sentences and findings made in summary proceedings as they apply in relation to convictions, sentences and findings made in solemn proceedings, and may for that purpose make in such an order such amendments to the provisions of this Part as appear to him to be necessary or expedient.

(2) An order under this section shall be made by statutory instrument, and shall not have effect unless a draft of it has been laid before and approved by a resolution of each House of Parliament.

NOTE

[1]Inserted by s.25 of the Crime and Punishment (Scotland) Act 1997 with effect from April 1, 1999 as provided by the Crime and Punishment (Scotland) Act 1997 (Commencement No. 5 and Transitional Provisions and Savings) Order 1999 (S.I. 1999 No. 652).

Further powers

[1]**194F.** The Commission may take any steps which they consider appropriate for assisting them in the exercise of any of their functions and may, in particular—

(a) themselves undertake inquiries and obtain statements, opinions or reports; or

(b) request the Lord Advocate or any other person to undertake such inquiries or obtain such statements, opinions and reports.

NOTE

[1]Inserted by s.25 of the Crime and Punishment (Scotland) Act 1997 with effect from April 1, 1999 as provided by the Crime and Punishment (Scotland) Act 1997 (Commencement No. 5 and Transitional Provisions and Savings) Order 1999 (S.I. 1999 No. 652).

Supplementary provision

[1]**194G.**—(1) The Secretary of State may by order make such incidental, consequential, transitional or supplementary provisions as may appear to him to be necessary or expedient for the purpose of bringing this Part of this Act into operation, and, without prejudice to the generality of the foregoing, of dealing with any cases being considered by him under section 124 of this Act at the time when this Part comes into force, and an order under this section may make different provision in relation to different cases or classes of case.

(2) An order under this section shall be made by statutory instrument subject to annulment in pursuance of a resolution of either House of Parliament.

NOTE

[1]Inserted by s.25 of the Crime and Punishment (Scotland) Act 1997 with effect from April 1, 1999 as provided by the Crime and Punishment (Scotland) Act 1997 (Commencement No. 5 and Transitional Provisions and Savings) Order 1999 (S.I. 1999 No. 652).

Powers of investigation of Commission

Power to request precognition on oath

[1]**194H.**—(1) Where it appears to the Commission that a person may have information which they require for the purposes of carrying out their functions, and the person refuses to make any statement to them, they may apply to the sheriff under this section.

(2) On an application made by the Commission under this section, the sheriff may, if he is satisfied that it is reasonable in the circumstances, grant warrant to cite the person concerned to appear before the sheriff in chambers at such time or place as shall be specified in the citation, for precognition on oath by a member of the Commission or a person appointed by them to act in that regard.

(3) Any person who, having been duly cited to attend for precognition under subsection (2) above and having been given at least 48 hours notice, fails without reasonable excuse to attend shall be guilty of an offence and liable on summary conviction to a fine not exceeding level 3 on the standard scale or to imprisonment for a period not exceeding 21 days; and the court may issue a warrant for the apprehension of the person concerned ordering him to be brought before a sheriff for precognition on oath.

(4) Any person who, having been duly cited to attend for precognition under subsection (2) above, attends but—

(a) refuses to give information within his knowledge or to produce evidence in his possession; or

(b) prevaricates in his evidence,

shall be guilty of an offence and shall be liable to be summarily subjected to a fine not exceeding level 3 on the standard scale or to imprisonment for a period not exceeding 21 days.

NOTE
[1]Inserted by s.25 of the Crime and Punishment (Scotland) Act 1997 with effect from April 1, 1999 as provided by the Crime and Punishment (Scotland) Act 1997 (Commencement No. 5 and Transitional Provisions and Savings) Order 1999 (S.I. 1999 No. 652).

Power to obtain documents etc.

[1]**194I.**—(1) Where the Commission believe that a person or a public body has possession or control of a document or other material which may assist them in the exercise of any of their functions, they may apply to the High Court for an order requiring that person or body—

(a) to produce the document or other material to the Commission or to give the Commission access to it; and

(b) to allow the Commission to take away the document or other material or to make and take away a copy of it in such form as they think appropriate,

and such an order may direct that the document or other material must not be destroyed, damaged or altered before the direction is withdrawn by the Court.

(2) The duty to comply with an order under this section is not affected by any obligation of secrecy or other limitation on disclosure (including any such obligation or limitation imposed by or by virtue of any enactment) which would otherwise prevent the production of the document or other material to the Commission or the giving of access to it to the Commission.

(3) The documents and other material covered by this section include, in particular, any document or other material obtained or created during any investigation or proceedings relating to—

(a) the case in relation to which the Commission's function is being or may be exercised; or

(b) any other case which may be in any way connected with that case (whether or not any function of the Commission could be exercised in relation to that other case).

(4) In this section—

"Minister" means a Minister of the Crown as defined by section 8 of the Ministers of the Crown Act 1975;

"police force" means any police force maintained for a local government area under section 1(1) of the Police (Scotland) Act 1967 and references to a chief constable are references to the chief constable of such a force within the meaning of that Act; and

"public body" means

(a) any police force;

(b) any government department, local authority or other body constituted for the purposes of the public service, local government or the administration of justice; or

[2](c) any other body whose members are appointed by Her Majesty, any Minister, the Scottish Minister or any government department or whose revenues consist wholly or mainly of money provided by Parliament.

NOTES

[1]Inserted by s.25 of the Crime and Punishment (Scotland) Act 1997 with effect from April 1, 1999 as provided by the Crime and Punishment (Scotland) Act 1997 (Commencement No. 5 and Transitional Provisions and Savings) Order 1999 (S.I. 1999 No. 652).

[2]As amended by the Scotland Act 1998 (Consequential Modifications) (No. 2) Order 1999 (S.I. 1999 No. 1820) art. 4 and Sched. 2, para. 122(2) (effective July 1, 1999).

Disclosure of information

Offence of disclosure

[1]**194J.**—(1) A person who is or has been a member or employee of the Commission shall not disclose any information obtained by the Commission in the exercise of any of their functions unless the disclosure of the information is excepted from this section by section 194K of this Act.

(2) A member of the Commission shall not authorise the disclosure by an employee of the Commission of any information obtained by the Commission in the exercise of any of their functions unless the authorisation of the disclosure of the information is excepted from this section by section 194K of this Act.

(3) A person who contravenes this section is guilty of an offence and liable on summary conviction to a fine of an amount not exceeding level 5 on the standard scale.

NOTE

[1]Inserted by s.25 of the Crime and Punishment (Scotland) Act 1997 with effect from April 1, 1999 as provided by the Crime and Punishment (Scotland) Act 1997 (Commencement No. 5 and Transitional Provisions and Savings) Order 1999 (S.I. 1999 No. 652).

Exceptions from obligations of non-disclosure

[1]**194K.**—(1) The disclosure of information, or the authorisation of the disclosure of information, is excepted from section 194J of this Act by this section if the information is disclosed, or is authorised to be disclosed—

(a) for the purposes of any criminal, disciplinary or civil proceedings;

(b) in order to assist in dealing with an application made to the Secretary of State for compensation for a miscarriage of justice;

(c) by a person who is a member or an employee of the Commission to another person who is a member or an employee of the Commission;

(d) in any statement or report required by this Act;

(e) in or in connection with the exercise of any function under this Act; or

(f) in any circumstances in which the disclosure of information is permitted by an order made by the Secretary of State.

(2) The disclosure of information is also excepted from section 194J of this Act by this section if the information is disclosed by an employee of the Commission who is authorised to disclose the information by a member of the Commission.

(3) The disclosure of information, or the authorisation of the disclosure of information, is also excepted from section 194J of this Act by this section if the information is disclosed, or is authorised to be disclosed, for the purposes of—

(a) the investigation of an offence; or

(b) deciding whether to prosecute a person for an offence,

unless the disclosure is or would be prevented by an obligation or other limitation on disclosure (including any such obligation or limitation imposed by, under or by virtue of any enactment) arising otherwise than under that section.

(4) Where the disclosure of information is excepted from section 194J of this Act by subsection (1) or (2) above, the disclosure of the information is not prevented by any obligation of secrecy or other limitation on disclosure (including any such obligation or limitation imposed by, under or by virtue of any enactment) arising otherwise than under that section.

(5) The power to make an order under subsection (1)(f) above is exercisable by statutory instrument which shall be subject to annulment in pursuance of a resolution of either House of Parliament.

NOTE

[1]Inserted by s.25 of the Crime and Punishment (Scotland) Act 1997 with effect from April 1, 1999 as provided by the Crime and Punishment (Scotland) Act 1997 (Commencement No. 5 and Transitional Provisions and Savings) Order 1999 (S.I. 1999 No. 652).

Consent of disclosure

[1]**194L.**—(1) Where a person or body is required by an order under section 194I of this Act to produce or allow access to a document or other material to the Commission and notifies them that any information contained in the document or other material to which the order relates is not to be disclosed by the Commission without his or its prior consent, the Commission shall not disclose the information without such consent.

(2) Such consent may not be withheld unless—

(a) (apart from section 194I of this Act) the person would have been prevented by any obligation of secrecy or other limitation on disclosure from disclosing the information without such consent; and

(b) it is reasonable for the person to withhold his consent to disclosure of the information by the Commission.

(3) An obligation of secrecy or other limitation on disclosure which applies to a person only where disclosure is not authorised by another person shall not be taken for the purposes of subsection (2)(a) above to prevent the disclosure by the person of information to the Commission unless—

(a) reasonable steps have been taken to obtain the authorisation of the other person; or

(b) such authorisation could not reasonably be expected to be obtained.".

NOTE

[1]Inserted by s.25 of the Crime and Punishment (Scotland) Act 1997 with effect from April 1, 1999 as provided by the Crime and Punishment (Scotland) Act 1997 (Commencement No. 5 and Transitional Provisions and Savings) Order 1999 (S.I. 1999 No. 652).

PART XI

SENTENCING

General

Remit to High Court for sentence

195.—(1) Where at any diet in proceedings on indictment in the sheriff court, sentence falls to be imposed but the sheriff holds that any competent sentence which he can impose is inadequate so that the question of sentence is appropriate for the High Court, he shall—
   (a) endorse upon the record copy of the indictment a certificate of the plea or the verdict, as the case may be;
   (b) by interlocutor written on the record copy remit the convicted person to the High Court for sentence; and
   (c) append to the interlocutor a note of his reasons for the remit,
and a remit under this section shall be sufficient warrant to bring the accused before the High Court for sentence and shall remain in force until the person is sentenced.

(2) Where under any enactment an offence is punishable on conviction on indictment by imprisonment for a term exceeding three years but the enactment either expressly or impliedly restricts the power of the sheriff to impose a sentence of imprisonment for a term exceeding three years, it shall be competent for the sheriff to remit the accused to the High Court for sentence under subsection (1) above; and it shall be competent for the High Court to pass any sentence which it could have passed if the person had been convicted before it.

(3) When the Clerk of Justiciary receives the record copy of the indictment he shall send a copy of the note of reasons to the convicted person or his solicitor and to the Crown Agent.

(4) Subject to subsection (3) above, the note of reasons shall be available only to the High Court and the parties.

Sentence following guilty plea

196.—(1) In determining what sentence to pass on, or what other disposal or order to make in relation to, an offender who has pled guilty to an offence, a court may take into account—
   (a) the stage in the proceedings for the offence at which the offender indicated his intention to plead guilty, and
   (b) the circumstances in which that indication was given.

(2) Where the court is passing sentence on an offender under section 205B(2) of this Act and that offender has pled guilty to the offence for which he is being so sentenced, the court may, after taking into account the matters mentioned in paragraphs (a) and (b) of subsection (1) above, pass a sentence of less than seven years imprisonment or, as the case may be, detention but any such sentence shall not be of a term of imprisonment or period of detention of less than five years, two hundred and nineteen days.

NOTE
[1]Inserted by the Crime and Punishment (Scotland) Act 1997 (c. 48) s.2(2) with effect from October 20, 1997 in terms of the Crime and Punishment (Scotland) Act 1997 (Commencement No. 2 and Transitional Provisions) Order 1997 (S.I. 1997 No. 2323) Art. 3 and Sched. 1.

Sentencing guidelines

197. Without prejudice to any rule of law, a court in passing sentence shall have regard to any relevant opinion pronounced under section 118(7) or section 189(7) of this Act.

Form of sentence

198.—(1) In any case the sentence to be pronounced shall be announced by the judge in open court and shall be entered in the record in the form prescribed by Act of Adjournal.

(2) In recording a sentence of imprisonment, it shall be sufficient to minute the term of imprisonment to which the court sentenced the accused, without specifying the prison in which the sentence is to be carried out; and an entry of sentence, signed by the clerk of court, shall be full warrant and authority for any subsequent execution of the sentence and for the clerk to issue extracts for the purposes of execution or otherwise.

(3) In extracting a sentence of imprisonment, the extract may be in the form set out in an Act of Adjournal or as nearly as may be in such form.

Power to mitigate penalties

199.—(1) Subject to subsection (3) below, where a person is convicted of the contravention of an enactment and the penalty which may be imposed involves—

(a) imprisonment;

(b) the imposition of a fine;

(c) the finding of caution for good behaviour or otherwise whether or not imposed in addition to imprisonment or a fine,

subsection (2) below shall apply.

(2) Where this subsection applies, the court, in addition to any other power conferred by statute, shall have power—

(a) to reduce the period of imprisonment;

(b) to substitute for imprisonment a fine (either with or without the finding of caution for good behaviour);

(c) to substitute for imprisonment or a fine the finding of caution;

(d) to reduce the amount of the fine;

(e) to dispense with the finding of caution.

(3) Subsection (2) above shall not apply—

(a) in relation to an enactment which carries into effect a treaty, convention, or agreement with a foreign state which stipulates for a fine of a minimum amount;

(b) to proceedings taken under any Act relating to any of Her Majesty's regular or auxiliary forces; or

[1] (c) to any proceedings in which the court on conviction is under a duty to impose a sentence under section 205A(2) or 205B(2) of this Act.

(4) Where, in summary proceedings, a fine is imposed in substitution for imprisonment, the fine—

(a) in the case of an offence which is triable either summarily or on indictment, shall not exceed the prescribed sum; and

(b) in the case of an offence triable only summarily, shall not exceed level 4 on the standard scale.

(5) Where the finding of caution is imposed under this section—

(a) in respect of an offence which is triable only summarily, the amount shall not exceed level 4 on the standard scale and the period shall not exceed that which the court may impose under this Act; and

(b) in any other case, the amount shall not exceed the prescribed sum and the period shall not exceed 12 months.

NOTE

[1]Inserted by the Crime and Punishment (Scotland) Act 1997 with effect from October 20, 1997 as provided by the Crime and Punishment (Scotland) Act 1997 (Commencement No. 2) and Transitional and Consequential Provisions) Order 1997 (S.I. 1997 No. 2323).

Pre-sentencing procedure

Remand for inquiry into physical or mental condition

200.—(1) Without prejudice to any powers exercisable by a court under section 201 of this Act, where—
   (a) the court finds that an accused has committed an offence punishable with imprisonment; and
   (b) it appears to the court that before the method of dealing with him is determined an inquiry ought to be made into his physical or mental condition,
subsection (2) below shall apply.
   (2) Where this subsection applies the court shall—
   (a) for the purpose of inquiry solely into his physical condition, remand him in custody or on bail;
   (b) for the purpose of inquiry into his mental condition (whether or not in addition to his physical condition), remand him in custody or on bail or, where the court is satisfied—
      (i) on the written or oral evidence of a medical practitioner, that the person appears to be suffering from a mental disorder; and
      (ii) that a hospital is available for his admission and suitable for his detention,
   make an order committing him to that hospital,
for such period or periods, no single period exceeding three weeks, as the court thinks necessary to enable a medical examination and report to be made.
   (3) where the court is of the opinion that a person ought to continue to be committed to hospital for the purpose of inquiry into his mental condition following the expiry of the period specified in an order for committal to hospital under paragraph (b) of subsection (2) above, the court may—
   (a) if the condition in sub-paragraph (i) of that paragraph continues to be satisfied and a suitable hospital is available for his continued detention, renew the order for such further period not exceeding three weeks as the court thinks necessary to enable a medical examination and report to be made; and
   (b) in any other case, remand the person in custody or on bail in accordance with subsection (2) above.
   (4) An order under subsection (3)(a) above may, unless objection is made by or on behalf of the person to whom it relates, be made in his absence.
   (5) Where, before the expiry of the period specified in an order for committal to hospital under subsection (2)(b) above, the court considers, on an application made to it, that committal to hospital is no longer required in relation to the person, the court shall revoke the order and may make such other order, under subsection (2)(a) above or any other provision of this Part of this Act, as the court considers appropriate.
   (6) Where an accused is remanded on bail under this section, it shall be a condition of the order granting bail that he shall—
   (a) undergo a medical examination by a duly qualified registered medical practitioner or, where the inquiry is into his mental condition, and the order granting bail so specifies, two such practitioners; and
   (b) for the purpose of such examination, attend at an institution or place, or on any such practitioner specified in the order granting bail and, where the inquiry is into his mental condition, comply with any directions which may be given to him for the said purpose by any person so specified or by a person of any class so specified,
and, if arrangements have been made for his reception, it may be a condition

of the order granting bail that the person shall, for the purpose of the examination, reside in an institution or place specified as aforesaid, not being an institution or place to which he could have been remanded in custody, until the expiry of such period as may be so specified or until he is discharged therefrom, whichever first occurs.

(7) On exercising the powers conferred by this section to remand in custody or on bail the court shall—

    (a) where the person is remanded in custody, send to the institution or place in which he is detained; and

    (b) where the person is released on bail, send to the institution or place at which or the person by whom he is to be examined,

a statement of the reasons for which it appears to the court that an inquiry ought to be made into his physical or mental condition, and of any information before the court about his physical or mental condition.

(8) On making an order of committal to hospital under subsection (2)(b) above the court shall send to the hospital specified in the order a statement of the reasons for which the court is of the opinion that an inquiry ought to be made into the mental condition of the person to whom it relates, and of any information before the court about his mental condition.

(9) A person remanded under this section may appeal against the refusal of bail or against the conditions imposed and a person committed to hospital under this section may appeal against the order of committal within 24 hours of his remand or, as the case may be, committal, by note of appeal presented to the High Court, and the High Court, either in court or in chambers, may after hearing parties—

    (a) review the order and grant bail on such conditions as it thinks fit; or

    (b) confirm the order; or

    (c) in the case of an appeal against an order of committal to hospital, revoke the order and remand the person in custody.

(10) The court may, on cause shown, vary an order for committal to hospital under subsection (2)(b) above by substituting another hospital for the hospital specified in the order.

(11) Subsection (2)(b) above shall apply to the variation of an order under subsection (10) above as it applies to the making of an order for committal to hospital.

Power of court to adjourn case before sentence

201.—(1) Where an accused has been convicted or the court has found that he committed the offence and before he has been sentenced or otherwise dealt with, subject to subsection (3) below, the court may adjourn the case for the purpose of enabling inquiries to be made or of determining the most suitable method of dealing with his case.

(2) Where the court adjourns a case solely for the purpose mentioned in subsection (1) above, it shall remand the accused in custody or on bail or ordain him to appear at the adjourned diet.

(3) A court shall not adjourn the hearing of a case as mentioned in subsection (1) above for any single period exceeding—

    (a) where the accused is remanded in custody, three weeks; and

    (b) where he is remanded on bail or ordained to appear, four weeks or, on cause shown, eight weeks.

(4) An accused who is remanded under this section may appeal against the refusal of bail or against the conditions imposed within 24 hours of his remand, by note of appeal presented to the High Court, and the High Court, either in court or in chambers, may, after hearing parties—

    (a) review the order appealed against and either grant bail on such conditions as it thinks fit or ordain the accused to appear at the adjourned diet; or

(b) confirm the order.

Deferred sentence

202.—(1) It shall be competent for a court to defer sentence after conviction for a period and on such conditions as the court may determine.

(2) If it appears to the court which deferred sentence on an accused under subsection (1) above that he has been convicted during the period of deferment, by a court in any part of Great Britain of an offence committed during that period and has been dealt with for that offence, the court which deferred sentence may—

(a) issue a warrant for the arrest of the accused; or

(b) instead of issuing such a warrant in the first instance, issue a citation requiring him to appear before it at such time as may be specified in the citation,

and on his appearance or on his being brought before the court it may deal with him in any manner in which it would be competent for it to deal with him on the expiry of the period of deferment.

(3) Where a court which has deferred sentence on an accused under subsection (1) above convicts him of another offence during the period of deferment, it may deal with him for the original offence in any manner in which it would be competent for it to deal with him on the expiry of the period of deferment, as well as for the offence committed during the said period.

Reports

203.—(1) Where a person specified in section 27(1)(b)(i) to (vi) of the Social Work (Scotland) Act 1968 commits an offence, the court shall not dispose of the case without obtaining from the local authority in whose area the person resides a report as to—

(a) the circumstances of the offence; and

(b) the character of the offender, including his behaviour while under the supervision, or as the case may be subject to the order, so specified in relation to him.

(2) In subsection (1) above, "the court" does not include a district court.

(3) Where, in any case, a report by an officer of a local authority is made to the court with a view to assisting the court in determining the most suitable method of dealing with any person in respect of an offence, a copy of the report shall be given by the clerk of the court to the offender or his solicitor.

Imprisonment, etc.

Restrictions on passing sentence of imprisonment or detention

204.—(1) A court shall not pass a sentence of imprisonment or of detention in respect of any offence, nor impose imprisonment, or detention, under section 214(2) of this Act in respect of failure to pay a fine, on an accused who is not legally represented in that court and has not been previously sentenced to imprisonment or detention by a court in any part of the United Kingdom, unless the accused either—

(a) applied for legal aid and the application was refused on the ground that he was not financially eligible; or

(b) having been informed of his right to apply for legal aid, and having had the opportunity, failed to do so.

[1](2) A court shall not pass a sentence of imprisonment on a person of or over twenty-one years of age who has not been previously sentenced to imprisonment or detention by a court in any part of the United Kingdom

unless the court considers that no other method of dealing with him is appropriate ...

[2](2A) For the purpose of determining under subsection (2) above whether any other method of dealing with such a person is appropriate, the court shall take into account—

(a) such information as it has been able to obtain from an officer of a local authority or otherwise about his circumstances;

(b) any information before it concerning his character and mental and physical condition;

(c) its power to make a hospital direction in addition to imposing a sentence of imprisonment.

(3) Where a court of summary jurisdiction passes a sentence of imprisonment on any such person as is mentioned in subsection (2) above, the court shall state the reason for its opinion that no other method of dealing with him is appropriate, and shall have that reason entered in the record of the proceedings.

(4) The court shall, for the purpose of determining whether a person has been previously sentenced to imprisonment or detention by a court in any part of the United Kingdom—

(a) disregard a previous sentence of imprisonment which, having been suspended, has not taken effect under section 23 of the Powers of Criminal Courts Act 1973 or under section 19 of the Treatment of Offenders Act (Northern Ireland) 1968;

(b) construe detention as meaning—

(i) in relation to Scotland, detention in a young offenders institution or detention centre;

(ii) in relation to England and Wales a sentence of youth custody, borstal training or detention in a young offender institution or detention centre; and

(iii) in relation to Northern Ireland, detention in a young offenders centre.

(5) This section does not affect the power of a court to pass sentence on any person for an offence the sentence for which is fixed by law.

(6) In this section—

"legal aid" means legal aid for the purposes of any part of the proceedings before the court;

"legally represented" means represented by counsel or a solicitor at some stage after the accused is found guilty and before he is dealt with as referred to in subsection (1) above.

NOTES

[1]Words deleted by s.6(3) of the Crime and Punishment (Scotland) Act 1997 with effect from January 1, 1998 as provided by the Crime and Punishment (Scotland) Act 1997 (Commencement No. 2 and Transitional and Consequential Provisions) Order 1997 (S.I. 1997 No. 2323) Art. 4 and Sched. 2.

[2]Inserted by s.6(3) of the above Act and commenced on January 1, 1998 in terms of the above Order.

Restriction on consecutive sentences for released prisoners

[1]**204A.** A court sentencing a person to imprisonment or other detention shall not order or direct that the term of imprisonment or detention shall commence on the expiration of any other such sentence from which he has been released at any time under the existing or new provisions within the meaning of Schedule 6 to the Prisoners and Criminal Proceedings (Scotland) Act 1993.

NOTE

[1]Inserted by the Crime and Disorder Act 1998 (c. 37) s.112 (effective September 30, 1998: S.I. 1998 No. 2327).

Punishment for murder

205.—(1) Subject to subsections (2) and (3) below, a person convicted of murder shall be sentenced to imprisonment for life.

(2) Where a person convicted of murder is under the age of 18 years he shall not be sentenced to imprisonment for life but to be detained without limit of time and shall be liable to be detained in such place, and under such conditions, as the Secretary of State may direct.

(3) Where a person convicted of murder has attained the age of 18 years but is under the age of 21 years he shall not be sentenced to imprisonment for life but to be detained in a young offenders institution and shall be liable to be detained for life.

(4) On sentencing any person convicted of murder a judge may make a recommendation as to the minimum period which should elapse before, under section 1(4) of the Prisoners and Criminal Proceedings (Scotland) Act 1993, the Secretary of State releases that person on licence.

(5) When making a recommendation under subsection (4) above, the judge shall state his reasons for so recommending.

(6) Notwithstanding subsection (2) of section 106 of this Act it shall be competent to appeal under paragraph (b) or (f) of subsection (1) of that section against a recommendation made under subsection (4) above; and for the purposes of such appeal (including the High Court's power of disposal under section 118(4)(b) of this Act) the recommendation shall be deemed part of the sentence passed on conviction.

Minimum sentence for third conviction of certain offences relating to drug trafficking

¹**205B.**—(1) This section applies where—

(a) a person is convicted on indictment in the High Court of a class A drug trafficking offence committed after the commencement of section 2 of the Crime and Punishment (Scotland) Act 1997;

(b) at the time when that offence was committed, he had attained the age of at least 18 years and had been convicted in any part of the United Kingdom of two other class A drug trafficking offences, irrespective of—

   (i) whether either of those offences was committed before or after the commencement of section 2 of the Crime and Punishment (Scotland) Act 1997;

   (ii) the court in which any such conviction was obtained; and

   (iii) his age at the time of the commission of either of those offences; and

(c) one of the offences mentioned in paragraph (b) above was committed after he had been convicted of the other.

(2) Subject to subsection (3) below, where this section applies the court shall sentence the person—

(a) where he has attained the age of 21 years, to a term of imprisonment of at least seven years; and

(b) where he has attained the age of 18 years but is under the age of 21 years, to detention in a young offenders institution for a period of at least seven years.

(3) The court shall not impose the sentence otherwise required by subsection (2) above where it is of the opinion that there are specific circumstances which—

(a) relate to any of the offences or to the offender; and

(b) would make that sentence unjust.

(4) For the purposes of section 106(2) of this Act a sentence passed under subsection (2) above in respect of a conviction for a class A drug trafficking offence shall not be regarded as a sentence fixed by law for that offence.

(5) In this section "class A drug trafficking offence" means a drug trafficking offence committed in respect of a class A drug; and for this purpose—

> "class A drug" has the same meaning as in the Misuse of Drugs Act 1971;
>
> "drug trafficking offence" means a drug trafficking offence within the meaning of—
>> (i) the Drug Trafficking Act 1994;
>> (ii) the Proceeds of Crime (Scotland) Act 1995; or
>> (iii) the Proceeds of Crime (Northern Ireland) Order 1996.

NOTE

[1]Inserted by the Crime and Punishment (Scotland) Act 1997 (c. 48), s.2 with effect from January 20, 1998 as provided by the Crime and Punishment (Scotland) Act 1997 (Commencement No. 2 and Transitional and Consequential Provisions) Order 1997 (S.I. 1997 No. 2323) Art. 3, Sched. 1.

Meaning of "conviction" for purposes of sections 205A and 205B

[1]**205C.**—(1) For the purposes of paragraph (b) of subsection (1) of each sections 205A and 205B of this Act "conviction" includes—

(a) a finding of guilt in respect of which the offender was admonished under section 181 of the Criminal Procedure (Scotland) Act 1975 (admonition); and

(b) a conviction for which an order is made placing the offender on probation,

and related expressions shall be construed accordingly.

NOTE

[1]Inserted by the Crime and Punishment (Scotland) Act 1997 (c. 48), s.3 (in part) with effect from October 20, 1997 as provided by the Crime and Punishment (Scotland) Act 1997 (Commencement No. 2 and Transitional and Consequential Provisions) Order 1997 (S.I. 1997 No. 2323) Art. 3, Sched. 1.

Minimum periods of imprisonment

206.—(1) No person shall be sentenced to imprisonment by a court of summary jurisdiction for a period of less than five days.

(2) Where a court of summary jurisdiction has power to impose imprisonment on an offender, it may, if any suitable place provided and certified as mentioned in subsection (4) below is available for the purpose, sentence the offender to be detained therein, for such period not exceeding four days as the court thinks fit, and an extract of the finding and sentence shall be delivered with the offender to the person in charge of the place where the offender is to be detained and shall be a sufficient authority for his detention in that place in accordance with the sentence.

(3) The expenses of the maintenance of offenders detained under this section shall be defrayed in like manner as the expenses of the maintenance of prisoners under the Prisons (Scotland) Act 1989.

(4) The Secretary of State may, on the application of any police authority, certify any police cells or other similar places provided by the authority to be suitable places for the detention of persons sentenced to detention under this section, and may by statutory instrument make regulations for the inspection of places so provided, the treatment of persons detained therein and generally for carrying this section into effect.

(5) No place certified under this section shall be used for the detention of females unless provision is made for their supervision by female officers.

(6) In this section the expression "police authority" has the same meaning as in the Police (Scotland) Act 1967.

Detention of young offenders

207.—(1) It shall not be competent to impose imprisonment on a person under 21 years of age.

[1](2) Subject to section 205(2) and (3), 205A(2)(b) and 205B(2)(b) of this Act and to subsections (3) and (4) below, a court may impose detention (whether by way of sentence or otherwise) on a person, who is not less than 16 but under 21 years of age, where but for subsection (1) above the court would have power to impose a period of imprisonment; and a period of detention imposed under this section on any person shall not exceed the maximum period of imprisonment which might otherwise have been imposed.

(3) The court shall not under subsection (2) above impose detention on an offender unless it is of the opinion that no other method of dealing with him is appropriate; and the court shall state its reasons for that opinion, and, except in the case of the High Court, those reasons shall be entered in the record of proceedings.

(4) To enable the court to form an opinion under subsection (3) above, it shall obtain from an officer of a local authority or otherwise such information as it can about the offender's circumstances; and it shall also take into account any information before it concerning the offender's character and physical and mental condition.

[2](4A) In forming an opinion under subsection (3) above the court shall take into account its power to make a hospital direction in addition to imposing a period of detention.

(5) A sentence of detention imposed under this section shall be a sentence of detention in a young offenders institution.

Notes
[1]Inserted by the Crime and Punishment (Scotland) Act 1997 (c. 48), Shed. 1, para. 21(25) with effect from October 20, 1997 by the Crime and Punishment (Scotland) Act 1997 (Commencement No. 2 and Transitional and Consequential Provisions) Order 1997 (S.I. 1997 No. 2323) Art. 3, Sched. 1.
[2]Inserted by the Crime and Punishment (Scotland) Act 1997 s.6(4) with effect from January 1, 1998 in terms of the Crime and Punishment (Scotland) Act 1997 (Commencement No. 2 and Transitional and Consequential Provisions) Order 1997 (S.I. 1997 No. 2323) Art. 4 and Sched. 2.

Detention of children convicted on indictment

208. Subject to section 205 of this Act, where a child is convicted on indictment and the court is of the opinion that no other method of dealing with him is appropriate, it may sentence him to be detained for a period which it shall specify in the sentence; and the child shall during that period be liable to be detained in such place and on such conditions as the Secretary of State may direct.

Supervised release orders

[1]**209.**—(1) Where a person is convicted on indictment of an offence other than a sexual offence within the meaning of section 210A of this Act and is sentenced to imprisonment for a term of less than four years, the court on passing sentence may, if it considers that it is necessary to do so to protect the public from serious harm from the offender on his release, make such order as is mentioned in subsection (3) below.

(2) A court shall, before making an order under subsection (1) above, consider a report by a relevant officer of a local authority about the offender and his circumstances and, if the court thinks it necessary, hear that officer.

(3) The order referred to in subsection (1) above (to be known as a "supervised release order") is that the person, during a relevant period—
    (a) be under the supervision either of a relevant officer of a local authority or of an officer of a local probation board appointed for or

assigned to a petty sessions area (such local authority or the justices for such area to be designated under section 14(4) or 15(1) of the Prisoners and Criminal Proceedings (Scotland) Act 1993);

(b) comply with;

(i) such requirements as may be imposed by the court in the order; and

(ii) such requirements as that officer may reasonably specify,

for the purpose of securing the good conduct of the person or preventing, or lessening the possibility of, his committing a further offence (whether or not an offence of the kind for which he was sentenced); and

(c) comply with the standard requirements imposed by virtue of subsection (4)(a)(i) below.

(4) A supervised release order—

(a) shall—

(i) without prejudice to subsection (3)(b) above, contain such requirements (in this section referred to as the "standard requirements"); and

(ii) be as nearly as possible in such form,

as may be prescribed by Act of Adjournal;

(b) for the purposes of any appeal or review constitutes part of the sentence of the person in respect of whom the order is made; and

(c) shall have no effect during any period in which the person is subject to a licence under Part I of the said Act of 1993.

(5) Before making a supervised release order as respects a person the court shall explain to him, in as straightforward a way as is practicable, the effect of the order and the possible consequences for him of any breach of it.

(6) The clerk of the court by which a supervised release order is made in respect of a person shall—

(a) forthwith send a copy of the order to the person and to the Secretary of State; and

(b) within seven days after the date on which the order is made, send to the Secretary of State such documents and information relating to the case and to the person as are likely to be of assistance to a supervising officer.

[1](7) In this section—

"relevant officer" has the same meaning as in Part I of the Prisoners and Criminal Proceedings (Scotland) Act 1993;

"relevant period" means such period as may be specified in the supervised release order, being a period—

(a) not exceeding twelve months after the date of the person's release; and

(b) no part of which is later than the date by which the entire term of imprisonment specified in his sentence has elapsed; and

"supervising officer" means, where an authority has or justices have been designated as is mentioned in subsection (3)(a) above for the purposes of the order, any relevant officer or, as the case may be, officer of a local probation board who is for the time being supervising for those purposes the person released.

[2](7A) Where a person—

(a) is serving a sentence of imprisonment and on his release from that sentence will be subject to a supervised release order; and

(b) is sentenced to a further term of imprisonment, whether that term is to run consecutively or concurrently with the sentence mentioned in paragraph (a) above,

the relevant period for any supervised release order made in relation to him shall begin on the date when he is released from those terms of imprisonment; and where there is more than one such order he shall on his release be subject to whichever of them is for the longer or, as the case may be, the longest period.

(8) This section applies to a person sentenced under section 207 of this Act as it applies to a person sentenced to a period of imprisonment.

NOTES

[1]As amended by the Crime and Disorder Act 1998 (c. 37), s.86(2) (effective September 30, 1998: S.I. 1998 No. 2327).

[2]Inserted by the Crime and Punishment (Scotland) Act 1997, Sched. 1, para. 21(26) (effective April 1, 1999: S.I. 1999 No. 652).

[3]As amended by the Criminal Justice and Court Services Act 2000 (c. 43), s.74 and Sched. 7, para. 4. Brought into force by the Criminal Justice and Court Services Act 2000 (Commencement No. 4) Order 2001 (S.I. 2001 No. 919 (C. 33)), art. 2(f)(ii) (effective April 1, 2001).

[4]As amended by the Criminal Justice and Court Services Act 2000 (c. 43), s.74 and Sched. 7, para. 121. Brought into force as above.

Consideration of time spent in custody

210.—(1) A court, in passing a sentence of imprisonment or detention on a person for an offence, shall—

[1](a) in determining the period of imprisonment or detention, have regard to any period of time spent in custody by the person on remand awaiting trial or sentence, or spent in custody awaiting extradition to the United Kingdom, or spent in hospital awaiting trial or sentence by virtue of an order made under section 52, 53 or 200 of this Act;

(b) specify the date of commencement of the sentence; and

(c) if the person—

    (i) has spent a period of time in custody on remand awaiting trial or sentence; or

    (ii) is an extradited prisoner for the purposes of this section, or

    [1](iii) has spent a period of time in hospital awaiting trial or sentence by virtue of an order under section 52, 53 or 200 of this Act,

and the date specified under paragraph (b) above is not earlier than the date on which sentence was passed, state its reasons for not specifying an earlier date.

(2) A prisoner is an extradited prisoner for the purposes of this section if—

(a) he was tried for the offence in respect of which his sentence of imprisonment was imposed—

    (i) after having been extradited to the United Kingdom; and

    (ii) without having first been restored to the state from which he was extradited or having had an opportunity of leaving the United Kingdom; and

(b) he was for any period in custody while awaiting such extradition.

(3) In this section "extradited to the United Kingdom" means returned to the United Kingdom—

(a) in pursuance of extradition arrangements (as defined in section 3 of the Extradition Act 1989);

(b) under any law which corresponds to that Act and is a law of a designated Commonwealth country (as defined in section 5(1) of that Act);

(c) under that Act as extended to a colony or under any corresponding law of a colony;

(d) in pursuance of arrangements with a foreign state in respect of which an Order in Council under section 2 of the Extradition Act 1870 is in force; or

(e) in pursuance of a warrant of arrest endorsed in the Republic of Ireland under the law of that country corresponding to the Backing of Warrants (Republic of Ireland) Act 1965.

NOTE
[1]Inserted by the Crime and Punishment (Scotland) Act 1997 (c. 48), s.12 and commenced on August 1, 1997 by the Crime and Punishment (Scotland) Act 1997 (Commencement and Transitional Provisions) Order 1997 (S.I. 1997 No. 1712) para. 3.

Sexual or violent offenders

Extended sentences for sex and violent offenders

[1]**210A.**—(1) Where a person is convicted on indictment of a sexual or violent offence, the court may, if it—
  (a) intends, in relation to—
        (i) a sexual offence, to pass a determinate sentence of imprisonment; or
        (ii) a violent offence, to pass such a sentence for a term of four years or more; and
  (b) considers that the period (if any) for which the offender would, apart from this section, be subject to a licence would not be adequate for the purpose of protecting the public from serious harm from the offender,
pass an extended sentence on the offender.
  (2) An extended sentence is a sentence of imprisonment which is the aggregate of—
  (a) the term of imprisonment ("the custodial term") which the court would have passed on the offender otherwise than by virtue of this section; and
  (b) a further period ("the extension period") for which the offender is to be subject to a licence and which is, subject to the provisions of this section, of such length as the court considers necessary for the purpose mentioned in subsection (1)(b) above.
  (3) The extension period shall not exceed, in the case of—
  (a) a sexual offence, ten years; and
  (b) a violent offence, five years.
  (4) A court shall, before passing an extended sentence, consider a report by a relevant officer of a local authority about the offender and his circumstances and, if the court thinks it necessary, hear that officer.
  (5) The term of an extended sentence passed for a statutory offence shall not exceed the maximum term of imprisonment provided for in the statute in respect of that offence.
  (6) Subject to subsection (5) above, a sheriff may pass an extended sentence which is the aggregate of a custodial term not exceeding the maximum term of imprisonment which he may impose and an extension period not exceeding three years.
  (7) The Secretary of State may by order—
  (a) amend paragraph (b) of subsection (3) above by substituting a different period, not exceeding ten years, for the period for the time being specified in that paragraph; and
  (b) make such transitional provision as appears to him to be necessary or expedient in connection with the amendment.
  (8) The power to make an order under subsection (7) above shall be exercisable by statutory instrument; but no such order shall be made unless a draft of the order has been laid before, and approved by a resolution of, each House of Parliament.
  (9) An extended sentence shall not be imposed where the sexual or violent offence was committed before the commencement of section 86 of the Crime and Disorder Act 1998.
  (10) For the purposes of this section—

"licence" and "relevant officer" have the same meaning as in Part I of
the Prisoners and Criminal Proceedings (Scotland) Act 1993;
"sexual offence" means—
  (i) rape;
  (ii) clandestine injury to women;
  (iii) abduction of a woman or girl with intent to rape or ravish;
  (iv) assault with intent to rape or ravish;
  (v) indecent assault;
  (vi) lewd, indecent or libidinous behaviour or practices;
  (vii) shameless indecency;
  (viii) sodomy;
  (ix) an offence under section 170 of the Customs and Excise
     Management Act 1979 in relation to goods prohibited to be
     imported under section 42 of the Customs Consolidation Act
     1876, but only where the prohibited goods include indecent
     photographs of persons;
  (x) an offence under section 52 of the Civic Government (Scot-
     land) Act 1982 (taking and distribution of indecent images of
     children);
  (xi) an offence under section 52A of that Act (possession of
     indecent images of children);
  (xii) an offence under section 1 of the Criminal Law (Consoli-
     dation) (Scotland) Act 1995 (incest);
  (xiii) an offence under section 2 of that Act (intercourse with a
     stepchild);
  (xiv) an offence under section 3 of that Act (intercourse with child
     under 16 by person in position of trust);
  (xv) an offence under section 5 of that Act (unlawful intercourse
     with girl under 16);
  (xvi) an offence under section 6 of that Act (indecent behaviour
     towards girl between 12 and 16);
  (xvii) an offence under section 8 of that Act (abduction of girl under
     18 for purposes of unlawful intercourse);
  (xviii) an offence under section 10 of that Act (person having
     parental responsibilities causing or encouraging sexual activity
     in relation to a girl under 16);
  (xix) an offence under subsection (5) of section 13 of that Act
     (homosexual offences); and
  [2](xx) an offence under section 3 of the Sexual Offences (Amend-
     ment) Act 2000 (abuse of position of trust);
"imprisonment" includes—
  (i) detention under section 207 of this Act; and
  (ii) detention under section 208 of this Act; and
"violent offence" means any offence (other than an offence which is a
  sexual offence within the meaning of this section) inferring
  personal violence.
(11) Any reference in subsection (10) above to a sexual offence includes—
(a) a reference to any attempt, conspiracy or incitement to commit that
  offence; and
(b) except in the case of an offence in paragraphs (i) to (viii) of the
  definition of "sexual offence" in that subsection, a reference to aiding
  and abetting, counselling or procuring the commission of that offence.

NOTES
[1]Inserted by the Crime and Disorder Act 1998 (c. 37), s.86 (effective September 30, 1998: S.I.
1998 No. 2327).

[2]Inserted by the Sexual Offences (Amendment) Act 2000 (c. 44), s.6(2).

Fines

Fines

211.—(1) Where an accused who is convicted on indictment of any offence (whether triable only on indictment or triable either on indictment or summarily other than by virtue of section 292(6) of this Act) would apart from this subsection be liable to a fine of or not exceeding a specified amount, he shall by virtue of this subsection be liable to a fine of any amount.

(2) Where any Act confers a power by subordinate instrument to make a person liable on conviction on indictment of any offence mentioned in subsection (1) above to a fine or a maximum fine of a specified amount, or which shall not exceed a specified amount, the fine which may be imposed in the exercise of that power shall by virtue of this subsection be a fine of an unlimited amount.

(3) Any sentence or decree for any fine or expenses pronounced by a sheriff court or district court may be enforced against the person or effects of any party against whom the sentence or decree was awarded—

    (a) in the district where the sentence or decree was pronounced; or

    (b) in any other such district.

(4) A fine imposed by the High Court shall be remitted for enforcement to, and shall be enforceable as if it had been imposed by—

    (a) where the person upon whom the fine was imposed resides in Scotland, the sheriff for the district where that person resides; and

    (b) where that person resides outwith Scotland, the sheriff before whom he was brought for examination in relation to the offence for which the fine was imposed.

(5) Any fine imposed in the High Court on the accused, and on a juror for non-attendance, and any forfeiture for non-appearance of a party, witness or juror in the High Court shall be payable to and recoverable by the Treasury, except where the High Court orders that the whole or any part of the fine shall be otherwise disposed of.

(6) All fines and expenses imposed in summary proceedings under this Act shall be paid to the clerk of court to be accounted for by him to the person entitled to such fines and expenses, and it shall not be necessary to specify in any sentence the person entitled to payment of such fines or expenses unless it is necessary to provide for the division of the penalty.

(7) A court in determining the amount of any fine to be imposed on an offender shall take into consideration, amongst other things, the means of the offender so far as known to the court.

Fines in summary proceedings

212.—(1) Where a court of summary jurisdiction imposes a fine on an offender, the court may order him to be searched, and any money found on him on apprehension or when so searched or when taken to prison or to a young offenders institution in default of payment of the fine, may, unless the court otherwise directs and subject to subsection (2) below, be applied towards payment of the fine, and the surplus if any shall be returned to him.

(2) Money shall not be applied as mentioned in subsection (1) above if the court is satisfied that it does not belong to the person on whom it was found or that the loss of the money will be more injurious to his family than his imprisonment or detention.

(3) When a court of summary jurisdiction, which has adjudged that a sum of money shall be paid by an offender, considers that any money found on the offender on apprehension, or after he has been searched by order of the court, should not be applied towards payment of such sum, the court, shall make a direction in writing to that effect which shall be written on the extract

of the sentence which imposes the fine before it is issued by the clerk of the court.

(4) An accused may make an application to such a court either orally or in writing, through the governor of the prison in whose custody he may be at that time, that any sum of money which has been found on his person should not be applied in payment of the fine adjudged to be paid by him.

(5) A person who alleges that any money found on the person of an offender is not the property of the offender, but belongs to that person, may apply to such court either orally or in writing for a direction that the money should not be applied in payment of the fine adjudged to be paid, and the court after enquiry may so direct.

(6) A court of summary jurisdiction, which has adjudged that a sum of money shall be paid by an offender, may order the attendance in court of the offender, if he is in prison, for the purpose of ascertaining the ownership of money which has been found on his person.

(7) A notice in the form prescribed by Act of Adjournal, or as nearly as may be in such form, addressed to the governor of the prison in whose custody an offender may be at the time, signed by the judge of a court of summary jurisdiction shall be a sufficient warrant to the governor of such prison for conveying the offender to the court.

Remission of fines

213.—(1) A fine may at any time be remitted in whole or in part by—
- (a) in a case where a transfer of fine order under section 222 of this Act is effective and the court by which payment is enforceable is, in terms of the order, a court of summary jurisdiction in Scotland, that court; or
- (b) in any other case, the court which imposed the fine or, where that court was the High Court, by which payment was first enforceable.

(2) Where the court remits the whole or part of a fine after imprisonment has been imposed under section 214(2) or (4) of this Act, it shall also remit the whole period of imprisonment or, as the case may be, reduce the period by an amount which bears the same proportion to the whole period as the amount remitted bears to the whole fine.

(3) The power conferred by subsection (1) above shall be exercisable without requiring the attendance of the accused.

Fines: time for payment and payment by instalments

214.—(1) Where a court has imposed a fine on an offender or ordered him to find caution the court shall, subject to subsection (2) below, allow him at least seven days to pay the fine or the first instalment thereof or, as the case may be, to find caution; and any reference in this section and section 216 of this Act to a failure to pay a fine or other like expression shall include a reference to a failure to find caution.

(2) If on the occasion of the imposition of a fine—
- (a) the offender appears to the court to possess sufficient means to enable him to pay the fine forthwith; or
- (b) on being asked by the court whether he wishes to have time for payment, he does not ask for time; or
- (c) he fails to satisfy the court that he has a fixed abode; or
- (d) the court is satisfied for any other special reason that no time should be allowed for payment,

the court may refuse him time to pay the fine and, if the offender fails to pay, may exercise its power to impose imprisonment and, if it does so, shall state the special reason for its decision.

(3) In all cases where time is not allowed by a court for payment of a fine, the reasons of the court for not so allowing time shall be stated in the extract of the finding and sentence as well as in the finding and sentence itself.

(4) Where time is allowed for payment of a fine or payment by instalments is ordered, the court shall not, on the occasion of the imposition of a fine, impose imprisonment in the event of a future default in paying the fine or an instalment thereof unless the offender is before it and the court determines that, having regard to the gravity of the offence or to the character of the offender, or to other special reason, it is expedient that he should be imprisoned without further inquiry in default of payment; and where a court so determines, it shall state the special reason for its decision.

(5) Where a court has imposed imprisonment in accordance with subsection (4) above, then, if at any time the offender asks the court to commit him to prison, the court may do so notwithstanding subsection (1) of this section.

(6) Nothing in the foregoing provisions of this section shall affect any power of the court to order a fine to be recovered by civil diligence.

(7) Where time has been allowed for payment of a fine imposed by the court, it may, on an application by or on behalf of the offender, and after giving the prosecutor an opportunity of being heard, allow further time for payment.

(8) Without prejudice to subsection (2) above, where a court has imposed a fine on an offender, the court may, of its own accord or on the application of the offender, order payment of that fine by instalments of such amounts and at such time as it may think fit.

(9) Where the court has ordered payment of a fine by instalments it may—

(a) allow further time for payment of any instalment thereof;

(b) order payment thereof by instalments of lesser amounts, or at longer intervals, than those originally fixed,

and the powers conferred by this subsection shall be exercisable without requiring the attendance of the accused.

Application for further time to pay fine

215.—(1) An application by an offender for further time in which to pay a fine imposed on him by a court, or of instalments thereof, shall be made, subject to subsection (2) below, to that court.

(2) Where a transfer of fine order has been made under section 222 of this Act, section 90 of the Magistrates' Courts Act 1980 or Article 95 of the Magistrates' Courts (Northern Ireland) Order 1981, an application under subsection (1) above shall be made to the court specified in the transfer order, or to the court specified in the last transfer order where there is more than one transfer.

(3) A court to which an application is made under this section shall allow further time for payment of the fine or of instalments thereof, unless it is satisfied that the failure of the offender to make payment has been wilful or that the offender has no reasonable prospect of being able to pay if further time is allowed.

(4) An application made under this section may be made orally or in writing.

Fines: restriction on imprisonment for default

216.—(1) Where a court has imposed a fine or ordered the finding of caution without imposing imprisonment in default of payment, subject to subsection (2) below, it shall not impose imprisonment on an offender for failing to make payment of the fine or, as the case may be, to find caution, unless on an occasion subsequent to that sentence the court has enquired into in his presence the reason why the fine has not been paid or, as the case may be, caution has not been found.

(2) Subsection (1) above shall not apply where the offender is in prison.

(3) A court may, for the purpose of enabling enquiry to be made under this section—

(a) issue a citation requiring the offender to appear before the court at a time and place appointed in the citation; or

(b) issue a warrant of apprehension.

(4) On the failure of the offender to appear before the court in response to a citation under this section, the court may issue a warrant of apprehension.

(5) The citation of an offender to appear before a court in terms of subsection (3)(a) above shall be effected in like manner, *mutatis mutandis*, as the citation of an accused to a sitting or diet of the court under section 141 of this Act, and—

(a) the citation shall be signed by the clerk of the court before which the offender is required to appear, instead of by the prosecutor; and

(b) the forms relating to the citation of an accused shall not apply to such citation.

(6) The following matters shall be, or as nearly as may be, in such form as is prescribed by Act of Adjournal—

(a) the citation of an offender under this section;

(b) if the citation of the offender is effected by an officer of law, the written execution, if any, of that officer of law;

(c) a warrant of apprehension issued by a court under subsection (4) above; and

(d) the minute of procedure in relation to an enquiry into the means of an offender under this section.

(7) Where a child would, if he were an adult, be liable to be imprisoned in default of payment of any fine the court may, if it considers that none of the other methods by which the case may legally be dealt with is suitable, order that the child be detained for such period, not exceeding one month, as may be specified in the order in a place chosen by the local authority in whose area the court is situated.

Fines: supervision pending payment

217.—(1) Where an offender has been allowed time for payment of a fine, the court may, either on the occasion of the imposition of the fine or on a subsequent occasion, order that he be placed under the supervision of such person, in this section referred to as the "supervising officer", as the court may from time to time appoint for the purpose of assisting and advising the offender in regard to payment of the fine.

(2) An order made in pursuance of subsection (1) above shall remain in force so long as the offender to whom it relates remains liable to pay the fine or any part of it unless the order ceases to have effect or is discharged under subsection (3) below.

(3) An order under this section shall cease to have effect on the making of a transfer of fine order under section 222 of this Act in respect of the fine or may be discharged by the court that made it without prejudice, in either case, to the making of a new order.

(4) Where an offender under 21 years of age has been allowed time for payment of a fine, the court shall not order the form of detention appropriate to him in default of payment of the fine unless—

(a) he has been placed under supervision in respect of the fine; or

(b) the court is satisfied that it is impracticable to place him under supervision.

(5) Where a court, on being satisfied as mentioned in subsection (4)(b) above, orders the detention of a person under 21 years of age without an order under this section having been made, the court shall state the grounds on which it is so satisfied.

(6) Where an order under this section is in force in respect of an offender, the court shall not impose imprisonment in default of the payment of the fine unless before doing so it has—

(a) taken such steps as may be reasonably practicable to obtain from the supervising officer a report, which may be oral, on the offender's conduct and means, and has considered any such report; and

(b) in a case where an enquiry is required by section 216 of this Act, considered such enquiry.

(7) When a court appoints a different supervising officer under subsection (1) above, a notice shall be sent by the clerk of the court to the offender in such form, as nearly as may be, as is prescribed by Act of Adjournal.

(8) The supervising officer shall communicate with the offender with a view to assisting and advising him in regard to payment of the fine, and unless the fine or any instalment thereof is paid to the clerk of the court within the time allowed by the court for payment, the supervising officer shall report to the court without delay after the expiry of such time, as to the conduct and means of the offender.

Fines: supplementary provisions as to payment

218.—(1) Where under the provisions of section 214 or 217 of this Act a court is required to state a special reason for its decision or the grounds on which it is satisfied that it is undesirable or impracticable to place an offender under supervision, the reason or, as the case may be, the grounds shall be entered in the record of the proceedings along with the finding and sentence.

(2) Any reference in the said sections 214 and 217 to imprisonment shall be construed, in the case of an offender on whom by reason of his age imprisonment may not lawfully be imposed, as a reference to the lawful form of detention in default of payment of a fine appropriate to that person, and any reference to prison shall be construed accordingly.

(3) Where a warrant has been issued for the apprehension of an offender for non-payment of a fine, the offender may, notwithstanding section 211(6) of this Act, pay such fine in full to a constable; and the warrant shall not then be enforced and the constable shall remit the fine to the clerk of court.

Fines: periods of imprisonment for non-payment

219.—(1) Subject to sections 214 to 218 of this Act—

(a) a court may, when imposing a fine, impose a period of imprisonment in default of payment; or

(b) where no order has been made under paragraph (a) above and a person fails to pay a fine, or any part or instalment of a fine, by the time ordered by the court (or, where section 214(2) of this Act applies, immediately) the court may, subject to section 235(1) of this Act, impose a period of imprisonment for such failure either with immediate effect or to take effect in the event of the person failing to pay the fine or any part or instalment of it by such further time as the court may order,

whether or not the fine is imposed under an enactment which makes provision for its enforcement or recovery.

(2) Subject to the following subsections of this section, the maximum period of imprisonment which may be imposed under subsection (1) above or for failure to find caution, shall be as follows—

Amount of Fine or Caution	Maximum Period of Imprisonment
Not exceeding £200	7 days
Exceeding £200 but not exceeding £500	14 days
Exceeding £500 but not exceeding £1,000	28 days
Exceeding £1,000 but not exceeding £2,500	45 days
Exceeding £2,500 but not exceeding £5,000	3 months
Exceeding £5,000 but not exceeding £10,000	6 months
Exceeding £10,000 but not exceeding £20,000	12 months
Exceeding £20,000 but not exceeding £50,000	18 months
Exceeding £50,000 but not exceeding £100,000	2 years
Exceeding £100,000 but not exceeding £250,000	3 years
Exceeding £250,000 but not exceeding £1 Million	5 years
Exceeding £1 Million	10 years

(3) Where an offender is fined on the same day before the same court for offences charged in the same indictment or complaint or in separate indictments or complaints, the amount of the fine shall, for the purposes of this section, be taken to be the total of the fines imposed.

(4) Where a court has imposed a period of imprisonment in default of payment of a fine, and—

(a) an instalment of the fine is not paid at the time ordered; or

(b) part only of the fine has been paid within the time allowed for payment,

the offender shall be liable to imprisonment for a period which bears to the period so imposed the same proportion, as nearly as may be, as the amount outstanding at the time when warrant is issued for imprisonment of the offender in default bears to the original fine.

(5) Where no period of imprisonment in default of payment of a fine has been imposed and—

(a) an instalment of the fine is not paid at the time ordered; or

(b) part only of the fine has been paid within the time allowed for payment,

the offender shall be liable to imprisonment for a maximum period which bears, as nearly as may be, the same proportion to the maximum period of imprisonment which could have been imposed by virtue of the Table in subsection (2) above in default of payment of the original fine as the amount outstanding at the time when he appears before the court bears to the original fine.

(6) If in any sentence or extract sentence the period of imprisonment inserted in default of payment of a fine or on failure to find caution is in excess of that competent under this Part of this Act, such period of imprisonment shall be reduced to the maximum period under this Part of this Act applicable to such default or failure, and the judge who pronounced the sentence shall have power to order the sentence or extract to be corrected accordingly.

(7) The provisions of this section shall be without prejudice to the operation of section 220 of this Act.

(8) Where in any case—

(a) the sheriff considers that the imposition of imprisonment for the number of years for the time being specified in section 3(3) of this Act would be inadequate; and

(b) the maximum period of imprisonment which may be imposed under subsection (1) above (or under that subsection as read with either or

both of sections 252(2) of this Act and section 14(2) of the Proceeds of Crime (Scotland) Act 1995) exceeds that number of years,
he shall remit the case to the High Court for sentence.

Fines: part payment by prisoners

220.—(1) Where a person committed to prison or otherwise detained for failure to pay a fine imposed by a court pays to the governor of the prison, under conditions prescribed by rules made under the Prisons (Scotland) Act 1989, any sum in part satisfaction of the fine, the term of imprisonment shall be reduced (or as the case may be further reduced) by a number of days bearing as nearly as possible the same proportion to such term as the sum so paid bears to the amount of the fine outstanding at the commencement of the imprisonment.

(2) The day on which any sum is paid as mentioned in subsection (1) above shall not be regarded as a day served by the prisoner as part of the said term of imprisonment.

(3) All sums paid under this section shall be handed over on receipt by the governor of the prison to the clerk of the court in which the conviction was obtained, and thereafter paid and applied *pro tanto* in the same manner and for the same purposes as sums adjudged to be paid by the conviction and sentence of the court, and paid and recovered in terms thereof, are lawfully paid and applied.

(4) In this section references to a prison and to the governor thereof shall include respectively references to any other place in which a person may be lawfully detained in default of payment of a fine, and to an officer in charge thereof.

Fines: recovery by civil diligence

221.—(1) Where any fine falls to be recovered by civil diligence in pursuance of this Act or in any case in which a court may think it expedient to order a fine to be recovered by civil diligence, there shall be added to the finding of the court imposing the fine a warrant for civil diligence in a form prescribed by Act of Adjournal which shall have the effect of authorising—

(a) the charging of the person who has been fined to pay the fine within the period specified in the charge and, in the event of failure to make such payment within that period, the execution of an earnings arrestment and the poinding of articles belonging to him and, if necessary for the purpose of executing the poinding, the opening of shut and lockfast places;

(b) an arrestment other than an arrestment of earnings in the hands of his employer,

and such diligence, whatever the amount of the fine imposed, may be executed in the same manner as if the proceedings were on an extract decree of the sheriff in a summary cause.

(2) Subject to subsection (3) below, proceedings by civil diligence under this section may be taken at any time after the imposition of the fine to which they relate.

(3) No such proceedings shall be authorised after the offender has been imprisoned in consequence of his having defaulted in payment of the fine.

(4) Where proceedings by civil diligence for the recovery of a fine or caution are taken, imprisonment for non-payment of the fine or for failure to find such caution shall remain competent and such proceedings may be authorised after the court has imposed imprisonment for, or in the event of, the non-payment or the failure but before imprisonment has followed such imposition.

Transfer of fine orders

222.—(1) Where a court has imposed a fine on a person convicted of an offence and it appears to the court that he is residing—

(a) within the jurisdiction of another court in Scotland; or

(b) in any petty sessions area in England and Wales; or

(c) in any petty sessions district in Northern Ireland,

the court may order that payment of the fine shall be enforceable by that other court or in that petty sessions area or petty sessions district as the case may be.

(2) An order under this section (in this section referred to as a "transfer of fine order") shall specify the court by which or the petty sessions area or petty sessions district in which payment is to be enforceable and, where the court to be specified in a transfer of fine order is a court of summary jurisdiction, it shall, in any case where the order is made by the sheriff court, be a sheriff court.

(3) Subject to subsections (4) and (5) below, where a transfer of fine order is made with respect to any fine under this section, any functions under any enactment relating to that sum which, if no such order had been made, would have been exercisable by the court which made the order or by the clerk of that court shall cease to be so exercisable.

(4) Where—

(a) the court specified in a transfer of fine order is satisfied, after inquiry, that the offender is not residing within the jurisdiction of that court; and

(b) the clerk of that court, within 14 days of receiving the notice required by section 223(1) of this Act, sends to the clerk of the court which made the order notice to that effect,

the order shall cease to have effect.

(5) Where a transfer of fine order ceases to have effect by virtue of subsection (4) above, the functions referred to in subsection (3) above shall again be exercisable by the court which made the order or, as the case may be, by the clerk of that court.

(6) Where a transfer of fine order under this section, section 90 of the Magistrates' Courts Act 1980 or Article 95 of the Magistrates' Courts (Northern Ireland) Order 1981 specifies a court of summary jurisdiction in Scotland, that court and the clerk of that court shall have all the like functions under this Part of this Act in respect of the fine or the sum in respect of which that order was made (including the power to make any further order under this section) as if the fine or the sum were a fine imposed by that court and as if any order made under this section, the said Act of 1980 or the said Order of 1981 in respect of the fine or the sum before the making of the transfer of fine order had been made by that court.

(7) The functions of the court to which subsection (6) above relates shall be deemed to include the court's power to apply to the Secretary of State under any regulations made by him under section 24(1)(a) of the Criminal Justice Act 1991 (power to deduct fines etc. from income support).

(8) Where a transfer of fine order under section 90 of the Magistrates' Courts Act 1980, Article 95 of the Magistrates' Courts (Northern Ireland) Order 1981, or this section provides for the enforcement by a sheriff court in Scotland of a fine imposed by the Crown Court, the term of imprisonment which may be imposed under this Part of this Act shall be the term fixed in pursuance of section 31 of the Powers of Criminal Courts Act 1973 by the Crown Court or a term which bears the same proportion to the term so fixed as the amount of the fine remaining due bears to the amount of the fine imposed by that court, notwithstanding that the term exceeds the period applicable to the case under section 219 of this Act.

Transfer of fines: procedure for clerk of court

223.—(1) Where a court makes a transfer of fine order under section 222 of this Act, the clerk of the court shall send to the clerk of the court specified in the order—

   (a) a notice in the form prescribed by Act of Adjournal, or as nearly as may be in such form;

   (b) a statement of the offence of which the offender was convicted; and

   (c) a statement of the steps, if any, taken to recover the fine,

and shall give him such further information, if any, as, in his opinion, is likely to assist the court specified in the order in recovering the fine.

(2) In the case of a further transfer of fine order, the clerk of the court which made the order shall send to the clerk of the court by which the fine was imposed a copy of the notice sent to the clerk of the court specified in the order.

(3) The clerk of the court specified in a transfer of fine order shall, as soon as may be after he has received the notice mentioned in subsection (1)(a) above, send an intimation to the offender in the form prescribed by Act of Adjournal or as nearly as may be in such form.

(4) The clerk of court specified in a transfer of fine order shall remit or otherwise account for any payment received in respect of the fine to the clerk of the court by which the fine was imposed, and if the sentence has been enforced otherwise than by payment of the fine, he shall inform the clerk of court how the sentence was enforced.

Discharge from imprisonment to be specified

224. All warrants of imprisonment in default of payment of a fine, or on failure to find caution, shall specify a period at the expiry of which the person sentenced shall be discharged, notwithstanding the fine has not been paid, or caution found.

Penalties: standard scale, prescribed sum and uprating

225.—(1) There shall be a standard scale of fines for offences triable only summarily, which shall be known as "the standard scale".

(2) The standard scale is shown below—

Level on the scale	Amount of Fine
1	£ 200
2	£ 500
3	£1,000
4	£2,500
5	£5,000

(3) Any reference in any enactment, whenever passed or made, to a specified level on the standard scale shall be construed as referring to the amount which corresponds to that level on the standard scale referred to in subsection (2) above.

(4) If it appears to the Secretary of State that there has been a change in the value of money since the relevant date, he may by order substitute for the sum or sums for the time being specified in the provisions mentioned in subsection (5) below such other sum or sums as appear to him justified by the change.

(5) The provisions referred to in subsection (4) above are—

(a) subsection (2) above;
(b) subsection (8) below;
(c) section 219(2) of this Act;
(d) column 5 or 6 of Schedule 4 to the Misuse of Drugs Act 1971 so far as the column in question relates to the offences under provisions of that Act specified in column 1 of that Schedule in respect of which the maximum fines were increased by Part II of Schedule 8 to the Criminal Justice and Public Order Act 1994.

(6) In subsection (4) above "the relevant date" means—
(a) in relation to the first order made under that subsection, the date the last order was made under section 289D(1) of the Criminal Procedure (Scotland) Act 1975; and
(b) in relation to each subsequent order, the date of the previous order.

(7) An order under subsection (4) above—
(a) shall be made by statutory instrument subject to annulment in pursuance of a resolution of either House of Parliament and may be revoked by a subsequent order thereunder; and
(b) without prejudice to Schedule 14 to the Criminal Law Act 1977, shall not affect the punishment for an offence committed before that order comes into force.

(8) In this Act "the prescribed sum" means £5,000 or such sum as is for the time being substituted in this definition by an order in force under subsection (4) above.

Penalties: exceptionally high maximum fines

226.—(1) The Secretary of State may by order amend an enactment specifying a sum to which this subsection applies so as to substitute for that sum such other sum as appears to him—
(a) to be justified by a change in the value of money appearing to him to have taken place since the last occasion on which the sum in question was fixed; or
(b) to be appropriate to take account of an order altering the standard scale which has been made or is proposed to be made.

(2) Subsection (1) above applies to any sum which—
(a) is higher than level 5 on the standard scale; and
(b) is specified as the fine or the maximum fine which may be imposed on conviction of an offence which is triable only summarily.

(3) The Secretary of State may by order amend an enactment specifying a sum to which this subsection applies so as to substitute for that sum such other sum as appears to him—
(a) to be justified by a change in the value of money appearing to him to have taken place since the last occasion on which the sum in question was fixed; or
(b) to be appropriate to take account of an order made or proposed to be made altering the statutory maximum.

(4) Subsection (3) above applies to any sum which—
(a) is higher than the statutory maximum; and
(b) is specified as the maximum fine which may be imposed on summary conviction of an offence triable either on indictment or summarily.

(5) An order under this section—
(a) shall be made by statutory instrument subject to annulment in pursuance of a resolution of either House of Parliament; and
(b) shall not affect the punishment for an offence committed before that order comes into force.

(6) In this section "enactment" includes an enactment contained in an Act or subordinate instrument passed or made after the commencement of this Act.

Caution

227. Where a person is convicted on indictment of an offence (other than an offence the sentence for which is fixed by law) the court may, instead of or in addition to imposing a fine or a period of imprisonment, ordain the accused to find caution for good behaviour for a period not exceeding 12 months and to such amount as the court considers appropriate.

Probation

Probation orders

228.—(1) Subject to subsection (2) below, where an accused is convicted of an offence (other than an offence the sentence for which is fixed by law) the court if it is of the opinion that it is expedient to do so—
- (a) having regard to the circumstances, including the nature of the offence and the character of the offender; and
- (b) having obtained a report as to the circumstances and character of the offender,

may, instead of sentencing him, make an order requiring the offender to be under supervision for a period to be specified in the order of not less than six months nor more than three years; and such an order is, in this Act, referred to as a "probation order".

(2) A court shall not make a probation order under subsection (1) above unless it is satisfied that suitable arrangements for the supervision of the offender can be made—
- (a) in a case other than that mentioned in paragraph (b) below, by the local authority in whose area he resides or is to reside; or
- ¹(b) in a case where, by virtue of section 234(1) of this Act, subsections (3) and (4) below would not apply, by the local probation board for the area which contains the petty sessions area which would be named in the order.

(3) A probation order shall be as nearly as may be in the form prescribed by Act of Adjournal, and shall—
- (a) name the local authority area in which the offender resides or is to reside; and
- (b) subject to subsection (4) below, make provision for the offender to be under the supervision of an officer of the local authority of that area.

(4) Where the offender resides or is to reside in a local authority area in which the court which makes the order has no jurisdiction, the court shall name the appropriate court (being such a court as could have been named in any amendment of the order in accordance with Schedule 6 to this Act) in the area of residence or intended residence, and the appropriate court shall require the local authority for that area to arrange for the offender to be under the supervision of an officer of that authority.

(5) Before making a probation order, the court shall explain to the offender in ordinary language—
- (a) the effect of the order, including any additional requirements proposed to be inserted under section 229 or 230 of this Act; and
- (b) that if he fails to comply with the order or commits another offence during the probation period he will be liable to be sentenced for the original offence,

and the court shall not make the order unless the offender expresses his willingness to comply with the requirements thereof.

(6) The clerk of the court by which a probation order is made or of the appropriate court, as the case may be, shall—

(a) cause copies of the probation order to be given to the officer of the local authority who is to supervise the probationer and to the person in charge of any institution or place in which the probationer is required to reside under the probation order; and

(b) cause a copy thereof to be given to the probationer or sent to him by registered post or by the recorded delivery service; and an acknowledgement or certificate of delivery of a letter containing such copy order issued by the Post Office shall be sufficient evidence of the delivery of the letter on the day specified in such acknowledgement or certificate.

NOTE

[1]As amended by the Criminal Justice and Court Services Act 2000 (c. 43), s.74 and Sched. 7, para. 122. Brought into force by the Criminal Justice and Court Serivces Act 2000 (Commencement No. 4) Order 2001 (S.I. 2001 No. 919 (C. 33)), art. 2(f)(ii) (effective April 1, 2001).

Probation orders: additional requirements

229.—(1) Subject to section 230 of this Act, a probation order may require the offender to comply during the whole or any part of the probation period with such requirements as the court, having regard to the circumstances of the case, considers—

(a) conducive to securing the good conduct of the offender or for preventing a repetition by him of the offence or the commission of other offences; or

(b) where the probation order is to include such a requirement as is mentioned in subsection (4) or (6) below, conducive to securing or, as the case may be, preventing the matters mentioned in paragraph (a) above.

(2) Without prejudice to the generality of subsection (1) above, a probation order may, subject to subsection (3) below, include requirements relating to the residence of the offender.

(3) In relation to a probation order including a requirement such as is mentioned in subsection (2) above—

(a) before making the order, the court shall consider the home surroundings of the offender; and

(b) if the order requires the offender to reside in any institution or place, the name of the institution or place and the period for which he is so required to reside shall be specified in the order, and that period shall not extend beyond 12 months from the date of the requirement or beyond the date when the order expires.

(4) Without prejudice to the generality of subsection (1) above, where an offender has been convicted of an offence punishable by imprisonment and a court which is considering making a probation order—

(a) is satisfied that the offender is of or over 16 years of age and that the conditions specified in paragraphs (a) and (c) of section 238(2) of this Act for the making of a community service order have been met;

(b) has been notified by the Secretary of State that arrangements exist for persons who reside in the locality where the offender resides, or will be residing when the probation order comes into force, to perform unpaid work as a requirement of a probation order; and

(c) is satisfied that provision can be made under the arrangements mentioned in paragraph (b) above for the offender to perform unpaid work under the probation order,

it may include in the probation order, in addition to any other requirement, a requirement that the offender shall perform unpaid work for such number of hours (being in total not less than 40 nor more than 240) as may be specified in the probation order.

(5) Sections 238 (except subsections (1), (2)(b) and (d) and (4)(b)), 239(1) to (3), and 240 of this Act shall apply, subject to any necessary modifications, to a probation order including a requirement such as is mentioned in subsection (4) above as they apply to a community service order, and in the application of subsection (5) of the said section 238 for the words "subsection (1) above" there shall be substituted the words "subsection (4) of section 229 of this Act".

(6) Without prejudice to the generality of subsection (1) above, where a court is considering making a probation order it may include in the probation order, in addition to any other requirement, a requirement that the offender shall pay compensation either in a lump sum or by instalments for any personal injury, loss or damage caused (whether directly or indirectly) by the acts which constituted the offence; and the following provisions of this Act shall apply to such a requirement as if any reference in them to a compensation order included a reference to a requirement to pay compensation under this subsection—

section 249(3) to (5), (8) to (10);
section 250(2);
section 251(1) and (2)(b);
section 253.

(7) Where the court imposes a requirement to pay compensation under subsection (6) above—

(a) it shall be a condition of a probation order containing such a requirement that payment of the compensation shall be completed not more than 18 months after the making of the order or not later than two months before the end of the period of probation, whichever first occurs;

(b) the court, on the application of the offender or the officer of the local authority responsible for supervising the offender, may vary the terms of the requirement, including the amount of any instalments, in consequence of any change which may have occurred in the circumstances of the offender; and

(c) in any proceedings for breach of a probation order where the breach consists only in the failure to comply with a requirement to pay compensation, a document purporting to be a certificate signed by the clerk of the court for the time being having jurisdiction in relation to the order that the compensation or, where payment by instalments has been allowed, any instalment has not been paid shall be sufficient evidence of such breach.

Probation orders: requirement of treatment for mental condition

[1]**230.**—(1) Where the court is satisfied, on the evidence of a registered medical practitioner approved for the purposes of section 20 or 39 of the Mental Health (Scotland) Act 1984, that the mental condition of an offender is such as requires and may be susceptible to treatment but is not such as to warrant his detention in pursuance of a hospital order under Part V of that Act, or under this Act, the court may, if it makes a probation order, include a requirement that the offender shall submit, for such period, not extending beyond 12 months from the date of the requirement, as may be specified in the order, to treatment by or under the direction of a registered medical practitioner or chartered psychologist with a view to the improvement of the offender's mental condition.

(2) The treatment required by virtue of subsection (1) above shall be such one of the following kinds of treatment as may be specified in the order, that is to say—

    (a) treatment as a resident patient in a hospital within the meaning of the said Act of 1984, not being a State hospital within the meaning of the Act;

    (b) treatment as a non-resident patient at such institution or place as may be specified in the order; or

    (c) treatment by or under the direction of such registered medical practitioner or chartered psychologist as may be specified in the order,

but otherwise the nature of the treatment shall not be specified in the order.

(3) A court shall not make a probation order containing a requirement under subsection (1) above unless it is satisfied that arrangements have been made for the treatment intended to be specified in the order, and, if the offender is to be treated as a resident patient, for his reception.

(4) Where the registered medical practitioner or chartered psychologist by whom or under whose direction a probationer is receiving any of the kinds of treatment to which he is required to submit in pursuance of a probation order is of the opinion—

    (a) that the probationer requires, or that it would be more appropriate for him to receive, a different kind of treatment (whether in whole or in part) from that which he has been receiving, being treatment of a kind which subject to subsection (5) below could have been specified in the probation order; or

    (b) that the treatment (whether in whole or in part) can be more appropriately given in or at a different institution or place from that where he has been receiving treatment in pursuance of the probation order,

he may, subject to subsection (6) below, make arrangements for the probationer to be treated accordingly.

(5) Arrangements made under subsection (4) above may provide for the probationer to receive his treatment (in whole or in part) as a resident patient in an institution or place notwithstanding that it is not one which could have been specified for that purpose in the probation order.

(6) Arrangements shall not be made under subsection (4) above unless—

    (a) the probationer and any officer responsible for his supervision agree;

    (b) the treatment will be given by or under the direction of a registered medical practitioner or chartered psychologist who has agreed to accept the probationer as his patient; and

    (c) where such treatment entails the probationer's being a resident patient, he will be received as such.

(7) Where any such arrangements as are mentioned in subsection (4) above are made for the treatment of a probationer—

    (a) any officer responsible for the probationer's supervision shall notify the appropriate court of the arrangements; and

    (b) the treatment provided for by the arrangements shall be deemed to be treatment to which he is required to submit in pursuance of the probation order.

(8) Subsections (3) to (5) of section 61 of this Act shall apply for the purposes of this section as if for the reference in subsection (3) to section 58(1)(a) of this Act there were substituted a reference to subsection (1) above.

(9) Except as provided by this section, a court shall not make a probation order requiring a probationer to submit to treatment for his mental condition.

Probation orders: amendment and discharge

231.—(1) Schedule 6 to this Act shall have effect in relation to the discharge and amendment of probation orders.

(2) Where, under section 232 of this Act, a probationer is sentenced for the offence for which he was placed on probation, the probation order shall cease to have effect.

Probation orders: failure to comply with requirement

232.—(1) If, on information from—

(a) the officer supervising the probationer;

(b) the chief social work officer of the local authority whose officer is supervising the probationer; or

(c) an officer appointed by the chief social work officer to act on his behalf for the purposes of this subsection,

it appears to the court which made the probation order or to the appropriate court that the probationer has failed to comply with any requirement of the order, that court may issue a warrant for the arrest of the probationer, or may, if it thinks fit, instead of issuing such a warrant in the first instance, issue a citation requiring the probationer to appear before the court at such time as may be specified in the citation.

(2) If it is proved to the satisfaction of the court before which a probationer appears or is brought in pursuance of subsection (1) above that he has failed to comply with a requirement of the probation order, the court may—

(a) except in the case of a failure to comply with a requirement to pay compensation and without prejudice to the continuance in force of the probation order, impose a fine not exceeding level 3 on the standard scale; or

(b) sentence the offender for the offence for which the order was made; or

(c) vary any of the requirements of the probation order, so however that any extension of the probation period shall terminate not later than three years from the date of the probation order; or

(d) without prejudice to the continuance in force of the probation order, in a case where the conditions required by sections 238 to 244 of this Act are satisfied, make a community service order, and those sections shall apply to such an order as if the failure to comply with the requirement of the probation order were the offence in respect of which the order had been made.

(3) For the purposes of subsection (2) above, evidence of one witness shall be sufficient evidence.

(4) A fine imposed under this section in respect of a failure to comply with the requirements of a probation order shall be deemed for the purposes of any enactment to be a sum adjudged to be paid by or in respect of a conviction or a penalty imposed on a person summarily convicted.

(5) A probationer who is required by a probation order to submit to treatment for his mental condition shall not be deemed for the purpose of this section to have failed to comply with that requirement on the ground only that he has refused to undergo any surgical, electrical or other treatment if, in the opinion of the court, his refusal was reasonable having regard to all the circumstances.

(6) Without prejudice to section 233 of this Act, a probationer who is

convicted of an offence committed during the probation period shall not on that account be liable to be dealt with under this section for failing to comply with any requirement of the probation order.

(7) The citation of a probationer to appear before a court of summary jurisdiction in terms of subsection (1) above or section 233(1) of this Act shall be effected in like manner, *mutatis mutandis*, as the citation of an accused to a sitting or diet of the court under section 141 of this Act.

Probation orders: commission of further offence

233.—(1) If it appears to—

(a) the court which made a probation order; or, as the case may be,

(b) the appropriate court,

in this section referred to as "the court", that the probationer to whom the order relates has been convicted by a court in any part of Great Britain of an offence committed during the probation period and has been dealt with for that offence, the court may issue a warrant for the arrest of the probationer, or may, if it thinks fit, instead of issuing such a warrant in the first instance issue a citation requiring the probationer to appear before the court at such time as may be specified in the citation, and on his appearance or on his being brought before the court, the court may, if it thinks fit, deal with him under section 232(2)(b) of this Act.

(2) Where a probationer is convicted by the court of an offence committed during the probation period, the court may, if it thinks fit, deal with him under section 232(2)(b) of this Act for the offence for which the order was made as well as for the offence committed during the period of probation.

(3) Where—

(a) a court has, under section 229(4) of this Act, included in a probation order a requirement that an offender shall perform unpaid work; and

(b) the offender is convicted of an offence committed in the circumstances mentioned in subsection (4) below,

the court which sentences him for the offence shall, in determining the appropriate sentence for that offence, have regard to the fact that the offence was committed in those circumstances.

(4) The circumstances referred to in subsection (3) above are that the offence was committed—

(a) during the period that the offender was subject to a requirement to perform unpaid work or within the period of three months following the expiry of that period; and

(b) in any place where the unpaid work was being or had previously been performed.

(5) The court shall not, under subsection (3) above, have regard to the fact that the offence was committed in the circumstances mentioned in subsection (4) above unless that fact is libelled in the indictment or, as the case may be, specified in the complaint.

¹(6) The fact that the offence mentioned in subsection (3)(b) above was committed in the circumstances mentioned in subsection (4) above shall, unless challenged—

(a) in the case of proceedings on indictment, by giving notice of a preliminary objection under paragraph (b) of section 72(1) of this Act or under that paragraph as applied by section 71(2) of this Act; or

(b) in summary proceedings, by preliminary objection before his plea is recorded,

be held as admitted.

NOTE

¹Inserted by the Crime and Punishment (Scotland) Act 1997 (c. 48) s.26(1) and given effect from August 1, 1997 by the Crime and Punishment (Scotland) Act 1997 (Commencement and Transitional Provisions) Order 1997 (S.I. 1997 No. 1712) para. 3.

Probation orders: persons residing in England and Wales

234.—(1) Where the court which made a probation order to which this subsection applies is satisfied that the offender has attained the age of 16 years and resides or will reside in England and Wales, subsections (3) and (4) of section 228 of this Act shall not apply to the order, but—

    (a) the order shall contain a requirement that he be under the supervision of a probation officer appointed for or assigned to the petty sessions area in which the offender resides or will reside; and

    (b) that area shall be named in the order,

and where the order includes a requirement that the probationer performs unpaid work for a number of hours, the number specified shall not exceed one hundred.

    [2,8](2) Subsection (1) above applies to a probation order which is made under the said section 228 but does not include a requirement which would, if made, correspond to a requirement mentioned in paragraph 2 or 3 of Schedule 2 to the 2000 Act, but would, if included in a community rehabilitation order made under that Act, fail to accord with a restriction as to days of presentation, participation or attendance mentioned in paragraph 2(4)(a) or (6)(a), or as the case may be 3(4)(a), of that Schedule.

    (3) Where a probation order has been made under the said section 228 and the court in Scotland which made the order or the appropriate court is satisfied—

    (a) that the probationer has attained the age of 16 years;

    (b) that he proposes to reside, or is residing, in England and Wales; and

    [8](c) that suitable arrangements for his supervision can be made by the local probation board for the area which contains the petty sessions area in which he resides or will reside,

the power of that court to amend the order under Schedule 6 to this Act shall include power to insert the provisions required by subsection (1) above or to vary any requirement for performance of unpaid work so that such hours as remain to be worked do not exceed one hundred, and the court may so amend the order without summoning the probationer and without his consent.

    [3](4) A probation order made or amended by virtue of this section may, notwithstanding section 230(9) of this Act, include a requirement that the probationer shall submit to treatment for his mental condition, and—

    [8](a) subsections (1), (3) and (8) of the said section 230 and paragraph 5(3) of Schedule 2 to the 2000 Act (all of which regulate the making of probation orders or, as the case may be, community rehabilitation orders which include any such requirement) shall apply to the making of an order which includes any such requirement by virtue of this subsection as they apply to the making of an order which includes any such requirement by virtue of the said section 230 and paragraph 5 of the said Schedule 2 respectively; and

    (b) sub-paragraphs (5) to (7) of the said paragraph 5 (functions of supervising officer and registered medical practitioner where such a requirement has been imposed) shall apply in relation to a probationer who is undergoing treatment in England and Wales in pursuance of a requirement imposed by virtue of this subsection as they apply in relation to a probationer undergoing such treatment in pursuance of a requirement imposed by virtue of that section.

    [4,8](5) Sections 231(1) and 232(1) of this Act shall not apply to any order made or amended under this section; but subject to subsection (6) below, Schedule 3 to the 2000 Act shall apply to the order—

    (a) except in the case mentioned in paragraph (b) below, as if that order were a community rehabilitation order made under section 41 of that Act; and

(b) in the case of an order which contains a requirement such as is mentioned in section 229(4) of this Act, as if it were a community punishment and rehabilitation order made under section 51 of that Act.

[5](6) Part III of Schedule 3 to the 2000 Act shall not apply as mentioned in subsection (5) above; and sub-paragraphs (4) and (5) of paragraph 4 of that Schedule shall so apply as if for the first reference in the said sub-paragraph (4) to the Crown Court there were substituted a reference to a court in Scotland and for other references in those sub-paragraphs to the Crown Court there were substituted references to the court in Scotland.

(7) If it appears on information to a justice acting for the petty sessions area named in a probation order made or amended under this section that the person to whom the order relates has been convicted by a court in any part of Great Britain of an offence committed during the period specified in the order he may issue—

(a) a summons requiring that person to appear, at the place and time specified in the summons, before the court in Scotland which made the probation order; or

(b) if the information is in writing and on oath, a warrant for his arrest, directing that person to be brought before the last-mentioned court.

(8) If a warrant for the arrest of a probationer issued under section 233 of this Act by a court is executed in England and Wales and the probationer cannot forthwith be brought before that court, the warrant shall have effect as if it directed him to be brought before a magistrates' court for the place where he is arrested; and the magistrates' court shall commit him to custody or release him on bail (with or without sureties) until he can be brought or appear before the court in Scotland.

[1](9) The court by which a probation order is made or amended in accordance with the provisions of this section shall send three copies of the order to the clerk to the justices for the petty sessions area named in the order, together with such documents and information relating to the case as it considers likely to be of assistance to the court acting for that petty sessions area.

[6,8](10) Where a probation order which is amended under subsection (3) above is an order to which the provisions of this Act apply by virtue of paragraph 6 of Schedule 4 to the 2000 Act (which relates to community rehabilitation orders under that Act relating to persons residing in Scotland) then, notwithstanding anything in that Schedule or this section, the order shall, as from the date of the amendment, have effect in all respects as if it were an order made under section 41 of that Act in the case of a person residing in England and Wales.

[7](11) In this section "the 2000 Act" means the Powers of Criminal Courts (Sentencing) Act 2000.

NOTES

[1]Prospectively amended by the Access to Justice 1999 (c.22), s.90 and Sched. 13, para.175.

[2]As amended by the Powers of Criminal Courts (Sentencing) Act 2000 (c.6), s.165 and Sched. 9, para. 176(2)(a) and (b).

[3]As amended by the Powers of Criminal Courts (Sentencing) Act 2000 (c.6), s.165 and Sched. 9, para. 176(3)(a) and (b).

[4]As amended by the Powers of Criminal Courts (Sentencing) Act 2000 (c.6), s.165 and Sched. 9, para. 176(4)(a), (b) and (c).

[5]As amended by the Powers of Criminal Courts (Sentencing) Act 2000 (c.6), s.165 and Sched. 9, para. 176(5)(a), (b) and (c).

[6]As amended by the Powers of Criminal Courts (Sentencing) Act 2000 (c.6), s.165 and Sched. 9, para. 176(6)(a) and (b).

[7]As substituted by the Powers of Criminal Courts (Sentencing) Act 2000 (c.6), s.165 and Sched. 9, para. 176(7).

[8]As amended by the Criminal Justice and Court Services Act 2000 (c. 43), s.74 and Sched. 7, para. 123. Brought into force by the Criminal Justice and Court Services Act 2000 (Commencement No. 4) Order 2001 (S.I. 2001 No. 919 (C. 33)), art. 2(f)(ii) (effective April 1, 2001).

Non-harassment orders

[1]**234A.**—(1) Where a person is convicted of an offence involving harassment of a person ("the victim"), the prosecutor may apply to the court to make a non-harassment order against the offender requiring him to refrain from such conduct in relation to the victim as may be specified in the order for such period (which includes an indeterminate period) as may be so specified, in addition to any other disposal which may be made in relation to the offence.

(2) On an application under subsection (1) above the court may, if it is satisfied on a balance of probabilities that it is appropriate to do so in order to protect the victim from further harassment, make a non-harassment order.

(3) A non-harassment order made by a criminal court shall be taken to be a sentence for the purposes of any appeal and, for the purposes of this subsection "order" includes any variation or revocation of such an order made under subsection (6) below.

(4) Any person who is found to be in breach of a non-harassment order shall be guilty of an offence and liable—

- (a) on conviction on indictment, to imprisonment for a term not exceeding 5 years or to a fine, or to both such imprisonment and such fine; and
- (b) on summary conviction, to imprisonment for a period not exceeding 6 months or to a fine not exceeding the statutory maximum, or to both such imprisonment and such fine.

[2](5) ...

(6) The person against whom a non-harassment order is made, or the prosecutor at whose instance the order is made, may apply to the court which made the order for its revocation or variation and, in relation to any such application the court concerned may, if it is satisfied on a balance of probabilities that it is appropriate to do so, revoke the order or vary it in such manner as it thinks fit, but not so as to increase the period for which the order is to run.

(7) For the purposes of this section "harassment" shall be construed in accordance with section 8 of the Protection from Harassment Act 1997.

NOTES

[1]Inserted by the Protection from Harassment Act 1997 (c. 40), s.11.
[2]Repealed by the Crime and Punishment (Scotland) Act 1997 (c. 48), s.62(1) and Sched. 1, para. 21(30) with effect from August 1, 1997 in terms of the Crime and Punishment (Scotland) Act 1997 (Commencement and Transitional Provisions) Order (S.I. 1997 No. 1712) para. 3.

Drug treatment and testing order

[1]**234B.**—(1) This section applies where a person of 16 years of age or more is convicted of an offence, other than one for which the sentence is fixed by law, committed on or after the date on which section 89 of the Crime and Disorder Act 1998 comes into force.

(2) Subject to the provisions of this section, the court by or before which the offender is convicted may, if it is of the opinion that it is expedient to do so instead of sentencing him, make an order (a "drug treatment and testing order") which shall—

(a) have effect for a period specified in the order of not less than six months nor more than three years ("the treatment and testing period"); and

(b) include the requirements and provisions mentioned in section 234C of this Act.

(3) A court shall not make a drug treatment and testing order unless it—

(a) has been notified by the Secretary of State that arrangements for implementing such orders are available in the area of the local authority proposed to be specified in the order under section 234C(6) of this Act and the notice has not been withdrawn;

(b) has obtained a report by, and if necessary heard evidence from, an officer of the local authority in whose area the offender is resident about the offender and his circumstances; and

(c) is satisfied that—

> (i) the offender is dependent on, or has a propensity to misuse, drugs;
>
> (ii) his dependency or propensity is such as requires and is susceptible to treatment; and
>
> (iii) he is a suitable person to be subject to such an order.

(4) For the purpose of determining for the purposes of subsection (3)(c) above whether the offender has any drug in his body, the court may by order require him to provide samples of such description as it may specify.

(5) A drug treatment and testing order or an order under subsection (4) above shall not be made unless the offender expresses his willingness to comply with its requirements.

(6) The Secretary of State may by order—

(a) amend paragraph (a) of subsection (2) above by substituting a different period for the minimum or the maximum period for the time being specified in that paragraph; and

(b) make such transitional provisions as appear to him necessary or expedient in connection with any such amendment.

(7) The power to make an order under subsection (6) above shall be exercisable by statutory instrument; but no such order shall be made unless a draft of the order has been laid before and approved by resolution of each House of Parliament.

(8) A drug treatment and testing order shall be as nearly as may be in the form prescribed by Act of Adjournal.

NOTE
[1]Inserted by the Crime and Disorder Act 1998 (c. 37), s.89 (effective September 30, 1998: S.I. 1998 No. 2327).

Requirements and provisions of drug treatment and testing orders

[1]**234C.**—(1) A drug treatment and testing order shall include a requirement ("the treatment requirement") that the offender shall submit, during the whole of the treatment and testing period, to treatment by or under the direction of a specified person having the necessary qualifications or experience ("the treatment provider") with a view to the reduction or elimination of the offender's dependency on or propensity to misuse drugs.

(2) The required treatment for any particular period shall be

(a) treatment as a resident in such institution or place as may be specified in the order; or

(b) treatment as a non-resident in or at such institution or place, and at such intervals, as may be so specified;

but the nature of the treatment shall not be specified in the order except as mentioned in paragraph (a) or (b) above.

(3) A court shall not make a drug treatment and testing order unless it is satisfied that arrangements have been made for the treatment intended to be

specified in the order (including arrangements for the reception of the offender where he is required to submit to treatment as a resident).

(4) A drug treatment and testing order shall include a requirement ("the testing requirement") that, for the purpose of ascertaining whether he has any drug in his body during the treatment and testing period, the offender shall provide during that period, at such times and in such circumstances as may (subject to the provisions of the order) be determined by the treatment provider, samples of such description as may be so determined.

(5) The testing requirement shall specify for each month the minimum number of occasions on which samples are to be provided.

(6) A drug treatment and testing order shall specify the local authority in whose area the offender will reside when the order is in force and require that authority to appoint or assign an officer (a "supervising officer") for the purposes of subsections (7) and (8) below.

(7) A drug treatment and testing order shall—
(a) provide that, for the treatment and testing period, the offender shall be under the supervision of a supervising officer;
(b) require the offender to keep in touch with the supervising officer in accordance with such instructions as he may from time to time be given by that officer, and to notify him of any change of address; and
(c) provide that the results of the tests carried out on the samples provided by the offender in pursuance of the testing requirement shall be communicated to the supervising officer.

(8) Supervision by the supervising officer shall be carried out to such extent only as may be necessary for the purpose of enabling him—
(a) to report on the offender's progress to the appropriate court;
(b) to report to that court any failure by the offender to comply with the requirements of the order; and
(c) to determine whether the circumstances are such that he should apply to that court for the variation or revocation of the order.

NOTE
[1]Inserted by the Crime and Disorder Act 1998 (c. 37), s.90 (effective September 30, 1998: S.I. 1998 No. 2327).

Procedural matters relating to drug treatment and testing orders

[1]**234D.**—(1) Before making a drug treatment and testing order, a court shall explain to the offender in ordinary language—
(a) the effect of the order and of the requirements proposed to be included in it;
(b) the consequences which may follow under section 234G of this Act if he fails to comply with any of those requirements;
(c) that the court has power under section 234E of this Act to vary or revoke the order on the application of either the offender or the supervising officer; and
(d) that the order will be periodically reviewed at intervals provided for in the order.

(2) Upon making a drug treatment and testing order the court shall—
(a) give, or send by registered post or the recorded delivery service, a copy of the order to the offender;
(b) send a copy of the order to the treatment provider;
(c) send a copy of the order to the chief social work officer of the local authority specified in the order in accordance with section 234C(6) of this Act; and
(d) where it is not the appropriate court, send a copy of the order (together with such documents and information relating to the case as are considered useful) to the clerk of the appropriate court.

(3) Where a copy of a drug treatment and testing order has under

subsection (2)(a) been sent by registered post or by the recorded delivery service, an acknowledgement or certificate of delivery of a letter containing a copy order issued by the Post Office shall be sufficient evidence of the delivery of the letter on the day specified in such acknowledgement or certificate.

NOTE
[1]Inserted by the Crime and Disorder Act 1998 (c. 37), s.91 (effective September 30, 1998: S.I. 1998 No. 2327).

Amendment of drug treatment and testing order

[1]**234E.**—(1) Where a drug treatment and testing order is in force either the offender or the supervising officer may apply to the appropriate court for variation or revocation of the order.

(2) Where an application is made under subsection (1) above by the supervising officer, the court shall issue a citation requiring the offender to appear before the court.

(3) On an application made under subsection (1) above and after hearing both the offender and the supervising officer, the court may by order, if it appears to it in the interests of justice to do so—

(a) vary the order by—
    (i) amending or deleting any of its requirements or provisions;
    (ii) inserting further requirements or provisions; or
    (iii) subject to subsection (4) below, increasing or decreasing the treatment and testing period; or
(b) revoke the order.

(4) The power conferred by subsection (3)(a)(iii) above shall not be exercised so as to increase the treatment and testing period above the maximum for the time being specified in section 234B(2)(a) of this Act, or to decrease it below the minimum so specified.

(5) Where the court, on the application of the supervising officer, proposes to vary (otherwise than by deleting a requirement or provision) a drug treatment and testing order, sections 234B(5) and 234D(1) of this Act shall apply to the variation of such an order as they apply to the making of such an order.

(6) If an offender fails to appear before the court after having been cited in accordance with subsection (2) above, the court may issue a warrant for his arrest.

NOTE
[1]Inserted by the Crime and Disorder Act 1998 (c. 37), s.92 (effective September 30, 1998: S.I. 1998 No. 2327).

Periodic review of drug treatment and testing order

[1]**234F.**—(1) A drug treatment and testing order shall—
(a) provide for the order to be reviewed periodically at intervals of not less than one month;
(b) provide for each review of the order to be made, subject to subsection (5) below, at a hearing held for the purpose by the appropriate court (a "review hearing");
(c) require the offender to attend each review hearing;
(d) provide for the supervising officer to make to the court, before each review, a report in writing on the offender's progress under the order; and
(e) provide for each such report to include the test results communicated to the supervising officer under section 234C(7)(c) of this Act and the views of the treatment provider as to the treatment and testing of the offender.

(2) At a review hearing the court, after considering the supervising officer's report, may amend any requirement or provision of the order.

(3) The court—

(a) shall not amend the treatment or testing requirement unless the offender expresses his willingness to comply with the requirement as amended;

(b) shall not amend any provision of the order so as reduce the treatment and testing period below the minimum specified in section 234B(2)(a) of this Act or to increase it above the maximum so specified; and

(c) except with the consent of the offender, shall not amend any requirement or provision of the order while an appeal against the order is pending.

(4) If the offender fails to express his willingness to comply with the treatment or testing requirement as proposed to be amended by the court, the court may revoke the order.

(5) If at a review hearing the court, after considering the supervising officer's report, is of the opinion that the offender's progress under the order is sastisfactory, the court may so amend the order as to provide for each subsequent review to be made without a hearing.

(6) A review without a hearing shall take place in chambers without the parties being present.

(7) If at a review without a hearing the court, after considering the supervising officer's report, is of the opinion that the offender's progress is no longer satisfactory, the court may issue a warrant for the arrest of the offender or may, if it thinks fit, instead of issuing a warrant in the first instance, issue a citation requiring the offender to appear before that court as such time as may be specified in the citation.

(8) Where an offender fails to attend—

(a) a review hearing in accordance with a requirement contained in a drug treatment and testing order; or

(b) a court at the time specified in a citation under subsection (7) above, the court may issue a warrant for his arrest.

(9) Where an offender attends the court at a time specified by a citation issued under subsection (7) above—

(a) the court may exercise the powers conferred by this section as if the court were conducting a review hearing; and

(b) so amend the order as to provide for each subsequent review to be made at a review hearing.

NOTE
[1]Inserted by the Crime and Disorder Act 1998 (c. 37), s.92 (effective September 30, 1998: S.I. 1998 No. 2327).

Breach of drug treatment testing order

[1]**234G.**—(1) If at any time when a drug treatment and testing order is in force it appears to the appropriate court that the offender has failed to comply with any requirement of the order, the court may issue a citation requiring the offender to appear before the court at such time as may be specified in the citation or, if it appears to the court to be appropriate, it may issue a warrant for the arrest of the offender.

(2) If it is proved to the satisfaction of the appropriate court that the offender has failed without reasonable excuse to comply with any requirement of the order, the court may by order—

(a) without prejudice to the continuation in force of the order, impose a fine not exceeding level 3 on the standard scale;

(b) vary the order; or

(c) revoke the order.

(3) For the purposes of subsection (2) above, the evidence of one witness shall be sufficient evidence.

(4) A fine imposed under this section in respect of a failure to comply with the requirements of a drug treatment and testing order shall be deemed for the purposes of any enactment to be a sum adjudged to be paid by or in respect of a conviction or a penalty imposed on a person summarily convicted.

NOTE
[1]Inserted by the Crime and Disorder Act 1998 (c. 37), s.93 (effective September 30, 1998: S.I. 1998 No. 2327).

Disposal on revocation of drugs treatment and testing order

[1]**234H.**—(1) Where the court revokes a drugs treatment and testing order under section 234E(3)(b), 234F(4) or 234G(2)(c) of this Act, it may dispose of the offender in any way which would have been competent at the time when the order was made.

(2) In disposing of an offender under subsection (1) above, the court shall have regard to the time for which the order has been in operation.

(3) Where the court revokes a drug treatment and testing order as mentioned in subsection (1) above and the offender is subject to—

(a) a probation order, by virtue of section 234J of this Act; or
(b) a restriction of liberty order, by virtue of section 245D of this Act; or
(c) a restriction of liberty order and a probation order, by virtue of the said section 245D,

the court shall, before disposing of the offender under subsection (1) above—

(i) where he is subject to a probation order, discharge that order;
(ii) where he is subject to a restriction of liberty order, revoke that order; and
(iii) where he is subject to both such orders, discharge the probation order and revoke the restriction of liberty order.

NOTE
[1]Inserted by the Crime and Disorder Act 1998 (c. 37), s.93 (effective September 30, 1998: S.I. 1998 No. 2327).

Concurrent drug treatment and testing and probation orders

[1]**234J.**—(1) Notwithstanding sections 228(1) and 234B(2) of this Act, where the court considers it expedient that the offender should be subject to a drug treatment and testing order and to a probation order, it may make both such orders in respect of the offender.

(2) In deciding whether it is expedient for it to exercise the power conferred by subsection (1) above, the court shall have regard to the circumstances, including the nature of the offence and the character of the offender and to the report submitted to it under section 234B(3)(b) of this Act.

(3) Where the court makes both a drug treatment and testing order and a probation order by virtue of subsection (1) above, the clerk of the court shall send a copy of each of the orders to the following—

(a) the treatment provider within the meaning of section 234C(1);
(b) the officer of the local authority who is appointed or assigned to be the supervising officer under section 234C(6) of this Act; and
(c) if he would not otherwise receive a copy of the order, the officer of the local authority who is to supervise the probationer.

(4) Where the offender by an act or omission fails to comply with a requirement of an order made by virtue of subsection (1) above—

(a) if the failure relates to a requirement contained in a probation order and is dealt with under section 232(2)(c) of this Act, the court may, in addition, exercise the power conferred by section 234G(2)(b) of this Act in relation to the drug treatment and testing order; and

(b) if the failure relates to a requirement contained in a drug treatment and testing order and is dealt with under section 234G(2)(b) of this Act, the court may, in addition, exercise the power conferred by section 232(2)(c) of this Act in relation to the probation order.

(5) Where an offender by an act or omission fails to comply with both a requirement contained in a drug treatment and testing order and in a probation order to which he is subject by virtue of subsection (1) above, he may, without prejudice to subsection (4) above, be dealt with as respects that act or omission either under section 232(2) of this Act or under section 234G(2) of this Act but he shall not be liable to be otherwise dealt with in respect of that act or omission.

(2) Schedule 6 to this Act (Part I of which makes further provision in relation to the combination of drug treatment and testing orders with other orders and Part II of which makes provision in relation to appeals) shall have effect.

NOTE

[1]Inserted by the Crime and Disorder Act 1998 (c. 37), s.94 (effective September 30, 1998: S.I. 1998 No. 2327).

Drug treatment and testing orders: interpretation

[1]**234K.** In sections 234B to 234J of this Act—

"the appropriate court" means—

(a) where the drug treatment and testing order has been made by the High Court, that court;

(b) in any other case, the court having jurisdiction in the area of the local authority for the time being specified in the order under section 234C(6) of this Act, being a sheriff or district court according to whether the order had been made by a sheriff or district court, but in a case where an order has been made by a district court and there is no district court in that area, the sheriff court; and

"local authority" means a council constituted under section 2 of the Local Government etc. (Scotland) Act 1994 and any reference to the area of such an authority is a reference to the local government area within the meaning of that Act for which it is so constituted.

NOTE

[1]Inserted in terms of the Crime and Disorder Act 1998 (c. 37), s.95(1) (effective September 30, 1998: S.I. 1998 No. 2327).

Supervised attendance

Supervised attendance orders

235.—(1) A court may make a supervised attendance order in the circumstances specified in subsection (3) below and shall, subject to paragraph 1 of Schedule 7 to this Act, make such an order where subsection (4) below applies.

(2) A supervised attendance order is an order made by a court in respect of an offender requiring him—

(a) to attend a place of supervision for such period, being a period of not less than 10 hours and not more than—

(i) where the amount of the fine, part or instalment which the offender has failed to pay does not exceed level 1 on the standard scale, 50 hours; and

(ii) in any other case, 100 hours, as is specified in the order; and

(b) during that period, to carry out such instructions as may be given to him by the supervising officer.

(3) The circumstances referred to in subsection (1) above are where—

(a) the offender is of or over 18 years of age; and

(b) having been convicted of an offence, he has had imposed on him a fine which (or any part or instalment of which) he has failed to pay and the court, but for this section, would also have imposed on him a period of imprisonment under subsection (1) of section 219 of this Act; and

(c) the court considers a supervised attendance order more appropriate than the serving of or, as the case may be, imposition of such a period of imprisonment.

(4) This subsection applies where—

(a) the court is a court prescribed for the purposes of this subsection by order made by the Secretary of State;

(b) the offender is of or over 18 years of age and is not serving a sentence of imprisonment;

(c) having been convicted of an offence, he has had imposed on him a fine which (or any part or instalment of which) he has failed to pay and the court, but for this section, would have imposed on him a period of imprisonment under section 219(1)(b) of this Act; and

(d) the fine, or as the case may be, the part or instalment, is of an amount not exceeding level 2 on the standard scale.

(5) An order under subsection (4)(a) above shall be made by statutory instrument, which shall be subject to annulment in pursuance of a resolution of either House of Parliament.

(6) The coming into force of a supervised attendance order shall have the effect of discharging the fine referred to in subsection (3)(b) or (4)(c) above or, as the case may be, section 236(3)(a) or 237(1) of this Act.

(7) Schedule 7 to this Act has effect for the purpose of making further and qualifying provision as to supervised attendance orders.

(8) In this section—

"imprisonment" includes detention;

"place of supervision" means such place as may be determined for the purposes of a supervised attendance order by the supervising officer; and

"supervising officer", in relation to a supervised attendance order, means a person appointed or assigned under Schedule 7 to this Act by the local authority whose area includes the locality in which the offender resides or will be residing when the order comes into force.

Supervised attendance orders in place of fines for 16 and 17 year olds

236.—(1) This section applies where a person of 16 or 17 years of age is convicted of an offence by a court of summary jurisdiction and the court considers that, but for this section, the appropriate sentence is a fine.

(2) Where this section applies, the court shall determine the amount of the fine and shall consider whether the person is likely to pay a fine of that amount within 28 days.

(3) If the court considers that the person is likely to pay the fine as mentioned in subsection (2) above, it shall—

(a) impose the fine; and

(b) subject to paragraph 1 of Schedule 7 to this Act, make a supervised attendance order in default of payment of the fine within 28 days.

(4) A supervised attendance order made under subsection (3)(b) above—

(a) shall come into force on such date, not earlier than 28 days after the making of the order, as may be specified in the order, unless the person pays the fine within that period;

(b) shall, for the purposes of the said Schedule 7, be deemed to be made on the date when it comes into force.

(5) Where, before the coming into force of a supervised attendance order made under subsection (3)(b) above, the person pays part of the fine, the period specified in the order shall be reduced by the proportion which the part of the fine paid bears to the whole fine, the resulting figure being rounded up or down to the nearest 10 hours; but this subsection shall not operate to reduce the period to less than 10 hours.

(6) If the court considers that the person is not likely to pay the fine as mentioned in subsection (2) above, it shall, subject to paragraph 1 of Schedule 7 to this Act, make a supervised attendance order in respect of that person.

(7) Sections 211(3), 213, 214(1) to (7), 215, 216(1) to (6), 217 to 219, 222 and 223 of this Act shall not apply in respect of a person to whom this section applies.

(8) For the purposes of any appeal or review, a supervised attendance order made under this section is a sentence.

(9) In this section "supervised attendance order" means an order made in accordance with section 235(2), (7) and (8) of this Act.

Supervised attendance orders where court allows further time to pay fine

237.—(1) Where a court, on an application to it under section 215(1) of this Act, allows a person further time for payment of a fine or instalments thereof it may, in addition, subject to paragraph 1 of Schedule 7 to this Act, impose a supervised attendance order in default of payment of the fine or any instalment of it on the due date.

(2) A supervised attendance order made under subsection (1) above shall—

(a) if the person fails to pay the fine or any instalment of it on the due date, come into force on the day after the due date; and

(b) for the purposes of the said Schedule 7, be deemed to be made on the date when it comes into force.

(3) Where, before the coming into force of a supervised attendance order under subsection (1) above, the person pays part of the fine, the period specified in the order shall be reduced by the proportion which the part of the fine paid bears to the whole fine, the resulting figure being rounded up or down to the nearest 10 hours; but this subsection shall not operate to reduce the period to less than 10 hours.

(4) In this section "supervised attendance order" means an order made in accordance with section 235(2), (7) and (8) of this Act.

Community service by offenders

Community service orders

238.—[1](1) Subject to the provisions of this Act, where a person of or over 16 years of age is convicted of an offence punishable by imprisonment, other than an offence the sentence for which is fixed by law, the court may, instead of imposing on him a sentence of, or including, imprisonment or any other form of detention, make an order (in this Act referred to as "a community service order") requiring him to perform unpaid work for such number of hours (being in total not less than 80 nor more than 300 on conviction on indictment, and not less than 80 nor more than 240 in any other case) as may be specified in the order.

(2) A court shall not make a community service order in respect of any offender unless—

(a) the offender consents;

(b) the court has been notified by the Secretary of State that arrangements exist for persons who reside in the locality in which the offender resides, or will be residing when the order comes into force, to perform work under such an order;

(c) the court is satisfied, after considering a report by an officer of a local authority about the offender and his circumstances, and, if the court thinks it necessary, hearing that officer, that the offender is a suitable person to perform work under such an order; and

(d) the court is satisfied that provision can be made under the arrangements mentioned in paragraph (b) above for the offender to perform work under such an order.

(3) A copy of the report mentioned in subsection (2)(c) above shall be supplied to the offender or his solicitor.

(4) Before making a community service order the court shall explain to the offender in ordinary language—

(a) the purpose and effect of the order and in particular the obligations on the offender as specified in subsections (1) to (3) of section 239 of this Act;

(b) the consequences which may follow under subsections (4) to (6) of that section if he fails to comply with any of those requirements; and

(c) that the court has under section 240 of this Act the power to review the order on the application either of the offender or of an officer of the local authority in whose area the offender for the time being resides.

(5) The Secretary of State may by order direct that subsection (1) above shall be amended by substituting, for the maximum or minimum number of hours specified in that subsection as originally enacted or as subsequently amended under this subsection, such number of hours as may be specified in the order; and an order under this subsection may specify a different maximum or minimum number of hours for different classes of case.

(6) An order under subsection (5) above shall be made by statutory instrument, but no such order shall be made unless a draft of it has been laid before, and approved by a resolution of, each House of Parliament; and any such order may be varied or revoked by a subsequent order under that subsection.

(7) Nothing in subsection (1) above shall be construed as preventing a court which makes a community service in respect of any offence from—

(a) imposing any disqualification on the offender;

(b) making an order for forfeiture in respect of the offence;

(c) ordering the offender to find caution for good behaviour.

(8) A community service order shall—

(a) specify the locality in which the offender resides or will be residing when the order comes into force;

(b) require the local authority in whose area the locality specified under paragraph (a) above is situated to appoint or assign an officer (referred to in this section and sections 239 to 245 of this Act as "the local authority officer") who will discharge the functions assigned to him by those sections; and

(c) state the number of hours of work which the offender is required to perform.

(9) Where, whether on the same occasion or on separate occasions, an offender is made subject to more than one community service order, or to both a community service order and a probation order which includes a requirement that that offender shall perform any unpaid work, the court may direct that the hours of work specified in any of those orders shall be concurrent with or additional to those specified in any other of those orders, but so that at no time shall the offender have an outstanding number of hours of work to perform in excess of the maximum provided for in subsection (1) above.

(10) Upon making a community service order the court shall—

(a) give, or send by registered post or the recorded delivery service, a copy of the order to the offender;

(b) send a copy of the order to the chief social work officer of the local authority in whose area the offender resides or will be residing where the order comes into force; and

(c) where it is not the appropriate court, send a copy of the order (together with such documents and information relating to the case as are considered useful) to the clerk of the appropriate court.

(11) Where a copy of a community service order has, under subsection (10)(a) above, been sent by registered post or by the recorded delivery service, an acknowledgement or certificate of delivery of a letter containing the copy order issued by the Post Office shall be sufficient evidence of the delivery of the letter on the day specified in such acknowledgement or certificate.

NOTE

[1] Substituted by the Community Service by Offenders (Hours of Work) (Scotland) Order 1996 (S.I. 1996 No. 1938), para. 3.

Community service orders: requirements

239.—(1) An offender in respect of whom a community service order is in force shall—

(a) report to the local authority officer and notify him without delay of any change of address or in the times, if any, at which he usually works; and

(b) perform for the number of hours specified in the order such work at such times as the local authority officer may instruct.

(2) Subject to section 240(1) of this Act, the work required to be performed under a community service order shall be performed during the period of 12 months beginning with the date of the order; but, unless revoked, the order shall remain in force until the offender has worked under it for the number of hours specified in it.

(3) The instructions given by the local authority officer under this section shall, so far as practicable, be such as to avoid any conflict with the offender's religious beliefs and any interference with the times, if any, at which he normally works or attends a school or other educational establishment.

(4) If at any time while a community service order is in force in respect of any offender it appears to the appropriate court, on information from the local authority officer, that that offender has failed to comply with any of the requirements of subsections (1) to (3) above (including any failure satisfactorily to perform the work which he has been instructed to do), that court may issue a warrant for the arrest of that offender, or may, if it thinks fit, instead of issuing a warrant in the first instance issue a citation requiring that offender to appear before that court at such time as may be specified in the citation.

(5) If it is proved to the satisfaction of the court before which an offender appears or is brought in pursuance of subsection (4) above that he has failed without reasonable excuse to comply with any of the requirements of the said subsections (1) to (3), that court may—

(a) without prejudice to the continuance in force of the order, impose on him a fine not exceeding level 3 on the standard scale;

(b) revoke the order and deal with that offender in any manner in which he could have been dealt with for the original offence by the court which made the order if the order had not been made; or

(c) subject to section 238(1) of this Act, vary the number of hours specified in the order.

(6) The evidence of one witness shall, for the purposes of subsection (5) above, be sufficient evidence.

Community service orders: amendment and revocation etc.

240.—(1) Where a community service order is in force in respect of any offender and, on the application of that offender or of the local authority officer, it appears to the appropriate court that it would be in the interests of justice to do so having regard to circumstances which have arisen since the order was made, that court may—

(a) extend, in relation to the order, the period of 12 months specified in section 239(2) of this Act;

(b) subject to section 238(1) of this Act, vary the number of hours specified in the order;

(c) revoke the order; or

(d) revoke the order and deal with the offender for the original offence in any manner in which he could have been dealt with for that offence by the court which made the order if the order had not been made.

(2) If the appropriate court is satisfied that the offender proposes to change, or has changed, his residence from the locality for the time being specified under section 238(8)(a) of this Act to another locality and—

(a) that court has been notified by the Secretary of State that arrangements exist for persons who reside in that other locality to perform work under community service orders; and

(b) it appears to that court that provision can be made under those arrangements for him to perform work under the order,

that court may, and on the application of the local authority officer shall, amend the order by substituting that other locality for the locality for the time being specified in the order; and sections 238 to 245 of this Act shall apply to the order as amended.

(3) Where the court proposes to exercise its powers under subsection (1)(a), (b) or (d) above otherwise than on the application of the offender, it shall issue a citation requiring him to appear before the court and, if he fails to appear, may issue a warrant for his arrest.

Community service order: commission of offence while order in force

241.—(1) Where—

(a) a court has made a community service order in respect of an offender; and

(b) the offender is convicted of an offence committed in the circumstances mentioned in subsection (2) below,

the court which sentences him for that offence shall, in determining the appropriate sentence for that offence, have regard to the fact that the offence was committed in those circumstances.

(2) The circumstances referred to in subsection (1) above are that the offence was committed—

(a) during the period when the community service order was in force or within the period of three months following the expiry of that order; and

(b) in any place where unpaid work under the order was being or had previously been performed.

(3) The court shall not, under subsection (1) above, have regard to the fact that the offence was committed in the circumstances mentioned in subsection (2) above unless that fact is libelled in the indictment or, as the case may be, specified in the complaint.

[1](4) The fact that the offence mentioned in subsection (1)(b) above was committed in the circumstances mentioned in subsection (2) above shall, unless challenged—

(a) in the case of proceedings on indictment, by giving notice of a preliminary objection under paragraph (b) of section 72(1) of this Act or under that paragraph as applied by section 71(2) of this Act; or

(b) in summary proceedings, by preliminary objection before his plea is
      recorded,
be held as admitted.

NOTE

[1]Inserted by the Crime and Punishment (Scotland) Act 1997 (c. 48) s.26(2) with effect from
August 1, 1997 in terms of the Crime and Punishment (Scotland) Act 1997 (Commencement
and Transitional Provisions) Order 1997 (S.I. 1997 No. 1712) para. 3.

Community service orders: persons residing in England and Wales

242.—(1) Where a court is considering the making of a community service
order and it is satisfied that the offender has attained the age of 16 years and
resides, or will be residing when the order comes into force, in England or
Wales, then—

[1,4](a) section 238 of this Act shall have effect as if subsection (2) were
      amended as follows—
    (i) paragraph (b) shall be omitted;
    (ii) in paragraph (c) for the words "such an order" there shall be
substituted the words "a community punishment order"; and
    (iii) for paragraph (d) there shall be substituted the following
paragraph—
    "(d) it appears to that court that provision can be made for the
      offender to perform work under the order made under
      subsection (1) above under the arrangements which exist
      in the petty sessions area in which he resides or will be
      residing for persons to perform work under community
      punishment orders made under section 46 of the Powers
      of Criminal Courts (Sentencing) Act 2000;"; and
(b) the order shall specify that the unpaid work required to be performed
      by the order shall be performed under the arrangements mentioned in
      section 238(2)(d) of this Act as substituted by paragraph (a) above.
(2) Where a community service order has been made and—
(a) the appropriate court is satisfied that the offender has attained the age
      of 16 years and proposes to reside or is residing in England or Wales;
      and
[2,4](b) it appears to that court that provision can be made for the offender to
      perform work under the order made under the arrangements which
      exist in the petty sessions area in which he proposes to reside or is
      residing for persons to perform work under community punishment
      orders made under section 46 of the Powers of Criminal Courts
      (Sentencing) Act 2000,
it may amend the order by specifying that the unpaid work required to be
performed by the order shall be performed under the arrangements
mentioned in paragraph (b) of this subsection.
(3) A community service order made under section 238(1) as amended by
or in accordance with this section shall—
(a) specify the petty sessions area in England or Wales in which the
      offender resides or will be residing when the order or the amendment
      comes into force; and
[3,4](b) require the local probation board for that area to appoint or assign an
      officer of the board who will discharge in respect of the order the
      functions in respect of community punishment orders conferred on
      responsible officers by the Powers of Criminal Courts (Sentencing)
      Act 2000.

NOTES

[1]As amended by the Powers of Criminal Courts (Sentencing) Act 2000 (c.6), s.165 and Sched.
9, para. 177(2).

²As amended by the Powers of Criminal Courts (Sentencing) Act 2000 (c.6), s.165 and Sched. 9, para. 177(3).

³As amended by the Powers of Criminal Courts (Sentencing) Act 2000 (c.6), s.165 and Sched. 9, para. 177(4).

⁴As amended by the Criminal Justice and Court Services Act 2000 (c. 43), s.74 and Sched. 7, para. 124. Brought into force by the Criminal Justice and Court Services Act 2000 (Commencement No. 4) Order 2001 (S.I. 2001 No. 919 (C. 33)), art. 2(f)(ii) (effective April 1, 2001).

Community service orders: persons residing in Northern Ireland

243.—(1) Where a court is considering the making of a community service order and it is satisfied that the offender resides, or will be residing when the order comes into force, in Northern Ireland, then—

    (a) section 238 of this Act shall have effect as if subsection (2) were amended as follows—

        (i) paragraph (b) shall be omitted;

        (ii) for paragraph (d) there shall be substituted the following paragraph—

            "(d) it appears to the court that provision can be made by the Probation Board for Northern Ireland for him to perform work under such an order;";

    (b) the order shall specify that the unpaid work required to be performed by the order shall be performed under the provision made by the Probation Board for Northern Ireland and referred to in section 238(2)(d) of this Act as substituted by paragraph (a) above.

    (2) Where a community service order has been made and—

    (a) the appropriate court is satisfied that the offender proposes to reside or is residing in Northern Ireland; and

    (b) it appears to that court that provision can be made by the Probation Board for Northern Ireland for him to perform work under the order,

it may amend the order by specifying that the unpaid work required to be performed by the order shall be performed under the provision made by the Probation Board for Northern Ireland and referred to in paragraph (b) of this subsection.

    (3) A community service order made under section 238(1) of this Act as amended by or in accordance with this section shall—

    (a) specify the petty sessions district in Northern Ireland in which the offender resides or will be residing when the order or the amendment comes into force; and

    (b) require the Probation Board for Northern Ireland to select an officer who will discharge in respect of the order the functions in respect of community service orders conferred on the relevant officer by the Treatment of Offenders (Northern Ireland) Order 1976.

Community service orders: general provisions relating to persons living in England and Wales or Northern Ireland

244.—(1) Where a community service order is made or amended in the circumstances specified in section 242 or 243 of this Act, the court which makes or amends the order shall send three copies of it as made or amended to the home court, together with such documents and information relating to the case as it considers likely to be of assistance to that court.

    (2) In this section—

    "home court" means—

        (a) if the offender resides in England or Wales, or will be residing in England or Wales at the relevant time, the magistrates' court acting for the petty sessions area in which he resides or proposes to reside; and

    (b) if he resides in Northern Ireland, or will be residing in Northern Ireland, at the relevant time, the court of summary jurisdiction acting for the petty sessions district in which he resides or proposes to reside; and

"the relevant time" means the time when the order or the amendment to it comes into force.

[3](3) Subject to the following provisions of this section—

(a) a community service order made or amended in the circumstances specified in section 242 shall be treated as if it were a community punishment order made in England and Wales and the legislation relating to community punishment orders which has effect in England and Wales shall apply accordingly; and

(b) a community service order made or amended in the circumstances specified in section 243 shall be treated as if it were a community service order made in Northern Ireland and the legislation relating to community service orders which has effect in Northern Ireland shall apply accordingly.

[2](4) Before making or amending a community service order in those circumstances the court shall explain to the offender in ordinary language—

(a) the requirements of the legislation relating to community service orders or, as the case may be, community punishment orders which has effect in the part of the United Kingdom in which he resides or will be residing at the relevant time;

(b) the powers of the home court under that legislation, as modified by this section; and

(c) its own powers under this section,

and an explanation given in accordance with this section shall be sufficient without the addition of an explanation under section 238(4) of this Act.

[2](5) The home court may exercise in relation to the community service order any power which it could exercise in relation to a community service order or, as the case may be, a community punishment order made by a court in the part of the United Kingdom in which the home court exercises jurisdiction, by virtue of the legislation relating to such orders which has effect in that part of the United Kingdom, except—

(a) a power to vary the order by substituting for the number of hours' work specified in it any greater number than the court which made the order could have specified;

(b) a power to revoke the order; and

(c) a power to revoke the order and deal with the offender for the offence in respect of which it was made in any manner in which he could have been dealt with for that offence by the court which made the order if the order had not been made.

[2](6) If at any time while legislation relating to community service orders or, as the case may be, community punishment orders which has effect in one part of the United Kingdom applies by virtue of subsection (3) above to a community service order made in another part—

(a) it appears to the home court—

    (i) if that court is in England or Wales, on information to a justice of the peace acting for the petty sessions area for the time being specified in the order; or

    (ii) if it is in Northern Ireland, upon a complaint being made to a justice of the peace acting for the petty sessions district for the time being specified in the order,

that the offender has failed to comply with any of the requirements of the legislation applicable to the order; or

¹(b) it appears to the home court on the application of—
   (i) the offender; or
   (ii) if that court is in England and Wales, the responsible officers by the Powers of Criminal Courts (Sentencing) Act 2000; or
   (iii) if that court is in Northern Ireland, the relevant officer under the Treatment of Offenders (Northern Ireland) Order 1976,
that it would be in the interests of justice to exercise a power mentioned in subsection (5)(b) or (c) above,
the home court may require the offender to appear before the court by which the order was made.

(7) Where an offender is required by virtue of subsection (6) above to appear before the court which made a community service order, that court—

(a) may issue a warrant for his arrest; and

(b) may exercise any power which it could exercise in respect of the community service order if the offender resided in the part of the United Kingdom where the court has jurisdiction,

and any enactment relating to the exercise of such powers shall have effect accordingly.

NOTES
¹As amended by the Powers of Criminal Courts (Sentencing) Act 2000 (c.6), s.165 and Sched. 9, para. 178.
²As amended by the Criminal Justice and Court Services Act 2000 (c. 43), s.74 and Sched. 7, para. 125. Brought into force by the Criminal Justice and Court Services Act 2000 (Commencement No. 4) Order 2001 (S.I. 2001 No. 919 (C. 33)), art. 2(f)(ii) (effective April 1, 2001).
³Substituted by the Criminal Justice and Court Services Act 2000 (c. 43), s.74 and Sched. 7, para. 125. Brought into force as above.

Community service orders: rules, annual report and interpretation

245.—(1) The Secretary of State may make rules for regulating the performance of work under community service orders or probation orders which include a requirement that the offender shall perform unpaid work.

(2) Without prejudice to the generality of subsection (1) above, rules under this section may—

(a) limit the number of hours' work to be done by a person under such an order on any one day;

(b) make provision as to the reckoning of time worked under such orders;

(c) make provision for the payment of travelling and other expenses in connection with the performance of work under such orders;

(d) provide for records to be kept of the work done by any person under such an order.

(3) Rules under this section shall be made by statutory instrument subject to annulment in pursuance of a resolution of either House of Parliament.

(4) The Secretary of State shall lay before Parliament each year, or incorporate in annual reports he already makes, a report of the working of community service orders.

(5) In sections 238 to 243 of this Act, "the appropriate court" means—

(a) where the relevant community service order has been made by the High Court, the High Court;

(b) in any other case, the court having jurisdiction in the locality for the time being specified in the order under section 238(8)(a) of this Act, being a sheriff or district court according to whether the order has been made by a sheriff or a district court, but in a case where the order has been made by a district court and there is no district court in that locality, the sheriff court.

Restriction of liberty orders

[1]**245A.**—(1) Without prejudice to section 245D of this Act, where a person of 16 years of age or more is convicted of an offence (other than an offence the sentence for which is fixed by law) the court, if it is of opinion that it is the most appropriate method of disposal, may make an order under this section (in this Act referred to as a "restriction of liberty order") in respect of him; and in this section and sections 245B to 245I of this Act any reference to an "offender" is a reference to a person in respect of whom an order has been made under this subsection.

(2) A restriction of liberty order may restrict the offender's movements to such extent as the court thinks fit and, without prejudice to the generality of the foregoing, may include provision—

(a) requiring the offender to be in such place as may be specified for such period or periods in each day or week as may be specified;

(b) requiring the offender not to be in such place or places, or such class or classes of place or places, at such time or during such periods, as may be specified,

but the court may not, under paragraph (a) above, require the offender to be in any place or places for a period of periods totalling more than 12 hours in any one day.

(3) A restriction of liberty order may be made for any period up to 12 months.

(4) Before making a restriction of liberty order, the court shall explain to the offender in ordinary language—

(a) the effect of the order, including any requirements which are to be included in the order under section 245C of this Act;

(b) the consequences which may follow any failure by the offender to comply with the requirements of any order; and

(c) that the court has power under section 245E of this Act to review the order on the application either of the offender or of any person responsible for monitoring the order,

and the court shall not make the order unless the offender agrees to comply with its requirements.

(5) The clerk of the court by which a restriction of liberty order is made shall—

(a) cause a copy of the order to be sent to any person who is to be responsible for monitoring the offender's compliance with the order; and

(b) cause a copy of the order to be given to the offender or sent to him by registered post or by the recorded delivery service; and an acknowledgment or certificate of delivery of a letter containing such copy order issued by the Post Office shall be sufficient evidence of the delivery of the letter on the day specified in such acknowledgment or certificate.

(6) Before making a restriction of liberty order which will require the offender to remain in a specified place or places the court shall obtain and consider information about that place or those places, including information as to the attitude of persons likely to be affected by the enforced presence there of the offender.

(7) A restriction of liberty order shall be taken to be a sentence for the purposes of this Act and of any appeal.

[2](8) The Secretary of State may by regulations prescribe—

(a) which courts, or class or classes of courts, may make restriction of liberty orders;

(b) what method or methods of monitoring compliance with such orders may be specified in any such order by any such court; and

(c) the class or classes of offenders in respect of which restriction of liberty orders may be made,

and different provision may be made in relation to the matters mentioned in paragraphs (b) and (c) above in relation to different courts or classes of court.

²(9) Without prejudice to the generality of subsection (8) above, in relation to district courts, regulations under that subsection may make provision as respects such courts by reference to whether the court is constituted by a stipendiary magistrate or by one or more justices.

²(10) Regulations under subsection (8) above may make such transitional and consequential provisions, including provision in relation to the continuing effect of any restriction of liberty order in force when new regulations are made, as the Secretary of State considers appropriate.

²(11) A court shall not make a restriction of liberty order which requires an offender to be in or, as the case may be, not to be in, a particular place or places unless it is satisfied that his compliance with that requirement can be monitored by the means of monitoring which it intends to specify in the order.

²(12) The Secretary of State may by regulations substitute for the period of—

(a) hours for the time being mentioned in subsection (2) above; or

(b) months for the time being mentioned in subsection (3) above,

such period of hours or, as the case may be, months as may be prescribed in the regulations.

²(13) Regulations under this section shall be made by statutory instrument.

²(14) A statutory instrument containing regulations made under subsection (8) above shall be subject to annulment in pursuance of a resolution of either House of Parliament.

²(15) No regulations shall be made under subsection (12) above unless a draft of the regulations has been laid before, and approved by a resolution of, each House of Parliament.

NOTES

¹Inserted by the Crime and Punishment (Scotland) Act 1997 (c. 48), s.5 (in part) with (effective July 1, 1998: S.I. 1997 No. 2323).

²Inserted by the Crime and Punishment (Scotland) Act 1997 (c. 48), s.5 (in part) with effect from October 20, 1997 in terms of the Crime and Punishment (Scotland) Act 1997 (Commencement No. 2 and Transitional and Consequential Provisions) Order 1997 (S.I. 1997 No. 2323 (S.155)) art. 3, Sched. 1.

Monitoring of restriction of liberty orders

¹**245B.**—(1) Where the Secretary of State, in regulations made under section 245A(8) of this Act, empowers a court or a class of court to make restriction of liberty orders he shall notify the court or each of the courts concerned of the person or class or description of persons who may be designated by that court for the purpose of monitoring an offender's compliance with any such order.

(2) A court which makes a restriction of liberty order in respect of an offender shall include provision in the order for making a person notified by the Secretary of State under subsection (1) above, or a class or description of persons so notified, responsible for the monitoring of the offender's compliance with it.

(3) Where the Secretary of State changes the person or class or description

of persons notified by him under subsection (1) above, any court which has made a restriction of liberty order shall, if necessary, vary the order accordingly and shall notify the variation to the offender.

NOTE
[1]Inserted by the Crime and Punishment (Scotland) Act 1997 (c. 48), s.5 (effective July 1, 1998: S.I. 1997 No. 2323).

Remote monitoring

[1]**245C.**—(1) The Secretary of State may make such arrangements, including contractual arrangements, as he considers appropriate with such persons, whether legal or natural, as he thinks fit for the remote monitoring of the compliance of offenders with restriction of liberty orders, and different arrangements may be made in relation to different areas or different forms of remote monitoring.

(2) A court making a restriction of liberty order which is to be monitored remotely may include in the order a requirement that the offender shall, either continuously or for such periods as may be specified, wear or carry a device for the purpose of enabling the remote monitoring of his compliance with the order to be carried out.

(3) The Secretary of State shall by regulations specify devices which may be used for the purpose of remotely monitoring the compliance of an offender with the requirements of a restriction of liberty order.

(4) Regulations under this section shall be made by statutory instrument subject to annulment in pursuance of a resolution of either House of Parliament.

NOTE
[1]Inserted by the Crime and Punishment (Scotland) Act 1997 (c. 48), s.5 (effective July 1, 1998: S.I. 1997 No. 2323).

Concurrent probation and restriction of liberty orders

[1]**245D.**—(1) Notwithstanding sections 228(1) and 245A(1) of this Act, where the court—

(a) intends to make a restriction of liberty order under section 245A(1); and

(b) considers it expedient—
    (i) having regard to the circumstances, including the nature of the offence and the character of the offender; and
    (ii) having obtained a report as to the circumstances and character of the offender,
that the offender should also be subject to a probation order made under section 228(1) of this Act,
it may make both such orders in respect of the offender.

(2) Where the court makes both a restriction of liberty order and a probation order by virtue of subsection (1) above, the clerk of the court shall send a copy of each order to both—

(a) any person responsible for monitoring the offender's compliance with the restriction of liberty order; and

(b) the officer of the local authority who is to supervise the probationer.

(3) Where the offender by an act or omission fails to comply with a requirement of an order made by virtue of subsection (1) above—

(a) if the failure relates to a requirement contained in a probation order and is dealt with under section 232(2)(c) of this Act, the court may, in addition, exercise the power conferred by section 245F(2)(b) of this Act in relation to the restriction of liberty order; and

(b) if the failure relates to a requirement contained in a restriction of liberty order and is dealt with under section 245F(2)(b) of this Act, the court may, in addition, exercise the power conferred by section 232(2)(c) in relation to the probation order.

(4) Where the offender by an act or omission fails to comply with both a requirement contained in a probation order and a requirement contained in a restriction of liberty order to which he is subject by virtue of subsection (1) above, he may, without prejudice to subsection (3) above, be dealt with as respects that act or omission either under section 232(2) of this Act or under section 245F(2) of this Act but he shall not be liable to be otherwise dealt with in respect of that act or omission.

NOTE
[1]Inserted by the Crime and Punishment (Scotland) Act 1997 (c. 48), s.5 (effective July 1, 1998: S.I. 1997 No. 2323).

Variation of restriction of liberty order

245E.—(1) Where a restriction of liberty order is in force either the offender or any person responsible for monitoring his compliance with the order may apply to the court which made the order for a review of it.

(2) On an application made under subsection (1) above, and after hearing both the offender and any person responsible for monitoring his compliance with the order, the court may by order, if it appears to it to be in the interests of justice to do so—

(a) vary the order by—
    (i) amending or deleting any of its requirements;
    (ii) inserting further requirements; or
    (iii) subject to subsection (3) of section 245A of this Act, increasing the period for which the order has to run; or
(b) revoke the order.

(3) Where the court, on the application of a person other than the offender, proposes to—

(a) exercise the power conferred by paragraph (a) of subsection (2) above to vary (otherwise than by deleting a requirement) a restriction of liberty order, it shall issue a citation requiring the offender to appear before the court and section 245A(4) shall apply to the variation of such an order as it applies to the making of an order; and

(b) exercise the power conferred by subsection (2)(b) above to revoke such an order and deal with the offender under section 245G of this Act, it shall issue a citation requiring him to appear before the court.

(4) If an offender fails to appear before the court after having been cited in accordance with subsection (3) above, the court may issue a warrant for his arrest.

NOTE
[1]Inserted by the Crime and Punishment (Scotland) Act 1997 (c. 48), s.5 (effective July 1, 1998: S.I. 1997 No. 2323).

Breach of restriction of liberty order

[1]**245F.**—(1) If at any time when a restriction of liberty order is in force it appears to the court which made the order that the offender has failed to comply with any of the requirements of the order the court may issue a citation requiring the offender to appear before the court at such time as may be specified in the citation or, if it appears to the court to be appropriate, it may issue a warrant for the arrest of the offender.

(2) If it is proved to the satisfaction of the court that the offender has failed without reasonable excuse to comply with any of the requirements of the order the court may by order—

(a) without prejudice to the continuance in force of the order, impose a fine not exceeding level 3 on the standard scale;

(b) vary the restriction of liberty order; or
(c) revoke that order.

A fine imposed under this section in respect of a failure to comply with the requirements of a restriction of liberty order shall be deemed for the purposes of any enactment to be a sum adjudged to be paid by or in respect of a conviction or a penalty imposed on a person summarily convicted.

(4) Where the court varies a restriction of liberty order under subsection (2) above it may do so in any of the ways mentioned in paragraph (a) of section 245E(2) of this Act.

NOTE
[1] Inserted by the Crime and Punishment (Scotland) Act 1997 (c. 48), s.5 (effective July 1, 1998: S.I. 1997 No. 2323).

Disposal on revocation of restriction of liberty order

[1]**245G.**—(1) Where the court revokes a restriction of liberty order under section 245E(2)(b) or 245F(2) of this Act, it may dispose of the offender in any way which would have been competent at the time when the order was made, but in so doing the court shall have regard to the time for which the order has been in operation.

(2) Where the court revokes a restriction of liberty order as mentioned in subsection (1) above, and the offender is, by virtue of section 245D(1) of this Act, subject to a probation order, it shall, before disposing of the offender under subsection (1) above, discharge the probatin order.

NOTE
[1] Inserted by the Crime and Punishment (Scotland) Act 1997 (c. 48), s.5 (effective July 1, 1998: S.I. 1997 No. 2323).

Documentary evidence in proceedings under section 245F

[1]**245H.**—(1) Evidence of the presence or absence of the offender at a particular place at a particular time may, subject to the provisions of this section, be given by the production of a document or documents bearing to be—

(a) a statement automatically produced by a device specified in regulations made under section 245C of this Act, by which the offender's whereabouts were remotely monitored; and
(b) a certificate signed by a person nominated for the purpose of this paragraph by the Secretary of State that the statement relates to the whereabouts of the person subject to the order at the dates and times shown in the statement.

(2) The statement and certificate mentioned in subsection (1) above shall, when produced at a hearing, be sufficient evidence of the facts set out in them.

(3) Neither the statement nor the certificate mentioned in subsection (1) above shall be admissible in evidence unless a copy of both has been served on the offender prior to the hearing and, without prejudice to the foregoing, where it appears to the court that the offender has had insufficient notice of the statement or certificate, it may adjourn a hearing or make any order which it thinks appropriate in the circumstances.

NOTE
[1] Inserted by the Crime and Punishment (Scotland) Act 1997 (c. 48), s.5 (effective July 1, 1998: S.I. 1997 No. 2323).

Procedure on variation or revocation of restriction of liberty order

[1]**245I.** Where a court exercises any power conferred by sections 232(3A), 245E(2) or 245F(2)(b) or (c) of this Act, the clerk of the court shall forthwith

give copies of the order varying or revoking the restriction of liberty order to any person responsible for monitoring the offender's compliance with that order and that person shall give a copy of the order to the offender.".

NOTE
[1]Inserted by the Crime and Punishment (Scotland) Act 1997 (c. 48), s.5 (effective July 1, 1998: S.I. 1997 No. 2323).

Admonition and absolute discharge

Admonition and absolute discharge

246.—(1) A court may, if it appears to meet the justice of the case, dismiss with an admonition any person convicted by the court of any offence.

(2) Where a person is convicted on indictment of an offence (other than an offence the sentence for which is fixed by law), if it appears to the court, having regard to the circumstances including the nature of the offence and the character of the offender, that it is inexpedient to inflict punishment and that a probation order is not appropriate it may instead of sentencing him make an order discharging him absolutely.

(3) Where a person is charged before a court of summary jurisdiction with an offence (other than an offence the sentence for which is fixed by law) and the court is satisfied that he committed the offence, the court, if it is of the opinion, having regard to the circumstances including the nature of the offence and the character of the offender, that it is inexpedient to inflict punishment and that a probation order is not appropriate may without proceeding to conviction make an order discharging him absolutely.

Effect of probation and absolute discharge

247.—(1) Subject to the following provisions of this section, a conviction of an offence for which an order is made placing the offender on probation or discharging him absolutely shall be deemed not to be a conviction for any purpose other than the purposes of the proceedings in which the order is made and of laying it before a court as a previous conviction in subsequent proceedings for another offence.

(2) Without prejudice to subsection (1) above, the conviction of an offender who is placed on probation or discharged absolutely as aforesaid shall in any event be disregarded for the purposes of any enactment which imposes any disqualification or disability upon convicted persons, or authorises or requires the imposition of any such disqualification or disability.

(3) Subsections (1) and (2) above shall not affect any right to appeal.

(4) Where a person charged with an offence has at any time previously been discharged absolutely in respect of the commission by him of an offence it shall be competent, in the proceedings for that offence, to lay before the court the order of absolute discharge in like manner as if the order were a conviction.

(5) Where an offender is discharged absolutely by a court of summary jurisdiction, he shall have the like right of appeal against the finding that he committed the offence as if that finding were a conviction.

(6) Where an offender, being not less than 16 years of age at the time of his conviction of an offence for which he is placed on probation as mentioned in subsection (1) above, is subsequently sentenced under this Act for that offence, the provisions of that subsection shall cease to apply to the conviction.

Disqualification where vehicle used to commit offence

248.—(1) Where a person is convicted of an offence (other than one triable only summarily) and the court which passes sentence is satisfied that a motor vehicle was used for the purposes of committing or facilitating the commission of that offence, the court may order him to be disqualified for such a period as the court thinks fit from holding or obtaining a licence to drive a motor vehicle granted under Part III of the Road Traffic Act 1988.

(2) A court which makes an order under this section disqualifying a person from holding or obtaining a licence shall require him to produce any such licence held by him and its counterpart.

(3) Any reference in this section to facilitating the commission of an offence shall include a reference to the taking of any steps after it has been committed for the purpose of disposing of any property to which it relates or of avoiding apprehension or detection.

(4) In relation to licences which came into force before 1st June 1990, the reference in subsection (2) above to the counterpart of a licence shall be disregarded.

General power to disqualify offenders

[1]**248A.**—(1) Subject to subsection (2) below, the court by or before which a person is convicted of an offence may, in addition to or instead of dealing with him in any other way, order him to be disqualified from holding or obtaining a licence to drive a motor vehicle granted under Part III of the Road Traffic Act 1988 for such period as it thinks fit.

(2) Where the person is convicted of an offence for which the sentence is fixed by law, subsection (1) above shall have effect as if the words "or instead of" were omitted.

(3) Subsections (2) and (4) of section 248 of this Act shall apply for the purposes of this section as they apply for the purposes of that section.

NOTE
[1]Inserted by the Crime and Punishment (Scotland) Act 1997 (c. 48) s.15 with effect from January 1, 1998 in terms of the Crime and Punishment (Scotland) Act 1977 (Commencement No. 2 and Transitional and Consequential Provisions) Order 1997 (S.I. 1997 No. 2323) Art. 3, Sched. 1.

Power to disqualify fine defaulters

[1]**248B.**—(1) This section applies where the court has power to impose a period of imprisonment in default of payment of a fine, or any part or instalment of a fine.

(2) Where this section applies, the court may, instead of imposing such a period of imprisonment as is mentioned in subsection (1) above, order that where the offender is in default he shall be disqualfied from holding a licence to drive a motor vehicle granted under Part III of the Road Traffic Act 1988 for such period not exceeding twelve months as the court thinks fit.

(3) Where an order has been made under subsection (2) above in default of payment of any fine, or any part or instalment of a fine—

(a) on payment of the fine to any person authorised to receive it, the order shall cease to have effect; and

(b) on payment of any part of that fine to any such person, the period of disqualification to which the order relates shall be reduced (or, as the case may be, further reduced) by a number of days bearing as nearly as possible the same proportion to such period as the sum so paid bears to the amount of the fine outstanding at the commencement of that period.

(4) Subsections (2) and (4) of section 248 of this Act shall apply for the purposes of this section as they apply for the purposes of that section.

(5) Section 19 of the Road Traffic Offenders Act 1988 (proof of disqualification in Scottish proceedings) shall apply to an order under subsection (2) above as it applies to a conviction or extract conviction.

(6) The Secretary of State may by order made by statutory instrument vary the period specified in subsection (2) above; but not such order shall be made unless a draft of the order has been laid before, and approved by a resolution of, each House of Parliament.

NOTE
[1]Inserted by the Crime and Punishment (Scotland) Act 1997 (c. 48) s.15 with effect from January 1, 1998 in terms of the Crime and Punishment (Scotland) Act 1997 (Commencement No. 2 and Transitional and Consequential Provisions) Order 1997 (S.I. 1997 No. 2323) Art. 3, Sched. 1.

Application of sections 248A and 248B

[1]**248C.**—(1) The Secretary of State may by order prescribe which courts, or class or classes of courts, may make orders under section 248A or 248B of this Act and, without prejudice to that generality, in relation to district courts an order under this subsection may make provision as respects such courts by reference to whether the court is constituted by a stipendiary magistrate or by one or more justices.

(2) An order made under subsection (1) above shall be made by statutory instrument and any such instrument shall be subject to annulment in pursuance of a resolution of either House of Parliament.

(3) Where an order has been made under subsection (1) above, section 248(1) of this Act shall not apply as respects any court, or class or classes of court prescribed by the order.

NOTE
[1]Inserted by the Crime and Punishment (Scotland) Act 1997 (c. 48) s.15 with effect from October 20, 1997 in terms of the Crime and Punishment (Scotland) Act 1997 (Commencement No. 2 and Transitional and Consequential Provisions) Order 1997 (S.I. 1997 No. 2323) Art. 3, Sched. 1.

Compensation

Compensation order against convicted person

249.—(1) Subject to subsections (2) and (4) below, where a person is convicted of an offence the court, instead of or in addition to dealing with him in any other way, may make an order (in this Part of this Act referred to as "a compensation order") requiring him to pay compensation for any personal injury, loss or damage caused, whether directly or indirectly, by the acts which constituted the offence.

(2) It shall not be competent for a court to make a compensation order—
(a) where, under section 246(2) of this Act, it makes an order discharging him absolutely;
(b) where, under section 228 of this Act, it makes a probation order; or
(c) at the same time as, under section 202 of this Act, it defers sentence.

(3) Where, in the case of an offence involving dishonest appropriation, or the unlawful taking and using of property or a contravention of section 178(1) of the Road Traffic Act 1988 (taking motor vehicle without authority etc.) the property is recovered, but has been damaged while out of the owner's possession, that damage, however and by whomsoever it was in fact

caused, shall be treated for the purposes of subsection (1) above as having been caused by the acts which constituted the offence.

(4) No compensation order shall be made in respect of—

(a) loss suffered in consequence of the death of any person; or

(b) injury, loss or damage due to an accident arising out of the presence of a motor vehicle on a road, except such damage as is treated, by virtue of subsection (3) above, as having been caused by the convicted person's acts.

(5) In determining whether to make a compensation order against any person, and in determining the amount to be paid by any person under such order, the court shall take into consideration his means so far as known to the court.

(6) For the purposes of subsection (5) above, in assessing the means of a person who is serving, or is to serve, a period of imprisonment or detention, no account shall be taken of earnings contingent upon his obtaining employment after release.

(7) In solemn proceedings there shall be no limit on the amount which may be awarded under a compensation order.

(8) In summary proceedings—

(a) a sheriff, or a stipendiary magistrate appointed under section 5 of the District Courts (Scotland) Act 1975, shall have power to make a compensation order awarding in respect of each offence an amount not exceeding the prescribed sum;

(b) a judge of a district court (other than such stipendiary magistrate) shall have power to make a compensation order awarding in respect of each offence an amount not exceeding level 4 on the standard scale.

(9) Payment of any amount under a compensation order shall be made to the clerk of the court who shall account for the amount to the person entitled thereto.

(10) Only the court shall have power to enforce a compensation order.

Compensation orders: supplementary provisions

250.—(1) Where a court considers that in respect of an offence it would be appropriate to impose a fine and to make a compensation order but the convicted person has insufficient means to pay both an appropriate fine and an appropriate amount in compensation the court should prefer a compensation order.

(2) Where a convicted person has both been fined and had a compensation order made against him in respect of the same offence or different offences in the same proceedings, a payment by the convicted person shall first be applied in satisfaction of the compensation order.

(3) For the purposes of any appeal or review, a compensation order is a sentence.

(4) Where a compensation order has been made against a person, a payment made to the court in respect of the order shall be retained until the determination of any appeal in relation to the order.

Review of compensation order

251.—(1) Without prejudice to the power contained in section 213 of this Act, (as applied by section 252 of this Act), at any time before a compensation order has been complied with or fully complied with, the court, on the application of the person against whom the compensation order was made, may discharge the compensation order or reduce the amount that remains to be paid if it appears to the court that—

(a) the injury, loss or damage in respect of which the compensation order was made has been held in civil proceedings to be less than it was taken to be for the purposes of the compensation order; or

(b) that property the loss of which is reflected in the compensation order has been recovered.

(2) In subsection (1) above "the court" means—

(a) in a case where, as respects the compensation order, a transfer of fine order under section 222 of this Act (as applied by the said section 252) is effective and the court by which the compensation order is enforceable is in terms of the transfer of fine order a court of summary jurisdiction in Scotland, that court; or

(b) in any other case, the court which made the compensation order or, where that court was the High Court, by which the order was first enforceable.

Enforcement of compensation orders: application of provisions relating to fines

252.—(1) The provisions of this Act specified in subsection (2) below shall, subject to any necessary modifications and to the qualifications mentioned in that subsection, apply in relation to compensation orders as they apply in relation to fines; and section 91 of the Magistrates' Courts Act 1980 and article 96 of the Magistrates' Courts (Northern Ireland) Order 1981 shall be construed accordingly.

(2) The provisions mentioned in subsection (1) above are—

section 211(3), (4) and (7) to (9) (enforcement of fines);

section 212 (fines in summary proceedings);

section 213 (power to remit fines), with the omission of the words "or (4)" in subsection (2) of that section;

section 214 (time for payment) with the omission of—
  (a) the words from "unless" to "its decision" in subsection (4); and
  (b) subsection (5);

section 215 (further time for payment);

section 216 (reasons for default);

section 217 (supervision pending payment of fine);

section 218 (supplementary provisions), except that subsection (1) of that section shall not apply in relation to compensation orders made in solemn proceedings;

subject to subsection (3) below, section 219(1)(b), (2), (3), (5), (6) and (8) (maximum period of imprisonment for non-payment of fine);

section 220 (payment of fine in part by prisoner);

section 221 (recovery by civil diligence);

section 222 (transfer of fine orders);

section 223 (action of clerk of court on transfer of fine order);[1]

section 224 (discharge from imprisonment to be specified)[1]; and

[2]section 248B (driving disqualification for fine defaulters) so far as it relates to the power conferred by section 219(1)(b).

(3) In the application of the provisions of section 219 of this Act mentioned in subsection (2) above for the purposes of subsection (1) above—

(a) a court may impose imprisonment in respect of a fine and decline to impose imprisonment in respect of a compensation order but not vice versa; and

(b) where a court imposes imprisonment both in respect of a fine and of a compensation order the amounts in respect of which imprisonment is imposed shall, for the purposes of subsection (2) of the said section 219, be aggregated.

NOTES

[1]Amended by the Crime and Punishment (Scotland) Act 1997 (c. 48) s.15(2) with effect from January 1, 1998 in terms of the Crime and Punishment (Scotland) Act 1997 (Commencement

No. 2 and Transitional and Consequential Provisions) Order 1997 (S.I. 1997 No. 2323) art. 4 and Sched. 2.

²Inserted by the above provisions.

Effect of compensation order on subsequent award of damages in civil proceedings

253.—(1) This section shall have effect where a compensation order or a service compensation order or award has been made in favour of any person in respect of any injury, loss or damage and a claim by him in civil proceedings for damages in respect thereof subsequently falls to be determined.

(2) The damages in the civil proceedings shall be assessed without regard to the order or award; but where the whole or part of the amount awarded by the order or award has been paid, the damages awarded in the civil proceedings shall be restricted to the amount (if any) by which, as so assessed, they exceed the amount paid under the order or award.

(3) Where the whole or part of the amount awarded by the order or award remains unpaid and damages are awarded in a judgment in the civil proceedings, then, unless the person against whom the order or award was made has ceased to be liable to pay the amount unpaid (whether in consequence of an appeal, or of his imprisonment for default or otherwise), the court shall direct that the judgment—

    (a) if it is for an amount not exceeding the amount unpaid under the order or award, shall not be enforced; or

    (b) if it is for an amount exceeding the amount unpaid under the order or award, shall not be enforced except to the extent that it exceeds the amount unpaid,

without the leave of the court.

(4) In this section a "service compensation order or award" means—

    (a) an order requiring the payment of compensation under paragraph 11 of—

        (i) Schedule 5A to the Army Act 1955;

        (ii) Schedule 5A to the Air Force Act 1955; or

        (iii) Schedule 4A to the Naval Discipline Act 1957; or

    (b) an award of stoppages payable by way of compensation under any of those Acts.

Forfeiture

Search warrant for forfeited articles

254. Where a court has made an order for the forfeiture of an article, the court or any justice may, if satisfied on information on oath—

    (a) that there is reasonable cause to believe that the article is to be found in any place or premises; and

    (b) that admission to the place or premises has been refused or that a refusal of such admission is apprehended,

issue a warrant of search which may be executed according to law.

PART XII

EVIDENCE

Special capacity

Special capacity

255. Where an offence is alleged to be committed in any special capacity, as by the holder of a licence, master of a vessel, occupier of a house, or the like, the fact that the accused possesses the qualification necessary to the commission of the offence shall, unless challenged—

    (a) in the case of proceedings on indictment, by giving notice of a preliminary objection under paragraph (b) of section 72(1) of this Act or under that paragraph as applied by section 71(2) of this Act; or

    (b) in summary proceedings, by preliminary objection before his plea is recorded,

be held as admitted.

Proof of age

[1]**255A.** Where the age of any person is specified in an indictment or complaint, it shall, unless challenged—

    (a) in the case of proceedings on indictment by giving notice of a preliminary objection under paragraph (b) of section 72(1) of this Act or under that paragraph as applied by section 71(2) of this Act; or

    (b) in summary proceedings—

        (i) by preliminary objection before the plea of the accused is recorded; or

        (ii) by objection at such later time as the court may in special circumstances allow,

be held as admitted.

NOTE

[1]Inserted by the Crime and Punishment (Scotland) Act 1997 (c. 48) s.27 with effect from August 1, 1997 by the Crime and Punishment (Scotland) Act 1997 (Commencement and Transitional Provisions) Order 1997 (S.I. 1997 No. 1712) para. 3.

Agreed evidence

Agreements and admissions as to evidence

256.—(1) In any trial it shall not be necessary for the accused or for the prosecutor—

    (a) to prove any fact which is admitted by the other; or

    (b) to prove any document, the terms and application of which are not in dispute between them,

and, without prejudice to paragraph 1 of Schedule 8 to this Act, copies of any documents may, by agreement of the parties, be accepted as equivalent to the originals.

(2) For the purposes of subsection (1) above, any admission or agreement shall be made by lodging with the clerk of court a minute in that behalf signed—

    (a) in the case of an admission, by the party making the admission or, if that party is the accused and he is legally represented, by his counsel or solicitor; and

    (b) in the case of an agreement, by the prosecutor and the accused or, if he is legally represented, his counsel or solicitor.

(3) Where a minute has been signed and lodged as aforesaid, any facts and documents admitted or agreed thereby shall be deemed to have been duly proved.

Duty to seek agreement of evidence

257.—(1) Subject to subsection (2) below, the prosecutor and the accused (or each of the accused if more than one) shall each identify any facts which are facts—

    (a) which he would, apart from this section, be seeking to prove;

    (b) which he considers unlikely to be disputed by the other party (or by any of the other parties); and

(c) in proof of which he does not wish to lead oral evidence,
and shall, without prejudice to section 258 of this Act, take all reasonable steps to secure the agreement of the other party (or each of the other parties) to them; and the other party (or each of the other parties) shall take all reasonable steps to reach such agreement.

(2) Subsection (1) above shall not apply in relation to proceedings as respects which the accused (or any of the accused if more than one) is not legally represented.

(3) The duty under subsection (1) above applies—

(a) in relation to proceedings on indictment, from the date of service of the indictment until the swearing of the jury or, where intimation is given under section 76 of this Act, the date of that intimation; and

(b) in relation to summary proceedings, from the date on which the accused pleads not guilty until the swearing of the first witness or, where the accused tenders a plea of guilty at any time before the first witness is sworn, the date when he does so.

Uncontroversial evidence

258.—(1) This section applies where, in any criminal proceedings, a party (in this section referred to as "the first party") considers that facts which that party would otherwise be seeking to prove are unlikely to be disputed by the other parties to the proceedings.

(2) Where this section applies, the first party may prepare and sign a statement—

(a) specifying the facts concerned; or

(b) referring to such facts as set out in a document annexed to the statement,

and shall, not less than 14 days before the trial diet, serve a copy of the statement and any such document on every other party.

(3) Unless any other party serves on the first party, not more than seven days after the date of service of the copy on him under subsection (2) above or by such later time as the court may in special circumstances allow, a notice that he challenges any fact specified or referred to in the statement, the facts so specified or referred to shall be deemed to have been conclusively proved.

(4) Where a notice is served under subsection (3) above, the facts specified or referred to in the statement shall be deemed to have been conclusively proved only in so far as unchallenged in the notice.

(5) Subsections (3) and (4) above shall not preclude a party from leading evidence of circumstances relevant to, or other evidence in explanation of, any fact specified or referred to in the statement.

(6) Notwithstanding subsections (3) and 94) above, the court—

(a) may, on the application of any party, where it is satisfied that there are special circumstances; and

(b) shall, on the joint application of all the parties,

direct that the presumptions in those subsections shall not apply in relation to such fact specified or referred to in the statement as is specified in the direction.

(7) An application under subsection (6) above may be made at any time after the commencement of the trial and before the commencement of the prosecutor's address to the court on the evidence.

(8) Where the court makes a direction under subsection (6) above it shall, unless all the parties otherwise agree, adjourn the trial and may, without prejudice to section 268 of this Act, permit any party to lead evidence as to any such fact as is specified in the direction, notwithstanding that a witness or production concerned is not included in any list lodged by the parties and that the notice required by sections 67(5) and 78(4) of this Act has not been given.

opy of a statement or a notice required, under this section, to be
any party shall be served in such manner as may be prescribed by
ljournal; and a written execution purporting to be signed by the
person who served such copy or notice together with, where appropriate, the
relevant post office receipt shall be sufficient evidence of such service.

Exceptions to the rule that hearsay evidence is inadmissible

259.—(1) Subject to the following provisions of this section, evidence of a
statement made by a person otherwise than while giving oral evidence in
court in criminal proceedings shall be admissible in those proceedings as
evidence of any matter contained in the statement where the judge is
satisfied—

(a) that the person who made the statement will not give evidence in the
proceedings of such matter for any of the reasons mentioned in
subsection (2) below;

(b) that evidence of the matter would be admissible in the proceedings if
that person gave direct oral evidence of it;

(c) that the person who made the statement would have been, at the time
the statement was made, a competent witness in such proceedings;
and

(d) that there is evidence which would entitle a jury properly directed, or
in summary proceedings would entitle the judge, to find that the
statement was made and that either—

(i) it is contained in a document; or

(ii) a person who gave oral evidence in the proceedings as to the
statement has direct personal knowledge of the making of the
statement.

(2) The reasons referred to in paragraph (a) of subsection (1) above are
that the person who made the statement—

(a) is dead or is, by reason of his bodily or mental condition, unfit or
unable to give evidence in any competent manner;

(b) is named and otherwise sufficiently identified, but is outwith the
United Kingdom and it is not reasonably practicable to secure his
attendance at the trial or to obtain his evidence in any other
competent manner;

(c) is named and otherwise sufficiently identified, but cannot be found
and all reasonable steps which, in the circumstances, could have been
taken to find him have been so taken;

(d) having been authorised to do so by virtue of a ruling of the court in the
proceedings that he is entitled to refuse to give evidence in connection
with the subject matter of the statement on the grounds that such
evidence might incriminate him, refuses to give such evidence; or

(e) is called as a witness and either—

(i) refuses to take the oath or affirmation; or

(ii) having been sworn as a witness and directed by the judge to
give evidence in connection with the subject matter of the
statement refuses to do so,

and in the application of this paragraph to a child, the reference to a
witness refusing to take the oath or affirmation or, as the case may be,
to having been sworn shall be construed as a reference to a child who
has refused to accept an admonition to tell the truth or, having been so
admonished, refuses to give evidence as mentioned above.

(3) Evidence of a statement shall not be admissible by virtue of subsection
(1) above where the judge is satisfied that the occurrence of any of the
circumstances mentioned in paragraphs (a) to (e) of subsection (2) above, by
virtue of which the statement would otherwise be admissible, is caused by—

(a) the person in support of whose case the evidence would be given; or

(b) any other person acting on his behalf,
for the purpose of securing that the person who made the statement does not give evidence for the purposes of the proceedings either at all or in connection with the subject matter of the statement.

(4) Where in any proceedings evidence of a statement made by any person is admitted by reference to any of the reasons mentioned in paragraphs (a) to (c) and (e)(i) of subsection (2) above—

 (a) any evidence which, if that person had given evidence in connection with the subject matter of the statement, would have been admissible as relevant to his credibility as a witness shall be admissible for that purpose in those proceedings;

 (b) evidence may be given of any matter which, if that person had given evidence in connection with the subject matter of the statement, could have been put to him in cross-examination as relevant to his credibility as a witness but of which evidence could not have been adduced by the cross-examining party; and

 (c) evidence tending to prove that that person, whether before or after making the statement, made in whatever manner some other statement which is inconsistent with it shall be admissible for the purpose of showing that he has contradicted himself.

(5) Subject to subsection (6) below, where a party intends to apply to have evidence of a statement admitted by virtue of subsection (1) above he shall, before the trial diet, give notice in writing of—

 (a) that fact;

 (b) the witnesses and productions to be adduced in connection with such evidence; and

 (c) such other matters as may be prescribed by Act of Adjournal,

to every other party to the proceedings and, for the purposes of this subsection, such evidence may be led notwithstanding that a witness or production concerned is not included in any list lodged by the parties and that the notice required by sections 67(5) and 78(4) of this Act has not been given.

(6) A party shall not be required to give notice as mentioned in subsection (5) above where—

 (a) the grounds for seeking to have evidence of a statement admitted are as mentioned in paragraph (d) or (e) of subsection (2) above; or

 (b) he satisfies the judge that there was good reason for not giving such notice.

(7) If no other party to the proceedings objects to the admission of evidence of a statement by virtue of subsection (1) above, the evidence shall be admitted without the judge requiring to be satisfied as mentioned in that subsection.

(8) For the purposes of the determination of any matter upon which the judge is required to be satisfied under subsection (1) above—

 (a) except to the extent that any other party to the proceedings challenges them and insists in such challenge, it shall be presumed that the circumstances are as stated by the party seeking to introduce evidence of the statement; and

 (b) where such a challenge is insisted in, the judge shall determine the matter on the balance of probabilities, and he may draw any reasonable inference—

  (i) from the circumstances in which the statement was made or otherwise came into being; or

  (ii) from any other circumstances, including, where the statement is contained in a document, the form and contents of the document.

(9) Where evidence of a statement has been admitted by virtue of subsection (1) above on the application of one party to the proceedings,

without prejudice to anything in any enactment or rule of law, the judge may permit any party to lead additional evidence of such description as the judge may specify, notwithstanding that a witness or production concerned is not included in any list lodged by the parties and that the notice required by sections 67(5) and 78(4) of this Act has not been given.

(10) Any reference in subsections (5), (6) and (9) above to evidence shall include a reference to evidence led in connection with any determination required to be made for the purposes of subsection (1) above.

Admissibility of prior statements of witnesses

260.—(1) Subject to the following provisions of this section, where a witness gives evidence in criminal proceedings, any prior statement made by the witness shall be admissible as evidence of any matter stated in it of which direct oral evidence by him would be admissible if given in the course of those proceedings.

(2) A prior statement shall not be admissible under this section unless—

(a) the statement is contained in a document;

(b) the witness, in the course of giving evidence, indicates that the statement was made by him and that he adopts it as his evidence; and

(c) at the time the statement was made, the person who made it would have been a competent witness in the proceedings.

(3) For the purposes of this section, any reference to a prior statement is a reference to a prior statement which, but for the provisions of this section, would not be admissible as evidence of any matter stated in it.

(4) Subsections (2) and (3) above do not apply to a prior statement—

(a) contained in a precognition on oath; or

(b) made in other proceedings, whether criminal or civil and whether taking place in the United Kingdom or elsewhere,

and, for the purposes of this section, any such statement shall not be admissible unless it is sufficiently authenticated.

Statements by accused

261.—(1) Subject to the following provisions of this section, nothing in sections 259 and 260 of this Act shall apply to a statement made by the accused.

(2) Evidence of a statement made by an accused shall be admissible by virtue of the said section 259 at the instance of another accused in the same proceedings as evidence in relation to that other accused.

(3) For the purposes of subsection (2) above, the first mentioned accused shall be deemed—

(a) where he does not give evidence in the proceedings, to be a witness refusing to give evidence in connection with the subject matter of the statement as mentioned in paragraph (e) of subsection (2) of the said section 259; and

(b) to have been, at the time the statement was made, a competent witness in the proceedings.

(4) Evidence of a statement shall not be admissible as mentioned in subsection (2) above unless the accused at whose instance it is sought to be admitted has given notice of his intention to do so as mentioned in subsection (5) of the said section 259; but subsection (6) of that section shall not apply in the case of notice required to be given by virtue of this subsection.

Construction of sections 259 to 261

262.—(1) For the purposes of sections 259 to 261 of this Act, a "statement" includes—

(a) any representation, however made or expressed, of fact or opinion; and

(b) any part of a statement,

but does not include a statement in a precognition other than a precognition on oath.

(2) For the purposes of the said sections 259 to 261 a statement is contained in a document where the person who makes it—

(a) makes the statement in the document personally;

(b) makes a statement which is, with or without his knowledge, embodied in a document by whatever means or by any person who has direct personal knowledge of the making of the statement; or

(c) approves a document as embodying the statement.

(3) In the said sections 259 to 261—

"criminal proceedings" include any hearing by the sheriff of an application made under Chapter 3 of Part II of the Children (Scotland) Act 1995 for a finding as to whether grounds for the referral of a child's case to a children's hearing are established, in so far as the application relates to the commission of an offence by the child, or for a review of such a finding;

"document" includes, in addition to a document in writing—

(a) any map, plan, graph or drawing;

(b) any photograph;

(c) any disc, tape, sound track or other device in which sounds or other data (not being visual images) are recorded so as to be capable (with or without the aid of some other equipment) of being reproduced therefrom; and

(d) any film, negative, tape, disc or other device in which one or more visual images are recorded so as to be capable (as aforesaid) of being reproduced therefrom;

"film" includes a microfilm;

"made" includes allegedly made.

(4) Nothing in the said sections 259 to 261 shall prejudice the admissibility of a statement made by a person other than in the course of giving oral evidence in court which is admissible otherwise than by virtue of those sections.

Witnesses

Examination of witnesses

263.—(1) In any trial, it shall be competent for the party against whom a witness is produced and sworn *in causa* to examine such witness both in cross and *in causa*.

(2) The judge may, on the motion of either party, on cause shown order that the examination of a witness for that party ("the first witness") shall be interrupted to permit the examination of another witness for that party.

(3) Where the judge makes an order under subsection (2) above he shall, after the examination of the other witness, permit the recall of the first witness.

(4) In a trial, a witness may be examined as to whether he has on any specified occasion made a statement on any matter pertinent to the issue at the trial different from the evidence given by him in the trial; and evidence may be led in the trial to prove that the witness made the different statement on the occasion specified.

(5) In any trial, on the motion of either party, the presiding judge may permit a witness who has been examined to be recalled.

Spouse of accused a competent witness

264.—(1) The spouse of an accused may be called as a witness—

(a) by the accused;

(b) by a co-accused or by the prosecutor without the consent of the accused.

(2) Nothing in this section shall—

(a) make the spouse of an accused a compellable witness for a co-accused or for the prosecutor in a case where such spouse would not be so compellable at common law;

(b) compel a spouse to disclose any communication made between the spouses during the marriage.

(3) The failure of the spouse of an accused to give evidence shall not be commented on by the defence or the prosecutor.

(4) The spouse of a person charged with bigamy may be called as a witness either for the prosecution or the defence and without the consent of the person charged.

Witnesses not excluded for conviction, interest, relationship, etc.

265.—(1) Every person adduced as a witness who is not otherwise by law disqualified from giving evidence, shall be admissible as a witness, and no objection to the admissibility of a witness shall be competent on the ground of—

(a) conviction of or punishment for an offence;

(b) interest;

(c) agency or partial counsel;

(d) the absence of due citation to attend; or

(e) his having been precognosced subsequently to the date of citation.

(2) Where any person who is or has been an agent of the accused is adduced and examined as a witness for the accused, it shall not be competent for the accused to object, on the ground of confidentiality, to any question proposed to be put to such witness on matter pertinent to the issue of the guilt of the accused.

(3) No objection to the admissibility of a witness shall be competent on the ground that he or she is the father, mother, son, daughter, brother or sister, by consanguinity or affinity, or uncle, aunt, nephew or niece, by consanguinity of any party adducing the witness in any trial.

(4) It shall not be competent for any witness to decline to be examined and give evidence on the ground of any relationship mentioned in subsection (3) above.

Accused as witness

266.—(1) Subject to subsections (2) to (8) below, the accused shall be a competent witness for the defence at every stage of the case, whether the accused is on trial alone or along with a co-accused.

(2) The accused shall not be called as a witness in pursuance of this section except upon his own application or in accordance with subsection (9) or (10) below.

(3) An accused who gives evidence on his own behalf in pursuance of this section may be asked any question in cross-examination notwithstanding that it would tend to incriminate him as to the offence charged.

(4) An accused who gives evidence on his own behalf in pursuance of this section shall not be asked, and if asked shall not be required to answer, any question tending to show that he has committed, or been convicted of, or

been charged with, any offence other than that with which he is then charged, or is of bad character, unless—

(a) the proof that he has committed or been convicted of such other offence is admissible evidence to show that he is guilty of the offence with which he is then charged; or

(b) the accused or his counsel or solicitor has asked questions of the witnesses for the prosecution with a view to establishing the accused's good character or impugning the character of the complainer, or the accused has given evidence of his own good character, or the nature or conduct of the defence is such as to involve imputations on the character of the prosecutor or of the witnesses for the prosecution or of the complainer; or

(c) the accused has given evidence against any other person charged in the same proceedings.

(5) In a case to which paragraph (b) of subsection (4) above applies, the prosecutor shall be entitled to ask the accused a question of a kind specified in that subsection only if the court, on the application of the prosecutor, permits him to do so.

(6) An application under subsection (5) above in proceedings on indictment shall be made in the course of the trial but in the absence of the jury.

(7) In subsection (4) above, references to the complainer include references to a victim who is deceased.

(8) Every person called as a witness in pursuance of this section shall, unless otherwise ordered by the court, give his evidence from the witness box or other place from which the other witnesses give their evidence.

(9) The accused may—

(a) with the consent of a co-accused, call that other accused as a witness on the accused's behalf; or

(b) ask a co-accused any question in cross-examination if that co-accused gives evidence,

but he may not do both in relation to the same co-accused.

(10) The prosecutor or the accused may call as a witness a co-accused who has pleaded guilty to or been acquitted of all charges against him which remain before the court (whether or not, in a case where the co-accused has pleaded guilty to any charge, he has been sentenced) or in respect of whom the diet has been deserted; and the party calling such co-accused as a witness shall not require to give notice thereof, but the court may grant any other party such adjournment or postponement of the trial as may seem just.

(11) Where, in any trial, the accused is to be called as a witness he shall be so called as the first witness for the defence unless the court, on cause shown, otherwise directs.

Witnesses in court during trial

267.—(1) The court may, on an application by any party to the proceedings, permit a witness to be in court during the proceedings or any part of the proceedings before he has given evidence if it appears to the court that the presence of the witness would not be contrary to the interests of justice.

(2) Without prejudice to subsection (1) above, where a witness has, without the permission of the court and without the consent of the parties to the proceedings, been present in court during the proceedings, the court may, in its discretion, admit the witness, where it appears to the court that the presence of the witness was not the result of culpable negligence or criminal intent, and that the witness has not been unduly instructed or

influenced by what took place during his presence, or that injustice will not be done by his examination.

Additional evidence, etc.

Additional evidence

268.—(1) Subject to subsection (2) below, the judge may, on a motion of the prosecutor or the accused made—
  (a) in proceedings on indictment, at any time before the commencement of the speeches to the jury;
  (b) in summary proceedings, at any time before the prosecutor proceeds to address the judge on the evidence,
permit him to lead additional evidence.

(2) Permission shall only be granted under subsection (1) above where the judge—
  (a) considers that the additional evidence is *prima facie* material; and
  (b) accepts that at the commencement of the trial either—
      (i) the additional evidence was not available and could not reasonably have been made available; or
      (ii) the materiality of such additional evidence could not reasonably have been foreseen by the party.

(3) The judge may permit the additional evidence to be led notwithstanding that—
  (a) in proceedings on indictment, a witness or production concerned is not included in any list lodged by the parties and that the notice required by sections 67(5) and 78(4) of this Act has not been given; or
  (b) in any case, a witness must be recalled.

(4) The judge may, when granting a motion in terms of this section, adjourn or postpone the trial before permitting the additional evidence to be led.

(5) In this section "the commencement of the trial" means—
  (a) in proceedings on indictment, the time when the jury is sworn; and
  (b) in summary proceedings, the time when the first witness for the prosecution is sworn.

Evidence in replication

269.—(1) The judge may, on a motion of the prosecutor made at the relevant time, permit the prosecutor to lead additional evidence for the purpose of—
  (a) contradicting evidence given by any defence witness which could not reasonably have been anticipated by the prosecutor; or
  (b) providing such proof as is mentioned in section 263(4) of this Act.

(2) The judge may permit the additional evidence to be led notwithstanding that—
  (a) in proceedings on indictment, a witness or production concerned is not included in any list lodged by the parties and that the notice required by sections 67(5) and 78(4) of this Act has not been given; or
  (b) in any case, a witness must be recalled.

(3) The judge may when granting a motion in terms of this section, adjourn or postpone the trial before permitting the additional evidence to be led.

(4) In subsection (1) above, "the relevant time" means—
  (a) in proceedings on indictment, after the close of the defence evidence and before the commencement of the speeches to the jury; and
  (b) in summary proceedings, after the close of the defence evidence and before the prosecutor proceeds to address the judge on the evidence.

Evidence of criminal record and character of accused

270.—(1) This section applies where—

(a) evidence is led by the defence, or the defence asks questions of a witness for the prosecution, with a view to establishing the accused's good character or impugning the character of the prosecutor, of any witness for the prosecution or of the complainer; or

(b) the nature or conduct of the defence is such as to tend to establish the accused's good character or to involve imputations on the character of the prosecutor, of any witness for the prosecution or of the complainer.

(2) Where this section applies the court may, without prejudice to section 268 of this Act, on the application of the prosecutor, permit the prosecutor to lead evidence that the accused has committed, or has been convicted of, or has been charged with, offences other than that for which he is being tried, or is of bad character, notwithstanding that, in proceedings on indictment, a witness or production concerned is not included in any list lodged by the prosecutor and that the notice required by sections 67(5) and 78(4) of this Act has not been given.

(3) In proceedings on indictment, an application under subsection (2) above shall be made in the course of the trial but in the absence of the jury.

(4) In subsection (1) above, references to the complainer include references to a victim who is deceased.

Evidence of children

Evidence of vulnerable persons: special provisions

[1]**271.**—(1) Subject to subsections (7) and (8) below, where a vulnerable person has been or could be cited to give evidence in a trial the court may appoint a commissioner to take the evidence of that person if—

(a) in solemn proceedings, at any time before the oath is administered to the jury;

(b) in summary proceedings, at any time before the first witness is sworn;

(c) in exceptional circumstances in either solemn or summary proceedings, during the course of the trial,

application is made in that regard; but to be so appointed a person must be, and for a period of five years have been, a member of the Faculty of Advocates or a solicitor.

(2) Proceedings before a commissioner appointed under subsection (1) above shall be recorded by video recorder.

(3) An accused shall not, except by leave of the commissioner, be present in the room where such proceedings are taking place but shall be entitled by such means as seem suitable to the commissioner to watch and hear the proceedings.

(4) Subsections (2) to (6), (8) and (9) of section 272 of this Act shall apply to an application under subsection (1) above and evidence taken by a commissioner appointed under that subsection as those subsections apply to an application under subsection (1) of that section and evidence taken by a commissioner appointed on such an application.

(5) Subject to subsections (7) and (8) below, where a vulnerable person has been or is likely to be cited to give evidence in a trial, the court may, on an application being made to it, authorise the giving of evidence by that person by means of a live television link.

(6) Subject to subsections (7) and (8) below, where a vulnerable person has been or is likely to be cited to give evidence in a trial, the court may, on

application being made to it, authorise the use of a screen to conceal the accused from the sight of that person while that person is present to give evidence; but arrangements shall be made to ensure that the accused is able to watch and hear as the evidence is given by the vulnerable person.

(7) The court may grant an application under subsection (1), (5) or (6) above only on cause shown having regard in particular to—

(a) the possible effect on the vulnerable person if required to give evidence, no such application having been granted;

(b) whether it is likely that the vulnerable person would be better able to give evidence if such an application were granted; and

(c) the views of the vulnerable person.

(8) In considering whether to grant an application under subsection (1), (5) or (6) above the court may take into account, where appropriate, any of the following—

(a) the nature of the alleged offence;

(b) the nature of the evidence which the vulnerable person is likely to be called upon to give;

(c) the relationship, if any, between the person and the accused; and

(d) where the person is a child, his age and maturity.

(9) Where a sheriff to whom an application has been made under subsection (1), (5) or (6) above would have granted the application but for the lack of accommodation or equipment necessary to achieve the purpose of the application, he may by order transfer the case to any sheriff court which has such accommodation and equipment available, being a sheriff court in the same sheriffdom.

(10) The sheriff court to which a case has been transferred under subsection (9) above shall be deemed to have granted an application under, as the case may be, subsection (1), (5) or (6) above in relation to the case.

(11) Where a court has or is deemed to have granted an application under subsection (1), (5) or (6) above in relation to a vulnerable person, and the vulnerable person gives evidence that he recalls having identified, prior to the trial, a person alleged to have committed an offence, the evidence of a third party as to the identification of that person by the vulnerable person prior to the trial shall be admissible as evidence as to such identification.

(12) In this section—

"child" means a person under the age of 16 years;

"court" means the High Court or the sheriff court;

"trial" means a trial under solemn or under summary procedure; and

"vulnerable person" means—

(a) any child; and

(b) any person of or over the age of 16 years—

(i) who is subject to an order made in consequence of a finding of a court in any part of the United Kingdom that he is suffering from mental disorder within the meaning of section 1(2) of the Mental Health (Scotland) Act 1984, section 1(2) of the Mental Health Act 1983, or Article 3(1) of the Mental Health (Northern Ireland) Order 1986 (application of enactment); or

(ii) who is subject to a transfer direction under section 71(1) of the 1984 Act, section 47 of the 1983 Act, or Article 53 of the 1986 Order (transfer directions); or

(iii) who otherwise appears to the court to suffer from significant impairment of intelligence and social functioning.

NOTE

[1]Substituted by the Crime and Punishment (Scotland) Act 1997 (c. 48) s.29 with effect from August 1, 1997 in terms of the Crime and Punishment (Scotland) Act 1997 (Commencement and Transitional Provisions) Order 1997 (S.I. 1997 No. 1712) para. 3.

Evidence on commission and from abroad

Evidence by letter of request or on commission

272.—(1) In any criminal proceedings in the High Court or the sheriff court the prosecutor or the defence may, at an appropriate time, apply to a judge of the court in which the trial is to take place (or, if that is not yet known, to a judge of the High Court) for—

  (a) the issue of a letter of request to a court, or tribunal, exercising jurisdiction in a country or territory outside the United Kingdom, Channel Islands and Isle of Man for the examination of a witness resident in that country or territory; or

  (b) the appointment of a commissioner to examine, at any place in the United Kingdom, Channel Islands, or Isle of Man, a witness who—

    (i) by reason of being ill or infirm is unable to attend the trial diet; or

    (ii) is not ordinarily resident in, and is, at the time of the trial diet, unlikely to be present in, the United Kingdom, Channel Islands or the Isle of Man.

(2) A hearing, as regards any application under subsection (1) above by a party, shall be conducted in chambers but may be dispensed with if the application is not opposed.

(3) An application under subsection (1) above may be granted only if the judge is satisfied that—

  (a) the evidence which it is averred the witness is able to give is necessary for the proper adjudication of the trial; and

  (b) there would be no unfairness to the other party were such evidence to be received in the form of the record of an examination conducted by virtue of that subsection.

(4) Any such record as is mentioned in paragraph (b) of subsection (3) above shall, without being sworn to by witnesses, be received in evidence in so far as it either accords with the averment mentioned in paragraph (a) of that subsection or can be so received without unfairness to either party.

(5) Where any such record as is mentioned in paragraph (b) of subsection (3) above, or any part of such record, is not a document in writing, that record or part shall not be received in evidence under subsection (4) above unless it is accompanied by a transcript of its contents.

(6) The procedure as regards the foregoing provisions of this section shall be prescribed by Act of Adjournal; and without prejudice to the generality of the power to make it, such an Act of Adjournal may provide for the appointment of a person before whom evidence may be taken for the purposes of this section.

Evidence on commission and from abroad

Evidence by letter of request or on commission

272.—(1) In any criminal proceedings in the High Court or the sheriff court the prosecutor or the defence may, at an appropriate time, apply to a judge of the court in which the trial is to take place (or, if that is not yet known, to a judge of the High Court) for—

  (a) the issue of a letter of request to a court, or tribunal, exercising jurisdiction in a country or territory outside the United Kingdom, Channel Islands and Isle of Man for the examination of a witness resident in that country or territory; or

  (b) the appointment of a commissioner to examine, at any place in the United Kingdom, Channel Islands, or Isle of Man, a witness who—

    (i) by reason of being ill or infirm is unable to attend the trial diet; or

    (ii) is not ordinarily resident in, and is, at the time of the trial diet, unlikely to be present in, the United Kingdom, Channel Islands or the Isle of Man.

(2) A hearing, as regards any application under subsection (1) above by a party, shall be conducted in chambers but may be dispensed with if the application is not opposed.

(3) An application under subsection (1) above may be granted only if the judge is satisfied that—

(a) the evidence which it is averred the witness is able to give is necessary for the proper adjudication of the trial; and

(b) there would be no unfairness to the other party were such evidence to be received in the form of the record of an examination conducted by virtue of that subsection.

(4) Any such record as is mentioned in paragraph (b) of subsection (3) above shall, without being sworn to by witnesses, be received in evidence in so far as it either accords with the averment mentioned in paragraph (a) of that subsection or can be so received without unfairness to either party.

(5) Where any such record as is mentioned in paragraph (b) of subsection (3) above, or any part of such record, is not a document in writing, that record or part shall not be received in evidence under subsection (4) above unless it is accompanied by a transcript of its contents.

(6) The procedure as regards the foregoing provisions of this section shall be prescribed by Act of Adjournal; and without prejudice to the generality of the power to make it, such an Act of Adjournal may provide for the appointment of a person before whom evidence may be taken for the purposes of this section.

(7) In subsection (1) above, "appropriate time" means as regards—

(a) solemn proceedings, any time before the oath is administered to the jury;

(b) summary proceedings, any time before the first witness is sworn,

or (but only in relation to an application under paragraph (b) of that subsection) any time during the course of the trial if the circumstances on which the application is based had not arisen, or would not have merited such application, within the period mentioned in paragraph (a) or, as the case may be, (b) of this subsection.

(8) In subsection (3) and (4) above, "record" includes, in addition to a document in writing—

(a) any disc, tape, soundtrack or other device in which sounds or other data (not being visual images) are recorded so as to be capable (with or without the aid of some other equipment) of being reproduced therefrom; and

(b) any film (including microfilm), negative, tape, disc or other device in which one or more visual images are recorded so as to be capable (as aforesaid) of being reproduced therefrom.

(9) This section is without prejudice to any existing power at common law to adjourn a trial diet to the place where a witness is.

Television link evidence from abroad

273.—(1) In any solemn proceedings in the High Court or the sheriff court a person other than the accused may give evidence through a live television link if—

(a) the witness is outside the United Kingdom;

(b) an application under subsection (2) below for the issue of a letter of request has been granted; and

(c) the court is satisfied as to the arrangements for the giving of evidence in that manner by that witness.

(2) The prosecutor or the defence in any proceedings referred to in subsection (1) above may apply to a judge of the court in which the trial is to

take place (or, if that court is not yet known, to a judge of the High Court) for the issue of a letter of request to—

(a) a court or tribunal exercising jurisdiction in a country or territory outside the United Kingdom where a witness is ordinarily resident; or

(b) any authority which the judge is satisfied is recognised by the government of that country or territory as the appropriate authority for receiving requests for assistance in facilitating the giving of evidence through a live television link,

requesting assistance in facilitating the giving of evidence by that witness through a live television link.

(3) An application under subsection (2) above shall be granted only if the judge is satisfied that—

(a) the evidence which it is averred the witness is able to give is necessary for the proper adjudication of the trial; and

(b) the granting of the application—

(i) is in the interests of justice; and

(ii) in the case of an application by the prosecutor, is not unfair to the accused.

Evidence relating to sexual offences

Restrictions on evidence relating to sexual offences

274.—(1) In any trial of a person on any charge to which this section applies, subject to section 275 of this Act, the court shall not admit, or allow questioning designed to elicit, evidence which shows or tends to show that the complainer—

(a) is not of good character in relation to sexual matters;

(b) is a prostitute or an associate of prostitutes; or

(c) has at any time engaged with any person in sexual behaviour not forming part of the subject matter of the charge.

(2) This section applies to a charge of committing or attempting to commit any of the following offences, that is to say—

(a) rape;

(b) sodomy;

(c) clandestine injury to women;

(d) assault with intent to rape;

(e) indecent assault;

(f) indecent behaviour (including any lewd, indecent or libidinous practice or behaviour);

(g) an offence under section 106(1)(a) or 107 of the Mental Health (Scotland) Act 1984 (unlawful sexual intercourse with mentally handicapped female or with patient); or

(h) an offence under any of the following provisions of the Criminal Law (Consolidation) (Scotland) Act 1995—

(i) sections 1 to 3 (incest and related offences);

(ii) section 5 (unlawful sexual intercourse with girl under 13 or 16);

(iii) section 6 (indecent behaviour toward girl between 12 and 16);

(iv) section 7(2) and (3) (procuring by threats etc.);

(v) section 8 (abduction and unlawful detention);

(vi) section 13(5) (homosexual offences).

(3) In this section "complainer" means the person against whom the offence referred to in subsection (2) above is alleged to have been committed.

(4) This section does not apply to questioning, or evidence being adduced, by the Crown.

Exceptions to restrictions under section 274

275.—(1) Notwithstanding section 274 of this Act, in any trial of an a accused on any charge to which that section applies, where the court is satisfied on an application by the accused—

(a) that the questioning or evidence referred to in subsection (1) of that section is designed to explain or rebut evidence adduced, or to be adduced, otherwise than by or on behalf of the accused;

(b) that the questioning or evidence referred to in paragraph (c) of that subsection—

    (i) is questioning or evidence as to sexual behaviour which took place on the same occasion as the sexual behaviour forming the subject matter of the charge; or

    (ii) is relevant to the defence of incrimination; or

(c) that it would be contrary to the interests of justice to exclude the questioning or evidence referred to in that subsection,

the court shall allow the questioning or, as the case may be, admit the evidence.

(2) Where questioning or evidence is or has been allowed or admitted under this section, the court may at any time limit as it thinks fit the extent of that questioning or evidence.

(3) Any application under this section shall be made in the course of the trial but in the absence of the jury, the complainer, any person cited as a witness and the public.

Biological material

Evidence of biological material

276.—(1) Evidence as to the characteristics and composition of any biological material deriving from human beings or animals shall, in any criminal proceedings, be admissible notwithstanding that neither the material nor a sample of it is lodged as a production.

(2) A party wishing to lead such evidence as is referred to in subsection (1) above shall, where neither the material nor a sample of it is lodged as a production, make the material or a sample of it available for inspection by the other party unless the material constitutes a hazard to health or has been destroyed in the process of analysis.

Transcripts and records

Transcript of police interview sufficient evidence

277.—(1) Subject to subsection (2) below, for the purposes of any criminal proceedings, a document certified by the person who made it as an accurate transcript made for the prosecutor of the contents of a tape (identified by means of a label) purporting to be a recording of an interview between—

(a) a police officer and an accused person; or

(b) a person commissioned, appointed or authorised under section 6(3) of the Customs and Excise Management Act 1979 and an accused person,

shall be received in evidence and be sufficient evidence of the making of the transcript and of its accuracy.

(2) Subsection (1) above shall not apply to a transcript—

(a) unless a copy of it has been served on the accused not less than 14 days before his trial; or

(b) if the accused, not less than six days before his trial, or by such later time before his trial as the court may in special circumstances allow, has served notice on the prosecutor that the accused challenges the making of the transcript or its accuracy.

(3) A copy of the transcript or a notice under subsection (2) above shall be served in such manner as may be prescribed by Act of Adjournal; and a written execution purporting to be signed by the person who served the transcript or notice, together with, where appropriate, the relevant post office receipt shall be sufficient evidence of such service.

(4) Where subsection (1) above does not apply to a transcript, if the person who made the transcript is called as a witness his evidence shall be sufficient evidence of the making of the transcript and of its accuracy.

Record of proceedings at examination as evidence

278.—(1) Subject to subsection (2) below, the record made, under section 37 of this Act (incorporating any rectification authorised under section 38(1) of this Act), of proceedings at the examination of an accused shall be received in evidence without being sworn to by witnesses, and it shall not be necessary in proceedings on indictment to insert the names of any witnesses to the record in any list of witnesses, either for the prosecution or for the defence.

(2) On the application of either an accused or the prosecutor—

(a) in proceedings on indictment, subject to sections 37(5) and 72(1)(b) (iv) of this Act, the court may determine that the record or part of the record shall not be read to the jury; and

(b) in summary proceedings, subject to the said section 37(5) and to subsection (4) below, the court may refuse to admit the record or some part of the record as evidence.

(3) At the hearing of an application under subsection (2) above, it shall be competent for the prosecutor or the defence to adduce as witnesses the persons who were present during the proceedings mentioned in subsection (1) above and for either party to examine those witnesses upon any matters regarding the said proceedings.

(4) In summary proceedings, except on cause shown, an application under subsection (2)(b) above shall not be heard unless notice of at least 10 clear days has been given to the court and to the other parties.

(5) In subsection (2) above, the "record" comprises—

(a) as regards any trial of an indictment, each record included, under section 68(1) of this Act, in the list of productions; and

(b) as regards a summary trial, each record which it is sought to have received under subsection (1) above.

Documentary evidence

Evidence from documents

279. Schedule 8 to this Act, which makes provision regarding the admissibility in criminal proceedings of copy documents and of evidence contained in business documents, shall have effect.

Evidence from certain official documents

[1]**279A.**—[2](1) Any letter, minute or other official document issuing from the office of or in custody of any of the departments of state or government in the United Kingdom or any part of the Scottish Administration which—

(a) is required to be produced in evidence in any prosecution; and

(b) according to the rules and regulations applicable to such departments may competently be so produced,

shall when so produced be *prima facie* evidence of the matters contained in it without being produced or sworn to by any witness.

(2) A copy of any such document as is mentioned in subsection (1) above bearing to be certified by any person having authority to certify it shall be treated as equivalent to the original of that document and no proof of the

signature of the person certifying the copy or of his authority to certify it shall be necessary.

[2](3) Any order made by any of the departments of state or government or the Scottish Parliament or any local authority or public body made under powers conferred by any statute or a print or a copy of such order, shall when produced in a prosecution be received as evidence of the due making, confirmation, and existence of the order without being sworn to by any witness and without any further or other proof.

(4) Subsection (3) above is without prejudice to any right competent to the accused to challenge any order such as is mentioned in that subsection as being *ultra vires* of the authority making it or any other competent ground.

(5) Where an order such as is mentioned in subsection (3) above is referred to in the indictment or, as the case may be, the complaint, it shall not be necessary to enter it in the record of the proceedings as a documentary production.

(6) The provisions of this section are in addition to, and not in derogation of, any powers of proving documents conferred by statute or existing at common law.

NOTES

[1]Inserted by the Crime and Punishment (Scotland) Act 1997 (c. 48) s.28(2); commenced with effect from August 1, 1997 in terms of the Crime and Punishment (Scotland) Act 1997 (Commencement and Transitional Provisions) Order 1997 (S.I. 1997 No. 1712) para. 3.

[2]As amended by the Scotland Act 1998 (Consequential Modifications) (No. 2) Order 1999 (S.I. 1999 No. 1820) art. 4 and Sched. 2, para.122(4) (effective July 1, 1999).

Routine evidence

Routine evidence

280.—(1) For the purposes of any proceedings for an offence under any of the enactments specified in column 1 of Schedule 9 to this Act, a certificate purporting to be signed by a person or persons specified in column 2 thereof, and certifying the matter specified in column 3 thereof shall, subject to subsection (6) below, be sufficient evidence of that matter and of the qualification or authority of that person or those persons.

(2) The Secretary of State may by order—
(a) amend or repeal the entry in Schedule 9 to this Act in respect of any enactment; or
(b) insert in that Schedule an entry in respect of a further enactment.

(3) An order under subsection (2) above may make such transitional, incidental or supplementary provision as the Secretary of State considers necessary or expedient in connection with the coming into force of the order.

(4) For the purposes of any criminal proceedings, a report purporting to be signed by two authorised forensic scientists shall, subject to subsection (5) below, be sufficient evidence of any fact or conclusion as to fact contained in the report and of the authority of the signatories.

(5) A forensic scientist is authorised for the purposes of subsection (4) above if—
(a) he is authorised for those purposes by the Secretary of State; or
(b) he—
    (i) is a constable or is employed by a police authority under section 9 of the Police (Scotland) Act 1967;
    (ii) possesses such qualifications and experience as the Secretary of State may for the purposes of that subsection by order prescribe; and
    (iii) is authorised for those purposes by the chief constable of the police force maintained for the police area of that authority.

(6) Subsections (1) and (4) above shall not apply to a certificate or, as the case may be, report tendered on behalf of the prosecutor or the accused—

(a) unless a copy has been served on the other party not less than fourteen days before the trial; or

[1](b) where the other party, not more than seven days after the date of service of the copy on him under paragraph (a) above or by such later time as the court may in special circumstances allow, has served notice on the first party that he challenges the matter, qualification or authority mentioned in subsection (1) above or as the case may be the fact, conclusion or authority mentioned in subsection (4) above.

(7) A copy of a certificate or, as the case may be, report required by subsection (6) above, to be served on the accused or the prosecutor or of a notice required by that subsection or by subsection (1) or (2) of section 281 of this Act to be served on the prosecutor shall be served in such manner as may be prescribed by Act of Adjournal; and a written execution purporting to be signed by the person who served such certificate or notice, together with, where appropriate, the relevant post office receipt shall be sufficient evidence of service of such a copy.

(8) Where, following service of a notice under subsection (6)(b) above, evidence is given in relation to a report referred to in subsection (4) above by both of the forensic scientists purporting to have signed the report, the evidence of those forensic scientists shall be sufficient evidence of any fact (or conclusion as to fact) contained in the report.

(9) At any trial of an offence it shall be presumed that the person who appears in answer to the complaint is the person charged by the police with the offence unless the contrary is alleged.

(10) An order made under subsection (2) or (5)(b)(ii) above shall be made by statutory instrument.

(11) No order shall be made under subsection (2) above unless a draft of the order has been laid before, and approved by a resolution of, each House of Parliament.

(12) A statutory instrument containing an order under subsection (5)(b)(ii) above shall be subject to annulment pursuant to a resolution of either House of Parliament.

NOTE

[1]Amended by the Crime and Punishment (Scotland) Act 1997 (c. 48) s.62(1) and Sched. 1, para. 21(32) with effect from August 1, 1997 in terms of the Crime and Punishment (Scotland) Act (Commencement and Transitional Provisions) Order 1997 (S.I. 1997 No. 1712), para. 3.

Routine evidence: autopsy and forensic science reports

281.—(1) Where in a trial an autopsy report is lodged as a production by the prosecutor it shall be presumed that the body of the person identified in that report is the body of the deceased identified in the indictment or complaint, unless the accused not less than six days before the trial, or by such later time before the trial as the court may in special circumstances allow, gives notice that the contrary is alleged.

(2) At the time of lodging an autopsy or forensic science report as a production the prosecutor may intimate to the accused that it is intended that only one of the pathologists or forensic scientists (whom the prosecutor shall specify) purporting to have signed the report shall be called to give evidence in respect thereof; and the evidence of that pathologist or forensic scientist shall be sufficient evidence of any fact or conclusion as to fact contained in the report and of the qualifications of the signatories, unless the accused, not less than six days before the trial or by such later time before the trial as the court may in special circumstances allow, serves notice on the prosecutor that he requires the attendance at the trial of the other pathologist or forensic scientist also.

(3) Where, following service of a notice by the accused under subsection (2) above, evidence is given in relation to an autopsy or forensic science

report by both of the pathologists or forensic scientists purporting to have signed the report, the evidence of those pathologists or forensic scientists shall be sufficient evidence of any fact (or conclusion as to fact) contained in the report.

Sufficient evidence

Evidence as to controlled drugs and medicinal products

282.—(1) For the purposes of any criminal proceedings, evidence given by an authorised forensic scientist, either orally or in a report purporting to be signed by him, that a substance which satisfies either of the conditions specified in subsection (2) below is—

(a) a particular controlled drug or medicinal product; or

(b) a particular product which is listed in the British Pharmacopoeia as containing a particular controlled drug or medicinal product,

shall, subject to subsection (3) below, be sufficient evidence of that fact notwithstanding that no analysis of the substance has been carried out.

(2) Those conditions are—

(a) that the substance is in a sealed container bearing a label identifying the contents of the container; or

(b) that the substance has a characteristic appearance having regard to its size, shape, colour and manufacturer's mark.

(3) A party proposing to rely on subsection (1) above ("the first party") shall, not less than 14 days before the trial diet, serve on the other party ("the second party")—

(a) a notice to that effect; and

(b) where the evidence is contained in a report, a copy of the report,

and if the second party serves on the first party, not more than seven days after the date of service of the notice on him, a notice that he does not accept the evidence as to the identity of the substance, subsection (1) above shall not apply in relation to that evidence.

(4) A notice or copy report served in accordance with subsection (3) above shall be served in such manner as may be prescribed by Act of Adjournal; and a written execution purporting to be signed by the person who served the notice or copy together with, where appropriate, the relevant post office receipt shall be sufficient evidence of such service.

(5) In this section—

"controlled drug" has the same meaning as in the Misuse of Drugs Act 1971; and

"medicinal product" has the same meaning as in the Medicines Act 1968.

Evidence as to time and place of video surveillance recordings

283.—(1) For the purposes of any criminal proceedings, a certificate purporting to be signed by a person responsible for the operation of a video surveillance system and certifying—

(a) the location of the camera;

(b) the nature and extent of the person's responsibility for the system; and

(c) that visual images recorded on a particular video tape are images, recorded by the system, of events which occurred at a place specified in the certificate at a time and date so specified,

shall, subject to subsection (2) below, be sufficient evidence of the matters contained in the certificate.

(2) A party proposing to rely on subsection (1) above ("the first party") shall, not less than 14 days before the trial diet, serve on the other party ("the second party") a copy of the certificate and, if the second party serves on the first party, not more than seven days after the date of service of the copy

certificate on him, a notice that he does not accept the evidence contained in the certificate, subsection (1) above shall not apply in relation to that evidence.

(3) A copy certificate or notice served in accordance with subsection (2) above shall be served in such manner as may be prescribed by Act of Adjournal; and a written execution purporting to be signed by the person who served the copy or notice together with, where appropriate, the relevant post office receipt shall be sufficient evidence of such service.

(4) In this section, "video surveillance system" means apparatus consisting of a camera mounted in a fixed position and associated equipment for transmitting and recording visual images of events occurring in any place.

Evidence in relation to fingerprints

284.—[1](1) For the purposes of any criminal proceedings, a certificate purporting to be signed by a person authorised in that behalf by a chief constable and certifying that relevant physical data (within the meaning of section 18(7A) of this Act) was taken from or provided by thereon were taken from a person designated in the certificate at a time, date and place specified therein shall, subject to subsection (2) below, be sufficient evidence of the facts contained in the certificate.

[2](2) A party proposing to rely on subsection (1) above ("the first party") shall, not less than 14 days before the trial diet, serve on any other party to the proceedings a copy of the certificate, and such other party shall not be entitled to challenge the sufficiency of the evidence contained within the certificate.

[2](2A) Where the first party does not serve a copy of the certificate on any other party as mentioned in subsection (2) above, he shall not be entitled to rely on subsection (1) above as respects that party.

(3) A copy certificate or notice served in accordance with subsection (2) above shall be served in such manner as may be prescribed by Act of Adjournal; and a written execution purporting to be signed by the person who served the copy or notice together with, where appropriate, the relevant post office receipt shall be sufficient evidence of such service.

NOTES

[1]Substituted by the Crime and Punishment (Scotland) Act 1997 s.47(4)(a) with effect from August 1, 1997 in terms of the Crime and Punishment (Scotland) Act 1997 (Commencement and Transitional Provisions) Order 1997 (S.I. 1997 No. 1712) para. 3.

[2]Substituted by s.47(4)(b) of the 1997 and effected by the Order specified above.

Proof of previous convictions

Previous convictions: proof, general

285.—(1) A previous conviction may be proved against any person in any criminal proceedings by the production of such evidence of the conviction as is mentioned in this subsection and subsections (2) to (6) below and by showing that his fingerprints and those of the person convicted are the fingerprints of the same person.

[1](2) A certificate purporting to be signed by or the Secretary of State or by a person authorised by him to sign such a certificate or the Commissioner of Police of the Metropolis, containing particulars relating to a conviction extracted from the criminal records kept in pursuance of a service provided and maintained by the Secretary of State under or by virtue of Section 36 of the Police (Scotland) Act 1967 or by or on behalf of the Commissioner of Police of the Metropolis, and certifying that the copies of the fingerprints contained in the certificate are copies of the fingerprints appearing from the

said records to have been taken in pursuance of rules for the time being in force under sections 12 and 39 of the Prisons (Scotland) Act 1989, or regulations for the time being in force under section 16 of the Prison Act 1952, from the person convicted on the occasion of the conviction or on the occasion of his last conviction, shall be sufficient evidence of the conviction or, as the case may be, of his last conviction and of all preceding convictions and that the copies of the fingerprints produced on the certificate are copies of the fingerprints of the person convicted.

(3) Where a person has been apprehended and detained in the custody of the police in connection with any criminal proceedings, a certificate purporting to be signed by the chief constable concerned or a person authorised on his behalf, certifying that the fingerprints produced thereon were taken from him while he was so detained, shall be sufficient evidence in those proceedings that the fingerprints produced on the certificate are the fingerprints of that person.

(4) A certificate purporting to be signed by or on behalf of the governor of a prison or of a remand centre in which any person has been detained in connection with any criminal proceedings, certifying that the fingerprints produced thereon were taken from him while he was so detained, shall be sufficient evidence in those proceedings that the fingerprints produced on the certificate are the fingerprints of that person.

²(5) A certificate purporting to be signed by the Secretary of State or by a person authorised by him to sign such a certificate, and certifying that the fingerprints, copies of which are certified as mentioned in subsection (2) above by the Secretary of State or by a person authorised by him to sign such a certificate or by or on behalf of or the Commissioner of Police of the Metropolis to be copies of the fingerprints of a person previously convicted and the fingerprints certified by or on behalf of a chief constable or a governor as mentioned in subsection (3) or (4) above, or otherwise shown, to be the fingerprints of the person against whom the previous conviction is sought to be proved, are the fingerprints of the same person, shall be sufficient evidence of the matter so certified.

(6) An extract conviction of any crime committed in any part of the United Kingdom bearing to have been issued by an officer whose duties include the issue of extract convictions shall be received in evidence without being sworn to by witnesses.

(7) It shall be competent to prove a previous conviction or any fact relevant to the admissibility of the conviction by witnesses, although the name of any such witness is not included in the list served on the accused; and the accused shall be entitled to examine witnesses with regard to such conviction or fact.

(8) An official of any prison in which the accused has been detained on such conviction shall be a competent and sufficient witness to prove its application to the accused, although he may not have been present in court at the trial to which such conviction relates.

(9) The method of proving a previous conviction authorised by this section shall be in addition to any other method of proving the conviction.

³(10) In this section "fingerprint" includes any record of the skin of a person's finger created by a device approved by the Secretary of State under section 18(7B) of this Act.

NOTES
¹Substituted by the Crime and Punishment (Scotland) Act 1997 (c. 48) s.59(2) with effect from August 1, 1997 as enacted by the Crime and Punishment (Scotland) Act 1997 (Commencement and Transitional Provisions) Order 1997 (S.I. 1997 No. 1712) para. 3.
²Substituted by the 1997 Act s.59(3) and enacted from August 1, 1997 by the above Order.

[3]Inserted by the 1997 Act s.47(5) and enacted from August 1, 1997 by the above Order.

Previous convictions: proof in support of substantive charge

286.—(1) Without prejudice to section 285(6) to (9) or, as the case may be, section 166 of this Act, where proof of a previous conviction is competent in support of a substantive charge, any such conviction or an extract of it shall, if—

    (a) it purports to relate to the accused and to be signed by the clerk of court having custody of the record containing the conviction; and

    (b) a copy of it has been served on the accused not less than 14 days before the trial diet,

be sufficient evidence of the application of the conviction to the accused unless, within seven days of the date of service of the copy on him, he serves notice on the prosecutor that he denies that it applies to him.

(2) A copy of a conviction or extract conviction served under subsection (1) above shall be served on the accused in such manner as may be prescribed by Act of Adjournal, and a written execution purporting to be signed by the person who served the copy together with, where appropriate, the relevant post office receipt shall be sufficient evidence of service of the copy.

PART XIII

MISCELLANEOUS

Lord Advocate

Demission of office by Lord Advocate

287.—(1) All indictments which have been raised by a Lord Advocate shall remain effective notwithstanding his subsequently having died or demitted office and may be taken up and proceeded with by his successor.

(2) During any period when the office of Lord Advocate is vacant it shall be lawful to indict accused persons in name of the Solicitor General then in office.

(3) The advocates depute shall not demit office when a Lord Advocate dies or demits office but shall continue in office until their successors receive commissions.

(4) The advocates depute and procurators fiscal shall have power, notwithstanding any vacancy in the office of Lord Advocate, to take up and proceed with any indictment which—

    (a) by virtue of subsection (1) above, remains effective; or

    (b) by virtue of subsection (2) above, is in the name of the Solicitor General.

(5) For the purposes of this Act, where, but for this subsection, demission of office by one Law Officer would result in the offices of both being vacant, he or, where both demit office on the same day, the person demitting the office of Lord Advocate shall be deemed to continue in office until the warrant of appointment of the person succeeding to the office of Lord Advocate is granted.

[1](6) The Lord Advocate shall enter upon the duties of his office immediately upon the grant of his warrant of appointment.

NOTE

[1]As amended by the Scotland Act 1998 (Consequential Modifications) (No. 1) Order 1999 (S.I. 1999 No. 1042) art. 4 and Sched. 2, para. 11 and Sched. 2, Pt III.

Intimation of proceedings in High Court to Lord Advocate

288.—(1) In any proceeding in the High Court (other than a proceeding to which the Lord Advocate or a procurator fiscal is a party) it shall be competent for the court to order intimation of such proceeding to the Lord Advocate.

(2) On intimation being made to the Lord Advocate under subsection (1) above, the Lord Advocate shall be entitled to appear and be heard in such proceeding.

Devolution issues

Rights of appeal for Advocate General: devolution issues

¹**288A.**—(1) This section applies where—

(a) a person is acquitted or convicted of a charge (whether on indictment or in summary proceedings), and

(b) the Advocate General for Scotland was a party to the proceedings in pursuance of paragraph 6 of Schedule 6 to the Scotland Act 1998 (devolution issues).

(2) The Advocate General for Scotland may refer any devolution issue which has arisen in the proceedings to the High Court for their opinion; and the Clerk of Justiciary shall send to the person acquitted or convicted and to any solicitor who acted for that person at the trial, a copy of the reference and intimation of the date fixed by the Court for a hearing.

(3) The person may, not later than seven days before the date so fixed, intimate in writing to the Clerk of Justiciary and to the Advocate General for Scotland either—

(a) that he elects to appear personally at the hearing, or

(b) that he elects to be represented by counsel at the hearing,

but, except by leave of the Court on cause shown, and without prejudice to his right to attend, he shall not appear or be represented at the hearing other than by and in conformity with an election under this subsection.

(4) Where there is no intimation under subsection (3)(b), the High Court shall appoint counsel to act at the hearing as amicus curiae.

(5) The costs of representation elected under subsection (3)(b) or of an appointment under subsection (4) shall, after being taxed by the Auditor of the Court of Session, be paid by the Advocate General for Scotland out of money provided by Parliament.

(6) The opinion on the point referred under subsection (2) shall not affect the acquittal or (as the case may be) conviction in the trial.

NOTE
¹Inserted by the Scotland Act 1998 (c. 46) Sched. 8, para. 32 and brought into force by the Scotland Act 1998 (Commencement) Order 1998, Art. 2, Sched. 3 (S.I. 1998 No. 3178: effective May 6, 1999).

Appeals to Judicial Committee of the Privy Council

¹**288B.**—(1) This section applies where the Judicial Committee of the Privy Council determines an appeal under paragraph 13(a) of Schedule 6 to the Scotland Act 1998 against a determination of a devolution issue by the High Court in the ordinary course of proceedings.

(2) The determination of the appeal shall not affect any earlier acquittal or earlier quashing of any conviction in the proceedings.

(3) Subject to subsection (2) above, the High Court shall have the same powers in relation to the proceedings when remitted to it by the Judicial Committee as it would have if it were considering the proceedings otherwise than as a trial court.

NOTE
¹Inserted by the Scotland Act 1998 (c. 46) Sched. 8, para. 32 and brought into force by the Scotland Act 1998 (Commencement) Order 1998, Art. 2, Sched. 3 (S.I. 1998 No. 3178: effective May 6, 1999).

Treason trials

Procedure and evidence in trials for treason

289. The procedure and rules of evidence in proceedings for treason and misprision of treason shall be the same as in proceedings according to the law of Scotland for murder.

Certain rights of accused

Accused's right to request identification parade

290.—(1) Subject to subsection (2) below, the sheriff may, on an application by an accused at any time after the accused has been charged with an offence, order that, in relation to the alleged offence, the prosecutor shall hold an identification parade in which the accused shall be one of those constituting the parade.

(2) The sheriff shall make an order in accordance with subsection (1) above only after giving the prosecutor an opportunity to be heard and only if—

    (a) an identification parade, such as is mentioned in subsection (1) above, has not been held at the instance of the prosecutor;

    (b) after a request by the accused, the prosecutor has refused to hold, or has unreasonably delayed holding, such an identification parade; and

    (c) the sheriff considers the application under subsection (1) above to be reasonable.

Precognition on oath of defence witnesses

291.—(1) The sheriff may, on the application of an accused, grant warrant to cite any person (other than a co-accused), who is alleged to be a witness in relation to any offence of which the accused has been charged, to appear before the sheriff in chambers at such time or place as shall be specified in the citation, for precognition on oath by the accused or his solicitor in relation to that offence, if the court is satisfied that it is reasonable to require such precognition on oath in the circumstances.

(2) Any person who, having been duly cited to attend for precognition under subsection (1) above and having been given at least 48 hours notice, fails without reasonable excuse to attend shall be guilty of an offence and shall be liable on summary conviction to a fine not exceeding level 3 on the standard scale or to imprisonment for a period not exceeding 21 days; and the court may issue a warrant for the apprehension of the person concerned, ordering him to be brought before a sheriff for precognition on oath.

(3) Any person who, having been duly cited to attend for precognition under subsection (1) above, attends but—

    (a) refuses to give information within his knowledge or to produce evidence in his possession; or

    (b) prevaricates in his evidence,

shall be guilty of an offence and shall be liable to be summarily subjected forthwith to a fine not exceeding level 3 on the standard scale or to imprisonment for a period not exceeding 21 days.

Mode of trial

Mode of trial of certain offences

292.—(1) Subject to subsection (6) below, the offences mentioned (and broadly described) in Schedule 10 to this Act shall be triable only summarily.

(2) An offence created by statute shall be triable only summarily if—

(a) the enactment creating the offence or any other enactment expressly so provides (in whatever words); or

(b) subject to subsections (4) and (5)(a) below, the offence was created by an Act passed on or before 29 July 1977 (the date of passing of the Criminal Law Act 1977) and the penalty or maximum penalty in force immediately before that date, on any conviction of that offence, did not include any of the following—

    (i) a fine exceeding £400;

    (ii) subject to subsection (3) below, imprisonment for a period exceeding 3 months;

    (iii) a fine exceeding £50 in respect of a specified quantity or number of things, or in respect of a specified period during which a continuing offence is committed.

(3) In the application of paragraph (b)(ii) of subsection (2) above, no regard shall be paid to the fact that section 5(3) of this Act permits the imposition of imprisonment for a period exceeding 3 months in certain circumstances.

(4) An offence created by statute which is triable only on indictment shall continue only to be so triable.

(5) An offence created by statute shall be triable either on indictment or summarily if—

(a) the enactment creating the offence or any other enactment expressly so provides (in whatever words); or

(b) it is an offence to which neither subsection (2) nor subsection (4) above applies.

(6) An offence which may under any enactment (including an enactment in this Act or passed after this Act) be tried only summarily, being an offence which, if it had been triable on indictment, could competently have been libelled as an additional or alternative charge in the indictment, may (the provisions of this or any other enactment notwithstanding) be so libelled, and tried accordingly.

(7) Where an offence is libelled and tried on indictment by virtue of subsection (6) above, the penalty which may be imposed for that offence in that case shall not exceed that which is competent on summary conviction.

Art and part and attempt

Statutory offences: art and part and aiding and abetting

293.—(1) A person may be convicted of, and punished for, a contravention of any enactment, notwithstanding that he was guilty of such contravention as art and part only.

(2) Without prejudice to subsection (1) above or to any express provision in any enactment having the like effect to this subsection, any person who aids, abets, counsels, procures or incites any other person to commit an offence against the provisions of any enactment shall be guilty of an offence and shall be liable on conviction, unless the enactment otherwise requires, to the same punishment as might be imposed on conviction of the first-mentioned offence.

Attempt at crime

294.—(1) Attempt to commit any indictable crime is itself an indictable crime.

(2) Attempt to commit any offence punishable on complaint shall itself be an offence punishable on complaint.

Legal custody

Legal custody

295. Any person required or authorised by or under this Act or any other enactment to be taken to any place, or to be detained or kept in custody shall, while being so taken or detained or kept, be deemed to be in legal custody.

Warrants

Warrants for search and apprehension to be signed by judge

296. Any warrant for search or apprehension granted under this Act shall be signed by the judge granting it, and execution upon any such warrant may proceed either upon the warrant itself or upon an extract of the warrant issued and signed by the clerk of court.

Execution of warrants and service of complaints, etc.

297.—(1) Any warrant granted by a justice may, without being backed or endorsed by any other justice, be executed throughout Scotland in the same way as it may be executed within the jurisdiction of the justice who granted it.

(2) Any complaint, warrant, or other proceeding for the purposes of any summary proceedings under this Act may without endorsation be served or executed at any place within Scotland by any officer of law, and such service or execution may be proved either by the oath in court of the officer or by production of his written execution.

(3) A warrant issued in the Isle of Man for the arrest of a person charged with an offence may, after it has been endorsed by a justice in Scotland, be executed there by the person bringing that warrant, by any person to whom the warrant was originally directed or by any officer of law of the sheriff court district where the warrant has been endorsed in like manner as any such warrant issued in Scotland.

(4) In subsection (3) above, "endorsed" means endorsed in the like manner as a process to which section 4 of the Summary Jurisdiction (Process) Act 1881 applies.

(5) The Indictable Offences Act Amendment Act 1868 shall apply in relation to the execution in Scotland of warrants issued in the Channel Islands.

Trial judge's report

Trial judge's report

298.—(1) Without prejudice to sections 113 and 186(3)(b) of this Act, the High Court may, in relation to—

 [1](a) an appeal under section 106(1), 108, 108A or 175(2) to (4) of this Act;
 (b) an appeal by way of bill of suspension or advocation; or
 (c) a petition to the nobile officium,

at any time before the appeal is finally determined or, as the case may be, petition finally disposed of, order the judge who presided at the trial, passed sentence or otherwise disposed of the case to provide to the Clerk of Justiciary a report in writing giving the judge's opinion on the case generally or in relation to any particular matter specified in the order.

 [2](2) The Clerk of Justiciary shall send a copy of a report provided under subsection (1) above to the convicted person or his solicitor, the Crown Agent and, in relation to cases referred under Part XA of this Act, the Commission.

(3) Subject to subsection (2) above, the report of the judge shall be

available only to the High Court, the parties and, on such conditions as may be prescribed by Act of Adjournal, such other persons or classes of persons as may be so prescribed.

NOTES

[1]Inserted by the Crime and Punishment (Scotland) Act 1997 (c. 48), Sched. 1, para. 21(33)(a) with effect from October 20, 1997 in terms of the Crime and Punishment (Scotland) Act 1997 (Commencement No. 2 and Transitional and Consequential Provisions) Order 1997 (S.I. 1997 No. 2323) Art. 3 and Sched. 1.

[2]As amended by the Crime and Punishment (Scotland) Act 1997 (c. 48), Sched. 1, para. 21(33)(b) (effective April 1, 1999: SI. 1999 No. 652).

Correction of entries

Correction of entries

299.—(1) Subject to the provisions of this section, it shall be competent to correct any entry in—

(a) the record of proceedings in a prosecution; or

(b) the extract of a sentence passed or an order of court made in such proceedings,

in so far as that entry constitutes an error of recording or is incomplete.

(2) An entry mentioned in subsection (1) above may be corrected—

(a) by the clerk of the court, at any time before either the sentence or order of the court is executed or, on appeal, the proceedings are transmitted to the Clerk of Justiciary;

(b) by the clerk of the court, under the authority of the court which passed the sentence or made the order, at any time after the execution of the sentence or order of the court but before such transmission as is mentioned in paragraph (a) above; or

(c) by the clerk of the court under the authority of the High Court in the case of a remit under subsection (4)(b) below.

(3) A correction in accordance with paragraph (b) or (c) of subsection (2) above shall be intimated to the prosecutor and to the former accused or his solicitor.

(4) Where during the course of an appeal, the High Court becomes aware of an erroneous or incomplete entry, such as is mentioned in subsection (1) above, the court—

(a) may consider and determine the appeal as if such entry were corrected; and

(b) either before or after the determination of the appeal, may remit the proceedings to the court of first instance for correction in accordance with subsection (2)(c) above.

(5) Any correction under subsections (1) and (2) above by the clerk of the court shall be authenticated by his signature and, if such correction is authorised by a court, shall record the name of the judge or judges authorising such correction and the date of such authorisation.

Amendment of records of conviction and sentence in summary proceedings

300.—(1) Without prejudice to section 299 of this Act, where, on an application in accordance with subsection (2) below, the High Court is satisfied that a record of conviction or sentence in summary proceedings inaccurately records the identity of any person, it may authorise the clerk of the court which convicted or, as the case may be, sentenced the person to correct the record.

(2) An application under subsection (1) above shall be made after the determination of the summary prosecution and may be made by any party to the summary proceedings or any other person having an interest in the correction of the alleged inaccuracy.

(3) The High Court shall order intimation of an application under subsection (1) above to such persons as it considers appropriate and shall not determine the application without affording to the parties to the summary proceedings and to any other person having an interest in the correction of the alleged inaccuracy an opportunity to be heard.

(4) The power of the High Court under this section may be exercised by a single judge of the High Court in the same manner as it may be exercised by the High Court, and subject to the same provisions.

Rights of audience

Rights of audience

301.—(1) Without prejudice to section 103(8) of this Act, any solicitor who has, by virtue of section 25A (rights of audience) of the Solicitors (Scotland) Act 1980, a right of audience in relation to the High Court of Justiciary shall have the same right of audience in that court as is enjoyed by an advocate.

(2) Any person who has complied with the terms of a scheme approved under section 26 of the Law Reform (Miscellaneous Provisions) (Scotland) Act 1990 (consideration of applications made under section 25) shall have such rights of audience before the High Court of Justiciary as may be specified in an Act of Adjournal made under subsection (7)(b) of that section.

Fixed penalties

Fixed penalty: conditional offer by procurator fiscal

302.—(1) Where a procurator fiscal receives a report that a relevant offence has been committed he may send to the alleged offender a notice under this section (referred to in this section as a conditional offer); and where he issues a conditional offer the procurator fiscal shall notify the clerk of court specified in it of the issue of the conditional offer and of its terms.

(2) A conditional offer—

(a) shall give such particulars of the circumstances alleged to constitute the offence to which it relates as are necessary for giving reasonable information about the alleged offence;

(b) shall state—

(i) the amount of the appropriate fixed penalty for that offence;

(ii) the amount of the instalments by which the penalty may be paid; and

(iii) the intervals at which such instalments should be paid;

(c) shall indicate that if, within 28 days of the date on which the conditional offer was issued, or such longer period as may be specified in the conditional offer, the alleged offender accepts the offer by making payment of the fixed penalty or of the first instalment thereof to the clerk of court specified in the conditional offer at the address therein mentioned, any liability to conviction of the offence shall be discharged;

(d) shall state that proceedings against the alleged offender shall not be commenced in respect of that offence until the end of a period of 28 days from the date on which the conditional offer was issued, or such longer period as may be specified in the conditional offer; and

(e) shall state that acceptance of the offer in the manner described in paragraph (c) above by the alleged offender shall not be a conviction nor be recorded as such.

(3) A conditional offer may be made in respect of more than one relevant offence and shall, in such a case, state the amount of the appropriate fixed penalty for all the offences in respect of which it is made.

(4) Where payment of the appropriate fixed penalty or of the first instalment has not been made to the clerk of court, he shall, upon the expiry of the period of 28 days referred to in subsection (2)(c) above or such longer period as may be specified in the conditional offer, notify the procurator fiscal who issued the conditional offer that no payment has been made.

(5) Proceedings shall not be brought against any person for the offence to which a conditional offer relates until the procurator fiscal receives notification from the clerk of court in accordance with subsection (4) above.

(6) Where an alleged offender makes payment of the appropriate fixed penalty or of the first instalment to the clerk of court specified in the conditional offer no proceedings shall be brought against the alleged offender for the offence.

(7) The Secretary of State shall, by order, prescribe a scale of fixed penalties for the purpose of this section, the amount of the maximum penalty on the scale being a sum not exceeding level 1 on the standard scale.

(8) An order under subsection (7) above—

(a) may contain provision as to the payment of fixed penalties by instalments; and

(b) shall be made by statutory instrument, which shall be subject to annulment in pursuance of a resolution of either House of Parliament.

(9) In this section—

(a) "a relevant offence" means any offence in respect of which an alleged offender could competently be tried before a district court, but shall not include a fixed penalty offence within the meaning of section 51 of the Road Traffic Offenders Act 1988 nor any other offence in respect of which a conditional offer within the meaning of sections 75 to 77 of that Act may be sent; and

(b) "the appropriate fixed penalty" means such fixed penalty on the scale prescribed under subsection (7) above as the procurator fiscal thinks fit having regard to the circumstances of the case.

Fixed penalty: enforcement

303.—(1) Subject to subsection (2) below, where an alleged offender accepts a conditional offer by paying the first instalment of the appropriate fixed penalty, any amount of the penalty which is outstanding at any time shall be treated as if the penalty were a fine imposed by the court, the clerk of which is specified in the conditional offer.

(2) In the enforcement of a penalty which is to be treated as a fine in pursuance of subsection (1) above—

(a) any reference, howsoever expressed, in any enactment whether passed or made before or after the coming into force of this section to—

(i) the imposition of imprisonment or detention in default of payment of a fine shall be construed as a reference to enforcement by means of civil diligence;

(ii) the finding or order of the court imposing the fine shall be construed as a reference to a certificate given in pursuance of subsection (3) below;

(iii) the offender shall be construed as a reference to the alleged offender;

(iv) the conviction of the offender shall be construed as a reference to the acceptance of the conditional offer by the alleged offender;

(b) the following sections of this Act shall not apply—
section 211(7);

section 213(2);
section 214(1) to (6);
section 216(7);
section 219, except subsection (1)(b);
section 220;
section 221(2) to (4);
section 222(8); and
section 224.

(3) For the purposes of any proceedings in connection with, or steps taken for, the enforcement of any amount of a fixed penalty which is outstanding, a document purporting to be a certificate signed by the clerk of court for the time being responsible for the collection or enforcement of the penalty as to any matter relating to the penalty shall be conclusive of the matter so certified.

(4) The Secretary of State may, by order made by statutory instrument subject to annulment in pursuance of a resolution of either House of Parliament, make such provision as he considers necessary for the enforcement in England and Wales or Northern Ireland of any penalty, treated in pursuance of subsection (1) above as a fine, which is transferred as a fine to a court in England and Wales or, as the case may be, Northern Ireland.

Transfer of rights of appeal of deceased person

[1]**303A.**—(1) Where a person convicted of an offence has died, any person may, subject to the provisions of this section, apply to the High Court for an order authorising him to institute or continue any appeal which could have been or has been instituted by the deceased.

(2) An application for an order under this section may be lodged with the Clerk of Justiciary within three months of the deceased's death or at such later time as the Court may, on cause shown, allow.

(3) Where the Commission makes a reference to the High Court under section 194B of this Act in respect of a person who is deceased, any application under this section must be made within one month of the reference.

(4) Where an application is made for an order under this section and the applicant—
(a) is an executor of the deceased; or
(b) otherwise appears to the Court to have a legitimate interest,
the Court shall make an order authorising the applicant to institute or continue any appeal which could have been instituted or continued by the deceased; and, subject to the provisions of this section, any such order may include such ancillary or supplementary provision as the Court thinks fit.

(5) The person in whose favour an order under this section is made shall from the date of the order be afforded the same rights to carry on the appeal as the deceased enjoyed at the time of his death and, in particular, where any time limit had begun to run against the deceased the person in whose favour an order has been made shall have the benefit of only that portion of the time limit which remained unexpired at the time of the death.

(6) In this section "appeal" includes any sort of application, whether at common law or under statute, for the review of any conviction, penalty or other order made in respect of the deceased in any criminal proceedings whatsoever.

NOTE
[1]Inserted by the Crime and Punishment (Scotland) Act 1997 (c. 48), s.20 with effect from August 1, 1997 in terms of the Crime and Punishment (Scotland) Act 1997 (Commencement and Transitional Provisions) Order 1997 (S.I. 1997 No. 1712) para. 3.

Part XIV

General

Criminal Courts Rules Council

304.—(1) There shall be established a body, to be known as the Criminal Courts Rules Council (in this section referred to as "the Council") which shall have the functions conferred on it by subsection (9) below.

(2) The Council shall consist of—

(a) the Lord Justice General, the Lord Justice Clerk and the Clerk of Justiciary;

(b) a further Lord Commissioner of Justiciary appointed by the Lord Justice General;

(c) the following persons appointed by the Lord Justice General after such consultation as he considers appropriate—

(i) two sheriffs;

(ii) two members of the Faculty of Advocates;

(iii) two solicitors;

(iv) one sheriff clerk; and

(v) one person appearing to him to have a knowledge of the procedures and practices of the district court;

(d) two persons appointed by the Lord Justice General after consultation with the Lord Advocate, at least one of whom must be a procurator fiscal;

(e) two persons appointed by the Lord Justice General after consultation with the Secretary of State, at least one of whom must be a person appearing to the Lord Justice General to have—

(i) a knowledge of the procedures and practices of the courts exercising criminal jurisdiction in Scotland; and

(ii) an awareness of the interests of victims of crime and of witnesses in criminal proceedings; and

(f) any persons appointed under subsection (3) below.

(3) The Lord Justice General may appoint not more than two further persons, and the Secretary of State may appoint one person, to membership of the Council.

(4) The chairman of the Council shall be the Lord Justice General or such other member of the Council, being a Lord Commissioner of Justiciary, as the Lord Justice General may nominate.

(5) The members of the Council appointed under paragraphs (b) to (f) of subsection (2) above shall, so long as they retain the respective qualifications mentioned in those paragraphs, hold office for three years and be eligible for reappointment.

(6) Any vacancy in the membership of the Council by reason of the death or demission of office, prior to the expiry of the period for which he was appointed, of a member appointed under any of paragraphs (b) to (f) of subsection (2) above shall be filled by the appointment by the Lord Justice General or, as the case may be, the Secretary of State, after such consultation as is required by the paragraph in question, of another person having the qualifications required by that paragraph, and a person so appointed shall hold office only until the expiry of that period.

(7) The Council shall meet—

(a) at intervals of not more than 12 months; and

(b) at any time when summoned by the chairman or by three members of the Council,

but shall, subject to the foregoing, have power to regulate the summoning of its meetings and the procedure at such meetings.

(8) At any meeting of the Council six members shall be a quorum.

(9) The functions of the Council shall be—

(a) to keep under general review the procedures and practices of the courts exercising criminal jurisdiction in Scotland (including any matters incidental or relating to those procedures or practices); and

(b) to consider and comment on any draft Act of Adjournal submitted to it by the High Court, which shall, in making the Act of Adjournal, take account to such extent as it considers appropriate of any comments made by the Council under this paragraph.

(10) In the discharge of its functions under subsection (9) above the Council may invite representations on any aspect of the procedures and practices of the courts exercising criminal jurisdiction in Scotland (including any matters incidental or relating to those procedures or practices) and shall consider any such representations received by it, whether or not submitted in response to such an invitation.

Acts of Adjournal

305.—(1) The High Court may by Act of Adjournal—

(a) regulate the practice and procedure in relation to criminal procedure;

(b) make such rules and regulations as may be necessary or expedient to carry out the purposes and accomplish the objects of any enactment (including an enactment in this Act) in so far as it relates to criminal procedure;

(c) subject to subsection (5) below, to fix and regulate the fees payable in connection with summary criminal proceedings; and

(d) to make provision for the application of sums paid under section 220 of this Act and for any matter incidental thereto.

(2) The High Court may by Act of Adjournal modify, amend or repeal any enactment (including an enactment in this Act) in so far as that enactment relates to matters with respect to which an Act of Adjournal may be made under subsection (1) above.

(3) No rule, regulation or provision which affects the governor or any other officer of a prison shall be made by Act of Adjournal except with the consent of the Secretary of State.

(4) The Clerk of Justiciary may, with the sanction of the Lord Justice General and the Lord Justice Clerk, vary the forms set out in an Act of Adjournal made under subsection (1) above or any other Act whether passed before or after this Act from time to time as may be found necessary for giving effect to the provisions of this Act relating to solemn procedure.

(5) Nothing in paragraph (c) of subsection (1) above shall empower the High Court to make any regulation which the Secretary of State is empowered to make by the Courts of Law Fees (Scotland) Act 1895.

Information for financial and other purposes

306.—(1) The Secretary of State shall in each year publish such information as he considers expedient for the purpose of—

(a) enabling persons engaged in the administration of criminal justice to become aware of the financial implications of their decisions; or

(b) facilitating the performance by such persons of their duty to avoid discriminating against any persons on the ground of race or sex or any other improper ground.

(2) Publication under subsection (1) above shall be effected in such manner as the Secretary of State considers appropriate for the purpose of bringing the information to the attention of the persons concerned.

Interpretation

307.—(1) In this Act, unless the context otherwise requires—

"appropriate court" means a court named as such in pursuance of section 228(4) of this Act or of Schedule 6 to this Act in a probation order or in an amendment of any such order made on a change of residence of a probationer;

"bail" means release of an accused or an appellant on conditions, or conditions imposed on bail, as the context requires;

"chartered psychologist" means a person for the time being listed in the British Psychological Society's Register of Chartered Psychologists;

"child", except in section 46(3) of and Schedule 1 to this Act, has the meaning assigned to that expression for the purposes of Chapters 2 and 3 of Part II of the Children (Scotland) Act 1995;

"children's hearing" has the meaning assigned to it in Part II of the Children (Scotland) Act 1995;

"Clerk of Justiciary" shall include assistant clerk of justiciary and shall extend and apply to any person duly authorised to execute the duties of Clerk of Justiciary or assistant clerk of justiciary;

"commit for trial" means commit until liberation in due course of law;

"community service order" means an order made under section 238 of this Act;

"complaint" includes a copy of the complaint laid before the court;

"constable" has the same meaning as in the Police (Scotland) Act 1967;

"court of summary jurisdiction" means a court of summary criminal jurisdiction;

"court of summary criminal jurisdiction" includes the sheriff court and district court;

"crime" means any crime or offence at common law or under any Act of Parliament whether passed before or after this Act, and includes an attempt to commit any crime or offence;

[6]"devolution issue" has the same meaning as in Schedule 6 to the Scotland Act 1988;

"diet" includes any continuation of a diet;

[5]"drug treatment and testing order" has the meaning assigned to it in section 234B(2) of this Act;

"enactment" includes an enactment contained in a local Act and any order, regulation or other instrument having effect by virtue of an Act;

"examination of facts" means an examination of facts held under section 55 of this Act;

"existing" means existing immediately before the commencement of this Act;

"extract conviction" and "extract of previous conviction" include certified copy conviction, certificate of conviction, and any other document lawfully issued from any court of justice of the United Kingdom as evidence of a conviction;

"fine" includes—

    (a) any pecuniary penalty, (but not a pecuniary forfeiture or pecuniary compensation); and

    (b) an instalment of a fine;

"governor" means, in relation to a contracted out prison within the meaning of section 106(4) of the Criminal Justice and Public Order Act 1994, the director of the prison;

"guardian", in relation to a child, includes any person who, in the opinion of the court having cognizance of any case in relation to the child or in which the child is concerned, has for the time being the charge of or control over the child;

"guardianship order" has the meaning assigned to it by section 58 of this Act;

"High Court" and "Court of Justiciary" shall mean "High Court of Justiciary" and shall include any court held by the Lords Commissioners of Justiciary, or any of them;

"hospital" means—

 (a) any hospital vested in the Secretary of State under the National Health Service (Scotland) Act 1978;

 [1](aa) any hospital managed by a National Health Service Trust established under section 12A of that Act;

 (b) any private hospital registered under Part IV of the Mental Health (Scotland) Act 1984; and

 (c) any State hospital;

[2]"hospital direction" has the meaning assigned to it by section 59A(1) of this Act.

"hospital order" has the meaning assigned to it by section 58 of this Act;

"impose detention" or "impose imprisonment" means pass a sentence of detention or imprisonment, as the case may be, or make an order for committal in default of payment of any sum of money or for contempt of court;

"indictment" includes any indictment whether in the sheriff court or the High Court framed in the form set out an Act of Adjournal or as nearly as may be in such form;

"judge", in relation to solemn procedure, means a judge of a court of solemn criminal jurisdiction and, in relation to summary procedure, means any sheriff or any judge of a district court;

"justice" includes the sheriff and any stipendiary magistrate or justice of the peace;

"justice of the peace" means any of Her Majesty's justices of the peace for any commission area in Scotland within such commission area;

"legalised police cells" has the like meaning as in the Prisons (Scotland) Act 1989;

"local authority" has the meaning assigned to it by section 1(2) of the Social Work (Scotland) Act 1968;

[7]"local probation board" means a local probation board established under section 4 of the Criminal Justice and Court Services Act 2000;

"Lord Commissioner of Justiciary" includes Lord Justice General and Lord Justice Clerk;

"offence" means any act, attempt or omission punishable by law;

"officer of law" includes, in relation to the service and execution of any warrant, citation, petition, indictment, complaint, list of witnesses, order, notice, or other proceeding or document—

 (a) any macer, messenger-at-arms, sheriff officer or other person having authority to execute a warrant of the court;

 (b) any constable;

 [3](ba) any person commissioned by the Commissioners of Customs and Excise;

 (c) any person who is employed under section 9 of the Police (Scotland) Act 1967 for the assistance of the constables of a police force and who is authorised by the chief constable of that police force in relation to service and execution as mentioned above;

 (d) where the person upon whom service or execution is effected is in prison at the time of service on him, any prison officer; and

 [4](e) any person or class of persons authorised in that regard for the time being by the Lord Advocate or by the Secretary of State;

"order" means any order, byelaw, rule or regulation having statutory authority;

"patient" means a person suffering or appearing to be suffering from mental disorder;

"place of safety", in relation to a person not being a child, means any police station, prison or remand centre, or any hospital the board of management of which are willing temporarily to receive him, and in relation to a child means a place of safety within the meaning of Part II of the Children (Scotland) Act 1995;

"the prescribed sum" has the meaning given by section 225(8) of this Act;

"prison" does not include a naval, military or air force prison;

"prison officer" and "officer of a prison" means, in relation to a contracted out prison within the meaning of section 106(4) of the Criminal Justice and Public Order Act 1994, a prisoner custody officer within the meaning of section 114(1) of that Act;

"probationer" means a person who is under supervision by virtue of a probation order or who was under such supervision at the time of the commission of any relevant offence or failure to comply with such order;

"probation order" has the meaning assigned to it by section 228 of this Act;

"probation period" means the period for which a probationer is placed under supervision by a probation order;

"procurator fiscal" means the procurator fiscal for a sheriff court district, and includes assistant procurator fiscal and procurator fiscal depute and any person duly authorised to execute the duties of the procurator fiscal;

"prosecutor"—

    (a) for the purposes of proceedings other than summary proceedings, includes Crown Counsel, procurator fiscal, any other person prosecuting in the public interest and any private prosecutor; and

    (b) for the purposes of summary proceedings, includes procurator fiscal, and any other person prosecuting in the public interest and complainer and any person duly authorised to represent or act for any public prosecutor;

"remand" means an order adjourning the proceedings or continuing the case and giving direction as to detention in custody or liberation during the period of adjournment or continuation and references to remanding a person or remanding in custody or on bail shall be construed accordingly;

"remand centre" has the like meaning as in the Prisons (Scotland) Act 1989;

"residential establishment" means an establishment within the meaning of that expression for the purposes of the Social Work (Scotland) Act 1968 or, as the case may be, of Part II of the Children (Scotland) Act 1995;

"responsible medical officer" has the meaning assigned to it by section 59 of the Mental Health (Scotland) Act 1984;

"restriction order" has the meaning assigned to it by section 59 of this Act;

"sentence", whether of detention or of imprisonment, means a sentence passed in respect of a crime or offence and does not include an order for committal in default of payment of any sum of money or for contempt of court;

"sheriff clerk" includes sheriff clerk depute, and extends and applies to any person duly authorised to execute the duties of sheriff clerk;

"sheriff court district" extends to the limits within which the sheriff has jurisdiction in criminal matters whether by statute or at common law;

"State hospital" has the meaning assigned to it in Part VIII of the Mental Health (Scotland) Act 1984;

"statute" means any Act of Parliament, public general, local, or private, and any Provisional Order confirmed by Act of Parliament;

"supervision requirement" has the meaning assigned to it in Part II of the Children (Scotland) Act 1995;

"training school order" has the same meaning as in the Social Work (Scotland) Act 1968;

"witness" includes haver;

"young offenders institution" has the like meaning as in the Prisons (Scotland) Act 1989.

(2) References in this Act to a court do not include references to a court-martial; and nothing in this Act shall be construed as affecting the punishment which may be awarded by a court-martial under the Naval Discipline Act 1957, the Army Act 1955 or the Air Force Act 1955 for a civil offence within the meaning of those Acts.

(3) For the purposes of this Act, except section 228(6), where a probation order has been made on appeal, the order shall be deemed to have been made by the court from which the appeal was brought.

(4) Any reference in this Act to a previous sentence of imprisonment shall be construed as including a reference to a previous sentence of penal servitude; any such reference to a previous sentence of Borstal training shall be construed as including a reference to a previous sentence of detention in a Borstal institution.

(5) Any reference in this Act to a previous conviction or sentence shall be construed as a reference to a previous conviction by a court in any part of the United Kingdom and to a previous sentence passed by any such court.

(6) References in this Act to an offence punishable with imprisonment shall be construed, in relation to any offender, without regard to any prohibition or restriction imposed by or under any enactment, including this Act, upon the imprisonment of offenders of his age.

(7) Without prejudice to section 46 of this Act, where the age of any person at any time is material for the purposes of any provision of this Act regulating the powers of a court, his age at the material time shall be deemed to be or to have been that which appears to the court, after considering any available evidence, to be or to have been his age at that time.

(8) References in this Act to findings of guilty and findings that an offence has been committed shall be construed as including references to pleas of guilty and admissions that an offence has been committed.

NOTES

[1]Inserted by the Crime and Punishment (Scotland) Act 1997 (c. 48), s.62(1) and Sched. 1, para. 21(34)(b) with effect from August 1, 1997 in terms of the Crime and Punishment (Scotland) Act 1997 (Commencement and Transitional Provisions) Order 1997 (S.I. 1997 No. 1712) para. 3.

[2]Inserted by the Crime and Punishment (Scotland) Act 1997 (c. 48), s.6(5) with effect from January 1, 1998 in terms of the Crime and Punishment (Scotland) Act 1997 (Commencement No. 2 and Transitional and Consequential Provisions) Order 1997 (S.I. 1997 No. 2323) Sched. 2.

[3]Inserted by the Crime and Disorder Act 1998 (c. 37), Sched. 8, para. 124 (effective September 30, 1998: S.I. 1998 No. 2327).

[4]Amended as above.

[5]Inserted by the Crime and Disorder Act 1998 (c. 37), s.95.

[6]Inserted by the Scotland Act 1998 (c. 46), s.125(1) and Sched. 8, para. 31(3).

[7]Inserted by the Criminal Justice and Court Services Act 2000 (c. 43), s.74 and Sched. 7, para.

126. Brought into force by the Criminal Justice and Court Services Act 2000 (Commencement No. 4) Order 2001 (S.I. 2001 No. 919 (C. 33)), art. 2(f)(ii) (effective April 1, 2001).

Construction of enactments referring to detention etc.

308. In any enactment—
(a) any reference to a sentence of imprisonment as including a reference to a sentence of any other form of detention shall be construed as including a reference to a sentence of detention under section 207 of this Act; and
(b) any reference to imprisonment as including any other form of detention shall be construed as including a reference to detention under that section.

Short title, commencement and extent

309.—(1) This Act may be cited as the Criminal Procedure Act 1995.
(2) This Act shall come into force on 1 April 1996.
(3) Subject to subsections (4) and (5) below, this Act extends to Scotland only.
(4) The following provisions of this Act and this section extend to England and Wales—
section 44;
section 47;
section 209(3) and (7);
section 234(4) to (11);
section 244;
section 252 for the purposes of the construction mentioned in subsection (1) of that subsection;
section 303(4).
(5) The following provisions of this Act and this section extend to Northern Ireland—
section 44;
section 47;
section 244;
section 252 for the purposes of the construction mentioned in subsection (1) of that subsection;
section 303(4).

(6) Section 297(3) and (4) of this Act and this section also extend to the Isle of Man.

SCHEDULES

SCHEDULE 1

Offences Against Children Under the Age of 17 Years to which Special Provisions Apply

1. Any offence under Part I of the Criminal Law (Consolidation) (Scotland) Act 1995.
2. Any offence under section 12, 15, 22 or 33 of the Children and Young Persons (Scotland) Act 1937.
3. Any other offence involving bodily injury to a child under the age of 17 years.

4. Any offence involving the use of lewd, indecent or libidinous practice or behaviour towards a child under the age of 17 years.

Sections 34 & 64(2) SCHEDULE 2

EXAMPLES OF INDICTMENTS

"A.B. (*name and address, that given in the declaration being sufficient*), you are indicted at the instance of A. F. R. (*name of Lord Advocate*), Her Majesty's Advocate, and the charge against you is that on 20th 199, in a shop in George Street, Edinburgh, occupied by John Cruikshank, draper, you did steal a shawl and a boa."

"...You did rob Charles Doyle, a cattle dealer, of Biggar, Lanarkshire, of a watch and chain and £36 of money..."

"...You did break into the house occupied by Andrew Howe, banker's clerk, and did there steal twelve spoons, a ladle, and a candlestick..."

"...You did force open (*or* attempt to force open) a lockfast cupboard and did thus attempt to steal therefrom..."

"...You did place your hand in one of the packets of Thomas Kerr, commercial traveller, 115 Main Street, Perth, and did thus attempt to steal..."

"...You did assault Lewis Mann, station-master of Earlston, and compress his throat and attempt to take from him a watch and chain..."

"...You did, while in the employment of James Pentland, accountant in Frederick Street, Edinburgh, embezzle £4,075 of money..."

"...You did, while acting as commercial traveller to Brown and Company, merchants in Leith, at the times and places specified in the inventory hereto subjoined, receive from the persons therein set forth the respective sums of money therein specified for the said Brown and Company, and did embezzle the same (*or* did embezzle £470 of money, being part thereof)..."

"...You did pretend to Norah Omond, residing there, that you were a collector of subscriptions for a charitable society, and did thus induce her to deliver to you £15 of money as a subscription thereto, which you appropriated to your own use..."

"...You did reset a watch and chain, pocket book and £15.55 of money, the same having been dishonestly appropriated by theft or robbery..."

"...You did utter as genuine a bill, on which the name of John Jones bore to be signed as acceptor, such signature being forged by (*here describe in general terms how the bill was uttered, and add where the bill is produced*), and said bill of exchange is No. of the productions lodged herewith..."

"...You did utter as genuine a letter bearing to be a certificate of character of you, as a domestic servant, by Mary Watson, of 15 Bon Accord Street, Aberdeen, what was written above the signature of Mary Watson having been written there by some other person without her authority by handing it to Ellen Chisholm of Panmore Street, Forfar, to whom you were applying for a situation (*here add when the letter is produced*), and said letter is No. of the productions lodged herewith..."

"...You did utter a cheque signed by Henry Smith for £8 sterling, which had been altered without his authority by adding the letter Y to eight and the figure 0 to figure 8, so as to make it read as a cheque for XC11,480 sterling, by presenting such altered cheque for payment to Allen Brown, Cashier of the Bank of Scotland at Callander (*here add when the cheque is produced*), and said cheque is No. of the productions lodged herewith..."

"...You did, when examined under section 45 of the Bankruptcy (Scotland) Act 1985 before Hubert Hamilton Esquire, sheriff of the Lothians and Borders, depone (*here state the general nature of the false statement*), in order to defraud your creditors..."

"...You did, sequestration having been awarded on your estate on the 20th March 1991, conceal property consisting of (*here state generally the property concealed*), falling under your sequestration, in order to defraud your creditor, by burying it in the garden of your house in Troon Street, Kilmarnock (*or* by removing it to the house of James Kidd, your son, No. 17 Greek Street, Port-Glasgow)..."

"...You did set fire to a warehouse occupied by Peter Cranston in Holly Lane, Greenock, and the fire took effect on said warehouse, and this you did wilfully (*or* culpably and recklessly)..."

"...You did set fire to the shop in Brown Street, Blairgowrie, occupied by you, with intent to defraud the Liverpool, London, and Globe Insurance Company, and the fire took effect on said shop..."

"...You did assault Theresa Unwin, your wife, and did beat her and did murder her..."

"...You did stab Thomas Underwood, baker, of Shiels Place, Oban, and did murder him..."

"...You did administer poison to Vincent Wontner, your son, and did murder him..."

"...You did strangle Mary Shaw, mill-worker, daughter of John Shaw, residing at Juniper Green, in the county of Midlothian, and did murder her..."

"...You were delivered of a child now dead or amissing, and you did conceal your pregnancy and did not call for or use assistance at the birth, contrary to the Concealment of Birth (Scotland) Act 1809..."

"...You did assault Hector Morrison, carter, of 20 Buccleuch Street, Dalkeith, and did beat him with your fists and with a stick, and did break his arm..."

"...You did ravish Harriet Cowan, mill-worker, of 27 Tweed Row, Peebles..."

"...You did attempt to ravish Jane Peters, servant, at Glen House, near Dunbar..."

"...You did, when acting as railway signalman, cancel a danger signal and allow a train to enter on a part of the line protected by the signals under your charge, and did cause a collision, and did kill William Peters, commercial traveller, of Brook Street, Carlisle, a passenger in said train..."

"...You formed part of a riotous mob, which, acting of common purpose, obstructed A. B., C. D., and E. F., constables of the Northern constabulary on duty, and assaulted them, and forcibly took two persons whom they had arrested from their custody..."

"...You did, being the lawful husband of Helen Hargreaves, of 20 Teviot Row, Edinburgh, and she being still alive, bigamously marry Dorothy Rose, a widow, of 7 Blacks Row, Brechin, and did cohabit with her as her husband..."

"...You being sworn as a witness in a civil cause, then proceeding in the sheriff court, deponed (*here set forth the statements said to be false*) the truth as you knew being that (*here state the true facts*)..."

"...You did suborn James Carruthers, scavenger, 12 Hercles Street, Edinburgh, to depone as a witness in the sheriff court of Edinburgh, that (*here set forth the statements said to be false*), and he did (*time and place*) depone to that effect, the truth as you knew being (*here state the true facts*)..."

"...You did deforce John Macdonald, a sheriff officer of Renfrewshire, and prevent him serving a summons issued by the sheriff of Renfrewshire upon Peter M'Innes, market gardener in Renfrew..."

Sections 64(6) and 138(4)   SCHEDULE 3

INDICTMENTS AND COMPLAINTS

1. An accused may be named and designed—
(a) according to the existing practice; or
(b) by the name given by him and designed as of the place given by him as his residence when he is examined or further examined; or
(c) by the name under which he is committed until liberated in due course of law.

2. It shall not be necessary to specify by any *nomen juris* the offence which is charged, but it shall be sufficient that the indictment or complaint sets forth facts relevant and sufficient to constitute an indictable offence or, as the case may be, an offence punishable on complaint.

3. It shall not be necessary to allege that any act or commission or omission charged was done or omitted to be done "wilfully" or "maliciously", or "wickedly and feloniously", or "falsely and fraudulently" or "knowingly", or "culpably and recklessly", or "negligently", or in "breach of duty", or to use such words as "knowing the same to be forged", or "having good reason to know", or "well knowing the same to have been stolen", or to use any similar words or expressions qualifying any act charged, but such qualifying allegation shall be implied in every case.

4.—(1) The latitude formerly used in stating time shall be implied in all statements of time where an exact time is not of the essence of the charge.

(2) The latitude formerly used in stating any place by adding to the word "at", or to the word "in", the words "or near", or the words "or in the near neighbourhood thereof" or similar words, shall be implied in all statements of place where the actual place is not of the essence of the charge.

(3) Subject to sub-paragraph (4) below, where the circumstances of the offence charged make it necessary to take an exceptional latitude in regard to time or place it shall not be necessary to set forth the circumstances in the indictment, or to set forth that the particular time or the particular place is to the prosecutor unknown.

(4) Where exceptional latitude is taken as mentioned in sub-paragraph (3) above, the court shall, if satisfied that such exceptional latitude was not reasonable in the circumstances of the case, give such remedy to the accused by adjournment of the trial or otherwise as shall seem just.

(5) Notwithstanding sub-paragraph (4) above, nothing in any rule of law shall prohibit the amendment of an indictment or, as the case may be, a complaint to include a time outwith the

exceptional latitude if it appears to the court that the amendment would not prejudice the accused.

(6) The latitude formerly used in describing quantities by the words "or thereby", or the words "or part thereof", or the words "or some other quantity to the prosecutor unknown" or similar words, shall be implied in all statements of quantities.

(7) The latitude formerly used in stating details connected with the perpetration of any act regarding persons, things or modes by inserting general alternative statements followed by the words "to the prosecutor unknown" or similar words, shall be implied in every case.

(8) In this paragraph references to latitude formerly used are references to such use before the commencement of—

(a) in the case of proceedings on indictment, the Criminal Procedure (Scotland) Act 1887; and

(b) in the case of summary proceedings, the Summary Jurisdiction (Scotland) Act 1908.

5. The word "money" shall include cheques, banknotes, postal orders, money orders and foreign currency.

6. Any document referred to shall be referred to by a general description and, where it is to be produced in proceedings on indictment, by the number given to it in the list of productions for the prosecution.

7. In an indictment which charges a crime importing personal injury inflicted by the accused, resulting in death or serious injury to the person, the accused may be lawfully convicted of the aggravation that the assault or other injurious act was committed with intent to commit such crime.

8.—(1) In an indictment or a complaint charging the resetting of property dishonestly appropriated—

(a) having been taken by theft or robbery; or

(b) by breach of trust, embezzlement or falsehood, fraud and wilful imposition,

it shall be sufficient to specify that the accused received the property, it having been dishonestly appropriated by theft or robbery, or by breach of trust and embezzlement, or by falsehood, fraud and wilful imposition, as the case may be.

(2) Under an indictment or a complaint for robbery, theft, breach of trust and embezzlement or falsehood, fraud and wilful imposition, an accused may be convicted of reset.

(3) Under an indictment or a complaint for robbery, breach of trust and embezzlement, or falsehood, fraud and wilful imposition, an accused may be convicted of theft.

(4) Under an indictment or a complaint for theft, an accused may be convicted of breach of trust and embezzlement, or of falsehood, fraud and wilful imposition, or may be convicted of theft, although the circumstances proved may in law amount to robbery.

(5) The power conferred by sub-paragraphs (2) to (4) above to convict a person of an offence other than that with which he is charged shall be exercisable by the sheriff court before which he is tried notwithstanding that the other offence was committed outside the jurisdiction of that sheriff court.

9.—(1) Where two or more crimes or acts of crime are charged cumulatively, it shall be lawful to convict of any one or more of them.

(2) Any part of the charge in an indictment or complaint which itself constitutes an indictable offence or, as the case may be an offence punishable on complaint, shall be separable and it shall be lawful to convict the accused of that offence.

(3) Where any crime is charged as having been committed with a particular intent or with particular circumstances of aggravation, it shall be lawful to convict of the crime without such intent or aggravation.

10.—(1) Under an indictment or, as the case may be, a complaint which charges a completed offence, the accused may be lawfully convicted of an attempt to commit the offence.

(2) Under an indictment or complaint charging an attempt, the accused may be convicted of such attempt although the evidence is sufficient to prove the completion of the offence said to have been attempted.

(3) Under an indictment or complaint which charges an offence involving personal injury inflicted by the accused, resulting in death or serious injury to the person, the accused may be lawfully convicted of the assault or other injurious act, and may also be lawfully convicted of the aggravation that the assault or other injurious act was committed with intent to commit such offence.

11. In an indictment or complaint charging a contravention of an enactment the description of the offence in the words of the enactment contravened, or in similar words, shall be sufficient.

12. In a complaint charging a contravention of an enactment—

(a) the statement that an act was done contrary to an enactment shall imply a statement—

(i) that the enactment applied to the circumstances existing at the time and place of the offence;

(ii) that the accused was a person bound to observe the enactment;

(iii) that any necessary preliminary procedure had been duly gone through; and

(iv) that all the circumstances necessary to a contravention existed,

and, in the case of the contravention of a subordinate instrument, such statement shall imply a statement that the instrument was duly made, confirmed, published and generally made effectual according to the law applicable, and was in force at the time and place in question; and

(b) where the offence is created by more than one section of one or more statutes or subordinate instruments, it shall be necessary to specify only the leading section or one of the leading sections.

13. In the case of an offence punishable under any enactment, it shall be sufficient to allege that the offence was committed contrary to the enactment and to refer to the enactment founded on without setting out the words of the enactment at length.

14. Where—

(a) any act alleged in an indictment or complaint as contrary to any enactment is also criminal at common law; or

(b) where the facts proved under the indictment or complaint do not amount to a contravention of the enactment, but do amount to an offence at common law,

it shall be lawful to convict of the common law offence.

15. Where the evidence in a trial is sufficient to prove the identity of any person, corporation or company, or of any place, or of anything, it shall not be a valid objection to the sufficiency of the evidence that any particulars specified in the indictment or complaint relating to such identity have not been proved.

16. Where, in relation to an offence created by or under an enactment any exception, exemption, proviso, excuse, or qualification, is expressed to have effect whether by the same or any other enactment, the exception, exemption, proviso, excuse or qualification need not be specified or negatived in the indictment or complaint, and the prosecution is not required to prove it, but the accused may do so.

17. It shall be competent to include in one indictment or complaint both common law and statutory charges.

18. In any proceedings under the Merchant Shipping Acts it shall not be necessary to produce the official register of the ship referred to in the proceedings in order to prove the nationality of the ship, but the nationality of the ship as stated in the indictment or, as the case may be, complaint shall, in the absence of evidence to the contrary, be presumed.

19. In offences inferring dishonest appropriation of property brought before a court whose power to deal with such offences is limited to cases in which the value of such property does not exceed level 4 on the standard scale it shall be assumed, and it shall not be necessary to state in the charge, that the value of the property does not exceed that sum.

Section 57(5)   SCHEDULE 4

SUPERVISION AND TREATMENT ORDERS

PART I

PRELIMINARY

1.—(1) In this Schedule "supervision and treatment order" means an order requiring the person in respect of whom it is made ("the supervised person")—

(a) to be under the supervision of a social worker who is an officer of the local authority for the area where the supervised person resides or is to reside (in this Schedule referred to as "the supervising officer") for such period, not being more than three years, as is specified in the order;

(b) to comply during that period with instructions given to him by the supervising officer regarding his supervision; and

(c) to submit during that period to treatment by or under the direction of a medical practitioner with a view to the improvement of his mental condition.

(2) The Secretary of State may by order amend sub-paragraph (1) above by substituting, for the period for the time being specified in that sub-paragraph, such period as may be specified in the order.

(3) An order under sub-paragraph (2) above may make any amendment to paragraph 8(2) below which the Secretary of State considers necessary in consequence of the order.

(4) The power of the Secretary of State to make orders under sub-paragraph (2) above shall

be exercisable by statutory instrument subject to annulment in pursuance of a resolution of either House of Parliament.

PART II

MAKING AND EFFECT OF ORDERS

Circumstances in which orders may be made

2.—(1) The court shall not make a supervision and treatment order unless it is satisfied—

(a) that, having regard to all the circumstances of the case, the making of such an order is the most suitable means of dealing with the person; and

(b) on the written or oral evidence of two or more medical practitioners approved for the purposes of section 20 or 39 of the Mental Health (Scotland) Act 1984, that the mental condition of the person—

(i) is such as requires and may be susceptible to treatment; but

(ii) is not such as to warrant the making of an order under paragraph (a) of subsection (2) of section 57 of this Act (whether with or without an order under paragraph (b) of that subsection) or an order under paragraph (c) of that subsection.

(2) The court shall not make a supervision and treatment order unless it is also satisfied—

(a) that the supervising officer intended to be specified in the order is willing to undertake the supervision; and

(b) that arrangements have been made for the treatment intended to be specified in the order.

(3) Subsections (3) to (5) of section 61 of this Act shall have effect with respect to proof of a person's mental condition for the purposes of sub-paragraph (1) above as they have effect with respect to proof of an offender's mental condition for the purposes of section 58(1)(a) of this Act.

Making of orders and general requirements

3.—(1) A supervision and treatment order shall specify the local authority area in which the supervised person resides or will reside.

(2) Before making such an order, the court shall explain to the supervised person in ordinary language—

(a) the effect of the order (including any requirements proposed to be included in the order in accordance with paragraph 5 below); and

(b) that the sheriff court for the area in which the supervised person resides or will reside (in this Schedule referred to as "the relevant sheriff court") has power under paragraphs 6 to 8 below to review the order on the application either of the supervised person or of the supervising officer.

(3) After making such an order, the court shall forthwith give a copy of the order to—

(a) the supervised person;

(b) the supervising officer; and

[1](bb) the medical practitioner by whom or under whose supervision the supervised person is to be treated under the order;

(c) the person in charge of any institution in which the supervised person is required by the order to reside.

(4) After making such an order, the court shall also send to the relevant sheriff court—

(a) a copy of the order; and

(b) such documents and information relating to the case as it considers likely to be of assistance to that court in the exercise of its functions in relation to the order.

(5) Where such an order is made, the supervised person shall comply with such instructions as he may from time to time be given by the supervising officer regarding his supervision and shall keep in touch with that officer and notify him of any change of address.

Obligatory requirements as to medical treatment

4.—(1) A supervision and treatment order shall include a requirement that the supervised person shall submit, during the period specified in the order, to treatment by or under the direction of a medical practitioner with a view to the improvement of his mental condition.

(2) The treatment required by the order shall be such one of the following kinds of treatment as may be specified in the order, that is to say—

(a) treatment as a non-resident patient at such institution or place as may be specified in the order; and

(b) treatment by or under the direction of such medical practitioner as may be so specified;

but the nature of the treatment shall not be specified in the order except as mentioned in paragraph (a) or (b) above.

(3) Where the medical practitioner by whom or under whose direction the supervised person is being treated for his mental condition in pursuance of a supervision and treatment order is of the opinion that part of the treatment can be better or more conveniently given at an institution or place which—

(a) is not specified in the order; and

(b) is one at which the treatment of the supervised person will be given by or under the direction of a medical practitioner,

he may, with the consent of the supervised person, make arrangements for him to be treated accordingly.

(4) Where any such arrangements as are mentioned in sub-paragraph (3) above are made for the treatment of a supervised person—

(a) the medical practitioner by whom the arrangements are made shall give notice in writing to the supervising officer, specifying the institution or place at which the treatment is to be carried out; and

(b) the treatment provided for by the arrangements shall be deemed to be treatment to which he is required to submit in pursuance of the supervision and treatment order.

Optional requirements as to residence

5.—(1) Subject to sub-paragraphs (2) to (4) below, a supervision and treatment order may include requirements as to the residence of the supervised person.

(2) Such an order may not require the supervised person to reside as a resident patient in a hospital.

(3) Before making such an order containing any such requirement, the court shall consider the home surroundings of the supervised person.

(4) Where such an order requires the supervised person to reside in any institution, the period for which he is so required to reside shall be specified in the order.

PART III

REVOCATION AND AMENDMENT OF ORDERS

Revocation of order in interests of health or welfare

6. Where a supervision and treatment order is in force in respect of any person and, on the application of the supervised person or the supervising officer, it appears to the relevant sheriff court that, having regard to circumstances which have arisen since the order was made, it would be in the interests of the health or welfare of the supervised person that the order should be revoked, the court may revoke the order.

Amendment of order by reason of change of residence

7.—(1) This paragraph applies where, at any time while a supervision and treatment order is in force in respect of any person, the relevant sheriff court is satisfied that—

(a) the supervised person proposes to change, or has changed, his residence from the area specified in the order to the area of another local authority;

(b) a social worker who is an officer of the other local authority ("the new supervising officer") is willing to undertake the supervision; and

(c) the requirements of the order as respects treatment will continue to be complied with.

(2) Subject to sub-paragraph (3) below the court may, and on the application of the supervising officer shall, amend the supervision and treatment order by substituting the other area for the area specified in the order and the new supervising officer for the supervising officer specified in the order.

(3) Where a supervision and treatment order contains requirements which, in the opinion of the court, can be complied with only if the supervised person continues to reside in the area specified in the order, the court shall not amend the order under this paragraph unless it also, in accordance with paragraph 8 below, either—

(a) cancels those requirements; or

(b) substitutes for those requirements other requirements which can be complied with if the supervised person ceases to reside in that area.

Amendment of requirements of order

8.—(1) Without prejudice to paragraph 7 above, but subject to sub-paragraph (2) below, the relevant sheriff court may, on the application of the supervised person or the supervising officer, by order amend a supervision and treatment order—

(a) by cancelling any of the requirements of the order; or

(b) by inserting in the order (either in addition to or in substitution for any such requirement) any requirement which the court could include if it were the court by which the order was made and were then making it.

(2) The power of the court under sub-paragraph (1) above shall not include power to amend an order by extending the period specified in it beyond the end of three years from the date of the original order.

Amendment of requirements in pursuance of medical report

9.—(1) Where the medical practitioner by whom or under whose direction the supervised person is being treated for his mental condition in pursuance of any requirement of a supervision and treatment order—

(a) is of the opinion mentioned in sub-paragraph (2) below; or

(b) is for any reason unwilling to continue to treat or direct the treatment of the supervised person,

he shall make a report in writing to that effect to the supervising officer and that officer shall apply under paragraph 8 above to the relevant sheriff court for the variation or cancellation of the requirement.

(2) The opinion referred to in sub-paragraph (1) above is—

(a) that the treatment of the supervised person should be continued beyond the period specified in the supervision and treatment order;

(b) that the supervised person needs different treatment, being treatment of a kind to which he could be required to submit in pursuance of such an order;

(c) that the supervised person is not susceptible to treatment; or

(d) that the supervised person does not require further treatment.

Supplemental

10.—²(1) On the making under paragraph 6 above of an order revoking a supervision and treatment order, the sheriff clerk shall forthwith give a copy of the revoking order to the supervising officer and to the medical practitioner by whom or under whose supervision the supervised person was treated under the supervision and treatment order.

(2) On receipt of a copy of the revoking order the supervising officer shall give a copy to the supervised person and to the person in charge of any institution in which the supervised person was required by the order to reside.

11.—(1) On the making under paragraph 7 or 8 above of an order amending a supervision and treatment order, the sheriff clerk shall forthwith—

²(a) if the order amends the supervision and treatment order otherwise than by substituting a new area or a new place for the one specified in that order, give a copy of the amending order to the supervising officer and to the medical practitioner by whom or under whose supervision the supervised person has been treated under the supervision and treatment order;

(b) if the order amends the supervision and treatment order in the manner excepted by paragraph (a) above, send to the new relevant sheriff court—

(i) a copy of the amending order; and

(ii) such documents and information relating to the case as he considers likely to be of assistance to that court in exercising its functions in relation to the order;

and in a case falling within paragraph (b) above, the sheriff clerk shall give a copy of the amending order to the supervising officer.

(2) On receipt of a copy of an amending order the supervising officer shall give a copy to the supervised person and to the person in charge of any institution in which the supervised person is or was required by the order to reside.

12. On the making, revocation or amendment of a supervision and treatment order the supervising officer shall give a copy of the order or, as the case may be, of the order revoking or amending it, to the Mental Welfare Commission for Scotland.

[1]Inserted by the Crime and Punishment (Scotland) Act 1997 (c. 48), Sched. 1, para. 21(35) with effect from January 1, 1998 as provided by The Crime and Punishment (Scotland) Act 1997 (Commencement No. 2 and Transitional and Consequential Provisions) Order 1997 (S.I. 1997 No. 2323) Art. 4, Sched. 2.

[2]As amended by the above provisions with effect from January 1, 1998.

Section 138(2)   SCHEDULE 5

Forms of Complaint and Charges

The following Forms are additional to those contained in Schedule 2 to this Act, all of which, in so far as applicable to charges which may be tried summarily, are deemed to be incorporated in this Schedule:—

You did assault A.L. and strike him with your fists.

You did conduct yourself in a disorderly manner and commit a breach of the peace.

You did threaten violence to the lieges and commit a breach of the peace.

You did fight and commit a breach of the peace.

You did publicly expose your person in a shameless and indecent manner in presence of the lieges.

You did obtain from A.N. board and lodging to the value of £16 without paying and intending not to pay therefor.

You did maliciously knock down 20 metres of the coping of a wall forming the fence between two fields on the said farm.

You did maliciously place a block of wood on the railway line and attempt to obstruct a train.

You did drive a horse and cart recklessly to the danger of the lieges.

You did break into a poultry house and steal three fowls.

You did steal a coat which you obtained from R.O. on the false representation that you had been sent for it by her husband.

having received from D.G. £6 to hand to E.R., you did on (date) at (place) steal the said sum.

having received from G.R. a watch in loan, you did on at, sell it to E.G., and steal it.

having found a watch, you did, without trying to discover its owner, sell it on at, to O.R., and steal it.

You did acquire from K.O., a private in the Third Battalion a military jacket and waist belt, contrary to section 195 of the Army Act 1955.

You, being a person whose estate has been sequestrated, did obtain credit from W.A. to the extent of £260 without informing him that your estate had been sequestrated and that you had not received your discharge, contrary to section 67(9) of the Bankruptcy (Scotland) Act 1985.

You, being the occupier of the said house, did use the same for the purpose of betting with persons resorting thereto, contrary to section 1 of the Betting, Gaming and Lotteries Act 1963.

You did frequent and loiter in the said street for the purpose of betting and receiving bets, contrary to section 8 of the Betting, Gaming and Lotteries Act 1963.

You did assault L.S., a constable of the Police, while engaged in the execution of his duty, and with a stick strike him on the face to the great effusion of blood contrary to section 41 of the Police (Scotland) Act 1967.

You did cruelly ill-treat a horse by causing it to draw a cart while it was suffering from a sore on its back under the saddle, contrary to section 1 of the Protection of Animals (Scotland) Act 1912.

You did wilfully neglect your children K.I., aged seven years; J.I., aged five years; and H.I., aged three years, by failing to provide them with adequate food and clothing, and by keeping them in a filthy and verminous condition, contrary to section 12 of the Children and Young Persons (Scotland) Act 1937.

You are the owner of a dog which is dangerous and not kept under proper control, and which on in did chase a flock of sheep, contrary to section 2 of the Dogs Act 1871, section 2, as amended by section 1 of the Dogs Act 1906, whereby you are liable to be ordered to keep the said dog under proper control or to destroy it.

You, being a parent of D.U., a child of school age, aged, who has attended school, and the said child having failed, between and, without reasonable excuse, to attend regularly at the said school, you are thereby guilty of an offence against section 35 of the Education (Scotland) Act 1980.

being an unauthorised place you did keep for sale 75 kilograms of gunpowder, contrary to the Explosives Act 1875, section 5.

You did keep 78 kilograms of gunpowder, and did not keep it in a fireproof safe, contrary to the Explosives Act 1875, section 22 and section 3, subsection (1), Mode B, of the Order in Council dated 26th October 1896.

You did sell and deliver to N.C. to his prejudice an article of food namely; gallons of sweet milk which was not of the nature, substance and quality of the article demanded by him and was not genuine sweet milk in respect that it was deficient in milk fat to the extent of per cent, or thereby in that it contained only per cent, of milk fat, conform to certificate of analysis granted on (date) by A.N. analytical chemist (address), public analyst for (a copy of which certificate of analysis is annexed hereto) of a sample of the said milk taken (specify time and place) by L.O., duly appointed sampling officer for, acting under the direction of the local authority for the said burgh, while the said milk was in course of delivery to the said N.C. contrary to the Food Act 1984, and the Sale of Milk Regulations 1901.

You did take part in gaming in the street contrary to sections 5 and 8 of the Gaming Act 1968.

You did by night enter on the said land with nets for the purpose of taking game, contrary to section 1 of the Night Poaching Act 1828; or

You did by night unlawfully take six rabbits, contrary to, etc.

You did in the daytime trespass on the said land in search of pursuit of game (*or* rabbits), contrary to section 1 of the Game (Scotland) Act 1832.

You were found in the possession of five hares, a net and six net pins, which hares you had obtained by unlawfully going on land in search or pursuit of game, and which net and nets pins you had used for unlawfully killing or taking game, or you had been accessory thereto, contrary to section 2 of the Poaching Prevention Act 1862.

You did present or cause to be presented to W.E., Assessors for a return in which you falsely stated that the yearly rent of your House. No. Street, was £20, instead of £30, contrary to section 7 of the Lands Valuation (Scotland) Act 1854.

You did sell a half gill of whisky to J.M., who was then a drunken person, contrary to your certificate and section 76 of the Licensing (Scotland) Act 1976.

You were found drunk and incapable of taking care of yourself, and not under the care or protection of some suitable person, contrary to section 74(2) of the Licensing (Scotland) Act 1976.

You did drive a motor car recklessly contrary to section 2 of the Road Traffic Act 1988.

You did act as a pedlar without having obtained a certificate, contrary to section 4 of the Pedlars' Act 1871.

You did place in a Post Office letter box a lighted match, contrary to section 60 of the Post Office Act 1953.

You did travel in a railway carriage without having previously paid your fare, and with intent to avoid payment thereof, contrary to section 5(3)(a) of the Regulation of Railways Act 1889.

Having on within the house No. Street, given birth to a female child, you did fail, within twenty-one days thereafter, to attend personally and give information to C.W., registrar of births, deaths, and marriages for (Registration District), of the particulars required to be registered concerning the birth, contrary to sections 14 and 53 of the Registration of Births, Deaths, and Marriages (Scotland) Act 1965.

You did take two salmon during the annual close time by means of cobles and sweep nets, contrary to section 15 of the Salmon Fisheries (Scotland) Act 1868.

You had in your possession for use for trade a counter balance which was false, and two weights, which were unjust, contrary to the Weights and Measures Act 1985, section 17.

Section 231(1)   SCHEDULE 6

DISCHARGE OF AND AMENDMENT TO PROBATION ORDERS

Discharge

1. A probation order may on the application of the officer supervising the probationer or of the probationer be discharged—
   (a) by the appropriate court; or
   (b) if no appropriate court has been named in the original or in any amending order, by the court which made the order.

Amendment

2.—(1) If the court by which a probation order was made, or the appropriate court, is satisfied that the probationer proposes to change or has changed his residence from the area of a local authority named in the order to the area of another local authority, the court may, and if application is made in that behalf by the officer supervising the probationer shall, by order, amend the probation order by—

(a) substituting for the area named therein that other area; and

(b) naming the appropriate court to which all the powers of the court by which the order was made shall be transferred and shall require the local authority for that other area to arrange for the probationer to be under the supervision of an officer of that authority.

(2) Subject to sub-paragraphs (3) and (4) below, the court to be named as the appropriate court in any amendment of a probation order in pursuance of sub-paragraph (1) above shall be a court exercising jurisdiction in the place where the probationer resides or is to reside and shall be a sheriff court or district court according to whether the probation order was made by a sheriff court or district court.

(3) If the probation order was made by a district court and there is no district court exercising jurisdiction in the place mentioned in sub-paragraph (2) above, the court to be named shall be the sheriff court.

(4) If the probation order contains requirements which in the opinion of the court cannot be complied with unless the probationer continues to reside in the local authority area named in the order, the court shall not amend the order as mentioned in sub-paragraph (2) above unless, in accordance with the following provisions of this Schedule, it cancels those requirements or substitutes therefor other requirements which can be so complied with.

(5) Where a probation order is amended under this paragraph, the clerk of the court amending it shall send to the clerk of the appropriate court four copies of the order together with such documents and information relating to the case as the court amending the order considers likely to be of assistance to the appropriate court, and the clerk of that court shall send one copy of the probation order to the local authority of the substituted local authority area and two copies to the officer supervising the probationer, one of which the supervising officer shall give to the probationer.

(6) The foregoing provisions of this paragraph shall, in a case where the probation order was made by the High Court, have effect subject to the following modifications—

(a) the court shall not name an appropriate court, but may substitute for the local authority named in the order, the local authority for the area in which the probationer is to reside;

(b) the Clerk of Justiciary shall send to the chief social work officer of that area in which the probationer is to reside three copies of the amending order together with such documents and information relating to the case as is likely to be of assistance to the chief social work officer, and the chief social work officer shall send two copies of the amending order to the officer supervising the probationer, one of which the supervising officer shall give to the probationer.

3.—(1) Without prejudice to paragraph 2 above, the court by which a probation order was made or the appropriate court may, upon application made by the officer supervising the probationer or by the probationer, subject to sub-paragraph (2) below, by order amend a probation order by cancelling any of the requirements thereof or by inserting therein (either in addition to or in substitution for any such requirement) any requirement which could be included in the order if it were then being made by that court in accordance with sections 228 to 230 of this Act.

(2) The court shall not amend a probation order under sub-paragraph (1) above—

(a) by reducing the probation period, or by extending that period beyond the end of three years from the date of the original order;

(b) so that the probationer is thereby required to reside in any institution or place, or to submit to treatment for his mental condition, for any period or periods exceeding 12 months in all;

(c) by inserting in it a requirement that the probationer shall submit to treatment for his mental condition unless the amending order is made within three months after the date of the original order.

4. Where the medical practitioner or chartered psychologist by whom or under whose direction a probationer is being treated for his mental condition in pursuance of any requirement of the probation order is of the opinion—

(a) that the treatment of the probationer should be continued beyond the period specified for that purpose in the order; or

(b) that the probationer needs a different kind of treatment (whether in whole or in part) from that which he has been receiving in pursuance of the probation order, being treatment of a kind which could have been specified in the probation order but to which the probationer or his supervising officer has not agreed under section 230(6) of this Act; or

(c) that the probationer is not susceptible to treatment; or

(d) that the probationer does not require further treatment, or where the practitioner or psychologist is for any reason unwilling to continue to treat or direct the treatment of the probationer, he shall make a report in writing to that effect to the officer supervising the probationer and the supervising officer shall apply to the court which made the order or to the appropriate court for the variation or cancellation of the requirement.

General

5.—(1) Where the court which made the order or the appropriate court proposes to amend a probation order under this Schedule, otherwise than on the application of the probationer, it shall cite him to appear before the court; and the court shall not amend the probation order unless the probationer expresses his willingness to comply with the requirements of the order as amended.

(2) Sub-paragraph (1) above shall not apply to an order cancelling a requirement of the probation order or reducing the period of any requirement, or substituting a new area of a local authority for the area named in the probation order.

6. On the making of an order discharging or amending a probation order, the clerk of the court shall forthwith give copies of the discharging or amending order to the officer supervising the probationer; and the supervising officer shall give a copy to the probationer and to the person in charge of any institution in which the probationer is or was required by the order to reside.

Section 235   SCHEDULE 7

SUPERVISED ATTENDANCE ORDERS: FURTHER PROVISIONS

1.—(1) A court shall not make a supervised attendance order in respect of any offender unless—
  (a) the court has been notified by the Secretary of State that arrangements exist for persons of a class which includes the offender who reside in the locality in which the offender resides, or will be residing when the order comes into force, to carry out the requirements of such an order.
  (b) the court is satisfied that provision can be made under the arrangements mentioned in sub-sub-paragraph (a) above for the offender to carry out such requirements.

(2) Before making a supervised attendance order, the court shall explain to the offender in ordinary language—
  (a) the purpose and effect of the order and in particular the obligations on the offender as specified in paragraph 3 below;
  (b) the consequences which may follow under paragraph 4 below if he fails to comply with any of those requirements; and
  (c) that the court has, under paragraph 5 below, the power to review the order on the application either of the offender or of an officer of the local authority in whose area the offender for the time being resides.

(3) The Secretary of State may by order direct that subsection (2) of section 235 of this Act shall be amended by substituting, for any number of hours specified in that subsection such other number of hours as may be specified in the order; and an order under this subsection may in making such amendment specify different such numbers of hours for different classes of case.

(4) An order under sub-paragraph (3) above shall be made by statutory instrument, but no such order shall be made unless a draft of it has been laid before, and approved by a resolution of, each House of Parliament.

2.—(1) A supervised attendance order shall—
  (a) specify the locality in which the offender resides or will be residing when the order comes into force; and
  (b) require the local authority in whose area the locality specified under sub-sub-paragraph (a) above is situated to appoint or assign a supervising officer.

(2) Where, whether on the same occasion or on separate occasions, an offender is made subject to more than one supervised attendance order, the court may direct that the requirements specified in any of those orders shall be concurrent with or additional to those specified in any other of those orders, but so that at no time shall the offender have an outstanding number of hours during which he must carry out the requirements of these orders in excess of the largest number specified in section 235 of this Act.

(3) Upon making a supervised attendance order the court shall—
  (a) give, or send by registered post or by the recorded delivery service, a copy of the order to the offender;
  (b) send a copy of the order to the chief social work officer of the local authority in whose area the offender resides or will be residing when the order comes into force; and

(c) where it is not the appropriate court, send a copy of the order (together with such documents and information relating to the case as are considered useful) to the clerk of the appropriate court.

(4) Where a copy of a supervised attendance order has, under sub-paragraph (3)(a) above, been sent by registered post or by the recorded delivery service, an acknowledgement or certificate of delivery of a letter containing the copy order issued by the Post Office shall be sufficient evidence of the delivery of the letter on the day specified in such acknowledgement or certificate.

3.—(1) An offender in respect of whom a supervised attendance order is in force shall report to the supervising officer and notify him without delay of any change of address or in the times, if any, at which he usually works.

(2) Subject to paragraph 5(1) below, instructions given under a supervised attendance order shall be carried out during the period of twelve months beginning with the date of the order; but, unless revoked, the order shall remain in force until the offender has carried out the instructions given under it for the number of hours specified in it.

(3) The instructions given by the supervising officer under the order shall, so far as practicable, be such as to avoid any conflict with the offender's religious beliefs and any interference with the times, if any, at which he normally works or attends a school or other educational establishment.

4.—(1) If at any time while a supervised attendance order is in force in respect of any offender it appears to the appropriate court, on information from the supervising officer, that that offender has failed to comply with any of the requirements of paragraph 3 above or of the order (including any failure satisfactorily to carry out any instructions which he has been given by the supervising officer under the order), the court may issue a warrant for the arrest of that offender, or may, if it thinks fit, instead of issuing a warrant in the first instance issue a citation requiring the offender to appear before that court at such time as may be specified in the citation.

(2) If it is proved to the satisfaction of the court before which an offender is brought or appears in pursuance of sub-paragraph (1) above that he has failed without reasonable excuse to comply with any of the requirements of paragraph 3 above or of the order (including any failure satisfactorily to carry out any instructions which he has been given by the supervising officer under the order) the court may—

(a) revoke the order and impose such period of imprisonment not exceeding—
    (i) in the case of a sheriff court, three months; and
    (ii) in the case of a district court, 60 days,
  as the court considers appropriate; or

(b) subject to section 235 of this Act and paragraph 2(2) above, vary the number of hours specified in the order.

(3) The evidence of one witness shall, for the purposes of sub-paragraph (2) above, be sufficient evidence.

5.—(1) Where a supervised attendance order is in force in respect of any offender and, on the application of that offender or of the supervising officer, it appears to the appropriate court that it would be in the interests of justice to do so having regard to circumstances which have arisen since the order was made, that court may—

(a) extend, in relation to the order, the period of twelve months specified in paragraph 3 above;

(b) subject to section 235 of this Act and paragraph 2(2) above, vary the numbers of hours specified in the order;

(c) revoke the order; or

(d) revoke the order and impose such period of imprisonment not exceeding—
    (i) in the case of a sheriff court, three months; and
    (ii) in the case of a district court, 60 days,
  as the court considers appropriate.

(2) If the appropriate court is satisfied that the offender proposes to change, or has changed, his residence from the locality for the time being specified under paragraph 2(1)(a) above to another locality and—

(a) that court has been notified by the Secretary of State that arrangements exist for persons who reside in that other locality to carry out instructions under supervised attendance orders; and

(b) it appears to that court that provision can be made under those arrangements for him to carry out instructions under the order,

that court may, and on application of the supervising officer shall, amend the order by substituting that other locality for the locality for the time being specified in the order; and section 235 of this Act and this Schedule shall apply to the order as amended.

(3) Where the court proposes to exercise its powers under sub-paragraph (1)(a), (b) or (d) above otherwise than on the application of the offender, it shall issue a citation requiring him to appear before the court and, if he fails to appear, may issue a warrant for his arrest.

6.—(1) The Secretary of State may make rules for regulating the carrying out of the requirements of supervised attendance orders.

(2) Without prejudice to the generality of sub-paragraph (1) above, rules under this paragraph may—

(a) limit the number of hours during which the requirements of an order are to be met on any one day;

(b) make provision as to the reckoning of time for the purposes of the carrying out of these requirements;

(c) make provision for the payment of travelling and other expenses in connection with the carrying out of these requirements;

(d) provide for records to be kept of what has been done by any person carrying out these requirements.

(3) Rules under this paragraph shall be made by statutory instrument subject to annulment in pursuance of a resolution of either House of Parliament.

7. The Secretary of State shall lay before Parliament each year, or incorporate in annual reports he already makes, a report of the operation of section 235 of this Act and this Schedule.

8. In this Schedule—

"the appropriate court" in relation to a supervised attendance order, means the court having jurisdiction in the locality for the time being specified in the order under paragraph 2(1)(a) above, being a sheriff or district court according to whether the order has been made by a sheriff or district court, but in the case where an order has been made by a district court and there is no district court in that locality, the sheriff court;

"supervising officer" has the same meaning as in section 235 of this Act.

Section 279   SCHEDULE 8

DOCUMENTARY EVIDENCE IN CRIMINAL PROCEEDINGS

Production of copy documents

1.—(1) For the purposes of any criminal proceedings a copy of, or of a material part of, a document, purporting to be authenticated in such manner and by such person as may be prescribed, shall unless the court otherwise directs, be—

(a) deemed a true copy; and

(b) treated for evidential purposes as if it were the document, or the material part, itself, whether or not the document is still in existence.

(2) For the purposes of this paragraph it is immaterial how many removes there are between a copy and the original.

(3) In this paragraph "copy" includes a transcript or reproduction.

Statements in business documents

2.—(1) Except where it is a statement such as is mentioned in paragraph 3(b) and (c) below, a statement in a document shall be admissible in criminal proceedings as evidence of any fact or opinion of which direct oral evidence would be admissible, if the following conditions are satisfied—

(a) the document was created or received in the course of, or for the purposes of, a business or undertaking or in pursuance of the functions of the holder of a paid or unpaid office;

(b) the document is, or at any time was, kept by a business or undertaking or by or on behalf of the holder of such an office; and

(c) the statement was made on the basis of information supplied by a person (whether or not the maker of the statement) who had, or may reasonably be supposed to have had, personal knowledge of the matters dealt with in it.

(2) Sub-paragraph (1) above applies whether the information contained in the statement was supplied directly or indirectly unless, in the case of information supplied indirectly, it appears to the court that any person through whom it was so supplied did not both receive and supply it in the course of a business or undertaking or as or on behalf of the holder of a paid or unpaid office.

(3) Where in any proceedings a statement is admitted as evidence by virtue of this paragraph—

(a) any evidence which, if—

         (i) the maker of the statement; or

         (ii) where the statement was made on the basis of information supplied by another person, such supplier,

had been called as a witness, would have been admissible as relevant to the witness's credibility shall be so admissible in those proceedings;

(b) evidence may be given of any matter which, if the maker or as the case may be the supplier had been called as a witness, could have been put to him in cross-examination as relevant to his credibility but of which evidence could not have been adduced by the cross-examining party; and

(c) evidence tending to prove that the maker or as the case may be the supplier, whether before or after making the statement or supplying the information on the basis of which the statement was made, made (in whatever manner) some other representation which is inconsistent with the statement shall be admissible for the purpose of showing that he has contradicted himself.

(4) In sub-paragraph (3)(c) above, "representation" does not include a representation in a precognition.

3. A statement in a document shall be admissible in criminal proceedings as evidence of the fact that the statement was made if—

(a) the document satisfies the conditions mentioned in sub-paragraph (1)(a) and (b) of paragraph 2 above;

(b) the statement is made, whether directly or indirectly, by a person who in those proceedings is an accused; and

(c) the statement, being exculpatory only, exculpates the accused.

Documents kept by businesses etc.

4. Unless the court otherwise directs, a document may in any criminal proceedings be taken to be a document kept by a business or undertaking or by or on behalf of the holder of a paid or unpaid office if it is certified as such by a docquet in the prescribed form and purporting to be authenticated, in such manner as may be prescribed—

(a) by a person authorised to authenticate such a docquet on behalf of the business or undertaking by which; or

(b) by, or by a person authorised to authenticate such a docquet on behalf of, the office-holder by whom,

the document was kept.

Statements not contained in business documents

5.—(1) In any criminal proceedings, the evidence of an authorised person that—

(a) a document which satisfies the conditions mentioned in paragraph 2(1)(a) and (b) above does not contain a relevant statement as to a particular matter; or

(b) no document, within a category of documents satisfying those conditions, contains such a statement,

shall be admissible evidence whether or not the whole or any part of that document or of the documents within that category and satisfying those conditions has been produced in the proceedings.

(2) For the purposes of sub-paragraph (1) above, a relevant statement is a statement which is of the kind mentioned in paragraph 2(1)(c) above and which, in the ordinary course of events—

(a) the document; or

(b) a document within the category and satisfying the conditions mentioned in that sub-paragraph,

might reasonably have been expected to contain.

(3) The evidence referred to in sub-paragraph (1) above may, unless the court otherwise directs, be given by means of a certificate by the authorised person in the prescribed form and purporting to be authenticated in such manner as may be prescribed.

(4) In this paragraph, "authorised person" means a person authorised to give evidence—

(a) on behalf of the business or undertaking by which; or

(b) as or on behalf of the office-holder by or on behalf of whom,

the document is or was kept.

Additional evidence where evidence from business documents challenged

6.—(1) This sub-paragraph applies where—

(a) evidence has been admitted by virtue of paragraph 2(3) above; or

(b) the court has made a direction under paragraph 1(1), 4 or 5(3) above.

(2) Where sub-paragraph (1) above applies the judge may, without prejudice to sections 268 and 269 of this Act—

(a) in solemn proceedings, on a motion of the prosecutor or defence at any time before the commencement of the speeches to the jury;

(b) in summary proceedings, on such a motion at any time before the prosecutor proceeds to address the judge on the evidence,

permit him to lead additional evidence of such description as the judge may specify.

(3) Subsections (3) and (4) of section 268 of this Act shall apply in relation to sub-paragraph (2) above as they apply in relation to subsection (1) of that section.

General

7.—(1) Nothing in this Schedule—

(a) shall prejudice the admissibility of a statement made by a person other than in the course of giving oral evidence in court which is admissible otherwise than by virtue of this Schedule;

(b) shall affect the operation of the Bankers' Books Evidence Act 1879;

(c) shall apply to—

(i) proceedings commenced; or

(ii) where the proceedings consist of an application to the sheriff by virtue of section 42(2)(c) of the Social Work (Scotland) Act 1968, an application made,

before this Schedule comes into force.

For the purposes of sub-paragraph (1)(c)(i) above, solemn proceedings are commenced when the indictment is served.

8. In this Schedule—

"business" includes trade, profession or other occupation;

"criminal proceedings" includes any hearing by the sheriff under section 62 of the Children (Scotland) Act 1995 of an application for a finding as to whether grounds for the referral of a child's case to a children's hearing are established, in so far as the application relates to the commission of an offence by the child;

"document" includes, in addition to a document in writing—

(a) any map, plan, graph or drawing;

(b) any photograph;

(c) any disc, tape, sound track or other device in which sounds or other data (not being visual images) are recorded so as to be capable, with or without the aid of some other equipment, of being reproduced therefrom; and

(d) any film, negative, tape, disc or other device in which one or more visual images are recorded so as to be capable (as aforesaid) of being produced therefrom;

"film" includes a microfilm;

"made" includes allegedly made;

"prescribed" means prescribed by Act of Adjournal;

"statement" includes any representation (however made or expressed) of fact or opinion, including an instruction, order or request, but, except in paragraph 7(1)(a) above, does not include a statement which falls within one or more of the following descriptions—

(a) a statement in a precognition;

(b) a statement made for the purposes of or in connection with—

(i) pending or contemplated criminal proceedings; or

(ii) a criminal investigation; or

(c) a statement made by an accused person in so far as it incriminates a co-accused;

and

"undertaking" includes any public or statutory undertaking, any local authority and any government department.

Sections 34 & 64(2)

SCHEDULE 9

CERTIFICATES AS TO PROOF OF CERTAIN ROUTINE MATTERS

Enactment	Persons who may purport to sign certificates	Matters which may be certified
The Parks Regulations Acts 1872 to 1974.	An officer authorised to do so by the Secretary of State.	That, on a date specified in the certificate— (a) copies of regulations made under those Acts, prohibiting such activity as may be so specified, were displayed at a location so specified; (b) in so far as those regulations prohibited persons from carrying out a specified activity in the park without written permission, such permission had not been given to a person so specified.
The Wireless Telegraphy Act 1949 (c. 54) Section 1 in so far as it relates to the installation or use of a television receiver (within the meaning of that Act); and section 1A in so far as it relates to an intended such use.	A person authorised to do so by the British Broadcasting Corporation.	In relation to an address specified in the certificate, whether on a date so specified any television licence (within the meaning of that Act) was, in records maintained on behalf of the Corporation in relation to such licences, recorded as being in force; and, if so, particulars so specified of such record of that licence.
The Building (Scotland) Act 1959 (c. 24) Section 6(1) (prohibition of construction, demolition or change of use of building without warrant).	An officer of a local authority authorised to do so by the authority.	In relation to a building specified in the certificate, that on a date so specified, there had not been obtained a warrant under section 6 of that Act for construction, demolition or, as the case may be, change of use.
Section 9(5) (offence of occupying or using a building before certificate of completion issued).	An officer of a local authority authorised to do so by the authority.	That, on a date specified in the certificate— (a) a certificate of completion under section 9 of that Act had not been issued in respect of a building so specified; and (b) written permission for occupation or use of the building so specified, had not been granted under subsection (6) of that section by the local authority.

Enactment	Persons who may purport to sign certificates	Matters which may be certified
The Firearms Act 1968 (c. 27).	[1]As respects the matters specified in paragraph (a) of column 3, a constable or a person employed by a police authority, if the constable or person is authorised to do so by the chief constable of the police force maintained for the authority's area; and as respects the matters specified in paragraph (b) of column 3, an officer authorised to do so by the Secretary of State or a member of staff of the Scottish Administration who is authorised to do so by the Scottish Ministers.	In relation to a person identified in the certificate, that on a date specified therein— (a) he held, or as the case may be did not hold, a firearm certificate or shotgun certificate (within the meaning of that Act); [1](b) he possessed, or as the case may be did not possess, an authority (which as regards a possessed authority, shall be described in the certificate) given under section 5 of that Act by the Secretary of State or, by virtue of provision made under section 63 of the Scotland Act 1998, the Scottish Ministers.
The Misuse of Drugs Act 1971 (c. 38) Sections 4, 5, 6, 8, 9, 12, 13, 19 and 20 (various offences concerning controlled drugs).	Two analysts who have analysed the substance and each of whom is either a person possessing the qualifications (qualifying persons for appointments as public analysts) prescribed by regulations made under section 76 of the Food Act 1984 (c. 30), or section 30 of the Food Safety Act 1990 (c. 16), or a person authorised by the Secretary of State to make analyses for the purposes of the provisions of the Misuse of Drugs Act 1971 mentioned in column 1.	The type, classification, purity, weight and description of any particular substance identified in the certificate by reference to a label or otherwise, which is alleged to be a controlled drug within the meaning of section 2 of the Act referred to in column 1.

NOTE
[1] As amended by the Scotland Act 1998 (Consequential Modifications) (No. 2) Order 1999 (S.I. 1999 No. 1820) art. 4 and Sched. 2, para.122(5) (effective July 1, 1999).

Enactment	Persons who may purport to sign certificates	Matters which may be certified
The Immigration Act 1971 (c. 77) Section 24(1)(a) in so far as it relates to entry in breach of a deportation order, section 24(1)(b) and section 26(1)(f) in so far as it relates to a requirement of regulations (various offences concerning persons entering, or remaining in, the United Kingdom).	An officer authorised to do so by the Secretary of State.	In relation to a person identified in the certificate— (a) the date, place or means of his arrival in, or any removal of him from, the United Kingdom; (b) any limitation on, or condition attached to, any leave for him to enter or remain in the United Kingdom; (c) the date and method of service of any notice of, or of variations of conditions attached to, such leave.
The Control of Pollution Act 1974 (c. 40) [1]Section 30F (pollution offences), 32(1) (permitting trade effluent or sewage effluent to be discharged into such waters, etc.) or 49(1)(a) (causing accumulated deposit to be carried away in suspension in inland waters) or regulations under section 31(4) (prohibition on carrying on without consent certain activities likely to pollute waters in designated areas).	[1]Two persons authorised to do so by the Scottish Environment Protection Agency.	That they have analysed a sample identified in the certificate (by label or otherwise) and that the sample is of a nature and composition specified in the certificate.
The Licensing (Scotland) Act 1976 (c. 66).	A person authorised to do so by the Secretary of State.	In relation to a person identified in the certificate, that on a date specified therein he held, or as the case may be did not hold, a licence granted under that Act.
Customs and Excise Management Act 1979 The following provisions in so far as they have effect in relation to the prohibitions contained in sections 20 and 21 of the Forgery and Counterfeiting Act 1981 namely— Sections 50(2) and (3) Section 68; and Section 170 (various offences committed in connection with contraventions of prohibitions on the import and export of counterfeits or currency notes or protected coins).	Two officials authorised to do so by the Secretary of State, being officials of the authority or body which may lawfully issue the currency notes or protected coins referred to in column 3 hereof.	That the coin or note identified in the certificate by reference to a label or otherwise is a counterfeit of a currency note or protected coin; where "currency note" has the meaning assigned to it by section 27(1)(a) of the Forgery and Counterfeiting Act 1981, and "protected coin" means any coin which is customarily use as money in the United Kingdom, any of the Channel Islands, the Isle of Man or the Republic of Ireland.

Enactment	Persons who may purport to sign certificates	Matters which may be certified
The Forgery and Counterfeiting Act 1981 Sections 14 to 16 (certain offences relating to counterfeiting).	Two officials authorised to do so by the Secretary of State, being officials of the authority or body which may lawfully issue the currency notes or protected coins referred to in column 3 hereof.	That the coin or note identified in the certificate by reference to a label or otherwise is a counterfeit of a currency note or protected coin: where "currency note" has the meaning assigned to it by section 27(1)(a) of the Forgery and Counterfeiting Act 1981, and "protected coin" means any coin which is customarily used as money in the United Kingdom, any of the Channel Islands, the Isle of Man or the Republic of Ireland.
The Wildlife and Countryside Act 1981 (c. 69) Sections 1, 5, 6(1) to (3), 7, 8, 9(1), (2), (4) and (5), 11(1) and (2), 13(1) and (2) and 14 (certain offences relating to protection of wild animals or wild plants).	An officer of the appropriate authority (within the meaning of section 16(9) of that Act) authorised to do so by the authority.	In relation to a person specified in the certificate that, on a date so specified, he held, or as the case may be did not hold, a licence under section 16 of that Act and, where he held such a licence— (a) the purpose for which the licence was granted; and (b) the terms and conditions of the licence.
The Civic Government (Scotland) Act 1982 (c. 45).	A person authorised to do so by the Secretary of State.	In relation to a person identified in the certificate, that on a date specified therein he held, or as the case may be, did not hold, a licence under a provision so specified of that Act.
The Road Traffic Regulation Act 1984 (c. 27).	Two police officers who have tested the apparatus.	The accuracy of any particular— (a) speedometer fitted to a police vehicle; (b) odometer fitted to a police vehicle; (c) radar meter; or (d) apparatus for measuring speed, time or distance, identified in the certificate by reference to its number or otherwise.

Enactment	Persons who may purport to sign certificates	Matters which may be certified
The Video Recordings Act 1984 (c. 39) Sections 9 to 14 (offences relating to the supply and possession of video recordings in contravention of that Act).	[1]A person authorised to do so by the Secretary of State, being a person who has examined the record maintained in pursuance of arrangements made by the designated authority and in the case of a certificate in terms of— (a) sub-paragraph (a) in column 3, the video work mentioned in that sub-paragraph; (b) sub-paragraph (b) in that column, both video works mentioned in that sub-paragraph.	[1]That the record shows any of the following— (a) in respect of a video work (or part of a video work) contained in a video recording identified by the certificate, that by a date specified no classification certificate has been issued; (b) in respect of a video work which is the subject of a certificate under sub-paragraph (a) above, that the video work differs in a specified way from another video work contained in a video recording identified in the certificate under this sub-paragraph and that, on a date specified, a classification certificate was issued in respect of that other video work; (c) that, by a date specified, no classification certificate had been issued in respect of a video work having a particular title; (d) that, on a date specified, a classification certificate was issued in respect of a video work having a particular title and that a document which is identified in the certificate under this sub-paragraph is a copy of the classification certificate so issued; expressions used in column 2, or in this column, of this entry being construed in accordance with that Act; and in each of sub-paragraphs (a) to (d) above "specified" means specified in the certificate under that sub-paragraph.

NOTE

[1]Substituted by the Crime and Punishment (Scotland) Act 1997 (c. 48), s.30 with effect from August 1, 1997 in terms of the Crime and Punishment (Scotland) Act 1997 (Commencement and Transitional Provisions) Order 1997 (S.I. 1997 No. 1712) para. 3.

Enactment	Persons who may purport to sign certificates	Matters whcih may be certified
The Road Traffic Act 1988 (c. 52) Section 165(3) (offence of failure to give name and address and to produce vehicle documents when required by constable).	A constable.	In relation to a person specified in the certificate, that he failed, by such date as may be so specified, to produce such documents as may be so specified at a police station so specified.
The Control of Pollution (Amendment) Act 1989 (c. 14) Section 1 (offence of transporting controlled waste without registering)	An officer of a regulation authority within the meaning of that Act authorised to do so by the authority.	In relation to a person specified in the certificate, that on a date so specified he was not a registered a carrier of controlled waste within the meaning of that Act.
The Environmental Protection Act 1990 (c. 43) Section 33(1)(a) and (b) (prohibition on harmful depositing, treatment or disposal of waste).	An officer of a waste regulation authority within the meaning of that Act authorised to do so by the authority.	In relation to a person specified in the certificate that, on a date so specified, he held, or as the case may be he did not hold, a waste management licence.
Section 34(1)(c) (duty of care as respects transfer of waste)	An officer of a waste regulation authority within the meaning of that Act authorised to do so by the authority.	In relation to a person specified in the certificate, that on a date so specified he was not an authorised person within the meaning of section 34(3)(b) or (d) of that Act.
The Social Security Administration Act 1992 (c. 5) Section 112(1) (false statements etc. to obtain payments)	Any officer authorised to do so by the Secretary of State.	In relation to a person identified in the certificate— (a) the assessment, award, or nature of any benefit applied for by him; (b) the transmission or handing over of any payment to him.

NOTE
[1] Amended by the Criminal Procedure and Investigations Act 1996 (c. 25) s.73(4).

A–445

Enactment	Persons who may purport to sign certificates	Matters which may certified
The Criminal Justice and Public Order Act 1994 (c. 33)		
Paragraph 5 of Schedule 6 (offence of making false statements to obtain certification as prisoner custody officer).	An officer authorised to do so by the Secretary of State.	That— (a) on a date specified in the certificate, an application for a certificate under section 114 of that Act was received from a person so specified; (b) the application contained a statement so specified; (c) a person so specified made, on a date so specified, a statement in writing in terms so specified.
This Act Sections 24(3) to (8), 25 and 27 to 29.	The Clerk of Justiciary or the clerk of court.	In relation to a person specified in the certificate, that— (a) an order granting bail under that Act was made on a date so specified by a court so specified; (b) the order or a condition of it so specified was in force on a date so specified; (c) notice of the time and place appointed for a diet so specified was given to him in a manner so specified; (d) as respects a diet so specified, he failed to appear.
Section 150(8) (offence of failure of accused to appear at diet after due notice).	The clerk of court.	That, on a date specified in the certificate, he gave a person so specified, in a manner so specified, notice of the time and place appointed for a diet so specified.

"SCHEDULE 9A

THE COMMISSION: FURTHER PROVISIONS

Membership

1. Her Majesty shall, on the recommendation of the Secretary of State, appoint one of the members of the Commission to be the chairman of the Commission.

2.—(1) Subject to the following provisions of this paragraph, a person shall hold and vacate office as a member of the Commission, or as chairman of the Commission, in accordance with the terms of his appointment.

(2) An appointment as a member of the Commission may be full-time or part-time.

(3) The appointment of a person as a member of the Commission, or as chairman of the Commission, shall be for a fixed period of not longer than five years.

(4) Subject to sub-paragraph (5) below, a person whose term of appointment as a member of the Commission, or as chairman of the Commission, expires shall be eligible for re-appointment.

(5) No person may hold office as a member of the Commission for a continuous period which is longer than ten years.

(6) A person may at any time resign his office as a member of the Commission, or as chairman of the Commission, by notice in writing addressed to Her Majesty.

(7) Her Majesty may at any time remove a person from office as a member of the Commission if satisfied—

(a) that he has without reasonable excuse failed to discharge his functions as a member for a continuous period of three months beginning not earlier than six months before that time;

(b) that he has been convicted of a criminal offence;

(c) that a bankruptcy order has been made against him, or his estate has been sequestrated, or he has made a composition or arrangement with or granted a trust deed for, his creditors; or

(d) that he is unable or unfit to discharge his functions as a member.

(8) If the chairman of the Commission ceases to be a member of the Commission he shall also cease to be chairman.

Members and employees

3.—(1) The Commission shall—

(a) pay to members of the Commission such remuneration;

(b) pay to or in respect of members of the Commission any such allowances, fees, expenses and gratuities; and

(c) pay towards the provisons of pensions to or in respect of members of the Commission any such sums,

as the Commission are required to pay by or in accordance with directions given by the Secretary of State.

(2) Where a member of the Commission was, immediately before becoming a member, a participant in a scheme under section 1 of the Superannuation Act 1972, the Minister for the Civil Service may determine that his term of office as a member shall be treated for the purposes of the scheme as if it were service in the employment or office by reference to which he was a participant in the scheme; and his rights under the scheme shall not be affected by sub-paragraph (1)(c) above.

(3) Where—

(a) a person ceases to hold office as a member of the Commission otherwise than on the expiry of his term of appointment; and

(b) it appears to the Secretary of State that there are special circumstances which make it right for him to receive compensation,

the Secretary of State may direct the Commission to make to him a payment of such amount as the Secretary of State may determine.

4.—(1) The Commission may appoint a chief executive and such other employees as the Commission think fit, subject to the consent of the Secretary of State as to their number and terms and conditions of service.

(2) The Commisison shall—

(a) pay to employees of the Commission such remuneration; and

(b) pay to or in respect of employees of the Commission any such allowances, fees, expenses and gratuities,

as the Commission may, with the consent of the Secretary of State determine.

(3) Employment by the Commission shall be included among the kinds of employment to which a scheme under section 1 of the Superannuation Act 1972 may apply.

5. The Commission shall pay to the Minister for the Civil Service, at such times as he may direct, such sums as he may determine in respect of any increase attributable to paragraph 3(2) or 4(3) above in the sums payable out of money provided by Parliament under the Superannuation Act 1972.

Procedure

6.—(1) The arrangements for the procedure of the Commission including the quorum for meetings) shall be such as the Commission may determine.

(2) The arrangements may provide for the discharge, under the general direction of the Commission, of any function of the Commission—

(a) in the case of the function specified in sub-paragraph (3) below, by a committee consisting of not fewer than three members of the Commission; and

(b) in any other case, by any committee of, or by one or more of the members or employees of, the Commission.

(3) The function referred to in sub-paragraph (2)(a) above is making a reference to the High Court under section 194B of this Act.

(4) The validity of any proceedings of the Commission (or of any committee of the Commission) shall not be affected by—

(a) any vacancy among the members of the Commission or in the office of chairman of the Commission; or

(b) any defect in the appointment of any person as a member of the Commission or as chairman of the Commission.

(5) Where—

(a) a document or other material has been produced to the Commission under section 194I of this Act, or they have been given access to a document or other material under that section, and the Commission have taken away the document or other material (or a copy of it); and

(b) the person who produced the document or other material to the Commission, or gave them access to it, has notified the Commission that he considers that its disclosure to others may be contrary to the interests of national security, the Commission shall, after consulting that person, deal with the document or material (or copy) in a manner appropriate for safeguarding the interests of national security.

Evidence

7. A document purporting to be—

(a) duly executed under the seal of the Commission; or

(b) signed on behalf of the Commission,

shall be received in evidence and, unless the contrary is proved, taken to be so executed or signed.

Annual reports and accounts

8.—(1) As soon as possible after the end of each financial year of the Commission, the Commission shall send to the Secretary of State a report on the discharge of their functions during that year.

(2) Such a report may include an account of the working of the provisions of Part XA of this Act and recommendations relating to any of those provisions.

(3) The Secretary of State shall lay before each House of Parliament, and cause to be published, a copy of every report sent to him under sub-paragraph (1).

9.—(1) The Commission shall—

(a) keep proper accounts and proper records in relation to the accounts; and

(b) prepare a statement of accounts in respect of each financial year of the Commission.

²(2) The statement of accounts shall contain such information and shall be in such form as the Secretary of State may direct.

³(3) The Commission shall send the statement of accounts to the Secretary of State within such period after the end of the financial year to which the statement relates as the Secretary of State may direct.

⁴(3A) The Scottish Ministers shall send the statement of accounts to the Auditor General for Scotland for auditing.

(4) [*Repealed by the Public Finance and Accountability (Scotland) Act (asp 1), s.26 and Sched. 4, para. 14(c).*]

10. For the purposes of this Schedule the Commission's financial year shall be the period of twelve months ending with 31st March; but the first financial year of the Commission shall be

the period beginning with the date of establishment of the Commission and ending with the first 31st March which falls at least six months after that date.

Expenses

11. The Secretary of State shall defray the expenses of the Commission up to such amount as may be approved by him.".

NOTES
[1]Inserted by s.25 of the Crime and Punishment (Scotland) Act 1997 with effect from April 1, 1999 as provided by the Crime and Punishment (Scotland) Act 1997 (Commencement No. 5 and Transitional Provisions and Savings) Order 1999 (S.I. 1999 No. 652).
[2]As amended by the Scotland Act 1998 (Consequential Modifications) (No. 2) Order 1999 (S.I. 1999 No. 1820) art. 4 and Sched. 2, para.122(3) (effective July 1, 1999).
[3]As amended by the Public Finance and Accountability (Scotland) Act (asp 1), s.26 and Sched. 4, para. 14(a).
[4]As inserted by the Public Finance and Accountability (Scotland) Act (asp 1), s.26 and Sched. 4, para. 14(b).

Section 292(1)   SCHEDULE 10

CERTAIN OFFENCES TRIABLE ONLY SUMMARILY

Night Poaching Act 1828 (c. 69)

1. Offences under section 1 of the Night Poaching Act 1828 (taking or destroying game or rabbits by night or entering land for that purpose).

Public Meeting Act 1908 (c. 66)

2. Offences under section 1(1) of the Public Meeting Act 1908 (endeavour to break up a public meeting).

Post Office Act 1953 (c. 36)

3. Offences under section 56 of the Post Office Act 1953 (criminal diversions of letters from addressee).

Betting, Gaming and Lotteries Act 1963 (c. 2)

4. Offences under the following provisions of the Betting, Gaming and Lotteries Act 1963—
(a) section 7 (restriction of betting on dog racecourses);
(b) section 10(5) (advertising licensed betting offices);
(c) section 11(6) (person holding bookmaker's or betting agency permit employing a person disqualified from holding such a permit);
(d) section 18(2) (making unauthorised charges to bookmakers on licensed track);
(e) section 19 (occupiers of licensed tracks not to have any interest in bookmaker thereon);
(f) section 21 (betting with young persons); and
(g) section 22 (betting circulars not to be sent to young persons).

Theatres Act 1968 (c. 54)

5. Offences under section 6 of the Theatres Act 1968 (provocation of breach of the peace by means of public performance of play).

Criminal Law (Consolidation) (Scotland) Act 1995 (c. 39)

6. Offences under section 12(1) of the Criminal Law (Consolidation) (Scotland) Act 1995 (allowing child under 16 to be in brothel).

TABLE OF DERIVATIONS

Notes: 1. This Table shows the derivation of the provisions of the Bill.
2. The following abbreviations are used in the Table:

Acts of Parliament

1975	= Criminal Procedure (Scotland) Act 1975 (c. 21)
1977	= Criminal Law Act 1977 (c. 45)
1978	= Community Service by Offenders (Scotland) Act 1978 (c. 49)
1980B	= Bail (Scotland) Act 1980 (c. 4)
1980LR	= Law Reform (Miscellaneous Provisions) (Scotland) Act 1980 (c. 55)
1980CJ	= Criminal Justice (Scotland) Act 1980 (c. 62)
1982	= Criminal Justice Act 1982 (c. 48)
1983	= Mental Health (Amendment) (Scotland) Act 1983 (c. 39)
1984	= Mental Health (Scotland) Act 1984 (c. 36)
1985	= Law Reform (Miscellaneous Provisions) (Scotland) Act 1985 (c. 73)
1987	= Criminal Justice (Scotland) Act 1987 (c. 41)
1988	= Criminal Justice Act 1988 (c. 33)
1990	= Law Reform (Miscellaneous Provisions) (Scotland) Act 1990 (c. 40)
1991	= Criminal Justice Act 1991 (c. 53)
1993P	= Prisoners and Criminal Proceedings (Scotland) Act 1993 (c. 9)
1993CJ	= Criminal Justice Act 1993 (c. 36)
1994	= Criminal Justice and Public Order Act 1994 (c. 33)
1995	= Criminal Justice (Scotland) Act 1995 (c. 20)
1995C	= Children (Scotland) Act 1995 (c. 36)

Provision	Derivation
1(1)	Court of Session (Scotland) Act 1830 (11 Geo 4 & 1 Will 4 c. 69) s. 18.
(2)	1975 s.113(1).
(3)	1975 s.113(2).
(4), (5)	1975 s.113(4).
2	1975 s.114; 1987 s.57(2).
3(1)	1975 s.2(1).
(2)	1975 s.112; 1987 s.57(1).
(3) to (5)	1975 s.2(2) to (4); 1987 s.58(1).
(6)	1975 s.8; Drafting.
4(1)	1975 ss.3(1), 288(1).
(2)	1975 ss.3(4), 288(5); 1990 s.60; drafting.
(3)	1975 ss.3(2), 288(2).
(4)	1975 s.288(4); drafting.
5(1)	Drafting.
(2)	1975 s.289; 1977 Sch. 11 §44.
(3)	1975 s.290.
(4)	1975 s.291(2), (3); 1980 s.38.
6(1)	District Courts (Scotland) Act 1975 (1975 c. 20) s.2(1), (1A).
(2)	District Courts (Scotland) Act 1975 (1975 c. 20) s.2(2).
(3)	District Courts (Scotland) Act 1975 (1975 c. 20)(1) (part).
(4)	District Courts (Scotland) Act 1975 (1975 c.20) s.6(2) (part), (3) (part).
(5)	District Courts (Scotland) Act 1975 (1975 c. 20) s.6(9).
(6)	Drafting.
7(1)	District Courts (Scotland) Act 1975 (1975 c. 20) s.3(1).
(2)	District Courts (Scotland) Act 1975 (1975 c. 20) s.3(4).
(3)	1980CJ s.7(1); 1995 s.60.
4(4)	1980CJ s.7(3); 1982 Sch. 7 §14.
(5)	District Courts (Scotland) Act 1975 (1975 c. 20) s.3(2).
(6)	1975 s.284; 1977 Sch. 11 §3; 1982 Sch. 7 §§4, 5.
(7)	1980CJ s.7(1A); 1995 s.60.
(8)	1975 c.285; 1980CJ s.7(3); 1982 Sch. 7 §6.
(9), (10)	1975 s.286.
8	1980B s.10; 1985 s.21.
9(1)	1975 ss.4(1), 3(3), 287(1).
(2)	1975 ss.4(2), 287(2).
(3)	1975 ss.4(3), 287(3).
(4), (5)	1975 ss.4(4), (5), 287(4), (5).

Provision	Derivation
10	1975 s.5; 1987 Sch. 1 §4.
11(1), (2)	1975 s.6(1), (2).
4(3)	1975 s.6(3); 1995 Sch. 6 §7.
(4)	1975 ss.7(1), (2), 292(1), (2).
12	1975 ss.9, 293.
13	1980CJ s.1.
14(1)	1980CJ s.2(1); 1994 s.129(1).
(2)	1980CJ s.2(2); 1987 Sch. 1 §16(a), (b), 1993P Sch. 7.
(3)	1980CJ s.2(3).
(4)	1980CJ s.2(3A); 1987 Sch. 1 §16(c); 1994 Sch. 10 §47; 1995 s.59.
(5)	1980CJ s.2(3B); 1994 Sch. 10 §47.
(6)	1980CJ s.2(4); 1994 s.129(2).
(7) to (9)	1980CJ s.2(5) to (7).
15(1), (2)	1980CJ s.3(1); 1994 s.129(3).
4(3) to (5)	1980CJ s.3(2) to (4).
(6)	1980CJ s.3(5); 1985 Sch. 2 §23.
16	1980CJ s.5.
17(1)	1975 ss.19(1), 305; 1980CJ Sch. 7 §25; 1995 Sch. 6 §§11, 106.
(2)	1975 ss.19(2), 305; 1995 Sch. 6 §§11, 106.
18(1), (2)	1993P s.28(1), (2).
(3)	1993P s.28(3); 1995 s.58(2), Sch. 6 §179(5).
(4)	1993P s.28(3A), (3C); 1995 s.58(3).
(5)	1993P s.28(3B); 1995 s.58(3).
(6)	1993P s.28(4); 1995 s.58(4).
(7), (8)	1993P s.28(5), (6).
19	1993P s.28A; 1995 s.58(5).
20	1993P s.28B; 1995 s.58(5).
21(1)	1975 ss.18(1), 294(1).
(2) to (5)	1975 ss.18(2) to (5), 294(2) to (5); 1980B s.7(1), (2).
22(1) to (3)	1975 s.295(1), (2); 1980B s.8.
(4), (5)	1975 ss.294(4), (5), 295(3); 1980B ss.7(2), 8.
23(1)	1975 s.26(2); 1995 Sch. 6 §15(a).
(2)	1975 s.26(3); 1995 Sch. 6 §15(b).
(3)	1975 s.26(4).
(4)	1975 s.27.
(5)	1975 s.28(1).
(6)	1975 s.298(1) (part).
(7)	1975 ss.28(2), 298(2).
(8)	1975 ss.28(3), 298(3); 1980CJ Sch. 7 §§26, 51.
24(1)	1975 ss.26(1), 298(1) (part).
(2)	1975 s.35.
(3)	1980B s.1(1); drafting.
(4) to (8)	1980B s.1(2) to (5); 1995 s.1.
25	1980B s.2.
26	1975 s.28A; 1995 s.3.
27(1), (2)	1980B s.3(1), (2); 1995 s.2(2), (3).
(3) to (6)	1980B s.3(2A) to (2D); 1995 s.2(4).
(7) to (10)	1980B s.3(3) to (6).
(11)	1980B s.3(12).
28	1980B s.3(7) to (11).
29	1980B s.4.
30(1)	1975 ss.30(1), 299(1); 1980B s.1(4).
(2)	1975 ss.30(2), 299(2); 1980B Sch. 1 §§4, 6.
(3)	1975 ss.30(3), 299(3).
(4)	1975 ss.30(4), 299(4); 1980B s.1(4).
31	1975 ss.30A, 299A; 1995 s.4.
32(1)	1975 ss.31(1), 300(1) (part).
(2)	1975 ss.31(2), 300(1) (part); 1987 s.62(4)(a).
(3), (4)	1975 ss.31(3), (4), 300(2), (3).

Provision	Derivation
32(5)	1975 ss.31(4A), 300(3A); 1995 Sch. 6 §§16, 105(a).
(6)	1975 ss.31(5), 300(6) (part).
(7), (8)	1975 ss.33(1), 300(4); 1995 Sch. 6 §§17(a), 105(b).
(9)	1975 s.300(4A); 1987 s.62(4)(b).
(10)	1975 s.33(2); 1995 Sch.6 §17(b).
33	1975 s.32, 300(6)(part).
34(1)	1975 s.12.
(2)	1975 s.74(7).
35(1), (2)	1975 s.19(2) (part), (3), s.305(3).
(3)	1975 s.20(1); 1980CJ s.6(1).
(4)	1975 s.20(3); 1980CJ s.6(1).
(5) to (7)	1975 s.20(3A) to (3C); 1980CJ s.6(1).
(8)	1975 s.20(4).
36(1) to (4)	1975 s.20A(1); 1980CJ s.6(2); 1995 s.10(2).
(5)	1975 s.20A(2); 1980CJ s.6(2).
(6)	1975 s.20A(3), (3A); 1980CJ s.6(2); 1995 s.10(3).
(7)	1975 s.20A(4); 1980CJ s.6(2).
(8)	1975 s.20A(5); 1980CJ s.6(2).
(9)	1975 s.20A(6); 1980CJ s.6(2).
(10), (11)	1975 s.20A(7), (8); 1995 s.10(4).
37(1)	1975 s.20B(1); 1980CJ s.6(2); 1993P Sch. 6 §1(2).
(2) to (4)	1975 s.20B(1A) to (1C); 1993P Sch. 5 §1(2).
(5)	1975 s.20B(2); 1993P Sch. 5 §1(2).
(6)	1975 s.20B(3); 1980CJ s.6(2).
(7), (8)	1975 s.20B(5); 1980CJ s.6(2).
(9)	1975 s.20B(6); 1980CJ s.6(2).
(10)	1975 s.20B(9); 1980CJ s.6(2); 1995 Sch. 6 §13.
38	1975 s.20B(4), (7) and (8); 1980CJ s.6(2).
39	1975 s.21.
40	1975 s.22.
41	1975 ss.170, 369.
42(1)	Social Work (Scotland) Act 1968 (1968 c. 49) s.31(1); Health and Social Services and Social Security Adjudications Act 1983 (1983 c. 41) Sch. 2 §7.
(2) to (4)	1975 ss.39(1) to (3), 307(1) to (3).
(5), (6)	1975 ss.39(4), (5), 307(4), (5); 1995C Sch. 4 §24(5), (11).
(7), (8)	1975 ss.40(1), (2), 308(1), (2).
(9), (10)	1975 ss.38, 306.
43(1) to (3)	1975 s.296(1); 1980B s.9(a); 1995 Sch. 6 §104.
(4)	1975 s.296(2); 1995 Sch. 6 §104.
(5), (6)	1975 s.296(3), (4); 1995C Sch.4 §24(9).
(7), (8)	1975 s.296(5), (6); 1980B s.9(b).
44(1)	1975 s.413(1); 1987 s.59(1); 1993P Sch. 5 §1(32); 1995 Sch. 6 §141; 1995C Sch. 4 §24(17).
(2)	1975 s.413(2); 1987 s.59(1).
(3), (4)	1975 s.413(3A), (4); 1987 s.59(1); 1995C Sch. 4 §24(17).
(5)	1975 s.413(5); 1993P s.8.
(6) to (8)	1975 s.413(6A) to (6C); 1993P s.8; 1995C Sch. 4 §24(17).
(9)	1975 s.413(7); 1987 s.59(1); 1993P Sch.5 §1(32).
(10)	1975 s.413(3); 1987 s.59(1).
45(1) to (4)	1975 ss.37(1) to (3), 304(1) to (3).
(5)	1975 ss.37(4), 304(4); 1995C Sch. 4 §24(4), (10).
46(1), (2)	1975 ss.171(1), (2), 368(1), (2); 1995C Sch. 4 §24(7), (15); drafting.
(3)	1975 ss.171(3), 368(3); Sexual Offences (Scotland) Act (c. 67) Sch. 1; Incest and Related Offences (Scotland) Act 1986 (c. 36) Sch. 1 §§1, 3; 1988 Sch. 15 §48.
(4)	1975 ss.171(4), 368(4).
(5), (6)	1975 ss.171(1), (2), 368(1), (2); 1995C Sch. 4 §24(7), (15).
(7)	1975 ss.171(6), 368(6).
47(1) to (3)	1975 ss.169(1), 374(1), 1980CJ s.22.

Provision	Derivation
47(4)	1975 ss.169(2), 374(2); 1980CJ s.22; Cable and Broadcasting Act 1986 (c. 46) Sch. 5 §30; Broadcasting Act 1990 (c. 42) Sch. 20 §21.
(5), (6)	1975 ss.169(3), (4), 374(3), (4); 1980CJ s.22.
48	1975 ss.168, 364; 1980CJ Sch. 7 §§34, 57; 1995C Sch. 4 §24(6), (14).
49(1)	1975 ss.173(1), 372(1); Local Government etc. (Scotland) Act 1994 (c. 39) Sch. 13 §97(2).
(2)	1975 ss.173(2), 372(2).
(3)	1975 ss.173(3), 372(3); 1980CJ Sch. 7 §35; Local Government etc. (Scotland) Act 1994 (c. 39) Sch. 13 §97(2).
(4), (5)	1975 ss.173(4), (5), 372(4), (5).
(6), (7)	1975 s.373; Local Government etc. (Scotland) Act 1994 (c. 39) Sch. 13 §97(2).
50(1), (2)	1975 ss.165, 361.
(3), (4)	1975 ss.166(1), (2), 362(1), (2); 1995 Sch. 6 §64.
(5)	1975 ss.167, 363.
(6)	1975 ss.172, 371.
51(1)	1975 ss.23(1), s.329(1); 1987 s.62(2); 1995 Sch. 6 §14; 1995C Sch. 4 §24(13).
(2) to (4)	1975 ss.23(2) to (4), 329(2) to (4); 1995 Sch. 6 §14; 1995C Sch. 4 §24(13).
52(1)	1975 ss.175(2), 376(5).
(2)	1975 ss.25(1), 330(1).
(3)	1975 ss.25(2), 330(2); 1984 Sch. 3 §§24, 31.
(4), (5)	1975 ss.25(3), (4), 330(3), (4).
(6), (7)	1975 ss.25(5), (6), 330(5), (6); 1995 s.53.
53(1)	1974 ss.174A(1) (part), 375A(1) (part); 1983 s.34(a); 1984 Sch. 3 §§25, 32.
(2) to (10)	1975 ss.174A(2) to (10), 375A(3) to (11); 1983 s.34(a).
(11), (12)	1975 ss.174A(1) (part), 375A(1) (part), (2); 1983 s.34(a).
54(1) to (4)	1975 ss.174(1) to (1C), 375(2) to (2C); 1995 s.47(1).
(5)	1975 ss.174(5), 375(4).
(6)	1975 ss.174(2), 375(3A); 1995 s.48, Sch. 6 §65.
(7)	1975 s.375(3); 1995 Sch. 6 §132.
(8)	Drafting.
55	1975 ss.174ZA, 375ZA; 1995 s.49(1), (2).
56	1975 ss.174ZB, 375ZB; 1995 s.49(1), (2).
57(1) to (4)	1975 ss.174ZC, 375ZC; 1995 s.50(1), (2).
(5)	Drafting.
58(1), (2)	1975 ss.175(1), 376(1); 1983 Sch. 2 §§31, 34(a); 1984 Sch. 3 §§26, 33.
(3)	1975 s.376(3); 1995 Sch. 6 §133(b).
(4)	1975 ss.175(3), 376(6).
(5)	1975 ss.175(4), 376(7).
(6)	1975 ss.175(5), 376(8); 1983 Sch. 2 §§31, 34.
(7)	1975 ss.175(6), 376(9); 1983 Sch. 2 §§31, 34.
(8)	1975 ss.175(7), 376(10); 1983 Sch. 2 §§31, 34.
(9)	1975 ss.177, 378; 1995C Sch. 4 §24(8), (16).
(10)	1975 s.376(4).
59(1)	1975 ss.178(1), 379(1); 1983 s.22(2); 1984 Sch. 3 §§28, 35; 1995 s.54.
(2)	1975 ss.178(2), 379(2); 1983 Sch. 2 §§33, 36; 1984 Sch. 3 §§28, 35.
(3)	1975 ss.178(3), 379(3); 1983 Sch. 2 §§33, 36; 1984 Sch. 3 §§28, 35; 1995 Sch. 6 §§67, 135.
60	1975 ss.280, 443; 1980CJ Sch. 2 §32, Sch. 3 §2; 1983 s.34(b), (d).
61(1)	1975 ss.176(1), 377(1); 1983 Sch. 2 §§32, 35; 1984 Sch. 3 §§27, 34; 1995 Sch. 6 §§66(a), 134(a).
(2)	1975 ss.176(1A), 377(1A); 1983 s.35(a), (b).
(3)	1975 ss.176(2), 377(2); 1995 Sch. 6 §§66(b), 134(b).
(4)	1975 ss.176(3), 377(3).
(5)	1975 ss.176(4), 377(4); 1995 Sch. 6 §§66(c), 134(c).
62	1975 ss.174ZD, 375ZD, 1995 s.51.
63(1) to (5)	1975 ss.174ZE, 375ZE; 1995 s.52.
(6)	Drafting.
64(1) to (4)	1975 s.41.
(5)	1975 s.57.
(6)	Drafting.

Provision	Derivation
65(1) to (3)	1975 s.101(1); 1980CJ s.14(1).
(4) to (9)	1975 s.101(2) to (6); 1980CJ s.14(1).
(10)	1975 s.101(1A); 1995 s.15.
66(1), (2)	1975 s.69(1); 1980CJ Sch. 4 §2; 1995 Sch. 6 §26(a).
(3)	1975 s.69(2); 1995 Sch. 6 §26(b).
(4)	1975 s.70.
(5)	1975 s.78(1); 1980CJ Sch. 4 §8; 1995 Sch. 6 §30.
(6)	1975 s.75; 1980CJ Sch. 4 §4; 1995 s.13(1).
(7)	1975 s.71; 1980CJ Sch. 7 §27.
(8)	1975 s.73(1); 1995 Sch. 6 §28.
(9)	1975 s.72(1); 1995 Sch. 5 §27(a), (b).
(10)	1975 s.72(2); 1995 Sch. 6 §27(c).
(11)	1975 s.73(2).
(12) to (14)	1975 s.58; 1995 Sch. 6 §22.
67(1)	1975 s.79(1) (part); 1995 Sch. 6 §31.
(2)	1975 s.79(2).
(3)	1975 s.80(1); 1980CJ Sch. 4 §9; 1995 Sch. 6 §32.
(4)	1975 s.80(2); 1980CJ Sch. 4 §9.
(5)	1975 s.81; 1980CJ Sch. 7 §28; 1995 Sch. 6 §33.
(6)	1975 s.82A; 1980CJ s.27.
68(1)	1975 s.78(2); 1980CJ Sch. 4 §8.
(2)	1975 s.83; 1980CJ Sch. 4 §11.
(3), (4)	1975 s.84; 1980CJ Sch. 4 §12; 1995 s.23.
69(1)	1975 s.68(1).
(2)	1975 s.68(2); 1995 Sch. 6 §25.
(3)	1975 s.68(3) (part); 1980CJ Sch. 4 §1.
(4)	1975 s.68(4) (part); 1995 Sch. 6 §25.
(5)	1975 s.68(3) (part) and (4) (part); 1980CJ Sch. 4 §1; 1995 Sch. 6 §25.
70(1)	Drafting.
4(2), (3)	1975 s.74(1).
(4)	1975 s.74(2).
(5)	1975 s.74(4); 1980CJ Sch. 4 §3(b).
(6)	1975 s.74(5).
(7)	1975 ss.74(6), 103(4).
(8)	1975 s.74(8).
71	1975 s.75A; 1995 s.13(2).
72(1)	1975 s.76(1) (part) and (2), s.108(1) (part); 1980CJ Sch. 4 §5, §19; 1985 Sch. 2 §18; 1993P s.39(2), Sch. 5 §1(3); 1995 s.13(3)(a), Sch. 6 §39.
(2)	1975 s.76(1) (part); 1980CJ Sch. 4 §5.
(3) to (6)	1975 s.76(3) to (5), (7).
73(1), (2)	1975 s.76(6) (part).
(3) to (6)	1975 s.76(6A) to (6D); 1995 s.13(3)(b).
(7)	1975 s.109 (part).
(8)	1975 s.76(6) (part); drafting.
74	1975 s.76A; 1980CJ Sch. 4 §5; 1995 s.13(4).
75	1975 s.111A; 1980CJ Sch. 7 §31.
76	1975 s.102; 1980CJ s.16.
77(1)	1975 s.103(1) and (4), s.124 (part); 1980CJ Sch. 4 §14; 1995 Sch. 6 §38.
(2), (3)	1975 s.103(2), (3); 1980CJ Sch. 4 §14.
78(1)	1975 s.82(1) (part); Act of Adjournal (Consolidation) 1988 (S.I. 1988/110) s.68 (part); 1980CJ s.13; 1995 Sch. 6 §34(a).
(2)	1975 s.82(1A); 1995 s.11.
(3)	1975 s.82(1) (part); Act of Adjournal (Consolidation) 1988 (S.I. 1988/110) s.68 (part); 1980CJ s.13; 1995 Sch. 6 §34(a).
(4)	1975 s.82(2); 1980CJ Sch. 4 §10; 1995 Sch. 6 §34(b).
78(5)	1975 s.82(3); 1980CJ Sch. 4 §10.
79(1)	1975 s.108(1) (part) and (2); 1980CJ Sch. 4 §19; 1985 Sch. 2 §18; 1995 Sch. 6 §39.
(2)	1975 s.108(1) (part); 1980CJ Sch. 4 §19; 1985 Sch. 2 §18; 1995 Sch. 6 §39.

Provision	Derivation
80(1)	1975 s.77; 1980CJ Sch. 4 §6; 1995 Sch. 6 §29.
(2) to (4)	1975 s.77A(1) to (3); 1980CJ Sch. 4 §7.
(5), (6)	1975 s.77A(4), drafting; 1980CJ Sch. 4 §7.
81(1)	1975 s.127(1); 1980CJ Sch. 4 §27; 1995 Sch. 6 §44(a).
4(2)	1975 s.127(1ZA); 1995 Sch. 6 §44(b).
(3)	1975 s.127(1A); 1980CJ s.18(1).
4(4) to (6)	1975 s.127(2) to (4); 1995 Sch. 6 §44(c).
(7)	1975 s.127(5); 1995 Sch. 6 §44(d).
82	1975 s.111.
83	1975 s.114A; 1995 Sch. 6 §41.
84(1)	1975 s.85; 1995 Sch. 6 §35.
(2)	1975 s.86(1); 1987 Sch. 1 §5.
(3)	1975 s.86(2); 1987 Sch. 1 §5.
(4)	1975 s.89; 1985 Sch. 2 §16.
(5)	1975 s.90; 1985 Sch. 2 §16.
(6)	1975 s.91; 1980LR Sch. 2 §6; 1985 Sch. 2 §16.
(7)	1975 s.92.
(8)	1975 s.93; 1995 Sch. 6 §36.
(9)	1975 s.94.
(10)	1975 s.95.
85(1)	1975 s.96(1); 1980CJ Sch. 4 §13.
(2)	1975 s.96(2).
(3)	1975 s.97.
(4), (5)	1975 s.98; 1980CJ Sch. 7 §29; 1985 Sch. 2 §17.
(6), (7)	1975 s.99; 1980LR s.2(3).
(8)	1975 s.100(1); 1995 Sch. 6 §37.
86(1)	1975 s.130(3A); 1995 s.8.
(2)	1975 s.130(4).
(3)	1975 s.130(5); 1980LR Sch. 2 §7.
(4)	1975 s.130(6).
87	1975 s.128; 1995 s.30(2), (3).
88(1)	1975 s.125; 1995 Sch. 6 §43.
(2)	1975 s.129 (part); 1987 Sch. 1 §7; 1995 Sch. 6 §45.
(3)	1975 s.131, drafting.
(4)	1975 s.132(1).
(5), (6)	1975 s.135(1); 1995 Sch. 6 §48(a), (b); drafting.
(7)	1975 s.133.
4(8)	1975 s.137.
89	1975 s.135(2) to (4); 1995 Sch. 6 §48(c).
90	1975 s.134; 1995 Sch. 6 §47.
91	1975 s.136.
92(1), (2)	1975 s.145(1); 1980CJ s.21.
(3)	1975 s.145(3).
93	1975 s.274; 1980CJ Sch. 8; 1995 Sch. 6 §98.
94	1975 s.275; 1993P Sch. 5 §1(27).
95	1975 s.137A; 1993P Sch. 1 §1(5).
96	1975 s.123.
97(1)	1975 s.140A(1); 1980CJ s.19(1); 1995 Sch.6 §49.
(2), (3)	1975 s.140A(3), (4); 1980CJ s.19(1).
(4)	1975 s.140A(2); 1980CJ s.19(1).
98	1975 s.152.
99(1)	1975 s.153(2); 1980CJ s.24(1).
(2), (3)	1975 s.153(3); 1980CJ s.24(1); 1995 Sch. 6 §57(b).
(4)	1975 s.153(3A); 1980CJ s.24(1).
(5)	1975 s.153(4).
(6)	1975 s.155A; 1993P s.40(1).
100(1), (2)	1975 s.154; 1980CJ s.24(2).
(3)	1975 s.155 (part); drafting.
101(1)	1975 s.160(1).
(2)	1975 ss.160(2), 161(5); 1995 s.24(3).
(3)	1975 s.161(1).
(4), (5)	1975 s.161(2).

Provision	Derivation
100(6)	1975 s.161(4).
(7)	1975 s.159(2)
(8)	1975 s.161(3).
102(1)	1975 s.156(1) and (2); 1995 Sch. 6 §58.
(2)	1975 s.157(1); 1995 Sch. 6 §59.
(3)	1975 ss.156(3) and 157(3).
(4)	1975 s.156(6).
4(5)	1975 s.158.
103(1)	1975 s.245(2); 1987 Sch. 1 §13(2); drafting.
(2)	1975 s.245(1); 1987 Sch. 1 §13(1); 1995 s.43(1).
(3)	1975 s.245(1A); 1995 s.43(1).
(4)	1975 s.245(3); 1980CJ Sch. 8.
(5)	1975 ss.247 (part), 248; 1980CJ Sch. 2 §15, Sch. 8.
(6)	1975 s.247 (part); 1980CJ Sch. 2 §15, Sch. 8.
(7)	1975 s.249.
(8)	1975 s.250.
104(1)	1975 s.252; 1980CJ Sch. 2 §16; 1993P Sch. 5 §1(18).
(2), (3)	1975 s.253; 1980CJ Sch. 8.
105(1) to (4)	1975 s.251(1) to (4).
(5)	1975 s.251(5); 1980CJ Sch. 7 §44.
(6)	1975 s.251(6).
106(1), (2)	1975 s.228(1); 1980CJ Sch. 2 §1; 1993CJ s.68(1); 1995 s.42(1).
(3)	1975 s.228(2); 1980CJ Sch. 2 §1.
(4)	1975 s.270(1).
(5) to (9)	1975 s.270(2) to (4); 1980CJ Sch. 2 §26; 1995 Sch. 6 §96.
107	1975 s.230A; 1995 s.42(2).
108	1975 s.228A; 1993P s,42(1); 1993CJ s.68(2).
109(1)	1975 s.231(1) (part) and (2); 1980CJ Sch. 2 §3; 1987 s.45(6)(a).
(2)	1975 s.231(1) (part); 1980CJ Sch. 2 §3; 1987 s.45(6)(a).
(3)	1975 s.231(3); 1980CJ Sch. 2 §3.
(4), (5)	1975 s.231(4); 1987 s.45(6)(b).
(6)	1975 s.231(5); 1987 s.45(6)(c).
110(1), (2)	1975 s.233(1); 1980CJ Sch. 2 §5; 1993P Sch. 5 §1(9); 1993CJ Sch. 5 §2(4).
(3), (4)	1975 s.233(2), (3); 1980CJ Sch. 2 §5.
(5)	1975 s.233(3A); 1995 s.42(3).
(6)	1975 s.233(4); 1980CJ Sch. 2§5; 1993CJ Sch. 5 §2(4).
111	1975 s.236B; 1980CJ Sch. 2 §8; 1993P Sch. 5 §1(11).
112(1)	1975 s.238(1); 1993CJ Sch. 5 §2(5); 1995 s.5(2).
(2)	1975 s.2338(1A); 1995 s.5(3).
(3), (4)	1975 s.238(2); 1980CJ Sch. 2 §10(a); 1995 Sch. 6 §81.
(5)	1975 s.238(3); 1980CJ Sch. 2 §10(b).
113	1975 s.236A; 1980CJ Sch. 2 §8; 1995 Sch. 6 §78.
114	1975 s.235; 1995 Sch. 6 §77.
115(1), (2)	1975 s.234(1); 1980CJ Sch. 8.
(3), (4)	1975 s.234(2), (3); 1980CJ Sch. 8.
116(1)	1975 s.244(1); 1980CJ Sch. 2 §13.
(2)	1975 s.244(2); 1980CJ Sch. 2 §13; 1993CJ Sch. 5 §2(6).
117(1), (2)	1975 s.241; 1980CJ Sch. 7 §41.
(3)	1975 s.240; 1993P Sch. 5 §1(15); 1995 Sch. 6 §83.
(4), (5), (6)	1975 s.242; 1980CJ Sch. 7 §42.
(7)	1975 s.242A; 1993P Sch. 5 §1(16).
(8)	1975 s.243; 1980CJ Sch. 7; 1993P Sch. 5 §1(17).
(9)	1975 s.239(1); 1980CJ Sch. 2 §11; 1993 Sch. 5 §1(14); 1995 Sch. 6 §82.
118(1), (2)	1975 s.254(1); 1980CJ Sch. 2 §18; 1993CH Sch. 5 §2(7).
(3)	1975 s.254(2); 1993CJ Sch. 5 §2(7).
(4)	1975 s.254(3), (4A); 1993CJ Sch. 5 §2(7).
(5)	1975 s.254(4); 1993CJ Sch. 5 §2(7); 1995 Sch. 6 §85.
(6)	1975 s.254(5); 1995 Sch. 6 §85.
(7)	1975 s.254A(1); 1995 s.34(1).

Provision	Derivation
118(8)	1975 s.254B; 1995 Sch. 6 §86.
119(1)	1975 s.255(1) (part); 1980CJ Sch. 2 §19; 1995 s.46(1).
(2)	1975 s.255(1A); 1995 s.46(1).
(3)	1975 s.255(1) (part), 1980CJ Sch. 2 §19; 1995 s.46(1).
(4)	1975 s.255(2); 1980CJ Sch. 2 §19.
(5)	1975 s.255(3) (part); 1980 Sch. 2 §19.
(6)	1975 s.255(1B); 1995 s.46(1).
(7)	1975 s.255(1C); 1995 s.46(1).
(8)	1975 s.255(3) (part); 1980CJ Sch. 2 §19.
(9)	1975 s.255(4); 1980CJ Sch. 2 §19.
(10), (11)	1975 s.255(5), (6); 1995 s.46(1)(c)
120(1)	1975 s.257; 1980CJ Sch. 8; 1995 Sch. 6 §88.
(2)	1975 s.258; 1993P Sch. 5 §1(19).
(3)	1975 s.260.
(4)	1975 s.261; 1980CJ Sch. 7 §45; 1993P Sch. 5 §1(20).
121(1), (2)	1975 s.264(1), (2); 1980CJ Sch. 2 §23; 1995 Sch. 6 §92(a).
(3)	1975 s.264(3); 1987 s.68(3).
(4)	1975 s.264(4); 1995 Sch. 6 §92(b).
22(1), (2)	1975 s.265(1), (2); 1995 Sch. 6 §93.
(3)	1975 s.265(4).
(4)	1975 s.265(4A); 1993P Sch. 5 §1(22).
123	1975 s.263A; 1980CJ s.37; 1995 Sch. 6 §91.
124(1)	1975 s.263(1) (part); 1980CJ Sch. 2 §22.
(2)	1975 ss.262, 281.
(3)	1975 s.263(1) (part); 1980CJ Sch. 2 §22.
(4)	1975 s.263(2); 1987 Sch. 2.
(5)	1975 s.263(3); 1995 Sch. 6 §90.
125(1)	1975 s.268(1); 1987 Sch. 1 §14(1); 1993P Sch. 5 §1(23); 1993CJ Sch. 5 §2(8).
(2)	1975 s.268(2); 1987 Sch. 1 §14(2); 1993P Sch. 5 §1(23); 1993CJ Sch. 5 §2(8).
(3)	1975 s.268(3); 1987 Sch. 1 §14(3); 1993P Sch. 5 §1(23).
(4)	1975 s.268(4); 1980CJ Sch. 7 §46; 1995 Sch. 6 §94.
126	1975 s.269; 1980CJ Sch. 2 §25; 1993P Sch. 5 §1(24); 1995 Sch. 6 §95.
127	1975 s.271; 1980CJ Sch. 2 §27; 1985 Sch. 2 §19.
128	1975 ss.266, 267.
129(1), (2)	1975 s.277(1); 1980CJ Sch. 8.
(3)	1975 s.277(2); 1980 CJ Sch. 2 §31, Sch. 8; 1995 Sch. 6 §100.
(4)	1975 s.277(1) (part).
130	1975 s.230.
131	1975 s.280A; 1980CJ s.35.
132	1975 s.279.
133(1)	1975 s.283(1); 1995 Sch. 6 §102.
(2)	1975 s.283(1A); 1995 Sch. 6 §102.
(3)	1975 s.283(2) (part).
(4)	1975 s.283(3); drafting.
(5)	1975 s.310A; 1995 s.63.
134	1975 s.310; 1995 Sch. 6 §108; drafting.
135(1)	1975 s.321(1); 1995 Sch. 6 §117(a).
(2)	1975 s.321(2).
(3), (4)	1975 s.321(3); 1980B Sch. 1 §7; 1995 Sch. 6 §117(b).
(5)	1975 s.321(4).
136	1975 s.331; Incest and Related Offences (Scotland) Act 1986 (1986 c. 36) Sch. 1 §2; 1995 s.62.
137(1)	1975 s.314(3); 1980CJ Sch. 8.
(2)	1975 s.314(4); 1980CJ s.11.
(3)	1975 s.314(4A); 1995 Sch. 6 §111(b).
(4), (5)	1975 s.314(5), (6); 1980CJ s.11.
138(1)	1975 s.311(1) (part) & (2); 1995 Sch. 6 §109; drafting.
(2)	1975 s.312 (part); drafting.

Provision	Derivation
138(3)	1975 s.311(3).
(4)	1975 s.312(a)–(z), drafting.
139(1)	1975 s.314(1); 1995 Sch. 6 §111(a).
(2)	1975 s.314(2); 1980CJ s.11.
140	1975 s.315; 1995 Sch. 6 §112.
141(1)	1975 s.316(1) & (2) (part).
(2)	1975, s.316(2) (part).
(3), (4)	1975 s.316(3); 1995 Sch. 6 §113.
(5)	1975 s.316(4).
(6), (7)	1975 s.319; 1995 Sch. 6 §115; drafting.
142(1)	1975 s.366(1); 1995 Sch. 6 §131.
(2) to (4)	1975 s.367.
(5)	1975 s.370; 1980CJ Sch. 7 §58.
143	1975 s.333.
144(1)	1975 s.334(1) (part); 1980CJ Sch. 7 §54(a); 1993P Sch. 5 §1(30).
(2), (3)	1975 s.334(3).
(4), (5)	1975 s.334(1) (part) & (2) (part); 1980CJ Sch. 7 §54(b).
(6) to (8)	1974 s.334(4) to (6).
(9)	1975 s.334(1) (part); 1980CJ Sch. 7 §54(a); drafting.
145	1975 s.333A; 1993P s.38(1).
146(1)	1975 s.337 (part).
(2)	1975 s.337(a); 1980B Sch. 2.
(3)	1975 s.337(b).
(4), (5)	1975 s.337(c).
(6)	1975 s.337(d); 1980B Sch. 1 §8; 1987 s.62(3).
(7) to (9)	1975 s.337(f) to (h).
147	1975 s.331A; 1980CJ s.14(2).
148	1975 s.337A; 1980CJ s.15; 1995 s.14; drafting.
149	1975 s.339; 1995 Sch. 6 §121.
150(1)	1975 s.338(1) (part); 1995 Sch. 6 §120.
(2)	1975 s.338(1)(a) (part).
(3)	1975 s.338(1)(c).
(4)	1975 s.338(1)(a) (part).
(5), (6), (7)	1975 s.338(1)(b).
(8), (9), (10)	1975 s.338(2) to (4); 1980CJ s.17.
151	1975 s.331B; 1995 s.30(4).
152	1975 s.338A; 1980CJ s.18(2).
153	1975 s.337B; 1995 s.31.
154	1975 s.353.
155(1)	1975 s.344(1); 1980CJ s.46(1)(c); 1982 Sch. 7 §7; 1995 Sch. 6 §122.
(2), (3)	1975 s.344(2), (3).
(4)	1975 s.344(4); 1980CJ Sch. 7 §55.
156(1), (2)	1975 s.320; 1995 Sch. 6 §117.
(3), (4)	1975 s.321(5), (6); 1995 Sch. 6 §117.
157	1975 s.359; 1995 Sch. 6 §128.
158	1975 s.360A(1); 1993P s.40(2); 1995 Sch. 6 §130.
159	1975 s.335; 1995 Sch. 6 §118.
160	1975 345A; 1980CJ s.19(2).
161	1975 s.351.
162	1975 s.355.
163(1)	1975 s.440; 1995 Sch. 6 §145.
(2)	1975 s.441; 1995 Sch. 6 §146.
164	1975 s.427.
165	1975 s.429.
166(1) to (6)	1975 s.357(1); 1980CJ s.40; 1995 Sch. 6 §127(a).
(7)	1975 s.356(2).
(8)	1975 s.357(5); 1995 s.24(6).

Provision	Derivation
167(1)	1975 s.433.
(2), (3), (4)	1975 s.430(1); 1995 Sch. 6 §142(a).
(5), (6)	1975 s.430(2), (3).
(7)	1975 s.430(4); 1995 Sch. 6 §142(b).
(8)	1975 s.434.
168	1975 s.303(1).
169	1975 s.424; 1980CJ Sch. 7 §68.
170	1975 s.456.
171	1975 s.332.
172(1)	1975 s.309(1); 1995 Sch. 6 §107.
(2), (3)	1975 s.309(2) (part), (3).
173	1975 s.451A; 1995 s.43(2).
174	1975 s.334(2A) to (2D); 1980CJ s.36.
175(1) to (4)	1975 s.442(1); 1980 Sch. 3 §1; 1993CJ s.68(3); 1995 s.42(4).
(5), (6)	1974 s.442(2), (3); 1980 Sch. 3 §1.
175(7), (8)	1975 s.442A(1), (2); 1980CJ Sch. 3 §1.
(9)	1975 s.442B; 1980CJ Sch. 3 §1; 1993CJ Sch. 5 §2(1).
(10)	1975 s.283(2) (part).
176(1)	1975 s.444(1); 1980CJ Sch. 3 §3; 1993CJ Sch. 5 §2(12); 1995 Sch. 6 §148.
(2)	1975 s.444(1A); 1980CJ Sch. 3 §3.
(3)	1975 s.444(1B); 1980CJ Sch. 3 §3.
(4)	1975 s.444(2).
(5)	1975 s.450; 1980CJ Sch. 3 §9; drafting.
177(1)	1975 s.446(1); 1980CJ Sch. 3 §5.
(2), (3)	1975 S.446(2).
(4)	1975 s.446(3).
(5) to (7)	1975 s.446(4) to (6); 1995 Sch. 6 §149.
178(1)	1975 s.447(1); 1980CJ Sch. 3 §6; 1985 Sch. 2 §20.
(2)	1975 s.447(2); 1980CJ Sch. 8.
179	1975 s.448(1)–(5); 1980CJ Sch. 3 §7; 1985 Sch. 4.
180	1975 s.442ZA; 1995 s.42(5).
181(1), (2)	1975 ss.444(3), (4), 448(6), (7); 1980CJ Sch. 3 §7.
(3)	1975 ss.444(5), 448(8); 1980B Sch. 1 §10, §12; 1980CJ Sch. 3 §3, §7.
182	1975 s.452; 1980CJ Sch. 3 §11; 1995 s.42(6).
183(1), (2)	1975 s.452A(1); 1980CJ Sch. 3 §11; 1993P Sch. 5 §1(35).
(3)	1975 s.452A(2) (part); 1980CJ Sch. 3 §11; 1993P Sch. 5 §1(35)(b); 1993CJ Sch. 5 §2(13).
(4)	1975 s.452A(3); 1980CJ Sch. 3 §11.
(5)	1975 s.452A(2) (part); 1980CJ Sch. 3 §11; 1993P Sch. 5 §1(35)(b); 1993CJ Sch. 5 §2(13).
(6), (7)	1975 s.452A(7); 1980CJ Sch. 3 §11.
(8)	1975 s.452A(4A); 1993CJ Sch. 5 §2(13).
(9)	1975 s.452A(5); 1980CJ Sch. 3 §11.
(10)	1975 s.452A(6); 1980CJ Sch. 3 §11.
184	1975 s.449; 1980CJ Sch. 3 §8.
185(1)	1975 s.452B(1) (part); 1980CJ Sch. 3 §11; 1995 s.46(2).
(2)	1975 s.452B(1A); 1995 s.46(2).
(3)	1975 s.452B(1) (part); 1980CJ Sch. 3 §11.
(4)	1975 s.452B(2); 1980CJ Sch. 3 §11.
(5)	1975 s.452B(3) (part); 1980CJ Sch. 3 §11.
(6), (7)	1975 s.452B(1B), (1C); 1995 s.46(2).
(8)	1975 s.452B(3) (part); 1980CJ Sch. 3 §11.
(9)	1975 s.452B(4); 1980CJ Sch. 3 §11.
(10)	1975 s.452B(5); 1995 s.46(2)(c).
186(1), (2)	1975 s.453B(1), (2); 1980CJ Sch. 3 §13; 1993P Sch. 5 §1(36); 1993CJ Sch. 5 §2(14).
(3)	1975 s.453B(3); 1980CJ Sch. 3 §13; 1993CJ Sch. 5 §2(14).
(4), (5)	1975 s.453B(4); 1980CJ Sch. 3 §13; 1993CJ Sch. 5 §2(14); 1995 s.45(2).
(6)	1975 s.453B(4A); 1995 Sch. 6 §152.

Provision	Derivation
186(7)	1975 s.453B(5); 1980CJ Sch. 3 §13; 1993P Sch. 5 §1(36).
(8), (9)	1975 s.453B(6), (7); 1980CJ Sch. 3 §13; 1993P Sch. 5 §1(36); 1993CJ Sch. 5 §2(14).
(10)	1975 s.453B(8); 1980CJ Sch. 3 §13.
187	1975 s.453AA; 1995 s.42(7).
188(1)	1975 s.453(1); 1993P s.43; 1995 Sch. 6 §151(2).
(2), (3)	1975 s.453 (2), (3); 1993P s.43.
(4)	1975 s.453(4); 1993P s.43; 1995 Sch. 6 §151(3).
(5). (6), (7)	1975 s.453(5), (6), (7); 1993P s.43.
189(1), (2)	1975 s.453C(1); 1980CJ Sch. 3 §13.
(3)	1975 s.453C(2); 1980 Sch. 3 §13.
(4)	1975 s.453C(3); 1980CJ Sch. 3 §13; 1993P Sch. 5 §1(37); 1993CJ Sch. 5 §2(15).
(5), (6)	1975 s.453C(4), (5); 1993CJ Sch. 5 §2(15).
(7)	1975 s.455A(1); 1995 s.34(2).
190	1975 s.453D; 1980CJ Sch. 3 §13; 1995 Sch. 6 §153.
191(1), (2)	1975 s.453A(1); 1980CJ Sch. 3 §13.
(3), (4)	1975 s.453A(2), (3); 1980CJ Sch. 3 §13.
192(1), (2)	1975 s.453E; 1980CJ Sch. 3 §13.
(3)	1975 s.454(1); 1995 Sch. 6 §154.
(4), (5)	1975 s.455(1), (2).
193(1), (2)	1975 s.443A(1), (2); 1987 s.68(1); 1993CJ Sch. 5 §2(11).
(3)	1975 s.443A(3); 1995 Sch. 6 §147.
194(1)	1975 s.451(1); 1980CJ Sch. 3 §10.
(2)	1975 s.451(2); 1980CJ Sch. 3 §10; 1995 s.45(1).
(3)	1975 s.451(3); 1980CJ Sch. 3 §10; 1995 Sch. 6 §150.
195(1)	1975 s.104(1); 1980CJ Sch. 4 §15.
(2)	1975 s.104(1A); 1987 s.58(2).
(3), (4)	1975 s.104(2), (3); 1980CJ Sch. 4 §15.
196	1975 ss.217A, 430A; 1995 s.33.
197	1975 ss.254A(2), 455A(2); 1995 s.34.
198(1)	1975 s.217(1) (part); drafting.
(2), (3)	1975 s.217(2), (3); drafting.
199	1975 ss.193, 394; 1977 Sch. 13 §7; 1980CJ s.46(2), Sch. 8; 1982 Sch. 7 §10; drafting.
200(1), (2)	1975 ss.180(1) (part), 381(1) (part); 1995 s.55(2).
(3), (4), (5)	1975 ss.180(1A) to (1C), 381(1A) to (1C); 1995 s.55(3).
(6)	1975 ss.180(2), 381(2); 1980B Sch. 1 §5, Sch. 2.
(7)	1975 ss.180(4), 381(4); 1995 s.55(4).
(8)	1975 ss.180(4A), 381(4A); 1995 s.55(5).
(9)	1975 ss.180(5), 381(5); 1980B s.6(b); 1995 s.55(6).
(10), (11)	1975 ss.180(6), (7), 381(6), (7); 1995 s.55(7).
201(1) to (3)	1975 ss.179(1), 380(1); 1980B s.5(a); 1980CJ Sch. 7 §36(a), §59(a); 1995 Sch. 6 §68.
(4)	1975 s.179(2), s.380(2); 1980B s.5(b); 1980CJ Sch. 7 §36(b), §59(b).
202	1975 ss.219, 432; 1980CJ s.54; 1995 Sch. 6 §143.
203(1)	1975 ss.179A, 380A(1); 1995 s.37.
(2)	1975 s.380A(2); 1995 s.37(2).
(3)	1975 ss.192 (part), 393 (part); 1995 Sch. 6 §74.
204(1)	1980CJ s.41(1).
(2)	1980 s.42(1).
(3)	1980CJ s.42(2).
(4)	1980CJ ss.41(2), 42(3) (part); 1987 Sch. 1 §17; 1988 Sch. 9 §5.
(5)	1980CJ ss.41(3), 42(3) (part).
(6)	1980CJ s.41(4).
205(1) to (3)	1975 s.205(1) to (3); 1980CJ s.43.
(4) to (6)	1975 s.205A(1) to (3); 1980CJ s.43.

Provision	Derivation
206	1975 s.425.
207(1) to (4)	1975 ss.207(1) to (4), 415(1) to (4); 1980CJ s.45(1).
(5)	1975 ss.207(5), 415(5); 1980CJ ss.45(1); 1985 s.43(a); 1988 s.124.
208	1975 s.206; 1980CJ s.44; Prisons (Scotland) Act 1989 (1989 c.45) Sch. 2 §12.
209(1)	1975 s.212A(1); 1993P s.14(1).
(2)	1975 s.212A(1A); 1995 s.36.
(3), (4)	1975 s.212A(2), (3); 1993P s.14(1); 1995 s.132.
(5) to (7)	1975 s.212A(4) to (6).
(8)	1975 s.212A(7); 1993CJ s.69.
210(1)	1975 ss.218(1), 431(1); 1980 Sch. 7 §70, Sch. 8; 1993P s.41.
(2), (3)	1975 ss.218(2), (3), 431(2), (3); 1993P s.41.
211(1)	1975 s.193A(1); 1977 Sch. 11 §1; 1980CJ Sch. 7 §37; 1982 Sch. 15 §17.
(2)	1975 s.193A(2); 1982 Sch. 15 §17.
(3)	1975 s.196(1), 402; 1995 Sch. 6 §75.
(4)	1975 s.196(2); 1980CJ s.48.
(5)	1975 s.203.
(6)	1975 s.412.
(7)	1975 ss.194, 395(1).
212(1), (2)	1975 s.395(2) (part); 1980CJ Sch. 7 §60.
(3) to (7)	1975 s.395(3) to (7).
(8), (9)	1975 s.395(2) (part); 1980CJ Sch. 7 §60.
213	1975 ss.194, 395A(1) to (3); 1980CJ ss.47, 49.
214(1) to (6)	1975 ss.194, 396(1) to (6); 1980CJ s.47; drafting.
(7)	1975 ss.194, 396(7); 1980CJ s.47; 1995 Sch. 6 §137.
(8)	1975 ss.194, 399(1); 1980CJ s.47.
(9)	1975 ss.194, 399(2) & (3); 1980CJ s.47, Sch. 7 §62(b).
215(1), (2)	1975 ss.194, 397; 1977 Sch. 11 §8; Magistrates' Courts Act 1980 (1980 c.43) Sch. 7 §136; 1980CJ s.47.
(3), (4)	1975 ss.194, 397(2), (3); 1980CJ s.47.
216(1), (2)	1975 ss.194, 398(1); 1980CJ s.47, Sch. 7 §61; 1995 Sch. 6 §138.
(3)	1975 ss.194, 398(2); 1980CJ s.47.
(4)	1975 ss.194, 398(3); 1980CJ s.47.
(5)	1975 ss.194, 318(1); 1980CJ s.47.
(6)	1975 ss.194, 318(2) & (3), 398(4) & (5); 1980CJ s.47; 1995 Sch. 6 §114.
(7)	1975 ss.194, 406; 1980CJ s.47; 1995 Sch. 6 §139.
217	1975 ss.194, 400; 1980CJ s.47.
218(1), (2)	1975 ss.194, 401(1), (2); 1980CJ s.47.
(3)	1975 ss.194, 401(3); 1980CJ s.47, Sch. 7 §63.
219(1)	1975 ss.194, 407(1); 1980CJ ss.47, 50; 1990 Sch. 7 §27(3).
(2)	1975 ss.194, 407(1A); 1980CJ ss.47, 50; 1985; 1987 s.67(1); 1991 s.23(2).
(3) to (5)	1975 ss.194, 407(1B) to (1D); 1980CJ s.47, 50.
(6)	1975 ss.194, 407(2); 1980CJ s.47.
(7)	1975 ss.194, 407(4); 1980CJ s.47.
(8)	1975 ss.194, 407(5); 1980CJ s.47; 1987 s.67(2).
220(1), (2)	1975 ss.194, 409(1); 1980CJ s.47, Sch. 7 §65.
(3)	1975 s.194, Sch. 7; 1980CJ s.47.
(4)	1975 ss.194, 409(2); 1980CJ s.47.
221(1)	1975 ss.194, 411(1); 1980CJ s.47; Debtors (Scotland) Act 1987 (1987 c. 18) Sch. 6 §18.
(2), (3)	1975 ss.194, 411(3); 1980CJ s.47.
(4)	1980CJ s.52 (part).
222(1)	1975 ss.194, 403(1); 1977 Sch. 7 §2; 1980CJ s.47.
(2)	1975 ss.194, 403(2); 1980CJ s.47.
(3)	1975 ss.194, 403(3); 1980CJ s.47; 1995 s.67(2).
(4)	1975 ss.194, 403(3A); 1980CJ s.47; 1995 s.67(3).
(5)	1975 ss.194, 403(3B); 1980CJ s.47; 1995 s.67(3).
(6)	1975 ss.194, 403(4); 1977 Sch. 7 §2; 1980CJ s.47.

Provision	Derivation
222(7)	1975 ss.194, 403(4A); 1980CJ s.47; 1994 s.47(4).
(8)	1975 ss.194, 403(6); 1977 Sch. 7 §2; 1980CJ s.47.
223	1975 s.404.
224	1975 ss.194, 408; 1980CJ s.47; 1995 Sch. 6 §140.
225(1)	1975 s.289G(1); 1982 s.54.
(2)	1975 s.289G(2); 1982 s.54; S.I. 1984/526; 1991 s.17(1).
(3)	1975 s.289G(3); 1982 s.54.
(4)	1975 s.289D(1); 1977 Sch. 11 §5; 1982 s.53(a).
(5)	1975 s.289D(1A); 1982 s.53(a); 194 s.157(7).
(6)	1975 s.289D(1B); 1982 s.53(a); drafting.
(7)	1975 s.289D(4); 1977 Sch. 11 §5; 1987 Sch. 2.
(8)	1975 s.289B(6) (part); drafting.
226	1975 s.289GB; 1987 s.66(2).
227	1975 s.182A; 1995 Sch. 6 §69.
228(1)	1975 ss.183(1), 384(1); 1980CJ s.53(1); 1987 Sch. 1 §10; 1990 s.61(1); 1995 s.38(3)(a).
(2)	1975 ss.183(1A), 384(1A); 1990 s.61; 1991 Sch. 3 §7(2).
(3), (4)	1975 ss.183(2), 384(2).
(5)	1975 ss.183(6), 384(6); 1987 s.65(4); 1995 s.38(3)(c).
(6)	1975 ss.183(7), 384(7); 1995 Sch. 6 §70.
229(1)	1975 ss.183(4), 384(4); 1978 s.7; 1987 s.65(3); 1990 s.61(1).
(2), (3)	1975 ss.183(5), 384(5).
(4), (5)	1975 ss.183(5A), 384(5A); 1978 s.7; 1982 Sch. 13 §3; 1995 s.38(1), (3)(b); drafting.
(6), (7)	1975 ss.183(5B), (5C), 384(5B), (5C); 1987 s.65.
230(1)	1975 ss.184(1), 385(1); 1984 Sch. 3 §§29, 36; 1995 s.39(1).
(2)	1975 ss.184(2), 385(2); 1984 Sch. 3 §§29, 36; 1995 s.39(1).
(3)	1975 ss.184(3), 385(3).
(4)	1975 ss.184(5), 385(5); 1983 s.36(2); 1995 s.39(1).
(5)	1975 ss.184(5A), 385(5A); 1983 s.36(2).
(6)	1975 ss.184(5B), 385(5B); 1983 s.36(2); 1995 s.39(1).
(7)	1975 ss.184(6), 385(6); 1983 s.36(3).
(8), (9)	1975 ss.184(7), (8), 385(7), (8).
231	1975 ss.185, 386.
232(1)	1975 ss.186(1), 387(1); 1978 s.8; 1990 s.61(2); Local Government etc. (Scotland) Act 1994 (c. 39) Sch. 13 §97(3); 1995 Sch. 6 §671.
(2)	1975 ss.186(2), 387(2); 1978 s.8; 1980CJ s.46(1); 1982 Sch. 7 §§3, 9; 1987 s.65(5); 1995 s.38(2).
(3)	1975 ss.186(2A), 387(2A); 1993P Sch. 5 §1(7).
(4) to (6)	1975 ss.186(3) to (5), 387(3) to (5).
(7)	1975 s.317.
233(1), (2)	1975 ss.187(1), (2), 388(1), (2).
(3) to (5)	1975 ss.187(3) to (5), 388(3) to (5); 1995 s.40(1), (2).
234(1), (2)	1975 ss.188(1), 389(1); 1978 Sch. 2 §2, 3; 1991 Sch. 3 §7(3).
(3) to (10)	1975 ss.188(2) to (8), 389(2) to (8); 1991 Sch. 3 §7(3).
(11)	Drafting.
235	1990 s.62; 1995 s.35(2) to (7).
236	1975 s.412A; 1995 s.35(11).
237	1975 s.412B; 1995 s.35(11).
238(1)	1978 s.1(1); 1990 s.61(3).
(2) to (7)	1978 s.1(2) to (7).
(8), (9)	1978 s.2(1), (2).
(10), (11)	1978 s.2(3), (4); 1995 Sch. 6. §161.
239(1) to (3)	1978 s.3(1) to (3).
(4)	1978 s.4(1); 1995 Sch. 6 §162.
(5)	1978 s.4(2); 1982 Sch. 7 §12.
(6)	1978 s.4(3); 1990 Sch. 8 §28.
240	1978 s.5.

Provision	Derivation
241	1978 s.5A; 1995 s.40(3).
242	1978 s.6; 1982 Sch. 13 §4.
243(1)	1978 s.6A(1); 1982 Sch. 13 §5.
(2)	1978 s.6A(2); 1982 Sch. 13 §5; S.I. 1989/1345.
(3)	1978 s.6A(3); 1982 Sch. 13 §5.
244	1978 s.6B; 1982 Sch. 13 §5.
245(1) to (3)	1978 s.10(1) to (3).
(4)	1978 s.11.
(5)	1978 s.12(1).
246(1)	1975 ss.181, 382; 1993CJ Sch. 5 §2(2).
(2)	1975 s.182.
(3)	1975 s.383.
247(1)	1975 ss.191(1) (part), 392(1) (part).
(2)	1975 ss.191(2), 392(2).
(3)	1975 ss.191(3) (part), 392(3) (part), 392(3); 1993CJ Sch. 5 §2(3), (9).
(4)	1975 ss.191(4), 392(5); 1995 Sch. 6 §§73, 136.
(5)	1975 s.392(4); 1995 Sch. 6 §136.
(6)	1975 ss.191(1) (part), 392(1) (part).
248(1) to (4)	1975 ss.223A, 436A; Road Traffic Act 1991 (c. 40) s.39.
249(1), (2)	1980CJ s.58(1).
(3), (4)	1980CJ s.58(2), (3).
(5), (6)	1980CJ s.59(1).
(7), (8)	1980CJ s.59(2), (3).
(9), (10)	1980CJ s.60(1), (2).
250(1)	1980CJ s.61.
(2)	1980CJ s.62.
(3), (4)	1980CJ s.63(1), (2).
251	1980CJ s.64.
252	1980CJ s.66.
253	1980CJ s.67; Armed Forces Act 1991 (c. 62) Sch. 2) Sch. 2 §9(2).
254	1975 ss.224, 437.
255	1975 ss.67, 312(x); drafting.
256(1)	1975 ss.150(1), 354(1); 1995 Sch. 6 §§55(a), 126; drafting.
(2)	1975 ss,150(2), 354(2) (part); 1995 Sch. 6 §55(b).
(3)	1975 ss.150(3), 354(2) (part); drafting.
257	1975 ss.84A, 333B; 1995 s.12.
258	1995 s.16.
259	1995 s.17.
260	1995 s.18.
261	1995 s.19.
262	1995 s.20.
263(1) to (3)	1975 ss.148(1) to (3), 340(1) to (3); 1995 Sch. 6 §54.
(4)	1975 ss. 147, 349.
(5)	1975 ss.148A, 349A; 1982 s.73(1), (2).
264(1) to (3)	1975 ss.143(1) to (3), 348(1) to (3); 1980CJ s.29.
(4)	Criminal Justice Administration Act 1914 (c. 58) s.28(3).
265(1)	1975 ss.138(1), (2), 341(1), (2).
(2)	1975 ss.138(4), 341(4).
(3), (4)	1975 ss.139, 342.
266(1)	1975 ss.141(1) (part), 346(1) (part); Criminal Evidence Act 1979 (1979 c. 16) s.1(1); 1980CJ s.28, Sch. 7 §56; 1995 s.24.
(2)	1975 ss.141(1)(a), 346(1)(a).
(3)	1975 ss.141(1)(e), 346(1)(e).
(4)	1975 ss.141(1)(f), 346(1)(f); Criminal Evidence Act 1979 (c. 16) s.1(1); 1995 s.24(1)(a), (4)(a).
(5)	1975 ss.141(1A), 346(1A): 1995 s.24(1)(b), (4)(b).

Provision	Derivation
266(6)	1975 s.141(1B); 1995 s.24(1)(b).
(7)	1975 ss.141(1C), 346(1B); 1995 s.24(1)(c), (4)(b).
(8)	1975 ss.141(1)(g), 346(1)(g).
(9)	1975 ss.141(2), 346(2); 1980CJ s.28.
(10)	1975 ss.141(3), 346(3); 1980CJ s.28.
(11)	1975 ss.142, 347; 1995 Sch. 6 §§50, 124.
267(1)	1975 ss.139A, 342A; 1987 s.63.
(2)	1975 ss.140, 343.
268(1), (2)	1975 ss.149(1), 350(1); 1980CJ s.30; 1985 s.37; 1987 Sch. 1 §9; 1993P Sch. 5 §1(31).
(3), (4)	1975 ss.149(2), (3), 350(2), (3); 1980CJ s.30.
(5)	Drafting.
269(1)	1975 ss.149A(1), 350A(2); 1980CJ s.30; 1985 s.37.
(2), (3)	1975 ss.149A(2), (3), 350A(2), (3); 1980CJ s.30.
(4)	Drafting.
270(1), (2)	1975 ss.141ZA(1), (2), 346ZA(1), (2); 1995 s.24(2), (5).
(3)	1975 s.141ZA(3); 1995 s.24(2).
(4)	1975 ss.141ZA(4), 346ZA(3); 1995 s.24(2), (5).
271(1) to (3)	1993P s.33(1) to (3).
(4)	1993P s.33(4); 1995 Sch. 6 §179(6).
(5)	1990 s.56(1); 1995 Sch. 6 §175(a).
(6)	1993P s.34; 1995 Sch. 6 §179(7).
(7)	1990 s.56(2); 1995 Sch. 6 §175(b).
(8)	1990 s.56(3).
(9)	1990 s.57(1).
(10)	1990 s.57(2).
(11)	1990 s.58; 1995 Sch. 6 §176.
(12)	1990 s.59.
272(1)	1980CJ s.32(1); 1987 s.61.
(2), (3)	1980CJ s.32(2).
(4)	1980CJ s.32(3).
(5)	1980CJ s.32(3A); 1993P s.30.
(6)	1980CJ s.32(4); 1987 s.61.
(7)	1980CJ s.32(5).
(8)	1980CJ s.32(5A); 1993P s.30
(9)	1980CJ s.32(6).
273	1980CJ s.32A; 1993P s.32.
274(1)	1975 ss.141A(1), 346A(1); 1985 s.36.
(2)	1975 ss.141A(2), 346A(2); 1985 s.36; 1995 s.28.
(3), (4)	1975 ss.141A(3), (4), 346A(3), (4); 1985 s.36.
275	1975 ss.141B, 346B; 1985 s.36.
276	1995 s.21.
277(1)	1987 s.60(1); 1993P s.31.
(2)	1987 s.60(2).
(3)	1987 s.60(3); 1995 Sch. 6 §170.
(4)	1987 s.60(4).
278(1)	1975 ss.151(1), 352(1); 1980CJ s.6.
(2), (3)	1975 ss.151(2), 352(2); 1995 Sch. 6 §§56, 125.
(4)	1975 s.352(4).
(5)	1975 ss.151(3), 352(3).
279	1993P s.29.
280(1)	1980CJ s.26(1).
(2), (3)	1980 s.26(1A), (1B); 1995 s.22(2).
(4)	1980 CJ s.26(2); 1995 s.22(3).
(5)	1980CJ s.26(2A); 1995 s.22(4).
(6)	1980CJ s.26(3); 1995 s.22(5).
(7)	1980CJ s.26(4); 1995 s.22(6), Sch. 6 §163.
(8)	1980CJ s.26(4A); 1995 s.22(7).
(9)	1980CJ s.26(5); 1995 s.22(8).

Provision	Derivation
279(10) to (12)	1980 s.26(7B) to (7D); 1995 s.22(9).
281(1), (2)	1980CJ s.26(6), (7).
(3)	1980CJ s.26(7A); 1995 s.22(9).
282	1995 s.25.
283	1995 s.26.
284	1995 s.27.
285(1) to (5)	1975 ss.164(1) to (5) 358(1) to (5).
(6)	1975 ss.162(1), 357(2) (part).
(7)	1975 s.162(2).
(8)	1975 ss.162(3), 357(2) (part); 1995 Sch. 6 §§62, 127(b).
(9)	1975 ss.164(6), 357(2) (part), 358(6).
286	1975 ss.162(4), (5), 357(6), (7); 1995 s.29.
287	1975 s.42; 1995 Sch. 6 §18.
288(1)	1975 s.10.
(2)	1975 s.11.
289	1980CJ s.39.
290	1980CJ s.10(1), (2).
291(1)	1980CJ s.9(1).
(2)	1980CJ s.9(2); 1982 Sch. 6 §64.
(3)	1980CJ s.9(3); 1982 Sch. 7.
292(1)	1975 ss.283A(1), (2); 1977 Sch. 11 §2; 1980CJ Sch. 7 §49.
(2) to (7)	1975 s.457A(1) to (4); 1982 s.55(1).
293	1975 ss.216, 428; 1987 s.64(1).
294(1)	1975 s.63(1) (part).
(2)	1975 s.312(o) (part).
295	1975 ss.215, 426; 1980CJ Sch. 7 §§39, 69; 1987 Sch. 1 §12.
296	1975 ss.15A, 309(2) (part); 1995 Sch. 6 §9.
297(1)	1975 ss.15, 327; 1995 s.9.
(2)	1975 s.326(1) (part).
(3), (4)	1975 ss.16(1), (2), 324(1), (2).
(5)	1975 s.326(1) (part).
298	1995 s.44.
299	1975 ss.227A, 439; 1980CJ s.20.
300	1975 s.439A; 1995 s.41.
301(1)	1975 s.282A; 1990 Sch. 8 §27.
(2)	1975 s.282B; 1990 Sch. 8 §27.
302(1)	1987 s.56(1).
(2)	1987 s.56(3); 1995 s.61(3).
(3)	1987 s.56(3A); 1995 s.61(4).
(4) to (6)	1987 s.56(4) to (6); 1995 s.61(5).
(7), (8)	1987 s.56(7), (7A); 1995 s.61(6).
(9)	1987 s.56(2), (2A); Road Traffic (Consequential Provisions) Act 1988 (1988 c. 54) Sch. 3 §34; 1995 s.61(2).
303(1) to (4)	1987 s.56(8) to (11); 1995 s.61(8).
304	1995 s.56(1) to (10).
305(1)	1975 ss.409(3), 457ZA(1) (part); Summary Jurisdiction (Scotland) Act 194 (c. 48) s.76(1)(d); 1995 Sch. 6 §156.
(2)	1975 s.457ZA(2); 1995 Sch. 6 §156.
(3)	1975 s.457ZA(1) (part); 1995 Sch. 6 §156.
(4)	1975 s.278.
(5)	Summary Jurisdiction (Scotland) Act 1954 (1954 c. 48) s.76(3).
306	1995 s.57.
307(1)	1975 s.462(1); 1977 Sch. 11 §10; National Health Service (Scotland) Act 1978 (1978 c. 29) Sch. 16 §41; 1980B Sch. 1 §14; 1980CJ s.25, Sch. 7 §76; 1982 Sch. 15 §19; 1983 Sch. 2 §37; 1984 Sch. 3 §37; National Health Service and Community Care Act 1990 (c. 19) Sch. 9 §14; 1995 s.39(2), Sch. 6 §157; 1995C Sch. 4 §24(18).

Provision	Derivation
307(2)	1975 s.462(2).
(3) to (8)	1975 s.462(4) to (9).
308	1975 ss.458, 459; 1980CJ Sch. 7 §§73, 74.
309	Drafting.
Sch. 1	1975 Sch. 1; Sexual Offences (Scotland) Act 1976 (1976 c. 67) Schs. 1, 2; 1988 Sch. 15 §§50, 51.
Sch. 2	Criminal Procedure (Scotland) Act 1887 (c. 35) Sch. 1
Sch. 3	
§1	1975 ss.43 (part), 312(a).
§2	1975 ss.44, 312(b).
§3	1975 ss.48, 312(e).
§4(1)	1975 ss.50(1), 312(f) (part).
(2)	1975 ss.50(2), 312(f) (part).
(3)	1975 ss.50(3) (part), 312(f) (part).
(4)	1975 ss.50(3) (part), 312(f) (part).
(5)	1975 ss.50(4), 312(f) (part); 1995 Sch. 6 §§20, 110(a).
(6)	1975 ss.51 (part), 312(g) (part).
(7)	1975 ss.51 (part), 312(g) (part).
(8)	Drafting.
	1975 ss.54, 312(j); 1995 Sch. 6 §§21, 110(b).
§6	1975 ss.55, 312(k).
§7	1975 s.63(2).
(1)	1975 ss.59 (part), 312(l) (part).
(2)	1975 ss.60(1), 312(m) (part).
(3)	1975 ss.60(2), 312(m) (part).
(4)	1975 ss.60(3), 312(m) (part).
(5)	1975 ss.60(4), 312(m) (part).
§9(1)	1975 ss.61(l), 312(n) (part).
(2)	1975 ss.61(2), 312(n) (part).
(3)	1975 ss.61(3), 312(n) (part).
§10(1)	1975 ss.63(1) (part), 312(o) (part).
§14(2)	1975 ss.63(1) (part), 312(o) (part).
(3)	1975 ss.63(2), 312(o) (part).
§11	1975 ss.48B, 312(p); 1995 Sch. 6 §19.
§12	1975 s.312(q), (r).
§13	1975 ss.49, 312(s).
§14	1975 ss.64, 312(t).
§15	1975 ss.65, 312(u).
§16	1975 ss.66, 312(v).
§17	1975 ss.48A, 312(w); 1995 Sch. 6 §19.
§18	1975 ss.60A, 312(y); 1995 Sch. 6 §23.
§19	1975 s.312(z); 1977 Sch. 11 §6; 1980CJ s.46(b); 1982 Sch. 7 §7.
Sch. 4	1975 Sch. 5A; 1995 Sch. 2.
Sch. 5	Summary Jurisdiction (Scotland) Act 1954 (c. 48) Sch. 2 Part II.
Sch. 6	
§1	1975 Sch. 5 §1.
§2	1975 Sch. 5 §2.
§3	1975 Sch. 5 §3.
§4	1975 Sch. 5 §4; 1983 s.36(4); 1995 Sch. 6 §158.
§5	1975 Sch. 5 §5.
§6	1975 Sch. 5 §6.
Sch. 7	
§1	1990 Sch. 6 §1; 1995 s.35(8)(a).
§2	1990 Sch. 6 §2; 1995 Sch. 6 §177(a).
§3	1990 Sch. 6 §3.
§4	1990 Sch. 6 §4; 1995 s.35(8)(b), Sch. 6 §177(b).
§5	1990 Sch. 6 §5; 1995 s.35(8)(c).
§6	1990 Sch. 6 §6.

Provision	Derivation
§7	1990 Sch. 6 §7.
§8	1990 Sch. 6 §9.
Sch. 8	1993P Sch. 3; 1995 Sch. 6 §179(8).
Sch. 9	1980CJ Sch. 1; Forgery and Counterfeiting Act 1981 (1981 c. 45) s.26; Road Traffic Regulation Act 1984 (1984 c. 27) Sch. 13 §37; Video Recording Act 1984 (1984 c. 39) s.20; 1987 Sch. 1 §18(2); 1993P Sch. 4; 1995 Sch. 1.
Sch. 10	1975 Sch. 7A; 1977 Sch. 11 §11.

TABLE OF DESTINATIONS

COURT OF SESSION (SCOTLAND) ACT 1830
(11 GEO. 4 & 1 WILL. 4 C.69)

1830	1995
s.18	s.1(1)

CRIMINAL PROCEDURE (SCOTLAND) ACT 1887
(c.35)

1887	1995
Sched.A	Sched.2

CRIMINAL JUSTICE ADMINISTRATION ACT 1914
(c.58)

1914	1995
s.28(3)	s.264(4)

SUMMARY JURISDICTION (SCOTLAND) ACT 1954
(c.48)

1954	1995
s.76(1)(d)	s.305(1)
76(3)	305(5)
Sched.2, Pt.II	Sched.5

SOCIAL WORK (SCOTLAND) ACT 1968
(c.49)

1968	1995
s.31(1)	s.42(1)

DISTRICT COURTS (SCOTLAND) ACT 1975
(c.20)

1975	1995
s.2(1)	s.6(1)
2(1A)	6(1)
(2)	6(2)
3(1)	7(1)
(2)	7(5)
(4)	7(2)
6(1) part	6(3)
(2) part	6(4)
(3) part	6(4)
(9)	6(5)

CRIMINAL PROCEDURE (SCOTLAND) ACT 1975
(c.21)

2

1975	1995	1975	1995	1975	1995
s.375(4)	s.54(5)	s.392(5)	s.247(4)	s.433	s.167(1)
375A(1) part	53(11), (12)	393 part	203(3)	434	167(8)
	53(11), (12)	394	199	436A	281(1)–(4)
(3)–(11)	53(2)–(10)	395(1)	211(7)	437	254
375ZA	55	(2) part	212(1), (2),	439	299
375ZB	56		(8), (9)	439A	300
375ZC	57(1)–(4)	(3)–(7)	212(3)–(7)	440	163(1)
375ZD	62	395A(1)–(3)	213	441	163(2)
375ZE	63(1)–(5)	396(1)–(6)	214(1)–(6)	442(1)	175(1)–(4)
376(1)	58(1), (2)	(7)	214(7)	(2), (3)	175(5), (6)
(3)	58(5)	397	215(1), (2)	442A(1), (2)	175(7), (8)
(4)	58(10)		215(3), (4)	422B	175(9)
(5)	52(1)	398(1)	216(1), (2)	442ZA	180
(6)	52(4)	(2)	216(3)	443	60
(7)	52(5)	(3)	216(4)	443A(1), (2)	193(1), (2)
(8)	52(6)	(4)	216(6)	(3)	193(3)
(9)	52(7)	(5)	216(6)	444(1)	176(1)
(10)	52(8)	399(1)	214(8)	(1A)	176(2)
377(1)	61(1)	(2)	214(9)	(1B)	176(3)
(1A)	61(2)	(3)	214(9)	(2)	176(4)
(2)	61(3)	400	217	(3)	181(1), (2)
(3)	61(4)	401(1), (2)	218(1), (2)	(4)	181(1), (2)
(4)	61(5)	(3)	218(3)	(5)	181(3)
378	52(9)	402	211(3)	446(1)	177(1)
379(1)	59(1)	403(1)	222(1)	(2)	177(2), (3)
(2)	59(2)		222(2)	(3)	177(4)
(3)	59(3)	(3)	222(3)	(4)–(6)	177(5)–(7)
380(1)	201(1)–(3)	(3A)	222(4)	447(1)	178(1)
(2)	201(4)	(3B)	222(5)	(2)	178(2)
380A(1)	203(1)	(4)	222(6)	448(1)–(5)	179
(2)	203(2)	(4A)	222(7)	(6)	181(1), (2)
381(1) part	200(1), (2)	(6)	222(8)	(7)	181(1), (2)
(1A)–(1C)	200(3)–(5)	404	223	(8)	181(3)
(2)	200(6)	406	216(7)	449	184
(4)	200(7)	407(1)	219(1)	450	176(5)
(4A)	200(8)	(1A)	219(2)	451(1)	194(1)
(5)	200(9)	(1B)–(1D)	219(3)–(5)	(2)	194(2)
(6), (7)	200(10), (11)	(2)	219(6)	(3)	194(3)
382	246(1)	(4)	219(7)	451A	173
383	246(3)	(5)	219(8)	452	182
384(1)	228(1)	408	224	452A(1)	183(1), (2)
(1A)	228(2)	409(1)	220(1), (2)	(2) part	183(3), (5)
(2)	228(3), (4)	(2)	220(4)	(3)	183(4)
(4)	229(1)	(3)	305(1)	(4A)	183(8)
(5)	229(2), (3)	411(1)	221(1)	(5)	183(9)
(5A	229(4), (5)	(3)	221(2), (3)	(6)	183(10)
(5B),		412	211(6)	(7)	183(6), (7)
384(5C)	229(6), (7)	412A	236	452B(1) part	185(1), (3)
(6)	228(5)	412B	237	(1A)	185(2)
384(7)	228(6)	413(1)	44(1)	(1B), (C)	185(6), (7)
385(1)	230(1)	(2)	44(2)	(2)	185(4)
(2)	230(2)	(3)	44(10)	(3) part	185(5), (8)
(3)	230(3)	(3A), (4)	44(3), (4)	(4)	185(9)
(5)	230(4)	(5)	44(5)	(5)	185(10)
(5A)	230(5)	(6A)–(6C)	44(6)–(8)	453(1)	188(1)
(5B)	230(6)	(7)	44(9)	(2), (3)	188(2), (3)
(6)	230(7)	415(1)–(4)	207(1)–(4)	(4)	188(4)
(7), (8)	230(8), (9)	(5)	207(5)	(5)–(7)	188(5), (6),
s.386	231	424	169		(7)
387(1)	232(1)	425	206	453A(1)	191(1), (2)
(2)	232(2)	426	295	(2)	191(3), (4)
(2A)	232(3)	427	164	453B(1), (2)	186(1), (2)
(3)–(5)	232(4)–(6)	428	293	(3)	186(3)
388(1), (2)	233(1), (2)	429	165	(4)	186(4), (5)
(3)–(5)	233(3)–(5)	430(1)	167(2)–(4)	(4A)	186(6)
389(1)	234(1), (2)	(2), (3)	167(5), (6)	(5)	186(7)
(2)–(8)	234(3)–(10)	(4)	167(7)	(6), (7)	186(8), (9)
392(1) part	247(1), (6)	430A	196	(8)	186(10)
(2)	247(2)	431(1)	210(1)	453C(1)	189(1), (2)
(3) part	247(3)	(2), (3)	210(2), (3)	(2)	189(3)
(4)	247(5)	432	202	(3)	189(4)

SEXUAL OFFENCES (SCOTLAND) ACT 1976
(c.67)

CRIMINAL LAW ACT 1977
(c.45)

NATIONAL HEALTH SERVICE (SCOTLAND) ACT 1978
(c.29)

COMMUNITY SERVICE BY OFFENDERS (SCOTLAND) ACT 1978
(c.49)

1978	1995	1978	1995	1978	1995
s.1(1)	s.238(1)	s.5A	s.241	s.10(1)–(3)	s.245(1)–(3)
(2)–(7)	238(2)–(7)	6	242	11	245(4)
2(1), (2)	238(8), (9)	6A(1)	243(1)	12(1)	245(5)
(3), (4)	238(10), (11)	(2)	243(2)	Sched.2,	
3(1)–(3)	239(1)–(3)	(3)	243(3)	para.2	234(1), (2)
4(1)	239(4)	6B	244	para.3	234(1), (2)
(2)	239(5)	7	229(1), (4), (5)		
(3)	239(6)				
5	240	8	232(1), (2)		

CRIMINAL EVIDENCE ACT 1979
(c.16)

1979	1995
s.1(1)	s.266(1), (4)

BAIL (SCOTLAND) ACT 1980
(c.4)

1980	1995	1980	1995	1980	1995
s.1(1)	s.24(3)	s.4	s.29	Sched.1,	
1(2)–(3)	24(4)–(8)	5(a)	201(1)–(3)	para.4	30(2)
1(4)	24(4)–(8), 30(1), (4)	5(b)	201(4)	para.5	200(6)
1(5)	24(4)–(8)	6(b)	200(9)	para.6	30(2)
2	25	7(1)	21(2)–(5)	para.7	135(3), (4)
3(1), (2)	27(1), (2)	7(2)	ss.21(2)–(5), 22(4), (5)	para.8	146(6)
3(2A)–(2D)	27(3)–(6)	8	22(1)–(3), (4), (5)	para.10	181(3)
3(3)–(6)	27(7)–(10)			para.12	181(3)
3(7)–(11)	28	9(a)	43(1)–(3)	para.14	307(1)
3(12)	27(11)	9(b)	43(7)–(8)	Sched.2	ss.146(2), 200(6)
		10	8		

MAGISTRATES' COURTS ACT 1980
(c.43)

1980	1995
Sched.7,	
para.136	215(1), (2)

LAW REFORM (MISCELLANEOUS PROVISIONS) (SCOTLAND) ACT 1980
(c.55)

1980	1995
s.2(3)	85(6), (7)
Sched.2,	
para.6	84(6)
para.7	86(3)

A–475

CRIMINAL JUSTICE ACT (SCOTLAND) ACT 1980
(c.62)

1980	1995	1980	1995	1980	1995
Sched.7—*cont.*		Sched.7—*cont.*		Sched.7—*cont.*	
para.42	117(4)–(6)	para.57	48	para.68	169
para.44	105(5)	para.58	142(5)	para.69	295
para.45	120(4)	para.59(a)......	201(1)–(3)	para.73	308
para.46	125(4)	para.59(b)......	201(4)	para.74	308
para.49	292(1)	para.60	212(1), (2),	para.76	307(1)
para.51	23(1)		(8), (9)	Sched.8.............	ss.93, 103(4)–
para.54(a)......	144(1), (9)	para.61	216(1), (2)		(6), 104(2), (3),
para.54(b)......	144(4), (5)	para.62(b)......	214(9)		115(1)–(4),
para.55	155(4)	para.63	218(3)		120(1), 129(1)–
para.56	266(1)	para.65	220(1), (2)		(3), 137(1),
					178(2), 199

FORGERY AND COUNTERFEITING ACT 1981
(c.45)

1981	1995
s.267...............	Sched.9

CRIMINAL JUSTICE ACT 1982
(c.48)

1982	1995	1982	1995	1982	1995
s.53(a)	s.225(4)–(6)	Sched.7—*cont.*		Sched.13	
54.....................	225(1)–(3)	para.5	7(6)	para.3	229(4), (5)
55(1)	292(2)–(7)	para.6	7(8)	para.4	242
73(1), (2)........	263(5)	para.7	155(1),	para.5	ss.243(1)–(3),
Sched.6			Sched.3, para.19		244
para.64	291(2)	para.9	232(2)	Sched.15,	
Sched.7..............	291(3)	para.10	199	para.17	211(1), (2)
para.4	7(6)	para.12	239(5)	para.19	307(1)
para.3	232(2)	para.14	7(4)		

MENTAL HEALTH (AMENDMENT) (SCOTLAND) ACT 1983
(c.39)

1983	1995	1983	1995	1983	1995
s.22(2)	s.59(1)	s.36(3)	s.230(7)	Sched. 2—*cont.*	
34(a)	53(1), (2)–	36(4)	Sched.6,	para.33	59(2), (3)
	(10), (11), (12),		para.4	para.34	58(6)–(8)
	58(1), (2)	Sched.2		para.35	61(1)
34(b), (d)	60	para.31	58(1), (2),	para.36	59(2), (3)
35(a), (b)	61(2)		(6)–(8)	para.37	307(1)
36(2)	230(4)–(6)	para.32	61(1)		

HEALTH AND SOCIAL SERVICES AND SOCIAL SECURITIES ADJUDICATIONS ACT 1983
(c.41)

1983	1995
Sched.2	
para.7	42(1)

ROAD TRAFFIC REGULATION ACT 1984
(c.27)

1984	1995
Sched.13,	
para.37	Sched.9

MENTAL HEALTH (SCOTLAND) ACT 1984
(c.36)

1984	1995
Sched.3,	
para.24	52(3)
para.25	53(1)
para.26	58(1)
para.27	61(1)
para.28	59(1)–(3)
para.29	230(1), (2)
para.31	52(3)
para.32	53(1)
para.33	58(1)
para.34	61(1)
para.35	59(1)–(3)
para.36	230(1), (2)
para.37	307(1)

VIDEO RECORDING ACT 1984
(c.39)

1984	1995
s.20	Sched.9

LAW REFORMS (MISCELLANEOUS PROVISIONS) (SCOTLAND) ACT 1985
(c.73)

1985	1995
s.21	s.8
36	ss.274(1), (2), (3), (4), 275
37	ss.268(1), (2), 269(1)
43(a)	207(5)
Sched.2,	
para.16	84(4)–(6)
para.17	85(4), (5)
para.18	ss.72(1), 79(1), (2)
para.19	127
para.20	178(1)
para.23	15(6)
Sched.4	179

INCEST AND RELATED OFFENCES (SCOTLAND) ACT 1986
(c.36)

1986	1995
Sched.1,	
para.1	46(3)
para.2	136
para.3	46(3)

TABLE OF DESTINATIONS

CABLE AND BROADCASTING ACT 1986
(c.46)

1986	1995
Sched.5,	
para.30	47(4)

DEBTORS (SCOTLAND) ACT 1987
(c.18)

1987	1995
Sched.6,	
para.18	221(1)

CRIMINAL JUSTICE (SCOTLAND) ACT 1987
(c.41)

1987	1995	1987	1995	1987	1995
s.45(6)(a)	s.109(1), (2)	s.60(4)	277(4)	Sched. 1—*cont.*	
45(6)(b)	109(4), (5)	61	272(1), (6)	para.7	88(2)
(6)(c)...........	109(6)	62(3)	146(6)	para.9	268(1), (2)
56(1)	302(1)	(4)(a)	32(2)	para.10	228(1)
(2), (2A)	302(9)	(b)	32(9)	para.12	295
(3)	302(2)	63	267(1)	para.13(1)......	103(2)
(3A)...........	302(3)	64(1)	293	para.13(2)......	103(1)
(4)–(6)........	302(4)–(6)	65	229(6), (7)	para.14(1)......	125(1)
(7), (7A)	302(7), (8)	(3)	229(1)	para.14(2)......	125(2)
(8)–(11).......	303(1)–(4)	(4)	228(5)	para.14(3)......	125(3)
57(1)	3(2)	(5)	232(2)	para.16(a),	
(2)	2	66(2)	226	(b)	14(2)
58(1)	3(3)–(5)	67(1)	219(2)	para.16(c)......	14(4)
(2)	195(2)	(2)	219(8)	para.17	204(4)
59(1)	44(1)–(4), (9),	68(1)	193(1), (2)	para.18(2)......	Sched.9
	(10)	(3)	121(3)	Sched.2.............	ss.124(4),
60(1)	277(1)	Sched.1,			225(7)
(2)	277(2)	para.4	10		
(3)	277(3)	para.5	84(2), (3)		

CRIMINAL JUSTICE ACT 1988
(c.33)

1988	1995
s.124...............	s.207(5)
Sched.9,	
para.5	204(4)
Sched.15,	
para.48	46(3)
para.50	Sched.1
para.51	Sched.1

ROAD TRAFFIC (CONSEQUENTIAL PROVISIONS) ACT 1988
(c.54)

1988	1995
Sched.3,	
para 34	s.302(9)

PRISONS (SCOTLAND) ACT 1989
(c.45)

1989	1995
Sched.2,	
para.12	s.208

NATIONAL HEALTH SERVICE AND COMMUNITY CARE ACT 1990
(c.19)

1990	1995
Sched.9,	
para.14	s.307(1)

LAW REFORM (MISCELLANEOUS PROVISIONS) (SCOTLAND) ACT 1990
(c.40)

1990	1995	1990	1995	1990	1995
s.56(1)	271(5)	s.61(1)	229(1)	Sched.6—*cont.* ..	Sched.7—*cont.*
(2)	271(7)	(2)	232(1)	para.5	para.5
(3)	271(8)	(3)	238(1)	para.6	para.6
57(1)	271(9)	62	235	para.7	para.7
(2)	271(10)	Sched.6,	Sched.7	para.9	para.8
58	271(11)	para.1	para.1	Sched.8,	
59	271(12)	para.2	para.2	para.27	301(1), (2)
60	4(2)	para.3	para.3	para.27(3)	219(1)
61	228(1), (2)	para.4	para.4	para.28	239(6)

BROADCASTING ACT 1990
(c.42)

1990	1995
Sched.20,	
para.21	47(4)

ROAD TRAFFIC ACT 1991
(c.40)

1991	1995
s.39	s.248(1)–(4)

CRIMINAL JUSTICE ACT 1991
(c.53)

1991	1995
s.17(1)	s.225(2)
23(2)	219(2)
Sched.3,	
para.7(2)	228(2)
para.7(3)	234(1)–(10)

ARMED FORCES ACT 1991
(c.62)

1991	1995
Sched.2,	
para.9(2)	253

CRIMINAL JUSTICE (SCOTLAND) ACT 1995
(C.20)

CHILDREN (SCOTLAND) ACT 1995
(c.36)

INCREASE OF CRIMINAL PENALTIES ETC. (SCOTLAND) ORDER 1984
(S.I. 1984/526)

ACT OF ADJOURNAL (CONSOLIDATION) 1988
(S.I. 1988/110)

TABLE OF DESTINATIONS

CRIME AND PUNISHMENT (SCOTLAND) ACT 1997

(1997 c. 48)

ARRANGEMENT OF SECTIONS

PART I

SENTENCING

Automatic sentences

PART II

CRIMINAL PROCEDURE

Appeals

An Act to make provision as respects Scotland in relation to criminal appeals, the disposal of offenders, criminal procedure, evidence in criminal proceedings, the treatment and early release of prisoners, offences committed by newly released prisoners, criminal legal assistance, the police, confiscation of alcohol from persons under 18, sex offenders and the payment by the Lord Advocate of grants for the provision of forensic medical services; to enable courts in England and Wales and Northern Ireland to remit offenders to courts in Scotland in certain circumstances; to make amendments consequential upon the provisions of this Act to the law in other parts of the United Kingdom; and for connected purposes.

[21st March 1997]

PART I

SENTENCING

Automatic sentences

Imprisonment for life on further conviction for certain offences

1.—(1) After section 205 of the 1995 Act there shall be inserted the following section—

"Imprisonment for life on further conviction for certain offences
205A.—(1) This section applies where a person—

A–487

(a) is convicted on indictment in the High Court of a qualifying offence committed after the relevant date; and

(b) at the time when the offence mentioned in paragraph (a) above was committed, he had attained the age of at least 18 years and had a conviction for a qualifying offence which was obtained on indictment in the High Court or for any relevant offence, irrespective of—

    (i) whether that offence was committed before or after the relevant date; and

    (ii) his age at the time of the commission of that offence.

(2) Subject to subsection (3) below, where this section applies the High Court shall sentence the person—

(a) where he has attained the age of 21 years, to imprisonment for life;

(b) where he has attained the age of 18 years but is under the age of 21 years, to be detained for life, and a person so sentenced shall be liable to be detained in a young offenders institution.

(3) Notwithstanding subsection (2) above, if the High Court is of the opinion that it would be in the interests of justice for it to pass a sentence other than the sentence which that subsection would require it to pass, it may decline to pass that sentence and may instead pass any sentence which it otherwise has power to pass in respect of a conviction for that offence.

(4) For the purposes of section 106(2) of this Act a sentence passed under subsection (2) above in respect of a conviction for a qualifying offence shall not be regarded as a sentence fixed by law for that offence.

(5) In this section—

"qualifying offence" means any offence mentioned in Part I of Schedule 5A to this Act;

"the relevant date" means the date on which section 1 of the Crime and Punishment (Scotland) Act 1997 comes into force; and

"relevant offence" means any offence mentioned in Part II of Schedule 5A to this Act.".

(2) After Schedule 5 to the 1995 Act, there shall be inserted the following Schedule—

"SCHEDULE 5A

OFFENCES FOR THE PURPOSES OF SECTION 205A OF THIS ACT

PART I

QUALIFYING OFFENCES

1. Culpable homicide.

2. Attempted murder, incitement to commit murder or conspiracy to commit murder.

3. Rape or attempted rape.

4. Clandestine injury to women or an attempt to cause such injury.

5. Sodomy or attempted sodomy where, in either case, the complainer, that is to say the person against whom the offence was committed, did not consent.

6. Assault, where the assault—

(a) is aggravated because it was carried out to—

      (i) the victim's severe injury; or

      (ii) the danger of the victim's life; or

  (b) was carried out with an intention to rape or to ravish the victim.

7. Robbery, where, at some time during the commission of the offence, the offender had in his possession a firearm or an imitation firearm.

8. Any offence committed by contravention of—

  (a) section 16 (possession of a firearm with intent to endanger life or cause serious injury);

  (b) section 17 (use of firearm to resist arrest); or

  (c) section 18 (having a firearm for purpose of committing an offence listed in Schedule 2),

of the Firearms Act 1968.

9. Lewd, indecent or libidinous behaviour or practices.

10. Any offence committed by contravention of section 5(1) of the Criminal Law (Consolidation) (Scotland) Act 1995 (unlawful intercourse with a girl under the age of thirteen years).

PART II

RELEVANT OFFENCES

11. Any of the following offences committed in England and Wales, namely—

  (a) an attempt to commit murder, a conspiracy to commit murder or an incitement to murder;

  (b) an offence under section 4 of the Offences Against the Person Act 1861 (soliciting murder);

  (c) manslaughter;

  (d) an offence under section 18 of the Offences Against the Person Act 1861 (wounding, or causing grievous bodily harm, with intent);

  (e) rape or an attempt to commit rape;

  (f) an offence under section 5 of the Sexual Offences Act 1956 (intercourse with a girl under 13);

  (g) any offence committed by contravention of—

      (i) section 16 (possession of a firearm with intent to endanger life or cause serious injury);

      (ii) section 17 (use of firearm to resist arrest); or

      (iii) section 18 (carrying a firearm with criminal intent) of the Firearms Act 1968;

  (h) robbery, where, at some time during the commission of the offence the offender had in his possession a firearm or imitation firearm.

12. Any of the following offences committed in Northern Ireland, namely—

  (a) an offence mentioned in sub-paragraphs (a) to (e) of paragraph 11 above;

  (b) an offence under section 4 of the Criminal Law Amendment Act 1885 (intercourse with a girl under 14);

  (c) an offence under Article 17 (possession of a firearm with intent to injure), Article 18(1) (use of a firearm to resist arrest) or Article 19 (carrying a firearm with criminal intent) of the Firearms (Northern Ireland) Order 1981; and

  (d) robbery, where, at some time during the commission of the offence, the offender had in his possession a firearm or imitation firearm within the meaning of that Order.

Part III

Interpretation

13. In paragraphs 7 and 11(h) above "firearm" and "imitation firearm" have the meanings respectively given to them by section 57 of the Firearms Act 1968.".

Minimum sentence for third conviction of certain offences relating to drug trafficking

2.—(1) [Inserts s.205B into the 1995 Act].
(2) [Inserts s.196(2) into the 1995 Act].

Meaning of "conviction"

3. [*Inserts s.205C into the 1995 Act.*]

Imposition of supervised release orders on conviction of qualifying offence

4.—[*Repealed by the Crime and Disorder Act 1998 (c. 37), Sched. 8, para. 140.*]

Restriction of liberty orders

Restriction of liberty orders

5. After section 245 of the 1995 Act there shall be inserted the following sections—

"Restriction of liberty orders

Restriction of liberty orders

245A.—(1) Without prejudice to section 245D of this Act, where a person of 16 years of age or more is convicted of an offence (other than an offence the sentence for which is fixed by law) the court, if it is of opinion that it is the most appropriate method of disposal, may make an order under this section (in this Act referred to as a "restriction of liberty order") in respect of him; and in this section and sections 245B to 245I of this Act any reference to an "offender" is a reference to a person in respect of whom an order has been made under this subsection.

(2) A restriction of liberty order may restrict the offender's movements to such extent as the court thinks fit and, without prejudice to the generality of the foregoing, may include provision—

(a) requiring the offender to be in such place as may be specified for such period or periods in each day or week as may be specified;

(b) requiring the offender not to be in such place or places, or such class or classes of place or places, at such time or during such periods, as may be specified,

but the court may not, under paragraph (a) above, require the offender to be in any place or places for a period or periods totalling more than 12 hours in any one day.

(3) A restriction of liberty order may be made for any period up to 12 months.

(4) Before making a restriction of liberty order, the court shall explain to the offender in ordinary language—

(a) the effect of the order, including any requirements which are to be included in the order under section 245C of this Act;

(b) the consequences which may follow any failure by the offender to comply with the requirements of any order; and

(c) that the court has power under section 245E of this Act to review the order on the application either of the offender or of any person responsible for monitoring the order,

and the court shall not make the order unless the offender agrees to comply with its requirements.

(5) The clerk of the court by which a restriction of liberty order is made shall—

(a) cause a copy of the order to be sent to any person who is to be responsible for monitoring the offender's compliance with the order; and

(b) cause a copy of the order to be given to the offender or sent to him by registered post or by the recorded delivery service; and an acknowledgment or certificate of delivery of a letter containing such copy order issued by the Post Office shall be sufficient evidence of the delivery of the letter on the day specified in such acknowledgment or certificate.

(6) Before making a restriction of liberty order which will require the offender to remain in a specified place or places the court shall obtain and consider information about that place or those places, including information as to the attitude of persons likely to be affected by the enforced presence there of the offender.

(7) A restriction of liberty order shall be taken to be a sentence for the purposes of this Act and of any appeal.

(8) The Secretary of State may by regulations prescribe—

(a) which courts, or class or classes of courts, may make restriction of liberty orders;

(b) what method or methods of monitoring compliance with such orders may be specified in any such order by any such court; and

(c) the class or classes of offenders in respect of which restriction of liberty orders may be made,

and different provision may be made in relation to the matters mentioned in paragraphs (b) and (c) above in relation to different courts or classes of court.

(9) Without prejudice to the generality of subsection (8) above, in relation to district courts, regulations under that subsection may make provision as respects such courts by reference to whether the court is constituted by a stipendiary magistrate or by one or more justices.

(10) Regulations under subsection (8) above may make such transitional and consequential provisions, including provision in relation to the continuing effect of any restriction of liberty order in force when new regulations are made, as the Secretary of State considers appropriate.

(11) A court shall not make a restriction of liberty order which requires an offender to be in or, as the case may be, not to be in, a particular place or places unless it is satisfied that his compliance with that requirement can be monitored by the means of monitoring which it intends to specify in the order.

(12) The Secretary of State may by regulations substitute for the period of—

(a) hours for the time being mentioned in subsection (2) above; or

(b) months for the time being mentioned in subsection (3) above,

such period of hours or, as the case may be, months as may be prescribed in the regulations.

(13) Regulations under this section shall be made by statutory instrument.

(14) A statutory instrument containing regulations made under subsection (8) above shall be subject to annulment in pursuance of a resolution of either House of Parliament.

(15) No regulations shall be made under subsection (12) above unless a draft of the regulations has been laid before, and approved by a resolution of, each House of Parliament.

Monitoring of restriction of liberty orders

245B.—(1) Where the Secretary of State, in regulations made under section 245A(8) of this Act, empowers a court or a class of court to make restriction of liberty orders he shall notify the court or each of the courts concerned of the person or class or description of persons who may be designated by that court for the purpose of monitoring an offender's compliance with any such order.

(2) A court which makes a restriction of liberty order in respect of an offender shall include provision in the order for making a person notified by the Secretary of State under subsection (1) above, or a class or description of persons so notified, responsible for the monitoring of the offender's compliance with it.

(3) Where the Secretary of State changes the person or class or description of persons notified by him under subsection (1) above, any court which has made a restriction of liberty order shall, if necessary, vary the order accordingly and shall notify the variation to the offender

Remote monitoring

245C.—(1) The Secretary of State may make such arrangements, including contractual arrangements, as he considers appropriate with such persons, whether legal or natural, as he thinks fit for the remote monitoring of the compliance of offenders with restriction of liberty orders, and different arrangements may be made in relation to different areas or different forms of remote monitoring.

(2) A court making a restriction of liberty order which is to be monitored remotely may include in the order a requirement that the offender shall, either continuously or for such periods as may be specified, wear or carry a device for the purpose of enabling the remote monitoring of his compliance with the order to be carried out.

(3) The Secretary of State shall by regulations specify devices which may be used for the purpose of remotely monitoring the compliance of an offender with the requirements of a restriction of liberty order.

(4) Regulations under this section shall be made by statutory instrument subject to annulment in pursuance of a resolution of either House of Parliament.

Concurrent probation and restriction of liberty orders

245D.—(1) Notwithstanding sections 228(1) and 245A(1) of this Act, where the court—

(a) intends to make a restriction of liberty order under section 245A(1); and

(b) considers it expedient—

(i) having regard to the circumstances, including the nature of the offence and the character of the offender; and

(ii) having obtained a report as to the circumstances and character of the offender,

that the offender should also be subject to a probation order made under section 228(1) of this Act,

it may make both such orders in respect of the offender.

(2) Where the court makes both a restriction of liberty order and a probation order by virtue of subsection (1) above, the clerk of the court shall send a copy of each order to both—

(a) any person responsible for monitoring the offender's compliance with the restriction of liberty order; and

(b) the officer of the local authority who is to supervise the probationer.

(3) Where the offender by an act or omission fails to comply with a requirement of an order made by virtue of subsection (1) above—

(a) if the failure relates to a requirement contained in a probation order and is dealt with under section 232(2)(c) of this Act, the court may, in addition, exercise the power conferred by section 245F(2)(b) of this Act in relation to the restriction of liberty order; and

(b) if the failure relates to a requirement contained in a restriction of liberty order and is dealt with under section 245F(2)(b) of this Act, the court may, in addition, exercise the power conferred by section 232(2)(c) in relation to the probation order.

(4) Where the offender by an act or omission fails to comply with both a requirement contained in a probation order and a requirement contained in a restriction of liberty order to which he is subject by virtue of subsection (1) above, he may, without prejudice to subsection (3) above, be dealt with as respects that act or omission either under section 232(2) of this Act or under section 245F(2) of this Act but he shall not be liable to be otherwise dealt with in respect of that act or omission.

Variation of restriction of liberty order

245E.—(1) Where a restriction of liberty order is in force either the offender or any person responsible for monitoring his compliance with the order may apply to the court which made the order for a review of it.

(2) On an application made under subsection (1) above, and after hearing both the offender and any person responsible for monitoring his compliance with the order, the court may by order, if it appears to it to be in the interests of justice to do so—

(a) vary the order by—

(i) amending or deleting any of its requirements;

(ii) inserting further requirements; or

(iii) subject to subsection (3) of section 245A of this Act, increasing the period for which the order has to run; or

(b) revoke the order.

(3) Where the court, on the application of a person other than the offender, proposes to—

(a) exercise the power conferred by paragraph (a) of subsection (2) above to vary (otherwise than by deleting a requirement) a restriction of liberty order, it shall issue a citation requiring the offender to appear before the court and section 245A(4) shall apply to the variation of such an order as it applies to the making of an order; and

(b) exercise the power conferred by subsection (2)(b) above to revoke such an order and deal with the offender under section 245G of this Act, it shall issue a citation requiring him to appear before the court.

(4) If an offender fails to appear before the court after having been cited in accordance with subsection (3) above, the court may issue a warrant for his arrest.

Breach of restriction of liberty order

245F.—(1) If at any time when a restriction of liberty order is in force it appears to the court which made the order that the offender has failed to comply with any of the requirements of the order the court may issue a citation requiring the offender to appear before the court at such time as may be specified in the citation or, if it appears to the court to be appropriate, it may issue a warrant for the arrest of the offender.

(2) If it is proved to the satisfaction of the court that the offender has failed without reasonable excuse to comply with any of the requirements of the order the court may by order—

(a) without prejudice to the continuance in force of the order, impose a fine not exceeding level 3 on the standard scale;

(b) vary the restriction of liberty order; or

(c) revoke that order.

(3) A fine imposed under this section in respect of a failure to comply with the requirements of a restriction of liberty order shall be deemed for the purposes of any enactment to be a sum adjudged to be paid by or in respect of a conviction or a penalty imposed on a person summarily convicted.

(4) Where the court varies a restriction of liberty order under subsection (2) above it may do so in any of the ways mentioned in paragraph (a) of section 245E(2) of this Act.

Disposal on revocation of restriction of liberty order

245G.—(1) Where the court revokes a restriction of liberty order under section 245E(2)(b) or 245F(2) of this Act, it may dispose of the offender in any way which would have been competent at the time when the order was made, but in so doing the court shall have regard to the time for which the order has been in operation.

(2) Where the court revokes a restriction of liberty order as mentioned in subsection (1) above, and the offender is, by virtue of section 245D(1) of this Act, subject to a probation order, it shall, before disposing of the offender under subsection (1) above, discharge the probation order.

Documentary evidence in proceedings under section 245F

245H.—(1) Evidence of the presence or absence of the offender at a particular place at a particular time may, subject to the provisions of this section, be given by the production of a document or documents bearing to be—

(a) a statement automatically produced by a device specified in regulations made under section 245C of this Act, by which the offender's whereabouts were remotely monitored; and

(b) a certificate signed by a person nominated for the purpose of this paragraph by the Secretary of State that the statement relates to the whereabouts of the person subject to the order at the dates and times shown in the statement.

(2) The statement and certificate mentioned in subsection (1) above shall, when produced at a hearing, be sufficient evidence of the facts set out in them.

(3) Neither the statement nor the certificate mentioned in subsection (1) above shall be admissible in evidence unless a copy of both has been served on the offender prior to the hearing and, without prejudice to the foregoing, where it appears to the court that the offender has had insufficient notice of the statement or certificate, it may adjourn a hearing or make any order which it thinks appropriate in the circumstances.

Procedure on variation or revocation of restriction of liberty order

245I. Where a court exercises any power conferred by sections 232(3A), 245E(2) or 245F(2)(b) or (c) of this Act, the clerk of the court shall forthwith give copies of the order varying or revoking the restriction of liberty order to any person responsible for monitoring the offender's compliance with that order and that person shall give a copy of the order to the offender.".

Mentally disordered offenders

Disposal in cases of mentally disordered offenders

6.—(1) [Inserts s.59A into the 1995 Act].
(2) [Amends s.60 of the 1995 Act].
(3) [Amends s.204(2) of the 1995 Act and inserts subs.(2A) therein].
(4) [Inserts subs.(4A) into s.207 of the 1995 Act].
(5) [Amends s.307 of the 1995 Act].

Effect of hospital direction

7.—(1) After section 62 of the 1984 Act, there shall be inserted the following section—

"Effect of hospital direction

62A.—(1) A hospital direction made under section 59A of the Criminal Procedure (Scotland) Act 1995 shall be sufficient authority—

(a) for a constable, a mental health officer, an officer on the staff of the hospital specified in the direction or other person directed to do so by the court to convey the person in respect of whom the direction has been made to the hospital specified in the direction within a period of 7 days; and

(b) for the managers of the hospital so specified to admit him at any time within that period and thereafter to detain him in accordance with the provisions of this Act.

(2) Where the managers of a hospital specified in a hospital direction propose to admit the patient to a hospital unit in that hospital, they shall, if that unit was not so specified, notify the Secretary of State and the Mental Welfare Commission of the patient's proposed admission to and detention in that unit; and the patient shall not be so admitted unless the Secretary of State has consented to the proposed admission.

(3) If within the period of 7 days referred to in subsection (1) of this section it appears to the Secretary of State that by reason of an emergency or other special circumstance it is not practicable for the person to whom the hospital direction relates to be received into the hospital specified in the direction, he may give a direction under this subsection for the admission of that person to such other hospital as appears to be appropriate in lieu of the hospital so specified.

(4) Where a direction is given by the Secretary of State under subsection (3) of this section, he shall cause the person having custody of the person to whom the hospital direction relates to be informed, and the hospital direction shall have effect as if the hospital specified in the direction under subsection (3) of this section were substituted for the hospital specified in the hospital direction.

(5) Where a patient has been admitted to a hospital under a hospital direction—

(a) none of the provisions of Part V of this Act relating to the duration, renewal and expiration of authority for the detention of patients shall apply, and the patient shall continue to be liable to be detained by virtue of the relevant hospital direction until he is remitted to prison in accordance with section 65(2) or 74(3) of this Act or he is discharged in accordance with section 74(8B) of this Act;

(b) the following powers shall be exercisable only with the consent of the Secretary of State, that is to say—

(i) power to grant leave of absence to the patient under section 27 of this Act;

(ii) power to transfer the patient under section 29 of this Act;

and if leave of absence is granted under the said section 27 the power to recall shall be vested in the Secretary of State as well as in the responsible medical officer;

(c) the power to take the patient into custody and return him under section 28 of this Act may be exercised at any time,

and in relation to any such patient the provisions of the said Part V specified in Part II of the Second Schedule to this Act shall have effect subject to the exceptions and modifications set out in that Part and the remaining provisions of Part V shall not apply.".

(2) In section 63 of that Act (rights of appeal of restricted patients)—

(a) in subsection (1)—

(i) in the definition of "restricted patient" after the word "order" there shall be substituted the words ", to a hospital direction"; and

(ii) for the definition of "relevant hospital order" and "relevant transfer direction" there shall be substituted the following definition—

" "relevant hospital order", "relevant hospital direction" and "relevant transfer direction", in relation to a restricted patient, mean the hospital order, hospital direction or transfer direction by virtue of which he is liable to be detained in a hospital."; and

(b) in subsection (2), in paragraph (a), after the word "order" there shall be inserted the words ", hospital direction".

(3) In section 65 of that Act (appeal where person is subject to restriction direction)—

(a) in subsection (1), after the word "subject" there shall be inserted the words "to a hospital direction or";

(b) in subsection (2)—

(i) in paragraph (a) for the words "removed to hospital" there shall be substituted the words "conveyed under a relevant hospital direction or removed under a relevant transfer direction to a hospital specified in the direction" and for the words "so removed" there shall be substituted the words "so conveyed or removed"; and

(ii) the words after paragraph (b) shall cease to have effect; and

(c) after subsection (2) there shall be inserted the following subsection—

"(3) Where a direction has been given under subsection (2) of this section, on the person's arrival in the prison or other institution or place to which he has been remitted by virtue of such a direction the relevant hospital direction or, as the case may be, the relevant transfer direction together with the restriction direction given in respect of the person shall cease to have effect.".

(4) In section 74 of that Act (further provision as to transfer directions and restriction directions)—

(a) after subsection (1), there shall be inserted the following subsection—

"(1A) This subsection applies if the Secretary of State is satisfied as regards a person who has been conveyed to a hospital under a hospital direction as to the matters mentioned in subsection (2) below at a time when the person, by virtue of a sentence of imprisonment imposed on him at the time that direction was made, would but for that direction be in prison or being detained other than in a hospital.":

(b) in subsection (2), after the words "subsection (1)" there shall be inserted the words "and (1A)";

(c) in subsection (3)—

(i) after the words "subsection (1)" there shall be inserted the words "or (1A)";

(ii) after the word "been", where it occurs for the second time, there shall be inserted the words "conveyed or"; and

(iii) for the words "so removed" there shall be substituted the words "so conveyed or removed";

(d) in subsection (4), after the words "subsection (1)" there shall be inserted the words "or (1A)";

(e) in subsection (5), after the words "restriction direction" there shall be inserted the words "or, as the case may be, the hospital direction";

(f) after subsection (8), there shall be inserted the following subsections—

"(8A) This subsection applies where a hospital direction has been made in respect of a person and he has thereafter been released under the Crime and Punishment (Scotland) Act 1997.

(8B) Where subsection (8A) above applies—

(a) the hospital direction shall forthwith cease to have effect; and

(b) the person shall thereupon be discharged from hospital unless a report is furnished in respect of him under subsection (9) below.";

(g) in subsection (9)—

(i) after the word "before" there shall be inserted—

"- (a)"; and

(ii) after the word "above" there shall be inserted the following paragraph—

"; or

(b) a hospital direction ceases to have effect,";

(h) in subsection (10), after the words "restriction direction", in both places where they occur, there shall be inserted the words "or, as the case may be, hospital direction"; and

(i) in subsection (11), after the words "transfer direction" there shall be inserted the words "or, as the case may be, hospital direction".

(5) In section 125 of that Act (interpretation), after the definition of "hospital" there shall be inserted the following definition—

" "hospital direction" has the meaning assigned to it by section 59A(1) of the Criminal Procedure (Scotland) Act 1995;".

Remand of persons suffering from mental disorder to private hospital

8. In section 70 of the 1984 Act (removal to hospital of persons on remand), the words "(not being a private hospital)" shall cease to have effect.

Power to specify hospital unit

9.—(1) Subject to subsection (2) below, any power to specify a hospital which is conferred by—

(a) section 57(2)(a) of the 1995 Act (disposal where accused insane);

(b) section 58 of the 1995 Act (hospital orders);

(c) section 59A of the 1995 Act (hospital directions); or

(d) section 71 of the 1984 Act (transfer direction),

includes a power to specify a hospital unit; and where such a unit is specified in relation to any person in the exercise of such a power, any reference in any enactment (including one contained in this Act) to him being, or being liable to be, detained in a hospital shall be construed accordingly.

(2) In subsection (1) above—

(a) paragraph (a) shall not apply unless the court also makes an order under paragraph (b) of section 57(2) of the 1995 Act;

(b) paragraph (b) shall not apply unless the court also makes an order under section 59 of the 1995 Act;

(c) paragraph (d) shall not apply unless the Secretary of State also gives a direction under section 72 of the 1984 Act.

(3) In this section—

"hospital", in relation to the exercise of a power, has the same meaning as in the enactment which confers the power;

"hospital unit" means any part of a hospital which is treated as a separate unit.

Medical evidence in relation to mentally disordered offenders

10.—(1) [Amends subss. (1) and (2) of s.53 of the 1995 Act].

(2) [Amends s.61(1) of the 1995 Act, inserts subss. (1A) and (6) therein and amends subss. (2), (3) and (5)].

Increase in maximum period of interim hospital orders

11. In section 53 of the 1995 Act (interim hospital orders), in subsection (6), for the words "six months" there shall be substituted the words "twelve months".

Sentence calculation where remand spent in hospital

12. [Amends s.210 of the 1995 Act].

Increases in sentencing powers and penalties

Increase in sentences available to sheriff and district courts

13.—(1) In section 3 of the 1995 Act (jurisdiction and powers of solemn courts)—

(a) in subsection (3), for the words "three years" there shall be substituted the words "five years";

(b) in subsection (4), for the words "three years" there shall be substituted "five years";

(c) after subsection (4) there shall be inserted the following subsection—

"(4A) Subject to subsection (5) below, where under any enactment passed or made after 1st January 1988 but before the commencement of section 13 of the Crime and Punishment (Scotland) Act 1997 (increase in sentencing powers of sheriff courts) an offence is punishable on conviction on indictment for a term exceeding three years but the enactment either expressly or impliedly restricts the power of the sheriff to impose a sentence of imprisonment for a term exceeding three years, it shall be competent for the sheriff to impose a sentence of imprisonment for a term exceeding three but not exceeding five years."; and

(d) in subsection (5), for the words "subsection (4)" there shall be substituted the words "subsections (4) and (4A)".

(2) In section 5 of the 1995 Act (powers of sheriff when sitting as summary court)—

(a) in subsection (2)(d), for the words "three months" there shall be substituted the words "six months"; and

(b) in subsection (3), for the words "six months" there shall be substituted the words "twelve months".

(3) In section 195(2) of the 1995 Act (remit to High Court for sentence where sheriff's power limited by statute) for the words "three years", in both places where they occur, there shall be substituted the words "five years".

(4) In paragraph 12 of Schedule 3 to the Criminal Procedure (Consequential Provisions) (Scotland) Act 1995 (construction of references to penal

servitude and hard labour), in sub-paragraph (3), for the words "two years" there shall be substituted the words "five years".

Increase in maximum penalty for certain sexual offences

14.—(1) [Amends s.5 of the Criminal Law (Consolidation) Act 1997].
(2) [Amends s.6 of the Criminal Law (Consolidation) Act 1997].

Powers of court to disqualify from driving

Driving disqualifications

15.—(1) [Inserts ss.248A, 248B and 248C in the Act in relation to offences committed on or after January 1, 1998].
(2) [Amends s.252(2) of the 1995 Act].
(3) [Inserts s.14(2)(h) into the Proceeds of Crime (Scotland) Act 1995].

Miscellaneous

Designated life prisoners

16.—(1) [Substitutes s.2(1) of the Prisoners and Criminal Proceedings (Scotland) Act 1993].
(2) This subsection applies where, in the case of a person sentenced, prior to the coming into force of this section, in respect of a murder committed by him before he attained the age of 18 years, the Lord Justice General, whom failing the Lord Justice Clerk, after consultation with the trial judge, if available, certifies his opinion that, if section 2 of the 1993 Act, as amended by this Act, had been in force at the time when the prisoner was sentenced, the court by which he was sentenced would have ordered that that section should apply to him as soon as he had served a part of his sentence specified in the certificate.
(3) In a case to which subsection (2) above applies, Part I of the 1993 Act, except sections 1(4) and 2(9), shall apply as if—
  (a) the life prisoner concerned were a designated life prisoner within the meaning of section 2 of that Act; and
  (b) the designated part of his sentence within the meaning of that section were the part specified in the certificate.
(4) Where a person is serving two or more sentences of imprisonment for life or detention without limit of time or for life—
  (a) he shall be treated as a designated life prisoner within the meaning of section 2 of the 1993 Act only if the requirements of subsection (2) above are satisfied in respect of each of those sentences; and
  (b) notwithstanding the terms of any certificate under that subsection, subsections (4) and (6) of that section shall not apply to him until he has served the designated part of each of those sentences.

PART II

CRIMINAL PROCEDURE

Appeals

Right of appeal

17.—(1) [Inserted as s.106(3) to (3D) of the 1995 Act].
(2) [Inserted as s.175(5) to (5E) of the 1995 Act].

Automatic sentences: jurisdiction and appeals

18.—(1) [Inserted (under deletion of references to ss.205 and 209(1A) as) s.106(1)(bb) of the 1995 Act].

(2) [Inserted (under deletion of references to ss.205A(3) and 209(1A) as) s.108A of the 1995 Act].
(3) [Amends s.112(1)(b) of the 1995 Act].
(4) [Amends s.116 of the 1995 Act].
(5) [Amends s.118(4) and inserts s.118(4A) of the 1995 Act].
(6) [Amends s.121 of the 1995 Act].
(7) [Amends s.125 of the 1995 Act].
(8) [Amends s.126 of the 1995 Act].

Appeal against automatic sentence where earlier conviction quashed

19.—(1) [Inserts s.106A(2), (4) and (5) into the 1995 Act and s.106A(3) (under deletion of reference to s.205A(2))].
(2) [Amends s.110(1)(a) of the 1995 Act].

Transfer of rights of appeal of deceased person

20. [Inserted as s.303A of the 1995 Act].

Increased rights of appeal of prosecutor

21.—(1) [Substituted as s.108(1) and (2) of the 1995 Act].
(2) [Substituted as s.175(4) and (4A) of the 1995 Act].

Appeal by prosecutor against hospital orders etc.

22. [Inserted as s.60A of the 1995 Act].

Appeals against orders under section 49 of the 1995 Act

23. It shall be competent for a convicted person or a prosecutor to appeal against a decision made under section 49 of the 1995 Act (reference or remit to children's hearing) to remit a case to the Principal Reporter and, accordingly—
(a) [Inserted in s.49(4) of the 1995 Act].
(b) [Inserted as s.106(1)(da) of the 1995 Act].
(c) [Inserted as s.175(2)(ca) of the 1995 Act].

Suspension of certain sentences pending determination of appeal

24.—(1) [Inserted as s.121A of the 1995 Act].
(2) [Inserted as s.193A of the 1995 Act].

The Scottish Criminal Cases Review Commission

Scottish Criminal Cases Review Commission

25.—(1) [Inserted Part XA and Sched. 9A into the 1995 Act].

Evidential provisions

Evidence concerning certain orders

26.—(1) [Inserted as s.233(6) of the 1995 Act].
(2) [Inserted as s.241(4) of the 1995 Act].

Proof of age

27. [Inserted as s.255A of the 1995 Act].

Evidence from certain official documents

28.—(1) Section 154 of the 1995 Act shall cease to have effect.
(2) [Inserted as s.279A of the 1995 Act].

Evidence of vulnerable persons: special provisions

29.[Substituted as s.271 of the 1995 Act].

Routine evidence

30.—(1) [Inserted in Schedule 9 of the 1995 Act].
(2) [Inserted in Schedule 9 of the 1995 Act].
(3) [Inserted in Schedule 9 of the 1995 Act].
(4) Section 5 of the Video Recordings Act 1993 shall cease to have effect.
(5) In Schedule 22 of the Environment Act 1995 (minor and consequential amendments), paragraph 35 shall cease to have effect.

Previous convictions in solemn proceedings

31. In section 101 of the 1995 Act (previous convictions in solemn proceedings), subsection (5) shall cease to have effect.

Supervision and care of persons diverted from prosecution or subject to supervision requirement

32. In section 27(1) of the Social Work (Scotland) Act 1968 (supervision and care of persons put on probation or released from prisons etc.)—
   (a) after paragraph (a) there shall be inserted the following paragraph—
      "(aa) making available to any children's hearing such reports relating to persons aged 16 and 17 years in relation to the commission of an offence as the hearing may require for the disposal of a case;";
   (b) after paragraph (a) there shall be inserted the following paragraph—
      "(ab) making available to any procurator fiscal or the Lord Advocate such reports as the procurator fiscal or the Lord Advocate may request in relation to persons who are charged with an offence;";
   (c) after sub-paragraph (iv) of paragraph (b) there shall be inserted the following sub-paragraph—
      "(v) without prejudice to sub-paragraphs (i) to (iv) above, persons in their area who are subject to a supervision and treatment order under section 57(2)(d) of the Criminal Procedure (Scotland) Act 1995;";
   (d) after sub-paragraph (iv) of paragraph (b) there shall be inserted the following sub-paragraph—
      "(vi) persons in their area aged 16 and 17 years who are subject to a supervision requirement imposed in relation to the commission of any offence by that person;"; and
   (e) after sub-paragraph (iv) of paragraph (b) there shall be inserted the following sub-paragraph—
      "(vii) persons in their area who are charged with, but not prosecuted for, any offence and are referred to the local authority by the procurator fiscal or the Lord Advocate; and".

PART III

PRISONERS

CHAPTER I

EARLY RELEASE

Early release

Application of provisions with respect to early release

33.—[*Repealed by the Crime and Disorder Act 1998 (c. 37), Sched. 10 (effective September 30, 1998: S.I. 1998 No. 2327, art. 2(3)(y)).*]

Early release

34.—[*Repealed by the Crime and Disorder Act 1998 (c. 37), Sched. 10 (effective September 30, 1998: S.I. No. 2327, art. 2(3)(y)).*]

Prisoners held on remand

35.—[*Repealed by the Crime and Disorder Act 1998 (c. 37), Sched. 10 (effective September 30, 1998: S.I. No. 2327, art. 2(3)(y)).*]

Amendments to 1989 Act

36.—[*Repealed by the Crime and Disorder Act 1998 (c. 37), Sched. 10 (effective September 30, 1998: S.I. No. 2327, art. 2(3)(y)).*]

Suspension of period of early release

37.—[*Repealed by the Crime and Disorder Act 1998 (c. 37), Sched. 10 (effective September 30, 1998: S.I. No. 2327, art. 2(3)(y)).*]

Commission of offence within certain period of release from prison to be aggravation

38.—[*Repealed by the Crime and Disorder Act 1998 (c. 37), Sched. 10 (effective September 30, 1998: S.I. No. 2327, art. 2(3)(y)).*]

Application of early release provisions in certain cases

Fine defaulters and persons convicted of contempt of court

39.—[*Repealed by the Crime and Disorder Act 1998 (c. 37), Sched. 10 (effective September 30, 1998: S.I. No. 2327, art. 2(3)(y)).*]

Persons liable to removal from the United Kingdom

40.—[*Repealed by the Crime and Disorder Act 1998 (c. 37), Sched. 10 (effective September 30, 1998: S.I. No. 2327, art. 2(3)(y)).*]

Mentally disordered offenders

41.—[*Repealed by the Crime and Disorder Act 1998 (c. 37), Sched. 10 (effective September 30, 1998: S.I. No. 2327, art. 2(3)(y)).*]

CHAPTER II

TREATMENT OF PRISONERS

Testing of prisoners for alcohol

42. After section 41B of the 1989 Act there shall be inserted the following section—

"**Testing of prisoners for alcohol**
    41C.—(1) If an authorisation is in force for the prison, any officer of the prison may, at the prison, in accordance with rules under section 39 of this Act, require any prisoner who is confined in the prison, and whom he reasonably believes to have taken alcohol, to provide a sample of breath for the purpose of ascertaining whether he has any alcohol in his body.
    (2) If the authorisation so provides, the power conferred by subsection (1) above shall include the power to require a prisoner to provide a sample of any other description specified in the authorisation, not being an intimate sample, whether instead of or in addition to a sample of breath.

(3) In this section—

"authorisation" means an authorisation by the governor; and
"intimate sample" means a sample of blood, semen or other tissue fluid, saliva or pubic hair, or a swab taken from a person's body orifice.".

Medical services in prisons

43.—(1) In section 3(1) of the 1989 Act (general superintendence of prisons) the words from "including" to the end shall cease to have effect.

(2) After section 3 of the 1989 Act there shall be inserted the following section—

"Medical services in prisons

3A.—(1) Without prejudice to section 11(2) of this Act, the Secretary of State shall secure the provision of appropriate medical services within prisons.

(2) The Secretary of State may perform the duty imposed by subsection (1) above by—

(a) appointing for a prison one or more medical officers, each of whom shall be a registered medical practitioner;

(b) entering into an arrangement with any person for the provision of appropriate medical services in relation to any prison or prisons; or

(c) both making any such appointment as is mentioned in paragraph (a) above and by entering such an arrangement as is mentioned in paragraph (b) above.

(3) In this section "appropriate medical services" means such services in relation to—

(a) routine and emergency health care for prisoners; and

(b) the provision of advice to the governor on matters related to the medical treatment and health of prisoners generally,

as the Secretary of State considers appropriate for the prison in which they are to be provided; and such services shall be provided by or under the supervision of a registered medical practitioner.

(4) Any medical officer appointed under subsection (2)(a) above shall, for the purposes of this Act, be an officer of the prison.

(5) A registered medical practitioner providing, or supervising the provision of, appropriate medical services in accordance with an arrangement made under subsection (2)(b) above shall be deemed to be a medical officer for the prison for the purposes of—

(a) section 27(5) of this Act (so far as that section continues to have effect by virtue of Schedule 6 to the Prisoners and Criminal Proceedings (Scotland) Act 1993 (existing provisions which continue to have effect in relation to prisoners sentenced before 1st October 1993)); and

(b) any rules or directions made or issued under section 39 of this Act;

unless such rules or directions otherwise provide or the context otherwise requires.

(6) Subject to subsection (7) below, rules under section 39 of this Act may make provision for the governor to authorise the carrying out by officers of the prison of a search of any person who is in or is seeking to enter the prison for the purpose of providing appropriate medical services in accordance with an arrangement made under subsection (2)(b) above.

(7) Nothing contained in rules made by virtue of subsection (6) above shall permit the governor to authorise an officer of a prison to require a

person to remove any of his clothing other than an outer coat, jacket, headgear, gloves and footwear.".

(3) In section 19(4) of the 1989 Act (application of enactments to young offenders institutions and remand centres)—

(a) in paragraph (a), after the word "sections" there shall be inserted the words "3A,"; and

(b) in paragraph (b), for the words "1 to 7" there shall be substituted the words "1 to 3, 4 to 7".

(4) For section 107(6) of the Criminal Justice and Public Order Act 1994 (medical officers in contracted out prisons), there shall be substituted the following subsections—

"(6) Without prejudice to section 11(2) of the 1989 Act (direction by Secretary of State for prisoner to be taken hospital for treatment), the contractor shall secure the provision of appropriate medical services within the prison by—

(a) appointing one or more registered medical practitioners to the prison;

(b) entering into an arrangement with any person for the provision of such services in relation to the prison; or

(c) both making any such appointment as is mentioned in paragraph (a) above and entering into such an arrangement as is mentioned in paragraph (b) above.

(7) In subsection (6) above "appropriate medical services" means such services in relation to—

(a) routine and emergency health care for prisoners; and

(b) the provision of advice to the director on matters related to the medical treatment and health of prisoners generally,

as the Secretary of State may direct or, in the absence of such a direction, as the contractor considers appropriate for the prison in which they are to be provided; and such services shall be provided by or under the supervision of a registered medical practitioner.

(8) In subsections (6) and (7) above "contractor", where the contract provides for the running of prison by a sub-contractor, means that sub-contractor.".

(5) In section 110 of that Act (application of enactments)—

(a) in subsection (3), after the word "sections" there shall be inserted the words "3A(6) (power to authorise searches of persons providing medical services),";

(b) in subsection (4), after the word "sections" there shall be inserted the words "3A(6) (power to carry out searches of persons providing medical services),";

(c) after subsection (4) there shall be inserted the following subsection—

"(4A) A registered medical practitioner appointed to a contracted out prison or providing, or supervising the provision of, appropriate medical services in accordance with an arrangement made under section 107(6)(b) of this Act shall be deemed to be a medical officer for the prison for the purposes of—

(a) section 111(3)(c) of this Act;

(b) section 27(5) of the 1989 Act (so far as that section continues to have effect by virtue of Schedule 6 to the Prisoners and Criminal Proceedings (Scotland) Act 1993 (existing provisions which continue to have effect in relation to prisoners sentenced before 1st October 1993)); and

(c) any rules or directions made or issued under section 39 of the 1989 Act,

unless such rules or directions otherwise provide or the context otherwise requires."; and

(d) in subsection (6), after the word "Sections" there shall be inserted the words "3A(1) to (5)(medical services),".

(6) In section 112(4) of that Act (contracted out functions at directly managed prisons)—

(a) before paragraph (a) there shall be inserted the following paragraph—

"(aa) section 3A(6) and (7) of the 1989 Act (searches of persons providing medical services);"; and

(b) in paragraph (a) for the words "the 1989" there shall be substituted the word "that".

Unlawful disclosure of information

44.—(1) After section 41B of the 1989 Act there shall be inserted the following section—

"Unlawful disclosure of information by medical officer

41D.—(1) This section applies to—

(a) a registered medical practitioner appointed under paragraph (a) of section 107(6) of the Criminal Justice and Public Order Act 1994 (medical services in contracted out prisons);

(b) a registered medical practitioner providing appropriate medical services under an arrangement entered into under section 3A(2)(b) of this Act or paragraph (b) of the said section 107(6); and

(c) any person acting under the supervision of such a practitioner.

(2) Any person to whom this section applies who discloses, otherwise than in the course of his duty or as authorised by the Secretary of State, any information relating to a particular prisoner which he has acquired in the course of carrying out his duties shall be guilty of an offence.

(3) A person guilty of an offence under subsection (2) above shall be liable—

(a) on conviction on indictment, to imprisonment for a term not exceeding two years or a fine or both;

(b) on summary conviction, to imprisonment for a term not exceeding six months or a fine not exceeding the statutory maximum or both.".

PART IV

POLICE

Police funding and organisation

Police grant

45.—(1) For section 32 of the Police (Scotland) Act 1967 there shall be substituted the following section—

"Police grant

32.—(1) Subject to the following provisions of this section, the Secretary of State shall for the financial year 1997–98 and for each subsequent financial year make grants out of money provided by Parliament for police purposes to police authorities and joint police boards.

(2) Where a grant is made under subsection (1) above to a joint police board, no grant under that subsection shall be payable to a constituent authority.

(3) For each financial year the Secretary of State shall with the approval of the Treasury by order determine—

(a) the aggregate amount of grants to be made under subsection (1) above; and

(b) the amount of the grant to be made to each police authority or joint police board,

and any determination under this subsection for any financial year may be varied or revoked by a subsequent such determination for that year.

(4) In making a determination under subsection (3)(b) above, the Secretary of State may exclude certain categories of expenditure for police purposes from a grant made under subsection (1) above.

(5) A grant made to a police authority or to a joint police board by virtue of an order made under subsection (3) above may be subject to such conditions and shall be paid at such times and in such manner as the Secretary of State may with the approval of the Treasury by order determine; and any such time may fall within or after the financial year concerned.

(6) The Secretary of State shall prepare a report stating the considerations which he took into account in making the determinations mentioned in subsection (3) above.

(7) The considerations which the Secretary of State takes into account in making a determination under subsection (3)(b) above may be different for different authorities or different joint police boards.

(8) A statutory instrument containing an order made under subsection (3) above shall be subject to annulment in pursuance of a resolution of either House of Parliament.

(9) A copy of a report prepared under subsection (6) above shall be laid before each House of Parliament at the time at which the statutory instrument containing the order made under subsection (3) above to which it relates is so laid.

(10) Where in consequence of the variation or revocation of an order made under subsection (3) above the amount of a police authority's or a joint police board's grant is less than the amount already paid to it for the year concerned, a sum equal to the difference shall be paid by the authority or, as the case may be, board to the Secretary of State on such day as he may specify.

(11) In this section "financial year" has the meaning assigned to it by section 116 of the Local Government Finance Act 1992.".

(2) A determination made under section 32(3) (police grant) of the Police (Scotland) Act 1967 (as inserted into that Act by subsection (1) above) for the financial year 1997–98 may, notwithstanding that this section comes into force after the beginning of that financial year, relate to the whole of that year; and the first such determination shall take effect in place of any determination made for that year under section 32(1) of that Act as it had effect prior to the coming into force of this section.

Common police services

46.—(1) For section 36 of the Police (Scotland) Act 1967 there shall be substituted the following section—

"Common police services

36.—(1) The Secretary of State may—

(a) himself—

(i) provide and maintain facilities and services; or

(ii) establish and maintain institutions and organisations; or

(b) contribute, by way of financial assistance, grant or otherwise, to—

(i) the provision and maintenance of facilities and services; or

(ii) the establishment and maintenance of institutions and organisations,
by others,
where he considers that to do so is necessary or expedient for promoting the efficiency or effectiveness of the police.

(2) The Secretary of State may by regulations make provision for requiring all police forces in Scotland to use specified facilities or services, or facilities or services of a specified description (whether or not provided under subsection (1) above), if he considers that it would be in the interests of the efficiency or effectiveness of the police for them to do so.

(3) The Secretary of State may recover from police authorities and joint police boards the whole or any part of any expenditure which he incurs under subsection (1) above and, for that purpose, he may—

  (a) fix charges to be paid to him in respect of the use by police forces of any facilities or services such as are mentioned in subsection (1) above; and

  (b) determine amounts to be paid to him by police authorities and joint police boards, and he may determine different amounts in respect of different police authorities and joint police boards.

(4) Before exercising the powers conferred by any of subsections (1) to (3) above the Secretary of State shall consult the Joint Central Committee and such bodies or associations as appear to him to be representative of police authorities or of chief constables or superintendents.

(5) Any sum due by a police authority or joint police board to the Secretary of State under this section—

  (a) may be deducted by him from the amount of police grant payable to that authority or board under section 32 of this Act; or

  (b) failing such deduction, shall be defrayed in like manner as other expenses incurred for the purposes of this Act by that authority or board.".

(2) In section 38(5) of that Act (central service on police duties), for the definition of "central service" there shall be substituted the following definition—

" "central service" means temporary service under the Crown, with the consent of the appropriate authority, in connection with—

    (a) facilities and services provided and maintained by the Secretary of State under section 36(1)(a)(i) of this Act;

    (b) facilities and services provided by organisations or institutions established and maintained by the Secretary of State under section 36(1)(a)(ii) of this Act; and

    (c) research or other services connected with the police provided by the Secretary of State,

and temporary service under section 34 of this Act.".

(3) Section 36, and the definition of "central services" in section 38(5), of the Police (Scotland) Act 1967, as substituted respectively by subsections (1) and (2) above, shall come into force or, if this section comes into force after that date, be deemed to have come into force, on 1st April 1997.

(4) The first determination made by the Secretary of State under section 36(3) of that Act, as so substituted, for the recovery of any expenditure incurred by him under that section—

  (a) may be applied by him in relation to any expenditure so incurred during the period beginning on 1st April 1997 and ending on the date on which the determination is made; and

  (b) subject to subsection (5) below, shall take effect in place of any provision for such recovery made in an order under the said section 36 as it had effect prior to the coming into force of this section.

(5) Nothing in subsection (4) above shall entitle the Secretary of State to recover a higher proportion of his expenditure in relation to the period mentioned in that subsection than he would have been entitled to recover in relation to that period under any such order.

Collection and use of records

Record of evidence taken from external parts of body

47.—(1) In section 18 of the 1995 Act (prints and samples in criminal investigations)—
  (a) [Amends subs. (2) in s.18 of the 1995 Act].
  (b) [Amends subs. (3) in s.18 of the 1995 Act].
  (c) subsection (7) shall cease to have effect; and
  (d) [Inserts subs. (7A) and (7B) in s.18 of the 1995 Act].
(2) [Amends subss. (1), (2) and (4) of s.19 of the 1995 Act].
(3) [Amends s.20 of the 1995 Act].
(4) [Amends subss. (1) and (2) and inserts subs. (2A) of s.284 of the 1995 Act].
(5) [Inserts subs. (10) in s.285 of the 1995 Act].

Samples etc. from persons convicted of sexual and violent offences

48.—(1) In section 19 of the 1995 Act (taking of prints and samples after conviction) in subsection (1) for the word "This" there shall be substituted the words "Without prejudice to any power exercisable under section 19A of this Act, this".
(2) After section 19 of the 1995 Act there shall be inserted the following sections—

"Samples etc. from persons convicted of sexual and violent offences
  19A.—(1) This section applies where a person—
  (a) is convicted on or after the relevant date of a relevant offence and is sentenced to imprisonment;
  (b) was convicted before the relevant date of a relevant offence, was sentenced to imprisonment and is serving that sentence on or after the relevant date;
  (c) was convicted before the relevant date of a specified relevant offence, was sentenced to imprisonment, is not serving that sentence on that date or at any time after that date but was serving it at any time during the period of five years ending with the day before that date.
  (2) Subject to subsections (3) and (4) below, where this section applies a constable may—
  (a) take from the person or require the person to provide him with such relevant physical data as the constable reasonably considers appropriate; and
  (b) with the authority of an officer of a rank no lower than inspector, take from the person any sample mentioned in any of paragraphs (a) to (d) of subsection (6) of section 18 of this Act by the means specified in that paragraph in relation to that sample.
  (3) The power conferred by subsection (2) above shall not be exercised where the person has previously had taken from him or been required to provide relevant physical data or any sample under section 19(1)(a) of this Act or under this section unless the data so taken or required have been or, as the case may be, the sample so taken or required has been lost or destroyed.

(4) Where this section applies by virtue of—

(a) paragraph (a) or (b) of subsection (1) above, the powers conferred by subsection (2) above may be exercised at any time when the person is serving his sentence; and

(b) paragraph (c) of the said subsection (1), those powers may only be exercised within a period of three months beginning on the relevant date.

(5) Where a person in respect of whom the power conferred by subsection (2) above may be exercised—

(a) is no longer serving his sentence of imprisonment, subsections (3)(a), (5) and (6);

(b) is serving his sentence of imprisonment, subsection (3)(b),

of section 19 of this Act shall apply for the purposes of subsection (2) above as they apply for the purposes of subsection (2) of that section.

(6) In this section—

"conviction" includes—

(a) an acquittal, by virtue of section 54(6) or 55(3) of this Act, on the ground of the person's insanity at the time at which he committed the act constituting the relevant offence;

(b) a finding under section 55(2) of this Act,

and "convicted" shall be construed accordingly;

"relevant date" means the date on which section 48 of the Crime and Punishment (Scotland) Act 1997 is commenced;

"relevant offence" means any relevant sexual offence or any relevant violent offence;

"relevant sexual offence" means any of the following offences—

(a) rape;

(b) clandestine injury to women;

(c) abduction of a woman with intent to rape;

(d) assault with intent to rape or ravish;

(e) indecent assault;

(f) lewd, indecent or libidinous behaviour or practices;

(g) shameless indecency;

(h) sodomy; and

(i) any offence which consists of a contravention of any of the following statutory provisions—

(i) section 52 of the Civic Government (Scotland) Act 1982 (taking and distribution of indecent images of children);

(ii) section 52A of that Act (possession of indecent images of children);

(iii) section 106 of the Mental Health (Scotland) Act 1984 (protection of mentally handicapped females);

(iv) section 107 of that Act (protection of patients);

(v) section 1 of the Criminal Law (Consolidation)(Scotland) Act 1995 (incest);

(vi) section 2 of that Act (intercourse with step-child);

(vii) section 3 of that Act (intercourse with child under 16 years by person in position of trust);

(viii) section 5(1) or (2) of that Act (unlawful intercourse with girl under 13 years);

(ix) section 5(3) of that Act (unlawful intercourse with girl aged between 13 and 16 years);

(x) section 6 of that Act (indecent behaviour towards girl between 12 and 16 years);

(xi) section 7 of that Act (procuring);

(xii) section 8 of that Act (abduction and unlawful detention of women and girls);

(xiii) section 9 of that Act (permitting use of premises for unlawful sexual intercourse);

(xiv) section 10 of that Act (liability of parents etc. in respect of offences against girls under 16 years);

(xv) section 11(1)(b) of that Act (soliciting for immoral purpose);

(xvi) section 13(5)(b) and (c) of that Act (homosexual offences);

"relevant violent offence" means any of the following offences—

(a) murder or culpable homicide;

(b) uttering a threat to the life of another person;

(c) perverting the course of justice in connection with an offence of murder;

(d) fire raising;

(e) assault;

(f) reckless conduct causing actual injury;

(g) abduction; and

(h) any offence which consists of a contravention of any of the following statutory provisions—

(i) sections 2 (causing explosion likely to endanger life) or 3 (attempting to cause such an explosion) of the Explosive Substances Act 1883;

(ii) section 12 of the Children and Young Persons (Scotland) Act 1937 (cruelty to children);

(iii) sections 16 (possession of firearm with intent to endanger life or cause serious injury), 17 (use of firearm to resist arrest) or 18 (having a firearm for purpose of committing an offence listed in Schedule 2) of the Firearms Act 1968;

(iv) section 6 of the Child Abduction Act 1984 (taking or sending child out of the United Kingdom); and

"sentence of imprisonment" means the sentence imposed in respect of the relevant offence and includes—

(a) a hospital order, a restriction order, a hospital direction and any order under section 57(2)(a) or (b) of this Act; and

(b) a sentence of detention imposed under section 207 or 208 of this Act,

and "sentenced to imprisonment" shall be construed accordingly; and any reference to a person serving his sentence shall be construed as a reference to the person being detained in a prison, hospital or other place in pursuance of a sentence of imprisonment; and

"specified relevant offence" means—

(a) any relevant sexual offence mentioned in paragraphs (a), (b), (f) and (i)(viii) of the definition of that expression and any such offence as is mentioned in paragraph (h) of that definition where the person against whom the offence was committed did not consent; and

(b) any relevant violent offence mentioned in paragraph (a) or (g) of the definition of that expression and any such offence as is mentioned in paragraph (e) of that definition where the assault is to the victim's severe injury,

but, notwithstanding subsection (7) below, does not include—

(i) conspiracy or incitement to commit; and

(ii) aiding and abetting, counselling or procuring the commission of,

any of those offences.

(7) In this section—
(a) any reference to a relevant offence includes a reference to any attempt, conspiracy or incitement to commit such an offence; and
(b) any reference to—
(i) a relevant sexual offence mentioned in paragraph (i); or
(ii) a relevant violent offence mentioned in paragraph (h),
of the definition of those expressions in subsection (6) above includes a reference to aiding and abetting, counselling or procuring the commission of such an offence.

Power of constable in obtaining relevant physical data etc.
19B. A constable may use reasonable force in—
(a) taking any relevant physical data from a person or securing a person's compliance with a requirement made under section 18(2), 19(2)(a) or 19A(2)(a) of this Act;
(b) exercising any power conferred by section 18(6), 19(2)(b) or 19A(2)(b) of this Act.".

PART V

CRIMINAL LEGAL ASSISTANCE

Criminal legal assistance

49. After Part IV of the 1986 Act there shall be inserted the following Part—

"PART IVA

CRIMINAL LEGAL ASSISTANCE

Registration

Criminal Legal Assistance Register
25A.—(1) The Board shall, in accordance with the provisions of this section, establish and maintain a Criminal Legal Assistance Register ("the Register") of—
(a) solicitors who are eligible to provide criminal legal assistance; and
(b) subject to subsection (4) below, the firms with which the solicitors mentioned in paragraph (a) above are connected.
(2) A sole solicitor who wishes to provide criminal legal assistance shall require to be registered both as a solicitor and as a firm.
(3) Only those solicitors whose names appear on the Register may provide criminal legal assistance; and, subject to subsection (4) below, a solicitor may provide criminal legal assistance only when working in the course of a connection with a registered firm.
(4) A solicitor employed by the Board under section 28A of this Act shall require to be registered, and the entry relating to his name on the Register shall include a note that he is so employed; but the Board shall not be regarded as a firm for the purposes of this section, and shall not itself require to be registered.
(5) An application for entry on the Register shall be made in such form as the Board may determine, and shall be accompanied by such documents as the Board may specify, which shall include, in the case of a solicitor, a copy of his practising certificate.

(6) Before making any decisions as to the matters mentioned in subsection (5) above the Board shall—

(a) send to the Law Society and to such other persons and bodies as it considers appropriate a draft of its proposals in that regard, inviting their comments on those proposals within such period, being not less than 8 weeks from the date on which the draft is sent, as it may specify; and

(b) consider any such comments timeously received by it,

but, where it amends those proposals in the light of any such comments, it shall not be required to re-intimate the amended proposals to any of those who were invited to comment.

(7) Subject to subsection (15) below, where a solicitor is connected with a firm the Board shall not consider his application unless the firm—

(a) is already registered; or

(b) has also applied for registration.

(8) On receipt of an application the Board shall make such enquiries as it thinks appropriate for the purpose of determining whether the applicant complies with the relevant provisions of the code; and it may for that purpose use the powers conferred on it by section 35A of this Act.

(9) Subject to subsection (10) below, where the Board is satisfied that an applicant complies with the code and, in the case of a solicitor, is not otherwise disqualified from providing criminal legal assistance, it shall make the appropriate entry on the Register.

(10) Subject to subsection (15) below, where a solicitor is connected with a firm, the Board shall not enter his name on the Register unless the firm's name is already entered on the Register.

(11) Where a solicitor is connected with a firm or firms, the name or names of which appear on the Register, the entry relating to that solicitor shall include the name of that firm or those firms.

(12) Where the Board decides to refuse an application it shall forthwith intimate that decision to the applicant, and shall as soon as practicable thereafter send him or them, by recorded delivery, a written note of its reasons.

(13) An applicant aggrieved by a decision of the Board to refuse registration may, within 21 days of the receipt of the notification of the Board's reasons under subsection (12) above, appeal to the Court of Session against that decision.

(14) An appeal under subsection (13) above may be on questions of both fact and law and the court, after hearing such evidence and representations as it considers appropriate, may make such order as it thinks fit.

(15) Where a solicitor who is seeking registration, or is registered, is connected with more than one firm the requirements of subsections (7) and (10) above shall be satisfied if one of those firms has applied for registration or, as the case may be, is registered.

Code of practice

Code of practice in relation to criminal legal assistance

25B.—(1) The Board shall prepare a draft code of practice in relation to the carrying out by solicitors of their functions with regard to the provision of criminal legal assistance and, without prejudice to the generality of the foregoing, the code may include provision as to—

(a) the conditions to be complied with in order to qualify for registration, including—

(i) the attendance by the solicitor at a sufficient number of specified courses relevant to the provision of criminal legal assistance, including courses in criminal law, evidence and pleading and professional ethics;

(ii) the keeping of records in a particular format;

(b) the standards of conduct expected of a solicitor providing or proposing to provide criminal legal assistance;

(c) the manner in which a solicitor should conduct a case and represent his client, including—

(i) the passage of timeous and accurate information to the client in relation to his case;

(ii) the frequency of meetings with the client;

(iii) the giving of advice to the client as to the consequences of any decision made by the client in relation to his defence;

(iv) the taking of such precognitions as may be necessary;

(v) the conduct of relations with the prosecution;

(d) the manner in which applications for criminal legal assistance are to be presented;

(e) the monitoring of a solicitor's performance with a view to a decision by the Board as to whether he should continue to be registered, including—

(i) periodic review of his handling of particular cases by other solicitors or by the Board;

(ii) the extent to which he attends courses relevant to the provision of criminal legal assistance, including courses in criminal law, evidence and pleading and professional ethics;

(f) the manner in which records are kept, including—

(i) maintaining books of account, and presentation of accounts to the Board, in a specified format;

(ii) office procedures;

(iii) time recording systems;

(iv) instructions given to the staff,

and any other matter relating to the organisation of or accounting for criminal legal assistance which appears to the Board to be relevant.

(2) The code may make different provision in relation to firms and solicitors including, in relation to solicitors employed by the Board by virtue of section 28A of this Act, different provision to reflect the fact that they are so employed.

(3) The Board shall—

(a) send a copy of the draft code prepared by it under subsection (1) above to the Law Society and to such other persons and bodies as it considers appropriate, inviting their comments on the draft within such period, being not less than 8 weeks from the date on which the draft is sent, as it may specify; and

(b) consider any such comments timeously received by it,

but, where it amends the draft code in the light of any such comments, it shall not be required to re-intimate the amended code to any of those who were invited to comment.

(4) After carrying out the consultation mentioned in subsection (3) above the Board shall submit the draft code to the Secretary of State for his approval.

(5) The Secretary of State may approve the draft code, with or without modifications.

(6) When the Secretary of State has approved the draft code under subsection (5) above he shall—

(a) return the draft to the Board; and

(b) specify the date upon which it is to come into force and how the Board is to publish it.

(7) The Board—

(a) shall make and publish the code by the date and in the manner specified by the Secretary of State under subsection (6) above; and

(b) may make a copy of the code available to any person requesting one, on payment of such sum, if any, towards the cost of preparation, publication and, where relevant, postage, as it considers appropriate.

(8) The Board shall keep under review the code prepared under this section and may from time to time revise it, and the provisions of this section shall apply in relation to any revision of the code as they apply in relation to the version originally prepared.

Supervision of registered solicitors and firms

25C.—(1) Solicitors and firms whose names appear on the Register ("registered solicitors" and "registered firms") shall comply with the requirements of the code.

(2) The Board shall monitor the carrying out by registered solicitors and firms of their duty under subsection (1) above.

(3) For the purpose of carrying out its duty under subsection (2) above the Board may use the powers conferred on it by sections 35A and 35B of this Act.

Removal of name from Register

Removal of name from Register following failure to comply with code

25D.—(1) Where it appears to the Board (whether or not following a complaint made to it) that a registered firm or solicitor may not be complying with the code, it shall investigate the matter in such manner as it thinks fit, and shall give the firm or solicitor concerned an opportunity to make representations.

(2) For the purpose of carrying out its duty under subsection (1) above the Board may use the powers conferred on it by sections 35A and 35B of this Act.

(3) Following an investigation under subsection (1) above, the Board may give the firm or solicitor concerned an opportunity, within such time as it may specify, to remedy any defect in their or his compliance with the code.

(4) Where, after carrying out the procedures mentioned in subsection (1) above and, where a time limit has been set under subsection (3) above, after the expiry of that time limit, the Board is satisfied that—

(a) the firm are not complying with the code, it shall remove the names of the firm and, subject to subsection (5) below, of any registered solicitors connected with the firm from the Register;

(b) the solicitor is not complying with the code, it shall remove his name from the Register.

(5) Where a registered solicitor mentioned in subsection (4)(a) above is also connected with another registered firm, the Board shall not remove his name from the Register, but shall alter the entry against his name in the Register so as to remove therefrom the name of the firm whose name has been removed from the Register.

(6) Where the Board removes the name of a solicitor from the Register the solicitor shall—

(a) in accordance with arrangements approved by the Board, forthwith, and without waiting for the resolution of any appeal, transfer—

(i) any work currently being undertaken by him for any client by way of criminal legal assistance; and

(ii) notwithstanding any lien to which he might otherwise be entitled, any documents connected with any such work,

to a registered solicitor; and

(b) in accordance with section 25A(3) of this Act, stop providing criminal legal assistance.

(7) Where the Board removes the name of a firm or solicitor from the Register it shall forthwith intimate that removal to the firm or solicitor concerned, and shall as soon as practicable thereafter send them or him, by recorded delivery, a written note of its reasons for its decision.

(8) A firm or solicitor aggrieved by a decision of the Board under subsection (4) above may, within 21 days of the receipt of the notification under subsection (7) above, appeal to the Court of Session against that decision.

(9) An appeal under subsection (8) above may be on questions of both fact and law and the court, after hearing such evidence and representations as it considers appropriate, may make such order as it thinks fit; but the making of such an appeal shall not have the effect of restoring the firm's or solicitor's name to the Register.

Further provision as to removal of name from Register

25E.—(1) Where the Board is satisfied, whether on being so informed by the solicitor concerned or not, that a registered solicitor—

(a) has become connected with an unregistered firm; and

(b) is no longer connected with a registered firm,

it shall remove his name from the Register.

(2) Subsections (6) to (9) of section 25D of this Act apply in relation to a solicitor whose name is removed from the Register under subsection (1) above as they apply in relation to a solicitor whose name is removed from the Register under subsection (4) of that section.

Publication of Register

25F.—(1) The Board shall make available for inspection, without charge—

(a) the Register;

(b) any decision refusing an application for entry on the Register; and

(c) any decision removing the name of a firm or solicitor from the Register,

and the publication of a decision such as is mentioned in paragraphs (b) or (c) above shall be accompanied by a statement of the reasons for the decision.

(2) The Board shall, as soon as is practicable after 1st December in each year, send a copy of the current Register to the Secretary of the Law Society.

(3) When any change is made to the Register in the course of a year, the Board shall, as soon as is practicable, send written notice of that change to the Secretary of the Law Society.".

Employment of solicitors

Employment of solicitors in relation to criminal legal assistance

50. After section 28 of the 1986 Act there shall be inserted the following section—

"Power of Board to employ solicitors to provide criminal assistance

28A.—(1) The Secretary of State may, in accordance with the provisions of this section, provide for the carrying out of a study into the feasibility of providing criminal legal assistance by means of solicitors employed directly by the Board and, accordingly, may by regulations made under this section empower the Board to employ solicitors for the purpose of providing criminal legal assistance.

(2) The Board shall not, by virtue of this section, employ more solicitors than are necessary to enable it to maintain at all times a working staff of such number of full-time or part-time solicitors as will equal six full-time solicitors; and any solicitor employed by the Board on a casual or temporary basis to fill a vacancy left by the absence on leave or because of illness of a permanent appointee shall require to be a registered solicitor.

(3) The Secretary of State may authorise the Board to make such preparations for the feasibility study as will enable it to begin the study as soon as regulations under subsection (1) above come into force; and such preparations may relate to the purchase and equipping of heritable and moveable property and the employment of staff including, but only for the purposes of training, solicitors.

(4) The provisions of paragraph 8 of Schedule 1 to this Act shall apply to solicitors employed by the Board by virtue of this section as they apply to employees appointed by the Board under that paragraph.

(5) Regulations made by the Secretary of State under this section may make such provision as appears to him to be appropriate for the purposes of this section and, without prejudice to the generality of the foregoing, may—

(a) specify in which area or areas employed solicitors are to be used; and

(b) make different provision in relation to different areas.

(6) Regulations under this section may provide that where the Board has by virtue of this section employed solicitors to provide criminal legal assistance in any area, the Board may, subject to subsection (7) below, require as many of the persons seeking criminal legal assistance in that area as it considers appropriate to instruct the solicitors employed by it.

(7) In requiring persons seeking criminal legal assistance to instruct solicitors employed by the Board, the Board shall, where there is or may be a conflict of interest, make provision for any particular person to be re-allocated to another solicitor or, where registration is in force, to a registered solicitor in the area.

(8) Regulations made under this section may make such transitional and consequential provisions and savings as appear to the Secretary of State to be necessary or expedient.

(9) Sections 26, 27 and 28 of this Act shall not apply in relation to solicitors employed by the Board by virtue of this section.

(10) Within three years of the date on which regulations made under subsection (1) above first come into effect, the Secretary of State shall lay before each House of Parliament a report on the results of the feasibility study.

(11) This section, and the provisions of this Act mentioned in subsection (12) below, shall cease to have effect five years after the date on which regulations made under subsection (1) above first come into effect.

(12) The provisions referred to in subsection (11) above are—

(a) in section 4, subsection (2)(aa) and (3)(ab);

(b) in section 11—

    (i) in subsection (1) the words "or (3)"; and

    (ii) subsections (3) and (4);

(c) in section 12(2), the words "; but does not apply to the salary payable to a solicitor employed by the Board by virtue of section 28A of this Act.";

(d) section 25A(4);

(e) in section 25B(2), the words from "including" to the end; and

(f) in section 31(1A), paragraph (c).

(13) Prior to the date on which this section ceases to have effect the Board shall make arrangements for the transfer to solicitors or, where registration is in force, registered solicitors not employed by it of any work currently being undertaken by way of criminal legal assistance by solicitors employed by it by virtue of this section.

(14) On the date when this section ceases to have effect the Board shall remove from the Register the name of any solicitor employed by it by virtue of this section who is not otherwise entitled to be registered.".

Fixed payments for criminal legal assistance

Fixed payments

51. In section 33 of the 1986 Act (fees and outlays of counsel and solicitors), after subsection (3) there shall be inserted the following subsections—

"(3A) The Secretary of State may by regulations under this section prescribe fixed payments to be made to a solicitor in respect of—

(a) his professional services in providing criminal legal assistance; and

(b) such outlays as may be so prescribed.

(3B) A solicitor who provides any criminal legal assistance in respect of which a fixed payment has been prescribed in regulations made under subsection (3A) above shall not be entitled to any other payment out of the Fund in respect of the professional services and outlays mentioned in that subsection, but shall be entitled to reimbursement of any other outlays which he has properly incurred.".

Contracts for the provision of criminal legal assistance

52. After section 33 of the 1986 Act there shall be inserted the following section—

"Contracts for the provision of criminal legal assistance

Contracts for the provision of criminal legal assistance

33A.—(1) The Secretary of State may by regulations made under this section empower the Board to enter into contracts with registered firms for the provision by registered solicitors connected with those firms of criminal legal assistance.

(2) Regulations under this section may prescribe—

(a) the procedures to be followed by the Board in awarding any such contract; and

(b) subject to subsection (3) below, any terms and conditions which are to be included in any such contract.

(3) Regulations under this section shall provide that any contract entered into by virtue of this section shall include a provision that, in the event of the termination of the contract, or a breach of it by the registered firm concerned, the Board may—

(a) withhold payments under the contract; and

(b) require the firm to secure the transfer of—

(i) any work currently being undertaken by any solicitor connected with them for any client by way of criminal legal assistance; and

(ii) notwithstanding any lien to which any such solicitor might otherwise be entitled, any documents connected with any such work, to a registered solicitor.

(4) Regulations under this section may provide that where the Board has by virtue of this section entered into contracts with any registered firms for the provision of criminal legal assistance in any area, then, unless it seems to the Board to be inappropriate in a particular case, any person seeking such assistance in that area shall be required to instruct a registered solicitor connected with one of those firms.

(5) Any money due to a firm under a contract made by virtue of this section shall be paid to the firm—

(a) firstly, out of any amount payable by the client in accordance with section 11(2) of this Act;

(b) secondly, in priority to all other debts, out of any expenses which by virtue of an order of a criminal court are payable to that client by any other person in respect of the matter in connection with which the criminal legal assistance was given; and

(c) thirdly, by the Board out of the Fund.

(6) For the purposes of sections 32 and 33 of this Act, the money paid to a firm, as provided in subsection (5) above, in respect of a contract made by virtue of this section shall be taken to be a payment made in accordance with this Act, and no solicitor connected with such a firm shall be entitled to any other payment out of the Fund in respect of any work done by him by virtue of such a contract.".

Powers of investigation

Power of investigation of Scottish Legal Aid Board

53. After section 35 of the 1986 Act there shall be inserted the following sections—

"Power of Board to require information

35A.—(1) The Board may, for the purpose of determining whether—

(a) a solicitor or any employee of him or of his firm may be committing a criminal offence in connection with criminal legal assistance; or

(b) a solicitor may be seeking, in relation to criminal legal assistance, to recover from the Fund money to which he is not entitled, as, for example, by performing unnecessary work; or

(c) a registered firm or solicitor is or may not be complying with the code,

require any solicitor or firm to produce such information and documents relating wholly or partly to the provision of criminal legal assistance as it may specify, at such time and place as it may specify.

(2) If it appears to the Board that there is good reason to do so, it may authorise any of its officers to require any solicitor or firm to produce forthwith any such information or documents as are mentioned in subsection (1) above.

(3) An officer of the Board acting under subsection (2) above shall, if requested to do so, produce evidence of his authorisation by the Board.

(4) The power under this section to require production of information and documents includes power—

(a) to require any person, who is a present or past partner or employee of any such solicitor or firm and who appears to the Board or one of its officers to have any information or documents, to produce them;

(b) if any documents are produced—

(i) to take copies of them or extracts from them; and

(ii) to require the person producing them, or any other

person who is a present or past partner or employee of the solicitor or firm in question, to provide an explanation of them;

(c) if any document or information is held other than in legible form, to require the production of a copy of it in legible form; and

(d) if documents are not produced, to require the person who was required to produce them to state, to the best of his knowledge and belief, where they are.

(5) Where any person claims a lien over any documents required to be produced under this section the production is without prejudice to the lien.

(6) Any person who is required under this section to produce information or documents shall, notwithstanding any duty of confidentiality, comply with that requirement; and if he fails to comply he shall be guilty of an offence and liable—

(a) on conviction on indictment, to a fine; and

(b) on summary conviction, to a fine not exceeding the statutory maximum.

(7) Where a person is charged with an offence under subsection (6) above in respect of a requirement to produce documents, it shall be a defence for him to prove that they were not in his possession or under his control and that it was not reasonably practicable for him to comply with the requirement.

(8) No information or documents obtained by the Board by virtue of this section or section 35B of this Act shall be used by it or by any of its employees for any purpose other than the purposes mentioned in subsection (1) above.

(9) Section 34 of this Act applies in relation to a contravention of subsection (8) above as it applies in relation to a contravention of subsection (1) of that section.

Power of entry

Power of Board to enter premises and investigate

35B.—(1) Where a sheriff is satisfied, by evidence on oath given on behalf of the Board by a person authorised by the Board for that purpose, that there are reasonable grounds for believing that—

(a) a solicitor or any employee of him or his firm may be committing a criminal offence in connection with criminal legal assistance; or

(b) a solicitor may be seeking, in relation to criminal legal assistance, to recover from the Fund money to which he is not entitled, as, for example, by performing unnecessary work; or

(c) a registered firm or solicitor may not be complying with the code; or

(d) there are on any premises documents the production of which has been required under section 35A of this Act and which have not been produced in accordance with that requirement,

he may issue a warrant under this section to a person authorised for that purpose by the Board.

(2) A person holding a warrant under this section may—

(a) search the premises named in the warrant;

(b) take possession of any documents which appear to him to relate, wholly or partly, to any criminal legal assistance provided in or from those premises;

(c) take copies of any such documents;

(d) take any other steps which appear to him to be necessary for preserving those documents or preventing their destruction or interference with them; and

(e) require any person named in the warrant to provide an explanation of the documents or to state where they may be found.

(3) The duty to produce documents and to provide explanations applies notwithstanding any duty of confidentiality, but where any person claims a lien over any documents the production is without prejudice to that lien.

(4) A warrant under this section shall continue in force for the period of one month from the date when it is issued.

(5) The Board may retain any documents which it has obtained under this section for—

(a) a period of not more than 12 months; or

(b) where, within that period, proceedings to which the documents are relevant are commenced by the Board, the Law Society or a prosecutor, until the conclusion of those proceedings.

(6) Any person who intentionally obstructs the execution of a warrant issued under this section or who fails without reasonable excuse to comply with any requirement imposed in accordance with subsection (2)(e) above shall be guilty of an offence, and liable—

(a) on conviction on indictment, to a fine; and

(b) on summary conviction, to a fine not exceeding the statutory maximum.

Suspension or payments to solicitor

Suspension of payments to solicitor

35C.—(1) Where it appears to the Board that any solicitor has, in connection with the provision of criminal legal assistance, acted in such a way as to justify action being taken against him by the Law Society or the Scottish Solicitors' Discipline Tribunal it shall refer the matter to either of those bodies so that they can consider whether to take action under section 31(3) of this Act.

(2) Where it appears to the Board that any solicitor may have been guilty of a criminal offence it shall refer the matter to the police or the procurator fiscal, so that they can consider whether any criminal offence may have been committed.

(3) Where the Board refers a matter to any of the bodies mentioned in subsections (1) or (2) above, it may disclose to that body any information or documents which it has obtained from the solicitor concerned under this Act.

(4) Where the Board has referred a matter to any of the bodies mentioned in subsections (1) or (2) above it may—

(a) suspend the solicitor concerned from providing criminal legal assistance; and

(b) withhold payment of any fees due to him in respect of such work, pending the outcome of the investigation by the body or bodies to which the matter has been referred.

(5) A solicitor who is suspended from providing criminal legal assistance under subsection (4)(a) above shall, in accordance with arrangements approved by the Board, transfer—

(a) any work currently being undertaken by him for any client by way of criminal legal assistance; and

(b) notwithstanding any lien to which he might otherwise be entitled, any documents connected with any such work,

to a solicitor (or, where registration is in force, a registered solicitor).".

Regulations in relation to criminal legal assistance

54. After section 41 of the 1986 Act there shall be inserted the following section—

"Regulations in relation to criminal legal assistance

41A.—(1) The Secretary of State may by regulations made under this section provide that any reference in, under or by virtue of this Act to "criminal legal assistance" shall relate, for any of the purposes of this Act, to such class or classes of criminal legal assistance as he thinks appropriate.

(2) Without prejudice to the generality of subsection (1) above, the power conferred by that subsection may be exercised by reference to—

   (a) the class or classes of person who are to receive criminal legal assistance;

   (b) the class or classes of case in respect of which such assistance is to be given;

   (c) the nature of the work;

   (d) the place or places where the assistance is to be provided;

   (e) the period for which it is to be provided,

or to any combination of the foregoing; and different provision may be made under that subsection for different purposes, or in relation to different areas or different periods.".

PART VI

MISCELLANEOUS AND GENERAL

Miscellaneous

Liberation of child by police

55.—(1) Section 43 of the 1995 Act (arrangements where child arrested) shall be amended in accordance with this section.

(2) [Inserted in s.43 of the 1995 Act].

(3) [Amends s.43(b) of the 1995 Act].

Powers of the court on remand or committal of children and young persons

56.—(1) Section 51 of the 1995 Act (remand or committal of children and young persons) shall be amended in accordance with this section.

(2)–(4) [Inserted in s.51 of the 1995 Act].

Precognitions

57.—(1) [Inserted as s.67A of the 1995 Act].

(2) [Amends s.140(1) of the 1995 Act].

Information concerning jurors

58. [Amends s.85 of the 1995 Act and inserts therein subss. (2A) to (2C)].

Certification of previous convictions in criminal proceedings

59. [Amends s.285 of the 1995 Act].

Grants for forensic medical services

60. The Lord Advocate may out of money provided by Parliament make grants of such amount and on such conditions as he considers appropriate to any person for the provision to him by that person of forensic medical services.

Confiscation of alcohol from persons under 18

61.—(1) Where a constable has reasonable grounds for suspecting that a person in a public place—

A–521

    (a) is under the age of 18; and

    (b) is in possession of alcoholic liquor, within the meaning of the Licensing (Scotland) Act 1976,

he may require that person to surrender that liquor to him, and may dispose of it in such manner as he considers appropriate; and he may also require that person to supply him with his name and address.

(2) Where a constable has reasonable grounds for suspecting that a person of or over the age of 18 has alcoholic liquor in his possession in a public place and that that person—

    (a) has supplied such liquor to a person under the age of 18 for consumption in a public place; or

    (b) intends that that liquor should be consumed in a public place by a person under the age of 18,

the constable may require the person in possession of the liquor to surrender it to him, and may dispose of it in such manner as he considers appropriate; and he may also require that person to supply him with his name and address.

(3) Subject to subsection (4) below, it shall be an offence punishable on summary conviction by a fine not exceeding level 2 on the standard scale for a person to fail to comply with a requirement made under subsection (1) or (2) above.

(4) Where a constable makes a requirement such as is mentioned in subsection (1) or (2) above he shall inform the person concerned—

    (a) of his suspicion; and

    (b) of the fact that failure to comply with a requirement made under either of those provisions is an offence.

    (5) A constable may arrest without warrant any person who fails to comply with a requirement made under subsection (1) or (2) above.

(6) In this section "public place" includes—

    (a) any place to which the public have access for the time being (whether on payment of a fee or otherwise); and

    (b) any place to which the public do not have access but to which the persons mentioned in subsection (1) or (2) have unlawfully gained access,

but does not include licensed premises within the meaning of the Licensing (Scotland) Act 1976.

General

Minor and consequential amendments, and repeals

    62.—(1) The enactments mentioned in Schedule 1 to this Act shall have effect subject to the amendments specified therein, being minor amendments and amendments consequential upon the provisions of this Act.

(2) The enactments mentioned in Schedule 3 to this Act are repealed to the extent specified in the third column of that Schedule.

Financial provisions

    63.—(1) There shall be paid out of money provided by Parliament any expenses incurred—

    (a) by the Secretary of State, under—

        (i) section 245C(1) of the 1995 Act (remote monitoring of restriction of liberty orders) (as inserted by section 5 of this Act);

        (ii) Part XA of the 1995 Act (Scottish Criminal Cases Review Commission) (as inserted by section 25 of this Act);

        (iii) section 36(1) of the Police (Scotland) Act 1967 (common police services) (as inserted by section 46 of this Act); or

    (b) by the Scottish Legal Aid Board under—

(i) section 28A(1) of the 1986 Act (power of Board to employ solicitors for criminal legal assistance) (as inserted by section 50 of this Act); or

(ii) section 33A(1) of the 1986 Act (power of Board to enter into contracts for provision of criminal legal assistance) (as inserted by section 52 of this Act); or

(c) by the Lord Advocate under section 60 of this Act.

(2) There shall be paid out of money provided by Parliament any increase attributable to this Act in the sums payable out of money so provided under any other Act.

Interpretation

64. In this Act, unless the context otherwise requires—

"supervised release order" has the same meaning as in section 209 of the 1995 Act (supervised release orders);

"the 1984 Act" means the Mental Health (Scotland) Act 1984;

"the 1986 Act" means the Legal Aid (Scotland) Act 1986;

"the 1989 Act" means the Prisons (Scotland) Act 1989;

"the 1993 Act" means the Prisoners and Criminal Proceedings (Scotland) Act 1993;

"the 1995 Act" means the Criminal Procedure (Scotland) Act 1995.

Short title, commencement and extent

65.—(1) This Act may be cited as the Crime and Punishment (Scotland) Act 1997.

(2) This Act, except sections 45 and 46, shall come into force on such day as the Secretary of State may by order made by statutory instrument appoint, and different days may be appointed for different purposes.

(3) In an order under subsection (2) above made in respect of any provision of sections 49 to 54 of this Act, or of paragraph 12 of Schedule 1 to this Act—

(a) different days may be appointed for different provisions;

(b) different days may be appointed for different areas; and

(c) different provisions may be brought into force in relation to different areas.

(4) An order under subsection (2) above may contain such transitional and consequential provisions and savings as appear to the Secretary of State to be necessary or expedient in connection with the provisions brought into force.

(5) Subject to subsections (6) and (7) below, this Act shall extend to Scotland only.

(6) Section 4(3) and (5) of this Act shall extend to England and Wales, and section 37(4) of this Act shall extend to England and Wales and Northern Ireland.

(7) The amendment or repeal of any enactment by Schedules 1 or 3 to this Act shall have the same extent as the enactment so amended or, as the case may be, repealed.

SCHEDULES

SCHEDULE 1

Section 62(1)

MINOR AND CONSEQUENTIAL AMENDMENTS

The Public Records Act 1958 (c. 51)

1. [*Repealed by the Crime and Disorder Act 1998 (c. 37), Sched. 8, para. 141 (effective September 30, 1998: S.I. 1998 No. 2327.*]

The Police (Scotland) Act 1967 (c. 77)

2.—(1) The Police (Scotland) Act 1967 shall be amended in accordance with this paragraph.
(2) Section 6(2) (application of certain provisions to appointments of ranks below assistant chief constable) shall cease to have effect.
(3) In section 17 (general functions and duties of constables)—
(a) in subsection (1), for the words "section 321(1) of the Criminal Procedure (Scotland) Act 1975" there shall be substituted the words "section 135(3) and (4) of the Criminal Procedure (Scotland) Act 1995"; and
(b) in subsection (7)(a) after the word "agreements" there shall be inserted the words "or of section 98 of the Police Act 1996 (cross-border aid of one police force by another)".
(4) In section 19(3) (amalgamation schemes) for the words from "reimbursed" to the end there shall be substituted the words "provided for by a grant made to the board under section 32 of this Act".
(5) In section 41(1)(b)(ii) (penalty for assaults on constables) for the words "section 289B of the Criminal Procedure (Scotland) Act 1975" there shall be substituted the words "section 225(8) of the Criminal Procedure (Scotland) Act 1995".
(6) In section 46(1)(b) (rewards) after the word "agreements" there shall be inserted the words "or of section 98 of the Police Act 1996 (cross-border aid of one police force by another)".

The Firearms Act 1968 (c. 27)

3. In section 51 of the Firearms Act 1968 (penalties for offences), after subsection (2) there shall be inserted the following subsection—
"(2A) Nothing in subsection (2) above or Schedule 6 to this Act shall prejudice the operation of section 205A of the Criminal Procedure (Scotland) Act 1995 (imprisonment for life on further conviction of certain offences).".

The Superannuation Act 1972 (c. 11)

4. In Schedule 1 to the Superannuation Act 1972 (kinds of employment to which a scheme under section 1 of that Act may apply), at the end of the list of "Royal Commissions and other Commissions" insert—
"Scottish Criminal Cases Review Commission.".

The House of Commons Disqualification Act 1975 (c. 24)

5. In the House of Commons Disqualification Act 1975, in Part II of Schedule 1 (bodies of which all members are disqualified), at the appropriate place insert—
"The Scottish Criminal Cases Review Commission.".

The Sexual Offences (Scotland) Act 1976 (c. 67)

6.—(1) The Sexual Offences (Scotland) Act 1976 shall cease to have effect.
(2) This paragraph shall be deemed to have come into force on 1st April 1996 and the Sexual Offences (Scotland) Act 1976 shall for the purposes of the Criminal Procedure (Consequential Provisions) (Scotland) Act 1995 be regarded as a repealed enactment within the meaning of that Act.

The Law Reform (Miscellaneous Provisions) (Scotland) Act 1980 (c. 55)

7. In Part I of Schedule 1 to the Law Reform (Miscellaneous Provisions) (Scotland) Act 1980 (persons ineligible for jury service), in Group B, after paragraph (w) insert—
"(wa) members and employees of the Scottish Criminal Cases Review Commission;".

The Criminal Justice (Scotland) Act 1980 (c. 62)

8. In section 3D(1)(b) of the Criminal Justice (Scotland) Act 1980 (interpretation of sections 3A to 3C), for the words "section 3 of this Act" there shall be substituted the words "section 15(6) of the Criminal Procedure (Scotland) Act 1995".

The Mental Health (Scotland) Act 1984 (c. 36.)

9.—(1) The Mental Health (Scotland) Act 1984 shall be amended in accordance with this paragraph.
(2) In section 60 (effect of hospital orders)—

(a) in subsection (1)(a)—
            (i) after the word "officer" there shall be inserted the words ", an officer on the staff of the hospital specified in the order"; and
            (ii) for the words "28" there shall be substituted the word "7";
(b) in subsection (4), for the words "28" there shall be substituted the word "7".
    (3) In section 62 (restriction orders)—
(a) after subsection (1) there shall be inserted the following subsection—
    "(1A) Where the managers of a hospital specified in a restriction order propose to admit the patient to a hospital unit in that hospital, they shall, if that unit was not so specified, notify the Secretary of State and the Mental Welfare Commission of the patient's proposed admission to and detention in that unit; and the patient shall not be so admitted unless the Secretary of State has consented to the proposed admission."; and
(b) in subsection (3), for the words "section 178(3) and 379(3) of the said Act of 1975" there shall be substituted the words "section 59(3) of the said Act of 1995".
    (4) In section 71 (removal to hospital of persons serving sentences of imprisonment and other persons), in subsection (4) at the beginning there shall be inserted the following words "Subject to section 71A of this Act,".
    (5) After section 71 there shall be inserted the following section—

"Further provision as to persons removed to hospital under section 71
    71A.—(1) Where the Secretary of State is satisfied, in relation to a person in respect of whom he has made a transfer direction under section 71(1) of this Act, that—
    (a) either—
            (i) the person is not suffering from mental disorder of a nature or degree which makes it appropriate for him to be liable to be detained in a hospital for medical treatment; or
            (ii) it is not necessary for the health or safety of the person or for the protection of other persons that he should receive such treatment; and
    (b) it is not appropriate for the person to remain liable to be recalled to hospital for further treatment,
he shall by warrant direct that the person be remitted to any prison or other institution or place in which he might have been detained had he not been removed to hospital and that he be dealt with there as if he had not been so removed.
    (2) Where the Secretary of State is satisfied as to the matters mentioned in subsection (1)(a) above, but not as to the matters mentioned in subsection (1)(b) above, he may either—
    (a) by warrant give such direction as is mentioned in subsection (1) above; or
    (b) decide that the person shall continue to be detained in hospital.
    (3) If a direction is given under subsection (1) or (2)(a) above, then on the person's arrival in the prison or other institution or place to which he is remitted by virtue of that subsection the transfer direction shall cease to have effect.".
    (6) In section 72(2) (restriction directions) for the words "section 178 or 379 of the Criminal Procedure (Scotland) Act 1975" there shall be substituted the words "section 59 of the Criminal Procedure (Scotland) Act 1995".
    (7) [*Repealed by the Crime and Disorder Act 1998 (c. 37), Sched. 8, para. 141 (effective September 30, 1998: S.I. 1998 No. 2327).*]
    (8) In section 77 (transfers to England and Wales), after subsection (5) there shall be inserted the following subsection—
    "(5A) Where a patient removed under this section was immediately before his removal liable to be detained under this Act by virtue of a hospital direction made by a court in Scotland, he shall be treated as if any sentence of imprisonment passed at the time at which the hospital direction was made had been imposed by a court in England and Wales.".
    (9) In section 80 (transfers to Northern Ireland), after subsection (6), there shall be inserted the following subsection—
    "(6A) Where a patient removed under this section was immediately before his removal liable to be detained under this Act by virtue of a hospital direction made by a court in Scotland, he shall be treated as if any sentence of imprisonment passed at the time at which the hospital direction was made had been imposed by a court in Northern Ireland.".
    (10) In section 82(2) (removal of certain patients from the Channel Islands), for the words "section 174 of the Criminal Procedure (Scotland) Act 1975" there shall be substituted the words "section 57(2)(a) and (b) of the Criminal Procedure (Scotland) Act 1995".
    (11) In section 96 (application of provisions relating to consent to treatment), in paragraph (b) for the words "section 177 or 378 of the Criminal Procedure (Scotland) Act 1975" there shall be substituted the words "section 58(9) of the Criminal Procedure (Scotland) Act 1995".

(12) In section 106(4) (protection of mentally handicapped patients), for the words "Section 18 of the Sexual Offences (Scotland) Act 1976" there shall be substituted the words "Section 16 of the Criminal Law (Consolidation)(Scotland) Act 1995".

(13) In section 107(3) (further protection of patients), for the words "section 80(6) of the Criminal Justice (Scotland) Act 1980" there shall be substituted the words "section 13(4) of the Criminal Law (Consolidation) (Scotland) Act 1995".

(14) In section 121A (warrants for arrest of escaped patients)—

(a) in subsection (1), for the words "section 30 or 108 of the Mental Health Act (Northern Ireland) 1961" there shall be substituted the words "Articles 29, 45(6) and 132 of the Mental Health (Northern Ireland) Order 1986";

(b) in subsection (3), for the words "section 107 of the Mental Health Act (Northern Ireland) 1961" there shall be substituted the words "Article 131 of the Mental Health (Northern Ireland) Order 1986"; and

(c) in subsection (4)—

(i) in the definition of "convicted mental patient", for the words "the Mental Health Act (Northern Ireland) 1961" there shall be substituted the words "the Mental Health (Northern Ireland) Order 1986"; and

(ii) in the definition of "place of safety", for the words "the said Act of 1961" there shall be substituted the words "the said Order of 1986".

(15) In section 125(1), after the definition of "hospital order" there shall be inserted the following definition—

" "hospital unit" means any part of a hospital which is treated as a separate unit;".

(16) In Part II of Schedule 2 (application of provisions of Part V to restricted patients), for paragraph 6 there shall be substituted the following paragraph—

"6. In section 29—

(a) for subsection (1) there shall be substituted—

"(1) A patient who is for the time being detained in a hospital or a hospital unit specified in a restriction order or a hospital direction or notified to the Secretary of State under section 62(1A) or 62A(2) of this Act may, with the consent of the Secretary of State, be transferred by the managers of the hospital—

(a) to another hospital, with the consent of the managers of that hospital: or

(b) to another hospital unit—

(i) in the hospital managed by them; or

(ii) in another hospital with the consent of the managers of that hospital.";

(b) in subsection (2)—

(i) after the word "hospital" there shall be inserted the words "within which or"; and

(ii) the words after "transferred" shall be omitted; and

(c) in subsection (3) for the words from "as follows" to the end of the subsection there shall be substituted the words "as if the order or direction by virtue of which he was liable under Part VI of this Act to be detained before being transferred were an order or direction for his admission or removal to the hospital or hospital unit to which he is transferred.".

The Repatriation of Prisoners Act 1984 (c. 47)

10.—(1) The Repatriation of Prisoners Act 1984 shall be amended in accordance with this paragraph.

(2) In section 2(4)(b) (transfer of prisoners out of the United Kingdom)—

(a) [*Repealed by the Crime and Disorder Act 1998 (c. 37), Sched. 8, para. 141 (effective September 30, 1998: S.I. 1998 No. 2327).*]

(b) after sub-paragraph (ii) there shall be inserted the following sub-paragraph—

"(iia) released subject to a supervised release order made under section 209 of the Criminal Procedure (Scotland) Act 1995;".

(3) In section 3(9) (transfer of prisoners into the United Kingdom)—

(a) the words "or section 10", in the second place where they occur, shall cease to have effect; and

(b) after the word "sentence", in the second place where it occurs, there shall be inserted the words "or by virtue of section 10 as the designated part of his sentence".

The Foster Children (Scotland) Act 1984 (c. 56)

11. In section 13 of the Foster Children (Scotland) Act, for the words "section 47 of the Children and Young Persons (Scotland) Act 1937" to the end there shall be substituted the words "section 55 of the Children (Scotland) Act 1995 (child assessment orders) as giving the

local authority reasonable cause for the suspicion mentioned in subsection (1)(a) of that section".

The Legal Aid (Scotland) Act 1986 (c. 47)

12.—(1) The Legal Aid (Scotland) Act 1986 shall be amended in accordance with this paragraph.

(2) In section 4 (Scottish Legal Aid Fund)—

(a) in subsection (2)—

(i) in paragraph (a), for the words "by him" there shall be substituted the words "or in respect of payments made in accordance with regulations made under section 33(3A) of this Act";

(ii) after paragraph (a) there shall be inserted the following paragraphs—

"(aa) any expenses incurred by the Board in connection with the provision of criminal legal assistance by solicitors employed by it by virtue of section 28A of this Act;

"(ab) any sums payable by the Board under contracts made by virtue of section 33A of this Act;"; and

(b) in subsection (3), after paragraph (a) there shall be inserted the following paragraphs—

"(aa) any contribution payable to the Board by any person in pursuance of section 11 of this Act;

"(ab) any award of expenses made by a criminal court to a person to whom criminal legal assistance has been provided by a solicitor employed by the Board by virtue of section 28A of this Act;".

(3) In section 11 (clients' contributions)—

(a) in subsection (1), after the words "subsection (2)" there shall be inserted the words "or (3)"; and

(b) after subsection (2) there shall be inserted the following subsections—

"(3) Where a client to whom paragraphs (a) and (b) of subsection (2) above apply receives criminal legal assistance from a solicitor employed by the Board by virtue of section 28A of this Act, he shall pay to the Board such contribution in respect of that assistance as the Board may, subject to subsection (4) below, determine.

(4) The amount determined by the Board under subsection (3) above shall not exceed the amount which could have been charged in respect of the assistance in question by a solicitor.".

(4) In section 12 (payment of fees or outlays otherwise than through clients' contributions)—

(a) at the end of subsection (2) there shall be inserted the words—

"; but does not apply to the salary payable to a solicitor employed by the Board by virtue of section 28A of this Act."; and

(b) for the word "contribution", where it appears in subsection (3)(a), there shall be substituted the word "amount".

(5) In section 21 (scope and nature of criminal legal aid), in subsection (1)(aa), for the word "discretionary" there shall be substituted the word "designated".

(6) In section 22 (automatic availability of legal aid), at the end of subsection (1) there shall be inserted the words—

"and, in relation to paragraph (dc) above, "accused person" includes a person authorised to institute or continue an appeal under section 303A(4) of the Criminal Procedure (Scotland) Act 1995 (transfer of rights of appeal of deceased person).".

(7) After section 25 (legal aid in appeals) there shall be inserted the following section—

"Legal aid in respect of appeals under section 303A of the 1995 Act

25AA.—(1) Subject to the provisions of this section, section 25 of this Act applies to any appeal, within the meaning of section 303A of the Criminal Procedure (Scotland) Act 1995 (transfer of rights of appeal of deceased person), instituted or continued by a person (an "authorised person") authorised under subsection (4) of the said section 303A.

(2) Where an authorised person is continuing an appeal which has been instituted by the deceased person, and criminal legal aid, within the meaning of section 25, has been awarded to the deceased person in connection with any proceedings, such legal aid shall continue to be made available to the authorised person in respect of those proceedings.

(3) Where—

(a) the deceased person had applied for criminal legal aid within the meaning of section 25, but the application had not been determined prior to his death; or

(b) the deceased person had not applied for such legal aid,

the authorised person shall be regarded as the applicant and, in a case to which paragraph (b) applies, may apply for such legal aid.

(4) Notwithstanding subsection (3) above—

   (a) in section 25(2)(a) of this Act, where the authorised person is the executor of the deceased, any reference to—

      (i) the financial circumstances of the applicant shall be construed as a reference to the value of the deceased person's estate; and

      (ii) the applicant's dependants shall be construed as a reference to the beneficiaries of the deceased's estate; and

   (b) any reference in section 25(2)(c) or (2A) of this Act to whether it is in the interests of justice that the applicant should receive legal aid shall be construed as a reference to whether it would have been in the interests of justice that the deceased should have received legal aid.".

(8) In section 31 (solicitors and counsel)—

(a) in subsection (1), for the words from the beginning to "below" there shall be substituted the words "Subject to subsection (1A) below,";

(b) after subsection (1) there shall be inserted the following subsection—

   "(1A) Subsection (1) above is subject to—

   (a) section 25A(3) of this Act;

   (b) section 30(2) of this Act;

   (c) regulations made under section 28A(6) of this Act;

   (d) regulations made under section 33A(4) of this Act; and

   (e) regulations made under subsection (9) below.".

(9) In section 33 (fees and outlays of counsel and solicitors), in subsection (1), at the beginning there shall be inserted the words "Subject to subsections (3A) and (3B) below,".

(10) In section 41 (interpretation)—

(a) after the definition of "civil legal aid" there shall be inserted the following definition—

   " "the code" means the code of practice in relation to criminal legal assistance for the time being in force under section 25B of this Act;";

(b) after the definition of "criminal legal aid" there shall be inserted the following definitions—

   " "criminal legal assistance" means criminal legal aid and advice and assistance in relation to criminal matters;

   "document" includes information recorded in any form;

   "firm" includes an incorporated practice, a sole solicitor and a law centre;";

(c) after the definition of "incorporated practice" there shall be inserted the following definition—

   " "law centre" means a body—

      (a) established for the purpose of providing legal services to the public generally as well as to individual members of the public; and

      (b) which does not distribute any profits made either to its members or otherwise, but reinvests any such profits for the purposes of the law centre;" and

(d) after the definition of "person" there shall be inserted the following definitions—

   " "the Register" means the Register established and maintained under section 25A of this Act;

   "registered firm" means a firm whose name appears on the Register;

   "registered solicitor" means a solicitor whose name appears on the Register;

   "sole solicitor" means a solicitor practising under his own name or as a single solicitor under a firm name; and

   "solicitor connected with a firm" includes a sole solicitor and a solicitor who is a partner, director or employee of a firm, and cognate expressions shall be construed accordingly.".

The Prisons (Scotland) Act 1989 (c. 45)

13.—(1) The Prisons (Scotland) Act 1989 shall be amended in accordance with this paragraph.

(2) In section 19(4) (application of enactments to young offenders institutions and remand centres), in paragraph (b)—

(a) for the words "and 41B" there shall be substituted the words ", 41B, 41C"; and

(b) before the word "of" there shall be inserted the words "and 41D".

(3) [*Repealed by the Crime and Disorder Act 1998 (c. 37), Sched. 8, para. 141 (effective September 30, 1998: S.I. 1998 No. 2327).*]

(4) In section 27(5) (power of the Secretary of State to discharge prisoners not to affect duties of medical officer) (so far as that subsection continues to have effect by virtue of Schedule 6 to the Prisoners and Criminal Proceedings (Scotland) Act 1993 (existing provisions which

continue to have effect in relation to prisoners sentenced before 1st October 1993)) for the word "the", where it occurs for the second time, there shall be substituted the word "any".

The Prisoners and Criminal Proceedings (Scotland) Act 1993 (c. 9)

14.—(1) The Prisoners and Criminal Proceedings (Scotland) Act 1993 shall be amended in accordance with this paragraph.

(2) In section 1 (release of prisoners)—

(a) [*Repealed by the Crime and Disorder Act 1998 (c. 37), Sched. 8, para. 141 (effective September 30, 1998: S.I. 1998 No. 2327).*]

(b) in subsection (4), for the word "discretionary" there shall be substituted the word "designated".

(3) In section 2 (duty to release discretionary life prisoners)—

(a) in subsection (2)—

    (i) for the words "subsection (1)(b)" there shall be substituted the words "subsection (1)"; and

    (ii) before the word "life", in both places where it occurs, there shall be inserted the word "designated";

(b) in subsection (3), for the words "subsection (1)(a)" there shall be substituted the words "subsection (1)";

(c) for the word "relevant", where it occurs in subsections (2), (8) and (9), there shall be substituted the word "designated";

(d) for the word "discretionary" where it occurs in subsections (4), (6), (8) and (9) there shall be substituted the word "designated"; and

(e) [*Repealed by the Crime and Disorder Act 1998 (c. 37) Sched. 8, para. 141 (effective September 30, 1998: S.I. 1998 No. 2327).*]

(4) [*Repealed by the Crime and Disorder Act 1998 (c. 37), Sched. 8, para. 141 (effective September 30, 1998: S.I. 1998 No. 2327).*]

(8) In section 10 (life prisoners transferred to Scotland)—

(a) for subsection (1) there shall be substituted the following subsection—

"(1) In a case where a transferred life prisoner transferred from England and Wales (whether before or after the commencement of this enactment) is a life prisoner to whom section 28 of the Crime (Sentences) Act 1997 (duty to release certain life prisoners) applies, this Part of this Act except sections 1(4) and 2(9) shall apply as if—

    (a) the prisoner were a designated life prisoner within the meaning of section 2 of this Act; and

    (b) the designated part of his sentence within the meaning of that section were the relevant part specified in an order or direction made under the said section 28.";

(b) in subsection (3)(a), for the word "discretionary" there shall be substituted the word "designated";

(c) in subsection (3)(b), for the word "relevant" there shall be substituted the word "designated";

(d) in subsection (5)(a), for the word "discretionary" there shall be substituted the word "designated"; and

(e) in subsection (5)(b), for the words "section 34 of the said Act of 1991" there shall be substituted the words "the said section 28 of the Crime (Sentences) Act 1997".

(9) [*Repealed by the Crime and Disorder Act 1998 (c. 37), Sched. 8, para. 141 (effective September 30, 1998: S.I. 1998 No. 2327).*]

(10) In section 12(3) (insertion, variation and cancellation of conditions in licences)—

(a) [*Repealed by the Crime and Disorder Act 1998 (c. 37), Sched. 8, para. 141 (effective September 30, 1998: S.I. 1998 No. 2327).*]

(b) for the word "discretionary" there shall be substituted the word "designated".

(11) In section 14 (supervised release orders)—

(a) in subsection (2)—

    (i) the words from the beginning to "209(1) of the 1995 Act" shall cease to have effect; and

    (ii) after the words "prison in Scotland" there shall be inserted the words "under Schedule 1 to the Crime (Sentences) Act 1997 in an unrestricted transfer within the meaning of that Schedule"; and

(b) [*Repealed by the Crime and Disorder Act 1998 (c. 37), Sched. 8, para. 141 (effective September 30, 1998: S.I. 1998 No. 2327).*]

(12) Section 16 shall cease to have effect.

(13) [*Repealed by the Crime and Disorder Act 1998 (c. 37), Sched. 8, para. 141 (effective September 30, 1998: S.I. 1998 No. 2327).*]

[1](16) In section 27(1) (interpretation), in the definition of "supervised release order" the words "(as inserted by secton 14 of this Act)" shall cease to have effect.

(17) [*Repealed by the Crime and Disorder Act 1998 (c. 37), Sched. 8, para. 141 (effective September 30, 1998: S.I. 1998 No. 2327).*]

(18) In Schedule 6 (transitional provisions and savings)—

(a) for the word "relevant" in each place where it occurs in paragraph 6(2) and (3) and 6A(2), there shall be substituted the word "designated"; and

(b) for the word "discretionary" in each place where it occurs in paragraphs 6, 6A(2) and 7, there shall be substituted the word "designated".

NOTE

[1]As substituted by the Crime and Disorder Act 1998 (c. 37), Sched. 8, para. 141 (effective September 30, 1998: S.I. 1998 No. 2327).

The Criminal Justice and Public Order Act 1994 (c. 33)

15. In section 110 of the Criminal Justice and Public Order Act 1994 (modifications of the Prisons (Scotland) Act 1989 in its application to contracted out prisons)—

(a) in subsection (3) for the words "and 41B(3) (testing prisoners for drugs)" there shall be substituted the words ", 41B(3) (testing prisoners for drugs) and 41C(3) (testing prisoners for alcohol)"; and

(b) in subsection (4) for the words "and 41B(1) (testing prisoners for drugs)" there shall be substituted the words ", 41B(1) (testing prisoners for drugs) and 41C(1) (testing prisoners for alcohol)".

The Criminal Justice (Scotland) Act 1995 (c. 20)

16. Section 66 of the Criminal Justice (Scotland) Act 1995 shall cease to have effect.

The Children (Scotland) Act 1995 (c. 36)

17. In Schedule 4 to the Children (Scotland) Act 1995, paragraph 35(6) shall cease to have effect.

The Criminal Law (Consolidation) (Scotland) Act 1995 (c. 39)

18.—(1) The Criminal Law (Consolidation) (Scotland) Act 1995 shall be amended in accordance with this paragraph.

(2) In section 5 (unlawful sexual intercourse with a girl under the age of 13 years)—

(a) in subsection (1), at the beginning there shall be inserted the words "Subject to section 205A of the Criminal Procedure (Scotland) Act 1995 (imprisonment for life on further conviction of certain offences),"; and

(b) in subsection (6) (definition of "like offence" for purposes of that section), for the words "section 10(1) of this Act" there shall be substituted the words "section 9(1) of this Act".

(3) In section 7(3) (deemed rape where husband impersonated) after the word "with" there shall be inserted the word "her".

(4) In section 19(3) (vehicles in relation to which certain offences relating to alcohol at sporting events may be committed), for the word "principle" there shall be substituted the word "principal".

(5) In section 21 (police powers in relation to control of alcohol etc. at sporting events), in paragraph (e), after sub-paragraph (ii) there shall be inserted the following sub-paragraph—

"; or

(iii) a controlled article or substance as defined in section 20(8) of this Act.".

(6) In section 23 (interpretation of Part II), after the definition of "keeper" there shall be inserted the following definition—

" "motor vehicle" means a mechanically propelled vehicle intended or adapted for use on roads;".

(7) In section 26(11) (interpretation of powers of Customs and Excise officers to detain persons in connection with drug smuggling) for the definition of superior officer there shall be substituted the following definition—

" "superior officer" means an officer whose title is specified for the purposes of this section by the Treasury in an order made by statutory instrument subject to annulment in pursuance of a resolution of either House of Parliament.".

(8) In section 45(1) (aiding and abetting offences under section 44), for the word "principle" there shall be substituted the word "principal".

The Criminal Procedure (Consequential Provisions) (Scotland) Act 1995 (c. 40)

19.—(1) The Criminal Procedure (Consequential Provisions) (Scotland) Act 1995 shall be amended in accordance with this paragraph.

(2) In Part II of Schedule 2 (increase in certain penalties), the entry relating to section 1 of the Protection of Animals (Scotland) Act 1912 shall cease to have effect.

(3) In Schedule 4 (minor and consequential amendments)—

(a) paragraph 6(4)(a) and (d) shall cease to have effect;

(b) paragraph 16 shall cease to have effect;

(c) paragraph 50(7)(b) shall cease to have effect; and

(d) paragraph 53(3) shall cease to have effect.

The Proceeds of Crime (Scotland) Act 1995 (c. 43)

20. In section 42(1) of the Proceeds of Crime (Scotland) Act 1995 (power to make Order in Council with respect to enforcement of orders in England and Wales), in paragraph (a) after the word "offence" there shall be inserted the words ", other than a drug trafficking offence,".

The Criminal Procedure (Scotland) Act 1995 (c. 46)

21.—(1) The 1995 Act shall be amended as follows.

(2) In section 15 (rights of persons arrested or detained), in subsection (6)(b), for the words "actual custody" there shall be substituted the word "care".

(3) In section 44 (detention of children in summary proceedings)—

(a) in subsection (4), the words ", subject to subsection (6) below,";

(b) subsections (6) to (9); and

(c) in subsection (10), the words "or (8)",

shall cease to have effect.

(4) In section 46 (presumption and determination of age of child)—

(a) in subsection (1), after the word "offence" there shall be inserted the words ", whose age is not specified in the indictment or complaint in relation to that offence,";

(b) in subsection (3) at the beginning there shall be inserted the words "Without prejudice to section 255A of this Act,".

(5) In section 53 (power to make interim hospital order)—

(a) in subsection (1), after the word "way" there shall be inserted the words ", including imposing a sentence of imprisonment and making a hospital direction,";

(b) in subsection (3), for the words "28" there shall be substituted the word "7";

(c) in subsection (4), after the word "not" there shall be inserted the words "at that time";

(d) in subsection (5), for the words "28" there shall be substituted the word "7";

(e) after subsection (5), there shall be inserted the following subsection—

"(5A) Subsections (1) and (4) of section 60 of the Mental Health (Scotland) Act 1984 shall apply to an interim hospital order as they apply to a hospital order."; and

(f) in subsection (6), after the word "way" there shall be inserted the words ", including imposing a sentence of imprisonment and making a hospital direction".

(6) In section 58 (hospital orders)—

(a) in subsection (4), for the words "28" there shall be substituted the word "7"; and

(b) in subsection (9), for the words "28" there shall be substituted the word "7".

(7) In section 62(6)(b) (disposal in appeals by accused in cases involving insanity), for the words "or order" there shall be substituted the words ", order or other disposal".

(8) In section 63 (appeals by prosecutor in cases involving insanity)—

(a) in subsection (1), paragraph (d) shall cease to have effect;

(b) in subsection (2)(b)(ii), the words "or (d)" shall cease to have effect; and

(c) in subsection (5)(b)—

(i) for the words "or order", in the first place where they occur, there shall be substituted the words "order or disposal"; and

(ii) for the words "or order", in the second place where they occur, there shall be substituted the words "or acquittal".

(9) In section 65 (prevention of delay), after subsection (3) there shall be inserted the following subsection—

"(3A) An application under subsection (3) shall not be made at any time when an appeal made with leave under section 74(1) of this Act has not been disposed of by the High Court.".

(10) In section 74(4) (disposal of appeals in connection with preliminary diets)—

(a) the word "and" after paragraph (a) shall cease to have effect; and

(b) after paragraph (b) there shall be inserted the following words "; and

    (c) may on cause shown extend the period mentioned in section 65(1) of this Act.".

(11) In section 81(6) (list of jurors where trial does not take place)—

(a) the word ", signed" shall cease to have effect; and

(b) for the words "85(1) and (2)" there shall be substituted the words "85(2)".

(12) In section 83 (transfer of sheriff court solemn proceedings)—

(a) in subsection (1), for the words "transfer the case to a sheriff court" there shall be substituted the words "adjourn the trial and transfer it to a sitting of a sheriff court, appointed as mentioned in section 66(1) of this Act,";

(b) in subsection (2)—

        (i) before the word "make" there shall be inserted the words "adjourn the trial and"; and

        (ii) for the word "case" there shall be substituted the words "trial as mentioned in subsection (1) above"; and

(c) after subsection (2), there shall be inserted the following subsection—

    "(3) Where a warrant to cite any person to attend a sitting of the sheriff court has been issued by the sheriff clerk under section 66(1) of this Act and the trial has been adjourned and transferred by an order under subsection (2) above, the warrant shall have effect as if the trial diet had originally been fixed for the court, and the date of the sitting of that court, to which the trial is so transferred.".

(13) In section 103 (appeal sittings)—

(a) in subsection (3), for the words "subsection (1)" there shall be substituted the words "subsection (2)";

(b) in subsection (4), for the words "and (2)" there shall be substituted the words "to (3)"; and

(c) in subsection (7), after the words "subsection (5)" there shall be inserted the words "and (6)".

(14) In subsection (1)(b) of section 104 (power of High Court in appeals) the word "additional" shall cease to have effect.

(15) In section 107(4) (application where leave to appeal refused), for the words "subsection (7)" there shall be substituted the words "subsection (10)".

(16) In section 113(2)(c) (recipients of copy of judge's report) for the words "section 124(3) of this Act, to the Secretary of State" there shall be substituted the words "Part XA of this Act, to the Commission".

(17) In section 118 (disposal of appeals)—

(a) in subsection (4)(b), the word "additional" shall cease to have effect; and

(b) after subsection (8) there shall be inserted the following subsection—

    "(9) The High Court may give its reasons for the disposal of any appeal in writing without giving those reasons orally.".

(18) In section 124 (finality of proceedings and Secretary of State's reference)—

(a) in subsection (1), after "this Part" there shall be inserted the words "or Part XA";

(b) in subsection (2), for the words "subsection (3) below" there shall be substituted the words "Part XA of this Act"; and

(c) subsections (3) to (5) shall cease to have effect.

(19) In section 141 (manner of citation)—

(a) in subsection (3)—

        (i) the words "signed by the prosecutor and" shall cease to have effect;

        (ii) in paragraph (a), after the word "accused," there shall be inserted the words "signed by the prosecutor and"; and

        (iii) in paragraph (b), after the word "sent" there shall be inserted the words "by or on behalf of the prosecutor"; and

(b) after subsection (5) there shall be inserted the following subsection—

    "(5A) The citation of a witness to a sitting or diet or adjourned sitting or diet as mentioned in subsection (1) above shall be effective if it is sent by the accused's solicitor by ordinary post to the dwelling house or place of business of the witness or, if he has no known dwelling house or place of business, to any other place in which he may be resident at the time.".

(20) In section 179(2) (stated case: adjustment and signature) the word "additional" shall cease to have effect.

(21) In subsection (5)(b) of section 182 (stated case: hearing of appeal) the word "additional" shall cease to have effect.

(22) In subsection (1)(b) of section 189 (disposal of appeal against sentence) the word "additional" shall cease to have effect.

(23) In section 199 (power to mitigate penalties), in subsection (3) after paragraph (b) there shall be inserted the following paragraph—

"; or

(c) to any proceedings in which the court on conviction is under a duty to impose a sentence under section 205A(2) or 205B(2) of this Act.".

(24) In section 202(1) (deferral of sentence) at the beginning there shall be inserted the words "Subject to section 205A of this Act,".

(25) In section 207(2) (detention of young offenders)—

(a) for the words "section 205(2) and (3)" there shall be substituted the words "sections 205(2) and (3), 205A(2)(b) and 205B(2)(b)"; and

(b) for the word "exceed" there shall be substituted the words "be less than the minimum nor more than".

(26) In section 209 (supervised release orders), after subsection (7) there shall be inserted the following subsection—

"(7A) Where a person—

(a) is serving a sentence of imprisonment and on his release from that sentence will be subject to a supervised release order; and

(b) is sentenced to a further term of imprisonment, whether that term is to run consecutively or concurrently with the sentence mentioned in paragraph (a) above,

the relevant period for any supervised release order made in relation to him shall begin on the date when he is released from those terms of imprisonment; and where there is more than one such order he shall on his release be subject to whichever of them is for the longer or, as the case may be, the longest period.".

(27) In section 228(1) (probation orders), after the word "below" there shall be inserted the words "and without prejudice to section 245D of this Act".

(28) In section 232 (failure to comply with requirements of probation order), after subsection (3) there shall be inserted the following subsection—

"(3A) Where the court intends to sentence an offender under subsection (2)(b) above, and the offender is by virtue of section 245D of this Act subject to a restriction of liberty order, it shall, before sentencing the offender under that paragraph, revoke the restriction of liberty order.".

(29) In section 233 (commission of further offence while subject to probation order), after subsection (5) there shall be added the following subsection—

"(6) This section shall not apply where the offence in respect of which the order was made and the offence committed during the probation period are qualifying offences within the meaning of section 205A of this Act.".

(30) In section 234A (non-harassment orders), subsection (5) shall cease to have effect.

(31) In section 246(1) (admonition), at the beginning, there shall be inserted the words "Subject to sections 205A and 205B of this Act,".

(32) In section 280 (routine evidence), in subsection (6)(b), for the words "the accused" there shall be substituted the word "he".

(33) In section 298 (trial judge's report)—

(a) in subsection (1)(a), after the words "108" there shall be inserted the words ", 108A"; and

(b) in subsection (2), for the words "section 124(3) of this Act, the Secretary of State" there shall be substituted the words "Part XA of this Act, the Commission".

(34) In section 307(1) (interpretation)—

(a) after the definition of "Clerk of Justiciary" insert—

"the Commission" has the meaning given by section 194A(1) of this Act;"; and

(b) after paragraph (a) of the definition of "hospital", there shall be inserted the following paragraph—

"(aa) any hospital managed by a National Health Service Trust established under section 12A of that Act;".

(35) In Schedule 4 (supervision and treatment orders)—

(a) in paragraph 3(3), after the word "officer;" there shall be inserted the following sub-paragraph—

"(bb) the medical practitioner by whom or under whose supervision the supervised person is to be treated under the order;";

(b) in paragraph 10(1), after the word "officer" there shall be inserted the words "and to the medical practitioner by whom or under whose supervision the supervised person was treated under the supervision and treatment order";

(c) in paragraph 11(1)(a), after the word "officer" there shall be inserted the words "and to the medical practitioner by whom or under whose supervision the supervised person has been treated under the supervision and treatment order".

Division A—Legislation

SCHEDULE 2

TRANSITIONAL PROVISIONS WITH RESPECT TO EARLY RELEASE

1.—16 [*Repealed by the Crime and Disorder Act 1998 (c. 37), Sched. 8, para. 142 (effective September 30, 1998: S.I. 1998 No. 2327).*]

SCHEDULE 3

[1]REPEALS

Chapter	Short title	Extent of repeal
1967 c. 77.	The Police (Scotland) Act 1967.	Section 6(2).
1968 c. 49.	The Social Work (Scotland) Act 1968.	In section 27(1)(b), the word "and" where it appears after sub-paragraph (iv).
1976 c. 67.	The Sexual Offences (Scotland) Act 1976.	The whole Act.
1984 c. 36.	The Mental Health (Scotland) Act 1984.	In section 65(2), the words after paragraph (b). In section 70(1), the words "(not being a private hospital)".
1984 c. 47.	The Repatriation of Prisoners Act 1984.	In section 3(9), the words "or section 10" in the second place where they occur.
1989 c. 45.	The Prisons (Scotland) Act 1989.	In section 3(1), the words from "including" to the end.
1993 c. 9.	The Prisoners and Criminal Proceedings (Scotland) Act 1993.	In section 2(2), the word "and". In section 14, in subsection (2), the words from the beginning to "209(1) of the 1995 Act". In section 27, in subsection (1), in the definition of "supervised release order" the words "(as inserted by section 14 of this Act)".
1993 c. 24.	The Video Recordings Act 1993.	Section 5.
1995 c. 20.	The Criminal Justice (Scotland) Act 1995.	Section 66.
1995 c. 25.	The Environment Act 1995.	In Schedule 22, paragraph 35.
1995 c. 36.	The Children (Scotland) Act 1995.	In Schedule 4, paragraph 35(6).
1995 c. 40.	The Criminal Procedure (Consequential Provisions) (Scotland) Act 1995.	In Part II of Schedule 2, the entry relating to section 1(1) of the Protection of Animals (Scotland) Act 1912. In Schedule 4, paragraphs 6(4)(a) and (d), 16, 50(7)(b) and 53(3).
1995 c. 46.	The Criminal Procedure (Scotland) Act 1995.	In section 18, subsection (7). In section 19(4)(b), the words ", print or impression". In section 53, in subsection (1), the words "subsection (2) below and", and subsection (2). In section 63, subsection (1)(d) and in subsection (2)(b)(ii) the words "or (d)". In section 74(4), the word "and" after paragraph (a). In section 81(6), the word ", signed". In section 85(1), the words from "but" to the end. Section 101(5). In section 104(1)(b), the word "additional". In section 118(4)(b), the word "additional". In section 124, subsections (3) to (5). Section 140(3).

Chapter	Short title	Extent of repeal
		In section 141(3), the words "signed by the prosecutor and".
		Section 154.
		In section 179(2), the word "additional".
		In section 182(5)(b), the word "additional".
		In section 189(1)(b), the word "additional".
		In section 204(2), the words from "and" to the end.
		In section 234A, subsection (5).
		In section 252(2), the word "and", in the third place where it occurs.

[1] As amended by the Crime and Disorder Act 1998 (c. 37), Sched. 10 (effective September 30, 1998: S.I. 1998 No. 2327)

Table of Derivations

Provision	Derivation	Effective from
Prisoners and Criminal Proceedings (Scotland) Act 1993		
2(1)	1997 Act s.16(1)(a)	20.10.97
(2)	1997 Act s.16(1)(b)	20.10.97
Criminal Law (Consolidation) (Scotland) Act 1995		
5(2)	1997 s.14(1)	1.8.97[1]
(3)	1997 s.14(1)	1.8.97[1]
(6)	1997 Sched. 1, para. 18(2)	1.8.97
6	1997 s.14(2)	1.8.97[1]
7(3)	1997 Sched. 1, para. 18(3)	1.8.97
19(3)	1997 Sched. 1, para. 18(4)	1.8.97
21	1997 Sched. 1, para. 18(5)	1.8.97
23	1997 Sched. 1, para. 18(6)	1.8.97
26(11)	1997 Sched. 1, para. 18(7)	1.8.97
45(1)	1997 Sched. 1, para. 18(8)	1.8.97
Criminal Procedure (Consequential Provisions) (Scotland) Act 1995		
Sched. 2, Pt. II	1997 Sched. 1, para. 19(2)	1.8.97
Sched. 4, para. 6(4)	1997 Sched. 1, para. 19(3)	1.8.97
para. 16	1997 Sched. 1, para. 19(3)	1.8.97
para. 50(7)	1997 Sched. 1, para. 19(3)	1.8.97
para. 53(3)	1997 Sched. 1, para. 19(3)	1.8.97
Proceeds of Crime (Scotland) Act 1995		
14(2)	1997 s. 15(3)	1.1.98[2]
42(1)	1997 Sched. 1, para. 20	1.8.97
Criminal Procedure (Scotland) Act 1995		
15(6)(b)	1997 Sched. 1, para. 21(2)	1.8.97
18(2)	1997 s.47(1)(a)	1.8.97
(3)	1997 s.47(1)(b)	1.8.97
(7)(a) & (b)	1997 s.47(1)(d)	1.8.97
19(1)	1997 s.47(2)(a)	1.8.97
(2)(a)	1997 s.47(2)(b)	1.8.97
(4)(b)	1997 s.47(2)(c)	1.8.97

NOTES

[1] Applies only to offences committed on or after August 1, 1997.
[2] Applies only to offences committed on or after January 1, 1998.

Provision	Derivation	Effective from
20	1997 s.47(3)(a) & (b)	1.8.97
43(1)	1997 s.55(2)	1.8.97
(6)	1997 s.55(3)	1.8.97
46(1)	1997 Sched. 1, para. 21(4)	1.8.97
(3)	1997 Sched. 1, para. 21(4)	1.8.97
49(4)	1997 s.23(a)	1.8.97
51(1)(a)	1997 s.56(2)	1.8.97
(1)(aa)	1997 s.56(2)	1.8.97
(1)(b)	1977 s.56(2)	1.8.97
(4)	1997 s.56(3)	1.8.97
(4A)	1997 s.56(4)	1.8.97
53(1)	1997 s.10(1)	1.1.98
	1997 Sched. 1, para. 21(5)	1.1.98
(2)	1997 s.10(1)	1.1.98
(3)	1997 Sched. 1, para. 21(5)	1.1.98
(4)	1997 Sched. 1, para. 21(5)	1.1.98
(5)	1997 Sched. 1, para. 21(5)	1.1.98
53(5A)	1997 Sched. 1, para. 21(5)	1.1.98
(6)	1997 s.11	1.1.98
	1997 Sched. 1, para. 21(5)	1.1.98
58(4)	1997 Sched. 1, para. 21(6)	1.1.98
(9)	1997 Sched. 1, para. 21(6)	1.1.98
59A	1997 s.6(1)	1.1.98
60	1997 s.6(2)	1.1.98
60A	1997 s.22	1.1.98
61	1997 s.10(2)(a)	1.1.98
(1A)	1997 s.10(2)(b)	1.1.98
(2)	1997 s.10(2)(c)	1.1.98
(3)	1997 s.10(2)(d)	1.1.98
(6)	1997 s.10(2)(e)	1.1.98
62(6)(b)	1997 Sched. 1, para. 21(7)	1.1.98
63(1)	1997 Sched. 1, para. 21(8)	1.1.98
(2)(b)(ii)	1997 Sched. 1, para. 21(8)	1.1.98
(5)(b)	1997 Sched. 1, para. 21(8)	1.1.98
65(3A)	1997 Sched. 1, para. 21(9)	1.8.97
67A	1997 s.57(1)	1.8.97[1]
74(4)	1997 Sched. 1, para. 21(10)	1.8.97
81(6)	1997 Sched. 1, para. 21(11)	1.8.97
83(1)	1997 Sched. 1, para. 21(12)	1.8.97
(2)	1997 Sched. 1, para. 21(12)	1.8.97
(3)	1997 Sched. 1, para. 21(12)	1.8.97
85(1)	1997 s.58(2)	1.8.97
(2)	1997 s.58(3)	1.8.97
(2A)–(2C)	1997 s.58(3)	1.8.97
101	1997 s.31	1.8.97
103(3)	1997 Sched. 1, para. 21(13)	1.8.97
(4)	1997 Sched. 1, para. 21(13)	1.8.97
(7)	1997 Sched. 1, para. 21(13)	1.8.97
104(1)(b)	1997 Sched. 1, para. 21(14)	1.8.97
106(1)(bb)	1997 s.18(1)(pt)	20.10.97
(1)(da)	1997 s.23(b)	1.8.97
(3)	1997 s.17(1)	1.8.97
(3A)–(3D)	1997 s.17(1)	1.8.97
106A(2)–(5)	1997 s.19(1)(pt)	20.10.97
107(4)	1997 Sched. 1, para. 21(15)	1.8.97
108	1997 s.21(1)	1.8.97
108A	1997 s.18(2)	20.10.97

NOTE
[1] Applies only in relation to citations served on or after August 1, 1997.

Provision	Derivation	Effective from
110(1)	1997 s.19(2)	20.10.97
112(1)	1997 s.18(3)	20.10.97
116(2)	1997 s.18(4)	20.10.97
118(4)	1997 s.18(5)	20.10.97
(4)(b)	1997 Sched. 1, para. 21(17)	1.8.97
(4A)	1997 s.18(5)	20.10.97
(9)	1997 Sched. 1, para. 21(17)	1.8.97
121(1)	1997 s.18(6)	20.10.97
(2)	1997 s.18(6)	20.10.97
(4)	1997 s.18(6)	20.10.97
121A(1)	1997 s.24(1)	1.8.97
(2)	1997 s.24(1)	1.8.97
(3)	1997 s.24(1)	1.8.97
(4)(a)–(c)	1997 s.24(1)	1.8.97
125(1)	1997 s.18(7)	20.10.97
(2)	1997 s.18(7)	20.10.97
126	1997 s.18(8)	20.10.97
140(1)	1997 s.57(2)	1.8.97
(3)	1997 s.57(2)	1.8.97
141(3)	1997 Sched. 1, para. 21(19)	1.8.97
(5A)	1997 Sched. 1, para. 21(19)	1.8.97
154	1997 s.28(1)	1.8.97
175(2)(ca)	1997 s.23(c)	1.8.97
(4)	1997 s.21(2)	1.8.97
(4A)	1997 s.21(2)	1.8.97
(5)	1997 s.17(2)	1.8.97
(5A)–(5E)	1997 s.17(2)	1.8.97
179(2)	1997 Sched. 1, para. 21(20)	1.8.97
182(5)(b)	1997 Sched. 1, para. 21(21)	1.8.97
189(1)(b)	1997 Sched. 1, para. 21(22)	1.8.97
193A(1)	1997 s.24(2)	1.8.97
(2)	1997 s.24(2)	1.8.97
(3)	1997 s.24(2)	1.8.97
(4)(a)–(c)	1997 s.24(2)	1.8.97
196(2)	1997 s.2(2)	20.10.97
199	1997 Sched. 1, para. 21(23)	20.10.97
204(2)	1997 s.6(3)	1.1.98
(2A)	1997 s.6(3)	1.1.98
205B	1997 s.2(1)	20.10.97
205C(1)	1997 s.3(pt)	20.10.97
207(2)	1997 Sched. 1, para. 21(25)	20.10.97
(4A)	1997 s.6(4)	1.1.98
210	1997 s.12	1.8.97
233(6)	1997 s.26(1)	1.8.97
234A	1997 Sched. 1, para. 21(30)	1.8.97
241(4)	1997 s.26(2)	1.8.97
245A(1)–(7)	1997 s.5	1.7.98
(8)	1997 s.5(pt)	20.10.97
(9)–(15)	1997 s.5	1.7.98
245B–245I	1997 s.5	1.7.98
246(1)	1997 Sched. 1, para. 21(31)	20.10.97
248A	1997 s.15(1)	1.1.98[1]
248B	1997 s.15(1)	1.1.98[1]
248C(1)	1997 s.15(1)(pt)	20.10.97
(2)	1997 s.15(1)(pt)	20.10.97
252(2)	1997 s.15(2)	1.1.98
255A	1997 s.27	1.8.97

NOTE
[1]Applies only in relation to offences committed on or after January 1, 1998.

Provision	Derivation	Effective from
271	1997 s.29	1.8.97
279A	1997 s.28(2)	1.8.97
280(6)(b)	1997 Sched. 1, para. 21(32)	1.8.97
285(2)	1997 s.59(2)	1.8.97
(5)	1997 s.59(3)	1.8.97
298	1997 Sched. 1, para. 21(33)	20.10.97
303A(1)	1997 s.20	1.8.97
(2)	1997 s.20	1.8.97
(4)	1997 s.20	1.8.97
(5)	1997 s.20	1.8.97
(6)	1997 s.20	1.8.97
307	1997 Sched. 1, para. 21(34)(b)	1.8.97
	1997 s.6(5)	1.1.98
Schedule 4, para. 3(3)	1997 Sched. 1, para. 21(35)	1.1.98
para. 10(1)	1997 Sched. 1, para. 21(35)	1.1.98
para. 11(1)(a)	1997 Sched. 1, para. 21(35)	1.1.98
Schedule 9	1997 s.30(1)	1.8.97

CRIME AND DISORDER ACT 1998

(1998 c. 37)

Division A—Miscellaneous Legislation

An Act to make provision for preventing crime and disorder; to create certain racially-aggravated offences; to abolish the rebuttable presumption that a child is doli incapax and to make provision as to the effect of a child's failure to give evidence at his trial; to abolish the death penalty for treason and piracy; to make changes to the criminal justice system; to make further provision for dealing with offenders; to make further provision with respect to remands and committals for trial and the release and recall of prisoners; to amend Chapter I of Part II of the Crime (Sentences) Act 1997 and to repeal Chapter I of Part III of the Crime and

Punishment (Scotland) Act 1997; to make amendments designed to facilitate, or otherwise desirable in connection with, the consolidation of certain enactments; and for connected purposes.   [31st July 1998]

PART I

PREVENTION OF CRIME AND DISORDER

CHAPTER I

ENGLAND AND WALES

Crime and disorder: general

. . .

CHAPTER II

SCOTLAND

Anti-social behaviour orders

19.—(1) A local authority may make an application for an order under this section if it appears to the authority that the following conditions are fulfilled with respect to any person of or over the age of 16, namely—

(a) that the person has—
> (i) acted in an anti-social manner, that is to say, in a manner that caused or was likely to cause alarm or distress; or
> (ii) pursued a course of anti-social conduct, that is to say, pursued a course of conduct that caused or was likely to cause alarm or distress,

to one or more persons not of the same household as himself in the authority's area (and in this section "anti-social acts" and "anti-social conduct" shall be construed accordingly); and

(b) that such an order is necessary to protect persons in the authority's area from further anti-social acts or conduct by him.

(2) An application under subsection (1) above shall be made by summary application to the sheriff within whose sheriffdom the alarm or distress was alleged to have been caused or to have been likely to be caused.

(3) On an application under subsection (1) above, the sheriff may, if he is satisfied that the conditions mentioned in that subsection are fulfilled, make an order under this section (an "anti-social behaviour order") which, for the purpose of protecting persons in the area of the local authority from further anti-social acts or conduct by the person against whom the order is sought, prohibits him from doing anything described in the order.

(4) For the purpose of determining whether the condition mentioned in subsection (1)(a) is fulfilled, the sheriff shall disregard any act of the person in respect of whom the application is made which that person shows was reasonable in the circumstances.

(5) This section does not apply in relation to anything done before the commencement of this section.

(6) Nothing in this section shall prevent a local authority from instituting any legal proceedings otherwise than under this section against any person in relation to any anti-social act or conduct.

(7) In this section "conduct" includes speech and a course of conduct must involve conduct on at least two occasions.

(8) In this section and section 21 below "local authority" means a council constituted under section 2 of the Local Government etc. (Scotland) Act 1994 and any reference to the area of such an authority is a reference to the local government area within the meaning of that Act for which it is so constituted.

Sex offender orders

20.—(1) An application for an order under this section may be made by a chief constable if it appears to him that the conditions mentioned in subsection (2) below are fulfilled with respect to any person in the area of his police force.

(2) The conditions are—

(a) that the person in respect of whom the application for the order is made is—

(i) of or over the age of 16 years; and

(ii) a sex offender; and

(b) that the person has acted, since the relevant date, in such a way as to give reasonable cause to believe that an order under this section is necessary to protect the public from serious harm from him.

(3) An application under subsection (1) above shall be made by summary application to the sheriff within whose sheriffdom the person is alleged to have acted as mentioned in subsection (2)(b) above.

(4) On an application under subsection (1) above the sheriff may—

(a) pending the determination of the application, make any such interim order as he considers appropriate; and

(b) if he is satisfied that the conditions mentioned in subsection (2) above are fulfilled, make an order under this section ("a sex offender order") which prohibits the person in respect of whom it is made from doing anything described in the order.

(5) The prohibitions that may be imposed by an order made under subsection (4) above are those necessary for the purpose of protecting the public from serious harm from the person in respect of whom the order is made.

(6) While a sex offender order has effect, Part I of the Sex Offenders Act 1997 shall have effect as if—

(a) the person in respect of whom the order has been obtained were subject to the notification requirements of that Part; and

(b) in relation to that person, the relevant date (within the meaning of that Part) were the date on which the copy of the order was given or delivered to that person in accordance with subsections (8) and (9) of section 21 below.

(7) Section 3 above applies for the purposes of this section as it applies for the purposes of section 2 above with the following modifications—

(a) any reference in that section to the defendant shall be construed as a reference to the person in respect of whom the order is sought; and

(b) in subsection (2) of that section, the reference to subsection (1) of the said section 2 shall be construed as a reference to subsection (2)(b) of this section.

(8) A constable may arrest without warrant a person whom he reasonably suspects of doing, or having done, anything prohibited by an order under subsection (4)(a) above or a sex offender order.

Procedural provisions with respect to orders

21.—(1) Before making an application under—

(a) section 19(1) above;

(b) subsection (7)(b)(i) below,

the local authority shall consult the relevant chief constable.

(2) Before making an application under section 20(1) above or subsection (7)(b)(i) below, the chief constable shall consult the local authority within whose area the person in respect of whom the order is sought is for the time being.

(3) In subsection (1) above "relevant chief constable" means the chief constable of the police force maintained under the Police (Scotland) Act

1967 the area of which includes the area of the local authority making the application.

(4) A failure to comply with subsection (1) or (2) above shall not affect the validity of an order made on any application to which either of those subsections applies.

(5) A record of evidence shall be kept on any summary application under section 19 or 20 above or subsection (7)(b) below.

(6) Subsections (7) to (9) below apply to anti-social behaviour orders and sex offender orders and subsections (8) and (9) below apply to an order made under section 20(4)(a) above.

(7) An order to which this subsection applies—

(a) shall have effect for a period specified in the order or indefinitely; and

(b) may at any time be varied or revoked on a summary application by—

    (i) the local authority or, as the case may be, chief constable who obtained the order; or

    (ii) the person subject to the order.

(8) The clerk of the court by which an order to which this subsection applies is made or varied shall cause a copy of the order as so made or varied to be—

(a) given to the person named in the order; or

(b) sent to the person so named by registered post or by the recorded delivery service.

(9) An acknowledgement or certificate of delivery of a letter sent under subsection (8)(b) above issued by the Post Office shall be sufficient evidence of the delivery of the letter on the day specified in such acknowledgement or certificate.

(10) Where an appeal is lodged against the determination of an application under section 19 or 20 above or subsection (7)(b) above, any order made on the application shall, without prejudice to the determination of an application under subsection (7)(b) above made after the lodging of the appeal, continue to have effect pending the disposal of the appeal.

Offences in connection with breach of orders

22.—(1) Subject to subsection (3) below, if without reasonable excuse a person breaches an anti-social behaviour order by doing anything which he is prohibited from doing by the order, he shall be guilty of an offence and shall be liable—

(a) on summary conviction, to a term of imprisonment not exceeding six months or to a fine not exceeding the statutory maximum or to both; or

(b) on conviction on indictment, to imprisonment for a term not exceeding five years or to a fine or to both.

(2) Subsection (3) applies where—

(a) the breach of the anti-social behaviour order referred to in subsection (1) above consists in the accused having acted in a manner prohibited by the order which constitutes a separate offence (in this section referred to as the "separate offence"); and

(b) the accused has been charged with that separate offence.

(3) Where this subsection applies, the accused shall not be liable to be proceeded against for an offence under subsection (1) above that, subject to subsection (4) below, the court which sentences him for that separate offence shall, in determining the appropriate sentence or disposal for that offence, have regard to—

(a) the fact that the offence was committed by him while subject to an anti-social behaviour order;

(b) the number of such orders to which he was subject at the time of the commission of the offence;

    (c) any previous conviction of the accused of an offence under subsection (1) above; and

    (d) the extent to which the sentence or disposal in respect of any such previous conviction of the accused differed, by virtue of this subsection, from that which the court would have imposed but for this subsection.

(4) The court shall not, under subsection (3) above, have regard to the fact that the separate offence was committed while the accused was subject to an anti-social behaviour order unless that fact is libelled in the indictment or, as the case may be, specified in the complaint.

(5) The fact that the separate offence was committed while the accused was subject to an anti-social behaviour order shall, unless challenged—

    (a) in the case of proceedings on indictment, by giving notice of a preliminary objection under paragraph (b) of section 72 of the Criminal Procedure (Scotland) Act 1995 ("the 1995 Act") or under that paragraph as applied by section 71(2) of that Act; or

    (b) in summary proceedings, by preliminary objection before his plea is recorded,

be held as admitted.

(6) Subject to subsection (7) below, subsections (1) to (5) above apply in relation to an order under section 20(4) above and to a sex offender order as they apply in relation to an anti-social behaviour order.

(7) Subsection (2) above as applied for the purposes of subsection (6) above shall have effect with the substitution of the words "at the time at which he committed" for the words "which constitutes".

Anti-social behaviour as ground of eviction

23.—(1) Schedule 3 to the Housing (Scotland) Act 1987 (grounds of eviction in relation to secure tenancies) shall be amended in accordance with subsections (2) and (3) below.

(2) For paragraph 2 there shall be substituted the following paragraph—

    "2.—(1) The tenant, a person residing or lodging in the house with the tenant or a person visiting the house has been convicted of—

    (a) using or allowing the house to be used for immoral or illegal purposes; or

    (b) an offence punishable by imprisonment committed in, or in the locality of, the house.

    (2) In sub-paragraph (1) above "tenant" includes any one of joint tenants and any sub-tenant."

(3) For paragraph 7 there shall be substituted the following paragraph—

    "7.—(1) The tenant, a person residing or lodging in the house with the tenant or a person visiting the house has—

    (a) acted in an anti-social manner in relation to a person residing, visiting or otherwise engaging in lawful activity in the locality; or

    (b) pursued a course of anti-social conduct in relation to such a person as is mentioned in head (a) above,

and it is not reasonable in all the circumstances that the landlord should be required to make other accommodation available to him.

    (2) In sub-paragraph (1) above—

    "anti-social", in relation to an action or course of conduct, means causing or likely to cause alarm, distress, nuisance or annoyance;

    "conduct" includes speech and a course of conduct must involve conduct on at least two occasions; and

    "tenant" includes any one of joint tenants and any sub-tenant."

(4) For Ground 15 in Schedule 5 to the Housing (Scotland) Act 1988 (eviction on ground of use of premises for immoral or illegal purposes etc.) there shall be substituted the following—

"Ground 15

The tenant, a person residing or lodging in the house with the tenant or a person visiting the house has—

    (a) been convicted of—

        (i) using or allowing the house to be used for immoral or illegal purposes; or

        (ii) an offence punishable by imprisonment committed in, or in the locality of, the house; or

    (b) acted in an anti-social manner in relation to a person residing, visiting or otherwise engaging in lawful activity in the locality; or

    (c) pursued a course of anti-social conduct in relation to such a person as is mentioned in head (b) above.

In this Ground "anti-social", in relation to an action or course of conduct, means causing or likely to case alarm, distress, nuisance or annoyance, "conduct" includes speech and a course of conduct must involve conduct on at least two occasions and "tenant" includes any one of joint tenants."

(5) No person shall be liable to eviction under paragraph 2 or 7 of Schedule 3 to the Housing (Scotland) Act 1987 or Ground 15 in Schedule 5 to the Housing (Scotland) Act 1988 as substituted respectively by subsection (2), (3) and (4) above in respect of any act or conduct before the commencement of this section unless he would have been liable to be evicted under those paragraphs or, as the case may be, that Ground as they had effect before that substitution.

Noise-making equipment: police power of seizure

24.—(1) The Civic Government (Scotland) Act 1982 shall be amended in accordance with this section.

(2) In section 54 (offence of playing instruments, etc.), after subsection (2) there shall be inserted the following subsections—

"(2A) Where a constable reasonably suspects that an offence under subsection (1) above has been committed in relation to a musical instrument or in relation to such a device as is mentioned in paragraph (c) of that subsection, he may enter any premises on which he reasonably suspects that instrument or device to be and seize any such instrument or device he finds there.

(2B) A constable may use reasonable force in the exercise of the power conferred by subsection (2A) above.

(2C) Schedule 2A to this Act (which makes provision in relation to the retention and disposal of property seized under subsection (2A) above) shall have effect."

(3) In section 60 (powers of search and seizure)—

    (a) in subsection (5)—

        (i) after the words "Nothing in" there shall be inserted the words "section 54(2A) of this Act or"; and

        (ii) for the words from "which" to the end there shall be substituted the words "which is otherwise exercisable by a constable"; and

    (b) in subsection (6)—

        (i) in paragraph (a), for the words from "in pursuance" to the word "vessel" there shall be substituted the words—

"to enter and search—

        (i) any premises in pursuance of section 54(2A) of this Act or of subsection (1) above; or

        (ii) any vehicle or vessel in pursuance of the said subsection (1),"; and

        (ii) in paragraph (c), after "under" there shall be inserted the words "section 54(2A) of this Act or".

(4) After Schedule 2 there shall be inserted the Schedule set out in Schedule 1 to this Act.

CHAPTER III

GREAT BRITAIN

Powers to require removal of masks etc.

25.—(1) After subsection (4) of section 60 (powers to stop and search in anticipation of violence) of the Criminal Justice and Public Order Act 1994 ("the 1994 Act") there shall be inserted the following subsection—

"(4A) This section also confers on any constable in uniform power—
    (a) to require any person to remove any item which the constable reasonably believes that person is wearing wholly or mainly for the purpose of concealing his identity;
    (b) to seize any item which the constable reasonably believes any person intends to wear wholly or mainly for that purpose."

(2) In subsection (5) of that section, for the words "those powers" there shall be substituted the words "the powers conferred by subsection (4) above".

(3) In subsection (8) of that section, for the words "to stop or (as the case may be) to stop the vehicle" there shall be substituted the following paragraphs—

"(a) to stop, or to stop a vehicle; or
(b) to remove an item worn by him,".

Retention and disposal of things seized

26. After section 60 of the 1994 Act there shall be inserted the following section—

Retention and disposal of things seized under section 60

60A.—(1) Any things seized by a constable under section 60 may be retained in accordance with regulations made by the Secretary of State under this section.

(2) The Secretary of State may make regulations regulating the retention and safe keeping, and the disposal and destruction in prescribed circumstances, of such things.

(3) Regulations under this section may make different provisions for different classes of things or for different circumstances.

(4) The power to make regulations under this section shall be exercisable by statutory instrument which shall be subject to annulment in pursuance of a resolution of either House of Parliament.

Power of arrest for failure to comply with requirement

27.—(1) In section 24(2) (arrestable offences) of the Police and Criminal Evidence Act 1984 ("the 1984 Act"), after paragraph (n) there shall be inserted—

"(o) an offence under section 60(8)(b) of the Criminal Justice and Public Order Act 1994 (failing to comply with requirement to remove mask etc.);".

(2) After section 60A of the 1994 Act there shall be inserted the following section—

"Arrest without warrant for offences under section 60: Scotland
   60B. In Scotland, where a constable reasonably believes that a person has committed or is committing an offence under section 60(8) he may arrest that person without warrant."

PART II

CRIMINAL LAW

Racially-aggravated offences: England and Wales

...

Racially-aggravated offences: Scotland

33. [*Inserted s.50A into the Criminal Law (Consolidation) (Scotland) Act 1995.*]

PART IV

DEALING WITH OFFENDERS

CHAPTER I

ENGLAND AND WALES

Sexual or violent offenders

...

CHAPTER II

SCOTLAND

Sexual or violent offenders

Extended sentences for sex and violent offenders
86.—(1) [*Inserted s.210A into the 1995 Act.*]
   (2) [*Amends s.209 of the 1995 Act.*]

Further provision as to extended sentences
87. [*Inserted s.26A into the 1993 Act.*]

Re-release of prisoner's serving extended sentences
88. [*Inserted s.3A into the 1993 Act.*]

Offenders dependent etc. on drugs.

Drug treatment and testing orders
89. [*Inserted s.234B into the 1995 Act.*]

Requirements and Provisions to be included in drug treatment and testing orders
90. [*Inserted s.234C into the 1995 Act.*]

Procedural matters relating to drug treatment and testing orders
91. [*Inserted s.234D into the 1995 Act.*]

Amendment and periodic review of drug treatment and testing orders
92. [*Inserted ss.234E and 234F into the 1998 Act.*]

Consequences of breach of drug treatment and testing order

93. [*Inserted s.234G into the 1995 Act.*]

Combination of orders

94. [*Inserted s.234J into the 1995 Act.*]
(2) Schedule 6 to this Act (Part I of which makes further provision in relation to the combination of drug treatment and testing orders with other orders and Part II of which makes provision in relation to appeals) shall have effect.

Interpretation provision in relation to drug treatment and testing orders

95.—(1) [*Inserted s.234K into the 1995 Act.*]
(2) [*Inserted into s.307(1) of the 1995 Act.*]

Racial aggravation

Offences racially aggravated

96.—(1) The provisions of this section shall apply where it is—
(a) libelled in an indictment; or
(b) specified in a complaint,
and, in either case, proved that an offence has been racially aggravated.
(2) An offence is racially aggravated for the purposes of this section if—
(a) at the time of committing the offence, or immediately before or after doing so, the offender evinces towards the victim (if any) of the offence malice and ill-will based on the victim's membership (or presumed membership) of a racial group; or
(b) the offence is motivated (wholly or partly) by malice and ill-will towards members of a racial group based on their membership of that group.
and evidence from a single source shall be sufficient evidence to establish, for the purposes of this subsection, that an offence is racially aggravated.
(3) In subsection (2)(a) above—
"membership", in relation to a racial group, includes association with members of that group;
"presumed" means presumed by the offender.
(4) It is immaterial for the purposes of paragraph (a) or (b) of subsection (2) above whether or not the offender's malice and ill-will is also based, to any extent, on—
(a) the fact or presumption that any person or group of persons belongs to any religious group; or
(b) any other factor not mentioned in that paragraph.
(5) Where this section applies, the court shall, on convicting a person, take the aggravation into account in determining the appropriate sentence.
(6) In this section "racial group" means a group of persons defined by reference to race, colour, nationality (including citizenship) or ethnic or national origins.

PART V

MISCELLANEOUS AND SUPPLEMENTAL

Remands and committals

...

Release and recall of prisoners

...

...

Repeal of Chapter I of Part III of Crime and Punishment (Scotland) Act 1997

108. Chapter I of Part III of the Crime and Punishment (Scotland) Act 1997 (early release of prisoners) shall cease to have effect.

Transitional provisions in relation to certain life prisoners

109.—(1) Section 16 of the Crime and Punishment (Scotland) Act 1997 (designated life prisoners) shall have effect and shall be deemed always to have had effect with the amendments made by subsections (2) and (3) below.

(2) [*Inserted in s.16(2) of the Crime and Punishment (Scotland) Act 1997 (c. 48).*]

(3) [*Inserted as s.16(3A) to 16(3C) of the above Act.*]

(4) Where, prior to the commencement of this section, a certificate has been issued under subsection (2) of section 16 of the Crime and Punishment (Scotland) Act 1997 in respect of a case to which subsection (3A) of that section applies, the certificate shall be disregarded.

Calculation of period of detention at customs office etc. where person previously detained

110. In section 24 of the Criminal Law (Consolidation) (Scotland) Act 1995 (detention and questioning by customs officers), in subsection (4)—
  (a) for the words from "he" to "be" there shall be substituted the words "and is"; and
  (b) after the word "detention" there shall be inserted the words ", the period of six hours mentioned in subsection (2) above shall be reduced by the length of that earlier detention".

Early release in Scotland: two or more sentences

111.—(1) [*Inserted s.1A into the 1993 Act.*]

(2) [*Inserted s.16(8) into the 1993 Act.*]

(3) [*Substituted s.27(5) of the 1993 Act.*]

(4) In sub-paragraph (1) of paragraph 6B of Schedule 6 to the 1993 Act (aggregation of old and new sentences)—
  (a) for the words "a prisoner" there shall be substituted the words "an existing prisoner";
  (b) the word "and" after head (a) shall cease to have effect;
  (c) in head (b), for the words "that date" there shall be inserted the words "the date on which section 111 of the Crime and Disorder Act 1998 comes into force"; and
  (d) after head (b) there shall be inserted the following—
      "; and
    (c) he has not at any time prior to the passing of the sentence or sentences mentioned in head (b) above been released from the sentence or sentences mentioned in head (a) above under the existing provisions."

(5) [*Inserted s.6C into Sched. 6 of the 1993 Act.*]

(6) Subject to subsection (7) below, the amendments made by subsections (1) to (5) above apply where one or more of the sentences concerned was passed after the commencement of this section.

(7) Where the terms of two or more sentences passed before the commencement of this section have been treated, by virtue of section 27(5) of, or paragraph 6B of Schedule 6 to, the 1993 Act, as a single term for the purposes of Part I of that Act, they shall continue to be so treated after that commencement.

(8) In relation to a prisoner released on licence at any time under section 16(7)(b) of the 1993 Act, section 17(1)(a) of that Act shall have effect as if after the word "Act" there were inserted the words "or a short term prisoner has been released on licence by virtue of section 16(7)(b) of this Act".

Restriction on consecutive sentences for released prisoners: Scotland

112. [*Inserted s.204A into the 1995 Act.*]

Deputy authorising officer under Part III of Police Act 1997

113.—(1) [1][*Repealed by s.82 of and Sched. 5 to the Regulation of Investigatory Powers Act 2000 (c. 23)*]

(2) In subsection (3) of that section, for paragraphs (a) and (b) there shall be substituted the words "he holds the rank of assistant chief constable in that Service or Squad".

(3) [1][*Repealed by s.82 of and Sched. 5 to the Regulation of Investigatory Powers Act 2000 (c. 23)*]

(d) in the case of an authorising officer within paragraph (h) of section 93(5), means the customs officer designated by the Commissioners of Customs and Excise to act in his absence for the purposes of this paragraph."

NOTE
[1]Repealed by the Regulation of Investigatory Powers Act 2000 (c. 23), s.82 and Sched. 5. Brought into force by the Regulation of Investigatory Powers Act 2000 (Commencement No. 1 and Transitional Provisions) Order 2000 (S.I. 2000 No. 2543 (C.71)).

Supplemental

Orders and regulations

114.—(1) Any power of a Minister of the Crown to make an order or regulations under this Act—
(a) is exercisable by statutory instrument; and
(b) includes power to make such transitional provision as appears to him necessary or expedient in connection with any provision made by the order or regulations.

(2) A statutory instrument containing an order under section 5(2) or (3) or 10(6) above, or regulations under paragraph 1 of Schedule 3 to this Act, shall be subject to annulment in pursuance of a resolution of either House of Parliament.

[1](3) No order under section 38(5) or 41(6) above shall be made unless a draft of the order has been laid before and approved by a resolution of each House of Parliament.

NOTE
[1]As amended by the Powers of Criminal Courts (Sentencing) Act 2000 (c. 6), s.165 and Sched. 9, para. 199.

Disclosure of information

115.—(1) Any person who, apart from this subsection, would not have power to disclose information—
(a) to a relevant authority; or
(b) to a person acting on behalf of such an authority,
shall have power to do so in any case where the disclosure is necessary or expedient for the purposes of any provision of this Act.

(2) In subsection (1) above "relevant authority" means—
(a) the chief officer of police for a police area in England and Wales;
(b) the chief constable of a police force maintained under the Police (Scotland) Act 1967;

   (c) a police authority within the meaning given by section 101(1) of the
Police Act 1996;

   (d) a local authority, that is to say—

         (i) in relation to England, a county council, a district council, a
London borough council or the Common Council of the City of
London;

         (ii) in relation to Wales, a county council or a county borough
council;

         (iii) in relation to Scotland, a council constituted under section 2
of the Local Government etc. (Scotland) Act 1994;

[1](e) a local probation board in England and Wales;

   (f) a health authority.

NOTE

[1]As amended by the Criminal Justice and Court Services Act 2000 (c. 43), s.74 and Sched. 7,
para. 151. Brought into force by the Criminal Justice and Court Services Act 2000
(Commencement No. 4) Order 2001 (S.I. 2001 No. 919 (C. 33)), art. 2(f)(ii) (effective April 1,
2001).

General interpretation

117.—(1) In this Act—

"the 1933 Act" means the Children and Young Persons Act 1933;

"the 1969 Act" means the Children and Young Persons Act 1969;

"the 1973 Act" means the Powers of Criminal Courts Act 1973;

"the 1980 Act" means the Magistrates' Courts Act 1980;

"the 1982 Act" means the Criminal Justice Act 1982;

"the 1984 Act" means the Police and Criminal Evidence Act 1984;

"the 1985 Act" means the Prosecution of Offences Act 1985;

"the 1989 Act" means the Children Act 1989;

"the 1991 Act" means the Criminal Justice Act 1991;

"the 1994 Act" means the Criminal Justice and Public Order Act 1994;

"the 1997 Act" means the Crime (Sentences) Act 1997;

"caution" has the same meaning as in Part V of the Police Act 1997;

"child" means a person under the age of 14;

"commission area" has the same meaning as in the Justices of the Peace
Act 1997;

[1]"custodial sentence" has the same meaning as in the Powers of
Criminal Courts (Sentencing) Act 2000;

"guardian" has the same meaning as in the 1933 Act;

[2]"local probation board" means a local probation board established
under section 4 of the Criminal Justice and Court Services Act
2000;

"prescribed" means prescribed by an order made by the Secretary of
State;

"young person" means a person who has attained the age of 14 and is
under the age of 18;

"youth offending team" means a team established under section 39
above.

(2) In this Act—

"the 1993 Act" means the Prisoners and Criminal Proceedings (Scotland) Act 1993; and

"the 1995 Act" means the Criminal Procedure (Scotland) Act 1995.

(3) For the purposes of this Act, the age of a person shall be deemed to be
that which it appears to the court to be after considering any available
evidence.

NOTES

[1]As amended by the Powers of Criminal Courts (Sentencing) Act 2000 (c. 6), s.165 and Sched.
9, para. 200.

[2] As amended by the Criminal Justice and Court Services Act 2000 (c. 43), s.74 and Sched. 7, para. 152. Brought into force by the Criminal Justice and Court Services Act 2000 (Commencement No. 4) Order 2001 (S.I. 2001 No. 919 (C. 33)), art. 2(f)(ii) (effective April 1, 2001).
...

Transitional provisions, savings and repeals

120.—(1) The transitional provisions and savings contained in Schedule 9 to this Act shall have effect; but nothing in this subsection shall be taken as prejudicing the operation of sections 16 and 17 of the Interpretation Act 1978 (which relate to the effect of repeals).

(2) The enactments specified in schedule 10 to this Act, which include some that are spent, are hereby repealed to the extent specified in the third column of that Schedule.

Short title, commencement and extent

121.—(1) This Act may be cited as the Crime and Disorder Act 1998.

(2) This Act, except this section, sections 109 and 111(8) above and paragraphs 55, 99 and 117 of Schedule 8 to this Act, shall come into force on such day as the Secretary of State may by order appoint; and different days may be appointed for different purposes or different areas.

(3) Without prejudice to the provisions of Schedule 9 to this Act, an order under subsection (2) above may make such transitional provisions and savings as appear to the Secretary of State necessary or expedient in connection with any provision brought into force by the order.

(4) Subject to subsections (5) to (12) below, this Act extends to England and Wales only.

(5) The following provisions extend to Scotland only, namely—

(a) Chapter II of Part I;
(b) section 33;
(c) Chapter II of Part IV;
(d) sections 108 to 112 and 117(2); and
(e) paragraphs 55, 70, 71, 98 to 108, 115 to 124 and 140 to 143 of Schedule 8 and section 119 above so far as relating to those paragraphs.

(6) The following provisions also extent to Scotland, namely—

(a) Chapter III of Part I;
(b) section 36(3) to (5);
(c) section 65(9);
(d) section 115;
(e) paragraph 3 of Schedule 3 to this Act and section 52(6) above so far as relating to that paragraph;
(f) [*Repealed by the Powers of Criminal Courts (Sentencing) Act 2000 (c. 6), s.165 and Sched. 12, Part I*]
(g) paragrapha 1, 7(1) and (3), 14(1) and (2), 35, 36, 45, 135, 136 and 138 of Schedule 8 to this Act and section 119 above so far as relating to those paragraphs; and
(h) this section.

(7) Sections 36(1), (2)(a), (b) and (d) and (6)(b) and section 118 above extend to Northern Ireland only.

(8) Section 36(3)(b), (4) and (5) above, paragraphs 7(1) and (3), 45, 135 and 138 of Schedule 8 to this Act, section 119 above so far as relating to those paragraphs and this section also extend to Northern Ireland.

(9) Section 36(5) above, paragraphs 7(1) and (3), 45 and 134 of Schedule 8 to this Act, section 119 above so far as relating to those paragraphs and this section also extend to the Isle of Man.

(10) Section 36(5) above, paragraphs 7(1) and (3), 45 and 135 of Schedule 8 to this Act, section 119 above so far as relating to those paragraphs and this section also extend to the Channel Islands.

(11) The repeals in Schedule 10 to this Act, and section 120(2) above so far as relating to those repeals, have the same extent as the enactments on which the repeals operate.

(12) Section 9(4) of the Repatriation of Prisoners Act 1984 (power to extend Act to Channel Islands and Isle of Man) applies to the amendments of that Act made by paragraphs 56 to 60 of Schedule 8 to this Act; and in Schedule 1 to the 1997 Act—

    (a) paragraph 14 (restricted transfers between the United Kingdom and the Channel Islands) as applied in relation to the Isle of Man; and

    (b) paragraph 19 (application of Schedule in relation to the Isle of Man), apply to the amendments of that Schedule made by paragraph 135 of Schedule 8 to this Act.

SCHEDULES

Section 24(4)   SCHEDULE 1

SCHEDULE 2A TO THE CIVIC GOVERNMENT (SCOTLAND) ACT 1982

Section 54(2C)   "Schedule 2A

RETENTION AND DISPOSAL OF PROPERTY SEIZED UNDER SECTION 54(2A) OF THIS ACT

Application

1. This schedule applies to property seized under section 54(2A) of this Act.

Retention

2.—(1) Subject to sub-paragraph (2) below, property to which this Schedule applies may be retained for a period of twenty-eight days beginning with the day on which it was seized.

(2) Where proceedings for an offence are instituted within the period specified in sub-paragraph (1) above against any person, the property may be retained for a period beginning on the day on which it was seized and ending on the day when—

    (a) the prosecutor certifies that the property is not, or is no longer, required as a production in criminal proceedings or for any purpose relating to such proceedings;

    (b) the accused in such proceedings—

        (i) is sentenced or otherwise dealt with for the offence; or

        (ii) is acquitted of the offence; or

    (c) the proceedings are expressly abandoned by the prosecutor or are deserted *simpliciter*.

Arrangements for custody of property

3.—(1) Subject to the proviso to section 17(3)(b) of the Police (Scotland) Act 1967 (duty to comply with instructions received from prosecutor), the chief constable shall, in accordance with the provisions of this Schedule, make such arrangements as he considers appropriate for the care, custody, return or disposal of property to which this Schedule applies.

(2) Any reference in this Schedule to property being in the possession of, delivered by or disposed of by, the chief constable includes a reference to its being in the possession of, delivered by or disposed of by, another person under arrangements made under sub-paragraph (1) above.

Disposal

4. Where the period of retention permitted by paragraph 2 above expires and the chief constable has reason to believe that the person from whom the property was seized is not the owner or the person having right to possession of it, he shall take reasonable steps to ascertain the identity of the owner or of the person with that right and to notify him of the procedures determined under paragraph 5(1) below.

5.—(1) Subject to sub-paragraphs (5) and (6) below, the owner or any person having right to possession of any property to which this Schedule applies and which, at the expiry of the period of retention permitted by paragraph 2 above, is in the possession of the chief constable may at any time prior to its disposal under paragraph 6 below claim that property in accordance with such procedure as the chief constable may determine.

(2) Subject to sub-paragraphs (3), (5) and (6) below, where the chief constable considers that the person making a claim in accordance with the procedure determined under sub-paragraph

(1) above is the owner of the property or has a right to possession of it, he shall deliver the property to the claimant.

(3) Subject to sub-paragraph (4) below, the chief constable may impose such conditions connected with the delivery to the claimant of property under sub-paragraph (2) above as he thinks fit and, without prejudice to that generality, such conditions may relate to the payment of such reasonable charges (including any reasonable expenses incurred in relation to the property by or on behalf of him) as he may determine.

(4) No condition relating to the payment of any charge shall be imposed by the chief constable on the owner or person having right of possession of the property where he is satisfied that that person did not know, and had no reason to suspect, that the property to which this Schedule applies was likely to be used in a manner which gave rise to its seizure.

(5) This paragraph does not apply where the period of retention expires in such manner as is mentioned in paragraph 2(2)(b)(i) above and the court by which he was convicted has made a suspended forfeiture order or a restraint order in respect of the property to which this Schedule applies.

(6) This paragraph shall cease to apply where at any time—

(a) the property to which this Schedule applies—

      (i) is seized under any other power available to a constable; or

      (ii) passes into the possession of the prosecutor; or

(b) proceedings for an offence are instituted, where the property to which this Schedule applies is required as a production.

6.—(1) Where this sub-paragraph applies, the chief constable may—

(a) sell property to which this Schedule applies; or

(b) if in his opinion it would be impracticable to sell such property, dispose of it.

(2) Sub-paragraph (1) above applies—

(a) at any time after the expiry of the relevant period where, within that period—

      (i) no claim has been made under paragraph 5 above; or

      (ii) any such a claim which has been made has been rejected by the chief constable; and

(b) where a claim has been made under paragraph 5 above and not determined within the relevant period, at any time after the rejection of that claim by the chief constable.

(3) In sub-paragraph (2) above, the "relevant period" means a period of six months beginning with the day on which the period of retention permitted by paragraph 2 above expired.

(4) Sections 71, 72 and 77(1) of this Act shall apply to a disposal under this paragraph as they apply to a disposal under section 68 of this Act.

Appeals

7.—(1) A claimant under sub-paragraph (2) of paragraph 5 above may appeal to the sheriff against any decision of the chief constable made under that paragraph as respects the claim.

(2) The previous owner of any property disposed of for value under paragraph 6 above may appeal to the sheriff against any decision of the chief constable made under section 72 of this Act as applied by sub-paragraph (4) of that paragraph.

(3) Subsections (3) to (5) of section 76 of this Act shall apply to an appeal under this paragraph as they apply to an appeal under that section.

Interpretation

8. In this Schedule—

"chief constable" means the chief constable for the police area in which the property to which this Schedule applies was seized, and includes a constable acting under the direction of the chief constable for the purposes of this Schedule;

"restraint order" shall be construed in accordance with section 28(1) of the Proceeds of Crime (Scotland) Act 1995;

"suspended forfeiture order" shall be construed in accordance with section 21(2) of that Act."

...

Section 94(2)   SCHEDULE 6

DRUG TREATMENT AND TESTING ORDERS: AMENDMENT OF THE 1995 ACT

PART I

AMENDMENTS RELATING TO COMBINATION OF ORDERS

1. In section 228(1) (probation orders), for the words "section 245D" there shall be substituted the words "sections 234J and 245D".

2.—(1) Section 232 (failure to comply with requirements of probation orders) shall be amended as follows.

(2) In subsection (3A)—

(a) for the words "a restriction of liberty order" there shall be substituted—

"(a) a restriction of liberty order; or

(b) a restriction of liberty order and a drug treatment and testing order,"; and

(b) at the end there shall be added the words "or, as the case may be, the restriction of liberty order and the drug treatment and testing order."

(3) After that subsection there shall be inserted the following subsection—

"(3B) Where the court intends to sentence an offender under subsection (2)(b) above and the offender is by virtue of section 234J of this Act subject to a drug treatment and testing order, it shall, before sentencing the offender under that paragraph, revoke the drug treatment and testing order."

3. For section 245D there shall be substituted the following section—

"Combination of restriction of liberty order with other orders

245D.—(1) Subsection (3) applies where the court—

(a) intends to make a restriction of liberty order under section 245A(1) of this Act; and

(b) considers it expedient that the offender should also be subject to a probation order made under section 228(1) of this Act or to a drug treatment and testing order made under section 234B(2) of this Act or to both such orders.

(2) In deciding whether it is expedient to make a probation order or a drug treatment and testing order by virtue of paragraph (b) of subsection (1) above, the court shall—

(a) have regard to the circumstances, including the nature of the offence and the character of the offender; and

(b) obtain a report as to the circumstances and character of the offender.

(3) Where this subsection applies, the court, notwithstanding sections 228(1), 234B(2) and 245A(1) of this Act, may make a restriction of liberty order and either or both of a probation order and a drug treatment and testing order.

(4) Where the court makes a restriction of liberty order and a probation order by virtue of subsection (3) above, the clerk of the court shall send a copy of each order to—

(a) any person responsible for monitoring the offender's compliance with the restriction of liberty order; and

(b) the officer of the local authority who is to supervise the probationer.

(5) Where the court makes a restriction of liberty order and a drug treatment and testing order by virtue of subsection (3) above, the clerk of the court shall send a copy of each order to—

(a) any person responsible for monitoring the offender's compliance with the restriction of liberty order;

(b) the treatment provider, within the meaning of section 234C(1) of this Act; and

(c) the officer of the local authority who is appointed or assigned to be the supervising officer under section 234C(6) of this Act.

(6) Where the court makes a restriction of liberty order, a probation order and a drug treatment and testing order the clerk of the court shall send copies of each of the orders to the persons mentioned—

(a) in subsection (4) above;

(b) in paragraph (b) of subsection (5) above; and

(c) in paragraph (c) of that subsection, if that person would not otherwise receive such copies.

(7) Where the offender by an act or omission fails to comply with a requirement of an order made by virtue of subsection (3) above—

(a) if the failure relates to a requirement contained in a probation order and is dealt with under section 232(2)(c) of this Act, the court may, in addition, exercise the powers conferred by section 234G(2)(b) of this Act in relation to a drug treatment and testing order to which the offender is subject by virtue of subsection (3) above and by section 245F(2) of this Act in relation to the restriction of liberty order;

(b) if the failure relates to a requirement contained in a drug treatment and testing order and is dealt with under section 234G(2)(b) of this Act, the court may, in addition, exercise the powers conferred by section 232(2)(c) of this Act in relation to a probation order to which the offender is subject by virtue of subsection (3) above and by section 245F(2)(b) of this Act in relation to the restriction of liberty order; and

(c) if the failure relates to a requirement contained in a restriction of liberty order and is dealt with under section 245F(2)(b) of this Act, the court may, in addition, exercise the powers conferred by section 232(2)(c) of this Act in relation to a probation order and by section 234G(2)(b) of this Act in relation to a drug treatment and testing order to which, in either case, the offender is subject by virtue of subsection (3) above.

(8) In any case to which this subsection applies, the offender may, without prejudice to subsection (7) above, be dealt with as respects that case under section 232(2) or, as the case may be, section 234G or section 245F(2) of this Act but he shall not be liable to be otherwise dealt with as respects that case.

(9) Subsection (8) applies in a case where—

(a) the offender by an act or omission fails to comply with both a requirement contained in a restriction of liberty order and in a probation order to which he is subject by virtue of subsection (3) above;

(b) the offender by an act or omission fails to comply with both a requirement contained in a restriction of liberty order and in a drug treatment and testing order to which he is subject by virtue of subsection (3) above;

(c) the offender by an act or omission fails to comply with a requirement contained in each of a restriction of liberty order, a probation order and a drug treatment and testing order to which he is subject by virtue of subsection (3) above."

4.—(1) Section 245G (disposal on revocation of restriction of liberty order) shall be amended as follows.

(2) In subsection (2), for the words from "by" to the end there shall be substituted the words "by virtue of section 245D(3) of this Act, subject to a probation order or a drug treatment and testing order or to both such orders, it shall, before disposing the offender under subsection (1) above—

(a) where he is subject to a probation order, discharge that order;

(b) where he is subject to a drug treatment and testing order, revoke that order; and

(c) where he is subject to both such orders, discharge the probation order and revoke the drug treatment and testing order."

(3) After subsection (2) there shall be added—

"(3) Where the court orders a probation order discharged or a drug treatment and testing order revoked the clerk of the court shall forthwith give copies of that order to the persons mentioned in subsection (4) or, as the case may be, (5) of section 245D of this Act.

(4) Where the court orders a probation order discharged and a drug treatment and testing order revoked, the clerk of the court shall forthwith give copies of that order to the persons mentioned in section 245D(6) of this Act."

Part II

Amendments relating to appeals

5. In section 106 (solemn appeals), in paragraph (d), after the words "probation order" there shall be inserted the words ", drug treatment and testing order".

6.—(1) Section 108 (right of appeal of prosecutor) shall be amended as follows.

(2) In subsection (1), after paragraph (d) there shall be inserted the following paragraph—

"(dd) a drug treatment and testing order;".

(3) In subsection (2)(b)(iii), for the word "or", where it first occurs, there shall be substituted the word "to".

7.—(1) Section 175 (appeals in summary cases) shall be amended as follows.

(2) In subsection (2)(c), after the words "probation order" there shall be inserted the words ", drug treatment and testing order".

(3) In subsection (4), after paragraph (d) there shall be inserted the following paragraph—

"(dd) a drug treatment and testing order;".

(4) In subsection (4A)(b)(iii), for the word "or", where it first occurs, there shall be substituted the word "to".

. . .

Section 119   SCHEDULE 8

Minor and consequential amendments

Children and Young Persons Act 1933 (c. 12)

1. In subsection (4A) of section 49 of the 1933 Act (restrictions on reports of proceedings), for paragraph (e) there shall be substituted the following paragraph—

"(e) where a detention and training order is made, the enforcement of any requirements imposed under seection 76(6)(b) of the Crime and Disorder Act 1998."
[*Paras 2–4 repealed by the Powers of Criminal Courts (Sentencing) Act 2000 (c. 6), s.165 and Sched. 12, Part I*]

Administration of Justice (Miscellaneous Provisions) Act 1933 (c. 36)

5.—(1) In subsection (2) of section 2 of the Administration of Justice (Miscellaneous Provisions) Act 1933 (procedure for indictment of offenders)—
(a) after paragraph (ab) there shall be inserted the following paragraph—
"(ac) the person charged has been sent for trial for the offence under section 51 (no criminal proceedings for indictable-only offences) of the Crime and Disorder Act 1998 ("the 1998 Act"); or"; and
(b) after paragraph (b) there shall be inserted the words "or
(c) the bill is preferred under section 22B(3)(a) of the Prosecution of Offences Act 1985."
(2) After paragraph (iA) of the proviso to that subsection there shall be inserted the following paragraph—
"(iB) in a case to which paragraph (ac) above applies, the bill of indictment may include, either in substitution for or in addition to any count charging an offence specified in the notice under section 51(7) of the 1998 Act, any counts founded on material which, in pursuance of regulations made under paragraph 1 of Schedule 3 to that Act, was served on the person charged, being counts which may be lawfully joined in the same indictment;".

Prison Act 1952 (c. 52)

6. In subsection (1) of section 43 of the Prison Act 1952 (which enables certain institutions for young offenders to be provided and applies provisions of the Act to them), for paragraph (d) there shall be substituted the following paragraph—
"(d) secure training centres, that is to say places in which offenders in respect of whom detention and training orders have been made under section 73 of the Crime and Disorder Act 1998 may be detained and given training and education and prepared for their release."
7.—(1) In subsection (1) of section 49 of that Act (persons unlawfully at large), for the words from "imprisonment" to "secure training centre" there shall be substituted the words "imprisonment or custody for life or ordered to be detained in secure accommodation or in a young offenders institution".
(2) In subsection (2) of that section—
(a) for the words from "imprisonment" to "secure training centre" there shall be substituted the words "imprisonment, or ordered to be detained in secure accommodation or in a young offenders institution"; and
(b) for the words from "in a prison" to "secure training centre" there shall be substituted the words "in a prison or remand centre, in secure accommodation or in a young offenders institution".
(3) After subsection (4) of that section there shall be inserted the following subsection—
"(5) In this section "secure accommodation" means—
(a) a young offender institution;
(b) a secure training centre; or
(c) any other accommodation that is secure accommodation within the meaning given by section 75(7) of the Crime and Disorder Act 1998 (detention and training orders)."

Criminal Procedure (Attendance of Witnesses) Act 1965 (c. 69)

8. In subsection (4) of section 2 of the Criminal Procedure (Attendance of Witnesses) Act 1965 (issue of witness summons on application to Crown Court), after the words "committed for trial" there shall be inserted the words ", or sent for trial under section 51 of the Crime and Disorder Act 1998,".

Criminal Justice Act 1967 (c. 80)

[*Paras 9 and 10 repealed by the Powers of Criminal Courts (Sentencing) Act 2000 (c. 6), s.165 and Sched. 12, Part I*]
11. At the end of subsection (2) of section 104 of that Act (general provisions as to interpretation) there shall be inserted the words "if—

(a) the sentences were passed on the same occasion; or
(b) where they were passed on different occasions, the person has not been released under
  Part II of the Criminal Justice Act 1991 at any time during the period beginning with the
  first and ending with the last of those occasions."

Criminal Appeal Act 1968 (c. 19)

12. In subsection (2) of section 9 of the Criminal Appeal Act 1968 (appeal against sentence
following conviction on indictment), after the words "for either way offence)" there shall be
inserted the words "or paragraph 6 of Schedule 3 to the Crime and Disorder Act 1998 (power of
Crown Court to deal with summary offence where person sent for trial for indictable-only
offence)".

13.—(1) In subsection (2) of section 10 of that Act (appeal against sentence in other cases
dealt with at Crown Court), the words "(other than a supervision order within the meaning of
that Part)" shall cease to have effect.

(2) In subsection (3) of that section, after paragraph (c) there shall be inserted the following
paragraph—
"(cc) where the court makes such an order with regard to him as is mentioned in section 40(3A)
  of the Criminal Justice Act 1991."

Firearms Act 1968 (c. 27)

14.—(1) In subsection (2) of section 21 of the Firearms Act 1968 (possession of firearms by
persons previously convicted of crime), after the words "a secure training order" there shall be
inserted the words "or a detention and training order".

(2) In subsection (2A) of that section, after paragraph (b) there shall be inserted the following
paragraph—
"(c) in the case of a person who has been subject to a detention and training order—
  (i) the date on which he is released from detention under the order;
  (ii) the date on which he is released from detention ordered under section 77 of
  the Crime and Disorder Act 1998; or
  (iii) the date of the half-way point of the term of the order, whichever is the later."

15. In subsection (1) of section 52 of that Act (forfeiture and disposal of firearms), for the
words "secure training order" there shall be substituted the words "detention and training
order".

Children and Young Persons Act 1969 (c. 54)

[*Paras 16–21 repealed by the Powers of Criminal Courts (Sentencing) Act 2000 (c. 6), s.165 and
Sched. 12, Part I*]

Superannuation Act 1972 (c. 11)

24. In Schedule 1 to the Superannuation Act 1972 (kinds of employment to which a scheme
under section 1 of that Act may apply), at the end of the list of "Other Bodies" there shall be
inserted the following entry—
"Youth Justice Board for England and Wales."

Powers of Criminal Courts Act 1973 (c. 62)

[*Paras 25–34 repealed by the Powers of Criminal Courts (Sentencing) Act 2000 (c. 6), s.165 and
Sched. 12, Part I*]

Rehabilitation of Offenders Act 1974 (c. 53)

35. After subsection (6) of section 5 of the Rehabilitation of Offenders Act 1974
(rehabilitation periods for particular sentences) there shall be inserted the following
subsection—
"(6A) Where in respect of a conviction a detention and training order was made under
section 73 of the Crime and Disorder Act 1998, the rehabilitation period applicable to the
sentence shall be—
(a) in the case of a person aged fifteen years or over at the date of his conviction, five
  years if the order was, and three and a half years if the order was not, for a term
  exceeding six months;
(b) in the case of a person aged under fifteen years at the date of his conviction, a period
  beginning with that date and ending one year after the date on which the order ceases
  to have effect."

36. In subsection (2) of section 7 of that Act (limitations on rehabilitation under Act etc.), after paragraph (b) there shall be inserted the following paragraph—

"(bb) in any proceedings on an application for a sex offender order under section 2 or, as the case may be, 20 of the Crime and Disorder Act 1998 or in any appeal against the making of such an order;".

Bail Act 1976 (c. 63)

37. After subsection (8A) of section 3 of the Bail Act 1976 (general provisions) there shall be inserted the following subsection—

"(8B) Subsection (8) above applies where a court has sent a person on bail to the Crown Court for trial under section 51 of the Crime and Disorder Act 1998 as it applies where a court has commited a person on bail to the Crown Court for trial."

38. In paragraph 8(1) of Schedule 1 to that Act (persons entitled to bail: supplementary provisions), after the words "subsection (6)(d)" there shall be inserted the words "or (e)".

Magistrates' Courts Act 1980 (c. 43)

39. In subsection (3) of section 11 of the 1980 Act (certain sentences and orders not to be made in absence of accused), for the words "secure training order" there shall be substituted the words "detention and training order".

40.—(1) In subsection (1)(a) of section 24 of the 1980 Act (summary trial of information against child or young person for indictable offence), for the words "that subsection" there shall be substituted the words "subsection (3) of that section".

(2) In subsection (2) of that section, for the words from "that other offence" to the end there shall be substituted the words "the charges for both offences could be joined in the same indictment".

41. Section 37 of the 1980 Act (committal to Crown Court with a view to greater term of detention in a young offender institution) shall cease to have effect.

42. In subsection (1) of section 65 of the 1980 Act (meaning of "family proceedings"), after paragraph (p) there shall be inserted the following paragraph—

"(q) sections 11 and 12 of the Crime and Disorder Act 1998;".

43. In subsection (2) of section 108 of the 1980 Act (right of appeal to the Crown Court), the words "a probation order or" shall cease to have effect.

[1]44. In subsection (4)(c) of section 125 of the 1980 Act (warrants)—

(a) the word "and" at the end of sub-paragraph (ii) shall cease to have effect;

(b) in sub-paragraph (iii), for the words "or 97 above" there shall be substituted the words ", 97 or 97A above; and"; and

(c) after that sub-paragraph there shall be inserted the following sub-paragraph—

"(iv) paragraph 4 of Schedule 3 to the Crime and Disorder Act 1998."

NOTE

[1]Prospectively repealed by the Access to Justice 1999 (c.22), s.106 and Sched. 15, Pt V(8).

---

45. In section 126 of the 1980 Act (execution of certain warrants outside England and Wales)—

(a) the word "and" at the end of paragraph (c) shall cease to have effect;

(b) after that paragraph there shall be inserted the following paragraph—

"(cc) warrants of arrest issued under section 97A above;"; and

(c) after paragraph (d) there shall be inserted the words "; and

(e) warrants of arrest issued under paragraph 4 of Schedule 3 to the Crime and Disorder Act 1998."

46. *[Repealed by the Powers of Criminal Courts (Sentencing) Act 2000 (c. 6), s.165 and Sched. 12, Part I]*

Supreme Court Act 1981 (c. 54)

47. *[Repealed by the Powers of Criminal Courts (Sentencing) Act 2000 (c. 6), s.165 and Sched. 12, Part I]*

48. In subsection (1)(a) of section 81 of the Supreme Court Act 1981 (bail), after the words "Criminal Justice Act 1987" there shall be inserted the words "or who has been sent in custody to the Crown Court for trial under section 51 of the Crime and Disorder Act 1998".

Criminal Justice Act 1982 (c. 48)

[*Paras 49–53 repealed by the Powers of Criminal Courts (Sentencing) Act 2000 (c. 6), s.165 and Sched. 12, Part I*]

Mental Health Act 1983 (c. 20)

54. In subsection (8) of section 37 of the Mental Health Act 1983 (powers of courts to order hospital admission or guardianship), for the words from "pass sentence of imprisonment" to "in respect of the offender" there shall be inserted the following paragraphs—
   "(a) pass a sentence of imprisonment, impose a fine or make a community order (within the meaning of Part I of the Criminal Justice Act 1991) in respect of the offence; or
   (b) make an order under section 58 of that Act (binding over of parent or guardian) in respect of the offender,".

Mental Health (Scotland) Act 1984 (c. 36)

55.—(1) In subsection (8A) of section 74 of the Mental Health (Scotland) Act 1984 (effect of certain directions), for the words "the Crime and Punishment (Scotland) Act 1997" there shall be substituted the words "Part I of the Prisoners and Criminal Proceedings (Scotland) Act 1993".

(2) The amendment made by sub-paragraph (1) above shall be deemed to have had effect from 1 January 1998.

Repatriation of Prisoners Act 1984 (c. 47)

56. In subsection (4)(b) of section 2 (transfer of prisoners out of United Kingdom) of the Repatriation of Prisoners Act 1984, for sub-paragraph (i) there shall be substituted the following sub-paragraph—
   "(i) released on licence under section 33(1)(b), (2) or (3), 33A(2), 34A(3) or 35(1) of the Criminal Justice Act 1991 or section 28(5) or 29(1) of the Crime (Sentences) Act 1997;".
57. In subsection (9) of section of that Act (transfer of prisoners into United Kingdom)—
   (a) for the words "section 48 of the Criminal Justice Act 1991 (discretionary life prisoners transferred to England and Wales)" there shall be substituted the words "section 33 of the Crime (Sentences) Act 1997 (life prisoner transferred to England and Wales)"; and
   (b) for the words "section 34 of that Act (duty of Secretary of State to release discretionary life prisoners)" there shall be substituted the words "section 28 of that Act (duty to release certain life prisoners)".
58.—(1) Paragraph 2 of the Schedule to that Act as it has effect, and is deemed always to have had effect, by virtue of paragraph 2 of Schedule 2 to the 1997 Act shall be amended as follows.

(2) In sub-paragraph (4), for the definition of "the enactments relating to release on licence" there shall be substituted the following definition—
   ""the enactments relating to release on licence" means sections 33(1)(b), (2) and (3), 33A(2), 34A(3), 35(1) and 37(1) and (2) of the Criminal Justice Act 1991 and section 28(5) and (7) of the Crime (Sentences) Act 1997;".
59.—(1) Paragraph 2 of the Schedule to that Act (operation of certain enactments in relation to the prisoner) as it has effect by virtue of paragraph 3 of Schedule 2 to the 1997 Act—
   (a) shall have effect in relation to all prisoners repatriated to England and Wales after the commencement of Schedule 2; and
   (b) as it so has effect, shall be amended as follows.

(2) In sub-paragraph (2), for the words "34(3) and (5) and 35(1) of the Criminal Justice Act 1991" there shall be substituted the words "35(1) of the Criminal Justice Act 1991 and section 28(5) and (7) of the Crime (Sentences) Act 1997".

(3) In sub-paragraph (4), for the definition of "the enactments relating to release on licence" there shall be substituted the following definition—
   ""the enactments relating to release on licence" means sections 33(1)(b), (2) and (3), 33A(2), 34A(3), 35(1) and 37(1) and (2) of the Criminal Justice Act 1991 and section 28(5) and (7) of the Crime (Sentences) Act 1997;".
60. For paragraph 3 of the Schedule to that Act there shall be substituted the following paragraph—

"Life imprisonment

3. Where the relevant provisions include provision equivalent to a sentence in relation to which subsection (1) of section 29 of the Crime (Sentences) Act 1997 (power to release certain life prisoners etc.) applies, that subsection shall have effect as if the reference to consultation with the trial judge if available were omitted."

Police and Criminal Evidence Act 1984 (c. 60)

61. After subsection (4) of section 27 of the 1984 Act (fingerprinting of certain offenders and recording of offences) there shall be inserted the following subsection—
"(4A) In subsection (4) above "conviction" includes—
(a) a caution within the meaning of Part V of the Police Act 1997; and
(b) a reprimand or warning given under section 65 of the Crime and Disorder Act 1998."
62. After section 47 of the 1984 Act there shall be inserted the following section—

"Early administrative hearings conducted by justices' clerks

47A. Where a person has been charged with an offence at a police station, any requirement imposed under this Part for the person to appear or be brought before a magistrates' court shall be taken to be satisfied if the person appears or is brought before the clerk to the justices for a petty sessions area in order for the clerk to conduct a hearing under section 50 of the Crime and Disorder Act 1998 (early administrative hearings)."

Prosecution of Offences Act 1985 (c. 23)

63. In subsection (2) of section 23 of the 1985 Act (discontinuance of proceedings), after paragraph (b) there shall be inserted the following paragraph—
"(c) in the case of any offence, any stage of the proceedings after the accused has been sent for trial under section 51 of the Crime and Disorder Act 1998 (no committal proceedings for indictable-only and related offences)."
64. After that section there shall be inserted the following section—

"Discontinuance of proceedings after accused has been sent for trial
23A.—(1) This section applies where—
(a) the Director of Public Prosecutions, or a public authority (within the meaning of section 17 of this Act), has the conduct of proceedings for an offence; and
(b) the accused has been sent for trial under section 51 of the Crime and Disorder Act 1998 for the offence.
(2) Where, at any time before the indictment is preferred, the Director or authority gives notice under this section to the Crown Court sitting at the place specified in the notice under section 51(7) of the Crime and Disorder Act 1998 that he or it does not want the proceedings to continue, they shall be discontinued with effect from the giving of that notice.
(3) The Director or authority shall, in any notice given under subsection (2) above, give reasons for not wanting the proceedings to continue.
(4) On giving any notice under subsection (2) above the Director or authority shall inform the accused of the notice; but the Director or authority shall not be obliged to give the accused any indication of his reasons for not wanting the proceedings to continue.
(5) The discontinuance of any proceedings by virtue of this section shall not prevent the institution of fresh proceedings in respect of the same offence."

Criminal Justice Act 1987 (c. 38)

65. After subsection (3) of section 4 of the Criminal Justice Act 1987 (notices of transfer in serious fraud cases) there shall be inserted the following subsection—
"(4) This section and sections 5 and 6 below shall not apply in any case in which section 51 of the Crime and Disorder Act 1998 (no committal proceedings for indictable-only offences) applies."

Criminal Justice Act 1988 (c. 33)

66. In subsection (1) of section 40 of the Criminal Justice Act 1988 (power to join in indictment count for common assault etc.), at the end there shall be inserted the words "or are disclosed by material which, in pursuance of regulations made under paragraph 1 of Schedule 3 to the Crime and Disorder Act 1998 (procedure where person sent for trial under section 51), has been served on the person charged".

Legal Aid Act 1988 (c. 34)

¹67.—(1) In subsection (4) of section 20 of the Legal Aid Act 1988 (competent authorities to grant representation under Part V), after paragraph (a) there shall be inserted the following paragraph—

"(aa) which sends a person for trial under section 51 of the Crime and Disorder Act 1998 (no committal proceedings for indictable-only offences),".

(2) After subsection (5) of that section there shall be inserted the following subsection—

"(5A) A magistrates' court which has a duty or a power to send a person for trial under section 51 of the Crime and Disorder Act 1998 is also competent, before discharging that duty or (as the case may be) deciding whether to exercise that power, as respects any proceedings before the Crown Court on the person's trial."

(3) In subsection (3)(a) of section 21 of that Act (availability of representation under Part V), after the word "committed" there shall be inserted the words "or sent".

(4) In subsection (4) of that section, after the word "commits" there shall be inserted the words "or sends".

NOTE
¹Prospectively repealed by the Access to Justice 1999 (c.22), s.106 and Sched. 15, Pt V(8).

Children Act 1989 (c. 41)

68. In subsection (4) of section 8 of the 1989 Act (which defines "family proceedings"), after paragraph (h) there shall be inserted the following paragraph—

"(i) sections 11 and 12 of the Crime and Disorder Act 1998."

69. In subsection (3) of section 47 of the 1989 Act (local authority's duty to investigate), after the words "this Act" there shall be inserted the words "or section 11 of the Crime and Disorder Act 1998 (child safety orders)".

Prisons (Scotland) Act 1989 (c. 45)

70.—(1) Section 16 of the Prisons (Scotland) Act 1989 (discharge of prisoners) which, notwithstanding its repeal by the Prisoners and Criminal Proceedings (Scotland) Act 1993, is an "existing provision" for the purposes of Schedule 6 to that Act of 1993, shall for those purposes be amended as follows.

(2) In subsection (1), for the words "or Sunday" there shall be substituted the words "Sunday or public holiday".

(3) At the end there shall be inserted the following subsection—

"(3) For the purposes of this section "public holiday" means any day on which, in the opinion of the Secretary of State, public offices or other facilities likely to be of use to the prisoner in the area in which he is likely to be following his discharge from prison will be closed."

71. In section 39 of that Act (rules for the management of prisons)—

(a) in subsection (7)—

(i) at the beginning there shall be inserted the words "Subject to subsection (7A) below,";

(ii) for the words "a short-term or long-term prisoner within the meaning of" there shall be substituted the words "any person who is, or is treated as, a long-term or short-term prisoner for the purposes of any provision of"; and

(iii) the words from "and the foregoing" to the end shall cease to have effect; and

(b) after that subsection there shall be inserted the following subsections—

"(7A) Additional days shall not be awarded under rules made under subsection (7) above in respect of a sentence where the prisoner has at any time been released on licence, in relation to that sentence, under Part I of the Prisoners and Criminal Proceedings (Scotland) Act 1993; and any reference to a sentence in such rules shall be construed in accordance with section 27(5) of that Act.

(7B) In the application of subsection (7) above to a prisoner subject to an extended sentence within the meaning of section 210A of the 1995 Act, the reference to his sentence shall be construed as a reference to the custodial term of that extended sentence."

Criminal Justice Act 1991 (c. 53)

[Paras 72–78 repealed by the Powers of Criminal Courts (Sentencing) Act 2000 (c. 6), s.165 and Sched. 12, Part I]

79.—(1) In subsection (1)(b) of section 32 of the 1991 Act (Parole Board), for the words "the functions conferred by Part II of the Crime (Sentences) Act 1997 ("Part II")" there shall be substituted the words "the functions conferred by this Part in respect of long-term and short-term prisoners and by Chapter II of Part II of the Crime (Sentences) Act 1997 ("Chapter II") in respect of life prisoners within the meaning of that Chapter".

(2) In subsections (3), (4) and (6) of that section, for the words "Part II" there shall be substituted the words "this Part of Chapter II".

80.—(1) In subsection (3) of section 33 of the 1991 Act (duty to release short-term and long-term prisoners)—

(a) in paragraph (a), for the words "subsection (1)(b) or (2) above or section 35 or 36(1) below" there shall be substituted the words "this Part"; and

(b) in paragraph (b), for the words "38(2) or 39(1)" there shall be substituted the words "39(1) or (2)".

(2) After that subsection there shall be inserted the following subsection—

"(3A) In the case of a prisoner to whom section 44A below applies, it shall be the duty of the Secretary of State to release him on licence at the end of the extension period (within the meaning of section 58 of the Crime and Disorder Act 1998)."

(3) Subsection (4) of that section shall cease to have effect.

81. After that section there shall be inserted the following section—

"Duty to release prisoners: special cases

33A.—(1) As soon as a prisoner—

(a) whose sentence is for a term of less than twelve months; and

(b) who has been released on licence under section 34A(3) or 36(1) below and recalled to prison under section 38A(1) or 39(1) or (2) below,

would (but for his release) have served one-half of his sentence, it shall be the duty of the Secretary of State to release him unconditionally.

(2) As soon as a prisoner—

(a) whose sentence is for a term of twelve months or more; and

(b) who has been released on licence under section 34A(3) below and recalled to prison under section 38A(1) below,

would (but for his release) have served one-half of his sentence, it shall be the duty of the Secretary of State to release him on licence.

(3) In the case of a prisoner who—

(a) has been released on licence under this Part and recalled to prison under section 39(1) or (2) below; and

(b) has been subsequently released on licence under section 33(3) or (3A) above and recalled to prison under section 39(1) or (2) below,

section 33(3) above shall have effect as if for the words "three-quarters" there were substituted the words "the whole" and the words "on licence" were omitted."

82. In subsection (1) of section 36 of the 1991 Act (power to release prisoners on compassionate grounds), for word "prisoner" there shall be substituted the words "short-term or long-term prisoner".

83.—(1) In subsection (1) of section 37 of the 1991 Act (duration and conditions of licences)—

(a) for the words "subsection (2)" there shall be substituted the words "subsections (1A), (1B) and (2)"; and

(b) the words "any suspension under section 38(2) below or, as the case may be," shall cease to have effect.

(2) After subsection (1A) of that section there shall be inserted the following subsection—

"(1B) Where a prisoner whose sentence is for a term of twelve months or more is released on licence under section 33A(2) or 34A(3) above, subsection (1) above shall have effect as if for the reference to three-quarters of his sentence there were substituted a reference to the difference between—

(a) that proportion of his sentence; and

(b) the duration of the curfew condition to which he is or was subject."

(3) In subsection (2) of that section, for the words "section 36(1) above" there shall be substituted the words "section 34A(3) or 36(1) above".

(4) In subsection (4) of that section—

(a) after the words "a licence" there shall be inserted the words "under this Part"; and

(b) the words "(which shall include on his release conditions as to his supervision by a probation officer)" shall cease to have effect.

(5) After that subsection there shall be inserted the following subsection—

"(4A) The conditions so specified may in the case of a person released on licence under section 34A above whose sentence is for a term of less than twelve months, and shall in any other case, include on the person's release conditions as to his supervision by—

(a) a probation officer appointed for or assigned to the petty sessions area within which the person resides for the time being; or

(b) where the person is under the age of 18 years, a member of a youth offending team established by the local authority within whose area the person resides for the time being."

(6) For subsection (5) of that section there shall be substituted the following subsection—

"(5) The Secretary of State shall not include on release, or subsequently insert, a condition in the licence of a long-term prisoner, or vary or cancel any such condition, except after consultation with the Board."

84. After subsection (5) of section 39 of the 1991 Act (recall of prisoners while on licence) there shall be inserted the following subsection—

"(5A) In the case of a prisoner to whom section 44A below applies, subsections (4)(b) and (5) of that section apply in place of subsection (5) above."

85. [*Repealed by the Powers of Criminal Courts (Sentencing) Act 2000 (c. 6), s.165 and Sched. 12, Part I*]

¹86.—(1) For subsections (1) and (2) of section 41 of the 1991 Act (remand time to count towards time served) there shall be substituted the following subsections—

"(1) Where a person is sentenced to imprisonment for a term in respect of an offence, this section applies to him if the court directs under section 9.87 of the Powers of Criminal Courts (Sentencing) Act 2000 that the number of days for which he was remanded in custody in connection with—

(a) the offence; or

(b) any other offence the charge for which was founded on the same facts or evidence,

shall count as time served by him as part of the sentence.

(2) For the purpose of determining for the purposes of this Part whether a person to whom this section applies—

(a) has served, or would (but for his release) have served, a particular proportion of his sentence; or

(b) has served a particular period,

the number of days specified in the direction shall, subject to subsections (3) and (4) below, be treated as having been served by him as part of that sentence or period."

(2) After subsection (3) of that section there shall be inserted the following subsection—

"(4) Where the period for which a licence granted under section 33A(2), 34A(3) or 36(1) above to a short-term prisoner remains in force cannot exceed one-quarter of his sentence, nothing in subsection (2) above shall have the effect of reducing that period."

87.—(1) In subsection (3) of section 43 of the 1991 Act (young offenders), for the words "subsections (1)" there shall be substituted the words "subsection (1)".

(2) In subsection (5) of that section, for the words "section 37(4)" there shall be substituted the words "section 37(4A)".

88.—(1) In subsection (1) of section 45 of the 1991 Act (fine defaulters and contemnors), for the words "except sections 35 and 40" there shall be substituted the words "except sections 33A, 34A, 35 and 40".

(2) In subsection (3) of that section—

(a) for the words "subsections (1) to (4)" there shall be substituted the words "subsections (1) to (3)"; and

(b) for the words "section 38(2) or 39(1)" there shall be substituted the words "section 39(1) or (2)".

(3) In subsection (4) of that section—

(a) the words "any suspension under section 38(2) below; or" shall cease to have effect; and

(b) for the words "section 39(1)" there shall be substituted the words "section 39(1) or (2)".

89. In subsection (2) of section 46 of the 1991 Act (persons liable to removal from the United Kingdom), for the words from "section 37(4)" to the end there shall be substituted the words "section 37 above shall have effect as if subsection (4A) were omitted".

90. For subsection (2) of section 47 of the 1991 Act (persons extradited to the United Kingdom) there shall be substituted the following subsection—

"(2) In the case of an extradited prisoner, section 9 of the Crime (Sentences) Act 1997 (crediting of periods of remand in custody) shall have effect as if the days for which he was kept in custody while awaiting extradition were days for which he was remanded in custody in connection with the offence, or any other offence the charge for which was founded on the same facts or evidence."

91. In section 50 of the 1991 Act (transfer by order of certain functions to Board), for subsection (3) (including that subsection as applied by any order under subsection (1) of that section) there shall be substituted the following subsection—

"(3) In section 37 above, in subsection (5) for the words "after consultation with the Board" there shall be substituted the words "in accordance with recommendations of the Board", and subsection (6) shall be omitted."

92. [*Repealed by the Powers of Criminal Courts (Sentencing) Act 2000 (c. 6), s.165 and Sched. 12, Part I*]

93. After subsection (7) of section 53 of the 1991 Act (notices of transfer in certain cases involving children) there shall be inserted the following subsection—

"(8) This section shall not apply in any case in which section 51 of the Crime and Disorder Act 1998 (no committal proceedings for indictable-only offences) applies."

94.—(1) In subsection (1) of section 65 of the 1991 Act (supervision of young offenders after release), for the words from "a probation officer" to the end there shall be substituted the following paragraphs—

"(a) a probation officer;

(b) a social worker of a local authority social services department; or

(c) in the case of a person under the age of 18 years on his release, a member of a youth offending team."

(2) After that subsection there shall be inserted the following subsections—

"(1A) Where the supervision is to be provided by a probation officer, the probation officer shall be an officer appointed for or assigned to the petty sessions area within which the offender resides for the time being.

(1B) Where the supervision is to be provided by—

(a) a social worker of a local authority social services department; or

(b) a member of a youth offending team,

the social worker or member shall be a social worker of, or a member of a youth offending team established by, the local authority within whose area the offender resides for the time being."

95. In subsection (1) of section 99 of the 1991 Act (general interpretation), after the definition of "young person" there shall be inserted the following definition—

""youth offending team" means a team established under section 39 of the Crime and Disorder Act 1998."

96. [*Repealed by the Powers of Criminal Courts (Sentencing) Act 2000 (c. 6), s.165 and Sched. 12, Part I*]

97. In paragraph 1(2) of Schedule 5 to the 1991 Act (Parole Board: supplementary provisions), for the words "its functions under Part II of this Act" there shall be substituted the following paragraphs—

"(a) its functions under this Part in respect of long-term and short-term prisoners; and

(b) its functions under Chapter II of Part II of the Crime (Sentences) Act 1997 in respect of life prisoners within the meaning of that Chapter".

NOTE
[1]As amended by the Powers of Criminal Courts (Sentencing) Act 2000 (c. 6), s.165 and Sched. 19, para. 202.

Prisoners and Criminal Proceedings (Scotland) Act 1993 (c. 9)

98.—(1) In subsection (1) of section 1 of the 1993 Act (release of short-term, long-term and life prisoners), at the beginning there shall be inserted the words "Subject to section 26A(4) of thist Act,".

(2) In subsection (2) of that section, at the end there shall be added the words "unless he has before that time been so released, in relation to that sentence, under any provision of this Act".

(3) After subsection (3) of that section there shall be inserted the following subsection—

"(3A) Subsections (1) to (3) above are subject to section 1A of this Act."

99.—(1) After subsection (1) of section 4 of the 1993 Act (persons detained under the Mental Health (Scotland) Act 1984) there shall be inserted the following subsection—

"(1A) This Part of this Act shall apply to a person conveyed to and detained in a hospital pursuant to a hospital direction under section 59A of the 1995 Act as if, while so detained, he was serving the sentence of imprisonment imposed on him at the time at which that direction was made."

(2) The amendment made by sub-paragraph (1) above shall be deemed to have had effect from 1 January 1998.

100. In section 5 of the 1993 Act (fine defaulters and persons in contempt of court)—

(a) in subsection (1), for the words "and (3)" there shall be substituted the words "to (4)"; and

(b) after subsection (3) there shall be inserted the following subsection—

"(4) Where a person has had imposed on him two or more terms of imprisonment or detention mentioned in subsection (1)(a) or (b) above, sections 1A and 27(5) of this Act shall apply to those terms as if they were terms of imprisonment."

101. In section 7 of the 1993 Act (children detained in solemn proceedings)—

(a) in subsection (1)(b), at the end there shall be added the words "unless he has before that time been so released, in relation to that sentence, under any provision of this Act";

(b) after that subsection there shall be inserted the following subsections—

"(2A) This subsection applies where a child detained under section 208 of the 1995 Act is sentenced, while so detained, to a determinate term of detention in a young offenders institution or imprisonment and, by virtue of section 27(5) of this Act, such terms of detention or imprisonment are treated as single term.

(2B) In a case where subsection (2A) applies and the single term mentioned in that subsection is less than four years, the provisions of this section shall apply.

(2C) In a case where subsection (2A) applies and the single term mentioned in that subsection is of four or more years—

(a) section 6 of this Act shall apply to him as if the single term were an equivalent sentence of detention in a young offenders institution, if that term is served in such an institution; and

(b) the provisions of this Act shall apply to him as if the single term were an equivalent sentence of imprisonment, if that term is served in a remand centre or a prison.";

(c) after subsection (4) there shall be inserted the following subsection—

"(4A) Where an order under subsection (3) above is made, the making of the order shall, if there is in force a licence relating to the person in respect of whom the order is made, have the effect of revoking that licence."; and

(d) in subsection (5), after the word "construed" there shall be inserted the words "and sections 1A and 27 shall apply".

102. In section 11 of the 1993 Act (duration of licences), subsections (3)(b) and (4) shall cease to have effect.

103. In section 14 of the 1993 Act (supervised release of short-term prisoners), subsections (2) and (3) shall cease to have effect.

104.—(1) In subsection (1) of section 16 of the 1993 Act (orders for return to prison after commission of further offence), after the word "released" there shall be inserted the words "at any time".

(2) In paragraph (a) of subsection (7) of that section, after the word "shall" there shall be inserted the words, ", if the licence is in force when the order is made,".

(3) Paragraph (b) of that subsection shall cease to have effect.

105. In section 17 of the 1993 Act (revocation of licence), after subsection (4) there shall be inserted the following subsection—

"(4A) Where the case of a prisoner to whom section 3A of this Act applies is referred to the Parole Board under subsection (3) above, subsection (4) of that section shall apply to that prisoner in place of subsection (4) above."

106. In section 20 of the 1993 Act (Parole Board for Scotland), at the end of subsection (4) there shall be inserted the words—

"and rules under this section may make different provision for different classes of prisoner."

107. After subsection (7) of section 27 of the 1993 Act (interpretation) there shall be inserted the following subsection—

"(8) For the purposes of this section "public holiday" means any day on which, in the opinion of the Secretary of State, public offices or other facilities likely to be of use to the prisoner in the area in which he is likely to be following his discharge from prison will be closed."

108. In Schedule 6 to the 1993 Act (transitional provisions), after paragraph 6C there shall be inserted the following paragraph—

"6D. Where a prisoner released on licence is treated by virtue of the provisions of this or any other enactment as a prisoner whose licence was granted under section 2(4) of this Act, the validity of his licence shall not be affected by the absence in the licence of such a condition as is specified in section 12(2) of this Act."

Probation Service Act 1993 (c. 47)

109. [*Repealed by the Powers of Criminal Courts (Sentencing) Act 2000 (c. 6), s.165 and Sched. 12, Part I*]

110.—(1) In subsection (1) of section 17 of that Act (probation committee expenditure), for the words "(5) and (5A)" there shall be substituted the words "and (5)".

(2) Subsection (5A) of that section shall cease to have effect.

Criminal Justice and Public Order Act 1994 (c. 33)

111. In subsection (3) of section 12 of the 1994 Act (escort arrangements and officers), after the words "secure training orders" there shall be inserted the words "or detention and training orders".

112. [*Repealed by the Powers of Criminal Courts (Sentencing) Act 2000 (c. 6), s.165 and Sched. 12, Part I*]

113.—(1) In sub-paragraph (1) of paragraph 3 of Schedule 2 to the 1994 Act (certification of custody officers: England and Wales)—

(a) in paragraph (b), for the words "person in charge" there shall be substituted the word "monitor"; and

(b) in paragraph (c), for the words "person in charge" there shall be substituted the word "governor".

(2) In sub-paragraph (2) of that paragraph, for the words "or person in charge" there shall be substituted the words ", monitor or governor".

Drug Trafficking Act 1994 (c. 37)

114. In subsection (7) of section 2 of the Drug Trafficking Act 1994 (confiscation orders), paragraph (a) shall cease to have effect.

Proceeds of Crime (Scotland) Act 1995 (c. 43)

115. At the end of section 18 of the Proceeds of Crime (Scotland) Act 1995 (order to make material available) there shall be added the following subsection—

"(12) In this section "constable" includes a person commissioned by the Commissioners of Customs and Excise."

116. In subsection (6) of section 19 of that Act (authority for search)—

(a) for the words "subsection (10)" there shall be substituted the words "subsections (10) and (12)"; and

(b) for the words "it applies" there shall be substituted the words "they apply".

Criminal Procedure (Scotland) Act 1995 (c. 46)

117.—(1) For section 18(3) of the 1995 Act (prints and samples) there shall be substituted the following subsection—

"(3) Subject to subsection (4) below, all record of any relevant physical data taken from or provided by a person under subsection (2) above, all samples taken under subsection (6) below and all information derived from such samples shall be destroyed as soon as possible following a decision not to institute criminal proceedings against the person or on the conclusion of such proceedings otherwise than with a conviction or an order under section 246(3) of this Act."

(2) The amendment made by sub-paragraph (1) above shall be deemed to have had effect from 1 August 1997.

118. In subsection (3) of section 49 of the 1995 Act (references to children's hearings), in paragraph (b), after the words "the sheriff" there shall be inserted the words "or district".

119. In section 106(1)(bb) of the 1995 Act (appeals against automatic sentences), which is prospectively inserted by section 18(1) of the Crime and Punishment (Scotland) Act 1997, for the words "205B(3) or 209(1A)" there shall be substituted the words "or 205B(3)".

120. In section 108A of the 1995 Act (prosecutor's right of appeal against refusal to impose

automatic sentence), which is prospectively inserted by section 18(2) of the Crime and Punishment (Scotland) Act 1997, for the words "205B(3) or 209(1A)" there shall be substituted the words "or 205B(3)".

121. In section 118(4A) of the 1995 Act (disposal of appeals), which is prospectively inserted by section 18(5) of the Crime and Punishment (Scotland) Act 1997, in paragraph (c), sub-paragraph (iii) shall cease to have effect.

122. In section 167 of the 1995 Act (findings and sentences in summary proceedings), in subsection (7), at the beginning there shall be inserted the words "Subject to section 204A of this Act,".

123. In subsection (5C) of section 175 of the 1995 Act (right of appeal in summary proceedings), the words "paragraph (a) of" shall be omitted.

124. In subsection (1) of section 307 of the 1995 Act (interpretation), in the definition of "officer of law"—

    (a) after paragraph (b) there shall be inserted the following paragraph—

        "(ba) any person commissioned by the Commissioners of Customs and Excise;"; and

    (b) in paragraph (e), for the words "class or persons" there shall be substituted the words "class of persons".

Criminal Procedure and Investigations Act 1996 (c. 25)

125. In subsection (2) of section 1 of the Criminal Procedure and Investigations Act 1996 (application of Part I of that Act)—

    (a) after paragraph (c) there shall be inserted the following paragraph—

        "(cc) a person is charged with an offence for which he is sent for trial under section 51 (no committal proceedings for indictable-only offences) of the Crime and Disorder Act 1998,"; and

    (b) at the end there shall be inserted the words "or

        (f) a bill of indictment charging a person with an indictable offence is preferred under section 22B(3)(a) of the Prosecution of Offences Act 1985."

126. In section 5 of that Act (compulsory disclosure by accused), after subsection (3) there shall be inserted the following subsection—

    "(3A) Where this Part applies by virtue of section 1(2)(cc), this section does not apply unless—

        (a) copies of the documents containing the evidence have been served on the accused under regulations made under paragraph 1 of Schedule 3 to the Crime and Disorder Act 1998; and

        (b) a copy of the notice under subsection (7) of section 51 of that Act has been served on him under that subsection."

127. In subsection (1) of section 13 of that Act (time limits: transitional)—

    (a) [*Repealed by the Access to Justice 1999 (c.22), s.106 and Sched. 15, Pt III (effective September 27, 1999: s.108(3)).*]

    (b) after the words "section 1(2)(e)" there shall be inserted the words "or (f)".

128. In subsection (1)(a) of section 28 of that Act (introduction to Part III), after the words "committed for trial" there shall be inserted the words ", or sent for trial under section 51 of the Crime and Disorder Act 1998,".

129. In subsection (1) of section 39 of that Act (meaning of pre-trial hearing), after the words "committed for trial for the offence concerned" there shall be inserted the words ", after the accused has been sent for trial for the offence under section 51 of the Crime and Disorder Act 1998,".

Crime (Sentences) Act 1997 (c. 43)

130.—(1) In subsection (3) of section 28 of the 1997 Act (duty to release certain life prisoners), after paragraph (b) there shall be inserted the words "and

    (c) the provisions of this section as compared with those of sections 33(2) and 35(1) of the Criminal Justice Act 1991 ("the 1991 Act")".

    (2) In subsection (7) of that section, in paragraph (c), for the words from "the time when" to the end there shall be substituted the words "he has served one-half of that sentence".

131.—(1) In subsection (2) of section 31 of the 1997 Act (duration and conditions of licences), the words "(which shall include on his release conditions as to his supervision by a probation officer)" shall cease to have effect.

    (2) After that subsection there shall be inserted the following subsection—

        "(2A) The conditions so specified shall include on the prisoner's release conditions as to his supervision by—

    (a) a probation officer appointed for or assigned to the petty sessions area within which the prisoner resides for the time being;

    (b) where the prisoner is under the age of 22, a social worker of the social services department of the local authority within whose area the prisoner resides for the time being; or

    (c) where the prisoner is under the age of 18, a member of a youth offending team established by that local authority under section 39 of the Crime and Disorder Act 1998."

(3) In subsection (6) of that section, for the words "section 24(2) above" there shall be substituted the words "section 46(3) of the 1991 Act", and for the words "the words in parentheses" there shall be substituted the words "subsection (2A) above".

132.—(1) In subsection (1) of section 35 of the 1997 Act (fine defaulters: general), for the words "the 1980 Act" there shall be substituted the words "the Magistrates' Courts Act 1980 ("the 1980 Act")".

(2) [*Repealed by the Powers of Criminal Courts (Sentencing) Act 2000 (c. 6), s.165 and Sched. 12, Part I*].

(3) [*Repealed by the Powers of Criminal Courts (Sentencing) Act 2000 (c. 6), s.165 and Sched. 12, Part I*].

133. In section 54 of the 1997 Act (general interpretation), subsection (2) shall cease to have effect.

134. Subsection (5)(b) of section 57 of the 1997 Act (short title, commencement and extent) shall have effect as if the reference to the Channel islands included a reference to the Isle of Man.

135.—(1) Schedule 1 to the 1997 Act (transfer of prisoners within the British Islands) shall be amended as follows.

(2) In sub-paragraph (3) of paragraph 6—

(a) after paragraph (a) there shall be inserted the following paragraph—

    "(aa) in relation to a person who is supervised in pursuance of a detention and training order, being ordered to be detained for any fialure to comply with requirements under section 76(6)(b) of the Crime and Disorder Act 1998;"; and

(b) in paragraph (b), for the words "recalled to prison under the licence" there shall be substituted the words "recalled or returned to prison".

(3) In paragraph 8—

(a) in sub-paragraph (2), for the words from "sections 10" to "27 of this Act" there shall be substituted the words "sections 33 to 39, 41 to 46 and 65 of the 1991 Act, paragraphs 8, 10 to 13 and 19 of Schedule 12 of that Act and sections 75 to 77 of the Crime and Disorder Act 1998";

(b) in sub-paragraph (4), for the words from "sections 16" to "27 of this Act" there shall be substituted the words "sections 37 to 39, 43 to 46 and 65 of the 1991 Act, paragraphs 8, 10 to 13 and 19 of Schedule 12 to that Act and sections 76 and 77 of the Crime and Disorder Act 1998";

(c) in sub-paragraph (5), after the words "Any provision of" there shall be inserted the words "Part II of the 1991 Act or"; and

(d) after sub-paragraph (5) there shall be inserted the following sub-paragraphs—

    "(6) Section 41 of the 1991 Act, as applied by sub-paragraph (2) or (4) above, shall have effect as if section 67 of the Criminal Justice Act 1967 (computation of sentences of imprisonment passed in England and Wales) or, as the case may require, section 9 of this Act extended to Scotland.

    (7) Section 65(7)(b) of the 1991 Act, as applied by sub-paragraph (2) or (4) above, shall have effect as if the reference to a young offender institution were a reference to a young offenders institution."

(4) In paragraph 9–

(a) in sub-paragraph (1), paragraph (a) and, in paragraph (b), the words "to that and" shall cease to have effect;

(b) in sub-paragraph (2), for the words from "sections 10" to "27 of this Act" there shall be substituted the words "sections 33 to 46 and 65 of the 1991 Act, paragraphs 8, 10 to 13 and 19 of Schedule 12 to that Act and sections 75 to 77 of the Crime and Disorder Act 1998";

(c) in sub-paragraph (4), for the words from "section 16" to "27 of this Act" there shall be substituted the words "sections 37 to 40A, 43 to 46 and 65 of the 1991 Act, paragraphs 8, 10 to 13 and 19 of Schedule 12 to that Act and sections 76 and 77 of the Crime and Disorder Act 1998";

(d) sub-paragraph (5) shall cease to have effect;

(e) in sub-paragraph (6), after the words "Any provision of" there shall be inserted the words "Part II of the 1991 Act or"; and

(f) after sub-paragraph (6) there shall be inserted the following sub-paragraphs—

"(7) Section 41 of the 1991 Act, as applied by sub-paragraph (2) or (4) above, shall have effect as if section 67 of the Criminal Justice Act 1967 or, as the case may require, section 9 of this Act extended to Northern Ireland.

(8) Section 65(7)(b) of the 1991 Act, as applied by sub-paragraph (1), (2) or (4) above, shall have effect as if the reference to a young offender institution were a reference to a young offenders centre."

(5) In paragraph 10—

(a) in sub-paragraph (2)(a)—

(10) In sub-paragraph (1) of paragraph 20, in the definition of "supervision", after the word "purpose" there shall be inserted the words "or a detention and training order".

136. In Schedule 2 to the 1997 Act (repatriation of prisoners to the British Islands), paragraphs 4 and 8 are hereby repealed.

137. In Schedule 4 to the 1997 Act (minor and consequential amendments), the following provisions are hereby repealed, namely—

(a) in paragraph 6, sub-paragraph (1)(b);

(b) paragraphs 9 and 11; and

(c) in paragraph 12, sub-paragraph (4).

138.—(1) In Schedule 5 to the 1997 Act (transitional provisions and savings), paragraphs 1 to 4 and 6 are hereby repealed and the following provisions shall cease to have effect, namely—

(a) paragraph 5(2);

(b) paragraphs 8, 9(1) and 10(1);

(c) in paragraph 11, sub-paragraph (1), in sub-paragraph (2)(c), the words "or Part III of the 1997 Act" and, in sub-paragraph (3), the words from the beginning to "1995; and"; and

(d) in paragraph 12, sub-paragraph (1) and, in sub-paragraph (2)(c), the words "or Part III of the 1997 Act".

(2) In paragraph 11(2) of that Schedule—

(a) in paragraph (a)—

(i) for the words from "sections 15" to "1997 Act" there shall be substituted the words "sections 1, 1A, 3, 3A, 5, 6(1)(a), 7, 9, 11 to 13, 15 to 21, 26A and 27 of, and Schedules 2 and 6 to, the Prisoners and Criminal Proceedings (Scotland) Act 1993 ("the 1993 Act")"; and

(ii) for the words "the 1989 Act" there shall be substituted the words "the Prisons (Scotland) Act 1989 ("the 1989 Act")"; and

(b) in paragraph (b), for the words from "sections 15" to "1997 Act" there shall be substituted the words "sections 1A, 2(4), 3A, 11 to 13, 15 to 21, 26A and 27 of, and Schedules 2 and 6 to, the 1993 Act".

(3) In paragraph 12(2) of that Schedule—

(a) in paragraph (a)—

(i) for the words from "sections 15" to "1997 Act" there shall be substituted the words "sections 1, 1A, 3, 3A, 5, 6(1)(a), 7, 9, 11 to 13, 15 to 21, 26A and 27 of, and Schedules 2 and 6 to, the Prisoners and Criminal Proceedings (Scotland) Act ("the 1993 Act")"; and

(ii) for the words "the 1989 Act" there shall be substituted the words "the Prisons (Scotland) Act 1989 ("the 1989 Act"); and

(b) in paragraph (b), for the words from "sections 15" to "1997 Act" there shall be substituted the words "sections 1A, 2(4), 3A, 11 to 13, 15 to 21, 26A and 27 of, and Schedules 2 and 6 to, the 1993 Act".

139. In Schedule 6 to the 1997 (repeals), the entries relating to sections 33 to 51 and 65 of the 1991 Act are hereby repealed.

Crime and Punishment (Scotland) Act 1997 (c. 48)

140. Section 4 of the Crime and Punishment (Scotland) Act 1997 (supervised release orders) is hereby repealed.

141.—(1) In Schedule 1 to that Act (minor and consequential amendments), the following provisions are hereby repealed, namely—

(a) paragraphs 1, 9(7), 10(2)(a), 13(3) and 21(3); and

(b) in paragraph 15, sub-paragraphs (2)(a), (3)(e), (4) to (7), (9), (10)(a), (11)(b), (12), (13) to (15) and (17).

(2) In paragraph 14 of that Schedule, for sub-paragraph (16) there shall be substituted the following sub-paragraph—

"(16) In section 27(1) (interpretation), in the definition of "supervised release order" the words "(as inserted by section 14 of this Act)" shall cease to have effect."

142. Schedule 2 to that Act (transitional provisions) is hereby repealed.

143.—(1) Schedule 3 to that Act (repeals) shall be amended in accordance with this paragraph.

(2) In the entry relating to the Prisons (Scotland) Act 1989, in the third column, the words "In section 39, subsection (7)" are hereby repealed.

(3) In the entry relating to the Prisoners and Criminal Proceedings (Scotland) Act 1993—

(a) the words relating to sections 1, 3(2), 5, 6(1), 7, 9, 12(3), 16, 17(1), 20, 24, and Schedule 1;

(b) in the words relating to section 14, the words "and in subsection (4), the words "short-term"";

(c) in the words relating to 27(1)—

(i) the words "the definitions of "short term prisoner" and "long-term prisoner" and";

(ii) in the words relating to the definition of "supervised release order" the words "and the words from "but" to the end"; and

(d) the words relating to section 27(2), (3), (5) and (6),

are hereby repealed.

(4) In the entry relating to the Criminal Procedure (Scotland) Act 1995, in the third column, the words relating to section 44 are hereby repealed.

Sex Offenders Act 1997 (c. 51)

144. In subsection (1)(a) of section 4 of the Sex Offenders Act 1997 (young sex offenders), after the word "under" there shall be inserted the words "a detention and training order or".

SCHEDULE 10

Section 120(2)

REPEALS

Chapter	Short title	Extent of repeal
30 Geo 3 c. 48.	Treason Act 1790.	The whole Act.
36 Geo 3 c. 7.	Treason Act 1795.	The whole Act.
36 Geo 3 c. 31.	Treason by Women Act (Ireland) 1796.	The whole Act.
57 Geo 3 c. 6.	Treason Act 1817.	The whole Act.
11 & 12 Vict c. 12.	Treason Felony Act 1848.	Section 2.
21 & 22 Geo 5 c. 24.	Sentence of Death (Expectant Mothers) Act 1931.	The whole Act.
23 Geo 5 c. 12.	Children and Young Persons Act 1933.	In section 47(2), the words from the beginning to "court; and". In Schedule 2, in paragraph 15(a), the word "shall", in the second place where it occurs, and, in paragraph 17, the words "or, if a metropolitan stipendiary magistrate, may sit alone".
1945 c. 15 (N.I.).	Criminal Justice Act (Northern Ireland) 1945.	Sections 32 and 33.
1967 c. 80.	Criminal Justice Act 1967.	In section 56, subsections (3), (6) and (13).
1968 c. 19.	Criminal Appeal Act 1968.	In section 10(2), the words "(other than a supervision order within the meaning of that Part)".
1969 c. 54.	Children and Young Persons Act 1969.	Section 12D. Section 13(2). In section 16, subsection (10) and, in subsection (11), the words "seventeen or". Section 23(14)(a). In section 34, in subsection (1), paragraph (a) and, in paragraph (c), the words "7(7), 7(8),". Section 69(5). In Schedule 6, the entries relating to sections 55, 56(1) and 59(1) of the Children and Young Persons Act 1933.

Chapter	Short title	Extent of repeal
1972 c. 71.	Criminal Justice Act 1972.	Section 49.
1973 c. 62.	Powers of Criminal Courts Act 1973.	In section 1, in subsections (8)(b) and (8A) the words "37 or".
		Section 1B(10).
		In section 1C(1), paragraph (b) and the word "and" immediately preceding it.
		In section 2(1), the words "by a probation officer" and the words from "For the purposes" to "available evidence".
		Section 11.
		Section 14(8).
		In section 31, in subsection (3A), the words "Subject to subsections (3B) and (3C) below,", subsections (3B) and (3C), in subsection (4), the words "4 or" and, in subsection (6), the words "about committal by a magistrates' court to the Crown Court".
		Section 32(5).
		Section 42(2).
		In Schedule 1A, paragraph 6(7).
		In Schedule 5, paragraph 35.
1976 c. 63.	Bail Act 1976.	In section 3(5), the words "If it appears that he is unlikely to remain in Great Britain until the time appointed for him to surrender to custody".
1980 c. 43.	Magistrates' Courts Act 1980.	
		Section 37.
		In sections 38(2) and 38A(2), the words ", in accordance with section 56 of the Criminal Justice Act 1967,".
		In section 108(2), the words "a probation order or".
		In section 125(4)(c), the word "and" at the end of sub-paragraph (ii).
		In section 126, the word "and" at the end of paragraph (c).
		In Schedule 7, paragraph 120(b).
1982 c. 48.	Criminal Justice Act 1982.	Section 1A(4A).
		Section 1B.
		In section 1C(2), the words "but if he is under 18 at the time of the direction, only for a temporary purpose".
		In section 3(1)(a), the words "under section 1A above".
		Section 18(7).
		In section 19, in subsection (3)(a), the words "revoke it and" and, in subsection (5), the words "revoke the attendance centre order and".
		Section 66(3).
		In Schedule 14, paragraph 28.
1987 c. 42.	Family Law Reform Act 1987.	
		Section 8(1).
		In Schedule 2, paragraph 26.
1988 c. 33.	Criminal Justice Act 1988.	Section 69(2).
		In Schedule 15, paragraph 40.
1989 c. 45.	Prisons (Scotland) Act 1989.	
		In section 39(7), the words from "and the foregoing" to the end.

Chapter	Short title	Extent of repeal
1991 c. 53.	Criminal Justice Act 1991.	In section 6(4), the word "and" immediately following paragraph (e). In section 31(1), in the definition of "custodial sentence", in paragraph (b), the words "or a secure training order under section 1 of the Criminal Justice and Public Order Act 1994". Section 33(4). In section 37, in subsection (1), the words "any suspension under section 38(2) below or, as the case may be," and, in subsection (4), the words "(which shall include on his release conditions as to his supervision by a probation officer)". Section 38. In section 45(4), the words "any suspension under section 38(2) below; or". In section 61(1), paragraph (b) and the word "or" immediately preceding that paragraph. Section 62. In Schedule 2, in paragraphs 3(1)(d) and 4(1)(d), the words "revoke the order and" and, in paragraph 17(1), the words from "and the court" to the end. In Schedule 11, paragraphs 10, 11 and 14. In Schedule 12, paragraph 17(3).
1993 c. 9.	Prisoners and Criminal Proceedings (Scotland) Act 1993.	Section 11(3)(b) and (4). Section 14(2) and (3). Section 16(7)(b). In paragraph 6B(1) of Schedule 6, the word "and" after head (a).
1993 c. 47.	Probation Service Act 1993.	Section 17(5A).
1994 c. 33.	Criminal Justice and Public Order Act 1994.	Sections 1 to 4. Section 20. In section 35, in subsection (1), the words "who has attained the age of fourteen years" and subsection (6). Section 130(4). In Schedule 10, paragraph 42.
1994 c. 37.	Drug Trafficking Act 1994.	Section 2(7)(a).
1995 c. 46.	Criminal Procedure (Scotland) Act 1995.	Section 118(4A)(c)(iii). In section 175(5C), the words "paragraph (a) of". In section 209(1), the words "not less than twelve months but".
1997 c. 43.	Crime (Sentences) Act 1997.	Section 1. Section 8. Sections 10 to 27. In section 31(2), the words "(which shall include on his release conditions as to his supervision by a probation officer)". In section 35, in subsection (5), paragraph (c) and the word "and" at the end of paragraph (d), and in subsection (8), in paragraph (a), the words "to revoke the

Chapter	Short title	Extent of repeal
		order and deal with an offender for the offence in respect of which the order was made" and the word "and" at the end of that paragraph. Section 43(4). Section 54(2). In Schedule 1, in paragraph 9(1), paragraph (a) and, in paragraph (b), the words "to that and", paragraph 9(5), paragraph 10(4), in paragraph 11(6), the words "or Part III of the 1997 Act", in paragraph 12(5), in the Table, the entry relating to the expression "prison rules" and, in paragraph 13(5), in the Table, the entry relating to the expression "prison rules". In Schedule 2, paragraphs 4 and 8. In Schedule 4, paragraph 6(1)(b), paragraphs 9 and 11 and paragraph 12(4). In Schedule 5, paragraphs 1 to 4, paragraph 5(2), paragraph 6, paragraph 8, paragraph 9(1), paragraph 10(1), in paragraph 11, sub-paragraph (1), in sub-paragraph (2)(c), the words "or Part III of the 1997 Act" and, in sub-paragraph (3), the words from the beginning to "1995; and", and in paragraph 12, sub-paragraph (1) and, in sub-paragraph (2)(c), the words "or Part III of the 1997 Act". In Schedule 6, the entries relating to sections 33 to 51 and 65 of the Criminal Justice Act 1991.
1997 c. 48.	Crime and Punishment (Scotland) Act 1997.Section 4.	Chapter I of Part III. In Schedule 1, paragraph 1, paragraph 9(7), paragraph 10(2)(a), paragraph 13(3), in paragraph 14, sub-paragraphs (2)(a), (3) (e), (4) to (7), (9), (10)(a), (11)(b), (12), (13) to (15) and (17), and paragraph 21(3). Schedule 2. In Schedule 3, in the entry relating to the Prisons (Scotland) Act 1989, the words "In section 39, subsection (7)", in the entry relating to the Prisoners and Criminal Proceedings (Scotland) Act 1993, the words relating to sections 1, 3(2), 5, 6(1), 7, 9, 12(3), 16, 17(1), 20, 24, 27(2), (3), (5) and (6) and Schedule 1, in the words relating to section 14, the words "and, in subsection (4), the words "short-term"", in the words relating to section 27(1), the words "the definitions of "short term prisoner" and "long-term prisoner" and" and "and the words from "but" to the end" and, in the entry relating to the Criminal Procedure (Scotland) Act 1995, the words relating to section 44.
1997 c. 50.	Police Act 1997.	In section 94(4), the word "and" immediately preceding paragraph (c).

Division A

Part II

Miscellaneous Statutes

CONTENTS

SHERIFF COURTS AND LEGAL OFFICERS (SCOTLAND) ACT 1927

(1927 c. 35)

ARRANGEMENT OF SECTIONS

PART I

SHERIFF CLERKS, PROCURATORS FISCAL, ETC.

PART II

MISCELLANEOUS PROVISIONS

An Act to amend the law relating to the offices of Sheriff Clerk, Procurator Fiscal, and Commissary Clerk in Scotland, and to make further provisions regarding Sheriff Courts.   [22nd December 1927]

PART I

Sheriff Clerks, Procurators Fiscal, etc.

Appointment of sheriff clerk and procurator fiscal

[1]**1.**—(1) The right of appointing to and removing from office of Sheriff Clerk shall be vested in one of His Majesty's Principal Secretaries of State. There shall be a sheriff clerk for each sheriffdom in Scotland as heretofore, provided that it shall be lawful for the Secretary of State, where the division of sheriff court districts or other circumstances appear to him to render such a course expedient, to appoint a sheriff clerk for an area other than a sheriffdom whether situated entirely within one sheriffdom or not.

[2](2) The right of appointing to and removing from the office of procurator fiscal shall be vested in the Lord Advocate, and the Lord Advocate may from time to time fix the number of procurators fiscal in Scotland, and the limits of the districts for which such procurators shall act.

[3, 4](3) Notwithstanding anything in either of the foregoing subsections but subject to subsections (4) and (5) below, no sheriff clerk or procurator fiscal shall be removed from his office except upon a report by the Lord President of the Court of Session and the Lord Justice Clerk:

> Provided that no such report shall be required in any case of retirement of a sheriff clerk or procurator fiscal in circumstances which would qualify him for an award under the principal civil service pension scheme within the meaning of section 2 of the Superannuation Act 1972

and for the time being in force, or in consequence of the operation of an age limit.

[5](4) The right vested—

(a) in the Secretary of State under subsection (1) above shall include the right to transfer the sheriff clerk of one sheriff clerk court district to an office, whether of sheriff clerk or (however styled) or sheriff clerk depute, in another sheriff court district;

(b) in the Lord Advocate under subsection (2) above shall include the right to transfer the procurator fiscal of one district to an office, whether of procurator fiscal or (however styled) of procurator fiscal depute, in another district

where in the opinion of the Secretary of State or, as the case may be, of the Lord Advocate the transfer is for the purpose of securing efficient organisation and administration.

(5) It is hereby declared that, for the purposes of subsection (3) above, a transfer under subsection (4) above is not a removal from office.

NOTES

[1]As amended by the Sheriff Court (Scotland) Act 1971 (c. 58), Sched. 1, para. 1.
[2]As amended by the Scotland Act 1998 (c. 46), Sched. 8 and Sched. 9.
[3]As amended by Law Reform (Miscellaneous Provisions) (Scotland) Act 1985 (c. 73), s.47(1).
[4]As amended by Superannuation Act 1972 (c. 11), s.29, Sched. 6, para. 9.
[5]Subsection inserted by Law Reform (Miscellaneous Provisions) (Scotland) Act 1985 (c. 73), s.47(2).

Appointment of sheriff clerk and procurator fiscal deputes

[1]**2.** In each sheriffdom or district the Secretary of State and the Lord Advocate may respectively appoint such sheriff clerk deputes or procurator fiscal deputes as may be necessary.

NOTE

[1]As amended by virtue of Sheriff Courts (Scotland) Act 1971 (c. 58), Sched. 1, para. 1 and by Scotland Act 1998 (c. 46), Sched. 8 and Sched. 9.

Whole-time sheriff clerks and procurators fiscal and deputes

[1]**3.** The Secretary of State in the case of the office of any sheriff clerk or sheriff clerk depute, and the Lord Advocate in the case of the office of any procurator fiscal or procurator fiscal depute, may from time to time, having regard to the amount of business to be performed, determine that such office shall be a whole-time office; and no person appointed to any such office under this Act (in this Act referred to as a whole-time officer) shall engage directly or indirectly in practice as a law agent or carry on any employment of such nature as will, in the opinion of the Secretary of State or of the Lord Advocate as the case may be, interfere with the due discharge of the duties of his office.

NOTE

[1]As amended by Scotland Act 1998 (c. 46), Sched. 8 and Sched. 9.

Vacancy in office of sheriff clerk, procurator fiscal or deputes

4. In the case of a vacancy in the office of sheriff clerk, sheriff clerk depute, procurator fiscal or procurator fiscal depute, or in the case of the incapacity of any such officer, it shall be lawful for the Secretary of State and the Lord Advocate respectively to give directions for the discharge during the vacancy or incapacity of the duties of such officer by any other officer in the sheriff clerk or procurator fiscal service respectively, or by any other fit person.

Whole-time clerks

[1]**5.** The Secretary of State and the Lord Advocate may respectively appoint such whole-time clerks or other whole-time assistants to a sheriff clerk or procurator fiscal as may be deemed necessary, and such clerks or other assistants are in this Act referred to as whole-time clerks.

NOTE
[1]As amended by Scotland Act 1998 (c. 46), Sched. 8 and Sched. 9.

Tenure of whole-time officers

6. [*Repealed by the Scotland Act 1998 (Consequential Modifications) (No. 2) Order 1999 (S.I. 1999 No. 1820) art.4, Sched.2, para.14 and Pt IV (effective July 1, 1999).*]
...

Secretary of State may issue instructions etc.

[1]**8.**—(1) The Secretary of State as regards sheriff clerks and the Lord Advocate as regards procurators fiscal may from time to time issue such instructions as may be deemed necessary for the purpose of giving effect to the provisions of this Act.

[2](2) The Secretary of State may from time to time by order make such modifications and adaptations of the provisions of any enactment as may be necessary in consequence of the exercise of the power vested in him by subsection (1) of section 1 of this Act to appoint a sheriff clerk for an area other than a sheriffdom.

NOTES
[1]As amended by the Sheriff Courts (Scotland) Act 1971 (c. 58), s.20.
[2]As amended by the Sheriff Courts (Scotland) Act 1971 (c. 58), Sched. 1, para. 1.

Deputation by sheriff clerk or procurator fiscal

9. Notwithstanding anything contained in section 2 of this Act, it shall be lawful for a sheriff clerk with the consent of the Secretary of State, and for a procurator fiscal with the consent of the Lord Advocate, to grant a deputation to a fit person for whose actings (except in the case where such person is a whole-time clerk) he shall be responsible.

Prosecutions at instance of procurator fiscal

[1]**12.** It shall be lawful for the Lord Advocate, by Order to direct in the case of any Act of Parliament that, notwithstanding anything therein contained all proceedings in the sheriff court under the Summary Jurisdiction (Scotland) Acts for a contravention of or an offence against such Act of Parliament shall be taken by and at the instance of the procurator fiscal.

NOTE
[1]As amended by the Scotland Act 1998 (c. 46), Sched. 8 and Sched. 9; as amended by the Scotland Act 1998 (Consequential Modifications) (No. 2) Order 1999 (S.I. 1999 No. 1820) art.4, Sched.2, para.14 and Pt IV (effective July 1, 1999).

Expenses

13. [*Repealed by the Scotland Act 1998 (Consequential Modifications) (No. 2) Order 1999 (S.I. 1999 No. 1820) art.4, Sched.2, para.14 and Pt IV (effective July 1, 1999).*]
...

PART II

Miscellaneous provisions

Summary of [sic] complaints at instance of procurator fiscal

20. A complaint under the Summary Jurisdiction (Scotland) Acts at the instance of a person discharging the duties of procurator fiscal for any district, may, in the event of that person dying or ceasing to be entitled to discharge the duties of procurator fiscal for such district, be taken up and proceeded with by any other person entitled to discharge such duties.

POLICE (SCOTLAND) ACT 1967

(1967 c. 77)

ARRANGEMENT OF SECTIONS

PART I

ORGANISATION OF POLICE FORCES

Police areas, police authorities and police forces

PART III

MISCELLANEOUS AND GENERAL

Offences and legal proceedings

Supplemental

An Act to consolidate certain enactments relating to police forces in Scotland and to the execution of warrants in the border counties of England and Scotland and to repeal certain provisions relating to the police in Scotland which have ceased to have any effect.

[27th July 1967]

PART I

ORGANISATION OF POLICE FORCES

Police areas, police authorities and police forces

Establishment of police forces

3.—(1) A police force shall consist of a chief constable and—
(a) permanent and probationary whole-time constables (thereafter in this Act referred to as "regular constables") and
(b) part-time constables (hereafter in this Act referred to as "special constables").
not exceeding such number in each case as may from time to time be

authorised by the police authority with the consent of the Secretary of State, and may in addition include temporary whole-time constables (hereafter in this Act referred to as "temporary constables") not exceeding such number as may be so authorised.

PART III

Offences and legal proceedings

Assaults on constables, etc.

41.—(1) Any person who—

(a) assaults, resists, obstructs, molests or hinders a constable in the execution of his duty or a person assisting a constable in the execution of his duty, or;

(b) rescues or attempts to rescue, or assists or attempts to assist the escape of any person in custody,

shall be guilty of an offence and on summary conviction shall be liable—

[1](i) where he has not within the period of two years immediately preceding the commission of the said offence, been convicted of an offence against this section, to a fine not exceeding level 4 on the standard scale or to imprisonment for a period not exceeding three months or to both such fine and such imprisonment;

[2](ii) where he has, within the first-mentioned period, been convicted of an offence against this section, to imprisonment for a period not exceeding nine months or to a fine not exceeding the prescribed sum within the meaning of section 225(8) of the Criminal Procedure (Scotland) Act 1995, or to both.

(2) The reference in subsection (1) of this section to a person in custody shall be construed as a reference to a person—

(a) who is in the lawful custody of a constable or any person assisting a constable in the execution of his duty, or

[3](b) who is in the act of eluding or escaping from such custody, whether or not he has actually been arrested.

[4](3) This section also applies to a constable who is a member of a police force maintained in England and Wales or in Northern Ireland when he is executing a warrant or otherwise acting in Scotland by virtue of any enactment conferring powers on him in Scotland.

NOTES

[1]Amended by s.289G of the Criminal Procedure (Scotland) Act 1975 (c. 21) as replaced by s.22(2) of the Criminal Procedure (Scotland) Act 1995 (c. 46).

[2]Added by s.57 of the Criminal Justice (Scotland) Act 1980 as replaced by s.225(8) of the Criminal Procedure (Scotland) Act 1995 (c. 46).

[3]Section 295 of the Criminal Procedure (Scotland) Act 1995 (c. 46) provides that any person required or authorised by or under that Act *or any other enactment* to be taken to any place, or to be detained or kept in custody, shall while being so taken or detained or kept, be deemed to be in legal custody.

[4]Inserted by s.168(2) and Sched. 10 of the Criminal Justice and Public Order Act 1994 (c. 33).

Causing disaffection

42.—[1](1) Any person who causes, or attempts to cause, or does any act calculated to cause, disaffection amongst the constables of any police force, or who induces, or attempts to induce, or does any act calculated to induce, any constable to withhold his services, shall be guilty of an offence, and shall be liable—

[2](a) on summary conviction, to a fine not exceeding level 4 on the standard scale or to imprisonment for a period not exceeding three months or to both such fine and such imprisonment.

A–584

(b) on conviction on indictment, to imprisonment for a period not exceeding two years.

(2) Any person convicted of an offence against this section shall be permanently disqualified from becoming or remaining a constable.

NOTES
[1]As amended by s.93 and Sched. 9 of the Police and Magistrates' Court Act 1994 (c. 29).
[2]As amended by s.289G of the Criminal Procedure (Scotland) Act 1975 as replaced by s.225(2) of the Criminal Procedure (Scotland) Act 1995 (c. 46).

Impersonation etc.

43.—[1](1) Subject to the provisions of this section, any person who—

(a) takes the name, designation or character of a constable for the purpose of obtaining admission into any house or other place or of doing or procuring to be done any act which such person would not be entitled to do or procure to be done of his own authority, or for any other unlawful purpose, or

(b) wears any article of police uniform without the permission of the police authority for the police area in which he is, or

(c) has in his possession any article of police uniform without being able to account satisfactorily for his possession thereof.

shall be guilty of an offence and on summary conviction shall be liable to a fine not exceeding level 4 of the standard scale or to imprisonment for a period not exceeding three months.

(2) Nothing in subsection (1) of this section shall make it an offence to wear any article of police uniform in the course of taking part in a stage play, or music hall or circus performance, or of performing in or producing a cinematograph film or television broadcast.

(3) In this section "article of police uniform" means any article of uniform or any distinctive badge or mark usually issued by any police authority to constables, or any article having the appearance of such article, badge or mark.

NOTE
[1]As amended by s.3(2) and Sched. 2 of the Criminal Procedure (Consequential Provisions) (Scotland) Act 1995, (c. 40).

Offences by constables

44.—(1) Any constable who wilfully absents himself from duty otherwise than in accordance with regulations made under Part II of this Act shall be guilty of an offence.

(2) Any constable who neglects or violates his duty shall be guilty of an offence.

(3) Any constable who fails without reasonable excuse to return to his chief constable (or other person appointed by the chief constable for the purpose), immediately upon being ordered to do so, any accoutrements or clothing which have been issued to him for the execution of his duty shall be guilty of an offence.

(4) Any person who has been a constable of a police force and has failed without reasonable excuse to return to the chief constable of that force (or other person appointed by the chief constable for the purpose), when he ceased to be constable of the force, any accoutrements or clothing which were issued to him for the execution of his duty shall be guilty of an offence.

[1](5) Any person guilty of an offence against this section shall, without prejudice to the operation of any regulations made under this Act, or to any civil proceedings, be liable on summary conviction to a fine not exceeding level 3 on the standard scale or to imprisonment for a period not exceeding sixty days.

Warrant to search for police accoutrements and clothing

45.—(1) If a sheriff, justice of the peace or magistrate of a burgh is satisfied on information on oath that there has been a failure to return duly any accoutrements or clothing issued to a constable for the execution of his duty, and that any of the said accoutrements or clothing are in any premises or place, he may grant a warrant to any constable named therein to enter and search the said premises or place at any reasonable hour, if necessary by force, and to seize and detain any of the said accoutrements or clothing which he may find therein.

General interpretation

51.—(1) In this Act unless the context otherwise requires the following expressions shall have the meanings hereby assigned to them respectively, that is to say—

> ...
> [1]"constable" means a constable (including the chief constable) of a police force;

NOTE
[1]The original distinction made reference to s.3(1) of the 1967 Act, but the definition was repealed in part by s.93 and Sched. 9 of the Police and Magistrates' Courts Act 1994.

DISTRICT COURTS (SCOTLAND) ACT 1975

(1975 c. 20)

ARRANGEMENT OF SECTIONS

PART I

DISTRICT COURTS

PART II

JUSTICES AND CLERKS OF THE PEACE

Justices of the peace

Clerks of the peace

PART III

MISCELLANEOUS AND GENERAL

Miscellaneous

General

An Act to make provision as respects district courts and justices of the peace in Scotland, to amend sections 28 and 29 of the Licensing (Scotland) Act 1959; and for connected purposes.

[27th March 1975]

NOTE

Any reference in any provision to government departments; or to, or to any part or officer of, any government department (however described in that provision) is to be read, so far as the effect of the Scotland Act 1998 Act (c. 46) makes it necessary or expedient to do so, as including or being a reference to, or to any corresponding part or member of the staff of, the Scottish Administration: effective July 1, 1999 by the Scotland Act 1998 (Consequential Modifications) (No. 2) Order 1999 (S.I.1999 No.1820), art. 2.

PART I

DISTRICT COURTS

Abolition of existing inferior courts and establishment of district courts

¹**1.**—(1) On 16th May 1975 the inferior courts in Scotland immediately before that date (in this Act referred to as "the existing courts") shall cease to exist, and on that date be established. in accordance with the provisions of this Act, a district court for each commission area except in the case of a commission area in respect of which the Secretary of State otherwise directs, having regard to the likely lack of business for such a court.

In this subsection, "inferior courts " means all justice of the peace courts. quarter sessions, burgh courts, police courts, and the court of the bailie of the river and firth of Clyde.

(2) On and after that date, all functions of burgh magistrates, not otherwise provided for, shall be exercisable by a justice of the peace.

(3) Where proceedings wore instituted before that date in any existing court and those proceedings have not been completed by that date, then, for the purpose of enabling those proceedings to be continued on and after that date, and for preserving in other respects the continuity of the administration of justice —

(a) the district court having jurisdiction in the area where the proceedings were instituted shall be treated as succeeding to, and being the same court as, the existing court concerned. and any verdict, sentence, order, complaint, notice, citation, warrant, bail bond or other proceedings or document shall have effect accordingly; and

(b) the clerk and the prosecutor of the existing court shall transfer all records, productions and documents relating to those proceedings to the clerk or, as the case may be, the prosecutor of the district court concerned.

(4) Where proceedings were instituted after 14th May 1969 in any existing court and were completed on or before 15th May 1975, the clerk of that court shall transfer all complaints, minutes and other records relating thereto to the clerk of the district concerned.

(5) In the case of any other record or document relating to proceedings in the existing courts, the person having custody of it shall, on request by or on behalf of a district court, release it to that court for the purpose of proceedings in that court, and any record or document so released shall be returned to the person who released it as soon as may be after it has ceased be required for the said purposes.

NOTE

¹Reference to the "Secretary of State" shall be read as a reference to the "Scottish Ministers" by reason of s.53 of the Scotland Act 1998 (c.46).

Further provision as to establishment and disestablishment of district courts

[1]**1A.**—(1) Where it appears to the Secretary of State that—

(a) there is insufficient business or the district court in a particular commission area; and

(b) such insufficiency of business is likely to continue,

he may by order provide that the district court for that area cease to exit on a specified date.

(2) Where it appears to the Secretary of State that, in a commission area in which there is no district court, there is likely to be a sufficient business to justify the establishment of such a court, he may by order provide for the establishment of such a court in that area on a specified date.

(3) An order under subsection (1) or (2) above may contain all such provisions as appear to the Secretary of State to be necessary or expedient for rendering the order of full effect and any incidental, supplemental or consequential provisions which appear to him to be necessary or expedient for the purposes of the order, including, but without prejudice to the generality of the foregoing words, provisions amending, repealing or revoking any enactment (whether passed or made before or after the commencement of this enactment).

[3](4) Before making an order under subsection (1) or (2) above, the Secretary of State shall consult the local authority council for the area concerned, and such other persons as appear to him to have an interest in the proposed order.

(5) Orders under subsection (1) or (2) above shall be made by statutory instrument, which shall be subject to annulment in pursuance of a resolution of either House of Parliament.

NOTES

[1]Inserted by the Law Reform (Miscellaneous Provisions)(Scotland) Act 1985 (c.73), s.33.

[2]Reference to the "Secretary of State" shall be read as a reference to the "Scottish Ministers" by reason of s.53 of the Scotland Act 1998 (c.46).

[3]As amended by the Local Government etc. (Scotland) Act 1994 (c39), s.180(1) and Sched.

District of, and exercise of jurisdiction by, district court

2. [*Amended by the Bail etc (Scotland) Act 1980 (c.40), s.10(3) then repealed by the Criminal Procedure (Consequential Provisions)(Scotland) Act 1995 (c.40), s.6 and Sched. 5 and was consolidated in the Criminal Procedure (Scotland) Act 1995 (c.40), s.6.*]

Jurisdiction and powers of district court

3. [*Repealed by the Criminal Procedure (Consequential Provisions) (Scotland) Act 1995 (c.40), s.6 and Sched.5 and thereafter consolidated in the Criminal Procedure (Scotland) Act 1995(c.46), s.7.*]

Procedure and practice in the district court

4. [*Repealed by the Criminal Procedure (Consequential Provisions) (Scotland) Act 1995 (c.40), s.6 and Sched.5 and was then consolidated in the Criminal Procedure (Scotland) Act 1995 (c.46), s.8.*]

Stipendiary magistrates

[1]**5.**—(1) Subject to subsections (2) and (3) below, a local authority may appoint a stipendiary magistrate to sit in a district court, and the terms and conditions of such an appointment, including superannuation and other benefits, shall be those applicable to a service in a local government.

(2) A person shall not be appointed to be a stipendiary magistrate unless he is, and has been for at least five years, legally qualified, and for the

purposes of this subsection a person shall be legally qualified if he is an advocate or a solicitor.

(3) A person shall not be appointed to be a stipendiary magistrate until the Secretary of State approves—

(a) the establishment of the office of stipendiary magistrate in the district court concerned;

(b) the salary which it is proposed should pertain to that office; and

(c) the appointment of the person proposed for that office.

(4) Where it appears to the Secretary of State that it is expedient so to do in order to avoid delays in the administration of justice in any district court, he may direct the local authority concerned to appoint a person qualified to be so appointed to act as stipendiary magistrate in that court during such period as the Secretary of State thinks fit.

(5) Any person who immediately before 16th May 1975 holds office as stipendiary magistrate for any area shall, on that date, become stipendiary magistrate in the district court having jurisdiction in that area and shall be deemed in all respects to have been appointed by virtue of this section.

(6) The salary of any such stipendiary magistrate as is mentioned in subsection (5) above shall not be less than that payable to him immediately before 16th May 1975

(7) Every stipendiary magistrate shall, by virtue of his office, be a justice of the peace for the commission area in which he is appointed.

(8) Section 12 of the Sheriff Courts (Scotland) Act 1971 (removal from the office of sheriff) shall apply in relation to a stipendiary magistrate as it applies in relation to a sheriff.

NOTE

[1] Reference to the "Secretary of State" shall be read as a reference to the "Scottish Ministers" by reason of s.53 of the Scotland Act 1998 (c.46).

District prosecutor

6. [*Repealed by the Criminal Procedure (Consequential Provisions) (Scotland) Act 1995 (c.40), s.6 and Sched.5 and was consolidated in the Criminal Procedure (Scotland) Act 1995 (c.46), s.6.*]

Clerk of District Court

7.—(1) It shall be the duty of each local authority to appoint and employ, whether on a full-time or part-time basis, an officer to act as clerk of the district court for their area, who shall also act as legal assessor in that court, and any person so appointed shall be an advocate or a solicitor.

(2) There shall be transferred to the clerks of the district courts all functions hitherto exercisable by clerks of the existing courts.

(3) [*Repealed by the Local Government etc (Scotland) Act 1994 (c.39), s.180(1) and Sched.13, para. 96(3) and Sched.14.*]

Court houses for district court

8.—(1) Every local authority shall provide suitable and sufficient premises and facilities for the purposes of the district court.

(2) Without prejudice to subsection (1) above, every regional, islands or district council having control of premises used to any extent for the purposes of the existing courts as at 15th may 1975 shall make those premises available for the purpose of the district court, and, where those premises include accommodation used by the prosecutor in the existing courts or in the district courts, that accommodation shall be made available to any procurator fiscal appointed by the Lord Advocate to serve in the district court for such period and at such times as the fiscal require.

PART II

JUSTICES AND CLERKS OF THE PEACE

Justices of the peace

Appointment and removal of justices

[1]**9.**—(1) Subject to the provisions of this section, there shall, in Scotland, be a commission of the peace for each commission area; and the commission for any commission area shall be a commission under the Great Seal addressed generally, and not by name, to all such persons as may from time to time hold office as justices of the peace for the commission area.

[2](2) Justices of the peace for any commission area, other than stipendiary magistrates and ex officio justices, shall be appointed by name on behalf and in the name of Her Majesty by instrument under the hand of the Secretary of State.

[7](2A) That instrument shall specify whether the appointment is as a full justice or as a signing justice, and the name of any signing justice so appointed shall be entered in the supplemental list.

[7](2B) A signing justice may, subject to sections 9A, 12 and 15(1) of this Act, be appointed under subsection (2) above as a full justice.

[7](2C) A signing justice may, in the name of Her Majesty and by instrument under the hand of the Scottish Ministers, be removed from office.

(3) Subject to subsection (4) below and section 10 of this Act, a person shall not be appointed to hold office as a justice of the peace for any commission area under subsection (2) above and shall not act as a justice for that area unless he lives in or within 15 miles of that area.

(4) The residential requirements mentioned in subsection (3) above shall not apply in any case where it appears to the Secretary of State to be in the public interest that those requirements should not apply and he so directs; and, where any such direction relates to the appointment of any person as a justice for any commission area, it shall have effect, and shall be treated for the purposes of this Act, as an instrument appointing that person to hold office as a justice for that area in accordance with subsection (2) above.

(5) A direction given under subsection (4) above may be made subject to such conditions as the Secretary of State thinks fit.

[3](6) Where a direction given under subsection (4) above is rescinded by a further direction and at that time the justice to whom it relates does not meet the residential requirements mentioned in subsection (3) above, that further direction shall have effect, and shall be treated for the purposes of this Act, as if it were an instrument made under subsection (7) below removing the justice from office.

[4](7) Where a person appointed justice of the peace for any area is not qualified under the foregoing provisions of this section to act by virtue of the appointment, he shall be removed from office by an instrument in the name of Her Majesty under the hand of the Scottish Minister, if they are of the opinion that the appointment ought not to continue having regard to the probable duration and other circumstances of the want of qualification.

(8) No appointment of a justice of the peace nor any act of a justice shall be invalidated by reason only of the fact that a justice of the peace so appointed or so acting does not meet the residential requirements mentioned in subsection (3) above, or does not comply with any condition imposed by the Secretary of State under subsection (5) above.

[8](8A) In making appointments of justices of the peace, the Scottish Ministers shall comply with such requirements as to procedure and consultation as may be prescribed by regulations made by them.

[8](8B) Regulations under subsection (8A) above shall be made by statutory instrument.

[8](8C) No such regulations shall be made unless laid in draft before, and approved by resolution of, the Scottish Parliament.

[5](9) There shall be kept and maintained by Secretary of State—

(a) a record of all persons for the time being holding office as a justice of the peace;

(b) the instruments of appointment (if any) of those persons;

(bb) a record of orders under section 9A(1) of this Act which have come into operation;

(c) the instruments of removal (if any) of those who have held that office ; and

(d) the supplemental list provided for by section 15 below.

[6](10) The Secretary of State shall cause to be transmitted to the clerk for each commission area a copy of any instrument appointing or removing a justice of the peace for that area in accordance with subsection (2), (2C) or (7) above or section 11(7) of this Act and notification of the names of any justices whose names have been entered in the supplemental list.

(11) Subject to any express amendment or repeal made by this Act, any enactment passed or instrument made before the passing of this Act shall have effect on and after 16th May 1975 as if—

(a) any reference to a person appointed justice by a commission of the peace or to a person being removed from a commission of the peace were a reference to his being appointed or removed from office in accordance with the provisions of this Act; and

(b) any reference to a supplemental list in connection with the commission of peace for any area were a reference to the supplemental list kept by virtue of this Act.

[9](12) In this section—

a "full justice" means a justice of the peace who is qualified as a justice to do any act (including any function of a judicial nature) or to be a member of any committee or other body; and

a "signing justice" means a justice of the peace who is qualified only to do all or any of the acts as a justice set out in section 15(9) of this Act.".

NOTES

[1]Reference to the "Secretary of State" shall be read as a reference to the "Scottish Ministers" by reason of s.53 of the Scotland Act 1998 (c.46).

[2]As amended by the Bail, Judicial Appointments etc. (Scotland) Act 2000 (asp 9), s.12 and Sched., para. 2(1)(a).

[3]As amended by the Bail, Judicial Appointments etc. (Scotland) Act 2000 (asp 9), s.12 and Sched., para. 2(1)(b).

[4]As amended by the Bail, Judicial Appointments etc. (Scotland) Act 2000 (asp 9), s.12 and Sched., para. 2(1)(c).

[5]Inserted by the Bail, Judicial Appointments etc. (Scotland) Act 2000 (asp 9), s.12 and Sched., para. 2(1)(d).

[6]As amended by the Bail, Judicial Appointments etc. (Scotland) Act 2000 (asp 9), s.12 and Sched., para. 2(1)(e).

[7]Inserted by the Bail, Judicial Appointments etc. (Scotland) Act 2000 (asp 9), s.8(a).

[8]Inserted by the Bail, Judicial Appointments etc. (Scotland) Act 2000 (asp 9), s.8(b).

[9]Inserted by the Bail, Judicial Appointments etc. (Scotland) Act 2000 (asp 9), s.8(c).

Removal, restriction of functions and suspension of justices

[1]**9A.**—(1) A full justice may be removed from office or be restricted to having the functions of a signing justice by, and only by, order of the tribunal constituted by and under subsection (3) below (the "tribunal"); but this subsection is without prejudice to sections 9(4) (as read with (6)) and (7), 12(2) and 15(1) of this Act.

(2) The tribunal may make an order under subsection (1) above only if,

after investigation carried out at the request of the Scottish Ministers, it finds that the full justice is, by reason of inability, neglect of duty or misbehaviour—

    (a) unfit for office as such; or, as the case may be,

    (b) unfit for performing functions of a judicial nature.

(3) The tribunal shall consist of the following three members, who shall be appointed by the Lord President of the Court of Session—

    (a) a sheriff principal (who shall preside);

    (b) a person who is, and has been for at least ten years, legally qualified within the meaning of section 5(2) of this Act; and

    (c) one other person.

(4) Except in a case to which subsection (5) below applies, the sheriff principal shall be the sheriff principal for the sheriffdom which includes the commission area for which the justice who is the subject of the investigation was appointed.

(5) This subsection applies where it appears to the Lord President of the Court of Session to be inappropriate for that sheriff principal to be a member of the tribunal.

(6) The sheriff principal referred to in subsection (3)(a) above shall not be a temporary sheriff principal.

(7) Regulations, made by the Scottish Ministers—

    (a) may make provision enabling the tribunal, at any time during an investigation, to suspend a full justice from office or from performing functions of a judicial nature and providing as to the effect and duration of such suspension;

    (b) shall make such further provision as respects the tribunal as the Scottish Ministers consider necessary or expedient, including provision for the procedure to be followed by and before it.

(8) Regulations under subsection (7) above shall be made by statutory instrument.

(9) No such regulations shall be made unless laid in draft before, and approved by resolution of, the Scottish Parliament.

(10) A person who has been removed under subsection (1) above from the office of justice shall be ineligible for re-appointment; and a justice whose functions have been restricted under that subsection to those of a signing justice shall be ineligible for re-appointment as a full justice.

(11) The name of a person who is the subject of an order under subsection (1) above, restricting that person's functions to those of a signing justice, shall be entered in the supplemental list.

(12) The Scottish Ministers shall send a copy of each order under subsection (1) above to the clerk of the peace for the commission area for which the justice who is the subject of the order was appointed.

(13) In this section, "full justice" and "signing justice" have the same meanings as in section 9 of this Act.".

NOTE
[1] Inserted by the Bail, Judicial Appointments etc. (Scotland) Act 2000 (asp 9), s.9(1).

Existing justices and magistrates

10.—(1) Subject to the Provisions of this section, any person holding office as justice of the peace for any area immediately before 16th May 1975 by virtue of the entry of his name in any commission of the peace—

    (a) who resides in the area to which that commission relates shall, on and after that date, hold that office for the commission area in which he resides at that date,

    (b) who does not so reside shall, on and after that date, hold that office for the commission area in which he resided at the time of his appointment under such commission.

(2) Any person holding office as a magistrate or judge of police of a burgh immediately before 16th May 1975 shall, on and after that date, hold office as justice of the peace for the commission area in which the burgh was situated.

(3) Any person holding office as justice of the peace for any commission area on or after 16th May 1975 by virtue of the provisions of subsection (1) or (2) above shall hold that office as if appointed in accordance with section 9(2) of this Act as a justice for that area.

(4) Where the Secretary of State is satisfied in all the circumstances that it is expedient that any such person as is mentioned in subsection (1) above should hold that office for another commission area, he may so direct, and any such direction shall have effect, and shall be treated for the purposes of this Act, as an instrument appointing that person in accordance with the said section 9(2) to hold office for such commission area as is mentioned in the direction.

(5) [*Repealed by the Licensing (Scotland) Act 1976 (c.66), s.136 and Sched.*]

NOTE

[1]Reference to the "Secretary of State" shall be read as a reference to the "Scottish Ministers" by reason of s.53 of the Scotland Act 1998 (c.46).

Ex officio justices

[1]**11.**—(1) Any person holding office as justice of the peace for any area immediately before 16th May 1975 by virtue of any other office for the time being held by him shall, on that date, cease to hold office as justice for that area, notwithstanding the provisions of any enactment or of any instrument in terms of which he holds that office.

(2) Each local authority may nominate up to one quarter of their members to serve as ex officio justices for their area, and any person so nominated shall hold office as ex officio justice from the date on which the local authority intimate their nomination to the Secretary of State and shall continue as such for the period during which he remains a member of the authority and continues to retrain the authority's nomination.

[3](2A) The name of a person appointed as an ex officio justice under subsection (2) above shall be entered in the supplemental list.

(3) Subject to subsection (4) below, any person nominated to serve as an ex officio justice shall, before acting as such a justice, take the oath of allegiance and judicial oath in accordance with the Promissory Oaths Act 1868 and the Promissory Oaths Act 1871.

(4) A person re-nominated to serve as an ex officio justice immediately after the expiry of a previous term as such shall not require to take again the oaths mentioned in subsection (3) above.

(5) Each local authority shall intimate to the Secretary of State the date on which a person duly nominated under subsection (2) above ceases to be a member of the authority or on which his nomination is terminated by the authority.

(6) A person duly nominated under subsection (2) above shall not be treated as having ceased to be a member of the local authority during any period when he is standing for re-election to that authority.

[2](7) Subject to section 12 of this Act, A person holding office as an ex officio justice by virtue of subsection (2) above shall hold office as if appointed in accordance with section 9(2) of this Act as a justice for the commission area concerned and not-withstanding that he remains a duly nominated member of the authority, may be removed from office by an instrument in the name of Her Majesty under the hand of the Scottish Ministers.

(8) [*Repealed by the Licensing (Scotland) Act 1976 (c.66), s.136 and Sched.8.*]

NOTES
[1]Reference to the "Secretary of State" shall be read as a reference to the "Scottish Ministers" by reason of s.53 of the Scotland Act 1998 (c.46).
[2]As amended by the Law Reform (Miscellaneous Provisions) Act l985 (c.73), s.34(a) and the Bail, Judicial Appointments etc. (Scotland) Act 2000 (asp 9), s.12 and Sched., para. 2(b).
[3]Inserted by the Bail, Judicial Appointments etc. (Scotland) Act 2000 (asp 9), s.12 and Sched., para. 2(a).

Disqualification in certain cases of justices who are members of local authorites

[1]**12.**—(1) A member of a local authority—
(a) shall not be appointed to hold office as a full justice;
(b) may be appointed as a signing justice.
(2) A full justice who—
(a) at the coming into force of section 9 of the Bail, Judicial Appointments etc. (Scotland) Act 2000 (asp 9) is; or
(b) at any time thereafter becomes,
a member of a local authority, shall thereupon become a signing justice.
(3) The name of a person—
(a) appointed as a justice under subsection (1)(b) above;
(b) who becomes a signing justice by virtue of the operation of subsection (2) above,
shall be entered in the supplemental list.
(4) In subsection (1) above—
"local authority" includes the Service Authority for the National Criminal Intelligence Service;
"full justice" and "signing justice" have the same meanings as in section 9 of this Act.

NOTE
[1]Substituted by the Bail, Judicial Appointments (Scotland) Act 2000 (asp 9), s.10.

Disqualification of solicitor who is a justice

13.—(1) Subject to the provisions of this section, it shall not be lawful for any solicitor who is a justice of the peace for any commission area, nor for any partner of his, nor for any member of his or his firm's staff, to act directly or indirectly as a solicitor in or in connection with any proceedings before—
(a) a district court for that area;
(b) *[Repealed by the Licensing (Scotland) Act 1976 (c.66), s.136 and Sched.8.]*
(2) The disqualification imposed by the foregoing subsection shall not apply to a solicitor who is a justice of the peace for any area and whose name is entered on the supplemental list.
(3) *[Repealed by the Licensing (Scotland) Act 1976 (c.66), s.136.]*

Disqualification in case of sequestration or bankruptcy

[1]**13A.**—(1) Subject to subsections (2) and (3) below, a person shall be disqualified for being appointed or acting as a justice of the peace if he is a person whose estate has been sequestrated in Scotland or who has been adjudged bankrupt elsewhere than in Scotland.
(2) Where a person is disqualified under this section by reason of his estate having been sequestrated, the disqualification shall cease if and when—
(a) the award of sequestration is recalled or reduced; or
(b) he is discharged under or by virtue of the Bankruptcy (Scotland) Act 1985.
(3) Where a person is disqualified under this section by reason of having been adjudged bankrupt, the disqualification shall cease if and when —

(a) the adjudication of bankruptcy against him is annulled; or
(b) he is discharged.

NOTE
[1]Inserted by the Statute Law (Repeals) Act 1989 (c43), s.1(2) and Sched. 2, Pt 1, para.2.

Courses for justice

14. The Secretary of State may make schemes and provide courses for the instruction of justices of peace, and shall be the duty of the justices' committee of a commission area to implement and administer any such schemes in accordance with arrangements approved by the Secretary of State.

NOTE
[1]Reference to the "Secretary of State" shall be read as a reference to the "Scottish Ministers" by reason of s.53 of the Scotland Act 1998 (c.46).

Supplemental List

[1]**15.**—(1) Subject to subsection (5) below, there shall be entered in the supplemental list the name of any justice of the peace who is of the age of 70 years or over.

(2) [*Repealed by the Bail, Judicial Appointments etc. (Scotland) Act (asp 9), s.12 and Sched., para. 2(3)(a)*]

(3) On a person's appointment as a justice of the peace for any area, the Secretary of State may direct that his name shall be entered in the supplemental list if that person is appointed a justice for that area on ceasing to be a justice for some other area (including any commission area within the meaning of the Administration of Justice Act 1973).

(4) The name of a justice of the peace shall be entered in the supplemental list if he applies for it to be entered and the application is approved by Secretary of State.

(5) Nothing in subsections (1) to (4) above shall apply to a person holding office as stipendiary magistrate.

(6) A person's name shall be removed from the supplemental list if he ceases to be a justice of the peace.

(7) [*Repealed by the Bail, Judicial Appointments etc. (Scotland) Act (asp 9), s.12 and Sched., para. 2(3)(a)*]

(8) Subject to the following subsections, a justice of the peace for any area, while his name is entered in the supplemental list, shall not, by reason of being a justice for that area, be qualified as a justice to do any act or to be a member of any committee or other body.

[3](8A) A justice whose name is, under this section, entered in the supplemental list is a signing justice within the meaning of section 9(12) of this Act.

(9) Subsection (8) above shall not preclude a justice from doing all or any of the following acts as a justice, that is to say—
(a) signing any document for the purpose of authenticating another person's signature ;
(b) taking and authenticating by his signature any written declaration ; and
(c) giving a certificate of facts within his knowledge or of his opinion as to any matter.

(10) No act or appointment shall be invalidated by reason of the disqualification under subsection (8) above of the person acting or appointed.

(11) Where immediately before 16th May 1975 a person's name is entered

in the supplemental list kept in connection with any commission of the peace by virtue of section 4 of the Justices of the Peace Act 1949, his name shall be treated as included in the supplemental list for Scotland under this section.

Justices' committees

[1]16.—(1) There shall be constituted in accordance with this section a justices' committee for every commission area which shall—
  (a) assist and advise the local authority concerned on any matter relating to the administration of the district court;
  (b) approve the duty rota of justices;
  (c) secure that adequate training arrangements for justices are made for their area in accordance with a scheme made under section 14 above, and that these arrangements are adhered to by justices ;
  (d) take such other steps as appear to them to be appropriate in order to secure the effective administration of justice in the district court.

(2) The clerk of the Peace for a commission area shall, before 16th June 1975 and during the month preceding 16th June in every following year, call a meeting of the justices for that area, at such place and time as he may consider convenient, to elect from their number a justices' committee.

[2](2A) For the purposes of subsection (2) above, "justices" includes signing justices who are or have become such by operation of section 12 of this Act.

(3) The Secretary of State may prescribe the upper and lower limits of the number of members of which a committee in any commission area may be composed.

(4) A stipendiary magistrate appointed to any commission area shall, by virtue of his office, be a member of the committee for that area.

(5) The members of a committee shall elect from among themselves a chairman, who shall preside at their meetings.

(6) The clerk of the peace for a commission area shall, by virtue of his office, be secretary to the committee for that area.

(7) A justices' committee may regulate their own procedure.

Allowance

[1]17.—(1) Subject to the provisions of this section, a justice of the peace shall be entitled to receive payments at the prescribed rates by way of travelling
allowance or subsistence allowance where expenditure on travelling or, as the case may be, on subsistence is necessarily incurred by him for the purpose of enabling him to perform any of his duties as a justice, and to receive payments at the prescribed rate by way of financial loss allowance where for that purpose there is incurred by him any other expenditure to which he would not otherwise be subject or there is suffered by him any loss of earnings or of benefit under the National Insurance Acts 1965 to 1973 which he would otherwise have made or received.

(2) [*Repealed by the Licensing (Scotland) Act 1976 (c.66), s.136 and Sched. 8.*]

(3) A justice attending a meeting of justices authorised by or under any enactment or approved by the Secretary of State for the purpose of this section shall be deemed to be acting in the performance of his duties as a justice.

(4) For the purposes of this section, a justice attending a course of instruction provided in accordance with arrangements made by the Secretary of State or by a justices' committee, by virtue of section 14 of this Act, or such other cause as may be approved by the Secretary of State, shall be deemed to be acting in the performance of his duties as a justice.

(5) A justice shall not be entitled to any payment under this section in respect of any duties if, in respect of those duties, a payment of the like nature may be paid to him under arrangement made apart from this section or if regulations provide that this section shall not apply.

(6) An allowance payable under this section to a justice for any area in respect of his duties as such shall be paid by the local authority concerned.

(7) Regulations may make provisions as to the manner in which this section is to be administered and, in particular—
- (a) for prescribing the rates of allowances and the forms to be used and the particulars to be provided for the purpose of claiming payment thereof;
- (b) for avoiding duplication between payments under this section and under other arrangements where expenditure is incurred for more than one purpose, and otherwise for preventing abuse.

(8) Regulations for this purpose of this section shall be made by the Secretary of State by statutory instrument, which shall be subject to annulment in pursuance of a resolution of either House of Parliament.

(9) The provisions of this section do not apply to stipendiary magistrates.

NOTE
[1]Reference to the "Secretary of State" shall be read as a reference to the "Scottish Ministers" by reason of s.53 of the Scotland Act 1998 (c.46).

Clerks of the Peace

Appointment and duties of clerk of peace

[1]**18.**—(1) Any person who immediately before 16th May 1975 holds office as clerk of the peace for any area shall, on that date, cease to hold that office, notwithstanding the provisions of any enactment or of any instrument in terms of which any person holds that office.

(2) On and after that date, the duties of clerk of the peace shall, subject to subsection (3) below, be performed in each commission area by an officer of the local authority concerned, and it shall be the duty of every such authority to appoint and employ, whether on a full-time or part-time basis, an officer to hold the office of clerk of the peace for their area for the purpose of performing those duties.

(3) [*Repealed by the Local Government etc (Scotland) Act 1984 (c.39), s.180(2) and Sched.14.*]

(4) It shall be the duty of the clerk of the peace for any commission area—
- (a) to advise and assist the justices in the performance of their functions;
- (b) to arrange meetings of the justices for that area;
- (c) to cause to be kept a record of—
  - (i) those for the time being holding office as a justice for that area, and
  - (ii) those having held that office who have ceased to do so, and to include in that record a copy of any instrument appointing or removing a justice for that area in accordance with section 9(2) of this Act;

(d) to cause to be kept a record of the justices in that area whose names are entered in the supplemental list;(e) to notify the Secretary of State of all deaths and resignations of justices in that area who has become incapable of exercising any function as a justice or who has ceased to meet the residential requirements mentioned in section 9(3) above;

(f) to carry out such further duties as may be prescribed.

NOTE
[1]Reference to the "Secretary of State" shall be read as a reference to the "Scottish Ministers" by reason of s.53 of the Scotland Act 1998 (c.46).

PART III

MISCELLANEOUS AND GENERAL

Miscellaneous

Compensation

19.—(1) The Secretary of State shall, by regulations made with the consent of the Minister for the Civil Service, provide for the payment by such person as may be prescribed, subject to such expectations and conditions as may be prescribed, of compensation to or in respect of persons who are or were clerks of the peace, justice of the peace, fiscals or the holders of such other office or employment as may be prescribed and who suffer loss of employment or loss or diminution of emoluments which is attributable to any provision of this Act.

(2) Regulations under this section may—

(a) include Provision as to the manner in which and the person to whom any claim for compensation is to be made, and for the determination of all questions arising under the regulations ;

(b) make different ' provisions for different classes of persons and for other different circumstances ;

(c) be framed so as to have effect from a date earlier than the making of the regulations, but not so as to place any person in a less favourable position than he would have been in if they had not been so framed.

(3) Any statutory instrument containing regulations under this section shall be subject to annulment in pursuance of a resolution of either House of Parliament.

NOTE
[1]Reference to the "Secretary of State" shall be read as a reference to the "Scottish Ministers" by reason of s.53 of the Scotland Act 1998 (c.46).

Custody of records

20.—(1) Subject to section 1 of .this Act and the provisions of this section, the clerk of the peace for any area shall, on or before 15th May 1975, transmit to the Keeper of the Records of Scotland all justice of the peace records, other than records relating to licensing under the Licensing Acts, being records of which at that date he has the custody under the Public Records (Scotland) Act 1937; and, for the purposes of this subsection, justice of the peace records shall be deemed to include the commission of the peace.

(2) Subject to subsections (3) and (4) below, records of county licensing courts and courts of appeal shall, on or before 15th May 1975, be transferred to and vest in the local authority concerned within whose area the court to which those records relate has jurisdiction.

(3) Where the area within which such a court has jurisdiction is divided so that the area falls within the areas of two or more districts, the records relating to that court shall be transferred to and vest in the district council

whose area includes, according to the latest census (not being a sample census), the greater part of the population of the area within which that court has jurisdiction.

(4) Where, under subsection (3) above, the records of a court have vested in a district council, that council shall make the records available for consultation to any other council to which that subsection relates.

(5) All records relating to the appointment of justices of the peace for any commission area under this Act, to their acts as justices for that area (whether under the Licensing Acts or not), and to their ceasing to hold office as justices for that area, shall be records of the local authority concerned; and shall be records belonging to that authority for the purposes of section 200(7) to (10) of the Local Government (Scotland) Act 1973.

(6) Any dispute as to the vesting of records under this section shall be referred to and determined by the Secretary of State, whose decision in the matter shall be final.

NOTE
[1]Reference to the "Secretary of State" shall be read as a reference to the "Scottish Ministers" by reason of s.53 of the Scotland Act 1998 (c.46).

Amendment of Legal Aid (Scotland) Act 1967 and Legal Advice and Assistance Act 1972

21. [*Repealed by the Legal Aid (Scotland) Act 1986 (c.47), s.45 and Sched.5.*]

Amendment of sections 28 and 29 of the Licensing (Scotland) Act 1959

22. [*Repealed by the Licensing (Scotland) Act 1976 (c.66), s.136 and Sched. 8.*]

District court and justice of peace expenses and destination fines

[1]**23.**—(1) All expenses in connection with the district court and justice of the peace business shall be defrayed by the local authority concerned.

(2) Except where otherwise provided, all fines imposed in the district court shall accrue to the local authority concerned.

(3) A local authority shall defray the expenses of any appeal in which the district prosecutor is involved in connection with proceedings brought by him in his capacity as district prosecutor.

(4) A local authority may defray the expenses of any action brought against the district prosecutor in connection with the exercise of his functions, and may relieve him from any liability imposed as a result of such an action.

(5) Having regard to the additional expenditure incurred or likely to be incurred by local authorities in the year 1975–76, which is attributable to the coming into operation of any provision of this Act, the Secretary of State may redetermine for that year the amount and proportion mentioned in section 2(2)(a) and (b) of the Local Government (Scotland) Act 1966, and by an order, made in the like manner and subject to the like provisions as a rate support grant order, increase the amount fixed by the relevant rate support grant order as the aggregate amount of the rate support grants and any element of the grants for that year.

(6) The provisions of sections 2 and 3 of' the said Act of 1966, relating to consultation and to a report of the considerations leading to a determination under the said section 2, shall apply to a redetermination under subsection (5) above as they apply to a determination under that section.

(7) Expressions used in subsections (5) and (6) above have the same meanings as in the said Act of 1966.

General

Amendments and repeals

[1]**24.**—(1) The enactments mentioned in Schedule 1 to this Act shall have effect subject to the amendments respectively specified in that Schedule, being minor amendments or amendments consequential on the provisions of this Act.

(2) The enactments specified in Schedule 2 to this Act (which includes certain obsolete or unnecessary enactments) are hereby repealed to the extent specified in the third column of that Schedule.

(3) The Secretary of State may by order amend, repeal or revoke any provision of an Act passed or an instrument under an Act made before 16th May 1975 if it appears to him that that provision is inconsistent with any provision of this Act or requires modification in consequence of this Act.

(4) Where any local enactment provides for any matter which is also provided for by any of this Act or of any order made thereunder, the Provision of this Act, or, as the case may be, of that order, shall have effect in substitution for the local enactment which shall cease to have effect.

(5) Any order made under this section shall be by statutory instrument, which shall be subject to annulment in pursuance of a resolution of either House of Parliament.

Expenses

25. There shall be defrayed out of moneys provided by Parliament—
(a) any expenses incurred by the Secretary of State under this Act ; and
(b) any increase attributable to the provisions of this Act in the sums payable out of moneys so provided under any other enactment.

Interpretation

26.—(1) In this Act, unless the context otherwise requires—
"clerk of the district court" includes such depute clerk as may be required for the purposes of any district court;
[1]"commission area" means the area of local authority;
"district prosecutor" includes such dispute or assistant district prosecutor as may be required for the purposes of any district court;
"justice" or "justice of the peace" means a justice of the peace appointed under section 9 of this Act or deemed to have been so appointed;
[[2]...]
[1]"local authority" means a council constituted under section 2 of the Local Government ect. (Scotland) Act 1994.
[3]"prescribed" means prescribed by regulations made by the [Scottish Ministers].

(2) Any power conferred by this Act to make an order shall include power, exercisable in like manner and subject to the same conditions, to vary or revoke the order by a subsequent order.

(3) Unless the context otherwise requires, any reference in this Act to any other enactment is a reference thereto as amended, extended or applied by or under any other enactment, including this Act.

NOTES

[1] As amended by the Local Government etc (Scotland) Act 1994 (c.39), s.180(1) and Sched.13, para.96.

[2] The definitions of "licensing court" and " court of appeal" were repealed by the Licensing (Scotland) Act 1976 (c.66), s.136 and Sched.8

[3] Reference to the "Secretary of State" shall be read as a reference to the "Scottish Ministers" by reason of s.53 of the Scotland Act 1998 (c.46).

Short title, extent and commencement

27.—(1)This Act may be cited as the District Courts (Scotland) Act 1975, and, except section 24(1) and subsection (2) below and the entries in Schedule 1 to this Act relating to the Magistrates' Courts Act 1952 and to section 18(1) of the Police (Scotland) Act 1967, extends to Scotland only.

(2) This Act, except sections 8, 10, 11, 14, 16, 17, 20, 23, 26 and this section, shall come into force on 16th May 1975.

SCHEDULES

[...]

LICENSED PREMISES (EXCLUSION OF CERTAIN PERSONS) ACT 1980

(1980 c. 32)

An Act to empower the courts to make orders excluding certain categories of convicted persons from licensed premises.

[30th June 1980]

Exclusion orders

1.—(1) Where a court by or before which a person is convicted of an offence committed on licensed premises is satisfied that in committing that offence he resorted to violence or offered or threatened to resort to violence, the court may, subject to subsection (2) below, make an order (in this Act referred to as an "exclusion order") prohibiting him from entering those premises or any other specified premises, without the express consent of the licensee of the premises or his servant or agent.

(2) An exclusion order may be made either—

(a) in addition to any sentence which is imposed in respect of the offence of which the person is convicted; or

(b) [*Not applicable in Scotland*]

(c) where the offence was committed in Scotland, notwithstanding the provisions of sections 182, 183, 191, 383, 384, and 392 of the Criminal Procedure (Scotland) Act 1975 (cases in which probation orders and absolute discharges may be made, and their effect), in addition to a probation order or an order discharging him absolutely;

but not otherwise.

(3) An exclusion order shall have effect for such period, not less than three months or more than two years, as is specified in the order, unless it is terminated under section 2(2) below.

Penalty for non-compliance with exclusion order

2.—(1) A person who enters any premises in breach of an exclusion order shall be guilty of an offence and shall be liable on summary conviction or, in Scotland, on conviction in a court of summary jurisdiction to a fine not exceeding £1,000 or to imprisonment for a term not exceeding one month or both.

(2) The court by which a person is convicted of an offence under subsection (1) above shall consider whether or not the exclusion order should continue in force, and may, if it thinks fit, by order terminate the exclusion order or vary it by deleting the name of any specified premises, but an exclusion order shall not otherwise be affected by a person's conviction for such an offence.

Power to expel persons from licensed premises

3.—Without prejudice to any other right to expel a person from premises, the licensee of licensed premises or his servant or agent may expel from those premises any person who has entered or whom he reasonably suspects of having entered the premises in breach of an exclusion order; and a constable shall on the demand of the licensee or his servant or agent help to expel from licensed premises any person whom the constable reasonably suspects of having entered in breach of an exclusion order.

Supplemental

4.—(1) In this Act—

"licensed premises", in relation to England and Wales, means premisesin respect of which there is in force a justices' onlicence (within the meaning of section 1of the Licensing Act 1964) and , in relation to Scotland, means premises in respect of which a licence under the Licensing (Scotland) Act 1976, other than off-sales licence or a license under Part III of that Act (licenses for seamen's canteens), is in force; and

"licensee" in relation to any licensed premises means the holder of the licence granted in respect of those premises; and

"specified premises", in relation to an exclusion order, means any licensed premises which the court may specify by name and address in the order.

(2) In the application of section 1 above to Scotland, the reference in subsection (1) of that section to a person's being convicted of an offence shall, in relation to proceedings in a court of summary jurisdiction in which the court, without proceeding to conviction, discharges him absolutely under section 383 of the Criminal Procedure (Scotland) Act 1975 or makes a probation order under section 384 of that Act, shall be construed as a reference to the court's being satisfied that he committed the offence.

(3) Where a court makes an exclusion order or an order terminating or varying an exclusion order the clerk of the court, or the appropriate officer of the Crown Court, as the case may be, shall send a copy of the order to the licensee of the premises to which the order relates.

Short title, citation and extent

5.—(1) This Act may be cited as the Licensed Premises (Exclusion of Certain Persons) Act 1980 and this Act, in its application to Scotland, and the Licensing (Scotland) Act 1976 may be cited together as the Licensing (Scotland) Acts 1976 to 1980.

(2) This Act shall not extend to Northern Ireland.

CIVIC GOVERNMENT (SCOTLAND) ACT 1982

(1982 c. 45)

ARRANGEMENT OF SECTIONS

PART IV

OFFENCES, POWERS OF CONSTABLES ETC.

Preventive offences

An Act to make provision as regards Scotland for the licensing and regulation of certain activities; for the preservation of public order and safety and the prevention of crime; for prohibiting the taking of and dealing with indecent photographs of children; as to certain powers of constables and others; as to lost and abandoned property and property in the possession of persons taken into police custody; as to the rights and duties of the owners and users of certain land, buildings and other structures; as to the making by local authorities of byelaws; and to enable them to make management rules applying to land or premises under their control; as to certain other functions of local authorities and their officers; as to the time when the Burgh Police (Scotland) Acts 1892 to 1911 and certain local statutory provisions cease to have effect; and for connected purposes.

[28th October 1982]

PART IV

OFFENCES, POWERS OF CONSTABLES ETC.

Preventive offences

Being in or on building etc. with intent to commit theft

57.—(1) Any person who, without lawful authority to be there, is found in or on a building or other premises, whether enclosed or not, or in its curtilage or in a vehicle or vessel so that, in all the circumstances, it may reasonably be inferred that he intended to commit theft there shall be guilty of an offence and liable, on summary conviction, to a fine not exceeding level 2 on the standard scale or to imprisonment for a period not exceeding 3 months or to both.

(2) In this section "theft" includes any aggravation of theft including robbery.

Convicted theft in possession

58.—(1) Any person who, being a person to whom this section applies—

(a) has or has recently had in his possession any tool or other object from the possession of which it may reasonably be inferred that he intended to commit theft or has committed theft; and

(b) is unable to demonstrate satisfactorily that his possession of such tool or other object is or was not for the purposes of committing theft

shall be guilty of an offence and liable, on summary conviction, to a fine not exceeding level 2 on the standard scale or to imprisonment for a period not exceeding 3 months or to both.

(2) For the purposes of subsection (1) above, a person shall have recently had possession of a tool or other object if he had possession of it within 14 days before the date of—

(a) his arrest without warrant for the offence of having so possessed it in contravention of subsection (1) above; or

(b) the issue of a warrant for his arrest for that offence; or

(c) if earlier, the service upon him of the first complaint alleging that he has committed that offence.

(3) Where a court convicts a person of an offence under this section or discharges him absolutely or makes a probation order in relation to him in respect of such an offence it may order the forfeiture of any tool or other object in respect of the possession of which he was convicted or discharged absolutely, or, as the case may be, the probation order was made.

(4) This section applies to a person who has two or more convictions for theft which are not, for the purposes of the Rehabilitation of Offenders Act 1974, spent convictions.

(5) In this section "theft" includes any aggravation of theft including robbery.

Powers of arrest and apprehension

59.—(1) Subject to subsection (2) below, a constable may, where it is necessary in the interests of justice to do so, arrest without warrant a person whom he finds committing an offence to which this section applies or a person who is delivered into his custody in pursuance of subsection (3) below.

(2) A constable who is not in uniform shall produce his identification if required to do so by any person whom he is arresting under subsection (1) above.

(3) The owner, tenant or occupier of any property in, upon, or in respect of, which an offence to which this section applies is being committed or any person authorised by him may apprehend any person whom the owner or, as the case may be, the tenant, occupier or authorised person finds committing that offence and detain the apprehended person until he can be delivered into the custody of a constable.

In this subsection "property" means heritable or moveable property.

(4) This section applies to offences under sections 50, 57 and 58 of this Act.

(5) This section shall not prejudice any power of arrest conferred by law apart from this section.

Powers of search and seizure

60.—(1) Subject to subsections (2) and (3) below, if a constable has reasonable grounds to suspect that a person is in possession of any stolen property, the constable may without warrant—

(a) search that person or anything in his possession, and detain him for as long as is necessary for the purpose of that search;

(b) enter and search any vehicle or vessel in which the constable suspects that that thing may be found, and for that purpose require the person in control of the vehicle or vessel to stop it and keep it stopped;

(c) enter and search any premises occupied by a second-hand dealer or a metal dealer for the purposes of his business;

(d) seize and detain anything found in the course of any such search which appears to the constable to have been stolen or to be evidence of the commission of the crime of theft

and may, in doing so, use reasonable force.

In this subsection "second-hand dealer" and "metal dealer" have the meanings respectively assigned to them by sections 24(2) and 37(1) of this Act.

(2) The power under subsection (1)(b) above to require the person in charge of a vehicle or vessel to stop it shall be exercisable only by a constable in uniform.

(3) A constable who is not in uniform shall not be entitled to exercise the powers which he may exercise under subsection (1)(a) to (c) above until he has produced his identification—

(a) in relation to the exercise of powers under subsection (1)(a) above, to the person in respect of whom the powers are exercised;

(b) in relation to the exercise of powers under subsections (1)(b) or (c) above, to the person for the time being in charge of the vehicle, vessel or premises and to any other person in or on the vehicle, vessel or premises who, having reasonable cause to do so, requests to see it.

(4) In subsection (1) above "theft" includes any aggravation of theft including robbery.

[1](5) Nothing in section 54(2A) of this Act or this section prejudices any power of entry or search or any power to seize or detain property or any power to require any vehicle or vessel to be stopped which is otherwise exercisable by a constable.

[2](6) Any person who, without reasonable excuse—

(a) fails to allow a constable to enter and search—

(i) any premises in pursuance of section 54(2A) of this Act or of subsection (1) above; or

(ii) any vehicle or vessel in pursuance of the said subsection (1), or seize and detain anything found in the course of such search;

(b) when required by a constable in pursuance of subsection (1) above to stop a vehicle or vessel and keep it stopped, fails to do so; or

(c) obstructs a constable in the exercise of his powers under section 54(2A) of this Act or subsection (1) above;

shall be guilty of an offence and liable, on summary conviction, to a fine not exceeding level 1 on the standard scale.

NOTES

[1]The amendments to s.60(5) are inserted by s.24(3)(a) of the Crime and Disorder Act 1998 (c. 37).

[2]The amendments to s.60(6) are inserted by s.24(3)(b) of the 1998 Act.

Protection of insecure premises

61.—(1) Where—

(a) any premises have been left open, unlocked or otherwise insecure; and

(b) in the opinion of a constable, the insecurity of the premises is likely to conduce to the commission of an offence,

the constable may take such reasonable steps as he may consider necessary to make the premises secure.

(2) Any reasonable expense incurred by a constable in making any premises secure under subsection (1) above may be recovered by the police authority from the occupier (or, where there is no occupier, from the tenant or, where there is no occupier or tenant, from the owner) of the premises.

EXTRADITION ACT 1989

(1989 c. 33)

ARRANGEMENT OF SECTIONS

PART I

General

PART II

RESTRICTIONS ON RETURN

PART III

PROCEDURE

General

Special extradition arrangements

Effect of delay

An Act to consolidate enactments relating to extradition under the Criminal Justice Act 1988, the Fugitive Offenders Act 1967 and the Extradition Acts 1870 to 1935, with amendments to give effect to recommendations of the Law Commission and the Scottish Law Commission.

[27th July 1989]

PART I

INTRODUCTION

General

Liability to extradition

1.—(1) Where extradition procedures under Part III of this Act are available as between the United Kingdom and a foreign state, a person in the United Kingdom who—
   (a) is accused in that state of the commission of an extradition crime; or
   (b) is alleged to be unlawfully at large after conviction of an extradition crime by a court in that state,
may be arrested and returned to that state in accordance with those procedures.

(2) Subject to the provisions of this Act, a person in the United Kingdom who is accused of an extradition crime—
   (a) in a Commonwealth country designated for the purposes of this subsection under section 5(1) below; or
   (b) in a colony,
or who is alleged to be unlawfully at large after conviction of such an offence in any such country or in a colony, may be arrested and returned to that country or colony in accordance with extradition procedures under Part III of this Act.

¹(2A) Subject to the provisions of this Act, a person in the United Kingdom who—
   (a) is accused in the Hong Kong Special Administrative Region of an extradition crime, or
   (b) is alleged to be unlawfully at large after conviction for such an offence in that Region,
may be arrested and returned to that Region in accordance with extradition procedures under Part III of this Act.

(3) Where an Order in Council under section 2 of the Extradition Act 1870 is in force in relation to a foreign state, Schedule 1 to this Act (the provisions of which derive from that Act and certain associated enactments) shall have effect in relation to that state, but subject to the limitations, restrictions, conditions, exceptions and qualifictions, if any, contained in the Order.

NOTE
¹As amended by the Hong Kong (Extradition) Order 1997 (S.I. 1997 No. 1178), Art. 2, Sched., para. 1.

Extradition crime

Meaning of "extradition crime"

2.—(1) In this Act, except in Schedule 1, "extradition crime" means—
³(a) conduct in the territory of a foreign state, a designated Commonwealth country, a colony or the Hong Kong Special Administrative Region which, if it occurred in the United Kingdom, would constitute

an offence punishable with imprisonment for a term of 12 months, or any greater punishment, and which, however described in the law of the foreign state, Commonwealth country or colony or of the Hong Kong Administrative Region, is so punishable under that law;

³(b) an extra-territorial offence against the law of a foreign state, designated Commonwealth country or colony or of the Hong Kong Special Administrative Region, which is punishable under that law with imprisonment for a term of 12 months, or any greater punishment, and which satisfies—

    (i) the condition specified in subsection (2) below; or

    (ii) all the conditions specified in subsection (3) below.

(2) The condition mentioned in subsection (1)(b)(i) above is that in corresponding circumstances equivalent conduct would constitute an extra-territorial offence against the law of the United Kingdom punishable with imprisonment for a term of 12 months, or any greater punishment.

(3) The conditions mentioned in subsection (1)(b)(ii) above are—

³(a) that the foreign state, Commonwealth country or colony or the Hong Kong Special Administrative Region bases its jurisdiction on the nationality of the offender;

(b) that the conduct constituting the offence occurred outside the United Kingdom; and

(c) that, if it occurred in the United Kingdom, it would constitute an offence under the law of the United Kingdom punishable with imprisonment for a term of 12 months, or any greater punishment; but

²(d) reference shall be made to the law of the colony or dependency of a foreign state or of a designated Commonwealth country, and not (where different) to the law of the foreign state or Commonwealth country, to determine the level of punishment applicable to conduct in that colony or dependency.

¹(4) For the purposes of this Act, except Schedule 1—

(a) the law of a foreign state, designated Commonwealth country or colony includes the law of any part of it and the law of the United Kingdom includes the law of any part of the United Kingdom;

(b) conduct in a colony or dependency of a foreign state or of a designated Commonwealth country, or a vessel, aircraft or hovercraft of a foreign state or of such a country, shall be treated as if it were conduct in the territory of that state or country;

(c) conduct in a vessel, aircraft or hovercraft of a colony of the United Kingdom shall be treated as if it were conduct in that colony; and

⁴(d) conduct in a vessel, aircraft or hovercraft of the Hong Kong Special Administrative Region shall be treated as if it were conduct in that Region.

NOTES

¹As amended by the Criminal Justice and Public Order Act 1994, Sched. 9, para. 37.

²Inserted by the above Act, Sched. 9, para. 37.

³As amended by the Hong Kong (Extradition) Order 1997 (S.I. 1997 No. 1178), Art. 2, Sched., para. 2.

⁴Inserted by the above Order, Art. 2, Sched., para. 2(4).

Return to foreign states

Arrangements for availability of Part III procedure

3.—(1) In this Act "extradition arrangements" means arrangements made with a foreign state under which extradition procedures under Part III of this Act will be available as between the United Kingdom and that state.

(2) For this purpose "foreign state" means any state other than—

(i) the United Kingdom;
(ii) a country mentioned in Schedule 3 to the British Nationality Act 1981 (countries whose citizens are Commonwealth citizens);
(iii) a colony;
(iv) the Republic of Ireland; or
[1](v) the Hong Kong Special Administrative Region.
but a state which is a party to the European Convention on Extradition done at Paris on 13th December 1957 may be treated as a foreign state.

(3) Extradition arrangements may be—

(a) arrangements of a general nature made with one or more states and relating to the operation of extradition procedures under Part III of this Act (in this Act referred to as "general extradition arrangements"); or

(b) arrangements relating to the operation of those procedures in particular cases (in this Act referred to as "special extradition arrangements") made with a state with which there are no general extradition arrangements.

NOTE
[1]Inserted by the Hong Kong (Extradition) Order 1997 (S.I. 1997 No. 1178), Art. 2, Sched., para. 3.

Orders in Council as to extradition

4.—(1) Where general extradition arrangements have been made, Her Majesty may, by Order in Council reciting or embodying their terms, direct that this Act, so far as it relates to extradition procedures under Part III of this Act, shall apply as between the United Kingdom and the foreign state, or any foreign state, with which they have been made, subject to the limitations, restrictions, exceptions and qualifictions, if any, contained in the Order.

(2) An Order in Council under this section shall not be made unless the general extradition arrangements to which it relates—

(a) provide for their determination after the expiration of a notice given by a party to them and not exceeding one year or for their denunciation by means of such a notice; and

(b) are in conformity with the provisions of this Act, and in particular with the restrictions on return contained in Part II of this Act.

(3) An Order in Council under this section shall be conclusive evidence that the arrangements therein referred to comply with this Act and that this Act, so far as it relates to extradition procedures under Part III of this Act, applies in the case of the foreign state, or any foreign state, mentioned in the Order.

(4) An Order in Council under this section shall be laid before Parliament after being made.

[1](5) An Order in Council under this section which does not provide that a person may only be returned to the foreign state requesting his return if the court of committal is satisfied that the evidence would be sufficient to make a case requiring an answer by that person if the proceedings the extradition crime had taken place within the jurisdiction of the court shall be subject to annulment in pursuance of a resolution of either House of Parliament.

NOTE
[1]As amended by Criminal Justice and Public Order Act 1994 (c. 33), s.158(2).

Return to Commonwealth countries and colonies

Procedure for designation etc.

5.—(1) Her Majesty may by Order in Council designate for the purposes of section 1(2) above any country for the time being mentioned in Schedule 3

to the British Nationality Act 1981 (countries whose citizens are Commonwealth citizens); and any country so designated is in this Act referred to as a
"designated Commonwealth country".

(2) This Act has effect in relation to all colonies.

(3) Her Majesty may by Order in Council direct that this Act shall have
effect in relation to the return of persons to, or in relation to persons
returned from, any designated Commonwealth country or any colony
subject to such exceptions, adaptations or modifications as may be specified
in the Order.

(4) Any Order under this section may contain such transitional or other
incidental and supplementary provisions as may appear to Her Majesty to be
necessary or expedient.

(5) For the purposes of any Order in Council under subsection (1) above,
any territory for the external relations of which a Commonwealth country is
responsible may be treated as part of that country or, if the Government of
that country so requests, as a separate country.

(6) Any Order in Council under this section, other than an Order to which
subsection (7) below applies, shall be subject to annulment in pursuance of a
resolution of either House of Parliament.

(7) No recommendation shall be made to Her Majesty in Council to make
an Order containing any such direction as is authorised by subsection (3)
above unless a draft of the Order has been laid before Parliament and
approved by resolution of each House of Parliament.

PART II

RESTRICTION ON RETURN

General restrictions on return

6.—(1) A person shall not be returned under Part III of this Act, or
committed or kept in custody for the purposes of return, if it appears to an
appropriate authority—

   (a) that the offence of which that person is accused or was convicted is an
     offence of a political character;

   (b) that it is an offence under military law which is not also an offence
     under the general criminal law;

   (c) that the request for his return (though purporting to be made on
     account of an extradition crime) is in fact made for the purpose of
     prosecuting or punishing him on account of his race, religion,
     nationality or political opinions; or

   (d) that he might, if returned, be prejudiced at his trial or punished,
     detained or restricted in his personal liberty by reason of his race,
     religion, nationality or political opinions.

[1](2) A person who is alleged to be unlawfully at large after conviction of an
extradition crime shall not be returned to a foreign state or to the Hong
Kong Special Administrative Region, or committed or kept in custody for
the purposes of return to a foreign state or to that Region, if it appears to an
appropriate authority—

   (a) that the conviction was obtained in his absence; and

   (b) that it would not be in the interest of justice to return him on the
     ground of that conviction.

(3) A person accused of an offence shall not be returned, or committed or
kept in custody for the purposes of return, if it appears to an appropriate
authority that if charged with that offence in the United Kingdom he would
be entitled to be discharged under any rule of law relating to previous
acquittal or conviction.

[1](4) A person shall not be returned, or committed or kept in custody for
the purposes of such return, unless provision is made by the relevant law, or

A–613

by an arrangement made with the relevant foreign state, Commonwealth country of colony or with the Hong Kong Special Administrative Region, for securing that he will not, unless he has first had an opportunity to leave it, be dealt with there for or in respect of any offence committed before his return to it other than—

(a) the offence in respect of which his return is ordered;

(b) an offence, other than an offence excluded by subsection (5) below, which is disclosed by the facts in respect of which his return was ordered; or

[2](c) subject to subsection (6) below, any other offence being an extradition crime in respect of which the Secretary of State or the Scottish Ministers may consent to his being dealt with.

(5) The offences excluded from paragraph (b) of subsection (4) above are offences in relation to which an order for the return of the person concerned could not lawfully be made.

[2,3](6) The Secretary of State or the Scottish Ministers may not give consent under paragraph (c) of that subsection in respect of an offence in relation to which it appears to him or them that an order for the return of the person concerned could not lawfully be made, or would not in fact be made.

[2](7) Any such arrangement as is mentioned in subsection (4) above which is made with a designated Commonwealth country or a colony may be an arrangement made for the particular case or an arrangement of a more general nature; and for the purposes of that subsection a certificate issued by or under the authority of the Secretary of State or the Scottish Ministers confirming the existence of an arrangement with a Commonwealth country or a colony and stating its terms shall be conclusive evidence of the matters contained in the certificate.

(8) In relation to a Commonwealth country or a colony the reference in subsection (1) above to an offence of a political character does not include an offence against the life or person of the Head of the Commonwealth or attempting or conspiring to commit, or assisting, counselling or procuring the commission of or being accessory before or after the fact to such an offence, or of impeding the apprehension or prosecution of persons guilty of such an offence.

(9) In this Act "appropriate authority" means—

[4](a) the court of committal;   (b)

(c) the High Court or High Court of Justiciary on an application for habeas corpus or for review of the order of committal.

(10) In this section, in relation to Commonwealth countries and colonies, "race" includes tribe.

NOTE

[1]As amended by the Hong Kong (Extradition) Order 1997 (S.I. 1997 No. 1178), Art. 2, Sched., para. 4.

[2] As amended by the Scotland Act 1998 (Transfer of Functions to the Scottish Ministers etc.) Order 1999 (S.I. 1999 No. 1750), art.6 and Sched. 5, para. 9(2)(a) (effective July 1, 1999).

[3] As amended by the Scotland Act 1998 (Transfer of Functions to the Scottish Ministers etc.) Order 1999 (S.I. 1999 No. 1750), art.6 and Sched. 5, para. 9(2)(b) (effective July 1, 1999).

[4] Substituted by the Scotland Act 1998 (Transfer of Functions to the Scottish Ministers etc.) Order 1999 (S.I. 1999 No. 1750), art.6 and Sched. 5, para. 9(2)(c) (effective July 1, 1999).

PART III

PROCEDURE

General

Extradition request and authority to proceed

7.—³,⁷(1) Subject to the provisions of this Act relating to provisional warrants, a person shall not be dealt with under this Part of this Act except in pursuance of an order of the Secretary of State or the Scottish Ministers (in this Act referred to as an "authority to proceed") issued in pursuance of a request (in this Act referred to as an "extradition request") for the surrender of a person under this Act made to the Secretary of State—

  (a) by—
      (i) an authority in a foreign state which appears to the Secretary of State to have the function of making extradition requests in that foreign state, or
      (ii) some person recognised by the Secretary of State as a diplomatic or consular representative of a foreign state; or
  (b) by or on behalf of the Government of a designated Commonwealth country, or the Governor of a colony; or
  ⁶(c) by or on behalf of the Government of the Hong Kong Special Administrative Region,
      and an extradition request may be made by facsimile transmission and an authority to proceed issued without waiting to receive the original.

(2) There shall be furnished with any such request—

  (a) particulars of the person whose return is requested;
  ¹(b) particulars of the offence of which he is accused or was convicted (including evidence or, in a case falling within subsection (2A) below, information sufficient to justify the issue of a warrant for his arrest under this Act);
  ³(c) in the case of a person accused of an offence, a warrant or a duly authenticated copy of a warrant for his arrest issued in the foreign state, Commonwealth country or colony or in the Hong Kong Special Administrative Region; and
  ³,⁵(d) in the case of a person unlawfully at large after conviction of an offence, a certificate or a duly authenticated copy of a warrant of the conviction and sentence.

and copies of them shall be served on the person whose return is requested before he is brought before the court of committal.

  ²(2A) Where—

  (a) the extradition request is made by a foreign state; and
  (b) an Order in Council falling within section 4(5) above is in force in relation to that state,

it shall be a sufficient compliance with subsection (2)(b) above to furnish information sufficient to justify the issue of a warrant for his arrest under this Act.

(3) Rules under section 144 of the Magistrates' Courts Act 1980 may make provision as to the procedure for service under subsection (2) above in England and Wales and the High Court of Justiciary may, by Act of Adjournal, make rules as to such procedure in Scotland.

⁷(4) On receipt of any such request the Secretary of State or the Scottish Ministers may issue an authority to proceed unless it appears to him them that an order for the return of the person concerned could not lawfully be made, or would not in fact be made, in accordance with the provisions of this Act.

⁷(5) An authority to proceed shall specify the offence or offences under

the law of the United Kingdom which it appears to the Secretary of State or the Scottish Ministers would be constituted by equivalent conduct in the United Kingdom.

(6) In this section "warrant", in the case of any foreign state, includes any judicial document authorising the arrest of a person accused of a crime.

(7) Where an extradition request is made by facsimile transmission this Act (including subsection (2) above) shall have effect as if the foreign documents so sent were the originals used to make the transmission and receivable in evidence accordingly.

NOTES
[1]As amended by the Criminal Justice and Public Order Act 1994 (c. 33), s.158(3).
[2]Inserted by the above Act, s.158(3)(b).
[3]As amended by the above Act, Sched. 9, para. 37(3).
[4]Inserted by the above Act, Sched. 9, para. 37(3)(c).
[5]As amended by the Hong Kong (Extradition) Order 1997 (S.I. 1997 No. 1178) Art. 2, Sched., para. 5.
[6]Inserted by the above Order, Art. 2, Sched., para. 5.
[7]As amended by the Scotland Act 1998 (Transfer of Functions to the Scottish Ministers etc.) Order 1999 (S.I. 1999 No. 1750), art.6 and Sched. 5, para. 9(3) (effective July 1, 1999).

Arrest for purposes of committal

8.—(1) For the purposes of this Part of this Act a warrant for the arrest of a person may be issued—
   [3](a) on receipt of an authority to proceed—
      (i) by the chief metropolitan stipendiary magistrate or a designated metropolitan magistrate;
      (ii) by the sheriff of Lothian and Borders;
   (b) without such an authority—
      [4](i) by a metropolitan magistrate;
      (ii) by a justice of the peace in any part of the United Kingdom; and
      (iii) in Scotland, by a sheriff,
upon information that the said person is or is believed to be in or on his way to the United Kingdom;
and any warrant issued by virtue of paragraph (b) above is in this Act referred to as a "provisional warrant".
   [4](2) In this Act—
      designated metropolitan magistrate" means a metropolitan stipendiary magistrate designated for the purposes of this Act by the Lord Chancellor; and
      "metropolitan magistrate" means the chief metropolitan stipendiary magistrate or a designated metropolitan magistrate.
   [1](3) A person empowered to issue warrants of arrest under this section may issue such a warrant if he is supplied with such evidence or, in a case following within subsection (3A) below, information as would in his opinion justify the issue of a warrant for the arrest of a person accused or, as the case may be, convicted within his jurisdiction and it appears to him that the conduct alleged would constitute an extradition crime.
   [2](3A) Where—
      (a) the extradition request or, where a provisional warrant is applied for, the request for the person's arrest is made by a foreign state; and
      (b) an Order in Council falling within section 4(5) above is in force in relation to that state.
it shall be sufficient for the purposes of subsection (3) above to supply such information as would, in the opinion of the person so empowered, justify the issue of a warrant of arrest.
   [5](4) Where a provisional warrant is issued under this section, the authority by whom it is issued shall forthwith give notice to the Secretary of State or the Scottish Ministers, and transmit to him or them the information and

evidence, or certified copies of the information and evidence, upon which it was issued; and the Secretary of State or the Scottish Ministers may in any case, and shall if he decides or, they decide not to issue an authority to proceed in respect of the person to whom the warrant relates, by order cancel the warrant and, if that person has been arrested under it, discharge him from custody.

(5) A warrant of arrest issued under this section may, without being backed, be executed in any part of the United Kingdom and may be so executed by any person to whom it is directed or by any constable.

(6) Where a warrant is issued under this section for the arrest of a person accused of an offence of stealing or receiving stolen property in a designated Commonwealth country or colony or any other offence committed in such a country or in a colony in respect of property, a justice of the peace in any part of the United Kingdom and in Scotland a sheriff shall have the like power to issue a warrant to search for the property as if the offence had been committed within his jurisdiction.

NOTES
[1]As amended by the Criminal Justice and Public Order Act 1994 (c. 33), s.158(4)(a).
[2]Inserted by the above Act, s.58(4)(b).
[3]Prospectively amended by the Access to Justice Act 1999 (c.11), s. 78 and Sched.11, para.32.
[4]Prospectively repealed by the Access to Justice Act 1999 (c.11), s.106 and Sched.15, Pt V(3).
[5]As amended by the Scotland Act 1998 (Transfer of Functions to the Scottish Ministers etc.) Order 1999 (S.I. 1999 No. 1750), art.6 and Sched.5, para.9(4) (effective July 1, 1999).

Proceedings for committal

9.—[4,5](1) A person arrested in pursuance of a warrant under section 8 above shall (unless previously discharged under subsection (4) of that section) be brought as soon as practicable before a court (in this Act referred to as "the court of committal") consisting of a metropolitan magistrate or the sheriff of Lothian and Borders, as may be directed by the warrant.

[1,4](2) For the purposes of proceedings under this section a court of committal in England and Wales shall have the like powers, as nearly as may be, including powers to adjourn the case and meanwhile to remand the person arrested under the warrant either in custody or on bail, as if the proceedings were the summary trial of an information against him; and section 16(1)(c) of the Prosecution of Offences Act 1985 (costs on dismissal) shall apply accordingly reading the reference to the dismissal of the information as a reference to the discharge of the person arrested.

[2](2A) If a court of committal in England and Wales exercises its power to adjourn the case it shall on so doing remand the person arrested in custody or on bail.

[3,4](3) For the purposes of proceedings under this section a court of committal in Scotland shall have the like powers, including power to adjourn the case and meanwhile to remand the person arrested under the warrant either in custody or on bail, and the proceedings shall be conducted as nearly as may be in the like manner, as if the proceedings were summary proceedings in respect of an offence alleged to have been committed by that person; and the provisions of the Legal Aid (Scotland) Act 1986 relating to such proceedings or any appellate proceedings following thereon shall apply accordingly to that person.

[1](4) Where—
(a) the extradition request is made by a foreign state; and
(b) an Order in Council such as is mentioned in subsection (8) below is in force in relation to that state,
there is no need to furnish the court of committal with evidence sufficient to make a case requiring an answer by the arrested person if the proceedings were the summary trial of an information against him.

[6](5) Where the person arrested is in custody by virtue of a provisional warrant and no authority to proceed has been received in respect of him, the court of committal may fix a period (of which the court shall give notice to the Secretary of State or the Scottish Minister) after which he will be discharged from custody unless such an authority has been received.

(6) In exercising the power conferred by subsection (5) above in a case where the extradition request is made under general extradition arrangements the court shall have regard to any period specified for the purpose in the Order in Council relating to the arrangements.

(7) Where—

(a) the extradition request is made under general extradition arrangements but no period is so specified; or

(b) the application is made under special extradition arrangements, the court of committal may fix a reasonable period.

[3](7A) In exercising the power conferred by subsection (5) above in a case where the extradition request is made by or on behalf of the Government of the Hong Kong Special Administrative Region the court shall not fix a period ending more than 60 days after the day of the person's arrest, unless the exceptional circumstances of the case justify a longer period.

(8) Where an authority to proceed has been issued in respect of the person arrested and the court of committal is satisfied, after hearing any representations made in support of the extradition request or on behalf of that person, that the offence to which the authority relates is an extradition crime, and is further satisfied—

[1](a) where that person is accused of the offence, unless an Order in Council giving effect to general extradition arrangements under which the extradition request was made otherwise provides, that the evidence would be sufficient to make a case requiring an answer by that person if the proceedings were the summary trial of an information against him;

(b) where that person is alleged to be unlawfully at large after conviction of the offence, that he has been so convicted and appears to be so at large,

the court, unless his committal is prohibited by any other provision of this Act, shall commit him to custody or on bail—

[7](i) to await the Secretary of State's or the Scottish Ministers decision as to his return; and

[7](ii) if the Secretary of State decides or the Scottish Ministers' decide that he shall be returned, to await his return.

(9) If the court commits a person under subsection (8) above, it shall issue a certificate of the offence against the law of the United Kingdom which would be constituted by his conduct.

(10) If the court commits a person to custody in the exercise of that power, it may subsequently grant bail if it considers it appropriate to do so.

(11) If—

(a) the court is not satisfied as mentioned in subsection (8) above in relation to the person arrested; or

(b) his committal is prohibited by a provision of this Act,

it shall discharge him.

Notes

[1]As amended by the Criminal Justice and Public Order Act 1994 (c. 33), s.158(5).

[2]Inserted by the above Act, s.158(5)(b).

[3]Inserted by the Hong Kong (Extradition) Order 1997 (S.I. 1997 No. 1178), Art. 2, Sched., para. 6.

[4]Prospectively amended by the Access to Justice Act 1999 (c.11), s. 78 and Sched.11, para.33.

[5]Prospectively amended by the Access to Justice Act 1999 (c.11), s.106 and Sched.15, Pt V(3).

[6]As amended by the Scotland Act 1998 (Transfer of Functions to the Scottish Ministers etc.) Order 1999 (S.I. 1999 No. 1750), art.6 and Sched.5, para.9(5) (effective July 1, 1999).

[7]As amended by the Scotland Act 1998 (Transfer of Functions to the Scottish Ministers etc.) Order 1999 (S.I. 1999 No. 1750), art.6 and Sched.5, para.9(6) (effective July 1, 1999).

Statement of case by court

10.—(1) If the court of committal refuses to make an order in relation to a person under section 9 above in respect of the offence or, as the case may be, any of the offences to which the authority to proceed relates, the foreign state, Commonwealth country or colony seeking the surrender of that person to it may question the proceeding on the ground that it is wrong in law by applying to the court to state a case for the opinion of the High Court or, in Scotland, the High Court of Justiciary on the question of law involved.

(2) If the state, country or colony seeking return immediately informs the court of committal that it intended to make such an application, the court shall make an order providing for the detention of the person to whom the authority to proceed relates, or directing that he shall not be released except on bail.

(3) Rules of Court may specify—

(a) a period within which such an application must be made unless the court grants a longer period; and

(b) a period within which the court of committal must comply with such an application.

(4) Where the court of committal fails to comply with an application under subsection (1) above within the period specified by Rules of Court, the High Court or, in Scotland, the High Court of Justiciary may, on the application of the state, country or colony that applied for the case to be stated, make an order requiring the court to state a case.

(5) The High Court or High Court of Justiciary shall have power—

(a) to remit the case to the court of committal to decide if according to the opinion of the High Court or High Court of Justiciary on the question of law; or

(b) to dismiss the appeal.

[4](6) Where the court dismisses an appeal relating to an offence, it shall by order declare that that offence is not an offence in respect of which the Secretary of State or the Scottish Ministers has power to make an order for return in respect of the person whose return was requested.

[3](7) An order made by a metropolitan magistrate under subsection (2) above shall cease to have effect if—

(a) the court dismisses the appeal in respect of the offence or all the offences to which it relates; and

(b) the foreign state, Commonwealth country or colony does not immediately—

(i) apply for leave to appeal to the House of Lords; or

(ii) inform the court that it intends to apply for leave.

(8) An order made by the sheriff of Lothian and Borders under subsection (2) above shall cease to have effect if the court dismisses the appeal in respect of the offence or all the offences to which it relates.

(9) In relation to a decision of a court on an appeal under this section, section 1 of the Administration of Justice Act 1960 (right of appeal to House of Lords) shall have effect as if so much of subsection (2) as restricts the grant of leave to appeal were omitted.

(10) The House of Lords may exercise any powers of the High Court under subsection (5) above and subsection (6) above shall apply to them as it applies to that Court.

(11) Subject to subsections (7) and (8) above, an order under subsection (2) above shall have effect so long as the case is pending.

(12) For the purposes of this section a case is pending (unless proceedings are discontinued) until (disregarding any power of a court to grant leave to

take any step out of time) there is no step that the state, country or colony can take.

[1](13) In the application of this section to Scotland subsections (9) and (10) above shall be omitted and in relation to an appeal under this section in Scotland the court may make an order providing for the detention of the person to whom it relates or it may grant bail; and section 177(2) and (3) of the Criminal Procedure (Scotland) Act 1995 shall apply for the purpose of such an appeal as it applies for the purpose of an appeal such as is mentioned in section 176 of that Act.

[2](14) This section shall apply to the Hong Kong Special Administrative Region in the same way as it applies to any foreign state, Commonwealth country or colony.

NOTES

[1]As amended by the Criminal Procedure (Consequential Provisions) (Scotland) Act 1995 (c. 40), Sched. 40, para. 73.

[2]Inserted by the Hong Kong (Extradition) Order 1997 (S.I. 1997 No. 1178), Art. 2, Sched., para. 7.

[3]Prospectively amended by the Access to Justice Act 1999 (c.11), s. 78 and Sched.11, para.34.

[4]As amended by the Scotland Act 1998 (Transfer of Functions to the Scottish Ministers etc.) Order 1999 (S.I. 1999 No. 1750), art.6 and Sched.5, para.9(7) (effective July 1, 1999).

Application for habeas corpus etc.

11.—[1](1) Where a person is committed under section 9 above, the court shall inform him in ordinary language of his right to make an application for habeas corpus, and shall forthwith give notice of the committal to the Secretary of State or the Scottish Minister.

(2) A person committed shall not be returned—

(a) in any case, until the expiration of the period of 15 days beginning with the day on which the order for his committal is made;

(b) if an application for habeas corpus is made in his case, so long as proceedings on that application is pending.

(3) Without prejudice to any jurisdiction of the High Court apart from this section, the court shall order the applicant's discharge if it appears to the court in relation to the offence, or each of the offences, in repect of which the applicant's return is sought, that—

(a) by reason of the trivial nature of the offence; or

(b) by reason of the passage of time since he is alleged to have committed it or to have become unlawfully at large, as the case may be; or

(c) because the accusation against him is not made in good faith in the interests of justice,

it would, having regard to all the circumstances, be unjust or oppressive to return him.

(4) On any such application the court may receive additional evidence relevant to the exercise of its jurisdiction under section 6 above or subsection (3) above.

(5) Proceedings on an application for habeas corpus shall be treated for the purposes of this section as pending (unless they are discontinued) until (disregarding any power of a court to grant leave to appeal out of time) there is no further possibility of an appeal.

(6) In the application of this section to Scotland references to an application for habeas corpus shall be construed as references to an application for review of the order of committal and references to the High Court shall be construed as references to the High Court of Justiciary.

NOTE

[1]As amended by the Scotland Act 1998 (Transfer of Functions to the Scottish Ministers etc.) Order 1999 (S.I. 1999 No. 1750), art.6 and Sched.5, para.9(8) (effective July 1, 1999).

Order for return

12.—[2](1) Where a person is committed under section 9 above and is not discharged by order of the High Court or the High Court of Justiciary, the Secretary of State or the Scottish Ministers may by warrant order him to be returned unless his return is prohibited, or prohibited for the time being, by this Act, or the Secretary of State decides or the Scottish Ministers' decide under this section to make no such order in his case.

[1,2](2) Without prejudice to his general discretion as to the making of an order for the return of a person to a foreign state, Commonwealth country or colony or to the Hong Kong Special Administrative Region—

(a) the Secretary of State shall not make an order in the case of any person if it appears to the Secretary of State or the Scottish Ministers in relation to the offence, or each of the offences, in respect of which his return is sought, that—

   (i) by reason of its trivial nature; or

   (ii) by reason of the passage of time since he is alleged to have committed it or to have become unlawfully at large, as the case may be; or

   (iii) because the accusation against him is not in good faith in the interests of justice,

it would, having regard to all the circumstances, be unjust or oppressive to return him; and

(b) the Secretary of State may decide to make no order for the return of a person accused or convicted of an offence not punishable with death in Great Britain if that person could be or has been sentenced to death for that offence in the country by which the request for his return is made.

(3) An order for return shall not be made in the case of a person who is serving a sentence of imprisonment or detention, or is charged with an offence, in the United Kingdom—

(a) in the case of a person serving such a sentence, until the sentence has been served;

(b) in the case of a person charged with an offence, until the charge is disposed of or withdrawn or unless an order is made for it to lie on the file and, if it results in his serving a term of imprisonment or detention, until the sentence has been served.

(4) In the application of this section to Scotland, the reference in subsection (3) above to an order being made for the charge to lie on the file shall be construed as a reference to the diet being deserted *pro loco et tempore*.

(5) The Secretary of State or the Scottish Ministers may decide to make no order under this section for the return of a person committed in consequence of an extradition request if another extradition request or a requisition under Schedule 1 to this Act has been made in respect of him and it appears to the Secretary of State, having regard to all the circumstances of the case and in particular—

(a) the relative seriousness of the offences in question;

(b) the date on which each such request was made; and

(c) the nationality or citizenship of the person concerned and his ordinary residence,

that preference should be given to that other request or requisition.

(6) Notice of the issue of a warrant under this section for the return of a person to a Commonwealth country or colony shall forthwith be given to the person to be returned.

NOTES
[1]As amended by the Hong Kong (Extradition) Order 1997 (S.I. 1997 No. 1178), Art. 2, Sched., para. 8.

[2]As amended by the Scotland Act 1998 (Transfer of Functions to the Scottish Ministers etc.) Order 1999 (S.I. 1999 No. 1750), art. 6 and Sched. 5, para. 9(9) (effective July 1, 1999).

Return to foreign states—supplementary

13.—[1,2](1) The Secretary of State or the Scottish Ministers shall give the person to whom an order under section 12(1) above for return to a foreign state or to the Hong Kong Special Administrative Region would relate notice in writing that he is contemplating making such an order.

(2) The person to whom such an order would relate shall have a right to make representations, at any time before the expiration of the period of 15 days commencing with the date on which the notice is given, as to why he should not be returned to the foreign state, and unless he waives that right, no such order shall be made in relation to him before the end of that period.

(3) A notice under subsection (1) above shall explain in ordinary language the right conferred by subsection (2) above.

[2](4) It shall be the duty of the Secretary of State or the Scottish Ministers to consider any representations made in the exercise of that right.

[1](5) Unless the person to whom it relates waives the right conferred on him by subsection (6) below, he shall not be returned to the foreign state or to the Hong Kong Special Administrative Region until the expiration of the period of seven days commencing with the date on which the warrant is issued or such longer period as—

(a) in England and Wales, rules under section 84 of the Supreme Court Act 1981 may provide; or

(b) in Scotland, the High Court of Justiciary may provide by Act of Adjournal.

[2](6) At any time within that period, he may apply for leave to seek judicial review of the Secretary of State's decision or the Scottish Ministers' decision to make the order.

(7) If he applies for judicial review, he may not be returned so long as the proceedings for judicial review are pending.

(8) Proceedings for judicial review shall be treated for the purposes of this section as pending (unless they are discontinued) until (disregarding any power of a court to grant leave to appeal out of time) there is no further possibility of an appeal.

(9) A warrant under section 12 above—

[2](a) shall state in ordinary language that the Secretary of State or the Scottish Minister has considered any representations made in the exercise of the right conferred by subsection (2) above; and

[1](b) shall explain in ordinary language the rights conferred by this section on a person whose return to a foreign state or to the Hong Kong Special Administrative Region has been ordered under section 12 above,

and a copy shall be given to the person to whom it relates as soon as the order for his return is made.

NOTES

[1]As amended by the Hong Kong (Extradition) Order 1997 (S.I. 1997 No. 1178), Art. 2, Sched., para. 9.

[2]As amended by the Scotland Act 1998 (Transfer of Functions to the Scottish Ministers etc.) Order 1999 (S.I. 1999 No. 1750), art. 6 and Sched. 5, para. 9 (effective July 1, 1999).

Simplified procedure

14.—(1) A person may give notice that he waives the rights conferred on him by section 11 above.

(2) A notice under this section shall be given in England and Wales in the manner prescribed by rules under section 144 of the Magistrates' Courts Act 1980, and without prejudice to the generality of subsection (1) of that

section, the power to make such rules shall include power to make provision for a magistrate to order the committal for return of a person with his consent at any time after his arrest.

(3) A notice under this section shall be given in Scotland in the manner prescribed by the High Court of Justiciary by Act of Adjournal and the sheriff may order the committal for return of a person with his consent at any time after his arrest.

(4) Where an order is made by virtue of this section, this Act shall cease to apply to the person in respect of whom it is made, except that, if he is not surrendered within one month after the order is made, the High Court or, in Scotland, the High Court of Justiciary, upon application by or on behalf of that person, may, unless reasonable cause is shown for the delay, order him to be discharged.

Special extradition arrangements

Special extradition arrangements

15.—(1) Where special extradition arrangements have been made in respect of a person, extradition procedures shall be available in the case of that person, as between the United Kingdom and the foreign state with which the arrangements have been made, subject to the limitations, restrictions, exceptions and qualifications, if any, contained in the arrangements.

(2) If the Secretary of State issues a certificate of special extradition arrangements, it shall be conclusive evidence of all matters stated in it.

(3) In subsection (2) above "certificate of special extradition arrangements" means a certificate—

    (a) that special extradition arrangements have been made in respect of a person as between the United Kingdom and a foreign state specified in the certificate; and

    (b) that extradition procedures are available in the case of that person as between the United Kingdom and the foreign state to the extent specified in the certificate.

Effect of delay

Discharge in case of delay

16.—(1) If a person committed under section 9 above is still in the United Kingdom after the expiration of the relevant period, he may apply to the High Court or High Court of Justiciary for his discharge.

(2) Unless he has instituted proceedings for judicial review of the Secretary of State's decision to order his return, the relevant period is—

    (a) the period of two months beginning with the very first day on which, having regard to section 11(2) above, he could have been returned;

    (b) where a warrant for his return has been issued under section 12 above, the period of one month beginning with the day on which that warrant was issued.

(3) If he has instituted such proceedings, the relevant period is the period expiring one month after they end.

(4) Proceedings for judicial review end for the purposes of this section—

    (a) if they are discontinued, on the day of discontinuance; and

    (b) if they are determined, on the day on which (disregarding any power of a court to grant leave to appeal out of time) there is no further possibility of an appeal.

(5) If upon an application under this section the court is satisfied that reasonable notice of the proposed application has been given to the Secretary of State, the court may, unless sufficient cause is shown to the

contrary, by order direct the applicant to be discharged and, if a warrant for his return has been issued under section 12 above, quash that warrant.

Custody

17.—(1) Any person remanded or committed to custody under this Part of this Act shall be committed to the like institution as a person charged with an offence before the court of committal.

(2) If any person who is in custody by virtue of a warrant under this Act escapes out of custody, he may be retaken in any part of the United Kingdom in like manner as a person escaping from custody under a warrant for his arrest issued in that part in respect of an offence committed in that part.

(3) Where a person, being in custody in any part of the United Kingdom whether under this Part of this Act or otherwise, is required to be removed in custody under this Act to another part of the United Kingdom and is so removed by sea or by air, he shall be deemed to continue in legal custody until he reaches the place to which he is required to be removed.

(4) A warrant for the return of any person shall be sufficient authority for all persons to whom it is directed and all constables to receive that person, keep him in custody and convey him into the jurisdiction to which he is to be returned.

...

PROTECTION FROM HARASSMENT ACT 1997

(1997 c. 40)

An Act to make provision for protecting persons from harassment and similar conduct.

[28th October 1982]

Scotland

Harassment

8.—(1) Every individual has a right to be free from harassment and, accordingly, a person must not pursue a course of conduct which amounts to harassment of another and—

(a) is intended to amount to harassment of that person; or
(b) occurs in circumstances where it would appear to a reasonable person that it would amount to harassment of that person.

(2) An actual or apprehended breach of subsection (1) may be the subject of a claim in civil proceedings by the person who is or may be the victim of the course of conduct in question; and any such claim shall be known as an action of harassment.

(3) For the purposes of this section—
"conduct" includes speech;
"harassment" of a person includes causing the person alarm or distress; and
a course of conduct must involve conduct on at least two occasions.

(4) It shall be a defence to any action of harassment to show that the course of conduct complained of—

(a) was authorised by, under or by virtue of any enactment or rule of law;
(b) was pursued for the purpose of preventing or detecting crime; or
(c) was, in the particular circumstances, reasonable.

(5) In an action of harassment the court may, without prejudice to any other remedies which it may grant—

(a) award damages;
(b) grant—
(i) interdict or interim interdict;
(ii) if it is satisfied that it is appropriate for it to do so in order to protect the person from further harassment, an order, to be known as a "non-harassment order", requiring the defender to refrain from such conduct in relation to the pursuer as may be specified in the order for such period (which includes an indeterminate period) as may be so specified,

A–625

but a person may not be subjected to the same prohibitions in an interdict or interim interdict and a non-harassment order at the same time.

(6) The damages which may be awarded in an action of harassment include damages for any anxiety caused by the harassment and any financial loss resulting from it.

(7) Without prejudice to any right to seek review of any interlocutor, a person against whom a non-harassment order has been made, or the person for whose protection the order was made, may apply to the court by which the order was made for revocation of or a variation of the order and, on any such application, the court may revoke the order or vary it in such manner as it considers appropriate.

(8) In section 10(1) of the Damages (Scotland) Act 1976 (interpretation), in the definition of "personal injuries", after "to reputation" there is inserted ", or injury resulting from harassment actionable under section 8 of the Protection from Harassment Act 1997".

Breach of non-harassment order

9.—(1) Any person who is found to be in breach of a non-harassment order made under section 8 is guilty of an offence and liable—

  (a) on conviction on indictment, to imprisonment for a term not exceeding five years or to a fine, or to both such imprisonment and such fine; and

  (b) on summary conviction, to imprisonment for a period not exceeding six months or to a fine not exceeding the statutory maximum, or to both such imprisonment and such fine.

(2) A breach of a non-harassment order shall not be punishable other than in accordance with subsection (1).

Limitation

10.—(1) After section 18A of the Prescription and Limitation (Scotland) Act 1973 there is inserted the following section—

  "**Actions of harassment**

  18B.—(1) This section applies to actions of harassment (within the meaning of section 8 of the Protection from Harassment Act 1997) which include a claim for damages.

  (2) Subject to subsection (3) below and to section 19A of this Act, no action to which this section applies shall be brought unless it is commenced within a period of 3 years after—

    (a) the date on which the alleged harassment ceased; or

    (b) the date, (if later than the date mentioned in paragraph (a) above) on which the pursuer in the action became, or on which, in the opinion of the court, it would have been reasonably practicable for him in all the circumstances to have become, aware, that the defender was a person responsible for the alleged harassment or the employer or principal of such a person.

  (3) In the computation of the period specified in subsectoin (2) above there shall be disregarded any time during which the person who is alleged to have suffered the harassment was under legal disability by reason of nonage or unsoundness of mind.".

(2) In subsection (1) of section 19A of that Act (power of court to override time-limits), for "section 17 or section 18 and section 18A" there is substituted "section 17, 18, 18A or 18B".

Non-harassment order following criminal offence

11. [*Inserted s.234A into the Criminal Procedure (Scotland) Act 1995.*]

General

National security, etc.

12.—(1) If the Secretary of State certifies that in his opinion anything done by a specified person on a specified occasion related to—

(a) national security,
(b) the economic well-being of the United Kingdom, or
(c) the prevention or detection of serious crime,

and was done on behalf of the Crown, the certificate is conclusive evidence that this Act does not apply to any conduct of that person on that occasion.

(2) In subsection (1), "specified" means specified in the certificate in question.

(3) A document purporting to be a certificate under subsection (1) is to be received in evidence and, unless the contrary is proved, be treated as being such a certificate.

Extent

14.—(1) Sections 1 to 7 extend to England and Wales only.

(2) Sections 8 to 11 extend to Scotland only.

(3) This Act (except section 13) does not extend to Northern Ireland.

Commencement

15.—(1) Sections 1, 2, 4, 5 and 7 to 12 are to come into force on such day as the Secretary of State may by order made by statutory instrument appoint.

Sections 3 and 6 are to come into force on such day as the Lord Chancellor may by order made by statutory instrument appoint.

(3) Different days may be appointed under this section for different purposes.

Short title

16. This Act may be cited as the Protection from Harassment Act 1997.

CRIMINAL JUSTICE (TERRORISM AND CONSPIRACY) ACT 1998

(1998 c. 40)

ARRANGEMENT OF SECTIONS

Proscribed organisations

An Act to make provision about procedure and forfeiture in relation to offences concerning proscribed organisations, and about conspiracy to commit offences outside the United Kingdom.

[4th September 1998]

Evidence and inferences: Great Britain

[1]**1.**—(1) The following sections shall be inserted after section 2 of the Prevention of Terrorism (Temporary Provisions) Act 1989—

"Evidence and inferences

2A.—(1) This section applies where a person is charged with an offence under section 2(1)(a) above; and references here to a specified organisation must be construed in accordance with section 2B below.

(2) Subsection (3) below applies if a police officer of or above the rank of superintendent states in oral evidence that in his opinion the accused—

(a) belongs to an organisation which is specified, or

(b) belonged at a particular time to an organisation which was then specified.

(3) If this subsection applies—

(a) the statement shall be admissible as evidence of the matter stated, but

(b) the accused shall not be committed for trial in England and Wales, or be found to have a case to answer or be convicted, solely on the basis of the statement.

(4) Subsection (6) below applies if evidence is given that—

(a) at any time before being charged with the offence the accused, on being questioned under caution by a constable, failed to mention a fact which is material to the offence and which he could reasonably be expected to mention, and

(b) before being questioned he was permitted to consult a solicitor.

(5) Subsection (6) below also applies if evidence is given that—

(a) on being charged with the offence or informed by a constable that he might be prosecuted for it the accused failed to mention a fact which is material to the offence and which he could reasonably be expected to mention, and

(b) before being charged or informed he was permitted to consult a solicitor.

(6) If this subsection applies—

(a) the court or jury, in considering any question whether the accused belongs or belonged at a particular time to a specified organisation, may draw from the failure inferences relating to that question, but

(b) the accused shall not be committed for trial in England and Wales, or be found to have a case to answer or be convicted, solely on the basis of the inferences.

(7) Subject to any directions by the court, evidence tending to establish the failure may be given before or after evidence tending to establish the fact which the accused is alleged to have failed to mention.

(8) This section does not—

(a) prejudice the admissibility of evidence admissible apart from this section;

(b) preclude the drawing of inferences which could be drawn apart from this section;

(c) prejudice an enactment providing (in whatever words) that an answer or evidence given by a person in specified circumstances is not admissible in evidence against him or some other person in any proceedings or class of proceedings (however described, and whether civil or criminal).

(9) In subsection (8)(c) above the reference to giving evidence is a reference to giving it in any manner (whether by giving information, making discovery or disclosure, producing documents or otherwise).

(10) In any proceedings in Scotland for an offence under section 2(1)(a) above in which the accused is charged with belonging to a specified organisation, where the court or jury draws an inference as mentioned in subsection (6) above any evidence that he belongs or, as the case may be, belonged to the organisation shall be sufficient evidence of that matter.

(11) In this section "police officer" means a member of—

(a) a police force within the meaning of the Police Act 1996 or the Police (Scotland) Act 1967, or

(b) the Royal Ulster Constabulary.

(12) This section does not apply to a statement made or failure occurring before the day on which the Criminal Justice (Terrorism and Conspiracy) Act 1998 was passed.

Specified organisations

2B.—(1) For the purposes of section 2A above an organisation is specified at a particular time if at that time—

(a) it is specified under section 3(8) of the Northern Ireland (Sentences) Act 1998 or under subsection (2) below, and

    (b) it is, or forms part of, an organisation which is proscribed for the purposes of this Act.

(2) If the condition in subsection (3) below is satisfied the Secretary of State may by order specify an organisation which is not specified under section 3(8) of the Northern Ireland (Sentences) Act 1998.

(3) The condition is that the Secretary of State believes that the organisation—

    (a) is concerned in terrorism connected with the affairs of Northern Ireland, or in promoting or encouraging it, and

    (b) has not established or is not maintaining a complete and unequivocal ceasefire.

(4) An order under this section shall be made by statutory instrument; and no order shall be made unless a draft has been laid before, and approved by resolution of, each House of Parliament."

(2) For the purposes of section 27 of the Prevention of Terrorism (Temporary Provisions) Act 1989 (duration etc.) sections 2A and 2B of that Act shall be treated as having been continued in force by the order under subsection (6) of section 27 which has effect when this Act is passed.

NOTE
[1]Prospectively amended by the Terrorism Act 2000 (c. 11), s.125 and Sched. 16, Part I.

Evidence and inferences: Northern Ireland

2. [Does not apply in Scotland.]

Arrest and detention

[1]**3.**—(1) In section 14(1)(a) of the Prevention of Terrorism (Temporary Provisions) Act 1989 (arrest and detention of persons suspected of certain offences etc.) after "above" there shall be inserted "or under section 30 of the Northern Ireland (Emergency Provisions) Act 1996".

(2) This section applies whether the offence is suspected to have been committed before or on or after the day on which this Act is passed.

NOTE
[1]Prospectively amended by the Terrorism Act 2000 (c. 11), s.125 and Sched. 16, Part I.

Forfeiture orders

[1]**4.**—(1) This section applies if—

    (a) a person is convicted of an offence under section 2 of the Prevention of Terrorism (Temporary Provision) Act 1989 (membership etc. of proscribed organisations), and

    (b) at the time of the offence he belonged to an organisation which was then a specified organisation for the purposes of section 2A of that Act.

(2) This section also applies if—

    (a) a person is convicted of an offence under section 30 of the Northern Ireland (Emergency Provisions) Act 1996 (membership etc. of proscribed organisations), and

    (b) at the time of the offence he belonged to an organisation which was then a specified organisation for the purposes of section 30A of that Act.

(3) The court by or before which the person is convicted may order the forfeiture of any money or other property if—

    (a) he had it in his possession or under his control at the time of the offence, and

    (b) it has been used in furtherance of or in connection with the activities of the specified organisation, or the court believes it may be so used unless forfeited.

(4) If a person other than the convicted person claims to be the owner of or otherwise interested in anything which can be forfeited by an order under this section, before making such an order in respect of it the court must give him an opportunity to be heard.

(5) The standard of proof required to determine any question arising as to whether subsection (1)(b), (2)(b) or (3)(a) or (b) is satisfied shall be that applicable in civil proceedings.

(6) For the purposes of this section property includes property wherever situated and whether real or personal, heritable or moveable, a thing in action or other intangible or incorporeal property.

(7) Schedule 4 to the Prevention of Terrorism (Temporary Provisions) Act 1989 shall apply in relation to orders under subsection (3) above, and in its application by virtue of this subsection—

(a) the references in paragraphs 1(1), 11(1) and 21(1) to section 13(2), (3) or (4) of that Act shall be treated as references to subsection (3) above;

(b) the references in paragraphs 1(1)(d), 11(1)(d) and 21(1)(d) to section 13(6) of that Act shall be treated as references to subsection (4) above.

(8) This section applies where the offence is committed on or after the day on which this Act is passed, and for this purpose an offence committed over a period of more than one day or at some time during a period of more than one day must be taken to be committed on the last of the days in the period.

(9) The following paragraphs apply so far as this section extends to England and Wales and Scotland—

(a) section 27(5) of the Prevention of Terrorism (Temporary Provisions) Act 1989 (duration) shall apply to this section;

(b) for the purposes of section 27 this section shall be treated as having been continued in force by the order under subsection (6) of section 27 which has effect when this Act is passed.

(10) So far as this section extends to Northern Ireland, for the purposes of section 62 of the Northern Ireland (Emergency Provisions) Act 1996 (duration etc.) it shall be treated as a temporary provision of that Act.

NOTE
[1]Prospectively amended by the Terrorism Act 2000 (c. 11), s.125 and Sched. 16, Part I.

Conspiracy to commit offences outside the United Kingdom

5. [Does not apply in Scotland.]

6. [Does not apply in Scotland.]

Scotland

7. [*Inserted s.11A into the Criminal Procedure (Scotland) Act 1995.*]

General

Report to Parliament

8. The Secretary of State shall lay before both Houses of Parliament at least once in every 12 months a report on the working of this Act.

Consequential amendments and repeals

9.—(1) Schedule 1 (consequential amendments) shall have effect.

(2) The enactments specified in Schedule 2 are hereby repealed or revoked to the extent specified.

(3) The amendments in Part II of Schedule 1, and the repeals and revocations in Part II of Schedule 2, shall have no effect—

    (a) in England and Wales and Northern Ireland, in relation to an agreement entered into before the day on which this Act is passed, or

    (b) in Scotland, in relation to an act done before the day on which this Act is passed.

Extent

10. A provision of this Act which amends, repeals or revokes an enactment shall have the same extent as the enactment which it amends, repeals or revokes.

Short title

11. This Act may be cited as the Criminal Justice (Terrorism and Conspiracy) Act 1998.

SCHEDULES

Section 9(1)   SCHEDULE 1

CONSEQUENTIAL AMENDMENTS

[1]PART I

PROSCRIBED ORGANISATIONS

Criminal Justice Act 1988 (c. 33)

1. In section 74(2) of the Criminal Justice Act 1988 (property not realisable) the word "or" at the end of paragraph (c) shall be omitted and at the end of paragraph (d) there shall be inerted "or

    (e) an order under section 4(3) of the Criminal Justice (Terrorism and Conspiracy) Act 1998 (forfeiture orders),".

Prevention of Terrorism (Temporary Provisions) Act 1989 (c. 4)

2. In Schedule 3 to the Prevention of Terrorism (Temporary Provisions) Act 1989 (supervision of detention and examination powers) in paragraph 3(3)(a)(i) for "(in the case of detention under section 14) or under section 8" there shall be substituted "or under section 30 of the Northern Ireland (Emergency Provisions) Act 1996 (in the case of detention under section 14 of this Act) or under section 8 of this Act".

Drug Trafficking Act 1994 (c. 37)

3. In section 6(3) of the Drug Trafficking Act 1994 (property not realisable) after paragraph (e) there shall be inserted—

    "(f) section 4(3) of the Criminal Justice (Terrorism and Conspiracy) Act 1998 (forfeiture orders)."

NOTE

  [1]Prospectively amended by the Terrorism Act 2000 (c. 11), s.125 and Sched. 16, Part I.

PART II

CONSPIRACY

Criminal Law Act 1977 (c. 45)

4. In section 1 of the Criminal Law Act 1977 (conspiracy) the following shall cease to have effect—

    (a) subsections (1A) and (1B),

    (b) in subsections (4), the words from "except that" to the end, and

    (c) subsections (5) and (6).

Criminal Attempts and Conspiracy (Northern Ireland) Order 1983 (S.I. 1983/1120 (N.I. 13))

5. In Article 9 of the Criminal Attempts and Conspiracy (Northern Ireland) Order 1983 (conspiracy) the following shall cease to have effect—

(a) paragraphs (1A) and (1B),
(b) in paragraph (4), the words from "except that" to the end, and
(c) paragraphs (5) and (6).

Computer Misuse Act 1990 (c. 18)

6.—(1) In section 8 of the Computer Misuse Act 1990 (relevance of external law)—
(a) subsection (2) shall cease to have effect,.
(b) in subsection (5), for "any of subsections (1) to (3)" there shall be substituted "subsection (1) or (3)", and
(c) subsection (6)(b) shall cease to have effect.
(2) Section 9(2)(b) of that Act (British citizenship immaterial: conspiracy) shall cease to have effect.
(3) In section 16 of that Act (application to Northern Ireland)—
(a) in subsection (4), for "Subsections (5) to (7) below apply in substitution for subsections (1) to (3) of section 7" there shall be substituted "Subsection (7) below shall apply in substitution for subsection (3) of section 7", and
(b) subsections (5), (6) and (8)(a) shall cease to have effect.

Criminal Justice Act 1993 (c. 36)

7.—(1) Section 5(1) of the Criminal Justice Act 1993 (conspiracy, attempt and incitement) shall cease to have effect.
(2) In section 6(1) of that Act (relevance of external law) the words "by virtue of section 1A of the Criminal Law Act 1977, or" shall cease to have effect.

Criminal Law (Consolidation) (Scotland) Act 1995 (c. 39)

8. Section 16A of the Criminal Law (Consolidation) (Scotland) Act 1995 (conspiracy or incitement to commit certain sexual acts outside the United Kingdom) shall be amended as follows—
(a) in subsection (1) omit the words "conspiracy or" and "the criminal purpose or, as the case may be,",
(b) in subsection (2) omit the words "the criminal purpose or, as the case may be," and "conspiracy or",
(c) in subsection (3) omit paragraph (a) and the words "(b) in the case of proceedings charging incitement", and
(d) in subsection (5) omit paragraph (a) and the words "(b) in relation to proceedings charging incitement".

Sexual Offences (Conspiracy and Incitement) Act 1996 (c. 29)

9.—(1) Section 1 of the Sexual Offences (Conspiracy and Incitement) Act 1996 (conspiracy to commit certain sexual acts outside the United Kingdom) shall cease to have effect.
(2) Section 3 of that Act (supplementary) shall be amended as follows—
(a) in subsection (1) for "sections 1 and 2" substitute "section 2",
(b) in subsection (2)—
   (i) omit "1(3) or", and
   (ii) for "the relevant conduct" substitute "what the accused had in view".
(c) omit subsection (3),
(d) in subsection (6) omit "1 or",
(e) omit subsection (7), and
(f) in subsection (9)—
   (i) for "Subsections (7) and (8) apply" substitute "Subsection (8) applies", and
   (ii) for "sections 1 and 2" substitute "section 2".
(3) Section 4(b) and (c) of that Act (application to Northern Ireland) shall cease to have effect.
(4) In section 7(3) of that Act (commencement), the word "1" shall cease to have effect.

Criminal Justice (Northern Ireland) Order 1996 (S.I. 1996/3160 (N.I. 24))

10.—(1) Article 42(1)(b) of the Criminal Justice (Northern Ireland) Order 1996 (attempt, conspiracy and incitement) shall cease to have effect.

(2) In Article 43(2) of that Order (relevance of external law) the words "by virtue of Article 9A of that Order, or" shall cease to have effect.

Section 9(2)   SCHEDULE 2

REPEALS AND REVOCATIONS

¹PART I

PROSCRIBED ORGANISATIONS

Chapter	Short title	Extent of repeal
1988 c. 33.	Criminal Justice Act 1988.	In section 74(2) the word "or" at the end of paragraph (c).

NOTE
¹Prospectively amended by the Terrorism Act 2000 (c. 11), s.125 and Sched. 16, Part I.

PART II

CONSPIRACY

Chapter	Short title	Extent of repeal
1977 c. 45.	Criminal Law Act 1977.	In section 1, subsections (1A) and (1B), the words in subsection (4) from "except that" to the end, and subsections (5) and (6).
S.I. 1983/1120 (N.I. 13).	Criminal Attempts and Conspiracy (Northern Ireland) Order 1983.	In Article 9, paragraphs (1A) and (1B), the words in paragraph (4) from "except that" to the end, and paragraphs (5) and (6).
1990 c. 18.	Computer Misuse Act 1990.	Section 7(1) and (2). Section 8(2) and (6)(b). Section 9(2b). Section 16(5), (6) and (8)(a).
1993 c. 36.	Criminal Justice Act 1993.	Section 5(1). In section 6(1), the words "by virtue of section 1A of the Criminal Law Act 1977, or".
1995 c. 39.	Criminal Law (Consolidation) (Scotland) Act 1995.	In section 16A, in subsection (1) the words "conspiracy or" and "the criminal purpose or, as the case may be,", in subsection (2) the words "the criminal purpose or, as the case may be," and "conspiracy or", in subsection (3) paragraph (a) and the words "(b) in the case of proceedings charging incitement" and in subsection (5) paragraph (a) and the words "(b) in relation to proceedings charging incitement".
1996 c. 29.	Sexual Offences (Conspiracy and Incitement) Act 1996.	Section 1. In section 3, the words "1(3) or" in subsection (2), subsection (3), the words "1 or" in subsection (6) and subsection (7). Section 4(b) and (c). In section 7(3) the word "1".
S.I. 1996/3160 (N.I. 24).	Criminal Justice (Northern Ireland) Order 1996.	Article 42(1)(b). In Article 43(2) the words "by virtue of Article 9A of that Order, or".

HUMAN RIGHTS ACT 1998

(1998 c. 42)

ARRANGEMENT OF SECTIONS

Introduction

Legislation

Public authorities

Remedial action

Other rights and proceedings

Derogations and reservations

Judges of the European Court of Human Rights

Parliamentary procedure

Supplemental

An Act to give further effect to rights and freedoms guaranteed under the European Convention on Human Rights; to make provision with respect to holders of certain judicial offices who become judges of the European Court of Human Rights; and for connected purposes.

[9th November 1998]

Introduction

The Convention Rights

1.—(1) In this Act "the Convention rights" means the rights and fundamental freedoms set out in—
 (a) Articles 2 to 12 and 14 of the Convention,
 (b) Articles 1 to 3 of the First Protocol, and
 (c) Articles 1 and 2 of the Sixth Protocol,
as read with Articles 16 to 18 of the Convention.

(2) Those Articles are to have effect for the purposes of this Act subject to any designated derogation or reservation (as to which see sections 14 and 15).

(3) The Articles are set out in Schedule 1.

(4) The Secretary of State may by order make such amendments to this Act as he considers appropriate to reflect the effect, in relation to the United Kingdom, of a protocol.

(5) In subsection (4) "protocol" means a protocol to the Convention—
 (a) which the United Kingdom has ratified; or
 (b) which the United Kingdom has signed with a view to ratification.

(6) No amendment may be made by an order under subsection (4) so as to come into force before the protocol concerned is in force in relation to the United Kingdom.

Interpretation of Convention rights

2.—(1) A court or tribunal determining a question which has arisen in connection with a Convention right must take into account any—
 (a) judgment, decision, declaration or advisory opinion of the European Court of Human Rights,
 (b) opinion of the Commission given in a report adopted under Article 31 of the Convention,
 (c) decision of the Commission in connection with Article 26 or 27(2) of the Convention, or
 (d) decision of the Committee of Ministers taken under Article 46 of the Convention,
whenever made or given, so far as, in the opinion of the court or tribunal, it is relevant to the proceedings in which that question has arisen.

(2) Evidence of any judgment, decision, declaration or opinion of which account may have to be taken under this section is to be given in proceedings before any court or tribunal in such manner as may be provided by rules.

(3) In this section "rules" means rules of court or, in the case of proceedings before a tribunal, rules made for the purposes of this section—
 (a) by the Lord Chancellor or the Secretary of State, in relation to any proceedings outside Scotland;
 (b) by the Secretary of State, in relation to proceedings in Scotland; or
 (c) by a Northern Ireland department, in relation to proceedings before a tribunal in Northern Ireland—

(i) which deals with transferred matters; and
(ii) for which no rules made under paragraph (a) are in force.

Legislation

Interpretation of legislation

3.—(1) So far as it is possible to do so, primary legislation and subordinate legislation must be read and given effect in a way which is compatible with the Convention rights.

(2) This section—

(a) applies to primary legislation and subordinate legislation whenever enacted;

(b) does not affect the validity, continuing operation or enforcement of any incompatible primary legislation; and

(c) does not affect the validity, continuing operation or enforcement of any incompatible subordinate legislation if (disregarding any possibility of revocation) primary legislation prevents removal of the incompatibility.

Declaration of incompatibility

4.—(1) Subsection (2) applies in any proceedings in which a court determines whether a provision of primary legislation is compatible with a Convention right.

(2) If the court is satisfied that the provision is incompatible with a Convention right, it may make a declaration of that incompatibility.

(3) Subsection (4) applies in any proceedings in which a court determines whether a provision of subordinate legislation, made in the exercise of a power conferred by primary legislation, is compatible with a Convention right.

(4) If the court is satisfied—

(a) that the provision is incompatible with a Convention right, and

(b) that (disregarding any possibility of revocation) the primary legislation concerned prevents removal of the incompatibility,

it may make a declaration of that incompatibility.

(5) In this section "court" means—

(a) the House of Lords;

(b) the Judicial Committee of the Privy Council;

(c) the Courts-Martial Appeal Court;

(d) in Scotland, the High Court of Justiciary sitting otherwise than as a trial court or the Court of Session;

(e) in England and Wales or Northern Ireland, the High Court or the Court of Appeal.

(6) A declaration under this section ("a declaration of incompatibility")—

(a) does not affect the validity, continuing operation or enforcement of the provision in respect of which it is given; and

(b) is not binding on the parties to the proceedings in which it is made.

Right of Crown to intervene

5.—(1) Where a court is considering whether to make a declaration of incompatibility, the Crown is entitled to notice in accordance with rules of court.

(2) In any case to which subsection (1) applies—

(a) a Minister of the Crown (or a person nominated by him),

(b) a member of the Scottish Executive,

(c) a Northern Ireland Minister,

(d) a Northern Ireland department,

is entitled, on giving notice in accordance with rules of court, to be joined as a party to the proceedings.

(3) Notice under subsection (2) may be given at any time during the proceedings.

(4) A person who has been made a party to criminal proceedings (other than in Scotland) as the result of a notice under subsection (2) may, with leave, appeal to the House of Lords against any declaration of incompatibility made in the proceedings.

(5) In subsection (4)—

"criminal proceedings" includes all proceedings before the Courts-Martial Appeal Court; and

"leave" means leave granted by the Court making the declaration of incompatibility or by the House of Lords.

Public authorities

Acts of public authorities

6.—(1) It is unlawful for a public authority to act in a way which is incompatible with a Convention right.

(2) Subsection (1) does not apply to an act if—

(a) as the result of one or more provisions of primary legislation, the authority could not have acted differently; or

(b) in the case of one or more provisions of, or made under, primary legislation which cannot be read or given effect in a way which is compatible with the Convention rights, the authority was acting so as to give effect to or enforce those provisions.

(3) In this section "public authority" includes—

(a) a court or tribunal, and

(b) any person certain of whose functions are functions of a public nature, but does not include either House of Parliament or a person exercising functions in connection with proceedings in Parliament.

(4) In subsection (3) "Parliament" does not include the House of Lords in its judicial capacity.

(5) In relation to a particular act, a person is not a public authority by virtue only of subsection (3)(b) if the nature of the act is private.

(6) "An act" includes a failure to act but does not include a failure to—

(a) introduce in, or lay before, Parliament a proposal for legislation; or

(b) make any primary legislation or remedial order.

Proceedings

7.—(1) A person who claims that a public authority has acted (or proposes to act) in a way which is made unlawful by section 6(1) may—

(a) bring proceedings against the authority under this Act in the appropriate court or tribunal, or

(b) rely on the Convention right or rights concerned in any legal proceedings,

but only if he is (or would be) a victim of the unlawful act.

(2) In subsection (1)(a) "appropriate court or tribunal" means such court or tribunal as may be determined in accordance with rules; and proceedings against an authority include a counterclaim or similar proceeding.

(3) If the proceedings are brought on an application for judicial review, the applicant is to be taken to have a sufficient interest in relation to the unlawful act only if he is, or would be, a victim of that act.

(4) If the proceedings are made by way of a petition for judicial review in Scotland, the applicant shall be taken to have title and interest to sue in relation to the unlawful act only if he is, or would be, a victim of that act.

(5) Proceedings under subsection (1)(a) must be brought before the end of—

    (a) the period of one year beginning with the date on which the act complained of took place; or

    (b) such longer period as the court or tribunal considers equitable having regard to all the circumstances,

but that is subject to any rule imposing a stricter time limit in relation to the procedure in question.

(6) In subsection (1)(b) "legal proceedings" includes—

    (a) proceedings brought by or at the instigation of a public authority; and

    (b) an appeal against the decision of a court or tribunal.

(7) For the purposes of this section, a person is a victim of an unlawful act only if he would be a victim for the purposes of Article 34 of the Convention if proceedings were brought in the European Court of Human Rights in respect of that act.

(8) Nothing in this Act creates a criminal offence.

(9) In this section "rules" means—

    (a) in relation to proceedings before a court or tribunal outside Scotland, rules made by the Lord Chancellor or the Secretary of State for the purposes of this section or rules of court,

    (b) in relation to proceedings before a court or tribunal in Scotland, rules made by the Secretary of State for those purposes,

    (c) in relation to proceedings before a tribunal in Northern Ireland—

        (i) which deals with transferred matters; and

        (ii) for which no rules made under paragraph (a) are in force,

    rules made by a Northern Ireland department for those purposes,

and includes provision made by order under section 1 of the Courts and Legal Services Act 1990.

(10) In making rules, regard must be had to section 9.

(11) The Minister who has power to make rules in relation to a particular tribunal may, to the extent he considers it necessary to ensure that the tribunal can provide an appropriate remedy in relation to an act (or proposed act) of a public authority which is (or would be) unlawful as a result of section 6(1), by order add to—

    (a) the relief or remedies which the tribunal may grant; or

    (b) the grounds on which it may grant any of them.

(12) An order made under subsection (11) may contain such incidental, supplemental, consequential or transitional provision as the Minister making it considers appropriate.

(13) "The Minister" includes the Northern Ireland department concerned.

Judicial remedies

8.—(1) In relation to any act (or proposed act) of a public authority which the court finds is (or would be) unlawful, it may grant such relief or remedy, or make such order, within its powers as it considers just and appropriate.

(2) But damages may be awarded only by a court which has power to award damages, or to order the payment of compensation, in civil proceedings.

(3) No award of damages is to be made unless, taking account of all the circumstances of the case, including—

    (a) any other relief or remedy granted, or order made, in relation to the act in question (by that or any other court), and

    (b) the consequences of any decision (of that or any other court) in respect of that act,

the court is satisfied that the award is necessary to afford just satisfaction to the person in whose favour it is made.

(4) In determining—
(a) whether to award damages, or
(b) the amount of an award,
the court must take into account the principles applied by the European Court of Human Rights in relation to the award of compensation under Article 41 of the Convention.

(5) A public authority against which damages are awarded is to be treated—
(a) in Scotland, for the purposes of section 3 of the Law Reform (Miscellaneous Provisions) (Scotland) Act 1940 as if the award were made in an action of damages in which the authority has been found liable in respect of loss or damage to the person to whom the award is made;
(b) for the purposes of the Civil Liability (Contribution) Act 1978 as liable in respect of damage suffered by the person to whom the award is made.

(6) In this section—
"court" includes a tribunal;
"damages" means damages for an unlawful act of a public authority; and
"unlawful" means unlawful under section 6(1).

Judicial acts

9.—(1) Proceedings under section 7(1)(a) in respect of a judicial act may be brought only—
(a) by exercising a right of appeal;
(b) on an application (in Scotland a petition) for judicial review; or
(c) in such other forum as may be prescribed by rules.

(2) That does not affect any rule of law which prevents a court from being the subject of judicial review.

(3) In proceedings under this Act in respect of a judicial act done in good faith, damages may not be awarded otherwise than to compensate a person to the extent required by Article 5(5) of the Convention.

(4) An award of damages permitted by subsection (3) is to be made against the Crown; but no award may be made unless the appropriate person, if not a party to the proceedings, is joined.

(5) In this section—
"appropriate person" means the Minister responsible for the court concerned, or a person or government department nominated by him;
"court" includes a tribunal;
"judge" includes a member of a tribunal, a justice of the peace and a clerk or other officer entitled to exercise the jurisdiction of a court;
"judicial act" means a judicial act of a court and includes an act done on the instructions, or on behalf, of a judge; and
"rules" has the same meaning as in section 7(9).

Remedial action

Power to take remedial action

10.—(1) This section applies if—
(a) a provision of legislation has been declared under section 4 to be incompatible with a Convention right and, if an appeal lies—
(i) all persons who may appeal have stated in writing that they do not intend to do so;
(ii) the time for bringing an appeal has expired and no appeal has been brought within that time; or

(iii) an appeal brought within that time has been determined or abandoned; or

(b) it appears to a Minister of the Crown or Her Majesty in Council that, having regard to a finding of the European Court of Human Rights made after the coming into force of this section in proceedings against the United Kingdom, a provision of legislation is incompatible with an obligation of the United Kingdom arising from the Convention.

(2) If a Minister of the Crown considers that there are compelling reasons for proceeding under this section, he may by order make such amendments to the legislation as he considers necessary to remove the incompatibility.

(3) If, in the case of subordinate legislation, a Minister of the Crown considers—

(a) that it is necessary to amend the primary legislation under which the subordinate legislation in question was made, in order to enable the incompatibility to be removed, and

(b) that there are compelling reasons for proceeding under this section,

he may by order make such amendments to the primary legislation as he considers necessary.

(4) This section also applies where the provision in question is in subordinate legislation and has been quashed, or declared invalid, by reason of incompatibility with a Convention right and the Minister proposes to proceed under paragraph 2(b) of Schedule 2.

(5) If the legislation is an Order in Council, the power conferred by subsection (2) or (3) is exercisable by Her Majesty in Council.

(6) In this section "legislation" does not include a Measure of the Church Assembly or of the General Synod of the Church of England.

(7) Schedule 2 makes further provision about remedial orders.

Other rights and proceedings

Safeguard for existing human rights

11. A person's reliance on a Convention right does not restrict—

(a) any other right or freedom conferred on him by or under any law having effect in any part of the United Kingdom; or

(b) his right to make any claim or bring any proceedings which he could make or bring apart from sections 7 to 9.

Freedom of expression

12.—(1) This section applies if a court is considering whether to grant any relief which, if granted, might affect the exercise of the Convention right to freedom of expression.

(2) If the person against whom the application for relief is made ("the respondent") is neither present nor represented, no such relief is to be granted unless the court is satisfied—

(a) that the applicant has taken all practicable steps to notify the respondent; or

(b) that there are compelling reasons why the respondent should not be notified.

(3) No such relief is to be granted so as to restrain publication before trial unless the court is satisfied that the applicant is likely to establish that publication should not be allowed.

(4) The court must have particular regard to the importance of the Convention right to freedom of expression and, where the proceedings relate to material which the respondent claims, or which appears to the court, to be journalistic, literary or artistic material (or to conduct connected with such material), to—

(a) the extent to which—

> (i) the material has, or is about to, become available to the public; or
> (ii) it is, or would be, in the public interest for the material to be published;

(b) any relevant privacy code.

(5) In this section—

"court" includes a tribunal; and

"relief" includes any remedy or order (other than in criminal proceedings).

Freedom of thought, conscience and religion

13.—(1) If a court's determination of any question arising under this Act might affect the exercise by a religious organisation (itself or its members collectively) of the Convention right to freedom of thought, conscience and religion, it must have particular regard to the importance of that right.

(2) In this section "court" includes a tribunal.

Derogations and reservations

Derogations

14.—(1) In this Act "designated derogation" means—

(a) the United Kingdom's derogation from Article 5(3) of the Convention; and

(b) any derogation by the United Kingdom from an Article of the Convention, or of any protocol to the Convention, which is designated for the purposes of this Act in an order made by the Secretary of State

(2) The derogation referred to in subsection (1)(a) is set out in Part I of Schedule 3.

(3) If a designated derogation is amended or replaced it ceases to be a designated derogation.

(4) But subsection (3) does not prevent the Secretary of State from exercising his power under subsection (1)(b) to make a fresh designation order in respect of the Article concerned.

(5) The Secretary of State must by order make such amendments to Schedule 3 as he considers appropriate to reflect—

(a) any designation order; or

(b) the effect of subsection (3).

(6) A designation order may be made in anticipation of the making by the United Kingdom of a proposed derogation.

Reservations

15.—(1) In this Act "designated reservation" means—

(a) the United Kingdom's reservation to Article 2 of the First Protocol to the Convention; and

(b) any other reservation by the United Kingdom to an Article of the Convention, or of any protocol to the Convention, which is designated for the purposes of this Act in an order made by the Secretary of State.

(2) The text of the reservation referred to in subsection (1)(a) is set out in Part II of Schedule 3.

(3) If a designated reservation is withdrawn wholly or in part it ceases to be a designated reservation.

(4) But subsection (3) does not prevent the Secretary of State from exercising his power under subsection (1)(b) to make a fresh designation order in respect of the Article concerned.

(5) The Secretary of State must by order make such amendments to this Act as he considers appropriate to reflect—

(a) any designation order; or

(b) the effect of subsection (3).

Period for which designated derogations have effect

16.—(1) If it has not already been withdrawn by the United Kingdom, a designated derogation ceases to have effect for the purposes of this Act—
- (a) in the case of the derogation referred to in section 14(1)(a), at the end of the period of five years beginning with the date on which section 1(2) came into force;
- (b) in the case of any other derogation, at the end of the period of five years beginning with the date on which the order designating it was made.

(2) At any time before the period—
- (a) fixed by subsection (1)(a) or (b), or
- (b) extended by any order under this subsection,

comes to an end, the Secretary of State may by order extend it by a further period of five years.

(3) An order under section 14(1)(b) ceases to have effect at the end of the period for consideration, unless a resolution has been passed by each House approving the order.

(4) Subsection (3) does not affect—
- (a) anything done in reliance on the order; or
- (b) the power to make a fresh order under section 14(1)(b).

(5) In subsection (3) "period for consideration" means the period of forty days beginning with the day on which the order was made.

(6) In calculating the period for consideration, no account is to be taken of any time during which—
- (a) Parliament is dissolved or prorogued; or
- (b) both Houses are adjourned for more than four days.

(7) If a designated derogation is withdrawn by the United Kingdom, the Secretary of State must by order make such amendments to this Act as he considers are required to reflect that withdrawal.

Periodic review of designated reservations

17.—(1) The appropriate Minister must review the designated reservation referred to in section 15(1)(a)—
- (a) before the end of the period of five years beginning with the date on which section 1(2) came into force; and
- (b) if that designation is still in force, before the end of the period of five years beginning with the date on which the last report relating to it was laid under subsection (3).

(2) The appropriate Minister must review each of the other designated reservations (if any)—
- (a) before the end of the period of five years beginning with the date on which the order designating the reservation first came into force; and
- (b) if the designation is still in force, before the end of the period of five years beginning with the date on which the last report relating to it was laid under subsection (3).

(3) The Minister conducting a review under this section must prepare a report on the result of the review and lay a copy of it before each House of Parliament.

Judges of the European Court of Human Rights

Appointment to European Court of Human Rights

¹**18.**—(1) In this section "judicial office" means the office of—
- (a) Lord Justice of Appeal, Justice of the High Court or Circuit judge, in England and Wales;

   (b) judge of the Court of Session or sheriff, in Scotland;

   (c) Lord Justice of Appeal, judge of the High Court or county court judge, in Northern Ireland.

   (2) The holder of a judicial office may become a judge of the European Court of Human Rights ("the Court") without being required to relinquish his office.

   (3) But he is not required to perform the duties of his judicial office while he is a judge of the Court.

   (4) In respect of any period during which he is a judge of the Court—

   (a) a Lord Justice of Appeal or Justice of the High Court is not to count as a judge of the relevant court for the purposes of section 2(1) or 4(1) of the Supreme Court Act 1981 (maximum number of judges) nor as a judge of the Supreme Court for the purposes of section 12(1) to (6) of that Act (salaries etc.);

   (b) a judge of the Court of Session is not to count as a judge of that court for the purposes of section 1(1) of the Court of Session Act 1988 (maximum number of judges) or of section 9(1)(c) of the Administration of Justice Act 1973 ("the 1973 Act") (salaries etc.);

   (c) a Lord Justice of Appeal or judge of the High Court in Northern Ireland is not to count as a judge of the relevant court for the purposes of section 2(1) or 3(1) of the Judicature (Northern Ireland) Act 1978 (maximum number of judges) nor as a judge of the Supreme Court of Northern Ireland for the purposes of section 9(1)(d) of the 1973 Act (salaries etc.);

   (d) a Circuit judge is not to count as such for the purposes of section 18 of the Courts Act 1971 (salaries etc.);

   (e) a sheriff is not to count as such for the purposes of section 14 of the Sheriff Courts (Scotland) Act 1907 (salaries etc.);

   (f) a county court judge of Northern Ireland is not to count as such for the purposes of section 106 of the County Courts Act (Northern Ireland) 1959 (salaries etc.).

   (5) If a sheriff principal is appointed a judge of the Court, section 11(1) of the Sheriff Courts (Scotland) Act 1971 (temporary appointment of sheriff principal) applies, while he holds that appointment, as if his office is vacant.

   (6) Schedule 4 makes provision about judicial pensions in relation to the holder of a judicial office who serves as a judge of the Court.

   (7) The Lord Chancellor or the Secretary of State may by order make such transitional provision (including, in particular, provision for a temporary increase in the maximum number of judges) as he considers appropriate in relation to any holder of a judicial office who has completed his service as a judge of the Court.

NOTE
[1] Brought into force by s.22(2): effective November 9, 1998.

Parliamentary procedure

Statements of compatibility

   [1] **19.**—(1) A Minister of the Crown in charge of a Bill in either House of Parliament must, before Second Reading of the Bill—

   (a) make a statement to the effect that in his view the provisions of the Bill are compatible with the Convention rights ("a statement of compatibility"); or

   (b) make a statement to the effect that although he is unable to make a statement of compatibility the government nevertheless wishes the House to proceed with the Bill.

   (2) The statement must be in writing and be published in such manner as the Minister making it considers appropriate.

NOTE
[1]Brought into force by S.I. 1998 No. 2882: effective November 24, 1998.

Supplemental

Orders etc. under this Act

[1]**20.**—(1) Any power of a Minister of the Crown to make an order under this Act is exercisable by statutory instrument.

(2) The power of the Lord Chancellor or the Secretary of State to make rules (other than rules of court) under section 2(3) or 7(9) is exercisable by statutory instrument.

(3) Any statutory instrument made under section 14, 15 or 16(7) must be laid before Parliament.

(4) No order may be made by the Lord Chancellor or the Secretary of State under section 1(4), 7(11) or 16(2) unless a draft of the order has been laid before, and approved by, each House of Parliament.

(5) Any statutory instrument made under section 18(7) or Schedule 4, or to which subsection (2) applies, shall be subject to annulment in pursuance of a resolution of either House of Parliament.

(6) The power of a Northern Ireland department to make—
(a) rules under section 2(3)(c) or 7(9)(c), or
(b) an order under section 7(11),
is exercisable by statutory rule for the purposes of the Statutory Rules (Northern Ireland) Order 1979.

(7) Any rules made under section 2(3)(c) or 7(9)(c) shall be subject to negative resolution; and section 41(6) of the Interpretation Act (Northern Ireland) 1954 (meaning of "subject to negative resolution") shall apply as if the power to make the rules were conferred by an Act of the Northern Ireland Assembly.

(8) No order may be made by a Northern Ireland department under section 7(11) unless a draft of the order has been laid before, and approved by, the Northern Ireland Assembly.

NOTE
[1]Brought into force by s.22(2): effective November 9, 1998.

Interpretation, etc.

21.—(1) In this Act—
"amend" includes repeal and apply (with or without modifications);
"the appropriate Minister" means the Minister of the Crown having charge of the appropriate authorised government department (within the meaning of the Crown Proceedings Act 1947);
"the Commission" means the European Commission of Human Rights;
"the Convention" means the Convention for the Protection of Human Rights and Fundamental Freedoms, agreed by the Council of Europe at Rome on 4th November 1950 as it has effect for the time being in relation to the United Kingdom;
"declaration of incompatibility" means a declaration under section 4;
"Minister of the Crown" has the same meaning as in the Ministers of the Crown Act 1975;
"Northern Ireland Minister" includes the First Minister and the deputy First Minister in Northern Ireland;
"primary legislation" means any—
(a) public general Act;
(b) local and personal Act;
(c) private Act;
(d) Measure of the Church Assembly;
(e) Measure of the General Synod of the Church of England;

 (f) Order in Council—
  (i) made in exercise of Her Majesty's Royal Prerogative;
  (ii) made under section 38(1)(a) of the Northern Ireland Constitution Act 1973 or the corresponding provision of the Northern Ireland Act 1998; or
  (iii) amending an Act of a kind mentioned in paragraph (a), (b) or (c);
and includes an order or other instrument made under primary legislation (otherwise than by the National Assembly for Wales, a member of the Scottish Executive, a Northern Ireland Minister or a Northern Ireland department) to the extent to which it operates to bring one or more provisions of that legislation into force or amends any primary legislation;

"the First Protocol" means the protocol to the Convention agreed at Paris on 20th March 1952;

"the Sixth Protocol" means the protocol to the Convention agreed at Strasbourg on 28th April 1983;

"the Eleventh Protocol" means the protocol to the Convention (restructuring the control machinery established by the Convention) agreed at Strasbourg on 11th May 1994;

"remedial order" means an order under section 10;

"subordinate legislation" means any—
 (a) Order in Council other than one—
  (i) made in exercise of Her Majesty's Royal Prerogative;
  (ii) made under section 38(1)(a) of the Northern Ireland Constitution Act 1973 or the corresponding provision of the Northern Ireland Act 1998; or
  (iii) amending an Act of a kind mentioned in the definition of primary legislation;
 (b) Act of the Scottish Parliament;
 (c) Act of the Parliament of Northern Ireland;
 (d) Measure of the Assembly established under section 1 of the Northern Ireland Assembly Act 1973;
 (e) Act of the Northern Ireland Assembly;
 (f) order, rules, regulations, scheme, warrant, byelaw or other instrument made under primary legislation (except to the extent to which it operates to bring one or more provisions of that legislation into force or amends any primary legislation);
 (g) order, rules, regulations, scheme, warrant, byelaw or other instrument made under legislation mentioned in paragraph (b), (c), (d) or (e) or made under an Order in Council applying only to Northern Ireland;
 (h) order, rules, regulations, scheme, warrant, byelaw or other instrument made by a member of the Scottish Executive, a Northern Ireland Minister or a Northern Ireland department in exercise of prerogative or other executive functions of Her Majesty which are exercisable by such a person on behalf of Her Majesty;

"transferred matters" has the same meaning as in the Northern Ireland Act 1998; and

"tribunal" means any tribunal in which legal proceedings may be brought.

(2) The references in paragraphs (b) and (c) of section 2(1) to Articles are to Articles of the Convention as they had effect immediately before the coming into force of the Eleventh Protocol.

(3) The reference in paragraph (d) of section 2(1) to Article 46 includes a reference to Articles 32 and 54 of the Convention as they had effect immediately before the coming into force of the Eleventh Protocol.

(4) The references in section 2(1) to a report or decision of the Commission or a decision of the Committee of Ministers include references to a report or decision made as provided by paragraphs 3, 4 and 6 of Article 5 of the Eleventh Protocol (transitional provisions).

[2](5) Any liability under the Army Act 1955, the Air Force Act 1955 or the Naval Discipline Act 1957 to suffer death for an offence is replaced by a liability to imprisonment for life or any less punishment authorised by those Acts; and those Acts shall accordingly have effect with the necessary modifications.

NOTE

[1]Brought into force early by s.22(2): effective November 9, 1998.

Short title, commencement, application and extent

22.—(1) This Act may be cited as the Human Rights Act 1998.

(2) Sections 18, 20 and 21(5) and this section come into force on the passing of this Act.

(3) The other provisions of this Act come into force on such day as the Secretary of State may by order appoint; and different days may be appointed for different purposes.

(4) Paragraph (b) of subsection (1) of section 7 applies to proceedings brought by or at the instigation of a public authority whenever the act in question took place; but otherwise that subsection does not apply to an act taking place before the coming into force of that section.

(5) This Act binds the Crown.

(6) This Act extends to Northern Ireland.

(7) Section 21(5), so far as it relates to any provision contained in the Army Act 1955, the Air Force Act 1955 or the Naval Discipline Act 1957, extends to any place to which that provision extends.

SCHEDULES

[1]SCHEDULE 1

THE ARTICLES

PART I

THE CONVENTION

RIGHTS AND FREEDOMS

Article 2

Right to Life

1. Everyone's right to life shall be protected by law. No one shall be deprived of his life intentionally save in the execution of a sentence of a court following his conviction of a crime for which this penalty is provided by law.

2. Deprivation of life shall not be regarded as inflicted in contravention of this Article when it results from the use of force which is no more than absolutely necessary:

(a) in defence of any person from unlawful violence;

(b) in order to effect a lawful arrest or to prevent the escape of a person lawfully detained;

(c) in action lawfully taken for the purpose of quelling a riot or insurrection.

Article 3

Prohibition of Torture

No one shall be subjected to torture or to inhuman or degrading treatment or punishment.

Article 4

Prohibition of Slavery and forced Labour

1. No one shall be held in slavery or servitude.
2. No one shall be required to perform forced or compulsory labour.
3. For the purpose of this Article the term "forced or compulsory labour" shall not include:
(a) any work required to be done in the ordinary course of detention imposed according to the provisions of Article 5 of this Convention or during conditional release from such detention;
(b) any service of a military character or, in case of conscientious objectors in countries where they are recognised, service exacted instead of compulsory military service;
(c) any service exacted in case of an emergency or calamity threatening the life or well-being of the community;
(d) any work or service which forms part of normal civic obligations.

Article 5

Right to Liberty and Security

1. Everyone has the right to liberty and security of person. No one shall be deprived of his liberty save in the following cases and in accordance with a procedure prescribed by law:
(a) the lawful detention of a person after conviction by a competent court;
(b) the lawful arrest or detention of a person for non-compliance with the lawful order of a court or in order to secure the fulfilment of any obligation prescribed by law;
(c) the lawful arrest or detention of a person effected for the purpose of bringing him before the competent legal authority on reasonable suspicion of having committed an offence or when it is reasonably considered necessary to prevent his committing an offence or fleeing after having done so;
(d) the detention of a minor by lawful order for the purpose of educational supervision or his lawful detention for the purpose of bringing him before the competent legal authority;
(e) the lawful detention of persons for the prevention of the spreading of infectious diseases, of persons of unsound mind, alcoholics or drug addicts or vagrants;
(f) the lawful arrest or detention of a person to prevent his effecting an unauthorised entry into the country or of a person against whom action is being taken with a view to deportation or extradition.
2. Everyone who is arrested shall be informed promptly, in a language which he understands, of the reasons for his arrest and of any charge against him.
3. Everyone arrested or detained in accordance with the provisions of paragraph 1(c) of this Article shall be brought promptly before a judge or other officer authorised by law to exercise judicial power and shall be entitled to trial within a reasonable time or to release pending trial. Release may be conditioned by guarantees to appear for trial.
4. Everyone who is deprived of his liberty by arrest or detention shall be entitled to take proceedings by which the lawfulness of his detention shall be decided speedily by a court and his release ordered if the detention is not lawful.
5. Everyone who has been the victim of arrest or detention in contravention of the provisions of this Article shall have an enforceable right to compensation.

Article 6

Right to a Fair Trial

1. In the determination of his civil rights and obligations or of any criminal charge against him, everyone is entitled to a fair and public hearing within a reasonable time by an independent and impartial tribunal established by law. Judgment shall be pronounced publicly but the press and public may be excluded from all or part of the trial in the interest of morals, public order or national security in a democratic society, where the interests of juveniles or the protection of the private life of the parties so require, or to the extent strictly necessary in the opinion of the court in special circumstances where publicity would prejudice the interests of justice.
2. Everyone charged with a criminal offence shall be presumed innocent until proved guilty according to law.
3. Everyone charged with a criminal offence has the following minimum rights:
(a) to be informed promptly, in a language which he understands and in detail, of the nature and cause of the accusation against him;

(b) to have adequate time and facilities for the preparation of his defence;

(c) to defend himself in person or through legal assistance of his own choosing or, if he has not sufficient means to pay for legal assistance, to be given it free when the interests of justice so require;

(d) to examine or have examined witnesses against him and to obtain the attendance and examination of witnesses on his behalf under the same conditions as witnesses against him;

(e) to have the free assistance of an interpreter if he cannot understand or speak the language used in court.

Article 7

No Punishment Without Law

1. No one shall be held guilty of any criminal offence on account of any act or omission which did not constitute a criminal offence under national or international law at the time when it was committed. Nor shall a heavier penalty be imposed than the one that was applicable at the time the criminal offence was committed.

2. This Article shall not prejudice the trial and punishment of any person for any act or omission which, at the time when it was committed, was criminal according to the general principles of law recognised by civilised nations.

Article 8

Right to Respect for Private and Family Life

1. Everyone has the right to respect for his private and family life, his home and his correspondence.

2. There shall be no interference by a public authority with the exercise of this right except such as is in accordance with the law and is necessary in a democratic society in the interests of national security, public safety or the economic well-being of the country, for the prevention of disorder or crime, for the protection of health or morals, or for the protection of the rights and freedoms of others.

Article 9

Freedom of Thought, Conscience and Religion

1. Everyone has the right to freedom of thought, conscience and religion; this right includes freedom to change his religion or belief and freedom, either alone or in community with others and in public or private, to manifest his religion or belief, in worship, teaching, practice and observance.

2. Freedom to manifest one's religion or beliefs shall be subject only to such limitations as are prescribed by law and are necessary in a democratic society in the interests of public safety, for the protection of public order, health or morals, or for the protection of the rights and freedoms of others.

Article 10

Freedom of Expression

1. Everyone has the right to freedom of expression. This right shall include freedom to hold opinions and to receive and impart information and ideas without interference by public authority and regardless of frontiers. This Article shall not prevent States from requiring the licensing of broadcasting, television or cinema enterprises.

2. The exercise of these freedoms, since it carries with it duties and responsibilities, may be subject to such formalities, conditions, restrictions or penalties as are prescribed by law and are necessary in a democratic society, in the interests of national security, territorial integrity or public safety, for the prevention of disorder or crime, for the protection of health or morals, for the protection of the reputation or rights of others, for preventing the disclosure of information received in confidence, or for maintaining the authority and impartiality of the judiciary.

Article 11

Freedom of Assembly and Association

1. Everyone has the right to freedom of peaceful assembly and to freedom of association with others, including the right to form and to join trade unions for the protection of his interests.

2. No restrictions shall be placed on the exercise of these rights other than such as are prescribed by law and are necessary in a democratic society in the interests of national security or public safety, for the prevention of disorder or crime, for the protection of health or morals or for the protection of the rights and freedoms of others. This Article shall not prevent the imposition of lawful restrictions on the exercise of these rights by members of the armed forces, of the police or of the administration of the State.

Article 12

Right to Marry

Men and women of marriageable age have the right to marry and to found a family, according to the national laws governing the exercise of this right.

Article 14

Prohibition of Discrimination

The enjoyment of the rights and freedoms set forth in this Convention shall be secured without discrimination on any ground such as sex, race, colour, language, religion, political or other opinion, national or social origin, association with a national minority, property, birth or other status.

Article 16

Restrictions on Political Activity of Aliens

Nothing in Articles 10, 11 and 14 shall be regarded as preventing the High Contracting Parties from imposing restrictions on the political activity of aliens.

Article 17

Prohibition of Abuse of Rights

Nothing in this Convention may be interpreted as implying for any State, group or person any right to engage in any activity or perform any act aimed at the destruction of any of the rights and freedoms set forth herein or at their limitation to a greater extent than is provided for in the Convention.

Article 18

Limitation on Use of Restrictions on Rights

The restrictions permitted under this Convention to the said rights and freedoms shall not be applied for any purpose other than those for which they have been prescribed.

PART II

THE FIRST PROTOCOL

Article 1

Protection of Property

Every natural or legal person is entitled to the peaceful enjoyment of his possessions. No one shall be deprived of his possessions except in the public interest and subject to the conditions provided for by law and by the general principles of international law.

The preceding provisions shall not, however, in any way impair the right of a State to enforce such laws as it deems necessary to control the use of property in accordance with the general interest or to secure the payment of taxes or other contributions or penalties.

Article 2

Right to Education

No person shall be denied the right to education. In the exercise of any functions which it assumes in relation to education and to teaching, the State shall respect the right of parents to ensure such education and teaching in conformity with their own religious and philosophical convictions.

Article 3

Right to Free Elections

The High Contracting Parties undertake to hold free elections at reasonable intervals by secret ballot, under conditions which will ensure the free expression of the opinion of the people in the choice of the legislature.

PART III

THE SIXTH PROTOCOL

Article 1

Abolition of the Death Penalty

The death penalty shall be abolished. No one shall be condemned to such penalty or executed.

Article 2

Death Penalty in Time of War

A State may make provision in its law for the death penalty in respect of acts committed in time of war or of imminent threat of war; such penalty shall be applied only in the instances laid down in the law and in accordance with its provisions. The State shall communicate to the Secretary General of the Council of Europe the relevant provisions of that law.

[1]SCHEDULE 2

REMEDIAL ORDERS

Orders

1.—(1) A remedial order may—
(a) contain such incidental, supplemental, consequential or transitional provision as the person making it considers appropriate;
(b) be made so as to have effect from a date earlier than that on which it is made;
(c) make provision for the delegation of specific functions;
(d) make different provision for different cases.
(2) The power conferred by sub-paragraph (1)(a) includes—
(a) power to amend primary legislation (including primary legislation other than that which contains the incompatible provision); and
(b) power to amend or revoke subordinate legislation (including subordinate legislation other than that which contains the incompatible provision).
(3) A remedial order may be made so as to have the same extent as the legislation which it affects.
(4) No person is to be guilty of an offence solely as a result of the retrospective effect of a remedial order.

Procedure

2. No remedial order may be made unless—
(a) a draft of the order has been approved by a resolution of each House of Parliament made after the end of the period of 60 days beginning with the day on which the draft was laid; or
(b) it is declared in the order that it appears to the person making it that, because of the urgency of the matter, it is necessary to make the order without a draft being so approved.

Orders laid in draft

3.—(1) No draft may be laid under paragraph 2(a) unless—
(a) the person proposing to make the order has laid before Parliament a document which contains a draft of the proposed order and the required information; and
(b) the period of 60 days, beginning with the day on which the document required by this sub-paragraph was laid, has ended.

(2) If representations have been made during that period, the draft laid under paragraph 2(a) must be accompanied by a statement containing—

(a) a summary of the representations; and

(b) if, as a result of the representations, the proposed order has been changed, details of the changes.

Urgent cases

4.—(1) If a remedial order ("the original order") is made without being approved in draft, the person making it must lay it before Parliament, accompanied by the required information, after it is made.

(2) If representations have been made during the period of 60 days beginning with the day on which the original order was made, the person making it must (after the end of that period) lay before Parliament a statement containing—

(a) a summary of the representations; and

(b) if, as a result of the representations, he considers it appropriate to make changes to the original order, details of the changes.

(3) If sub-paragraph (2)(b) applies, the person making the statement must—

(a) make a further remedial order replacing the original order; and

(b) lay the replacement order before Parliament.

(4) If, at the end of the period of 120 days beginning with the day on which the original order was made, a resolution has not been passed by each House approving the original or replacement order, the order ceases to have effect (but without that affecting anything previously done under either order or the power to make a fresh remedial order).

Definitions

5. In this Schedule—

"representations" means representations about a remedial order (or proposed remedial order) made to the person making (or proposing to make) it and includes any relevant Parliamentary report or resolution; and

"required information" means—

(a) an explanation of the incompatibility which the order (or proposed order) seeks to remove, including particulars of the relevant declaration, finding or order; and

(b) a statement of the reasons for proceeding under section 10 and for making an order in those terms.

Calculating periods

6. In calculating any period for the purposes of this Schedule, no account is to be taken of any time during which—

(a) Parliament is dissolved or prorogued; or

(b) both Houses are adjourned for more than four days.

¹7.—(1) This paragraph applies in relation to—

(a) any remedial order made, and any draft of such an order proposed to be made—

(i) by the Scottish Ministers; or

(ii) within devolved competence (within the meaning of the Scotland Act 1998) by Her Majesty in Council; and

(b) any document or statement to be laid in connection with such an order (or proposed order).

(2) This Schedule has effect in relation to any such order (or proposed order), document or statement subject to the following modifications.

(3) Any reference to Parliament, each House of Parliament or both Houses of Parliament shall be construed as a reference to the Scottish Parliament.

(4) Paragraph 6 does not apply and instead, in calculating any period for the purposes of this Schedule, no account is to be taken of any time during which the Scottish Parliament is dissolved or is in recess for more than four days.

NOTE

¹Inserted by the Scotland Act 1998 (Consequential Modifications) Order 2000 (S.I. 2000 No. 2040), art. 2 and Sched. 1, para. 21.

Human Rights Act 1998

DEROGATION AND RESERVATION

PART I

DEROGATION

The 1988 notification

The United Kingdom Permanent Representative to the Council of Europe presents his compliments to the Secretary General of the Council, and has the honour to convey the following information in order to ensure compliance with the obligations of Her Majesty's Government in the United Kingdom under Article 15(3) of the Convention for the Protection of Human Rights and Fundamental Freedoms signed at Rome on 4 November 1950.

There have been in the United Kingdom in recent years campaigns of organised terrorism connected with the affairs of Northern Ireland which have manifested themselves in activities which have included repeated murder, attempted murder, maiming, intimidation and violent civil disturbance and in bombing and fire raising which have resulted in death, injury and widespread destruction of property. As a result, a public emergency within the meaning of Article 15(1) of the Convention exists in the United Kingdom.

The Government found it necessary in 1974 to introduce and since then, in cases concerning persons reasonably suspected of involvement in terrorism connected with the affairs of Northern Ireland, or of certain offences under the legislation, who have been detained for 48 hours, to exercise powers enabling further detention without charge, for periods of up to five days, on the authority of the Secretary of State. These powers are at present to be found in Section 12 of the Prevention of Terrorism (Temporary Provisions) Act 1984, Article 9 of the Prevention of Terrorism (Supplemental Temporary Provisions) Order 1984 and Article 10 of the Prevention of Terrorism (Supplemental Temporary Provisions) (Northern Ireland) Order 1984.

Section 12 of the Prevention of Terrorism (Temporary Provisions) Act 1984 provides for a person whom a constable has arrested on reasonable grounds of suspecting him to be guilty of an offence under Section 1, 9 or 10 of the Act, or to be or to have been involved in terrorism connected with the affairs of Northern Ireland, to be detained in right of the arrest for up to 48 hours and thereafter, where the Secretary of State extends the detention period, for up to a further five days. Section 12 substantially re-enacted Section 12 of the Prevention of Terrorism (Temporary Provisions) Act 1976 which, in turn, substantially re-enacted Section 7 of the Prevention of Terrorism (Temporary Provisions) Act 1974.

Article 10 of the Prevention of Terrorism (Supplemental Temporary Provisions) (Northern Ireland) Order 1984 (S.I. 1984/417) and Article 9 of the Prevention of Terrorism (Supplemental Temporary Provisions) Order 1984 (S.I. 1984/418) were both made under Sections 13 and 14 of and Schedule 3 to the 1984 Act and substantially re-enacted powers of detention in Orders made under the 1974 and 1976 Acts. A person who is being examined under Article 4 of either Order on his arrival in, or on seeking to leave, Northern Ireland or Great Britain for the purpose of determining whether he is or has been involved in terrorism connected with the affairs of Northern Ireland, or whether there are grounds for suspecting that he has committed an offence under Section 9 of the 1984 Act, may be detained under Article 9 or 10, as appropriate, pending the conclusion of his examination. The period of this examination may exceed 12 hours if an examining officer has reasonable grounds for suspecting him to be or to have been involved in acts of terrorism connected with the affairs of Northern Ireland.

Where such a person is detained under the said Article 9 or 10 he may be detained for up to 48 hours on the authority of an examining officer and thereafter, where the Secretary of State extends the detention period, for up to a further five days.

In its judgment of 29 November 1988 in the Case of *Brogan and Others*, the European Court of Human Rights held that there had been a violation of Article 5(3) in respect of each of the applicants, all of whom had been detained under Section 12 of the 1984 Act. The Court held that even the shortest of the four periods of detention concerned, namely four days and six hours, fell outside the constraints as to time permitted by the first part of Article 5(3). In addition, the Court held that there had been a violation of Article 5(5) in the case of each applicant.

Following this judgment, the Secretary of State for the Home Department informed Parliament on 6 December 1988 that, against the background of the terrorist campaign, and the overriding need to bring terrorists to justice, the Government did not believe that the maximum period of detention should be reduced. He informed Parliament that the Government were examining the matter with a view to responding to the judgment. On 22 December 1988, the Secretary of State further informed Parliament that it remained the Government's wish, if it could be achieved, to find a judicial process under which extended detention might be reviewed and where appropriate authorised by a judge or other judicial officer. But a further period of reflection and consultation was necessary before the Government could bring forward a firm and final view.

Since the judgment of 29 November 1988 as well as previously, the Government have found it necessary to continue to exercise, in relation to terrorism connected with the affairs of Northern Ireland, the powers described above enabling further detention without charge for periods of up to 5 days, on the authority of the Secretary of State, to the extent strictly required by the exigencies of the situation to enable necessary enquiries and investigations properly to be completed in order to decide whether criminal proceedings should be instituted. To the extent that the exercise of these powers may be inconsistent with the obligations imposed by the Convention the Government has availed itself of the right of derogation conferred by Article 15(1) of the Convention and will continue to do so until further notice.

Dated 23 December 1988.

The 1989 notification

The United Kingdom Permanent Representative to the Council of Europe presents his compliments to the Secretary General of the Council, and has the honour to convey the following information.

In his communication to the Secretary General of 23 December 1988, reference was made to the introduction and exercise of certain powers under section 12 of the Prevention of Terrorism (Temporary Provisions) Act 1984, Article 9 of the Prevention of Terrorism (Supplemental Temporary Provisions) Order 1984 and Article 10 of the Prevention of Terrorism (Supplemental Temporary Provisions) (Northern Ireland) Order 1984.

These provisions have been replaced by section 14 of and paragraph 6 of Schedule 5 to the Prevention of Terrorism (Temporary Provisions) Act 1989, which make comparable provision. They came into force on 22 March 1989. A copy of these provisions is enclosed.

The United Kingdom Permanent Representative avails himself of this opportunity to renew to the Secretary General the assurance of his highest consideration.

23 March 1989.

PART II

RESERVATION

At the time of signing the present (First) Protocol, I declare that, in view of certain provisions of the Education Acts in the United Kingdom, the principle affirmed in the second sentence of Article 2 is accepted by the United Kingdom only so far as it is compatible with the provision of efficient instruction and training, and the avoidance of unreasonable public expenditure.

Dated 20 March 1952

Made by the United Kingdom Permanent Representative to the Council of Europe.

[1] SCHEDULE 4

JUDICIAL PENSIONS

[Not reproduced]

SCOTLAND ACT 1998

(1998 c. 46)

An Act to provide for the establishment of a Scottish Parliament and Administration and other changes in the government of Scotland; to provide for changes in the constitution and functions of certain public authorities; to provide for the variation of the basic rate of income tax in relation to income of Scottish taxpayers in accordance with a resolution of the Scottish Parliament; to amend the law about parliamentary constituencies in Scotland; and for connected purposes.

[19th November 1998]

Legislation

...

Acts of the Scottish Parliament

28.—(1) Subject to section 29, the Parliament may make laws, to be known as Acts of the Scottish Parliament.

(2) Proposed Acts of the Scottish Parliament shall be known as Bills; and a Bill shall become an Act of the Scottish Parliament when it has been passed by the Parliament and has received Royal Assent.

(3) A Bill receives Royal Assent at the beginning of the day on which Letters Patent under the Scottish Seal signed with Her Majesty's own hand signifying Her Assent are recorded in the Register of the Great Seal.

(4) The date of Royal Assent shall be written on the Act of the Scottish Parliament by the Clerk, and shall form part of the Act.

(5) The validity of an Act of the Scottish Parliament is not affected by any invalidity in the proceedings of the Parliament leading to its enactment.

(6) Every Act of the Scottish Parliament shall be judicially noticed.

(7) This section does not affect the power of the Parliament of the United Kingdom to make laws for Scotland.

Legislative competence

29.—(1) An Act of the Scottish Parliament is not law so far as any provision of the Act is outside the legislative competence of the Parliament.

(2) A provision is outside that competence so far as any of the following paragraphs apply—

(a) it would form part of the law of a country or territory other than Scotland, or confer or remove functions exercisable otherwise than in or as regards Scotland,

(b) it relates to reserved matters,

(c) it is in breach of the restrictions in Schedule 4,

(d) it is incompatible with any of the Convention rights or with Community law,

(e) it would remove the Lord Advocate from his position as head of the systems of criminal prosecution and investigation of deaths in Scotland.

(3) For the purposes of this section, the question whether a provision of an Act of the Scottish Parliament relates to a reserved matter is to be determined, subject to subsection (4), by reference to the purpose of the provision, having regard (among other things) to its effect in all the circumstances.

(4) A provision which—

(a) would otherwise not relate to reserved matters, but

(b) makes modifications of Scots private law, or Scots criminal law, as it applies to reserved matters,

is to be treated as relating to reserved matters unless the purpose of the provision is to make the law in question apply consistently to reserved matters and otherwise.

...

Ministers and their staff

The Scottish Executive

44.—(1) There shall be a Scottish Executive, whose members shall be—

(a) the First Minister,

(b) such Ministers as the First Minister may appoint under section 47, and
(c) the Lord Advocate and the Solicitor General for Scotland.
(2) The members of the Scottish Executive are referred to collectively as the Scottish Ministers.
(3) A person who holds a Ministerial office may not be appointed a member of the Scottish Executive; and if a member of the Scottish Executive is appointed to a Ministerial office he shall cease to hold office as a member of the Scottish Executive.
(4) In subsection (3), references to a member of the Scottish Executive include a junior Scottish Minister and "Ministerial office" has the same meaning as in section 2 of the House of Commons Disqualification Act 1975.
...

Ministerial functions

...

Community law and Convention rights

57.—(1) Despite the transfer to the Scottish Ministers by virtue of section 53 of functions in relation to observing and implementing obligations under Community law, any function of a Minister of the Crown in relation to any matter shall continue to be exercisable by him as regards Scotland for the purposes specified in section 2(2) of the European Communities Act 1972.
(2) A member of the Scottish Executive has no power to make any subordinate legislation, or to do any other act, so far as the legislation or act is incompatible with any of the Convention rights or with Community law.
(3) Subsection (2) does not apply to an act of the Lord Advocate—
(a) in prosecuting any offence, or
(b) in his capacity as head of the systems of criminal prosecution and investigation of deaths in Scotland,
which, because of subsection (2) of section 6 of the Human Rights Act 1998, is not unlawful under subsection (1) of that section.

Juridical

Devolution issues

98. Schedule 6 (which makes provision in relation to devolution issues) shall have effect.
...

SCHEDULE 6

Section 98

DEVOLUTION ISSUES

PART I

PRELIMINARY

1. In this Schedule "devolution issue" means—
(a) a question whether an Act of the Scottish Parliment or any provision of an Act of the Scottish Parliament is within the legislative competence of the Parliament,
(b) a question whether any function (being a function which any person has purported, or is proposing, to exercise) is a function of the Scottish Ministers, the First Minister or the Lord Advocate,
(c) a question whether the purported or proposed exercise of a function by a member of the Scottish Executive is, or would be, within devolved competence,
(d) a question whether a purported or proposed exercise of a function by a member of the Scottish Executive is, or would be, incompatible with any of the Convention rights or with Community law,
(e) a question whether a failure to act by a member of the Scottish Executive is incompatible with any of the Convention rights or with Community law,

(f) any other question about whether a function is exercisable within devolved competence or in or as regards Scotland and any other question arising by virtue of this Act about reserved matters.

PART II

PROCEEDINGS IN SCOTLAND

Application of Part II

3. This Part of this Schedule applies in relation to devolution issues in proceedings in Scotland.

Institution of proceedings

4.—(1) Proceedings for the determination of a devolution issue may be instituted by the Advocate General or the Lord Advocate.

(2) The Lord Advocate may defend any such proceeding instituted by the Advocate General.

(3) This paragraph is without prejudice to any power to institute or defend proceedings exercisable apart from this paragraph by any person.

Intimation of devolution issue

5. Intimation of any devolution issue which arises in any proceedings before a court or tribunal shall be given to the Advocate General and the Lord Advocate (unless the person to whom the intimation would be given is a party to the proceedings).

Reference of devolution issue to higher court

7. A court, other than the House of Lords or any court consisting of three or more judges of the Court of Session, may refer any devolution issue which arises in proceedings (other than criminal proceedings) before it to the Inner House of the Court of Session.

8. A tribunal from which there is no appeal shall refer any devolution issue which arises in proceedings before it to the Inner House of the Court of Session; and any other tribunal may make such a reference.

9. A court, other than any court consisting of two or more judges of the High Court of Justiciary, may refer any devolution issue which arises in criminal proceedings before it to the High Court of Justiciary.

References from superior courts to Judicial Committee

10. Any court consisting of three or more judges of the Court of Session may refer any devolution issue which arises in proceedings before it (otherwise than on a reference under paragraph 7 or 8) to the Judicial Committee.

11. Any court consisting of two or more judges of the High Court of Justiciary may refer any devolution issue which arises in proceedings before it (otherwise than on a reference under paragraph 9) to the Judicial Committee.

Appeals from superior courts to Judicial Committee

12. An appeal against a determination of a devolution issue by the Inner House of the Court of Session on a reference under paragraph 7 or 8 shall lie to the Judicial Committee.

13. An appeal against a determination of a devolution issue by—
(a) a court of two or more judges of the High Court of Justiciary (whether in the ordinary course of proceedings or on a reference under paragraph 9), or
(b) a court of three or more judges of the Court of Session from which there is no appeal to the House of Lords,
shall lie to the Judicial Committee, but only with leave of the court concerned or, failing such leave, with special leave of the Judicial Committee.

PART III

PROCEEDINGS IN ENGLAND AND WALES

Application of Part III

14. This Part of this Schedule applies in relation to devolution issues in proceedings in England and Wales.

Institution of proceedings

15.—(1) Proceedings for the determination of a devolution issue may be instituted by the Attorney General.

(2) The Lord Advocate may defend any such proceedings.

(3) This paragraph is without prejudice to any power to institute or defend proceedings exercisable apart from this paragraph by any person.

Notice of devolution issue

16. A court or tribunal shall order notice of any devolution issue which arises in any proceedings before it to be given to the Attorney General and the Lord Advocate (unless the person to whom the notice would be given is a party to the proceedings).

17. A person to whom notice is given in pursuance of paragraph 16 may take part as a party in the proceedings, so far as they relate to a devolution issue.

Reference of devolution issue to High Court or Court of Appeal

18. A magistrates' court may refer any devolution issue which arises in proceedings (other than criminal proceedings) before it to the High Court.

19.—(1) a court may refer any devolution issue which arises in proceedings (other than criminal proceedings) before it to the Court of Appeal.

(2) Sub-paragraph (1) does not apply to—

(a) a magistrates' court, the Court of Appeal or the House of Lords, or

(b) the High Court if the devolution issue arises in proceedings on a reference under paragraph 18.

20. A tribunal from which there is no appeal shall refer any devolution issue which arises in proceedings before it to the Court of Appeal; and any other tribunal may make such a reference.

21. A court, other than the House of Lords or the Court of Appeal, may refer any devolution issue which arises in criminal proceedings before it to—

(a) the High Court (if the proceedings are summary proceedings, or

(b) the Court of Appeal (if the proceedings are proceedings on indictment).

References from Court of Appeal to Judicial Committee

22. The Court of Appeal may refer any devolution issue which arises in proceedings before it (otherwise than on a reference under paragraph 19, 20 or 21) to the Judicial Committee.

Appeals from superior courts to Judicial Committee

23. An appeal against a determination of a devolution issue by the High Court or the Court of Appeal on a reference under paragraph 18, 19, 20 or 21 shall lie to the Judicial Committee, but only with leave of the High Court or (as the case may be) the Court of Appeal or, failing such leave, with special leave of the Judicial Committee.

PART IV

PROCEEDINGS IN NORTHERN IRELAND

Application of Part IV

24. This Part of this Schedule applies to devolution issues in proceedings in Northern Ireland.

Institution of proceedings

25.—(1) Proceedings for the determination of a devolution issue may be instituted by the Attorney General for Northern Ireland.

(2) The Lord Advocate may defend any such proceedings.

(3) This paragraph is without prejudice to any power to institute or defend proceedings exercisable apart from this paragraph by any person.

Notice of devolution issue

26. A court or tribunal shall order notice of any devolution issue which arises in any proceedings before it to be given to the Attorney General for Northern Ireland and the Lord Advocate (unless the person to whom the notice would be given is a party to the proceedings).

27. A person to whom notice is given in pursuance of paragraph 26 may take part as a party in the proceedings, so far as they relate to a devolution issue.

Reference of devolution issue to Court of Appeal

28. A court, other than the House of Lords or the Court of Appeal in Northern Ireland, may refer any devolution issue which arises in any proceedings before it to the Court of Appeal in Northern Ireland.

29. A tribunal from which there is no appeal shall refer any devolution issue which arises in any proceedings before it to the Court of Appeal in Northern Ireland; and any other tribunal may make such a reference.

References from Court of Appeal to Judicial Committee

30. The Court of Appeal in Northern Ireland may refer any devolution issue which arises in proceedings before it (otherwise than on a reference under paragraph 28 or 29) to the Judicial Committee.

Appeals from Court of Appeal to Judicial Committee

31. An appeal against a determination of a devolution issue by the Court of Appeal in Northern Ireland on a reference under paragraph 28 or 29 shall lie to the Judicial Committee, but only with leave of the Court of Appeal in Northern Ireland or, failing such leave, with special leave of the Judicial Committee.

PART V

GENERAL

Proceedings in the House of Lords

32. Any devolution issue which arises in judicial proceedings in the House of Lords shall be referred to the Judicial Committee unless the House considers it more appropriate, having regard to all the circumstances, that it should determine the issue.

Direct references to Judicial Committee

33. The Lord Advocate, the Advocate General, the Attorney General or the Attorney General for Northern Ireland may require any court or tribunal to refer to the Judicial Committee any devolution issue which has arisen in proceedings before it to which he is a party.

34. The Lord Advocate, the Attorney General, the Advocate General or the Attorney General for Northern Ireland may refer to the Judicial Committee any devolution issue which is not the subject of proceedings.

35.—(1) This paragraph applies where a reference is made under paragraph 34 in relation to a devolution issue which relates to the proposed exercise of a function by a member of the Scottish Executive.

(2) The person making the reference shall notify a member of the Scottish Executive of that fact.

(3) No member of the Scottish Executive shall exercise the function in the manner proposed during the period beginning with the receipt of the notification under sub-pararaph (2) and ending with the reference being decided or otherwise disposed of.

(4) Proceedings relating to any possible failure by a member of the Scottish Executive to comply with sub-paragraph (3) may be instituted by the Advocate General.

(5) Sub-paragraph (4) is without prejudice to any power to institute proceedings exercisable apart from that sub-paragraph by any person.

Expenses

36.—(1) A court or tribunal before which any proceedings take place may take account of any additional expense of the kind mentioned in sub-paragraph (3) in deciding any question as to costs or expenses.

(2) In deciding any such question, the court or tribunal may award the whole or part of the additional expense as costs or (as the case may be) expenses to the party who incurred it (whatever the decision on the devolution issue).

(3) The additional expense is any additional expense which the court or tribunal considers that any party to the proceedings has incurred as a result of the participation of any person in pursuance of paragraph 6, 17 or 27.

Procedure of courts and tribunals

37. Any power to make provision for regulating the procedure before any court or tribunal shall include power to make provision for the purposes of this Schedule including, in particular, provision—
   (a) for prescribing the stage in the proceedings at which a devolution issue is to be raised or referred,
   (b) for the sisting or staying of proceedings for the purpose of any proceedings under this Schedule, and
   (c) for determining the manner in which and the time within which any intimation or notice is to be given.

Interpretation

38. Any duty or power conferred by this Schedule to refer a devolution issue to a court shall be construed as a duty or (as the cae may be) power to refer the issue to the court for decision.

REGULATION OF INVESTIGATORY POWERS (SCOTLAND) ACT 2000

(2000 asp 11)

ARRANGEMENT OF SECTIONS

An Act of the Scottish Parliament to regulate surveillance and the use of covert human intelligence sources.

[28 September, 2000]

Conduct to which this Act applies

1.—(1) This Act applies to the following conduct—

(a) directed surveillance;

(b) intrusive surveillance; and

(c) the conduct and use of covert human intelligence sources.

(2) For the purposes of this Act surveillance is directed if it is covert but not intrusive and is undertaken—

(a) for the purposes of a specific investigation or a specific operation;

(b) in such a manner as is likely to result in the obtaining of private information about a person (whether or not one specifically identified for the purposes of the investigation or operation); and

(c) otherwise than by way of an immediate response to events or circumstances the nature of which is such that it would not be reasonably practicable for an authorisation under this Act to be sought for the carrying out of the surveillance.

(3) Subject to subsections (4) and (5) below, surveillance is intrusive for the purposes of this Act if, and only if, it is covert surveillance that—

(a) is carried out in relation to anything taking place on any residential premises or in any private vehicle; and

(b) involves the presence of an individual on the premises or in the vehicle or is carried out by means of a surveillance device.

(4) For the purposes of this Act surveillance is not intrusive to the extent that it is carried out by means only of a surveillance device designed or adapted principally for the purpose of providing information about the location of a vehicle.

(5) For the purposes of this Act surveillance which—

(a) is carried out by means of a surveillance device in relation to anything taking place on any residential premises or in any private vehicle; but

(b) is carried out without that device being present on the premises or in the vehicle,

is not intrusive unless the device is such that it consistently provides information of the same quality and detail as might be expected to be obtained from a device actually present on the premises or in the vehicle.

(6) In this Act—

(a) references to the conduct of a covert human intelligence source are references to any conduct of such a source which falls within any of paragraphs (a) to (c) of subsection (7) below, or is incidental to anything falling within any of those paragraphs; and

(b) references to the use of a covert human intelligence source are references to inducing, asking or assisting a person to engage in the conduct of such a source, or to obtain information by means of the conduct of such a source.

(7) For the purposes of this Act a person is a covert human intelligence source if the person—

(a) establishes or maintains a personal or other relationship with another person for the covert purpose of facilitating the doing of anything falling within paragraph (b) or (c) below;

(b) covertly uses such a relationship to obtain information or to provide access to any information to another person; or

(c) covertly discloses information obtained by the use of such a relationship or as a consequence of the existence of such a relationship.

(8) For the purposes of this section-

(a) surveillance is covert if, and only if, it is carried out in a manner that is calculated to ensure that persons who are subject to the surveillance are unaware that it is or may be taking place;

(b) a purpose is covert, in relation to the establishment or maintenance of a personal or other relationship, if and only if the relationship is conducted in a manner that is calculated to ensure that one of the parties to the relationship is unaware of the purpose; and

(c) a relationship is used covertly, and information obtained as mentioned in subsection (7)(c) above is disclosed covertly, if and only if it is used or, as the case may be, disclosed in a manner that is calculated to ensure that one of the parties to the relationship is unaware of the use or disclosure in question.

(9) In this section "private information", in relation to a person, includes any information relating to the person's private or family life.

(10) References in this section, in relation to a vehicle, to the presence of a surveillance device in the vehicle include references to its being located on or under the vehicle and also include references to its being attached to it.

Surveillance Commissioners

Surveillance Commissioners

2.—(1) The Scottish Ministers shall appoint for the purposes of this Act—

(a) a Chief Surveillance Commissioner; and

(b) such number of other Surveillance Commissioners as the Scottish Ministers think fit.

(2) The persons appointed under subsection (1) above shall be persons who hold or have held high judicial office within the meaning of the Appellate Jurisdiction Act 1876 (c.59).

(3) Subject to subsections (4) to (7) below, each Surveillance Commissioner shall hold and vacate office in accordance with the terms of his appointment.

(4) Each Surveillance Commissioner shall be appointed for a term of three years.

(5) A person who ceases to be a Surveillance Commissioner (otherwise than under subsection (7) below) may be reappointed under this section.

(6) Subject to subsection (7) below, a Surveillance Commissioner shall not be removed from office before the end of the term for which that Commissioner is appointed unless a resolution approving the removal has been passed by the Scottish Parliament.

(7) A Surveillance Commissioner may be removed from office by the Scottish Ministers if after his appointment—

(a) a bankruptcy order is made against the Commissioner or the Commissioner's estate is sequestrated or the Commissioner makes a composition or arrangement with, or grants a trust deed for, the Commissioner's creditors;

(b) a disqualification order under the Company Directors Disqualification Act 1986 (c.46) or Part II of the Companies (Northern Ireland) Order 1989 (S.I. 1989/2404 (N.I.18)), or an order under section 429(2)(b) (failure to pay under county court administration order) of the Insolvency Act 1986 (c.45), is made against the Commissioner; or

(c) the Commissioner is convicted in the United Kingdom, the Channel Islands or the Isle of Man of an offence and is sentenced to imprisonment (whether suspended or not).

(8) The Scottish Ministers shall pay to each Surveillance Commissioner such allowances as the Scottish Ministers consider appropriate.

(9) The Scottish Ministers may, after consultation with the Chief Surveillance Commissioner, provide the Commissioners with such staff as the Scottish Ministers consider necessary for the discharge of the Commissioners' functions.

(10) The decisions of the Chief Surveillance Commissioner or, subject to section 16 below, any other Surveillance Commissioner (including decisions

as to jurisdiction) shall not be subject to appeal or liable to be questioned in any court.

Assistant Surveillance Commissioners

3.—(1) The Scottish Ministers may, after consultation with the Chief Surveillance Commissioner as to numbers, appoint as Assistant Surveillance Commissioners such number of persons as the Scottish Ministers consider necessary (in addition to the ordinary Surveillance Commissioners) for the purpose of providing the Chief Surveillance Commissioner with assistance under this section.

(2) A person shall not be appointed as an Assistant Surveillance Commissioner unless that person holds or has held office as—

(a) a sheriff;

(b) a judge of the Crown Court in England and Wales or a Circuit judge there; or

(c) a county court judge in Northern Ireland.

(3) The Chief Surveillance Commissioner may require any ordinary Surveillance Commissioner or any Assistant Surveillance Commissioner to provide him with assistance in carrying out that Chief Surveillance Commissioner's functions under this Act.

(4) The assistance that may be provided under this section includes—

(a) the conduct on behalf of the Chief Surveillance Commissioner of the review of any matter; and

(b) the making of a report to the Chief Surveillance Commissioner about the matter reviewed.

(5) Subsections (3) to (8) of section 2 above apply in relation to a person appointed under this section as they apply in relation to a person appointed under that section.

Delegation of Commissioner's functions

4.—(1) Anything authorised or required by or under this Act to be done by a relevant Commissioner may be done by any member of the staff of that Commissioner who is authorised for the purpose (whether generally or specifically) by that Commissioner.

(2) In this section "relevant Commissioner" means any Surveillance Commissioner or Assistant Surveillance Commissioner.

Authorisation of surveillance and human intelligence sources

Lawful surveillance etc.

5.—(1) Conduct to which this Act applies shall be lawful for all purposes if—

(a) an authorisation under this Act confers an entitlement to engage in that conduct on the person whose conduct it is; and

(b) that person's conduct is in accordance with the authorisation.

(2) A person shall not be subject to any civil liability in respect of any conduct of that person which—

(a) is incidental to any conduct that is lawful by virtue of subsection (1) above; and

(b) is not itself conduct an authorisation or warrant for which is capable of being granted under a relevant enactment and might reasonably have been expected to have been sought in the case in question.

(3) In this section "relevant enactment" means—

(a) an enactment contained in this Act; or

(b) an enactment contained in Part III of the Police Act 1997 (c.50) (authorisation of interference with property and wireless telegraphy) in so far as relating to a police force.

Authorisation of directed surveillance

6.—(1) Subject to the following provisions of this Act, the persons designated for the purposes of this section shall each have power to grant authorisations for the carrying out of directed surveillance.

(2) A person shall not grant an authorisation for the carrying out of directed surveillance unless that person is satisfied—

    (a) that the authorisation is necessary on grounds falling within subsection (3) below; and

    (b) that the authorised surveillance is proportionate to what is sought to be achieved by carrying it out.

(3) An authorisation is necessary on grounds falling within this subsection if it is necessary—

    (a) for the purpose of preventing or detecting crime or of preventing disorder;

    (b) in the interests of public safety; or

    (c) for the purpose of protecting public health.

(4) The conduct that is authorised by an authorisation for the carrying out of directed surveillance is any conduct that—

    (a) consists in the carrying out of directed surveillance of any such description as is specified in the authorisation; and

    (b) is carried out in the circumstances described in the authorisation and for the purposes of the investigation or operation specified or described in the authorisation.

Authorisation of covert human intelligence sources

7.—(1) Subject to the following provisions of this Act, the persons designated for the purposes of this section shall each have power to grant authorisations for the conduct or the use of a covert human intelligence source.

(2) A person shall not grant an authorisation for the conduct or the use of a covert human intelligence source unless that person is satisfied—

    (a) that the authorisation is necessary on grounds falling within subsection (3) below;

    (b) that the authorised conduct or use is proportionate to what is sought to be achieved by that conduct or use; and

    (c) that arrangements exist for the source's case that satisfy the requirements of subsection (6) below and such other requirements as may be imposed by order made by the Scottish Ministers.

(3) An authorisation is necessary on grounds falling within this subsection if it is necessary—

    (a) for the purpose of preventing or detecting crime or of preventing disorder;

    (b) in the interests of public safety; or

    (c) for the purpose of protecting public health.

(4) The Scottish Ministers may by order—

    (a) prohibit the authorisation under this section of any such conduct or uses of covert human intelligence sources as may be described in the order; and

    (b) impose requirements, in addition to those provided for by subsection (2) above, that must be satisfied before an authorisation is granted under this section for any such conduct or uses of covert human intelligence sources as may be described.

(5) The conduct that is authorised by an authorisation for the conduct or the use of a covert human intelligence source is any conduct that—

    (a) is comprised in any such activities involving conduct of a covert human intelligence source, or the use of a covert human intelligence source, as are specified or described in the authorisation;

(b) consists in conduct by or in relation to the person who is so specified or described as the person to whose actions as a covert human intelligence source the authorisation relates; and

(c) is carried out for the purposes of, or in connection with, the investigation or operation so specified or described.

(6) For the purposes of this Act there are arrangements for the source's case that satisfy the requirements of this subsection if such arrangements are in force as are necessary for ensuring—

(a) that there will at all times be a person holding an office, rank or position with the relevant investigating authority who will have day-to-day responsibility for dealing with the source on behalf of that authority, and for the source's security and welfare;

(b) that there will at all times be another person holding an office, rank or position with the relevant investigating authority who will have general oversight of the use made of the source;

(c) that there will at all times be a person holding an office, rank or position with the relevant investigating authority who will have responsibility for maintaining a record of the use made of the source;

(d) that the records relating to the source that are maintained by the relevant investigating authority will always contain particulars of all such matters (if any) as may be specified for the purposes of this paragraph in regulations made by the Scottish Ministers; and

(e) that records maintained by the relevant investigating authority that disclose the identity of the source will not be available to persons except to the extent that there is a need for access to them to be made available to those persons.

(7) In this section "relevant investigating authority", in relation to an authorisation for the conduct or the use of an individual as a covert human intelligence source, means (subject to subsection (8) below) the public authority for whose benefit the activities of that individual as such a source are to take place.

(8) In the case of any authorisation for the conduct or the use of a covert human intelligence source whose activities are to be for the benefit of more than one public authority, the references in subsection (6) above to the relevant investigating authority are references to one of them (whether or not the same one in the case of each reference).

Persons entitled to grant authorisations under sections 6 and 7

8.—(1) Subject to subsection (2) below, the persons designated for the purposes of sections 6 and 7 above are the individuals holding such offices, ranks or positions with relevant public authorities as are prescribed for the purposes of this subsection by order made by the Scottish Ministers.

(2) The Scottish Ministers may by order impose restrictions—

(a) on the authorisations under sections 6 and 7 above that may be granted by any individual holding an office, rank or position with a specified public authority; and

(b) on the circumstances in which, or the purposes for which, such authorisations may be granted by any such individual.

(3) A public authority is a relevant public authority for the purposes of this section in relation to sections 6 and 7 above if it is—

(a) a police force;

(b) the Scottish Administration;

(c) a council constituted under section 2 of the Local Government etc. (Scotland) Act 1994 (c.39);

(d) the Common Services Agency for the Health Service;

(e) a health board;

(f) a special health board;

(g) a National Health Service trust established under section 12A of the National Health Service (Scotland) Act 1978 (c.29);

(h) the Scottish Environment Protection Agency.

(4) The Scottish Ministers may by order amend subsection (3) above by—

(a) adding a public authority to those enumerated in that subsection;

(b) removing a public authority therefrom;

(c) making any change consequential on any change in the name of a public authority enumerated therein

(5) No order shall be made under subsection (4)(a) above unless it has been laid in draft before and approved by resolution of the Scottish Parliament.

Special provision for the Scottish Crime Squads

9.—(1) In this Act, the "Scottish Crime Squad" means the joint operation known by that name and established by agreement among the chief constables of the Scottish police forces and police authorities made under section 12 of the Police (Scotland) Act 1967 (c.77) and in force at the date of Royal Assent to this Act or any other joint operation, howsoever named, established by agreement under that section and which fulfils purposes most or all of which consist of or include purposes which are the same as or similar to those fulfilled by the Scottish Crime Squad.

(2) Sections 6 to 8 above and 19 to 32 below apply to the Scottish Crime Squad and constables seconded to it as if it were a public authority specified in section 8(3) above.

(3) For the purposes of subsection (2) above, the Scottish Ministers shall prescribe, under subsection (1) of section 8 above, offices, ranks or positions with the Scottish Crime Squad corresponding to those they prescribe in relation to police forces under that subsection of that section.

(4) A person who is a designated person for the purposes of section 6 or 7 above by reference to the office, rank or position with the Scottish Crime Squad held by that person shall not grant an authorisation under that section except on an application made by a constable seconded to that Squad.

(5) For the purposes of subsections (2) and (3) above, references in this Act to a person's office, rank or position with the Scottish Crime Squad shall be taken as references to that person's office, rank or position with the police force from which that person is seconded.

(6) This section has effect only for the purposes of enabling and regulating the grant and cancellation of authorisations under this Act within the Scottish Crime Squad; accordingly, it does not otherwise affect the constitution of the Scottish Crime Squad, or the functions of constables seconded to it or the liabilities of the chief constables of the police forces from which those constables are seconded.

Authorisation of intrusive surveillance

10.—(1) Subject to the following provisions of this Act, the chief constable of every police force shall have power to grant authorisations for the carrying out of intrusive surveillance.

(2) No such authorisation shall be granted unless the chief constable granting it is satisfied—

(a) that the authorisation is necessary for the purpose of preventing or detecting serious crime; and

(b) that the authorised surveillance is proportionate to what is sought to be achieved by carrying it out

(3) The matters to be taken into account in considering whether the requirements of subsection (2) above are satisfied in the case of any authorisation shall include whether the information which it is thought

necessary to obtain by the authorised conduct could reasonably be obtained by other means.

(4) The conduct that is authorised by an authorisation for the carrying out of intrusive surveillance is any conduct that—

(a) consists in the carrying out of intrusive surveillance of any such description as is specified in the authorisation;

(b) is carried out in relation to the residential premises specified or described in the authorisation or in relation to the private vehicle so specified or described; and

(c) is carried out for the purposes of, or in connection with, the investigation or operation so specified or described.

Rules for grant of authorisations

11.—(1) A person who is a designated person for the purposes of section 6 or 7 above by reference to the office, rank or position with a police force held by that person shall not grant an authorisation under that section except on an application made by a member of the same force.

(2) A chief constable of a police force shall not grant an authorisation for the carrying out of intrusive surveillance except—

(a) on an application made by a member of the same force; and

(b) in the case of an authorisation for the carrying out of intrusive surveillance in relation to any residential premises, where those premises are in the area of operation of that force.

(3) A chief constable of a police force may grant an authorisation for the carrying out of intrusive surveillance on the application of a constable seconded to the Scottish Crime Squad if—

(a) in the case of an authorisation for the carrying out of intrusive surveillance in relation to any residential premises, those premises are in; and

(b) in the case of an authorisation for the carrying out of intrusive surveillance in relation to any private vehicle, the chief constable is satisfied that the surveillance operation will commence in,

the area of operation of that chief constable's police force.

(4) A single authorisation may combine both—

(a) an authorisation granted under this Act by, or on the application of, an individual who is a member of a police force; and

(b) an authorisation given by, or on the application of, that individual under Part III of the Police Act 1997 (c.50) (authorisation of interference with property and wireless telegraphy) insofar as relating to a police force,

but the provisions of this Act or the 1997 Act that are applicable in the case of each of the authorisations shall apply separately in relation to the part of the combined authorisation to which they are applicable.

(5) For the purposes of this section, the area of operation of a police force is the area for which that force is maintained.

Grant of authorisations in cases of urgency

12.—(1) This section applies in the case of an application for an authorisation for the carrying out of intrusive surveillance where the case is urgent.

(2) If it is not reasonably practicable, having regard to the urgency of the case—

(a) for the application to be considered by the chief constable of the police force in question; and

(b) for the application to be considered by a person (if there is one) who is entitled, as a designated deputy of that chief constable, to exercise the functions in relation to that application of that chief constable, the application may be made to and considered by any person who is entitled under subsection (4) below to act for that chief constable.

(3) A person who considers an application under subsection (1) above shall have the same power to grant an authorisation as the person for whom the person considering the application is entitled to act.

(4) For the purposes of this section a person is entitled to act for the chief constable of a police force if the person holds the rank of assistant chief constable in that force.

(5) In this section "designated deputy", in relation to a chief constable, means a person holding the rank of assistant chief constable who is designated to act under section 5(4) of the Police (Scotland) Act 1967 (c.77).

Notification of authorisations for intrusive surveillance

13.—(1) Where a person grants or cancels an authorisation for the carrying out of intrusive surveillance, the person shall give notice of the grant or cancellation to an ordinary Surveillance Commissioner.

(2) A notice given for the purposes of subsection (1) above—

(a) must be given in writing as soon as reasonably practicable after the grant or, as the case may be, cancellation of the authorisation to which it relates;

(b) must be given in accordance with any such arrangements made for the purposes of this paragraph by the Chief Surveillance Commissioner as are for the time being in force; and

(c) must specify such matters as the Scottish Ministers may by order prescribe.

(3) A notice under this section of the grant of an authorisation shall, as the case may be, either—

(a) state that the approval of a Surveillance Commissioner is required by section 14 below before the grant of the authorisation will take effect; or

(b) state that the case is one of urgency and set out the grounds on which the person granting the authorisation is satisfied that the case is one of urgency.

(4) Where a notice for the purposes of subsection (1) above of the grant of an authorisation has been received by an ordinary Surveillance Commissioner, the Commissioner shall, as soon as practicable—

(a) scrutinise the authorisation; and

(b) in a case where notice has been given in accordance with subsection (3)(a) above, decide whether or not to approve the authorisation.

(5) Subject to subsection (6) below, the Scottish Ministers shall not make an order under subsection (2)(c) above unless a draft of the order has been laid before and approved by a resolution of the Scottish Parliament.

(6) Subsection (5) above does not apply in the case of an order made on the first occasion on which the Scottish Ministers exercise their powers to make an order under subsection (2)(c) above.

(7) The order made on that occasion shall cease to have effect at the end of the period of 40 days beginning with the day on which it was made unless, before the end of that period, it has been approved by resolution of the Scottish Parliament.

(8) For the purposes of subsection (7) above—

(a) the order's ceasing to have effect shall be without prejudice to anything previously done or to the making of a new order; and

(b) in reckoning the period of 40 days, no account shall be taken of any period during which the Scottish Parliament is dissolved or is in recess for more than 4 days.

(9) Any notice that is required by any provision of this section to be given in writing may be given, instead, by being transmitted by electronic means.

Approval required for authorisations to take effect

14.—(1) Subject to subsection (2) below, an authorisation for the carrying out of intrusive surveillance shall not take effect until such time (if any) as—

   (a) the grant of the authorisation has been approved by an ordinary Surveillance Commissioner; and

   (b) written notice of the decision of that approval by that Commissioner has been given, in accordance with subsection (3) below, to the person who granted the authorisation.

(2) Where the person who grants the authorisation—

   (a) is satisfied that the case is one of urgency; and

   (b) gives notice in accordance with section 13(3)(b) above,

subsection (1) above shall not apply to the authorisation, and the authorisation shall have effect from the time of its grant.

(3) Where subsection (1) above applies to the authorisation—

   (a) a Surveillance Commissioner shall give approval under this section to the authorisation if, and only if, satisfied that there are reasonable grounds for being satisfied that the requirements of section 10(2)(a) and (b) above are satisfied in the case of the authorisation; and

   (b) a Surveillance Commissioner who makes a decision as to whether or not the authorisation should be approved shall, as soon as reasonably practicable after making that decision, give written notice of that decision to the person who granted the authorisation.

(4) If an ordinary Surveillance Commissioner decides not to approve an authorisation to which subsection (1) above applies, the Commissioner shall make a report of that decision and the Commissioner's findings to the most senior relevant person.

(5) In this section "the most senior relevant person" means—

   (a) in relation to an authorisation granted on the application of a member of a police force, the chief constable of that force; and

   (b) in relation to an authorisation granted on the application of a member of the Scottish Crime Squad, the chief constable of the police force—

     (i) who;

     (ii) whose designated deputy; or

     (iii) on whose behalf a person entitled under subsection (4) of section 12 above, granted it.

(6) Any notice that is required by any provision of this section to be given in writing may be given, instead, by being transmitted by electronic means.

(7) In this section "designated deputy" has the same meaning as in section 12 above.

Quashing of authorisations etc.

15.—(1) Where an ordinary Surveillance Commissioner is at any time satisfied that, at the time the authorisation for the carrying out of intrusive surveillance was granted or at any time when it was renewed, there were no reasonable grounds for being satisfied that the requirements of section 10(2)(a) and (b) above were satisfied, the Commissioner may quash the authorisation with effect, as the Commissioner thinks fit, from the time of the grant of the authorisation or from the time of any renewal of the authorisation.

(2) If an ordinary Surveillance Commissioner is satisfied at any time while the authorisation is in force that there are no longer any reasonable grounds for being satisfied that the requirements of section 10(2)(a) and (b) above are satisfied in relation to the authorisation, he may cancel the authorisation with effect from such time as appears to the Commissioner to be the time from which those requirements ceased to be so satisfied.

(3) Where, in the case of any authorisation of which notice has been given in accordance with section 13(3)(b) above, an ordinary Surveillance Commissioner is at any time satisfied that, at the time of the grant or renewal of the authorisation to which that notice related, there were no reasonable grounds for being satisfied that the case was one of urgency, the Commissioner may quash the authorisation with effect, as the Commissioner thinks fit, from the time of the grant of the authorisation or from the time of any renewal of the authorisation.

(4) Subject to subsection (6) below, where an ordinary Surveillance Commissioner quashes an authorisation under this section, the Commissioner may order the destruction of any records relating wholly or partly to information obtained by the authorised conduct after the time from which the decision of the Commissioner takes effect.

(5) Subject to subsection (6) below, where—

    (a) an authorisation has ceased to have effect (otherwise than by virtue of subsection (1) or (3) above); and

    (b) an ordinary Surveillance Commissioner is satisfied that there was a time while the authorisation was in force when there were no reasonable grounds for being satisfied that the requirements of section 10(2)(a) and (b) above continued to be satisfied in relation to the authorisation,

the Commissioner may order the destruction of any records relating, wholly or partly, to information obtained at such time by the authorised conduct.

(6) No order shall be made under this section for the destruction of any records required for pending criminal or civil proceedings.

(7) Where an ordinary Surveillance Commissioner exercises a power conferred by this section, the Commissioner shall, as soon as reasonably practicable, make a report of that exercise of that power and of the Commissioner's reasons for doing so—

    (a) to the most senior relevant person (within the meaning of section 14 above); and

    (b) to the Chief Surveillance Commissioner.

(8) Where an order for the destruction of records is made under this section, the order shall not become operative until such time (if any) as—

    (a) the period for appealing against the decision to make the order has expired; and

    (b) any appeal brought within that period has been dismissed by the Chief Surveillance Commissioner.

(9) No notice shall be required to be given under section 13(1) above in the case of a cancellation under subsection (2) above.

Appeals against decisions by Surveillance Commissioners

16.—(1) A chief constable of a police force may appeal to the Chief Surveillance Commissioner against any of the following—

    (a) any refusal of an ordinary Surveillance Commissioner to approve an authorisation for the carrying out of intrusive surveillance;

    (b) any decision of such a Commissioner to quash or cancel such an authorisation;

    (c) any decision of such a Commissioner to make an order under section 15 above for the destruction of records.

(2) A designated deputy of a chief constable or a person specified in or designated under subsection (4) of section 12 above, who granted an authorisation under that section, shall also be entitled to appeal under this section.

(3) An appeal under this section must be brought within the period of seven days beginning with the day on which the refusal or decision appealed against is reported to the appellant.

(4) Subject to subsection (5) below, the Chief Surveillance Commissioner, on an appeal under this section, shall allow the appeal—

    (a) if satisfied that there were reasonable grounds for being satisfied that the requirements of section 10(2)(a) and (b) above were satisfied in relation to the authorisation at the time in question; or

    (b) if not satisfied that the authorisation is one of which notice was given in accordance with section 13(3)(b) above without there being any reasonable grounds for being satisfied that the case was one of urgency.

(5) If, on an appeal falling within subsection (1)(b) above, the Chief Surveillance Commissioner—

    (a) is satisfied that grounds exist which justify the quashing or cancellation under section 15 above of the authorisation in question; but

    (b) considers that the authorisation should have been quashed or cancelled from a different time from that from which it was quashed or cancelled by the ordinary Surveillance Commissioner against whose decision the appeal is brought,

the Chief Surveillance Commissioner may modify the ordinary Surveillance Commissioner's decision to quash or cancel the authorisation, and any related decision for the destruction of records, so as to give effect to the decision under section 15 above that the Chief Surveillance Commissioner considers should have been made.

(6) Where, on appeal under this section against a decision to quash or cancel an authorisation, the Chief Surveillance Commissioner allows the appeal the Commissioner shall also quash any related order for the destruction of records relating to information obtained by the authorised conduct.

(7) In this section "designated deputy" has the same meaning as in section 12 above.

Appeals to the Chief Surveillance Commissioner: supplementary

17.—(1) On determining an appeal under section 16 above, the Chief Surveillance Commissioner shall give notice of the determination to both—

    (a) the person by whom the appeal was brought; and

    (b) the ordinary Surveillance Commissioner whose decision was appealed against.

(2) Where the determination of the Chief Surveillance Commissioner on an appeal under section 16 above is a determination to dismiss the appeal, the Chief Surveillance Commissioner shall make a report of the findings—

    (a) to the persons mentioned in subsection (1) above; and

    (b) to the Scottish Ministers.

(3) Subject to subsection (2) above, the Chief Surveillance Commissioner shall not give any reasons for any determination of the Commissioner on an appeal under section 16 above.

Information to be provided to Surveillance Commissioners

18. It shall be the duty of—

    (a) every member of a police force; and

    (b) every member of the Scottish Crime Squad,

to comply with any request of a Surveillance Commissioner for documents or information required by the Commissioner for the purpose of enabling the Commissioner to carry out the functions of such a Commissioner under sections 13 to 17 above.

General rules about grant, renewal and duration

19.—(1) An authorisation under this Act—
(a) may be granted or renewed orally in any urgent case in which the entitlement to act of the person granting or renewing it is not confined to urgent cases; and
(b) in any other case, must be in writing.
(2) A single authorisation may combine two or more different authorisations under this Act; but the provisions of this Act that are applicable in the case of each of the authorisations shall apply separately in relation to the part of the combined authorisation to which they are applicable
(3) Subject to subsections (4) and (8) below, an authorisation under this Act shall cease to have effect at the end of the following period—
(a) in the case of an authorisation which—
(i) has not been renewed and was granted either orally or by a person whose entitlement to act is confined to urgent cases; or
(ii) was last renewed either orally or by such a person,
the period of 72 hours beginning with the time when the grant of the authorisation or, as the case may be, its latest renewal takes effect;
(b) in a case not falling within paragraph (a) above in which the authorisation is for the conduct or the use of a covert human intelligence source, the period of 12 months beginning with the day on which the grant of the authorisation or, as the case may be, its latest renewal takes effect; and
(c) in any case not falling within paragraph (a) or (b) above, the period of three months beginning with the day on which the grant of the authorisation or, as the case may be, its latest renewal takes effect.
(4) Subject to subsection (6) below, an authorisation under this Act may be renewed, at any time before the time at which it ceases to have effect, by any person who would be entitled to grant a new authorisation in the same terms.
(5) Sections 6 to 18 above shall have effect in relation to the renewal of an authorisation under this Act as if references to the grant of an authorisation included references to its renewal.
(6) A person shall not renew an authorisation for the conduct or the use of a covert human intelligence source, unless the person—
(a) is satisfied that a review has been carried out of the matters mentioned in subsection (7) below; and
(b) has, for the purpose of deciding whether to renew the authorisation, considered the results of that review.
(7) The matters mentioned in subsection (6) above are—
(a) the use made of the source in the period since the grant or, as the case may be, latest renewal of the authorisation; and
(b) the tasks given to the source during that period and the information obtained from the conduct or the use of the source.
(8) The Scottish Ministers may by order provide, in relation to authorisations of such descriptions as may be specified in the order, that subsection (3) above is to have effect as if the period at the end of which an authorisation of a description so specified is to cease to have effect were such period, shorter than that provided for by that subsection, as may be fixed by or determined in accordance with that order.
(9) References in this section to the time at which, or the day on which, the grant or renewal of an authorisation takes effect are references—
(a) in the case of the grant of an authorisation to which paragraph (c) below does not apply, to the time at which or, as the case may be, day on which the authorisation is granted;

(b) in the case of the grant of the renewal of an authorisation to which paragraph (c) below does not apply, to the time at which or, as the case may be, day on which the authorisation would cease to have effect but for the renewal; and

(c) in the case of any grant or renewal that takes effect under subsection (1) of section 14 above at a time or on a day later than that given in paragraph (a) or (b) above, to the time at which or, as the case may be, the day on which the grant or renewal takes effect in accordance with that subsection.

Cancellation of authorisations

20.—(1) The person who granted or, as the case may be, last renewed an authorisation under this Act shall cancel it—

(a) if satisfied that the authorised conduct no longer satisfies the requirements of section 6(2)(a) and (b), 7(2)(a) and (b) or, as the case may be, 10(2)(a) and (b) above; or

(b) in the case of an authorisation under section 7 above, if satisfied that arrangements for the source's case that satisfy the requirements of subsection (2)(c) of that section no longer exist.

(2) Where an authorisation under this Act was granted or, as the case may be, last renewed—

(a) by a person entitled to act for any other person; or

(b) by the deputy of any other person,

that other person shall cancel the authorisation if satisfied as to either of the matters mentioned in subsection (1) above.

(3) Where an authorisation under this Act was granted or, as the case may be, last renewed by a person whose deputy had power to grant it and it is not reasonably practicable for that person to cancel it under subsection (1) above, that deputy shall cancel the authorisation if he is satisfied as to either of the matters mentioned in subsection (1) above.

(4) The Scottish Ministers may by regulations provide for the person by whom any duty imposed by this section is to be performed in a case in which it would otherwise fall on a person who is no longer available to perform it.

(5) Regulations under subsection (4) above may provide for the person on whom the duty is to fall to be a person appointed in accordance with the regulations.

(6) The references in this section to a person's deputy are references, in relation to a chief constable of a police force, to the designated deputy of the chief constable.

(7) In this section "designated deputy" has the same meaning as in section 12 above.

Chief Surveillance Commissioner

Functions of Chief Surveillance Commissioner

21.—(1) Subject to subsection (4) below, the Chief Surveillance Commissioner shall keep under review the exercise and performance, by the persons on whom they are conferred or imposed, of the powers and duties conferred or imposed by or under this Act.

(2) The Chief Surveillance Commissioner may require any ordinary Surveillance Commissioner to provide assistance in the carrying out of the former's functions under subsection (1) above, and that assistance may include—

(a) the conduct on behalf of the Chief Surveillance Commissioner of the review of any matter; and

(b) the making of a report to the Chief Surveillance Commissioner about the matter reviewed.

(3) The Chief Surveillance Commissioner shall give the Tribunal all such assistance (including the opinion of that Commissioner as to any issue falling to be determined by the Tribunal) as is appropriate—

(a) in connection with the investigation of any matter by the Tribunal; or

(b) otherwise for the purposes of the Tribunal's consideration or determination of any matter.

(4) It shall not be the function of the Chief Surveillance Commissioner to keep under review the exercise of any power of the Scottish Ministers to make, amend or revoke any subordinate legislation.

Co-operation with and reports by Commissioner

22.—(1) It shall be the duty of—

(a) every person by whom, or on whose application, there has been granted any authorisation the grant of which is subject to review by the Chief Surveillance Commissioner;

(b) every person who holds or has held any office, rank or position with the same public authority as a person falling within paragraph (a) above;

(c) every person who has engaged in any conduct with the authority of such an authorisation; and

(d) every person who holds or has held any office, rank or position with a public authority for whose benefit any such authorisation has been or may be granted,

to disclose or provide to that Commissioner all such documents and information as that Commissioner may require for the purpose of enabling that Commissioner to carry out that Commissioner's functions under this Act.

(2) If it at any time appears to the Chief Surveillance Commissioner—

(a) that there has been a contravention of the provisions of this Act in relation to any matter with which that Commissioner is concerned; and

(b) that the contravention has not been the subject of a report made to the Scottish Ministers by the Tribunal,

that Commissioner shall make a report to the Scottish Ministers with respect to that contravention.

(3) The Chief Surveillance Commissioner shall make an annual report to the Scottish Ministers with respect to the carrying out of that Commissioner's functions under this Act.

(4) The Scottish Ministers shall lay before the Scottish Parliament a copy of every annual report made by the Commissioner under subsection (3) above, together with a statement as to whether any matter has been excluded from that copy in pursuance of subsection (5) below.

(5) If it appears to the Scottish Ministers, after consultation with the Commissioner, that the publication of any matter in an annual report would be contrary to the public interest or prejudicial to—

(a) the prevention or detection of serious crime; or

(b) the continued discharge of the functions of any public authority whose activities include activities that are subject to review by that Commissioner,

the Scottish Ministers may exclude that matter from the copy of the report as laid before the Parliament.

Complaints by aggrieved persons

Complaints to the Tribunal

23.—(1) In this section, the "Tribunal" means the tribunal established under section 65 of the Regulation of Investigatory Powers Act 2000 (c.23).

(2) A person who is aggrieved by any conduct falling within subsection (3) below which the person believes—

    (a) to have taken place in relation to that person or to any property of that person; and

    (b) to have taken place in challengeable circumstances,
        is entitled to complain to the Tribunal.

(3) Conduct falls within this subsection if (whenever it occurred) it is conduct to which this Act applies.

(4) For the purposes of this section conduct takes place in challengeable circumstances if—

    (a) it takes place with the authority, or purported authority, of anything falling within subsection (5) below; or

    (b) the circumstances are such that (whether or not there is such authority) it would not have been appropriate for the conduct to take place without it, or at least without proper consideration having been given to whether such authority should be sought.

(5) The following fall within this subsection—

    (a) an authorisation under this Act;

    (b) an authorisation under section 93 of the Police Act 1997 (c.50) insofar as relating to a police force.
        Complaints to the Tribunal

Codes of practice

Issue and revision of codes of practice

24.—(1) The Scottish Ministers shall issue one or more codes of practice relating to the exercise and performance of the powers and duties mentioned in subsection (2) below.

(2) Those powers and duties are those (excluding any power to make subordinate legislation) that are conferred or imposed, by or under—

    (a) this Act; and

    (b) Part III of the Police Act 1997 (c.50) (authorisation of interference with property or wireless telegraphy) insofar as relating to a police force,

otherwise than on the Surveillance Commissioners appointed under this Act or the Commissioners holding office under section 91 of that Act.

(3) Before issuing a code of practice under subsection (1) above, the Scottish Ministers shall—

    (a) prepare and publish a draft of that code; and

    (b) consider any representations made to them about the draft,

and the Scottish Ministers may incorporate in the code finally issued any modifications made by them to the draft after its publication.

(4) The Scottish Ministers shall lay before the Scottish Parliament every draft code of practice prepared and published by them under this section.

(5) A code of practice issued by the Scottish Ministers under this section shall not be brought into force except in accordance with an order made by them.

(6) An order under subsection (5) above may contain such transitional provisions and savings as appear to the Scottish Ministers to be necessary or expedient in connection with the bringing into force of the code brought into force by that order.

(7) The Scottish Ministers may from time to time—

    (a) revise the whole or any part of a code issued under this section; and

    (b) issue the revised code.

(8) Subsections (3) to (6) above shall apply (with appropriate modifications) in relation to the issue of any revised code under this section as they apply in relation to the first issue of such a code.

(9) The Scottish Ministers shall not make an order containing provision

for any of the purposes of this section unless a draft of the order has been laid before, and approved by a resolution of the Parliament.

Interim codes of practice

25.—(1) The Scottish Ministers may, notwithstanding the provisions of section 24 above, issue one or more interim codes of practice relating to the exercise and performance of the powers and duties mentioned in subsection (2) of that section.

(2) An interim code issued under subsection (1) above shall have effect from its date of issue as if it were a code issued under subsection (1) of section 24 above which had been brought into force by an order under subsection (5) of that section.

(3) An interim notice issued under subsection (1) above shall cease to have effect insofar as it is superseded by a code issued and brought into force under section 24 above.

Effect of codes of practice

26.—(1) A person exercising or performing any power or duty in relation to which provision may be made by a code of practice under section 24 or 25 above shall, in doing so, have regard to the provisions (so far as they are applicable) of every code of practice for the time being in force under that section.

(2) A failure on the part of any person to comply with any provision of a code of practice for the time being in force under section 24 or 25 above shall not of itself render the person liable to any criminal or civil proceedings.

(3) A code of practice in force at any time under section 24 or 25 above shall be admissible in evidence in any criminal or civil proceedings.

(4) If any provision of a code of practice issued under section 24 or 25 or revised under section 24(7) above appears to—

(a) the court or tribunal conducting any civil or criminal proceedings;
(b) the Chief Surveillance Commissioner carrying out any of the functions of that Commissioner under this Act; or
(c) a Surveillance Commissioner carrying out the functions of that Commissioner under this Act insofar as relating to a police force,

to be relevant to any question arising in the proceedings, or in connection with the exercise of that jurisdiction or the carrying out of those functions, in relation to a time when it was in force, that provision of the code shall be taken into account in determining that question.

Supplementary provisions

Power to extend or modify authorisation provisions

27.—(1) The Scottish Ministers may by order do one or both of the following—

(a) apply this Act, with such modifications as they think fit, to any such surveillance, that is neither directed nor intrusive, as may be described in the order;
(b) provide for any description of directed surveillance to be treated for the purposes of this Act as intrusive surveillance.

(2) No order shall be made under this section unless a draft of it has been laid before and approved by resolution of the Scottish Parliament.

Orders and regulations

28.—(1) This section applies to any power of the Scottish Ministers to make any order or regulations under any provision of this Act.

(2) The powers to which this section applies shall be exercisable by statutory instrument.

(3) A statutory instrument containing any order or regulations made in exercise of a power to which this section applies, other than one containing—

(a) an order a draft of which has been approved for the purposes of section 8(5), 13(5) or (7), 24(9) and 27(2) above; or

(b) an order under section 32(2) below appointing a day,

shall be subject to annulment in pursuance of a resolution of the Scottish Parliament.

(4) An order or regulations made in exercise of a power to which this section applies may—

(a) make different provisions for different cases; and

(b) contain such incidental, supplemental, consequential and transitional provisions as the Scottish Ministers think fit.

Financial provision

29. The Scottish Ministers shall pay to the Secretary of State such amount as is agreed between them to be appropriate to reimburse the expenditure or increased expenditure incurred by the Secretary of State in consequence of this Act.

General saving for lawful conduct

30. Nothing in any of the provisions of this Act by virtue of which conduct of any description is or may be authorised, or by virtue of which information may be obtained in any manner, shall be construed—

(a) as making it unlawful to engage in any conduct of that description which is not otherwise unlawful under this Act and would not be unlawful apart from this Act;

(b) as otherwise requiring-

(i) the issue, grant or giving of such authorisation; or

(ii) the taking of any step for or towards obtaining the authority of such authorisation,

before any such conduct of that description is engaged in; or

(c) as prejudicing any power to obtain information by any means not involving conduct that may be authorised under this Act.

Interpretation

31.—(1) In this Act—

"apparatus" includes any equipment, machinery or device and any wire or cable;

"communication" includes—

(a) anything comprising speech, music, sounds, visual images, or data of any description; and

(b) signals serving either for the impartation of anything between persons, between a person and a thing or between things or for the actuation or control of any apparatus;

"covert human intelligence source" shall be construed in accordance with section 1(7) above;

"directed" and "intrusive", in relation to surveillance, shall be construed in accordance with section 1(2) to (5) above;

"ordinary Surveillance Commissioner" means a Surveillance Commissioner other than a Chief Surveillance Commissioner;

"police force" means any police force maintained under or by virtue of section 1 of the Police (Scotland) Act 1967 (c.77) (police areas);

"private vehicle" means (subject to subsection (9)(a) below) any vehicle which is used primarily for the private purposes of the person who owns it or of a person otherwise having the right to use it;

"residential premises" means (subject to subsection (9)(b) below) so much of any premises as is for the time being occupied or used by any person, however temporarily, for residential purposes or otherwise as living accommodation (including hotel or prison accommodation that is so occupied or used);

"surveillance" shall be construed in accordance with subsections (2) to (3) below;

"Surveillance Commissioner" means a Commissioner holding office under section 2 above and "Chief Surveillance Commissioner" shall be construed accordingly;

"surveillance device" means any apparatus designed or adapted for use in surveillance;

"the Tribunal" has the same meaning as in section 23(1) above.

(2) Subject to subsection (3) below, in this Act "surveillance" includes—

  (a) monitoring, observing or listening to persons, their movements, their conversations or their other activities or communications;

  (b) recording anything monitored, observed or listened to in the course of surveillance; and

  (c) surveillance by or with the assistance of a surveillance device.

(3) References in this Act to surveillance do not include references to—

  (a) any conduct of a covert human intelligence source for obtaining or recording (whether or not using a surveillance device) any information which is disclosed in the presence of the source;

  (b) the use of a covert human intelligence source for so obtaining or recording information; or

  (c) any such entry on or interference with property or with wireless telegraphy as would be unlawful unless authorised under Part III of the Police Act 1997 (c.50) (authorisation of interference with property or wireless telegraphy).

(4) References in this Act to an individual holding an office or position with a public authority include references to any member, official or employee of that authority.

(5) For the purposes of this Act the activities of a covert human intelligence source which are to be taken as activities for the benefit of a particular public authority include any of that source's conduct as such a source which is in response to inducements or requests made by or on behalf of that authority.

(6) In this Act—

  (a) references to crime are references to conduct which constitutes one or more criminal offences or is, or corresponds to, any conduct which, if it all took place in any one part of the United Kingdom would constitute one or more criminal offences; and

  (b) references to serious crime are references to crime that satisfies the test in subsection (7)(a) or (b) below.

(7) Those tests are—

  (a) that the offence or one of the offences that is or would be constituted by the conduct is an offence for which a person who has attained the age of 21 and has no previous convictions could reasonably be expected to be sentenced to imprisonment for a term of three years or more;

  (b) that the conduct involves the use of violence, results in substantial financial gain or is conduct by a large number of persons in pursuit of a common purpose.

(8) For the purposes of this Act, detecting crime shall be taken to include—

  (a) establishing by whom, for what purpose, by what means and generally in what circumstances any crime was committed; and

  (b) the apprehension of the person by whom any crime was committed, and any reference in this Act to preventing or detecting serious crime shall be construed accordingly.

(9) In subsection (1) above—

(a) the reference to a person having the right to use a vehicle does not, in relation to a motor vehicle, include a reference to a person whose right to use the vehicle derives only from having paid, or undertaken to pay, for the use of the vehicle and its driver for a particular journey; and

(b) the reference to premises occupied or used by any person for residential purposes or otherwise as living accommodation does not include a reference to so much of any premises as constitutes any common area to which the person has or is allowed access in connection with the person's use or occupation of any accommodation.

(10) In this section—

"premises" includes any vehicle or moveable structure and any other place whatever, whether or not occupied as land;

"vehicle" includes any vessel, aircraft or hovercraft.

Short title and commencement

32.—(1) This Act may be cited as the Regulation of Investigatory Powers (Scotland) Act 2000.

(2) The provisions of this Act shall come into force on such day as the Scottish Ministers may by order appoint; and different days may be appointed under this subsection for different purposes.

REGULATION OF INVESTIGATORY POWERS ACT 2000

(2000 c. 23)

ARRANGEMENT OF SECTIONS

PART I

COMMUNICATIONS

CHAPTER I

INTERCEPTION

CHAPTER II

ACQUISITION AND DISCLOSURE OF COMMUNICATIONS DATA

PART II

SURVEILLANCE AND COVERT HUMAN INTELLIGENCE SOURCES

Introductory

Division A—Miscellaneous Legislation

PART III

INVESTIGATION OF ELECTRONIC DATA PROTECTED BY ENCRYPTION ETC.

PART IV

SCRUTINY ETC. OF INVESTIGATORY POWERS AND OF THE FUNCTIONS OF THE INTELLIGENCE
SERVICES

Commissioners

The Tribunal

Codes of practice

PART V

MISCELLANEOUS AND SUPPLEMENTAL

Miscellaneous

Supplemental

An Act to make provision for and about the interception of communications, the acquisition and disclosure of data relating to communications,
the carrying out of surveillance, the use of covert human intelligence
sources and the acquisition of the means by which electronic data
protected by encryption or passwords may be decrypted or accessed; to
provide for Commissioners and a tribunal with functions and jurisdiction

in relation to those matters, to entries on and interferences with property or with wireless telegraphy and to the carrying out of their functions by the Security Service, the Secret Intelligence Service and the Government Communications Headquarters; and for connected purposes.

[28th July 2000]

PART I

COMMUNICATIONS

CHAPTER I

INTERCEPTION

Unlawful and authorised interception

Unlawful interception

1.—(1) It shall be an offence for a person intentionally and without lawful authority to intercept, at any place in the United Kingdom, any communication in the course of its transmission by means of—

    (a) a public postal service; or

    (b) a public telecommunication system.

(2) It shall be an offence for a person—

    (a) intentionally and without lawful authority, and

    (b) otherwise than in circumstances in which his conduct is excluded by subsection (6) from criminal liability under this subsection,

to intercept, at any place in the United Kingdom, any communication in the course of its transmission by means of a private telecommunication system.

(3) Any interception of a communication which is carried out at any place in the United Kingdom by, or with the express or implied consent of, a person having the right to control the operation or the use of a private telecommunication system shall be actionable at the suit or instance of the sender or recipient, or intended recipient, of the communication if it is without lawful authority and is either—

    (a) an interception of that communication in the course of its transmission by means of that private system; or

    (b) an interception of that communication in the course of its transmission, by means of a public telecommunication system, to or from apparatus comprised in that private telecommunication system.

(4) Where the United Kingdom is a party to an international agreement which—

    (a) relates to the provision of mutual assistance in connection with, or in the form of, the interception of communications,

    (b) requires the issue of a warrant, order or equivalent instrument in cases in which assistance is given, and

    (c) is designated for the purposes of this subsection by an order made by the Secretary of State,

it shall be the duty of the Secretary of State to secure that no request for assistance in accordance with the agreement is made on behalf of a person in the United Kingdom to the competent authorities of a country or territory outside the United Kingdom except with lawful authority.

(5) Conduct has lawful authority for the purposes of this section if, and only if—

    (a) it is authorised by or under section 3 or 4;

    (b) it takes place in accordance with a warrant under section 5 ("an interception warrant"); or

(c) it is in exercise, in relation to any stored communication, of any statutory power that is exercised (apart from this section) for the purpose of obtaining information or of taking possession of any document or other property;

and conduct (whether or not prohibited by this section) which has lawful authority for the purposes of this section by virtue of paragraph (a) or (b) shall also be taken to be lawful for all other purposes.

(6) The circumstances in which a person makes an interception of a communication in the course of its transmission by means of a private telecommunication system are such that his conduct is excluded from criminal liability under subsection (2) if—

(a) he is a person with a right to control the operation or the use of the system; or

(b) he has the express or implied consent of such a person to make the interception.

(7) A person who is guilty of an offence under subsection (1) or (2) shall be liable—

(a) on conviction on indictment, to imprisonment for a term not exceeding two years or to a fine, or to both;

(b) on summary conviction, to a fine not exceeding the statutory maximum.

(8) No proceedings for any offence which is an offence by virtue of this section shall be instituted—

(a) in England and Wales, except by or with the consent of the Director of Public Prosecutions;

(b) in Northern Ireland, except by or with the consent of the Director of Public Prosecutions for Northern Ireland.

Meaning and location of "interception" etc.

2.—(1) In this Act—

"postal service" means any service which—

(a) consists in the following, or in any one or more of them, namely, the collection, sorting, conveyance, distribution and delivery (whether in the United Kingdom or elsewhere) of postal items; and

(b) is offered or provided as a service the main purpose of which, or one of the main purposes of which, is to make available, or to facilitate, a means of transmission from place to place of postal items containing communications;

"private telecommunication system" means any telecommunication system which, without itself being a public telecommunication system, is a system in relation to which the following conditions are satisfied—

(a) it is attached, directly or indirectly and whether or not for the purposes of the communication in question, to a public telecommunication system; and

(b) there is apparatus comprised in the system which is both located in the United Kingdom and used (with or without other apparatus) for making the attachment to the public telecommunication system;

"public postal service" means any postal service which is offered or provided to, or to a substantial section of, the public in any one or more parts of the United Kingdom;

"public telecommunications service" means any telecommunications service which is offered or provided to, or to a substantial section of, the public in any one or more parts of the United Kingdom;

"public telecommunication system" means any such parts of a telecommunication system by means of which any public telecommunications service is provided as are located in the United Kingdom;

"telecommunications service" means any service that consists in the provision of access to, and of facilities for making use of, any telecommunication system (whether or not one provided by the person providing the service); and

"telecommunication system" means any system (including the apparatus comprised in it) which exists (whether wholly or partly in the United Kingdom or elsewhere) for the purpose of facilitating the transmission of communications by any means involving the use of electrical or electromagnetic energy.

(2) For the purposes of this Act, but subject to the following provisions of this section, a person intercepts a communication in the course of its transmission by means of a telecommunication system if, and only if, he—

(a) so modifies or interferes with the system, or its operation,

(b) so monitors transmissions made by means of the system, or

(c) so monitors transmissions made by wireless telegraphy to or from apparatus comprised in the system,

as to make some or all of the contents of the communication available, while being transmitted, to a person other than the sender or intended recipient of the communication.

(3) References in this Act to the interception of a communication do not include references to the interception of any communication broadcast for general reception.

(4) For the purposes of this Act the interception of a communication takes place in the United Kingdom if, and only if, the modification, interference or monitoring or, in the case of a postal item, the interception is effected by conduct within the United Kingdom and the communication is either—

(a) intercepted in the course of its transmission by means of a public postal service or public telecommunication system; or

(b) intercepted in the course of its transmission by means of a private telecommunication system in a case in which the sender or intended recipient of the communication is in the United Kingdom.

(5) References in this Act to the interception of a communication in the course of its transmission by means of a postal service or telecommunication system do not include references to—

(a) any conduct that takes place in relation only to so much of the communication as consists in any traffic data comprised in or attached to a communication (whether by the sender or otherwise) for the purposes of any postal service or telecommunication system by means of which it is being or may be transmitted; or

(b) any such conduct, in connection with conduct falling within paragraph (a), as gives a person who is neither the sender nor the intended recipient only so much access to a communication as is necessary for the purpose of identifying traffic data so comprised or attached.

(6) For the purposes of this section references to the modification of a telecommunication system include references to the attachment of any apparatus to, or other modification of or interference with—

(a) any part of the system; or

(b) any wireless telegraphy apparatus used for making transmissions to or from apparatus comprised in the system.

(7) For the purposes of this section the times while a communication is being transmitted by means of a telecommunication system shall be taken to include any time when the system by means of which the communication is being, or has been, transmitted is used for storing it in a manner that enables the intended recipient to collect it or otherwise to have access to it.

(8) For the purposes of this section the cases in which any contents of a communication are to be taken to be made available to a person while being transmitted shall include any case in which any of the contents of the communication, while being transmitted, are diverted or recorded so as to be available to a person subsequently.

(9) In this section "traffic data", in relation to any communication, means—

(a) any data identifying, or purporting to identify, any person, apparatus or location to or from which the communication is or may be transmitted,

(b) any data identifying or selecting, or purporting to identify or select, apparatus through which, or by means of which, the communication is or may be transmitted,

(c) any data comprising signals for the actuation of apparatus used for the purposes of a telecommunication system for effecting (in whole or in part) the transmission of any communication, and

(d) any data identifying the data or other data as data comprised in or attached to a particular communication,

but that expression includes data identifying a computer file or computer program access to which is obtained, or which is run, by means of the communication to the extent only that the file or program is identified by reference to the apparatus in which it is stored.

(10) In this section—

(a) references, in relation to traffic data comprising signals for the actuation of apparatus, to a telecommunication system by means of which a communication is being or may be transmitted include references to any telecommunication system in which that apparatus is comprised; and

(b) references to traffic data being attached to a communication include references to the data and the communication being logically associated with each other;and in this section "data", in relation to a postal item, means anything written on the outside of the item.

(11) In this section "postal item" means any letter, postcard or other such thing in writing as may be used by the sender for imparting information to the recipient, or any packet or parcel.

Lawful interception without an interception warrant.

3.—(1) Conduct by any person consisting in the interception of a communication is authorised by this section if the communication is one which, or which that person has reasonable grounds for believing, is both—

(a) a communication sent by a person who has consented to the interception; and

(b) a communication the intended recipient of which has so consented.

(2) Conduct by any person consisting in the interception of a communication is authorised by this section if—

(a) the communication is one sent by, or intended for, a person who has consented to the interception; and

(b) surveillance by means of that interception has been authorised under Part II.

(3) Conduct consisting in the interception of a communication is authorised by this section if—

(a) it is conduct by or on behalf of a person who provides a postal service or a telecommunications service; and

(b) it takes place for purposes connected with the provision or operation of that service or with the enforcement, in relation to that service, of any enactment relating to the use of postal services or telecommunications services.

(4) Conduct by any person consisting in the interception of a communication in the course of its transmission by means of wireless telegraphy is authorised by this section if it takes place—

(a) with the authority of a designated person under section 5 of the Wireless Telegraphy Act 1949 (misleading messages and interception and disclosure of wireless telegraphy messages); and

(b) for purposes connected with anything falling within subsection (5).

(5) Each of the following falls within this subsection—

(a) the issue of licences under the Wireless Telegraphy Act 1949;

(b) the prevention or detection of anything which constitutes inter-ference with wireless telegraphy; and

(c) the enforcement of any enactment contained in that Act or of any enactment not so contained that relates to such interference.

Power to provide for lawful interception.

4.—(1) Conduct by any person ("the interceptor") consisting in the interception of a communication in the course of its transmission by means of a telecommunication system is authorised by this section if—

(a) the interception is carried out for the purpose of obtaining infor-mation about the communications of a person who, or who the interceptor has reasonable grounds for believing, is in a country or territory outside the United Kingdom;

(b) the interception relates to the use of a telecommunications service provided to persons in that country or territory which is either—
  (i) a public telecommunications service; or
  (ii) a telecommunications service that would be a public telecom-munications service if the persons to whom it is offered or provided were members of the public in a part of the United Kingdom;

(c) the person who provides that service (whether the interceptor or another person) is required by the law of that country or territory to carry out, secure or facilitate the interception in question;

(d) the situation is one in relation to which such further conditions as may be prescribed by regulations made by the Secretary of State are required to be satisfied before conduct may be treated as authorised by virtue of this subsection; and

(e) the conditions so prescribed are satisfied in relation to that situation.

(2) Subject to subsection (3), the Secretary of State may by regulations authorise any such conduct described in the regulations as appears to him to constitute a legitimate practice reasonably required for the purpose, in connection with the carrying on of any business, of monitoring or keeping a record of—

(a) communications by means of which transactions are entered into in the course of that business; or

(b) other communications relating to that business or taking place in the course of its being carried on.

(3) Nothing in any regulations under subsection (2) shall authorise the interception of any communication except in the course of its transmission using apparatus or services provided by or to the person carrying on the business for use wholly or partly in connection with that business.

(4) Conduct taking place in a prison is authorised by this section if it is conduct in exercise of any power conferred by or under any rules made under section 47 of the Prison Act 1952, section 39 of the Prisons (Scotland) Act 1989 or section 13 of the Prison Act (Northern Ireland) 1953 (prison rules).

(5) Conduct taking place in any hospital premises where high security psychiatric services are provided is authorised by this section if it is conduct in pursuance of, and in accordance with, any direction given under section 17

of the National Health Service Act 1977 (directions as to the carrying out of their functions by health bodies) to the body providing those services at those premises.

(6) Conduct taking place in a state hospital is authorised by this section if it is conduct in pursuance of, and in accordance with, any direction given to the State Hospitals Board for Scotland under section 2(5) of the National Health Service (Scotland) Act 1978 (regulations and directions as to the exercise of their functions by health boards) as applied by Article 5(1) of and the Schedule to The State Hospitals Board for Scotland Order 1995 (which applies certain provisions of that Act of 1978 to the State Hospitals Board).

(7) In this section references to a business include references to any activities of a government department, of any public authority or of any person or office holder on whom functions are conferred by or under any enactment.

(8) In this section—

"government department" includes any part of the Scottish Administration, a Northern Ireland department and the National Assembly for Wales;

"high security psychiatric services" has the same meaning as in the National Health Service Act 1977;

"hospital premises" has the same meaning as in section 4(3) of that Act; and

"state hospital" has the same meaning as in the National Health Service (Scotland) Act 1978.

(9) In this section "prison" means—

(a) any prison, young offender institution, young offenders centre or remand centre which is under the general superintendence of, or is provided by, the Secretary of State under the Prison Act 1952 or the Prison Act (Northern Ireland) 1953, or

(b) any prison, young offenders institution or remand centre which is under the general superintendence of the Scottish Ministers under the Prisons (Scotland) Act 1989,and includes any contracted out prison, within the meaning of Part IV of the Criminal Justice Act 1991 or section 106(4) of the Criminal Justice and Public Order Act 1994, and any legalised police cells within the meaning of section 14 of the Prisons (Scotland) Act 1989.

Interception with a warrant.

5.—(1) Subject to the following provisions of this Chapter, the Secretary of State may issue a warrant authorising or requiring the person to whom it is addressed, by any such conduct as may be described in the warrant, to secure any one or more of the following—

(a) the interception in the course of their transmission by means of a postal service or telecommunication system of the communications described in the warrant;

(b) the making, in accordance with an international mutual assistance agreement, of a request for the provision of such assistance in connection with, or in the form of, an interception of communications as may be so described;

(c) the provision, in accordance with an international mutual assistance agreement, to the competent authorities of a country or territory outside the United Kingdom of any such assistance in connection with, or in the form of, an interception of communications as may be so described;

(d) the disclosure, in such manner as may be so described, of intercepted material obtained by any interception authorised or required by the warrant, and of related communications data.

(2) The Secretary of State shall not issue an interception warrant unless he believes—

(a) that the warrant is necessary on grounds falling within subsection (3); and

(b) that the conduct authorised by the warrant is proportionate to what is sought to be achieved by that conduct.

(3) Subject to the following provisions of this section, a warrant is necessary on grounds falling within this subsection if it is necessary—

(a) in the interests of national security;

(b) for the purpose of preventing or detecting serious crime;

(c) for the purpose of safeguarding the economic well-being of the United Kingdom; or

(d) for the purpose, in circumstances appearing to the Secretary of State to be equivalent to those in which he would issue a warrant by virtue of paragraph (b), of giving effect to the provisions of any international mutual assistance agreement.

(4) The matters to be taken into account in considering whether the requirements of subsection (2) are satisfied in the case of any warrant shall include whether the information which it is thought necessary to obtain under the warrant could reasonably be obtained by other means.

(5) A warrant shall not be considered necessary on the ground falling within subsection (3)(c) unless the information which it is thought necessary to obtain is information relating to the acts or intentions of persons outside the British Islands.

(6) The conduct authorised by an interception warrant shall be taken to include—

(a) all such conduct (including the interception of communications not identified by the warrant) as it is necessary to undertake in order to do what is expressly authorised or required by the warrant;

(b) conduct for obtaining related communications data; and

(c) conduct by any person which is conduct in pursuance of a requirement imposed by or on behalf of the person to whom the warrant is addressed to be provided with assistance with giving effect to the warrant.

Interception warrants

Application for issue of an interception warrant.

6.—(1) An interception warrant shall not be issued except on an application made by or on behalf of a person specified in subsection (2).(2) Those persons are—

(a) the Director-General of the Security Service;

(b) the Chief of the Secret Intelligence Service;

(c) the Director of GCHQ;

(d) the Director General of the National Criminal Intelligence Service;

(e) the Commissioner of Police of the Metropolis;

(f) the Chief Constable of the Royal Ulster Constabulary;

(g) the chief constable of any police force maintained under or by virtue of section 1 of the Police (Scotland) Act 1967;

(h) the Commissioners of Customs and Excise;

(i) the Chief of Defence Intelligence;

(j) a person who, for the purposes of any international mutual assistance agreement, is the competent authority of a country or territory outside the United Kingdom.

(3) An application for the issue of an interception warrant shall not be

made on behalf of a person specified in subsection (2) except by a person holding office under the Crown.

Issue of warrants.

7.—(1) An interception warrant shall not be issued except—
(a) under the hand of the Secretary of State; or
(b) in a case falling within subsection (2), under the hand of a senior official.
(2) Those cases are—
(a) an urgent case in which the Secretary of State has himself expressly authorised the issue of the warrant in that case; and
(b) a case in which the warrant is for the purposes of a request for assistance made under an international mutual assistance agreement by the competent authorities of a country or territory outside the United Kingdom and either—
　(i) it appears that the interception subject is outside the United Kingdom; or
　(ii) the interception to which the warrant relates is to take place in relation only to premises outside the United Kingdom.
(3) An interception warrant—
(a) must be addressed to the person falling within section 6(2) by whom, or on whose behalf, the application for the warrant was made; and
(b) in the case of a warrant issued under the hand of a senior official, must contain, according to whatever is applicable—
　(i) one of the statements set out in subsection (4); and
　(ii) if it contains the statement set out in subsection (4)(b), one of the statements set out in subsection (5).
(4) The statements referred to in subsection (3)(b)(i) are—
(a) a statement that the case is an urgent case in which the Secretary of State has himself expressly authorised the issue of the warrant;
(b) a statement that the warrant is issued for the purposes of a request for assistance made under an international mutual assistance agreement by the competent authorities of a country or territory outside the United Kingdom.
(5) The statements referred to in subsection (3)(b)(ii) are—
(a) a statement that the interception subject appears to be outside the United Kingdom;
(b) a statement that the interception to which the warrant relates is to take place in relation only to premises outside the United Kingdom.

Contents of warrants

8.—(1) An interception warrant must name or describe either—
(a) one person as the interception subject; or
(b) a single set of premises as the premises in relation to which the interception to which the warrant relates is to take place.
(2) The provisions of an interception warrant describing communications the interception of which is authorised or required by the warrant must comprise one or more schedules setting out the addresses, numbers, apparatus or other factors, or combination of factors, that are to be used for identifying the communications that may be or are to be intercepted.
(3) Any factor or combination of factors set out in accordance with subsection (2) must be one that identifies communications which are likely to be or to include—
(a) communications from, or intended for, the person named or described in the warrant in accordance with subsection (1); or
(b) communications originating on, or intended for transmission to, the premises so named or described.

(4) Subsections (1) and (2) shall not apply to an interception warrant if—

(a) the description of communications to which the warrant relates confines the conduct authorised or required by the warrant to conduct falling within subsection (5); and

(b) at the time of the issue of the warrant, a certificate applicable to the warrant has been issued by the Secretary of State certifying—

   (i) the descriptions of intercepted material the examination of which he considers necessary; and

   (ii) that he considers the examination of material of those descriptions necessary as mentioned in section 5(3)(a), (b) or (c).

(5) Conduct falls within this subsection if it consists in—

(a) the interception of external communications in the course of their transmission by means of a telecommunication system; and

(b) any conduct authorised in relation to any such interception by section 5(6).

(6) A certificate for the purposes of subsection (4) shall not be issued except under the hand of the Secretary of State.

Duration, cancellation and renewal of warrants

9.—(1) An interception warrant—

(a) shall cease to have effect at the end of the relevant period; but

(b) may be renewed, at any time before the end of that period, by an instrument under the hand of the Secretary of State or, in a case falling within section 7(2)(b), under the hand of a senior official.

(2) An interception warrant shall not be renewed under subsection (1) unless the Secretary of State believes that the warrant continues to be necessary on grounds falling within section 5(3).

(3) The Secretary of State shall cancel an interception warrant if he is satisfied that the warrant is no longer necessary on grounds falling within section 5(3).

(4) The Secretary of State shall cancel an interception warrant if, at any time before the end of the relevant period, he is satisfied in a case in which—

(a) the warrant is one which was issued containing the statement set out in section 7(5)(a) or has been renewed by an instrument containing the statement set out in subsection (5)(b)(i) of this section, and

(b) the latest renewal (if any) of the warrant is not a renewal by an instrument under the hand of the Secretary of State,

   that the person named or described in the warrant as the interception subject is in the United Kingdom.

(5) An instrument under the hand of a senior official that renews an interception warrant must contain—

(a) a statement that the renewal is for the purposes of a request for assistance made under an international mutual assistance agreement by the competent authorities of a country or territory outside the United Kingdom; and

(b) whichever of the following statements is applicable—

   (i) a statement that the interception subject appears to be outside the United Kingdom;

   (ii) a statement that the interception to which the warrant relates is to take place in relation only to premises outside the United Kingdom.

(6) In this section "the relevant period"—

(a) in relation to an unrenewed warrant issued in a case falling within section 7(2)(a) under the hand of a senior official, means the period ending with the fifth working day following the day of the warrant's issue;

(b) in relation to a renewed warrant the latest renewal of which was by an instrument endorsed under the hand of the Secretary of State with a statement that the renewal is believed to be necessary on grounds falling within section 5(3)(a) or (c), means the period of six months beginning with the day of the warrant's renewal; and

(c) in all other cases, means the period of three months beginning with the day of the warrant's issue or, in the case of a warrant that has been renewed, of its latest renewal.

Modification of warrants and certificates

10.—(1) The Secretary of State may at any time—

(a) modify the provisions of an interception warrant; or

(b) modify a section 8(4) certificate so as to include in the certified material any material the examination of which he considers to be necessary as mentioned in section 5(3)(a), (b) or (c).

(2) If at any time the Secretary of State considers that any factor set out in a schedule to an interception warrant is no longer relevant for identifying communications which, in the case of that warrant, are likely to be or to include communications falling within section 8(3)(a) or (b), it shall be his duty to modify the warrant by the deletion of that factor.

(3) If at any time the Secretary of State considers that the material certified by a section 8(4) certificate includes any material the examination of which is no longer necessary as mentioned in any of paragraphs (a) to (c) of section 5(3), he shall modify the certificate so as to exclude that material from the certified material.

(4) Subject to subsections (5) to (8), a warrant or certificate shall not be modified under this section except by an instrument under the hand of the Secretary of State or of a senior official.

(5) Unscheduled parts of an interception warrant shall not be modified under the hand of a senior official except in an urgent case in which—

(a) the Secretary of State has himself expressly authorised the modification; and

(b) a statement of that fact is endorsed on the modifying instrument.

(6) Subsection (4) shall not authorise the making under the hand of either—

(a) the person to whom the warrant is addressed, or

(b) any person holding a position subordinate to that person, of any modification of any scheduled parts of an interception warrant.

(7) A section 8(4) certificate shall not be modified under the hand of a senior official except in an urgent case in which—

(a) the official in question holds a position in respect of which he is expressly authorised by provisions contained in the certificate to modify the certificate on the Secretary of State's behalf; or

(b) the Secretary of State has himself expressly authorised the modification and a statement of that fact is endorsed on the modifying instrument.

(8) Where modifications in accordance with this subsection are expressly authorised by provision contained in the warrant, the scheduled parts of an interception warrant may, in an urgent case, be modified by an instrument under the hand of—

(a) the person to whom the warrant is addressed; or

(b) a person holding any such position subordinate to that person as may be identified in the provisions of the warrant.

(9) Where—

(a) a warrant or certificate is modified by an instrument under the hand of a person other than the Secretary of State, and

(b) a statement for the purposes of subsection (5)(b) or (7)(b) is endorsed on the instrument, or the modification is made under subsection (8),

that modification shall cease to have effect at the end of the fifth working day following the day of the instrument's issue.

(10) For the purposes of this section—

(a) the scheduled parts of an interception warrant are any provisions of the warrant that are contained in a schedule of identifying factors comprised in the warrant for the purposes of section 8(2); and

(b) the modifications that are modifications of the scheduled parts of an interception warrant include the insertion of an additional such schedule in the warrant; and references in this section to unscheduled parts of an interception warrant, and to their modification, shall be construed accordingly.

Implementation of warrants

11.—(1) Effect may be given to an interception warrant either—

(a) by the person to whom it is addressed; or

(b) by that person acting through, or together with, such other persons as he may require (whether under subsection (2) or otherwise) to provide him with assistance with giving effect to the warrant.

(2) For the purpose of requiring any person to provide assistance in relation to an interception warrant the person to whom it is addressed may—

(a) serve a copy of the warrant on such persons as he considers may be able to provide such assistance; or

(b) make arrangements under which a copy of it is to be or may be so served.

(3) The copy of an interception warrant that is served on any person under subsection (2) may, to the extent authorised—

(a) by the person to whom the warrant is addressed, or

(b) by the arrangements made by him for the purposes of that subsection,

omit any one or more of the schedules to the warrant.

(4) Where a copy of an interception warrant has been served by or on behalf of the person to whom it is addressed on—

(a) a person who provides a postal service,

(b) a person who provides a public telecommunications service, or

(c) a person not falling within paragraph (b) who has control of the whole or any part of a telecommunication system located wholly or partly in the United Kingdom,

it shall (subject to subsection (5)) be the duty of that person to take all such steps for giving effect to the warrant as are notified to him by or on behalf of the person to whom the warrant is addressed.

(5) A person who is under a duty by virtue of subsection (4) to take steps for giving effect to a warrant shall not be required to take any steps which it is not reasonably practicable for him to take.

(6) For the purposes of subsection (5) the steps which it is reasonably practicable for a person to take in a case in which obligations have been imposed on him by or under section 12 shall include every step which it would have been reasonably practicable for him to take had he complied with all the obligations so imposed on him.

(7) A person who knowingly fails to comply with his duty under subsection (4) shall be guilty of an offence and liable—

(a) on conviction on indictment, to imprisonment for a term not exceeding two years or to a fine, or to both;

(b) on summary conviction, to imprisonment for a term not exceeding six months or to a fine not exceeding the statutory maximum, or to both.

(8) A person's duty under subsection (4) to take steps for giving effect to a warrant shall be enforceable by civil proceedings by the Secretary of State

for an injunction, or for specific performance of a statutory duty under section 45 of the Court of Session Act 1988, or for any other appropriate relief.

(9) For the purposes of this Act the provision of assistance with giving effect to an interception warrant includes any disclosure to the person to whom the warrant is addressed, or to persons acting on his behalf, of intercepted material obtained by any interception authorised or required by the warrant, and of any related communications data.

Interception capability and costs

Maintenance of interception capability

12.—(1) The Secretary of State may by order provide for the imposition by him on persons who—
   (a) are providing public postal services or public telecommunications services, or
   (b) are proposing to do so,
of such obligations as it appears to him reasonable to impose for the purpose of securing that it is and remains practicable for requirements to provide assistance in relation to interception warrants to be imposed and complied with.

(2) The Secretary of State's power to impose the obligations provided for by an order under this section shall be exercisable by the giving, in accordance with the order, of a notice requiring the person who is to be subject to the obligations to take all such steps as may be specified or described in the notice.

(3) Subject to subsection (11), the only steps that may be specified or described in a notice given to a person under subsection (2) are steps appearing to the Secretary of State to be necessary for securing that that person has the practical capability of providing any assistance which he may be required to provide in relation to relevant interception warrants.

(4) A person shall not be liable to have an obligation imposed on him in accordance with an order under this section by reason only that he provides, or is proposing to provide, to members of the public a telecommunications service the provision of which is or, as the case may be, will be no more than—
   (a) the means by which he provides a service which is not a telecommunications service; or
   (b) necessarily incidental to the provision by him of a service which is not a telecommunications service.

(5) Where a notice is given to any person under subsection (2) and otherwise than by virtue of subsection (6)(c), that person may, before the end of such period as may be specified in an order under this section, refer the notice to the Technical Advisory Board.

(6) Where a notice given to any person under subsection (2) is referred to the Technical Advisory Board under subsection (5)—
   (a) there shall be no requirement for that person to comply, except in pursuance of a notice under paragraph (c)(ii), with any obligations imposed by the notice;
   (b) the Board shall consider the technical requirements and the financial consequences, for the person making the reference, of the notice referred to them and shall report their conclusions on those matters to that person and to the Secretary of State; and
   (c) the Secretary of State, after considering any report of the Board relating to the notice, may either—
      (i) withdraw the notice; or
      (ii) give a further notice under subsection (2) confirming its effect, with or without modifications.

(7) It shall be the duty of a person to whom a notice is given under subsection (2) to comply with the notice; and that duty shall be enforceable by civil proceedings by the Secretary of State for an injunction, or for specific performance of a statutory duty under section 45 of the Court of Session Act 1988, or for any other appropriate relief.

(8) A notice for the purposes of subsection (2) must specify such period as appears to the Secretary of State to be reasonable as the period within which the steps specified or described in the notice are to be taken.

(9) Before making an order under this section the Secretary of State shall consult with—

    (a) such persons appearing to him to be likely to be subject to the obligations for which it provides,

    (b) the Technical Advisory Board,

    (c) such persons representing persons falling within paragraph (a), and

    (d) such persons with statutory functions in relation to persons falling within that paragraph,

as he considers appropriate.

(10) The Secretary of State shall not make an order under this section unless a draft of the order has been laid before Parliament and approved by a resolution of each House.

(11) For the purposes of this section the question whether a person has the practical capability of providing assistance in relation to relevant interception warrants shall include the question whether all such arrangements have been made as the Secretary of State considers necessary—

    (a) with respect to the disclosure of intercepted material;

    (b) for the purpose of ensuring that security and confidentiality are maintained in relation to, and to matters connected with, the provision of any such assistance; and

    (c) for the purpose of facilitating the carrying out of any functions in relation to this Chapter of the Interception of Communications Commissioner;

but before determining for the purposes of the making of any order, or the imposition of any obligation, under this section what arrangements he considers necessary for the purpose mentioned in paragraph (c) the Secretary of State shall consult that Commissioner.

(12) In this section "relevant interception warrant"—

    (a) in relation to a person providing a public postal service, means an interception warrant relating to the interception of communications in the course of their transmission by means of that service; and

    (b) in relation to a person providing a public telecommunications service, means an interception warrant relating to the interception of communications in the course of their transmission by means of a telecommunication system used for the purposes of that service.

Technical Advisory Board

13.—(1) There shall be a Technical Advisory Board consisting of such number of persons appointed by the Secretary of State as he may by order provide.

(2) The order providing for the membership of the Technical Advisory Board must also make provision which is calculated to ensure—

    (a) that the membership of the Technical Advisory Board includes persons likely effectively to represent the interests of the persons on whom obligations may be imposed under section 12;

    (b) that the membership of the Board includes persons likely effectively to represent the interests of the persons by or on whose behalf applications for interception warrants may be made;

(c) that such other persons (if any) as the Secretary of State thinks fit may be appointed to be members of the Board; and

(d) that the Board is so constituted as to produce a balance between the representation of the interests mentioned in paragraph (a) and the representation of those mentioned in paragraph (b).

(3) The Secretary of State shall not make an order under this section unless a draft of the order has been laid before Parliament and approved by a resolution of each House.

Grants for interception costs

14.—(1) It shall be the duty of the Secretary of State to ensure that such arrangements are in force as are necessary for securing that a person who provides—

(a) a postal service, or

(b) a telecommunications service,

receives such contribution as is, in the circumstances of that person's case, a fair contribution towards the costs incurred, or likely to be incurred, by that person in consequence of the matters mentioned in subsection (2).

(2) Those matters are—

(a) in relation to a person providing a postal service, the issue of interception warrants relating to communications transmitted by means of that postal service;

(b) in relation to a person providing a telecommunications service, the issue of interception warrants relating to communications transmitted by means of a telecommunication system used for the purposes of that service;

(c) in relation to each description of person, the imposition on that person of obligations provided for by an order under section 12.

(3) For the purpose of complying with his duty under this section, the Secretary of State may make arrangements for payments to be made out of money provided by Parliament.

Restrictions on use of intercepted material etc.

General safeguards

15.—(1) Subject to subsection (6), it shall be the duty of the Secretary of State to ensure, in relation to all interception warrants, that such arrangements are in force as he considers necessary for securing—

(a) that the requirements of subsections (2) and (3) are satisfied in relation to the intercepted material and any related communications data; and

(b) in the case of warrants in relation to which there are section 8(4) certificates, that the requirements of section 16 are also satisfied.

(2) The requirements of this subsection are satisfied in relation to the intercepted material and any related communications data if each of the following—

(a) the number of persons to whom any of the material or data is disclosed or otherwise made available,

(b) the extent to which any of the material or data is disclosed or otherwise made available,

(c) the extent to which any of the material or data is copied, and

(d) the number of copies that are made,

is limited to the minimum that is necessary for the authorised purposes.

(3) The requirements of this subsection are satisfied in relation to the

intercepted material and any related communications data if each copy made of any of the material or data (if not destroyed earlier) is destroyed as soon as there are no longer any grounds for retaining it as necessary for any of the authorised purposes.

(4) For the purposes of this section something is necessary for the authorised purposes if, and only if—

(a) it continues to be, or is likely to become, necessary as mentioned in section 5(3);

(b) it is necessary for facilitating the carrying out of any of the functions under this Chapter of the Secretary of State;

(c) it is necessary for facilitating the carrying out of any functions in relation to this Part of the Interception of Communications Commissioner or of the Tribunal;

(d) it is necessary to ensure that a person conducting a criminal prosecution has the information he needs to determine what is required of him by his duty to secure the fairness of the prosecution; or

(e) it is necessary for the performance of any duty imposed on any person by the Public Records Act 1958 or the Public Records Act (Northern Ireland) 1923.

(5) The arrangements for the time being in force under this section for securing that the requirements of subsection (2) are satisfied in relation to the intercepted material or any related communications data must include such arrangements as the Secretary of State considers necessary for securing that every copy of the material or data that is made is stored, for so long as it is retained, in a secure manner.

(6) Arrangements in relation to interception warrants which are made for the purposes of subsection (1)—

(a) shall not be required to secure that the requirements of subsections (2) and (3) are satisfied in so far as they relate to any of the intercepted material or related communications data, or any copy of any such material or data, possession of which has been surrendered to any authorities of a country or territory outside the United Kingdom; but

(b) shall be required to secure, in the case of every such warrant, that possession of the intercepted material and data and of copies of the material or data is surrendered to authorities of a country or territory outside the United Kingdom only if the requirements of subsection (7) are satisfied.

(7) The requirements of this subsection are satisfied in the case of a warrant if it appears to the Secretary of State—

(a) that requirements corresponding to those of subsections (2) and (3) will apply, to such extent (if any) as the Secretary of State thinks fit, in relation to any of the intercepted material or related communications data possession of which, or of any copy of which, is surrendered to the authorities in question; and

(b) that restrictions are in force which would prevent, to such extent (if any) as the Secretary of State thinks fit, the doing of anything in, for the purposes of or in connection with any proceedings outside the United Kingdom which would result in such a disclosure as, by virtue of section 17, could not be made in the United Kingdom.

(8) In this section "copy", in relation to intercepted material or related communications data, means any of the following (whether or not in documentary form)—

(a) any copy, extract or summary of the material or data which identifies itself as the product of an interception, and

(b) any record referring to an interception which is a record of the identities of the persons to or by whom the intercepted material was sent, or to whom the communications data relates,

and "copied" shall be construed accordingly.

Extra safeguards in the case of certificated warrants

16.—(1) For the purposes of section 15 the requirements of this section, in the case of a warrant in relation to which there is a section 8(4) certificate, are that the intercepted material is read, looked at or listened to by the persons to whom it becomes available by virtue of the warrant to the extent only that it—

(a) has been certified as material the examination of which is necessary as mentioned in section 5(3)(a), (b) or (c); and

(b) falls within subsection (2).

(2) Subject to subsections (3) and (4), intercepted material falls within this subsection so far only as it is selected to be read, looked at or listened to otherwise than according to a factor which—

(a) is referable to an individual who is known to be for the time being in the British Islands; and

(b) has as its purpose, or one of its purposes, the identification of material contained in communications sent by him, or intended for him.

(3) Intercepted material falls within subsection (2), notwithstanding that it is selected by reference to any such factor as is mentioned in paragraph (a) and (b) of that subsection, if—

(a) it is certified by the Secretary of State for the purposes of section 8(4) that the examination of material selected according to factors referable to the individual in question is necessary as mentioned in subsection 5(3)(a), (b) or (c); and

(b) the material relates only to communications sent during a period of not more than three months specified in the certificate.

(4) Intercepted material also falls within subsection (2), notwithstanding that it is selected by reference to any such factor as is mentioned in paragraph (a) and (b) of that subsection, if—

(a) the person to whom the warrant is addressed believes, on reasonable grounds, that the circumstances are such that the material would fall within that subsection; or

(b) the conditions set out in subsection (5) below are satisfied in relation to the selection of the material.

(5) Those conditions are satisfied in relation to the selection of intercepted material if—

(a) it has appeared to the person to whom the warrant is addressed that there has been such a relevant change of circumstances as, but for subsection (4)(b), would prevent the intercepted material from falling within subsection (2);

(b) since it first so appeared, a written authorisation to read, look at or listen to the material has been given by a senior official; and

(c) the selection is made before the end of the first working day after the day on which it first so appeared to that person.

(6) References in this section to its appearing that there has been a relevant change of circumstances are references to its appearing either—

(a) that the individual in question has entered the British Islands; or

(b) that a belief by the person to whom the warrant is addressed in the individual's presence outside the British Islands was in fact mistaken.

Exclusion of matters from legal proceedings

17.—(1) Subject to section 18, no evidence shall be adduced, question asked, assertion or disclosure made or other thing done in, for the purposes of or in connection with any legal proceedings which (in any manner)—

(a) discloses, in circumstances from which its origin in anything falling within subsection (2) may be inferred, any of the contents of an intercepted communication or any related communications data; or

(b) tends (apart from any such disclosure) to suggest that anything falling within subsection (2) has or may have occurred or be going to occur.

(2) The following fall within this subsection—

(a) conduct by a person falling within subsection (3) that was or would be an offence under section 1(1) or (2) of this Act or under section 1 of the Interception of Communications Act 1985;

(b) a breach by the Secretary of State of his duty under section 1(4) of this Act;

(c) the issue of an interception warrant or of a warrant under the Interception of Communications Act 1985;

(d) the making of an application by any person for an interception warrant, or for a warrant under that Act;

(e) the imposition of any requirement on any person to provide assistance with giving effect to an interception warrant.

(3) The persons referred to in subsection (2)(a) are—

(a) any person to whom a warrant under this Chapter may be addressed;

(b) any person holding office under the Crown;

(c) any member of the National Criminal Intelligence Service;

(d) any member of the National Crime Squad;

(e) any person employed by or for the purposes of a police force;

(f) any person providing a postal service or employed for the purposes of any business of providing such a service; and

(g) any person providing a public telecommunications service or employed for the purposes of any business of providing such a service.

(4) In this section "intercepted communication" means any communication intercepted in the course of its transmission by means of a postal service or telecommunication system.

Exceptions to section 17

18.—(1) Section 17(1) shall not apply in relation to—

(a) any proceedings for a relevant offence;

(b) any civil proceedings under section 11(8);

(c) any proceedings before the Tribunal;

(d) any proceedings on an appeal or review for which provision is made by an order under section 67(8);

(e) any proceedings before the Special Immigration Appeals Commission or any proceedings arising out of proceedings before that Commission; or

(f) any proceedings before the Proscribed Organisations Appeal Commission or any proceedings arising out of proceedings before that Commission.

(2) Subsection (1) shall not, by virtue of paragraph (e) or (f), authorise the disclosure of anything—

(a) in the case of any proceedings falling within paragraph (e), to—

    (i) the appellant to the Special Immigration Appeals Commission; or

    (ii) any person who for the purposes of any proceedings so falling (but otherwise than by virtue of an appointment under section 6 of the Special Immigration Appeals Commission Act 1997) represents that appellant; or

(b) in the case of proceedings falling within paragraph (f), to—

     (i) the applicant to the Proscribed Organisations Appeal Commission;

    (ii) the organisation concerned (if different);

  (iii) any person designated under paragraph 6 of Schedule 3 to the Terrorism Act 2000 to conduct proceedings so falling on behalf of that organisation; or

  (iv) any person who for the purposes of any proceedings so falling (but otherwise than by virtue of an appointment under paragraph 7 of that Schedule) represents that applicant or that organisation.

(3) Section 17(1) shall not prohibit anything done in, for the purposes of, or in connection with, so much of any legal proceedings as relates to the fairness or unfairness of a dismissal on the grounds of any conduct constituting an offence under section 1(1) or (2), 11(7) or 19 of this Act, or section 1 of the Interception of Communications Act 1985.

(4) Section 17(1)(a) shall not prohibit the disclosure of any of the contents of a communication if the interception of that communication was lawful by virtue of section 1(5)(c), 3 or 4.

(5) Where any disclosure is proposed to be or has been made on the grounds that it is authorised by subsection (4), section 17(1) shall not prohibit the doing of anything in, or for the purposes of, so much of any legal proceedings as relates to the question whether that disclosure is or was so authorised.

(6) Section 17(1)(b) shall not prohibit the doing of anything that discloses any conduct of a person for which he has been convicted of an offence under section 1(1) or (2), 11(7) or 19 of this Act, or section 1 of the Interception of Communications Act 1985.

(7) Nothing in section 17(1) shall prohibit any such disclosure of any information that continues to be available for disclosure as is confined to—

  (a) a disclosure to a person conducting a criminal prosecution for the purpose only of enabling that person to determine what is required of him by his duty to secure the fairness of the prosecution; or

  (b) a disclosure to a relevant judge in a case in which that judge has ordered the disclosure to be made to him alone.

(8) A relevant judge shall not order a disclosure under subsection (7)(b) except where he is satisfied that the exceptional circumstances of the case make the disclosure essential in the interests of justice.

(9) Subject to subsection (10), where in any criminal proceedings—

  (a) a relevant judge does order a disclosure under subsection (7)(b), and

  (b) in consequence of that disclosure he is of the opinion that there are exceptional circumstances requiring him to do so,

he may direct the person conducting the prosecution to make for the purposes of the proceedings any such admission of fact as that judge thinks essential in the interests of justice.

(10) Nothing in any direction under subsection (9) shall authorise or require anything to be done in contravention of section 17(1).

(11) In this section "a relevant judge" means—

  (a) any judge of the High Court or of the Crown Court or any Circuit judge;

  (b) any judge of the High Court of Justiciary or any sheriff;

  (c) in relation to a court-martial, the judge advocate appointed in relation to that court-martial under section 84B of the Army Act 1955, section 84B of the Air Force Act 1955 or section 53B of the Naval Discipline Act 1957; or

  (d) any person holding any such judicial office as entitles him to exercise the jurisdiction of a judge falling within paragraph (a) or (b).

(12) In this section "relevant offence" means—

  (a) an offence under any provision of this Act;

(b) an offence under section 1 of the Interception of Communications Act 1985;

(c) an offence under section 5 of the Wireless Telegraphy Act 1949;

(d) an offence under section 45 of the Telegraph Act 1863, section 20 of the Telegraph Act 1868 or section 58 of the Post Office Act 1953;

(e) an offence under section 45 of the Telecommunications Act 1984;

(f) an offence under section 4 of the Official Secrets Act 1989 relating to any such information, document or article as is mentioned in subsection (3)(a) of that section;

(g) an offence under section 1 or 2 of the Official Secrets Act 1911 relating to any sketch, plan, model, article, note, document or information which incorporates or relates to the contents of any intercepted communication or any related communications data or tends to suggest as mentioned in section 17(1)(b) of this Act;

(h) perjury committed in the course of any proceedings mentioned in subsection (1) or (3) of this section;

(i) attempting or conspiring to commit, or aiding, abetting, counselling or procuring the commission of, an offence falling within any of the preceding paragraphs; and

(j) contempt of court committed in the course of, or in relation to, any proceedings mentioned in subsection (1) or (3) of this section.

(13) In subsection (12) "intercepted communication" has the same meaning as in section 17.

Offence for unauthorised disclosures

19.—(1) Where an interception warrant has been issued or renewed, it shall be the duty of every person falling within subsection (2) to keep secret all the matters mentioned in subsection (3).

(2) The persons falling within this subsection are—

(a) the persons specified in section 6(2);

(b) every person holding office under the Crown;

(c) every member of the National Criminal Intelligence Service;

(d) every member of the National Crime Squad;

(e) every person employed by or for the purposes of a police force;

(f) persons providing postal services or employed for the purposes of any business of providing such a service;

(g) persons providing public telecommunications services or employed for the purposes of any business of providing such a service;

(h) persons having control of the whole or any part of a telecommunication system located wholly or partly in the United Kingdom.

(3) Those matters are—

(a) the existence and contents of the warrant and of any section 8(4) certificate in relation to the warrant;

(b) the details of the issue of the warrant and of any renewal or modification of the warrant or of any such certificate;

(c) the existence and contents of any requirement to provide assistance with giving effect to the warrant;

(d) the steps taken in pursuance of the warrant or of any such requirement; and

(e) everything in the intercepted material, together with any related communications data.

(4) A person who makes a disclosure to another of anything that he is required to keep secret under this section shall be guilty of an offence and liable—

(a) on conviction on indictment, to imprisonment for a term not exceeding five years or to a fine, or to both;

    (b) on summary conviction, to imprisonment for a term not exceeding six months or to a fine not exceeding the statutory maximum, or to both.

(5) In proceedings against any person for an offence under this section in respect of any disclosure, it shall be a defence for that person to show that he could not reasonably have been expected, after first becoming aware of the matter disclosed, to take steps to prevent the disclosure.

(6) In proceedings against any person for an offence under this section in respect of any disclosure, it shall be a defence for that person to show that—

    (a) the disclosure was made by or to a professional legal adviser in connection with the giving, by the adviser to any client of his, of advice about the effect of provisions of this Chapter; and

    (b) the person to whom or, as the case may be, by whom it was made was the client or a representative of the client.

(7) In proceedings against any person for an offence under this section in respect of any disclosure, it shall be a defence for that person to show that the disclosure was made by a legal adviser—

    (a) in contemplation of, or in connection with, any legal proceedings; and

    (b) for the purposes of those proceedings.

(8) Neither subsection (6) nor subsection (7) applies in the case of a disclosure made with a view to furthering any criminal purpose.

(9) In proceedings against any person for an offence under this section in respect of any disclosure, it shall be a defence for that person to show that the disclosure was confined to a disclosure made to the Interception of Communications Commissioner or authorised—

    (a) by that Commissioner;

    (b) by the warrant or the person to whom the warrant is or was addressed;

    (c) by the terms of the requirement to provide assistance; or

    (d) by section 11(9).

Interpretation of Chapter I

Interpretation of Chapter I

20.—(1) In this Chapter—

"certified", in relation to a section 8(4) certificate, means of a description certified by the certificate as a description of material the examination of which the Secretary of State considers necessary;

"external communication" means a communication sent or received outside the British Islands;

"intercepted material", in relation to an interception warrant, means the contents of any communications intercepted by an interception to which the warrant relates;

"the interception subject", in relation to an interception warrant, means the person about whose communications information is sought by the interception to which the warrant relates;

"international mutual assistance agreement" means an international agreement designated for the purposes of section 1(4);

"related communications data", in relation to a communication intercepted in the course of its transmission by means of a postal service or telecommunication system, means so much of any communications data (within the meaning of Chapter II of this Part) as—

    (a) is obtained by, or in connection with, the interception; and

    (b) relates to the communication or to the sender or recipient, or intended recipient, of the communication;

"section 8(4) certificate" means any certificate issued for the purposes of section 8(4).

CHAPTER II

ACQUISITION AND DISCLOSURE OF COMMUNICATIONS DATA

Lawful acquisition and disclosure of communications data

21.—(1) This Chapter applies to—

(a) any conduct in relation to a postal service or telecommunication system for obtaining communications data, other than conduct consisting in the interception of communications in the course of their transmission by means of such a service or system; and

(b) the disclosure to any person of communications data.

(2) Conduct to which this Chapter applies shall be lawful for all purposes if—

(a) it is conduct in which any person is authorised or required to engage by an authorisation or notice granted or given under this Chapter; and

(b) the conduct is in accordance with, or in pursuance of, the authorisation or requirement.

(3) A person shall not be subject to any civil liability in respect of any conduct of his which—

(a) is incidental to any conduct that is lawful by virtue of subsection (2); and

(b) is not itself conduct an authorisation or warrant for which is capable of being granted under a relevant enactment and might reasonably have been expected to have been sought in the case in question.

(4) In this Chapter "communications data" means any of the following—

(a) any traffic data comprised in or attached to a communication (whether by the sender or otherwise) for the purposes of any postal service or telecommunication system by means of which it is being or may be transmitted;

(b) any information which includes none of the contents of a communication (apart from any information falling within paragraph (a)) and is about the use made by any person—

(i) of any postal service or telecommunications service; or

(ii) in connection with the provision to or use by any person of any telecommunications service, of any part of a telecommunication system;

(c) any information not falling within paragraph (a) or (b) that is held or obtained, in relation to persons to whom he provides the service, by a person providing a postal service or telecommunications service.

(5) In this section "relevant enactment" means—

(a) an enactment contained in this Act;

(b) section 5 of the Intelligence Services Act 1994 (warrants for the intelligence services); or

(c) an enactment contained in Part III of the Police Act 1997 (powers of the police and of customs officers).

(6) In this section "traffic data", in relation to any communication, means—

(a) any data identifying, or purporting to identify, any person, apparatus or location to or from which the communication is or may be transmitted,

(b) any data identifying or selecting, or purporting to identify or select, apparatus through which, or by means of which, the communication is or may be transmitted,

(c) any data comprising signals for the actuation of apparatus used for the purposes of a telecommunication system for effecting (in whole or in part) the transmission of any communication, and

(d) any data identifying the data or other data as data comprised in or attached to a particular communication, but that expression includes data identifying a computer file or computer program access to which is obtained, or which is run, by means of the communication to the extent only that the file or program is identified by reference to the apparatus in which it is stored.

(7) In this section—

(a) references, in relation to traffic data comprising signals for the actuation of apparatus, to a telecommunication system by means of which a communication is being or may be transmitted include references to any telecommunication system in which that apparatus is comprised; and

(b) references to traffic data being attached to a communication include references to the data and the communication being logically associated with each other;

and in this section "data", in relation to a postal item, means anything written on the outside of the item.

Obtaining and disclosing communications data

22.—(1) This section applies where a person designated for the purposes of this Chapter believes that it is necessary on grounds falling within subsection (2) to obtain any communications data.

(2) It is necessary on grounds falling within this subsection to obtain communications data if it is necessary—

(a) in the interests of national security;

(b) for the purpose of preventing or detecting crime or of preventing disorder;

(c) in the interests of the economic well-being of the United Kingdom;

(d) in the interests of public safety;

(e) for the purpose of protecting public health;

(f) for the purpose of assessing or collecting any tax, duty, levy or other imposition, contribution or charge payable to a government department;

(g) for the purpose, in an emergency, of preventing death or injury or any damage to a person's physical or mental health, or of mitigating any injury or damage to a person's physical or mental health; or

(h) for any purpose (not falling within paragraphs (a) to (g)) which is specified for the purposes of this subsection by an order made by the Secretary of State.

(3) Subject to subsection (5), the designated person may grant an authorisation for persons holding offices, ranks or positions with the same relevant public authority as the designated person to engage in any conduct to which this Chapter applies.

(4) Subject to subsection (5), where it appears to the designated person that a postal or telecommunications operator is or may be in possession of, or be capable of obtaining, any communications data, the designated person may, by notice to the postal or telecommunications operator, require the operator—

(a) if the operator is not already in possession of the data, to obtain the data; and

(b) in any case, to disclose all of the data in his possession or subsequently obtained by him.

(5) The designated person shall not grant an authorisation under subsection (3), or give a notice under subsection (4), unless he believes that obtaining the data in question by the conduct authorised or required by the authorisation or notice is proportionate to what is sought to be achieved by so obtaining the data.

(6) It shall be the duty of the postal or telecommunications operator to comply with the requirements of any notice given to him under subsection (4).

(7) A person who is under a duty by virtue of subsection (6) shall not be required to do anything in pursuance of that duty which it is not reasonably practicable for him to do.

(8) The duty imposed by subsection (6) shall be enforceable by civil proceedings by the Secretary of State for an injunction, or for specific performance of a statutory duty under section 45 of the Court of Session Act 1988, or for any other appropriate relief.

(9) The Secretary of State shall not make an order under subsection (2)(h) unless a draft of the order has been laid before Parliament and approved by a resolution of each House.

Form and duration of authorisations and notices

23.—(1) An authorisation under section 22(3)—
(a) must be granted in writing or (if not in writing) in a manner that produces a record of its having been granted;
(b) must describe the conduct to which this Chapter applies that is authorised and the communications data in relation to which it is authorised;
(c) must specify the matters falling within section 22(2) by reference to which it is granted; and
(d) must specify the office, rank or position held by the person granting the authorisation.

(2) A notice under section 22(4) requiring communications data to be disclosed or to be obtained and disclosed—
(a) must be given in writing or (if not in writing) must be given in a manner that produces a record of its having been given;
(b) must describe the communications data to be obtained or disclosed under the notice;
(c) must specify the matters falling within section 22(2) by reference to which the notice is given;
(d) must specify the office, rank or position held by the person giving it; and
(e) must specify the manner in which any disclosure required by the notice is to be made.

(3) A notice under section 22(4) shall not require the disclosure of data to any person other than—
(a) the person giving the notice; or
(b) such other person as may be specified in or otherwise identified by, or in accordance with, the provisions of the notice;
but the provisions of the notice shall not specify or otherwise identify a person for the purposes of paragraph (b) unless he holds an office, rank or position with the same relevant public authority as the person giving the notice.

(4) An authorisation under section 22(3) or notice under section 22(4)—
(a) shall not authorise or require any data to be obtained after the end of the period of one month beginning with the date on which the authorisation is granted or the notice given; and
(b) in the case of a notice, shall not authorise or require any disclosure after the end of that period of any data not in the possession of, or obtained by, the postal or telecommunications operator at a time during that period.

(5) An authorisation under section 22(3) or notice under section 22(4)

may be renewed at any time before the end of the period of one month applying (in accordance with subsection (4) or subsection (7)) to that authorisation or notice.

(6) A renewal of an authorisation under section 22(3) or of a notice under section 22(4) shall be by the grant or giving, in accordance with this section, of a further authorisation or notice.

(7) Subsection (4) shall have effect in relation to a renewed authorisation or renewal notice as if the period of one month mentioned in that subsection did not begin until the end of the period of one month applicable to the authorisation or notice that is current at the time of the renewal.

(8) Where a person who has given a notice under subsection (4) of section 22 is satisfied—

    (a) that it is no longer necessary on grounds falling within subsection (2) of that section for the requirements of the notice to be complied with, or

    (b) that the conduct required by the notice is no longer proportionate to what is sought to be achieved by obtaining communications data to which the notice relates,

he shall cancel the notice.

(9) The Secretary of State may by regulations provide for the person by whom any duty imposed by subsection (8) is to be performed in a case in which it would otherwise fall on a person who is no longer available to perform it; and regulations under this subsection may provide for the person on whom the duty is to fall to be a person appointed in accordance with the regulations.

Arrangements for payments

24.—(1) It shall be the duty of the Secretary of State to ensure that such arrangements are in force as he thinks appropriate for requiring or authorising, in such cases as he thinks fit, the making to postal and telecommunications operators of appropriate contributions towards the costs incurred by them in complying with notices under section 22(4).

(2) For the purpose of complying with his duty under this section, the Secretary of State may make arrangements for payments to be made out of money provided by Parliament.

Interpretation of Chapter II

25.—(1) In this Chapter—

"communications data" has the meaning given by section 21(4);

"designated" shall be construed in accordance with subsection (2);

"postal or telecommunications operator" means a person who provides a postal service or telecommunications service;

"relevant public authority" means (subject to subsection (4)) any of the following—

    (a) a police force;

    (b) the National Criminal Intelligence Service;

    (c) the National Crime Squad;

    (d) the Commissioners of Customs and Excise;

    (e) the Commissioners of Inland Revenue;

    (f) any of the intelligence services;

    (g) any such public authority not falling within paragraphs (a) to (f) as may be specified for the purposes of this subsection by an order made by the Secretary of State.

(2) Subject to subsection (3), the persons designated for the purposes of this Chapter are the individuals holding such offices, ranks or positions with relevant public authorities as are prescribed for the purposes of this subsection by an order made by the Secretary of State.

(3) The Secretary of State may by order impose restrictions—

(a) on the authorisations and notices under this Chapter that may be granted or given by any individual holding an office, rank or position with a specified public authority; and

(b) on the circumstances in which, or the purposes for which, such authorisations may be granted or notices given by any such individual.

(4) The Secretary of State may by order remove any person from the list of persons who are for the time being relevant public authorities for the purposes of this Chapter.

(5) The Secretary of State shall not make an order under this section that adds any person to the list of persons who are for the time being relevant public authorities for the purposes of this Chapter unless a draft of the order has been laid before Parliament and approved by a resolution of each House.

PART II

SURVEILLANCE AND COVERT HUMAN INTELLIGENCE SOURCES

Introductory

Conduct to which Part II applies

26.—(1) This Part applies to the following conduct—

(a) directed surveillance;

(b) intrusive surveillance; and

(c) the conduct and use of covert human intelligence sources.

(2) Subject to subsection (6), surveillance is directed for the purposes of this Part if it is covert but not intrusive and is undertaken—

(a) for the purposes of a specific investigation or a specific operation;

(b) in such a manner as is likely to result in the obtaining of private information about a person (whether or not one specifically identified for the purposes of the investigation or operation); and

(c) otherwise than by way of an immediate response to events or circumstances the nature of which is such that it would not be reasonably practicable for an authorisation under this Part to be sought for the carrying out of the surveillance.

(3) Subject to subsections (4) to (6), surveillance is intrusive for the purposes of this Part if, and only if, it is covert surveillance that—

(a) is carried out in relation to anything taking place on any residential premises or in any private vehicle; and

(b) involves the presence of an individual on the premises or in the vehicle or is carried out by means of a surveillance device.

(4) For the purposes of this Part surveillance is not intrusive to the extent that—

(a) it is carried out by means only of a surveillance device designed or adapted principally for the purpose of providing information about the location of a vehicle; or

(b) it is surveillance consisting in any such interception of a communication as falls within section 48(4).

(5) For the purposes of this Part surveillance which—

(a) is carried out by means of a surveillance device in relation to anything taking place on any residential premises or in any private vehicle, but

(b) is carried out without that device being present on the premises or in the vehicle,

is not intrusive unless the device is such that it consistently provides information of the same quality and detail as might be expected to be obtained from a device actually present on the premises or in the vehicle.

(6) For the purposes of this Part surveillance which—

   (a) is carried out by means of apparatus designed or adapted for the purpose of detecting the installation or use in any residential or other premises of a television receiver (within the meaning of section 1 of the Wireless Telegraphy Act 1949), and

   (b) is carried out from outside those premises exclusively for that purpose,

is neither directed nor intrusive.

  (7) In this Part—

   (a) references to the conduct of a covert human intelligence source are references to any conduct of such a source which falls within any of paragraphs (a) to (c) of subsection (8), or is incidental to anything falling within any of those paragraphs; and

   (b) references to the use of a covert human intelligence source are references to inducing, asking or assisting a person to engage in the conduct of such a source, or to obtain information by means of the conduct of such a source.

  (8) For the purposes of this Part a person is a covert human intelligence source if—

   (a) he establishes or maintains a personal or other relationship with a person for the covert purpose of facilitating the doing of anything falling within paragraph (b) or (c);

   (b) he covertly uses such a relationship to obtain information or to provide access to any information to another person; or

   (c) he covertly discloses information obtained by the use of such a relationship, or as a consequence of the existence of such a relationship.

  (9) For the purposes of this section—

   (a) surveillance is covert if, and only if, it is carried out in a manner that is calculated to ensure that persons who are subject to the surveillance are unaware that it is or may be taking place;

   (b) a purpose is covert, in relation to the establishment or maintenance of a personal or other relationship, if and only if the relationship is conducted in a manner that is calculated to ensure that one of the parties to the relationship is unaware of the purpose; and

   (c) a relationship is used covertly, and information obtained as mentioned in subsection (8)(c) is disclosed covertly, if and only if it is used or, as the case may be, disclosed in a manner that is calculated to ensure that one of the parties to the relationship is unaware of the use or disclosure in question.

  (10) In this section "private information", in relation to a person, includes any information relating to his private or family life.

  (11) References in this section, in relation to a vehicle, to the presence of a surveillance device in the vehicle include references to its being located on or under the vehicle and also include references to its being attached to it.

Authorisation of surveillance and human intelligence sources

Lawful surveillance, etc.

  27.—(1) Conduct to which this Part applies shall be lawful for all purposes if—

   (a) an authorisation under this Part confers an entitlement to engage in that conduct on the person whose conduct it is; and

   (b) his conduct is in accordance with the authorisation.

  (2) A person shall not be subject to any civil liability in respect of any conduct of his which—

   (a) is incidental to any conduct that is lawful by virtue of subsection (1); and

(b) is not itself conduct an authorisation or warrant for which is capable of being granted under a relevant enactment and might reasonably have been expected to have been sought in the case in question.

(3) The conduct that may be authorised under this Part includes conduct outside the United Kingdom.

(4) In this section "relevant enactment" means—

(a) an enactment contained in this Act;

(b) section 5 of the Intelligence Services Act 1994 (warrants for the intelligence services); or

(c) an enactment contained in Part III of the Police Act 1997 (powers of the police and of customs officers).

Authorisation of directed surveillance

28.—(1) Subject to the following provisions of this Part, the persons designated for the purposes of this section shall each have power to grant authorisations for the carrying out of directed surveillance.

(2) A person shall not grant an authorisation for the carrying out of directed surveillance unless he believes—

(a) that the authorisation is necessary on grounds falling within subsection (3); and

(b) that the authorised surveillance is proportionate to what is sought to be achieved by carrying it out.

(3) An authorisation is necessary on grounds falling within this subsection if it is necessary—

(a) in the interests of national security;

(b) for the purpose of preventing or detecting crime or of preventing disorder;

(c) in the interests of the economic well-being of the United Kingdom;

(d) in the interests of public safety;

(e) for the purpose of protecting public health;

(f) for the purpose of assessing or collecting any tax, duty, levy or other imposition, contribution or charge payable to a government department; or

(g) for any purpose (not falling within paragraphs (a) to (f)) which is specified for the purposes of this subsection by an order made by the Secretary of State.

(4) The conduct that is authorised by an authorisation for the carrying out of directed surveillance is any conduct that—

(a) consists in the carrying out of directed surveillance of any such description as is specified in the authorisation; and

(b) is carried out in the circumstances described in the authorisation and for the purposes of the investigation or operation specified or described in the authorisation.

(5) The Secretary of State shall not make an order under subsection (3)(g) unless a draft of the order has been laid before Parliament and approved by a resolution of each House.

Authorisation of covert human intelligence sources

29.—(1) Subject to the following provisions of this Part, the persons designated for the purposes of this section shall each have power to grant authorisations for the conduct or the use of a covert human intelligence source.

(2) A person shall not grant an authorisation for the conduct or the use of a covert human intelligence source unless he believes—

(a) that the authorisation is necessary on grounds falling within subsection (3);

(b) that the authorised conduct or use is proportionate to what is sought to be achieved by that conduct or use; and

(c) that arrangements exist for the source's case that satisfy the requirements of subsection (5) and such other requirements as may be imposed by order made by the Secretary of State.

(3) An authorisation is necessary on grounds falling within this subsection if it is necessary—

(a) in the interests of national security;

(b) for the purpose of preventing or detecting crime or of preventing disorder;

(c) in the interests of the economic well-being of the United Kingdom;

(d) in the interests of public safety;

(e) for the purpose of protecting public health;

(f) for the purpose of assessing or collecting any tax, duty, levy or other imposition, contribution or charge payable to a government department; or

(g) for any purpose (not falling within paragraphs (a) to (f)) which is specified for the purposes of this subsection by an order made by the Secretary of State.

(4) The conduct that is authorised by an authorisation for the conduct or the use of a covert human intelligence source is any conduct that—

(a) is comprised in any such activities involving conduct of a covert human intelligence source, or the use of a covert human intelligence source, as are specified or described in the authorisation;

(b) consists in conduct by or in relation to the person who is so specified or described as the person to whose actions as a covert human intelligence source the authorisation relates; and

(c) is carried out for the purposes of, or in connection with, the investigation or operation so specified or described.

(5) For the purposes of this Part there are arrangements for the source's case that satisfy the requirements of this subsection if such arrangements are in force as are necessary for ensuring—

(a) that there will at all times be a person holding an office, rank or position with the relevant investigating authority who will have day-to-day responsibility for dealing with the source on behalf of that authority, and for the source's security and welfare;

(b) that there will at all times be another person holding an office, rank or position with the relevant investigating authority who will have general oversight of the use made of the source;

(c) that there will at all times be a person holding an office, rank or position with the relevant investigating authority who will have responsibility for maintaining a record of the use made of the source;

(d) that the records relating to the source that are maintained by the relevant investigating authority will always contain particulars of all such matters (if any) as may be specified for the purposes of this paragraph in regulations made by the Secretary of State; and

(e) that records maintained by the relevant investigating authority that disclose the identity of the source will not be available to persons except to the extent that there is a need for access to them to be made available to those persons.

(6) The Secretary of State shall not make an order under subsection (3)(g) unless a draft of the order has been laid before Parliament and approved by a resolution of each House.

(7) The Secretary of State may by order—

(a) prohibit the authorisation under this section of any such conduct or uses of covert human intelligence sources as may be described in the order; and

(b) impose requirements, in addition to those provided for by subsection (2), that must be satisfied before an authorisation is granted under this section for any such conduct or uses of covert human intelligence sources as may be so described.

(8) In this section "relevant investigating authority", in relation to an authorisation for the conduct or the use of an individual as a covert human intelligence source, means (subject to subsection (9)) the public authority for whose benefit the activities of that individual as such a source are to take place.

(9) In the case of any authorisation for the conduct or the use of a covert human intelligence source whose activities are to be for the benefit of more than one public authority, the references in subsection (5) to the relevant investigating authority are references to one of them (whether or not the same one in the case of each reference).

Persons entitled to grant authorisations under ss. 28 and 29

30.—(1) Subject to subsection (3), the persons designated for the purposes of sections 28 and 29 are the individuals holding such offices, ranks or positions with relevant public authorities as are prescribed for the purposes of this subsection by an order under this section.

(2) For the purposes of the grant of an authorisation that combines—

(a) an authorisation under section 28 or 29, and

(b) an authorisation by the Secretary of State for the carrying out of intrusive surveillance,

the Secretary of State himself shall be a person designated for the purposes of that section.

(3) An order under this section may impose restrictions—

(a) on the authorisations under sections 28 and 29 that may be granted by any individual holding an office, rank or position with a specified public authority; and

(b) on the circumstances in which, or the purposes for which, such authorisations may be granted by any such individual.

(4) A public authority is a relevant public authority for the purposes of this section—

(a) in relation to section 28 if it is specified in Part I or II of Schedule 1; and

(b) in relation to section 29 if it is specified in Part I of that Schedule.

(5) An order under this section may amend Schedule 1 by—

(a) adding a public authority to Part I or II of that Schedule;

(b) removing a public authority from that Schedule;

(c) moving a public authority from one Part of that Schedule to the other;

(d) making any change consequential on any change in the name of a public authority specified in that Schedule.

(6) Without prejudice to section 31, the power to make an order under this section shall be exercisable by the Secretary of State.

(7) The Secretary of State shall not make an order under subsection (5) containing any provision for—

(a) adding any public authority to Part I or II of that Schedule, or

(b) moving any public authority from Part II to Part I of that Schedule, unless a draft of the order has been laid before Parliament and approved by a resolution of each House.

Orders under s. 30 for Northern Ireland

31.—(1) Subject to subsections (2) and (3), the power to make an order under section 30 for the purposes of the grant of authorisations for conduct in Northern Ireland shall be exercisable by the Office of the First Minister and deputy First Minister in Northern Ireland (concurrently with being exercisable by the Secretary of State).

(2) The power of the Office of the First Minister and deputy First Minister to make an order under section 30 by virtue of subsection (1) or (3) of that section shall not be exercisable in relation to any public authority other than—

(a) the Food Standards Agency;

(b) the Intervention Board for Agricultural Produce;

(c) an authority added to Schedule 1 by an order made by that Office;

(d) an authority added to that Schedule by an order made by the Secretary of State which it would (apart from that order) have been within the powers of that Office to add to that Schedule for the purposes mentioned in subsection (1) of this section.

(3) The power of the Office of the First Minister and deputy First Minister to make an order under section 30—

(a) shall not include power to make any provision dealing with an excepted matter;

(b) shall not include power, except with the consent of the Secretary of State, to make any provision dealing with a reserved matter.

(4) The power of the Office of the First Minister and deputy First Minister to make an order under section 30 shall be exercisable by statutory rule for the purposes of the Statutory Rules (Northern Ireland) Order 1979.

(5) A statutory rule containing an order under section 30 which makes provision by virtue of subsection (5) of that section for—

(a) adding any public authority to Part I or II of Schedule 1, or

(b) moving any public authority from Part II to Part I of that Schedule, shall be subject to affirmative resolution (within the meaning of section 41(4) of the Interpretation Act (Northern Ireland) 1954).

(6) A statutory rule containing an order under section 30 (other than one to which subsection (5) of this section applies) shall be subject to negative resolution (within the meaning of section 41(6) of the Interpretation Act (Northern Ireland) 1954).

(7) An order under section 30 made by the Office of the First Minister and deputy First Minister may—

(a) make different provision for different cases;

(b) contain such incidental, supplemental, consequential and transitional provision as that Office thinks fit.

(8) The reference in subsection (2) to an addition to Schedule 1 being within the powers of the Office of the First Minister and deputy First Minister includes a reference to its being within the powers exercisable by that Office with the consent for the purposes of subsection (3)(b) of the Secretary of State.

(9) In this section "excepted matter" and "reserved matter" have the same meanings as in the Northern Ireland Act 1998; and, in relation to those matters, section 98(2) of that Act (meaning of "deals with") applies for the purposes of this section as it applies for the purposes of that Act.

Authorisation of intrusive surveillance

32.—(1) Subject to the following provisions of this Part, the Secretary of State and each of the senior authorising officers shall have power to grant authorisations for the carrying out of intrusive surveillance.

(2) Neither the Secretary of State nor any senior authorising officer shall grant an authorisation for the carrying out of intrusive surveillance unless he believes—

(a) that the authorisation is necessary on grounds falling within subsection (3); and

(b) that the authorised surveillance is proportionate to what is sought to be achieved by carrying it out.

(3) Subject to the following provisions of this section, an authorisation is necessary on grounds falling within this subsection if it is necessary—

(a) in the interests of national security;

(b) for the purpose of preventing or detecting serious crime; or

(c) in the interests of the economic well-being of the United Kingdom.

(4) The matters to be taken into account in considering whether the requirements of subsection (2) are satisfied in the case of any authorisation shall include whether the information which it is thought necessary to obtain by the authorised conduct could reasonably be obtained by other means.

(5) The conduct that is authorised by an authorisation for the carrying out of intrusive surveillance is any conduct that—

(a) consists in the carrying out of intrusive surveillance of any such description as is specified in the authorisation;

(b) is carried out in relation to the residential premises specified or described in the authorisation or in relation to the private vehicle so specified or described; and

(c) is carried out for the purposes of, or in connection with, the investigation or operation so specified or described.

(6) For the purposes of this section the senior authorising officers are—

(a) the chief constable of every police force maintained under section 2 of the Police Act 1996 (police forces in England and Wales outside London);

(b) the Commissioner of Police of the Metropolis and every Assistant Commissioner of Police of the Metropolis;

(c) the Commissioner of Police for the City of London;

(d) the chief constable of every police force maintained under or by virtue of section 1 of the Police (Scotland) Act 1967 (police forces for areas in Scotland);

(e) the Chief Constable of the Royal Ulster Constabulary and the Deputy Chief Constable of the Royal Ulster Constabulary;

(f) the Chief Constable of the Ministry of Defence Police;

(g) the Provost Marshal of the Royal Navy Regulating Branch;

(h) the Provost Marshal of the Royal Military Police;

(i) the Provost Marshal of the Royal Air Force Police;

(j) the Chief Constable of the British Transport Police;

(k) the Director General of the National Criminal Intelligence Service;

(l) the Director General of the National Crime Squad and any person holding the rank of assistant chief constable in that Squad who is designated for the purposes of this paragraph by that Director General; and

(m) any customs officer designated for the purposes of this paragraph by the Commissioners of Customs and Excise.

Police and customs authorisations

Rules for grant of authorisations

33.—(1) A person who is a designated person for the purposes of section 28 or 29 by reference to his office, rank or position with a police force, the National Criminal Intelligence Service or the National Crime Squad shall not grant an authorisation under that section except on an application made by a member of the same force, Service or Squad.

(2) A person who is designated for the purposes of section 28 or 29 by reference to his office, rank or position with the Commissioners of Customs and Excise shall not grant an authorisation under that section except on an application made by a customs officer.

(3) A person who is a senior authorising officer by reference to a police force, the National Criminal Intelligence Service or the National Crime Squad shall not grant an authorisation for the carrying out of intrusive surveillance except—

(a) on an application made by a member of the same force, Service or Squad; and

(b) in the case of an authorisation for the carrying out of intrusive surveillance in relation to any residential premises, where those premises are in the area of operation of that force, Service or Squad.

(4) A person who is a senior authorising officer by virtue of a designation by the Commissioners of Customs and Excise shall not grant an authorisation for the carrying out of intrusive surveillance except on an application made by a customs officer.

(5) A single authorisation may combine both—

(a) an authorisation granted under this Part by, or on the application of, an individual who is a member of a police force, the National Criminal Intelligence Service or the National Crime Squad, or who is a customs officer; and

(b) an authorisation given by, or on the application of, that individual under Part III of the Police Act 1997;

but the provisions of this Act or that Act that are applicable in the case of each of the authorisations shall apply separately in relation to the part of the combined authorisation to which they are applicable.

(6) For the purposes of this section—

(a) the area of operation of a police force maintained under section 2 of the Police Act 1996, of the metropolitan police force, of the City of London police force or of a police force maintained under or by virtue of section 1 of the Police (Scotland) Act 1967 is the area for which that force is maintained;

(b) the area of operation of the Royal Ulster Constabulary is Northern Ireland;

(c) residential premises are in the area of operation of the Ministry of Defence Police if they are premises where the members of that police force, under section 2 of the Ministry of Defence Police Act 1987, have the powers and privileges of a constable;

(d) residential premises are in the area of operation of the Royal Navy Regulating Branch, the Royal Military Police or the Royal Air Force Police if they are premises owned or occupied by, or used for residential purposes by, a person subject to service discipline;

(e) the area of operation of the British Transport Police and also of the National Criminal Intelligence Service is the United Kingdom;

(f) the area of operation of the National Crime Squad is England and Wales;

and references in this section to the United Kingdom or to any part or area of the United Kingdom include any adjacent waters within the seaward limits of the territorial waters of the United Kingdom.

(7) For the purposes of this section a person is subject to service discipline—

(a) in relation to the Royal Navy Regulating Branch, if he is subject to the Naval Discipline Act 1957 or is a civilian to whom Parts I and II of that Act for the time being apply by virtue of section 118 of that Act ;

(b) in relation to the Royal Military Police, if he is subject to military law or is a civilian to whom Part II of the Army Act 1955 for the time being applies by virtue of section 209 of that Act; and

    (c) in relation to the Royal Air Force Police, if he is subject to air-force law or is a civilian to whom Part II of the Air Force Act 1955 for the time being applies by virtue of section 209 of that Act.

Grant of authorisations in the senior officer's absence

34.—(1) This section applies in the case of an application for an authorisation for the carrying out of intrusive surveillance where—

    (a) the application is one made by a member of a police force, of the National Criminal Intelligence Service or of the National Crime Squad or by a customs officer; and

    (b) the case is urgent.

(2) If—

    (a) it is not reasonably practicable, having regard to the urgency of the case, for the application to be considered by any person who is a senior authorising officer by reference to the force, Service or Squad in question or, as the case may be, by virtue of a designation by the Commissioners of Customs and Excise, and

    (b) it also not reasonably practicable, having regard to the urgency of the case, for the application to be considered by a person (if there is one) who is entitled, as a designated deputy of a senior authorising officer, to exercise the functions in relation to that application of such an officer,

the application may be made to and considered by any person who is entitled under subsection (4) to act for any senior authorising officer who would have been entitled to consider the application.

(3) A person who considers an application under subsection (1) shall have the same power to grant an authorisation as the person for whom he is entitled to act.

(4) For the purposes of this section—

    (a) a person is entitled to act for the chief constable of a police force maintained under section 2 of the Police Act 1996 if he holds the rank of assistant chief constable in that force;

    (b) a person is entitled to act for the Commissioner of Police of the Metropolis, or for an Assistant Commissioner of Police of the Metropolis, if he holds the rank of commander in the metropolitan police force;

    (c) a person is entitled to act for the Commissioner of Police for the City of London if he holds the rank of commander in the City of London police force;

    (d) a person is entitled to act for the chief constable of a police force maintained under or by virtue of section 1 of the Police (Scotland) Act 1967 if he holds the rank of assistant chief constable in that force;

    (e) a person is entitled to act for the Chief Constable of the Royal Ulster Constabulary, or for the Deputy Chief Constable of the Royal Ulster Constabulary, if he holds the rank of assistant chief constable in the Royal Ulster Constabulary;

    (f) a person is entitled to act for the Chief Constable of the Ministry of Defence Police if he holds the rank of deputy or assistant chief constable in that force;

    (g) a person is entitled to act for the Provost Marshal of the Royal Navy Regulating Branch if he holds the position of assistant Provost Marshal in that Branch;

    (h) a person is entitled to act for the Provost Marshal of the Royal Military Police or the Provost Marshal of the Royal Air Force Police if he holds the position of deputy Provost Marshal in the police force in question;

(i) a person is entitled to act for the Chief Constable of the British Transport Police if he holds the rank of deputy or assistant chief constable in that force;

(j) a person is entitled to act for the Director General of the National Criminal Intelligence Service if he is a person designated for the purposes of this paragraph by that Director General;

(k) a person is entitled to act for the Director General of the National Crime Squad if he is designated for the purposes of this paragraph by that Director General as a person entitled so to act in an urgent case;

(l) a person is entitled to act for a person who is a senior authorising officer by virtue of a designation by the Commissioners of Customs and Excise, if he is designated for the purposes of this paragraph by those Commissioners as a person entitled so to act in an urgent case.

(5) A police member of the National Criminal Intelligence Service or the National Crime Squad appointed under section 9(1)(b) or 55(1)(b) of the Police Act 1997 (police members) may not be designated under subsection (4)(j) or (k) unless he holds the rank of assistant chief constable in that Service or Squad.

(6) In this section "designated deputy"—

(a) in relation to a chief constable, means a person holding the rank of assistant chief constable who is designated to act under section 12(4) of the Police Act 1996 or section 5(4) of the Police (Scotland) Act 1967;

(b) in relation to the Commissioner of Police for the City of London, means a person authorised to act under section 25 of the City of London Police Act 1839;

(c) in relation to the Director General of the National Criminal Intelligence Service or the Director General of the National Crime Squad, means a person designated to act under section 8 or, as the case may be, section 54 of the Police Act 1997.

Notification of authorisations for intrusive surveillance

35.—(1) Where a person grants or cancels a police or customs authorisation for the carrying out of intrusive surveillance, he shall give notice that he has done so to an ordinary Surveillance Commissioner.

(2) A notice given for the purposes of subsection (1)—

(a) must be given in writing as soon as reasonably practicable after the grant or, as the case may be, cancellation of the authorisation to which it relates;

(b) must be given in accordance with any such arrangements made for the purposes of this paragraph by the Chief Surveillance Commissioner as are for the time being in force; and

(c) must specify such matters as the Secretary of State may by order prescribe.

(3) A notice under this section of the grant of an authorisation shall, as the case may be, either—

(a) state that the approval of a Surveillance Commissioner is required by section 36 before the grant of the authorisation will take effect; or

(b) state that the case is one of urgency and set out the grounds on which the case is believed to be one of urgency.

(4) Where a notice for the purposes of subsection (1) of the grant of an authorisation has been received by an ordinary Surveillance Commissioner, he shall, as soon as practicable—

(a) scrutinise the authorisation; and

(b) in a case where notice has been given in accordance with subsection (3)(a), decide whether or not to approve the authorisation.

(5) Subject to subsection (6), the Secretary of State shall not make an order under subsection (2)(c) unless a draft of the order has been laid before Parliament and approved by a resolution of each House.

(6) Subsection (5) does not apply in the case of the order made on the first occasion on which the Secretary of State exercises his power to make an order under subsection (2)(c).

(7) The order made on that occasion shall cease to have effect at the end of the period of forty days beginning with the day on which it was made unless, before the end of that period, it has been approved by a resolution of each House of Parliament.

(8) For the purposes of subsection (7)—

(a) the order's ceasing to have effect shall be without prejudice to anything previously done or to the making of a new order; and

(b) in reckoning the period of forty days no account shall be taken of any period during which Parliament is dissolved or prorogued or during which both Houses are adjourned for more than four days.

(9) Any notice that is required by any provision of this section to be given in writing may be given, instead, by being transmitted by electronic means.

(10) In this section references to a police or customs authorisation are references to an authorisation granted by—

(a) a person who is a senior authorising officer by reference to a police force, the National Criminal Intelligence Service or the National Crime Squad;

(b) a person who is a senior authorising officer by virtue of a designation by the Commissioners of Customs and Excise; or

(c) a person who for the purposes of section 34 is entitled to act for a person falling within paragraph (a) or for a person falling within paragraph (b).

Approval required for authorisations to take effect

36.—(1) This section applies where an authorisation for the carrying out of intrusive surveillance has been granted on the application of—

(a) a member of a police force;

(b) a member of the National Criminal Intelligence Service;

(c) a member of the National Crime Squad; or

(d) a customs officer.

(2) Subject to subsection (3), the authorisation shall not take effect until such time (if any) as—

(a) the grant of the authorisation has been approved by an ordinary Surveillance Commissioner; and

(b) written notice of the Commissioner's decision to approve the grant of the authorisation has been given, in accordance with subsection (4), to the person who granted the authorisation.

(3) Where the person who grants the authorisation—

(a) believes that the case is one of urgency, and

(b) gives notice in accordance with section 35(3)(b),

subsection (2) shall not apply to the authorisation, and the authorisation shall have effect from the time of its grant.

(4) Where subsection (2) applies to the authorisation—

(a) a Surveillance Commissioner shall give his approval under this section to the authorisation if, and only if, he is satisfied that there are reasonable grounds for believing that the requirements of section 32(2)(a) and (b) are satisfied in the case of the authorisation; and

(b) a Surveillance Commissioner who makes a decision as to whether or not the authorisation should be approved shall, as soon as reasonably practicable after making that decision, give written notice of his decision to the person who granted the authorisation.

(5) If an ordinary Surveillance Commissioner decides not to approve an authorisation to which subsection (2) applies, he shall make a report of his findings to the most senior relevant person.

(6) In this section "the most senior relevant person" means—

(a) where the authorisation was granted by the senior authorising officer with any police force who is not someone's deputy, that senior authorising officer;

(b) where the authorisation was granted by the Director General of the National Criminal Intelligence Service or the Director General of the National Crime Squad, that Director General;

(c) where the authorisation was granted by a senior authorising officer with a police force who is someone's deputy, the senior authorising officer whose deputy granted the authorisation;

(d) where the authorisation was granted by the designated deputy of the Director General of the National Criminal Intelligence Service or a person entitled to act for him by virtue of section 34(4)(j), that Director General;

(e) where the authorisation was granted by the designated deputy of the Director General of the National Crime Squad or by a person designated by that Director General for the purposes of section 32(6)(l) or 34(4)(k), that Director General;

(f) where the authorisation was granted by a person entitled to act for a senior authorising officer under section 34(4)(a) to (i), the senior authorising officer in the force in question who is not someone's deputy; and

(g) where the authorisation was granted by a customs officer, the customs officer for the time being designated for the purposes of this paragraph by a written notice given to the Chief Surveillance Commissioner by the Commissioners of Customs and Excise.

(7) The references in subsection (6) to a person's deputy are references to the following—

(a) in relation to—

(i) a chief constable of a police force maintained under section 2 of the Police Act 1996,

(ii) the Commissioner of Police for the City of London, or

(iii) a chief constable of a police force maintained under or by virtue of section 1 of the Police (Scotland) Act 1967,

to his designated deputy;

(b) in relation to the Commissioner of Police of the Metropolis, to an Assistant Commissioner of Police of the Metropolis; and

(c) in relation to the Chief Constable of the Royal Ulster Constabulary, to the Deputy Chief Constable of the Royal Ulster Constabulary;and in this subsection and that subsection "designated deputy" has the same meaning as in section 34.

(8) Any notice that is required by any provision of this section to be given in writing may be given, instead, by being transmitted by electronic means.

Quashing of police and customs authorisations etc

37.—(1) This section applies where an authorisation for the carrying out of intrusive surveillance has been granted on the application of—

(a) a member of a police force;

(b) a member of the National Criminal Intelligence Service;

(c) a member of the National Crime Squad; or

(d) a customs officer.

(2) Where an ordinary Surveillance Commissioner is at any time satisfied that, at the time when the authorisation was granted or at any time when it was renewed, there were no reasonable grounds for believing that the

requirements of section 32(2)(a) and (b) were satisfied, he may quash the authorisation with effect, as he thinks fit, from the time of the grant of the authorisation or from the time of any renewal of the authorisation.

(3) If an ordinary Surveillance Commissioner is satisfied at any time while the authorisation is in force that there are no longer any reasonable grounds for believing that the requirements of section 32(2)(a) and (b) are satisfied in relation to the authorisation, he may cancel the authorisation with effect from such time as appears to him to be the time from which those requirements ceased to be so satisfied.

(4) Where, in the case of any authorisation of which notice has been given in accordance with section 35(3)(b), an ordinary Surveillance Commissioner is at any time satisfied that, at the time of the grant or renewal of the authorisation to which that notice related, there were no reasonable grounds for believing that the case was one of urgency, he may quash the authorisation with effect, as he thinks fit, from the time of the grant of the authorisation or from the time of any renewal of the authorisation

(5) Subject to subsection (7), where an ordinary Surveillance Commissioner quashes an authorisation under this section, he may order the destruction of any records relating wholly or partly to information obtained by the authorised conduct after the time from which his decision takes effect.

(6) Subject to subsection (7), where—
(a) an authorisation has ceased to have effect (otherwise than by virtue of subsection (2) or (4)), and
(b) an ordinary Surveillance Commissioner is satisfied that there was a time while the authorisation was in force when there were no reasonable grounds for believing that the requirements of section 32(2)(a) and (b) continued to be satisfied in relation to the authorisation,

he may order the destruction of any records relating, wholly or partly, to information obtained at such a time by the authorised conduct.

(7) No order shall be made under this section for the destruction of any records required for pending criminal or civil proceedings.

(8) Where an ordinary Surveillance Commissioner exercises a power conferred by this section, he shall, as soon as reasonably practicable, make a report of his exercise of that power, and of his reasons for doing so—
(a) to the most senior relevant person (within the meaning of section 36); and
(b) to the Chief Surveillance Commissioner.

(9) Where an order for the destruction of records is made under this section, the order shall not become operative until such time (if any) as—
(a) the period for appealing against the decision to make the order has expired; and
(b) any appeal brought within that period has been dismissed by the Chief Surveillance Commissioner.

(10) No notice shall be required to be given under section 35(1) in the case of a cancellation under subsection (3) of this section.

Appeals against decisions by Surveillance Commissioners

38.—(1) Any senior authorising officer may appeal to the Chief Surveillance Commissioner against any of the following—
(a) any refusal of an ordinary Surveillance Commissioner to approve an authorisation for the carrying out of intrusive surveillance;
(b) any decision of such a Commissioner to quash or cancel such an authorisation;
(c) any decision of such a Commissioner to make an order under section 37 for the destruction of records.

(2) In the case of an authorisation granted by the designated deputy of a

senior authorising office or by a person who for the purposes of section 34 is entitled to act for a senior authorising officer, that designated deputy or person shall also be entitled to appeal under this section.

(3) An appeal under this section must be brought within the period of seven days beginning with the day on which the refusal or decision appealed against is reported to the appellant.

(4) Subject to subsection (5), the Chief Surveillance Commissioner, on an appeal under this section, shall allow the appeal if—

  (a) he is satisfied that there were reasonable grounds for believing that the requirements of section 32(2)(a) and

  (b) were satisfied in relation to the authorisation at the time in question; and

  (c) he is not satisfied that the authorisation is one of which notice was given in accordance with section 35(3)(b) without there being any reasonable grounds for believing that the case was one of urgency.

(5) If, on an appeal falling within subsection (1)(b), the Chief Surveillance Commissioner—

  (a) is satisfied that grounds exist which justify the quashing or cancellation under section 37 of the authorisation in question, but

  (b) considers that the authorisation should have been quashed or cancelled from a different time from that from which it was quashed or cancelled by the ordinary Surveillance Commissioner against whose decision the appeal is brought, he may modify that Commissioner's decision to quash or cancel the authorisation, and any related decision for the destruction of records, so as to give effect to the decision under section 37 that he considers should have been made.

(6) Where, on an appeal under this section against a decision to quash or cancel an authorisation, the Chief Surveillance Commissioner allows the appeal he shall also quash any related order for the destruction of records relating to information obtained by the authorised conduct.

(7) In this section "designated deputy" has the same meaning as in section 34.

Appeals to the Chief Surveillance Commissioner: supplementary

39.—(1) Where the Chief Surveillance Commissioner has determined an appeal under section 38, he shall give notice of his determination to both—

  (a) the person by whom the appeal was brought; and

  (b) the ordinary Surveillance Commissioner whose decision was appealed against.

(2) Where the determination of the Chief Surveillance Commissioner on an appeal under section 38 is a determination to dismiss the appeal, the Chief Surveillance Commissioner shall make a report of his findings—

  (a) to the persons mentioned in subsection (1); and

  (b) to the Prime Minister.

(3) Subsections (3) and (4) of section 107 of the Police Act 1997 (reports to be laid before Parliament and exclusion of matters from the report) apply in relation to any report to the Prime Minister under subsection (2) of this section as they apply in relation to any report under subsection (2) of that section.

(4) Subject to subsection (2) of this section, the Chief Surveillance Commissioner shall not give any reasons for any determination of his on an appeal under section 38.

Information to be provided to Surveillance Commissioners

40. It shall be the duty of—

  (a) every member of a police force,

(b) every member of the National Criminal Intelligence Service,
(c) every member of the National Crime Squad, and
(d) every customs officer,
to comply with any request of a Surveillance Commissioner for documents or information required by that Commissioner for the purpose of enabling him to carry out the functions of such a Commissioner under sections 35 to 39.

Other authorisations

Secretary of State authorisations

41.—(1) The Secretary of State shall not grant an authorisation for the carrying out of intrusive surveillance except on an application made by—
(a) a member of any of the intelligence services;
(b) an official of the Ministry of Defence;
(c) a member of Her Majesty's forces;
(d) an individual holding an office, rank or position with any such public authority as may be designated for the purposes of this section as an authority whose activities may require the carrying out of intrusive surveillance.

(2) Section 32 shall have effect in relation to the grant of an authorisation by the Secretary of State on the application of an official of the Ministry of Defence, or of a member of Her Majesty's forces, as if the only matters mentioned in subsection (3) of that section were—
(a) the interests of national security; and
(b) the purpose of preventing or detecting serious crime.

(3) The designation of any public authority for the purposes of this section shall be by order made by the Secretary of State.

(4) The Secretary of State may by order provide, in relation to any public authority, that an application for an authorisation for the carrying out of intrusive surveillance may be made by an individual holding an office, rank or position with that authority only where his office, rank or position is one prescribed by the order.

(5) The Secretary of State may by order impose restrictions—
(a) on the authorisations for the carrying out of intrusive surveillance that may be granted on the application of an individual holding an office, rank or position with any public authority designated for the purposes of this section; and
(b) on the circumstances in which, or the purposes for which, such authorisations may be granted on such an application.

(6) The Secretary of State shall not make a designation under subsection (3) unless a draft of the order containing the designation has been laid before Parliament and approved by a resolution of each House.

(7) References in this section to a member of Her Majesty's forces do not include references to any member of Her Majesty's forces who is a member of a police force by virtue of his service with the Royal Navy Regulating Branch, the Royal Military Police or the Royal Air Force Police.

Intelligence services authorisations

42.—(1) The grant by the Secretary of State on the application of a member of one of the intelligence services of any authorisation under this Part must be made by the issue of a warrant.

(2) A single warrant issued by the Secretary of State may combine both—
(a) an authorisation under this Part; and
(b) an intelligence services warrant;
but the provisions of this Act or the Intelligence Services Act 1994 that are applicable in the case of the authorisation under this Part or the intelligence

services warrant shall apply separately in relation to the part of the combined warrant to which they are applicable.

(3) Intrusive surveillance in relation to any premises or vehicle in the British Islands shall be capable of being authorised by a warrant issued under this Part on the application of a member of the Secret Intelligence Service or GCHQ only if the authorisation contained in the warrant is one satisfying the requirements of section 32(2)(a) otherwise than in connection with any functions of that intelligence service in support of the prevention or detection of serious crime.

(4) Subject to subsection (5), the functions of the Security Service shall include acting on behalf of the Secret Intelligence Service or GCHQ in relation to—

(a) the application for and grant of any authorisation under this Part in connection with any matter within the functions of the Secret Intelligence Service or GCHQ; and

(b) the carrying out, in connection with any such matter, of any conduct authorised by such an authorisation.

(5) Nothing in subsection (4) shall authorise the doing of anything by one intelligence service on behalf of another unless—

(a) it is something which either the other service or a member of the other service has power to do; and

(b) it is done otherwise than in connection with functions of the other service in support of the prevention or detection of serious crime.

(6) In this section "intelligence services warrant" means a warrant under section 5 of the Intelligence Services Act 1994.

Grant, renewal and duration of authorisations

General rules about grant, renewal and duration

43.—(1) An authorisation under this Part—

(a) may be granted or renewed orally in any urgent case in which the entitlement to act of the person granting or renewing it is not confined to urgent cases; and

(b) in any other case, must be in writing.

(2) A single authorisation may combine two or more different authorisations under this Part; but the provisions of this Act that are applicable in the case of each of the authorisations shall apply separately in relation to the part of the combined authorisation to which they are applicable.

(3) Subject to subsections (4) and (8), an authorisation under this Part shall cease to have effect at the end of the following period—

(a) in the case of an authorisation which—

(i) has not been renewed and was granted either orally or by a person whose entitlement to act is confined to urgent cases, or

(ii) was last renewed either orally or by such a person,

the period of seventy-two hours beginning with the time when the grant of the authorisation or, as the case may be, its latest renewal takes effect;

(b) in a case not falling within paragraph (a) in which the authorisation is for the conduct or the use of a covert human intelligence source, the period of twelve months beginning with the day on which the grant of the authorisation or, as the case may be, its latest renewal takes effect; and

(c) in any case not falling within paragraph (a) or (b), the period of three months beginning with the day on which the grant of the authorisation or, as the case may be, its latest renewal takes effect.

(4) Subject to subsection (6), an authorisation under this Part may be renewed, at any time before the time at which it ceases to have effect, by any person who would be entitled to grant a new authorisation in the same terms.

(5) Sections 28 to 41 shall have effect in relation to the renewal of an

authorisation under this Part as if references to the grant of an authorisation included references to its renewal.

(6) A person shall not renew an authorisation for the conduct or the use of a covert human intelligence source, unless he—

(a) is satisfied that a review has been carried out of the matters mentioned in subsection (7); and

(b) has, for the purpose of deciding whether he should renew the authorisation, considered the results of that review.

(7) The matters mentioned in subsection (6) are—

(a) the use made of the source in the period since the grant or, as the case may be, latest renewal of the authorisation; and

(b) the tasks given to the source during that period and the information obtained from the conduct or the use of the source.

(8) The Secretary of State may by order provide in relation to authorisations of such descriptions as may be specified in the order that subsection (3) is to have effect as if the period at the end of which an authorisation of a description so specified is to cease to have effect were such period shorter than that provided for by that subsection as may be fixed by or determined in accordance with that order.

(9) References in this section to the time at which, or the day on which, the grant or renewal of an authorisation takes effect are references—

(a) in the case of the grant of an authorisation to which paragraph (c) does not apply, to the time at which or, as the case may be, day on which the authorisation is granted;

(b) in the case of the renewal of an authorisation to which paragraph (c) does not apply, to the time at which or, as the case may be, day on which the authorisation would have ceased to have effect but for the renewal; and

(c) in the case of any grant or renewal that takes effect under subsection (2) of section 36 at a time or on a day later than that given by paragraph (a) or (b), to the time at which or, as the case may be, day on which the grant or renewal takes effect in accordance with that subsection.

(10) In relation to any authorisation granted by a member of any of the intelligence services, and in relation to any authorisation contained in a warrant issued by the Secretary of State on the application of a member of any of the intelligence services, this section has effect subject to the provisions of section 44.

Special rules for intelligence services authorisations

44.—(1) Subject to subsection (2), a warrant containing an authorisation for the carrying out of intrusive surveillance—

(a) shall not be issued on the application of a member of any of the intelligence services, and

(b) if so issued shall not be renewed,

except under the hand of the Secretary of State.

(2) In an urgent case in which—

(a) an application for a warrant containing an authorisation for the carrying out of intrusive surveillance has been made by a member of any of the intelligence services, and

(b) the Secretary of State has himself expressly authorised the issue of the warrant in that case,

the warrant may be issued (but not renewed) under the hand of a senior official.

(3) Subject to subsection (6), a warrant containing an authorisation for the carrying out of intrusive surveillance which—

   (a) was issued, on the application of a member of any of the intelligence
     services, under the hand of a senior official, and

   (b) has not been renewed under the hand of the Secretary of State,

shall cease to have effect at the end of the second working day following the
day of the issue of the warrant, instead of at the time provided for by section
43(3).

   (4) Subject to subsections (3) and (6), where any warrant for the carrying
out of intrusive surveillance which is issued or was last renewed on the
application of a member of any of the intelligence services, the warrant
(unless renewed or, as the case may be, renewed again) shall cease to have
effect at the following time, instead of at the time provided for by section
43(3), namely—

   (a) in the case of a warrant that has not been renewed, at the end of the
     period of six months beginning with the day on which it was issued;
     and

   (b) in any other case, at the end of the period of six months beginning with
     the day on which it would have ceased to have effect if not renewed
     again.

   (5) Subject to subsection (6), where—

   (a) an authorisation for the carrying out of directed surveillance is
     granted by a member of any of the intelligence services, and

   (b) the authorisation is renewed by an instrument endorsed under the
     hand of the person renewing the authorisation with a statement that
     the renewal is believed to be necessary on grounds falling within
     section 32(3)(a) or (c),

the authorisation (unless renewed again) shall cease to have effect at the end
of the period of six months beginning with the day on which it would have
ceased to have effect but for the renewal, instead of at the time provided for
by section 43(3).

   (6) The Secretary of State may by order provide in relation to authorisations of such descriptions as may be specified in the order that subsection
(3), (4) or (5) is to have effect as if the period at the end of which an
authorisation of a description so specified is to cease to have effect were such
period shorter than that provided for by that subsection as may be fixed by or
determined in accordance with that order.

   (7) Notwithstanding anything in section 43(2), in a case in which there is a
combined warrant containing both—

   (a) an authorisation for the carrying out of intrusive surveillance, and

   (b) an authorisation for the carrying out of directed surveillance, the
     reference in subsection (4) of this section to a warrant for the carrying
     out of intrusive surveillance is a reference to the warrant so far as it
     confers both authorisations.

Cancellation of authorisations

   45.—(1) The person who granted or, as the case may be, last renewed an
authorisation under this Part shall cancel it if—

   (a) he is satisfied that the authorisation is one in relation to which the
     requirements of section 28(2)(a) and (b), 29(2)(a) and (b) or, as the
     case may be, 32(2)(a) and (b) are no longer satisfied; or

   (b) in the case of an authorisation under section 29, he is satisfied that
     arrangements for the source's case that satisfy the requirements
     mentioned in subsection (2)(c) of that section no longer exist.

   (2) Where an authorisation under this Part was granted or, as the case may
be, last renewed—

   (a) by a person entitled to act for any other person, or

(b) by the deputy of any other person,

that other person shall cancel the authorisation if he is satisfied as to either of the matters mentioned in subsection (1).

(3) Where an authorisation under this Part was granted or, as the case may be, last renewed by a person whose deputy had power to grant it, that deputy shall cancel the authorisation if he is satisfied as to either of the matters mentioned in subsection (1).

(4) The Secretary of State may by regulations provide for the person by whom any duty imposed by this section is to be performed in a case in which it would otherwise fall on a person who is no longer available to perform it.

(5) Regulations under subsection (4) may provide for the person on whom the duty is to fall to be a person appointed in accordance with the regulations.

(6) The references in this section to a person's deputy are references to the following—

(a) in relation to—
  (i) a chief constable of a police force maintained under section 2 of the Police Act 1996,
  (ii) the Commissioner of Police for the City of London, or
  (iii) a chief constable of a police force maintained under or by virtue of section 1 of the Police (Scotland) Act 1967,
  to his designated deputy;

(b) in relation to the Commissioner of Police of the Metropolis, to an Assistant Commissioner of Police of the Metropolis;

(c) in relation to the Chief Constable of the Royal Ulster Constabulary, to the Deputy Chief Constable of the Royal Ulster Constabulary;

(d) in relation to the Director General of the National Criminal Intelligence Service, to his designated deputy; and

(e) in relation to the Director General of the National Crime Squad, to any person designated by him for the purposes of section 32(6)(l) or to his designated deputy.

(7) In this section "designated deputy" has the same meaning as in section 34.

Scotland

Restrictions on authorisations extending to Scotland

46.—(1) No person shall grant or renew an authorisation under this Part for the carrying out of any conduct if it appears to him—

(a) that the authorisation is not one for which this Part is the relevant statutory provision for all parts of the United Kingdom; and

(b) that all the conduct authorised by the grant or, as the case may be, renewal of the authorisation is likely to take place in Scotland.

(2) In relation to any authorisation, this Part is the relevant statutory provision for all parts of the United Kingdom in so far as it—

(a) is granted or renewed on the grounds that it is necessary in the interests of national security or in the interests of the economic well-being of the United Kingdom;

(b) is granted or renewed by or on the application of a person holding any office, rank or position with any of the public authorities specified in subsection (3);

(c) authorises conduct of a person holding an office, rank or position with any of the public authorities so specified;

(d) authorises conduct of an individual acting as a covert human intelligence source for the benefit of any of the public authorities so specified; or

(e) authorises conduct that is surveillance by virtue of section 48(4).

(3) The public authorities mentioned in subsection (2) are—

(a) each of the intelligence services;
(b) Her Majesty's forces;
(c) the Ministry of Defence;
(d) the Ministry of Defence Police;
(e) the Commissioners of Customs and Excise; and
(f) the British Transport Police.

(4) For the purposes of so much of this Part as has effect in relation to any other public authority by virtue of—
(a) the fact that it is a public authority for the time being specified in Schedule 1, or
(b) an order under subsection (1)(d) of section 41 designating that authority for the purposes of that section, the authorities specified in subsection (3) of this section shall be treated as including that authority to the extent that the Secretary of State by order directs that the authority is a relevant public authority or, as the case may be, is a designated authority for all parts of the United Kingdom.

Supplemental provision for Part II

Power to extend or modify authorisation provisions

47.—(1) The Secretary of State may by order do one or both of the following—
(a) apply this Part, with such modifications as he thinks fit, to any such surveillance that is neither directed nor intrusive as may be described in the order;
(b) provide for any description of directed surveillance to be treated for the purposes of this Part as intrusive surveillance.

(2) No order shall be made under this section unless a draft of it has been laid before Parliament and approved by a resolution of each House.

Interpretation of Part II

48.—(1) In this Part—
"covert human intelligence source" shall be construed in accordance with section 26(8);
"directed" and "intrusive", in relation to surveillance, shall be construed in accordance with section 26(2) to (6);
"private vehicle" means (subject to subsection (7)(a)) any vehicle which is used primarily for the private purposes of the person who owns it or of a person otherwise having the right to use it;
"residential premises" means (subject to subsection (7)(b)) so much of any premises as is for the time being occupied or used by any person, however temporarily, for residential purposes or otherwise as living accommodation (including hotel or prison accommodation that is so occupied or used);
"senior authorising officer" means a person who by virtue of subsection (6) of section 32 is a senior authorising officer for the purposes of that section;
"surveillance" shall be construed in accordance with subsections (2) to (4);
"surveillance device" means any apparatus designed or adapted for use in surveillance.

(2) Subject to subsection (3), in this Part "surveillance" includes—
(a) monitoring, observing or listening to persons, their movements, their conversations or their other activities or communications;
(b) recording anything monitored, observed or listened to in the course of surveillance; and
(c) surveillance by or with the assistance of a surveillance device.

(3) References in this Part to surveillance do not include references to—

(a) any conduct of a covert human intelligence source for obtaining or recording (whether or not using a surveillance device) any information which is disclosed in the presence of the source;

(b) the use of a covert human intelligence source for so obtaining or recording information; or

(c) any such entry on or interference with property or with wireless telegraphy as would be unlawful unless authorised under—

(i) section 5 of the Intelligence Services Act 1994 (warrants for the intelligence services); or

(ii) Part III of the Police Act 1997 (powers of the police and of customs officers).

(4) References in this Part to surveillance include references to the interception of a communication in the course of its transmission by means of a postal service or telecommunication system if, and only if—

(a) the communication is one sent by or intended for a person who has consented to the interception of communications sent by or to him; and

(b) there is no interception warrant authorising the interception.

(5) References in this Part to an individual holding an office or position with a public authority include references to any member, official or employee of that authority.

(6) For the purposes of this Part the activities of a covert human intelligence source which are to be taken as activities for the benefit of a particular public authority include any conduct of his as such a source which is in response to inducements or requests made by or on behalf of that authority.

(7) In subsection (1)—

(a) the reference to a person having the right to use a vehicle does not, in relation to a motor vehicle, include a reference to a person whose right to use the vehicle derives only from his having paid, or undertaken to pay, for the use of the vehicle and its driver for a particular journey; and

(b) the reference to premises occupied or used by any person for residential purposes or otherwise as living accommodation does not include a reference to so much of any premises as constitutes any common area to which he has or is allowed access in connection with his use or occupation of any accommodation.

(8) In this section—

"premises" includes any vehicle or moveable structure and any other place whatever, whether or not occupied as land;

"vehicle" includes any vessel, aircraft or hovercraft.

PART III

INVESTIGATION OF ELECTRONIC DATA PROTECTED BY ENCRYPTION ETC.

Power to require disclosure

Notices requiring disclosure

49.—(1) This section applies where any protected information—

(a) has come into the possession of any person by means of the exercise of a statutory power to seize, detain, inspect, search or otherwise to interfere with documents or other property, or is likely to do so;

(b) has come into the possession of any person by means of the exercise of any statutory power to intercept communications, or is likely to do so;

(c) has come into the possession of any person by means of the exercise of any power conferred by an authorisation under section 22(3) or under

A–732

Part II, or as a result of the giving of a notice under section 22(4), or is likely to do so;

(d) has come into the possession of any person as a result of having been provided or disclosed in pursuance of any statutory duty (whether or not one arising as a result of a request for information), or is likely to do so; or

(e) has, by any other lawful means not involving the exercise of statutory powers, come into the possession of any of the intelligence services, the police or the customs and excise, or is likely so to come into the possession of any of those services, the police or the customs and excise.

(2) If any person with the appropriate permission under Schedule 2 believes, on reasonable grounds—

(a) that a key to the protected information is in the possession of any person,

(b) that the imposition of a disclosure requirement in respect of the protected information is—

    (i) necessary on grounds falling within subsection (3), or

    (ii) necessary for the purpose of securing the effective exercise or proper performance by any public authority of any statutory power or statutory duty,

(c) that the imposition of such a requirement is proportionate to what is sought to be achieved by its imposition, and

(d) that it is not reasonably practicable for the person with the appropriate permission to obtain possession of the protected information in an intelligible form without the giving of a notice under this section,

the person with that permission may, by notice to the person whom he believes to have possession of the key, impose a disclosure requirement in respect of the protected information.

(3) A disclosure requirement in respect of any protected information is necessary on grounds falling within this subsection if it is necessary—

(a) in the interests of national security;

(b) for the purpose of preventing or detecting crime; or

(c) in the interests of the economic well-being of the United Kingdom.

(4) A notice under this section imposing a disclosure requirement in respect of any protected information—

(a) must be given in writing or (if not in writing) must be given in a manner that produces a record of its having been given;

(b) must describe the protected information to which the notice relates;

(c) must specify the matters falling within subsection (2)(b)(i) or (ii) by reference to which the notice is given;

(d) must specify the office, rank or position held by the person giving it;

(e) must specify the office, rank or position of the person who for the purposes of Schedule 2 granted permission for the giving of the notice or (if the person giving the notice was entitled to give it without another person's permission) must set out the circumstances in which that entitlement arose;

(f) must specify the time by which the notice is to be complied with; and

(g) must set out the disclosure that is required by the notice and the form and manner in which it is to be made;

and the time specified for the purposes of paragraph (f) must allow a period for compliance which is reasonable in all the circumstances.

(5) Where it appears to a person with the appropriate permission—

(a) that more than one person is in possession of the key to any protected information,

(b) that any of those persons is in possession of that key in his capacity as an officer or employee of any body corporate, and

(c) that another of those persons is the body corporate itself or another officer or employee of the body corporate,

a notice under this section shall not be given, by reference to his possession of the key, to any officer or employee of the body corporate unless he is a senior officer of the body corporate or it appears to the person giving the notice that there is no senior officer of the body corporate and (in the case of an employee) no more senior employee of the body corporate to whom it is reasonably practicable to give the notice.

(6) Where it appears to a person with the appropriate permission—

(a) that more than one person is in possession of the key to any protected information,

(b) that any of those persons is in possession of that key in his capacity as an employee of a firm, and

(c) that another of those persons is the firm itself or a partner of the firm,

a notice under this section shall not be given, by reference to his possession of the key, to any employee of the firm unless it appears to the person giving the notice that there is neither a partner of the firm nor a more senior employee of the firm to whom it is reasonably practicable to give the notice.

(7) Subsections (5) and (6) shall not apply to the extent that there are special circumstances of the case that mean that the purposes for which the notice is given would be defeated, in whole or in part, if the notice were given to the person to whom it would otherwise be required to be given by those subsections.

(8) A notice under this section shall not require the making of any disclosure to any person other than—

(a) the person giving the notice; or

(b) such other person as may be specified in or otherwise identified by, or in accordance with, the provisions of the notice.

(9) A notice under this section shall not require the disclosure of any key which—

(a) is intended to be used for the purpose only of generating electronic signatures; and

(b) has not in fact been used for any other purpose.

(10) In this section "senior officer", in relation to a body corporate, means a director, manager, secretary or other similar officer of the body corporate; and for this purpose "director", in relation to a body corporate whose affairs are managed by its members, means a member of the body corporate.

(11) Schedule 2 (definition of the appropriate permission) shall have effect.

Effect of notice imposing disclosure requirement

50.—(1) Subject to the following provisions of this section, the effect of a section 49 notice imposing a disclosure requirement in respect of any protected information on a person who is in possession at a relevant time of both the protected information and a means of obtaining access to the information and of disclosing it in an intelligible form is that he—

(a) shall be entitled to use any key in his possession to obtain access to the information or to put it into an intelligible form; and

(b) shall be required, in accordance with the notice imposing the requirement, to make a disclosure of the information in an intelligible form.

(2) A person subject to a requirement under subsection (1)(b) to make a disclosure of any information in an intelligible form shall be taken to have complied with that requirement if—

(a) he makes, instead, a disclosure of any key to the protected information that is in his possession; and

    (b) that disclosure is made, in accordance with the notice imposing the requirement, to the person to whom, and by the time by which, he was required to provide the information in that form.

    (3) Where, in a case in which a disclosure requirement in respect of any protected information is imposed on any person by a section 49 notice—

    (a) that person is not in possession of the information,

    (b) that person is incapable, without the use of a key that is not in his possession, of obtaining access to the information and of disclosing it in an intelligible form, or

    (c) the notice states, in pursuance of a direction under section 51, that it can be complied with only by the disclosure of a key to the information,

the effect of imposing that disclosure requirement on that person is that he shall be required, in accordance with the notice imposing the requirement, to make a disclosure of any key to the protected information that is in his possession at a relevant time.

    (4) Subsections (5) to (7) apply where a person ("the person given notice")—

    (a) is entitled or obliged to disclose a key to protected information for the purpose of complying with any disclosure requirement imposed by a section 49 notice; and

    (b) is in possession of more than one key to that information.

    (5) It shall not be necessary, for the purpose of complying with the requirement, for the person given notice to make a disclosure of any keys in addition to those the disclosure of which is, alone, sufficient to enable the person to whom they are disclosed to obtain access to the information and to put it into an intelligible form.

    (6) Where—

    (a) subsection (5) allows the person given notice to comply with a requirement without disclosing all of the keys in his possession, and

    (b) there are different keys, or combinations of keys, in the possession of that person the disclosure of which would, under that subsection, constitute compliance,

the person given notice may select which of the keys, or combination of keys, to disclose for the purpose of complying with that requirement in accordance with that subsection.

    (7) Subject to subsections (5) and (6), the person given notice shall not be taken to have complied with the disclosure requirement by the disclosure of a key unless he has disclosed every key to the protected information that is in his possession at a relevant time.

    (8) Where, in a case in which a disclosure requirement in respect of any protected information is imposed on any person by a section 49 notice—

    (a) that person has been in possession of the key to that information but is no longer in possession of it,

    (b) if he had continued to have the key in his possession, he would have been required by virtue of the giving of the notice to disclose it, and

    (c) he is in possession, at a relevant time, of information to which subsection (9) applies, the effect of imposing that disclosure requirement on that person is that he shall be required, in accordance with the notice imposing the requirement, to disclose all such information to which subsection (9) applies as is in his possession and as he may be required, in accordance with that notice, to disclose by the person to whom he would have been required to disclose the key.

    (9) This subsection applies to any information that would facilitate the obtaining or discovery of the key or the putting of the protected information into an intelligible form.

    (10) In this section "relevant time", in relation to a disclosure requirement imposed by a section 49 notice, means the time of the giving of the notice or

any subsequent time before the time by which the requirement falls to be complied with.

Cases in which key required

51.—(1) A section 49 notice imposing a disclosure requirement in respect of any protected information shall not contain a statement for the purposes of section 50(3)(c) unless—

(a) the person who for the purposes of Schedule 2 granted the permission for the giving of the notice in relation to that information, or

(b) any person whose permission for the giving of a such a notice in relation to that information would constitute the appropriate permission under that Schedule,

has given a direction that the requirement can be complied with only by the disclosure of the key itself.

(2) A direction for the purposes of subsection (1) by the police, the customs and excise or a member of Her Majesty's forces shall not be given—

(a) in the case of a direction by the police or by a member of Her Majesty's forces who is a member of a police force, except by or with the permission of a chief officer of police;

(b) in the case of a direction by the customs and excise, except by or with the permission of the Commissioners of Customs and Excise; or

(c) in the case of a direction by a member of Her Majesty's forces who is not a member of a police force, except by or with the permission of a person of or above the rank of brigadier or its equivalent.

(3) A permission given for the purposes of subsection (2) by a chief officer of police, the Commissioners of Customs and Excise or a person of or above any such rank as is mentioned in paragraph (c) of that subsection must be given expressly in relation to the direction in question.

(4) A person shall not give a direction for the purposes of subsection (1) unless he believes—

(a) that there are special circumstances of the case which mean that the purposes for which it was believed necessary to impose the requirement in question would be defeated, in whole or in part, if the direction were not given; and

(b) that the giving of the direction is proportionate to what is sought to be achieved by prohibiting any compliance with the requirement in question otherwise than by the disclosure of the key itself.

(5) The matters to be taken into account in considering whether the requirement of subsection (4)(b) is satisfied in the case of any direction shall include—

(a) the extent and nature of any protected information, in addition to the protected information in respect of which the disclosure requirement is imposed, to which the key is also a key; and

(b) any adverse effect that the giving of the direction might have on a business carried on by the person on whom the disclosure requirement is imposed.

(6) Where a direction for the purposes of subsection (1) is given by a chief officer of police, by the Commissioners of Customs and Excise or by a member of Her Majesty's forces, the person giving the direction shall give a notification that he has done so—

(a) in a case where the direction is given—

(i) by a member of Her Majesty's forces who is not a member of a police force, and

(ii) otherwise than in connection with activities of members of Her Majesty's forces in Northern Ireland,

to the Intelligences Services Commissioner; and

(b) in any other case, to the Chief Surveillance Commissioner.

(7) A notification under subsection (6)—

   (a) must be given not more than seven days after the day of the giving of the direction to which it relates; and

   (b) may be given either in writing or by being transmitted to the Commissioner in question by electronic means.

Contributions to costs

Arrangements for payments for disclosure

52.—(1) It shall be the duty of the Secretary of State to ensure that such arrangements are in force as he thinks appropriate for requiring or authorising, in such cases as he thinks fit, the making to persons to whom section 49 notices are given of appropriate contributions towards the costs incurred by them in complying with such notices.

(2) For the purpose of complying with his duty under this section, the Secretary of State may make arrangements for payments to be made out of money provided by Parliament.

Offences

Failure to comply with a notice

53.—(1) A person to whom a section 49 notice has been given is guilty of an offence if he knowingly fails, in accordance with the notice, to make the disclosure required by virtue of the giving of the notice.

(2) In proceedings against any person for an offence under this section, if it is shown that that person was in possession of a key to any protected information at any time before the time of the giving of the section 49 notice, that person shall be taken for the purposes of those proceedings to have continued to be in possession of that key at all subsequent times, unless it is shown that the key was not in his possession after the giving of the notice and before the time by which he was required to disclose it.(3) For the purposes of this section a person shall be taken to have shown that he was not in possession of a key to protected information at a particular time if—

   (a) sufficient evidence of that fact is adduced to raise an issue with respect to it; and

   (b) the contrary is not proved beyond a reasonable doubt.

(4) In proceedings against any person for an offence under this section it shall be a defence for that person to show—

   (a) that it was not reasonably practicable for him to make the disclosure required by virtue of the giving of the section 49 notice before the time by which he was required, in accordance with that notice, to make it; but

   (b) that he did make that disclosure as soon after that time as it was reasonably practicable for him to do so.

(5) A person guilty of an offence under this section shall be liable—

   (a) on conviction on indictment, to imprisonment for a term not exceeding two years or to a fine, or to both;

   (b) on summary conviction, to imprisonment for a term not exceeding six months or to a fine not exceeding the statutory maximum, or to both.

Tipping-off

54.—(1) This section applies where a section 49 notice contains a provision requiring—

   (a) the person to whom the notice is given, and

   (b) every other person who becomes aware of it or of its contents,

to keep secret the giving of the notice, its contents and the things done in pursuance of it.

(2) A requirement to keep anything secret shall not be included in a section 49 notice except where—

(a) it is included with the consent of the person who for the purposes of Schedule 2 granted the permission for the giving of the notice; or

(b) the person who gives the notice is himself a person whose permission for the giving of such a notice in relation to the information in question would have constituted appropriate permission under that Schedule.

(3) A section 49 notice shall not contain a requirement to keep anything secret except where the protected information to which it relates—

(a) has come into the possession of the police, the customs and excise or any of the intelligence services, or

(b) is likely to come into the possession of the police, the customs and excise or any of the intelligence services,

by means which it is reasonable, in order to maintain the effectiveness of any investigation or operation or of investigatory techniques generally, or in the interests of the safety or well-being of any person, to keep secret from a particular person.

(4) A person who makes a disclosure to any other person of anything that he is required by a section 49 notice to keep secret shall be guilty of an offence and liable—

(a) on conviction on indictment, to imprisonment for a term not exceeding five years or to a fine, or to both;

(b) on summary conviction, to imprisonment for a term not exceeding six months or to a fine not exceeding the statutory maximum, or to both.

(5) In proceedings against any person for an offence under this section in respect of any disclosure, it shall be a defence for that person to show that—

(a) the disclosure was effected entirely by the operation of software designed to indicate when a key to protected information has ceased to be secure; and

(b) that person could not reasonably have been expected to take steps, after being given the notice or (as the case may be) becoming aware of it or of its contents, to prevent the disclosure.

(6) In proceedings against any person for an offence under this section in respect of any disclosure, it shall be a defence for that person to show that—

(a) the disclosure was made by or to a professional legal adviser in connection with the giving, by the adviser to any client of his, of advice about the effect of provisions of this Part; and

(b) the person to whom or, as the case may be, by whom it was made was the client or a representative of the client.

(7) In proceedings against any person for an offence under this section in respect of any disclosure, it shall be a defence for that person to show that the disclosure was made by a legal adviser—

(a) in contemplation of, or in connection with, any legal proceedings; and

(b) for the purposes of those proceedings.

(8) Neither subsection (6) nor subsection (7) applies in the case of a disclosure made with a view to furthering any criminal purpose.

(9) In proceedings against any person for an offence under this section in respect of any disclosure, it shall be a defence for that person to show that the disclosure was confined to a disclosure made to a relevant Commissioner or authorised—

(a) by such a Commissioner;

(b) by the terms of the notice;

(c) by or on behalf of the person who gave the notice; or

(d) by or on behalf of a person who—

(i) is in lawful possession of the protected information to which the notice relates; and

    (ii) came into possession of that information as mentioned in section 49(1).

    (10) In proceedings for an offence under this section against a person other than the person to whom the notice was given, it shall be a defence for the person against whom the proceedings are brought to show that he neither knew nor had reasonable grounds for suspecting that the notice contained a requirement to keep secret what was disclosed.

    (11) In this section "relevant Commissioner" means the Interception of Communications Commissioner, the Intelligence Services Commissioner or any Surveillance Commissioner or Assistant Surveillance Commissioner.

Safeguards

General duties of specified authorities

    55.—(1) This section applies to—

    (a) the Secretary of State and every other Minister of the Crown in charge of a government department;

    (b) every chief officer of police;

    (c) the Commissioners of Customs and Excise; and

    (d) every person whose officers or employees include persons with duties that involve the giving of section 49 notices.

    (2) It shall be the duty of each of the persons to whom this section applies to ensure that such arrangements are in force, in relation to persons under his control who by virtue of this Part obtain possession of keys to protected information, as he considers necessary for securing—

    (a) that a key disclosed in pursuance of a section 49 notice is used for obtaining access to, or putting into an intelligible form, only protected information in relation to which power to give such a notice was exercised or could have been exercised if the key had not already been disclosed;

    (b) that the uses to which a key so disclosed is put are reasonable having regard both to the uses to which the person using the key is entitled to put any protected information to which it relates and to the other circumstances of the case;

    (c) that, having regard to those matters, the use and any retention of the key are proportionate to what is sought to be achieved by its use or retention;

    (d) that the requirements of subsection (3) are satisfied in relation to any key disclosed in pursuance of a section 49 notice;

    (e) that, for the purpose of ensuring that those requirements are satisfied, any key so disclosed is stored, for so long as it is retained, in a secure manner;

    (f) that all records of a key so disclosed (if not destroyed earlier) are destroyed as soon as the key is no longer needed for the purpose of enabling protected information to be put into an intelligible form.

    (3) The requirements of this subsection are satisfied in relation to any key disclosed in pursuance of a section 49 notice if—

    (a) the number of persons to whom the key is disclosed or otherwise made available, and

    (b) the number of copies made of the key,

are each limited to the minimum that is necessary for the purpose of enabling protected information to be put into an intelligible form.

    (4) Subject to subsection (5), where any relevant person incurs any loss or damage in consequence of—

    (a) any breach by a person to whom this section applies of the duty imposed on him by subsection (2), or

(b) any contravention by any person whatever of arrangements made in pursuance of that subsection in relation to persons under the control of a person to whom this section applies,

the breach or contravention shall be actionable against the person to whom this section applies at the suit or instance of the relevant person.

(5) A person is a relevant person for the purposes of subsection (4) if he is—

(a) a person who has made a disclosure in pursuance of a section 49 notice; or

(b) a person whose protected information or key has been disclosed in pursuance of such a notice;

and loss or damage shall be taken into account for the purposes of that subsection to the extent only that it relates to the disclosure of particular protected information or a particular key which, in the case of a person falling with paragraph (b), must be his information or key.

(6) For the purposes of subsection (5)—

(a) information belongs to a person if he has any right that would be infringed by an unauthorised disclosure of the information; and

(b) a key belongs to a person if it is a key to information that belongs to him or he has any right that would be infringed by an unauthorised disclosure of the key.

(7) In any proceedings brought by virtue of subsection (4), it shall be the duty of the court to have regard to any opinion with respect to the matters to which the proceedings relate that is or has been given by a relevant Commissioner.

(8) In this section "relevant Commissioner" means the Interception of Communications Commissioner, the Intelligence Services Commissioner, the Investigatory Powers Commissioner for Northern Ireland or any Surveillance Commissioner or Assistant Surveillance Commissioner.

Interpretation of Part III

56.—(1) In this Part—

"chief officer of police" means any of the following—

(a) the chief constable of a police force maintained under or by virtue of section 2 of the Police Act 1996 or section 1 of the Police (Scotland) Act 1967;

(b) the Commissioner of Police of the Metropolis;

(c) the Commissioner of Police for the City of London;

(d) the Chief Constable of the Royal Ulster Constabulary;

(e) the Chief Constable of the Ministry of Defence Police;

(f) the Provost Marshal of the Royal Navy Regulating Branch;

(g) the Provost Marshal of the Royal Military Police;

(h) the Provost Marshal of the Royal Air Force Police;

(i) the Chief Constable of the British Transport Police;

(j) the Director General of the National Criminal Intelligence Service;

(k) the Director General of the National Crime Squad;

"the customs and excise" means the Commissioners of Customs and Excise or any customs officer;

"electronic signature" means anything in electronic form which—

(a) is incorporated into, or otherwise logically associated with, any electronic communication or other electronic data;

(b) is generated by the signatory or other source of the communication or data; and

(c) is used for the purpose of facilitating, by means of a link between the signatory or other source and the communication or data, the establishment of the authenticity of the communication or data, the establishment of its integrity, or both;

"key", in relation to any electronic data, means any key, code, password, algorithm or other data the use of which (with or without other keys)—

    (a) allows access to the electronic data, or

    (b) facilitates the putting of the data into an intelligible form;

"the police" means—

    (a) any constable;

    (b) the Commissioner of Police of the Metropolis or any Assistant Commissioner of Police of the Metropolis; or

    (c) the Commissioner of Police for the City of London;

"protected information" means any electronic data which, without the key to the data—

    (a) cannot, or cannot readily, be accessed, or

    (b) cannot, or cannot readily, be put into an intelligible form;

"section 49 notice" means a notice under section 49;

"warrant" includes any authorisation, notice or other instrument (however described) conferring a power of the same description as may, in other cases, be conferred by a warrant.

(2) References in this Part to a person's having information (including a key to protected information) in his possession include references—

    (a) to its being in the possession of a person who is under his control so far as that information is concerned;

    (b) to his having an immediate right of access to it, or an immediate right to have it transmitted or otherwise supplied to him; and

    (c) to its being, or being contained in, anything which he or a person under his control is entitled, in exercise of any statutory power and without otherwise taking possession of it, to detain, inspect or search.

(3) References in this Part to something's being intelligible or being put into an intelligible form include references to its being in the condition in which it was before an encryption or similar process was applied to it or, as the case may be, to its being restored to that condition.

(4) In this section—

    (a) references to the authenticity of any communication or data are references to any one or more of the following—

        (i) whether the communication or data comes from a particular person or other source;

        (ii) whether it is accurately timed and dated;

        (iii) whether it is intended to have legal effect;

and

    (b) references to the integrity of any communication or data are references to whether there has been any tampering with or other modification of the communication or data.

PART IV

SCRUTINY ETC. OF INVESTIGATORY POWERS AND OF THE FUNCTIONS OF THE INTELLIGENCE SERVICES

Commissioners

Interception of Communications Commissioner

57.—(1) The Prime Minister shall appoint a Commissioner to be known as the Interception of Communications Commissioner.

(2) Subject to subsection (4), the Interception of Communications Commissioner shall keep under review—

(a) the exercise and performance by the Secretary of State of the powers and duties conferred or imposed on him by or under sections 1 to 11;

(b) the exercise and performance, by the persons on whom they are conferred or imposed, of the powers and duties conferred or imposed by or under Chapter II of Part I;

(c) the exercise and performance by the Secretary of State in relation to information obtained under Part I of the powers and duties conferred or imposed on him by or under Part III; and

(d) the adequacy of the arrangements by virtue of which—

   (i) the duty which is imposed on the Secretary of State by section 15, and

   (ii) so far as applicable to information obtained under Part I, the duties imposed by section 55,

   are sought to be discharged.

(3) The Interception of Communications Commissioner shall give the Tribunal all such assistance (including his opinion as to any issue falling to be determined by the Tribunal) as the Tribunal may require—

(a) in connection with the investigation of any matter by the Tribunal; or

(b) otherwise for the purposes of the Tribunal's consideration or determination of any matter.

(4) It shall not be the function of the Interception of Communications Commissioner to keep under review the exercise of any power of the Secretary of State to make, amend or revoke any subordinate legislation.

(5) A person shall not be appointed under this section as the Interception of Communications Commissioner unless he holds or has held a high judicial office (within the meaning of the Appellate Jurisdiction Act 1876).

(6) The Interception of Communications Commissioner shall hold office in accordance with the terms of his appointment; and there shall be paid to him out of money provided by Parliament such allowances as the Treasury may determine.

(7) The Secretary of State, after consultation with the Interception of Communications Commissioner, shall—

(a) make such technical facilities available to the Commissioner, and

(b) subject to the approval of the Treasury as to numbers, provide the Commissioner with such staff,

as are sufficient to secure that the Commissioner is able properly to carry out his functions.

(8) On the coming into force of this section the Commissioner holding office as the Commissioner under section 8 of the Interception of Communications Act 1985 shall take and hold office as the Interception of Communications Commissioner as if appointed under this Act—

(a) for the unexpired period of his term of office under that Act; and

(b) otherwise, on the terms of his appointment under that Act.

Co-operation with and reports by s. 57 Commissioner

58.—(1) It shall be the duty of—

(a) every person holding office under the Crown,

(b) every member of the National Criminal Intelligence Service,

(c) every member of the National Crime Squad,

(d) every person employed by or for the purposes of a police force,

(e) every person required for the purposes of section 11 to provide assistance with giving effect to an interception warrant,

(f) every person on whom an obligation to take any steps has been imposed under section 12,

    (g) every person by or to whom an authorisation under section 22(3) has been granted,

    (h) every person to whom a notice under section 22(4) has been given,

    (i) every person to whom a notice under section 49 has been given in relation to any information obtained under Part I, and

    (j) every person who is or has been employed for the purposes of any business of a person falling within paragraph (e), (f), (h) or (i),

to disclose or provide to the Interception of Communications Commissioner all such documents and information as he may require for the purpose of enabling him to carry out his functions under section 57.

(2) If it at any time appears to the Interception of Communications Commissioner—

    (a) that there has been a contravention of the provisions of this Act in relation to any matter with which that Commissioner is concerned, and

    (b) that the contravention has not been the subject of a report made to the Prime Minister by the Tribunal,

he shall make a report to the Prime Minister with respect to that contravention.

(3) If it at any time appears to the Interception of Communications Commissioner that any arrangements by reference to which the duties imposed by sections 15 and 55 have sought to be discharged have proved inadequate in relation to any matter with which the Commissioner is concerned, he shall make a report to the Prime Minister with respect to those arrangements.

(4) As soon as practicable after the end of each calendar year, the Interception of Communications Commissioner shall make a report to the Prime Minister with respect to the carrying out of that Commissioner's functions.

(5) The Interception of Communications Commissioner may also, at any time, make any such other report to the Prime Minister on any matter relating to the carrying out of the Commissioner's functions as the Commissioner thinks fit.

(6) The Prime Minister shall lay before each House of Parliament a copy of every annual report made by the Interception of Communications Commissioner under subsection (4), together with a statement as to whether any matter has been excluded from that copy in pursuance of subsection (7).

(7) If it appears to the Prime Minister, after consultation with the Interception of Communications Commissioner, that the publication of any matter in an annual report would be contrary to the public interest or prejudicial to—

    (a) national security,

    (b) the prevention or detection of serious crime,

    (c) the economic well-being of the United Kingdom, or

    (d) the continued discharge of the functions of any public authority whose activities include activities that are subject to review by that Commissioner,

the Prime Minister may exclude that matter from the copy of the report as laid before each House of Parliament.

Intelligence Services Commissioner

59.—(1) The Prime Minister shall appoint a Commissioner to be known as the Intelligence Services Commissioner.

(2) Subject to subsection (4), the Intelligence Services Commissioner shall keep under review, so far as they are not required to be kept under review by the Interception of Communications Commissioner—

(a) the exercise by the Secretary of State of his powers under sections 5 to 7 of the Intelligence Services Act 1994 (warrants for interference with wireless telegraphy, entry and interference with property etc.);

(b) the exercise and performance by the Secretary of State, in connection with or in relation to—

    (i) the activities of the intelligence services, and

    (ii) the activities in places other than Northern Ireland of the officials of the Ministry of Defence and of members of Her Majesty's forces,

of the powers and duties conferred or imposed on him by Parts II and III of this Act;

(c) the exercise and performance by members of the intelligence services of the powers and duties conferred or imposed on them by or under Parts II and III of this Act;

(d) the exercise and performance in places other than Northern Ireland, by officials of the Ministry of Defence and by members of Her Majesty's forces, of the powers and duties conferred or imposed on such officials or members of Her Majesty's forces by or under Parts II and III; and

(e) the adequacy of the arrangements by virtue of which the duty imposed by section 55 is sought to be discharged—

    (i) in relation to the members of the intelligence services; and

    (ii) in connection with any of their activities in places other than Northern Ireland, in relation to officials of the Ministry of Defence and members of Her Majesty's forces.

(3) The Intelligence Services Commissioner shall give the Tribunal all such assistance (including his opinion as to any issue falling to be determined by the Tribunal) as the Tribunal may require—

(a) in connection with the investigation of any matter by the Tribunal; or

(b) otherwise for the purposes of the Tribunal's consideration or determination of any matter.

(4) It shall not be the function of the Intelligence Services Commissioner to keep under review the exercise of any power of the Secretary of State to make, amend or revoke any subordinate legislation.

(5) A person shall not be appointed under this section as the Intelligence Services Commissioner unless he holds or has held a high judicial office (within the meaning of the Appellate Jurisdiction Act 1876).

(6) The Intelligence Services Commissioner shall hold office in accordance with the terms of his appointment; and there shall be paid to him out of money provided by Parliament such allowances as the Treasury may determine.

(7) The Secretary of State shall, after consultation with the Intelligence Services Commissioner and subject to the approval of the Treasury as to numbers, provide him with such staff as the Secretary of State considers necessary for the carrying out of the Commissioner's functions.

(8) Section 4 of the Security Service Act 1989 and section 8 of the Intelligence Services Act 1994 (Commissioners for the purposes of those Acts) shall cease to have effect.

(9) On the coming into force of this section the Commissioner holding office as the Commissioner under section 8 of the Intelligence Services Act 1994 shall take and hold office as the Intelligence Services Commissioner as if appointed under this Act—

(a) for the unexpired period of his term of office under that Act; and

(b) otherwise, on the terms of his appointment under that Act.

(10) Subsection (7) of section 41 shall apply for the purposes of this section as it applies for the purposes of that section.

Co-operation with and reports by s. 59 Commissioner

60.—(1) It shall be the duty of—
(a) every member of an intelligence service,
(b) every official of the department of the Secretary of State, and
(c) every member of Her Majesty's forces,
to disclose or provide to the Intelligence Services Commissioner all such documents and information as he may require for the purpose of enabling him to carry out his functions under section 59.

(2) As soon as practicable after the end of each calendar year, the Intelligence Services Commissioner shall make a report to the Prime Minister with respect to the carrying out of that Commissioner's functions.

(3) The Intelligence Services Commissioner may also, at any time, make any such other report to the Prime Minister on any matter relating to the carrying out of the Commissioner's functions as the Commissioner thinks fit.

(4) The Prime Minister shall lay before each House of Parliament a copy of every annual report made by the Intelligence Services Commissioner under subsection (2), together with a statement as to whether any matter has been excluded from that copy in pursuance of subsection (5).

(5) If it appears to the Prime Minister, after consultation with the Intelligence Services Commissioner, that the publication of any matter in an annual report would be contrary to the public interest or prejudicial to—
(a) national security,
(b) the prevention or detection of serious crime,
(c) the economic well-being of the United Kingdom, or
(d) the continued discharge of the functions of any public authority whose activities include activities that are subject to review by that Commissioner,
the Prime Minister may exclude that matter from the copy of the report as laid before each House of Parliament.

(6) Subsection (7) of section 41 shall apply for the purposes of this section as it applies for the purposes of that section.

Investigatory Powers Commissioner for Northern Ireland

61.—(1) The Prime Minister, after consultation with the First Minister and deputy First Minister in Northern Ireland, shall appoint a Commissioner to be known as the Investigatory Powers Commissioner for Northern Ireland.

(2) The Investigatory Powers Commissioner for Northern Ireland shall keep under review the exercise and performance in Northern Ireland, by the persons on whom they are conferred or imposed, of any powers or duties under Part II which are conferred or imposed by virtue of an order under section 30 made by the Office of the First Minister and deputy First Minister in Northern Ireland.

(3) The Investigatory Powers Commissioner for Northern Ireland shall give the Tribunal all such assistance (including his opinion as to any issue falling to be determined by the Tribunal) as the Tribunal may require—
(a) in connection with the investigation of any matter by the Tribunal; or
(b) otherwise for the purposes of the Tribunal's consideration or determination of any matter.

(4) It shall be the duty of—
(a) every person by whom, or on whose application, there has been given or granted any authorisation the function of giving or granting which is subject to review by the Investigatory Powers Commissioner for Northern Ireland,
(b) every person who has engaged in conduct with the authority of such an authorisation,

(c) every person who holds or has held any office, rank or position with the same public authority as a person falling within paragraph (a), and

(d) every person who holds or has held any office, rank or position with any public authority for whose benefit (within the meaning of Part II) activities which are or may be subject to any such review have been or may be carried out,

to disclose or provide to that Commissioner all such documents and information as he may require for the purpose of enabling him to carry out his functions.

(5) As soon as practicable after the end of each calendar year, the Investigatory Powers Commissioner for Northern Ireland shall make a report to the First Minister and deputy First Minister in Northern Ireland with respect to the carrying out of that Commissioner's functions.

(6) The First Minister and deputy First Minister in Northern Ireland shall lay before the Northern Ireland Assembly a copy of every annual report made by the Investigatory Powers Commissioner for Northern Ireland under subsection (5), together with a statement as to whether any matter has been excluded from that copy in pursuance of subsection (7).

(7) If it appears to the First Minister and deputy First Minister in Northern Ireland, after consultation with the Investigatory Powers Commissioner for Northern Ireland, that the publication of any matter in an annual report would be contrary to the public interest or prejudicial to—

(a) the prevention or detection of serious crime, or

(b) the continued discharge of the functions of any public authority whose activities include activities that are subject to review by that Commissioner,

they may exclude that matter from the copy of the report as laid before the Northern Ireland Assembly.

(8) A person shall not be appointed under this section as the Investigatory Powers Commissioner for Northern Ireland unless he holds or has held office in Northern Ireland—

(a) in any capacity in which he is or was the holder of a high judicial office (within the meaning of the Appellate Jurisdiction Act 1876); or

(b) as a county court judge.

(9) The Investigatory Powers Commissioner for Northern Ireland shall hold office in accordance with the terms of his appointment; and there shall be paid to him out of the Consolidated Fund of Northern Ireland such allowances as the Department of Finance and Personnel may determine.

(10) The First Minister and deputy First Minister in Northern Ireland shall, after consultation with the Investigatory Powers Commissioner for Northern Ireland, provide him with such staff as they consider necessary for the carrying out of his functions.

Additional functions of Chief Surveillance Commissioner

62.—(1) The Chief Surveillance Commissioner shall (in addition to his functions under the Police Act 1997) keep under review, so far as they are not required to be kept under review by the Interception of Communications Commissioner, the Intelligence Services Commissioner or the Investigatory Powers Commissioner for Northern Ireland—

(a) the exercise and performance, by the persons on whom they are conferred or imposed, of the powers and duties conferred or imposed by or under Part II;

(b) the exercise and performance, by any person other than a judicial authority, of the powers and duties conferred or imposed, otherwise than with the permission of such an authority, by or under Part III; and

(c) the adequacy of the arrangements by virtue of which the duties imposed by section 55 are sought to be discharged in relation to persons whose conduct is subject to review under paragraph (b).

(2) It shall not by virtue of this section be the function of the Chief Surveillance Commissioner to keep under review the exercise of any power of the Secretary of State to make, amend or revoke any subordinate legislation.

(3) In this section "judicial authority" means—

(a) any judge of the High Court or of the Crown Court or any Circuit Judge;

(b) any judge of the High Court of Justiciary or any sheriff;

(c) any justice of the peace;

(d) any county court judge or resident magistrate in Northern Ireland;

(e) any person holding any such judicial office as entitles him to exercise the jurisdiction of a judge of the Crown Court or of a justice of the peace.

Assistant Surveillance Commissioners

63.—(1) The Prime Minister may, after consultation with the Chief Surveillance Commissioner as to numbers, appoint as Assistant Surveillance Commissioners such number of persons as the Prime Minister considers necessary (in addition to the ordinary Surveillance Commissioners) for the purpose of providing the Chief Surveillance Commissioner with assistance under this section.

(2) A person shall not be appointed as an Assistant Surveillance Commissioner unless he holds or has held office as—

(a) a judge of the Crown Court or a Circuit judge;

(b) a sheriff in Scotland; or

(c) a county court judge in Northern Ireland.

(3) The Chief Surveillance Commissioner may—

(a) require any ordinary Surveillance Commissioner or any Assistant Surveillance Commissioner to provide him with assistance in carrying out his functions under section 62(1); or

(b) require any Assistant Surveillance Commissioner to provide him with assistance in carrying out his equivalent functions under any Act of the Scottish Parliament in relation to any provisions of such an Act that are equivalent to those of Part II of this Act.

(4) The assistance that may be provided under this section includes—

(a) the conduct on behalf of the Chief Surveillance Commissioner of the review of any matter; and

(b) the making of a report to the Chief Surveillance Commissioner about the matter reviewed.

(5) Subsections (3) to (8) of section 91 of the Police Act 1997 (Commissioners) apply in relation to a person appointed under this section as they apply in relation to a person appointed under that section.

Delegation of Commissioners' functions

64.—(1) Anything authorised or required by or under any enactment or any provision of an Act of the Scottish Parliament to be done by a relevant Commissioner may be done by any member of the staff of that Commissioner who is authorised for the purpose (whether generally or specifically) by that Commissioner.

(2) In this section "relevant Commissioner" means the Interception of Communications Commissioner, the Intelligence Services Commissioner,

the Investigatory Powers Commissioner for Northern Ireland or any Surveillance Commissioner or Assistant Surveillance Commissioner.

The Tribunal

The Tribunal

65.—(1) There shall, for the purpose of exercising the jurisdiction conferred on them by this section, be a tribunal consisting of such number of members as Her Majesty may by Letters Patent appoint.

(2) The jurisdiction of the Tribunal shall be—

(a) to be the only appropriate tribunal for the purposes of section 7 of the Human Rights Act 1998 in relation to any proceedings under subsection (1)(a) of that section (proceedings for actions incompatible with Convention rights) which fall within subsection (3) of this section;

(b) to consider and determine any complaints made to them which, in accordance with subsection (4), are complaints for which the Tribunal is the appropriate forum;

(c) to consider and determine any reference to them by any person that he has suffered detriment as a consequence of any prohibition or restriction, by virtue of section 17, on his relying in, or for the purposes of, any civil proceedings on any matter; and

(d) to hear and determine any other such proceedings falling within subsection (3) as may be allocated to them in accordance with provision made by the Secretary of State by order.

(3) Proceedings fall within this subsection if—

(a) they are proceedings against any of the intelligence services;

(b) they are proceedings against any other person in respect of any conduct, or proposed conduct, by or on behalf of any of those services;

(c) they are proceedings brought by virtue of section 55(4); or

(d) they are proceedings relating to the taking place in any challengeable circumstances of any conduct falling within subsection (5).

(4) The Tribunal is the appropriate forum for any complaint if it is a complaint by a person who is aggrieved by any conduct falling within subsection (5) which he believes—

(a) to have taken place in relation to him, to any of his property, to any communications sent by or to him, or intended for him, or to his use of any postal service, telecommunications service or telecommunication system; and

(b) to have taken place in challengeable circumstances or to have been carried out by or on behalf of any of the intelligence services.

(5) Subject to subsection (6), conduct falls within this subsection if (whenever it occurred) it is—

(a) conduct by or on behalf of any of the intelligence services;

(b) conduct for or in connection with the interception of communications in the course of their transmission by means of a postal service or telecommunication system;

(c) conduct to which Chapter II of Part I applies;

(d) conduct to which Part II applies;

(e) the giving of a notice under section 49 or any disclosure or use of a key to protected information;

(f) any entry on or interference with property or any interference with wireless telegraphy.

(6) For the purposes only of subsection (3), nothing mentioned in paragraph (d) or (f) of subsection (5) shall be treated as falling within that subsection unless it is conduct by or on behalf of a person holding any office, rank or position with—

(a) any of the intelligence services;
(b) any of Her Majesty's forces;
(c) any police force;
(d) the National Criminal Intelligence Service;
(e) the National Crime Squad; or
(f) the Commissioners of Customs and Excise;

and section 48(5) applies for the purposes of this subsection as it applies for the purposes of Part II.

(7) For the purposes of this section conduct takes place in challengeable circumstances if—

  (a) it takes place with the authority, or purported authority, of anything falling within subsection (8); or

  (b) the circumstances are such that (whether or not there is such authority) it would not have been appropriate for the conduct to take place without it, or at least without proper consideration having been given to whether such authority should be sought;

but conduct does not take place in challengeable circumstances to the extent that it is authorised by, or takes place with the permission of, a judicial authority.

(8) The following fall within this subsection—

  (a) an interception warrant or a warrant under the Interception of Communications Act 1985;

  (b) an authorisation or notice under Chapter II of Part I of this Act;

  (c) an authorisation under Part II of this Act or under any enactment contained in or made under an Act of the Scottish Parliament which makes provision equivalent to that made by that Part;

  (d) a permission for the purposes of Schedule 2 to this Act;

  (e) a notice under section 49 of this Act; or

  (f) an authorisation under section 93 of the Police Act 1997.

(9) Schedule 3 (which makes further provision in relation to the Tribunal) shall have effect.

(10) In this section—

  (a) references to a key and to protected information shall be construed in accordance with section 56;

  (b) references to the disclosure or use of a key to protected information taking place in relation to a person are references to such a disclosure or use taking place in a case in which that person has had possession of the key or of the protected information; and

  (c) references to the disclosure of a key to protected information include references to the making of any disclosure in an intelligible form (within the meaning of section 56) of protected information by a person who is or has been in possession of the key to that information;

and the reference in paragraph (b) to a person's having possession of a key or of protected information shall be construed in accordance with section 56.

(11) In this section "judicial authority" means—

  (a) any judge of the High Court or of the Crown Court or any Circuit Judge;

  (b) any judge of the High Court of Justiciary or any sheriff;

  (c) any justice of the peace;

  (d) any county court judge or resident magistrate in Northern Ireland;

  (e) any person holding any such judicial office as entitles him to exercise the jurisdiction of a judge of the Crown Court or of a justice of the peace.

Orders allocating proceedings to the Tribunal

66.—(1) An order under section 65(2)(d) allocating proceedings to the Tribunal—

(a) may provide for the Tribunal to exercise jurisdiction in relation to that matter to the exclusion of the jurisdiction of any court or tribunal; but

(b) if it does so provide, must contain provision conferring a power on the Tribunal, in the circumstances provided for in the order, to remit the proceedings to the court or tribunal which would have had jurisdiction apart from the order.

(2) In making any provision by an order under section 65(2)(d) the Secretary of State shall have regard, in particular, to—

(a) the need to secure that proceedings allocated to the Tribunal are properly heard and considered; and

(b) the need to secure that information is not disclosed to an extent, or in a manner, that is contrary to the public interest or prejudicial to national security, the prevention or detection of serious crime, the economic well-being of the United Kingdom or the continued discharge of the functions of any of the intelligence services.

(3) The Secretary of State shall not make an order under section 65(2)(d) unless a draft of the order has been laid before Parliament and approved by a resolution of each House.

Exercise of the Tribunal's jurisdiction

67.—(1) Subject to subsections (4) and (5), it shall be the duty of the Tribunal—

(a) to hear and determine any proceedings brought before them by virtue of section 65(2)(a) or (d); and

(b) to consider and determine any complaint or reference made to them by virtue of section 65(2)(b) or (c).

(2) Where the Tribunal hear any proceedings by virtue of section 65(2)(a), they shall apply the same principles for making their determination in those proceedings as would be applied by a court on an application for judicial review.

(3) Where the Tribunal consider a complaint made to them by virtue of section 65(2)(b), it shall be the duty of the Tribunal—

(a) to investigate whether the persons against whom any allegations are made in the complaint have engaged in relation to—

(i) the complainant,

(ii) any of his property,

(iii) any communications sent by or to him, or intended for him, or

(iv) his use of any postal service, telecommunications service or telecommunication system,

in any conduct falling within section 65(5);

(b) to investigate the authority (if any) for any conduct falling within section 65(5) which they find has been so engaged in; and

(c) in relation to the Tribunal's findings from their investigations, to determine the complaint by applying the same principles as would be applied by a court on an application for judicial review.

(4) The Tribunal shall not be under any duty to hear, consider or determine any proceedings, complaint or reference if it appears to them that the bringing of the proceedings or the making of the complaint or reference is frivolous or vexatious.

(5) Except where the Tribunal, having regard to all the circumstances, are satisfied that it is equitable to do so, they shall not consider or determine any complaint made by virtue of section 65(2)(b) if it is made more than one year after the taking place of the conduct to which it relates.

(6) Subject to any provision made by rules under section 69, where any proceedings have been brought before the Tribunal or any reference made

to the Tribunal, they shall have power to make such interim orders, pending their final determination, as they think fit.

(7) Subject to any provision made by rules under section 69, the Tribunal on determining any proceedings, complaint or reference shall have power to make any such award of compensation or other order as they think fit; and, without prejudice to the power to make rules under section 69(2)(h), the other orders that may be made by the Tribunal include—

    (a) an order quashing or cancelling any warrant or authorisation; and

    (b) an order requiring the destruction of any records of information which—

        (i) has been obtained in exercise of any power conferred by a warrant or authorisation; or

        (ii) is held by any public authority in relation to any person.

(8) Except to such extent as the Secretary of State may by order otherwise provide, determinations, awards, orders and other decisions of the Tribunal (including decisions as to whether they have jurisdiction) shall not be subject to appeal or be liable to be questioned in any court.

(9) It shall be the duty of the Secretary of State to secure that there is at all times an order under subsection (8) in force allowing for an appeal to a court against any exercise by the Tribunal of their jurisdiction under section 65(2)(c) or (d).

(10) The provision that may be contained in an order under subsection (8) may include—

    (a) provision for the establishment and membership of a tribunal or body to hear appeals;

    (b) the appointment of persons to that tribunal or body and provision about the remuneration and allowances to be payable to such persons and the expenses of the tribunal;

    (c) the conferring of jurisdiction to hear appeals on any existing court or tribunal; and

    (d) any such provision in relation to an appeal under the order as corresponds to provision that may be made by rules under section 69 in relation to proceedings before the Tribunal, or to complaints or references made to the Tribunal.

(11) The Secretary of State shall not make an order under subsection (8) unless a draft of the order has been laid before Parliament and approved by a resolution of each House.

(12) The Secretary of State shall consult the Scottish Ministers before making any order under subsection (8); and any such order shall be laid before the Scottish Parliament.

Tribunal procedure

68.—(1) Subject to any rules made under section 69, the Tribunal shall be entitled to determine their own procedure in relation to any proceedings, complaint or reference brought before or made to them.

(2) The Tribunal shall have power—

    (a) in connection with the investigation of any matter, or

    (b) otherwise for the purposes of the Tribunal's consideration or determination of any matter,

to require a relevant Commissioner appearing to the Tribunal to have functions in relation to the matter in question to provide the Tribunal with all such assistance (including that Commissioner's opinion as to any issue falling to be determined by the Tribunal) as the Tribunal think fit.

(3) Where the Tribunal hear or consider any proceedings, complaint or reference relating to any matter, they shall secure that every relevant

Commissioner appearing to them to have functions in relation to that matter—

  (a) is aware that the matter is the subject of proceedings, a complaint or a reference brought before or made to the Tribunal; and
  (b) is kept informed of any determination, award, order or other decision made by the Tribunal with respect to that matter.

(4) Where the Tribunal determine any proceedings, complaint or reference brought before or made to them, they shall give notice to the complainant which (subject to any rules made by virtue of section 69(2)(i)) shall be confined, as the case may be, to either—

  (a) a statement that they have made a determination in his favour; or
  (b) a statement that no determination has been made in his favour.

(5) Where—

  (a) the Tribunal make a determination in favour of any person by whom any proceedings have been brought before the Tribunal or by whom any complaint or reference has been made to the Tribunal, and
  (b) the determination relates to any act or omission by or on behalf of the Secretary of State or to conduct for which any warrant, authorisation or permission was issued, granted or given by the Secretary of State,

they shall make a report of their findings to the Prime Minister.

(6) It shall be the duty of the persons specified in subsection (7) to disclose or provide to the Tribunal all such documents and information as the Tribunal may require for the purpose of enabling them—

  (a) to exercise the jurisdiction conferred on them by or under section 65; or
  (b) otherwise to exercise or perform any power or duty conferred or imposed on them by or under this Act.

(7) Those persons are—

  (a) every person holding office under the Crown;
  (b) every member of the National Criminal Intelligence Service;
  (c) every member of the National Crime Squad;
  (d) every person employed by or for the purposes of a police force;
  (e) every person required for the purposes of section 11 to provide assistance with giving effect to an interception warrant;
  (f) every person on whom an obligation to take any steps has been imposed under section 12;
  (g) every person by or to whom an authorisation under section 22(3) has been granted;
  (h) every person to whom a notice under section 22(4) has been given;
  (i) every person by whom, or on whose application, there has been granted or given any authorisation under Part II of this Act or under Part III of the Police Act 1997;
  (j) every person who holds or has held any office, rank or position with the same public authority as a person falling within paragraph (i);
  (k) every person who has engaged in any conduct with the authority of an authorisation under section 22 or Part II of this Act or under Part III of the Police Act 1997;
  (l) every person who holds or has held any office, rank or position with a public authority for whose benefit any such authorisation has been or may be given;
  (m) every person to whom a notice under section 49 has been given; and
  (n) every person who is or has been employed for the purposes of any business of a person falling within paragraph (e), (f), (h) or (m).

(8) In this section "relevant Commissioner" means the Interception of Communications Commissioner, the Intelligence Services Commissioner, the Investigatory Powers Commissioner for Northern Ireland or any Surveillance Commissioner or Assistant Surveillance Commissioner.

Tribunal rules

69.—(1) The Secretary of State may make rules regulating—
(a) the exercise by the Tribunal of the jurisdiction conferred on them by or under section 65; and
(b) any matters preliminary or incidental to, or arising out of, the hearing or consideration of any proceedings, complaint or reference brought before or made to the Tribunal.

(2) Without prejudice to the generality of subsection (1), rules under this section may—
(a) enable the jurisdiction of the Tribunal to be exercised at any place in the United Kingdom by any two or more members of the Tribunal designated for the purpose by the President of the Tribunal;
(b) enable different members of the Tribunal to carry out functions in relation to different complaints at the same time;
(c) prescribe the form and manner in which proceedings are to be brought before the Tribunal or a complaint or reference is to be made to the Tribunal;
(d) require persons bringing proceedings or making complaints or references to take such preliminary steps, and to make such disclosures, as may be specified in the rules for the purpose of facilitating a determination of whether—
   (i) the bringing of the proceedings, or
   (ii) the making of the complaint or reference,
   is frivolous or vexatious;
(e) make provision about the determination of any question as to whether a person by whom—
   (i) any proceedings have been brought before the Tribunal, or
   (ii) any complaint or reference has been made to the Tribunal,
   is a person with a right to bring those proceedings or make that complaint or reference;
(f) prescribe the forms of hearing or consideration to be adopted by the Tribunal in relation to particular proceedings, complaints or references (including a form that requires any proceedings brought before the Tribunal to be disposed of as if they were a complaint or reference made to the Tribunal);
(g) prescribe the practice and procedure to be followed on, or in connection with, the hearing or consideration of any proceedings, complaint or reference (including, where applicable, the mode and burden of proof and the admissibility of evidence);
(h) prescribe orders that may be made by the Tribunal under section 67(6) or (7);
(i) require information about any determination, award, order or other decision made by the Tribunal in relation to any proceedings, complaint or reference to be provided (in addition to any statement under section 68(4)) to the person who brought the proceedings or made the complaint or reference, or to the person representing his interests.

(3) Rules under this section in relation to the hearing or consideration of any matter by the Tribunal may provide—
(a) for a person who has brought any proceedings before or made any complaint or reference to the Tribunal to have the right to be legally represented;
(b) for the manner in which the interests of a person who has brought any proceedings before or made any complaint or reference to the Tribunal are otherwise to be represented;
(c) for the appointment in accordance with the rules, by such person as may be determined in accordance with the rules, of a person to

represent those interests in the case of any proceedings, complaint or reference.

(4) The power to make rules under this section includes power to make rules—

(a) enabling or requiring the Tribunal to hear or consider any proceedings, complaint or reference without the person who brought the proceedings or made the complaint or reference having been given full particulars of the reasons for any conduct which is the subject of the proceedings, complaint or reference;

(b) enabling or requiring the Tribunal to take any steps in exercise of their jurisdiction in the absence of any person (including the person bringing the proceedings or making the complaint or reference and any legal representative of his);

(c) enabling or requiring the Tribunal to give a summary of any evidence taken in his absence to the person by whom the proceedings were brought or, as the case may be, to the person who made the complaint or reference;

(d) enabling or requiring the Tribunal to exercise their jurisdiction, and to exercise and perform the powers and duties conferred or imposed on them (including, in particular, in relation to the giving of reasons), in such manner provided for in the rules as prevents or limits the disclosure of particular matters.

(5) Rules under this section may also include provision—

(a) enabling powers or duties of the Tribunal that relate to matters preliminary or incidental to the hearing or consideration of any proceedings, complaint or reference to be exercised or performed by a single member of the Tribunal; and

(b) conferring on the Tribunal such ancillary powers as the Secretary of State thinks necessary for the purposes of, or in connection with, the exercise of the Tribunal's jurisdiction, or the exercise or performance of any power or duty conferred or imposed on them.

(6) In making rules under this section the Secretary of State shall have regard, in particular, to—

(a) the need to secure that matters which are the subject of proceedings, complaints or references brought before or made to the Tribunal are properly heard and considered; and

(b) the need to secure that information is not disclosed to an extent, or in a manner, that is contrary to the public interest or prejudicial to national security, the prevention or detection of serious crime, the economic well-being of the United Kingdom or the continued discharge of the functions of any of the intelligence services.

(7) Rules under this section may make provision by the application, with or without modification, of the provision from time to time contained in specified rules of court.

(8) Subject to subsection (9), no rules shall be made under this section unless a draft of them has first been laid before Parliament and approved by a resolution of each House.

(9) Subsection (8) does not apply in the case of the rules made on the first occasion on which the Secretary of State exercises his power to make rules under this section.

(10) The rules made on that occasion shall cease to have effect at the end of the period of forty days beginning with the day on which they were made unless, before the end of that period, they have been approved by a resolution of each House of Parliament.

(11) For the purposes of subsection (10)—

(a) the rules' ceasing to have effect shall be without prejudice to anything previously done or to the making of new rules; and

(b) in reckoning the period of forty days no account shall be taken of any period during which Parliament is dissolved or prorogued or during which both Houses are adjourned for more than four days.

(12) The Secretary of State shall consult the Scottish Ministers before making any rules under this section; and any rules so made shall be laid before the Scottish Parliament.

Abolition of jurisdiction in relation to complaints

70.—(1) The provisions set out in subsection (2) (which provide for the investigation etc. of certain complaints) shall not apply in relation to any complaint made after the coming into force of this section.

(2) Those provisions are—

(a) section 5 of, and Schedules 1 and 2 to, the Security Service Act 1989 (investigation of complaints about the Security Service made to the Tribunal established under that Act);

(b) section 9 of, and Schedules 1 and 2 to, the Intelligence Services Act 1994 (investigation of complaints about the Secret Intelligence Service or GCHQ made to the Tribunal established under that Act); and

(c) section 102 of, and Schedule 7 to, the Police Act 1997 (investigation of complaints made to the Surveillance Commissioners).

Codes of practice

Issue and revision of codes of practice

71.—(1) The Secretary of State shall issue one or more codes of practice relating to the exercise and performance of the powers and duties mentioned in subsection (2).

(2) Those powers and duties are those (excluding any power to make subordinate legislation) that are conferred or imposed otherwise than on the Surveillance Commissioners by or under—

(a) Parts I to III of this Act;

(b) section 5 of the Intelligence Services Act 1994 (warrants for interference with property or wireless telegraphy for the purposes of the intelligence services); and

(c) Part III of the Police Act 1997 (authorisation by the police or customs and excise of interference with property or wireless telegraphy).

(3) Before issuing a code of practice under subsection (1), the Secretary of State shall—

(a) prepare and publish a draft of that code; and

(b) consider any representations made to him about the draft;

and the Secretary of State may incorporate in the code finally issued any modifications made by him to the draft after its publication.

(4) The Secretary of State shall lay before both Houses of Parliament every draft code of practice prepared and published by him under this section.

(5) A code of practice issued by the Secretary of State under this section shall not be brought into force except in accordance with an order made by the Secretary of State.

(6) An order under subsection (5) may contain such transitional provisions and savings as appear to the Secretary of State to be necessary or expedient in connection with the bringing into force of the code brought into force by that order.

(7) The Secretary of State may from time to time—

(a) revise the whole or any part of a code issued under this section; and

(b) issue the revised code.

(8) Subsections (3) to (6) shall apply (with appropriate modifications) in

relation to the issue of any revised code under this section as they apply in relation to the first issue of such a code.

(9) The Secretary of State shall not make an order containing provision for any of the purposes of this section unless a draft of the order has been laid before Parliament and approved by a resolution of each House.

Effect of codes of practice

72.—(1) A person exercising or performing any power or duty in relation to which provision may be made by a code of practice under section 71 shall, in doing so, have regard to the provisions (so far as they are applicable) of every code of practice for the time being in force under that section.

(2) A failure on the part of any person to comply with any provision of a code of practice for the time being in force under section 71 shall not of itself render him liable to any criminal or civil proceedings.

(3) A code of practice in force at any time under section 71 shall be admissible in evidence in any criminal or civil proceedings.

(4) If any provision of a code of practice issued or revised under section 71 appears to—

(a) the court or tribunal conducting any civil or criminal proceedings,
(b) the Tribunal,
(c) a relevant Commissioner carrying out any of his functions under this Act,
(d) a Surveillance Commissioner carrying out his functions under this Act or the Police Act 1997, or
(e) any Assistant Surveillance Commissioner carrying out any functions of his under section 63 of this Act,

to be relevant to any question arising in the proceedings, or in connection with the exercise of that jurisdiction or the carrying out of those functions, in relation to a time when it was in force, that provision of the code shall be taken into account in determining that question.

(5) In this section "relevant Commissioner" means the Interception of Communications Commissioner, the Intelligence Services Commissioner or the Investigatory Powers Commissioner for Northern Ireland.

PART V

MISCELLANEOUS AND SUPPLEMENTAL

Miscellaneous

Conduct in relation to wireless telegraphy

73.—(1) Section 5 of the Wireless Telegraphy Act 1949 (misleading messages and interception and disclosure of wireless telegraphy messages) shall become subsection (1) of that section.

(2) In paragraph (b) of that subsection—
(a) for the words from "under the authority of" to "servant of the Crown," there shall be substituted "under the authority of a designated person"; and
(b) in sub-paragraph (i), for the words from "which neither" to the end of the sub-paragraph there shall be substituted "of which neither the person using the apparatus nor a person on whose behalf he is acting is an intended recipient,".

(3) In that section, after that subsection there shall be inserted—

"(2) The conduct in relation to which a designated person may give a separate authority for the purposes of this section shall not, except where he believes the conduct to be necessary on grounds falling within subsection (5) of this section, include—

    (a) any conduct which, if engaged in without lawful authority, constitutes an offence under section 1(1) or (2) of the Regulation of Investigatory Powers Act 2000;

    (b) any conduct which, if engaged in without lawful authority, is actionable under section 1(3) of that Act;

    (c) any conduct which is capable of being authorised by an authorisation or notice granted by any person under Chapter II of Part I of that Act (communications data);

    (d) any conduct which is capable of being authorised by an authorisation granted by any person under Part II of that Act (surveillance etc.).

(3) A designated person shall not exercise his power to give a separate authority for the purposes of this section except where he believes—

    (a) that the giving of his authority is necessary on grounds falling within subsection (4) or (5) of this section; and

    (b) that the conduct authorised by him is proportionate to what is sought to be achieved by that conduct.

(4) A separate authority for the purposes of this section is necessary on grounds falling within this subsection if it is necessary—

    (a) in the interests of national security;

    (b) for the purpose of preventing or detecting crime (within the meaning of the Regulation of Investigatory Powers Act 2000) or of preventing disorder;

    (c) in the interests of the economic well-being of the United Kingdom;

    (d) in the interests of public safety;

    (e) for the purpose of protecting public health;

    (f) for the purpose of assessing or collecting any tax, duty, levy or other imposition, contribution or charge payable to a government department; or

    (g) for any purpose (not falling within paragraphs (a) to (f)) which is specified for the purposes of this subsection by regulations made by the Secretary of State.

(5) A separate authority for the purposes of this section is necessary on grounds falling within this subsection if it is not necessary on grounds falling within subsection (4)(a) or (c) to (g) but is necessary for purposes connected with—

    (a) the issue of licences under this Act;

    (b) the prevention or detection of anything which constitutes interference with wireless telegraphy; or

    (c) the enforcement of any enactment contained in this Act or of any enactment not so contained that relates to such interference.

(6) The matters to be taken into account in considering whether the requirements of subsection (3) of this section are satisfied in the case of the giving of any separate authority for the purposes of this section shall include whether what it is thought necessary to achieve by the authorised conduct could reasonably be achieved by other means.

(7) A separate authority for the purposes of this section must be in writing and under the hand of—

    (a) the Secretary of State;

    (b) one of the Commissioners of Customs and Excise; or

    (c) a person not falling within paragraph (a) or (b) who is designated for the purposes of this subsection by regulations made by the Secretary of State.

(8) A separate authority for the purposes of this section may be general or specific and may be given—

    (a) to such person or persons, or description of persons,

(b) for such period, and

(c) subject to such restrictions and limitations,

as the designated person thinks fit.

(9) No regulations shall be made under subsection (4)(g) unless a draft of them has first been laid before Parliament and approved by a resolution of each House.

(10) For the purposes of this section the question whether conduct is capable of being authorised under Chapter II of Part I of the Regulation of Investigatory Powers Act 2000 or under Part II of that Act shall be determined without reference—

(a) to whether the person whose conduct it is is a person on whom any power or duty is or may be conferred or imposed by or under Chapter II of Part I or Part II of that Act; or

(b) to whether there are grounds for believing that the requirements for the grant of an authorisation or the giving of a notice under Chapter II of Part I or Part II of that Act are satisfied.

(11) References in this section to a separate authority for the purposes of this section are references to any authority for the purposes of this section given otherwise than by way of the issue or renewal of a warrant, authorisation or notice under Part I or II of the Regulation of Investigatory Powers Act 2000.

(12) In this section "designated person" means—

(a) the Secretary of State;

(b) the Commissioners of Customs and Excise; or

(c) any other person designated for the purposes of this section by regulations made by the Secretary of State."

(4) In section 16(2) of that Act (regulations and orders), after "the said powers" there shall be inserted ", other than one containing regulations a draft of which has been approved for the purposes of section 5(9),".

Warrants under the Intelligence Services Act 1994

74.—(1) In subsection (2) of section 5 of the Intelligence Services Act 1994 (the circumstances in which the Secretary of State may issue a warrant authorising interference with property or wireless telegraphy)—

(a) in paragraph (a), for "on the ground that it is likely to be of substantial value in" there shall be substituted "for the purpose of"; and

(b) for paragraph (b) there shall be substituted—

"(b) is satisfied that the taking of the action is proportionate to what the action seeks to achieve;".

(2) After that subsection, there shall be inserted—

"(2A) The matters to be taken into account in considering whether the requirements of subsection (2)(a) and (b) are satisfied in the case of any warrant shall include whether what it is thought necessary to achieve by the conduct authorised by the warrant could reasonably be achieved by other means."

(3) In each of sections 6(1)(b) and 7(5)(b) of that Act (warrants issued under the hand of a senior official of the Secretary of State's department), the words "of his department" shall be omitted.

(4) In section 11 of that Act (interpretation), for paragraph (1)(d) there shall be substituted—

"(d) "senior official" has the same meaning as in the Regulation of Investigatory Powers Act 2000;".

Authorisations under Part III of the Police Act 1997

75.—(1) Section 93 of the Police Act 1997 (authorisations to interfere with property etc.) shall be amended as follows.

(2) In subsection (1) (the action that the authorising officer may authorise), for "or" at the end of paragraph (a) there shall be substituted—
"(ab) the taking of such action falling within subsection (1A), in respect of property outside the relevant area, as he may specify, or".
(3) After that subsection there shall be inserted—
"(1A) The action falling within this subsection is action for maintaining or retrieving any equipment, apparatus or device the placing or use of which in the relevant area has been authorised under this Part or Part II of the Regulation of Investigatory Powers Act 2000 or under any enactment contained in or made under an Act of the Scottish Parliament which makes provision equivalent to that made by Part II of that Act of 2000.
(1B) Subsection (1) applies where the authorising officer is a customs officer with the omission of—
(a) the words "in the relevant area", in each place where they occur; and
(b) paragraph (ab)."
(4) In subsection (2) (the grounds on which action may be authorised)—
(a) in paragraph (a), for the words from "on the ground" to "detection of" there shall be substituted "for the purpose of preventing or detecting"; and
(b) for paragraph (b) there shall be substituted—
"(b) that the taking of the action is proportionate to what the action seeks to achieve."
(5) After subsection (2) there shall be inserted—
"(2A) Subsection (2) applies where the authorising officer is the Chief Constable or the Deputy Chief Constable of the Royal Ulster Constabulary as if the reference in subsection (2)(a) to preventing or detecting serious crime included a reference to the interests of national security.
(2B) The matters to be taken into account in considering whether the requirements of subsection (2) are satisfied in the case of any authorisation shall include whether what it is thought necessary to achieve by the authorised action could reasonably be achieved by other means."
(6) In subsection (5) (the meaning of authorising officer)—
(a) after paragraph (e) there shall be inserted—
"(ea) the Chief Constable of the Ministry of Defence Police;
(eb) the Provost Marshal of the Royal Navy Regulating Branch;
(ec) the Provost Marshal of the Royal Military Police;
(ed) the Provost Marshal of the Royal Air Force Police;
(ee) the Chief Constable of the British Transport Police;";
(b) in paragraph (g), after "National Crime Squad" there shall be inserted
", or any person holding the rank of assistant chief constable in that Squad who is designated for the purposes of this paragraph by that Director General"; and
(c) in paragraph (h), for the word "the", in the first place where it occurs, there shall be substituted "any".
(7) In subsection (6) (the meaning of relevant area), after paragraph (c) there shall be inserted—
"(ca) in relation to a person within paragraph (ea), means any place where, under section 2 of the Ministry of Defence Police Act 1987, the members of the Ministry of Defence Police have the powers and privileges of a constable;
(cb) in relation to a person within paragraph (ee), means the United Kingdom;".
(8) After that subsection there shall be inserted—
"(6A) For the purposes of any authorisation by a person within

paragraph (eb), (ec) or (ed) of subsection (5) property is in the relevant area or action in respect of wireless telegraphy is taken in the relevant area if, as the case may be—

    (a) the property is owned, occupied, in the possession of or being used by a person subject to service discipline; or

    (b) the action is taken in relation to the use of wireless telegraphy by such a person.

(6B) For the purposes of this section a person is subject to service discipline—

    (a) in relation to the Royal Navy Regulating Branch, if he is subject to the Naval Discipline Act 1957 or is a civilian to whom Parts I and II of that Act for the time being apply by virtue of section 118 of that Act ;

    (b) in relation to the Royal Military Police, if he is subject to military law or is a civilian to whom Part II of the Army Act 1955 for the time being applies by virtue of section 209 of that Act; and

    (c) in relation to the Royal Air Force Police, if he is subject to air-force law or is a civilian to whom Part II of the Air Force Act 1955 for the time being applies by virtue of section 209 of that Act."

Surveillance etc. operations beginning in Scotland

76.—(1) Subject to subsection (2), where—

    (a) an authorisation under the relevant Scottish legislation has the effect of authorising the carrying out in Scotland of the conduct described in the authorisation,

    (b) the conduct so described is or includes conduct to which Part II of this Act applies, and

    (c) circumstances arise by virtue of which some or all of the conduct so described can for the time being be carried out only outwith Scotland,

section 27 of this Act shall have effect for the purpose of making lawful the carrying out outwith Scotland of the conduct so described as if the authorisation, so far as is it relates to conduct to which that Part applies, were an authorisation duly granted under that Part.

(2) Where any such circumstances as are mentioned in paragraph (c) of subsection (1) so arise as to give effect outwith Scotland to any authorisation granted under the relevant Scottish legislation, that authorisation shall not authorise any conduct outwith Scotland at any time after the end of the period of three weeks beginning with the time when the circumstances arose.

(3) Subsection (2) is without prejudice to the operation of subsection (1) in relation to any authorisation on the second or any subsequent occasion on which any such circumstances as are mentioned in subsection (1)(c) arise while the authorisation remains in force.

(4) In this section "the relevant Scottish legislation" means an enactment contained in or made under an Act of the Scottish Parliament which makes provision, corresponding to that made by Part II, for the authorisation of conduct to which that Part applies.

Supplemental

Ministerial expenditure, etc.

77. There shall be paid out of money provided by Parliament—

    (a) any expenditure incurred by the Secretary of State for or in connection with the carrying out of his functions under this Act; and

    (b) any increase attributable to this Act in the sums which are payable out of money so provided under any other Act.

Orders, regulations and rules

78.—(1) This section applies to any power of the Secretary of State to make any order, regulations or rules under any provision of this Act.

(2) The powers to which this section applies shall be exercisable by statutory instrument.

(3) A statutory instrument which contains any order made in exercise of a power to which this section applies (other than the power to appoint a day under section 83(2)) but which contains neither—

    (a) an order a draft of which has been approved for the purposes of section 12(10), 13(3), 22(9), 25(5), 28(5), 29(6), 30(7), 35(5), 41(6), 47(2), 66(3), 67(11) or 71(9), nor

    (b) the order to which section 35(7) applies,

shall be subject to annulment in pursuance of a resolution of either House of Parliament.

(4) A statutory instrument containing any regulations made in exercise of a power to which this section applies shall be subject to annulment in pursuance of a resolution of either House of Parliament.

(5) Any order, regulations or rules made in exercise of a power to which this section applies may—

    (a) make different provisions for different cases;

    (b) contain such incidental, supplemental, consequential and transitional provision as the Secretary of State thinks fit.

Criminal liability of directors, etc.

79.—(1) Where an offence under any provision of this Act other than a provision of Part III is committed by a body corporate and is proved to have been committed with the consent or connivance of, or to be attributable to any neglect on the part of—

    (a) a director, manager, secretary or other similar officer of the body corporate, or

    (b) any person who was purporting to act in any such capacity,

he (as well as the body corporate) shall be guilty of that offence and liable to be proceeded against and punished accordingly.

(2) Where an offence under any provision of this Act other than a provision of Part III—

    (a) is committed by a Scottish firm, and

    (b) is proved to have been committed with the consent or connivance of, or to be attributable to any neglect on the part of, a partner of the firm,

he (as well as the firm) shall be guilty of that offence and liable to be proceeded against and punished accordingly.

(3) In this section "director", in relation to a body corporate whose affairs are managed by its members, means a member of the body corporate.

General saving for lawful conduct

80. Nothing in any of the provisions of this Act by virtue of which conduct of any description is or may be authorised by any warrant, authorisation or notice, or by virtue of which information may be obtained in any manner, shall be construed—

    (a) as making it unlawful to engage in any conduct of that description which is not otherwise unlawful under this Act and would not be unlawful apart from this Act;

    (b) as otherwise requiring—

        (i) the issue, grant or giving of such a warrant, authorisation or notice, or

        (ii) the taking of any step for or towards obtaining the authority of such a warrant, authorisation or notice,

before any such conduct of that description is engaged in; or

(c) as prejudicing any power to obtain information by any means not involving conduct that may be authorised under this Act.

General interpretation

81.—(1) In this Act—

"apparatus" includes any equipment, machinery or device and any wire or cable;

"Assistant Commissioner of Police of the Metropolis" includes the Deputy Commissioner of Police of the Metropolis;

"Assistant Surveillance Commissioner" means any person holding office under section 63;

"civil proceedings" means any proceedings in or before any court or tribunal that are not criminal proceedings;

"communication" includes—

(a) (except in the definition of "postal service" in section 2(1)) anything transmitted by means of a postal service;

(b) anything comprising speech, music, sounds, visual images or data of any description; and

(c) signals serving either for the impartation of anything between persons, between a person and a thing or between things or for the actuation or control of any apparatus;

"criminal", in relation to any proceedings or prosecution, shall be construed in accordance with subsection (4);

"customs officer" means an officer commissioned by the Commissioners of Customs and Excise under section 6(3) of the Customs and Excise Management Act 1979;

"document" includes a map, plan, design, drawing, picture or other image;

"enactment" includes—

(a) an enactment passed after the passing of this Act; and

(b) an enactment contained in Northern Ireland legislation;

"GCHQ" has the same meaning as in the Intelligence Services Act 1994;

"Her Majesty's forces" has the same meaning as in the Army Act 1955;

"intelligence service" means the Security Service, the Secret Intelligence Service or GCHQ;

"interception" and cognate expressions shall be construed (so far as it is applicable) in accordance with section 2;

"interception warrant" means a warrant under section 5;

"legal proceedings" means civil or criminal proceedings in or before any court or tribunal;

"modification" includes alterations, additions and omissions, and cognate expressions shall be construed accordingly;

"ordinary Surveillance Commissioner" means a Surveillance Commissioner other than the Chief Surveillance Commissioner;

"person" includes any organisation and any association or combination of persons;

"police force" means any of the following—

(a) any police force maintained under section 2 of the Police Act 1996 (police forces in England and Wales outside London);

(b) the metropolitan police force;

(c) the City of London police force;

(d) any police force maintained under or by virtue of section 1 of the Police (Scotland) Act 1967

(e) the Royal Ulster Constabulary;

    (f) the Ministry of Defence Police;
    (g) the Royal Navy Regulating Branch;
    (h) the Royal Military Police;
    (i) the Royal Air Force Police;
    (j) the British Transport Police;
"postal service" and "public postal service" have the meanings given by
    section 2(1);
"private telecommunication system", "public telecommunications ser-
    vice" and "public telecommunication system" have the meanings
    given by section 2(1);
"public authority" means any public authority within the meaning of
    section 6 of the Human Rights Act 1998 (acts of public authorities)
    other than a court or tribunal;
"senior official" means, subject to subsection (7), a member of the
    Senior Civil Service or a member of the Senior Management
    Structure of Her Majesty's Diplomatic Service;
"statutory", in relation to any power or duty, means conferred or
    imposed by or under any enactment or subordinate legislation;
"subordinate legislation" means any subordinate legislation (within the
    meaning of the Interpretation Act 1978) or any statutory rules
    (within the meaning of the Statutory Rules (Northern Ireland)
    Order 1979);
"Surveillance Commissioner" means a Commissioner holding office
    under section 91 of the Police Act 1997 and "Chief Surveillance
    Commissioner" shall be construed accordingly;
"telecommunication system" and "telecommunications service" have
    the meanings given by section 2(1);
"the Tribunal" means the tribunal established under section 65;
"wireless telegraphy" has the same meaning as in the Wireless
    Telegraphy Act 1949 and, in relation to wireless telegraphy,
    "interfere" has the same meaning as in that Act;
"working day" means any day other than a Saturday, a Sunday,
    Christmas Day, Good Friday or a day which is a bank holiday
    under the Banking and Financial Dealings Act 1971 in any part of
    the United Kingdom.
  (2) In this Act—
  (a) references to crime are references to conduct which constitutes one or
      more criminal offences or is, or corresponds to, any conduct which, if
      it all took place in any one part of the United Kingdom would
      constitute one or more criminal offences; and
  (b) references to serious crime are references to crime that satisfies the
      test in subsection (3)(a) or (b).
  (3) Those tests are—
¹(a) that the offence or one of the offences that is or would be constituted
      by the conduct is an offence for which a person who has attained the
      age of twenty-one and has no previous convictions could reasonably
      be expected to be sentenced to imprisonment for a term of three years
      or more;
  (b) that the conduct involves the use of violence, results in substantial
      financial gain or is conduct by a large number of persons in pursuit of a
      common purpose.
  (4) In this Act "criminal proceedings" includes—
  (a) proceedings in the United Kingdom or elsewhere before—
        (i) a court-martial constituted under the Army Act 1955, the Air
            Force Act 1955 or the Naval Discipline Act 1957; or
        (ii) a disciplinary court constituted under section 50 of the Act of
             1957;
  (b) proceedings before the Courts-Martial Appeal Court; and

(c) proceedings before a Standing Civilian Court;
and references in this Act to criminal prosecutions shall be construed accordingly.

(5) For the purposes of this Act detecting crime shall be taken to include—

(a) establishing by whom, for what purpose, by what means and generally in what circumstances any crime was committed; and

(b) the apprehension of the person by whom any crime was committed;
and any reference in this Act to preventing or detecting serious crime shall be construed accordingly, except that, in Chapter I of Part I, it shall not include a reference to gathering evidence for use in any legal proceedings.

(6) In this Act—

(a) references to a person holding office under the Crown include references to any servant of the Crown and to any member of Her Majesty's forces; and

(b) references to a member of a police force, in relation to the Royal Navy Regulating Branch, the Royal Military Police or the Royal Air Force Police, do not include references to any member of that Branch or Force who is not for the time being attached to or serving either with the Branch or Force of which he is a member or with another of those police forces.

(7) If it appears to the Secretary of State that it is necessary to do so in consequence of any changes to the structure or grading of the home civil service or diplomatic service, he may by order make such amendments of the definition of "senior official" in subsection (1) as appear to him appropriate to preserve, so far as practicable, the effect of that definition.

Amendments, repeals and savings etc

82.—(1) The enactments specified in Schedule 4 (amendments consequential on the provisions of this Act) shall have effect with the amendments set out in that Schedule.

(2) The enactments mentioned in Schedule 5 are hereby repealed to the extent specified in the third column of that Schedule.

(3) For the avoidance of doubt it is hereby declared that nothing in this Act (except paragraphs 1 and 2 of Schedule 4) affects any power conferred on the Post Office by or under any enactment to open, detain or delay any postal packet or to deliver any such packet to a person other than the person to whom it is addressed.

(4) Where any warrant under the Interception of Communications Act 1985 is in force under that Act at the time when the repeal by this Act of section 2 of that Act comes into force, the conduct authorised by that warrant shall be deemed for the period which—

(a) begins with that time, and

(b) ends with the time when that warrant would (without being renewed) have ceased to have effect under that Act,
as if it were conduct authorised by an interception warrant issued in accordance with the requirements of Chapter I of Part I of this Act.

(5) In relation to any such warrant, any certificate issued for the purposes of section 3(2) of the Interception of Communications Act 1985 shall have effect in relation to that period as if it were a certificate issued for the purposes of section 8(4) of this Act.

(6) Sections 15 and 16 of this Act shall have effect as if references to interception warrants and to section 8(4) certificates included references, respectively, to warrants under section 2 of the Interception of Communications Act 1985 and to certificates under section 3(2) of that Act; and references in sections 15 and 16 of this Act to intercepted or certified material shall be construed accordingly.

NOTE
[1]Prospectively amended by the Criminal Justice and Court Services Act 2000 (c. 43), s.74 and Sched. 7, para. 211.

Short title, commencement and extent

83.—(1) This Act may be cited as the Regulation of Investigatory Powers Act 2000.

(2) The provisions of this Act, other than this section, shall come into force on such day as the Secretary of State may by order appoint; and different days may be appointed under this subsection for different purposes.

(3) This Act extends to Northern Ireland.

SCHEDULES

SCHEDULE 1

RELEVANT PUBLIC AUTHORITIES

PART I

RELEVANT AUTHORITIES FOR THE PURPOSES OF ss.28 AND 29

Police forces etc.

1. Any police force.
2. The National Criminal Intelligence Service.
3. The National Crime Squad.
4. The Serious Fraud Office.

The intelligence services

5. Any of the intelligence services.

The armed forces

6. Any of Her Majesty's forces.

The revenue departments

7. The Commissioners of Customs and Excise.
8. The Commissioners of Inland Revenue.

Government departments

9. The Ministry of Agriculture, Fisheries and Food.
10. The Ministry of Defence.
11. The Department of the Environment, Transport and the Regions.
12. The Department of Health.
13. The Home Office.
14. The Department of Social Security.
15. The Department of Trade and Industry.

The National Assembly for Wales

16. The National Assembly for Wales.

Local authorities

17. Any local authority (within the meaning of section 1 of the Local Government Act 1999).

Other bodies

18. The Environment Agency.
19. The Financial Services Authority.
20. The Food Standards Agency.

21. The Intervention Board for Agricultural Produce.
22. The Personal Investment Authority.
23. The Post Office.

PART II

RELEVANT AUTHORITIES FOR THE PURPOSES ONLY OF S.28

The Health and Safety Executive

24. The Health and Safety Executive.

NHS bodies in England and Wales

25. A Health Authority established under section 8 of the National Health Service Act 1977.
26. A Special Health Authority established under section 11 of the National Health Service Act 1977.
27. A National Heath Service trust established under section 5 of the National Health Service and Community Care Act 1990.

The Royal Pharmaceutical Society of Great Britain

28. The Royal Pharmaceutical Society of Great Britain.

SCHEDULE 2

PERSONS HAVING THE APPROPRIATE PERMISSION

Requirement that appropriate permission is granted by a judge

1.—(1) Subject to the following provisions of this Schedule, a person has the appropriate permission in relation to any protected information if, and only if, written permission for the giving of section 49 notices in relation to that information has been granted—
(a) in England and Wales, by a Circuit judge;
(b) in Scotland, by a sheriff; or
(c) in Northern Ireland, by a county court judge.
(2) Nothing in paragraphs 2 to 5 of this Schedule providing for the manner in which a person may be granted the appropriate permission in relation to any protected information without a grant under this paragraph shall be construed as requiring any further permission to be obtained in a case in which permission has been granted under this paragraph.

Data obtained under warrant etc.

2.—(1) This paragraph applies in the case of protected information falling within section 49(1)(a), (b) or (c) where the statutory power in question is one exercised, or to be exercised, in accordance with—
(a) a warrant issued by the Secretary of State or a person holding judicial office; or
(b) an authorisation under Part III of the Police Act 1997 (authorisation of otherwise unlawful action in respect of property).
(2) Subject to sub-paragraphs (3) to (5) and paragraph 6(1), a person has the appropriate permission in relation to that protected information (without any grant of permission under paragraph 1) if—
(a) the warrant or, as the case may be, the authorisation contained the relevant authority's permission for the giving of section 49 notices in relation to protected information to be obtained under the warrant or authorisation; or
(b) since the issue of the warrant or authorisation, written permission has been granted by the relevant authority for the giving of such notices in relation to protected information obtained under the warrant or authorisation.
(3) Only persons holding office under the Crown, the police and customs and excise shall be capable of having the appropriate permission in relation to protected information obtained, or to be obtained, under a warrant issued by the Secretary of State.
(4) Only a person who—
(a) was entitled to exercise the power conferred by the warrant, or
(b) is of the description of persons on whom the power conferred by the warrant was, or could have been, conferred,
shall be capable of having the appropriate permission in relation to protected information obtained, or to be obtained, under a warrant issued by a person holding judicial office.

(5) Only the police and the customs and excise shall be capable of having the appropriate permission in relation to protected information obtained, or to be obtained, under an authorisation under Part III of the Police Act 1997.

(6) In this paragraph "the relevant authority"—

(a) in relation to a warrant issued by the Secretary of State, means the Secretary of State;

(b) in relation to a warrant issued by a person holding judicial office, means any person holding any judicial office that would have entitled him to issue the warrant; and

(c) in relation to protected information obtained under an authorisation under Part III of the Police Act 1997, means (subject to sub-paragraph (7)) an authorising officer within the meaning of section 93 of that Act.

(7) Section 94 of the Police Act 1997 (power of other persons to grant authorisations in urgent cases) shall apply in relation to—

(a) an application for permission for the giving of section 49 notices in relation to protected information obtained, or to be obtained, under an authorisation under Part III of that Act, and

(b) the powers of any authorising officer (within the meaning of section 93 of that Act) to grant such a permission,

as it applies in relation to an application for an authorisation under section 93 of that Act and the powers of such an officer under that section.

(8) References in this paragraph to a person holding judicial office are references to—

(a) any judge of the Crown Court or of the High Court of Justiciary;

(b) any sheriff;

(c) any justice of the peace;

(d) any resident magistrate in Northern Ireland; or

(e) any person holding any such judicial office as entitles him to exercise the jurisdiction of a judge of the Crown Court or of a justice of the peace.

(9) Protected information that comes into a person's possession by means of the exercise of any statutory power which—

(a) is exercisable without a warrant, but

(b) is so exercisable in the course of, or in connection with, the exercise of another statutory power for which a warrant is required,

shall not be taken, by reason only of the warrant required for the exercise of the power mentioned in paragraph (b), to be information in the case of which this paragraph applies.

Data obtained by the intelligence services under statute but without a warrant

3.—(1) This paragraph applies in the case of protected information falling within section 49(1)(a), (b) or (c) which—

(a) has come into the possession of any of the intelligence services or is likely to do so; and

(b) is not information in the case of which paragraph 2 applies.

(2) Subject to paragraph 6(1), a person has the appropriate permission in relation to that protected information (without any grant of permission under paragraph 1) if written permission for the giving of section 49 notices in relation to that information has been granted by the Secretary of State.

(3) Sub-paragraph (2) applies where the protected information is in the possession, or (as the case may be) is likely to come into the possession, of both—

(a) one or more of the intelligence services, and

(b) a public authority which is not one of the intelligence services,

as if a grant of permission under paragraph 1 were unnecessary only where the application to the Secretary of State for permission under that sub-paragraph is made by or on behalf of a member of one of the intelligence services.

Data obtained under statute by other persons but without a warrant

4.—(1) This paragraph applies—

(a) in the case of protected information falling within section 49(1)(a), (b) or (c) which is not information in the case of which paragraph 2 or 3 applies; and

(b) in the case of protected information falling within section 49(1)(d) which is not information also falling within section 49(1)(a), (b) or (c) in the case of which paragraph 3 applies.

(2) Subject to paragraph 6, where—

(a) the statutory power was exercised, or is likely to be exercised, by the police, the customs and excise or a member of Her Majesty's forces, or

(b) the information was provided or disclosed, or is likely to be provided or disclosed, to the police, the customs and excise or a member of Her Majesty's forces, or

(c) the information is in the possession of, or is likely to come into the possession of, the police, the customs and excise or a member of Her Majesty's forces,

the police, the customs and excise or, as the case may be, members of Her Majesty's forces have the appropriate permission in relation to the protected information, without any grant of permission under paragraph 1.

(3) In any other case a person shall not have the appropriate permission by virtue of a grant of permission under paragraph 1 unless he is a person falling within sub-paragraph (4).

(4) A person falls within this sub-paragraph if, as the case may be—

(a) he is the person who exercised the statutory power or is of the description of persons who would have been entitled to exercise it;

(b) he is the person to whom the protected information was provided or disclosed, or is of a description of person the provision or disclosure of the information to whom would have discharged the statutory duty; or

(c) he is a person who is likely to be a person falling within paragraph (a) or (b) when the power is exercised or the protected information provided or disclosed.

Data obtained without the exercise of statutory powers

5.—(1) This paragraph applies in the case of protected information falling within section 49(1)(e).

(2) Subject to paragraph 6, a person has the appropriate permission in relation to that protected information (without any grant of permission under paragraph 1) if—

(a) the information is in the possession of any of the intelligence services, or is likely to come into the possession of any of those services; and

(b) written permission for the giving of section 49 notices in relation to that information has been granted by the Secretary of State.

(3) Sub-paragraph (2) applies where the protected information is in the possession, or (as the case may be) is likely to come into the possession, of both—

(a) one or more of the intelligence services, and

(b) the police or the customs and excise,

as if a grant of permission under paragraph 1 were unnecessary only where the application to the Secretary of State for permission under that sub-paragraph is made by or on behalf of a member of one of the intelligence services.

General requirements relating to the appropriate permission

6.—(1) A person does not have the appropriate permission in relation to any protected information unless he is either—

(a) a person who has the protected information in his possession or is likely to obtain possession of it; or

(b) a person who is authorised (apart from this Act) to act on behalf of such a person.

(2) Subject to sub-paragraph (3), a constable does not by virtue of paragraph 1, 4 or 5 have the appropriate permission in relation to any protected information unless—

(a) he is of or above the rank of superintendent; or

(b) permission to give a section 49 notice in relation to that information has been granted by a person holding the rank of superintendent, or any higher rank.

(3) In the case of protected information that has come into the police's possession by means of the exercise of powers conferred by—

(a) section 44 of the Terrorism Act 2000 (power to stop and search), or

(b) section 13A or 13B of the Prevention of Terrorism (Temporary Provisions) Act 1989 (which had effect for similar purposes before the coming into force of section 44 of the Terrorism Act 2000),

the permission required by sub-paragraph (2) shall not be granted by any person below the rank mentioned in section 44(4) of that Act of 2000 or, as the case may be, section 13A(1) of that Act of 1989.

(4) A person commissioned by the Commissioners of Customs and Excise does not by virtue of paragraph 1, 4 or 5 have the appropriate permission in relation to any protected information unless permission to give a section 49 notice in relation to that information has been granted—

(a) by those Commissioners themselves; or

(b) by an officer of their department of or above such level as they may designate for the purposes of this sub-paragraph.

(5) A member of Her Majesty's forces does not by virtue of paragraph 1, 4 or 5 have the appropriate permission in relation to any protected information unless—

(a) he is of or above the rank of lieutenant colonel or its equivalent; or

(b) permission to give a section 49 notice in relation to that information has been granted by a person holding the rank of lieutenant colonel or its equivalent, or by a person holding a rank higher than lieutenant colonel or its equivalent.

Duration of permission

7.—(1) A permission granted by any person under any provision of this Schedule shall not entitle any person to give a section 49 notice at any time after the permission has ceased to have effect.

(2) Such a permission, once granted, shall continue to have effect (notwithstanding the cancellation, expiry or other discharge of any warrant or authorisation in which it is contained or to which it relates) until such time (if any) as it—

(a) expires in accordance with any limitation on its duration that was contained in its terms; or

(b) is withdrawn by the person who granted it or by a person holding any office or other position that would have entitled him to grant it.

Formalities for permissions granted by the Secretary of State

8. A permission for the purposes of any provision of this Schedule shall not be granted by the Secretary of State except—

(a) under his hand; or

(b) in an urgent case in which the Secretary of State has expressly authorised the grant of the permission, under the hand of a senior official.

SCHEDULE 3

THE TRIBUNAL

Membership of the Tribunal

1.—(1) A person shall not be appointed as a member of the Tribunal unless he is—

(a) a person who holds or has held a high judicial office (within the meaning of the Appellate Jurisdiction Act 1876);

(b) a person who has a ten year general qualification, within the meaning of section 71 of the Courts and Legal Services Act 1990;

(c) an advocate or solicitor in Scotland of at least ten years' standing; or

(d) a member of the Bar of Northern Ireland or solicitor of the Supreme Court of Northern Ireland of at least ten years' standing.

(2) Subject to the following provisions of this paragraph, the members of the Tribunal shall hold office during good behaviour.

(3) A member of the Tribunal shall vacate office at the end of the period of five years beginning with the day of his appointment, but shall be eligible for reappointment.

(4) A member of the Tribunal may be relieved of office by Her Majesty at his own request.

(5) A member of the Tribunal may be removed from office by Her Majesty on an Address presented to Her by both Houses of Parliament.

(6) If the Scottish Parliament passes a resolution calling for the removal of a member of the Tribunal, it shall be the duty of the Secretary of State to secure that a motion for the presentation of an Address to Her Majesty for the removal of that member, and the resolution of the Scottish Parliament, are considered by each House of Parliament.

President and Vice-President

2.—(1) Her Majesty may by Letters Patent appoint as President or Vice-President of the Tribunal a person who is, or by virtue of those Letters will be, a member of the Tribunal.

(2) A person shall not be appointed President of the Tribunal unless he holds or has held a high judicial office (within the meaning of the Appellate Jurisdiction Act 1876).

(3) If at any time—

(a) the President of the Tribunal is temporarily unable to carry out any functions conferred on him by this Schedule or any rules under section 69, or

(b) the office of President of the Tribunal is for the time being vacant,

the Vice-President shall carry out those functions.

(4) A person shall cease to be President or Vice-President of the Tribunal if he ceases to be a member of the Tribunal.

Members of the Tribunal with special responsibilities

3.—(1) The President of the Tribunal shall designate one or more members of the Tribunal as the member or members having responsibilities in relation to matters involving the intelligence services.

(2) It shall be the duty of the President of the Tribunal, in exercising any power conferred on him by rules under section 69 to allocate the members of the Tribunal who are to consider or hear any complaint, proceedings, reference or preliminary or incidental matter, to exercise that power in a case in which the complaint, proceedings or reference relates to, or to a matter involving—

(a) an allegation against any of the intelligence services or any member of any of those services, or

(b) conduct by or on behalf of any of those services or any member of any of those services, in such manner as secures that the allocated members consist of, or include, one or more of the members for the time being designated under sub-paragraph (1).

Salaries and expenses

4.—(1) The Secretary of State shall pay to the members of the Tribunal out of money provided by Parliament such remuneration and allowances as he may with the approval of the Treasury determine.

(2) Such expenses of the Tribunal as the Secretary of State may with the approval of the Treasury determine shall be defrayed by him out of money provided by Parliament.

Officers

5.—(1) The Secretary of State may, after consultation with the Tribunal and with the approval of the Treasury as to numbers, provide the Tribunal with such officers as he thinks necessary for the proper discharge of their functions.

(2) The Tribunal may authorise any officer provided under this paragraph to obtain any documents or information on the Tribunal's behalf.

Parliamentary disqualification

6. In Part II of Schedule 1 to the House of Commons Disqualification Act 1975 and in Part II of Schedule 1 to the Northern Ireland Assembly Disqualification Act 1975 (bodies whose members are disqualified) there shall be inserted (at the appropriate places) the following entry—

"The Tribunal established under section 65 of the Regulation of Investigatory Powers Act 2000".

SCHEDULE 4

CONSEQUENTIAL AMENDMENTS

The Post Office Act 1953 (c. 36)

1. In section 58(1) of the Post Office Act 1953 (opening or delaying of postal packets by officers of Post Office), after "the Interception of Communications Act 1985" there shall be inserted "or under the authority of an interception warrant under section 5 of the Regulation of Investigatory Powers Act 2000".

The Post Office Act 1969 (c. 48)

2. In paragraph 1(1) of Schedule 5 to the Post Office Act 1969 (repair of minor deficiencies in certain Acts), for the words from "in obedience" to the end of the sub-paragraph there shall be substituted "under the authority of an interception warrant under section 5 of the Regulation of Investigatory Powers Act 2000, under section 11(9) of that Act or in pursuance of a requirement imposed by the Interception of Communications Commissioner under section 58(1) of that Act or imposed by section 68(6) of that Act or by or in accordance with any rules under section 69 of that Act."

The Telecommunications Act 1984 (c. 12)

3. In section 45 of the Telecommunications Act 1984 (offence of disclosing of messages and use of telecommunication system), for subsections (2) and (3) there shall be substituted—

"(2) Subsection (1) above does not apply to any disclosure made—

(a) in accordance with the order of any court or for the purposes of any criminal proceedings;

(b) in accordance with any warrant, authorisation or notice issued, granted or given under any provision of the Regulation of Investigatory Powers Act 2000;

(c) in compliance with any requirement imposed (apart from that Act) in consequence of the exercise by any person of any statutory power exercisable by him for the purpose of obtaining any document or other information; or

(d) in pursuance of any duty under that Act of 2000, or under Part III of the Police Act 1997, to provide information or produce any document to the Interception of Communications Commissioner or to the tribunal established under section 65 of that Act of 2000.

(3) In subsection (2) above "criminal proceedings" and "statutory power" have the same meanings as in the Regulation of Investigatory Powers Act 2000."

The Security Service Act 1989 (c. 5)

4.—(1) In section 1 of the Security Service Act 1989 (functions of the Security Service), after subsection (4) there shall be inserted—

"(5) Section 81(5) of the Regulation of Investigatory Powers Act 2000 (meaning of "prevention" and "detection"), so far as it relates to serious crime, shall apply for the purposes of this Act as it applies for the purposes of the provisions of that Act not contained in Chapter I of Part I."

(2) In section 2(2)(a) of that Act (duty of Director General to secure that information not disclosed except for authorised purposes), for "preventing or detecting" there shall be substituted "the prevention or detection of".

The Official Secrets Act 1989 (c. 6)

5. In section 4(3)(a) of the Official Secrets Act 1989 (offence of disclosing interception information), after "1985" there shall be inserted "or under the authority of an interception warrant under section 5 of the Regulation of Investigatory Powers Act 2000".

The Intelligence Services Act 1994 (c. 13)

6. In section 11 of the Intelligence Services Act 1994 (interpretation), after subsection (1) there shall be inserted—

"(1A) Section 81(5) of the Regulation of Investigatory Powers Act 2000 (meaning of "prevention" and "detection"), so far as it relates to serious crime, shall apply for the purposes of this Act as it applies for the purposes of Chapter I of Part I of that Act."

The Criminal Procedure and Investigations Act 1996 (c. 25)

7.—(1) In each of sections 3(7), 7(6), 8(6) and 9(9) of the Criminal Procedure and Investigations Act 1996 (exceptions for interceptions from obligations to make disclosures to the defence), for paragraphs (a) and (b) there shall be substituted "it is material the disclosure of which is prohibited by section 17 of the Regulation of Investigatory Powers Act 2000."

(2) In section 23(6) of that Act (code of practice not to apply to material intercepted under the Interception of Communications Act 1985), after "1985" there shall be inserted "or under the authority of an interception warrant under section 5 of the Regulation of Investigatory Powers Act 2000".

The Police Act 1997 (c. 50)

8.—(1) In section 91(9) of the Police Act 1997 (staff for Surveillance Commissioners)—

(a) after "Chief Commissioner" there shall be inserted "and subject to the approval of the Treasury as to numbers"; and

(b) after "Commissioners" there shall be inserted "and any Assistant Surveillance Commissioners holding office under section 63 of the Regulation of Investigatory Powers Act 2000".

(2) In section 93(3) of that Act (persons who may make an application to an authorising officer within section 93(5))—

(a) in paragraph (a), for "(e)" there shall be substituted "(ea) or (ee)"; and

(b) after that paragraph there shall be inserted—

"(aa) if the authorising officer is within subsection (5)(eb) to (ed), by a member, as the case may be, of the Royal Navy Regulating Branch, the Royal Military Police or the Royal Air Force Police;".

(3) In section 94(1) of that Act (circumstances in which authorisations may be given in absence of authorising officer), in paragraph (b), for ", (f), (g) or (h)" there shall be substituted "or (f)", and after that paragraph there shall be inserted"or (c) if the authorising officer is within paragraph (g) of section 93(5), it is also not reasonably practicable for the application to be considered either—

(i) by any other person designated for the purposes of that paragraph; or

(ii) by the designated deputy of the Director General of the National Crime Squad."

(4) In section 94(2) of that Act (persons who may act in absence of the authorising officer)—

(a) after paragraph (d), there shall be inserted—

"(da) where the authorising officer is within paragraph (ea) of that subsection, by a person holding the rank of deputy or assistant chief constable in the Ministry of Defence Police;

(db) where the authorising officer is within paragraph (eb) of that subsection, by a person holding the position of assistant Provost Marshal in the Royal Navy Regulating Branch;

(dc) where the authorising officer is within paragraph (ec) or (ed) of that subsection, by a person holding the position of deputy Provost Marshal in the Royal Military Police or, as the case may be, in the Royal Air Force Police;

(dd) where the authorising officer is within paragraph (ee) of that subsection, by a person holding the rank of deputy or assistant chief constable in the British Transport Police;";

(b) in paragraph (e), the words "or (g)" and "or, as the case may be, of the National Crime Squad" shall be omitted; and

(c) after that paragraph, there shall be inserted—

"(ea) where the authorising officer is within paragraph (g) of that subsection, by a person designated for the purposes of this paragraph by the Director General of the National Crime Squad as a person entitled to act in an urgent case;".

(5) In section 94(3) of that Act (rank of police members of the National Crime Intelligence Squad and National Crime Squad entitled to act), after "(2)(e)" there shall be inserted "or (2)(ea)".

(6) In section 95 of that Act (authorisations: form and duration etc.)—

(a) in each of subsections (4) and (5), for the words from "the action" onwards there shall be substituted "the authorisation is one in relation to which the requirements of paragraphs (a) and (b) of section 93(2) are no longer satisfied."; and

(b) in subsection (6), for "or (e)" there shall be substituted ", (e) or (g)".

(7) In section 97 of that Act (authorisations requiring approval), in subsection (6), the words from "(and paragraph 7" onwards shall be omitted, and after that subsection there shall be inserted—

"(6A) The reference in subsection (6) to the authorising officer who gave the authorisation or in whose absence it was given shall be construed, in the case of an authorisation given by or in the absence of a person within paragraph (b), (e) or (g) of section 93(5), as a reference to the Commissioner of Police, Chief Constable or, as the case may be, Director General mentioned in the paragraph concerned."

(8) In section 103(7) of that Act (quashing authorisations), for the words from "and paragraph 7" onwards there shall be substituted "and subsection (6A) of section 97 shall apply for the purposes of this subsection as it applies for the purposes of subsection (6) of that section."

(9) In section 105 of that Act (appeals by authorising officers: supplementary), in subsection (1)(a), the word "and" shall be inserted at the end of sub-paragraph (i), and sub-paragraph (iii) and the word "and" immediately preceding it shall be omitted.

(10) In section 107 of that Act—

(a) in subsection (2) (report of Chief Surveillance Commissioner on the discharge of his functions under Part III of that Act)—

(i) for "the discharge of functions under this Part" there shall be substituted "the matters with which he is concerned"; and

(ii) for "any matter relating to those functions" there shall be substituted "anything relating to any of those matters";

(b) in subsection (4) (matters that may be excluded from a report), for "the prevention or detection of serious crime or otherwise" there shall be substituted "any of the purposes for which authorisations may be given or granted under this Part of this Act or Part II of the Regulation of Investigatory Powers Act 2000 or under any enactment contained in or made under an Act of the Scottish Parliament which makes provision equivalent to that made by Part II of that Act of 2000 or"; and

(c) after subsection (5) (duty to co-operate with the Chief Surveillance Commissioner) there shall be inserted the subsections set out in sub-paragraph (11).

(11) The subsections inserted after subsection (5) of section 107 of that Act are as follows—

"(5A) It shall be the duty of—

(a) every person by whom, or on whose application, there has been given or granted any authorisation the function of giving or granting which is subject to review by the Chief Commissioner,

(b) every person who has engaged in conduct with the authority of such an authorisation,

(c) every person who holds or has held any office, rank or position with the same public authority as a person falling within paragraph (a),

(d) every person who holds or has held any office, rank or position with any public authority for whose benefit (within the meaning of Part II of the Regulation of Investigatory Powers Act 2000) activities which are or may be subject to any such review have been or may be carried out, and

(e) every person to whom a notice under section 49 of the Regulation of Investigatory Powers Act 2000 (notices imposing a disclosure requirement in respect of information protected by a key) has been given in relation to any information obtained by conduct to which such an authorisation relates,

to disclose or provide to the Chief Commissioner all such documents and information as he may require for the purpose of enabling him to carry out his functions.

(5B) It shall be the duty of every Commissioner to give the tribunal established under section 65 of the Regulation of Investigatory Powers Act 2000 all such assistance (including his opinion as to any issue falling to be determined by that tribunal) as that tribunal may require—

(a) in connection with the investigation of any matter by that tribunal; or

(b) otherwise for the purposes of that tribunal's consideration or determination of any matter.

(5C) In this section "public authority" means any public authority within the meaning of section 6 of the Human Rights Act 1998 (acts of public authorities) other than a court or tribunal."

(12) In section 108(1) of that Act after "In this Part—" there shall be inserted—

""Assistant Commissioner of Police of the Metropolis" includes the Deputy Commissioner of Police of the Metropolis;".

(13) In Part VII of that Act, before section 134 there shall be inserted—

"Meaning of "prevention" and "detection".

133A. Section 81(5) of the Regulation of Investigatory Powers Act 2000 (meaning of "prevention" and "detection") shall apply for the purposes of this Act as it applies for the purposes of the provisions of that Act not contained in Chapter I of Part I."

The Northern Ireland Act 1998 (c. 47)

9. In paragraph 17(b) of Schedule 2 to the Northern Ireland Act 1998 (excepted matters), for "the Interception of Communications Act 1985" there shall be substituted "Chapter I of Part I of the Regulation of Investigatory Powers Act 2000".

The Electronic Communications Act 2000 (c. 7)

10. In section 4(2) of the Electronic Communications Act 2000 (exception to rules restricting disclosure of information obtained under Part I of that Act), for the word "or" at the end of paragraph (e) there shall be substituted—

"(ea) for the purposes of any proceedings before the tribunal established under section 65 of the Regulation of Investigatory Powers Act 2000; or".

The Financial Services and Markets Act 2000 (c. 8)

11. In section 394(7) of the Financial Services and Markets Act 2000 (exclusion of material from material of the Authority to which a person must be allowed access), for paragraphs (a) and (b) there shall be substituted—

"(a) is material the disclosure of which for the purposes of or in connection with any legal proceedings is prohibited by section 17 of the Regulation of Investigatory Powers Act 2000; or"

The Terrorism Act 2000 (c. 11)

12.—(1) In section 9(2)(d) of the Terrorism Act 2000 (proceedings under the Human Rights Act 1998), for "8" there shall be substituted "7".

(2) In each of paragraphs 6(3) and 7(5) of Schedule 3 to that Act (references to an

organisation and representative in paragraphs 5 and 8 of that Schedule), for "paragraphs 5 and 8" there shall be substituted "paragraph 5".

SCHEDULE 5

Repeals

Chapter	Short title	Extent of repeal
1975 c. 24.	The House of Commons Disqualification Act 1975.	In Part II of Schedule 1, the words "The Tribunal established under the Interception of Communications Act 1985", "The Tribunal established under the Security Service Act 1989", and "The Tribunal established under section 9 of the Intelligence Services Act 1994".
1975 c. 25.	The Northern Ireland Assembly Disqualification Act 1975.	In Part II of Schedule 1, the words "The Tribunal established under the Interception of Communications Act 1985", "The Tribunal established under the Security Service Act 1989", and "The Tribunal established under section 9 of the Intelligence Services Act 1994".
1985 c. 56.	The Interception of Communications Act 1985.	Sections 1 to 10. Section 11(3) to (5). Schedule 1.
1989 c. 5.	The Security Service Act 1989.	Sections 4 and 5. Schedules 1 and 2.
1989 c. 6.	The Official Secrets Act 1989.	In Schedule 1, paragraph 3.
1990 c. 41.	The Courts and Legal Services Act 1990.	In Schedule 10, paragraphs 62 and 74.
1994 c. 13.	The Intelligence Services Act 1994.	In section 6(1)(b), the words "of his department". In section 7(5)(b), the words "of his department". Sections 8 and 9. In section 11(1), paragraph (b). Schedules 1 and 2.
1997 c. 50.	The Police Act 1997.	In section 93(6), paragraph (f) and the word "and" immediately preceding it. In section 94(1), the word "or" at the end of paragraph (a). In section 94(2)(e), the words "or (g)" and "or, as the case may be, of the National Crime Squad". In section 94(4)— (a) the words "in his absence", in each place where they occur; and (b) paragraph (d) and the word "and" immediately preceding it. In section 97(6), the words from "(and paragraph 7" onwards. Sections 101 and 102. In section 104— (a) in subsection (1), paragraph (g); (b) in each of subsections (4), (5) and (6), paragraph (b) and the word "or" immediately preceding it; (c) in subsection (8), paragraph (b) and the word "and" immediately preceding it. In section 105(1)(a), sub-paragraph (iii) and the word "and" immediately preceding it. Section 106.

Chapter	Short title	Extent of repeal
		Section 107(6). Schedule 7.
1997 c. 68.	The Special Immigration Appeals Commission Act 1997.	Section 5(7).
1998 c. 37.	The Crime and Disorder Act 1998.	Section 113(1) and (3).
2000 c. 11.	The Terrorism Act 2000.	In Schedule 3, paragraph 8.

SEXUAL OFFENCES (AMENDMENT) ACT 2000

(2000 c. 44)

An Act to reduce the age at which, and to make provision with respect to the circumstances in which, certain sexual acts are lawful; to make it an offence for a person aged 18 or over to engage in sexual activity with or directed towards a person under that age if he is in a position of trust in relation to that person; and for connected purposes.

[30th November 2000]

. . .

3.—(1) Subject to subsections (2) and (3) below, it shall be an offence for a person aged 18 or over—
(a) to have sexual intercourse (whether vaginal or anal) with a person under that age; or
(b) to engage in any other sexual activity with or directed towards such a person,
if (in either case) he is in a position of trust in relation to that person.
(2) Where a person ("A") is charged with an offence under this section of having sexual intercourse with, or engaging in any other sexual activity with or directed towards, another person ("B"), it shall be a defence for A to prove that, at the time of the intercourse or activity—
(a) he did not know, and could not reasonably have been expected to know, that B was under 18;
(b) he did not know, and could not reasonably have been expected to know, that B was a person in relation to whom he was in a position of trust; or
(c) he was lawfully married to B.
(3) It shall not be an offence under this section for a person ("A") to have sexual intercourse with, or engage in any other sexual activity with or directed towards, another person ("B") if immediately before the commencement of this Act—
(a) A was in a position of trust in relation to B; and
(b) a sexual relationship existed between them.
(4) A person guilty of an offence under this section shall be liable—
(a) on summary conviction, to imprisonment for a term not exceeding six months, or to a fine not exceeding the statutory maximum, or to both;
(b) on conviction on indictment, to imprisonment for a term not exceeding five years, or to a fine, or to both.
(5) In this section, "sexual activity"—
(a) does not include any activity which a reasonable person would regard as sexual only with knowledge of the intentions, motives or feelings of the parties; but
(b) subject to that, means any activity which such a person would regard as sexual in all the circumstances.
4.—(1) For the purposes of section 3 above, a person aged 18 or over ("A") is in a position of trust in relation to a person under that age ("B") if any of the four conditions set out below, or any condition specified in an order made by the Secretary of State by statutory instrument, is fulfilled.

(2) The first condition is that A looks after persons under 18 who are detained in an institution by virtue of an order of a court or under an enactment, and B is so detained in that institution.

(3) The second condition is that A looks after persons under 18 who are resident in a home or other place in which—
> [1][...]

(c) accommodation is provided by an authority under section 26(1) of the Children (Scotland) Act 1995,

and B is resident, and is so provided with accommodation and maintenance or accommodation, in that place.

(4) The third condition is that A looks after persons under 18 who are accommodated and cared for in an institution which is—

(a) a hospital;

(b) a residential care home, nursing home, mental nursing home or private hospital;

(c) a community home, voluntary home, children's home or residential establishment; or

(d) a home provided under section 82(5) of the Children Act 1989,

and B is accommodated and cared for in that institution.

(5) The fourth condition is that A looks after persons under 18 who are receiving full-time education at an educational institution, and B is receiving such education at that institution.

(6) No order shall be made under subsection (1) above unless a draft of the order has been laid before and approved by a resolution of each House of Parliament.

(7) A person looks after persons under 18 for the purposes of this section if he is regularly involved in caring for, training, supervising or being in sole charge of such persons.

(8) For the purposes of this section a person receives full-time education at an educational institution if—

(a) he is registered or otherwise enrolled as a full-time pupil or student at the institution; or

(b) he receives education at the institution under arrangements with another educational institution at which he is so registered or otherwise enrolled.

(9) In this section, except where the context otherwise requires—

"authority" means—

(a) in relation to Great Britain, a local authority;
> [1][...]

"children's home" has—
> [1][...]

"community home" has the meaning given by section 53(1) of the Children Act 1989;

"hospital" has—
> [1][...]

(b) in relation to Scotland, the meaning given by section 108(1) of the National Health Service (Scotland) Act 1978; and
> [1][...]

"mental nursing home" has, in relation to England and Wales, the meaning given by section 22(1) of the Registered Homes Act 1984;

"nursing home"—
> [1][...]

(b) in relation to Scotland, means a nursing home registered under section 1 of the Nursing Homes Registration (Scotland) Act 1938; and
> [1][...]

"private hospital" has—
  (a) in relation to Scotland, the meaning given by section 12(2) of the Mental Health (Scotland) Act 1984; and
   ¹[...]
"residential care home"—
   ¹[...]
  (b) in relation to Scotland, means an establishment in respect of which a person is registered under section 62 or 63 of the Social Work (Scotland) Act 1968; and
   ¹[...]
"residential establishment" has the meaning given by section 93(1) of the Children (Scotland) Act 1995 as the meaning of that expression in relation to a place in Scotland;
"voluntary home" has—
   ¹[...]

NOTE
¹The definitions deleted apply to England and Wales, or to Northern Ireland, only.

5.—(1) Schedule 1 to the Sex Offenders Act 1997 (sexual offences to which Part I applies) shall be amended as follows.
(2) In paragraph 1 (offences under the law of England and Wales)—
 (a) in sub-paragraph (1), the word "and" immediately following paragraph (e) shall be omitted and after paragraph (f) there shall be inserted—
 "(g) an offence under section 3 of the Sexual Offences (Amendment) Act 2000 (abuse of position of trust)."; and
 (b) in sub-paragraph (2)(a), for the words "paragraph (a)(iii), (v) and (vi) does not" there shall be substituted the words "paragraphs (a)(iii), (v) and (vi) and (g) do not".
(3) In paragraph 2 (offences under the law of Scotland)—
 (a) in sub-paragraph (1), after paragraph (d) there shall be inserted—
 "(e) an offence under section 3 of the Sexual Offences (Amendment) Act 2000 (abuse of position of trust)."; and
 (b) in sub-paragraph (2), the word "and" immediately before paragraph (f) shall be omitted and after that paragraph there shall be inserted—
 "(g) paragraph (e) does not apply where the offender was under 20.".
(4) In paragraph 3 (offences under the law of Northern Ireland)—
 (a) in sub-paragraph (1), the word "and" immediately following paragraph (i) shall be omitted and after paragraph (j) there shall be inserted—
 "(k) an offence under section 3 of the Sexual Offences (Amendment) Act 2000 (abuse of position of trust)."; and
 (b) in sub-paragraph (2)(a), for the words "and (d)" there shall be substituted the words ", (d) and (k)".
6.—(1) In subsection (1) of section 31 of the Criminal Justice Act 1991 (interpretation of Part I), in the definition of "sexual offence"—
 (a) after paragraph (f) there shall be inserted—
 "(fa) an offence under section 3 of the Sexual Offences (Amendment) Act 2000;" and
 (b) in paragraph (g), for "(f)" there shall be substituted "(fa)".
(2) In subsection (10) of section 210A of the Criminal Procedure (Scotland) Act 1995 (extended sentences for sex and violent offenders), in the definition of "sexual offence" the word "and" immediately before paragraph (xix) shall be omitted and after that paragraph there shall be inserted "and

(xx) an offence under section 3 of the Sexual Offences (Amendment) Act 2000 (abuse of position of trust).".

7.—(1) This Act may be cited as the Sexual Offences (Amendment) Act 2000.

(2) For the purposes of the Scotland Act 1998, this Act shall be taken to be a pre-commencement enactment within the meaning of that Act.

(3) This Act shall come into force on such day as the Secretary of State may by order made by statutory instrument appoint; and different days may be appointed for different purposes.

(4) This Act extends to Northern Ireland.

DIVISION B

Acts of Adjournal, etc.

CONTENTS

HIGH COURT OF JUSTICIARY, SCOTLAND
SHERIFF COURT, SCOTLAND
SUMMARY JURISDICTION, SCOTLAND

ACT OF ADJOURNAL (CRIMINAL PROCEDURE RULES) 1996

(S.I. 1996 No. 513 (S.47))

Made	*29th February 1996*
Coming into force	*1st April 1996*

The Lord Justice General, Lord Justice-Clerk and Lords Commissioners of Justiciary under and by virtue of the powers conferred on them by section 305 of the Criminal Procedure (Scotland) Act 1995, the provisions specified in Schedule 1 to this Act of Adjournal and of all other powers enabling them in that behalf, do hereby enact and declare:

Citation and commencement

1.—(1) This Act of Adjournal may be cited as the Act of Adjournal (Criminal Procedure Rules) 1996 and shall come into force on 1st April 1996.

(2) This Act of Adjournal shall be inserted in the Books of Adjournal.

Criminal Procedure Rules

2. Schedule 2 to this Act of Adjournal shall have effect for the purpose of providing new rules of procedure in the High Court of Justiciary, in the sheriff court in exercise of its criminal jurisdiction, and in the district court.

Revocations

3. The Acts of Adjournal mentioned in Schedule 3 to this Act of Adjournal are revoked to the extent specified in the third column of that Schedule.

SCHEDULE 1

Preamble

POWERS UNDER AND BY VIRTUE OF WHICH THIS ACT OF ADJOURNAL IS MADE

Column 1 *Relevant enactment conferring power*	Column 2 *Relevant amending enactment*	Column 3 *Relevant provision in Schedule 2*
Section 1 of the Public Records (Scotland) Act 1937 (c. 43)		Rule 3.6
Section 2A(3) of the Backing of Warrants (Republic of Ireland) Act 1965 (c. 45)	Inserted by paragraph 5 of Schedule 1 to the Criminal Justice Act 1988 (c. 33) and continued by section 37(5) of the Extradition Act 1989 (c. 33)	Rule 30.3(2) and (6)
Section 8 of the Backing of Warrants (Republic of Ireland) Act 1965 (c. 45)	Amended by paragraph 5 of Schedule 4 to the Criminal Procedure (Consequential Provisions) (Scotland) Act 1995 (c. 40)	Chapter 30

Column 1 *Relevant enactment conferring power*	Column 2 *Relevant amending enactment*	Column 3 *Relevant provision in Schedule 2*
Section 38 of the Legal Aid (Scotland) Act 1986 (c. 47)		Chapter 33
Section 90(4) of the Debtors (Scotland) Act 1987 (c. 18)		Rule 20.8(2)
Section 10(3) of the Extradition Act 1989 (c. 33)		Rule 34.2(2) to (8)
Section 14(3) of, and paragraph 9(3) of Schedule 1 to, the Extradition Act 1989 (c. 33)		Rule 34.5
Section 8(5) of the Computer Misuse Act 1990 (c. 18)		Rule 35.1
Section 10 of the Criminal Justice (International Co-operation) Act 1990 (c. 5)		Chapter 36
Section 19(2) of the Prisoners and Criminal Proceedings (Scotland) Act 1993 (c. 9)		Rule 15.2(6)
Section 18(7) of the Proceeds of Crime (Scotland) Act 1995 (c. 43)		Rule 37.2

Paragraph 2

SCHEDULE 2

CRIMINAL PROCEDURE RULES 1996

ARRANGEMENT OF RULES

PART I

Preliminary and administration

CHAPTER 1

CITATION, INTERPRETATION ETC.

1.1. Citation of these Rules
1.2. Interpretation
1.3. Forms
1.4. Direction relating to Advocate General

CHAPTER 2

SERVICE OF DOCUMENTS

2.1. Service on Crown
2.2. Citation in solemn proceedings
2.3. General provisions for service
2.4. Service on witnesses
2.5. Service by post
2.6. Forms of execution of service
2.7. Proof of service furth of Scotland

CHAPTER 3

COURT RECORDS

PART II

General

CHAPTER 4

BAIL

CHAPTER 5

JUDICIAL EXAMINATION

CHAPTER 6

PROCEEDINGS INVOLVING CHILDREN

CHAPTER 7

MENTAL DISORDER

PART III

Solemn proceedings

CHAPTER 8

THE INDICTMENT

CHAPTER 9

FIRST DIETS AND PRELIMINARY DIETS

CHAPTER 10

PLEA OF GUILTY

CHAPTER 11

NOTICES BY ACCUSED IN RELATION TO DEFENCE

CHAPTER 12

ALTERATION AND POSTPONEMENT OF SOLEMN TRIAL DIET

CHAPTER 13

SUMMONING OF JURORS

CHAPTER 14

PROCEDURE AT TRIAL IN SOLEMN PROCEEDINGS

CHAPTER 15

APPEALS FROM SOLEMN PROCEEDINGS

PART IV

Summary proceedings

CHAPTER 16

COMPLAINTS

CHAPTER 17

SUMMARY PRE-TRIAL PROCEDURE

CHAPTER 18

PROCEDURE AT TRIAL IN SUMMARY PROCEEDINGS

CHAPTER 19

APPEALS FROM SUMMARY PROCEEDINGS

PART V

Sentencing

CHAPTER 20

SENTENCING

PART VI

Evidence

CHAPTER 21

UNCONTROVERSIAL EVIDENCE, HEARSAY AND PRIOR STATEMENTS

CHAPTER 22

EVIDENCE OF CHILDREN

CHAPTER 23

LETTERS OF REQUEST

CHAPTER 24

EVIDENCE ON COMMISSION

CHAPTER 25

RECORD OF JUDICIAL EXAMINATION AS EVIDENCE IN SOLEMN PROCEEDINGS

CHAPTER 26

DOCUMENTARY EVIDENCE

CHAPTER 27

ROUTINE EVIDENCE, SUFFICIENT EVIDENCE AND PROOF OF PREVIOUS CONVICTIONS

PART VII

Miscellaneous procedures

CHAPTER 28

IDENTIFICATION PARADES

CHAPTER 29

PRECOGNITION ON OATH OF DEFENCE WITNESSES

CHAPTER 30

PROCEEDINGS FOR THE EXECUTION OF IRISH WARRANTS

CHAPTER 31

REFERENCES TO THE EUROPEAN COURT OF JUSTICE

CHAPTER 32

ANNOYING CREATURES

CHAPTER 33

LEGAL AID

CHAPTER 34

EXTRADITION

CHAPTER 35

COMPUTER MISUSE ACT 1990

CHAPTER 36

CRIMINAL JUSTICE (INTERNATIONAL CO-OPERATION) ACT 1990

CHAPTER 37

PROCEEDINGS UNDER THE PROCEEDS OF CRIME (SCOTLAND) ACT 1995

CHAPTER 37A

PROCEEDINGS UNDER SECTION 7 OF THE KNIVES ACT 1997

CHAPTER 38

TRANSFER OF APPEAL OF DECEASED PERSONS

CHAPTER 39

PROCEEDINGS UNDER GENERAL LAW (CONSOLIDATION) (SCOTLAND) ACT 1995

CHAPTER 40

DEVOLUTION ISSUES

PART I

Preliminary and administration

CHAPTER 1

¹CITATION, INTERPRETATION ETC.

Citation of these Rules

1.1. These Rules may be cited as the Criminal Procedure Rules 1996.

Interpretation

1.2.—(1) In these Rules, unless the context otherwise requires—
"the Act of 1995" means the Criminal Procedure (Scotland) Act 1995;
"counsel" means a practising member of the Faculty of Advocates or a solicitor having a right of audience before the High Court by virtue of section 25A of the Solicitors (Scotland) Act 1980;
(2) Unless the context otherwise requires, a reference to a specified Chapter, Part, rule or form is a reference to the Chapter, Part, rule, or form in the appendix to these Rules, so specified in these Rules; and a reference to a specified paragraph, sub-paragraph or head is a reference to that paragraph of the rule or form, that sub-paragraph of the paragraph or that head of the sub-paragraph, in which the reference occurs.

Forms

1.3. Where there is a reference to the use of a form in these Rules, that form in the appendix to these Rules, or a form substantially to the same effect, shall be used with such variation as circumstances may require.

Direction relating to Advocate General

²**1.4.** The Lord Justice General may, by direction, specify such arrangements as he considers necessary for, or in connection with, the appearance in court of the Advocate General for Scotland.

NOTES
¹As amended by the Act of Adjournal (Criminal Procedure Rules Amendment No. 3) 1999 (S.I. 1999 No. 1387) para. 2(2)(a) (effective May 19, 1999).
²Inserted by the Act of Adjournal (Criminal Procedure Rules Amendment No. 3) 1999 (S.I. 1999 No. 1387) para. 2(2)(b) (effective May 19, 1999).

CHAPTER 2

SERVICE OF DOCUMENTS

Service on Crown

2.1. Any document that requires to be sent to or served on the Lord Advocate or the prosecutor under any enactment or rule of law shall be sent to or served on, as the case may be—
(a) if it relates to a case set down for trial in the High Court, the Crown Agent;

(b) if it relates to a case set down for trial in the sheriff court or district court, the appropriate procurator fiscal.

Citation in solemn proceedings

2.2.—(1) Subject to rule 2.4 (service on witnesses), this rule applies to the citation of, and service on, an accused under section 66 of the Act of 1995 (service and lodging of indictment, etc.).

(2) Service shall be effected by an officer of law—

(a) delivering the document to the accused personally;

(b) leaving the document in the hands of a member of the family of the accused or other occupier or employee at the proper domicile of citation of the accused;

(c) affixing the document to the door of, or depositing it in, the proper domicile of citation of the accused; or

(d) where the officer of law serving the document has reasonable grounds for believing that the accused, for whom no proper domicile of citation has been specified, is residing at a particular place but is unavailable—

   (i) leaving the document in the hands of a member of the family of the accused or other occupier or employee at that place; or

   (ii) affixing the document to the door of, or depositing it in, that place.

(3) In this rule, "proper domicile of citation" means the address at which the accused may be cited to appear at any diet relating to the offence with which he is charged or an offence charged in the same proceedings as that offence or to which any other intimation or document may be sent.

General provisions for service

2.3.—(1) Subject to the following paragraphs of this rule, the citation of, or the service of any document on, a person under or by virtue of the Act of 1995, these Rules or any other enactment shall, unless otherwise provided in the relevant enactment, be effected in the same manner, with the necessary modifications, as the citation of an accused in summary proceedings under section 141 of that Act (manner of citation) or under rule 2.2 of these Rules (citation in solemn proceedings).

(2) The citation of a probationer to appear before a court following a conviction on indictment under section 232 (probation orders: failure to comply with requirements), or section 233 (probation orders: commission of further offence), of the Act of 1995 shall be effected on the probationer in the same manner, with the necessary modifications, as the citation of an accused under rule 2.2 or by post.

(3) The citation in Form 29.3 of a person to attend a diet fixed for taking his precognition on oath under section 291 of the Act of 1995 (precognition on oath of defence witnesses) shall be made by personal service on him by an officer of law acting on the instructions of the accused or his solicitor.

Service on witnesses

2.4.—(1) Service of a citation by the prosecution or defence on a witness in any proceedings may, in the first instance, be by post.

(2) Where citation of a witness has been attempted by post but has not been effected, or the witness has not returned Form 8.2–D or Form 16.6–B, as the case may be, within the period prescribed in rule 8.2(3) or 16.6(1), as the case may be, citation of that witness shall be effected by an officer of law delivering the document to the witness personally.

Service by post

2.5.—(1) Subject to any provision in the Act of 1995, service by post shall be by registered post, ordinary first class post or the first class recorded delivery service.

(2) Where the citation of, or service on, any person is effected by post under these Rules, the date of citation shall be deemed to be the day after the date of posting.

Forms of execution of service

2.6.—(1) The execution of service of a citation and notice to appear of a person accused on indictment referred to in rule 8.2(1) (citation of accused and witnesses) shall be in Form 2.6–A.

(2) The execution of service of a complaint on an accused shall be in Form 2.6–B.

(3) The execution of personal service of a citation of a witness cited to appear at a trial on indictment shall be in Form 2.6–C.

(4) The execution of personal service of a citation of a witness cited to appear at a trial on summary complaint shall be in Form 2.6–D.

(5) The execution of a citation of a probationer under section 232(1) (failure to comply with requirement of probation order), or section 233(1) (commission of further offence while on probation), of the Act of 1995 shall be in Form 2.6–E.

(6) The execution of a citation or service under rule 2.3(1) (general provisions for service) shall, with the necessary modifications, be in Form 2.6–F.

Proof of service furth of Scotland

2.7. Where any citation of an accused is served in England, Wales or Northern Ireland by an officer effecting such service in accordance with section 39(3) of the Criminal Law Act 1977 (citation of person charged with crime or offence to appear before a court in Scotland), the evidence of—

(a) that officer on oath, or

(b) written execution of service by him,

shall be sufficient evidence of that service.

CHAPTER 3

COURT RECORDS

Books of Adjournal

3.1.—(1) The Edinburgh Book of Adjournal and the Book of Adjournal for cases heard outwith Edinburgh shall respectively contain—

(a) in the case of a trial in the High Court—

(i) the record copy of the indictment;

(ii) a summary of the proceedings in Form 3.1–A;

(iii) the relative printed list of assize;

(b) in the case of a petition to the High Court—

(i) the record copy of the petition;

(ii) a summary of the proceedings in Form 3.1–B.

(2) The Edinburgh Book of Adjournal shall contain the Acts of Adjournal.

(3) The summary of proceedings referred to in paragraph (1) shall be signed by the Clerk of Justiciary; and, on being so signed, shall have effect and shall be treated for all purposes, including extracts, as a true and sufficient record of the proceedings to which it relates.

Form of minuting in solemn proceedings

3.2. Subject to the provisions of any other enactment, the forms of minuting in solemn proceedings before the sheriff shall be in accordance with the forms used in the High Court.

Interlocutors in High Court to be signed by clerk of court

3.3. In the High Court, an interlocutor shall be distinctly minuted or entered in the record, and that entry shall be signed by the clerk of court.

Record copies of indictments etc. to be inserted in record books

3.4.—(1) The record copies of indictments brought before the High Court, and the record copies of all printed proceedings in that court, shall be inserted in the books of adjournal, either at their proper place in the body of such books, or at the end of the volume in which the relative procedure is recorded (in which case they shall be distinctly referred to as so appended); and the books of adjournal so made up and completed shall be and be taken to be and be used as the books of adjournal of that court.

(2) Where an indictment in solemn proceedings in a sheriff court is either wholly or partly printed, a copy of it, either wholly or partly printed, shall be inserted in the record book of court, either in its proper place in the body of that book or at the end of the volume in which the relative procedure is recorded (in which case it shall be distinctly referred to as so appended).

Form of recording warrants for remission of sentences

3.5. The Clerk of Justiciary shall cause all warrants under the royal sign manual for remission of sentences received by him to be bound in volumes and indexed, and a note of each warrant referring to a High Court sentence shall be entered in the margin of the minute book opposite the case to which it relates.

Registers kept by High Court

[1]**3.5A.** Any register kept by the High Court, whether or not under or by virtue of these Rules, may be kept either —
(a) in documentary form; or
(b) in electronic form (that is to say in a form accessible only by electronic means).

NOTE
[1]Inserted by the Act of Adjournal (Criminal Procedure Rules Amendment No. 3) 1999 (S.I. 1999 No. 1387) para. 2(3) (effective May 19, 1999).

Custody and transmission of records

3.6.—(1) Subject to the following provisions of this rule, the records of the High Court shall, after the Keeper of the Records of Scotland and the Clerk of Justiciary have consulted as to what records or parts of them may first be destroyed as not being considered to have a value for legal purposes or for historical or other research, be transmitted to the Keeper of the Records of Scotland under arrangements to be agreed between him and the Clerk of Justiciary.

(2) The Clerk of Justiciary and the Keeper of the Records of Scotland shall arrange for such transmissions at intervals of not less than five years nor more than 10 years from the date of the immediately preceding transmission and after similar consultation, for such periods as may be deemed by them to be appropriate.

(3) The Lord Justice General or Lord Justice-Clerk may make a direction from time to time in relation to the retention, disposal, transmission or

destruction by the Clerk of Justiciary of any document or category of document in the records of the High Court.

PART II

General

CHAPTER 4

BAIL

Application to alter address in bail order

4.1.—(1) An application under section 25(2) of the Act of 1995 (alteration of address specified in the order granting bail) shall—
   (a) include the following information—
      (i) identification of the proceedings in which the order was made;
      (ii) details of the new address; and
      (iii) reasons for the proposed change of address; and
   (b) be served on—
      (i) the clerk of the court which made the order; and
      (ii) the prosecutor.
(2) The prosecutor shall, within seven days of receipt of the copy of the application, notify the clerk of court in writing whether or not he intends to oppose the application.
(3) Where the prosecutor notifies the clerk of court that he does not intend to oppose the application, the court shall proceed to dispose of the application and may do so in the absence of the applicant.
(4) Where the prosecutor notifies the clerk of court that he intends to oppose the application, the clerk of court shall arrange a hearing before the court in chambers at which the applicant and the prosecutor may appear or be represented.
(5) The clerk of court shall give notice in writing of the decision of the court on an application referred to in paragraph (1) to—
   (a) the applicant;
   (b) the prosecutor; and
   (c) any co-accused.

CHAPTER 5

JUDICIAL EXAMINATION

Procedure in examination

5.1. Subject to the following provisions of this Chapter, the procedure to be followed in relation to examination of the accused under sections 35 to 39 of the Act of 1995 (which relate to judicial examination) on any charge shall be in accordance with existing law and practice.

Record of examination

5.2.—(1) The record of all proceedings under the sections of the Act of 1995 mentioned in rule 5.1 (procedure in examination) shall be kept by the sheriff clerk in Form 5.2, and shall be kept by him with the petition containing the charge or charges in respect of which the accused is brought before the sheriff for examination.
(2) The sheriff clerk shall transmit to the prosecutor a certified copy of the

petition under section 34 of the Act of 1995 (petition for warrant) and the record of proceedings—

(a) in relation to proceedings at which the accused is liberated in due course of law, on the conclusion of those proceedings; and

(b) in relation to any further examination, on the conclusion of that examination.

Verbatim record

5.3.—(1) Where the prosecutor provides a shorthand writer for the purposes of section 37(1) of the Act of 1995 (verbatim record of proceedings), the shorthand writer shall be—

(a) a person recognised by a court as a shorthand writer for the purposes of section 93 of the Act of 1995 (record of trial) or rule 29.18 of Schedule 1 to the Sheriff Courts (Scotland) Act 1907 (recording of evidence); or

(b) a person, other than a person mentioned in sub-paragraph (a) of this paragraph, who is skilled in the writing of shorthand (whether or not in the service of the prosecutor).

(2) In proceedings where a verbatim record is made by a person mentioned in paragraph (1)(b), a tape-recorded record of the proceedings shall also be made by the sheriff clerk in accordance with rule 5.4(1) and (2) (use of tape recorders).

(3) The name and address of the shorthand writer or the person recording the questions, answers and declarations by mechanical means shall be recorded in the record of proceedings.

(4) The shorthand writer shall record the whole proceedings relating to—

(a) the emitting by the accused of a declaration under section 35(4) of the Act of 1995; and

(b) any questions the accused is asked and any answers given including his declining to answer, under section 35(5) (accused brought before sheriff for further examination), or section 36 (judicial examination: questioning by prosecutor), of the Act of 1995.

(5) The shorthand writer shall not include in the transcript he makes of the proceedings any questions disallowed by the sheriff and any answers to such questions.

(6) The shorthand writer shall, in addition to the transcript of proceedings he makes under paragraph (4), also make such further transcript of the record made by him as either the judge at a first diet or, as the case may be, preliminary diet, or the High Court of Justiciary on an appeal, may direct for the purposes of considering an application under section 278(2) of the Act of 1995 (application that record of judicial examination not be read or be held inadmissible).

(7) The shorthand writer shall, as soon as possible after the conclusion of the proceedings, deliver to the prosecutor the transcript signed and certified by him in accordance with section 37(4)(b) of the Act of 1995.

Use of tape recorders

5.4.—(1) Any tape-recorded record of the proceedings made under rule 5.3(2), shall be made on two separate tapes simultaneously which shall be marked (and in this rule referred to as) "tape A" and "tape B" respectively.

(2) The sheriff clerk shall record on both tapes any proceedings mentioned in rule 5.3(5) (questions disallowed by sheriff), and for the purposes of maintaining a continuous record of the proceedings on both tapes, the proceedings may be interrupted at the instance of the sheriff clerk for such reasonable period as he may require.

(3) The sheriff clerk shall note in the record of proceedings the time of commencement and the time of termination of the tape-recording.

(4) On the conclusion of the proceedings in question, the sheriff clerk shall—
  (a) cause tape A to be sealed in an envelope or other similar container on which the following information shall be endorsed—
     (i) the name of the accused;
     (ii) the date of examination;
     (iii) the name of the presiding sheriff;
     (iv) the name of the shorthand writer;
     (v) the time of commencement and of termination of the tape; and
     (vi) the time and date of sealing of the tape; and
  (b) deliver tape B to the prosecutor.
(5) The sheriff clerk shall retain tape A until he is informed in writing by the prosecutor that the proceedings against the accused in respect of the charge or charges in relation to which he was examined have come to an end.
(6) The sheriff clerk shall not permit the seal on the container of tape A to be broken while he retains it except on being authorised to do so by a judge.
(7) On being so authorised the sheriff clerk shall only permit such access to tape A for such period as may be required for the purposes of the authorisation and, on the expiry of that period, shall again comply with the requirements of paragraphs (4)(a) and (5).
(8) The sheriff clerk shall, on being informed in writing by the prosecutor that the proceedings mentioned in paragraph (5) have come to an end, return tape A to the prosecutor.
(9) For the purposes of paragraph (8), the circumstances in which the proceedings have come to an end include—
  (a) a decision by the prosecutor to take no further action against the accused in respect of the charge in question;
  (b) following conviction and sentence of the accused in respect of the charge in question, the expiry of any statutory period of appeal without an appeal being taken; and
  (c) the final disposal of any appeal which has been taken.

Questions by prosecutor

5.5.—(1) The sheriff before whom the accused is brought for examination shall, if the prosecutor proposes to ask the accused questions regarding the alleged making by the accused of an extrajudicial confession to which section 36(3) of the Act of 1995 (confession in the hearing of constable) applies, be provided by the prosecutor before the commencement of the examination with a copy of the written record of the confession allegedly made.
(2) If the sheriff has not been provided with the written record required under paragraph (1), the prosecutor shall not ask the accused any such questions.
(3) The accused shall not be put on oath in the course of any proceedings on examination.
(4) The judge presiding at the trial of an accused who has declined to answer any question under section 36(1) of the Act of 1995 (prosecutor's questions as to matters in the charge or as to confession or declaration) may, in determining whether his having so declined may be commented upon by virtue of section 36(8) of the Act of 1995 (comments at trial), have regard to the terms of the charge to which the question related.
(5) The petition containing the terms of the charge to which the question referred to in paragraph (4) related, or a copy of the petition certified by the sheriff clerk as such, shall be sufficient evidence of the terms of that charge for the purposes of that paragraph; but the petition or a certified copy of the petition need not be included in any list of productions made available at the trial.
(6) The prosecutor shall, if the presiding judge proposes to have regard to

the terms of that charge for the purposes of paragraph (4), provide the presiding judge with the petition or certified copy of the petition referred to in paragraph (5).

Rectification of errors in transcript

5.6.—(1) A notice served under section 38(1)(a) of the Act of 1995 (notice of error or incompleteness in transcript) shall be in Form 5.6–A.

(2) The prosecutor shall, on serving or receiving such a notice, immediately lodge with the sheriff clerk the transcript certified in accordance with section 37(4)(b) of the Act of 1995.

(3) An application to the sheriff under section 38(1)(b) of the Act of 1995 (rectification of error or incompleteness) shall be in Form 5.6–B.

(4) The application referred to in paragraph (3) shall be lodged with the sheriff clerk with—

(a) a copy of the notice served under section 38(1)(a) of the Act of 1995; and

(b) an execution of service of that notice.

(5) Where the person on whom notice is served under section 38(1)(a) of the Act of 1995 agrees with the opinion to which that notice relates—

(a) he may intimate his agreement in Form 5.6–C to the person serving notice; and

(b) he shall, at the same time as intimating his agreement, send a copy of that form to the sheriff clerk.

(6) On the lodging of an application under paragraph (3), the sheriff shall, unless he dispenses with a hearing, by an order endorsed on the application—

(a) fix a date for a hearing; and

(b) order intimation of the date of the hearing to be made by the sheriff clerk to the prosecutor and to the accused person to whose examination the transcript relates.

(7) Where the sheriff authorises rectification of the transcript, he shall by an order endorsed on the application and signed by him specify the rectification authorised.

(8) The sheriff clerk shall give effect to any authorised rectification by amending the signed and certified transcript in accordance with the terms of the order of the sheriff and by initialling any amendment.

(9) On making any such amendment, the sheriff clerk shall—

(a) attach to the rectified transcript a copy of the order of the sheriff certified by the sheriff clerk;

(b) return the rectified transcript to the prosecutor;

(c) retain the application for rectification and the order of the sheriff made in respect of the application; and

(d) attach the documents mentioned in sub-paragraph (c) of this paragraph to the record of proceedings mentioned in rule 5.2 (record of examination).

Alteration of time limits by sheriff

5.7. Any direction made by the sheriff under section 37(7)(a) of the Act of 1995 (modifications as to time limits) shall be entered in the record of proceedings mentioned in rule 5.2 (record of examination) and authenticated by the sheriff subscribing his signature.

Postponement of trial diet by sheriff

5.8.—(1) The sheriff shall not make an order under section 37(7)(b) of the Act of 1995 (postponement of trial diet) in respect of a case set down for trial in the High Court.

(2) Any order by a sheriff under section 37(7)(b) of the Act of 1995 in a case not set down for trial in the High Court shall be—
  (a) endorsed on the record copy of the indictment;
  (b) authenticated by the signature of the sheriff; and
  (c) intimated—
      (i) by the prosecutor to any co-accused by serving on him an intimation of postponement in Form 5.8; and
      (ii) by the sheriff clerk to the governor of any institution in which any co-accused is detained.

Postponement of trial diet by High Court

5.9.—(1) If the sheriff considers that it may be appropriate to make an order under section 37(7)(b) of the Act of 1995 (postponement of trial diet) in respect of a case set down for trial in the High Court, he shall report the circumstances (including the making of any direction under section 37(7)(a) (modifications as to time limits)) to the Clerk of Justiciary.
  (2) The Clerk of Justiciary, on receiving the report of the sheriff, shall—
  (a) fix a diet (to which the trial diet shall be treated as being postponed) for the determination by a single judge of the High Court of the diet to which the trial shall be postponed; and
  (b) intimate that diet to the prosecutor, the accused and the governor of any institution in which any accused is detained.
  (3) The single judge of the High Court, in determining the diet to which the trial shall be postponed, shall have regard to the terms of the report of the sheriff.

Alteration of time limits by High Court

5.10.—(1) An application to the High Court for a direction to extend a time limit referred to in section 37(9) of the Act of 1995 shall be made by petition.
  (2) A petition under paragraph (1) shall be intimated to the other party and lodged with a certificate of intimation with the sheriff clerk.
  (3) The sheriff clerk shall, on the lodging of a petition, transmit it to the Clerk of Justiciary with a certified copy of the relative petition and record of proceedings.
  (4) A petition under paragraph (1) may be disposed of by a single judge of the High Court.
  (5) The Clerk of Justiciary shall, as soon as possible after he receives the petition—
  (a) fix a diet for the hearing; and
  (b) intimate the diet to the prosecutor and the accused.
  (6) The Clerk of Justiciary shall, on the disposal of the petition by the High Court, transmit a certified copy of the order of the High Court to the sheriff clerk.
  (7) The sheriff clerk shall, on receiving the certified copy of the order, attach it to the record of proceedings.

CHAPTER 6

PROCEEDINGS INVOLVING CHILDREN

Interpretation of this Chapter

6.1. In this Chapter—
  "the Act of 1937" means the Children and Young Persons (Scotland) Act 1937;
  "court" means the sheriff sitting as a court of summary jurisdiction.

Application of summary procedure

6.2. The procedure in summary proceedings shall apply, in relation to proceedings against a child as it applies to proceedings against an adult, subject to the provisions of the Act of 1937, the Act of 1995 and this Chapter.

Assistance for unrepresented child

6.3.—(1) Where a child is unrepresented in any proceedings, the parent or guardian of the child may assist him in conducting his defence.

(2) Where the parent or guardian of the child cannot be found, or cannot in the opinion of the court reasonably be required to attend, the court may allow a relative or other responsible person to assist the child in conducting his defence.

Procedure in summary proceedings

6.4. In a case where a child is brought before a court on a complaint, the sheriff—

(a) shall explain to the child the substance of the charge in simple language suitable to his age and understanding, and shall then ask the child whether he admits the charge;

(b) if satisfied, after trial or otherwise, that the child has committed an offence, shall so inform the child and—

    (i) the child and his parent, guardian, relative or other responsible person assisting the child, or the person representing the child, shall be given an opportunity to make a statement, and

    (ii) shall obtain such information as to the general conduct, home surroundings, school record, health and character of the child as may enable the sheriff to deal with the case in the best interests of the child and may remand the child for such enquiry as may be necessary; and

(c) if the sheriff considers it necessary in the interests of the child while considering disposal after conviction, may require the parent, guardian, relative or other responsible person assisting the child, or the person representing the child, or the child, as the case may be, to withdraw from the court.

Failure to comply with probation order

6.5.—(1) Any citation requiring the appearance of a child before the court in respect of a failure to comply with a probation order shall be accompanied by a notice—

(a) giving the reasons for the issue of such citation, and

(b) stating in what respects it is alleged that any one or more of the requirements of the probation order has or have not been complied with by him;

and, in any case where the child has been apprehended without prior citation, such a notice shall be handed to him in court.

(2) On the child appearing in court, the sheriff shall explain to the child in simple language suitable to his age and understanding the effect of the notice, and shall then ask him whether he admits having failed to comply with the requirements of the probation order as alleged.

(3) Where the child does not admit the alleged failure to comply with the requirements of the probation order, the proceedings shall thereafter be conducted and the matter shall be determined by the court in the same

manner as if the same were a matter which had arisen for determination on the original complaint.

Separation of children at sittings

6.6.—(1) The court shall take steps, so far as possible, to prevent children attending sittings of the court from mixing with one another.

(2) If this cannot be achieved by holding separate sittings or fixing different hours for the different cases and types of cases coming before it, the court may order additional waiting rooms to be brought into use or may provide for an attendant in the waiting room.

Restrictions on reports of proceedings involving children

6.7.—(1) Any direction made by a court under subsection (3)(a) (person under 16 is a witness only) of section 47 (restriction on report of proceedings involving children) of the Act of 1995 shall specify the person in respect of whom the direction is made.

(2) Any direction made by a court under subsection (3)(b) of section 47 of the Act of 1995 (restrictions dispensed with) shall specify the person in respect of whom the direction is made and the extent to which the provisions of the section are dispensed with in relation to that person.

(3) Any such direction shall be pronounced in open court and its terms shall be recorded in the record of proceedings; and the direction as so recorded shall be authenticated by the signature of the clerk of court.

CHAPTER 7

MENTAL DISORDER

Application for interim hospital orders

7.1.—(1) Where the court has made or renewed an interim hospital order under section 53 of the Act of 1995 and the responsible medical officer has intimated to the prosecutor that—

(a) he seeks a continuation of the order, or

(b) he seeks termination of the order before the date on which it would otherwise cease to have effect,

the prosecutor shall make an application in Form 7.1–A, to the court which made the order, to renew or terminate the order, as the case may be.

(2) Where an application is made under paragraph (1)—

(a) the court shall, by interlocutor in Form 7.1–B, appoint a diet for hearing the application and, where appropriate, grant warrant to authorised officers of the hospital, or officers of law, to bring the offender from the hospital to the court for that diet; and

(b) the clerk of court shall intimate the application and the diet to the offender or his solicitor.

(3) Where, in an application under paragraph (1)(a), the court renews an interim hospital order before the date on which the order would otherwise cease to have effect, the period of renewal shall commence from the date on which the order would otherwise cease to have effect.

(4) Where the court makes an order to renew or terminate an interim hospital order, before the date on which it would otherwise cease to have

effect, the adjourned diet fixed when the previous order of the court was made shall be treated as being discharged.

PART III

Solemn proceedings

CHAPTER 8

THE INDICTMENT

Appeals in relation to extension of time for trial

8.1.—(1) A note of appeal under section 65(8) of the Act of 1995 (appeal to High Court against grant or refusal of extension of time) in respect of an appeal from a decision under section 65(3) of that Act (extension of 12 months period for commencement of trial on indictment) shall be in Form 8.1–A.

(2) A note of appeal under section 65(8) of the Act of 1995 in respect of an appeal from a decision under section 65(5) or (7) of that Act (extension of 80 or 110 days period of committal) shall be in Form 8.1–B.

(3) A note of appeal mentioned in paragraph (1) or (2) shall be served by the appellant on—
   (a) the respondent;
   (b) any co-accused; and
   (c) the clerk of the court against the decision of which the appeal is taken.

(4) The appellant shall lodge with the Clerk of Justiciary—
   (a) the note of appeal; and
   (b) the execution of service in respect of the persons mentioned in paragraph (3).

(5) The clerk of the court against the decision of which the appeal is taken shall, as soon as practicable after being served with the note of appeal, transmit to the Clerk of Justiciary the original application and all the relative documents; and the Clerk of Justiciary shall, on receiving them, assign the appeal to the roll and intimate the date of the diet to the appellant and the respondent.

Further provision as respects extension of twelve months period for commencement of trial on indictment

[1]**8.1A.** Where all the parties join in an application to extend, by a specific length of time, the period mentioned in subsection (1) of section 65 of the Criminal Procedure (Scotland) Act 1995 (that is to say, the period of twelve months within which a trial is to be commenced) the court may proceed, under subsection (3) of that section, to hear the parties without the attendance of an accused who has signed a minute, lodged with the Clerk of Justiciary or as the case may be with the sheriff clerk, consenting to the extension applied for; but the court shall not, on so hearing the parties, grant an extension which exceeds the extension applied for.

NOTE
[1]Inserted by the Act of Adjournal (Criminal Procedure Rules) (Amendment) 1999 (S.I. 1999 No. 78: effective March 1, 1999).

Fresh indictment as alternative to serving notice fixing new trial diet

[1]**8.1B.** Where the court, under section 80(3) of the Criminal Procedure (Scotland) Act 1995 (discharge of trial diet), has given leave to the prosecutor to serve a notice fixing a new trial diet, the prosecutor may if he

thinks fit instead serve, under section 66 of that Act (service and lodging of indictment etc.), a further indictment containing the same, or amended, charges; but the list of witnesses and list of productions lodged under subsection (5) of the said section 66 with the record copy of the further indictment shall not include any witness, or as the case may be any production, not included in either—

    (a) the lists copies of which were so lodged with the record copy of the indictment which was not brought to trial; or

    (b) a written notice which was timeously given to the accused under section 67(5) of that Act (provision for examining any witness or putting in evidence any production not included in the lists lodged) before leave was given to the prosecutor as mentioned above.

NOTE

  [1]Inserted by the Act of Adjournal (Criminal Procedure Rules) (Amendment) 1999 (S.I. 1999 No. 78: effective March 1, 1999).

Citation of accused and witnesses

8.2.—(1) The warrant to cite a person accused on indictment and any witnesses to a diet of trial, under section 66(1) of the Act of 1995 (warrant to cite accused and witnesses), shall be in Form 8.2–A.

(2) The notice for the purposes of section 66(6) of the Act of 1995 (notice to accused to appear) to be served on a person accused on indictment shall be in Form 8.2–B.

(3) The form of postal citation of a witness on a warrant issued under section 66(1) of the Act of 1995 shall be in Form 8.2–C; and the witness shall complete and return Form 8.2–D to the procurator fiscal, or the accused person or his solicitor, as the case may be, in the pre-paid envelope provided within 14 days after the date of citation.

(4) The form of personal citation of a witness on a warrant issued under section 66(1) of the Act of 1995 shall be in Form 8.2–E.

Notice of previous convictions

8.3. Any notice to be served on an accused under section 69(2) of the Act of 1995 (notice of previous convictions) shall be in Form 8.3.

CHAPTER 9

FIRST DIETS AND PRELIMINARY DIETS

Minute giving written notice

9.1.—(1) Any notice given under section 71(2) (notice of preliminary matter), or section 72(1) (preliminary diet: notice), of the Act of 1995 shall be by minute in Form 9.1.

(2) Any such minute that relates to a case set down for trial in the High Court at a sitting outside Edinburgh shall specify any productions required for the preliminary diet.

(3) That minute shall be lodged—

    (a) if it relates to a case set down for trial in the High Court, with the Clerk of Justiciary, or

    (b) if it relates to a case set down for trial in the sheriff court, with the sheriff clerk.

Intimation of minute

9.2.—(1) A formal execution of prior intimation of the minute to all other parties shall be lodged at the same time as the minute.

(2) If an execution mentioned in paragraph (1) is not presented with the minute, the Clerk of Justiciary or the sheriff clerk, as the case may be, shall refuse to accept the minute for lodging.

Procedure on lodging minute

9.3. On the lodging of the minute, the Clerk of Justiciary or the sheriff clerk, as the case may be, shall—
  (a) endorse on it the time and date on which it was received; and
  (b) as soon as possible, place the minute before a judge.

Order for preliminary diet

9.4.—(1) On considering the minute in the absence of the parties or of any person acting on their behalf, or otherwise as he thinks fit, the judge—
  (a) if the minute raises a matter mentioned in paragraph (a) of subsection (1) of section 72 of the Act of 1995 (competency and relevancy, etc.), shall make an order for a preliminary diet specifying the date and time of the diet and the period (if any) for which the trial diet is postponed in terms of subsection (4) of that section; or
  (b) if the minute raises a matter mentioned in paragraph (b), (c) or (d) of subsection (1) of that section, may make or refuse to make such an order.

(2) An order made under paragraph (1) shall not be invalid by reason only of having been made in the absence of the parties or of any person acting on their behalf.

(3) Any such order shall be—
  (a) endorsed on the minute;
  (b) signed by the judge; and
  (c) attached with the minute to the record copy of the indictment.

Intimation of order for preliminary diet

9.5. The Clerk of Justiciary shall, as soon as possible after the making of any order under rule 9.4(1) (order for preliminary diet), intimate its terms to all parties and to the governor of any institution in which any accused is detained.

Order for preliminary diet to be warrant for citation

9.6. Any order made under rule 9.4(1) (order for preliminary diet) specifying the period for which the trial diet is postponed, and any order made under section 72(5) of the Act of 1995 (extension by High Court of period of postponement of trial diet), extending that period shall, for the purposes of section 66 of the Act of 1995 (service and lodging of indictment, etc.), be treated as being a warrant issued by the Clerk of Justiciary to officers of law to cite accused persons, witnesses and jurors for the date to which the trial diet has by virtue of that order been postponed; and any such order shall have effect for those purposes.

Calling postponed diet

9.7. If, in relation to any case a trial diet has been postponed by virtue of an order mentioned in rule 9.6 (order for preliminary diet to be warrant for citation), any requirement to call that diet at any sitting of the court shall have effect only in relation to a sitting on the date to which the diet has been postponed.

Warrant for conveyance and transmission

9.8. A copy of any order for a preliminary diet under rule 9.4(1) certified by the Clerk of Justiciary shall be warrant—

   (a) for the conveyance to the preliminary diet of any accused who is in custody; and

   (b) in a case set down for trial by the High Court at a sitting outside Edinburgh in respect of which the preliminary diet has been ordered to be heard in Edinburgh, for the transmission to the Clerk of Justiciary of any productions specified in the minute.

Abandonment of matter to be raised

9.9.—(1) Where a diet has been fixed for a preliminary diet under section 72 of the Act of 1995 and the party raising the matter decides not to proceed with it, he shall give written notice of abandonment.

   (2) The notice of abandonment shall be in Form 9.9.

   (3) The notice shall be intimated forthwith to the clerk of court and to all other parties and to the governor of any institution in which the accused is detained.

   (4) On such intimation, it shall not be necessary to convene the court for the preliminary diet unless another minute giving written notice under section 72(1) of the Act of 1995 has been lodged after the lodging of the first notice and before the notice of abandonment.

Procedure at first diet or preliminary diet

9.10.—(1) A first diet or preliminary diet shall commence on the diet being called.

   (2) For the purposes of the application of section 93 of the Act of 1995 (record of trial) to a first diet or preliminary diet, the whole proceedings at the preliminary diet shall be proceedings at the trial for the purposes of that section.

   (3) A record of those proceedings, including—

   (a) a note of the decision made by the court in respect of any notice placed before it,

   (b) any continuation or adjournment, and

   (c) the plea stated under section 71(6) or 73(1) of the Act of 1995 (accused to state how he pleads),

shall be kept in accordance with existing law and practice.

   (4) At any time after the commencement of the first diet or preliminary diet, the judge may make an order continuing or adjourning the diet to another time or place; but the judge shall not require to make an order continuing that diet to the trial diet.

   (5) A copy of an order continuing or adjourning the first diet or preliminary diet under paragraph (4) certified by the Clerk of Justiciary shall be warrant—

   (a) for the conveyance to the continued or adjourned diet of any accused who may be in custody; and

   (b) for the citation to that diet of any witnesses.

   (6) In this rule, "first diet" means a first diet to which section 71(2) of the Act of 1995 (notice of preliminary matter) applies.

Applications for leave to appeal

9.11.—(1) An application for leave to appeal to the High Court under section 74(1) of the Act of 1995 (appeals in connection with first diets or preliminary diets) shall be made by motion to the judge at that diet immediately following the making of the decision in question, and shall be granted or refused at that time.

   (2) Where leave to appeal is granted, the judge shall consider whether or not to postpone the diet of trial; and, if the judge decides that it is necessary or desirable to do so, he may discharge the trial diet and fix a new diet under section 80 of the Act of 1995 (alteration and postponement of trial diet).

(3) Rule 9.15 (intimation of order postponing trial diet) shall apply to an order postponing a trial diet under this rule as it applies to an order postponing a trial diet under that rule.

(4) An order made under this rule shall be recorded in the record of proceedings.

Note of appeal

9.12.—(1) An appeal under section 74(1) of the Act of 1995 (appeals in connection with first diets or preliminary diets) shall be made in Form 9.12.

(2) The note of appeal shall be lodged—

(a) in a case set down for trial in the High Court, with the Clerk of Justiciary, or

(b) in a case set down for trial in the sheriff court, with the sheriff clerk, not later than two days after the making of the decision in question.

Procedure on lodging note of appeal

9.13.—(1) On the lodging of a note of appeal with the sheriff clerk, he shall endorse on it a certificate that leave to appeal has been granted and the date and time of lodging.

(2) On the lodging of a note of appeal against a decision of a sheriff, the sheriff clerk shall, as soon as possible—

(a) send a copy of the note of appeal to the other parties or their solicitors;

(b) request a report on the circumstances relating to the decision from the sheriff; and

(c) transmit the note of appeal to the Clerk of Justiciary with a certified copy of—

(i) the indictment;

(ii) the record of proceedings; and

(iii) any relevant document.

Report of sheriff

9.14.—(1) The sheriff, on receiving a request for a report under rule 9.13(2)(b) (report on circumstances relating to decision), shall, as soon as possible, send his report to the Clerk of Justiciary.

(2) The Clerk of Justiciary shall, on receiving the report of the sheriff—

(a) send a copy of the report to the parties or their solicitors;

(b) arrange for a hearing of the appeal as soon as possible; and

(c) cause to be copied any documents necessary for the appeal.

Intimation of order postponing trial diet

9.15.—(1) Where, in relation to an appeal under section 74(1) of the Act of 1995 (appeals in connection with first diets or preliminary diets) in a case set down for hearing in the sheriff court, the High Court makes an order under section 74(3) of that Act postponing the trial diet, the Clerk of Justiciary shall send a copy of the order to—

(a) the sheriff clerk;

(b) all parties to the proceedings; and

(c) the governor of any institution in which any accused is detained.

(2) Rule 9.6 (order for preliminary diet to be warrant for citation) and rule 9.7 (calling postponed diet) shall apply to an order mentioned in paragraph (1) of this rule as they apply to an order mentioned in rule 9.6.

Orders of appeal court

9.16.—(1) The Clerk of Justiciary shall intimate to the sheriff clerk the decision of the High Court disposing of an appeal under section 74(1) of the Act of 1995 in relation to a first diet.

(2) Where the High Court in disposing of an appeal under section 74(1) of the Act of 1995 reverses a decision that dismisses the case against the accused, and makes a direction to the court of first instance that it fix a trial diet, that direction shall be authority to the Clerk of Justiciary or the sheriff clerk, as the case may be, to issue a fresh warrant for citation under section 66 of that Act (service and lodging of indictment, etc.).

Abandonment of appeal

9.17.—(1) An appellant who has taken an appeal under section 74(1) of the Act of 1995 (appeals in connection with first diets or preliminary diets) may abandon the appeal at any time before the hearing of the appeal.

(2) An abandonment of such an appeal shall be made by lodging a minute of abandonment with the Clerk of Justiciary in Form 9.17.

(3) The Clerk of Justiciary, on receiving such a minute of abandonment of an appeal in a case set down for trial in the sheriff court, shall inform the sheriff clerk and the other parties or their solicitors.

(4) The sheriff, on the sheriff clerk being so informed, may proceed as accords with the case.

CHAPTER 10

PLEA OF GUILTY

Procedure for plea of guilty

10.1.—(1) A notice to appear at a diet of the appropriate court served on an accused under section 76(1) of the Act of 1995 (procedure where accused desires to plead guilty) shall—

(a) if an indictment has not already been served, be in Form 10.1–A;

(b) if an indictment has already been served, be in Form 10.1–B.

(2) In any case set down for trial in the High Court, any diet fixed by virtue of section 76(1) of the Act of 1995 may be called before the High Court sitting in Edinburgh whether or not—

(a) the case has already been set down for trial at any sitting elsewhere, or

(b) any notice has already been served on the accused under section 66(6) of that Act (notice of first and trial diet).

(3) In the application of subsection (3) of section 76 of the Act of 1995, the court may postpone the trial diet under that section if, but only if—

(a) all the accused have been served with a notice in accordance with subsection (1) of that section;

(b) all the accused are present at the diet called by virtue of subsection (1) of that section; and

(c) a motion to postpone the trial diet is made to the court at that diet.

(4) Where the court grants that motion, the order granting it shall—

(a) be endorsed on the record copy of the indictment;

(b) be signed by the presiding judge;

(c) be entered in the record of proceedings; and

(d) have effect, for the purposes of subsections (1) to (3) of section 66 of the Act of 1995 (service and lodging of indictment, etc.), as a warrant of citation issued under that section by the Clerk of Justiciary or sheriff clerk, as the case may be, for the date to which the trial diet has, by virtue of that order, been postponed.

(5) A copy of the order shall be sent by the clerk of court to the governor of any institution in which any accused is detained.

(6) Any requirement to call the diet in any case where such an order has been made shall have effect only in relation to the postponed trial diet.

CHAPTER 11

NOTICES BY ACCUSED IN RELATION TO DEFENCE

Notices of special defence etc.

11.1.—(1) Where a notice under section 78(1) of the Act of 1995 (plea of special defence etc.) is to be served on a co-accused, that notice may be served on his solicitor.

Notices by accused of witnesses and productions

[1]**11.2.** Any notice given by an accused under section 78(4) of the Act of 1995 (notice of witnesses and productions) shall be served on any co-accused or his solicitor.

NOTE
[1] As amended by Act of Adjournal (Criminal Procedure Rules Amendment) (Miscellaneous) (S.I. 1996 No. 2147 (s.171)) (effective September 9, 1996).

CHAPTER 12

ALTERATION AND POSTPONEMENT OF SOLEMN TRIAL DIET

Alteration of trial diet

12.1.—(1) Where circumstances arise in which the court may adjourn the trial diet to a subsequent sitting under section 80(1) of the Act of 1995 (alteration and postponement of trial diet), and the prosecutor proposes such an adjournment, he may for that purpose require the trial diet to be called at the sitting for which it was originally fixed at such time as he thinks appropriate.

(2) If, on the trial being so called, the prosecutor—

(a) informs the court that a warrant for an appropriate subsequent sitting of the court has been issued, and

(b) moves the court to adjourn the trial diet to that subsequent sitting, the court shall grant his motion.

(3) The presence of the accused in court when the trial diet was so called and adjourned shall be sufficient intimation to him of the adjourned diet.

(4) If the trial diet was so called and adjourned in the absence of the accused, the prosecutor shall immediately serve on the accused an intimation of adjournment in Form 12.1.

(5) The calling and the adjournment of the trial diet including a record as to the presence or absence of the accused, as the case may be, shall be endorsed by the clerk of court on the record copy indictment and entered in the record of proceedings in accordance with existing law and practice.

(6) A copy of the order of the court adjourning the trial diet to a subsequent sitting under section 80(1) of the Act of 1995 shall be sent by the Clerk of Justiciary or sheriff clerk, as the case may be, to the governor of any institution in which the accused is detained.

Applications for postponement of trial diet

12.2.—(1) Subject to paragraph (2), an application under section 80(2) of the Act of 1995 (application for postponement of trial diet) shall be made by minute in Form 12.2–A.

(2) Where all the parties join in the application, the application shall be made by joint minute in Form 12.2–B.

(3) A minute under this rule shall be lodged—

(a) in a case set down for trial in the High Court, with the Clerk of Justiciary, or

(b) in a case set down for trial in the sheriff court, with the appropriate sheriff clerk.

Orders fixing diet for hearing of application to postpone trial diet

12.3. Where a minute referred to in rule 12.2 (applications for postponement of trial diet) has been lodged, the court shall, or, in a case in which all parties join in the application, may, make an order endorsed on the minute—

(a) fixing a diet for a hearing of the application; and

(b) for service of the minute with the date of the diet on all parties.

Calling of diet for hearing application

12.4.—(1) A diet fixed under rule 12.3 (orders fixing diet for hearing application to postpone trial diet) shall be held in open court in the presence of all parties (unless the court permits the hearing to proceed in the absence of the accused under section 80(5) of the Act of 1995), and shall be commenced by the calling of the diet.

(2) On the calling of the diet, the prosecutor shall inform the court—

(a) whether any other cases have been set down for trial at the sitting in respect of which the application for postponement of the trial diet is made; and

(b) whether a warrant has been issued under section 66(1) of the Act of 1995 (warrant to cite accused and witnesses for trial) for a subsequent sitting of the court.

Orders relating to postponed trial diet

12.5.—(1) Where the court is informed by the prosecutor that no other cases have been set down for trial at the sitting in respect of which the application for postponement of the trial diet is made and has granted the application under section 80(2) of the Act of 1995 (application for postponement of trial diet), the court shall make an order authorising—

(a) if citations have been issued to jurors for the original trial diet, the issue to those jurors of intimation that they are not required to attend at the original diet but are required to attend at the new diet; and

(b) if such citations have not been issued, the issue to the jurors shown on the original list of jurors of citations requiring them to attend at the new trial diet.

(2) Where the court is informed by the prosecutor that other cases have been set down for trial at that sitting and the court has granted the application under section 80(2) of the Act of 1995, the court shall, in fixing a new trial diet, have regard to the time required to issue citations to jurors who have not been summoned under section 84(3) of that Act (sitting of High Court at town in which it does not usually sit) for the sitting in which the new diet is being fixed.

(3) Where—

(a) the court is of opinion that the original trial diet should not proceed, and

(b) the court has been informed that a warrant has been issued under section 66(1) of the Act of 1995 (warrant to cite accused and witnesses for trial diet) for a subsequent sitting of the court within the period mentioned in relation to that court in section 80(1) of that Act (alteration and postponement of trial diet), the court may, without prejudice to the powers under section 80(3) of that Act (power to discharge trial diet and fix, or give leave to prosecutor to serve notice fixing, new trial diet), make an order postponing the trial diet to that subsequent sitting; and that order shall have effect as if it had been made under section 80(1) of that Act.

Notice fixing new trial diet

12.6.—(1) Where the court gives leave to the prosecutor to serve a notice fixing a new trial diet under section 80(3) of the Act of 1995, the prosecutor shall consult with the Clerk of Justiciary or sheriff clerk, as the case may be, as to an appropriate date before fixing that diet.

(2) A notice mentioned in paragraph (1) shall be in Form 12.6, and—

(a) shall be served by the prosecutor on all parties and on the governor of any institution in which the accused is detained; and

(b) a copy of the notice and certificate of execution of service shall be lodged by the prosecutor as soon as possible with the clerk of court.

(3) A notice served under paragraph (2) shall, for the purpose of section 66(1) of the Act of 1995 (warrant to cite accused and witnesses for trial diet), be treated as being a warrant issued by the Clerk of Justiciary or sheriff clerk, as the case may be, to officers of law to cite accused persons, witnesses and jurors for the date specified in the notice for the new trial diet, and shall have effect for those purposes.

(4) The clerk of court shall, on receiving a copy of such a notice, attach it to the record copy of the indictment.

Record of proceedings under this Chapter

12.7. The clerk of court shall record by endorsation on the record copy of the indictment—

(a) the calling of the diet of the hearing of an application under section 80(2) of the Act of 1995 (application for postponement of trial diet),

(b) the proceedings at the hearing, and

(c) the decision of the court;

and that record shall be signed by the judge, and entered in the record of proceedings.

Joint applications without hearing

12.8.—(1) Where, in the case of a joint application under subsection (2) of section 80 of the Act of 1995 (application for postponement of trial diet), the court proposes to proceed without hearing the parties by virtue of subsection (4) of that section (joint application for postponement of trial diet), the Clerk of Justiciary or sheriff clerk, as the case may be, shall on the lodging of the minute attach it to the record copy of the indictment and place it before a judge in chambers.

(2) The order made by the judge in chambers in respect of the joint application shall be—

(a) recorded by endorsation on the record copy of the indictment;

(b) signed by the clerk of court;

(c) entered in the record of proceedings; and

(d) intimated by the clerk of court to the applicants or their solicitors.

(3) The clerk of court shall send to the governor of any institution in which any accused is detained a copy of the following orders of the court—

(a) an order under rule 12.3 (order fixing diet for hearing of application to postpone trial diet);

(b) an order under section 80(3) of the Act of 1995 discharging a trial diet and fixing a new trial diet; and

(c) an order under rule 12.5(3) adjourning a trial diet to a subsequent sitting.

Calling of adjourned diet

12.9. If, in relation to any case, a trial diet has been discharged or adjourned under this Chapter, any requirement to call that diet at any sitting of the court shall have effect only in relation to the sitting at which the new trial diet has been fixed.

Form of notice of diet where trial does not take place

12.10. A notice referred to in section 81(1) of the Act of 1995 (procedure where trial does not take place) shall be in Form 8.2–B and signed by the prosecutor.

CHAPTER 13

SUMMONING OF JURORS

List of jurors

13.1.—(1) The clerk of the court before which the trial is to take place, in preparing a list of jurors for the trial diet for the purposes of section 84(1) of the Act of 1995, shall have regard, in determining the number of jurors to be listed, to the powers of postponing or adjourning any trial diet exercisable by the court under the following provisions of the Act of 1995—

section 73(5) (postponement of trial diet at preliminary diet),

section 74(3) (postponement of trial diet in appeals in connection with first diets or preliminary diets),

section 76(3) (postponement of trial diet where not guilty plea not accepted),

section 80 (alteration and postponement of trial diet).

Citation of jurors

13.2.—(1) The citation under section 85(4) of the Act of 1995 of a person summoned to serve as a juror shall be served on that person in Form 13.2–A.

(2) The execution of citation under section 85(4) of the Act of 1995 of persons summoned to serve as jurors shall be in Form 13.2–B.

CHAPTER 14

PROCEDURE AT TRIAL IN SOLEMN PROCEEDINGS

Recording of not guilty plea

14.1. Where the accused pleads not guilty, the clerk of court shall make an entry in the record of proceedings for the purposes of section 88(1) of the Act of 1995 (recording plea of not guilty and balloting jury) that, in respect that the accused pleaded not guilty, the accused was remitted to an assize and that the jurors were balloted for and duly sworn to try the libel.

Balloting of jurors

14.2.—(1) The clerk of court shall cause the name and address of each juror to be written on a separate piece of paper, all the pieces being of the same size, and shall cause the pieces to be folded up, as nearly as may be in the same shape, and to be put into a box or glass and mixed, and the clerk shall draw out the pieces of paper one by one from the box or glass.

(2) Where any of the persons whose names shall be so drawn does not appear, or is challenged (with or without cause assigned) and is set aside or,

before any evidence is led, is excused, then such further names shall be drawn until the number required for the trial is completed.

Form of oath or affirmation to jurors

14.3.—(1) Where the clerk of court administers the oath to the jury in terms of section 88(6) of the Act of 1995 (administration of oath in common form), he shall do so in accordance with the form in Form 14.3–A.

(2) In the case of any juror who elects to affirm, the clerk of court shall administer the affirmation in accordance with the form in Form 14.3–B.

(3) The oath or the affirmation administered in accordance with paragraph (1) or (2), as the case may be, shall be treated as having been administered for the purposes of section 88(6) of the Act of 1995.

Jurors chosen for one trial may continue to serve

14.4.—(1) Where the conditions in section 88(4) of the Act of 1995 (circumstances in which jurors for one trial may serve on another) are met, and subject to paragraph (2) of this rule, the clerk of court shall at the commencement of the first trial engross the names and addresses of the jurors in the record of proceedings; and in the record of proceedings of the subsequent trial it shall be sufficient to mention—

(a) that the jurors who served on the preceding trial also served on the assize of the accused then under trial; and

(b) that no objection was made to the contrary.

(2) The jurors referred to in paragraph (1) shall be sworn together in the presence of the accused in the subsequent trial.

Form of oath or affirmation to witnesses

14.5.—(1) Where the judge administers the oath to a witness, he shall do so in accordance with the form in Form 14.5–A.

(2) In the case of any witness who elects to affirm, the judge shall administer the affirmation in accordance with the form in Form 14.5–B.

(3) The oath or affirmation administered in accordance with paragraph (1) or (2), as the case may be, shall be treated as having been administered in common form.

Sheriff's notes of evidence

14.6. The sheriff who has presided at a trial on solemn procedure shall duly authenticate and preserve the notes of the evidence taken by him in the trial and, if called upon to do so by the High Court, shall produce them, or a certified copy of them, to the High Court.

Form of record of proceedings

14.7. Where the proceedings at a trial are recorded, the entry in the record of proceedings shall be signed by the clerk of court and shall be in the form in Form 14.7.

Interruption of trial for other proceedings

14.8.—(1) Where a trial is interrupted under section 102 of the Act of 1995 (interruption of trial for other proceedings), a minute of continuation of the diet of the interrupted trial shall be entered in the record of proceedings.

(2) Where a trial is interrupted under section 102 of the Act of 1995, the

trial shall be continued to a time later on the same day or to such other time as may be specified in the minute of proceedings.

Interruption of proceedings for conviction or sentence

14.9.—(1) On conviction of an accused in solemn proceedings, the presiding judge may, without adjourning those proceedings, interrupt them by—

   (a) considering a conviction against that accused in other proceedings pending before that court for which he has not been sentenced; or

   (b) passing sentence on that accused in respect of the conviction in those other proceedings.

(2) Where the judge has interrupted any proceedings under paragraph (1), he may, in passing sentence on an accused person in respect of a conviction in those proceedings, at the same time pass sentence on that person in respect of any other conviction he has considered.

(3) No interruption of any proceedings under paragraph (1) shall cause the instance to fall in respect of any person accused in those proceedings or shall otherwise affect the validity of those proceedings.

Issue of extract convictions

14.10.—(1) Subject to the following paragraphs, no extract of a conviction shall be issued during the period of four weeks after the day on which the conviction took place.

(2) An extract of a conviction may be issued at any time where it is required as a warrant for the detention of the person convicted under any sentence which shall have been pronounced against him.

(3) In the event of—

   (a) an appeal under section 108 (Lord Advocate's appeal against sentence),

   (b) an intimation of intention to appeal under section 109(1), or

   (c) a note of appeal under section 110 in respect of an appeal under section 106(1)(b) (appeal against sentence passed on conviction),

of the Act of 1995 being lodged, no extract of a conviction shall be issued until such appeal, if it is proceeded with, is determined.

(4) Where an accused is convicted on indictment in the sheriff court of any crime or offence and an extract of that conviction is subsequently required in evidence, such extract shall be issued at any time by the clerk of the court having the custody of the record copy of the indictment although the plea of the accused may have been taken and the sentence on him pronounced in another court.

CHAPTER 15

APPEALS FROM SOLEMN PROCEEDINGS

Register and lists of appeals

15.1.—(1) The Clerk of Justiciary shall keep a register, in such form as he thinks fit, of all cases in which he receives intimation of intention to appeal or, in the case of an appeal under section 106 (right of appeal) or section 108 (Lord Advocate's appeal against sentence) of the Act of 1995, a note of appeal under section 110 of that Act.

(2) The register kept under paragraph (1) shall be open for public inspection at such place and at such hours as the Clerk of Justiciary, subject to the approval of the Lord Justice General, considers convenient.

(3) The Clerk of Justiciary shall—

(a) prepare from time to time, a list of appeals to be dealt with by the High Court; and

(b) cause such list to be published in such manner as, subject to the approval of the Lord Justice General, he considers convenient for giving due notice to persons having an interest in the hearing of such appeals by the High Court.

Forms of appeal

15.2.—(1) Any intimation under section 109(1) of the Act of 1995 (written intimation of intention to appeal) shall be in Form 15.2–A.

(2) A note under section 110(1) of the Act of 1995 (written note of appeal) shall be in Form 15.2–B.

(3) An application under section 111(2) of the Act of 1995 (application to extend time) shall be made in Form 15.2–C.

(4) An application under section 112(1) of the Act of 1995 (application of appellant for bail) shall be made in Form 15.2–D.

(5) The following documents shall be signed by the appellant or by his counsel or solicitor—

(a) an intimation of intention to appeal under section 109(1) of the Act of 1995 except where the appellant is the Lord Advocate;

(b) an application under section 111(2) of the Act of 1995 (application to extend time); or

(c) a note of appeal.

(6) An appeal under section 19 of the Prisoners and Criminal Proceedings (Scotland) Act 1993 (appeals in respect of decisions relating to supervised release orders) shall be in Form 15.2–B.

Appeals against refusal of applications heard by single judge

15.3.—(1) Where an application has been dealt with by a single judge of the High Court by virtue of section 103(5) of the Act of 1995 (powers exercisable by single judge), the Clerk of Justiciary shall notify the decision to the applicant in Form 15.3–A.

(2) In the event of such judge refusing any such application, the Clerk of Justiciary on notifying such refusal to the applicant shall forward to him a form in Form 15.3–B to complete and return forthwith if he desires to have his application determined by the High Court as constituted for the hearing of appeals under Part VIII of the Act of 1995 (appeals from solemn proceedings).

Extension of time by Clerk of Justiciary

15.4. Where, under section 110(2) of the Act of 1995, the Clerk of Justiciary extends the period for lodging a note of appeal, the period of any such extension shall be recorded on the completed form of intimation of intention to appeal.

Intimation of appeal against sentence of death

15.5. The Clerk of Justiciary shall intimate an appeal against a conviction in respect of which sentence of death has been pronounced, and the determination in any such appeal, immediately on such intimation or determination, as the case may be, to—

(a) the Secretary of State for Scotland; and

(b) the governor of the prison in which the appellant is detained.

Abandonment of appeals

15.6. A notice of abandonment under section 116(1) of the Act of 1995 (abandonment of appeal) shall be in Form 15.6.

Note of proceedings at trial

15.7. In an appeal under section 106(1) of the Act of 1995 (right of appeal), the High Court may require the judge who presided at the trial to produce any notes taken by him of the proceedings at the trial.

Clerk to give notice of date of hearing

15.8.—(1) Where the High Court fixes the date for the hearing of an appeal or of an application under section 111(2) of the Act of 1995 (application to extend time), the Clerk of Justiciary shall give notice to the Crown Agent and to the solicitor of the convicted person, or to the convicted person himself if he has no known solicitor; and the appellant or applicant shall, within seven days before the hearing, lodge three copies (typed or printed) of the appeal or application for the use of the court.

(2) Where the powers of the court are to be exercised by a single judge under section 103(5) of the Act of 1995 (powers exercisable by single judge), a copy of the application to be determined shall be lodged for the use of the judge.

(3) A notice by the Clerk of Justiciary to the Secretary of State for the purposes of section 117(4) of the Act of 1995 (notice that appellant or applicant be present at a diet) shall be in Form 15.8.

Continuation of hearings

15.9.—(1) The High Court, or any single judge exercising the powers of the High Court under section 103(5) of the Act of 1995 (powers exercisable by single judge), may continue the hearing of any appeal or application to a date, fixed or not fixed.

(2) Any judge of the High Court, or the person appointed by the court to take additional evidence, may fix any diet or proof necessary for that purpose.

Note to be kept of appeal

15.10.—(1) The Clerk of Justiciary shall, in all cases of appeal from a conviction obtained or sentence pronounced in the High Court, note on the margin of the record of the trial the fact of an appeal having been taken and the result of the appeal.

(2) In the case of an appeal taken against any conviction obtained or sentence pronounced in the sheriff court on indictment, the Clerk of Justiciary shall notify the clerk of that court of the result of the appeal; and it shall be the duty of the clerk of that court to enter on the margin of the record of the trial a note of such result.

Suspension of disqualification from driving pending appeal

15.11.—(1) Where a person who has been disqualified from holding or obtaining a driving licence following a conviction on indictment appeals against that disqualification to the High Court, any application to suspend that disqualification pending the hearing of the appeal shall be made—

    (a) if the sentencing court was the sheriff, by application to the sheriff; or

    (b) if the sentencing court was the High Court, or if an application to the sheriff under subparagraph (a) has been refused, by petition to the High Court.

(2) An application to the sheriff under paragraph (1)(a) shall be—

    (a) in Form 15.11–A, and

    (b) lodged with the sheriff clerk with a copy of the note of appeal endorsed with the receipt of the Clerk of Justiciary;

and the sheriff clerk shall record the order made by the sheriff on the application in the minute of proceedings.

(3) A petition to the High Court under paragraph (1)(b) shall be—

(a) in Form 15.11–B; and
(b) lodged with the Clerk of Justiciary.

Provisions supplemental to rule 15.11(3)

15.12.—(1) The petitioner or his solicitor shall, on lodging a petition under rule 15.11(3), send a copy of it to—
    (a) the Crown Agent; and
    (b) if the sentencing court was the sheriff, the clerk of that court.
(2) The High Court may order such further intimation (including intimation to the Lord Advocate) as it thinks fit, and may dispose of the application in open court or in chambers.
(3) An order made by a single judge under paragraph (2) shall not be subject to review.
(4) On an order being made on a petition under rule 15.11(3), the Clerk of Justiciary shall, if the sentencing court was the sheriff, send a certified copy of the order to the clerk of that court.
(5) Where the order referred to in paragraph (4) suspends a disqualification from driving, the Clerk of Justiciary shall also send a certified copy of the order to the Secretary of State with such further information as the Secretary of State may require.
(6) The Clerk of Justiciary shall, on determination of the appeal against a disqualification from driving—
    (a) if the sentencing court was the sheriff, send the clerk of that court a certified copy of the order determining the appeal and the clerk of that court shall, if appropriate, make the appropriate endorsement on the appellant's driving licence and intimate the disqualification to the persons concerned; or
    (b) if the appeal against the disqualification is refused, make the appropriate endorsement on the appellant's driving licence and intimate the disqualification to the persons concerned.
(7) Where leave to appeal has been refused under section 107 of the Act of 1995, "determination" in paragraph (6) of this rule means—
    (a) the fifteenth day after the date of intimation to the appellant or his solicitor of refusal of leave under subsection (1)(b) of that section, unless the appellant applies to the High Court for leave to appeal; or
    (b) the day two days after the date of intimation to the appellant or his solicitor of the refusal of leave by the High Court under subsection (5)(b) of that section.

Suspension of sentence under s.121A of the Act of 1995

[1]**15.12A.**—(1) Where under section 109(1) of the Act of 1995 a person lodges intimation of intention to appeal, any application for suspension of a relevant sentence under section 121A of that Act shall be made by petition to the High Court in Form 15.12A–A.
(2) Where a convicted person or the prosecutor lodges a note of appeal in respect of an appeal under section 106(1)(b) to (e) or 108 of the Act of 1995, as the case may be, any application for suspension of a relevant sentence under section 121A of that Act shall be made by petition to the High Court in Form 15.12A–B.
(3) A petition to the High Court under paragraph (1) or (2) shall be lodged with the Clerk of Justiciary.
(4) The court shall grant or refuse any application under paragraph (1) or (2) within 7 days of the petition having been lodged as mentioned in paragraph (3).

(5) Where the court grants an application under paragraph (1) or (2) the Clerk of Justiciary shall, if the sentencing court was the sheriff, send a certified copy of the order to the clerk of that court.

(6) In any case where—

(a) intimation of intention to appeal is lodged under section 109(1) of the Act of 1995; and

(b) a relevant sentence is suspended under section 121A of that Act, but no note of appeal is lodged under section 110 of that Act, the order suspending *ad interim* the relevant sentence shall be recalled with effect from the seventh day after the date on which the Clerk of Justiciary intimates that the appeal is deemed to have been abandoned.

(7) In the application of section 121A of the Act of 1995 (suspension of certain sentences pending appeal) to a case in which leave to appeal has been refused under section 107 of that Act, the word "determined" in subsection (1) of the said section 121A shall be construed as meaning—

(a) the fifteenth day after the date of intimation to the appellant or his solicitor and to the Crown Agent of refusal of leave under subsection (1)(b) of section 107 of that Act, unless the appellant applies to the High Court for leave to appeal; or

(b) the seventh day after the date of intimation to the appellant or his solicitor and to the Crown Agent of the refusal of leave by the High Court under subsection (5)(b) of section 107 of that Act.

NOTE

[1]Inserted by Act of Adjournal (Criminal Procedure Rules Amendment No. 4) (S.I. 1997 No. 1834) (effective August 1, 1997).

Suspension of disqualification etc. under section 121 of the Act of 1995

[1]**15.13.**—In the application of section 121 of the Act of 1995 (suspension of disqualification, forfeiture, etc.) to a case in which leave to appeal has been refused under section 107 of the Act of 1995, the word "determined" in subsections (1) and (2) of section 121 of that Act shall be construed as meaning—

(a) the fifteenth day after the date of intimation to the appellant or his solicitor of refusal of leave under subsection (1)(b) of section 107 of that Act, unless the appellant applies to the High Court for leave to appeal; or

(b) the day seven days after the date of intimation to the appellant or his solicitor of the refusal of leave by the High Court under subsection (5)(b) of section 107 of that Act.

NOTE

[1]As amended by Act of Adjournal (Criminal Procedure Rules Amendment No. 3) 1997 (S.I. 1997 No. 1788) (effective August 11, 1997).

Remits in applications for leave to appeal

[1]**15.14.** The judge of the High Court considering an application for leave to appeal under section 107 of the Act of 1995 may, before deciding to grant or refuse leave, remit the case to the judge who presided at the trial for a supplementary report to be produced to him as soon as is reasonably practicable on any matter with respect to the grounds of appeal.

NOTE

[1]As inserted by Act of Adjournal (Criminal Procedure Rules Amendment) (Miscellaneous) (S.I. 1996 No. 2747 (s.171)) (effective September 9, 1996).

PART IV

Summary proceedings

CHAPTER 16

COMPLAINTS

Form of complaints and related notices and forms

16.1.—(1) The form of complaint referred to in section 138(1) of the Act of 1995 shall be in Form 16.1–A.

(2) The form of citation of an accused referred to in section 140(2) of the Act of 1995 shall be in Form 16.1–B.

(3) The procurator fiscal shall send to the accused with the citation in Form 16.1–B—
  (a) a reply form in Form 16.1–C for completion and return by him stating whether he pleads guilty or not guilty; and
  (b) a means form in Form 16.1–D for completion and return by him.

(4) The form of notice of previous convictions to be served on an accused under section 166(2) of the Act of 1995 shall be in Form 16.1–E.

Signature of prosecutor

16.2.—(1) The prosecutor shall sign the principal complaint and the citation to the accused.

(2) Any document sent with the citation to the accused including the copy complaint shall, for the purposes of such signature, be treated as part of the citation.

Effect of failure by prosecutor to comply with certain requirements

16.3. The validity of any proceedings against an accused shall not be affected by reason only of the failure of the prosecutor to comply in any respect with a requirement of rule 16.1(3) (reply and means forms).

Further procedural forms

16.4.—(1) The form of incidental application referred to in section 134 of the Act of 1995 (incidental applications) shall be in Form 16.4–A.

(2) The form of assignation of a diet shall be in Form 16.4–B.

(3) The form of minutes in the record of proceedings in summary proceedings shall be in Form 16.4–C.

Form of certain warrants

16.5.—(1) The form of warrant referred to in section 135 of the Act of 1995 (warrants of apprehension and search)—
  (a) to apprehend an accused shall be in Form 16.5–A;
  (b) to search the person, dwelling house and repositories of the accused shall be in Form 16.5–B.

(2) The form of order adjourning a diet and granting warrant to detain an accused shall be in Form 16.5–C.

Citation of witnesses

16.6.—(1) The form of postal citation of a person to appear as a witness at a trial on a summary complaint shall be in Form 16.6–A; and the witness shall complete and return Form 16.6–B to the procurator fiscal, or the accused or his solicitor, as the case may be, in the pre-paid envelope provided within 14 days after the date of citation.

(2) The form of personal citation of a witness at a trial on a summary complaint shall be in Form 16.6–C.

¹(3) In the case of a postal citation in Form 16.6–A by the prosecutor under section 141 of the Act of 1995, the citation may be signed by the prosecutor by use of an official stamp of his signature or by mechanical or electronic means.

Applications for alteration of diets

16.7.—(1) Where the prosecutor and the accused propose to make a joint application orally to the court under section 137(2) of the Act of 1995 (application for alteration of diet) for postponement of a diet that has been fixed, they may do so only at a diet which has been duly assigned and which has been called.

(2) An application by an accused under section 137(5) of the Act of 1995 (application to postpone or accelerate diet) shall be made in Form 16.7.

NOTE
¹ As inserted by Act of Adjournal (Criminal Procedure Rules Amendment) (Miscellaneous) (S.I. 1996 No. 2147 (s.171)) (effective September 9, 1996).

CHAPTER 17

SUMMARY PRE-TRIAL PROCEDURE

Appeals against extension of period of detention

17.1.—(1) A note of appeal presented to the High Court under section 147(3) of the Act of 1995 (appeal against grant or refusal of extension of 40 days detention) shall be made in Form 17.1

(2) Such a note of appeal shall be served by the appellant on—
(a) the respondent; and
(b) the clerk of the court against the decision of which the appeal is taken.

(3) The appellant in such a note of appeal shall lodge with the Clerk of Justiciary—
(a) the note of appeal; and
(b) the certificate of execution of service in respect of the persons mentioned in paragraph (2).

(4) The clerk of the court against the decision of which the appeal is taken shall, as soon as practicable after being served with the note of appeal, transmit to the Clerk of Justiciary the original application and all the relative documents; and the Clerk of Justiciary shall, on receipt of those documents, assign the appeal to the roll and intimate the date of the diet to the appellant and the respondent.

(5) The Clerk of Justiciary shall intimate the result of the appeal to the court against the decision of which the appeal was taken and to the governor of the institution in which the appellant is detained.

CHAPTER 18

PROCEDURE AT TRIAL IN SUMMARY PROCEEDINGS

Accused to plead personally and to receive intimation of diets

18.1.—(1) Subject to paragraph (2), in any summary proceedings where a person accused in those proceedings is present in court, that person shall personally plead to the charge against him whether or not he is represented.

(2) Where the judge is satisfied that the accused is not capable for any

reason of pleading personally to the charge against him, it shall be sufficient if the plea is tendered by a solicitor or by counsel on his behalf.

(3) Where an accused is not represented or not personally present and a court continues a diet without taking a plea from the accused, the prosecutor shall intimate the continuation and the date of the adjourned diet to the accused.

(4) Subject to section 150(2) of the Act of 1995 (adjournment to another diet), where an accused is not represented or not personally present, on the fixing of—
  (a) a diet of trial,
  (b) a diet after conviction, or
  (c) any diet after a plea from the accused has been recorded,
the sheriff clerk or clerk of the district court shall intimate the diet to the accused.

(5) Where the accused pleads guilty to the charge or to any part of it, and his plea is accepted by the prosecutor, the plea shall be recorded and signed by the judge or clerk of court, and the court shall thereafter dispose of the case at the same or any adjourned diet.

(6) The plea referred to in paragraph (5) and any sentence may be combined, in which case one signature shall be sufficient to authenticate both.

Form of oath or affirmation to witnesses

18.2.—(1) Where the judge administers the oath to a witness in summary proceedings, he shall do so in accordance with the form in Form 14.5–A.

(2) In the case of any witness who elects to affirm, the judge shall administer the affirmation in accordance with the form in Form 14.5–B.

(3) The oath or the affirmation administered in accordance with paragraph (1) or (2), as the case may be, shall be treated as having been administered in common form.

Warrant to apprehend witness who fails to appear

18.3. The form of warrant to apprehend a witness who has failed to appear at a diet in summary proceedings in answer to a citation shall be in Form 18.3.

Record of proceedings to be written or printed

18.4.—(1) The record of proceedings in summary proceedings may be in writing or printed, or may be partly written and partly printed.

(2) All forms of minute of proceedings or orders of the court may be on the same sheet of paper as the complaint or on a separate sheet attached to it.

[1](3) Where the record of proceedings or minute of proceedings or orders of the Court referred to in paragraph (1) or (2) are for whatever reason unavailable to the Court, it shall be competent for the Court to proceed with a copy certified as a true copy by the clerk of court.

NOTE
[1] As amended by the Act of Adjournal (Criminal Procedure Rules Amendment) (S.I. 1997 No. 63).

Interruption of proceedings after conviction

18.5.—(1) On conviction of an accused in summary proceedings, the judge may, without adjourning those proceedings, interrupt them by—
  (a) considering a conviction against that person in other proceedings pending before that court for which he has not been sentenced; or
  (b) passing sentence on that person in respect of the conviction in those other proceedings.
(2) When the judge has interrupted any proceedings under paragraph (1),

he may, in passing sentence on an accused person in respect of a conviction in those proceedings, at the same time pass sentence on that person in respect of any other conviction he has considered.

(3) No interruption of any proceedings under paragraph (1) shall cause the instance to fall in respect of any person accused in those proceedings or shall otherwise affect the validity of those proceedings.

Detention in precincts of court

18.6. An order under section 169(1) of the Act of 1995 (detention in precincts of court) shall be in Form 18.6.

CHAPTER 19

APPEALS FROM SUMMARY PROCEEDINGS

Appeals relating to preliminary pleas

19.1.—(1) If—
(a) an accused states an objection to the competency or relevancy of a complaint or the proceedings; and
(b) that objection is repelled,

he may apply for leave to appeal against that decision under section 174(1) of the Act of 1995 (appeals relating to preliminary pleas) only after stating how he pleads to the charge or charges set out in the complaint.

(2) Subject to paragraph (1), the accused shall apply for leave to appeal against any decision to which that paragraph applies; and the court which made the decision shall determine that application immediately following the decision in question.

(3) Where the court grants the application, the clerk of court shall enter in the minute of proceedings—
(a) details of the decision in question; and
(b) the granting of leave to appeal against it.

(4) An appeal to which this rule applies shall be made by note of appeal in Form 19.1–A.

(5) The note of appeal shall be lodged with the clerk of the court which granted leave to appeal not later than two days after the decision appealed against.

(6) The clerk of court shall, on the lodging of the note of appeal with him—
(a) send a copy to the respondent or his solicitor;
(b) request a report from the presiding judge; and
(c) transmit—
　　(i) the note of appeal,
　　(ii) two certified copies of the complaint and the minutes of proceedings, and
　　(iii) any other relevant documents,
　　to the Clerk of Justiciary.

(7) The presiding judge shall, as soon as possible after receiving a request for a report, send his report to the Clerk of Justiciary who shall send a copy to the appellant and respondent or their solicitors.

(8) The Clerk of Justiciary shall arrange for the High Court to hear the appeal as soon as possible, and shall cause to be copied any documents necessary for the High Court.

(9) Where the High Court makes any order postponing the trial diet under section 174(2) of the Act of 1995, or makes any such order and gives a direction under that section, the Clerk of Justiciary shall send a copy of that order and any direction to—
(a) the appropriate clerk of court;

(b) any accused who are not parties to the appeal or to their solicitors; and

(c) the governor of any institution in which any accused is detained.

(10) Any such appeal may be abandoned at any time prior to the hearing of the appeal.

(11) Where an appeal is abandoned, a minute of abandonment in Form 19.1–B shall be lodged with the Clerk of Justiciary.

(12) On the lodging of a minute of abandonment under paragraph (11), the Clerk of Justiciary shall inform the appropriate clerk of court and the respondent or his solicitor that the appeal has been abandoned.

Forms for appeals by stated case

19.2.—(1) An application under section 176(1) of the Act of 1995 (stated case: manner and time of appeal) shall be in Form 19.2–A.

(2) A stated case shall be in Form 19.2–B.

(3) The form of minutes of procedure in an appeal by stated case shall be in Form 19.2–C.

Forms for appeals against sentence only

19.3.—(1) A note of appeal under section 186(1) of the Act of 1995 (appeals against sentence only) shall be in Form 19.3–A.

(2) The form of minutes of procedure in an appeal under section 186(1) of the Act of 1995 shall be in Form 19.3–B.

Extension of time for appeals

19.4.—(1) An extension of time by the sheriff principal under section 186(5) (extension of time in appeal against sentence only), or section 194(2) (extension of time for stated case), of the Act of 1995 shall be in Form 19.4.

(2) Where, by virtue of subsection (8) of section 186 of the Act of 1995 (application of section 181 where appellant in appeal against sentence only fails to comply with a requirement), the court makes an order extending the period within which the note of appeal shall be lodged under subsection (2) of that section, the periods mentioned in subsections (2) and (4) of that section shall run from the date which is two days after the date on which the court makes that order and not from the date of the passing of the sentence.

Abandonment of appeals by stated case

19.5. A minute of abandonment of an appeal under section 184(1) of the Act of 1995 (abandonment of stated case before lodging it with the Clerk of Justiciary) shall be in Form 19.5.

Abandoning appeals against conviction only

19.6.—(1) This rule applies for the purpose of section 175(8) of the Act of 1995 (abandoning appeal against conviction and proceeding with appeal against sentence alone).

(2) An application to abandon an appeal under section 175(8) of the Act of 1995 shall be made by minute in Form 19.6 and intimated by the appellant to the respondent.

(3) Subject to paragraph (4), the minute shall be lodged with the clerk of the court which imposed the sentence being appealed against.

(4) Where, before the lodging of the minute, the stated case has been lodged with the Clerk of Justiciary, the minute shall be lodged with the Clerk of Justiciary who shall send a copy of the minute to the clerk of the court which imposed the sentence appealed against.

(5) Where, before the lodging of the minute, copies of the stated case and relative proceedings have been lodged with the Clerk of Justiciary, those copies shall be used for the purposes of the hearing of the appeal against sentence.

(6) On the lodging of the minute, section 186(3) to (9) of the Act of 1995 (provisions relating to appeal against sentence only) shall apply to the stated case as they apply to a note of appeal.

Abandonment of appeals against sentence only

19.7. A minute of abandonment under section 186(9) of the Act of 1995 (abandonment of appeal against sentence only) shall be in Form 19.7.

Intimation of abandonment

19.8. The Clerk of Justiciary or clerk of court, as the case may be, on the lodging with him of—
  (a) a minute abandoning an appeal under section 184(1) of the Act of 1995 (abandonment of appeal by stated case before lodging of case with the Clerk of Justiciary), or
  (b) a minute abandoning an appeal under section 186(9) of the Act of 1995 (abandonment of appeal against sentence only),
shall immediately notify the Crown Agent or the prosecutor, as the case may be, of the lodging of the minute; and the Clerk of Justiciary shall, where the minute is lodged with him, notify immediately the clerk of the appropriate court.

Applications for suspension of disqualification from driving in appeals

19.9.—(1) Where a person who has been disqualified from holding or obtaining a driving licence appeals against that disqualification under section 176(1) of the Act of 1995 by stated case, any application to suspend the disqualification shall be made with the application to the court to state a case for the opinion of the High Court.

(2) On an application being made under paragraph (1) to suspend a disqualification, the court shall grant or refuse to grant the application within seven days of it being made.

(3) Where the court refuses to grant the application and the appellant applies to the High Court to suspend the disqualification, any such application shall be made by note in Form 19.9.

(4) The note shall be lodged by the appellant or his solicitor with the Clerk of Justiciary.

(5) The appellant or his solicitor shall intimate the lodging of the note to the respondent and the clerk of the court which imposed the disqualification.

(6) The clerk shall, on receiving such intimation, forthwith send to the Clerk of Justiciary—
  (a) a certified copy of the complaint; and
  (b) a certified copy of the minute of proceedings.

(7) The High Court may order such further intimation (including intimation to the Lord Advocate) as it thinks fit, and may dispose of the application in open court or in chambers after such hearing as it thinks fit.

(8) On the High Court making an order on the note, the Clerk of Justiciary shall send a certified copy of the order to the clerk of the court which imposed the disqualification.

(9) Where the order suspends the disqualification, the Clerk of Justiciary shall also send a certified copy of the order to the Secretary of State with such further information as the Secretary of State may require.

(10) An order made by a single judge of the High Court under this rule shall not be subject to appeal or review.

Applications for suspension of disqualification from driving in bills of suspension

19.10.—(1) Where a person who has been disqualified from holding or obtaining a driving licence appeals against that disqualification by bill of suspension, an application to suspend the disqualification shall be made by requesting interim suspension of the disqualification in the prayer of the bill.

(2) Where the courts orders interim suspension, that order shall not have effect until—

(a) the bill has been served on the respondent; and

(b) the principal bill and first deliverance on the bill with an execution, or acceptance, of service—

    (i) have been shown to the clerk of the sentencing court and he has endorsed a certificate of exhibition; and

    (ii) they have been returned to the Clerk of Justiciary by the complainer or his solicitor.

(3) On certifying the bill under paragraph (2), the clerk of the court which imposed the disqualification shall send a certified copy of the complaint and the relative minute of proceedings to the Clerk of Justiciary.

(4) Paragraphs (2), (8), (9) and (10) of rule 19.9 (applications for suspension of disqualification from driving in appeals) apply to this rule as they apply to that rule.

Suspension of sentence under s.193A of the Act of 1995

[1]**19.10A.**—(1) Where a convicted person or the prosecutor appeals to the High Court under section 175 of the Act of 1995, any application to suspend a relevant sentence shall be made with—

(a) the application to the court to state a case for the opinion of the High Court; or

(b) the note of appeal, as the case may be.

(2) On an application being made under paragraph (1) to suspend a sentence the court shall grant or refuse to grant the application within seven days of its being made.

(3) In the application of section 193A of the Act of 1995 (suspension of certain sentences pending appeal) to a case in which leave to appeal has been refused under section 180 or 187 of that Act, the word "determined" in subsection (1) of the said section 193A shall be construed as meaning—

(a) the fifteenth day after the date of intimation to the appellant or his solicitor and to the Crown Agent of refusal of leave under subsection (1)(b) of section 180 or 187 of that Act, as the case may be, unless the appellant applies to the High Court for leave to appeal; or

(b) the seventh day after the date of intimation to the appellant or his solicitor and to the Crown Agent of the refusal of leave by the High Court under subsection (5)(b) of section 180 or subsection (4)(b) of section 187 of that Act, as the case may be.

(4) In chapter 22 (evidence of children)—

(a) in the heading, for "CHILDREN" substitute "VULNERABLE PERSONS";

(b) in the heading of rule 22.1, for "children" substitute "vulnerable persons" and in paragraph (1) of that rule—

    (i) for "child" substitute "vulnerable person"; and

    (ii) at the end insert "and, where the vulnerable person is subject to an order or transfer direction (being an order or transfer direction such as is mentioned in paragraph (b)(i) or (ii) of the definition of "vulnerable person" in section 271(12) of the Act of 1995) shall be accompanied by a copy of the order or transfer direction, as the case may be"; and

(c) in rule 22.2(1)(b), for "child's" substitute "vulnerable person's".

NOTE

[1]Inserted by Act of Adjournal (Criminal Procedure Rules Amendment No. 4) (S.I. 1997 No. 1834) effective August 1, 1997.

Solicitor entering appearance etc.

19.11.—(1) Where an appellant in an appeal is represented by a solicitor who does not practise in Edinburgh, that solicitor may appoint a solicitor who practises in Edinburgh to carry out the duties of solicitor to the appellant in relation to that appeal.

(2) In paragraph (1), "appeal" includes any appeal whether by stated case, note of appeal, bill of suspension or advocation.

(3) The solicitor for the appellant or if unrepresented, the appellant, shall enter appearance and comply with the provisions of section 179(9) of the Act of 1995 (lodging of stated case with Clerk of Justiciary).

Duty to print stated case etc.

19.12.—(1) The solicitor for the appellant or, if unrepresented, the appellant shall—
  (a) print the complaint, minutes of proceedings and stated case or bill of suspension;
  (b) not later than seven days before the hearing, return the process to the Clerk of Justiciary; and
  (c) provide—
      (i) the Clerk of Justiciary with four copies of the print; and
      (ii) the respondent or his solicitor with three copies of the print.

(2) Where the solicitor for the appellant or the appellant, as the case may be, cannot comply with any of the requirements of paragraph (1), he shall, not later than seven days before the hearing, so inform the Clerk of Justiciary in writing with reasons.

(3) On being so informed, the Clerk of Justiciary may in his discretion postpone the hearing by dropping the appeal from the Justiciary Roll.

(4) Where the Clerk of Justiciary does not drop the appeal from the roll under paragraph (3), the court may, at the hearing, allow the appeal to be dropped from the roll or may dismiss the appeal.

Duty of solicitor in bill of suspension

19.13. A solicitor who requests a first deliverance in a bill of suspension shall comply with the requirements of rule 19.12(1) and (2) (printing of stated case) whether or not he is the nominated solicitor for the purposes of legal aid.

List of appeals

19.14.—(1) The Clerk of Justiciary shall, after consultation with the Lord Justice General or Lord Justice-Clerk, issue a list of appeals with the respective dates of hearing on the Justiciary Roll.

(2) The Clerk of Justiciary shall give the respective solicitors representing parties to an appeal so listed at least 14 days notice of the date fixed for the hearing of the appeal.

Diet for interim suspension

19.15. Where a bill of suspension contains a prayer for interim suspension of any order or for interim liberation—
  (a) the judge before whom the bill is laid for a first deliverance shall assign a diet at which counsel for each party may be heard on the crave for the interim order; and
  (b) the Clerk of Justiciary shall forthwith give notice of that diet to the parties.

Intimation of determination of appeal

19.16.—(1) The Clerk of Justiciary shall send to the clerk of the sentencing court a certified copy of the order made on determination of the appeal from summary proceedings.

(2) Where the appeal against a disqualification from driving is refused or abandoned, the clerk of the sentencing court shall—

(a) make the appropriate endorsement on the driving licence of the appellant; and

(b) intimate the disqualification to the appropriate driving licence and police authorities.

(3) In this rule, "appeal" includes any appeal whether by stated case, note of appeal, bill of suspension or advocation.

Suspension of disqualification etc. under section 193 of the Act of 1995

[1]**19.17.** In the application of section 193 of the Act of 1995 (suspension of disqualification, forfeiture, etc.) to a case in which leave to appeal has been refused under section 180 or 187 of the Act of 1995, the word "determination" in subsection (1) of section 193 of that Act shall be construed as meaning—

(a) the fifteenth day after the date of intimation to the appellant or his solicitor of refusal of leave under subsection (1)(b) of section 180 or 187 of that Act, as the case may be, unless the appellant applies to the High Court for leave to appeal; or

(b) the day seven days after the date of intimation to the appellant or his solicitor of the refusal of leave by the High Court under subsection (5)(b) of section 180 or subsection (4)(b) of section 187 of that Act, as the case may be.

NOTE
[1]As amended by Act of Adjournal (Criminal Procedure Rules Amendment No. 3) (S.I. 1997 No. 1788) (effective August 11, 1997).

Remits in applications for leave to appeal

[1]**19.18.** The judge of the High Court considering an application for leave to appeal under section 180 (leave to appeal against conviction etc.), or section 187 (leave to appeal against sentence), of the Act of 1995 may, before deciding to grant or refuse leave, remit the case to the judge at first instance for a report or a supplementary report to be produced to him as soon as is reasonably practicable on any matter with respect to the grounds of appeal.

NOTE
[1]As inserted by Act of Adjournal (Criminal Procedure Rules Amendment) (Miscellaneous) (S.I. 1996 No. 2747 (s.171) (effective September 9 1996).

PART V

Sentencing

CHAPTER 20

SENTENCING

Form of sentence of death

20.1. [*Repealed by the Act of Adjournal (Criminal Procedure Rules Amendment No. 3) 1999 (S.I. 1999 No. 1387) para. 2(4) (effective May 19, 1999).*]

Detention in police custody instead of imprisonment

20.2. An order under section 206(2) of the Act of 1995 (detention in police custody instead of imprisonment) shall be in Form 20.2.

Form of supervised release orders

20.3. An order under section 209 of the Act of 1995 (supervised release orders) shall be in Form 20.3.

Sexual offences to which Part I of Sex Offenders Act 1997 applies

[1]**20.3A.**—(1) A certificate in terms of section 5(2) of the Sex Offenders Act 1997 (certificate for the purposes of Part I of that Act that an accused has been convicted of, found not guilty by reason of insanity of, or found to be under a disability and to have done an Act charged against him in respect of, a sexual offence to which that Part applies) shall be in Form 20.3A–A.

(2) Subject to paragraph (3) of this rule, when a certificate such as is mentioned in paragrpah (1) of this rule is prepared, the accused shall be given a copy of it by the clerk of the court, together with a notice in Form 20.3A–B.

(3) If the certificate is not prepared immediately after the statement in open court but is to be prepared subsequently, the clerk of the court shall forthwith give the accused the notice required by paragraph (2) of this rule and shall in due course send a copy of the certificate to the accused.

(4) The clerk of the court shall retain a copy of the notice given to the accused and shall record on that copy the fact that notice has been so given.

(5) The record made under paragraph (4) of this rule shall be sufficient evidence of the fact recorded; and a certificate of posting sufficient evidence of the sending of a copy under paragraph (3) of this rule.

NOTE
[1]Inserted by Act of Adjournal (Criminal Procedure Rules Amendment No. 5) (S.I. 1997 No. 2082) (effective September 1, 1997).

Application of money found on offender towards fine

20.4.—(1) A direction under section 212(1) of the Act of 1995 that money found on an offender should not be applied towards payment of a fine shall be in Form 20.4–A.

(2) A notice for the purposes of section 212(7) of the Act of 1995 (notice to governor of prison as warrant to convey offender to court) shall be in Form 20.4–B.

Extension of time for payment of fine

20.5. An order under section 214(7) or 215(3) of the Act of 1995 (order allowing further time for payment of fine) shall be in Form 20.5.

Forms for enquiry for non-payment of fine

20.6.—(1) The citation of an offender issued under section 216(3)(a) of the Act of 1995 (citation to appear for enquiry before imprisonment in default of payment of fine) shall be in Form 20.6–A.

(2) The execution of a citation referred to in paragraph (1) which is served other than by post shall be in Form 20.6–B.

(3) The—

(a) execution of a citation referred to in paragraph (1) which is served by post,

(b) warrant for apprehension of an offender issued under section 216(3)(b) of the Act of 1995, and

(c) record of proceedings at an enquiry under section 216 of that Act, shall be in Form 20.6–C.

Supervision of payment of fine

20.7. A notice to be sent to an offender under section 217(7) of the Act of 1995 (appointment of different supervising officer to offender allowed time to pay fine) shall be in Form 20.7.

Forms of warrant for execution and charge for payment of fine or other financial penalty

20.8.—(1) In every extract of a sentence of a fine or other financial penalty, there shall be included a warrant for execution in the following terms: "and the Lords [*or* sheriff *or* justice(s)] grant(s) warrant for all lawful execution hereon".

(2) The charge for payment of a fine or other financial penalty to be used by a sheriff officer under section 90 of the Debtors (Scotland) Act 1987 (provisions relating to charges for payment) shall be in Form 20.8.

Transfer of fines

20.9.—(1) A transfer of fine order under section 222(1), and a notice of it required by section 223(1), of the Act of 1995 shall be in Form 20.9–A.

(2) A transfer of fine order made by virtue of section 222(5) of the Act of 1995, and a notice of it required by section 223(1), shall be in Form 20.9–B.

(3) Where a notice of a transfer of fine order is received by a court in Scotland, the clerk of that court shall serve by post a notice to the offender in Form 20.9–C.

Probation orders

20.10.—(1) A probation order shall be in Form 20.10–A.

(2) The citation of a probationer to appear before a court under section 232(1) (failure to comply with requirement of probation order), or section 233(1) (commission of further offence while on probation), of the Act of 1995 shall be in Form 20.10–B.

Form and notification of non-harassment order

20.10A.—(1) A non-harassment order made under section 234A of the Act of 1995 shall be in Form 20.10A.

(2) A non-harassment order mentioned in paragraph (1) above shall be intimated by the clerk of the court, by which it is made to any person, other than the offender, who is named in the order.

Variation or revocation of non-harassment order

20.10B.—(1) This rule applies to an application under section 234(6) of the Act of 1995 (application for variation or revocation of non-harassment order).

(2) In this rule—
"the offender" means the offender subject to the order to which the application relates; and
"the prosecutor" means the prosecutor at whose instance the order was made.

(3) The application shall—
(a) identify the proceedings in which the order was made;
(b) state the reasons for which the applicant seeks the variation or revocation of the order;
(c) be, as nearly as may be, in Form 20.10B.

(4) The applicant shall serve a copy of the application on—

  (a) the clerk of the court which made the order;
  (b) any person, other than the offender, who is named in the order; and
  (c) where the applicant is—
       (i) the offender, the prosecutor; and
       (ii) the prosecutor, the offender,
       but the application may proceed notwithstanding that, having taken reasonable steps to do so, the applicant has been unable to effect service of it on the offender or any person such as is mentioned in sub-paragraph (b) above.

(5) Where the offender is the applicant, the prosecutor shall, within fourteen days of the receipt of the copy of the application, notify the clerk of court in writing whether he intends to oppose the application.

(6) Where the prosecutor is the applicant, the offender shall, within fourteen days of receipt of the copy of the application, notify the clerk of court in writing whether he intends to oppose the application.

(7) Where a person notifies the clerk of court under paragraph (5) or (6) above that he does not intend to oppose the application, or fails to make any notification, the court shall proceed to dispose of the application and may do so in the absence of the applicant.

(8) Where a person notifies the clerk of court under paragraph (5) or (6) above that he does intend to oppose the application, the clerk of court shall arrange a hearing before the court at which the prosecutor and the offender may appear or be represnted.

(9) The clerk of court shall give notice in writing of the decision of the court on the application to—
  (a) the applicant;
  (b) any person served with a copy of the application under sub-paragraph (b) or (c) of paragraph (4) above.

Form of supervised attendance orders

20.11.—(1) A supervised attendance order made under section 235(1) of the Act of 1995 shall be in Form 20.11–A.

(2) A supervised attendance order made under section 236 of the Act of 1995 (supervised attendance orders in place of fines for 16 and 17 year olds) shall be in Form 20.11–B.

Community service orders

20.12.—(1) A community service order made under section 238 of the Act of 1995 shall be in Form 20.12–A.

(2) The citation of an offender to appear before a court under section 239(4) (failure to comply with requirement of community service order), or section 240(3) (amendment or revocation of community service order), of the Act of 1995 shall be in Form 20.12–B.

Restriction of liberty orders

[1]**20.12A.**—(1) A restriction of liberty order made under section 245A(1) of the Act of 1995 shall be in form 20.12A–A.

(2) An application under section 245E(1) (application to review a restriction of liberty order) of that Act shall be in form 20.12A–B.

(3) The citation of an offender under section 245E(3) (citation to appear before a court which proposes to vary or revoke a restriction of liberty order) of that Act shall be in form 20.12A–C.

(4) The citation of an offender under section 245F(1) (citation for failure to comply with requirement of restriction of liberty order) of that Act shall be in form 20.12A–D.

NOTE

[1]Inserted by the Act of Adjournal (Criminal Procedure Rules Amendment) (Restriction of Liberty Orders) 1998 (S.I. 1998 No. 1842) (effective August 17, 1998).

Form and notification of drug treatment and testing orders

[1]**20.12B** A drug treatment and testing order made under section 234B of the Act of 1995 shall be in Form 20.12B.

NOTE

[1]Inserted by the Act of Adjournal (Criminal Procedure Rules Amendment No. 4) (Drug Treatment and Testing Orders) 1999 (S.S.I. 1999 No.191) para. 2 (effective December 20, 1999).

Terms of compensation orders in record of proceedings

20.13. Entries shall be made in the record of proceedings by the clerk of court on the making of a compensation order, specifying the terms of the order and in particular—
(a) the name of the convicted person required to pay compensation;
(b) the amount of compensation required to be paid by such person;
(c) the name of the person entitled to the compensation payable; and
(d) where there is more than one person entitled to compensation, the amount of compensation each is entitled to and the priority, if any, among those persons for payment.

Legal disability of person entitled to compensation

20.14.—(1) The prosecutor, if he knows that any person entitled to payment of compensation under a compensation order is under any legal disability, shall so inform the court immediately it makes any such order in respect of any such person, and that information shall be entered by the clerk of court in the record of proceedings.

(2) Where payment of any sum is made under a compensation order to the clerk of court in respect of a person known to be under a legal disability, Part IV (except rule 36.17(1) (receipt sufficient discharge)) of Chapter 36 of the Ordinary Cause Rules 1993 in Schedule 1 to the Sheriff Courts (Scotland) Act 1907 (management of damages payable to persons under legal disability) shall apply to the administration of that sum as they apply to the administration of a sum of money paid into court in respect of damages for such a person.

Variation of compensation orders

20.15.—(1) The court may, at any time before a compensation order is fully complied with, and after such further inquiry as the court may order, vary the terms of the order as it thinks fit.

(2) A variation made under paragraph (1) may be made in chambers and in the absence of the parties or any of them.

Discharge or reduction of compensation order

20.16.—(1) An application to discharge a compensation order or to reduce the amount that remains to be paid under section 251(1) of the Act of 1995 (review of compensation order) shall be made in writing to the clerk of the court which made the order.

(2) The clerk of court shall, on any such application being made to him, serve a copy of the application on the prosecutor by post.

(3) The court to which the application is made may dispose of the application after such inquiry as it thinks fit.

Use of certified copy documents in certain proceedings

20.17.—(1) Subject to paragraph (2), in proceedings relating to—
(a) an order which imposed a fine,
(b) a supervised attendance order,
(c) a community service order, or
(d) a probation order,
in a court other than the court which made the order, the principal indictment, complaint, record or minute of proceedings, or notice of previous convictions need not be before the court.

(2) The court to which paragraph (1) applies shall have before it a copy of the principal of each of such documents certified as a true copy by the clerk of the court which made the order.

Form of extract of sentence

20.18.—(1) An extract of a custodial sentence following a conviction on indictment, and warrant of detention and return of sentence, required for any purpose in connection with any case shall be in Form 20.18–A.

(2) An extract of a sentence of imprisonment, a fine or caution in summary proceedings under the Act of 1995 shall be in the appropriate form in Form 20.18–B.

(3) An extract issued in accordance with paragraph (1) or (2) shall be warrant and authority for execution.

Reduction of disqualification period for drink-drive offenders

20.19.—(1) In this rule—
"the Act of 1988" means the Road Traffic Offenders Act 1988;
"course organiser" has the meaning assigned in section 34C(2) of the Act of 1988;
"date specified" means the date specified in an order under section 34A of the Act of 1988;
"supervising court" has the meaning assigned in section 34C(2) of the Act of 1988.

(2) An application to the supervising court for a declaration under section 34B(6) of the Act of 1988 shall be—
(a) in Form 20.19–A;
(b) accompanied by a copy of the written notice required by section 34B(5) of the Act of 1988 intimating the course organiser's decision not to give a course completion certificate; and
(c) lodged with the clerk of court within 28 days after the date specified.

(3) An application to the supervising court for a declaration under section 34B(7) of the Act of 1988 shall be—
(a) in Form 20.19–B; and
(b) lodged with the clerk of court within 28 days after the date specified.

(4) On the lodging of an application under section 34B(6) or (7) of the Act of 1988—
(a) the sheriff or stipendiary magistrate, as the case may be, shall fix a date for hearing the application; and
(b) the clerk of court shall—
(i) notify the applicant of the date of hearing; and
(ii) serve a copy of the application, with notice of the hearing, on the course organiser and the procurator fiscal.

PART VI

Evidence

CHAPTER 21

UNCONTROVERSIAL EVIDENCE, HEARSAY AND PRIOR STATEMENTS

Notice of uncontroversial evidence

21.1.—(1) Where a party to criminal proceedings serves a copy of a statement and document on another party under section 258 of the Act of 1995 (uncontroversial evidence), he shall also serve with that statement and document a statement in Form 21.1–A.

(2) Where a document is annexed to a statement under section 258(2) of the Act of 1995 and is not described in the statement, a docquet in Form 21.1–B shall be endorsed on that document.

Notice of challenge of evidence as uncontroversial

21.2. A notice by a party under section 258(3) of the Act of 1995 (notice challenging fact in statement under section 258(2) of the Act of 1995) shall be in Form 21.2.

Notice of intention to have hearsay statement admitted

21.3. A notice under section 259(5) of the Act of 1995 (notice of intention to apply to have evidence of hearsay statement admitted) shall be in Form 21.3.

Authentication of certain prior statements of witnesses

21.4. A statement in a document which it is sought to be admitted in evidence under section 260(4) of the Act of 1995 (admissibility of certain prior statements of witnesses) shall be authenticated by a certificate in Form 21.4 endorsed on or attached to the first page of the statement.

CHAPTER 22

EVIDENCE OF CHILDREN

Applications for evidence of children by television link

22.1.—(1) An application to the court under section 271(5) of the Act of 1995 (authorisation of the giving of evidence by a child by means of a live television link) shall be made by petition in Form 22.1.

(2) A petition referred to in paragraph (1) shall—
(a) where it relates to proceedings in the High Court, be lodged with the Clerk of Justiciary, or
(b) where it relates to proceedings in the sheriff court, be lodged with the sheriff clerk,
not later than 14 days before the trial diet (except on special cause shown).

(3) The High Court or the sheriff, as the case may be, shall—
(a) order intimation of the petition to be made to the other party or parties to the proceedings; and
(b) fix a diet for hearing the petition on the earliest practicable date.

Orders and transfer of cases

22.2.—(1) After hearing the parties and allowing such further procedure as the court thinks fit—

(a) the High Court or the sheriff, as the case may be, may make an order granting or refusing the application; or

(b) where section 271(9) of the Act of 1995 (transfer of cases in which child's evidence is to be given through television link) applies, the sheriff may make an order under that section transferring the case to another sheriff court in the same sheriffdom.

(2) Where the sheriff makes an order under paragraph (1)(b) transferring the case to another sheriff court (the "receiving court"), the sheriff clerk shall forthwith transmit the record copy of the indictment or the complaint, the minute of proceedings, any productions and any relevant documents to the clerk of the receiving court.

CHAPTER 23

LETTERS OF REQUEST

Applications for letters of request

23.1.—(1) An application to the court by the prosecutor or the defence under section 272(1)(a) of the Act of 1995 (evidence by letter of request) for the issue of a letter of request shall be made by petition—

(a) where the accused has appeared on petition under Part IV of the Act of 1995 (petition procedure) but an indictment has not been served on him, in Form 23.1–A presented to the High Court; or

(b) where an indictment or a complaint has been served on the accused, in Form 23.1–B presented to the appropriate court.

(2) A petition referred to in paragraph (1) shall—

(a) where it relates to proceedings in the High Court or to proceedings in respect of which the court where the trial is to take place is not yet known, be lodged with the Clerk of Justiciary, or

(b) where it relates to proceedings in the sheriff court, be lodged with the sheriff clerk,

and shall be accompanied by a proposed letter of request in Form 23.1–C.

(3) An application to the court by the prosecutor or the defence under section 273(2) of the Act of 1995 (television link evidence from abroad) for the issue of a letter of request shall be in Form 23.1–D and shall be accompanied by a letter of request in Form 23.1–E.

(4) Such an application made to the High Court may be disposed of by a single judge of that court.

(5) The High Court or the sheriff, as the case may be, shall—

(a) order intimation on the other party or parties to the proceedings;

(b) subject to paragraph (6), allow such time for lodging answers as appears appropriate; and

(c) fix a diet for hearing the petition and answers (if any).

(6) The High Court or the sheriff, as the case may be, may dispense with answers to the petition on cause shown.

Powers of court in applications

23.2.—(1) The High Court or the sheriff, as the case may be, may, after considering the petition for the issue of a letter of request and any answers to it, grant the petition with or without modification or refuse it.

(2) On granting the petition, the High Court or the sheriff, as the case may be, shall—

(a) in relation to an application under section 272(1)(a) of the Act of 1995 (evidence by letter of request), allow interrogatories to be adjusted summarily;

(b) pronounce an order approving the terms—

    (i) of the letter of request to be sent;

    (ii) of any interrogatories and cross-interrogatories to be sent; and

(c) if English is not an official language of the body to which the letter of request is addressed, specify a period within which a translation of each of the letter, any interrogatories and cross-interrogatories, and any productions, are to be lodged.

Expenses

23.3.—(1) The solicitor for the petitioner or, if he is unrepresented, the petitioner shall be liable for the expenses of the petition for the issue of a letter of request.

(2) The High Court or the sheriff, as the case may be, may order the solicitor for the petitioner, or the petitioner, to consign into court such sum in respect of those expenses as may be specified, and on or before such date as may be specified, in the order.

(3) In the event of the sum so specified not being consigned into court on or before the date so specified, the petition shall be treated as having been abandoned.

Transmission of letters of request

23.4.—(1) On—

(a) the High Court or the sheriff, as the case may be, pronouncing an order under rule 23.2(2), or

(b) in a case where a translation requires to be lodged, on the lodging of the translation,

the Clerk of Justiciary or the sheriff clerk, as the case may be, shall send the letter of request and any documents to the Secretary of State for Foreign and Commonwealth Affairs for onward transmission to the body to which the letter of request is addressed.

(2) On sending the letter of request and any documents to the Secretary of State, the Clerk of Justiciary or sheriff clerk, as the case may be, shall note, on the petition, record copy of the indictment or in the minute of proceedings—

(a) the documents sent;

(b) to whom the documents were sent; and

(c) the date on which the documents were sent.

(3) On the relative documents being returned to him, the Clerk of Justiciary or sheriff clerk, as the case may be, shall—

(a) note—

    (i) the documents returned,

    (ii) by whom they were returned, and

    (iii) the date on which they were returned,

    on the application, the record copy of the indictment or in the minute of proceedings; and

(b) intimate what he has noted to all parties concerned.

Custody of documents

23.5.—(1) The Clerk of Justiciary or sheriff clerk, as the case may be, shall, subject to paragraph (2), keep the documents referred to in rule 23.4(3) in his custody.

(2) Where the petition for the issue of a letter of request was made to the High Court on the ground that the court in which the trial was to take place was not then known, the prosecutor shall, as soon as that court is known, inform the Clerk of Justiciary of that fact; and if that court is the sheriff court, the Clerk of Justiciary shall, as soon as is practicable, send to the sheriff clerk of that sheriff court the record of the evidence of the witness obtained by a letter of request under section 272(1)(a) of the Act of 1995.

(3) Where the record of the evidence of a witness is in the custody of the Clerk of Justiciary or a sheriff clerk under this rule and where intimation has been given to that effect under rule 23.4(3) to all the parties concerned in the proceedings, the name and address of that witness and the record of his evidence shall be treated as being within the knowledge of those parties; and no party shall be required, notwithstanding any enactment to the contrary—
  (a) to include the name of that witness in any list of witnesses; or
  (b) to include the record of his evidence in any list of productions.

Prohibition of reference to evidence without leave

23.6.—(1) No reference shall be made either directly or indirectly in any proceedings to the evidence, or any part of the evidence, of a witness whose evidence has been taken by virtue of a letter of request under section 272(1)(a) of the Act of 1995 unless the party seeking to make such reference has made a motion to the court to that effect and that motion has been granted.
  (2) The terms of any motion made under paragraph (1) and the grant or refusal of that motion by the court shall be noted by the clerk of court in the record or minute of proceedings.
  (3) On any such motion in solemn proceedings being granted—
  (a) the judge may direct copies of the evidence, to which he has granted leave for reference to be made, to be provided to the jury by the party making the motion; and
  (b) the clerk of court shall read the record of that evidence to the jury and shall then record that he has done so in the record of proceedings.

CHAPTER 24

EVIDENCE ON COMMISSION

Applications to take evidence on commission

24.1.—(1) An application to the court by the prosecutor or the defence under section 272(1)(b) of the Act of 1995 for the appointment of a commissioner to examine a witness to whom that section applies, shall be made by petition—
  (a) where the accused has appeared on petition under Part IV of the Act of 1995 (petition procedure) but an indictment has not been served on him, in Form 24.1–A presented to the High Court; or
  (b) where an indictment or a complaint has been served on the accused, in Form 24.1–B presented to the appropriate court.
  (2) A petition referred to in paragraph (1) shall—
  (a) where it relates to proceedings in the High Court or to proceedings in respect of which the court where the trial is to take place is not yet known, be lodged with the Clerk of Justiciary; or
  (b) where it relates to proceedings in the sheriff court, be lodged with the sheriff clerk.
  (3) A petition in relation to section 272(1)(b)(i) of the Act of 1995 (examination of witness ill or infirm) shall be accompanied by an appropriate medical certificate duly certified on soul and conscience by a qualified medical practitioner.
  (4) Such an application made to the High Court may be disposed of by a single judge of that court.
  (5) The High Court or the sheriff, as the case may be, shall—
  (a) order intimation on the other party or parties to the proceedings;
  (b) subject to paragraph (6), allow such time for lodging answers as appears appropriate; and

(c) fix a diet for hearing the petition and answers (if any).

(6) The High Court or the sheriff, as the case may be, may dispense with answers to the petition on cause shown.

Appointment of commissioner

24.2.—(1) The High Court or the sheriff, as the case may be, may, after considering the petition for the taking of evidence on commission and any answers to it, grant the petition with or without modifications or refuse it.

(2) On making an order granting the petition, the High Court or the sheriff, as the case may be, shall appoint—

(a) a commissioner to examine the witness to whom the order applies, and

(b) a clerk to assist the commissioner in the carrying out of his duties, and shall dispense with interrogatories.

(3) On the making of an order under paragraph (1), the Clerk of Justiciary or sheriff clerk, as the case may be, shall send the order to the commissioner or his clerk with the other relative documents.

(4) On sending the order to the commissioner or his clerk under paragraph (2), the Clerk of Justiciary or sheriff clerk, as the case may be, shall note on the petition, record copy of the indictment or in the minute of proceedings—

(a) the order and documents sent;

(b) to whom they were sent; and

(c) the date on which they were sent.

Expenses

24.3.—(1) The solicitor for the petitioner or, if he is unrepresented, the petitioner shall be liable for the expenses of the petition for the appointment of a commissioner to take the evidence of a witness on commission.

(2) The High Court or the sheriff, as the case may be, may order the solicitor for the petitioner, or the petitioner, to consign into court such sum in respect of those expenses as may be specified, and on or before such date as may be specified, in the order.

(3) In the event of the sum so specified not being consigned into court on or before the date so specified, the petition shall be treated as having been abandoned.

The commission

24.4.—(1) The commissioner shall, on receiving the order and documents mentioned in rule 24.2 (appointment of commissioner), determine the place and the date of the diet for the examination of the witness to whom the order of the court relates, and shall give reasonable notice of those matters to all the parties concerned.

(2) The commissioner may vary or revoke his determination or adjourn the examination of any witness to such other place, at such other date and time, as he may determine.

(3) If, in the course of the examination of a witness under this rule, any question arises as to the admissibility of any evidence, the commissioner shall not determine any such question but shall allow the evidence subject to all questions of competency and relevancy.

Commissioner's report

24.5.—(1) On the carrying out of his commission in accordance with the terms of the order appointing him, or otherwise on concluding his commission, the commissioner shall complete a written report of his commission, and he or his clerk shall return the report and relative documents to the Clerk of Justiciary or sheriff clerk, as the case may be.

(2) On the report and any documents being returned to him, the Clerk of Justiciary or sheriff clerk, as the case may be, shall—

  (a) note—
      (i) the documents returned,
      (ii) by whom they were returned, and
      (iii) the date on which they were returned,
    on the application, the record copy of the indictment or in the minute of proceedings; and
  (b) intimate what he has noted to all parties concerned.

Custody of documents

24.6.—(1) The Clerk of Justiciary or the sheriff clerk, as the case may be, shall, subject to paragraph (2), keep the documents referred to in rule 24.5(2) in his custody.

(2) In any case where the petition for the taking of evidence on commission was made to the High Court on the ground that the court in which the trial was to take place was not then known, the prosecutor shall, as soon as that court is known, inform the Clerk of Justiciary of that fact; and if that court is the sheriff court, the Clerk of Justiciary shall, as soon as is practicable, send to the sheriff clerk of that sheriff court the record of the evidence of the witness or witnesses.

(3) Where the record of the evidence of a witness is in the custody of the Clerk of Justiciary or a sheriff clerk under this rule and where intimation has been given to that effect under rule 24.5(2) to all the parties concerned in the proceedings, the name and address of that witness and the record of his evidence shall be treated as being within the knowledge of those parties; and no party shall be required, notwithstanding any enactment to the contrary—

  (a) to include the name of that witness in any list of witnesses; or
  (b) to include the record of his evidence in any list of productions.

Prohibition of reference to evidence without leave

24.7.—(1) No reference shall be made either directly or indirectly in any proceedings to the evidence, or any part of the evidence, of a witness whose evidence has been taken on commission under this Chapter unless the party seeking to make such reference has made a motion to the court to that effect and that motion has been granted.

(2) The terms of any motion made under paragraph (1) and the grant or refusal of that motion by the court shall be noted by the clerk of court in the record or minute of proceedings.

(3) On any such motion in solemn proceedings being granted—

  (a) the judge may direct copies of the evidence, to which he has granted leave for reference to be made, to be provided to the jury by the party making the motion; and
  (b) the clerk of court shall read the record of that evidence to the jury and shall then record that he has done so in the record of proceedings.

CHAPTER 25

RECORD OF JUDICIAL EXAMINATION AS EVIDENCE IN SOLEMN PROCEEDINGS

Use of transcript of judicial examination

25.1.—(1) The record made under section 37 of the Act of 1995 (judicial examination: record of proceedings) shall be received in evidence in accordance with section 278(1) of that Act by means of the clerk of court, subject to paragraph (2) of this rule, reading the record of those proceedings to the jury.

(2) The clerk of court shall not read to the jury such part of the record as the court refuses to allow to be read to the jury on an application under section 278(2) of the Act of 1995.

(3) The presiding judge may direct that copies of such part of the record as has been read to the jury shall be made available to them together with copies of any written record of a confession allegedly made and received by the accused under section 36(3) of the Act of 1995 (written record of confession allegedly made received from prosecutor or constable).

CHAPTER 26

DOCUMENTARY EVIDENCE

Authentication of copies of documents

26.1.—(1) For the purposes of paragraph 1(1) of Schedule 8 to the Act of 1995 (production of copy documents), a copy, or a copy of a material part, of a document shall be authenticated—
  (a) by a person who is—
      (i) the author of the original of it;
      (ii) a person in, or who has been in, possession and control of the original of it or a copy of it; or
      (iii) the authorised representative of the person in, or who has been in, possession and control of the original of it or a copy of it; and
  (b) by means of a signed certificate, certifying the copy as a true copy, which may be in Form 26.1–A—
      (i) endorsed on the copy; or
      (ii) attached to the copy.

(2) For the purposes of paragraph 4 of Schedule 8 to Act of 1995 (documents kept by businesses etc.), a document shall be certified by a docquet in Form 26.1–B—
  (a) endorsed on the document; or
  (b) attached to the document.

(3) For the purposes of paragraph 5(3) of Schedule 8 to the Act of 1995 (statements not contained in business documents), a certificate shall be in Form 26.1–C.

CHAPTER 27

ROUTINE EVIDENCE, SUFFICIENT EVIDENCE AND PROOF OF PREVIOUS CONVICTIONS

Notices in relation to use of autopsy and forensic science reports

27.1.—(1) Any notice given by an accused under subsection (1) or (2) of section 281 of the Act of 1995 (routine evidence: autopsy and forensic science reports) shall be in writing and shall be given to the prosecutor.

(2) For the purposes of the application of section 281(1) of the Act of 1995 to any summary proceedings, an autopsy report shall not be treated as having been lodged as a production by the prosecutor unless it has been lodged as a production not later than 14 days before the date of the trial diet.

(3) For the purposes of the application of subsection (2) of section 281 of the Act of 1995 to any summary proceedings, the prosecutor shall intimate his intention in accordance with that subsection by serving a copy of the autopsy or forensic science report lodged by him on the accused or his solicitor with a notice of his intention not later than 14 days before the date of the trial diet.

Form of certificates in relation to certain evidence

27.2. A certificate under any of the following provisions of the Act of 1995 shall be in Form 27.2:—

section 283(1) (certificate as to time and place of video surveillance recordings),

section 284(1) (certificate in relation to fingerprints),

section 285(2) (certificate relating to previous convictions),

section 285(4) (certificate relating to fingerprints),

section 285(5) (certificate relating to fingerprints of previously convicted person).

Form of notice in relation to certain evidential certificates

27.3. A notice under any of the following provisions of the Act of 1995 shall be in Form 27.3:—

section 282(3) (notice not accepting evidence as to controlled drugs or medicinal products),

section 283(2) (notice not accepting evidence as to video surveillance),

section 284(2) (notice not accepting evidence in relation to fingerprints),

section 286(1) (notice denying extract conviction applies to accused).

Notices under section 16A(4) of the Criminal Law (Consolidation) (Scotland) Act 1995

[1]**27.4.**—(1) A notice under section 16A(4) of the Criminal Law (Consolidation) (Scotland) Act 1995 (notice disputing that condition is satisfied and requiring prosecutor to prove such) shall be in Form 27.4.

(2) A notice by an accused under section 16A(4) of the Criminal Law (Consolidation) (Scotland) Act 1995 (notice disputing condition specified in section 16A(3)) may be served on the prosecutor by any of the methods of service in rule 2.3 (general provisions for service).

(3) At the same time as he serves a notice on the prosecutor under paragraph (2), the accused shall serve a copy of that notice on any co-accused or his solicitor.

[2](4) An accused shall serve a notice under paragraphs (2) or (3), no later than 21 days before the trial diet.

Notes

[1]As amended by the Act of Adjournal (Criminal Procedure Rules Amendment) 1997 (No. 63).

[2]As amended by Act of Adjournal (Criminal Procedure Rules Amendment No. 3) (S.I. 1997 No. 1788) (effective August 11, 1997).

Notice under section 16B(4) of Criminal Law (Consolidation) (Scotland) Act 1995

[1]**27.5.**—(1) Any notice under section 16B(4) of the Criminal Law (Consolidation) (Scotland) Act 1995 (notice served on prosecutor by person accused of sexual offence disputing whether an act done by him abroad constituted an offence under the law in force in the country or territory in question) shall be in Form 27.5 and may be served on the prosecutor by any of the methods of service mentioned in rule 2.3.

(2) Any such notice shall be served not later than 21 days before the trial diet; and when he serves such a notice the accused shall serve a copy of it on any co-accused or on the solicitor of any co-accused.

Note

[1]Inserted by Act of Adjournal (Criminal Procedure Rules Amendment No. 5) (S.I. 1997 No. 2082) (effective September 1, 1997).

PART VII

Miscellaneous procedures

CHAPTER 28

IDENTIFICATION PARADES

Applications for identification parade

28.1.—(1) An application to the sheriff made by an accused under section 290 of the Act of 1995 (application by accused for identification parade) shall be made—
  (a) to the sheriff in whose sheriffdom the proceedings in relation to which the order is sought have been commenced;
  (b) by petition—
      (i) where the accused has appeared on petition under Part IV of the Act of 1995 (petition procedure) but an indictment has not been served on him, in Form 28.1–A; or
      (ii) where an indictment or a complaint has been served on the accused, in Form 28.1.–B.

(2) On the petition referred to in paragraph (1) being lodged, the sheriff shall—
  (a) order intimation of the petition to be made to the prosecutor;
  (b) fix a diet for a hearing of the petition on the earliest practicable date; and
  (c) after giving the prosecutor an opportunity to be heard at the hearing and allowing such further procedure as he thinks fit, make an order granting or refusing the petition.

(3) If—
  (a) the prosecutor is not present at the hearing of the petition; and
  (b) the sheriff makes an order granting the petition,
the sheriff clerk shall issue a certified copy of the order to the petitioner or his solicitor.

(4) The sheriff clerk shall record the order made by the sheriff under paragraph (2)(c) in the minute of proceedings, and shall keep the petition and relative documents in his custody.

CHAPTER 29

PRECOGNITION ON OATH OF DEFENCE WITNESSES

Applications for warrant to cite for precognition

29.1.—(1) An application to the sheriff made by an accused under section 291(1) of the Act of 1995 (warrant to cite any person to appear for precognition on oath) shall be made—
  (a) to the sheriff in whose sheriffdom the proceedings, in respect of which the accused seeks the precognition of that person, have been commenced;
  (b) by petition—
      (i) where the accused has appeared on petition under Part IV of the Act of 1995 (petition procedure) but an indictment has not been served on him, in Form 29.1–A; or
      (ii) where an indictment or a complaint has been served on the accused, in Form 29.1–B.

(2) On a petition referred to in paragraph (1) being lodged, the sheriff shall—

(a) order intimation of the application to be made to the procurator fiscal; and

(b) fix a diet for a hearing of the application.

Orders for taking precognition

29.2. Where, after the hearing fixed under rule 29.1(2), the sheriff is satisfied that it is reasonable to require such precognition on oath in the circumstances, he shall—

(a) order the precognition to be taken;

(b) fix a diet for it to be taken; and

(c) grant warrant to cite the person from whom it is to be taken.

Citation to attend for precognition

29.3.—(1) Citation of a person to attend the diet fixed for taking his precognition on oath shall be in Form 29.3; and an execution of service shall be produced at the diet fixed under rule 29.1(2).

(2) Where a person fails to appear at a diet fixed for taking his precognition and the sheriff issues a warrant for his apprehension under section 291(2) of the Act of 1995, execution of that warrant—

(a) shall be made by an officer of law instructed by the accused or his solicitor; and

(b) may proceed on a copy of the petition and warrant duly certified by the sheriff clerk.

(3) The clerk shall immediately give notice of that person's failure to appear at the diet to the procurator fiscal.

Record of proceedings

29.4.—(1) Where a person appears before the sheriff to have his precognition taken on oath, the proceedings shall be recorded in shorthand by an official shorthand writer instructed by the accused or his solicitor.

(2) The shorthand writer shall extend his shorthand notes recording the proceedings, sign the transcript, and lodge it with the sheriff clerk.

(3) On the transcript being lodged, the sheriff clerk shall—

(a) send a copy to the solicitor for the accused or, it he is not represented, to the accused; and

(b) fix a diet for the person whose precognition has been taken on oath to attend before the sheriff to sign the precognition.

Fees of shorthand writer

29.5.—(1) The solicitor for the accused or, if he is not represented, the accused shall be liable for payment of—

(a) the fees of the shorthand writer, and

(b) the reasonable expenses of the person precognosed on oath;

and shall tender any such expenses in advance if required by that person to do so.

(2) Where the accused is not represented, the sheriff may, at the hearing of the application or at any time before the precognition is taken, order the accused to consign into court such sum as he may be required to pay under paragraph (1) in respect of fees and expenses on or before such date as the sheriff may specify in the order.

(3) If the sheriff orders the accused to consign a sum into court under paragraph (2) and that sum is not consigned by the date specified in the order, the petition shall be treated as abandoned.

CHAPTER 30

PROCEEDINGS FOR THE EXECUTION OF IRISH WARRANTS

Interpretation of this Chapter

30.1. In this Chapter, unless the context otherwise requires—
"the Act of 1965" means the Backing of Warrants (Republic of Ireland) Act 1965;
"judicial authority" means a court, judge or justice of a court, or peace commissioner.

Form of endorsement

30.2.—(1) The endorsement of a warrant for execution within any part of Scotland under section 1 of the Act of 1965 (endorsement of warrants issued in Republic of Ireland) shall be in Form 30.2–A.

(2) A warrant issued under section 4 of the Act of 1965 (provisional warrants) shall be in Form 30.2–B.

(3) Where a person has been remanded in custody under section 2(1) or 4(3) of the Act of 1965 (which relate to proceedings before the sheriff), the order of the court shall be endorsed by the court on the warrant and delivered to the prison governor to whose custody the person has been remanded.

(4) Where a person who has been ordered to be delivered in accordance with section 2(1) of the Act of 1965 is remanded on bail, the bail order shall contain a condition requiring him to surrender at a specified police station at a time and date to be notified to him by or on behalf of the officer in charge of that station.

Procedure in applications for stated case under section 2A of the Act of 1965

30.3.—(1) The sheriff clerk of a court which refused to order a person to be delivered under section 2 of the Act of 1965 (proceedings before sheriff) but made an order under section 2A(2) of that Act releasing that person on bail shall, on the procurator fiscal immediately informing the court that he intends to make an application to the court to state a case for the opinion of the High Court, forthwith send a copy of that order to the Crown Agent.

(2) Where a court refuses to make an order in relation to a person under section 2 of the Act of 1965, any application to the court under section 2A(1) of the Act of 1965 (application to state a case for the opinion of the High Court on ground that it is wrong in law) shall be made to the court by the procurator fiscal within 21 days after the day on which the order was refused, unless the court grants a longer period within which the application is to be made.

(3) Such an application shall be made in writing and shall identify the question of law on which the opinion of the High Court is sought.

(4) Within 21 days after receipt of an application to state a case under section 2A(1) of the Act of 1965, the sheriff clerk shall send a draft stated case to the procurator fiscal and to the person to whom the warrant relates or his solicitor; and the sheriff shall allow each party 21 days from the date of the sending of the draft stated case within which to lodge and intimate proposed adjustments.

(5) Within seven days after the latest date on which adjustments may be lodged, the sheriff shall on the motion of either party, or may of his own accord, hear parties on any such adjustments.

(6) Within 14 days after the latest date on which such hearing on adjustments may take place or, if there are no such adjustments, within 14 days after the latest date by which such adjustments could have been lodged,

the sheriff shall, after considering any such proposed adjustments and representations, state and sign the case; and the sheriff clerk shall—
   (a) forthwith transmit the case, with the application for the case and all other documents, to the Clerk of Justiciary; and
   (b) send a duplicate of the case to the procurator fiscal and to the person to whom the warrant relates or his solicitor.

(7) Where any period of time specified in paragraphs (4), (5) or (6) expires on a Saturday, Sunday or court holiday prescribed for the sheriff court concerned, the period shall be extended to expire on the next day which is not a Saturday, Sunday or such court holiday.

(8) Where the sheriff who refuses to make an order referred to in paragraph (2) becomes temporarily absent from duty for any cause, the sheriff principal of the sheriffdom in which the court is situated may extend any period of time specified in that paragraph for such period as he considers reasonable.

(9) Where the sheriff referred to in paragraph (4), (5) or (6) dies before signing the stated case, the applicant for the stated case may present a bill of suspension to the High Court and bring under the review of that court any matter which might have been brought under review by stated case.

Power of High Court to extend period of time

30.4.—(1) Without prejudice to any other power of relief which the High Court may have, where it appears to that court, on an application made in accordance with the following provisions of this rule, that a party has failed to comply with any of the requirements of paragraph (2) or (4) of rule 30.3 (procedure in applications for stated case under section 2A of the Act of 1965), the High Court may direct that such further period of time as it considers reasonable be afforded to such party to comply with any requirements of paragraph (2) or (4) of rule 30.3.

(2) An application for a direction under paragraph (1) shall be made in writing to the Clerk of Justiciary and shall state the grounds for the application; and notification of the application shall be made by the applicant to the sheriff clerk.

(3) On receipt of such notification, the sheriff clerk shall transmit a certified copy of the complaint, documentary productions and any other proceedings in the case to the Clerk of Justiciary.

(4) The High Court shall dispose of any application under paragraph (1) in the same manner as an appeal in respect of bail under section 32 of the Act of 1995.

(5) After the High Court has disposed of the application, the Clerk of Justiciary shall inform the sheriff clerk of the result.

Notice of consent to early removal

30.5.—(1) A notice given under section 3(1)(a) of the Act of 1965 (consent to removal earlier than is otherwise permitted) shall be in Form 30.5, and shall be signed in the presence of a sheriff, a justice of the peace or a sheriff clerk who shall also sign it.

(2) Any such notice given by a person who has been remanded in custody shall be delivered to the governor of the prison in which he is detained.

(3) Where a person remanded on bail gives such notice, he shall deliver or send it to the clerk of the court which so remanded him.

Handing over of warrant of arrest

30.6.—(1) Where a person has been ordered to be delivered under section 2(1) of the Act of 1965 (proceedings before the sheriff)—

(a) if the person is remanded on bail, the sheriff clerk, or

(b) if the person is detained in custody, the governor of the prison in which he is detained,

shall arrange for the warrant of arrest issued by a judicial authority in the Republic of Ireland and endorsed in accordance with section 1 of that Act to be given to the member of the police force of the Republic of Ireland into whose custody the person is delivered when the person is so delivered.

(2) Where a person ordered to be delivered under section 2(1) of the Act of 1965 is remanded on bail, the sheriff clerk shall send a copy of the bail order to the police station at which that person is to surrender.

Certification of warrant

30.7.—(1) A document purporting to be a warrant issued by a judicial authority in the Republic of Ireland shall, for the purposes of section 7(a) of the Act of 1965 (evidence as to warrants), be verified by a certificate purporting to be signed by a judicial authority, a clerk of a court or a member of the police force of the Republic of Ireland and certifying that the document is a warrant and is issued by a judicial authority.

(2) A document purporting to be a copy of a summons issued by a judicial authority in the Republic of Ireland shall, for the purposes of section 7(a) of the Act of 1965, be verified by a certificate purporting to be signed by a judicial authority, clerk of court or member of the police force of the Republic of Ireland and certifying that the document is a true copy of such a summons.

(3) A deposition purporting to have been made in the Republic of Ireland, or an affidavit or written statement purporting to have been sworn there, shall, for the purposes of section 7(c) of the Act of 1965 (admission of depositions), be verified by a certificate purporting to be signed by the person before whom it was sworn and certifying that it was so sworn.

CHAPTER 31

REFERENCES TO THE EUROPEAN COURT OF JUSTICE

Interpretation of this Chapter

31.1.—(1) In this Chapter, unless the context otherwise requires—

"the European Court" means the Court of Justice of the European Communities;

[1]"question" means a question or issue under Article 234 of the E.E.C. Treaty, Article 150 of the Euratom Treaty or Article 41 of the E.C.S.C. Treaty;

"reference" means a request to the European Court for a preliminary ruling on a question.

(2) The expressions "E.E.C. Treaty", "Euratom Treaty" and "E.C.S.C. Treaty" have the meanings assigned respectively in Schedule 1 to the European Communities Act 1972.

Notice of references in solemn proceedings

31.2.—(1) Where a question is to be raised in any proceedings on indictment (other than proceedings on appeal), notice of intention to do so shall be given to the court before which the trial is to take place and to the other parties not later than 14 days after service of the indictment.

(2) Where such a notice is given, a record of the notice shall be made on the record copy of the indictment or in the record of proceedings, as the case may be; and the court, in chambers, shall reserve consideration of the question to the trial diet.

(3) The court may order that witnesses and jurors are not cited to attend at the trial diet.

(4) At the trial diet, the court, after hearing the parties, may determine the question or may decide that a preliminary ruling should be sought.

(5) Where the court determines the question, the accused shall then (if appropriate) be called on to plead to the indictment; and, without prejudice to any other power available to it, the court—

(a) may prorogate the time for lodging any special defence;

(b) may continue the diet to a specified time and place; and

(c) in a case where witnesses and jurors have not been cited to attend at the trial diet, shall continue the diet and order the citation of witnesses and jurors to attend the continued diet.

(6) No period during which the diet is continued under paragraph (5) shall—

(a) subject to paragraph (7), be longer than 21 days; or

(b) be taken into account for the purposes of determining whether any time limit has expired.

(7) The court may, on the application of the prosecutor or defence, extend any period during which the diet is continued for such longer period than 21 days as it thinks fit on special cause shown.

Notice of references in summary proceedings

31.3.—(1) Where a question is to be raised in any summary proceedings (other than proceedings on appeal), notice of intention to do so shall be given before the accused is called on to plead to the complaint.

(2) Where such notice is given, a record of the notice shall be entered in the minute of proceedings and the court shall not then call on the accused to plead to the complaint.

(3) The court may hear parties on the question forthwith or may adjourn the case to a specified date for such hearing.

(4) After hearing parties, the court may determine the question or may decide that a preliminary ruling should be sought.

(5) Where the court determines the question, the accused shall then (where appropriate) be called on to plead to the complaint.

Proceedings on appeal etc.

31.4.—(1) Where a question is raised in the High Court in any proceedings on appeal or on a petition for the exercise of the *nobile officium*, the court shall proceed to make a reference.

(2) In paragraph (1), the reference to proceedings on appeal is a reference to proceedings on appeal under the Act of 1995 or on appeal by bill of suspension, bill of advocation or otherwise.

Preparation of case for reference

31.5.—(1) Where the court decides that a preliminary ruling should be sought, the court shall—

(a) give its reasons and cause those reasons to be recorded in the record or minute of proceedings, as the case may be; and

(b) continue the proceedings from time to time as necessary for the purposes of the reference.

(2) The reference—

(a) except in so far as the court may otherwise direct, shall be drafted in Form 31.5 and the court may give directions to the parties as to the manner in which and by whom the case is to be drafted and adjusted;

(b) shall thereafter if necessary, be further adjusted to take account of any adjustments required by the court; and

(c) after approval and the making of an appropriate order by the court, shall (after the expiry of the period for appeal) be transmitted by the clerk of court to the Registrar of the European Court with a certified copy of the record or minute of proceedings, as the case may be, and, where applicable, a certified copy of the relevant indictment or complaint.

[3](3) In preparing a reference, the parties shall have regard to the guidance set out in the annex to these Rules.

Procedure on receipt of preliminary ruling

31.6.—(1) Where a preliminary ruling has been given by the European Court on a question referred to it and the ruling has been received by the clerk of the court which made the reference, the ruling shall be laid by the clerk before the court.

(2) On the ruling being laid before the court, the court shall then give directions as to further procedure, which directions shall be intimated by the clerk, with a copy of the ruling, to each of the parties to the proceedings.

Appeals against references

31.7.—(1) Subject to paragraph (2), where an order making a reference is made,[1] any party to the proceedings who is aggrieved by the order may, within 14 days after the date of the order, appeal against the order to the High Court sitting as a court of appeal.

(2) Paragraph (1) shall not apply to such an order made in proceedings in the High Court sitting as a court of appeal or in proceedings on petition to that court for the exercise of its *nobile officium*.

(3) Any appeal under this rule shall be taken by lodging with the clerk of the court which made the order a note of appeal in Form 31.7 and signed by the appellant or his solicitor; and a copy of the note shall be served by the appellant on every other party to the proceedings.

(4) The clerk of court shall record the lodging of the note in the record or minute of proceedings, as the case may be, and shall forthwith transmit the note to the Clerk of Justiciary with the record or minute of proceedings and a certified copy of the relevant indictment or complaint.

(5) In disposing of an appeal under this rule, the High Court (sitting as a court of appeal) may—

(a) sustain or dismiss the appeal, and in either case remit the proceedings to the court of first instance with instructions to proceed as accords; and

(b) give such directions for other procedure as it thinks fit.

(6) Unless the court making the order otherwise directs, a reference shall not be transmitted to the Registrar of the European Court before the time allowed by this rule for appealing against the order has expired or before the appeal has been disposed of or abandoned.

NOTES

[1]As amended by the Act of Adjournal (Criminal Procedure Rules Amendment No. 2) 1999 (S.I. 1999 No.1282), para.2(2) (effective May 1, 1999).

[2]As amended by the Act of Adjournal (Criminal Procedure Rules Amendment No. 2) 1999 (S.I. 1999 No.1282), para.2(3)(a) (effective May 1, 1999).

[3]Inserted by the Act of Adjournal (Criminal Procedure Rules Amendment No. 2) 1999 (S.I. 1999 No.1282), para.2(3)(b) (effective May 1, 1999).

NOTE

[1]As amended by Act of Adjournal (Criminal Procedure Rules Amendment) (Miscellaneous) (S.I. 1996 No. 2147 (s.171)) (effective September 9, 1996).

CHAPTER 32

ANNOYING CREATURES

Interpretation of this Chapter

32.1. In this Chapter, "the Act of 1982" means the Civic Government (Scotland) Act 1982.

Form of application to district court and service

32.2.—(1) An application to a district court under section 49(3) of the Act of 1982 (annoying creatures) shall be made in Form 32.2.

(2) On the lodging of any such application, the district court shall make an order for service of a copy of the application on any person mentioned in the application as having the creature so mentioned in his charge or keeping the creature, and fixing a date and time for the hearing of the application.

(3) A copy of the application and of the order made under paragraph (2) shall be served on any such person by recorded delivery at the normal place of residence or place of business of that person, and such service shall be treated as sufficient notice to that person of the terms of the application and the order for the purposes of paragraph (4).

(4) If any person upon whom service has been made in accordance with paragraph (3) fails to appear or be represented at the time and date of the hearing specified in the order without reasonable excuse, the court may proceed to hear and decide the application in his absence.

(5) Where the court makes an order in respect of any person under section 49(2) of the Act of 1982, the clerk of court shall, within seven days after the date on which the order was made, serve on that person, by recorded delivery at the normal place of residence or place of business of that person, a copy of the order and a notice setting out the terms of section 49(4) of the Act of 1982.

CHAPTER 33

LEGAL AID

Interpretation of this Chapter

33.1. In this Chapter, unless the context otherwise requires—
"the Act of 1986" means the Legal Aid (Scotland) Act 1986;
"assisted person" means a person who is in receipt of criminal legal aid in the proceedings in question;
"the Regulations" means the Criminal Legal Aid (Scotland) Regulations 1987.

Legal aid in High Court

33.2. Where an application for legal aid is made to the High Court under section 23 of the Act of 1986 (power of the court to grant legal aid), the court may—
(a) determine the application itself; or
(b) remit the application to the sheriff court for determination.

Discontinuance of entitlement to legal aid

33.3.—(1) Where the court before which there are proceedings in which an assisted person is an accused or appellant is satisfied, after hearing that person—
(a) that he—

   (i) has without reasonable cause failed to comply with a proper request made to him by the solicitor acting for him to supply any information relevant to the proceedings,

   (ii) has delayed unreasonably in complying with any such request,

  (iii) has without reasonable cause failed to attend at a diet of the court at which he has been required to attend or at a meeting with the counsel or solicitor acting for him under the Act of 1986 at which he has reasonably and properly been required to attend,

  (iv) has conducted himself in connection with the proceedings in such a way as to make it appear to the court unreasonable that he should continue to receive criminal legal aid,

   (v) has wilfully or deliberately given false information for the purpose of misleading the court in considering his financial circumstances under section 23(1) of the Act of 1986, or

  (vi) has without reasonable cause failed to comply with a requirement of the Regulations, or

(b) that it is otherwise unreasonable for the solicitor to continue to act on behalf of the assisted person in the proceedings,

the court may direct that the assisted person shall cease to be entitled to criminal legal aid in connection with those proceedings.

(2) Where a direction is made under paragraph (1) of this rule in the course of proceedings to which section 22 of the Act of 1986 (automatic availability of criminal legal aid) applies, the accused shall not be entitled to criminal legal aid in relation to any later stages of the same proceedings before the court of first instance.

(3) Where a court issues a direction under paragraph (1), the clerk of court shall send notice of it to the Scottish Legal Aid Board.

(4) Where a court of first instance has made a direction under paragraph (1)(a), it shall instruct the clerk of court to report the terms of the finding made by the court to the Scottish Legal Aid Board for its consideration in any application for criminal legal aid in an appeal in connection with the proceedings in that court.

Statements on oath

33.4. In considering any matter in regard to the entitlement of a person to criminal legal aid, the court may require that person to make a statement on oath for the purpose of ascertaining or verifying any fact material to his entitlement to criminal legal aid.

Intimation of determination of High Court

33.5. The Clerk of Justiciary shall intimate to the Scottish Legal Aid Board any decision of the High Court made under section 25(2A) of the Act of 1986 (determination by High Court that applicant should receive legal aid).

CHAPTER 34

EXTRADITION

Interpretation of this Chapter

34.1. In this Chapter—

"the Act of 1989" means the Extradition Act 1989;

"court of committal" has the meaning assigned in section 9(1) of the Act of 1989.

Procedure in applications for stated case

34.2.—(1) Where—
(a) the court of committal refuses to make an order under section 9 of the Act of 1989 (proceedings for committal) in relation to a person in respect of the offence or, as the case may be, any of the offences to which the authority to proceed relates,
(b) the state, country or colony seeking the surrender of that person immediately informs the court that it intends to make an application to the court to state a case for the opinion of the High Court, and
(c) the court of committal makes an order under section 10(2) of the Act of 1989 (detention or bail where refusal of extradition order challenged) releasing that person on bail,
the sheriff clerk shall forthwith send a copy of that order to the Crown Agent.

(2) Where—
(a) the court of committal refuses to make an order under section 9 of the Act of 1989 in relation to a person in respect of the offence or, as the case may be, any of the offences to which the authority to proceed relates, and
(b) the state, country or colony seeking his surrender wishes to apply to that court to state a case for the opinion of the High Court under section 10(1) of the Act of 1989,
such an application shall be made to the court of committal within 21 days after the date on which that court refuses to make the order under section 9 of the Act of 1989 unless the sheriff grants a longer period within which the application is to be made.

(3) Such an application shall be made in writing and shall identify the question or questions of law on which the opinion of the High Court is sought.

(4) Within 21 days after receipt of an application to state a case under section 10(1) of the Act of 1989, the clerk of the court of committal shall send a draft stated case prepared by the sheriff to the solicitor for the state, country or colony and to the person whose surrender is sought or his solicitor; and the court of committal shall allow each party 21 days from the date of the sending of the draft stated case within which to lodge and intimate proposed adjustments.

(5) Within seven days after the latest date on which such adjustments may be lodged, the sheriff shall, on the motion of either party, or may of his own accord, hear parties or any such adjustments.

(6) Within 14 days after the latest date on which such hearing on adjustments may take place (or, if there are no such adjustments, within 14 days after the latest date by which such adjustments could have been lodged), the sheriff shall, after considering any such proposed adjustments and representations, state and sign the case; and the sheriff clerk shall—
(a) forthwith transmit the case, with the application for the case and all other documents in the case to the Clerk of Justiciary; and
(b) send a duplicate of the case to the solicitor for the state, country or colony and to the person whose surrender is sought or his solicitor.

(7) If any period of time specified in paragraph (4), (5) or (6) expires on a Saturday, Sunday or court holiday prescribed for the court of committal, the period shall be extended to expire on the next day which is not a Saturday, Sunday or such court holiday.

(8) Where the sheriff referred to in paragraph (4), (5) or (6) becomes temporarily absent from duty for any cause, the sheriff principal of the

sheriffdom of Lothian and Borders may extend any period of time specified in that paragraph for such period as he considers reasonable.

(9) Where the sheriff referred to in paragraph (4), (5) or (6) dies before signing the stated case, the applicant for the stated case may present a bill of suspension to the High Court and bring under the review of that court any matter which might have been brought under review by stated case.

Power of High Court to extend period of time

34.3.—(1) Without prejudice to any other power which the High Court may have, where it appears to that court, on an application made in accordance with the following provisions of this rule, that a party has failed to comply with any of the requirements of paragraph (2) or (4) of rule 34.2 (procedure in applications for stated case), the High Court may direct that such further period of time as it considers reasonable be afforded to such party to comply with any requirements of paragraph (2) or (4) of rule 34.2.

(2) An application for a direction under paragraph (1) shall be made in writing to the Clerk of Justiciary and shall state the grounds for the application; and notification of the application shall be made by the applicant to the sheriff clerk of the court of committal; and the sheriff clerk shall forthwith transmit one certified copy of all documents in the case to the Clerk of Justiciary.

(3) The High Court shall dispose of any application under paragraph (1) in the same manner as an appeal in respect of bail under section 32 of the Act of 1995 and, when the High Court has disposed of the application, the Clerk of Justiciary shall inform the clerk of the court of committal of the result.

Applications to High Court for order for stated case

34.4. An application to the High Court for an order under section 10(4) of the Act of 1989 (order requiring court of committal to state a case) shall be made in writing to the Clerk of Justiciary and shall state the grounds for the application, and notification of application shall be made by the applicant to the sheriff clerk of the court of committal; and the sheriff clerk shall forthwith transmit one certified copy of all documents in the case to the Clerk of Justiciary.

Notices of waiver of rights and consent

34.5.—(1) A notice given under section 14 of, or paragraph 9 of Schedule 1 to, the Act of 1989 (which relate to waiver of rights) shall be in Form 34.5.

(2) Such a notice shall be signed in the presence of a sheriff, sheriff clerk, justice of the peace or solicitor.

(3) Any such notice given by a person in custody shall be delivered to the governor of the prison in whose custody he is.

(4) Where a person on bail gives such notice he shall deliver it, or send it by post in a registered letter or by the first class recorded delivery service addressed, to the Crown Agent.

CHAPTER 35

COMPUTER MISUSE ACT 1990

Notices in relation to relevance of external law

35.1. A notice under section 8(5) of the Computer Misuse Act 1990 (notice by defence that conditions not satisfied) shall be served on the prosecutor not later than 14 days before the trial diet.

CHAPTER 36

CRIMINAL JUSTICE (INTERNATIONAL CO-OPERATION) ACT 1990

Interpretation of this Chapter

36.1. In this Chapter—
"the Act of 1990" means the Criminal Justice (International Co-operation) Act 1990; and
"document" means a document to which section 2 of the Act of 1990 (service of United Kingdom process overseas) applies.

Service of orders outside the United Kingdom

36.2. Where a document is to be served on a person outside the United Kingdom, it shall be sent by the Clerk of Justiciary or sheriff clerk, as the case may be, to the Crown Agent with a view to its being served in accordance with arrangements made by the Secretary of State.

Proof of service outside the United Kingdom

36.3. The service on any person of a document may be proved in any legal proceedings by a certificate given by or on behalf of the Secretary of State, and such a certificate shall be sufficient evidence of the facts stated in it.

Notice of applications for letters of request

36.4. An application under section 3(1) of the Act of 1990 (issue of letter of request)—
(a) shall be made in Form 36.4–A;
(b) shall be lodged with the Clerk of Justiciary or sheriff clerk, as the case may be; and
(c) shall—
  (i) be made in writing;
  (ii) state the particulars of the offence which it is alleged has been committed or the grounds on which it is suspected that an offence has been committed;
  (iii) state whether proceedings in respect of the offence have been instituted or the offence is being investigated; and
  (iv) include particulars of the assistance requested in a draft letter of request in Form 36.4–B.

Hearing of applications for letters of request

36.5.—(1) Where the prosecutor presents an application under section 3(1) of the Act of 1990 (issue of letter of request) before either the first appearance of the accused on petition or the service of a summary complaint, the High Court or sheriff, as the case may be, shall, without requiring intimation to any other party, proceed to consider the application.
(2) Where any party presents such an application following the first appearance of the accused on petition or the service of a summary complaint, the High Court or sheriff, as the case may be, may—
(a) before the lodging of an indictment, dispense on cause shown with intimation to any other party and proceed to consider the application; or
(b) fix a diet for hearing the application and order intimation of the diet and application to any other party.
(3) The High Court or sheriff, as the case may be, after considering any such application—
(a) may allow summary adjustment of the statement of assistance required in the letter of request;

(b) shall grant the application, with or without any modifications which it or he deems appropriate, or shall refuse it.

(4) On granting such application the High Court or sheriff, as the case may be, shall—
  (a) approve and sign the letter of request;
  (b) if English is not an official language of the body to which the letter of request is addressed, specify a period within which a translation of the letter of request and of any production is to be lodged.

Court register of applications for letters of request

36.6.—(1) A register shall be kept by the Clerk of Justiciary and by the sheriff clerk of applications under section 3(1) of the Act of 1990 (issue of letter of request).

(2) Save as authorised by the court, the register relating to applications mentioned in paragraph (1) above shall not be open to inspection by any person.

Letters of request in cases of urgency

36.7. Where, in a case of urgency, the court sends a letter of request direct to any court or tribunal in accordance with section 3(5) of the Act of 1990 (issue of letter of request), the Clerk of Justiciary or sheriff clerk, as the case may be, shall forthwith notify the Crown Agent and Secretary of State of this and send with the notification a copy of the letter of request.

Proceedings before a nominated court

36.8.—(1) In proceedings before a court nominated under section 4(2) of the Act of 1990 (nomination of court to receive evidence for use overseas)—
  (a) the procurator fiscal or Crown counsel shall participate in any hearing;
  (b) the prosecutor of the requesting country mentioned in the request under section 4(1) of the Act of 1990 may participate in any hearing;
  (c) where the request under section 4(1) of the Act of 1990 (request for assistance in obtaining evidence in United Kingdom) originates from current criminal proceedings any party to or persons with an interest in those proceedings may attend and, with the leave of the court, participate in any hearing;
  (d) a judge or investigating magistrate in the current criminal proceedings may participate in any hearing;
  (e) a lawyer or person with a right of audience from the requesting country who represents any party to the current criminal proceedings may participate in any hearing;
  (f) a solicitor or counsel instructed by any party may participate in any hearing;
  (g) any other person may, with the leave of the court, participate in any hearing;
  (h) a shorthand writer may be present to record the proceedings; and
  (i) the proceedings shall be in private.

(2) Where any person applies for leave to participate in any hearing the court shall, in determining such application, consider any relevant representations made by the party making the request under section 4(1) of the Act of 1990.

Court record of proceedings before a nominated court

36.9.—(1) Where a court receives evidence in proceedings by virtue of a notice under section 4(2) of the Act of 1990 (nomination of court to receive evidence for use overseas), the Clerk of Justiciary or sheriff clerk, as the case may be, shall record in the minute of proceedings—

(a) particulars of the proceedings; and
(b) without prejudice to the generality of (a) above—
    (i) which persons were present;
    (ii) which of those persons were represented and by whom; and
    (iii) whether any of those persons was denied the opportunity of cross-examining a witness as to any part of his testimony.

(2) Save as authorised by the Lord Advocate, or with the leave of the court, the minute of proceedings mentioned in paragraph (1) above shall not be open to inspection by any person.

(3) When so requested by the Lord Advocate, the sheriff clerk shall send to him a certified copy of the minute of proceedings as it relates to any proceedings mentioned in paragraph (1).

(4) The Clerk of Justiciary or sheriff clerk, as the case may be, shall comply with paragraph 5 of Schedule 1 to the Act of 1990 (transmission of evidence) with regard to the transmission of evidence received by the court.

CHAPTER 37

PROCEEDINGS UNDER THE PROCEEDS OF CRIME (SCOTLAND) ACT 1995

Orders to make material available

37.1.—[1](1) An application by the procurator fiscal to the sheriff for an order under section 18(2) of the Proceeds of Crime (Scotland) Act 1995 (order to make material available in investigation into whether a person has benefited from commission of an offence shall be made by petition; and section 134 (incidental applications) of the Act of 1995 shall apply to any such application as it applies to an application referred to in that section.

(2) The sheriff may make the order sought in the petition under paragraph (1) before intimation of the petition to the person who appears to him to be in possession of the material to which the application relates.

(3) An application by the procurator fiscal for an order under section 18(5) of the Proceeds of Crime (Scotland) Act 1995 (order to allow constable to enter premises to obtain access to material) may be made in the petition applying for an order under section 18(2); and paragraph (2) of this rule shall apply to an order in respect of a person who appears to the sheriff to be entitled to grant entry to the premises in question as it applies to an order in respect of the person mentioned in that paragraph.

Discharge and variation of orders

37.2.—[1](1) A person, in respect of whom an order has been made under section 18(2) or (5) of the Proceeds of Crime (Scotland) Act 1995 (which relate to orders to make material available in investigating whether a person has benefited from commission of a offence), may apply to the sheriff for discharge or variation of the order in question.

(2) The sheriff may, after hearing the parties, grant or refuse to grant the discharge or variation sought.

Warrants to search premises

37.3. An application by the procurator fiscal to the sheriff under section 19(1) of the Proceeds of Crime (Scotland) Act 1995 (authority for search) shall be made by petition; and section 134 (incidental applications) of the

Act of 1995 shall apply to any such application for a warrant as it applies to an application for a warrant referred to in that section.

Orders under sections 25 and 26

[2]**37.4.** An application under section 25 (recall etc. of suspended forfeiture order) or 26 (return of property wrongly confiscated etc.) of the Proceeds of Crime (Scotland) Act 1995 by a person other than the accused to the court shall be made by petition in Form 37.4.

Appeals under section 27

[2]**37.5.** An appeal under section 27 of the Proceeds of Crime (Scotland) Act 1995 (appeal against grant or refusal of application under section 25(1) or 26(1)) shall be in Form 37.5.

NOTES
  [1]As amended by Act of Adjournal (Criminal Procedure Rules Amendment) (Miscellaneous) (S.I. 1996 No. 2147 (s.171)) (effective September 9, 1996).
  [2]Inserted by Act of Adjournal (Criminal Procedure Rules Amendment No. 7) (S.I. 1997 No. 2653) (effective November 21, 1997).

[1]CHAPTER 37A

PROCEEDINGS UNDER SECTION 7 OF THE KNIVES ACT 1997

37A. An application to the sheriff under section 7(3) of the Knives Act 1997 (recovery order for delivery of property to applicant if it appears to court that he owns it) shall be made by petition in Form 37A.

NOTE
  [1]Inserted by Act of Adjournal (Criminal Procedure Rules Amendment No. 6) (S.I. 1997 No. 2081) (effective September 1, 1997).

[1]CHAPTER 38

TRANSFER OF RIGHTS OF APPEAL OF DECEASED PERSONS

Applications for transfer under section 303A of the Act of 1995

38. Any application to the High Court under section 303A of the Act of 1995 for an order authorising a person (the "applicant") as executor, or as the case may be by reason of his having a legitimate interest, to institute or continue any appeal which could have been or has been instituted by a deceased person shall be made in Form 38 and shall be accompanied by a copy of the confirmation of the applicant as executor or evidence of his legitimate interest, as the case may be.

NOTE
  [1]Inserted by Act of Adjournal (Criminal Procedure Rules Amendment No. 4) (S.I. 1997 No. 1834) (effective August 1, 1997).

[1]CHAPTER 39

PROCEEDINGS UNDER CRIMINAL LAW (CONSOLIDATION) (SCOTLAND) ACT 1995

Orders to make material available

[1]**39.1.**—(1) An application by the procurator fiscal to the sheriff for an order under section 31(2) of the Criminal Law (Consolidation) (Scotland)

Act 1995 (order to make material available in investigation into drug trafficking) shall be made by petition; and section 134 of the Act of 1995 (incidental applications) shall apply to an application under section 31(2) as it applies to an application under section 31(2) as it applies to an application to which section 134 applies.

(2) The sheriff may make the order sought in the petition under paragraph (1) before intimation of the petition to the person who appears to him to be in possession of the material to which the application relates.

(3) An application by the procurator fiscal for an order under section 31(5) of the Criminal Law (Consolidation) (Scotland) Act 1995 (order allowing constable or person commissioned by Customs and Excise access to premises to obtain material) may be made in the petition applying for an order under section 31(2) of that Act; and paragraph (2) shall apply to an order in respect of a person who appears to the sheriff to be entitled to grant entry to the premises in question as it applies to an order in respect of the person mentioned in that paragraph.

Discharge and variation of orders

[1]**39.2.**—(1) A person in respect of whom an order has been made under section 31(2) or (5) of the Criminal Law (Consolidation) (Scotland) Act 1995 may apply to the sheriff for discharge or variation of the order in question.

(2) The sheriff may, after hearing the parties, grant or refuse to grant the discharge or variation sought.

Warrants to search premises

[1]**39.3.** An application by the procurator fiscal to the sheriff under section 32(1) of the Criminal Law (Consolidation) (Scotland) Act 1995 (authority for search) shall be made by petition; and section 134 of the Act of 1995 (incidental applications) shall apply to an application under section 32(1) as it applies to an application to which section 134 applies.

Note
[1]Inserted by Act of Adjournal (Criminal Procedure Rules Amendment No. 7) (S.I. 1997 No. 2653) (effective November 21, 1997) as Chapter 38.

[1]CHAPTER 40

DEVOLUTION ISSUES

Interpretation of this Chapter

40.1.—(1) In this Chapter—
"Advocate General" means the Advocate General for Scotland;
"devolution issue" means a devolution issue within the meaning of—
    (a) Schedule 6 to the Scotland Act 1998;
    (b) Schedule 10 to the Northern Ireland Act 1998; or
    (c) Schedule 8 to the Government of Wales Act 1998,
    and any reference to Schedule 6, Schedule 10 or Schedule 8 is a reference to that Schedule to, respectively, the Scotland Act 1998, the Northern Ireland Act 1998 and the Government of Wales Act 1998;
"the Judicial Committee" means the Judicial Committee of the Privy Council;
"relevant authority" means the Advocate General and—
    (a) in the case of a devolution issue within the meaning of Schedule 6, the Lord Advocate;

    (b) in the case of a devolution issue within the meaning of Schedule 10, the Attorney General for Northern Ireland, and the First Minister and deputy First Minister acting jointly;

    (c) in the case of a devolution issue within the meaning of Schedule 8, the National Assembly for Wales.

(2) For the purposes of this Chapter, a trial shall be taken to commence—

    (a) in proceedings on indictment, when the oath is administered to the jury;

    (b) in summary proceedings, when the first witness is sworn.

(3) Rule 2.1 (service on the Crown) does not apply to any requirement to serve any document on or give any notice or intimation of any matter to the Lord Advocate in pursuance of this Chapter.

Raising devolution issues: proceedings on indictment

40.2.—(1) Where a party to proceedings on indictment proposes to raise a devolution issue he shall, not later than 7 days after the date of service of the indictment, give written notice of his intention to do so in Form 40.2A to the clerk of the court in which the trial is to take place; and a copy of the notice shall, at the same time, be served on the other parties to the proceedings and on the relevant authority.

(2) The copy notice served on the relevant authority under paragraph (1) shall be treated as intimation of the devolution issue arising in the proceedings as mentioned in paragraph 5 of Schedule 6 or, as the case may be, paragraph 23 of Schedule 10 or paragraph 14(1) of Schedule 8, unless the court determines that no devolution issue arises in the proceedings.

(3) Where a relevant authority wishes to become a party to the proceedings as mentioned in paragraph 6 of Schedule 6 or, as the case may be, paragraph 24 of Schedule 10 or paragraph 14(2) of Schedule 8, he shall, not later than 7 days after receipt of the notice served under paragraph (1), give notice in Form 40.2B to the clerk of the court in which the trial is to take place; and a copy of such notice shall be served on the Lord Advocate and every other party to the proceedings.

²(3a) Where a relevant authority does not become a party to the proceedings at first instance the court may allow him to become a party to any subsequent appeal or reference to a higher court.

(4) A record of any notice given under paragraph (1) or (3) shall be made on the record copy of the indictment or in the record of the proceedings, as the case may be.

(5) This Rule is without prejudice to any right of or requirement upon any party to the proceedings to raise any matter or objection or to make any submission or application under section 72 of the Act of 1995.

Raising devolution issues: summary proceedings

40.3.—(1) Where a party to summary proceedings proposes to raise a devolution issue he shall, before the accused or, where there is more than one accused, any accused is called upon to plead, give notice of his intention to raise the devolution issue in Form 40.3A to the clerk of court; and a copy of the notice shall, at the same time, be served on other parties to the proceedings and on the relevant authority.

(2) The copy notice served on the relevant authority under paragraph (1) shall be treated as intimation of the devolution issue arising in the proceedings as mentioned in paragraph 5 of Schedule 6 or, as the case may be, paragraph 23 of Schedule 10 or paragraph 14(1) of Schedule 8, unless the court determines that no devolution issue arises in the proceedings.

(3) Where notice is given under paragraph (1) the court, unless it determines that no devolution issue arises in the proceedings, shall adjourn the case under section 145 of the Act of 1995.

(4) Where a relevant authority wishes to become a party to the proceedings as mentioned in paragraph 6 of Schedule 6 or, as the case may be, paragraph 24 of Schedule 10 or paragraph 14(2) of Schedule 8, he shall, not later than 7 days after receipt of the notice served under paragraph (1), give notice to the clerk of court in Form 40.3B of his intention to do so: and he shall, at the same time, serve a copy of that notice on any other relevant authority and on every other party to the proceedings.

²(5) Where a relevant authority does not become a party to the proceedings at first instance the court may allow him to become a party to any subsequent appeal or reference to a higher court.

Raising devolution issues: other criminal proceedings

40.4.—(1) This Rule applies to criminal proceedings which are not proceedings on indictment or summary proceedings.

(2) Where a party to proceedings to which this Rule applies proposes to raise a devolution issue he shall give notice of his intention to raise the devolution issue in Form 40.4A to the clerk of court; and a copy of the notice shall, at the same time, be served on the other parties to the proceedings and on the relevant authority.

(3) The copy notice served on the relevant authority under paragraph (2) shall be treated as intimation of the devolution issue arising in the proceedings as mentioned in paragraph 5 of Schedule 6 or, as the case may be, paragraph 23 of Schedule 10 or paragraph 14(1) of Schedule 8, unless the court determines that no devolution issue arises in the proceedings.

(4) Where a relevant authority wishes to become a party to the proceedings as mentioned in paragraph 6 of Schedule 6 or, as the case may be, paragraph 24 of Schedule 10 or paragraph 14(2) of Schedule 8, he shall, not later than 7 days after receipt of the notice served under paragraph (1), give notice to the clerk of court in Form 40.4B of his intention to do so: and he shall, at the same time, serve a copy of that notice on any other relevant authority and on every other party to the proceedings.

²(5) Where a relevant authority does not become a party to the proceedings at first instance the court may allow him to become a party to any subsequent appeal or reference to a higher court.

Time for raising devolution issue

40.5.—(1) No party to criminal proceedings shall raise a devolution issue in those proceedings except as in accordance with Rule 40.2, 40.3 or 40.4, unless the court, on cause shown, otherwise determines.

(2) Where the court determines that a devolution issue may be raised as mentioned in paragraph (1), it shall make such orders as to the procedure to be followed as appear to it to be appropriate and, in particular, it shall make such orders—

(a) as are necessary to ensure that intimation of the devolution issue is given in writing to the relevant authority for the purposes of paragraph 5 of Schedule 6 or, as the case may be, paragraph 23 of Schedule 10 or paragraph 14(1) of Schedule 8; and

(b) as to the time in which any step is to be taken by any party in the proceedings.

Specification of the devolution issue

40.6. The notice given under paragraph (1) of Rule 40.2 or 40.3 or paragraph (2) of Rule 40.4 shall specify the facts and circumstances and contentions of law on the basis of which it is alleged that a devolution issue arises in the proceedings in sufficient detail to enable the court to determine, for the purposes of paragraph 2 of Schedule 6 or, as the case may be, of Schedule 10 or Schedule 8, whether a devolution issue arises in the proceedings.

Reference of devolution issue to the High Court

40.7.—(1) Where a court, other than a court consisting of two or more judges of the High Court of Justiciary, decides to refer a devolution issue to the High Court of Justiciary under paragraph 9 of Schedule 6 or, as the case may be, paragraph 27 of Schedule 10 or paragraph 17 of Schedule 8, the court shall—
- (a) pronounce an order giving directions to the parties about the manner and time in which the reference is to be drafted;
- (b) give its reasons for making the reference and cause those reasons to be recorded in the record or minutes of proceedings, as the case may be; and
- (c) continue the proceedings from time to time as necessary for the purpose of the reference.

(2) The reference—
- (a) shall then be adjusted at the sight of the court in such manner as the court may direct; and
- (b) after approval and the making of an appropriate order by the court shall (after the expiry of any period for appeal) be transmitted by the clerk of court to the Clerk of Justiciary with a certified copy of the record or minutes of proceedings, as the case may be, and, where applicable, a certified copy of the relevant indictment or complaint.

(3) Where the court determines that a devolution issue may be raised during a trial, the court shall not refer the devolution issue to the High Court but shall determine the issue itself.

Orders pending determination of devolution issue

40.8.—(1) In any case where a devolution issue arises in criminal proceedings (including proceedings where there is a reference of a devolution issue to the High Court of Justiciary or the Judicial Committee), the court or, in the case of a reference or an appeal to the Judicial Committee, the High Court of Justiciary may make such orders as it considers just and equitable in the circumstances pending the determination of the devolution issue, including—
- (a) postponing any diet, including a trial diet, fixed in the case;
- (b) making such order as it considers appropriate in relation to bail;
- (c) subject to paragraph (2), extending the period within which any step requires to be taken or event to have occurred.

(2) An order under paragraph (1)(c) extending a period which may be extended under section 65 or 147 of the Act of 1995 may be made only by a court which has power to do so under that section; and, for the purposes of that section, the fact that a devolution issue has been raised by the prosecutor shall not, without more, be treated as fault on the part of the prosecutor.

Reference of devolution issue to Judicial Committee

40.9.—(1) This Rule applies where—
- (a) a court consisting if two or more judges of the High Court of Justiciary decides to refer a devolution issue to the Judicial Committee under paragraph 11 of Schedule 6 or, as the case may be, paragraph 29 of Schedule 10 or paragraph 19 of Schedule 8; or
- (b) a court is required by a relevant authority to refer a devolution issue to the Judicial committee as mentioned in paragraph 33 of Schedule 6

or, as the case may be, paragraph 33 of Schedule 10 or paragraph 30(1) of Schedule 8.

(2) The court shall—

(a) pronounce an order giving directions to the parties about the manner and time in which the reference is to be drafted;

(b) give its reasons for making the reference and cause those reasons to be recorded in the record or minutes of proceedings, as the case may be; and

(c) continue the proceedings from time to time as necessary for the purpose of the reference.

(3) The reference shall include such matters as may be required by Rule 2.9 of the Judicial Committee (Devolution Issues) Rules 1999 and—

(a) shall be adjusted at the sight of the court in such manner as may be so directed; and

(b) after approval and the making of an appropriate order by the court, shall be transmitted by the clerk of court to the Registrar of the Judicial Committee with a certified copy of the record or minutes of proceedings, as the case may be, and, where applicable, a certified copy of the relevant indictment or complaint.

Procedure on receipt of determination of devolution issue

40.10.—(1) Where on a reference of a devolution issue the High Court of Justiciary or, as the case may be, the Judicial Committee has determined the issue and the determination has been received by the clerk of the court which made the reference, the determination shall be laid before the court.

(2) On the determination being laid before the court, the court shall then give directions as to further procedure, which directions shall be intimated by the clerk with a copy of the determination to each of the parties to the proceedings.

Procedure following disposal of appeal by Judicial Committee

40.11. The High Court of Justiciary shall, on the application of any party to the proceedings, fix a diet for the purpose of disposing of any matter in consequence of a judgment of the Judicial Committee on an appeal under paragraph 13(a) of Schedule 6 or, as the case may be, paragraph 31(a) of Schedule 10 or paragraph 21(a) of Schedule 8.

Orders mitigating the effect of certain decisions

40.12.—(1) In any proceedings where the court is considering making an order under—

(a) section 102 of the Scotland Act 1998;

(b) section 81 of the Northern Ireland Act 1998; or

(c) section 110 of the Government of Wales Act 1998,

(power of the court to vary or suspend the effect of certain decisions), the court shall order intimation of the fact to be made by the clerk of court to every person to whom intimation is required to be given by that section.

(2) Intimation as mentioned in paragraph (1) above shall—

(a) be made forthwith in Form 40.12 by first class recorded delivery post; and

(b) specify 7 days, or such other period as the court thinks fit, as the period within which a person may give notice of his intention to take part in the proceedings.

NOTES

[1]Inserted by the Act of Adjournal (Devolution Issues Rules) 1999 (S.I. 1999 No. 1346) (effective May 6, 1999).

[2]Inserted by the Act of Adjournal (Criminal Procedure Rules Amendment)(Miscellaneous) 2000 (S.S.I. 2000 No. 65), para.3 (effective April 7, 2000).

¹CHAPTER 41

HUMAN RIGHTS ACT 1998

Application and interpretation

41.1.—(1) This Chapter deals with various matters relating to the Human Rights Act 1998.

(2) In this Chapter—

"the 1998 Act" means the Human Rights Act 1998;

"declaration of incompatibility" has the meaning given by section 4 of the 1998 Act.

Evidence of judgments, etc.

41.2.—(1) Evidence of any judgment, decision, declaration or opinion of which account has to be taken by the court under section 2 of the 1998 Act shall be given by reference to any authoritative and complete report of the said judgment, decision, declaration or opinion and may be given in any manner.

(2) Evidence given in accordance with paragraph (1) shall be sufficient evidence of that judgment, decision, declaration or opinion.

Declaration of incompatibility

41.3.—(1) Where in any proceedings the court is considering whether to make a declaration of incompatibility it shall give notice of this in Form 41.3–A to such persons as the Lord Justice General may from time to time direct.

(2) Where any—

(a) Minister of the Crown (or person nominated by him);

(b) member of the Scottish Executive;

(c) Northern Ireland Minister;

(d) Northern Ireland department,

wishes to be joined as a party to proceedings in relation to which the Crown is entitled to receive notice under section 5 of the 1998 Act he or, as the case may be, it shall serve notice in Form 41.3–B to that effect on the Deputy Principal Clerk of Justiciary and shall serve a copy of the notice on all other parties to the proceedings.

41.4. Within 14 days after the date of service of the notice under rule 41.3(2), the person serving the notice shall lodge a minute in the proceedings in Form 41.4 and shall serve a copy of that minute on all other parties to the proceedings.

41.5. The court may fix a diet for a hearing on the question of incompatibility as a separate hearing from any other hearing in the proceedings and may sist the proceedings if it considers it necessary to do so while the question of incompatibility is being determined.

NOTE

¹Inserted by Act of Adjournal (Criminal Procedure Rules Amendment No.2) (Human Rights Act 1998) 2000 (S.S.I. 2000 No. 315) (effective October 2, 2000).

Rule 1.3   **APPENDIX**

Rule 2.6(1)   **FORM 2.6–A**

Form of execution of service of indictment and of citation of accused under section 66(2) of the Criminal Procedure (Scotland) Act 1995

EXECUTION OF SERVICE AND CITATION OF ACCUSED

I, (*name and designation*), on (*date*) duly served on (*name and address of accused*) the indictment against him, with a notice to appear attached to it for the diet in the High Court of Justiciary [*or* Sheriff Court] at (*place*) on (*date*).

This I did by (*state method of service*).

(*Signed*)   (*Signed*)
                                     Witness
                                     Officer of Law

Rule 2.6(2)   [1]**FORM 2.6–B**

Form of execution of service of complaint on accused

EXECUTION OF SERVICE OF COMPLAINT

I, (*name and designation*), on (*date*) lawfully summoned (*name and address of accused as in complaint*) to appear before the Sheriff [*or* District] Court at (*address*) on (*date*) at (*time*) to answer to a complaint at the instance of the procurator fiscal charging him with (*state offence*).

This I did by delivering a copy of the complaint with a citation attached to it by (*state method of service*). [I also delivered to him with the copy of the complaint a notice specifying his previous conviction[s].]

                               (*Signed*)
                               Officer of Law

NOTE
    As amended by Act of Adjournal (Criminal Procedure Rules Amendment No. 3) (S.I. 1997 No. 1788) (effective August 11, 1997).

Rule 2.6(3)   **FORM 2.6–C**

Form of execution of personal service of citation of a witness at a trial on indictment

EXECUTION OF PERSONAL SERVICE OF CITATION OF WITNESS

I, (*name and designation*), on (*date*) duly served on (*name and address of witness*) a citation to attend the sitting of the High Court of Justiciary [*or* Sheriff Court] at (*place*) on (*date*), as witness in the case Her Majesty's Advocate v [C.D.] by delivering to him [*or* her] personally a citation in Form 8.2–E of the Criminal Procedure Rules 1996.

                               (*Signed*)
                               Officer of Law

Rule 2.6(4) **FORM 2.6–D**

Form of execution of personal service of citation of witness to appear at summary trial

EXECUTION OF PERSONAL SERVICE OF CITATION OF WITNESS

I, (*name and designation*), on (*date*) lawfully cited (*name and address of witness*) to appear before the Sheriff [*or* District] Court at (*address*) on (*date*) to give evidence for the prosecution [*or* defence] in the complaint at the instance of the procurator fiscal against (*name and address of accused*).

This I did by delivering to him [*or* her] personally a citation in Form 16.6–C of the Criminal Procedure Rules 1996.

(*Signed*)
Officer of Law

Rule 2.6(5) **FORM 2.6–E**

Form of execution of service of citation on a probationer under section 232 or 233 of the Criminal Procedure (Scotland) Act 1995

EXECUTION OF SERVICE

I, (*name and designation*), on (*date*) lawfully summoned (*name and address of accused as in complaint*) to appear before the Sheriff [*or* District] Court at (*address*) on (*date*) at (*time*) to answer to an allegation that he [*or* she] has failed to comply with a requirement of a probation order [*or* has been convicted by a court in Great Britain of an offence committed during the probation period and has been dealt with for that offence].

This I did by delivering a copy of the order of the court with a citation attached to it in Form 20.10–B of the Criminal Procedure Rules 1996 by (*state method of service*).

(*Signed*)
Officer of Law

Rule 2.6(6) **FORM 2.6–F**

Form of execution of service under rule 2.3(1)

EXECUTION OF SERVICE

I, (*name and designation*), on (*date*) lawfully cited [*or* served on] (*name and address of person cited or served*) to appear before the High Court of Justiciary [*or* Sheriff [*or* District] Court] at (*address*) on (*date*) at (*time*) for the purpose of (*specify purpose*) [*or* the document a copy of which is attached to this execution [*or* otherwise refer to or describe the document*]] [*or* set out circumstances of the execution as may be required*].

This I did by (*state method of service*).

(*Signed*)
Officer of Law [*or* as the case may be]

FORM 3.1–A Rule 3.1(1)(a)(ii)

Form of summary of proceedings at trial in High Court in Book of Adjournal

SUMMARY OF PROCEEDINGS AT TRIAL

	CASE
1. Place and date 2. Judge 3. Procurator for Crown 4. Procurator for panel 5. Relevancy 6. Plea 7. Jury per list 8. Crown witnesses, per list 9. Panel's witnesses, per list 10. Verdict 11. Sentence 12. Previous convictions 13. Other facts of importance	

FORM 3.1–B Rule 3.1(1)(b)(ii)

Form of summary of proceedings in petition to the High Court in Book of Adjournal

SUMMARY OF PROCEEDINGS IN PETITION

	CASE
1. Date of final interlocutor 2. Judge(s) 3. Counsel for petitioner(s) 4. Counsel for respondent(s) 5. Import of petition	
6. Final interlocutor	

FORM 5.2   Rule 5.2(1)

Form of record of proceedings at judicial examination

RECORD OF PROCEEDINGS AT JUDICIAL EXAMINATION

SHERIFF COURT:
DATE:
SHERIFF:
NAME OF ACCUSED APPEARING:
FOR THE PETITIONER: PROCURATOR FISCAL/DEPUTE
FOR THE ACCUSED: SOLICITOR (*address*)

The sheriff, under section 35(2) [*or* 35(6)] of the Criminal Procedure (Scotland) Act 1995 delays the examination until (*date*) at (*time*) in order to allow time for the attendance of the accused's solicitor (*name and address*); and grants warrant to imprison the said accused in the Prison of (*place*) until that date.

(*Signed*)
Sheriff

*The accused intimated that he did not desire to emit a declaration.
*The accused intimated that he desired to emit a declaration.

VERBATIM RECORDER: (*name and address*)
                                        to whom the declaration *de fideli administratione officii* was administered.
                                        Operation of tape recorder, for these proceedings was commenced at (*time*).

Thereafter the accused, having been judicially admonished, emitted a declaration which was recorded by the verbatim recorder for subsequent transcription.

Thereafter the prosecutor questioned the accused by virtue of section 36 of the Criminal Procedure (Scotland) Act 1995 and the proceedings were recorded by the verbatim recorder for subsequent transcription.

Operation of tape recorder for these proceedings was terminated at (*time*).

(*Signed*)
Sheriff Clerk

The sheriff, having [again] considered the foregoing petition under section 34 of the Criminal Procedure (Scotland) Act 1995, on the motion of the prosecutor, grants warrant to imprison the accused in the Prison of (*place*) for further examination [or until liberated in due course of law].

(*Signed*
Sheriff

Delete whichever is not appropriate

FORM 5.6–A   Rule 5.6(1)

Form of notice of opinion as to error in or incompleteness of transcript of judicial examination under section 38(1)(a) of the Criminal Procedure (Scotland) Act 1995

NOTICE OF OPINION AS TO ERROR IN OR INCOMPLETENESS OF TRANSCRIPT OF JUDICIAL EXAMINATION

To: (*name and address*)

Sheriff Court:

Name of accused:

Date of examination:

Date of service of transcript:

TAKE NOTICE that the Procurator Fiscal [*or* above accused] is of the opinion that the transcript of the proceedings at the above examination contains an error and [, or,] is incomplete in respect that:

(*here give full specification of all alleged points of error or incompleteness*).

> (*Signed*)
> Procurator Fiscal
> [*or* Solicitor for accused]
>
> (*Address and telephone number*)

Place and date:

FORM 5.6–B   Rule 5.6(3)

Form of application for rectification of transcript of judicial examination under section 38(1)(b) of the Criminal Procedure (Scotland) Act 1995

APPLICATION FOR RECTIFICATION OF TRANSCRIPT OF JUDICIAL EXAMINATION

Sheriff Court:

Name of accused:

Date of examination:

Presiding sheriff:

Date of service of notice of opinion under section 38(1)(a)
of the Criminal Procedure (Scotland) Act 1995:

The Procurator Fiscal [*or* above accused] applies to the sheriff for rectification of the transcript of the proceedings relating to the above examination. Details of the alleged error and, or, incompleteness are specified in the notice of opinion a copy of which is attached to this application.

> (*Signed*)
> Procurator Fiscal
> [*or* Solicitor for accused]
>
> (*Address and telephone number*)

Place and date:

FORM 5.6–C Rule 5.6(5)(a)

Form of intimation of agreement for the purposes of section 38(1)(a) of the Criminal Procedure (Scotland) Act 1995

INTIMATION OF AGREEMENT WITH NOTICE OF OPINION

To: (*name and address*)

Sheriff Court:

Name of accused:

Date of examination:

Date of service of notice of opinion
under section 38(1)(a) of the
Criminal Procedure (Scotland) Act 1995:

The Procurator Fiscal [*or* above accused] agrees with the opinion expressed in the notice specified above.

A copy of this intimation has been sent to the sheriff clerk of the above court.

        (*Signed*)
        Procurator Fiscal
        [*or* Solicitor for accused]

        (*Address and telephone number*)

Place and date:

FORM 5.8 Rule 5.8(2)(c)(i)

Form of intimation by prosecutor of postponement of trial diet under section 37(7)(b) of the Criminal Procedure (Scotland) Act 1995

INTIMATION OF POSTPONEMENT OF TRIAL DIET

HER MAJESTY'S ADVOCATE against (*insert names of all accused*)

To: (*name and address*)

(1) On (*date*) the court, in exercise of its powers under section 37(7)(b) of the Criminal Procedure (Scotland) Act 1995, in your absence postponed the trial diet to the sitting commencing on (*date*);

(2) TAKE NOTICE THEREFORE that YOU ARE REQUIRED TO APPEAR at (*place*) Sheriff Court on (*date*) at (*time*) to answer to the indictment which has already been served upon you.

        BY AUTHORITY OF HER MAJESTY'S ADVOCATE

        (*Signed*)
        Procurator Fiscal

Place and date:

FORM 7.1–A   Rule 7.1(1)

Form of application for renewal or termination of interim hospital order for the purposes of section 53(6) of the Criminal Procedure (Scotland) Act 1995

UNTO THE RIGHT HONOURABLE THE LORD JUSTICE GENERAL, LORD JUSTICE-CLERK AND LORDS COMMISSIONERS OF JUSTICIARY

[*or* UNTO THE HONOURABLE THE SHERIFF
OF (*name of sheriffdom*) AT (*place*)]
APPLICATION

under

Section 53(6) of the Criminal Procedure
(Scotland) Act 1995

by

Her Majesty's Advocate

[<u>*or*</u> [A.B.]   Procurator Fiscal]

in respect of

[C.D.] presently a patient in (*name*)

Hospital

for

Renewal [*or* Termination] of an interim hospital order

1. On (*date*) the court made an interim hospital order in respect of [C.D.] [which order was renewed by the court on (*date*)].

2. The order expires on (*date*).

3. It is necessary to bring the case before the court before the date mentioned in paragraph 2 above for the following reasons:—

(*here state reasons*).

MAY IT THEREFORE please your Lordship[s] to fix a diet for the purpose of considering this application to renew the interim hospital order; [and for that purpose to grant warrant to authorised officers of the hospital [*or* officers of law] to bring [C.D.] before the court for that diet].

[*Or* MAY IT THEREFORE please your Lordship[s] to fix a diet for the purpose of considering this application and further information now available with a view to making a final disposal of the case; [and for that purpose to grant warrant to authorised officers of the hospital [*or* officers of law] to bring [C.D.] before the court for that diet].]

ACCORDING TO JUSTICE, etc.

(*Signed*)
for Her Majesty's Advocate
[*or* Procurator Fiscal (Depute)]

(*Place and date*)

FORM 7.1–B Rule 7.1(2)(a)

Form of order for diet of hearing and warrant to bring offender to court for hearing of application for renewal or termination of interim hospital order

(*Place and date.*) The Lord Commissioner of Justiciary [*or* The Sheriff] appoints (*date*) at (*time*) within (*place*) as a diet for hearing the foregoing application; grants warrant to authorised officers of hospital [*or* officers of law] to bring (*name of offender*) before the court for that diet.

(*Signed*)
Clerk of court

FORM 8.1–A Rule 8.1(1)

Form of note of appeal against grant or refusal of extension of 12 months period under section 65(8) of the Criminal Procedure (Scotland) Act 1995

UNTO THE RIGHT HONOURABLE THE LORD JUSTICE GENERAL, LORD JUSTICE-CLERK AND LORDS COMMISSIONERS OF JUSTICIARY

NOTE OF APPEAL
under section 65(8) of the
Criminal Procedure (Scotland) Act 1995

by

[A.B.]
[whose domicile of citation has been specified as   ]

Appellant

against

[HER MAJESTY'S ADVOCATE]

Respondent

HUMBLY SHEWETH:

1. That at the sheriff court of the (*name of sheriffdom and place of court*) on (*date*) the appellant [, along with (*name(s) of co-accused*),] appeared on petition at the instance of the procurator fiscal of that court on [a] charge[s] of (*specify*).

2. That the appellant was committed for trial on (*date*) and was released on bail on (*date*).

3. That an indictment has been served on the appellant to stand trial at the High Court of Justiciary [*or* sheriff court] at (*place*) on (*date*).

4. That an application under section 65(3) of the Criminal Procedure (Scotland) Act 1995 was presented to the High Court of Justiciary [*or* sheriff court] on (*date*) by or on behalf of Her Majesty's Advocate and heard in the High Court of Justiciary [*or* sheriff court] at (*place*) on (*date*).

5. That Lord [*or* Sheriff] (*name*) extended [*or* refused to extend] the period of 12 months which would have expired on (*date*) by (*number*) days.

6. That the grant [*or* refusal] of the extension is unreasonable in respect that (*here state shortly reasons for appeal*).

ACCORDING TO JUSTICE, etc.

(*Signed*)
[Solicitor for appellant]

(*Place and date*)

FORM 8.1–B   Rule 8.1(2)

Form of note of appeal against grant or refusal of extension of 80 or 110 days period of committal under section 65(8) of the Criminal Procedure (Scotland) Act 1995

UNTO THE RIGHT HONOURABLE THE LORD JUSTICE GENERAL, LORD JUSTICE-CLERK AND LORDS COMMISSIONERS OF JUSTICIARY

NOTE OF APPEAL
under section 65(8) of the
Criminal Procedure (Scotland) Act 1995

by

[A.B.]
[presently a prisoner in the Prison of (*place*)]

Appellant

against

[HER MAJESTY'S ADVOCATE]

Respondent

HUMBLY SHEWETH:

1. That at the sheriff court of the (*name of sheriffdom and place of court*) on (*date*) the appellant [, along with (*name(s) of co-accused*),] appeared on petition at the instance of the procurator fiscal of that court on [a] charge(s) of (*specify*).

2. That the appellant was committed until liberated in due course of law on (*date*) and remains in custody.

3. That an indictment has been served on the appellant [*or* That the appellant was indicted to stand trial within the High Court of Justiciary [*or* sheriff court] sitting at (*place*) on (*date*)].

4. That an application under section 65(5) [*or* 65(7)] of the Criminal Procedure (Scotland) Act 1995 was presented to the High Court of Justiciary sitting at Edinburgh on (*date*) by or on behalf of Her Majesty's Advocate and was heard in that court on (*date*).

5. That Lord (*name*) extended [*or* refused to extend] the period of 80 [*or* 110] days which would have expired on (*date*) by (*number*) days.

6. That the grant [*or* refusal] of the extension is unreasonable in respect that (*here state shortly reasons for appeal*).

ACCORDING TO JUSTICE, etc.

(*Signed*)
[Solicitor for Appellant]

(*Place and date*)

FORM 8.2–A   Rule 8.2(1)

Form of warrant to cite accused and witnesses under section 66(1) of the Criminal Procedure (Scotland) Act 1995

WARRANT FOR CITATION OF ACCUSED AND WITNESSES

Whereas the High Court of Justiciary [*or* sheriff of (*sheriffdom*)] is to hold a sitting for the trial of persons accused on indictment at (*place*) on (*date*) with continuation of days, warrant is hereby granted to all officers competent to cite all persons accused to that sitting, and to cite to the sitting witnesses both for the prosecutor and accused.

(*Signed*)
Clerk of Justiciary
[*or* Sheriff Clerk]

(*Place and date*)

FORM 8.2–B   Rules 8.2(2) and 12.10

Form of notice to accused to appear under section 66(6) of the Criminal Procedure (Scotland) Act 1995

To: (*name and address of accused*)

TAKE NOTICE THAT YOU MUST APPEAR at (*place*) High Court of Justiciary (*address*) on (*date*) at (*time*) for a diet of trial [*or* Sheriff Court (*address*) on (*date*) at (*time*) for a first diet and on (*date*) at (*time*) for a trial diet] at which you will be required to answer to the indictment which is attached to this notice.

Served on (*date*) by me (*name and designation*) by (*state method of service*).

(*Signed*)

(*Signed*)
Witness
Officer of Law

FORM 8.2–C   Rule 8.2(3)

Form of postal citation of witness to appear at a trial on indictment

IN THE HIGH COURT OF JUSTICIARY [*or* SHERIFF COURT]

AT (*place*)

CITATION

To: (*name and address of witness*)

Date of citation: (*day after the date of posting*)

YOU ARE HEREBY CITED to appear on (*date*) at (*time*) in the High Court of Justiciary [*or* Sheriff Court] at (*address*) to give evidence for the prosecution [*or* defence] in the case of Her Majesty's Advocate against (*name of accused*).

Please return the enclosed form to the Procurator Fiscal [*or* the accused *or* the solicitor for the accused] in the pre-paid envelope provided within 14 days after the date of citation stated at the top of this citation.

IF YOU DO NOT ATTEND COURT WITHOUT A LAWFUL EXCUSE THE COURT MAY ORDER THAT YOU BE APPREHENDED AND PUNISHED.

FORM 8.2–D   Rule 8.2(3)

Form of reply slip to be completed and returned by witness cited to appear at trial on indictment

To: Procurator Fiscal [*or accused or his solicitor*] (*address to be completed by person serving the citation*)

From: (*name to be printed by person serving the citation*)

Date:

I, (*name and address of witness to be completed by person serving the citation*), acknowledge that I have received the citation to appear as a witness for the prosecution/defence* in the case of Her Majesty's Advocate against (*name of accused to be completed by person serving the citation*) on (*date to be inserted by person serving the citation*) at (*place to be inserted by person serving the citation*).

I shall attend on that date.

(*Signed*)

* *Person serving citation to delete whichever is not applicable.*

B–91

FORM 8.2–E   Rule 8.2(4)

Form of personal citation of witness to appear at a trial on indictment

IN THE HIGH COURT OF JUSTICIARY [*or* SHERIFF COURT]

AT (*place*)

CITATION

To: (*name and address of witness*)

Date of citation: (*date of citation*)

YOU ARE HEREBY CITED to appear on (*date*) at (*time*) in the High Court of Justiciary [*or* Sheriff Court] at (*address*) to give evidence for the prosecution [*or* defence] in the case of Her Majesty's Advocate against (*name of accused*).

IF YOU DO NOT ATTEND COURT WITHOUT A LAWGFUL EXCUSE THE COURT MAY ORDER THAT YOU BE APPREHENDED AND PUNISHED.

> (*Signed*)
> Officer of Law

FORM 8.3   Rule 8.3

Form of notice of previous convictions in solemn proceedings

NOTICE OF PREVIOUS CONVICTIONS APPLYING TO (name of accused)

In the event of your being convicted of the charge(s) in the indictment to which this notice is attached, it is intended to place before the court the following previous conviction(s) applying to you.

Date	Place of Trial	Court	Offence	Sentence

(*Signed*)
Procurator Fiscal

Date:

FORM 9.1   Rule 9.1(1)

**Form of minute of notice under section 71(2) or section 72(1) of the Criminal Procedure
(Scotland) Act 1995**

*UNTO THE RIGHT HONOURABLE THE LORD JUSTICE GENERAL, LORD
JUSTICE-CLERK AND LORDS COMMISSIONERS OF JUSTICIARY*

[UNTO THE HONOURABLE THE SHERIFF OF (*name of sheriffdom*)
AT (*place*)]

MINUTE

by

[A.B.] (*address*)
[*or* Prisoner in the Prison of (*place*)]

HUMBLY SHEWETH:

1. That the minuter, [, along with (*name(s) of co-accused*),] has been indicted at the instance of
Her Majesty's Advocate for trial in the High Court of Justiciary sitting at (*place*) on (*date*) [*or*
sheriff court at (*place*) on (*date*) with a first diet on (*date*)].

2. That [A.B.] (*here specify the matter, grounds of submission or point which in the opinion of the
minuter requires to be dealt with at a first diet or preliminary diet*).

3. That a copy of this minute has been duly intimated to Her Majesty's Advocate [and to the said
(*name(s) of co-accused*)] conform to execution[s] attached to this minute.

MAY IT THEREFORE PLEASE YOUR LORDSHIP[S]:

[(a)] to order that there be a preliminary diet and to assign a date for that diet [*or* to consider
the above preliminary matter at the first diet] [;
 (b) to order that the following productions be made available at that diet].

IN RESPECT WHEREOF

[Solicitor for minuter]

(*Address and telephone number of solicitor*)

(*Place and date*)

FORM 9.9   Rule 9.9(2)

Form of notice of abandonment of matter to be raised at preliminary diet

IN THE HIGH COURT OF JUSTICIARY [*or* SHERIFF COURT]

AT (*place*)

HER MAJESTY'S ADVOCATE against [A.B.]

I, [A.B.], abandon the written notice of intention lodged by me on (*date*) in terms of section
72(1) of the Criminal Procedure (Scotland) Act 1995 for which a preliminary diet has been fixed
to be heard at (*place*) at (*time*).

(*Signed*)
[Solicitor [*or* Counsel] for [A.B.]]

(*Address and telephone number of solicitor*)

(*Place and date*)

FORM 9.12 Rule 9.12(1)

Form of note of appeal under section 74(1) of the Criminal Procedure (Scotland) Act 1995

UNTO THE RIGHT HONOURABLE THE LORD JUSTICE GENERAL, LORD JUSTICE-CLERK AND LORDS COMMISSIONERS OF JUSTICIARY

NOTE OF APPEAL

by

[A.B.] *(address)*
[*or* Prisoner in the Prison of *(place)*]

HUMBLY SHEWETH:

1. That in the High Court of Justiciary [*or* sheriff court] sitting at *(place)* on *(date)* a preliminary [*or* first] diet was held in the case of Her Majesty's Advocate against [A.B.] [and *(name(s) of co-accused)*].

2. That the diet appointed for the trial on the indictment is [*or* was] *(specify any postponement of the trial diet ordered in terms of section 72(4))*.

3. That the ground[s] of submission raised at the preliminary [*or* first] diet was [*or* were] *(specify)*.

4. That the decision of the court was *(specify)*.

5. That the court granted leave to appeal to the High Court of Justiciary against that decision.

6. That [A.B.] appeals to the High Court of Justiciary against that decision on the following grounds *(specify)*.

ACCORDING TO JUSTICE, etc.

(Signed)
[Solicitor for [A.B.]]

(Address and telephone number of solicitor)

(Place and date)

FORM 9.17 Rule 9.17(2)

Form of minute of abandonment of appeal made under section 74(1) of the Criminal Procedure (Scotland) Act 1995

NOTICE OF ABANDONMENT OF APPEAL

Name of appellant:

Date of birth:

Prisoner in the Prison of *(place)* [*or as the case may be*]

Crime or offence to which appeal relates:

Court:

The above named appellant, having lodged a note of appeal under section 74(1) of the Criminal Procedure (Scotland) Act 1995, abandons, as from this date, that appeal against the decision at the preliminary [*or* first] diet.

(Signed)
[Solicitor for appellant]

Place and date:

FORM 10.1–A   Rule 10.1(1)(a)

Form of notice of special diet where accused intends to plead guilty (where indictment not already served)

To: (*name and address of accused*)

TAKE NOTICE:

(1)   That the Crown Agent has received intimation that you intend to plead guilty to the charge(s) on which you have been committed for trial.

(2)   That YOU MUST THEREFORE APPEAR before the High Court of Justiciary at (*place*) [*or* (*place*) Sheriff Court (*address*)] on (*date*) at (*time*) to answer to the indictment to which this notice is attached.

Served on the   day of   by me
by (*here state method of service*)

(*Signed*)
Witness

(*Signed*)
Officer of Law

(*Designation*)

FORM 10.1–B   Rule 10.1(1)(b)

Form of notice of special diet where accused intends to plead guilty (where indictment already served)

To: (*name and address of accused*)

TAKE NOTICE:

(1)   That the Crown Agent has received intimation that you intend to plead guilty to the charge(s) contained in the indictment the trial of which is to take place at the High Court of Justiciary [*or* Sheriff Court] sitting at (*place*) on (*date*).

(2)   That YOU MUST THEREFORE APPEAR before the High Court of Justiciary at (*place*) [*or* (*place*) Sheriff Court (*address*)] on (*date*) at (*time*) to answer to the indictment which has already been served on you.

Served on the   day of   by me
by (*here state method of service*)

(*Signed*)
Witness

(*Signed*)
Officer of Law

(*Designation*)

FORM 12.1   Rule 12.1(4)

Form of intimation by prosecutor of adjournment of trial diet under section 80(1) of the Criminal Procedure (Scotland) Act 1995

HER MAJESTY'S ADVOCATE against (*here name all accused*)

To: (*name and address of accused*)

TAKE NOTICE:

(1)   That, when the above indictment was not brought to trial at the trial diet fixed for the sitting commencing on (*date*), the court in your absence adjourned the trial diet to the sitting commencing on (*date*);

(2)   That YOU ARE THEREFORE REQUIRED TO APPEAR at the High Court of Justiciary [*or* Sheriff Court] sitting at (*place*) on (*date*) at (*time*) to answer to the indictment which has already been served on you.

Served on the   day of   by me
by (*here state method of service*)

BY AUTHORITY OF HER MAJESTY'S ADVOCATE

Advocate Depute [*or* Procurator Fiscal]

(*Place and date*)

FORM 12.2–A   Rule 12.2(1)

Form of minute for postponement of trial diet under section 80(2) of the Criminal Procedure (Scotland) Act 1995

UNTO THE RIGHT HONOURABLE THE LORD JUSTICE GENERAL, LORD JUSTICE-CLERK AND LORDS COMMISSIONERS OF JUSTICIARY

[*or* UNTO THE HONOURABLE THE SHERIFF
OF (*name of sheriffdom*) AT (*place*)]

MINUTE

by

[A.B.] (*address*)
[*or* Prisoner in the Prison of (*place*)]

HUMBLY SHEWETH:

1. That the minuter [, along with (*name(s) of co-accused*) ,] has been indicted at the instance of Her Majesty's Advocate for trial in the High Court of Justiciary sitting [*or* in the sheriff court] at (*place*) on (*date*);

2. That the minuter applies to the court for postponement of the trial diet for the following reasons:—

(*here state reasons*).

MAY IT THEREFORE PLEASE YOUR LORDSHIP[S]:

    (a) to fix a diet for hearing this application and to order intimation of this application and the diet to all the parties;

    (b) thereafter, after hearing all the parties, to discharge the trial diet and either to fix a new trial diet or to give leave to the prosecutor to serve a notice fixing a new trial diet;

    (c) or to do otherwise as to your Lordship[s] shall seem proper.

IN RESPECT WHEREOF

(*Signed*)
[Solicitor for minuter]

(*Address and telephone number of solicitor*)

FORM 12.2–B   Rule 12.2(2)

Form of joint minute for postponement of trial diet under section 80(2) of the Criminal Procedure (Scotland) Act 1995

UNTO THE RIGHT HONOURABLE THE LORD JUSTICE GENERAL, LORD JUSTICE-CLERK AND LORDS COMMISSIONERS OF JUSTICIARY

[*or* UNTO THE HONOURABLE THE SHERIFF OF (*name of sheriffdom*) AT (*place*)]

JOINT MINUTE

by

(1) Her Majesty's Advocate and
(2) [A.B.] (*address*) [*or* Prisoner in the Prison of (*place*)]

MINUTERS

HUMBLY SHEWETH:

1. That [A.B.] has been indicted at the instance of Her Majesty's Advocate for trial in the High Court of Justiciary sitting [*or* in the sheriff court] at (*place*) on (*date*);

2. That the minuters apply to the court for postponement of the trial diet for the following reasons:—

(*here state reasons*).

MAY IT THEREFORE PLEASE YOUR LORDSHIP[S]:

    (a) to dispense with a hearing of this application;

(b) to discharge the trial diet and either to fix a new trial diet or to give leave to the prosecutor to serve a Notice fixing a new trial diet;

(c) or to do otherwise as to your Lordship[s] shall seem proper.

IN RESPECT WHEREOF

(*Signed*)
Advocate Depute [*or* Procurator Fiscal]
On behalf of Her Majesty's Advocate

[Solicitor for [A.B.]

(*Address and telephone number of solicitor*)]

FORM 12.6 Rule 12.6(2)

Form of notice by prosecutor fixing a new trial diet by virtue of section 80(3) of the Criminal Procedure (Scotland) Act 1995

HER MAJESTY'S ADVOCATE against (*here name all accused*)

To: (*name and address*)

(1) TAKE NOTICE that on (*date*) the court discharged the trial diet fixed for the sitting commencing on (*date*) and granted leave to the prosecutor to serve on you a notice fixing a new trial diet.

(2) That the new trial diet will take place within the High Court of Justiciary [*or* Sheriff Court] sitting at (*place*) on (*date*) at (*time*) when YOU ARE REQUIRED TO APPEAR to answer to the indictment which has already been served on you.

BY AUTHORITY OF HER MAJESTY'S ADVOCATE

Advocate Depute [*or* Procurator Fiscal]

(*Place and date*)

FORM 13.2–A Rule 13.2(1)

Form of citation of person summoned to serve as a juror under section 85(4) of the Criminal Procedure (Scotland) Act 1995

CITATION TO SERVE AS JUROR

The High Court of Justiciary [*or* sheriff of (*name of sheriffdom*)] is to hold a sitting for the trial of persons accused on indictment at (*place*) on (*date*) with continuation of days:

YOU ARE HEREBY REQUIRED TO ATTEND at that place on that date as a person who may be called on to serve as a juror.

(*Signed*)
Clerk of Justiciary
[*or* Sheriff Clerk]

(*Place and date*)

FORM 13.2–B   Rule 13.2(2)

Form of certificate of execution of service and citation of witness under section 85(4) of the Criminal Procedure (Scotland) Act 1995

EXECUTION OF CITATION OF JURORS

I, (*name and address*), on (*date*) duly served on each of the following persons:

(*here list names of jurors*)

a citation to attend the sitting of the High Court of Justiciary [*or* Sheriff Court] at (*place*) on (*date*), as jurors for that sitting by sending to or for each of them a notice of citation by first class recorded delivery post.

(*Signed*)
Sheriff Clerk

FORM 14.3–A   Rule 14.3(1)

Form of oath for jurors

The jurors to raise their right hands and the clerk of court to ask them: "Do you swear by Almighty God that you will well and truly try the accused and give a true verdict according to the evidence?"

The jurors to reply: "I do".

FORM 14.3–B   Rule 14.3(2)

Form of affirmation for juror

The juror to repeat after the clerk of court: "I, (*name*), do solemnly, sincerely and truly declare and affirm that I will well and truly try the accused and give a true verdict according to the evidence".

FORM 14.5–A   Rules 14.5(1) and 18.2(1)

Form of oath for witnesses

The witness to raise his right hand and repeat after the judge: "I swear by Almighty God that I will tell the truth, the whole truth and nothing but the truth".

FORM 14.5–B   Rules 14.5(2) and 18.2(2)

Form of affirmation for witnesses

The witness to repeat after the judge: "I solemnly, sincerely and truly declare and affirm that I will tell the truth, the whole truth and nothing but the truth".

FORM 14.7   Rule 14.7

Form of minute of recording of proceedings

The court directed that the whole proceedings in this case [*or* in all the cases] set down for trial at this sitting be recorded by means of (*specify means*) and appointed (*name, designation and address*) to do so.

FORM 15.2–A   Rule 15.2(1)

Form of intimation of intention to appeal under section 109(1) of the Criminal Procedure (Scotland) Act 1995

IN THE HIGH COURT OF JUSTICIARY

INTIMATION OF INTENTION TO APPEAL

under section 109(1) of the Criminal Procedure (Scotland) Act 1995

To: Clerk of Justiciary

Name of convicted person:

Date of birth:

Prisoner in the Prison of:

Date of final determination of the proceedings:

Crime or offence to which the appeal relates:

Court and name of judge:

Sentence:

Intimation is hereby given that the above named convicted person intends to appeal to the High Court of Justiciary against the foregoing *conviction/sentence/conviction and sentence.

> (*Signed by the convicted person, his counsel or solicitor*)
> [Counsel [*or* Solicitor] for appellant]
>
> (*Address and telephone number of solicitor*)

Date:

* *Delete whatever is not applicable.*

B–101

FORM 15.2–B   Rule 15.2(2) and (6)

Form of note of appeal under section 110(1) of the Criminal Procedure (Scotland) Act 1995 or section 19 of the Prisoners and Criminal Proceedings (Scotland) Act 1993

IN THE HIGH COURT OF JUSTICIARY

NOTE OF APPEAL

under section 110 of the
Criminal Procedure (Scotland)
Act 1995
[*or* section 19 of the Prisoners and Criminal
Proceedings (Scotland) Act 1993]

To: Clerk of Justiciary

Name of convicted person:

Date of birth:

Prisoner in the Prison of:

Date of final determination of the proceedings:

Crime or offence to which the appeal relates:

Court and name of judge:

Sentence:

The above named convicted person appeals against conviction [*or as the case may be*] on the following grounds:—[*here give full statement of all grounds of appeal*].

(*Signed by the convicted person, his counsel or solicitor*)
[Counsel [*or* Solicitor] for appellant]

(*Address and telephone number of solicitor*)

(*Date*)

FORM 15.2–C   Rule 15.2(3)

Form of application for extension of time under section 111(2) of the Criminal Procedure (Scotland) Act 1995

UNTO THE RIGHT HONOURABLE THE LORD JUSTICE GENERAL, LORD JUSTICE-CLERK and LORDS COMMISSIONERS OF JUSTICIARY

APPLICATION FOR EXTENSION OF TIME

under section 111(2) of the
Criminal Procedure (Scotland) Act 1995

Name of convicted person:

Date of birth:

Prisoner in the Prison of:

Date of final determination of the proceedings:

Crime or offence to which the appeal relates:

Court and name of judge:

Sentence:

Application is hereby made for extension of time within which to:—
  *intimate an intention to appeal against conviction
  *intimate an intention to appeal against conviction and sentence
  *lodge a note of appeal against sentence
  *lodge a note of appeal against conviction
  *lodge a note of appeal against conviction and sentence

for the following reasons:—
  [*here fully state the reasons for the failure to lodge timeously the intimation of intention to appeal or note of appeal as the case may be*].

        (*Signed by the convicted person, his counsel or solicitor*)
        [Counsel [*or* Solicitor] for applicant]

        (*Address and telephone number of solicitor*)

(*Date*)

* *Delete whatever is not applicable.*

FORM 15.2–D   Rule 15.2(4)

Form of petition to High Court of Justiciary for bail pending appeal

UNTO THE RIGHT HONOURABLE THE LORD JUSTICE GENERAL, LORD JUSTICE-CLERK and LORDS COMMISSIONERS OF JUSTICIARY

PETITION

of

[A.B.] presently a prisoner in the
Prison of (*place*)

             PETITIONER

HUMBLY SHEWETH:

1. That on (*date*) the petitioner was convicted in the High Court of Justiciary [*or* sheriff court] at (*place*) of (*state crime or offence*) and sentenced to (*state sentence*).

2. That on (*date*) the petitioner lodged an intimation of intention to appeal [*or* a note of appeal] to the High Court of Justiciary under the Criminal Procedure (Scotland) Act 1995.

3. That (*state the relevant facts in support of grant of bail and, where the petitioner has not lodged a note of appeal, the grounds of appeal*).

4. That the said crime [*or* offence] is bailable.

MAY IT THEREFORE please your Lordships to remit this petition and relative documents to the sheriff at (*place*) with a direction to admit the petitioner to bail under section 112(1) of the Criminal Procedure (Scotland) Act 1995 so far as detained under said sentence upon his formal acceptance and, or, fulfilment of such conditions as your Lordships shall fix.

ACCORDING TO JUSTICE, etc.

(*Signed by the convicted person, his counsel or solicitor*)
[Counsel [*or* Solicitor] for petitioner]

(*Address and telephone number of solicitor*)

(*Date*)

FORM 15.3–A

Rule 15.3(1)

Form of notification of decision of single judge under section 103(5) of the Criminal Procedure (Scotland) Act 1995

NOTIFICATION TO APPLICANT OF A DECISION OF A JUDGE
under section 103(5) of the Criminal Procedure (Scotland) Act 1995

To: (*name and address*)

I hereby give notice that a judge of the High Court of Justiciary having considered your application for:—

*extension of time within which an intimation of intention to appeal against *conviction/ conviction and sentence may be lodged,

*extension of time within which a note of appeal against *conviction/conviction and sentence/sentence may be lodged,

*permission to you to be present at the hearing of any proceedings in relation to your appeal *and/or application,

*admission to bail,

*refused/granted the application.

If you wish to have the above mentioned application(s) which *has/have been refused, determined by the High Court of Justiciary constituted as provided in the Criminal Procedure (Scotland) Act 1995 you are required to fill up the enclosed Form 15.3–B and return it to me within five days of its receipt by you, otherwise the decision of the single judge will be final.

(*Signed*)
Clerk of Justiciary

Date:

* *Delete whatever is not applicable.*

| **FORM 15.3–B** | Rule 15.3(2) |

Form of application for determination by High Court under section 103(6) of the Criminal Procedure (Scotland) Act 1995

APPLICATION

for

DETERMINATION BY THE HIGH COURT OF JUSTICIARY
OF APPLICATION(S) REFUSED BY A SINGLE JUDGE

under section 103(6) of the Criminal Procedure (Scotland)
Act 1995

To: Clerk of Justiciary

I, (*name in full*), having received your notification that my application(s) for:—
    *extension of time within which an intimation of intention to appeal against *conviction/ conviction and sentence may be lodged,
    *extension of time within which a note of appeal against *conviction/conviction and sentence/sentence may be lodged,
    *permission to me to be present at the hearing of any proceedings in relation to my appeal *and/or application,
    *admission to bail,
*has/have been refused, HEREBY GIVE NOTICE that I desire that the said application(s) be considered and determined by the High Court of Justiciary constituted as provided in section 103(6) of the Criminal Procedure (Scotland) Act 1995.

(*Signed*)
Applicant

Date:

Note:—If the applicant desires to be present at the hearing by the court in relation to the application(s), the following should completed and signed:—
    I, (*name in full*), *being/not being legally represented, desire to be present at the hearing of my application(s) above mentioned.

(*Signed*)
Applicant

Date:

* *Delete whatever is not applicable.*

| **FORM 15.6** | Rule 15.6 |

Form of notice of abandonment of appeal

ABANDONMENT OF APPEAL

under section 116(1) of the
Criminal Procedure (Scotland) Act 1995

Name of convicted person:

Date of birth:

Prisoner in the Prison of:

Crime or offence to which the appeal relates:

Court:

Sentence:

I, (*name in full*), abandon as from this date my appeal against:—
    *conviction.
    *conviction but proceed with my appeal against sentence.
    *conviction and sentence.
    *sentence.

(*Signed*)
Appellant

To:— The Clerk of Justiciary
      Parliament Square
      Edinburgh
      EH1 1RF

* *Delete whatever is not applicable.*

FORM 15.8   Rule 15.8(3)

Form of notice to Secretary of State for the purposes of section 117(4) of the Criminal Procedure (Scotland) Act 1995

IN THE HIGH COURT OF JUSTICIARY

NOTICE TO SECRETARY OF STATE

of

INTIMATION OF DIET
for the purposes of section 117(4) of the
Criminal Procedure (Scotland) Act 1995

To: Governor of H M Prison mentioned below for the Secretary of State for Scotland

Name of *appellant/applicant:

Date of birth:

Prisoner in the Prison of:

In respect of the—
    *appeal
    *continued appeal
    *petition for bail
    *appeal under section (*specify*) of the Criminal Procedure (Scotland) Act 1995
by the above-named *appellant/applicant:

TAKE NOTICE that the court has fixed (*day*) of (*month*) at 10.30 a.m. as a diet for hearing the above *appeal/petition.

(*Signed*)
Clerk of Justiciary

Date:

* *Delete whatever is not applicable.*

FORM 15.11–A   Rule 15.11(2)(a)

Form of application to sheriff for suspension of order for disqualification pending appeal

APPLICATION

for

SUSPENSION
OF ORDER FOR DISQUALIFICATION
FROM DRIVING PENDING APPEAL

by

[A.B.] (*address*)

[*or* Prisoner in the Prison of (*place*)]

APPELLANT

under

Section 41(2) of the Road Traffic Offenders Act 1988

HUMBLY SHEWETH:

1. That on (*date*) the appellant was convicted in the sheriff court at (*place*) and was, *inter alia*, ordered to be disqualified for a period of (*specify*) under section 34 of the Road Traffic Offenders Act 1988.

2. That on (*date*) the appellant lodged with the Clerk of Justiciary a note of appeal under section 110 of the Criminal Procedure (Scotland) Act 1995. A copy of that note is attached to this application and is endorsed as having been received by the Clerk of Justiciary.

3. That the appellant has served a copy of this application on the Procurator Fiscal at (*place*).

MAY IT THEREFORE please your Lordship under section 41(2) of the Road Traffic Offenders Act 1988 to suspend the disqualification on such terms as your Lordship thinks fit.

IN RESPECT WHEREOF

(*Signed*)
[Solicitor for Appellant]

(*Address and telephone number of solicitor*)

(*Place and date*)

FORM 15.11–B   Rule 15.11(3)(a)

Form of petition to High Court of Justiciary for suspension of order for disqualification from driving pending appeal

UNTO THE RIGHT HONOURABLE THE LORD JUSTICE GENERAL, LORD JUSTICE-CLERK and LORDS COMMISSIONERS OF JUSTICIARY

PETITION

of

[A.B.] (*address*)
[*or* Prisoner in the Prison of (*place*)]

PETITIONER

under

Section 41(2) of the Road Traffic Offenders Act 1988

HUMBLY SHEWETH:

1. That on (*date*) the petitioner was convicted in the High Court of Justiciary [*or* sheriff court] at (*place*) and was, *inter alia*, ordered to be disqualified for a period of (*specify*) under section 34 of the Road Traffic Offenders Act 1988.

2. That on (*date*) the petitioner lodged with the Clerk of Justiciary a note of appeal under section 110 of the Criminal Procedure (Scotland) Act 1995.

[3. That an application for suspension of the disqualification made under section 39(2) of the Road Traffic Offenders Act 1988 was refused by the sheriff on (*date*) and that the petitioner has served a copy of this petition on the sheriff clerk of the sheriff court at (*place*).]

[4.] That the petitioner has served a copy of this petition on the Crown Agent.

MAY IT THEREFORE please your Lordships under section 41(2) of the Road Traffic Offenders Act 1988 to suspend the disqualification on such terms as your Lordships think fit.

ACCORDING TO JUSTICE, etc.

(*Signed*)
[Solicitor for petitioner]

(*Address and telephone number of solicitor*)

¹**FORM 15.12A–A**   Rule 15.12A(1)

Form of petition to High Court of Justiciary for suspension of sentence where intimation of intention to appeal lodged

UNTO THE RIGHT HONOURABLE THE LORD JUSTICE GENERAL, LORD JUSTICE-CLERK and LORDS COMMISSIONERS OF JUSTICIARY

PETITION

of

[A.B.] (*address*)
[*or* Prisoner in the Prison of (*place*)]

PETITIONER

under

section 121A of the Criminal Procedure (Scotland) Act 1995

HUMBLY SHEWETH:

1. That on (*date*) the petitioner was convicted in the High Court of Justiciary [*or* sheriff court] at (*place*) of (*specify offence*) and was sentenced to (*specify relevant sentence*).

2. That on (*date*) the petitioner lodged with the Clerk of Justiciary an intimation of intention to appeal under section 109(1) of the Criminal Procedure (Scotland) Act 1995.

3. That (state facts relevant to application).

4. That the applicant has served a copy of this application on the Crown Agent.

MAY IT THEREFORE please your Lordships under section 121A of the Criminal Procedure (Scotland) Act 1995 to suspend *ad interim* the sentence.

ACCORDING TO JUSTICE, etc.

(*Signed*)
[Solicitor for petitioner]

(*Address and telephone number of solicitor*)

NOTE
¹Inserted by Act of Adjournal (Criminal Procedure Rules Amendment No. 4) (S.I. 1997 No. 1834) (effective August 1, 1997).

¹**FORM 15.12A–B** Rule 15.12A(2)

Form of petition to High Court of Justiciary for suspension of sentence pending appeal

UNTO THE RIGHT HONOURABLE THE LORD JUSTICE GENERAL, LORD JUSTICE-CLERK and LORDS COMMISSIONERS OF JUSTICIARY

PETITION

of

[A.B.] (*address*)
[*or* Prisoner in the Prison of (*place*)]
or Her Majesty's Advocate]

PETITIONER

under

section 121A of the Criminal Procedure (Scotland) Act 1995

HUMBLY SHEWETH:

1. That on (*date*) the petitioner [*or* [A.B.] (*address*) *or* Prisoner in the Place of (*place*) was convicted in the High Court of Justiciary [*or* sheriff court] at (*place*) of (*specify offence*) and was sentenced to (*specify relevant sentence*).

2. That on (*date*) the petitioner lodged with the Clerk of Justiciary [a note of appeal under section 110 of the Criminal Procedure (Scotland) Act 1995 in respect of an appeal under section 106(1)(b) to (e) of that Act] [*or* an appeal under section 108 of the Criminal Procedure (Scotland) Act 1995].

3. That the petitioner has served a copy of this petition on the Crown Agent [*or* [A.B.]].

MAY IT THEREFORE please your Lordships under section 121A of the Criminal Procedure (Scotland) Act 1995 to suspend *ad interim* the sentence.

ACCORDING TO JUSTICE, etc.

(*Signed*)
[Solicitor for petitioner]
[Advocate Depute [*or* Procurator Fiscal]
On behalf of Her Majesty's Advocate]

(*Address and telephone number of solicitor*)

NOTE
¹Inserted by Act of Adjournal (Criminal Procedure Rules Amendment No. 4) (S.I. 1997 No. 1834) (effective August 1, 1997).

FORM 16.1–A   Rule 16.1(1)

Form of complaint under setion 138(1) of the Criminal Procedure (Scotland) Act 1995

IN THHE SHERIFF [*or*** DISTRICT] COURT**

AT (*place*)

THE COMPLAINTY OF THE PROCURATOR FISCAL

AGAINST

(*name and address sufficient to distinguish person*)
[*or* at present in custody]

The charge against you is that on (*date*) in [*or* at] you did (*set forth charge as nearly as may be in the form set out in Schedule 5 to the Criminal Procedure (Scotland) Act 1995*).

(*Signed*)
Procurator Fiscal
[*or* Complainer *or* Solicitor for Complainer]

FORM 16.1–B   Rule 16.1(2)

Form of citation of accused in summary proceedings

CITATION OF ACCUSED PERSON

PF REF ....
(This number must be quoted on all correspondence)

A COPY COMPLAINT IS ENCLOSED
FROM THE PROCURATOR FISCAL   ....

YOUR CASE WILL BE HEARD ON   ....

IN THE SHERIFF COURT HOUSE   at ....
.... am [*or* pm]

PROCURATOR FISCAL DEPUTE   ....

WHAT MUST I DO?

You must answer the complaint on or before the date the case is to be heard.

HOW DO I ANSWER THE COMPLAINT?

There are 3 methods—
(1) Attend court personally.
(2) Arrange for your lawyer or some other person to attend.
(3) Write to the court (REPLY FORM and envelope attached).

WHAT WILL HAPPEN IF I DO NOTHING?

A warrant may be issued for your arrest.

WHAT ABOUT MY FINANCIAL CIRCUMSTANCES?

YOU DO NOT HAVE TO GIVE ANY INFORMATION ABOUT THESE: but if you are pleading guilty and you wish the court to consider your financial circumstances you should give as much information as you can on the enclosed form (INFORMATION ABOUT YOUR MEANS).

CAN I GET LEGAL AID?

In certain circumstances Legal Aid is granted. If you want to know more, apply to the clerk of court in the sheriff court where your case will be heard.

NAME AND ADDRESS OF ACCUSED ....

....

....

DATE OF BIRTH .....

Check that your name, address and date of birth are shown correctly.

FORM 16.1–C   Rule 16.1(3)(a)

Form of reply to complaint

REPLY FORM   PF REF ....
                                     COURT DATE ....
                                     SHERIFF COURT AT ....

PLEASE COMPLETE WHICHEVER SECTION APPLIES

---

1.   PLEADING NOT GUILTY

I PLEAD NOT GUILTY. Please send me a note of the date of trial.

Signed .... Date ....

PLEASE NOW RETURN THIS FORM IN THE ENVELOPE PROVIDED

---

2.   PLEADING GUILTY

I PLEAD GUILTY TO THE CHARGE(S)

except ....
....

Signed .... Date ....

PLEASE CONTINUE TO COMPLETE THIS FORM

MOTORING OFFENCES

If you are pleading guilty to a motoring offence PLEASE SEND YOUR DRIVING LICENCE (BUT NOT YOUR HGV LICENCE) WITH THIS FORM.

NAME AND ADDRESS
OF ACCUSED

DATE OF BIRTH ....

Check that your name, address and date of birth are shown correctly.

Please correct anything that is wrong.

ONLY COMPLETE THIS PAGE IF PLEADING GUILTY

PREVIOUS CONVICTIONS

If previous convictions are attached to your complaint please tick the appropriate box.

I ADMIT THE PREVIOUS CONVICTIONS

I DO NOT ADMIT THE PREVIOUS CONVICTIONS

I ADMIT THE PREVIOUS CONVICTIONS EXCEPT THOSE
LISTED BELOW

....

....

NOTE   If convictions are listed and you do not complete this section, the court will take it that you admit all of them.

CAN I SEND A WRITTEN EXPLANATION?

YES. If you want to, use the space below and continue on a separate sheet if required.

....
....
....
....
....
....
....

PLEASE CHECK YOU HAVE SIGNED THE FORM AT THE PROPER PLACE AND RETURN IT IN THE ENVELOPE PROVIDED.

FOR OFFICIAL USE ONLY

D.L.   Documents Returned

Other Documents

FORM 16.1–D   Rule 16.1(3)(b)

MEANS FORM

INFORMATION ABOUT YOUR
MEANS   PF REF ....

You are not required by law to return this form completed but it can help you and the court.

If you decide to plead guilty by letter please complete this and the reply form and send them to the court.

If you are found guilty and are fined the information you give here will help the court to set an amount which you can reasonably afford and to give you the time you need to pay.

If you decide to appear in court you may hand the form in when you appear.

If the information you have given below changes a great deal between now and the court hearing you should tell the clerk of court – he will give you another form to fill in.

The information you give on this form will not be used for any other purpose.

PERSONAL DETAILS (Please use BLOCK CAPITALS and tick the appropriate box where required).

1.   Your full name ....

2.   Your address ....

3.   Are you   Married   Single   Separated   Divorced   Widowed

4.   Are you the head of your household?   Yes   No

5.   How many children under 16 do you support ....

6.   Is there anyone else financially dependent on you?   Yes   No
     (a)   If YES what is their relationship to you ....

YOUR JOB

7.   Are you   Employed   Unemployed   Self-employed   Other
      (a)   If OTHER, please give details here ....
      (b)   If EMPLOYED, please give your job here ....

YOUR WEEKLY INCOME   **YOUR WEEKLY EXPENSES**

You may not receive your money or pay your bills weekly. Even so please try to work out what the weekly figures would be.

		£			£
8.(a)	Your usual weekly take-home pay including overtime (if self-employed give your usual earnings)	____	9.(a)	Housing (rent, rates, mortgage) (If you pay board and lodgings give the amount)	____
(b)	Usual total weekly take-home pay of other household earners	____	(b)	Fuel (electricity, coal, gas, etc.)	____
(c)	Total Social Security payments received in your household each week	____	(c)	Food	____
			(d)	Travel	____
(d)	Total pensions received in your household each week	____	(e)	Weekly cost of supporting anyone else (see questions 5 and 6)	____
(e)	Any other form of income (eg student grant, etc), per week	____	(f)	Other big weekly payments (such as hire purchase agreements or repayment of rent arrears)	____
Usual total WEEKLY household income		____	Usual total WEEKLY expenses		____

GENERAL DETAILS

10.   If the court decides to fine you how much do you think you could afford to pay each week?

       £ ....

11.   Please give any further information about your finances which you would like the court to know here. (You can continue over the page if you need.)

SIGNATURE BOX

12.   I declare that the information I have given in this form is true and complete.

Signed .... Date ....

FORM 16.1–E   Rule 16.1(4)

Form of notice of previous convictions in summary proceedings

NOTICE OF PREVIOUS CONVICTIONS APPLYING TO (*name of accused*)

In the event of your being convicted of the charge(s) in the complaint to which this notice is attached, it is intended to place before the court the following previous conviction(s) applying to you.

Date	Place of Trial	Court	Offence	Sentence

(*Signed*)
Procurator Fiscal

Date:

Act of Adjournal (Criminal Procedure Rules) 1996

FORM 16.4–A   Rule 16.4(1)

Form of incidental application in summary proceedings

UNTO THE HONOURABLE THE SHERIFF OF (*name of sheriffdom*)
AT (*place of court*)

PETITION

of

[A.B.] (*address*)
[*or* Prisoner in the Prison of   (*place*)]

under

section 134 of the Criminal Procedure (Scotland) Act 1995

PETITIONER

HUMBLY SHEWETH:

(*Here set out in numbered paragraphs the reasons for the order sought and the statutory process*)

MAY IT THEREFORE please your Lordship to (*set out orders sought*).

ACCORDING TO JUSTICE, etc.

(*Signed*)
[Solicitor for petitioner]
(*Address and telephone number of solicitor*)

FORM 16.4–B   Rule 16.4(2)

Form of assignation of a diet in summary proceedings

(*Place and date*). The court assigns (*date*) at (*time*) within the Sheriff Court House, (*address*), as a diet in this case.

(*Signed*)
Clerk of Court

FORM 16.4–C   Rule 16.4(3)

Form of minutes in minute of proceedings

(*Place and date*). (*Name of judge*), Sheriff [*or* District Judge].

Plea of guilty.—Compeared the accused and, in answer to the complaint, pled guilty.

Sentence.—Sentence: Twenty-one days' imprisonment.

(*Signed*)
Clerk of Court

Where different pleas tendered.—Compeared the accused and, in answer to the complaint, [C.D.] pled guilty and [E.F.] pled guilty to the third charge.

Sentence where more than one accused and different pleas.—Sentence: [C.D.] Twenty-one days' imprisonment. [E.F.] seven days' imprisonment.

(*Signed*)
Clerk of Court

Plea and sentence combined.—Compeared the accused and, in answer to the complaint, pled guilty (*or state to what extent plea tendered*), and was sentenced to   days' imprisonment (*or was fined £*   and in default of payment   days' imprisonment) (*or as the case may be*).

(*Signed*)
Clerk of Court

Plea of not guilty.—Compeared the accused who, in answer to the complaint, pled not guilty.

Adjournment.—The court adjourned the diet for trial to (*date*) at (*time*), and ordained the accused then to appear.

[*or* The court adjourned the diet for trial to (*date*) at (*time*), and ordered the accused to be imprisoned until that date.]

[*or* The court adjourned the diet for trial to (*date*) at (*time*), and ordered the accused to appear personally at that diet under a penalty of £   in default.]

(*Signed*)
Clerk of Court

Trial.—(*Place and date*). (*Name of judge*), Sheriff [*or* District Judge]. Compeared the accused [*or* the accused failed to appear after being duly cited *or* after receiving due intimation of this diet].

Finding.—The court found the accused guilty as libelled [*or* as first (*or* last) alternatively libelled, *or state to what extent found guilty*] [*or* not guilty], [*or* found the charge not proven], [*or* found [C.D.] guilty as libelled and [E.F.] guilty as second libelled (*or as the case may be*)].

(*Signed*)
Clerk of Court

Sentence. Imprisonment.—   day's imprisonment.

[*or Fine, time allowed.*—Fined £   , [*or £*   each],   days allowed for payment].

Fine, imprisonment imposed for future default.—Fine £   , [*or £*   each].   days allowed for payment. For the reason stated below   days imprisonment [*or*   days imprisonment each] imposed in default of payment within the time allowed:—

(*here state reason*)

[*or Fine, no time to pay.*—Fined £   , [*or £*   each], and in default of payment   days' imprisonment. For the reason stated below, no time allowed for payment:—]

(*here state reason*)

Caution.—To find £   caution for good behaviour,   days allowed for finding such caution.

Fine imposed on parent in lieu of child.—The court found the accused [C.D.] guilty as libelled and fined him [£   ], and, in respect that [E.F.] has conduced to the commission of the said offence by habitually neglecting to exercise due care of the said [C.D.], ordered the fine to be paid by the said [E.F.], and in default of payment sentenced the said [E.F.] to   days' imprisonment.

Sentence deferred.—Sentence deferred till (*date*) at (*time*), when accused ordained to appear.

Admonition.—Admonished and dismissed.

Desertion of diet.—The court, on the motion of the prosecutor, deserted the diet *pro loco et tempore*.

(*Signed*)
Clerk of Court

FORM 16.5–A   Rule 16.5(1)(a)

Form of warrant to apprehend an accused person referred to in section 135 of the Criminal Procedure (Scotland) Act 1995

(*Place and date*). The court grants warrant to apprehend the said accused.

(*Signed*)
Sheriff

FORM 16.5–B   Rule 16.5(1)(b)

Form of warrant to search referred to in section 135 of the Criminal Procedure (Scotland) Act 1995

(*Place and date*). The court grants warrants to search the person, dwelling-house, and repositories of the accused, and any place where he may be found, and to take possession of the property mentioned or referred to in the complaint, and all articles and documents likely to afford evidence of his guilt or of guilty participation.

(*Signed*)
Sheriff

FORM 16.5–C   Rule 16.5(2)

Form of warrant to detain accused in prison or adjourning the case against him

(*Place and date*). The court, on the motion of the prosecutor [*or* accused (*or as the case may be*)], continued the case against the accused until (*date*), and meantime grants warrant to detain the accused in prison until that time [; the accused meantime being liberated on bail conform to separate order attached].

FORM 16.6–A   Rule 16.6(1)

Form of postal citation of witness to appear in summary proceedings

IN THE SHERIFF [*or* DISTRICT] COURT

AT (*place*)

CITATION

To: (*name and address of witness*)

Date of citation: (*day after the date of posting*)

YOU ARE HEREBY CITED to appear on (*date*) at (*time*) in the Sheriff [*or* District] Court House at (*address*) to give evidence for the prosecution [*or* defence] in the complaint by the procurator fiscal against (*name of accused person(s)*).

B–119

Please return the enclosed form to the procurator fiscal [*or the accused person or the solicitor for the accused*] in the pre-paid envelope provided within 14 days after the date of citation stated at the top of this citation.

IF YOU DO NOT ATTEND COURT WITHOUT A LAWFUL EXCUSE THE COURT MAY ORDER THAT YOU BE APPREHENDED AND PUNISHED.

(*Signed*)
Prosecutor
[*or* Solicitor for accused]

FORM 16.6–B   Rule 16.6(1)

Form of reply slip to be completed and returned by witness cited to appear at trial on summary complaint

To: Procurator Fiscal [*or accused or his solicitor*] (*address to be completed by person serving the citation*)

From: (*name to be printed by person serving the citation*)
Date:

I, (*name and address of witness to be completed by person serving the citation*), acknowledge that I have received the citation to appear as a witness for the prosecution [*or defence*] on the complaint by the procurator fiscal against (*name of accused person(s) to be completed by person serving the citation*) on (*date to be inserted by person serving citation*) at (*place to be inserted by person serving the citation*).

I shall attend on that date.

(*Signed*)

FORM 16.6–C   Rule 16.6(2)

Form of personal citation of witness to appear at trial on summary complaint

IN THE SHERIFF [*or* DISTRICT] COURT

AT (*place*)

CITATION

To: (*name and address of witness*)
Date: (*date of citation*)

You are hereby cited to appear on (*date*) at (*time*) in the Sheriff [*or* District] Court House at (*address*) to give evidence for the prosecution [*or* defence] in the complaint by the procurator fiscal against (*name of accused person(s)*).

IF YOU DO NOT ATTEND COURT WITHOUT A LAWFUL EXCUSE THE COURT MAY ORDER THAT YOU BE APPREHENDED AND PUNISHED.

(*Signed*)
[Officer of Law]
(*Designation*)

FORM 16.7 Rule 16.7(2)

Form of petition to postpone or accelerate diet in summary proceedings

IN THE SHERIFF [*or* DISTRICT] COURT

AT (*place*)

PETITION

of

[A.B.] (*address*)
[*or* Prisoner in the Prison of (*place*)]

under section 137(5) of the Criminal Procedure (Scotland) Act 1995

PETITIONER

HUMBLY SHEWETH:

1. That the petitioner [, along with (*name(s) of co-accused*),] has been charged in the above court on a summary complaint at the instance of the procurator fiscal with the offence of (*specify*).

2. That a diet in the proceedings has been fixed for (*date*).

3. That (*narrate circumstances on which application is based*).

4. That the petitioner has intimated to [(*name(s) of any co-accused*) and] the procurator fiscal that he desired a postponement [*or* an acceleration] of the said trial diet.

5. That the procurator fiscal refuses [and][*or* (*names(s) of co-accused*) refuse*] to make a joint application to the court for that purpose.

THE PETITIONER THEREFORE craves the court:
   (a) to appoint intimation of this petition to be made to (*name(s) of co-accused*) [and] [*or* the Procurator Fiscal]
   (b) to appoint parties to be heard on this petition; and
   (c) thereafter, in terms of section 137(5) of the Criminal Procedure (Scotland) Act 1995, to discharge the said diet and to fix in lieu of that diet a later [*or* earlier] diet.

ACCORDING TO JUSTICE, etc

(*Signed*)
[Solicitor for petitioner]

(*Address and telephone number of solicitor*)

FORM 17.1   Rule 17.1(1)

Form of note of appeal against grant or refusal of extension of 40 days period under section 147(3) of the Criminal Procedure (Scotland) Act 1995

UNTO THE RIGHT HONOURABLE THE LORD JUSTICE GENERAL, LORD JUSTICE-CLERK AND LORDS COMMISSIONERS OF JUSTICIARY

NOTE OF APPEAL

by

[A.B.], prisoner in the Prison of (*place*)

under section 147(3) of the Criminal Procedure (Scotland) Act 1995

APPELLANT

HUMBLY SHEWETH:

1. That at the sheriff [*or* district] court at (*place*) on (*date*) the appellant [, along with (*names of any co-accused*),] appeared on a complaint at the instance of the procurator fiscal on charges of (*specify*).

2. That he pled not guilty and trial was fixed for (*date*) and the appellant was remanded in custody.

3. That an application in terms of section 147(3) of the Criminal Procedure (Scotland) Act 1995 was presented to the sheriff at (*place*) on (*date*) [*in district court cases add*:—he having concurrent territorial jurisdiction with the Lay Justices [*or* Stipendiary Magistrate(s)] of said district court]. The application was heard by Sheriff (*name of judge*) in the said sheriff court on (*date*).

4. That Sheriff (*name of judge*) extended the period of 40 days which would have expired on (*date*) by (*number*) days from that date.

5. That the granting of that extension is unreasonable in respect that (*here state shortly reasons for appeal*).

ACCORDING TO JUSTICE, etc.

(*Signed*)
[Solicitor for appellant]

(*Address and telephone number of solicitor*)

FORM 18.3   Rule 18.3

Form of warrant to apprehend witness who has failed to answer a citation

(*Place and date*). The court, in respect that [E.F.], a witness in the cause, has failed to appear after being duly cited, adjourns the diet till (*date*) at (*time*), and ordains the accused and witnesses to appear personally at the said diet, and grants warrant to apprehend [E.F.] and to detain him in any prison or in police cells until the said diet, or bring him before a justice for the purpose of fixing security for his appearance at all diets of the court.

(*Signed*)
Sheriff

FORM 18.6   Rule 18.6

Form of order of detention in precincts of court under section 169(1) of the Criminal Procedure (Scotland) Act 1995

The court ordered the accused [*or* offender] to be detained within the precincts of the court [*or* the police station at (*place*)] until (*state time*) of this day.

(Signed)
Clerk of Court

FORM 19.1–A   Rule 19.1(4)

Form of note of appeal against decision relating to a preliminary plea

IN THE COURT OF JUSTICIARY

NOTE OF APPEAL

under section 174(1) of the Criminal Procedure
(Scotland) Act 1995

by

[A.B.] (*address*)
[*or* Prisoner in the Prison of (*place*)]

APPELLANT

against

[The Procurator Fiscal]

RESPONDENT

To the Sheriff Clerk [*or* Clerk to the District Court] at (*place of court*)

Date of decision appealed against:

Date of trial:

The appellant appeals to the High Court of Justiciary in respect that:—

(1) (*State whether objection taken to competency or relevancy of the complaint or the proceedings or denial issued that the appellant was the person charged by the police with the offence and specify the terms of the objection or denial*).
(2) (*State the decision which it is desired to bring under review by the High Court*).
(3) (*State the grounds of appeal*).

(Signed)
[Solicitor for Appellant]

(*Address and telephone number of solicitor*)

Place and date:

FORM 19.1–B   Rule 19.1(11)

Form of minute of abandonment of appeal

IN THE HIGH COURT OF JUSTICIARY

MINUTE OF ABANDONMENT

of

appeal under section 174(1) of the
Criminal Procedure (Scotland) Act 1995

To: Clerk of Justiciary

Name of appellant:

Name of respondent:

Date of decision appealed against:

Date of appeal hearing:

The above-named appellant abandons his [*or* her *or* its] appeal.

> (*Signed*)
> [Solicitor for Appellant]
>
> (*Address and telephone number of solicitor*)
> [*or* Procurator Fiscal]

Place and date:

FORM 19.2–A   Rule 19.2(1)

Form of application for stated case

IN THE SHERIFF [*or* DISTRICT] COURT AT (*place of court*)

APPLICATION FOR STATED CASE

under section 176(1) of the
Criminal Procedure (Scotland) Act 1995

by

[C.D.] [*or* [A.B.], Procurator Fiscal, (*place*)]

in

The Procurator Fiscal

against

[C.D.] (*address*)
[*or* Prisoner in the Prison of (*place*)]

1. [C.D.] [*or* The Procurator Fiscal] craves the court to state a case for the opinion of the High Court of Justiciary in the above proceedings in which the date of final determination was (*date*).

2. The matter[s] which it is desired to bring under review is [*or* are]:—

(*here specify*)

[3. The appeal is also against sentence.]

¹[4. The said [C.D.] [*or* Procurator Fiscal] also craves the court to (*here insert any application for bail, for interim suspension of an order for disqualification imposed under the Road Traffic Acts for interim suspension of sentence under section 193A of the Criminal Procedure (Scotland) Act 1995, or for any other interim order under section 177(1) of the Criminal Procedure (Scotland) Act 1995*).]

(*Signed*)
[Solicitor for [C.D.]]

(*Address and telephone number of solicitor*)
[*or* Procurator Fiscal]

(*Place and date*)

NOTE
¹As amended by Act of Adjournal (Criminal Procedure Rules Amendment No. 4) (S.I. 1997 No. 1834) (effective August 1, 1997).

FORM 19.2–B   Rule 19.2(2)

Form of stated case

IN THE SHERIFF [*or* DISTRICT] COURT AT (*place*)

CASE
for the Opinion of the High Court of Justiciary at Edinburgh
stated by (*name of judge*)

in

[A.B.] (*address*) [*or* Prisoner in the Prison of (*place*)] [*or*
The Procurator Fiscal at (*place*)]

APPELLANT

against

[C.D.] (*address or as the case may be*)

RESPONDENT

The appellant [*or* respondent] was charged with (*here summarise the relevant charges*).

(*Here state concisely the relevant procedural history of the proceedings.*)

(*Here state the decision and disposal.*)

I [*or* We] found the following facts admitted or proved:—

(*Here set out in numbered paragraphs the facts admitted or proved.*)

(*Where the appeal is against a decision on a submission of no case to answer, identify and summarise the Crown evidence and inferences drawn.*)

(*Here state the reasons for the decision with reference to the evidence on which the facts were found admitted or proved, objections to the admission or rejection of evidence, the grounds of the decision, and any other matters necessary to be stated for the information of the superior court.*)

The question[s] submitted for the opinion of the court is [*or* are]:—(*here state the question or questions in numbered paragraphs for the opinion of the court*).

This case is stated by me [*or* us]

(*Signature of the judge(s)*)

(*Name of judge(s)*)

(*Append any additional material required by section 179(7) of the Criminal Procedure (Scotland) Act 1995.*)

(*Initials of the judge(s)*)

[1]**FORM 19.2–C**   Rule 19.2(3)

Form of minutes of procedure in appeal by stated case

(Date)	Application for stated case lodged.	Clerk of Court
(Date)	*(Name of judge.)* The court refused [*or* granted] bail conform to separate order attached.	Clerk of Court
(Date)	*(Name of judge.)* The court refused to suspend [*or ad interim* suspended] the order for disqualification under section 41(2) of the Road Traffic Offenders Act 1988.	Clerk of Court
(Date)	*(Name of judge.)* The court refused to suspend [*or ad interim* suspended] the appellant's sentence under section 193A of the Criminal Procedure (Scotland) Act 1995.	Clerk of Court
(Date)	Draft stated case issued to appellant['s solicitor] and duplicate of it issued to respondent['s solicitor]. Last date for receipt of adjustment is *(date)*.	Clerk of Court
(Date)	Adjustments for appellant [*or* respondent] received.	Clerk of Court
(Date)	Adjustments for appellant [*or* respondent] received.	Clerk of Court
(Date)	Intimation by appellant [*or* respondent] that no adjustments proposed.	Clerk of Court
(Date)	Intimation by appellant [*or* respondent] that no adjustments proposed.	Clerk of Court
(Date)	Appeal deemed to be abandoned under section 179(3) of the Criminal Procedure (Scotland) Act 1995, and so intimated to appellant['s solicitor] and to respondent['s solicitor].	Clerk of Court
(Date)	Hearing on adjustments and any intended alteration to the draft case to be held on *(date and time)*. Appellant['s solicitor] and Respondent['s solicitor] informed.	Clerk of Court

(Place and date.) *(Name(s) of judge(s))*

Appeared: *(specify)*

Parties heard on the adjustments and on intended alterations to the draft case.

Case adjusted.

The following adjustments rejected by judge:— *(here specify)*

The following alterations proposed by judge not accepted by the appellant [*or* respondent]:— *(here specify)*

                                                        Clerk of Court

(Date)	Case signed and sent to appellant['s solicitor] and duplicate sent to respondent['s solicitor]. Complaint, proceedings and all relevant documents transmitted to Clerk of Justiciary.	Clerk of Court

NOTE
[1]As amended by Act of Adjournal (Criminal Procedure Rules Amendment No. 4) (S.I. 1997 No. 1834) (effective August 1, 1997).

FORM 19.3–A   Rule 19.3(1)

Form of note of appeal against sentence under section 186(1) of the Criminal Procedure (Scotland) Act 1995

IN THE SHERIFF [*or* DISTRICT] COURT AT (*place*)

NOTE OF APPEAL
against sentence

by

[A.B.] (*address*)
[or presently prisoner in the Prison of (*place*)]

APPELLANT

against

The Procurator Fiscal

RESPONDENT

1. The appellant appeals to the High Court of Justiciary against the sentence of (*specify*) passed in the above court on (*date*).

2. The ground[s] of appeal is [*or* are]:—

(*here set out the grounds(s)*).

[3. The appellant also craves the court to (*here insert any application for bail, for interim suspension of any order for disqualification imposed under the Road Traffic Acts for interim suspension of sentence under section 193A of the Criminal Procedure (Scotland) Act 1995, or for any other interim order under section 177(1) by virtue of section 188(10) of the Criminal Procedure (Scotland) Act 1995*).]

(*Signed*)
[Solicitor for appellant]

(*Address and telephone number of solicitor*)

(*Place and date*)

NOTE
[1]As amended by Act of Adjournal (Criminal Procedure Rules Amendment No. 4) (S.I. 1997 No. 1834) (effective August 1, 1997).

FORM 19.3–B Rule 19.3(2)

Form of minutes of procedure in note of appeal against sentence alone under section 186(1) of the Criminal Procedure (Scotland) Act 1995

(*Date*) Note of appeal lodged.

Clerk of Court

Eo die Copy note of appeal sent to procurator fiscal.

Clerk of Court

Eo die Copies of note of appeal, complaint, minutes of proceedings and relevant documents sent to (*name of judge*) for report. Proceedings to be sent to Clerk of Justiciary no later than (*date*).

Clerk of Court

(*Date*) (*Name of judge.*) The court refused bail [*or* granted bail] conform to separate order attached.

Clerk of Court

(*Date*) (*Name of judge.*) The court refused to suspend [*or ad interim* suspended] the order for disqualification in terms of section 41(2) of the Road Traffic Offenders Act 1988.

Clerk of Court

(*Date*) Report received.

Clerk of Court

(*Date*) Copy report sent to [A.B.] [*or* [C.D.]] and the Procurator Fiscal.

Clerk of Court

Eo die Note of appeal, report and certified copy of the complaint, minutes of proceedings and relevant documents sent to Clerk of Justiciary.

Clerk of Court

FORM 19.4 Rule 19.4

Form of extension of time by sheriff principal

IN THE SHERIFF [*or* DISTRICT] COURT AT (*place*)

[A.B.] v [Procurator Fiscal]

(*Place of date.*) I, (*name*), Sheriff Principal of the Sheriffdom of (*name of sheriffdom*) by virtue of the powers vested in me by section 186(5) [*or* 194(2)] of the Criminal Procedure (Scotland) Act 1995, and in respect that (*name of judge*) is temporarily absent from duty, extend the period specified in section (*specify relevant section*) of that Act so that it will now expire on (*date*).

(*Signed*)

FORM 19.5   Rule 19.5

Form of minute abandoning appeal under section 184(1) of the Criminal Procedure (Scotland) Act 1995

IN THE SHERIFF [*or* DISTRICT] COURT AT (*place*)

MINUTE OF ABANDONMENT

in the

APPEAL BY STATED CASE

by

[A.B.] (*address*)
[*or* presently a prisoner in the Prison of (*place*)]

APPELLANT

against

[The Procurator Fiscal (*or as the case may be*)]

RESPONDENT

The appellant abandons his [*or* her *or* its] appeal as from this date against conviction [*or* conviction and sentence] [*or* the acquittal of the respondent] [*or* the sentence passed on the respondent].

Intimation of the foregoing abandonment has been made to the respondent.

(*Signed*)
[Solicitor for appellant]

(*Address and telephone number of solicitor*)

(*Place and date*)

FORM 19.6   Rule 19.6(2)

Form of minute abandoning appeal under section 175(8) of the Criminal Procedure (Scotland) Act 1995

IN THE HIGH COURT OF JUSTICIARY

MINUTE OF ABANDONMENT

in the

APPEAL BY STATED CASE

by

[A.B.] (*address*)
[*or* presently a prisoner in the Prison of (*place*)]

APPELLANT

against

The Procurator Fiscal

RESPONDENT

The appellant abandons his [*or* her *or* its] appeal as from this date against conviction but proceeds with the appeal against sentence.

Intimation of the foregoing abandonment has been made to the respondent.

(*Signed*)
[Solicitor for appellant]

(*Address and telephone number of solicitor*)

(*Place and date*)

FORM 19.7   Rule 19.7

Form of minute of abandonment of appeal against sentence alone under section 186(9) of the Criminal Procedure (Scotland) Act 1995

MINUTE OF ABANDONMENT

of

APPEAL AGAINST SENTENCE

under section 186(9) of the Criminal Procedure (Scotland) Act 1995

Name of appellant:

Date of birth:

Prisoner in the Prison of:

Crime or offence to which appeal relates:

Sheriff/District Court at:

Sentence:

The above named appellant having lodged a note of appeal abandons as from this date the appeal against sentence under section 186(9) of the Criminal Procedure (Scotland) Act 1995.

Intimation of the foregoing abandonment has been made to the respondent.

(*Signed*)
[Solicitor for appellant]

(*Address and telephone number of solicitor*)

(*Place and date*)

FORM 19.9   Rule 19.9(3)

Form of application to High Court for suspension of disqualification from driving

UNTO THE RIGHT HONOURABLE THE LORD JUSTICE GENERAL, LORD JUSTICE-CLERK AND LORDS COMMISSIONERS OF JUSTICIARY

NOTE OF APPLICATION

for

SUSPENSION OF DISQUALIFICATION

under section 41(2) of the Road Traffic Offenders Act 1988

in

SUMMARY COMPLAINT

in causa

The Procurator Fiscal

COMPLAINER AND RESPONDENT

against

[C.D.] (*address*)

APPLICANT AND APPELLANT

HUMBLY SHEWETH:

1. That the applicant and appellant, having been convicted on a complaint brought under the Criminal Procedure (Scotland) Act 1995 at the instance of the complainer and respondent of (*specify charge*), was on (*date*) in the sheriff [*or* district] court at (*place*) fined [*or* sentenced to (*specify*)] and ordered to be disqualified for a period of (*state period of disqualification*) in terms of section [34] of the Road Traffic Offenders Act 1988.

2. That on (*date*) the applicant and appellant applied to the said court to state a case for the opinion of the High Court of Justiciary under section 176 of the Act of 1995.

3. That the applicant and appellant thereafter requested the court to suspend the period of disqualification under section 39(2) of the Road Traffic Offenders Act 1988.

4. That the court, on (*date*), refused to suspend the disqualification.

5. That the applicant and appellant has served a copy of this note on the clerk of the said court and on the respondent.

MAY IT THEREFORE please your Lordships under section 41(2) of the Road Traffic Offenders Act 1988 to suspend the said disqualification on such terms as your Lordships think fit.

ACCORDING TO JUSTICE, etc.

[Solicitor for applicant and appellant]

(*Address and telephone number of solicitor*)

FORM 20.1

Rule 20.1(1)

Form of sentence of death

[Repealed by the Act of Adjournal (Criminal Procedure Rules Amendment No. 3) 1999 (S.I. 1999 No. 1387) para. 2(5) (effective May 19, 1999).]

FORM 20.2

Rule 20.2

Form of order of detention in police custody instead of imprisonment under section 206(2) of the Criminal Procedure (Scotland) Act 1995

The court ordered the offender to be detained in the custody of the police at (*place*) for (*number of days not exceeding four*).

(*Signed*)
Clerk of Court

¹FORM 20.3

Rule 20.3

Form of supervised release order under section 209 of the Criminal Procedure (Scotland) Act 1995

SUPERVISED RELEASE ORDER

under section 209 of the Criminal Procedure (Scotland) Act 1995

Court:

Date:

Offender:

Address:

Date of birth:

Offence(s) of which convicted:

Date of offence(s):

THE COURT, having sentenced the offender to imprisonment for a term of (*state period*) being less than four years:

AND being of the opinion that this order is necessary to protect the public from serious harm from the offender on his release:

AND having explained to the offender the effect of the order and the possible consequences for the offender of any breach of it including any failure to comply with requirements mentioned below:

ORDERS that the offender shall, during a period of (*insert period being a period not exceeding 12 months and not extending beyond the date by which the entire term of imprisonment will elapse*) after the date of his release, be under the supervision either of a relevant officer of a local authority or of a probation officer appointed for or assigned to a petty sessions area designated by the Scottish Ministers under section 14(4) or 15(1) of the Prisoners and Criminal Proceedings (Scotland) Act 1993 and shall be subject to—

    (a) the following standard requirements specified by virtue of section 209(4)(a) of the Criminal Procedure (Scotland) Act 1995:—
        (i) to report to the supervising officer in a manner and at intervals specified by that officer; and
        (ii) to notify that officer without delay of any change of address;
    (b) such reasonable requirements as may, by virtue of section 209(3)(b) of the Criminal Procedure (Scotland) Act 1995, be specified by the supervising officer; and
    (c) (*insert any requirements which the court may wish to specify, e.g., as to counselling on drug or alcohol abuse, staying away from victims, etc.*).

(*Signed*)
Clerk of Court

Copy to: Offender
Scottish Ministers

NOTE
[1]As amended by the Act of Adjournal (Criminal Procedure Rules Amendment)(Miscellaneous) 2000 (S.S.I. 2000 No. 65), para. 2 (effective April 7, 2000)

[1]**FORM 20.3A–A**   Rule 20.3A(1)

Form of a certificate in terms of section 5(2) of Sex Offenders Act 1997 of Conviction or of Finding

CERTIFICATE IN TERMS OF SECTION 5(2) OF SEX OFFENDERS ACT 1997 OF [CONVICTION] [FINDING]

.... Court   Date ....

Case No. ....

Name:
Address:
Date of birth:
Date of [conviction] [finding]:
Date of sentence if different:
Offence(s) and sentence(s):

I hereby certify, in terms of section 5(2) of the Sex Offenders Act 1997, that the above named accused was on the above date [convicted of] [found not guilty by reason of insanity of] [found to be under a disability and to have done the act[s] charged against him in respect of] the above offence[s]; that the [offence is a sexual offence] [offences are sexual offences] to which Part I of that Act applies; and that the court so stated in open court on that date.

....
CLERK OF THE COURT

NOTE
[1]Inserted by Act of Adjournal (Criminal Procedure Rules Amendment No. 5) (S.I. 1997 No. 2082) (effective September 1, 1997).

[1]**FORM 20.3A–B**   Rule 20.3A(2)

Form of notice of Requirement under section 2 of Sex Offenders Act 1997 to notify police of conviction or of finding

NOTICE OF REQUIREMENT TO NOTIFY POLICE

(This notice contains a summary of the notification requirements you must comply with. It is not a complete statement of the law. If you need further explanation or advice you should consult a solicitor.)

Case No. ....

You have been [convicted of] [found not guilty by reason of insanity of] [found to be under a disability and to have done the act charged against you in respect of] a sexual offence covered by the Sex Offenders Act 1997. The details are set out in the Certificate of [Conviction] [Finding] which [is attached to this notice] [will be sent to you].

This means that you are now required by law to:

- **Notify the police** within the next 14 days (or, if you are in custody, within 14 days after your release) of your name, any other names you use, your date of birth and your home address (*i.e.* your sole or main residence in the UK or, if you have no such residence, any premises in the UK which you regularly visit).

- **Notify the police** of any change of name or home address within 14 days after the date of the change.

- **Notify the police** of any address in the UK where you reside or stay longer than 14 days. This means either 14 days at a time, or a total of 14 days in any 12 months period.

You can give this notification either by going to a police station in the police area in which your home is situated and giving it in person or by sending notification in writing to a police station in that area. This requirement to give notice applies even if you are already registered as a result of an earlier requirement. If you don't know which police area your home is situated in, or which police stations are in that area, then ask at **any** police station.

These requirements apply to you from [*date of conviction or finding*]
and shall continue to apply [for 5 years] [for 7 years] [for 10 years] [indefinitely].

If you fail to comply with these requirements without a reasonable excuse, or give the police false information you could be fined, or sent to prison for up to 6 months, or both.

NOTE
[1]Inserted by Act of Adjournal (Criminal Procedure Rules Amendment, No. 5) (S.I. 1997 No. 2082) (effective September 1, 1997).

FORM 20.4–A   Rule 20.4(1)

Form of direction as to money found on offender under section 212(1) of the Criminal Procedure (Scotland) Act 1995

The court directed that the money found on the person (*name of offender*) should not be applied to payment of the fine of £   imposed on him on (*date*).

(*Signed*)
Judge

FORM 20.4–B   Rule 20.4(2)

Form of notice to governor of prison under section 212(7) of the Criminal Procedure (Scotland) Act 1995

To the Governor of the Prison of (*place*).

TAKE NOTICE that the attendance of (*name*), presently in your custody, is required at (*place and address of court*) on (*date*) at (*time*).

(*Signed*)
Judge

(*Place and date*)

FORM 20.5   Rule 20.5

Form of order for further time for payment of fine under section 214(7) or 215(3) of the Criminal Procedure (Scotland) Act 1995

The court, having considered the application of the offender for extension of time for payment of the fine of £   , allowed payment to be made within   days from this date.

(*Signed*)
Clerk of Court

FORM 20.6–A   Rule 20.6(1)

Form of citation to appear for enquiry under section 216(3)(a) of the Criminal Procedure (Scotland) Act 1995

Court

To: (*name and address*)		No.
		Date
		Fine
		Class of offence
		Rate of payment

Citation to attend for enquiry

Balance
outstanding £

On (*date*)

At (*time*)

In respect that you were fined as shown above, that you are in default of payment and that the outstanding balance of the fine is as shown above, you are ordained to appear personally at the time and date shown above in the Sheriff [*or* District] Court at (*place and address*) for an enquiry under section 216 of the Criminal Procedure (Scotland) Act 1995.

(*Place and date*)   (*Signed*)
                                       Clerk of Court

NOTES

(1) If you fail to appear personally at the enquiry court, the court may issue a warrant for your arrest.
(2) If you pay the whole outstanding balance of the fine before the enquiry court, it will not be necessary for you to appear.

Act of Adjournal (Criminal Procedure Rules) 1996

FORM 20.6–B Rule 20.6(2)

Form of execution of citation otherwise than by post of offender for enquiry for non-payment of fine

I, (*name and designation*), on (*date*), did lawfully cite (*name and address of offender in the citation*) to appear in person before the Sheriff [*or* District] Court at (*place and address*) on (*date*) at (*time*) for an enquiry under section 216 of the Criminal Procedure (Scotland) Act 1995. This I did by handing the citation to (*name*) personally [*or if not served personally, state other method of service*].

(*Signed*)
Officer of Law

FORM 20.6–C Rule 20.6(3)

Execution of citation by post, warrant to apprehend and record of proceedings at enquiry under section 216 of the Criminal Procedure (Scotland) Act 1995

(*Name and address of offender*)	No.
	Date
	Fine
	Class of offence
	Rate of payment

To attend for enquiry Balance outstanding £

on (*date*)

at (*time*)

Today I lawfully cited the above named offender to appear in person before the Sheriff [*or* District] Court, on the date and time shown above for an enquiry under section 216 of the Criminal Procedure (Scotland) Act 1995.

This I did by posting a copy of the citation to the offender addressed as shown above, by the recorded delivery service.

(*Signed*)
Clerk of Court

(*Place and date*)

(*Place and date*.) In respect that the above named offender has failed to pay the outstanding balance of the fine as shown above within the time allowed and has failed to appear in person for enquiry after being duly cited, the court grants warrant for the apprehension of the said offender for the purposes of his [*or* her] appearance before the court for enquiry under section 216 of the Criminal Procedure (Scotland) Act 1995.

(*Signed*)
Judge

Judge:

(*Place and date*)

Compeared the offender for enquiry. After enquiry, the court in relation to the fine referred to above—

(1) allowed payment of the fine to be made within   days from   ;
(2) allowed payment of the fine to be made by instalments of £   per week commencing on   19   ;
(3) imposed as an alternative to the fine   days' imprisonment to commence forthwith.

(Signed)
Clerk of Court

FORM 20.7   Rule 20.7

Form of notice of fines supervision order under section 217(7) of the Criminal Procedure (Scotland) Act 1995

Court:
To: (*name and address of offender*)

In respect that a fine of £   was imposed on you by the court at (*place*) on (*date*) and that fine [*or* balance of £   ] remains unpaid, the court today has placed you under the supervision of (*name of supervising officer*) who will assist you and advise you on the payment of the fine for so long as the fine remains unpaid or until the further order of court.

Payment of the fine is now to be made by weekly instalments of £   per week, the first instalment being due within   days from this date.

(Place and date)   (Signed)
                          Clerk of Court

Copy to: Chief Social Work Officer
(*Address*)

FORM 20.8   Rule 20.8(2)

Form of charge for payment of a fine or other financial penalty

CHARGE FOR PAYMENT OF FINE OR OTHER FINANCIAL PENALTY

instructed by the sheriff clerk (*address*) [*or* Clerk to the District Court (*address*)]

To: (*name and address of person fined or subject to the financial penalty*)

On (*date*) a fine [*or* financial penalty] (*give details and total amount of fine or other financial penalty*) was imposed on you in the High Court of Justiciary [*or* Sheriff Court *or* District Court] at (*place*)]

The court authorised recovery of the fine [*or specify other financial penalty*] on (*date*) and an extract conviction was issued in respect of the outstanding balance of £   .

I, (*name and address*), Messenger-at-Arms [*or* sheriff officer], by virtue of the extract conviction, in Her Majesty's name and authority and in the name and authority of the Lords Commissioners of Justiciary [*or* sheriff *or* justice] at (*place*), charge you to pay the total sum due within [14] days after the date of this charge to the sheriff clerk [*or* clerk to the District Court] (*address*).

If you do not pay this sum within [14] days you are liable to have further action taken against you.

This charge is served on you today by me by (*state method of service*) and is witnessed by (*name and address of witness*).

Dated the   day of

(*Signed*)

Witness   Messenger-at-Arms
                                     [or Sheriff Officer]

FORM 20.9–A   Rule 20.9(1)

Form of notice of transfer of fine order under section 222(1) of the Criminal Procedure (Scotland) Act 1995

IN THE SHERIFF [*or* DISTRICT] COURT

AT (*place*)   ·

(*Name of offender*)

Date of birth:

was on (*date*) convicted of (*crime or offence*) and was sentenced to pay a fine of £   , the fine to be paid by (*date*) [*or* by weekly (*or otherwise*) instalments of £   , the first instalment to be paid on (*date*)]; and that fine [*or* the balance of that fine as shown in the statement below] is still unpaid and (*state period*) of imprisonment has been fixed in the event of a future default in payment of the sum in question.

And as it appears that (*name of offender*) is now residing at (*address*) a transfer of fine order is hereby made under section 222(2) of the Criminal Procedure (Scotland) Act 1995, transferring to the (*specify the court*) at (*place*) and to the clerk of that court in respect of that fine all the functions referred to in section 222 of that Act.

(*Signed*)
Clerk of Court

Date:
STATEMENT REFERRED TO

Fine	£	
Instalment(s) paid to date of transfer	£	
Balance due		
In instalments of	£	

B–139

FORM 20.9–B   Rule 20.9(2)

Form of notice of further transfer of fine order by virtue of section 222(5) of the Criminal Procedure (Scotland) Act 1995

IN THE SHERIFF [*or* DISTRICT] COURT

AT (*place*)

(*Name of offender*)

Date of birth:

was on (*date*) at (*name of court*) convicted of (*offence*) and was sentenced to pay a fine of £   , the fine to be paid by (*date*) [*or* by weekly (*or otherwise*) instalments of £   , the first instalment to be paid on (*date*)];

By virtue of a Transfer of Fine Order dated (*insert date*) the functions of the sheriff [*or* district] court were transferred to (*specify the court*) at (*place*). The clerk of that court has sent a notice stating that (*name of offender*) is not residing within its jurisdiction.

The fine or the balance of the fine as shown in the statement below is still unpaid and (*state period*) of imprisonment has been fixed in the event of a future default in payment of the sum in question.

And as it appears that (*name of offender*) is now residing at (*address*) outwith the jurisdiction of this court, a further transfer of fine order is hereby made under section 222(1) of the Criminal Procedure (Scotland) Act 1995, transferring to the (*specify the court*) at (*place*) and to the clerk of that court in respect of the fine all the functions referred to in section 222 of that Act.

(*Signed*)
Clerk of Court

Date:

STATEMENT REFERRED TO

Fine	£	
Instalment(s) paid to date of transfer	£	
Balance due		
In instalments of	£	

FORM 20.9–C   Rule 20.9(3)

Form of notice to offender of transfer of fine order under section 222(1) of the Criminal Procedure (Scotland) Act 1995

IN THE SHERIFF [*or* DISTRICT] COURT

AT (*place*)

TO: (*name and address of offender*)

On (*date*), you were convicted by the (*specify the court*) at (*place*) and were sentenced to pay a fine of £   , to be paid by (*date*) [*or* by weekly (*or otherwise*) instalments of £   , the first instalment to be paid on (*date*)]. The fine has not been [fully] paid and (*state period*) of imprisonment has been fixed in the event of a future default in payment of the sum in question.

NOTICE IS HEREBY GIVEN TO YOU that in consequence of a transfer of fine order made by the (*specify the court*) at (*place*) on (*date*), the enforcement of the fine [*or* the balance of the fine] due by you as shown in the statement below, has become a matter for this court.

Payment of that fine [*or* the balance of that fine] due by you should therefore be made within the time [*or* times] ordered, either by post or personally to me (*clerk of court and address*).

If you cannot pay forthwith [*or* by (*date*)], you should at once make an application for further time to be granted. Such an application should be made either in person to this court or by letter addressed to me stating fully why you are unable to pay the sum due.

(*Signed*)
Clerk of Court

(*Address*)

Date:

NOTE: Any communication sent by post must be properly stamped.
Cash should not be sent in an unregistered envelope.

STATEMENT REFERRED TO

Fine	£	
Instalment(s) paid to date of transfer	£	
Balance due		
In instalments of	£	

FORM 20.10–A   Rule 20.10(1)

Form of probation order made under section 228 of the Criminal Procedure (Scotland) Act 1995

PROBATION ORDER

under section 228 of the Criminal Procedure (Scotland) Act 1995

COURT:
DATE:
OFFENDER:
Address:
Date of birth:

THE COURT, having convicted the offender, and being of the opinion that, having regard to the circumstances, including the nature of the offence and the character of the offender, it is expedient to make a probation order containing the undernoted requirements;

AND the court having explained to the offender the effect of the probation order (including the requirements set out below), and that if he or she fails to comply with the probation order, he may be brought before the court by his supervising officer for a breach of probation and may be fined or sentenced or dealt with for the original offence, and that, if he or she commits another offence during the period of the probation order, he or she may be dealt with for that offence;

AND the offender having expressed his or her willingness to comply with the requirements of the probation order;

ORDERS that for a period of (*specify period*) from the date of this order the offender who resides [*or* is to reside] in the local authority area of (*specify*) shall be under the supervision of an officer of that local authority allocated for the purpose [*or* allocated for the purpose as required

B–141

by the court] at (*place*) in the said local authority area; that the offender shall be notified in writing by the clerk of court of the name and official address of the officer who is to supervise him or her and be similarly notified if at any time such supervision is to be undertaken by another officer of the local authority allocated for the purpose; and that the offender shall comply with the following requirements, namely—

(1) to be of good behaviour;
(2) to conform to the directions of the supervising officer;
(3) to inform the supervising officer at once if he or she changes his residence or place of employment;
(4) (*here insert any additional requirements*).

(*Signed*)
Clerk of Court

Date:

Note: (*Name of supervising officer*) of (*name of local authority*) has been allocated as supervising officer in this case.

I confirm that I understand the conditions of the probation order.

Signature of offender:

Signature of supervising officer:

FORM 20.10–B   Rule 20.10(2)

Form of citation of probationer under section 232(1) or 233(1) of the Criminal Procedure (Scotland) Act 1995

IN THE HIGH COURT OF JUSTICIARY

[*or* IN THE SHERIFF [*or* DISTRICT] COURT]

AT (*place*)

CITATION

To: (*name and address of probationer*)

Date of citation: (*date of citation or, if citation by post, the day after the date of posting*)

YOU ARE HEREBY CITED to appear on (*date*) at (*time*) in the High Court of Justiciary [*or* Sheriff [*or* District] Court] at (*address*) because it has been reported to the court that you have failed to comply with a requirement of your probation order as alleged in the written information attached [*or* by (*specify the failure alleged*)] [*or* committed an offence while on probation, namely, (*specify*)].

IF YOU DO NOT ATTEND COURT WITHOUT A LAWFUL EXCUSE THE COURT MAY ORDER THAT YOU BE APPREHENDED AND PUNISHED

(*Signed*)
Officer of Law
[*or* Clerk of Court]

B–142

SCHEDULE

FORM 20.10A   Rule 20.10A

Form of non-harassment order made under section 234A of the Criminal Procedure (Scotland) Act 1995

NON HARASSMENT ORDER

Under section 234A of the Criminal Procedure (Scotland) Act 1995

COURT:
DATE:
OFFENDER:
Address:
Date of birth:

THE COURT, having convicted the offender of (*specify offence or offences*), being [an offence] [offences] involving harassment, within the meaning of section 8 of the Protection from Harassment Act 1997([*3*] of a person;

AND being satisfied, on the balance of probabilities, that it is appropriate to make an order to protect that person from further harassment;

ORDERS that [for a period of (*specify period*) from the date of this order] [until further order] the offender shall (*specify conduct from which offender is to refrain*).

(*Signed*)

CLERK OF COURT

FORM 20.10B   Rule 20.10B

Form of application under section 234A(6) of the Criminal Procedure (Scotland) Act 1995

UNTO THE RIGHT HONOURABLE THE LORD JUSTICE GENERAL, LORD JUSTICE-CLERK AND LORDS COMMISSIONERS OF JUSTICIARY

[or UNTO THE HONOURABLE THE SHERIFF
OF (*name of sheriffdom*) AT (*place*)]

[or UNTO THE JUSTICES in the DISTRICT COURT
OF (*name of district*) AT (*place*)]

APPLICATION

by

Her Majesty's Advocate [*or*
[A.B.] (*address*) [*or* Prisoner in the Prison of (*place*)]

APPLICANT

HUMBLY SHEWETH:

1. That a non-harassment order was made against [A.B.] on (*date*) in the High Court of Justiciary sitting [*or* in the sheriff court *or* in the district court] at (*place*) on (*date*) in terms of the non-harassment order annexed hereto,

2. That the applicant applies to the court in terms of section 234A(6) of the Act of 1995 to revoke [*or* vary] the non-harassment order for the following reasons:—

(*here state reasons*).

MAY IT THEREFORE PLEASE YOUR LORDSHIP[S] [OR THE COURT]:
    (a) to [revoke the non-harassment order] [vary the non-harassment order by (*here state terms of variation of order sought*)].
    (b) or to do otherwise as to your Lordship[s] [OR to the court] shall seem proper.

IN RESPECT WHEREOF

(*Signed*)
Advocate Depute [*or* Procurator Fiscal]
On behalf of Her Majesty's Advocate [*or*]
[Solicitor for [A.B.]
(*Address and telephone number of solicitor*)].

NOTE
    You must notify the clerk of Court within 14 days of the receipt of this application whether or not you intend to oppose it. Failure so to notify will result in the court disposing of the matter in your absence.

FORM 20.11–A   Rule 20.11(1)

Form of supervised attendance order under section 235(1) of the Criminal Procedure (Scotland) Act 1995

SUPERVISED ATTENDANCE ORDER

under section 235(1) of the Criminal Procedure (Scotland) Act 1995

COURT:
DATE:
OFFENDER:
Address:
Date of birth:

(1) THE COURT, being satisfied that the requirements of paragraphs (a), (b) and (c) of section 235(3) of the Criminal Procedure (Scotland) Act 1995 have been met;

AND having explained to the offender the purpose and effect of this order (including the requirements set out below), and that if the offender fails to comply with this order the offender may be brought before the court which may revoke this order and impose a period of imprisonment or may vary the number of hours specified in this order, and that the court has power to review this order on the application either of the offender or of an officer of the local authority in whose area the offender for the time being resides;

AND the offender having expressed his or her willingness to comply with this order;

IN RESPECT that the offender [resides] [*or* is to reside] in the District of (*specify district of local authority*) in the area of (*specify the local authority*), REQUIRES the said Council to appoint or assign an officer to discharge the functions assigned to him or her by virtue of section 235 of, and Schedule 7 to, the Criminal Procedure (Scotland) Act 1995 in respect of the offender and to notify the offender forthwith of the particulars of the officer;

ORDERS that the offender shall—
    (a) attend a place of supervision notified to him or her by the officer for (*specify number of hours*) hours during the period of 12 months from this date or until the stated hours of

attendance have been completed, whichever is the shorter, and while at that place of supervision carry out such instructions as may be given to him or her by the officer; and
  (b) report to the officer and notify the officer without delay of any change of residence or of any change in the times, if any, at which the offender usually works.

(2) IF for any reason the offender fails to carry out the instructions given under this order for the number of hours specified at (1)(a) above within the period of 12 months from the date of this order:—
  (a) this order will remain in force until the offender has carried out the said instruction for the number of hours specified in this order;
  (b) the offender's obligations stated above will continue; and
  (c) the officer shall bring the circumstances to the attention of the court.

(*Signed*)
Clerk of Court

Copy: Offender
Chief Social Work Officer
[Clerk of appropriate court]

FORM 20.11–B   Rule 20.11(2)

Form of supervised attendance order under section 236 of the Criminal Procedure (Scotland) Act 1995

SUPERVISED ATTENDANCE ORDER

under section 236 of the Criminal Procedure (Scotland) Act 1995

COURT:
DATE:
OFFENDER:
Address:
Date of birth:

(1) THE COURT, being satisfied that the offender is likely to pay the fine of £
imposed by the court [*or* is unlikely to pay the fine of £   imposed by the court];

AND having explained to the offender the purpose and effect of this order (including the requirements set out below), and that if the offender fails to comply with this order the offender may be brought before the court which may revoke this order and impose a period of imprisonment or may vary the number of hours specified in this order, and that the court has power to review this order on the application either of the offender or of an officer of the local authority in whose area the offender for the time being resides;

AND the offender having expressed his [*or* her] willingness to comply with this order;

IN RESPECT that the offender [resides] [*or* is to reside] in the District of (*specify district of local authority*) in the area of (*specify the local authority*), REQUIRES the said Council to appoint or assign an officer to discharge the functions assigned to him or her by virtue of Schedule 7 to the Criminal Procedure (Scotland) Act 1995 in respect of the offender and to notify the offender forthwith of the particulars of the officer;

ORDERS that the offender shall [in default of payment of the said fine within 28 days of (*date*)]—
  (a) attend a place of supervision notified to him or her by the officer for (*specify number of hours*) hours during the period of 12 months from this date or until the stated hours of attendance have been completed, whichever is the shorter, and while at that place of supervision carry out such instructions as may be given to him or her by the officer; and

(b) report to the officer and notify the officer without delay of any change of residence or of any change in the times, if any, at which the offender usually works.

(2) IF for any reason the offender fails to carry out the instructions given under this order for the number of hours specified at (1)(a) above within the period of 12 months from the date of this order:—

    (a) this order will remain in force until the offender has carried out the said instruction for the number of hours specified in this order;

    (b) the offender's obligations stated above will continue; and

    (c) the officer shall bring the circumstances to the attention of the court.

(Signed)
Clerk of Court

Copy: Offender
Chief Social Work Officer
[Clerk of appropriate court]

FORM 20.12–A   Rule 20.12(1)

Form of community service order under section 238 of the Criminal Procedure (Scotland) Act 1995

COMMUNITY SERVICE ORDER

under section 238 of the Criminal Procedure (Scotland) Act 1995

COURT:
DATE:
OFFENDER:
Address:
Date of birth:
Offence(s):

(1) THE COURT, being satisfied that the offender has committed the offence with which he or she is charged [*or* in view of the conviction of the offender], and being of the opinion that, having regard to the circumstances, including the nature of the offence and the character of the offender, it is expedient to make a community service order containing the undernoted requirements;

AND having explained to the offender the effect of the community service order (including the requirements set out below), and that if he or she fails to comply with the community service order, he or she may be brought before the court by his or her supervising officer for a breach of the community service order and may be fined or sentenced or dealt with for the original defence, and that, if he or she commits another offence during the period of the community service order, he or she may be dealt with for that offence;

IN RESPECT that the offender who resides [*or* is to reside] in the District of (*specify district of local authority*) in the area of (*specify the local authority*) has been convicted of the said offence(s) REQUIRES the said Council to appoint or assign an officer to discharge the functions assigned by sections 239 to 245 of the Criminal Procedure (Scotland) Act 1995 in respect of the offender and to notify the offender forthwith of the particulars of the officer;

ORDERS that the offender shall, during the period of twelve months from this date or until the performance of the hours of unpaid work specified at (2) below, whichever is shorter—

    (a) report to the local authority officer appointed or assigned to him or her and notify the said officer without delay of any change of address or of any change in the times, if any, at which the offender usually works; and

    (b) perform for (*specify number of hours*) hours such unpaid work at times as the local authority officer may instruct.

(2) If for any reason the offender fails to perform the unpaid work specified in paragraph (1)(a) above during the period of twelve months from the date of the order—
    (a) the order shall remain in force beyond the twelve month period;
    (b) the offender's obligation under paragraph (1) above will continue, and;
    (c) the local authority officer appointed under the order shall take whatever action is appropriate to bring the circumstances to the attention of the court.

(Signed)
Clerk of Court

Copy to: Offender
Chief Social Worker

FORM 20.12–B   Rule 20.12(2)

Form of citation of offender under section 239(4) or 240(3) of the Criminal Procedure (Scotland) Act 1995

IN THE HIGH COURT OF JUSTICIARY

[*or* IN THE SHERIFF [*or* DISTRICT] COURT]

AT (*place*)

CITATION

To: (*name and address of probationer*)

Date of citation: (*date of citation or day after the date of posting*)

YOU ARE HEREBY CITED to appear on (*date*) at (*time*) in the High Court of Justiciary [*or* Sheriff [*or* District] Court] at (*address*) because it has been reported to the court that you have failed to comply with a requirement of your community service order by (*specify the failure alleged*) [*or* that, on the application of the local authority officer, the community service order should be amended or revoked because (*specify*)].

IF YOU DO NOT ATTEND COURT WITHOUT A LAWFUL EXCUSE THE COURT MAY ORDER THAT YOU BE APPREHENDED AND PUNISHED.

(Signed)
Officer of Law
[*or* Clerk of Court]

[1]**FORM 20.12A–A**   Rule 20.12A(1)

RESTRICTION OF LIBERTY ORDER

under section 245A(1) of the Criminal Procedure (Scotland) Act 1995

COURT:
DATE:
OFFENDER'S NAME, ADDRESS AND DATE OF BIRTH:
OFFENCE FOR WHICH CONVICTED:

THE COURT, having convicted (*name of offender*) of (*specify offence*) and being satisfied that the most appropriate method of disposal is to make an order under subsection (1) of section 245A of the Criminal Procedure (Scotland) Act 1995;

AND having complied with any requirement imposed on it by subsection (6) of, and provided the offender with the explanation required by subsection (4) of, that section and obtained from him his agreement that he will comply with the requirements of the proposed order;

ORDERS that for (*specify, as respects a day [or week], a period in that day [or week]*) the offender shall be in (*specify a place*) [*or that at (specify a time)* [*or during (specify a period)*]] the offender shall not be in (*specify a place*)].

(*Signed*)
Clerk of Court.
Date:

Note: (*Name and address of monitor*) has been designated by the court, under section 245B(2) of the Criminal Procedure (Scotland) Act 1995, as the person responsible for monitoring the offender's compliance with this order.

I confirm that I understand the requirements of this order and will comply with them.

(*Signed*)
Offender.

NOTE
[1]Inserted by the Act of Adjournal (Criminal Procedure Rules Amendment) (Restriction of Liberty Orders) 1998 (S.I. 1998 No. 1842).

[1]**FORM 20.12A–B**   Rule 20.12A(2)

Form of application under section 245E(1) of the Criminal Procedure (Scotland) Act 1995

UNTO THE RIGHT HONOURABLE THE LORD JUSTICE GENERAL, LORD JUSTICE-CLERK AND LORDS COMMISSIONERS OF JUSTICIARY

[*or* Unto The Honourable The Sheriff of (*name of sheriffdom*)
At (*place*)]
[*or* Unto The Justices In The District Court Of (*name of district*) At (*place*)]
Application
by
(*name of offender*) (*address*) [*or* Prisoner
in the Prison of (*place*)]
[**or** *name and address of applicant with responsibility for monitoring offender's compliance with restriction of liberty order*]

APPLICANT
HUMBLY SHEWETH
1. That a restriction of liberty order, a copy of which is annexed to this application, was made in respect of (*name of offender*) on (*date*) in the High Court of Justiciary sitting [*or* in the sheriff court *or* in the district court] at (*place*).
2. That the applicant applies to the court in terms of subsection (1) of section 245E of the Criminal Procedure (Scotland) Act 1995 to revoke [*or* vary] the order for the following reason—

(*statement of reason*)

MAY IT THEREFORE PLEASE YOUR LORDSHIP[S] [*OR* THE COURT]:
  (a) to [revoke the restriction of liberty order] [vary the restriction of liberty order by (*statement of variation sought in terms of subsection (2)(a) of the said section 245E*)],

or
(b) to do otherwise as to your Lordship[s] [*or* to the court] shall seem proper.

IN RESPECT WHEREOF
(*Signed*)

Offender
[*or* Solicitor for offender]
[*or* applicant with responsibility
for monitoring compliance]
(*Where a solicitor signs, the
address and telephone number of
the solicitor*).

NOTE
[1]Inserted by the Act of Adjournal (Criminal Procedure Rules Amendment) (Restriction of Liberty Orders) 1998 (S.I. 1998 No. 1842).

[1]**FORM 20.12A–C**   Rule 20.12A(3)

Form of citation of offender under section 245E(3) of the Criminal Procedure (Scotland) Act 1995

IN THE HIGH COURT OF JUSTICIARY

[*or* IN THE SHERIFF [*or* DISTRICT] COURT]

AT (*place*)

CITATION

To: (*name and address of offender*)
Date of citation: (*date of citation or, if citation by post, the day after the date of posting*)
YOU ARE HEREBY CITED to appear on (*date*) at (*time*) in the High Court of Justiciary [*or* Sheriff [*or* District] Court] at (*address*) because it appears to the court to be in the interests of justice that the restriction of liberty order made in respect of you on (*date*) should be varied or revoked.

IF YOU FAIL TO ATTEND COURT WITHOUT A LAWFUL EXCUSE THE COURT MAY ISSUE A WARRANT FOR YOUR ARREST.

(*Signed*)

Advocate Depute [*or* Procurator Fiscal]
On behalf of Her Majesty's Advocate.

[1]**FORM 20.12A–D**   Rule 20.12A(4)

Form of citation of offender under section 245F(1) of the Criminal Procedure (Scotland) Act 1995

IN THE HIGH COURT OF JUSTICIARY

[or IN THE SHERIFF *[or* DISTRICT] COURT]

AT *(place)*

CITATION

To: *(name and address of offender)*
Date of citation: *(date of citation or, if citation by post, the day after the date of posting)*
YOU ARE HEREBY CITED to appear on *(date)* at *(time)* in the High Court of Justiciary *[or* Sheriff *[or* District] Court] at *(address)* because it has been reported to the court that you have failed to comply with a requirement of your restriction of liberty order by *(specify the failure alleged)*.

IF YOU FAIL TO ATTEND COURT WITHOUT A LAWFUL EXCUSE THE COURT MAY ISSUE A WARRANT FOR YOUR ARREST.

(Signed)

Advocate Depute *[or* Procurator Fiscal]
On behalf of Her Majesty's Advocate.

NOTE
[1]Inserted by the Act of Adjournal (Criminal Procedure Rules Amendment) (Restriction of Liberty Orders) 1998 (S.I. 1998 No. 1842).

[1]**FORM 20.12B**   Rule 20.12B

Form of drug treatment and testing order made under section 234B of the Criminal Procedure (Scotland) Act 1995

DRUG TREATMENT AND TESTING ORDER

under section 234B of the Criminal Procedure (Scotland) Act 1995

COURT:
DATE:
OFFENDER:
Address:
Date of birth:

THE COURT, having convicted the offender and being of the opinion that having regard to the circumstances, including the nature of the offence and the character of the offender, it is expedient to make a drug treatment and testing order containing the undernoted requirements;

AND the Court having explained to the offender the effect of the order (including the requirements set out below) and the consequences of failure to comply with the order or with any requirement thereof;

AND the offender having expressed willingness to comply with the requirements of the order;

REQUIRES, in respect that in terms of this order the offender is to reside in the local authority area of (*specify*), the said Council to appoint or assign an officer (the "supervising officer") to discharge the functions assigned by sections 234C and 234F of the Criminal Procedure (Scotland) Act 1995 in respect of the offender and to notify the offender forthwith of the particulars of the supervising officer, of any change in the particulars of the supervising officer and of any change of appointed or assigned supervising officer;

ORDERS that the offender shall, for a period of (*specify period*) from the date of the order, reside in the local authority area of (*specify*) under the supervision of the supervising officer at (*place*) in the said local authority area; and that he shall throughout that period comply with the following requirements, namely—

    (i) to submit to treatment (*specify whether as a resident or as a non-resident*) by or under the direction of (*name of treatment provider*) (the "treatment provider") at (*name of institution*) with a view to the reduction or elimination of dependency on or propensity to misuse drugs;

    (ii) to conform to the directions of the supervising officer and of the treatment provider;

    (iii) to inform the supervising officer immediately of any change of address;

    (iv) to provide for the purpose of ascertaining whether he has any drug in his body such samples, of such description, at such times, in such circumstances, as the treatment provider may determine;

    (v) to keep in touch with the supervising officer as instructed from time to time by that officer;

    (vi) to attend each review hearing;

    (vii) (*any additional requirement*).

ORDERS that the treatment provider shall communicate to the supervising officer the results of the tests carried out on the samples provided by the offender in pursuance of this order;

ORDERS that the supervising officer shall report in writing on the offender's progress under this order to the court conducting the review hearing; and that he shall include in each such report the results of the tests communicated to him by the treatment provider and the views of the treatment provider as to the treatment and testing of the offender;

FURTHER ORDERS that this Order shall be reviewed periodically at intervals of not less than one month at a hearing held for the purpose by (*specify the appropriate court*), the first such review to be heard on (*date*).

Signed

Clerk of Court

Date:

Note: (*name of supervising officer*) of (*name of local authority*) has been allocated as supervising officer in this case.

I confirm that I understand the conditions of this drug treatment and testing order.

Signature of offender:
Signature of supervising officer:

NOTE
[1]Inserted by the Act of Adjournal (Criminal Procedure Rules Amendment No. 4) (Drug Treatment and Testing Orders) 1999 (S.S.I. 1999 No. 191) para. 2(3) and Sched. I (effective December 20, 1999).

FORM 20.18–A   Rule 20.18(1)

Form of extract of custodial sentence following conviction on indictment, warrant of detention and return of sentence

PROCEEDINGS ON INDICTMENT

under the Criminal Procedure (Scotland) Act 1995

EXTRACT SENTENCE, WARRANT OF DETENTION AND RETURN OF SENTENCE

Court	Judge
Accused	Date of Sentence
Address (where known)	Method of conviction Jury trial Sec. 76 Plea Jury trial Sec. 195

Date of Birth	Marital Status	Occupation

Offence(s) for which sentenced

Sentence:

The court sentenced the accused to be imprisoned/detained as from this date for the period specified below and thereafter to be set at liberty.

Period of imprisonment/detention:

Total period: To date from:

Warrant:

In respect of the foregoing sentence, the court ordained the accused to be conveyed by officers of law to the Prison of

thereafter to be dealt with in due course of law.

Officers
to prove conviction

Previous record
(as per list attached)

Extracted by me (*name*)

                             (*Signed*)
                             Clerk of Justiciary
                             [*or* Sheriff Clerk]

FORM 20.18–B   Rule 20.18(2)

Forms of extract of sentence imposed in summary proceedings

In the Sheriff [*or* District] Court of   at (*place*)

Name of accused:
Date of conviction:
Offence of which convicted:

[*Imprisonment*] Sentence, Imprisonment   months [*or* days].
In respect of which sentence, warrant is hereby granted to officers of law to convey the accused to the prison of (*place*) and for the detention of the accused therein for   days from the date of imprisonment.

[*Fine or imprisonment immediate*] Sentence, £   fine or   months' [*or* days'] imprisonment. In respect of which sentence warrant is hereby granted to officers of law to convey the accused to the prison of (*place*) and for the detention of the accused therein until the said fine is paid, but not exceeding   months [*or* days] from the date of imprisonment.

[*Fine or imprisonment time allowed and expired*] Sentence, £   fine (payable within   days) or   months' [*or* days'] imprisonment.
In respect of which sentence, the period allowed for payment of the said fine having expired and the said fine not having been paid, warrant is hereby granted to officers of law to convey the accused to the prison of (*place*) and for the detention of the accused therein until the fine is paid, but not exceeding   months [*or* days] from the date of imprisonment.

[*Fine and surrender of accused for imprisonment*] Sentence, £   fine payable within   months [*or* days] or   months' [*or* days'] imprisonment.
In respect of which sentence the accused, having surrendered himself to the court and stated that he prefers immediate imprisonment to waiting for the expiry of the time allowed, warrant is hereby granted to officers of law to convey the accused to the prison of (*place*) and for the detention of the accused therein until such fine is paid, but not exceeding   days from the date of imprisonment.

[*Caution*] Sentence, £   caution for good behaviour for six months (from date of conviction) or   months' [*or* days'] imprisonment.
In respect of which sentence warrant is hereby granted to officers of law to convey the accused to the prison of (*place*) and for the detention of the accused therein until the said caution is found, but not exceeding   days from the date of imprisonment.

[*Fine and caution*] Sentence, £   fine or   months' [*or* days'] imprisonment and £   caution for good behaviour for   months (from payment of the fine or from the expiry of the period of imprisonment for non-payment) or   months' [*or* days'] imprisonment further.
In respect of which sentence warrant is hereby granted to officers of law to convey the accused to the prison of (*place*) and for the detention of the accused therein until the said fine is paid and the said caution is found, the detention for non-payment of the said fine not exceeding   months [*or* days] from the date of imprisonment, and the detention for failure to find the said caution not exceeding   months [*or* days] further from payment of the fine or from expiry of the term of imprisonment for non-payment thereof.

[*Imprisonment and caution*] Sentence, imprisonment   months [*or* days] and £   caution for good behaviour for   months thereafter, or   months' [*or* days'] imprisonment.

In respect of which sentence warrant is hereby granted to officers of law to convey the accused to the prison of (*place*) and for the detention of the accused therein for   months [*or* days] from the date of imprisonment and for his further detention thereafter until the said caution is found, but not exceeding   months [*or* days] further.

(*Signed*)
Clerk of Court

FORM 20.19–A   Rule 20.19(2)(a)

Form of application under section 34B(6) of the Road Traffic Offenders Act 1988

UNTO THE HONOURABLE THE SHERIFF OF (*name of sheriffdom*)
[*or* UNTO THE STIPENDIARY MAGISTRATE OF
THE CITY OF GLASGOW DISTRICT]
AT (*place*)

APPLICATION

under

section 34B(6) of the Road Traffic Offenders Act 1988

by

[A.B.] (*address*)

APPLICANT

HUMBLY SHEWETH:

1. That the applicant is (*name of applicant*), and resides at (*address*).

2. That the sheriff [*or* stipendiary magistrate] on (*date of order*) made an order under section 34A of the Road Traffic Offenders Act 1988 (hereinafter referred to as "the Act of 1988") that the period of disqualification imposed on the applicant under section 34 of the Act of 1988 shall be reduced, if, by the date specified in the order, the applicant has completed satisfactorily an approved course as specified in the order.

3. That the course organiser of the course specified in the order was (*name and address of course organiser*).

4. That the date specified in the order for satisfactory completion by the applicant of the course was (*insert date specified*).

5. That the course organiser has given to the applicant the written notice required by section 34B(5) of the Act of 1988, by means of the notice dated (*date of notice*) which is lodged with this application, that he has decided not to give a course completion certificate to the applicant.

6. That the course organiser's decision not to give a course completion certificate is contrary to section 34B(4) of the Act of 1988 because (*state grounds of application*).

MAY IT THEREFORE please Your Lordship [*or* Your Honour]:

 (1) to fix a date for hearing this application;

 (2) to order the clerk of court to serve this application, with notice of the hearing, on the course organiser and the procurator fiscal; and thereafter

 (3) to declare that the course organiser's decision not to give a course completion certificate is contrary to section 34B(4) of the Act of 1988.

Act of Adjournal (Criminal Procedure Rules) 1996

IN RESPECT WHEREOF

(Signed)
Applicant
[*or* Solicitor for applicant]

(Address and telephone number of solicitor)

(Date)

FORM 20.19–B   Rule 20.19(3)(a)

Form of application under section 34B(7) of the Road Traffic Offenders Act 1988

UNTO THE HONOURABLE THE SHERIFF OF (*name of sheriffdom*)
[*or* UNTO THE STIPENDIARY MAGISTRATE OF
THE CITY OF GLASGOW DISTRICT]
AT (*place*)

APPLICATION

under

section 34B(7) of the Road Traffic Offenders Act 1998

by

[A.B.] (*address*)

APPLICANT

HUMBLY SHEWETH:

1. That the applicant is (*name of applicant*), and resides at (*address*).

2. That the sheriff [*or* stipendiary magistrate] on (*date of order*) made an order under section 34A of the Road Traffic Offenders Act 1988 (hereinafter referred to as "the Act of 1988") that the period of disqualification imposed on the applicant under section 34 of the Act of 1988 shall be reduced, if, by the date specified in the order, the applicant has completed satisfactorily an approved course as specified in the order.

3. That the course organiser of the course specified in the order was (*name and address of course organiser*).

4. That the date specified in the order for satisfactory completion by the applicant of the course was (*insert date specified*).

5. That the course organiser has not given to the applicant either a course completion certificate under section 34B(1) and (4) of the Act of 1988 or the written notice required by section 34B(5) of the Act of 1988 that he has decided not to give a course completion certificate, and that accordingly the course organiser is in default.

MAY IT THEREFORE please Your Lordship [*or* Your Honour]:

    (1) to fix a date for hearing this application;

    (2) to order the clerk of court to serve this application, with notice of the hearing, on the course organiser and the procurator fiscal; and thereafter

    (3) to declare that the course organiser is in default.

IN RESPECT WHEREOF

(Signed)
Applicant
[*or* Solicitor for applicant]

(Address and telephone number of solicitor)

(Date)

FORM 21.1–A   Rule 21.1(1)

Form of statement of uncontroversial evidence under section 258 of the Criminal Procedure (Scotland) Act 1995

IN THE HIGH COURT OF JUSTICIARY

[*or* IN THE SHERIFF [*or* DISTRICT] COURT]

AT *(place)*

STATEMENT OF UNCONTROVERSIAL EVIDENCE

by

[A.B.] *(address)*
[*or* Prisoner in the Prison of *(place)*]

in

HER MAJESTY'S ADVOCATE [*or* THE PROCURATOR FISCAL, *(place)*]

against

(Insert name(s) of accused)

TAKE NOTICE:

1. That the fact[s] listed below has [*or* have] been identified by me [*or* us] as uncontroversial and capable of being agreed in advance of trial under section 258 of the Criminal Procedure (Scotland) Act 1995.

[*Or* (1) That the fact[s] set out in the [following] document(s) annexed to this statement has [*or* have] been identified as uncontroversial and capable of being agreed in advance of trial under section 258 of the Criminal Procedure (Scotland) Act 1995:—

(here describe the documents)].

2. That a failure to challenge [any of] the foregoing fact[s] within seven days of the date of service of this notice will result in the unchallenged fact being treated by the court as having been conclusively proved unless the court makes a direction under subsection (6) of section 258 of the above-mentioned Act.

Served on *(date)* by me [*or* as the case may be] by *(state method of service)*.

(Signed)
Procurator Fiscal
[*or* Accused]
[*or* Solicitor for [A.B.]

(Address and telephone number of solicitor)]

FORM 21.1–B   Rule 21.1(2)

Form of docquet to be endorsed on document annexed to, but not described in, statement of uncontroversial evidence

I, *(insert name and address of party serving the notice)*, hereby certify that this document is a document referred to in the foregoing statement of uncontroversial facts.

(*Signed*)

(*Date*)

FORM 21.2   Rule 21.2

Form of notice of challenge under section 258(3) of the Criminal Procedure (Scotland) Act 1995

NOTICE OF CHALLENGE OF FACT[S]
specified [*or* referred to] in statement under
section 258(2) of the Criminal Procedure (Scotland) Act 1995

by

[A.B.] (*address*)
[*or* Prisoner in the Prison of (*place*)]

in

HER MAJESTY'S ADVOCATE [*or* THE PROCURATOR FISCAL, (*place*)]

against

(*Insert name(s) of accused*)

NOTICE IS HEREBY GIVEN that the following document[s] [*or* fact[s]] specified [*or* referred to] in the statement of uncontroversial evidence under section 258(2) of the Criminal Procedure (Scotland) Act 1995 served on (*date*) is [*or* are] challenged by me:—

(*here state or refer to the statement(s), document(s) or fact(s) challenged*).

(*Signed*)
Accused
[*or* Solicitor for accused *or* Procurator Fiscal]

(*Address and telephone number of solicitor*)

(*Date*)

FORM 21.3   Rule 21.3

Form of notice under section 259(5) of the Criminal Procedure (Scotland) Act 1995

IN THE HIGH COURT OF JUSTICIARY
[*or* IN THE SHERIFF [*or* DISTRICT] COURT]
AT (*place*)

NOTICE

under

Section 259(5) of the Criminal Procedure (Scotland) Act 1995

by

[A.B.]

in

HER MAJESTY'S ADVOCATE [*or* THE PROCURATOR FISCAL, (*place*)]

against

(*Insert name(s) of accused*)

TAKE NOTICE:

1. That [A.B.] intends to apply to the court to have evidence of a statement by (*name and address of person not giving oral evidence*) admitted in evidence under section 259 of the Criminal Procedure (Scotland) Act 1995 and that evidence of that statement will be given—
   * orally to the court by (*name and address of witness who will give evidence of the statement of that person*). A copy of an affidavit stating what the witness will say is attached.
   * in the form of a document, a copy of which is attached.
   * in the form of a document, a copy of which is attached, made by (*insert name, designation and address of maker of document*).

2. That there is evidence that the statement referred to in paragraph 1 above was made and that the person who will give evidence about it has direct personal knowledge of the making of the statement as appears from the affidavit of that person attached to this notice [*or* that the statement is contained in the document, the copy of which is attached to this notice].

3. That the reason why this evidence is not to be given personally by (*name*) is that:—
   * He/She is dead. An extract death certificate (*or specify other means of proof*) is attached.
   * He/She is unfit by reason of *his/her bodily condition to give evidence in any other competent manner. A copy of a report to this effect by a certified medical practitioner is attached.
   * He/She is unfit by reason of *his/her mental condition to give evidence in any other competent manner. A copy of a report to this effect by a certified medical practitioner is attached.
   * He/She is outwith the United Kingdom and is at (*address*) and it is not reasonably practicable to secure *his/her attendance at trial because (*state steps which have been taken to secure attendance*). The evidence may not be obtained in any other competent manner because (*state why the evidence may not be obtained in any other competent manner*).
   * He/She cannot be found and the following steps which are all reasonable steps which, in the circumstances, could have been taken to find *him/her have been taken (*state steps which have been taken*).

4. That I, (*insert name and address of party serving the notice*), procurator fiscal [*or* solicitor

acting on behalf of (*specify*)] certify that, the information given above is accurate in every respect to the best of my knowledge.

Served on (*date*) by me [*or as the case may be*] by (*state method of service*).

(*Signed*)

(*Capacity in which signing*)

(*Date of service if not by post*)

* *Delete whatever is not applicable.*

FORM 21.4   Rule 21.4

Form of certificate of authentication of documents containing a prior statement for the purposes of section 260(4) of the Criminal Procedure (Scotland) Act 1995

I, (*insert name and designation of person authenticating*), HEREBY CERTIFY THAT this document [*or* the attached document], comprising [this and] the following (*insert number*) pages is a full and accurate record of evidence given by (*insert name and designation of person who gave the prior statement and brief details of the nature, place and date of the proceedings during which the statement was made*).

(*Signed*)

(*Date*)

¹**FORM 22.1**   Rule 22.1(1)

Form of petition for authorisation of the giving of evidence by a vulnerable person by means of a live television link

UNTO THE RIGHT HONOURABLE THE LORD JUSTICE GENERAL, LORD JUSTICE-CLERK AND LORDS COMMISSIONERS OF JUSTICIARY

[*or* UNTO THE HONOURABLE THE SHERIFF OF (*name of sheriffdom*) AT (*place*)]

PETITION

of

HER MAJESTY'S ADVOCATE [*or* THE PROCURATOR FISCAL, (*place*)]

[*or* [A.B.] (*address*)
[*or* Prisoner in the Prison of (*place*)]]

PETITIONER

HUMBLY SHEWETH:

1. That the petitioner [*or* [C.D.]] has appeared on petition [*or* been indicted] [*or* charged] in your Lordships' [*or* Lordship's] court at the instance of Her Majesty's Advocate [*or* the procurator fiscal at (*place*)] with the crime of [*or* on a summary complaint at the instance of the procurator fiscal with the crime [*or* offence] of] (*specify*).

2. That the trial of the petitioner [*or* [C.D.]] is to take place in your Lordships' [*or* Lordship's] court [sitting at (*place*)] on (*date*).

3. That [E.F.], a vulnerable person residing at (*address*) has been [*or* is likely to be] cited to give evidence at the trial.

4. That (*here state reasons for application*).

5. That accordingly it is appropriate under section 271(5) of the Criminal Procedure (Scotland) Act 1995 that the evidence of [E.F.] should be given by means of live television link.

[6. That your Lordship's court at (*place*) lacks the accommodation or equipment necessary to enable [E.F.] to give evidence by such means.

7. That the sheriff court at (*specify*) has such accommodation and equipment available.]

MAY IT THEREFORE please Your Lordship[s]:

(1) to appoint intimation of this petition to be made to (*specify*);

(2) to appoint parties to be heard on this petition on the earliest practicable date hereafter; [and]

(3) thereafter, on being satisfied in terms of section 271(7) of the Criminal Procedure (Scotland) Act 1995, to order that the evidence of [E.F.] shall be given by means of a live television link[; and

(4) thereafter, on being satisfied in terms of section 271(8) of the said Act, to order that the case shall be transferred to the court at (*specify*)].

ACCORDING TO JUSTICE, etc.

(*Signed*)
[Solicitor for petitioner]

(*Address and telephone number of solicitor*)

NOTE
[1]As amended by Act of Adjournal (Criminial Procedure Rules Amendment No. 4) (S.I. 1997 No. 1834) (effective August 1, 1997).

FORM 23.1–A   Rule 23.1(1)(a)

Form of petition for issue of letter of request in High Court before indictment served

UNTO THE RIGHT HONOURABLE THE LORD JUSTICE GENERAL, LORD JUSTICE-CLERK AND LORDS COMMISSIONERS OF JUSTICIARY

PETITION

of

HER MAJESTY'S ADVOCATE

[*or* [A.B.] (*address*)
[*or* Prisoner in the Prison of (*place*)]]

PETITIONER

HUMBLY SHEWETH:

1. That the petitioner [*or* [C.D.]] [, along with (*name(s) of co-accused*),] on (*date*) in the sheriff court at (*place*) was committed to prison till liberated in due course of law on a petition at the instance of the Procurator Fiscal [*or* the petitioner] in that court charging the petitioner [*or* [C.D.]] with the crime of (*specify*).

2. That no indictment has been served on the petitioner [*or* [C.D.]] in respect of the said crime and that accordingly the court in which any trial of the petitioner [*or* [C.D.]] in respect of the crime for which he stands committed is not yet known.

3. That (*name of witness*) residing at (*address*) is a witness whose evidence the petitioner intends to adduce in the course of the trial.

4. That the evidence to the effect specified in the schedule attached to this petition which it is averred that the said witness is able to give is necessary for the proper adjudication of the trial.

5. That there would be no unfairness to the prosecutor [*or as the case may be*] if such evidence were to be received in the form of the record of an examination conducted by virtue of section 272(1)(a) of the Criminal Procedure (Scotland) Act 1995.

6. That (*name of court*) is a court or tribunal exercising jurisdiction in the country or territory of (*specify*) in which the said witness resides being a country or territory outside the United Kingdom, Channel Islands or Isle of Man.

7. That English is [not] the official language or one of the official languages of the said country or territory.

MAY IT THEREFORE please your Lordships:

   (1) to appoint intimation of this petition and schedule to be made to (*specify*);

   (2) to appoint parties to be heard on the petition on the earliest practicable date hereafter; and

   (3) thereafter, on being duly satisfied in terms of section 272(3) of the Criminal Procedure (Scotland) Act 1995, to issue a letter of request to (*state judge or tribunal within whose jurisdiction the witness is resident*) to take the evidence of the said witness; and to do further or otherwise as to your Lordships shall seem proper.

ACCORDING TO JUSTICE, etc.

(*Signed*)
[Solicitor for petitioner]

(*Address and telephone number of solicitor*)

FORM 23.1–B   Rule 23.1(1)(b)

Form of petition for issue of letter of request where indictment served or in summary proceedings

UNTO THE RIGHT HONOURABLE THE LORD JUSTICE GENERAL, LORD JUSTICE-CLERK AND LORDS COMMISSIONERS OF JUSTICIARY

[*or* UNTO THE HONOURABLE THE SHERIFF OF (*name of sheriffdom*) AT (*place*)]

PETITION

of

HER MAJESTY'S ADVOCATE [*or* THE PROCURATOR FISCAL, (*place*)]

[*or* [A.B.] (*address*)
[*or* Prisoner in the Prison of (*place*)]]

PETITIONER

HUMBLY SHEWETH:

1. That the petitioner [*or* [C.D.]] [, along with (*name(s) of co-accused*),] has been indicted [*or* charged] in your Lordships' [*or* Lordship's] court at the instance of Her Majesty's Advocate [*or* the petitioner] with the crime of (*specify*) [*or* on a summary complaint at the instance of the procurator fiscal [*or* the petitioner] with the crime [*or* offence] of (*specify*)].

2. That the trial of the petitioner [*or* [C.D.]] is to take place in your Lordships' [*or* Lordship's] court [sitting at (*place*)] on (*date*).

3. That (*name of witness*) residing at (*address*) in the country or territory of (*specify*) is a witness whose evidence the petitioner intends to adduce in the course of the trial.

4. That the evidence to the effect specified in the schedule attached to this petition, which it is averred that the said witness is able to give, is necessary for the proper adjudication of the trial.

5. That there would be no unfairness to the prosecutor [*or as the case may be*] if such evidence were to be received in the form of the record of an examination conducted by virtue of section 272(1)(a) of the Criminal Procedure (Scotland) Act 1995.

6. That (*name of court*) is a court or tribunal exercising jurisdiction in the said country or territory of (*specify*) being a country or territory outside the United Kingdom, Channel Islands or Isle of Man.

7. That English is [not] the official language or one of the official languages of the said country or territory.

MAY IT THEREFORE please your Lordship[s]:

    (1) to appoint intimation of this petition and schedule to be made to (*specify*);

    (2) to appoint parties to be heard thereon on the earliest practicable date hereafter; and

    (3) thereafter, on being duly satisfied in terms of section 272(3) of the Criminal Procedure (Scotland) Act 1995, to issue a letter of request to (*state judge or tribunal within whose jurisdiction the witness is resident*) to take the evidence of the said witness; and to do further or otherwise as to your Lordship[s] shall seem proper.

ACCORDING TO JUSTICE, etc.

(*Signed*)
[Solicitor for petitioner]

(*Address and telephone number of solicitor*)

FORM 23.1–C   Rule 23.1(2)

Form of letter of request

LETTER OF REQUEST

(Items to be included in all letters of request)

1. Sender   .... *(identity and address)*
                                                ....
                                                ....

2. Central authority of the requested   .... *(identity and address)*
    State   ....
                                                ....

3. Person to whom the executed   .... *(identity and address)*
    request is to be returned   ....
                                                ....

4. The undersigned applicant has the   .... *(identity and address)*
    honour to submit the following   ....
    request: ....
    (a) Requesting judicial authority   .... *(the requested State)*
    (b) To the competent authority   ....
                                                ....

5. Names and addresses of the parties   ....
    and their representatives: ....
    (a) Prosecutor   ....
    (b) Accused   ....
                                                ....
                                                ....

6. Nature and purpose of the pro-   ....
    ceedings and summary of the facts   ....
                                                ....

7. Evidence to be obtained or other   ....
    judicial act to be performed   ....
                                                ....

(Items to be completed where applicable)

8. Identity and address of any person   ....
    to be examined   ....
                                                ....

9. Questions to be put to the persons   .... *(or see attached list)* ....
    to be examined or statement of the   ....
    subject-matter about which they   ....
    are to be examined

10. Documents or other property to be   *(specify whether it is to be produced, copied, valued,*
    inspected   *etc.)* ....
                                                ....
                                                ....
                                                ....

11. Any requirement that the evidence   *(in the event that the evidence cannot be taken in the*
    be given on oath or affirmation and   *manner requested, specify whether it is to be taken in*
    any special form to be used   *such manner as provided by local law for the formal*
                                                taking of evidence) ....
                                                ....
                                                ....

12. Special methods or procedure to be   ....
    followed   ....
                                           ....

13. Request for notification of time   ....
    and place for the execution of the   ....
    request and identity and address of   ....
    any person to be notified

14. Request for attendance or partici-   ....
    pation of judicial personnel of the   ....
    requesting authority at the   ....
    execution of the letter of request

15. Specification of privilege or duty to ....
    refuse to give evidence under the   ....
    law of the State of origin   ....

16. The fees and costs incurred will be   .... (*identity and address*)
    borne by   ....
                                          ....

(Items to be included in all letters of request)

17. Date of request   ....
                                          ....
                                          ....

18. Signature and seal of the request-   ....
    ing authority   ....
                                          ....

FORM 23.1–D   Rule 23.1(3)

**Form of petition for issue of letter of request under section 273(2) of the Criminal
Procedure (Scotland) Act 1995**

*UNTO THE RIGHT HONOURABLE THE LORD JUSTICE GENERAL, LORD
JUSTICE-CLERK AND LORDS COMMISSIONERS OF JUSTICIARY*

[*or* UNTO THE HONOURABLE THE SHERIFF OF (*name of sheriffdom*)
AT (*place*)]

PETITION

of

HER MAJESTY'S ADVOCATE
[*or* [A.B.] (*address*)
[*or* Prisoner in the Prison of (*place*)]]

PETITIONER

HUMBLY SHEWETH:

1. That the petitioner [*or* [C.D.]] [, along with (*name(s) of co-accused*),] has appeared on
petition [*or* been indicted] [*or* charged] in your Lordships' [*or* Lordship's] court at the instance
of Her Majesty's Advocate [*or* the procurator fiscal at (*place*)][*or* the petitioner] with the crime
of (*specify*).

2. That no indictment has been served on the petitioner [*or* [C.D.]] in respect of the said crime and that accordingly the court in which any trial of the petitioner [*or* [C.D.]] in respect of the said crime for which he stands committed is not yet known. [*or* That the trial of the petitioner [*or* [C.D.]] is to take place in your Lordships' [*or* Lordship's] court [sitting at (*place*)] on (*date*).]

3. That (*name of witness*) residing at (*address*) in the country or territory of (*specify*) is a witness whose evidence the petitioner intends to adduce in the course of the trial. He seeks to adduce that evidence through a live television link in that country or territory under section 273 of the Criminal Procedure (Scotland) Act 1995.

4. That the evidence to the effect specified in the schedule attached to this petition, which it is averred that the said witness is able to give, is necessary for the proper adjudication of the trial.

5. That (*name of court*) is a court or tribunal exercising jurisdiction in the said country or territory of (*specify*) being a country or territory outside the United Kingdom.

6. That English is [not] the official language or one of the official languages of the said country or territory.

[7. That there would be no unfairness to the accused if such evidence were to be given through a live television link.]

MAY IT THEREFORE please your Lordship[s]:

    (1) to appoint intimation of this petition and schedule to be made to (*specify*);

    (2) to appoint parties to be heard thereupon on the earliest practicable date hereafter; and

    (3) thereafter, on being duly satisfied in terms of section 273(3) of the Criminal Procedure (Scotland) Act 1995, to issue a letter of request to (*state judge or tribunal within whose jurisdiction the witness is resident*) for assistance in facilitating the giving of evidence by the said witness through a live television link; and to do otherwise as to your Lordship[s] shall seem proper.

ACCORDING TO JUSTICE, etc.

(*Signed*)
[Solicitor for petitioner]

(*Address and telephone number of solicitor*)

FORM 23.1–E   Rule 23.1(3)

Form of letter of request for evidence to be obtained by television link

IN THE HIGH COURT OF JUSTICIARY

[*or* IN THE SHERIFF COURT OF (*name of sheriffdom*)
AT (*place*)]

LETTER OF REQUEST

in the Indictment [*or*
Petition *or* Complaint]

at the instance of
THE RIGHT HONOURABLE [A.B.],
HER MAJESTY'S ADVOCATE
[*or* PROCURATOR FISCAL]

for the Public Interest

against

[C.D.] (*address*)
[*or* Prisoner in the Prison of (*place*)]

The Honourable Lord (*name*), one of the Lords Commissioners of Justiciary, [*or* (*name*), Sheriff of (*name of sheriffdom*) at (*place*)] presents his compliments to (*here specify the court, tribunal or authority to which the request is addressed*) and has the honour of informing it of the following facts:

1. The High Court of Justiciary, of which the Honourable Lord (*name*) is one of the judges, is the supreme criminal court in Scotland and exercises a jurisdiction as a trial court [*or* The Sheriff Court of which Sheriff (*name*) is one of the judges, is a criminal court in Scotland which exercises jurisdiction as a trial court and in pre-trial procedures in all prosecutions for crime].

2. (*Specify briefly the applicant's part in the proceedings including, where appropriate, his relationship to the investigating agency.*)

3. Criminal proceedings have been instituted before the High Court of Justiciary at the instance of the Right Honourable [A.B.], Her Majesty's Advocate, [*or*, before the Sheriff Court of (*name sheriffdom*) at (*place*), at the instance of [A.B.], Procurator Fiscal,] against [C.D.] (*specify the nationality of the accused*) who is presently charged that (*here narrate the charge on the indictment, petition or complaint*). [*In a case where the accused has appeared on petition but has not yet been indicted, insert the following if it is known in which court the case will be indicted:*—It is expected that in due course the trial of [C.D.] will take place in the High Court of Justiciary [*or* the Sheriff Court of (*name of sheriffdom*)] at (*place*).]

4. The crime of (*specify the nomen juris of the crime charged or under investigation*) is a criminal offence at common law in Scotland and is not contained in any statute. It consists of (*summarise the essential elements of the crime*) [*or* It is a criminal offence under (*narrate statutory provision and its terms and add any explanation beyond the bare words of the statute thought necessary in order to enable the foreign court, tribunal or authority to understand clearly the elements of the crime*)]. The penalties for conviction are (*specify*).

5. It has been shown to the Honourable Lord (*name*) on application by Her Majesty's Advocate [*or* [C.D.]] [*or* It has been shown to the Sheriff of (*name of sheriffdom*) at (*place*) on application by the procurator fiscal [*or* [C.D.]]], a copy of which is annexed to this request, that it is necessary for the proper adjudication of the trial that the evidence of (*name and address of witness*) be given through a live television link.

6. The Criminal Procedure (Scotland) Act 1995 empowers the High Court of Justiciary [*or* the Sheriff Court] to request your assistance in facilitating the giving of that evidence by (*name of witness*) who resides within your jurisdiction through a live television link.

7. [*Here specify arrangements to be made and name, address and telephone number of clerk of court with whom arrangements are to be made.*]

[8.] In thanking (*specify the court, tribunal or authority to which the request is addressed*) in advance for its co-operation in this case, the Honourable Lord (*name*) [*or* Sheriff (*name*)] avails himself [*or* herself] of this opportunity to renew the assurance of his [*or* her] high consideration.

(*Signed*)
Lord Commissioner of Justiciary
[*or* Sheriff of (*name of sheriffdom*) at (*place*)]

Dated this (*date*).

FORM 24.1–A   Rule 24.1(1)(a)

Form of petition for appointment of commissioner to examine a witness in High Court before indictment served

UNTO THE RIGHT HONOURABLE THE LORD JUSTICE GENERAL, LORD JUSTICE-CLERK AND LORDS COMMISSIONERS OF JUSTICIARY

PETITION

of

HER MAJESTY'S ADVOCATE
[*or* [A.B.] (*address*)
[*or* Prisoner in the Prison of (*place*)]]

PETITIONER

HUMBLY SHEWETH:

1. That the petitioner [*or* [C.D.]] [, along with (*name(s) of co-accused*),] on (*date*) in the sheriff court at (*place*) was committed to prison till liberated in due course of law on a petition at the instance of the procurator fiscal [*or* the petitioner] in the said court charging the petitioner with the crime of (*specify*).

2. That no indictment has been served on the petitioner [*or* [C.D.]] in respect of the said crime and that accordingly the court in which any trial of the petitioner [*or* [C.D.]] in respect of the crime for which he stands committed is not yet known.

3. That (*name of witness*) residing at (*address*) is a witness whose evidence the petitioner intends to adduce in the course of the trial. The witness is unable to attend the trial diet by reason of being ill [*or* infirm] as appears from the medical certificate produced with this petition [*or* the witness is not ordinarily resident, and is, at the time of the trial diet, unlikely to be present, in the United Kingdom, Channel Islands or Isle of Man].

4. That the evidence to the effect specified in the schedule attached to this petition, which it is averred that the said witness is able to give, is necessary for the proper adjudication of the trial.

5. That there would be no unfairness to the prosecutor [*or as the case may be*] if such evidence were to be received in the form of the record of an examination conducted by virtue of section 272(1)(b) of the Criminal Procedure (Scotland) Act 1995.

MAY IT THEREFORE please your Lordships—

    (1) to appoint intimation of this petition and schedule to be made to (*specify*);

    (2) to appoint parties to be heard on the petition on the earliest practicable date hereafter; and

    (3) thereafter, on being duly satisfied in terms of section 272(3) of the Criminal Procedure (Scotland) Act 1995, to appoint (*name of proposed commissioner*) or such other person as your Lordships shall think fit to be a commissioner to take evidence of the said witness within the United Kingdom, Channel Islands or Isle of Man and to report to your Lordships *quam primum*; and to do further or otherwise as to your Lordships shall seem proper.

ACCORDING TO JUSTICE, etc.

(*Signed*)
[Solicitor for petitioner]

(*Address and telephone number of solicitor*)

FORM 24.1–B   Rule 24.1(1)(b)

Form of petition for appointment of commissioner to examine a witness where indictment served or in summary proceedings

UNTO THE RIGHT HONOURABLE THE LORD JUSTICE GENERAL, LORD JUSTICE-CLERK AND LORDS COMMISSIONERS OF JUSTICIARY

[*or* UNTO THE HONOURABLE THE SHERIFF OF (*name of sheriffdom*)
AT (*place*)]

PETITION

of

HER MAJESTY'S ADVOCATE [*or* THE PROCURATOR FISCAL, (*place*)]

[*or* [A.B.] (*address*)
[*or* Prisoner in the Prison of (*place*)]]

PETITIONER

HUMBLY SHEWETH:

1. That the petitioner [*or* [C.D.]] [, along with (*name(s) of co-accused*),] has been indicted [*or* charged] in your Lordships' [*or* Lordship's] Court at the instance of Her Majesty's Advocate [*or* the petitioner] with the crime of (*specify*) [*or* on a summary complaint at the instance of the procurator fiscal [*or* the petitioner] with the crime [*or* offence] of (*specify*)].

2. That the trial of the petitioner [*or* [C.D.]] is to take place in your Lordships' [*or* Lordship's] court [sitting at (*place*)] on (*date*).

3. That (*name of witness*) residing at (*address*) is a witness whose evidence the petitioner intends to adduce in the course of the trial. The witness is unable to attend the trial diet by reason of being ill [*or* infirm] as appears from the medical certificate produced with this petition [*or* the witness is not ordinarily resident, and is, at the time of the trial diet, unlikely to be present, in the United Kingdom, Channel Islands or Isle of Man].

4. That the evidence to the effect specified in the schedule attached to this petition, which it is averred that the witness is able to give, is necessary for the proper adjudication of the trial.

5. That there would be no unfairness to the prosecutor [*or as the case may be*] if such evidence were to be received in the form of the record of an examination conducted by virtue of section 272(1)(b) of the Criminal Procedure (Scotland) Act 1995.

MAY IT THEREFORE please your Lordship[s]—

   (1) to appoint intimation of this petition and schedule to be made to (*specify*);

   (2) to appoint parties to be heard on the petition on the earliest practicable date hereafter; and

   (3) thereafter, on being duly satisfied in terms of section 272(3) of the Criminal Procedure (Scotland) Act 1995, to appoint (*name of proposed commissioner*) or such other person as your Lordship[s] shall think fit to be a commissioner to take the evidence of the said witness within the United Kingdom, Channel Islands or Isle of Man and to report to your Lordship[s] *quam primum*; and to do further or otherwise as to your Lordship[s] shall seem proper.

ACCORDING TO JUSTICE, etc.

(*Signed*)
[Solicitor for petitioner]

(*Address and telephone number of solicitor*)

FORM 26.1–A   Rule 26.1(1)(b)

Form of certificate of authentication of document

I, (*insert name, address and title of office held*), being
    the author
    [*or* the person in [*or* who was on (*date*) in] possession and control]
    [*or* the authorised representative of (*name and address*) who [*or* which] is in [*or* who [*or* which] was on (*date*) in] possession and control]
of
    the original(s)
    [*or* a copy [*or* copies] of the original(s)]
    [*or* a copy [*or* copies] of a material part [*or* material parts] of the original(s)]
of the copy document [*or* documents listed and described below] on which this certificate is endorsed [*or* to which this certificate is attached]
hereby certify that
    it is a true copy
    [*or* they are true copies]
of [*or* part(s) of]
    the original(s)
    [*or* the copy [*or* copies] of the original(s)]
    [*or* the copy [*or* copies] of the material part [*or* material parts] of the original(s)]
[of] which
    I am the author
    [*or* is [*or* are] [*or* was] [*or* were] in my possession and control]
    [*or* is [*or* are] [*or* was] [*or* were] in the possession and control of (*name and address*) of whom [*or* which] I am the authorised representative.]

                                      (*Signed*)
                                      (*Add authorised capacity in which certificate signed*)

Date: (*insert date*)

[*List and describe documents*]

¹FORM 26.1–B   Rule 26.1(2)

Form of docquet certifying a document as one kept by a business or undertaking

I, (*insert name and title of office held*), hereby certify that this document [*or* the documents listed and described below and to which this certificate is attached] is [*or* are] [*or* was] [*or* were] a document [*or* documents] kept by a business [*or* undertaking] [*or* by or on behalf of the holder of a paid [*or* unpaid] office], namely (*insert name and address of business, undertaking or office*).

                                      (*Signed*)
                                      (*Add authorised capacity in which certificate signed*)

Date: (*insert date*)

[*List and describe documents*]

NOTE
¹As amended by S.I. 1996 No. 2147.

¹**FORM 26.1–C**   Rule 26.1(3)

Form of certificate that statement not contained in business document

I, (*insert name and title of office held*), being a person authorised to give evidence on behalf of (*insert name and address of business or undertaking, or body of which the signatory is an officeholder*), hereby state that (*name and describe document*) being a document [*or that no document within the category of documents of* (*name and describe category*) *being documents*] in respect of which the conditions (*specified in paragraph 2(1)(a) and (b) of Schedule 8 to the Criminal Procedure (Scotland) Act 1995*) are satisfied does not contain [*or, where no documents within a category of documents satisfying those conditions contains such a statement, contains*] (*specify the relevant statement as to the particular matter not contained in the documents*).

> (*Signed*)
> (*Add authorised capacity in which certificate signed*)

Date: (*insert date*)

NOTE
¹As amended by Act of Adjournal (Criminal Procedure Rules Amendment No. 3) (S.I. 1997 No. 1788) (effective August 11, 1997).

FORM 27.2   Rule 27.2

Form of certificate under section 283(1), 284(1) or 285(2), (4) or (5) of the Criminal Procedure (Scotland) Act 1995

I, (*insert name, designation and capacity in which the certificate is given*), being a person who may sign a certificate under section 283(1) [*or* 284(1) *or* 285(2), (4) or (5)] of the Criminal Procedure (Scotland) Act 1995,

HEREBY CERTIFY THAT (*here insert the matter which is being certified and specify enactment in respect of which the evidence is given*).

[If a notice is not served by you, under section 283(2) [*or* 284(2)] not more than seven days after the date of service of this certificate, the evidence contained in this certificate shall be sufficient evidence of the facts contained in the certificate.]

> (*Signed*)

(*Date*)

FORM 27.3   Rule 27.3

Form of notice in relation to certain evidential certificates

IN THE HIGH COURT OF JUSTICIARY
[*or* IN THE SHERIFF [*or* DISTRICT] COURT]

AT (*place*)

NOTICE

by

[A.B.] (*address*) [*or* Prisoner in the Prison of (*place*)]

under section (*specify*)

of the Criminal Procedure (Scotland) Act 1995

To: (*name of person to whom notice sent*)

I HEREBY GIVE NOTICE under section (*specify*) that I [*or* [A.B.]] do [*or* does] not accept the evidence contained in the certificate under section (*specify*).

(*Signed*)
[A.B.]
[*or* Solicitor for [A.B.]]

(*Address and telephone number of Solicitor*)

¹**FORM 27.4**   Rule 27.4

Form of notice under section 16A(4) of the Criminal Law (Consolidation) (Scotland) Act 1995

IN THE HIGH COURT OF JUSTICIARY [*or* IN THE SHERIFF COURT]

AT (*place*)

NOTICE

by

[A.B.] (*address*) [or Prisoner in the Prison of (*place*)]

under

Section 16A(4) of the Criminal Law (Consolidation) (Scotland) Act 1995

To: (*name of prosecutor, or co-accused*)

I HEREBY GIVE NOTICE that under section 16A(4) of the Criminal Law (Consolidation) (Scotland) Act 1995 that on the facts as alleged with respect to the relevant conduct, the condition in section 16A(3)(r) [*or* (b)] of the Criminal Law (Consolidation) (Scotland) Act 1995 is not satisfied for the following reasons:—

(*here set out reasons for regarding condition as unsatisfied*)

I HEREBY REQUIRE (*insert name and designation of prosecutor*) to prove that the said condition is satisfied.

(*Signed*)
[A.B.]
[*or* Solicitor for [A.B.]]
(*Address and telephone number of Solicitor*)

NOTE
¹As added by the Act of Adjournal (Criminal Procedure Rules Amendment) 1997 (No. 63).

¹**FORM 27.5**

Form of notice under section 16B(4) of the Criminal Law (Consolidation) (Scotland) Act 1995

[IN THE HIGH COURT OF JUSTICIARY]

[IN THE SHERIFF COURT]

AT (*place*)

NOTICE

by

[A.B.] (*address*) [*or* prisoner in the Prison of (*place*)]

under

Section 16B(4) of the Criminal Law (Consolidation) (Scotland) Act 1995

To: (*name of prosecutor or co-accused*)

I HEREBY GIVE NOTICE under subsection (4) of section 16B of the Criminal Law (Consolidation) (Scotland) Act 1995 that on the facts as alleged with respect to the act described in the charge against me, the condition in subsection (1)(a) of that section is not satisfied for the following reason[s]:

(*here set out reason[s] for regarding condition as unsatisfied*)

I HEREBY REQUIRE (*insert name and designation of prosecutor*) to prove that the said condition is satisfied.

> (*Signed*)
> [A.B.]
> [*or* Solicitor for [A.B.]]
> (*Address and telephone number of Solicitor*)

NOTE
¹As inserted by Act of Adjournal (Criminal Procedure Rules Amendment No. 5) (S.I. 1997 No. 2082) (effective September 1, 1997).

FORM 28.1–A   Rule 28.1(1)(b)(i)

Form of petition for order to hold identification parade in solemn proceedings before serving of indictment under section 290(1) of the Criminal Procedure (Scotland) Act 1995

UNTO THE HONOURABLE THE SHERIFF OF (*name of sheriffdom*)

AT (*place*)

PETITION

of

[A.B.] (*address*)
[*or* Prisoner in the Prison of (*place*)]

PETITIONER

HUMBLY SHEWETH:

1. That the petitioner [, along with (*name(s) of co-accused*),] has been charged in your Lordship's court at (*place*) on a petition at the instance of the procurator fiscal with the offence of (*specify*).

2. That the trial of the petitioner is to take place in your Lordship's court [*or* the High Court of Justiciary sitting at (*place*)] on (*date*).

3. That an identification parade in which the petitioner was one of those constituting the parade has not been held.

4. That the petitioner has requested the prosecutor to hold such a parade but he has refused to hold, or has unreasonably delayed holding, such a parade.

5. That it is reasonable in the circumstances in relation to the alleged crime [*or* offence] that such an identification parade should be held (*specify circumstances*).

MAY IT THEREFORE please your Lordship—

    (1) to appoint intimation of this petition to be made to the procurator fiscal;

    (2) to appoint parties to be heard thereon on the earliest practicable date hereafter; and

    (3) thereafter, on being duly satisfied in terms of section 290(2) of the Criminal Procedure (Scotland) Act 1995, to order the prosecutor to hold an identification parade in which the petitioner shall be one of those constituting the parade, in relation to the offence referred to above with which the petitioner has been charged.

ACCORDING TO JUSTICE, etc.

(*Signed*)
[Solicitor for petitioner]

(*Address and telephone number of solicitor*)

FORM 28.1–B   Rule 28.1(1)(b)(ii)

Form of petition for order to hold identification parade where indictment served or in summary proceedings under section 290(1) of the Criminal Procedure (Scotland) Act 1995

UNTO THE HONOURABLE THE SHERIFF OF (*name of sheriffdom*)

AT (*place*)

PETITION

of

[A.B.] (*address*)
[*or* Prisoner in the Prison of (*place*)]

PETITIONER

HUMBLY SHEWETH:

1. That the petitioner [, along with (*name(s) of co-accused*),] has been indicted [*or* charged] in your Lordship's court [*or* the High Court of Justiciary sitting at (*place*)] [*or* the District Court at (*place*)] at the instance of Her Majesty's Advocate [*or* the procurator fiscal] with the crime [*or* offence] of (*specify*).

2. That the trial of the petitioner is to take place in your Lordship's court [*or* the High Court of Justiciary sitting at (*place*)] [*or* the District Court at (*place*)] on (*date*).

3. That an identification parade in which the petitioner was one of those constituting the parade has not been held.

4. That the petitioner has requested the prosecutor to hold such a parade but he has refused to hold, or has unreasonably delayed holding, such a parade.

5. That it is reasonable in the circumstances in relation to the alleged crime [*or* offence] that such an identification parade should be held (*specify circumstances*).

MAY IT THEREFORE please your Lordship—

(1) to appoint intimation of this petition to be made to Her Majesty's Advocate [*or* the procurator fiscal];

(2) to appoint parties to be heard thereon on the earliest practicable date hereafter; and

(3) thereafter, on being duly satisfied in terms of section 290(2) of the Criminal Procedure (Scotland) Act 1995, to order the prosecutor to hold an identification parade in which the petitioner shall be one of those constituting the parade, in relation to the offence referred to above with which the petitioner has been charged.

ACCORDING TO JUSTICE, etc.

(*Signed*)
[Solicitor for petitioner]

(*Address and telephone number of solicitor*)

FORM 29.1–A   Rule 29.1(1)(b)(i)

Form of petition to take precognition on oath before service of indictment under section 291(1) of the Criminal Procedure (Scotland) Act 1995

UNTO THE HONOURABLE THE SHERIFF OF (*name of sheriffdom*)

AT (*place*)

PETITION

of

[A.B.] (*address*)
[*or* Prisoner in the Prison of (*place*)]

PETITIONER

HUMBLY SHEWETH:

1. That the petitioner [, along with (*name(s) of co-accused*),] has been charged in your Lordship's court at (*place*) on a petition at the instance of the procurator fiscal with the crime [*or* offence] of (*specify*).

2. That the trial of the petitioner is to take place in your Lordship's court [*or* the High Court of Justiciary sitting at (*place*)] on (*date*).

3. That the petitioner believes that [C.D.] residing at (*address*) is a witness in relation to the said crime [*or* offence].

4. That (*narrate all steps taken to obtain precognition from the witness and, or, the circumstances justifying the taking of the precognition on oath*).

5. That the petitioner [*or* the solicitor for the petitioner] is unable to complete his [*or* her] investigation [on behalf of the petitioner] without precognosing [C.D.].

MAY IT THEREFORE please your Lordship—

(1) to appoint intimation of this petition to be made to the procurator fiscal;

(2) to appoint parties to be heard thereon on the earliest practicable date hereafter; and

(3) thereafter, on being duly satisfied in terms of section 291(1) of the Criminal Procedure (Scotland) Act 1995, that it is reasonable to require such precognition on oath, to grant warrant to cite [C.D.] to attend for precognition on oath before your Lordship on the earliest practicable date thereafter; and to do further or otherwise as to your Lordship shall seem proper.

ACCORDING TO JUSTICE, etc.

(*Signed*)
[Solicitor for petitioner]

(*Address and telephone number of solicitor*)

FORM 29.1–B   Rule 29.1(1)(b)(ii)

Form of petition to take precognition on oath where indictment served or in summary proceedings under section 291(1) of the Criminal Procedure (Scotland) Act 1995

UNTO THE HONOURABLE THE SHERIFF OF (*name of sheriffdom*)

AT (*place*)

PETITION

of

[A.B.] (*address*)
[*or* Prisoner in the Prison of (*place*)]

HUMBLY SHEWETH:

1. That the petitioner [, along with (*name(s) of co-accused*),] has been indicted [*or* charged] in your Lordship's court [*or* the High Court of Justiciary sitting at (*place*)] [*or* the District Court at (*place*)] at the instance of Her Majesty's Advocate [*or* the procurator fiscal] with the crime [*or* offence] of (*specify*).

2. That the trial of the petitioner is to take place in your Lordship's court [*or* the High Court of Justiciary sitting at (*place*)] [*or* the District Court at (*place*)] on (*date*).

3. That the petitioner believes that [C.D.] residing at (*address*) is a witness in relation to the said crime [*or* offence] [*or* is witness no. (*state number*) on the list of witnesses attached to the indictment].

4. That (*narrate all steps taken to obtain a precognition from the witness and, or, the circumstances justifying the taking of the precognition on oath*).

5. That the petitioner [*or* the solicitor for the petitioner] is unable to complete his [*or* her] investigation [on behalf of the petitioner] without precognosing [C.D.].

MAY IT THEREFORE please your Lordship—

(1) to appoint intimation of this petition to be made to Her Majesty's Advocate [*or* the procurator fiscal];

(2) to appoint parties to be heard thereupon on the earliest practicable date hereafter; and

(3) thereafter, on being duly satisfied in terms of section 291(1) of the Criminal Procedure (Scotland) Act 1995 that it is reasonable to require such precognition on oath, to grant warrant to cite [C.D.] to attend for precognition on oath before your Lordship on the earliest practicable date thereafter; and to do further or otherwise as to your Lordship shall seem proper.

ACCORDING TO JUSTICE, etc.

(*Signed*)
[Solicitor for petitioner]

(*Address and telephone number of solicitor*)

FORM 29.3   Rule 29.3(1)

Form of citation of person to attend a diet for taking his precognition on oath

IN THE SHERIFF COURT AT (*place*)

CITATION

To: (*name and address of witness*)

Date of citation: (*date of citation or, if citation by post, the day after the date of posting*)

YOU ARE HEREBY CITED to appear on (*date*) at (*time*) in the Sheriff Court House at (*address*) in chambers to be precognosed on oath for the accused, (*name*), in relation to the offence with which he has been charged.

IF YOU DO NOT ATTEND COURT WITHOUT A REASONABLE EXCUSE THE COURT MAY ORDER THAT YOU BE APPREHENDED AND PUNISHED.

(*Signed*)
Officer of Law
[*or* Solicitor for accused]

FORM 30.2–A   Rule 30.2(1)

Form of endorsement of warrant of arrest under section 1(1) of the Backing of Warrants (Republic of Ireland) Act 1965

I, (*name*), one of Her Majesty's justices of the peace in and for the commission area of (*specify*) [*or as the case may be*] being satisfied that this warrant may be endorsed under section 1 of the Backing of Warrants (Republic of Ireland) Act 1965, hereby authorise (*name*), who brings me this warrant, and all other constables in Scotland to execute the same and to bring him as soon as practicable before a sheriff.

Given under my hand this (*date*)

(*Signed*)
Justice of the Peace [*or as the case may be*]

FORM 30.2–B Rule 30.2(2)

Form of provisional warrant of arrest under section 4 of the Backing of Warrants (Republic of Ireland) Act 1965

WHEREAS a constable, (*name*), has stated to me on oath that he has reason to believe that a warrant has been issued by a judicial authority in the Republic of Ireland for the arrest of (*name*) (hereinafter called "the accused") who is accused [*or* has been convicted] of an indictable offence against the laws of the Republic of Ireland but that the warrant is not yet in his possession; and that he has received a request made on grounds of urgency by a member of the police force of the Republic of Ireland holding the rank of inspector or above for the issue in the United Kingdom of a warrant for the arrest of the accused; and that he has reason to believe that the accused is within the county of (*specify*); [(*words to be omitted when a provisional warrant is issued for the arrest of a person not yet convicted*) and that he has reason to believe the requirements of section 1(3) of the Backing of Warrants (Republic of Ireland) Act 1965 are satisfied].

THEREFORE, I, (*name*), one of Her Majesty's justices of the peace in and for the commission area of (*specify*) [*or as the case may be*], hereby grant warrant to and authorise all constables in Scotland to apprehend the accused within five days after issue of this warrant and to bring him as soon as practicable before a sheriff.

Given under my hand this (*date*)

(*Signed*)
Justice of the Peace [*or as the case may be*]

NOTE: This warrant is not authority for the making of an arrest more than five days after its issue.

FORM 30.5 Rule 30.5(1)

Form of consent to earlier return under section 3(1)(a) of the Backing of Warrants (Republic of Ireland) Act 1965

WHEREAS on the (*date*) the Sheriff of (*name of sheriffdom*) sitting at (*place*) ordered that I, (*name*), should be delivered into the custody of a member of the police force of the Republic of Ireland;

AND WHEREAS I understand that, unless I consent to an earlier removal, I cannot be so delivered until the end of the period of 15 days beginning with the date on which the order was made;

NOW, THEREFORE, I give notice that I consent to my removal before the said period of 15 days has expired.

(*Signed*)
This form was signed by the above-named person in my presence on (*date*)

(*Signed*)
Justice of the Peace for the commission area of (*specify*) [*or as the case may be*]

FORM 31.5

Rule 31.5(2)(a)

Form of reference to the European Court

THE HIGH COURT OF JUSTICIARY
[*or* SHERIFF [*or* DISTRICT] COURT] IN SCOTLAND
HER MAJESTY'S ADVOCATE [*or* THE PROCURATOR FISCAL]

against

[C.D.] (*address*)

[*or* Prisoner in the Prison of (*place*)]

[*Here set out a clear and succinct statement of the case giving rise to the request for the ruling of the European Court in order to enable the European Court to consider and understand the issues of Community law raised and to enable governments of Member States and other interested parties to submit observations. The statement of the case should include:*
  (a) *particulars of the parties;*
  (b) *the history of the dispute between the parties;*
  (c) *the history of the proceedings;*
  (d) *the relevant facts as agreed by the parties or found by the court or, failing such agreement or finding, the contentions of the parties on such facts;*
  (e) *the nature of the issues of law and fact between the parties;*
  (f) *the Scots law, so far as is relevant;*
  (g) *the Treaty provisions or other acts, instruments or rules of Community law concerned; and*
  (h) *an explanation of why the reference is being made.*]

The preliminary ruling of the Court of Justice of the European Communities is accordingly requested on the following questions:
1, 2, etc. [*Here set out the questions on which the ruling is sought, identifying the Treaty provisions or other acts, instruments or rules of Community law concerned.*]

Dated the   day of   19 .

NOTE
[1] Substituted by the Act of Adjournal (Criminal Procedure Rules Amendment No. 2) 1999 (S.I. 1999 No. 1282), para. 2(4) and Sched. 1 (effective May 1, 1999).

FORM 31.7

Rule 31.7(3)

Form of appeal to High Court from the making of a reference to the European Court of Justice

NOTE OF APPEAL

by

[C.D.]

APPELLANT

in

HER MAJESTY'S ADVOCATE [*or* THE PROCURATOR FISCAL, (*place*)]

against

[C.D.] (*address*)

[*or* Prisoner in the Prison of (*place*)]

1. The appellant appeals to the High Court of Justiciary sitting as a court of appeal against the order of (*name of judge*) in the High Court of Justiciary sitting at (*place*) [*or* the sheriff [*or* district] court at (*place*)] on (*date*).

2. The appellant appeals against the order on the following grounds:—

(*here set out the grounds of appeal*).

IN RESPECT WHEREOF

(*Signed*)
[Solicitor for appellant]

(*Address and telephone number of solicitor*)

(*Date*)

FORM 32.2   Rule 32.2(1)

Form of application under section 49 of the Civic Government (Scotland) Act 1982

IN THE DISTRICT COURT OF (*place*)

APPLICATION

under

section 49(2) and (3) Civic Government (Scotland) Act 1982

by

[A.B.] (*address*)

COMPLAINER

against

[C.D.] (*address*)

RESPONDENT

HUMBLY SHEWETH:

1. That the complainer is resident at (*address*).

2. That the respondent occupies premises at (*specify address or place*) being in the vicinity of (*specify complainer's address*).

3. That at those premises [C.D.] keeps (*here identify the creature and describe the circumstances in which the creature is kept*).

4. (*Here describe in detail in one or more paragraphs the circumstances in which it is alleged the creature is causing annoyance.*)

MAY IT THEREFORE please the court to order service of a copy of this application on the said [C.D.]; to fix a date for the hearing of this application no earlier than 14 days after such service; and thereafter to make an order on [C.D.] to take within such period as may be specified in the order such steps (short of destruction of the creature) as may be so specified to prevent the continuation of the annoyance.

IN RESPECT WHEREOF

(*Signed*)
[Solicitor for complainer]

(*Address and telephone number of solicitor*)

FORM 34.5   Rule 34.5(1)

Notice of waiver and consent under setion 14 of, or paragraph 9 of Schedule 1 to, the Extradition Act 1989

WHEREAS on (*date*), the Sheriff of Lothian and Borders sitting at (*place*) ordered that I, (*name*), be committed to await the Secretary of State's decision as to my return to (*name of foreign state, Commonwealth country or United Kingdom dependencey*) which has requested my extradition;

AND WHEREAS I understand that I have the right—

(a)   to apply for a review of the order of committal; and

(b)   not to be returned in any case until the expiry of the period of 15 days beginning with the date on which the order was made and, if I apply for a review of the order of committal, for so long as proceedings on that application are pending:

NOW, THEREFORE, I give notice:—

1.   That I waive my right to make an application for a review of the order of committal.

*2.   That I consent to my earlier return before the said period of 15 days has expired.

(*Signed*)

This form was signed by the above-named person in my presence on (*date*).

(*Signed*)
Sheriff [*or* sheriff clerk *or* justice of the peace *or* solicitor]

Delete if consent is not given.

FORM 36.4–A   Rule 36.4(a)

Form of application for letter of request under section 3(1) of the Criminal Justice (International Co-operation) Act 1990

UNTO THE RIGHT HONOURABLE THE LORD JUSTICE GENERAL, LORD JUSTICE-CLERK AND LORDS COMMISSIONERS OF JUSTICIARY

[*or* UNTO THE HONOURABLE THE SHERIFF OF (*name of sheriffdom*)

AT (*place*)

PETITION

of

THE RIGHT HONOURABLE [A.B.],
HER MAJESTY'S ADVOCATE
[*or* THE PROCURATOR FISCAL]
for the Public Interest [*or* [C.D.]
Accused Person]

PETITIONER

HUMBLY SHEWETH:

1. That [C.D.] born on (*specify accused's date of birth*), was on (*date*) in the sheriff court at (*place*) fully committed on a petition at the instance of the petitioner [*or as the case may be*] charging [C.D.] with (*specify the nomen juris of the charge*) as more particularly specified in the copy petition annexed to this petition. [*Insert the following if it is known in which court the case will be indicted*: It is expected that in due course the trial of [C.D.] will take place in the High Court of Justiciary [*or* the sheriff court of (*name of sheriffdom*)] sitting at (*place*).]

[*or* 1. That there are reasonable grounds for suspecting that an offence has been committed, namely, (*specify the nomen juris of or otherwise described the offence or specify the statute and section contravened*) in respect that on (*specify the date of the offence*) at (*specify the locus of the offence*) it is alleged that (*specify the modus of the offence*). Police officers [*or* Officers of Customs and Excise] acting on the instructions of the petitioner are investigating the alleged offence.]

2. That in order that justice may be done in the case against [C.D.] [*or* in order that the investigation may be completed], it is necessary that evidence be obtained from (*specify country to which the request is being sent*). The precise evidence required is (*specify*).

3. That section 3(1) and (2) of the Criminal Justice (International Co-operation) Act 1990 provides that where on an application made by a prosecuting authority or, where proceedings have been instituted, by the person charged in those proceedings, it appears to a judge or a sheriff (a) that an offence has been committed or that there are reasonable grounds for suspecting that an offence has been committed and (b) that proceedings in respect of the offence have been instituted or that the offence is being investigated, the prosecutor may issue a letter of request requesting assistance in obtaining outside the United Kingdom such evidence as is specified in the letter for use in the proceedings or investigation.

MAY IT THEREFORE please your Lordship[s] to issue a letter of request to (*specify the court, tribunal or authority to whom it is desired to have the request addressed*) to obtain the evidence specified herein; and to do further or otherwise as to your Lordship[s] shall seem proper.

ACCORDING TO JUSTICE, etc.

(*Signed*)
[Solicitor for petitioner]

(*Address and telephone number of solicitor*)

FORM 36.4–B   Rule 36.4(c)(iv)

Letter of request under section 3 of the Criminal Justice (International Co-operation) Act 1990

IN THE HIGH COURT OF JUSTICIARY

[*or* IN THE SHERIFF COURT OF (*name of sheriffdom*) AT (*place*)]

LETTER OF REQUEST

in the Indictment [*or*
Petition *or* Complaint]

at the instance of
THE RIGHT HONOURABE [A.B.],
HER MAJESTY'S ADVOCATE
[*or* THE PROCURATOR FISCAL]
for the Public Interest

against

[C.D.] (*address*)

[*or* LETTER OF REQUEST

In the Investigation into

(*here specify the crime
under investigation
eg. Murder of [E.F.]*)]

HUMBLY SHEWETH:

The Honourable Lord (*name*), one of the Lords Commissioners of Justiciary, [*or* (*name*), Sheriff of (*name of sheriffdom*) at (*place*)] presents his compliments to (*here specify the court, tribunal or authority to which the request is addressed*) and has the honour of informing it of the following facts:

1. The High Court of Justiciary, of which the Honourable Lord (*name*) is one of the judges, is the supreme criminal court in Scotland and exercises a jurisdiction as a trial court [*or* The Sheriff Court of which Sheriff (*name*) is one of the judges, is a criminal court in Scotland which exercises jurisdiction as a trial court and in pre-trial procedures in all prosecutions for crime].

2. (*Specify briefly the applicant's part in the proceedings including, where appropriate, his relationship to the investigating agency.*)

3. Criminal proceedings have been instituted before the High Court of Justiciary at the instance of the Right Honourable [A.B.], Her Majesty's Advocate, [*or*, before the Sheriff Court of (*name of sheriffdom*) at (*place*), at the instance of [A.B.], Procurator Fiscal,] against [C.D.] (*specify the nationality of the accused*) who is presently charged that (*here narrate the charge on the indictment, petition or complaint*). [*In a case where the accused has appeared on petition but has not yet been indicted, insert the following if it is known in which court the case will be indicted:*—It is expected that in due course the trial of [C.D.] will take place in the High Court of Justiciary [*or*, the Sheriff Court of (*name of sheriffdom*)] at (*place*).]

[*or* 3. There are reasonable grounds for suspecting that an offence has been committed, namely (*specify the nomen juris of or otherwise describe the offence or specify the statute and section contravened*) in respect that on (*specify the date of the offence*) at (*specify the locus of the offence*) it is alleged that (*specify the modus of the offence*). Police officers [*or* Officers of Customs and Excise] acting on the instructions of the procurator fiscal are investigating the alleged offence.]

4. The crime of (*specify the nomen juris of the crime charged or under investigation*) is a criminal offence at common law in Scotland and is not contained in any statute. It consists of (*summarise the essential elements of the crime*) [*or* It is a criminal offence under (*narrate statutory provision and its terms and add any explanation beyond the bare words of the statute thought necessary in order to enable the foreign court, tribunal or authority to understand clearly the elements of the crime*)]. The penalties for conviction are (*specify*).

[*Where relevant, insert:*— [5.] A person may be convicted of an attempt at crime where he has taken an overt step in pursuance of his criminal intention and has passed from the stage of preparation to the stage of perpetration but has not completed the crime. Paragraph 10 of Schedule 3 to the Criminal Procedure (Scotland) Act 1995 provides:—

> "(1) Under an indictment or, as the case may be, a complaint which charges a completed offence, the accused may be lawfully convicted of an attempt to commit the offence.
>
> (2) Under an indictment or complaint charging an attempt, the accused may be convicted of such attempt although the evidence is sufficient to prove the completion of the offence said to have been attempted.
>
> (3) Under an indictment or complaint which charges an offence involving personal injury inflicted by the accused, resulting in death or serious injury to the person, the accused may be lawfully convicted of the assault or other injurious act, and may also be lawfully convicted of the aggravation that the assault or other injurious act was committed with intent to commit such offence."

[*Where relevant, insert:*—The Law of Scotland makes no distinction between commission and accession, and by the common law of Scotland anyone who gives assistance to or otherwise acts in previous concert with the principal or who is guilty of concert, assistance or participation in the crime is liable to be convicted of the crime.]]

[6.] It has been shown to the Honourable Lord (*name*) on application by Her Majesty's Advocate [*or* [C.D.]] [*or*, it has been shown to the Sheriff of (*name of sheriffdom*) at (*place*) on application by the procurator fiscal [*or* [C.D.]]], a copy of which is annexed to this request, that in order that justice may be done in the proceedings [*or*, in order that the investigation may be completed] it is necessary that evidence be obtained from (*specify country to which the request is being sent*).

[7.] The circumstances giving rise to this request are as follows:—(*narrate fully such evidence as is known which has relevance to the request so that the foreign court, tribunal or authority will have a clear understanding of the subject-matter of the case and the need for the evidence they are requested to obtain*).

[8.] The Criminal Justice (International Co-operation) Act 1990 empowers the High Court of Justiciary [*or* the Sheriff Court] to seek from and to give to courts, tribunals and other authorities exercising criminal jurisdiction in countries or territories outside the United Kingdom reciprocal assistance in the obtaining of evidence and it is requested in the present case that (*specify the court, tribunal or authority to which the request is addressed*) give assistance in the obtaining of the evidence herein specified. In particular, it is requested that (*specify the assistance requested, whether that is by the interview of witnesses, recovery of documents or other articles, search of premises, issue of extracts or otherwise. If witnesses are to be interviewed, identify them clearly and state nationality if known. If relevant, state any privilege which the witness might be able to claim and provide for the witness to claim that privilege under interview but to be required to answer the question nevertheless, leaving the application of that privilege and the admissibility of the answers given for the determination of the trial court. Specify the subject-matter of the questions to be put or formulate questions as appropriate; also specify any special procedures desired to be followed (for example, It is desired that, where competent, a witness be interviewed on oath). Where it is sought to recover documents or other articles specify precisely what is sought and identify the holder of the documents and other articles. State any request for parties or their agents or counsel to be present at the execution of the request and state any other request made. Schedules may be used.*)

[9.] [*Here narrate any time limit to which the case is subject and, if appropriate, insert:* In view of the foregoing it is respectfully requested that this request be treated as urgent.]

[10.] Any evidence provided in response to this letter of request will not, without the consent of the appropriate authority in (*name the country*), be used for any purpose other than the said proceedings [*or* the said investigation and any criminal proceedings arising out of it].

[11.] In thanking (*specify the court, tribunal or authority to which the request is addressed*) in advance for its co-operation in this case, the Honourable Lord (*name*) [*or* Sheriff (*name*)] avails himself [*or* herself] of this opportunity to renew the assurance of his [*or* her] high consideration.

> (*Signed*)
> Lord Commissioner of Justiciary
> [*or* Sheriff of (*name of sheriffdom*) at
> (*place*)]

Dated this (*date*).

Rule 37.4   ¹**FORM 37.4**

Form of petition under section 25 or 26 of the Proceeds of Crime (Scotland) Act 1995

UNTO THE RIGHT HONOURABLE THE LORD JUSTICE GENERAL, THE LORD
JUSTICE-CLERK and LORDS COMMISSIONERS OF JUSTICIARY

[*or* UNTO THE HONOURABLE THE SHERIFF OF (*name of sheriffdom*)

AT (*place*)]

PETITION

of

[A.B.] (*address*)

PETITIONER

HUMBLY SHEWETH:

1. That the Petitioner is (*name*) and resides at (*address*).

2. That on (*date*) the court in the case of Her Majesty's Advocate [*or* Procurator Fiscal] against (*name and address*) made an order under section 21 of the Proceeds of Crime (Scotland) Act 1995 forfeiting (*specify property and, for heritable property in Scotland, state conveyancing description (unless already stated in suspended forfeiture order) and date and county of recording of a certified copy of the suspended forfeiture order in the General Register of Sasines or, as the case may be, the Title Number under which a certified copy of the suspended forfeiture order was registered in the Land Register of Scotland*).

3. That (*state the relevant facts in support of grant of order*).

MAY IT THEREFORE please your Lordship(s):

(1) to appoint intimation of this petition to be made to (*specify*);

(2) to appoint parties to be heard thereon on the earliest practicable date thereafter; and

(3) thereafter, on being duly satisfied in terms of section 25(1)(a) [*or* section 26(1)(a)] of the Proceeds of Crime (Scotland) Act 1995, to make an order under section 25 [*or* section 26] of that Act; and to do further or otherwise as to your Lordship(s) shall seem proper.

ACCORDING TO JUSTICE, etc.

(*Signed*)
Petitioner
[*or* Solicitor for Petitioner]

(*Address and telephone number of Solicitor*)

NOTE
¹Inserted by Act of Adjournal (Criminal Procedure Rules Amendment No. 7) (S.I. 1997 No. 7) (effective November 21, 1997).

Rule 37.5   [1]**FORM 37.5**

Form of note of appeal under section 27 of the Proceeds of Crime (Scotland) Act 1995

IN THE HIGH COURT OF JUSTICIARY

[*or* IN THE SHERIFF COURT]

AT

(*place*)

NOTE OF APPEAL

under the Proceeds of Crime (Scotland) Act 1995

by

[A.B.] (*address*)

APPELLANT

against

[C.D.] (*address*)

RESPONDENT

1. The appellant appeals to the High Court of Justiciary against the refusal of an application under section 25(1) [*or* the granting of an application under section 26(1)] of the Proceeds of Crime (Scotland) Act 1995 in the above court on (*date*).

2. The ground(s) of appeal is (are):

(*here set out the ground(s)*)

(*Signed*)
Appellant
[*or* Solicitor for appellant]

(*Address and telephone number of solicitor*)

(*Place and date*)

NOTE
[1]Inserted by Act of Adjournal (Criminal Procedure Rules Amendment No. 7) (S.I. 1997 No. 2081) (effective November 21, 1997).

Rule 37A   [1]**FORM 37A**

Form of petition to sheriff under section 7(3) of the Knives Act 1997

UNTO THE HONOURABLE THE SHERIFF OF (*name of sheriffdom*)

AT (*place*)

PETITION

of

[A.B.] (*address*)

PETITIONER

HUMBLY SHEWETH:

1. That the petitioner is (*name*) and resides at (*address*).

2. That on (*date*) the court in the case (*Procurator Fiscal*) against (*name and address*), accused, made an Order in terms of section 6 of the Knives Act 1997 forfeiting (*specify property forfeited*).

3. That (*state facts relevant to application*).

MAY IT THEREFORE please your Lordship:

(1) to appoint intimation of this petition to be made to (*specify*).

(2) to appoint parties to be heard thereon on the earliest practicable date thereafter; and

(3) thereafter, on being duly satisfied, to make an order in terms of section 7(3) of the Knives Act 1997; and to do further or otherwise as Your Lordship shall deem proper.

ACCORDING TO JUSTICE, etc.

(*Signed*)
[Solicitor for petitioner]

(*Address and telephone number of solicitor*)

NOTE
[1]Inserted by Act of Adjournal (Criminal Procedure Rules Amendment No. 6) (S.I. 1997 No. 2081) (effective September 1, 1997).

Rule 38 [1]**FORM 38**

Form of application to High Court for transfer of rights of appeal of deceased person

UNTO THE RIGHT HONOURABLE THE LORD JUSTICE GENERAL, LORD JUSTICE CLERK and LORDS COMMISSIONERS OF JUSTICIARY

APPLICATION

for

TRANSFER OF RIGHTS OF APPEAL OF DECEASED PERSON

by

[A.B.] (*address*)

APPLICANT

under

section 303A of the Criminal Procedure (Scotland) Act 1995

HUMBLY SHEWETH:—

1. That on (*date*) [C.D.] (*address*) was convicted in the High Court of Justiciary [*or* sheriff court or district court] at (*place*) of (*specify offence*) and sentenced to (*specify sentence*).

2. That [C.D.] did not institute any appeal in relation to that conviction or sentence [*or state details of any appeal instituted by* [C.D.]].

3. That [C.D.] died on (*date*) at (*place*).

4. That the applicant is executor of [C.D.] conform to attached copy confirmation [*or* has a legitimate interest (*specify nature of interest and attach supporting documents*)].

5. That the applicant has served a copy of this application on the Crown Agent.

MAY IT THEREFORE please your Lordships under section 303A of the Criminal Procedure (Scotland) Act 1995 to authorise the applicant to institute any appeal in relation to that conviction which [C.D.] could have instituted [*or* to continue the appeal instituted by [C.D.]].

ACCORDING TO JUSTICE, etc.

(*Signed*)
[Solicitor for applicant]

(*Address and telephone number of solicitor*)

NOTE
[1]Inserted by Act of Adjournal (Criminal Procedure Rules Amendment No. 4) (S.I. 1997 No. 1834) (effective August 1, 1997).

Rule 40.2(1)   **[1]FORM 40.2A**

Form of minute of notice of intention to raise a devolution issue

UNTO THE RIGHT HONOURABLE THE LORD JUSTICE GENERAL, LORD JUSTICE-CLERK AND LORDS COMMISSIONERS OF JUSTICIARY

[UNTO THE HONOURABLE THE SHERIFF OF (*name of sheriffdom*)

AT (*place*)]

MINUTE

by

[A.B.] (*address*)

[*or* Prisoner in the Prison of (*place*)]

HUMBLY SHEWETH:

1. That [*name of accused*] has been indicted at the instance of Her Majesty's Advocate for trial in the High Court of Justiciary sitting at (*place*) on (*date*) [*or* sheriff court at (*place*) on (*date*) with a first diet on (*date*)].

2. That [A.B.] intends to raise a devolution issue within the meaning of Schedule 6 to the Scotland Act 1998/Schedule 10 to the Northern Ireland Act 1998/Schedule 8 to the Government of Wales Act 1998 on the following grounds (*here specify the facts and circumstances and contentions of law which are alleged to give rise to the devolution issue*).

3. That a copy of this minute has been duly intimated to Her Majesty's Advocate [and to (*name(s) of co-accused*)] and to the relevant authority within the meaning of Rule 40.1 conform to execution[s] attached to this minute.

MAY IT THEREFORE PLEASE YOUR LORDSHIP[S]:

to order that there be a diet and to assign a date for that diet;

IN RESPECT WHEREOF

[Solicitor for minuter]

(Address and telephone number of solicitor)

(Place and date)

NOTE
   [1]Inserted by the Act of Adjournal (Devolution Issues Rules) 1999 (S.I. 1999 No. 1346) (effective May 6, 1999).

Rule 40.2(3)   [1]**FORM 40.2B**

Form of notice of intervention by relevant authority

UNTO THE RIGHT HONOURABLE THE LORD JUSTICE GENERAL, LORD JUSTICE-CLERK AND LORDS COMMISSIONERS OF JUSTICIARY

[UNTO THE HONOURABLE THE SHERIFF OF *(name of sheriffdom)*

AT *(place)*]

NOTICE

by

[C.D.] *(address)*

HUMBLY SHEWETH:

1. That [*name of accused*] has been indicted at the instance of Her Majesty's Advocate for trial in the High Court of Justiciary sitting at *(place)* on *(date)* [*or* sheriff court at *(place)* on *(date)* with a first diet on *(date)*].

2. That [C.D.] *(here specify the name and title of the relevant authority and the fact of the intimation of the devolution issue)* intends to take part in the proceedings so far as they relate to the devolution issue

3. That a copy of this notice has been duly intimated to Her Majesty's Advocate [and to said *(name(s) of accused)*] and to any other relevant authority within the meaning of Rule 40.1 conform to execution[s] attached to this minute.

IN RESPECT WHEREOF

[Solicitor for the relevant authority]

(Address and telephone number of solicitor)

(Place and date)

NOTE
   [1]Inserted by the Act of Adjournal (Devolution Issues Rules) 1999 (S.I. 1999 No. 1346) (effective May 6, 1999).

Act of Adjournal (Criminal Procedure Rules) 1996

Rule 40.3(1)   [1]**FORM 40.3A**

Form of minute of notice of intention to raise a devolution issue

UNTO THE HONOURABLE THE SHERIFF OF (*name of sheriffdom*)

AT (*place*)

[*or* UNTO THE JUSTICES in the DISTRICT COURT IF (*name of district*)

AT (*place*)]

MINUTE

by

[E.F.] (*address*)

[*or* Prisoner in the Prison of (*place*)]

HUMBLY SHEWETH:

1. That [*name of accused*] has been charged at the instance of [G.H.] procurator fiscal at (*place*) with the crime [*or* offence] of (*specify*) and a diet is fixed for (*specify date*).

2. That [E.F.] intends to raise a devolution issue within the meaning of Schedule 6 to the Scotland Act 1998/Schedule 10 to the Northern Ireland Act 1998/Schedule 8 to the Government of Wales Act 1998 on the following grounds (*here specify the facts and circumstances and contentions of law which are alleged to give rise to the devolution issue*).

3. That a copy of this minute has been duly intimated to the said G.H., procurator fiscal [and to said (*name(s) of co-accused*)] and to the relevant authority within the meaning of Rule 40.1 conform to execution[s] attached to this minute.

MAY IT THEREFORE PLEASE YOUR LORDSHIP [or THE COURT]:

to order that there be a diet and to determine the devolution issue and to assign a date for that diet;

IN RESPECT WHEREOF

[Solicitor for minuter]

(*Address and telephone number of solicitor*)

(*Place and date*)

NOTE
[1]Inserted by the Act of Adjournal (Devolution Issues Rules) 1999 (S.I. 1999 No. 1346) (effective May 6, 1999).

Rule 40.3(3)   [1]**FORM 40.3B**

Form of notice of intervention by relevant authority

UNTO THE HONOURABLE THE SHERIFF OF (*name of sheriffdom*)

AT (*place*)

[or UNTO THE JUSTICES in the DISTRICT COURT OF (*name of district*) AT (*place*)]

NOTICE

by

[J.K.] (*address*)

HUMBLY SHEWETH:

1. That [*name of accused*] has been charged at the instance of [G.H.], procurator fiscal at (*place*) with the crime [*or* offence] of (*specify*) and a diet has been fixed for (*specify date*).

2. That [J.K.] (*here specify the name and title of the relevant authority and the fact of the intimation of the devolution issue*) intends to take part in the proceedings so far as they relate to the devolution issue.

3. That a copy of this notice has been duly intimated to the said G.H., procurator fiscal [and to said (*name(s) of accused*)] and to any other relevant authority within the meaning of Rule 40.1 conform to execution[s] attached to this minute.

IN RESPECT WHEREOF

[Solicitor for the relevant authority]

(*Address and telephone number of solicitor*)

(*Place and date*)

NOTE
[1]Inserted by the Act of Adjournal (Devolution Issues Rules) 1999 (S.I. 1999 No. 1346) (effective May 6, 1999).

Rule 40.4(2)   [1]**FORM 40.4A**

Form of minute of notice of intention to raise a devolution issue

UNTO THE RIGHT HONOURABLE THE LORD JUSTICE GENERAL, LORD JUSTICE-CLERK AND LORDS COMMISSIONERS OF JUSTICIARY

[or UNTO THE HONOURABLE THE SHERIFF OF (*name of sheriffdom*)

AT (*place*)]

[or UNTO THE JUSTICES in the DISTRICT COURT OF (*name of district*) AT (*place*)]

MINUTE

by

[L.M.] (*address*)

[*or* Prisoner in the Prison of (*place*)]

HUMBLY SHEWETH:

1. That (*here specify the nature of the proceedings, the names of the parties and the date of the diet fixed*).

2. That [L.M.] intends to raise a devolution issue within the meaning of Schedule 6 to the Scotland Act 1998/Schedule 10 to the Northern Ireland Act 1998/Schedule 8 to the Government of Wales Act 1998 on the following grounds (*here specify the facts and circumstances and contentions of law which are alleged to give rise to the devolution issue*).

3. That a copy of this minute has been duly intimated to Her Majesty's Advocate [*and to (name(s) of any other parties to the proceedings)*] and to the relevant authority within the meaning of Rule 40.1 conform to execution[s] attached to this minute.

MAY IT THEREFORE PLEASE YOUR LORDSHIP[S] [OR THE COURT]:

to order that there be a diet and to assign a date for that diet;

IN RESPECT WHEREOF

[Solicitor for minuter]

(*Address and telephone number of solicitor*)

(*Place and date*)

NOTE
[1]Inserted by the Act of Adjournal (Devolution Issues Rules) 1999 (S.I. 1999 No. 1346) (effective May 6, 1999).

Rule 40.4(4)   **[1]FORM 40.4B**

Form of notice of intervention by relevant authority

UNTO THE RIGHT HONOURABLE THE LORD JUSTICE GENERAL, LORD JUSTICE-CLERK AND LORDS COMMISSIONERS OF JUSTICIARY

[UNTO THE HONOURABLE THE SHERIFF OF (*name of sheriffdom*)

AT (*place*)]

[or UNTO THE JUSTICES in the DISTRICT COURT OF (*name of district*) AT (*place*)]

NOTICE

by

[N.O.] (*address*)

HUMBLY SHEWETH:

1. That (*here specify the nature of the proceedings, the names of the parties and the date of any diet fixed*).

2. That [N.O.] (*here specify the name and title of the relevant authority and the fact of the intimation of the devolution issue*) intends to take part in the proceedings so far as they relate to the devolution issue.

3. That a copy of this notice has been duly intimated to Her Majesty's Advocate [and to said (*name(s) of other parties*)] and to any other relevant authority within the meaning of Rule 40.1 conform to execution[s] attached to this minute.

IN RESPECT WHEREOF

[Solicitor for the relevant authority]

(*Address and telephone number of solicitor*)

(*Place and date*)

NOTE
[1]Inserted by the Act of Adjournal (Devolution Issues Rules) 1999 (S.I. 1999 No. 1346) (effective May 6, 1999).

Rule 40.12   **[1]FORM 40.12**

Form of intimation to a relevant authority that the court is considering making an order under [section 102 of the Scotland Act 1998/section 81 of the Northern Ireland Act 1998/ section 110 of the Government of Wales Act 1998]

To: (*name and address of relevant authority*)

1. You are given notice that in criminal proceedings in the [High Court of Justiciary/Sheriff/

District Court at (*place*)], at the instance of (*name and title of prosecutor*) against (*name of accused*) the court has decided [that an Act/provision of an Act of the Scottish Parliament is not within the legislative competence of the Parliament] [a member of the Scottish Executive does not have the power to make, confirm or approve a provision of subordinate legislation he has purported to make, confirm or approve]. A copy of the relevant decision is enclosed.

2. The court is considering whether to make an order [removing or limiting the retrospective effect of the decision/suspending the effect of the decision to allow the defect to be corrected].

3. If you wish to take part as a party to the proceedings so far as they relate to the making of the order mentioned in paragraph 2 you must lodge with (*title and address of clerk of court*) a notice in writing stating that you intend to take part as a party in the proceedings. The notice must be lodged within 7 days of (*insert date on which intimation was given*).

Date (*insert date*)

(*Signed*)

Clerk of Court

NOTE
[1]Inserted by the Act of Adjournal (Devolution Issues Rules) 1999 (S.I. 1999 No. 1346) (effective May 6, 1999).

Rule 41.3(1)   [1]**FORM 41.3A**

Form of notice to Crown under section 5(1) of the 1998 Act

IN THE HIGH COURT OF JUSTICIARY

AT (*place*)

IN

HER MAJESTY'S ADVOCATE

against

[C.D.] (*address* or *Prisoner in the Prison of {place}*)

Date: (*date of posting or other method of service*)

To: (*specify Minister or other person on whom notice is to be served*)

TAKE NOTICE
That the court is considering whether or not to make a declaration under section (*specify section 4(2), in relation to primary legislation or section 4(4) in relation to subordinate legislation*) of the Human Rights Act 1998 that (*specify the primary or subordinate legislation which is the subject of the proposed declaration*) is incompatible with (*specify the Convention right*) for the following reasons:

(*set out the reasons in summary*).

You may apply to become a party to the proceedings. If you wish to do so you should notify the Deputy Principal Clerk of Justiciary in Form 41.3–B.

(Signed)

Deputy Principal Clerk of Justiciary

NOTE
[1]Inserted by the Act of Adjournal (Criminal Procedure Rules Amendment No.2) (Human Rights 1998) 2000 (S.S.I. 2000 No. 315) (effective October 2, 2000).

Rule 41.3(2)   **¹FORM 41.3–B**

Form of notice to court under section 5(2) of the 1998 Act

IN THE HIGH COURT OF JUSTICIARY

in

HER MAJESTY'S ADVOCATE

against

[C.D.] (address or Prisoner in the Prison of {place})

To the Deputy Principal Clerk of Justiciary

The (*specify Minister or other person*) intends to join as a party to these proceedings.

(Signed)

Solicitor for (specify Minister of other person)

(Address)

NOTE
¹Inserted by the Act of Adjournal (Criminal Procedure Rules Amendment No.2) (Human Rights 1998) 2000 (S.S.I. 2000 No. 315) (effective October 2, 2000).

Rule 41.4   **¹FORM 41.4**

Form of minute under Rule 41.4

IN THE HIGH COURT OF JUSTICIARY

IN

HER MAJESTY'S ADVOCATE

against

[C.D.] (*address* or *Prisoner in the Prison of* {*place*})

To the Deputy Principal Clerk of Justiciary

(*set out the basis on which the court is considering whether or not to make a declaration of incompatibility including where appropriate a summary of any facts on which it proposes to rely, of any proposition of law which it proposes to enforce, and of any argument which it proposes to make*)

(Signed)

Solicitor for (*specify Minister or other person*).

NOTE
¹Inserted by the Act of Adjournal (Criminal Procedure Rules Amendment No.2) (Human Rights 1998) 2000 (S.S.I. 2000 No. 315) (effective October 2, 2000).

¹ANNEX
NOTES FOR COMPLETION OF FORM 31.5

Guidance of the Court of Justice of the European Communities
The development of the Community legal order is largely the result of co-operation between the Court of Justice of the European Communities and national courts and tribunals through

the preliminary ruling procedure under Article 177 of the EC Treaty and the corresponding provisions of the ECSC and Euratom Treaties.[1]

In order to make this co-operation more effective, and so enable the Court of Justice better to meet the requirements of national courts by providing helpful answers to preliminary questions, this Note for Guidance is addressed to all interested parties, in particular to all national courts and tribunals.

It must be emphasised that the Note is for information only and has no binding or interpretative effect in relation to the provisions governing the preliminary ruling procedure. It merely contains practical information which, in the light of experience in applying the preliminary ruling procedure, may help to prevent the kind of difficulties which the Court has sometimes encountered.

1. Any court or tribunal of a Member State may ask the Court of Justice to interpret a rule of Community law, whether contained in the Treaties or in acts of secondary law, if it considers that this is necessary for it to give judgment in a case pending before it.

Courts or tribunals against whose decisions there is no judicial remedy under national law must refer questions of interpretation arising before them to the Court of Justice, unless the Court has already ruled on the point or unless the correct application of the rule of Community law is obvious.[2]

2. The Court of Justice has jurisdiction to rule on the validity of acts of the Community institutions. National courts or tribunals may reject a plea challenging the validity of such an act. But where a national court (even one whose decision is still subject to appeal) intends to question the validity of a Community act, it must refer that question to the Court of Justice.[3]

Where, however, a national court or tribunal has serious doubts about the validity of a Community act on which a national measure is based, it may, in exceptional cases, temporarily suspend application of the latter measure or grant other interim relief with respect to it. It must then refer the question of validity to the Court of Justice, stating the reasons for which it considers that the Community act is not valid.[4]

3. Questions referred for a preliminary ruling must be limited to the interpretation or validity of a provision of Community law, since the Court of Justice does not have jurisdiction to interpret national law or assess its validity. It is for the referring court or tribunal to apply the relevant rule of Community law in the specific case pending before it.

4. The order of the national court or tribunal referring a question to the Court of Justice for a preliminary ruling may be in any form allowed by national procedural law. Reference of a question or questions to the Court of Justice generally involves stay of the national proceedings until the Court has given its ruling, but the decision to stay proceedings is one which it is for the national court alone to take in accordance with its own national law.

5. The order for reference containing the question or questions referred to the Court will have to be translated by the Court's translators into the other official languages of the Community. Questions concerning the interpretation or validity of Community law are frequently of general interest and the Member States and Community institutions are entitled to submit observations. It is therefore desirable that the reference should be drafted as clearly and precisely as possible.

6. The order for reference should contain a statement of reasons which is succinct but sufficiently complete to give the Court, and those to whom it must be notified (the Member States, the Commission and in certain cases the Council and the European Parliament), a clear understanding of the factual and legal context of the main proceedings.[5]

In particular, it should include a statement of the facts which are essential to a full understanding of the legal significance of the main proceedings, an exposition of the national law which may be applicable, a statement of the reasons which have prompted the national court to refer the question or questions to the Court of Justice and, where appropriate, a summary of the arguments of the parties. The aim should be to put the Court of Justice in a position to give the national court an answer which will be of assistance to it.

The order for reference should also be accompanied by copies of any documents needed for a proper understanding of the case, especially the text of the applicable national provisions. However, as the case-file or documents annexed to the order for reference are not always translated in full into the other official languages of the Community, the national court should ensure that the order for reference itself includes all the relevant information.

7. A national court or tribunal may refer a question to the Court of Justice as soon as it finds that a ruling on the point or points of interpretation or validity is necessary to enable it to give judgment. It must be stressed, however, that it is not for the Court of Justice to decide issues of fact or to resolve disputes as to the interpretation or application of rules of national law. It is therefore desirable that a decision to refer should not be taken until the national proceedings have reached a stage where the national court is able to define, if only as a working hypothesis, the factual and legal context of the question; on any view, the administration of justice is likely to be best served if the reference is not made until both sides have been heard.[6]

8. The order for reference and the relevant documents should be sent by the national court directly to the Court of Justice, by registered post (addressed to the Registry of the Court of Justice of the European Communities, L-2925 Luxembourg, telephone (352) 43031). The Court Registry will remain in contact with the national court until judgment is given, and will send copies of the various documents (written observations, Report for the Hearing, Opinion of the Advocate General). The Court will also send its judgment to the national court. The Court would appreciate being informed about the application of its judgment in the national proceedings and being sent a copy of the national court's final decision.

9. Proceedings for a preliminary ruling before the Court of Justice are free of charge. The Court does not rule on costs.

NOTE
[1]Inserted by the Act of Adjournal (Criminal Procedure Rules Amendment No. 2) 1999 (S.I. 1999 No. 1282), para. 2(5) and Sched. 2 (effective May 1, 1999).

Paragraph 3   SCHEDULE 3

ACTS OF ADJOURNAL REVOKED

Statutory Instrument Year and Number	Title of Act of Adjournal	Extent of Revocation
1988/110	Act of Adjournal (Consolidation) 1988	The whole Act of Adjournal
1989/48	Act of Adjournal (Consolidation Amendment) (Reference to European Court) 1989	The whole Act of Adjournal
1989/1020	Act of Adjournal (Consolidation Amendment No.2) (Forms of Warrant for Execution and Charge for Payment of Fine or Other Financial Penalty) 1989	The whole Act of Adjournal
1990/718	Act of Adjournal (Consolidation Amendment No.2) (Drug Trafficking) 1990	The whole Act of Adjournal
1990/2106	Act of Adjournal (Consolidation Amendment No.2) (Miscellaneous) 1990	The whole Act of Adjournal
1991/19	Act of Adjournal (Consolidation Amendment) (Extradition Rules and Backing of Irish Warrants) 1991	The whole Act of Adjournal
1991/847	Act of Adjournal (Consolidation Amendment No.1) 1991	The whole Act of Adjournal
1991/1916	Act of Adjournal (Consolidation Amendment No.2) (Evidence of Children) 1991	The whole Act of Adjournal
1991/2676	Act of Adjournal (Consolidation Amendment No.3) 1991	The whole Act of Adjournal
1991/2677	Act of Adjournal (Consolidation Amendment No.4) (Supervised Attendance Orders) 1991	The whole Act of Adjournal

Statutory Instrument Year and Number	Title of Act of Adjournal	Extent of Revocation
1992/1489	Act of Adjournal (Consolidation Amendment) (Criminal Justice International Co-operation Act 1990) 1992	The whole Act of Adjournal
1993/1955	Act of Adjournal (Consolidation Amendment) (Courses for Drink-drive Offenders) 1993	The whole Act of Adjournal
1993/2391	Act of Adjournal (Consolidation Amendment No.2) (Miscellaneous) 1993	The whole Act of Adjournal
1994/1769	Act of Adjournal (Consolidation Amendment) (Miscellaneous) 1994	The whole Act of Adjournal
1995/1875	Act of Adjournal (Consolidation Amendment) (Supervised Release Orders) 1995	The whole Act of Adjournal

Table of Derivations

(This Table is not part of the Act of Adjournal)

Note.   In this Table—
"A.A. 1988" means the Act of Adjournal (Consolidation) 1988 (S.I. 1988 No.110);
"CJSA 1949" means the Criminal Justice (Scotland) Act 1949 (c.94);
"C.P.R. 1996" means the Criminal Procedure Rules 1996 in Schedule 2 to this Act of Adjournal;
"CPSA 1887" means the Criminal Procedure (Scotland) Act 1887 (c.35);
"CPSA 1975" means the Criminal Procedure (Scotland) Act 1975 (c.21);
"SJ(S)A 1954" means the Summary Jurisdiction (Scotland) Act 1954 (c.48).

C.P.R. 1996		Derivation (r. = rule in A.A. 1988)
Chapter 1	r. 1.2(1)	r. 2(1)
	r. 1.2(2)	r. 2(2)
	r. 1.3	r. 2(3)
Chapter 2	r. 2.1	r. 166
	r. 2.2(1), (2)	r. 167 as amended by S.I. 1990/718
	r. 2.7	r. 91
Chapter 3	r. 3.1	r. 158
	r. 3.2	r. 157
	r. 3.3	s.225 CPSA 1975
	r. 3.4(1)	s.226 CPSA 1975
	r. 3.4(2)	s.227 CPSA 1975
	r. 3.5	r. 159
	r. 3.6(1), (2)	r. 160(1), (2)
Chapter 4	r. 4.1	r. 4 and r. 92
Chapter 5	r. 5.1	r. 14
	r. 5.2	r. 15
	r. 5.3(1)	r. 16(1) (part)
	r. 5.3(2)	r. 16(1) (part)
	r. 5.3(3)	r. 16(3) as amended by S.I. 1993/2391
	r. 5.3(4)	r. 16(4) as amended by S.I. 1993/2391
	r. 5.3(5)–(7)	r. 16(5)–(7)
	r. 5.4	r. 17
	r. 5.5	r. 18
	r. 5.6(1)	r. 19(1)
	r. 5.6(2)	r. 19(2) as amended by S.I. 1993/2391
	r. 5.6(3)–(9)	r. 19(3)–(9)
	r. 5.7	r. 20
	r. 5.8	r. 21
	r. 5.9	r. 22
	r. 5.10	r. 23
Chapter 6	r. 6.1	r. 140
	r. 6.2	r. 141
	r. 6.3	r. 143
	r. 6.4(a)	r. 144(a)
	r. 6.4(b)	r. 144(f)(i), (ii)
	r. 6.4(c)	r. 144(h)
	r. 6.5(1)	r. 145(b)
	r. 6.5(2)	r. 145(c) (part)
	r. 6.5(3)	r. 145(d)
	r. 6.6	r. 147
	r. 6.7	r. 71 and r. 120
Chapter 7	r. 7.1	r. 62 and r. 112
Chapter 8	r. 8.1(1)	r. 50(1) (part)
	r. 8.1(2)	r. 50(1) (part)
	r. 8.1(3)	r. 50(2)
	r. 8.1(4)	r. 50(3)
	r. 8.1(5)	r. 50(4)
	r. 8.2	r. 10(1) (part)
Chapter 9	r. 9.1	r. 24

C.P.R. 1996		Derivation (r. = rule in A.A. 1988)
	r. 9.2	r. 25
	r. 9.3	r. 26(1)
	r. 9.4(1)	r. 26(2)
	r. 9.4(2)	r. 27(1)
	r. 9.4(3)	r. 27(2)
	r. 9.5	r. 28(1)
	r. 9.6	r. 29
	r. 9.7	r. 30
	r. 9.8	r. 31
	r. 9.9	r. 32
	r. 9.10(1)–(5)	r. 33
	r. 9.11	r. 34
	r. 9.12	r. 35
	r. 9.13	r. 36
	r. 9.14	r. 37
	r. 9.15	r. 38
	r. 9.16	r. 39
	r. 9.17	r. 40
Chapter 10	r. 10.1	r. 12
Chapter 12	r. 12.1	r. 41
	r. 12.2	r. 42
	r. 12.3	r. 43
	r. 12.4	r. 44
	r. 12.5	r. 45
	r. 12.6	r. 46
	r. 12.7	r. 47
	r. 12.8	r. 48
	r. 12.9	r. 49
Chapter 13	r. 13.1	r. 11
	r. 13.2(1)	r. 10(1) (part)
Chapter 14	r. 14.1	s.125 CPSA 1975
	r. 14.2(1)	s.129 (part) CPSA 1975 as amended by the Criminal Justice (Scotland) Act 1987 (c.41), Sch. 1 para. 7
	r. 14.2(2)	s.129 (part) CPSA 1975 as amended by the Criminal Justice (Scotland) Act 1987 (c.41), Sch. 1 para. 7
	r. 14.3	r. 69
	r. 14.4(1)	s.132 (part) CPSA 1975
	r. 14.4(2)	s.132 (part) CPSA 1975
	r. 14.5	r. 70
	r. 14.6	s.146 CPSA 1975
	r. 14.7	s.276 (part) CPSA 1975 as amended by the Prisoners and Criminal Proceedings (Scotland) Act 1993 (c.9), Sch. 5 para. 1(28)
	r. 14.8(1)	s.156(4) (part) CPSA 1975
	r. 14.8(2)	s.156(4) (part) CPSA 1975
	r. 14.9	r. 74
	r. 14.10(1)–(3)	s.269 CPSA 1975 as amended by the Criminal Justice (Scotland) Act 1980 (c.62), Sch. 2 and the Prisoners and Criminal Proceedings (Scotland) Act 1993 (c.9), Sch. 5 para. 1(24)
Chapter 15	r. 15.1(1), (2)	s.273(1) CPSA 1975 as amended by the Criminal Justice (Scotland) Act 1980 (c.62), Sch. 2 and 8, and by the Prisoners and Criminal Proceedings (Scotland) Act 1993 (c.9), Sch. 5 para. 1(26)
	r. 15.1(3)	s.273(2) CPSA 1975 as amended by the Criminal Justice (Scotland) Act 1980 (c.62), Sch. 2 and 8
	r. 15.2(1)–(5)	r. 84(1) (part); as amended by S.I. 1991/2676
	r. 15.2(6)	r. 84(3) inserted by S.I. 1993/2391
	r. 15.3	r. 84(1), as amended by S.I. 1991/2676
	r. 15.4	r. 84(2)
	r. 15.5	r. 85
	r. 15.6	r. 84(1) as amended by S.I. 1991/2676

C.P.R. 1996		Derivation (r. = rule in A.A. 1988)
	r. 15.7	s. 237 CPSA 1975 substituted by the Criminal Justice (Scotland) Act 1980 (c.62), Sch. 2
	r. 15.8(1)	s. 239(1) CPSA 1975 as amended by the Criminal Justice (Scotland) Act 1980 (c.62), Sch. 2 and 8, and the Prisoners and Criminal Proceedings (Scotland) Act 1993 (c.9), Sch. 5 para. 1(14)
	r. 15.8(2)	s. 239(2) CPSA 1975 as amended by the Criminal Justice (Scotland) Act 1980 (c.62), Sch. 2 and 8
	r. 15.8(3)	r. 84(1) as amended by S.I. 1991/2676
	r. 15.9(1)	s. 259 (part) CPSA 1975
	r. 15.9(2)	s. 259 (part) CPSA 1975
	r. 15.10(1), (2)	s. 272 CPSA 1975 as amended by the Criminal Justice (Scotland) Act 1980 (c.62), Sch. 2 and 8
	r. 15.11(1)	r. 86(1) (part)
	r. 15.11(2)	r. 86(2) and (3)
	r. 15.11(3)	r. 86(1) (part) and r. 86(4)
	r. 15.12(1)	r. 86(5)
	r. 15.12(2)	r. 86(6)
	r. 15.12(3)	r. 86(7)
	r. 15.12(4)	r. 86(8)
	r. 15.12(5)	r. 86(9)
	r. 15.12(6)	r. 86(10)
Chapter 16	r. 16.1(1)	r. 87(1)
	r. 16.1(2)	r. 87(3)
	r. 16.1(3)	r. 88
	r. 16.1(4)	r. 87(4)
	r. 16.2(1)	r. 89 (part)
	r. 16.2(2)	r. 89 (part)
	r. 16.3	r. 90
	r. 16.4(1)–(3)	s. 309(1) CPSA 1975
	r. 16.5(1), (2)	s. 309(1) CPSA 1975
	r. 16.7	r. 99
Chapter 17	r. 17.1(1)–(4)	r. 100
Chapter 18	r. 18.1(1)	r. 119(1)
	r. 18.1(2)	r. 119(2)
	r. 18.1(3)	r. 119(3)
	r. 18.1(4)	r. 119(4)
	r. 18.2	r. 121
	r. 18.3	s. 321(1) CPSA 1975
	r. 18.4(1), (2)	s. 360 CPSA 1975
	r. 18.5	r. 123
	r. 18.6	r. 124(1)
Chapter 19	r. 19.1	r. 128
	r. 19.2	r. 127
	r. 19.3	r. 127
	r. 19.4(1)	r. 127
	r. 19.4(2)	r. 130(1)
	r. 19.5	r. 127
	r. 19.6	r. 129
	r. 19.7	r. 127
	r. 19.8	r. 131 as amended by S.I. 1990/2106
	r. 19.9	r. 132
	r. 19.10	r. 133
	r. 19.11	r. 135 as amended by S.I. 1991/2676
	r. 19.12	r. 136 as amended by S.I. 1991/2676
	r. 19.13	r. 138(2) as amended by S.I. 1991/2676
	r. 19.14(1)	r. 137(1)
	r. 19.14(2)	r. 137(2) as amended by S.I. 1991/2676
	r. 19.15	r. 139 as amended by S.I. 1991/2676
	r. 19.16(1)	r. 134(1)
	r. 19.16(2)	r. 134(2) as amended by S.I. 1990/2106

C.P.R. 1996		Derivation (r. = rule in A.A. 1988)
Chapter 20	r. 20.1	r. 75
	r. 20.2	r. 124(1)
	r. 20.3	r. 83E, inserted by S.I. 1993/2391
	r. 20.4	r. 124(1)
	r. 20.5	r. 124(1)
	r. 20.6	r. 124(1)
	r. 20.7	
	r. 124(1)	
	r. 20.8	r. 83A inserted by S.I. 1989/1020, and r. 126A inserted by S.I. 1989/1020
	r. 20.9	r. 124(1)
	r. 20.10(1)	r. 76 and r. 126
	r. 20.11(1)	r. 83C inserted by S.I. 1991/2677 and r. 126C inserted by S.I. 1991/2677
	r. 20.13	r. 78 and r. 125(2)
	r. 20.14(1)	r. 79(1) and r. 125(3)
	r. 20.14(2)	r. 82 and r. 125(10)
	r. 20.15(1)	r. 80(1) and r. 125(5)
	r. 20.15(2)	r. 80(2) and r. 125(6)
	r. 20.16(1)	r. 81(1) and r. 125(7)
	r. 20.16(2)	r. 81(2) and r. 125(8)
	r. 20.16(3)	r. 81(3) and r. 125(9)
	r. 20.17(1)	r. 83B (part) inserted by S.I. 1991/2676 and r. 126B (part) inserted by S.I. 1991/2676
	r. 20.17(2)	r. 83B (part) inserted by S.I. 1991/2676 and r. 126B (part) inserted by S.I. 1991/2676
	r. 20.18(1)	r. 83(2)
	r. 20.18(2)	s.430(1) CPSA 1975 (part)
	r. 20.18(3)	r. 83(3)
	r. 20.19	r. 83D inserted by S.I. 1993/1955 and r. 126D inserted by S.I. 1993/1955
Chapter 22	r. 22.1(1)–(3)	r. 61A(1)–(3) inserted by S.I. 1991/1916 and r. 111A(1)–(3) inserted by S.I. 1991/1916
	r. 22.2(1), (2)	r. 61A(4), (5) inserted by S.I. 1991/1916 and r. 111A(4), (5) inserted by S.I. 1991/1916
Chapter 23	r. 23.1(1)	r. 51(1) and r. 101(1)
	r. 23.1(2)	r. 51(2) and r. 101(2)
	r. 23.1(4)	r. 51(3)
	r. 23.1(5)	r. 51(4) and r. 102(1)
	r. 23.1(6)	r. 51(5) and r. 102(2)
	r. 23.2(1)	r. 52(1) and r. 102(3)
	r. 23.2(2)	r. 52(2) and r. 102(4)
	r. 23.3	r. 53 and r. 103
	r. 23.4	r. 54 and r. 104
	r. 23.5(1)	r. 55(1) and r. 105(1)
	r. 23.5(2)	r. 55(2)
	r. 23.5(3)	r. 55(3) and r. 105(2)
	r. 23.6(1)	r. 56(1) and r. 106(1)
	r. 23.6(2)	r. 56(2) and r. 106(2)
	r. 23.6(3)	r. 56(3)
Chapter 24	r. 24.1(1)	r. 57(1) and r. 107(1)
	r. 24.1(2)	r. 57(2) and r. 107(2)
	r. 24.1(3)	r. 57(3) inserted by S.I. 1990/2106 and r. 107(3) inserted by S.I. 1990/2106
	r. 24.1(4)	r. 51(3) and r. 61
	r. 24.1(5)	r. 51(4) and r. 61; and r. 102(1) and r. 111
	r. 24.1(6)	r. 51(5) and r. 61; and r. 102(2) and r. 111
	r. 24.2(1)	r. 52(1) and r. 61; and r. 102(3) and r. 111
	r. 24.2(2)	r. 58(1) and r. 108(1)
	r. 24.2(3)	r. 58(2) and r. 108(2)
	r. 24.2(4)	r. 58(3) and r. 108(3)
	r. 24.3	r. 53 and r. 61; and r. 103 and r. 111

C.P.R. 1996		Derivation (r. = rule in A.A. 1988)
	r. 24.4	r. 59 and r. 109
	r. 24.5(1)	r. 60 and r. 110
	r. 24.5(2)	r. 54(3) and r. 61; and r. 104(3) and r. 111
	r. 24.6(1)	r. 55(1) and r. 61; and r. 105(1) and r. 111
	r. 24.6(2)	r. 55(2) and r. 61
	r. 24.6(3)	r. 55(3) and r. 61; and r. 105(2) and r. 111
	r. 24.7(1)	r. 56(1) and r. 61; and r. 106(1) and r. 111
	r. 24.7(2)	r. 56(2) and r. 61; and r. 106(2) and r. 111
	r. 24.7(3)	r. 56(3) and r. 61
Chapter 25	r. 25.1	r. 73
Chapter 26	r. 26.1	r. 73A inserted by S.I. 1993/2391, and amended by S.I. 1994/1769 and r. 122A inserted by S.I. 1993/2391 and amended by S.I. 1994/1769
Chapter 27	r. 27.1(1)	r. 72 and r. 122(3)
	r. 27.1(2)	r. 122(1)
	r. 27.1(3)	r. 122(2)
Chapter 28	r. 28.1	r. 13 and r. 98
Chapter 29	r. 29.1	r. 5 and r. 93
	r. 29.2	r. 6 and r. 94
	r. 29.3	r. 7 and r. 95
	r. 29.4	r. 8 and r. 96
	r. 29.5	r. 9 and r. 97
Chapter 30	r. 30.1	r. 148
	r. 30.2	r. 149
	r. 30.3(1)–(5)	r. 149A inserted by S.I. 1991/19
	r. 30.3(6)	r. 149A(6) inserted by S.I. 1991/19 and as amended by S.I. 1991/847
	r. 30.3(7)–(9)	r. 149A(7)–(9) inserted by S.I. 1991/19
	r. 30.4(1)	r. 149B(1) inserted by S.I. 1991/19, as amended by S.I. 1991/847
	r. 30.4(2)	r. 149B(2) (part) inserted by S.I. 1991/19
	r. 30.4(3)	r. 149B(2) (part) inserted by S.I. 1991/19
	r. 30.4(4)	r. 149B(3) (part) inserted by S.I. 1991/19
	r. 30.4(5)	r. 149B(3) (part) inserted by S.I. 1991/19
	r. 30.5	r. 150
	r. 30.6	r. 151
	r. 30.7	r. 152
Chapter 31	r. 31.1(1)	r. 63 and r. 113
	r. 31.2	r. 64
	r. 31.3	r. 114
	r. 31.4	r. 64A inserted by S.I. 1989/48 and r. 115
	r. 31.5	r. 65 and r. 116
	r. 31.6(1)	r. 66 (part) and r. 117 (part)
	r. 31.6(2)	r. 66 (part) and r. 117 (part)
	r. 31.7(1)	r. 67(1) (part) and r. 118(1) (part)
	r. 31.7(2)	r. 67(1) (part) and r. 118(1) (part)
	r. 31.7(3)	r. 67(2) and r. 118(2)
	r. 31.7(4)	r. 67(3) and r. 118(3)
	r. 31.7(5)	r. 67(4) and r. 118(4)
	r. 31.7(6)	r. 67(5) and r. 118(5)
Chapter 32	r. 32.2	r. 153
Chapter 33	r. 33.1	r. 162
	r. 33.2	r. 163
	r. 33.3	r. 164
	r. 33.4	r. 165
Chapter 34	r. 34.1	r. 156A inserted by S.I. 1991/19
	r. 34.2(1)–(5)	r. 156B(1)–(5) inserted by S.I. 1991/19
	r. 34.2(6)	r. 156B(6) inserted by S.I. 1991/19, as amended by S.I. 1991/847
	r. 34.2(7)–(9)	r. 156B(7)–(9) inserted by S.I. 1991/19
	r. 34.3(1)	r. 156C(1) inserted by S.I. 1991/19 as amended by S.I. 1991/847

C.P.R. 1996		Derivation (r. = rule in A.A. 1988)
	r. 34.3(2)	r. 156C(2) inserted by S.I. 1991/19
	r. 34.3(3)	r. 156C(3) inserted by S.I. 1991/19
	r. 34.4	r. 156D inserted by S.I. 1991/19
	r. 34.5	r. 156E inserted by S.I. 1991/19
Chapter 35	r. 35.1	r. 68A inserted by S.I. 1991/847 and r. 118A inserted by S.I. 1991/847
Chapter 36	r. 36.1	r. 168
	r. 36.2	r. 169
	r. 36.3	r. 170
	r. 36.4	r. 171
	r. 36.5	r. 172
	r. 36.6	r. 173
	r. 36.7	r. 174
	r. 36.8	r. 175
	r. 36.9	r. 176
Chapter 37	r. 37.1	r. 154 as amended by S.I. 1990/718
	r. 37.2	r. 155 as amended by S.I. 1990/718
	r. 37.3	r. 156 as amended by S.I. 1990/718
Appendix:	Form 2.6–A	Form 4
	Form 2.6–C	CPSA 1887 Sch. D
	Form 3.1–A	Form 85
	Form 3.1–B	Form 86
	Form 5.2	Form 10 as amended by S.I. 1993/2391
	Form. 5.6–A	Form 11
	Form 5.6–B	Form 12
	Form 5.6–C	Form 13
	Form 5.8	Form 14
	Form 7.1–A	Form 29
	Form 7.1–B	Form 30
	Form 8.1–A	Form 23
	Form 8.1–B	Forms 24 and 25
	Form 8.2–A	Form 3 (part)
	Form 8.2–B	Form 5
	Form 8.2–D	CPSA 1887 Sch. N
	Form 8.3	CJSA 1949 Sch. 7 as amended by SJ(S)A 1954 Sch. 4
	Form 9.1	Form 15
	Form 9.9	Form 16
	Form 9.12	Form 17
	Form 9.17	Form 18
	Form 10.1–A	Form 6
	Form 10.1–B	Form 7
	Form 12.1	Form 19
	Form 12.2–A	Form 20
	Form 12.2–B	Form 21
	Form 12.6	Form 22
	Form 13.2–B	CPSA 1887 Sch. E
	Form 14.3–A	Form 33 Part 1
	Form 14.3–B	Form 33 Part 2
	Form 14.5–A	Form 33 Part 3
	Form 14.5–B	Form 33 Part 4
	Form 14.7	CPSA 1975 s.276 (part) as amended by the Prisoners and Criminal Proceedings (Scotland) Act 1993 (c.9), Sch. 5 para. 1(28)
	Form 15.2–A	Form 37
	Form 15.2–B	Form 38 as amended by S.I. 1993/2391
	Form 15.2–C	Form 39
	Form 15.2–D	Form 40
	Form 15.3–A	Form 42
	Form 15.3–B	Form 43
	Form 15.6	Form 41
	Form 15.8	Form 40A inserted by S.I. 1991/2676
	Form 15.11–A	Form 44A

C.P.R. 1996	Derivation (r. = rule in A.A. 1988)
Form 15.11–B	Form 44 as amended by S.I. 1991/2677
Form 16.1–A	Form 45
Form 16.1–B	Form 47
Form 16.1–C	Form 49
Form 16.1–D	Form 50
Form 16.1–E	Form 48
Form 16.4–A	SJ(S)A 1954 Sch. 2 Part I (incidental applications)
Form 16.4–B	SJ(S)A 1954 Sch. 2 Part IV (assignation of diet) as amended by S.I. 1964/249
Form 16.4–C	SJ(S)A 1954 Sch. 2 Part V (minutes of procedure) as amended by S.I. 1964/249
Form 16.5–A	SJ(S)A 1954 Sch. 2 Part IV (warrant of apprehension) as amended by S.I. 1964/249
Form 16.5–B	SJ(S)A 1954 Sch. 2 Part IV (warrant to search) as amended by S.I. 1964/249
Form 16.5–C	SJ(S)A 1954 Sch. 2 Part IV (form of adjournment for inquiry) as amended by S.I. 1964/249
Form 16.7	Form 53
Form 17.1	Form 54
Form 18.3	SJ(S)A 1954 Sch. 2 Part IV (apprehension of witness) as amended by S.I. 1964/249
Form 18.6	Form 67
Form 19.1–A	Form 78 as amended by S.I. 1991/2676
Form 19.1–B	Form 79
Form 19.2–A	Form 71
Form 19.2–B	Form 72
Form 19.2–C	Form 73
Form 19.3–A	Form 76
Form 19.3–B	Form 74
Form 19.4	Form 75
Form 19.5	Form 70 (part)
Form 19.6	Form 70 (part)
Form 19.7	Form 77
Form 19.9	Form 80 as amended by S.I. 1991/2676
Form 20.1	Form 34
Form 20.2	Form 68
Form 20.3	Form 96 inserted by S.I. 1993/2391 and substituted by S.I. 1995/1875
Form 20.4–A	Form 66
Form 20.4–B	Form 61
Form 20.5	Form 69
Form 20.6–A	Form 57
Form 20.6–B	Form 58
Form 20.6–C	Form 59
Form 20.7	Form 60
Form 20.8	Form 36A inserted by S.I. 1989/1020
Form 20.9–A	Forms 62 and 63
Form 20.9–B	Form 64
Form 20.9–C	Form 65
Form 20.10–A	Form 35 as amended by S.I. 1991/2677
Form 20.11–A	Form 36B inserted by S.I. 1991/2677
Form 20.18–A	Form 36
Form 20.18–B	SJ(S)A 1954 Sch. 2 Part V (extract) as amended by S.I. 1964/249
Form 20.19–A	Form 91 inserted by S.I. 1993/1955
Form 20.19–B	Form 92 inserted by S.I. 1993/1955
Form 22.1	Form 28D(1) inserted by S.I. 1991/1916, Form 28D(2) inserted by S.I. 1991/1916 and Form 56A inserted by S.I. 1991/1916
Form 23.1–A	Form 26B
Form 23.1–B	Forms 26A, 26C and 55
Form 23.1–C	Form 27

C.P.R. 1996	Derivation (r. = rule in A.A. 1988)
Form 24.1–A	Form 28B as amended by S.I. 1990/2106
Form 24.1–B	Form 28A as amended by S.I. 1990/2106, 28C as amended by S.I. 1990/2106 and Form 56 as amended by S.I. 1990/2106
Form 26.1–A	Form 93 inserted by S.I. 1993/2391; substituted by S.I. 1994/1769
Form 26.1–B	Form 94 inserted by S.I. 1993/2391
Form 26.1–C	Form 95 inserted by S.I. 1993/2391
Form 28.1–A	Form 8
Form 28.1–B	Forms 9 and 52
Form 29.1–A	Form 2
Form 29.1–B	Forms 1 and 51
Form 30.2–A	Form 81
Form 30.2–B	Form 82
Form 30.5	Form 83
Form 31.5	Form 31
Form 31.7	Form 32
Form 32.2	Form 84
Form 34.5	Form 88 inserted by S.I. 1991/19
Form 36.4–A	Form 89 inserted by S.I. 1992/1489
Form 36.4–B	Form 90 inserted by S.I. 1992/1489

Act of Adjournal (Criminal Procedure Rules) 1996

Table of Destinations

(This Table is not part of the Act of Adjournal)

Note.   In this Table, "C.P.R. 1996" means the Criminal Procedure Rules 1996 in Schedule 2 to this Act of Adjournal.

Part, section, Schedule or rule of enactment	Destination in C.P.R. 1996

Criminal Procedure (Scotland) Act 1887 (c.35)

Sch. D	Form 2.6–C
Sch. E	Form 13.2–B
Sch. N	Form 8.2–D

Criminal Justice (Scotland) Act 1949 (c.94)

Sch. 7	Form 8.3

Summary Jurisdiction (Scotland) Act 1954 (c.48)

Schedule 2		
Part I	(incidental applications)	Form 16.4–A
Part IV	(assignation of diet)	Form 16.4–B
	(warrant of apprehension)	Form 16.5–A
	(warrant to search)	Form 16.5–B
	(form of adjournment for inquiry)	Form 16.5–C
	(apprehension of witness)	Form 18.3
Part V	(minutes of procedure)	Form 16.4–C
	(extract)	Form 20.18–B

Criminal Procedure (Scotland) Act 1975 (c.21)

s.125	r. 14.1
s.129	r. 14.2(1) and (2)
s.132	r. 14.4(1) and (2)
s.146	r. 14.6
s.156(4)	r. 14.8(1) and (2)
s.225	r. 3.3
s.226	r. 3.4(1)
s.227	r. 3.4(2)
s.237	r. 15.7
s.239	r. 15.8(1) and (2)
s.259	r. 15.9
s.269	r. 14.10(1)–(3)
s.272	r. 15.10(1) and (2)
s.273(1)	r. 15.1(1) and (2)
s.273(2)	r. 15.1(3)
s.276	r. 14.7 and Form 14.7
s.309(1)	r. 16.4 and r. 16.5
s.321(1)	r. 18.3
s.360	r. 18.4(1) and (2)
s.430(1)	r. 20.18(2)

Act of Adjournal (Consolidation) 1988 [S.I. 1988/110]

r. 2(1)	r. 1.2(1)
r. 2(2)	r. 1.2(2)
r. 2(3)	r. 1.3
r. 4	r. 4.1
r. 5	r. 29.1

Part, section, Schedule or rule of enactment	Destination in C.P.R. 1996
r. 6	r. 29.2
r. 7	r. 29.3
r. 8	r. 29.4
r. 9	r. 29.5
r. 10(1)	r. 8.2 and r. 13.2(1)
r. 11	r. 13.1
r. 12	r. 10.1
r. 13	r. 28.1
r. 14	r. 5.1
r. 15	r. 5.2
r. 16(1)	r. 5.3(1) and (2)
r. 16(3)	r. 5.3(3)
r. 16(4)	r. 5.3(4)
r. 16(5)	r. 5.3(5)
r. 16(6)	r. 5.3(6)
r. 16(7)	r. 5.3(7)
r. 17	r. 5.4
r. 18	r. 5.5
r. 19	r. 5.6
r. 20	r. 5.7
r. 21	r. 5.8
r. 22	r. 5.9
r. 23	r. 5.10
r. 24	r. 9.1
r. 25	r. 9.2
r. 26(1)	r. 9.3
r. 26(2)	r. 9.4(1)
r. 27(1)	r. 9.4(2)
r. 27(2)	r. 9.4(3)
r. 28(1)	r. 9.5
r. 29	r. 9.6
r. 30	r. 9.7
r. 31	r. 9.8
r. 32	r. 9.9
r. 33	r. 9.10(1)–(5)
r. 34	r. 9.11
r. 35	r. 9.12
r. 36	r. 9.13
r. 37	r. 9.14
r. 38	r. 9.15
r. 39	r. 9.16
r. 40	r. 9.17
r. 41	r. 12.1
r. 42	r. 12.2
r. 43	r. 12.3
r. 44	r. 12.4
r. 45	r. 12.5
r. 46	r. 12.6
r. 47	r. 12.7
r. 48	r. 12.8
r. 49	r. 12.9
r. 50(1)	r. 8.1(1) and (2)
r. 50(2)	r. 8.1(3)
r. 50(3)	r. 8.1(4)
r. 50(4)	r. 8.1(5)
r. 51	r. 23.1(1), (2), (4), (5), (6) and r. 24.1(4)–(6)
r. 52	r. 23.2 and r. 24.2(1)
r. 53	r. 23.3 and r. 24.3
r. 54	r. 23.4 and r. 24.5(2)
r. 55	r. 23.5 and r. 24.6

Part, section, Schedule or rule of enactment	Destination in C.P.R. 1996
r. 56	r. 23.6 and r. 24.7
r. 57(1)	r. 24.1(1)
r. 57(2)	r. 24.1(2)
r. 57(3)	r. 24.1(3)
r. 58(1)	r. 24.2(2)
r. 58(2)	r. 24.2(3)
r. 58(3)	r. 24.2(4)
r. 59	r. 24.4
r. 60	r. 24.5(1)
r. 61	r. 24.1(4)–(6), r. 24.2(1), r. 24.3, r. 24.5(2), r. 24.6 and r. 24.7
r. 61A(1)	r. 22.1(1)
r. 61A(2)	r. 22.1(2)
r. 61A(3)	r. 22.1(3)
r. 61A(4)	r. 22.2(1)
r. 61A(5)	r. 22.2(2)
r. 62	r. 7.1
r. 63	r. 31.1(1)
r. 64	r. 31.2
r. 64A	r. 31.4
r. 65	r. 31.5
r. 66	r. 31.6(1) and (2)
r. 67(1)	r. 31.7(1) and (2)
r. 67(2)	r. 31.7(3)
r. 67(3)	r. 31.7(4)
r. 67(4)	r. 31.7(5)
r. 67(5)	r. 31.7(6)
r. 68A	r. 35.1
r. 69	r. 14.3
r. 70	r. 14.5
r. 71	r. 6.7
r. 72	r. 27.1(1)
r. 73	r. 25.1
r. 73A	r. 26.1
r. 74	r. 14.9
r. 75	r. 20.1
r. 76	r. 20.10
r. 78	r. 20.13
r. 79(1)	r. 20.14(1)
r. 80	r. 20.15
r. 81	r. 20.16
r. 82	r. 20.14(2)
r. 83(2)	r. 20.18(1)
r. 83(3)	r. 20.18(3)
r. 83A	r. 20.8
r. 83B	r. 20.17(1) and (2)
r. 83C	r. 20.11(1)
r. 83D	r. 20.19
r. 83E	r. 20.3
r. 84(1)	r. 15.2(1)–(5), r. 15.3, r. 15.6 and r. 15.8(3)
r. 84(2)	r. 15.4
r. 84(3)	r. 15.2(6)
r. 85	r. 15.5
r. 86(1)	r. 15.11(1) and (3) (part)
r. 86(2)	r. 15.11(2) (part)
r. 86(3)	r. 15.11(2) (part)
r. 86(4)	r. 15.11(3) (part)
r. 86(5)	r. 15.12(1)
r. 86(6)	r. 15.12(2)
r. 86(7)	r. 15.12(3)

Part, section, Schedule or rule of enactment	Destination in C.P.R. 1996
r. 86(8)	r. 15.12(4)
r. 86(9)	r. 15.12(5)
r. 86(10)	r. 15.12(6)
r. 87(1)	r. 16.1(1)
r. 87(3)	r. 16.1(2)
r. 87(4)	r. 16.1(4)
r. 88	r. 16.1(3)
r. 89	r. 16.2(1) and (2)
r. 90	r. 16.3
r. 91	r. 2.7
r. 92	r. 4.1
r. 93	r. 29.1
r. 94	r. 29.2
r. 95	r. 29.3
r. 96	r. 29.4
r. 97	r. 29.5
r. 98	r. 28.1
r. 99	r. 16.7
r. 100	r. 17.1(1)–(4)
r. 101(1)	r. 23.1(1)
r. 101(2)	r. 23.1(2)
r. 102(1)	r. 23.1(5) and r. 24.1(5)
r. 102(2)	r. 23.1(6) and r. 24.1(6)
r. 102(3)	r. 23.2(1) and r. 24.2(1)
r. 102(4)	r. 23.2(2), r. 24.1(5), (6) and r. 24.2(3)
r. 103	r. 23.3 and r. 24.3
r. 104	r. 23.4 and r. 24.5(2)
r. 105(1)	r. 23.5(1) and r. 24.6(1)
r. 105(2)	r. 23.5(3) (part) and r. 24.6(3)
r. 106(1)	r. 23.6(1) and r. 24.7(1)
r. 106(2)	r. 23.6(2) and r. 24.7(2)
r. 107(1)	r. 24.1(1)
r. 107(2)	r. 24.1(2) (part)
r. 107(3)	r. 24.1(3)
r. 108(1)	r. 24.2(2)
r. 108(2)	r. 24.2(3)
r. 108(3)	r. 24.2(4)
r. 109	r. 24.4
r. 110	r. 24.5(1)
r. 111	r. 24.1(5), (6), r. 24.2(1), r. 24.3, r. 24.5(2), r. 24.6(1), (3) and r. 24.7(1), (2)
r. 111A(1)	r. 22.1(1)
r. 111A(2)	r. 22.1(2)
r. 111A(3)	r. 22.1(3)
r. 111A(4)	r. 22.2(1)
r. 111A(5)	r. 22.2(2)
r. 112	r. 7.1
r. 113	r. 31.1(1)
r. 114	r. 31.3
r. 115	r. 31.4
r. 116	r. 31.5
r. 117	r. 31.6(1) and (2)
r. 118(1)	r. 31.7(1) and (2)
r. 118(2)	r. 31.7(3)
r. 118(3)	r. 31.7(4)
r. 118(4)	r. 31.7(5)
r. 118(5)	r. 31.7(6)
r. 118A	r. 35.1
r. 119(1)	r. 18.1(1)
r. 119(2)	r. 18.1(2)

Part, section, Schedule or rule of enactment	Destination in C.P.R. 1996
r. 119(3)	r. 18.1(3)
r. 119(4)	r. 18.1(4)
r. 120	r. 6.7
r. 121	r. 18.2
r. 122(1)	r. 27.1(2)
r. 122(2)	r. 27.1(3)
r. 122(3)	r. 27.1(1)
r. 122A	r. 26.1
r. 123	r. 18.5
r. 124(1)	r. 18.6, r. 20.2, r. 20.4, r. 20.5, r. 20.6, r. 20.7 and r. 20.9
r. 125(2)	r. 20.13
r. 125(3)	r. 20.14(1)
r. 125(5)	r. 20.15(1)
r. 125(6)	r. 20.15(2)
r. 125(7)	r. 20.16(1)
r. 125(8)	r. 20.16(2)
r. 125(9)	r. 20.16(3)
r. 125(10)	r. 20.14(2)
r. 126	r. 20.10
r. 126A	r. 20.8
r. 126B	r. 20.17(1) and (2)
r. 126C	r. 20.11(1)
r. 126D	r. 20.19
r. 127	r. 19.2, r. 19.3, r. 19.4(1), r. 19.5, r. 19.6(2) and r. 19.7
r. 128	r. 19.1
r. 129	r. 19.6
r. 130(1)	r. 19.4(2)
r. 131	r. 19.8
r. 132	r. 19.9
r. 133	r. 19.10
r. 134	r. 19.16(1) and (2)
r. 135	r. 19.11
r. 136	r. 19.12
r. 137	r. 19.14
r. 138(2)	r. 19.13
r. 139	r. 19.15
r. 140	r. 6.1
r. 141	r. 6.2
r. 143	r. 6.3
r. 144(a), (f)(i) and (ii), and (h)	r. 6.4
r. 145(b)	r. 6.5(1)
r. 145(c) (part)	r. 6.5(2)
r. 145(d)	r. 6.5(3)
r. 147	r. 6.6
r. 148	r. 30.1
r. 149	r. 30.2
r. 149A	r. 30.3
r. 149B(1)	r. 30.4(1)
r. 149B(2)	r. 30.4(2) and (3)
r. 149B(3)	r. 30.4(4) and (5)
r. 150	r. 30.5
r. 151	r. 30.6
r. 152	r. 30.7
r. 153	r. 32.2
r. 154	r. 37.1
r. 155	r. 37.2
r. 156	r. 37.3
r. 156A	r. 34.1

Part, section, Schedule or rule of enactment	Destination in C.P.R. 1996
r. 156B	r. 34.2
r. 156C	r. 34.3
r. 156D	r. 34.4
r. 156E	r. 34.5
r. 157	r. 3.2
r. 158	r. 3.1
r. 159	r. 3.5
r. 160(1) and (2)	r. 3.6(1) and (2)
r. 162	r. 33.1
r. 163	r. 33.2
r. 164	r. 33.3
r. 165	r. 33.4
r. 166	r. 2.1
r. 167	r. 2.2(1) and (2)
r. 168	r. 36.1
r. 169	r. 36.2
r. 170	r. 36.3
r. 171	r. 36.4
r. 172	r. 36.5
r. 173	r. 36.6
r. 174	r. 36.7
r. 175	r. 36.8
r. 176	r. 36.9
Form 1	Form 29.1–B
Form 2	Form 29.1–A
Form 3	Form 8.2–A (part)
Form 4	Form 2.6–A
Form 5	Form 8.2–B
Form 6	Form 10.1–A
Form 7	Form 10.1–B
Form 8	Form 28.1–A
Form 9	Form 28.1–B
Form 10	Form 5.2
Form 11	Form 5.6–A
Form 12	Form 5.6–B
Form 13	Form 5.6–C
Form 14	Form 5.8
Form 15	Form 9.1
Form 16	Form 9.9
Form 17	Form 9.12
Form 18	Form 9.17
Form 19	Form 12.1
Form 20	Form 12.2–A
Form 21	Form 12.2–B
Form 22	Form 12.6
Form 23	Form 8.1–A
Form 24	Form 8.1–B
Form 25	Form 8.1–B
Form 26A	Form 23.1–B
Form 26B	Form 23.1–A
Form 26C	Form 23.1–B
Form 27	Form 23.1–C
Form 28A	Form 24.1–B
Form 28B	Form 24.1–A
Form 28C	Form 24.1–B
Form 28D(1)	Form 22.1
Form 28D(2)	Form 22.1
Form 29	Form 7.1–A
Form 30	Form 7.1–B
Form 31	Form 31.5

Part, section, Schedule or rule of enactment	Destination in C.P.R. 1996
Form 32	Form 31.7
Form 33(1)	Form 14.3–A
Form 33(2)	Form 14.3–B
Form 33(3)	Form 14.5–A
Form 33(4)	Form 14.5–B
Form 34	Form 20.1
Form 35	Form 20.10–A
Form 36	Form 20.18–A
Form 36A	Form 20.8
Form 36B	Form 20.11–A
Form 37	Form 15.2–A
Form 38	Form 15.2–B
Form 39	Form 15.2–C
Form 40	Form 15.2–D
Form 40A	Form 15.8
Form 41	Form 15.6
Form 42	Form 15.3–A
Form 43	Form 15.3–B
Form 44	Form 15.11–B
Form 44A	Form 15.11–A
Form 45	Form 16.1–A
Form 47	Form 16.1–B
Form 48	Form 16.1–E
Form 49	Form 16.1–C
Form 50	Form 16.1–D
Form 51	Form 29.1–B
Form 52	Form 28.1–B
Form 53	Form 16.7
Form 54	Form 17.1
Form 55	Form 23.1–B
Form 56	Form 24.1–B
Form 56A	Form 22.1
Form 57	Form 20.6–A
Form 58	Form 20.6–B
Form 59	Form 20.6–C
Form 60	Form 20.7
Form 61	Form 20.4–B
Form 62	Form 20.9–A
Form 63	Form 20.9–A
Form 64	Form 20.9–B
Form 65	Form 20.9–C
Form 66	Form 20.4–A
Form 67	Form 18.6
Form 68	Form 20.2
Form 69	Form 20.5
Form 70	Form 19.5 (part) and Form 19.6 (part)
Form 71	Form 19.2–A
Form 72	Form 19.2–B
Form 73	Form 19.2–C
Form 74	Form 19.3–B
Form 75	Form 19.4
Form 76	Form 19.3–A
Form 77	Form 19.7
Form 78	Form 19.1–A
Form 79	Form 19.1–B
Form 80	Form 19.9
Form 81	Form 30.2–A
Form 82	Form 30.2–B
Form 83	Form 30.5
Form 84	Form 32.2

Part, section, Schedule or rule of enactment	Destination in C.P.R. 1996
Form 85	Form 3.1–A
Form 86	Form 3.1–B
Form 88	Form 34.5
Form 89	Form 36.4–A
Form 90	Form 36.4–B
Form 91	Form 20.19–A
Form 92	Form 20.19–B
Form 93	Form 26.1–A
Form 94	Form 26.1–B
Form 95	Form 26.1–C
Form 96	Form 20.3

SHERIFF COURT, SCOTLAND
ACT OF SEDERUNT (PROCEEDS OF CRIME RULES) 1996

S.I. 1996 No. 2446 (S.191)

Made – – – –	*12th September, 1996*
Coming into force	*7th October, 1996*

The Lords of Council and Session, under and by virtue of the powers conferred on them by section 32 of the Sheriff Courts (Scotland) Act 1971, sections 31(5) and 48 of, and paragraph 11 of Schedule 1 to, the Proceeds of Crime (Scotland) Act 1995 and of all other powers enabling them in that behalf, having approved, with modifications, draft rules submitted to them by the Sheriff Court Rules Council in accordance with section 34 of the said Act of 1971, do hereby enact and declare:

Citation, commencement and interpretation

1.—(1) This Act of Sederunt may be cited as the Act of Sederunt (Proceeds of Crime Rules) 1996 and shall come into force on 7th October 1996.

(2) This Act of Sederunt shall be inserted in the Books of Sederunt.

(3) In this Act of Sederunt—

"the Act of 1995" means the Proceeds of Crime (Scotland) Act 1995;
"administrator" means the person appointed under paragraph 1(1) of Schedule 1 to the Act of 1995.

Applications for compensation

2. An application to the sheriff under section 17(1) of the Act of 1995 (compensation) shall be made by summary application.

Applications for restraint orders

3.—(1) An application to the sheriff under section 28(1) of the Act of 1995 (application for restraint order) shall by summary application.

(2) Where the sheriff pronounces an interlocutor making a restraint order, the prosecutor shall serve a copy of that interlocutor on every person named in the interlocutor as restrained by the order.

Recall or variation of restraint orders

4.—(1) An application to the sheriff under any of the following provisions of the Act of 1995 shall be made by note in the process containing the interlocutor making the restraint order to which the application relates:—

(a) section 29(4) or (5) (recall of restraint orders in relation to realisable property);
(b) section 30(3) or (4) (recall of restraint orders in relation to forfeitable property);
(c) section 31(1) (variation or recall of restraint order).
(2) In respect of an application by note under paragraph (1)(c) above by a person having an interest for an order for variation or recall under section 31(1)(b) of the Act of 1995—
(a) the note shall be lodged in process within 21 days after service of the restraint order on that person or within such other period as the sheriff thinks fit; and
(b) the period of notice for lodging answers to the note shall be 14 days or such other period as the sheriff thinks fit.

Applications for interdict

5.—(1) An application to the sheriff under section 28(8) of the Act of 1995 (interdict) may be made—
(a) in the summary application under section 28(1) of the Act of 1995; or
(b) if made after a restraint order has been made, by note in the process of the application for that order.
(2) An application under section 28(8) of the Act of 1995 by note under paragraph (1)(b) above shall not be intimated, served or advertised before that application is granted.

Applications in relation to arrestment

6.—(1) An application to the sheriff under section 33(1) of the Act of 1995 (arrestment of property affected by restraint order) by the prosecutor for warrant for arrestment may be made—
(a) in the summary application under section 28(1) of the Act of 1995; or
(b) if made after a restraint order has been applied for, by note in the process of the application for that order.
(2) An application to the sheriff under section 33(2) of the Act of 1995, to loose, restrict or recall an arrestment shall be made by note in the process of the application for the restraint order.
(3) An application to the sheriff under section 33(4) of the Act of 1995 (recall or restriction of arrestment) shall be made by note in the process containing the interlocutor making the restraint order to which the application relates.

Appeals to the Court of Session

7.—(1) This rule applies to appeals against an interlocutor of the sheriff refusing, varying or recalling or refusing to vary or recall a restraint order.
(2) An appeal to which this rule applies shall be marked within 14 days after the date of the interlocutor concerned.
(3) An appeal to which this rule applies shall be marked by writing a note of appeal on the interlocutor sheet, or other written record containing the interlocutor appealed against, or on a separate sheet lodged with the sheriff clerk, in the following terms:— "The applicant appeals to the Court of Session.".
(4) A note of appeal to which this rule applies shall—
(a) be signed by the appellant;
(b) bear the date on which it is signed; and
(c) where the appellant is represented, specify the name and address of the solicitor or other agent who will be acting for him in the appeal.
(5) The sheriff clerk shall transmit the process within 4 days after the appeal is marked to the Deputy Principal Clerk of Session.

(6) Within the period specified in paragraph (5) above, the sheriff clerk shall—

(a) send written notice of the appeal to every other party; and

(b) certify on the interlocutor sheet that he has done so.

(7) Failure of the sheriff clerk to comply with paragraph (6) above shall not invalidate the appeal.

Applications for appointment of administrators

8.—(1) An application to the sheriff under paragraph 1 of Schedule 1 to the Act of 1995 (appointment of administrators) shall be made—

(a) where made after a restraint order has been made, by note in the process of the application for that order; or

(b) in any other case, by summary application.

(2) The notification to be made by the sheriff clerk under paragraph 1(3)(a) of Schedule 1 to the Act of 1995 shall be made by intimation of a copy of the interlocutor to the person required to give possession of property to an administrator.

Incidental applications in an administration

9.—(1) An application to the sheriff under any of the following provisions of Schedule 1 to the Act of 1995 shall be made by note in the process of the application for appointment of the administrator:—

(a) paragraph 1(1) with respect to an application after appointment of an administrator to require a person to give property to him;

(b) paragraph 1(4) (making or altering a requirement or removal of administrator);

(c) paragraph 1(5) (appointment of new administrator on death, resignation or removal of administrator);

(d) paragraph 2(1)(n) (directions as to functions of administrator);

(e) paragraph 4 (directions for application of proceeds).

(2) An application to the sheriff under any of the following provisions of Schedule 1 to the Act of 1995 shall be made in the application for appointment of an administrator under paragraph 1(1) of that Schedule or, if made after the application has been made, by note in that process:—

(a) paragraph 2(1)(o) (special powers of administrator);

(b) paragraph 2(3) (vesting of property in administrator);

(c) paragraph 12 (order to facilitate the realisation of property).

Requirements where order to facilitate realisation of property considered

10. Where the sheriff considers making an order under paragraph 12 of Schedule 1 to the Act of 1995 (order to facilitate the realisation of property)—

(a) the sheriff shall fix a date for a hearing in the first instance; and

(b) the applicant or noter, as the case may be, shall serve a notice in the Form set out in the Schedule to this Act of Sederunt (or in a form substantially to the same effect) on any person who has an interest in the property.

Documents for Accountant of Court

11.—(1) A person who has lodged any document in the process of an application for the appointment of an administrator shall forthwith send a copy of that document to the Accountant of Court.

(2) The sheriff clerk shall transmit to the Accountant of Court any part of the process as the Accountant of Court may request in relation to an administration which is in dependence before the sheriff unless such part of the process is, at the time of request, required by the sheriff.

Procedure for fixing and finding caution

12. Rules 9 to 12 of the Act of Sederunt (Judicial Factors Rules) 1992 (fixing and finding caution in judicial factories) shall, with the necessary modifications, apply to the fixing and finding of caution by an administrator under these Rules as they apply to the fixing and finding of caution by a judicial factor.

Administrator's title to act

13. An administrator appointed under these Rules shall not be entitled to act until he has obtained a copy of the interlocutor appointing him.

Duties of administrator

14.—(1) The administrator shall, as soon as possible, but within three months after the date of his appointment, lodge with the Accountant of Court—
- (a) an inventory of the property in respect of which he has been appointed;
- (b) all vouchers, securities, and other documents which are in his possession; and
- (c) a statement of that property which he has in his possession or intends to realise.

(2) An administrator shall maintain accounts of his intromissions with the property in his charge and shall, subject to paragraph (3) below—
- (a) within six months after the date of his appointment, and
- (b) at six monthly intervals after the first account during the subsistence of his appointment,

lodge with the Accountant of Court an account of his intromissions in such form, with such supporting vouchers and other documents, as the Accountant of Court may require.

(3) The Accountant of Court may waive the lodging of an account where the administrator certifies that there have been no intromissions during a particular accounting period.

State of funds and scheme of division

15.—(1) The administrator shall—
- (a) where there are funds available for division, prepare a state of funds after application of sums in accordance with paragraph 4(2) of Schedule 1 to the Act of 1995, and a scheme of division amongst those who held property which has been realised under the Act of 1995 and lodge them and all relevant documents with the Accountant of Court; or
- (b) where there are no funds available for division, prepare a state of funds only and lodge it with the Accountant of Court, and give to the Accountant of Court such explanations as he shall require.

(2) The Accountant of Court shall—
- (a) make a written report on the state of funds and any scheme of division including such observations as he considers appropriate for consideration by the sheriff; and
- (b) return the state of funds and any scheme of division to the administrator with his report.

(3) The administrator shall, on receiving the report of the Accountant of Court—
- (a) lodge in process the report, the state of funds and any scheme of division;
- (b) intimate a copy of it to the prosecutor; and
- (c) intimate to each person who held property which has been realised under the Act of 1995 a notice stating—

(i) that the state of funds and scheme of division or the state of funds only, as the case may be, and the report of the Accountant of Court, have been lodged in process; and

(ii) the amount for which that person has been ranked, and whether he is to be paid in full, or by a dividend, and the amount of it, or that no funds are available for payment.

Objections to scheme of division

16.—(1) A person wishing to be heard by the sheriff in relation to the distribution of property under paragraph 4(3) of Schedule 1 to the Act of 1995 shall lodge a note of objection in the process to which the scheme of division relates within 21 days of the date of the notice intimated under rule 15(3)(c) above.

(2) After the period for lodging a note of objection has expired and no note of objection has been lodged, the administrator may apply by motion for approval of the scheme of division and state of funds, or the state of funds only, as the case may be.

(3) After the period for lodging a note of objection has expired and a note of objection has been lodged, the sheriff shall dispose of such objection after hearing any objector and the administrator and making such inquiry as he thinks fit.

(4) If any objection is sustained to any extent, the necessary alterations shall be made to the state of funds and any scheme of division and shall be approved by the sheriff.

Application for discharge of administrator

17.—(1) Where the scheme of division is approved by the sheriff and the administrator has paid, delivered or conveyed to the persons entitled the sums or receipts allocated to them in the scheme, the administrator may apply for his discharge.

(2) An application to the sheriff for discharge of the administrator shall be made by note in the process of the application under paragraph 1(1) of Schedule 1 to the Act of 1995.

Appeals against determination of outlays and remuneration

18. An appeal to the sheriff under paragraph 6(2) of Schedule 1 to the Act of 1995 (appeal against a determination by the Accountant of Court) shall be made by note in the process of the application in which the administrator was appointed.

SCHEDULE

Rule 10(b)

Form of notice to person with interest in property subject to an application for an order under paragraph 12 of Schedule 1 to the Proceeds of Crime (Scotland) Act 1995

(Cause reference number)
IN THE SHERIFF COURT
in the
PETITION [*or* NOTE]
of
[A.B.] *(name and address)*
for an order under paragraph 12 of Schedule 1
to the Proceeds of Crime (Scotland) Act 1995

in respect of the estates of [C.D.] *(address)*

Date: *(date of posting or other method of service)*
To: *(name and address of person on whom notice is to be served)*

This Notice—
    (a) gives you warning that an application has been made to the sheriff court for an order which may affect your interest in property; and
    (b) informs you that you have an opportunity to appear and make representations to the court before the application is determined.

TAKE NOTICE

1. That on *(date)* in the sheriff court at *(place)* a confiscation order was made under section 1 of the Proceeds of Crime (Scotland) Act 1995 in respect of [C.D.] *(address)*.

2. That on *(date)* the administrator appointed under paragraph 1(1)(a) of Schedule 1 to the Proceeds of Crime (Scotland) Act 1995 on *(date)* was empowered to realise property belonging to [C.D.].

or

2. That on *(date)* the administrator was appointed under paragraph 1(1)(b) of Schedule 1 to the Proceeds of Crime (Scotland) Act 1995 on *(date)* to realise property belonging to [C.D.].

3. That application has been made by petition [*or* note] for an order under paragraph 12 of Schedule 1 to the Proceeds of Crime (Scotland) Act 1995 *(here set out briefly the nature of the order sought)*. A copy of the petition [*or* note] is attached.

4. That you have the right to appear before the court in person or by counsel or other person having a right of audience and make such representations as you may have in respect of the order applied for. The court has fixed *(insert day and date fixed for hearing the application)*, at *(insert time and place fixed for hearing)* as the time when you should appear to do this.

5. That if you do not appear or are not represented on the above date, the order applied for may be made in your absence.

IF YOU ARE UNCERTAIN ABOUT THE EFFECT OF THIS NOTICE, you should consult a Solicitor, Citizens Advice Bureau or other local advice agency or adviser immediately.

(Signed)
Sheriff Officer
[*or* Solicitor [*or* Agent] for petitioner
[*or* noter]]
(Address)

HIGH COURT OF JUSTICIARY (PROCEEDINGS IN THE NETHERLANDS) (UNITED NATIONS) ORDER 1998

HIGH COURT OF JUSTICIARY (PROCEEDINGS IN THE NETHERLANDS) (UNITED NATIONS) ORDER 1998

(S.I. 1998 No. 2251)

Made	*16th September 1998*
Laid before Parliament	*17th September 1998*
Coming into force	*18th September 1998L*

At the Court at Heathrow, the 16th day of September 1998

Present,

The Queen's Most Excellent Majesty in Council

Whereas under Article 41 of the Charter of the United Nations the Security Council of the United Nations has, by a resolution adopted on 27th August 1998, called upon Her Majesty's Government in the United Kingdom to take certain actions to facilitate the conducting of criminal proceedings under Scots law in the Netherlands:

Now therefore, Her Majesty, in exercise of the powers conferred on Her by section 1 of the United Nations Act 1946, is pleased, by and with the advice of Her Privy Council, to order, and it is hereby ordered:—

Citation and commencement

1. This Order may be cited as the High Court of Justiciary (Proceedings in the Netherlands) (United Nations) Order 1998 and shall come into force on 18th September 1998.

Interpretation

2.—(1) In this Order, the following expressions have, except where otherwise expressly provided, the meanings hereby assigned to them, that is to say—

"the 1995 Act" means the Criminal Procedure (Scotland) Act 1995;
"Lord Commissioner of Justiciary" includes a person appointed under—
  (a) section 22 of the Law Reform (Miscellaneous Provisions) (Scotland) Act 1985 (re-employment of retired judges); or
  (b) section 35(3) of the Law Reform (Miscellaneous Provisions) (Scotland) Act 1990 (temporary judges);
"premises of the court" means any premises in the Netherlands made available by the Government of the Netherlands for the purposes of proceedings conducted by virtue of this Order; and
"proceedings" includes anything which requires to be done or may be done in relation to proceedings by any person at any time.
(2) Expressions used in this Order and the 1995 Act have the meaning assigned to them by that Act.

Proceedings before High Court of Justiciary in the Netherlands

3.—(1) For the purpose of conducting criminal proceedings on indictment against Abdelbaset Ali Mohmed Al Megrahi and Al Amin Khalifa Fhimah (in this Order referred to as "the accused") on the charges of conspiracy to murder, murder and contravention of the Aviation Security Act 1982 specified in the petition upon which warrant for arrest was issued by the Sheriff of South Strathclyde, Dumfries and Galloway on 13th November 1991, the High Court of Justiciary may, in accordance with the provisions of this Order, sit in the Netherlands.

(2) Except as provided for in this Order, proceedings before the High Court of Justiciary sitting in the Netherlands shall be conducted in accordance with the law relating to proceedings on indictment before the High Court of Justiciary in Scotland.

Initiation of proceedings conducted by virtue of this Order

4.—(1) The Lord Advocate may give a notice under this article to the Lord Justice Clerk where it appears to him that both of the accused are present in the Netherlands.

(2) On receipt of a notice given by the Lord Advocate under paragraph (1) above the Lord Justice Clerk shall forthwith direct that, in respect of the proceedings against the accused and subject to articles 6 and 14 of this Order, the High Court of Justiciary shall sit in the Netherlands at the premises of the court.

(3) Without prejudice to paragraph (4) below, a notice given or a direction made under this article shall not be called in question otherwise than in the proceedings for which a court shall have been constituted under article 5 of this Order.

(4) Where the Lord Advocate withdraws a notice under paragraph (1) above by a further notice to the Lord Justice Clerk, the Lord Justice Clerk shall withdraw any direction he has made.

(5) Anything which the Lord Justice General requires, or has power, to do in relation to criminal proceedings shall, in relation to proceedings conducted by virtue of this Order, be done by the Lord Justice Clerk.

Constitution of court

5.—(1) After he has made a direction under article 4 of this Order, the Lord Justice Clerk shall appoint three Lords Commissioners of Justiciary to constitute a court for the purposes of any trial to be held in the course of proceedings to be conducted by virtue of this Order, and shall nominate one of them to preside.

(2) The determination of any question of law arising in any such trial shall be according to the votes of the majority of the members of the court, including the presiding judge.

(3) The court shall conduct any such trial without a jury.

(4) For the purposes of any such trial, the court shall have all the powers, authorities and jurisdiction which it would have had if it had been sitting with a jury in Scotland, including power to determine any question and to make any finding which would, apart from this article, be required to be determined or made by a jury, and references in any enactment or other rule of law to a jury or the verdict or finding of a jury shall be construed accordingly.

(5) At the conclusion of any such trial, the court shall retire to consider its verdict, which shall be determined by a majority and delivered in open court by the presiding judge.

(6) In the event of a verdict of guilty—

    (a) the presiding judge shall pass sentence; and

    (b) without prejudice to its power apart from this paragraph to give a judgment, the court shall, at the time of conviction or as soon as practicable thereafter, give a judgment in writing stating the reasons for the conviction.

(7) Any reference in any enactment or other rule of law to—
    (a) the commencement of the trial; or
    (b) the swearing of the jury,
shall be taken to be a reference to the reading of the indictment to the court by the clerk.

(8) In the application of section 87 of the 1995 Act (non-availability of judge) to such proceedings, any reference to the clerk of court includes a reference to the senior remaining judge.

NOTE

An application was made to a single judge to broadcast the trial of Megrahi and Fhimah on television. It was held that the fact that there was to be no jury was not a sufficient ground from departing from the prohibition of live transmission. In any event, the onus was on the broadcasters to show that doing so would involve no risk to the administration of justice. It was not for the Crown or the accused to demonstrate that there would be such a risk: *BBC, Petrs, The Times Law Reports* April 11, 2000.

Questions arising prior to trial

6.—(1) Questions arising in proceedings conducted by virtue of this Order prior to the reading of the indictment to the court by the clerk shall be dealt with in the ordinary way.

(2) Any such question shall be heard and determined at the premises of the court, unless the accused are not entitled, or have intimated that they do not wish, to be present, when it may be heard and determined at a sitting of the High Court of Justiciary in Edinburgh.

Additional judge

7.—(1) When he makes appointments under article 5 of this Order, the Lord Justice Clerk shall also appoint a Lord Commissioner of Justiciary (in this Article referred to as an "additional judge") to sit with the court.

(2) Subject to paragraph (3) below, the additional judge shall sit with the judges of the court, and shall participate in all their deliberations, but shall not vote in any decision which is required to be taken.

(3) Where one of the judges originally appointed to form part of the court—
    (a) has died; or
    (b) is absent, and it appears to the senior remaining judge that the absence will be prolonged,
the senior remaining judge shall so certify in writing, and the additional judge shall thereafter assume the functions of the deceased or absent judge.

Constables and officers of law

8. Anything which, under or by virtue of any enactment or other rule of law, requires to be done or may be done by a constable or officer of law in relation to criminal proceedings may, in relation to proceedings conducted by virtue of this Order, be done at the premises of the court.

Execution of warrant

9. For the purposes of any enactment or other rule of law relating to criminal proceedings in Scotland, the detention of the accused shall not begin prior to the execution of the warrant to arrest them at the premises of the court.

Powers of sheriff

10. Anything which, under or by virtue of any enactment or other rule of law, requires to be done or may be done by a sheriff in relation to criminal proceedings may, in relation to proceedings conducted by virtue of this Order, be done—

(a) by any sheriff who would have jurisdiction if the proceedings were taking place in Scotland; and
(b) at the premises of the court.

Productions

11. Productions shall be made available for inspection—
(a) by the accused, at the premises of the court; or
(b) by their representatives, at such address or addresses in the United Kingdom as may be intimated to the accused by the Clerk of Justiciary.

Witnesses

12.—(1) Witnesses in the United Kingdom who are cited to appear for the purpose of proceedings being conducted by virtue of this Order may be cited to appear at the premises of the court.

(2) Any warrant for the arrest of a witness shall be authority for him to be transferred, under arrangements made in that regard by the Secretary of State, to the premises of the court.

(3) It shall be competent for witnesses who are outwith the United Kingdom to be cited to appear before the High Court of Justiciary sitting in the Netherlands in the same way as if the court had been sitting in Scotland and, accordingly, subsection (1)(b) of section 2 of the Criminal Justice (International Co-operation) Act 1990 (service of United Kingdom process overseas) shall have effect as if the reference to a court in the United Kingdom included the High Court of Justiciary sitting, by virtue of this Order, in the Netherlands.

Offences committed in course of proceedings

13.—(1) The High Court of Justiciary shall have jurisdiction in relation to any contempt of court or other offence committed in the course of, or in relation to, proceedings being conducted by virtue of this Order, whether at the premises of the court or elsewhere in the Netherlands.

(2) Where an offence in relation to which the High Court of Justiciary has jurisdiction by virtue of paragraph (1) above is not dealt with summarily by that court sitting in the Netherlands, it may be dealt with at a later date by way of petition and complaint or on indictment at a sitting of the High Court of Justiciary in Scotland.

Appeals

14.—(1) For the purpose of hearing any appeal (including any application to the *nobile officium*) in relation to any proceedings to which this Order applies, the High Court of Justiciary may sit either at the premises of the court or in Scotland; but where either of the accused is entitled to attend any such appeal and intimates that he wishes to do so, it shall be heard at the premises of the court.

(2) Where the appeal is from a decision of the court constituted under article 5 of this Order, the quorum of the High Court of Justiciary sitting for the purposes of paragraph (1) above shall be five Lords Commissioners of Justiciary.

(3) The Lords Commissioners of Justiciary who are to constitute the court for the purposes of paragraph (1) above shall be appointed by the Lord Justice Clerk.

Place of confinement of accused

15.—(1) Where a warrant for the arrest or imprisonment of the accused has been executed, they shall be confined in the premises of the court until the conclusion of proceedings conducted by virtue of this Order.

(2) Any enactment or other rule of law applying to prisons or prisoners in Scotland shall, subject to article 16 of this Order, apply in relation to the premises of the court and the persons confined there as if, in so far as they are used for that purpose, the premises were a prison in Scotland.

(3) Anything which, under or by virtue of any enactment or other rule of law, requires to be done or may be done by an officer of a prison may be done by such an officer at the premises of the court.

Modification of enactments relating to prisons

16.—(1) The following provisions of the Prisons (Scotland) Act 1989 shall not apply, namely—

section 3(2) (appointment of chaplains),
section 7 (powers of inspection of prisons),
section 8 (visiting committees),
section 9 (appointment of prison ministers),
sections 36 to 38 (provisions relating to acquisition and disposal of prisons and land),
sections 40 and 40A (persons unlawfully at large),
section 41 (prohibited articles), and
section 41A (search by authorised employee).

(2) Section 3A of that Act (medical services) shall have effect as if any reference to a registered medical practitioner included a reference to any person in the Netherlands holding any diploma, certificate or other evidence of formal qualification entitled to recognition under Article 2 of Council Directive 93/16 to facilitate the free movement of doctors and the mutual recognition of their diplomas, certificates and other evidence of formal qualifications

(3) Section 34 of that Act (notification of death of prisoner) shall have effect as if—

(a) the reference to the procurator fiscal were a reference to the Lord Advocate; and

(b) the reference to the visiting committee were omitted.

(4) The following provisions of the Prisons and Young Offenders Institutions (Scotland) Rules 1994 shall not apply, namely—

(a) rules 36 to 38 (chaplains, visiting ministers and religious services);

(b) rule 71 (provision of work for remand prisoners);

(c) rules 104 to 110 (complaints);

(d) Part 13 (transfer and discharge of prisoners);

(e) Part 16 (visiting committees),

and, in applying the remainder of the Rules, the Governor may make such adaptations of the prisons regime as appear to him to be necessary, having regard to the circumstances of the premises of the court and of the persons confined there.

(5) Section 10 of the Prisons (Scotland) Act 1989 (place of confinement of prisoners) and Schedule 1 to the Crime (Sentences) Act 1997 (transfer of prisoners) shall not apply to the accused while they are confined in the premises of the court for the purpose of proceedings conducted by virtue of this Order.

Powers of Lord Advocate and Secretary of State

17. Without prejudice to any powers which he may have under any other enactment or other rule of law, the Lord Advocate or the Secretary of State may do anything, whether within or outwith the United Kingdom, which appears to him to be necessary or expedient for the purposes of this Order.